THE OXFORD HANDBOOK OF

CONTEMPORARY
PHILOSOPHY

THE OXFORD HANDBOOK OF

CONTEMPORARY PHILOSOPHY

Edited by

FRANK JACKSON

AND

MICHAEL SMITH

OXFORD
UNIVERSITY PRESS

OXFORD
UNIVERSITY PRESS

Great Clarendon Street, Oxford OX2 6DP

Oxford University Press is a department of the University of Oxford.
It furthers the University's objective of excellence in research, scholarship,
and education by publishing worldwide in

Oxford New York

Auckland Cape Town Dar es Salaam Hong Kong Karachi
Kuala Lumpur Madrid Melbourne Mexico City Nairobi
New Delhi Shanghai Taipei Toronto

With offices in

Argentina Austria Brazil Chile Czech Republic France Greece
Guatemala Hungary Italy Japan Poland Portugal Singapore
South Korea Switzerland Thailand Turkey Ukraine Vietnam

Oxford is a registered trade mark of Oxford University Press
in the UK and in certain other countries

Published in the United States
by Oxford University Press Inc., New York

British Library Cataloguing in Publication Data

Data available

Library of Congress Cataloging in Publication Data

The Oxford handbook of contemporary philosophy / edited by Frank Jackson
and Michael Smith.
p. cm.
Includes bibliographical references and index.
1. Philosophy, Modern—Handbooks, manuals, etc. I. Jackson,
Frank, 1943– . II. Smith, Michael, 1954 July 23– . III. Title:
Handbook of contemporary philosophy.
B790.094 2005
190'.9'05—dc22   2005019433

Typeset by Newgen Imaging Systems (P) Ltd., Chennai, India
Printed in Great Britain
on acid-free paper by
Ashford Colour Press Limited,
Gosport, Hampshire

ISBN 0–19–924295–X   978–0–19–924295–5

1 3 5 7 9 10 8 6 4 2

PREFACE

When Peter Momtchiloff invited us to edit *The Oxford Handbook of Contemporary Philosophy* we sat down (over a glass of wine, truth be known) and asked ourselves how best to produce a volume that, while not being an encyclopedia, was not a handbook of one or another area of philosophy. We wanted a volume that would give readers a sense of the range and excitement of contemporary analytic philosophy (excluding formal logic) and would inform them of some of the most interesting recent developments, while being something they could hold in one hand or maybe cradle in two.

We also wanted a volume that would be a contribution to the subject. With this in mind, we invited our contributors to take the opportunity to set agendas for future discussions of the subject matters of their chapters. They were asked to produce chapters that gave a good sense of the philosophical geography of their assigned topic, but we gave them maximum flexibility in how to structure their chapters and made it clear that they were free to focus the discussion on the issues they judged to be most central and to express their own opinions. We were looking not for a mini-encyclopedia but, if you like, for a series of very high-quality opinion pieces. We were delighted with the response. Reading the chapters as they came in was an education in the contemporary philosophical scene for both of us.

Although we gave our contributors maximum flexibility, we were intrusive when it came to the topics within the various parts (moral philosophy, social and polit-ical philosophy, philosophy of mind and action, philosophy of language, meta-physics, epistemology, and philosophy of the sciences). For each part we made a judgement concerning the topics of most interest and fertility, and of course drew on our knowledge of who was working on what. For example, in the philosophy of the sciences it seemed to us that realism, laws, physics, and biology were four topics that stood out for inclusion, and we were delighted to attract four major players on those topics as contributors. Similar remarks apply to the other parts.

An example of where we drew on our knowledge of who was working on what is the chapter by John Doris and Stephen Stich, 'As a Matter of Fact: Empirical Perspectives on Ethics'. We had heard versions of the challenging ideas in this chapter as presentations. But in fact most of the invitations to our contributors were prompted in one way or another by personal acquaintance with their work. There are also a number of chapters that we knew were in someone's head and that what was needed to make the highly desirable transfer from head to page was the right invitation.

There are topics we wish we could have included but could not find room for—or the right contributor for; and, of course, other editors would have made different choices. That's life.

Producing this volume has been a lot of work—perhaps rather more than we had expected. We are very grateful to our contributors for their contributions and in some cases their extraordinary patience, and to Peter Momtchiloff and Laurien Berkeley of Oxford University Press.

F. J. and M. S.

Contents

Notes on the Contributors   xi

PART I MORAL PHILOSOPHY

1. Meta-Ethics   3
   MICHAEL SMITH

2. Normative Ethics   31
   JULIA DRIVER

3. Moral Epistemology   63
   KAREN JONES

4. Moral Psychology   86
   R. JAY WALLACE

5. As a Matter of Fact: Empirical Perspectives on Ethics   114
   JOHN M. DORIS AND STEPHEN P. STICH

PART II SOCIAL AND POLITICAL PHILOSOPHY

6. Liberalism and Diversity   155
   LINDA BARCLAY

7. Law   181
   JEREMY WALDRON

8. Democratic Theory   208
   DAVID ESTLUND

9. Feminism in Philosophy   231
   RAE LANGTON

10. The Feasibility Issue 258
GEOFFREY BRENNAN AND PHILIP PETTIT

PART III PHILOSOPHY OF MIND AND ACTION

11. Intentionality 283
GABRIEL SEGAL

12. Consciousness 310
FRANK JACKSON

13. Action 334
ALFRED R. MELE

14. Cognitive Science 358
MARTIN DAVIES

PART IV PHILOSOPHY OF LANGUAGE

15. Reference and Description 397
SCOTT SOAMES

16. Meaning and Understanding 427
IAN RUMFITT

17. Truth 454
PAUL HORWICH

18. Pragmatics 468
DAN SPERBER AND DEIRDRE WILSON

PART V METAPHYSICS

19. Causation 505
NED HALL

20. Modality 534
LLOYD HUMBERSTONE

21. Time   615
    D. H. MELLOR

22. Constitution   636
    MARK JOHNSTON

PART VI EPISTEMOLOGY

23. Knowledge and Scepticism   681
    TIMOTHY WILLIAMSON

24. Perception   701
    M. G. F. MARTIN

25. The A Priori   739
    CHRISTOPHER PEACOCKE

PART VII PHILOSOPHY OF THE SCIENCES

26. Scientific Realism   767
    MICHAEL DEVITT

27. Laws   792
    NANCY CARTWRIGHT AND ANNA ALEXANDROVA WITH
    SOPHIA EFSTATHIOU, ANDREW HAMILTON, AND IOAN MUNTEAN

28. Philosophy of Biology   819
    PHILIP KITCHER

29. The Foundations of Physics   848
    DAVID ALBERT

Index   881

Notes on the Contributors

David Albert is Professor of Philosophy and Director of the MA Program in the Philosophical Foundations of Physics at Columbia University.

Anna Alexandrova is a graduate student in the Department of Philosophy and Science Studies at the University of California, San Diego.

Linda Barclay is a Lecturer in the Department of Philosophy at Aarhus University.

Geoffrey Brennan is Professor in the Social and Political Theory Group, Research School of Social Sciences, at the Australian National University, and holds a part-time joint position in the Political Science Department at Duke University and the Philosophy Department at the University of North Carolina at Chapel Hill.

Nancy Cartwright is Professor of Philosophy in the Department of Philosophy, Logic and Scientific Method at the London School of Economics and Political Science, and the Philosophy Department at the University of California, San Diego.

Martin Davies is Professor of Philosophy at the Australian National University.

Michael Devitt is Distinguished Professor of Philosophy at the Graduate Center of the City University of New York.

John M. Doris is Associate Professor, Philosophy–Neuroscience–Psychology Program and Department of Philosophy, Washington University in St Louis.

Julia Driver is Professor of Philosophy at Dartmouth College.

Sophia Efstathiou is a graduate student in Philosophy and Science Studies at the University of California, San Diego.

David Estlund is Professor of Philosophy at Brown University.

Ned Hall is Professor of Philosophy at Harvard University.

Andrew Hamilton is a graduate student in Philosophy and Science Studies at the University of California, San Diego.

Paul Horwich is Professor of Philosophy at New York University.

Lloyd Humberstone is a Reader in the Philosophy Department, School of Philosophy and Bioethics, at Monash University.

Frank Jackson is Distinguished Professor of Philosophy at the Australian National University.

Mark Johnston is Walter Cerf Professor of Philosophy at Princeton University.

Karen Jones is a Lecturer in the Department of Philosophy at the University of Melbourne.

Philip Kitcher is John Dewey Professor of Philosophy at Columbia University.

Rae Langton is Professor of Philosophy in the Department of Linguistics and Philosophy at the Massachusetts Institute of Technology.

M. G. F. Martin is a Professor at University College London.

Alfred R. Mele is the William H. and Lucyle T. Werkmeister Professor of Philosophy at Florida State University.

D. H. Mellor is Emeritus Professor of Philosophy at the University of Cambridge.

Ioan Muntean is a graduate student in the Department of Philosophy at the University of California, San Diego.

Christopher Peacocke is Professor of Philosophy at Columbia University.

Philip Pettit is William Nelson Cromwell Professor of Politics and Human Values at Princeton University.

Ian Rumfitt is Professor of Philosophy at Birkbeck College, University of London.

Gabriel Segal is Professor of Philosophy at King's College London.

Michael Smith is Professor of Philosophy at Princeton University.

Scott Soames is Professor of Philosophy at the University of Southern California.

Dan Sperber is a researcher at the Institut Jean Nicod in Paris.

Stephen P. Stich is Board of Governors Professor of Philosophy and Cognitive Science at Rutgers University.

Jeremy Waldron is University Professor in the School of Law at Columbia University and Director of Columbia's Center for Law and Philosophy.

R. Jay Wallace is Professor of Philosophy at the University of California, Berkeley.

Timothy Williamson is Wykeham Professor of Logic at the University of Oxford.

Deirdre Wilson is Professor of Linguistics at University College London.

PART I

MORAL PHILOSOPHY

CHAPTER 1

META-ETHICS

MICHAEL SMITH

1. INTRODUCTION

When we judge actions to be morally right or wrong, or people to be morally good
or bad, or outcomes to be just or unjust, we engage in the practice of moral
appraisal. But this practice raises all sorts of puzzling questions. Certain of these
questions are familiar substantive moral questions. To which principles do people
implicitly or explicitly commit themselves when they engage in moral appraisal?
Are the principles consequentialist or deontological in character, or is moral
thought less general and more particularistic? Should we be monists about the
good or pluralists? Are the goods all neutrally characterizable, or are some egocentric? Is justice a matter of equality, or is it rather a matter of giving priority to the
worst off? Questions of these kinds address issues in *normative ethics*. (For further
discussion of issues in normative ethics, see the next chapter, by Julia Driver.)

These moral questions are substantive in the sense that answers to them provide
us with specific normative recommendations about how to act or what to prefer.
Though sceptics about normative ethics might think that such recommendations
amount to little more than sounding off, Rawls's detailed description of the method
that we ordinarily use in justifying our answers to these substantive questions in
normative ethics—the method of reflective equilibrium—did much to quarantine
this kind of scepticism (Rawls 1951).[1] Very roughly, Rawls's idea is that we begin

---

[1] For further developments of the idea of reflective equilibrium, see Rawls (1971) and Daniels
(1979). For opposing views, see Hare (1971) and Singer (1974).

with those specific moral judgements about which we are most confident and try to provide them with a compelling and comprehensive underlying justification. We then amend our initial attempt to provide a comprehensive justification in the light of our specific judgements when we are more confident about our specific judgements; we amend our specific judgements in the light of the attempted comprehensive justification when we are more confident about the comprehensive justification; and so on and so forth until, eventually, we achieve a reflective equilibrium: a point at which we deem no further mutual adjustments to be required. Rawls's suggestion is that when we have achieved such a reflective equilibrium, we are in a position to have confidence not just in the resulting comprehensive justification and the specific judgements that they entail, but also about the results of using the comprehensive justification to give answers on those substantive normative issues about which we were, antecedently, less confident. (For further discussion of the epistemology of moral judgement, see Chapter 3, by Karen Jones.)

But though this might reassure us, to some extent at least, that normative ethics isn't simply a domain in which we sound off—the normative judgements that survive the reflective equilibrium procedure meet certain epistemic standards, after all— there is still plainly an unstated anti-sceptical assumption lurking in the background. In terms of Rawls's method of reflective equilibrium, the assumption is that there are no considerations that undermine our confidence in all of our moral judgements at once. However, this assumption can be questioned. For at the other extreme from familiar substantive questions in normative ethics lie much more general and abstract questions about the nature of moral judgements themselves. These are questions that we can at least attempt to answer while remaining neutral about substantive questions in normative ethics. However, they are also questions the answers to which have the potential to undermine our commitment to morality itself. Let me give some examples.

The main question of this kind that has preoccupied moral philosophers in recent years is whether, when we make moral judgements, we express beliefs about the way the world is morally, or instead express some sort of non-belief state, a desire (say) that the world be a certain way in non-moral respects. This is the all-important question that divides *cognitivists* from *non-cognitivists*.[2] This question is all-important because the answer we give to it reveals radically different ontological commitments. While the former view presupposes that in making moral judgements we commit ourselves to the existence of a distinctive realm of moral facts, the latter suggests that we have no such commitment. On the view that moral

---

[2] Cognitivists include Moore (1903), Frankena (1958), Nagel (1970), Foot (1972), Harman (1977), Mackie (1977), McDowell (1979, 1981, 1985), Wiggins (1987, 1990–1), Sturgeon (1985), Boyd (1988), Brink (1984, 1989), Railton (1986), Dreier (1990), Dancy (1993), Smith (1994), Jackson and Pettit (1995), Jackson (1998), and Shafer-Landau (2003). Non-cognitivists include Ayer (1936), Stevenson (1944), Hare (1952, 1963, 1981), Blackburn (1984, 1993, 1998), Gibbard (1990, 2003), and Timmons (1998).

judgements express desires, although we go in for talk of 'moral facts' and 'moral beliefs', such talk is simply a loose manner of speaking. Strictly speaking there are no moral facts and no moral beliefs at all. There are merely desires that gain expression in syntactically complex sentences, where expression must be understood to be exactly the same relation as holds between emotions and exclamations such as 'Boo!' and 'Hurray!' On the view that moral judgements express beliefs, by contrast, talk of moral facts and moral beliefs is no mere manner of speaking. Absent a realm of moral facts, all such beliefs are false (Mackie 1977).

This all-important question suggests a range of related questions. For example, we can ask what the constitutive features of moral judgements are that tell in favour of one or another answer to the central question. Which features make them appear belief-like and which make them appear desire-like?[3] If moral judgements express desires, we can ask how we are to understand the syntactically complex semantics of the sentences we use when we make moral judgements. Why do such sentences look for all the world like fact-stating sentences, sentences that are typically used to express beliefs, and nothing like the exclamations that are typically used to express emotions?[4] And if moral judgements express beliefs, we can ask whether any such beliefs are true, and, if so, what makes them true. For example, if there are moral facts, then what differentiates them from facts of other kinds? Do moral facts require the existence of properties alien to science? If so, then do we have any reason to believe in the existence of such properties?[5]

It should be clear how these questions connect back to the earlier discussion of reflective equilibrium as a method of justification in normative ethics. For if moral facts require the existence of properties alien to science, and if for general metaphysical reasons we have no reason to believe that there are any such properties, then these considerations look as if they might well undermine our confidence in *all* of our moral judgements at once. And if that happens, then further questions suggest themselves. We can ask whether this would undermine the entire point of going in for moral appraisal, or whether we could happily go on as before by (say) simply pretending that our moral judgements are true. In other words, we can ask whether morality is nothing more than a useful fiction. If so, what is the use of the fiction?[6]

---

[3] This is the issue that divides internalists and externalists. Internalists include Hare (1952), Nagel (1970), Blackburn (1984), McDowell (1985), Korsgaard (1986), and Smith (1994). Externalists include Frankena (1958), Foot (1972), Railton (1986), and Brink (1986).

[4] This is the issue that divides quasi-realists—non-cognitivists who think that they can explain why moral language looks for all the world as if it expresses belief—and their opponents. Quasi-realists include Blackburn (1984, 1993) and Gibbard (1990, 2003). Opponents of quasi-realism include Hale (1986, 1993), who focuses on Blackburn, and Dreier (1996, 1999), who focuses on Gibbard.

[5] This is the issue that divides naturalists from their opponents. Naturalists include Railton (1986, 1993a,b), Boyd (1988), Jackson (1998), and Sturgeon (2003). Those who oppose naturalism include Moore (1903), Dancy (1986), Wiggins (1993a,b), and Shafer-Landau (2003).

[6] For contrasting views, see Nietzsche (1887), Mackie (1977), and Joyce (2001). See also Wallace (forthcoming).

These quite general questions address issues in *meta-ethics*. As the list indicates, in meta-ethics the focus is not on the substance of morality—not on specific recommendations about how to act or what to prefer or the principles that guide such recommendations—but is rather on a range of interrelated semantic, meta-physical, psychological, and epistemological questions about the practice of making moral judgements themselves. Moreover, to repeat, these are questions that we seem able to raise and answer without paying too much regard to the substance of morality. They are therefore questions on which we might hope to make progress even while remaining ignorant of that substance. Indeed, it is an important part of the methodology of meta-ethics that we do not unnecessarily prejudge any substantive issues in normative ethics.

In recent years the arguments given in favour of different answers to the meta-ethical questions outlined above have become highly articulated.[7] This has not, however, brought about much in the way of agreement. Even positions that were once regarded as having been decisively refuted are now finding new adherents.[8] Moreover, as arguments for positions in meta-ethics have become increasingly more sophisticated and subtle, there has been a noticeable shift in the attention of some meta-ethicists.[9] The idea seems to be that meta-ethics has erred in taking the standard picture of human psychology for granted. Future advances in meta-ethics will, some seem to think, come from a more explicit and nuanced account of the nature of the psychological states and capacities that make it possible for agents to deliberate and act morally: that we need a better story about the nature of belief and desire and the ways in which each of these is regulated not just by the other but also, perhaps, by perception and emotion. (For further discussion of issues in moral psychology, see Chapter 4, by R. Jay Wallace.)

As I hope this sketch of the current state of play in meta-ethics makes clear, contemporary meta-ethics has reached a kind of plateau. My own hunch is that what is needed is not so much a new theory, or a new argument in favour of an old theory, as a pause while we all take stock. We need to remind ourselves of some of the more general underlying questions that hover in the background of meta-ethical discussions without always being made explicit, questions whose answers provide us with the more general orientation from which we give the answers we do to the standard meta-ethical questions. To be sure, some of these questions are psychological in nature. To this extent I agree with those meta-ethicists who think we should focus more explicitly on issues concerning the nature of our psychological

---

[7] See especially the naturalistic version of cognitivism defended by Jackson (1998) and the most recent version of non-cognitivism defended by Gibbard (2003).

[8] I have in mind the resuscitation of an older form of non-naturalism in Shafer-Landau (2003).

[9] See e.g. the papers in Cullity and Gaut (1997), Korsgaard (1996), Little (1997), Blackburn (1998), Scanlon (1998, ch. 1), Dancy (2000), Gibbard (2003), Arpaly (2003), Railton (2003, pt. III), Smith (2004a, pt. I), and D'Arms and Jacobson (forthcoming).

states and capacities. But there are other questions as well, and it is vitally important that we do not lose sight of them.

The aim of the current chapter is to bring some of these more general underlying questions into the foreground and then to suggest some answers. My hope is that, if we explicitly address these more general underlying questions, we will eventually find ourselves able to return to the standard questions already committed to answers, answers on which there might well be more prospect of agreement. Failing that, we might find that we agree about so much already that our residual disagreements are far less troubling.

2. WHY META-ETHICISTS SHOULD FOCUS ON META-LEVEL QUESTIONS ABOUT REASONS AND RATIONALITY

An initial question that hovers in the background of discussions in meta-ethics is why we bother thinking about meta-ethical questions in the first place, as opposed to meta-level questions about other normative domains. Coming up with an answer to this question forces us to address a fundamental issue about the normative force of moral claims.

It is uncontroversial that there are multiple systems of norms. There are norms of rationality, norms of morality, legal norms, norms of etiquette, professional codes of conduct, norms that govern games, and so on. Just as we can ask meta-ethical questions, we can ask meta-level questions in each of these other domains. For example, we can ask meta-legal questions about the nature of legal judgments. Are judgements about what the law is expressions of our beliefs about a domain of legal facts, or are they rather expressions of some non-belief state, our desires (say) about the way the world is to be in non-legal respects? If they express beliefs, then what would the truth-makers of legal judgments have to be like and are there any such truth-makers? And we could ask the same sorts of questions about normative judgements in each of the other systems as well.

Viewed from this perspective, meta-ethics is just one area in which we can raise the host of interrelated semantic, metaphysical, psychological, and epistemological questions described earlier. So the question is why we concern ourselves with these questions in meta-*ethics* as opposed to the similar questions that arise in meta-*rationality*, or meta-*law*, or meta-*etiquette*. One natural answer is that ethics purports to be, in some yet to be specified sense, a more basic normative system than the others. For example, the norms in each of these other domains, or the most important of them, might be thought to reduce, *inter alia*, to moral norms. If this were so, then it would be clear why we should begin by answering meta-ethical questions rather than the meta-level questions in the other domains, for the only way we could fully answer the other meta-level questions would in that case be by first answering those same questions in meta-ethics. Moreover, it does seem that, on at least some views about these other normative systems, moral norms do enjoy this more basic status.

For example, a central issue in jurisprudence, the area in which meta-legal questions are addressed in so far as they are addressed at all, is whether the legal norms of a jurisdiction are simply disguised moral norms. Advocates of natural law insist that they are (Finnis 1980; Dworkin 1986). Advocates of legal positivism insist that they are not (Hart 1961; Raz 1979). Thus, for example, Ronald Dworkin holds that a certain norm is a legal norm of a jurisdiction just in case it is entailed by the set of moral principles that best justifies the practices of that jurisdiction. Put in terms of judgements, Dworkin's view is that legal judgments are a subclass of moral judgements: when we say that such-and-such is a law we thereby make a moral judgement. If Dworkin is right, then it follows that, in order to say whether in making legal judgments we express beliefs or desires, we must first know whether in making moral judgements we express beliefs or desires. The two answers are tied together, with the meta-ethical question being more basic.

The trouble, however, is that if this is a good reason for supposing that we should answer meta-ethical questions prior to answering questions in meta-law, then a similar argument shows that we should answer meta-level questions about ration-ality before we answer meta-ethical questions. For a central issue in meta-ethics is similarly whether moral claims are just disguised claims about what there is reason to do, or perhaps disguised claims about what it is rational to do (for the time being I will not distinguish these two questions). The issue, in other words, is whether moral norms reduce to norms of reason or rationality. Advocates of ration-alism, like Kant (1786), hold that they do, whereas advocates of anti-rationalism, such as Hume (1740), insist that they do not.[10] But if the rationalists are right, then in order to say whether in making moral judgements we express beliefs or desires we must first know whether in making judgements about what there is reason to do or judgements about what is rational to do, we express beliefs or desires. The two answers are once again tied, but this time the meta-level questions about reason and rationality are more basic than the meta-ethical questions. We answer the meta-ethical questions only by first answering the meta-level questions about norms of reason and rationality.

There is another reason for thinking that we should focus initially on meta-level questions about reason and rationality, one that parallels a reason that is often

---

[10] A modern defence of rationalism can be found in Korsgaard (1996) and a modern defence of anti-rationalism can be found in Blackburn (1998).

given within jurisprudence for supposing that legal norms reduce to moral norms. As advocates of natural law point out, the law purports to be *authoritative* in a way that other systems of norms do not. One attraction of Dworkin's suggestion that a certain norm is a legal norm of a jurisdiction just in case it is entailed by the set of moral principles that best justifies the legal practices of that jurisdiction, for example, is that it seems to capture this authoritative element of law. The authoritative element of law thus seems to tell in favour of a reduction of legal norms to moral norms (Goldsworthy 1990).[11] Other institutionalized systems of norms, norms such as norms of etiquette, are not similarly authoritative. Their normative force seems to reside entirely in the brutely coercive power of those who are in a position to extract compliance: in the case of etiquette, the social elite whose interests are served by the enforcement of such norms (Foot 1972).

Whatever the merits of this line of argument within jurisprudence, the crucial point is that a strikingly similar case can be made for supposing that moral norms reduce to norms of reason or rationality. For if moral norms don't reduce to norms of reason or rationality, then we must ask in what sense moral norms could be authoritative. Are we supposed to think that people are morally obliged to act in ways that they have no reason to act, or ways it would be irrational for them to act? That seems absurd, on the face of it. How can we blame people for doing what they have every reason to do? We can, of course, make sense of the suggestion if we model moral norms on (say) norms of etiquette. But that merely underscores the difficulty. For if it is unattractive to suppose that legal norms are brutely coercive like norms of etiquette, then it is all that much more unattractive to suppose that moral norms are brutely coercive. The claim of moral norms to be authoritative is, after all, that much more secure (Korsgaard 1996).

The upshot is that those who are interested in meta-ethics should adopt the working hypothesis that moral norms reduce to norms of reason or rationality. They should focus their attention, initially at any rate, on meta-level questions about norms of reason and rationality. Nor should this be surprising. For though there are many systems of norms, the most basic and authoritative norms are plainly the norms of reason and rationality. As creatures with beliefs and desires we are, as such, subject to norms of reason and rationality. Belief and desire are defined in terms of their functional roles, where these functional roles mirror the rational liaisons that these states enter into. Norms of reason and rationality are thus, quite literally, inescapable (Lewis 1974; Davidson 1984). If moral norms too are supposed to be basic and authoritative, then the most straightforward way for this to be so would be for them to reduce to norms of reason or rationality.

If this is right, we should welcome the fact that some meta-ethicists have turned their attention to issues in moral psychology. For in looking for a better story about

---

[11] For more on this issue, see Postema (1996), Holton (1998), and Smith (1999).

the nature of belief and desire and the ways in which each is regulated by the other, these theorists willy-nilly address questions about the nature and scope of the norms of reason and rationality. The important point to emphasize, however, is that these theorists must keep a vivid sense of the meta-level questions that thereby arise. For example, are the claims that these theorists make about the substantive norms of reason and rationality expressions of belief or desire? What features of such judgements count in favour of one or another answer to this question? What are the ontological commitments of the different answers? Are these ontological commitments credible?

3. Deontic Concepts versus Evaluative Concepts

How should we proceed? Within normative domains in general, and in the domain of reason and rationality in particular, common sense distinguishes between two broad families of concepts. On the one hand there are *evaluative* concepts and on the other there are *deontic* concepts. The crucial task of the theorist is to say how these two families of concepts are related (Ross 1930; Brandt 1979; Rawls 1971). Let me first say something about this distinction. I will then explain why focusing on this distinction fixes how we should proceed.

It is easy enough to give lists of evaluative and deontic concepts. The concepts of the good and the bad, the desirable and the undesirable, the better and the worse, and so on, are evaluative concepts, and the concepts of the obligatory, the forbidden, and the permissible are deontic. The distinction is, in other words, a generalization of the well-known distinction between the right and the good. But though it is easy enough to provide these lists, it is much more difficult to give a precise characterization of the principle by which these lists get generated. On all accounts, however, the principle has something to do with the possibility of holding people responsible. Roughly speaking, those normative claims that entail the possibility of holding some agent responsible are deontic, whereas normative claims that do not entail such a possibility are evaluative.

Thus, for example, when people do something that they shouldn't do, it follows more or less immediately that they are candidates for being held responsible. There may be exemptions or excuses, so we may not hold them responsible in fact, but they are at least candidates. It was up to them to act in the relevant way, so the question of their responsibility arises. When someone or something is good or bad, by contrast, this question does not immediately arise. This is most obvious when we consider things that are good and bad that are not states of agents: sunsets and flowers, for example. But even when we consider examples of goods and bads that are states of agents, it is important to note that no issue about anyone's responsibility for those things arises *immediately*. For example, someone's experiencing pain may be a bad thing, but it doesn't follow from this that the person experiencing pain is a candidate for responsibility for his own pain because we don't yet have any reason to think that his experiencing pain was up to him. I will have more to say about how we might make this distinction more precise in what follows. For the time being, however, this rough characterization will suffice.

Concepts of both these sorts are in play in the domain of reason and rationality. When we talk of what agents rationally should or should not believe or desire or do, we seem to be in the realm of the deontic. Those who are subject to rational requirements are candidates for being held responsible for their successes and failures to live up to their obligations. It is up to people to believe and desire what they should believe and desire. Likewise, when we talk of what agents have reason to do, we once again seem to be in the realm of the deontic. It follows from the fact that someone has a reason to do something that they must account for their acting or failing to act on their reason: it is, in some sense, up to them to do what they have reason to do.

But evaluative concepts are plainly in play in the domain of reason and rationality as well. When we ask agents to defend their claim to have a reason to act in a certain way, what we require of them is, as Anscombe (1957) and Davidson (1963) emphasize, that they specify some 'desirability characteristic' possessed by their action (scc also McDowell 1978). They must tell us something good or desirable that they will thereby bring about, and here we seem to be in a realm with the potential, at any rate, to be purely evaluative. For many of the things that agents would mention when asked to provide such a desirability characteristic—their own pleasure or desire satisfaction, for example—look as if they could well come about completely by happenstance. For example, if pleasure and desire satisfaction are features of an agent's actions that make them good or desirable, then it looks as if they are equally features of random events that just happen to bring them about that make those events good or desirable. They are still good or desirable, but in that case no one would be accountable for bringing them about.

Armed with this common-sense distinction between evaluative and deontic concepts, we face an initial set of meta-level questions about how these concepts are to be defined. For example, within the family of evaluative concepts we can ask what the relationship is between something's being good or bad, on the one hand, and its being better or worse than something else, on the other. The answer to this question is, I take it, relatively straightforward, at least to a first approximation. Goodness and badness come in degrees and are arranged on a scale ordered by the better and worse relations. More goodness is better than less, some goodness is better than none, no goodness and no badness is better than some badness, and less badness is better than more. But here we note something crucially important. For the fact that we can identify a part of the scale to do with goodness, and a part to do with badness, and a point in between these two parts that is neither good nor bad, suggests that the concepts of goodness and badness are prior to the concepts of better and worse. There is more information on the scale than mere information about the ordering in terms of better and worse.

Likewise, within the deontic, we can ask what the relationship is between something's being obligatory, forbidden, and permissible. The key in this case is, I take it, relatively straightforward. We could begin with the concept of the obligatory. An act that is forbidden is an act that we are obliged not to perform, and an act that is permissible is an act that we are not obliged not to perform. Or we could begin with the concept of the forbidden. An act that is obligatory is an act that we are forbidden not to perform, and an act that is permissible is an act that we are not forbidden to perform. Or we could begin with the concept of the permissible. An act that is forbidden is one that is not permissible, and acts that are obligatory are acts that are uniquely permissible. In the case of deontic concepts, then, it seems that we can take any concept we like to be prior.

Definitional questions about the relationship *between* evaluative concepts and deontic concepts are, however, much more difficult to adjudicate. Are evaluative concepts definitionally prior to deontic concepts? Or are deontic concepts definitionally prior to evaluative concepts? Or are the concepts interdefinable, with neither enjoying definitional priority over the other? Or do we have two completely independent families of concepts, with neither being definable in terms of the other? It is not at all obvious how we should answer these meta-level questions. Such meta-level questions would, however, seem to be of the first importance. For meta-level questions about the kind of mental state that we express when we make normative claims must be asked about those claims that employ the definitionally most basic normative concepts.

In order to see that this is so, imagine for a moment that evaluative concepts are definitionally basic, and that deontic concepts are defined in terms of evaluative concepts together with some straightforwardly descriptive concepts. In that case, if we were to focus on the normative claims we make that are framed in terms of deontic concepts, what we would discover is that there is at least a straightforwardly factual element, an element expressive of belief, namely, that element specified in terms of straightforwardly descriptive concepts. But it would be wrong to conclude on this basis that normative claims in the domain of reason and rationality as such are expressive of belief. For the crucial question would still be left unanswered. Is the most basic element, the element framed in terms of evaluative concepts, also expressive of belief? Only confusion will result from asking meta-level questions about anything but the definitionally most basic normative concepts.

It is now clear how we should proceed. We should proceed by asking whether, within the normative domain of reason and rationality, evaluative concepts or deontic concepts are definitionally prior. Since to my knowledge this question hasn't ever been explicitly addressed with regard to this particular domain— indeed, to my knowledge the question hasn't been explicitly formulated—we will take our lead from similar discussions in the moral domain.

4. Moore's Definition of the Deontic

In *Principia Ethica* G. E. Moore (1903) argues that there is the following analytic connection between the fact that an act is our duty—an act that we ought to perform—and facts about the goodness and badness of that action's outcome.[12]

> $(x)(x$ ought to ϕ in circumstances C iff ϕ-ing is the unique action of those that x can perform in C that has the best outcome).

Moore's suggestion readily adapts to the normative domain of reasons and rationality. The idea would be that an agent has all-things-considered reason to ϕ in circumstances C if and only if ϕ-ing is the unique action of those she can perform in C that has the best outcome, where outcomes in turn are ranked in terms of their possession of various desirability characteristics.

Given Moore's definition of 'ought', note that we can readily define what it is for someone's acting in a certain way to be permissible (this is a matter of her acting in that way's being one among several acts she can perform that has the best outcome), and we can also readily define what it is for her acting in a certain way to be forbidden (this is a matter of the action's being one she perform that has less than the best outcome). According to Moore, there are thus two crucial elements in the definition of deontic concepts. One element is evaluative: being obligatory, permissible, and forbidden are all a matter of an act's standing in a certain relation to the *best* outcome. The other element concerns our capacities: we are obliged, permitted, and forbidden to act in certain ways only if *we can* act in those ways.

In this way Moore's definition purports to make it transparent why evaluative concepts and deontic concepts differ in the way we described earlier. It suggests that the application of a deontic concept entails the possibility of holding someone responsible because responsibility follows in the wake of having the *option* or the *capacity* to bring about a good outcome. If an agent has the option of bringing about a good outcome, rather than a bad outcome, then we expect her to bring about the good outcome: she is a candidate for praise if she succeeds and for blame

---

[12] Though he still thought that the connection was a priori, under the influence of Russell (1910), Moore (1942) ultimately gave up on the suggestion that the connection is analytic.

if she fails. But the mere application of an evaluative concept entails nothing about the object of evaluation having been the outcome of an action that was one of an agent's options, so no issue of responsibility arises. The fact that someone experiences pain is a bad thing, but it is not as such responsibility-implicating because there is so far nothing for the person to give an account of. The fact that someone brings about his own experience of pain when he had the option of acting so as not to have this experience, by contrast, is responsibility-implicating. This is, I think, a great virtue of the Moorean definition.

Moreover, Moore's definition trades on an apparent truism about the relationship between the desirability characteristics possessed by an agent's options and that agent's being a candidate for praise and blame. For suppose an agent has the option of acting in one of two ways and that one of these possesses more in the way of desirable characteristics than the other. Suppose further that she takes the option of producing (say) a less desirable outcome. It would seem to follow analytically that the agent is a candidate for blame, rather than praise. For what could possibly be said in favour of producing an outcome that is worse when you have the option of producing one that is better? If, as Anscombe and Davidson suggest, all reasons for action have the backing of desirability characteristics, then the answer is quite literally that nothing can be said. For no reason could be given that doesn't bring a desirability characteristic in its wake.

But Moore's definition has some other much less attractive features as well. Most obviously, since his definition entails that the evaluative cannot be spelled out in deontic terms, it follows that either the evaluative has to be defined in terms that are neither evaluative nor deontic—that is, in terms that are not normative at all—or that the evaluative is simply indefinable. Moore himself argued on the basis of the Open Question Argument that it is implausible to suppose that the evaluative is definable in non-normative terms, so he drew the conclusion that the evaluative is indefinable. But few were prepared to follow him down this path (Darwall *et al.* 1992).

Moore's definition has another unattractive feature. His definition is inconsistent with the truth of certain very standard views about the substance of the norms of reason and rationality, views that characterize what we have reason to do in egocentric terms. Consider the view that agents each have all-things-considered reason to act so as to satisfy their own current desires. On the methodological assumption mentioned earlier that in answering meta-level questions about reason and rationality we should try as much as possible not to rule out any views about the substance of these norms, we would have to hope that this standard view can at least be formulated in Moorean terms. For only then could its truth be a matter of substantive debate. Unfortunately, however, this standard view looks as if it can't be given a coherent formulation if we accept Moore's definition of the deontic in terms of the evaluative.

Suppose we ask what A and B have all-things-considered reason to do. According to Moore's definition they should each perform the unique act of those available to them that is best. The substantive view that agents have all-things-considered reason to satisfy their own current desires is a view about the nature of the good-making features of acts: an agents' acts are good to the extent that they satisfy their own current desires. In Anscombe's and Davidson's terms, the satisfaction of one's own current desires is the *desirable characteristic* possessed by an agent's actions (Anscombe 1957; Davidson 1963). So far, then, it seems that the view should be straightforwardly formulable in Moorean terms. We need simply to plug the substantive claim about what is desirable into the Moorean definition. Unfortunately, however, matters are not so straightforward.

If we accept Moore's definition, then how do we limit the good-making features of an agent's actions to the satisfaction of *that agent's own current* desires? After all, if the extent to which A's act at an earlier time satisfies A's earlier-current desires is a good-making feature of A's act at the earlier time, and the extent to which A's act at a later time satisfies A's later-current desires is a good-making feature of A's act at the later time, it would seem to follow that there is at least some goodness to be found in the satisfaction of A's earlier desires and some goodness to be found in the satisfaction of his later desires. To the extent that A at the earlier time acts so as to satisfy his own current desires, then, and not the desires that he will have later, it would seem to follow that he ignores something that he has to admit is good that he could bring about by his acts, namely, the satisfaction of his own later-current desires. It would therefore seem to be inconsistent to hold that the good-making features of an agent's actions could be limited to the satisfaction of that agent's own *current* desires.

Similarly, it seems inconsistent to suppose that the good-making features of an agent's actions could be limited to the satisfaction of *that agent's own* current desires. After all, if the extent to which A's act satisfies A's current desires is a good-making feature of A's act, and the extent to which B's act satisfies B's current desires is a good-making feature of B's act, then both A and B are in a position to recognize that there is at least some goodness in the satisfaction of A's current desires and some goodness in the satisfaction of B's current desires. To the extent that A and B act so as to satisfy their own current desires, and not the current desires that each other has as well, it would therefore seem to follow that they too ignore some of the things that are good that they could bring about by their acts, namely, in A's case, the satisfaction of B's current desires, and in B's case, the satisfaction of A's current desires.

The upshot is that, if we accept the Moorean definition, those who think that agents have all-things-considered reason to act so as to satisfy their own current desires seem to be guilty of focusing on only a *part* of the good, not *the whole* of the good. And since such a restricted focus is ad hoc, their view seems to suffer from a kind of incoherence. They are committed, by their own lights, to the quite different view that agents have all-things-considered reason to satisfy desires period, without regard to whose desires they are or when they are possessed: a form of preference utilitarianism. Moore embraced the general form of this argument wholeheartedly. He held that once we properly understand the definitional relations between deontic and evaluative concepts, a thesis established at the meta-level, we see that this has direct implications for which substantive normative views are coherent and which are not. Indeed, he himself argued against egoism and in favour of utilitarianism on precisely these grounds.

It must be said that this is a powerful line of argument if it works. However, most people who contemplate this argument are so convinced that the conclusion is false that they take the argument to be a *reductio* of the premiss (Broad 1942). In other words, they conclude that since Moore's definition of the deontic in terms of the evaluative really does entail that no reasons need to be characterized in egocentric terms, this means that the evaluative must not be definitionally prior to the deontic. But this reaction to Moore's argument is in fact totally misconceived. There is a flaw in Moore's argument all right, but the flaw leaves his definition of the deontic in terms of the evaluative firmly intact. What is called into question is not Moore's definition of the deontic in terms of the evaluative, but rather his assumption that goodness is metaphysically simple.

5. SIDGWICK'S DEFINITION OF THE EVALUATIVE

In holding that the evaluative is definitionally prior to the deontic, Moore thereby committed himself to the view that goodness is not itself further analysable in deontic terms. But of course Moore also held the much more radical view that goodness is metaphysically simple: goodness is not only not further analysable in deontic terms, but not further analysable in any terms whatsoever. In this respect it is worth comparing Moore's view with one of the theories he was reacting to at the time he was writing.

According to Henry Sidgwick (1907), the good is not metaphysically simple, but is rather a matter of what we ought to desire (Hurka 2003). More precisely, the Sidgwickian definition of 'good' can be formulated in the following terms.

$$(x)(t)(p \text{ is good}_{x,t} \text{ iff } x \text{ at } t \text{ ought to desire that } p).$$

Similarly, according to the Sidgwickian definition of 'bad', something is bad just in case we ought to be averse to it.

$$(x)(t)(p \text{ is bad}_{x,t} \text{ iff } x \text{ at } t \text{ ought to be averse to } p).$$

On the surface the Sidgwickian definitions seem to reverse the direction of definitional priority. But that isn't quite accurate. For there are many deontic concepts, and while Moore was defining one of these in terms of 'good', the Sidgwickian definition of 'good' appeals to another quite different concept.

Moore's definition, at least as we have interpreted it, specifies in evaluative terms what it means to say that an agent has all-things-considered reason to act in a certain way: an agent's reasons for action are defined in terms of the values of the outcomes of the actions that the agent can perform. The Sidgwickian definition, by contrast, defines what it is for something to be of value in terms of a quite different concept: something's being of value is defined in terms of those desires that are possessed by one whose psychology is ideal, that is, a psychology that meets all rational requirements and other ideals of reason. But the concept of *an agent's having all-things-considered reason to act in a certain way* and the concept of *an agent's psychology's meeting all rational requirements and ideals of reason* are quite different, though related, concepts. They are different but related concepts because, in a Moorean spirit, we can define the former in terms of the latter.

> $(x)(t)(x$ at t has all-things-considered reason to ϕ in circumstances C iff ϕ-ing is the unique action of those x can perform at t that brings about what x would desire most happens in C if his psychology met all rational requirements and ideals of reason)

or, more simply:

> $(x)(t)(x$ at t ought to ϕ in circumstances C iff ϕ-ing is the unique action of those x can perform at t that brings about the best$_{x,t}$ outcome in C).

Somewhat surprisingly, the Sidgwickian definition of 'good' and the Moorean definition of 'ought' are therefore consistent with each other.

The Sidgwickian definition of 'good' should sound familiar, for it bears a striking similarity to a whole range of theories of value that have been much discussed over the years: the fitting attitude theory (Ewing 1947, 1959), the ideal observer theory (Firth 1952), views that insist that values are like secondary qualities (McDowell 1985; Wiggins 1987), different versions of the dispositional theory (Lewis 1989; Smith 1994), and response-dependent theories (Johnston 1989). In common with all of these theories, the Sidgwickian definition of 'good' is, in Scanlon's (1998) terms, a *buck-passing* theory (see also the various theories discussed in Rabinowicz and Rønow-Rasmussen 2004). It entails that there is no metaphysically independent property of goodness, but rather that something's being good is a matter of its being an object of the desires that the subject would have if that subject had an idealized psychology. The definitional buck is in this way passed from the concept of goodness to the concept of an idealized psychology: the latter is the definitionally basic concept.[13]

---

[13] Scanlon says that the buck is passed from the concept of the good to the concept of a reason: that the concept of a reason is the definitionally basic concept. His idea is presumably that an idealized

Moreover, the Sidgwickian definition just given is illuminating because it brings out a crucial feature of buck-passing theories. If goodness is a matter of what ought to be desired—or, to put it more carefully, if intrinsic goodness is a matter of what ought to be intrinsically desired—then it follows that our ordinary talk of this or that's being good is potentially misleading. Though such talk makes it look as if goodness could be, as Moore thought it was, metaphysically simple, when we talk of a thing's being good we must, at least implicitly, be talking about that thing's being good *relative to people and times*, namely, all of those who ought, at those times, to desire that thing. The subscripts on 'good' in the definition are markers of this fact. So if we follow Sidgwick, it turns out that, contrary to Moore, goodness cannot be a simple property. Goodness has *structure* (Smith 2003).

This is important because the Moorean argument given earlier for the conclusion that it cannot be the case that each of us has all-things-considered reason to act so as to satisfy our own current desires can now be seen to be driven entirely by the assumption that goodness is metaphysically simple, and hence not structured in this way. For suppose that goodness is structured in the way that the Sidgwickian definition suggests. There is then no conceptual barrier to the following's being true:

$(x)(t)(x$ at t ought to desire the satisfaction of the desires x has at $t)$.

In other words, it could well be the case that people ought to desire the satisfaction of their own current desires. But if this is right then it would follow that:

$(x)(t)($the satisfaction of the desires that x has at t is good$_{x,t})$.

And if this is so then the Moorean argument considered earlier collapses.

Consider the argument given for insisting that agents must consider more than *their own* current desires. From the fact that the satisfaction of the desires that A has at t is good$_{A,t}$ and the satisfaction of the desires that B has at t is good$_{B,t}$ we cannot derive the conclusion that there are two good things where we understand goodness as being relative to the same person and time in each case. There is just one thing that is good$_{A,t}$, namely the satisfaction of the desires that A has at t, and one thing that is good$_{B,t}$, namely the satisfaction of the desires that B has at t. To suppose otherwise is to imagine that we can move from the premiss that each person ought to desire the satisfaction of their own current desires to the conclusion that each person ought to desire the satisfaction of everyone's current desires. But this

---

psychology is simply a psychology in which one's desires are suitably sensitive to reasons. But this assumes, unjustifiably, that the only way in which desires could be subject to rational requirements is if these rational requirements were, in turn, characterizable in terms of a sensitivity to reasons (Smith forthcoming). But that is simply false. Requirements of means–end rationality, for example, are not characterizable in terms of a sensitivity to reasons (Smith 2004b). The definitional buck may therefore be passed to the concept of a rational requirement without thereby being passed to the concept of a reason.

move is substantive. It is not licensed merely by the meaning of 'ought', but by a substantive claim about what we ought to desire.

The argument given for supposing that agents must consider more than the satisfaction of their own *current* desires is similarly shown to be defective. For agents can perfectly consistently hold that their own current desire satisfaction is good$_{\text{them,now}}$ and that their later desire satisfaction is good$_{\text{them,now}}$ without holding that their later desire satisfaction is good$_{\text{them,now}}$. To suppose otherwise is to imagine that we can move from the premiss that each person ought to desire the satisfaction of their own current desires to the conclusion that each person ought to desire the satisfaction of their own future desires. But this is also a substantive claim. It is not licensed merely by the meaning of 'ought', but by a substantive claim about what we ought to desire. However, the fact that the nature of the good things is in this way dependent on substantive claims about what ought to be desired is completely invisible if you think, as Moore does, that goodness is metaphysically simple. It is therefore no surprise that Moore found his own argument so convincing.

But though the Sidgwickian definition in this way enables us to diagnose the flaw in the Moorean argument given earlier for the conclusion that it cannot be the case that each of us has all-things-considered reason to act so as to satisfy our own current desires, it is important to note that it does not itself commit us to the opposite conclusion either. It is perfectly consistent with the Sidgwickian definition of 'good' that:

$$(x)(y)(t)(t')(x \text{ at } t \text{ ought to desire the satisfaction of the desires } y \text{ has at } t').$$

In other words, it is perfectly consistent with the Sidgwickian definition that desire satisfaction is of value quite independently of whose desire it is that is satisfied or when that desire is possessed. The Sidgwickian definition of 'good', unlike the Moorean definition, would thus seem so far to be in accord with the methodological constraint mentioned earlier, the constraint that in taking views at the meta-level we do not thereby rule out any substantive views at the normative level. If good-making features require egocentric characterization, then one attraction of the Sidgwickian definition of 'good' is that it allows such characterizations. But it does not require that good-making features be given an egocentric characterization. This is an additional attraction of the Sidgwickian definition.

The fact that the Sidgwickian definition of 'good' in terms of 'ought' blocks the Moorean argument for the conclusion that no all-things-considered reason needs to be characterized in egocentric terms should be reason enough to prefer it to Moore's suggestion that goodness is metaphysically simple. But the Sidgwickian definition has more to recommend it than just that. For when Anscombe (1957) and Davidson (1963) say that agents who claim to have reasons to act in a certain way must be prepared to specify some desirable feature brought about by their acting in that way, it is just very plausible to interpret this as the demand that people explain why the thing that they claim to have reason to do is something that they ought to desire: as the demand, in other words, that they would desire that thing if their psychology met rational requirements and other ideals of reason. This is both very plausible in its own right—undermining the claim that someone has reason to act in a certain way seems to be one and the same task as showing that their desire to do it doesn't fit into a coherent psychological profile (Williams 1980; Smith 1995)—and is made even more plausible because so understanding the demand explains why goodness and badness stand in the logical relationships in which they do. Let me explain this last idea.

We noted earlier that goods and bads come in degrees and are at opposite ends of a scale ordered by the 'better than' relation with neither good nor bad as its mid-point. We noted that everyone must come up with some sort of explanation of why goods and bads stand in these logical relationships to each other. Those who accept a definition of 'good' along Sidgwickian lines have a plausible explanation. The explanation is that goodness and badness stand in these logical relationships because desires and aversions—where aversion can be thought of as desiring the absence of something—are states with different strengths and can therefore be put in an isomorphic ordering with indifference as its mid-point. In this way the structure of goodness and badness can be seen as a shadow cast by the structure of desire and aversion.

Suppose, for example, that a subject S at a time t desires very strongly that p, a little less strongly that q, that he is indifferent to r neither desiring it to obtain nor desiring it not to obtain, that he has a weak desire that u not obtain, and that he desires very strongly that v not obtain. Now suppose further that these are all desires that the subject ought to have: they are part of a psychology that meets all rational requirements and other ideals of reason. The Sidgwickian then has the materials with which to explain the logical relationships between the goods and the bads. For the pattern of the subject's desires, given that these are all desires that the subject ought to have, together with the Sidgwickian definition of good and bad, entails that while p and q are both good$_{S,t}$, p is even better$_{S,t}$ than q; that q is better$_{S,t}$ than r, which is neither good$_{S,t}$ nor bad$_{S,t}$; that r is better$_{S,t}$ than both u and v, which are both bad$_{S,t}$; and that v is even worse$_{S,t}$ than u. If facts about goodness and badness are simply facts about the relative strength of the desires that are part of a psychology that meets all rational requirements and other ideals of reason, then it comes as no surprise at all that goodness and badness can be ordered in terms of better and worse with neither good nor bad as a mid-point.[14]

Finally, the Sidgwickian definition of 'good' makes it plain why facts about goods and bads are not responsibility-implicating in the way in which facts about reasons for action are responsibility-implicating. Agents are, after all, capable of desiring

---

[14] Here I assume that we can characterize indifference dispositionally in a way that makes it quite different from the psychological state of someone who simply hasn't given the matter any thought. For further discussion of this difficult issue, see Dreier (forthcoming).

things that they cannot bring about. So if agents ought to have such desires, then it follows that the class of good things is much broader than the class of things that an agent has reason to do: indeed, the class of things that the agent has reason to do is a subclass of the things that are good, namely, that subclass of good things that the agent can bring about. This, in turn, explains why facts about goods and bads *as such* are not responsibility-implicating. They are not responsibility-implicating because they may or may not be things that agents can bring about. In this way we can see that it may not be up to anyone to make things better as such, or to prevent things from getting worse as such. What is rather up to agents is to act on such reasons as they have: to take the option of making things better, or to prevent things from getting worse, when they have the option.

To sum up, though the Sidgwickian definition of 'good' is given in deontic terms, the deontic terms to which it appeals are very different from the deontic terms that Moore is trying to define with his definition of 'ought'. The Moorean definition of 'ought' and the Sidgwickian definition of 'good' can therefore be happily combined. This in turn means that the Sidgwickian definition of 'good' can be used to help diagnose the flaw in the argument we considered earlier from the Moorean definition of 'ought' to the conclusion that all reasons for action are characterizable in non-egocentric terms. Finally, as we have seen, the Sidgwickian definition of 'good' is immensely plausible in its own right and is made even more plausible by its ability to explain why goodness and badness are structured in the way they are and why facts about goodness and badness differ from facts about reasons for action in the way that they do.

The upshot is that we have now found the definitionally most basic concepts on which we need to focus at the meta-level in our discussion of norms of reason and rationality. The most basic normative judgement is the claim that an agent's psychology meets all rational requirements and ideals of reason. It is therefore time to ask the all-important meta-level question within this domain.

6. COGNITIVISM OR NON-COGNITIVISM?

Is the judgement that an agent's psychology meets all rational requirements and ideals of reason the expression of a belief or a desire? In other words, should we be cognitivists or non-cognitivists about judgements such as these? Let me begin by offering what I take to be the completely flat-footed answer to this question. To anticipate, the flat-footed answer supports cognitivism and the objections to be considered will all be found wanting. This means that, at the end of the day, the flat-footed answer stands.

It is immensely difficult to provide a comprehensive list of all of the rational requirements to which a psychology is subject or an account of what all of the ideals of reason are. Though most would agree that these requirements include the requirements and ideals of coherence, unity, and informedness, as soon as any concrete proposal is made about what these requirements amount to, the proposals are hotly contested (Gibbard 1990; Blackburn 1998). Even so, the arguments for and against any concrete proposal are a priori arguments—the arguments do not themselves turn on empirical claims—and this means that there is some structure within a psychology—some specific non-normative way in which a psychology has to be when it exhibits coherence, unity, and informedness—from which it follows, a priori, that a psychology that is so structured is a psychology that meets all rational requirements and ideals of reason. In arguing for specific proposals about what coherence, unity, and informedness amount to, after all, we thereby argue in favour of the significance of certain sorts of non-normative features over others. But since the judgement that a psychology that is so structured in non-normative terms is plainly the expression of a belief, indeed a belief with a metaphysically innocent content, and since it follows a priori from some such judgement that the psychology is one that meets all rational requirements and ideals of reason, it follows that the claim that a psychology meets all rational requirements and ideals of reason is itself an expression of belief, and, indeed, a belief with a metaphysically innocent content (compare Jackson 2003).

As I understand it, this argument might be resisted for one of two kinds of reason. The first calls into question the premiss that it follows a priori from some specific claim about the way in which a psychology is structured that that psychology is one that meets all rational requirements and ideals of reason.[15] After all, the objection goes, many very, very smart people have spent a lot of time thinking about what these requirements and ideals are, and, notwithstanding their best efforts, they have not yet been able to come to an agreement. Not only do Kantians and Humeans disagree about the rationality of specific violations of the categorical imperative, even hard-nosed decision theorists disagree with each other about the rationality of choosing one box rather than two boxes when faced with Newcomb's Problem (Campbell and Sowden 1985).[16] In order to suppose that this is a

[15] This is a version of the familiar argument from disagreement: see Mackie (1977) and Gibbard (1990). For earlier replies, see Brink (1984) and Nagel (1986).

[16] The classic statement is found in Nozick (1969). There are two players: a predictor and a chooser. The chooser is presented with two boxes: an open box containing $1,000, and a closed box that contains either $1 million or $0 (he doesn't know which). The chooser must decide whether she wants to be given the contents of both boxes, or just the contents of the closed box. The chooser knows that the day before, the predictor predicted how she will choose. If he predicted that the chooser will take only the closed box, then he put $1 million in the closed box. If he predicted that the chooser will take both boxes, he left that box empty. Suppose that the predictor has been 100 per cent accurate in his many predictions in similar cases in the past and that the chooser knows this. Should the chooser take just the one closed box or take both boxes?

disagreement about a matter of fact that is a priori accessible, we must therefore suppose either that those who have been arguing about such matters for years have yet to canvass the crucial arguments that would bring agreement about, or that they aren't really as smart as they seem to be: that in not being convinced by some argument on offer that is, by hypothesis, convincing, some of them are being irrational. In other words, some of them are thereby shown to have psychologies that are themselves inappropriately structured.

But, the suggestion goes, neither of these hypotheses is credible. We seem to have canvassed all of the arguments and the people doing the canvassing really do seem to be very, very smart. So the only credible conclusion for us to draw is that the move from a specific claim about the way in which a psychology is structured to the conclusion that that psychology is one that meets all rational requirements and ideals of reason is not a priori, but is rather a matter of decision. We make the specific claim and then, if we have the relevant kind of desire that people have psychologies that are so structured, we express our desire in the form of a judgement to the effect that psychologies of that kind meet all rational requirements and ideals of reason. Those who lack such a desire are not disposed to make that judgement. But this reveals no failure in their ability to reason in an a priori manner. In this way we find that we are committed to a non-cognitivist account of the definitionally most basic concepts in the domain of norms of reason and rationality, not a cognitivist account.

However, the trouble with this response is that it too easily overgeneralizes. If this really were a good reason to be a non-cognitivist about judgements to the effect that certain psychologies meet all rational requirements and ideals of reason, it would be an equally good reason to be a non-cognitivist about large parts of philosophy itself: all of those parts on which smart philosophers disagree. I take that to be a *reductio*. More to the point, it simply isn't implausible to suppose either that we have yet to discover some crucial argument in favour of the claim that a psychology that is structured in a certain way is one that meets the requirements and ideals of reason, or that some of those whom we deem to be very, very smart philosophers are in fact incapable of appreciating certain sorts of arguments. Indeed, I would have thought that professional philosophers are all too vividly aware of the possibility that they are themselves incapable of appreciating the very arguments that they should find compelling.

The second reason that might be given for resisting the flat-footed argument just given is that, if the judgement that a psychology that exhibits a certain kind of structure thereby meets all requirements and ideals of reason were the expression of a belief, then this would make it mysterious how judgements of that kind are able to play the role that they play in our psychological economy.[17] After all, the

---

[17] This is a version of the familiar motivation argument: see Hume (1740: 456–8) and Blackburn (1984, ch. 6).

suggestion goes, those who make such judgements are disposed, in so far as they are rational, to make their psychologies exhibit that kind of structure. Yet how could this be so unless their judgements were the expression of a psychological state that is itself capable of playing this motivational role? Desires are the obvious kind of psychological state that are capable of playing this motivational role. So we should suppose that those judgements express desires, not beliefs. This provides us with a second independent reason for giving a non-cognitivist account of the definitionally most basic concepts in the domain of norms of reason and rationality.

But the trouble with this response is that it reveals a radically mistaken view of what it is to be a rational creature. No one should suppose that *desires* play the crucial role of enabling psychologies to evolve so as to meet requirements and ideals of reason. For imagine someone who desires a certain end and believes that acting in a particular way is a way of achieving that end. His having this desire and means–end belief is not enough to guarantee that he has a desire for the means, because he may be means–end irrational: his psychology may not have evolved so as to meet the requirements of instrumental rationality. His desire and means–end belief must be put together in the way required for desiring the means. But how is this putting together of desire and means–end belief accomplished? Let's suppose, for *reductio*, that what's needed is a desire to have a psychology that meets requirements and ideals of reason. How would having this desire help? For it too must work in the normal means–end way. The person we have imagined must therefore not only desire to have a psychology that meets requirements and ideals of reason, but he must also believe that, since he desires a certain end and believes that a particular means is a means to that end, so having a desire for that means would give him a psychology that meets requirements and ideals of reason, and then . . . and then what? The possession of this particular desire and means–end belief is not enough to guarantee that the person we are imagining desires the means to this particular end either. In other words, we still have no guarantee that his psychology evolves so as to meet the requirements of instrumental rationality. His desire to have a psychology that meets requirements and ideals of reason and his belief to the effect that desiring the means would give him a psychology that meets requirements and ideals of reason must themselves be put together in the way required for desiring the means. But how is the putting together of this particular desire and means–end belief accomplished? If we suppose that the person must have a further desire, then we are off on an infinite regress.

The proper conclusion to draw is therefore that we have misconceived the way in which psychologies evolve to meet requirements and ideals of reason. This is not underwritten by a desire to have a certain sort of psychology. Rather, it is underwritten by a distinct capacity to have a psychology that meets requirements and ideals of reason, a capacity that is of a piece with the kinds of inferential capacities to which Lewis Carroll drew our attention in his famous discussion of Achilles and the Tortoise (1895). Agents have and exercise such capacities in a way that requires no mediation by beliefs about the manner of their own exercise. So even if we concede that those who judge that a psychology that exhibits a certain kind of structure thereby meets all requirements and ideals of reason are disposed, in so far as they are rational, to make their psychologies exhibit that kind of structure, this would not tell in favour of their judgement's being the expression of a desire. Their judgement may, for all that, be the expression of a desire, but it may also be the expression of a belief instead. The crucial point is simply that *whatever* psychological state their judgement expresses, its role in our psychological economy is secured by the agents' possession and exercise of the capacity to have a psychology that meets the requirements and ideals of reason. It is this capacity that they have in so far as they are rational, not a desire to have a certain sort of psychology.

The upshot is that we have been given no good reason to doubt the completely flat-footed reason given at the outset for supposing that the judgement that an agent's psychology meets all rational requirements and ideals of reason expresses a belief rather than a desire. Moreover, and just as importantly, the flat-footed reason we gave for this conclusion didn't require us to deny the obvious fact that it is hotly contested what exactly these requirements and ideals are. Nothing that was said entails that there are any such requirements and ideals, of course. For all that's been said we might even be massively deceived about the very coherence of the concept of requirements and ideals of reason. But, absent some concrete reason to think that these concepts are incoherent, it seems that we can in good conscience embrace cognitivism about such judgements and dismiss the idea that we are massively in error. Moreover, since we can use these concepts to give a Sidgwickian definition of the good, and then use our Sidgwickian concept of the good to give a Moorean definition of an all-things-considered reason to act in a certain way, it follows that we can in good conscience embrace cognitivism about these judgements and dismiss the idea that we are massively in error about them too.

7. CONCLUSION

The suggestion made at the outset was that meta-ethicists should adopt the working hypothesis that moral norms reduce to norms of reason and rationality. The pay-off of doing so is, I hope, now apparent. For we have seen good reason to be cognitivists about normative judgements within the domain of norms of reason and rationality. If moral norms reduce to norms of reason and rationality, then it seems that we have equally good reason to be cognitivists about moral judgements as well.

Moreover, we have seen that judgements about what we have all-things-considered reason to do, understood in the Moorean terms in which we have understood them, have a familiar consequentialist structure. This in turn suggests that, when we reduce moral norms to norms of reason and rationality, that consequentialist structure will be preserved. Meta-ethicists should therefore adopt not just the working hypothesis that moral norms reduce to norms of reason and rationality, but that all moral theories are, at bottom, forms of consequentialism. Given our Sidgwickian understanding of goodness and badness, the kind of consequentialism on offer is of course consistent with some, or even all, goods and bads being ego-centric. To this extent the consequentialism on offer is quite different from the standard forms of consequentialism discussed in the normative ethics literature, for according to these theories goods and bads are all neutral. But the conclusion is still a striking one, one which promises all sorts of advantages within normative ethics (Dreier 1993; Jackson and Smith forthcoming).

Some dissenters will no doubt want to take issue with one or another of the claims on which we have built our meta-ethical defence of cognitivism and consequentialism. But the theoretical reasons for accepting these claims—the comprehensive, systematic, and unified picture of the twin normative domains of morality and reason to which they give rise, and the benefits that would come from a consequentialist regimentation of the various theories on offer in normative ethics—not to mention the arguments given in their favour, should at least give such dissenters pause for thought.

REFERENCES

Anscombe, G. E. M. (1957). *Intention*. Oxford: Blackwell.

Arpaly, Nomy (2003). *Unprincipled Virtue*. New York: Oxford University Press.

Ayer, A. J. (1936). *Language, Truth and Logic*. London: Gollancz.

Blackburn, Simon (1984). *Spreading the Word*. Oxford: Oxford University Press.

—— (1993). *Essays in Quasi-Realism*. Oxford: Oxford University Press.

—— (1998). *Ruling Passions*. Oxford: Oxford University Press.

Boyd, Richard (1988). 'How to Be a Moral Realist', in Geoffrey Sayre McCord (ed.), *Essays on Moral Realism*. Ithaca, NY: Cornell University Press.

Brandt, Richard (1979). *A Theory of the Right and the Good*. Oxford: Clarendon Press.

Brink, David O. (1984). 'Moral Realism and the Sceptical Arguments from Disagreement and Queerness'. *Australasian Journal of Philosophy*, 62: 111–25.

—— (1986). 'Externalist Moral Realism', *Southern Journal of Philosophy*, suppl. vol., 24: 23–42.

—— (1989). *Moral Realism and the Foundations of Ethics*. New York: Cambridge University Press.

Broad, C. D. (1942). 'Certain Features of Moore's Ethical Doctrines', in P. A. Schilpp (ed.), *The Philosophy of G. E. Moore*. Evanston, Ill.: Northwestern University Press.

Campbell, Richmond, and Sowden, Lanning (eds.) (1985). *Paradoxes of Rationality and Cooperation*. Vancouver: University of British Columbia Press.

Carroll, Lewis (1895). 'What the Tortoise Said to Achilles', *Mind*, 4: 278–80.

Cullity, Garrett, and Gaut, Berys (eds.) (1997). *Ethics and Practical Reason*. Oxford: Oxford University Press.

Dancy, Jonathan (1986). 'Two Conceptions of Moral Realism', *Proceedings of the Aristotelian Society*, suppl. vol., 60: 167–87.

——(1993). *Moral Reasons*. Oxford: Blackwell.

——(2000). *Practical Reality*. Oxford: Oxford University Press.

Daniels, Norman (1979). 'Wide Reflective Equilibrium and Theory Acceptance in Ethics', *Journal of Philosophy*, 76: 256–82.

D'Arms, Justin, and Jacobson, Daniel (forthcoming). 'Sensibility Theory and Projection', in David Copp (ed.), *Oxford Handbook of Ethical Theory*. Oxford: Oxford University Press.

Darwall, Stephen, Gibbard, Allan, and Railton, Peter (1992). 'Toward *Fin de Siècle* Ethics: Some Trends', *Philosophical Review*, 101: 115–89.

Davidson, Donald (1963). 'Actions, Reasons and Causes', repr. in Davidson, *Essays on Actions and Events*. Oxford: Oxford University Press, 1980.

——(1984). *Inquiries into Truth and Interpretation*. Oxford: Oxford University Press.

Dreier, James (1990). 'Internalism and Speaker Relativism', *Ethics*, 101: 6–26.

——(1993). 'Structures of Normative Theories', *The Monist*, 76: 22–40.

——(1996). 'Expressivist Embeddings and Minimalist Truth', *Philosophical Studies*, 83: 29–51.

——(1999). 'Transforming Expressivism', *Noûs*, 33: 558–72.

——(forthcoming). 'Negation for Expressivists', in Russ Shafer-Landau (ed.), *Oxford Studies in Metaethics*, i. Oxford: Oxford University Press.

Dworkin, Ronald (1986). *Law's Empire*. Cambridge, Mass.: Harvard University Press.

Ewing, A. C. (1947). *The Definition of Good*. London: Macmillan.

——(1959). *Second Thoughts in Moral Philosophy*. London: Routledge & Kegan Paul.

Finnis, John (1980). *Natural Law and Natural Rights*. Oxford: Clarendon Press.

Firth, Roderick (1952). 'Ethical Absolutism and the Ideal Observer', *Philosophy and Phenomenological Research*, 12: 317–45.

Foot, Philippa (1972). 'Morality as a System of Hypothetical Imperatives', repr. in Foot, *Virtues and Vices*. Berkeley: University of California Press, 1978.

Frankena, William (1958). 'Obligation and Motivation in Recent Moral Philosophy', in A. I. Melden (ed.), *Essays on Moral Philosophy*. Seattle: University of Washington Press.

Gibbard, Allan (1990). *Wise Choices, Apt Feelings*. Oxford: Clarendon Press.

——(2003). *Thinking How to Live*. Cambridge, Mass.: Harvard University Press.

Goldsworthy, Jeff (1990). 'The Self-Destruction of Legal Positivism', *Oxford Journal of Legal Studies*, 10: 449–86.

Hale, Bob (1986). 'The Compleat Projectivist', *Philosophical Quarterly*, 36: 65–84.

——(1993). 'Can There Be a Logic of Attitudes?', in John Haldane and Crispin Wright (eds.), *Reality, Representation, and Projection*. Oxford: Oxford University Press.

Hare, R. M. (1952). *The Language of Morals*. Oxford: Oxford University Press.

——(1963). *Freedom and Reason*. Oxford: Oxford University Press.

——(1971). 'The Argument from Received Opinion', in Hare, *Essays on Philosophical Method*. London: Macmillan.

Hare, R. M. (1981). *Moral Thinking*. Oxford: Oxford University Press.

Harman, Gilbert (1977). *The Nature of Morality*. New York: Oxford University Press.

Hart, H. L. A. (1961). *The Concept of Law*. Oxford: Clarendon Press.

Holton, Richard (1998). 'Positivism and the Internal Point of View', *Law and Philosophy*, 17: 597–625.

Hume, David (1740). *A Treatise of Human Nature*, ed. L. A. Selby-Bigge. Oxford: Clarendon Press, 1968.

Hurka, Thomas (2003). 'Moore in the Middle', *Ethics*, 113: 599–628.

Jackson, Frank (1998). *From Metaphysics to Ethics*. Oxford: Oxford University Press.

—— (2003). 'Cognitivism, A Priori Deduction, and Moore', *Ethics*, 113: 557–75.

—— and Pettit, Philip (1995). 'Moral Functionalism and Moral Motivation', *Philosophical Quarterly*, 45: 20–40.

—— and Smith, Michael (forthcoming). 'Absolutist Moral Theories and Uncertainty'.

Johnston, Mark (1989). 'Dispositional Theories of Value', *Proceedings of the Aristotelian Society*, suppl. vol., 63: 139–74.

Joyce, Richard (2001). *The Myth of Morality*. Cambridge: Cambridge University Press.

Kant, Immanuel (1786). *Groundwork of the Metaphysics of Morals*. London: Hutchinson.

Korsgaard, Christine (1986). 'Scepticism About Practical Reason', *Journal of Philosophy*, 83: 5–25.

—— (1996). *The Sources of Normativity*. Cambridge: Cambridge University Press.

Lewis, David (1974). 'Radical Interpretation', *Synthese*, 27: 331–44.

—— (1989). 'Dispositional Theories of Value', *Proceedings of the Aristotelian Society*, suppl. vol., 63: 113–37.

Little, Margaret (1997). 'Virtue as Knowledge: Objections from the Philosophy of Mind', *Noûs*, 31: 59–79.

McDowell, John (1978). 'Are Moral Requirements Hypothetical Imperatives?', *Proceedings of the Aristotelian Society*, suppl. vol., 52: 13–29.

—— (1979). 'Virtue and Reason', *The Monist*, 62: 331–50.

—— (1981). 'Non-Cognitivism and Rule-Following', in Steven Holtzman and Christopher Leich (eds.), *Wittgenstein: To Follow a Rule*. London: Routledge.

—— (1985). 'Values and Secondary Qualities', in Ted Honderich (ed.), *Morality and Objectivity*. London: Routledge & Kegan Paul.

Mackie, J. L. (1977). *Ethics: Inventing Right and Wrong*. Harmondsworth: Penguin.

Moore, G. E. (1903). *Principia Ethica*. Cambridge: Cambridge University Press.

—— (1942). 'A Reply to my Critics', in P. A. Schilpp (ed.), *The Philosophy of G. E. Moore*. Evanston, Ill.: Northwestern University.

Nagel, Thomas (1970). *The Possibility of Altruism*. Princeton: Princeton University Press.

—— (1986). *The View from Nowhere*. Oxford: Oxford University Press.

Nietzsche, Friedrich (1887). *On the Genealogy of Morals/Ecce Homo*, ed. Walter Kaufmann, trans. Walter Kaufmann and R. J. Hollingdale. New York: Vintage Books, 1989.

Nozick, Robert (1969). 'Newcomb's Problem and Two Principles of Choice', in Nicholas Rescher (ed.), *Essays in Honour of Carl G. Hempel*. Dordrecht: Reidel.

Postema, Gerald J. (1996). 'Law's Autonomy and Public Practical Reason', in Robert P. George (ed.), *The Autonomy of Law: Essays on Legal Positivism*. Oxford: Clarendon Press.

Rabinowicz, Woldek, and Rønow-Rasmussen, Toni (2004). 'The Demon Strikes Back: On Fitting Pro-Attitudes and Value', *Ethics*, 114: 391–423.

Railton, Peter (1986). 'Moral Realism', *Philosophical Review*, 95: 163–207.

—— (1993*a*). 'What the Noncognitivist Helps Us to See the Naturalist Must Help Us to Explain', in John Haldane and Crispin Wright (eds.), *Reality, Representation, and Projection*. Oxford: Oxford University Press.

—— (1993*b*). 'Reply to David Wiggins', in John Haldane and Crispin Wright (eds.), *Reality, Representation, and Projection*. Oxford: Oxford University Press.

—— (1997). 'On the Hypothetical and Non-Hypothetical in Reasoning About Action', in Garrett Cullity and Berys Gaut (eds.), *Ethics and Practical Reason*. Oxford: Oxford University Press.

—— (2003). *Facts, Values, and Norms*. New York: Cambridge University Press.

Rawls, John (1951). 'Outline of a Decision Procedure for Ethics', *Philosophical Review*, 60: 177–97.

—— (1971). *A Theory of Justice*. Cambridge, Mass.: Harvard University Press.

Raz, Joseph (1979). *The Authority of Law*. Oxford: Clarendon Press.

Ross, W. D. (1930). *The Right and the Good*. Oxford: Oxford University Press.

Russell, B. (1910). 'The Elements in Ethics', repr. in Russell, *Philosophical Essays*. London: Routledge, 1944.

Scanlon, T. M. (1998). *What we Owe to Each Other*. Cambridge, Mass.: Harvard University Press.

Shafer-Landau, Russ (2003). *Moral Realism: A Defence*. Oxford: Oxford University Press.

Sidgwick, Henry (1907). *The Methods of Ethics*. Indianapolis: Hackett, 1981.

Singer, Peter (1974). 'Sidgwick and Reflective Equilibrium', *The Monist*, 58: 490–517.

Smith, Michael (1994). *The Moral Problem*. Oxford: Blackwell.

—— (1995). 'Internal Reasons', *Philosophy and Phenomenological Research*, 55: 109–31.

—— (1999). 'Morality and Law', in Christopher B. Gray (ed.), *The Philosophy of Law: An Encyclopedia*. New York: Garland.

—— (2003). 'Neutral and Relative Value After Moore', *Ethics*, 113: 576–98.

—— (2004*a*). *Ethics and the A Priori: Selected Essays in Moral Psychology and Meta-Ethics*. New York: Cambridge University Press.

—— (2004*b*). Instrumental Desires, Instrumental Rationality', *Proceedings of the Aristotelian Society*, suppl. vol., 78: 93–109.

—— (forthcoming). 'Is there a Nexus Between Reasons and Rationality?', in Sergio Tenenbaum (ed.), *Poznan Studies in the Philosophy of Science and Humanities: New Trends in Moral Psychology*. Amsterdam: Rodophi.

Stevenson, Charles (1944). *Ethics and Language*. New Haven: Yale University Press.

Sturgeon, Nicholas (1985). 'Moral Explanations', in David Copp and David Zimmerman (eds.), *Morality, Reason and Truth*. Totowa, NJ: Rowman & Allanheld.

—— (2003). 'Moore on Ethical Naturalism', *Ethics*, 113: 528–56.

Timmons, Mark (1998). *Morality without Foundations*. New York: Oxford University Press.

Wallace, R. Jay (forthcoming). '*Ressentiment*, Value, and Self-Vindication: Making Sense of Nietzsche's Slave Revolt', in Brian Leiter and Neil Sinhababu (eds.), *Nietzsche and Morality*. Oxford: Oxford University Press.

Wiggins, David (1987). 'A Sensible Subjectivism', in Wiggins, *Needs, Values, Truth*. Oxford: Blackwell.

—— (1990–1). 'Moral Cognitivism, Moral Relativism, and Motivating Moral Belief', *Proceedings of the Aristotelian Society*, 91: 61–86.

Wiggins, David (1993*a*). 'Cognitivism, Naturalism, and Normativity: A Reply to Peter Railton', in John Haldane and Crispin Wright (eds.), *Reality, Representation, and Projection*. Oxford: Oxford University Press.

——(1993*b*). 'A Neglected Position?', in John Haldane and Crispin Wright (eds.), *Reality, Representation, and Projection*. Oxford: Oxford University Press.

Williams, Bernard (1980). 'Internal and External Reasons', repr. in Williams, *Moral Luck*. Cambridge: Cambridge University Press, 1981.

CHAPTER 2

NORMATIVE ETHICS

JULIA DRIVER

1. INTRODUCTION

'Normative ethics' is an enormous field. It is concerned with the articulation and the justification of the fundamental principles that govern the issues of how we should live and what we morally ought to do. Its most general concerns are providing an account of moral evaluation and, possibly, articulating a decision procedure to guide moral action. Though both these aims rely on articulating the correct set of moral principles that govern evaluation and that can also be used in articulating a decision procedure or rule, they are not coextensive. Recent critical work, especially on the part of particularists and virtue ethicists, has generated more pressure to clearly separate the two.[1]

More specific concerns have to do with investigating the nature of value, for example, and related issues of weighing goods, incommensurability, and the nature of virtue and vice. Indeed, some of these projects, which began as ones peripheral to an understanding of moral evaluation and action guidance, have taken on a life of their own and have been responsible for generating connections between normative ethics and epistemology, economics, and psychology.

Normative ethical theories have traditionally been divided into teleological or deontological categories. Teleological theories are thought to be those that define moral quality in terms of the achievement of some good or avoidance of some bad. Thus, for these accounts, a theory of value is extremely important because it will

---

[1] For utilitarianism specifically, Eugene Bales (1971) made this distinction.

provide substance to what the theory recommends. Deontological accounts are those that specify moral quality—not in terms of goodness achieved, but rather as a function of something else, such as a duty that binds, no matter the consequences, or the adherence to principles that are agreed upon by rational agents. This is not to say that an account of value is not important to deontological approaches—it is. But these approaches do not define the right in terms of the good, so to speak.[2] A teleological theory does.

2. VALUE

Any teleological account of right or virtuous action will need to develop a theory of value—that is, a theory of the good that is to be caused or accomplished by the action or person. It is important to keep in mind that the theory of value, however, is only a portion of a full-fledged normative ethical theory. Such theories of value, for example, can also be appealed to in accounts of prudence or rationality.

In normative ethics, well-being is often taken to be the ultimate good for a person. It had been hoped that an elegant, simple, unified theory of value could be developed. However, it is possible that any kind of truly unified value theory is hopeless. As Thomas Nagel writes: 'I do not believe that the source of value is unitary—displaying apparent multiplicity only in its application to the world. I believe that value has fundamentally different kinds of sources, and that they are reflected in the classification of values into types. Not all values represent the pursuit of some single good in a variety of settings' (1979: 131–2). As we shall see, there are good reasons for Nagel's pessimism. A fragmented account of value would have serious implications for any ethical theory, and also have implications for views on moral dilemmas.[3] Nagel believes that not only are values plural, they are incommensurable or 'incomparable'. If so, that would mean that some moral dilemmas have no resolution.

Yet, a variety of unified theories of value have been proposed, the most well known being hedonism and desire satisfaction accounts of "good" and "good for".

Though few currently accept evaluative hedonism as the correct theory of value, it is certainly worth discussing in this context since most writers define their views relative to a rejection of hedonism. Hedonism is the view that pleasure is the only intrinsic good and pain the only intrinsic bad.[4] A number of writers have presented

---

[2] See Rawls (1971) for a discussion of this way of drawing the distinction.

[3] See e.g. the discussion in Sinnott-Armstrong (1988).

[4] Much recent work has been done that attempts to clarify the notion of "intrinsic good" or "intrinsic value" and the contrast with extrinsic and instrumental good or value. Christine Korsgaard, for example,

compelling counter-examples to this claim. Nozick's 'experience machine' example asks us to consider the following choice (Nozick 1974: 42–5): Suppose one could plug into a machine that could generate pleasurable experiences for the rest of one's life. Thus, one could believe one was actually doing whatever one wanted— sitting on a beach in Cancun, eating a great meal in Paris, or winning the Nobel Peace Prize. Would it be "good for" one to choose to be plugged into this experi- ence machine, even assuming that it will guarantee a greater balance of pleasurable experiences through one's life? Nozick, of course, believed not. And many others have the same intuition: experiences that are veridical (reflect reality) have greater value than experiences that are merely pleasurable. Thus, an objective feature seems relevant to the value of the experience.

Theoretical advantages to hedonism were thought to involve its relative simplicity: with just one basic good, the problem of weighing incommensurable goods can be avoided. However, even hedonism, which is relatively simple, cannot avoid the problem altogether. Most accounts of pleasure note that pleasure can be measured along certain distinct parameters—intensity and duration are just two examples.[5] The weighing problem will emerge in comparing pleasures along varying parameters of measurement.[6] The problem of interpersonal comparisons of "utility" occurs here as well.[7]

Thus, the theoretical advantage is not as profound. Given the counter-intuitive aspect of this account of value, alternatives that are more complicated do a better job of conforming to our considered judgements. There is by no means universal agreement on this, however. For example, Fred Feldman attempts to develop a more sophisticated version of hedonism, propositional hedonism, which is an improvement over the classical view.[8] Also, some writers have noted that Nozick's experience machine thought experiment gets its force from intuitions formed under normal circumstances, and those circumstances do not include experience machines (Railton 1989).

Other subjective or quasi-subjective accounts replace pleasure with preference or desire satisfaction. But these approaches also suffer from the problem that what we

argues that though intrinsic is often contrasted with instrumental, this is mistaken; instead, the con- trast is with extrinsic or relational good or value. Instrumental is instead contrasted with final good, or the value a thing has as an end in itself. Intrinsic value is the value something has "in itself", the value it carries with it, so to speak, and is non-relational. See Korsgaard (1983: 169–95). While Korsgaard has pointed out an important confusion, usage is such that I will still use "intrinsic" to refer to final good.

  [5] Jeremy Bentham famously lists a host of other parameters for measuring pleasure. See his discussion in Bentham (1823).   [6] Walter Sinnott-Armstrong (1988) makes this point.

  [7] John Broome (1991) takes up a discussion of the problems associated with weighing. He also discusses one of the major problems of ethical theory (and not just consequentialist theories), which is how to deal with risk or uncertainty. Space precludes a full discussion of this very important issue, but I refer the reader to Broome's book, particularly the discussion in ch. 6. For a discussion of ethical decision-making and uncertainty, see also Ted Lockhart (2000).

  [8] See his essays on hedonism in p. II, 'Hedonism', of Feldman (1997).

seem to find valuable is objective states of affairs existing independently. Thus, one might believe that certain aesthetic features, like beauty, have value even in the absence of any appreciation of beauty (Moore 1988). There is the additional problem that desire satisfaction views tend to reverse the connection between what is good and what is desired. The intuition is that x is not good for a because a desires x; rather, a desires x because x is good for a.[9]

These considerations have led some to reject the view that well-being is captured by appeal to subjective states—and thus reject both hedonism and desire or preference satisfaction approaches to value—in favour of some sort of objective list theory. Some things are good even if they don't cause pleasure, and are independent of our desires and/or preferences. Candidates will include not only beauty, but also things like knowledge. How do we decide what goes on this list? Recently, Tom Hurka (1993) has suggested a form of perfectionism. It is those things that constitute perfections of human nature that are constituents of human well-being. One might argue, then, that it is in our nature to seek knowledge, for example, and develop our rational capacities. Thus, knowledge forms a part of our well-being. Note that on this view, however, it is possible for something to be good for one even if one does not want it or even if it would not lead to one experiencing a pleasurable response.

Since some argue that the very point of morality is well-being, this issue is of enduring interest. It is of crucial importance, of course, to the so-called "teleological" accounts of moral evaluation, which we turn to next.[10]

3. CONSEQUENTIALISM

Consequentialist moral theories are those that determine the rightness of an action, appropriateness of blame, and so on, solely by a consideration of the consequences generated by the action in question.[11] The most prominent version of consequentialism is utilitarianism, which holds that the right action maximizes the good.

---

[9] A number of people have raised this criticism. For example, see David Brink's discussion (1989).

[10] However, it is worth noting that teleological theories such as utilitarianism don't have a lock on the view that well-being is of central importance to morality. Indeed, Gary Watson argues that contractualism can better account for the intuition that well-being is central to normative ethical theory while accommodating our intuitions about deontological constraints on action. See Watson (1998).

[11] Shelly Kagan makes use of a distinction that, unfortunately, space considerations prevent me from fully utilizing in this chapter. Kagan classifies theories as "teleological" or "deontological" at two different levels: the factoral and the foundational. Given this, it should be noted that the intuitionistic deontologist is deontological at the factoral level (the level of figuring out what to do) but is non-foundational since there is no deeper theoretical level to appeal to in providing justification for the principles used to help us figure out what to do. See Kagan (1998).

Classical act utilitarianism held that the right action maximized pleasure. While utilitarianism dominated analytic normative ethics for most of the last century, few modern writers accepted the classical version of the theory as proposed by Bentham and Mill in the nineteenth century. Problems with their commitment to hedonism led to a rejection of the value theory (discussed in the previous section). However, aside from this concern, problems were also raised for the theory's commitment to maximization or *promotion* of the good.[12] For example, utilitarianism seems insensitive to distribution issues and the distinctness of persons; it fails to reflect our intuitions regarding desert; it is too demanding; and it has been accused of ignoring agent-relative reasons through a commitment to agent-neutrality.[13] Each of these criticisms has prompted a response that has led to a modification.

One problem is that of understanding what, exactly, the principle of utility will recommend in terms of aggregating the good. A question arises as to whether the theory recommends that we strive to maximize average utility or total utility. The contrast is noted by a number of writers. Smart summarizes the choice this way:

Would you be quite indifferent between (a) a universe containing only one million happy sentient beings, all equally happy, and (b) a universe containing two million happy beings, each neither more nor less happy than any in the first universe? Or would you, as a humane and sympathetic person, give a preference to the second universe? (Smart and Williams 1973)

Smart himself favours the second, where the total is greater, though he thinks that in point of fact the distinction will have little practical import. Other writers, however, are not as optimistic. Total utilitarianism runs the risk of endorsing Parfit's (1984) famous "repugnant conclusion"—that is, it would seem committed to recommending a world with millions of marginally happy people over one with a much smaller group of quite happy people, because the total amount of happiness would be greater. But the average option, which avoids this implication, at least superficially, may run afoul of "mere addition".[14]

Another problem is the issue of justice or fairness. This problem comes up in a variety of contexts, and there are numerous examples offered to show that

[12] Philip Pettit in part characterizes consequentialist approaches, of which utilitarianism is the best known, as theories that hold that rightness is a matter of promoting the good as opposed to honouring the good. See e.g. Pettit (1997).

[13] I believe that it is misleading to characterize consequentialist theories as committed to agent-neutrality. As John Skorupski notes, what a consequentialist does is define rightness in relation to a theory of intrinsic value. But 'a theory of intrinsic value may generate agent-neutral or (as with Sidgwick's rational egoist) agent-relative reasons'. See his discussion in Skorupski (1995).

[14] Parfit plausibly argues that lowering average utility by 'mere addition' cannot be bad. He writes: 'There is *Mere Addition* when, in one of two outcomes, there exist extra people (1) who have lives worth living, (2) who affect no one else, and (3) whose existence does not involve social injustice'

utilitarianism is flawed because it will recommend to the agent that she perform acts that are obviously unjust. The classic example is this: Suppose that, to stop a spate of horrific murders, it proves necessary to frame an innocent person for one of the crimes in such a way that all would be convinced. If this act deterred future crimes, then it looks as though the utilitarian must recommend that the innocent person be sacrificed to save the other innocent persons.[15] Yet this seems quite incompatible with justice. Of course, to the utilitarian, if the act is what promotes the good, then it is right, so it would be a misdescription to say that the utilitarian tells us to do what is wrong if that will maximize the good.[16]

Utilitarianism is also criticized for its demandingness. For example, it would seem that an agent's time would be better spent working for Oxfam as opposed to taking a vacation. Thus, taking the vacation is wrong. This issue has generated a good deal of anti-consequentialist sentiment. The problem, again, is with the *maximizing* or *optimizing* element of the theory. Given that x is good, it does, intuitively, seem plausible to hold that more of x is better than less. Indeed, that seems only rational.

Some utilitarians simply bite the bullet, Singer (1972) and Kagan (1989) being examples of those who hold that morality just *is* demanding. Wishing it weren't so doesn't make it so. Those searching for a justification for a suburban-style ethics are searching in vain.[17] It should be noted as well that this concern is related to a separate criticism, that utilitarianism makes morality *all-pervasive*. For example, how can eating an apple as opposed to an orange be a *moral* issue or choice? This sort of challenge is distinct from both the overriding and the demandingness issues.

(1984: 420). If we compare A and A+, A+ seems to be better even though the additional persons lower the average.

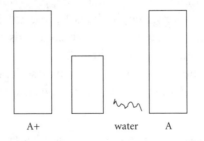

A+   water   A

This is just a part of his presentation of the mere addition paradox. For a discussion of the entire paradox and not merely this claim, see Parfit (1984: 420 ff.).

[15] This *type* of case was presented in Carritt (1947) and discussed by Rawls (1955), and in McCloskey's discussion of Rawls's article (1957).   [16] See also, for this point, Cummiskey (1996).

[17] A number of writers have argued that impartial ethics makes too many demands in viewing moral reasons as overriding (thus, this isn't simply a problem for utilitarianism). See e.g. Susan Wolf's excellent (1982) for more on this issue.

Many find the demandingness of utilitarianism problematic and try to offer alternative consequentialist views. For example, satisficers can avoid the problem by jettisoning the maximizing condition.[18] And, because satisficers can also be consequentialist, it seems mistaken to equate consequentialism with maximizing views. But the satisficing approach suffers from severe problems; namely, as noted above, it just seems irrational to prefer less good to more. The sorts of cases used to motivate the view can be readily explained as ones that are oversimplified. If ice cream is good, but more ice cream can sometimes be worse than less, then that shows that maximizing can't be right. But really all that shows is that maximizing ice cream can't be right. Ice cream is not a final good. And, as Philip Pettit points out, a consequentialist can motivate some 'satisficing' policies—ones that promote efficiency, for example. But 'unmotivated sub-optimizing' does seem quite irrational.[19]

One troubling aspect of demandingness is that the demand made on the individual in light of non-compliance by others—indeed, non-compliance by the vast majority of others—can be very weighty. It seems unjust that I should have to donate all of my assets to famine relief to help save starving people when it is also true that if everyone donated a bit of their income the starvation problem would be greatly alleviated. Why should my responsibility be greater simply because others fail to live up to theirs? Liam Murphy has suggested a 'collective principle of beneficence' that would avoid the problem by recommending that everyone do what is optimal of the options available, except in situations of non-compliance. That is, in situations of partial compliance 'a person's maximum level of required sacrifice is that which will reduce her level of expected well-being to the level it would be, all other aspects of her situation remaining the same, if there were to be full compliance from that point on'. This view, which presents a limited constraint on maximizing, clashes with our intuitions about rescue situations, as Murphy himself notes. If I can rescue more than one person, but my "fair share" given that others are present and also able to help is only one, it looks like Murphy says that I've fulfilled my obligation after the first rescue. But it seems counter-intuitive to say that I have lived up to my obligations, though I let people drown whom I could have easily saved (Murphy 2000: 117).[20]

This concern can be expanded upon by noting that utilitarians are committed to negative responsibility. That is, intuitively, one can be held responsible for what happens as a result of one's failure to act. Bernard Williams is the writer most associated with this criticism of utilitarianism. Negative responsibility becomes problematic, on his view, when another agent is in a position to affect the morality

---

[18] See Slote (1984) and Philip Pettit's response (1984).

[19] Again, see the discussion in Pettit (1984). See also Philip Pettit and Michael Smith's discussion of global versus local consequentialism in (2000).

[20] For critical discussion of this approach, see Mulgan (2001).

of one's actions. He asks us to imagine a scenario in which Jim, travelling through a remote village, comes across an evil dictator whose captain, Pedro, plans to execute twenty innocent villagers. Jim is offered the opportunity to kill one villager, in which case Pedro will spare the remaining nineteen. If, however, Jim refuses, all twenty will be executed. While it *may* be true that Jim is obligated to kill, Williams baulks at the view that if Jim fails to kill the one, he is thereby responsible for the death of the nineteen. True, Jim could have prevented their deaths, but the responsibility rests with Pedro. As problematic as this may seem, it is important to note that our intuitions in these sorts of cases seem to vary widely. Even something like changing the perspective from which the story is told has this effect. For example, one of the villagers whose life is at stake might well feel that Jim is responsible, at least in part. Indeed, we have these intuitions in structurally similar cases in which the agent is in a position to save a life by doing something that would normally be considered immoral, such as telling a lie. If an agent could save a life by telling a lie and does not do it, then it would seem appropriate to hold him responsible, at least in part.

Within consequentialism perhaps the most promising way to avoid the demandingness problem and related problems is to develop either an indirect form of the theory, such as rule consequentialism or motive consequentialism, or an objective view, such as that suggested by Railton.[21]

3.1 The Two-Levels View

R. M. Hare suggested one consequentialist approach that was intended to accommodate our intuitions about fairness as well as special obligations. Hare distinguishes two levels of moral thinking: the level of theory (or the critical level) and the level of actual practice (or the intuitive level). The intuitive level is the level of rules the agent follows, by and large; the critical level is the explicitly act utilitarian level. Which rules produce the best acts? They are those rules that are not too complicated or too hard to inculcate and teach. They guide us in our day-to-day practical decision-making, but they are by no means absolute. Instead, they function like overridable heuristics. There will be situations in which the agent must appeal to the critical level. For example, when selecting the principles to follow at the intuitive level—that is, the ones to inculcate and teach—we must try

---

[21] Rule consequentialism will be discussed in more detail in what follows, as will the objective approach. For another indirect approach, see Adams (1976). Philip Pettit and Michael Smith discuss local forms of consequentialism, motive utilitarianism being one example, and contrast this form with global consequentialism. Their view is that global consequentialism is superior in that it does not privilege any one evaluand (e.g. motives, rules, etc.) over another: if consequentialism offers a sound form of evaluation for one, why not the others? See Pettit and Smith (2000).

to operate at the critical level. Also, rules at the intuitive level may conflict, or an odd case may not be clearly covered by a rule, or there may be a situation in which there would be some massive loss of utility if the rule were followed, and so on. So, we must sometimes step back and think critically. Thinking at this level is to think as the ideal utilitarian would—the level of what Hare calls 'the Archangel'. The Archangel is not biased or prejudiced, and has full information and perfect reason. The truly right act is the one the Archangel would advise. However, in real life there are no archangels, so ordinary people must make do with the intuitive level, though, again, there will be circumstances in which it pays to try to adopt the critical level.

Hare argues, in a manoeuvre now fairly familiar to consequentialists, that efficiently acting at the intuitive level or efficient practical deliberation will involve the agent having the appropriate character and dispositions. These will be the dispositions, or virtues, that will enhance the agent's chances of acting optimifically. He makes this manoeuvre as a way of trying to avoid the self-defeating objection and the schizophrenia objection (described later).[22]

Hare holds that the cost of internalizing principles must be factored into overall efficiency considerations, and there are costs associated with violating rules that are effective when inculcated (at the intuitive level). Indirect versions of this theory such as rule utilitarianism also consider this factor.

3.2 Rule Consequentialism

One initially appealing strategy for dealing with the problems of fairness, demandingness, and conflicts with intuitions regarding justice is to argue that right action should be understood in terms of *rules* that maximize the good. Thus, the right action would be that action (among the alternatives) performed in accordance with the set of rules that maximizes utility. One could then argue that the utilitarian is *not* committed to the rightness of unjust acts. The reason why handing over an innocent person to a mob is wrong is because such an act conflicts with a rule that is part of a set of rules that maximize utility. Brandt (1979) nicely developed this alternative. However, the standard objection to this approach is that it is either guilty of absolutism, and thus shares familiar problems with Kant's ethics, or collapses into act utilitarianism.[23] More recently, Brad Hooker has developed an

---

[22] The latter is discussed by Michael Stocker (1976).

[23] David Lyons, for example, notes that though act and rule utilitarianism may be intensionally non-equivalent, expanding the content of the "rules" to avoid counter-intuitive absolutism will make them extensionally equivalent. Thus, for all practical purposes, rule utilitarianism collapses in act utilitarianism. See his discussion in Lyons (1965). See also J. J. C. Smart's discussion of the collapse problem in Smart and Williams (1973: 3–74).

alternative that he hopes will avoid these problems. On his view, a *wrong* action is defined in the following way:

An act is wrong if and only if it is forbidden by the code of rules whose internalization by the overwhelming majority of everyone everywhere in each new generation has maximum expected value in terms of well-being (with some priority for the worst off). The calculation of a code's expected value includes all costs of getting the code internalized. If in terms of expected value two or more codes are better than the rest but equal to one another, the one closest to conventional morality determines what acts are wrong. (Hooker 2000)

Hooker believes that his approach avoids the above-mentioned dilemma for rule consequentialism by building in internalization of the rules. The optimal system would not simply reduce to 'Maximize the good' for two reasons. First, it is too vague. Secondly, if persons came to believe that this was the one and only operative rule, they would lose confidence in the capacity of others not to steal, to keep their promises, and so forth. This system avoids rigidity with a 'prevent disaster' rule that will compete with the other rules and allow for some rules to be abandoned when there is a conflict with the directive to 'prevent disaster'.

   Of course, the act consequentialist need not deny rules a very significant place in morality. But those rules are rules of thumb that may be overridden by a consideration of consequences. The act utilitarian could argue that Hooker's escape clause of 'prevent disaster' simply performs basically the same overriding function. While this may make his account superior to a standard rule utilitarian view, it doesn't mark an improvement over act consequentialism.

3.3 Objective Consequentialism

In 'Alienation, Consequentialism, and the Demands of Morality' (Railton 1984) Peter Railton introduced a distinction between subjective and objective consequentialism:

Subjective consequentialism is the view that whenever one faces a choice of actions, one should attempt to determine which act of those available would most promote the good, and should then try to act accordingly . . . *Objective consequentialism* is the view that the criterion of the rightness of an act or course of action is whether it in fact would most promote the good of those acts available to the agent.

The subjective consequentialist holds that the moral agent must consciously try to maximize the good, whereas the objective consequentialist need not recommend a particular mode of decision-making since all that matters is actually getting it right, whatever decision procedure is used. Thus, if one opts for the objective formulation of the theory, one can solve a host of problems for the view. The theory is not weirdly self-defeating.[24] It allows the theory to bypass

---

[24] See Derek Parfit's presentation of this problem in Parfit (1984).

Michael Stocker's criticism, levelled against ethical theories more generally, that they are schizophrenic since the agent needn't be directly motivated by the value that itself justifies the motivation. Further, a variety of permissions and constraints can be justified on consequentialist grounds. That is, as Railton notes, it may well be permissible for a husband to spend money to see his wife who is away from home rather than send the money to Oxfam, because partial concern for one's spouse is something that promotes overall well-being. We want people, in general, to have such a partial concern because it is something that, given the facts of human psychology, makes for happier people. One gives an impartial justification for partial concern.[25] This also offers at least a partial solution to the demandingness problem. I needn't give all my assets to Oxfam if, incompatible with partial concern, that would have a negative impact on those 'near and dear'.

4. DEONTOLOGICAL ETHICS

Deontological approaches are standardly contrasted with consequentialist approaches in that the right is not defined in terms of the good. Instead, while consequences may or may not be *relevant* to a determination of rightness, consequences are not the sole determinant. Further, the deontologist will recognize certain "agent-relative" factors or elements as relevant to determinations of rightness. These features are often said to contrast with consequentialism, though I view this issue as irrelevant in marking the distinction since constraints and options can be given a consequentialist justification.[26] Thus, the range of theories covered by this category is quite broad: Kantian ethics, intuitionistic approaches, and contractarianism and contractualism. The natural law approach offers another alternative, and some writers—such as Bernard Gert, who develops a Hobbesian approach to morality—view themselves within this tradition.[27]

[25] Thus, the account I offer of consequentialism, and the account I believe is supported by Skorupski's discussion of agent-neutrality and consequentialism, is not *necessarily* incompatible with that offered by Michael Smith (2001: 174) when he writes that 'a distinctive mark of a consequentialist theory, as opposed to a non-consequentialist theory, is that it takes moral values to be neutral, as opposed to relative'. On the objective approach discussed here, agent-relative factors are justified by appeal to neutral reasons: these factors help to promote overall well-being.

[26] See Skorupski (1995).

[27] Gert views himself as advocating a natural law approach in which the moral rules are discovered by human reason in the sense that they are the rules all rational persons accept; See Gert (1998). For critical discussion of Gert's claims, see Audi and Sinnott-Armstrong (2002).

4.1 Kantian Ethics

While there is some debate about whether Kant truly counts as a deontologist, his work is generally classified as deontological since he holds that a person's duty or moral obligation is determined by adherence to a given principle that does not appeal for its justification to actual or expected consequences to be produced.[28] Kant's view is notoriously contrasted with consequentialism. Kant believed that the morally appropriate course of action must pass the test of the Categorical Imperative. There is in Kant's ethics the idea that the fundamental basis for moral duty is that there is some end that has *unconditional* value, and, for him, what has unconditional value is rational nature. Rational nature is an "end in itself". Rational beings are autonomous beings, ones free to choose actions and thus free to follow rules: their behaviour, unlike that of non-rational animals, is free and not determined by instinct or mere desire. Rational beings can follow the Categorical Imperative. Only rational beings can be moral agents, and, more controversially, only rational beings are the sorts of beings that can be *acted on* morally or immorally. A non-rational being, on Kant's view, deserves no moral respect.

The Categorical Imperative itself has several formulations, though the two most usually discussed are (1) the universalizability formulation, 'Act only according to that maxim by which you can at the same time will that it should become a universal law' (Kant 1969: 44), and (2) the principle of humanity, 'Act so that you treat humanity, whether in your own person or in that of another, always as an end and never as a means only' (Kant 1969: 54).

The Categorical Imperative is contrasted with hypothetical imperatives that specify what one ought to do given that one has certain goals. The binding force of the Categorical Imperative does not depend on the agent's goals or desires. Space precludes a detailed discussion of the fairly standard problems raised in connection with understanding the content of the formulations and applying them. However, significant questions arise in connection with formulation of the maxim tested against the Categorical Imperative. Is this an all-pervasive procedure— need I be constantly testing maxims to be sure my behaviour conforms to the Categorical Imperative? If so, Kantian ethics would in its own way be very demanding.

Barbara Herman argues that it isn't specific maxims that get tested against the Categorical Imperative; rather, it is "generic" maxims that, having met the demands

---

[28] For example, Barbara Herman is uncomfortable with this classification since it seems to hold that Kant's ethics does not have a firm grounding in value—a claim with which she strongly disagrees. However, she does agree that in some of the weaker senses of "deontological"—i.e. as simply being opposed to maximizing the good, or as being committed to the moral significance of certain distinctions independent of a consideration of consequences—Kant's theory is "deontological". See Herman (1993: 208–40).

of the Categorical Imperative, establish a presumption against a certain type of act (though this presumption can be defeated by some other consideration):

The idea is that we are to think of the CI [Categorical Imperative] procedure as applying not to actual maxims of action but to a type of action–justification pair: to do x-type action for y-type reason. I call these pairs 'generic maxims.' . . . The rejection of a generic maxim by the CI procedure shows that a certain kind of action may not be done for a certain kind of reason. This in effect establishes a principle of moral judgment that can set terms for moral deliberation. (Herman 1993: 147)

However, Kantian ethics, like utilitarianism, has come under attack from critics for its impartiality and oversimplification. Further, Kant's ethics—in contrast to virtue ethics, for example—seems cold and antiseptic. To Kant, the emotions have no intrinsic worth or moral significance in ethics, in deference to the role of reason and duty, whatever one's feelings. This line of attack has been pushed by writers such as Michael Stocker. Stocker (1976, 1990) presents the case of a person who is called upon to visit a sick friend in the hospital. On the Kantian view, it looks as though the morally appropriate motive for visiting one's friend would be duty, yet this seems to conflict with the ideal of friendship.

Marcia Baron, however, defends the Kantian approach here, noting that Kant's emphasis on the value of acting from duty should be seen as an acknowledgement or endorsement of the view that one's conduct should be regulated by a commitment to do what morality demands of one. She believes that the value of duty lies in its regulative role (Baron 1995: 118 ff.). It is misleading to interpret Kant as presenting an all-pervasive morality.

Virtue ethicists have also picked up on this feature of Kant's ethics, noting that Kant seems to put significance on strength of will as a primary virtue, whereas someone with a more Aristotelian view might argue for temperance.[29] Kant's unhappy agent, who must force himself to act well, contrasts with Aristotle's perfectly virtuous person, whose desires and moral beliefs are in harmony. Kant seems to hold that the continent person is a prime example of a morally good person. This feature of Kant's ethics has generated a large literature.[30] More recently, writers have been trying to argue that Kant and Aristotle are more similar on the topic of virtue than they might initially appear.[31] Intuitions in this regard may simply turn on how or what we are evaluating. For example, a common complaint against the Kantian view is that it seems to hold as a paradigm someone with unsavoury appetites who nevertheless manages to control them. The contrary intuition is: isn't it better, *pace* Aristotle, just not to have those appetites in the first place? But the question of who is the better person is distinct from the question of who has an important quality that we can admire: we may admire will-power while also valuing the people who have no need of it.

---

[29] Though not a virtue ethicist, Onora O'Neill covers this issue in O'Neill (1996).

[30] See e.g. Herman (1993: 1–22).   [31] See e.g. Korsgaard (1996).

Even more problematic is the seemingly absolutist quality of Kant's ethics. He notoriously holds lying to be immoral even for altruistic motives and for an excellent end, such as to save another's life. Christine Korsgaard, however, has argued (1986) that Kant's view would offer us a plausible way to deal with evil.

One telling contrast between Kant and the utilitarians on value can be encapsulated by their account of the status of animals. On a Kantian view, animals have no independent moral status whatsoever. On the classical utilitarian view they do, simply in virtue of being sentient—that is, in virtue of possessing the capacity for experiencing pleasure and pain. This is not to say that Kant believes that "anything goes" with respect to animals: if one is cruel to them, then one runs the risk of corruption. One may become more likely to engage in cruel acts against other persons.[32] Thus, we have an indirect duty to be kind to animals, since this will reinforce our duties to other persons. This instrumentalist rationale for kindness to animals, which, incidentally, looks rather consequentialist in form, strikes many as unsatisfactory. They regard cruelty to an animal as something morally problematic because it harms *the animal*, not simply because it may lead to further harms for human beings. Kant's justification seems to miss the point.

However, one significant theoretical advantage of the internalist strategy pursued by Kant is its strategy for avoiding moral luck problems. Writers such as Thomas Nagel and Bernard Williams have highlighted the problem. Nagel discusses the case of a truck driver who runs over a child, and who is blamed, contrasted with a case that is identical except for the fact that the truck driver, through good luck, happens not to run over anyone, and thus is not blamed. Luck is the only difference, yet our moral practice is such that we do seem to regard the first case as worse than the second. On a Kantian view, however, both truck drivers, if exhibiting negligence, are equally blameworthy because they both exhibit a bad will, though we may have difficulty *knowing* this, based on the evidence available to us. What actually happens, on Kant's view, is irrelevant. It is worth noting, however, that a subjective consequentialist would also share this "advantage" with the Kantian, or anyone else who took a purely internalist approach to moral evaluation.

4.2 Intuitionistic Approaches

Another body of deontological approaches tries to arrive at substantive principles on the basis of intuitive reactions to cases. There is no theoretical underpinning to these principles aside from the appeal to intuition.[33] One can be either a pluralist

[32] I discuss this issue more in Driver (1992).

[33] Of course, our intuitions about particular cases make up the basic data of ethical theory. However, most theories leave open the possibility that intuitions are mistaken, and that theory can provide the tools for evaluation of the intuitions themselves. The intuitionist approach does not appeal to an underlying theory.

or a monist with respect to this approach. The basic idea behind the former is that there may be a variety of factors that go into making an action right or wrong, and it is not possible to reduce these factors to a form that can be presented as a *single*, basic, principle of morality, or a comprehensive moral theory. Thus, no theory such as consequentialism or contractualism grounds the basic principles of morality. This makes the view extremely broad—a huge variety of principles have been articulated and defended by intuitionist deontologists. It will not be possible to cover all the variation here, but I will look at the most significant.[34]

One might be convinced by a kind of Rossian pluralism that there are a *variety* of different duties, the weight of which cannot be attributed to factors like production of consequences (Ross 1988). One category discussed by Ross and pursued by contemporary writers is that of our special obligations or duties. Indeed, the existence of these duties—i.e. duties to one's family and friends that seem more weighty than duties to strangers—has provided the fodder for much criticism of both utilitarian and Kantian ethics, which advocate impartiality. One needn't be a Rossian pluralist to see the force of these considerations. We do seem to owe more to the near and dear than to others.

Again, one can be a pluralist or a monist. However the intuitionism goes, though, the position is often understood in contrast to consequentialism, in terms of a commitment to some principle(s) with justificatory force independent of an exclusive consideration of consequences.

4.3 Doing and Allowing

Deontologists will frequently hold that one factor with intrinsic moral weight is *doing* harm to others. Doing harm is thought to be much worse than simply allowing harm, even though the effects of both may be completely the same. Further, against consequentialism, there will be situations in which it is wrong to harm someone even if that harm would result in greater good. Suppose that "greater good" could be achieved by killing one innocent person. For example, Alan is a wealthy miser whose wealth, were he to die before squandering it, would be distributed in such a way as to improve the lives of many other people. It would not be permissible, and certainly not obligatory, to kill Alan to ensure the timely redistribution of his assets.[35] Thus, deontological critics of utilitarianism will point to the fact that there must be an 'agent-centred

---

[34] It should also be noted that some of these principles have also, historically, been grounded in the natural law tradition, which holds very roughly that moral principles have an authority based on human nature, or what's natural for human beings. This, of course, doesn't distinguish the natural law approach completely. While it needn't have a religious basis, it often does. Indeed, the classical presentation of the approach is in Thomas Aquinas's *Summa Theologica*, where he holds that natural law is the "divine" law that is discoverable by human reason. However, more recent presentations of this approach can be found in John Finnis's work, particularly Finnis (1980). See also George (1993).

[35] This case is a modification of one presented in Kagan (1989).

constraint' (I will just use plain 'constraint') against harming in some circumstances.[36] Indeed, some writers characterize deontological approaches in contrast to consequentialist approaches in terms of this one factor. This is a mistake, since the objective consequentialist can argue for constraints on consequentialist grounds.[37] Further, because of the demandingness problem standardly levelled against consequentialism, many deontologists recognize a permission or an option to fail to maximize the good. One need not, for example, give the bulk of one's assets to charity. Such an action would be permitted and even supererogatory, but not required.

Some have noted that there is a morally significant distinction between doing harm and allowing harm. There are circumstances in which agents may permissibly allow harm, though they may not do it. We can refer to this as the doctrine of doing and allowing (DDA).

Philippa Foot has argued for a version of DDA, and against the doctrine of double effect (next section). Her view (Foot 1978) is that there is a morally significant distinction or difference between '(i) initiating or sustaining a harmful causal sequence' and '(ii) (a) allowing or enabling a harmful causal sequence to run its course (b) diverting a harmful causal sequence'.

So, for example, one would not be permitted to run one's car over one person even if doing so were necessary to get to five people in need of rescue. Killing (doing harm) is worse than letting die (allowing harm). Foot would like to offer an account that could accommodate our intuitions regarding two central cases, which were later expanded on by Judith Jarvis Thomson and together constitute 'the trolley problem'. To use Thomson's cases, consider the case of David, a great transplant surgeon, who could save the lives of five patients by sacrificing an innocent person—basically, by taking the life of one person and using his body parts to save the lives of the five. This seems clearly impermissible. But compare this scenario with the case of Edward, the driver of a trolley. The trolley's brakes have failed, and he sees ahead of him on the track five people who are unable to get off the track in time to avoid being hit by the trolley. However, Edward has enough time to turn the trolley onto another track, though, sadly, there is one person on that track who will also not be able to get off in time. Most think that it is morally permissible for Edward to turn the trolley onto the other track, even though that means he will be killing one to save the five. Thus, we have cases that seem to be structurally similar yet intuitively very dissimilar (Thomson 1976). For Foot there are negative and positive duties, negative duties being duties to avoid harm and positive ones being duties to provide aid. The former, she argues, are weightier than the latter. The trolley case differs from the transplant case (or similar cases) in that, in that case, two negative duties conflict; in the transplant case, in contrast, there is a negative duty in conflict with positive duties, and the negative duty trumps.

[36] See, in particular, Scheffler (2000).
[37] To use Kagan's terminology, one might be a deontologist at the factoral level in terms of recognizing constraints, but consequentialist at the foundational level.

Thomson modifies the trolley case by according the agency not to the trolley driver but to a bystander. She then argues that Foot's analysis can't handle the case, since the bystander would be killing one to save five. She contrasts this with the case of a fat man who is pushed onto the trolley tracks to keep it from killing the five. Clearly, she believes, the latter act is immoral; although it involves killing one to save five, it does so in a way that uses another person as a means to saving the five. What makes this action immoral is that the agent is doing something to a person in order to redistribute a threat: 'what matters in these cases in which a threat is to be distributed is whether the agent distributes it by doing something to it, or whether he distributes it by doing something to a person' (Thomson 1976: 16).

Warren Quinn is another example of a philosopher who has argued in favour of the distinction between doing and allowing, against consequentialism (Quinn 1993). Quinn uses several thought experiments to motivate the view that it may sometimes be permissible to allow a harm to befall another person, though not, under the same circumstances, actively to bring about that harm. Quinn's analysis hinges upon noting that there's a difference between positive and negative rights. Negative rights are the rights we have against being harmed by others; positive rights are the rights to actual aid from others. He agrees with Foot's view that negative rights are ones that are more difficult to override than positive ones, but explains this somewhat differently. He argues, against a consequentialist view, that negative rights are more important because respect for negative rights is crucial to our sense of self and moral autonomy:

A person is constituted by his body and mind. They are parts or aspects of him. For that very reason, it is fitting that he have primary say over what may be done to them—not because such an arrangement best promotes overall human welfare, but because any arrangement that denied him that say would be a grave indignity. . . . if your life is yours then there must be decisions concerning it that are yours to make—decisions protected by negative rights. (Quinn 1993: 309)

James Rachels, however, has attacked the distinction. He has noted (Rachels 1975) that we can come up with cases in which, holding everything constant but the killing versus letting die aspect, our intuitions are such that we do not hold the killing to be worse than the letting die. What seems to be at the basis of our intuitions about such cases has to do with the agent's intentions; malevolence is worse than indifference.

4.4 Intending Harm

Because of these and other problems, some have argued that the distinction between doing and allowing is not morally significant. Rather, the real distinction is between intending harm and merely foreseeing harm. The constraint, then, is best thought of as a constraint against intending to harm. The doctrine of double effect (DDE) captures this distinction. The DDE holds that it may sometimes be permissible to bring about a harm that is simply foreseen—as a side-effect of some action that is intended to bring about some good end—though it would be wrong to intend that harm as a means to the very same good end. Thus, there is a morally significant distinction between intention and foresight. The classic case summoned to motivate this doctrine is that of a bomber pilot during wartime who has no intention of killing innocent civilians when he drops a bomb on a military target, though he can certainly foresee that some innocent civilians will be killed as an unintended side-effect of the bombing. This may be perfectly permissible, given certain constraints. For example, the bad effect that is merely foreseen must not be out of proportion to the good effect that is intended, and the action itself must not be inherently wrong. However, it would not be permissible for the pilot intentionally to target innocent civilians.

But numerous problems arise. For example, it can prove difficult to maintain a sharp distinction between intention and foresight. To use a case from Alison McIntyre:

> suppose that I divert the trolley off a track with a rare wildflower about to bloom on it and onto a track with one track workman on it, because I judge that perpetuating a nearly extinct species is a more important goal. Would we say that the harm to the workman is a merely foreseen side effect of saving the wildflower, something wholly unintended? Or would it seem right to say that I intended that the harm fall on him, because I value preserving the flower more? (McIntyre 2001: 236)

McIntyre thinks that a wholesale rejection of intention–foresight would be mistaken. However, her view is that it is impossible to isolate just one way in which the intention–foresight distinction matters morally, and that the various attempts to do so in the literature simply lead to confusion.

As I mentioned earlier, a large number of deontological principles have been suggested as offering a way to navigate these sorts of cases. F. M. Kamm, for example, argues for the principle of permissible harm:

> The basic idea is that it is permissible for (i) greater good and (ii) means that have greater good as their noncausal flip side to cause lesser evil, but not permissible to (iii) intend lesser evil as a means to greater good or to (iv) intend means that cause lesser evil as a foreseen side effect and have greater good as a mere causal effect unmediated by (ii). By 'noncausal flip side,' I mean that the greater good occurring is, in essence, another way of describing the situation in which the means occur. (Kamm 2000: 213–14)

Kamm's idea is that this deontological principle can avoid certain problems. For example, it would sometimes permit harming some to help others: 'Suppose by directing gas into a room we can save five people. However, their breathing normally— the greater good—alters the air flow in the room, redirecting germs, killing an innocent person. In this case it is permissible to use the gas to save five people, because it is the greater good itself which causes the death' (2000: 214). The person who dies in this scenario is not being used as a means. Persons are inviolable on Kamm's approach.

Recently, these approaches have come under fire from moral psychologists co-opting work in psychology. For example, there is compelling evidence that moral intuitions in specific cases are heavily influenced by framing effects, and that various heuristics may have evolved to influence our decision-making by making it adaptive but might have little to offer in terms of reflecting some deep moral truth.[38] The trolley versus transplant cases help to illustrate this finding. Our intuitions about cases that are structurally similar are quite at odds. While there may be a way to resolve the conflict in this particular instance, numerous other cases can be concocted to show that our intuitions are often confused and inconsistent. Thus, simple reliance on intuitionistic responses to cases can be challenged.[39] Authors working within an explicitly theoretical framework have the resources at least to provide an error theory for some intuitions.

The methodology used has also been criticized. Shelly Kagan, for example, points out that the contrast strategy employed by these authors assumes a ubiquity thesis that seems unfounded. Instead of trying, intuitively, to isolate particular morally relevant factors, we are better off relying on foundational moral theory and putting our efforts into developing that alternative (Kagan 1988).[40] As the proposed deontological principles become ever more baroque in order to respond to cases, there is also the suspicion that the principles merely describe our intuitions and have no prescriptive force.

Thus, a variety of other authors find some theoretical approach, whether consequentialism, Kantian ethics, contractualism, or virtue ethics, to provide a more satisfactory systematic account of moral phenomena.

---

[38] Gilbert Harman, in discussing morality's conventionalism and the "intuitive" principle that harming is worse than not helping, writes that our intuitions have been shaped by social reality, that is, a kind of tacit understanding that the poor will not harm the wealthy in exchange for a weaker commitment to a norm of mutual benefit: 'The rich and powerful do not need much help and are often in the best position to give it; so, if a strong principle of mutual aid were adopted, they would gain little and lose a great deal . . . . On the other hand, the poor and weak might refuse to agree to a principle of noninterference or noninjury unless they also reached some agreement on mutual aid. We would therefore expect a compromise . . . . In the present case, the expected compromise would involve a strong principle of noninjury and a much weaker principle of mutual aid—which is just what we now have' (Harman 1977: 110–1).

[39] See also Tamara Horowitz's excellent (1998). Here Horowitz attacks Quinn's reliance on thought experiments alone to reveal moral norms, but the case she makes has broader implications. Her view is that prospect theory in psychology accounts for our intuitive distinction between doing and allowing, and that this distinction is, therefore, not morally significant. Prospect theory is developed by Daniel Kahneman and Amos Tversky (1979). Horowitz writes in her essay, 'I do not see why anyone would think the distinction is morally significant . . . If the distinction is not morally significant, then Quinn's thought experiments cannot play the role in his argument that he intends for them to play . . . . But to the extent that the intuitions elicited by Quinn's thought experiments are explained by prospect theory, they are not moral intuitions at all' (1998: 381). For responses to Horowitz, see Kamm (1998) and van Roojen (1999).   [40] For a response to Kagan, see Malm (1992).

4.5 Contractarian and Contractualist Ethics

These approaches could be considered deontological since they also treat the right as prior to the good. The contractarian approach has generally been concerned with issues in political philosophy, though some writers have felt that it could be extended more broadly to cover norms regulating individual and personal conduct as well. Fairly recently, a distinction has been drawn between contractarian and contractualist ethics.

The contractarian approach proceeds with the acknowledgement that normative ethics guides action in a social world. This purpose is achieved by acceptance on the part of rational persons within a given society of reasonable rules to guide action. Thus, the justification for the rules is a kind of contract or agreement between rational people. The contract is not based on the view that morality aims at a particular good, and thus is not teleological. This agreement is generally not regarded as "actual"; rather, the principles governing right action are those that would be agreed upon by rational self-interested persons through a process of negotiation. If the agreement needed to be historical fact and actual agreement, then it would not bind currently existing people: the obligations incurred by our ancestors are not ours. Thus, the contract is generally understood as "hypothetical"—what rational persons would agree to under certain circumstances. But the notion of a binding hypothetical contract has been attacked by Dworkin, who argues:

Suppose that I did not know the value of my painting on Monday; if you had offered me $100 for it then I would have accepted. On Tuesday I discovered it was valuable. You cannot argue that it would be fair for the courts to make me sell it to you for $100 on Wednesday. It may be my good fortune that you did not ask me on Monday, but that does not justify coercion against me later. (Dworkin 1977: 152)

One contractarian, David Gauthier (1986), follows Hobbes. Gauthier takes a central feature of morality to be the issue of *justified constraint*. Contractarianism gives an account of this feature in terms of what rational agents would agree to. The just moral constraints on behaviour are those that rational persons would agree to in recognition of the fact that they interact with other agents. Gauthier tries to bypass Dworkin's concern by noting that appealing to a contract is a way of providing a thought experiment that gets us to recognize what rationality demands.

For Gauthier, the bargainers are characterized as self-interested. Thus, the consent to abide by moral principles and the content of those principles is driven by self-interest. So for Gauthier the contract is a bargain in which each of the bargainers tries to negotiate the rules that best achieve his or her utility. However, he is willing to make a concession to solve the "compliance problem". To solve this problem he argues in favour of a principle of "minimax concession" (or "maximin relative bene-fit") according to which the rational bargainer will be concerned to minimize the maximum relative concessions she makes in the bargaining process.[41] The bargainer must perceive her concessions to be reasonable, and this is judged relative to what others are willing to give up or concede. She needs to perceive that she is optimizing the outcome for herself in such a way as to secure compliance from others. A major difficulty of this approach, however, is that in order to guarantee compliance after the contract is adopted, Gauthier argues that rational individuals will make a choice to be constrained maximizers of self-interest. He believes that they will choose to cultivate dispositions to keep their agreements, etc., and leave to one side self-interest in situations where they perceive that others are so acting. This can lead to situations in which the commitment to do what one says one will do can have apocalyptic results. Gauthier's most recent position tries to avoid this problem by holding that it is rational to act on a prior intention if and only if the expected outcome is as good as the expected outcome of not having formed that intention. But Joe Mintoff (1997) points out that while this formulation gets Gauthier out of the problem of apocalyptic retaliation strategies, it leaves him with other problems. Consider a variation on the famous toxin puzzle, presented by Gregory Kavka (1983). In this case, you are to imagine that an eccentric tycoon presents you with a vial of toxin and tells you that if you drink it you will not be caused permanent damage, but you will experience one day of intense illness. However, he also tells you that if at midnight tonight you form the intention to drink the toxin at eight tomorrow morning, he will pay you $1 million. You need not actually drink the toxin to get the money; you need only form the intention to do so. If you change your mind after forming the intention, you still get the money. It seems that on Gauthier's account it is rational for you to go ahead nevertheless and drink the toxin.[42]

Again, on the contractarian approach the right action will be specified according to rules of cooperation between reasonable persons. The spirit of the approach is to determine what rules would be in everyone's interests. Which principles bind us is a matter of agreement or contract. Theoretically, this would be a matter of negotiation.

And this is where contractarians and contractualists part company. One problem is that merely negotiated principles intuitively seem to have no binding moral force. Negotiation is not a legitimate basis for *moral* principles because those principles would then simply be arbitrary: Suppose it was agreed that the weakest members of a community be killed. Again, just intuitively, it seems that this can't be right; and, *even if* it were right, it's not right on the basis of an agreement. Contractualists do hold that moral principles are agreed upon, but they are inspired in making this claim by Kant's notion of equal respect between persons.

[41] See also his essays in Gauthier (1990), particularly 'Justice as a Social Choice' and 'Bargaining and Justice'.
[42] Mintoff points out a variety of other problems for Gauthier's account and then offers his own contractarian account of rational choice; see Mintoff (1997).

Principles agreed upon merely as the result of bargaining have no binding force. The legitimate principles are those that would be agreed to from the point of view of 'free and equal persons' operating under conditions of mutual respect. Rawls's methodology in *A Theory of Justice* embraces this Kantian approach. Though Rawls is limiting the scope of his work to justice, and is not offering a comprehensive theory of morality, one could see how the methodology could be employed to that end.[43] The correct principles of justice are those agreed upon by free and equal persons under conditions that ensure fairness of choice—that is, behind a "veil of ignorance" in what Rawls dubs the "original position" since it refers to the initial bargaining point. The agreement is hypothetical. He argues that rational agents will agree to two principles of justice under these conditions (Rawls 1971). The first principle is 'Each person is to have an equal right to the most extensive total system of equal basic liberties compatible with a similar system of liberty for all.' The second principle is more complicated, but basically holds that inequalities are to be arranged so that they are 'to the greatest benefit of the least advantaged . . . and . . . attached to offices and positions open to all under conditions of fair equality of opportunity'. Numerous criticisms have been made of this approach, in terms of both the methodology and the content of some of Rawls's assumptions.

One such criticism is that Rawls is not really offering a contractualist approach at all—that the method of reflective equilibrium is sufficient to generate the intuitions Rawls is counting on in support of his principles of justice. Recall Dworkin's criticism of the hypothetical contract as a basis for obligation. Because of this criticism Dworkin believes that Rawls's argument is best understood as simply drawing our attention to some other argument for the two principles of justice. Rawls seems to acknowledge this when he writes that his argument is one that seeks 'to draw solely upon basic intuitive ideas that are embedded in the political institutions of a constitutional democratic regime and the public traditions of their interpretation' (Rawls 1985: 225). Thus, we don't need a bargaining situation at all—just one rational individual reflecting on what would be reasonable.[44] But the notion that Rawls employs here also comes under attack. Rawls believes that the maximin principle is the rational principle to employ in the original position. Critics have noted that this is to assume that human beings are risk-averse, or that we ought to be risk-averse if we are rational (at least, in certain narrowly specified contexts).

One line of attack is to point out that the streamlined individual in Rawls's original position, behind the veil of ignorance, is no individual at all—disembodied and sexless.[45] This general line of attack is also developed by communitarian critics. For example, Michael Sandel (1982) argues that Rawls's conception of the self

---

[43] And, indeed, David Richards (1971) does this.   [44] See Sandel (1982).
[45] See Pateman (1988).

doesn't reflect the reality of how selves are formed by their goals, which are discovered by individuals within a shared community. Sandel writes: 'the Rawlsian self is not only a subject of possession, but an antecedently individuated subject, standing always at a certain distance from the interests it has. One consequence of this distance is to put the self beyond the reach of experience, to make it invulnerable, to fix its identity once and for all' (1982: 62).

This means, on Sandel's view, that Rawls's account rules out views of the self not committed to some 'antecedently individuated self'.

Be that as it may, Rawls's invocation of Kantian elements was responsible for generating a novel approach within this tradition—one currently labelled contractualism.

Central to some articulations of contractualism is the view that agents are accountable to others. Thus, these principles must be ones that can be justified to others. They must be ones that others could not reasonably reject. As Scanlon puts it: 'An act is wrong if its performance under the circumstances would be disallowed by any system of rules for the general regulation of behavior which no one could reasonably reject as a basis for informed, unforced, general agreement' (Scanlon 1982: 153).

And, later (1998): 'an act is wrong if it would be disallowed by any *principle* that no one could reasonably reject'. Note that on this view, as opposed to the consequentialist view, well-being is not given a central role (Scanlon 1998: 215 ff.). It is not the case that well-being is irrelevant—of course consideration of well-being will figure into the reasonable rejection of principles—it is just that well-being is not foundational to this account in the way it is to consequentialism. This avoids problems, Scanlon maintains, that a consequentialist will have through privileging well-being over other significant factors.

While the contractualist approach avoids a serious intuitive difficulty associated with the contractarian approach, they both share the view that agreement is crucial to determining moral principles and rules, and, thus, to giving an account of right action. This overall approach is hampered by an inclusion problem. Some writers have pointed out that contractarianism–contractualism has a general problem with including the vulnerable. Persons who are not in a position to negotiate or engage in rational reflection because they lack the requisite capacities are left out.[46] This problem applies to animals as well. Scanlon tries to address this problem by distinguishing broad and narrow conceptions of morality: contractualism is only a narrow conception that deals specifically with the norms governing interactions between rational beings. This is the relevant scope of his account. Animals fall outside that scope, but that is not to say they have no moral standing whatsoever. However, that would require a different argument. Scanlon's theory is at best incomplete. The problem that most critics focus on is its redundancy. The basic

---

[46] See Kittay (1999).

idea is that the appeal that Scanlon makes to what no one could 'reasonably reject' makes his account redundant, since we might just as well make direct reference to the grounds of reasonable rejection for our criterion or criteria for wrongness.[47] Thus, the appeal to what would be reasonably rejected does no work. In the end, we have a direct appeal to moral value that actually does the work.

These approaches have also been the target of many attacks from feminist philosophers and virtue ethicists, since the inclusion problem has historically been associated with the exclusion of women, for example, from the agreement. Of course, exclusion of groups of persons could not be endorsed by the theory: any contractualist is committed to including all rational persons. This may be more of a problem for the contractarian, since there seems to be no principled way for arguing that the scope of the agreement *must* include all persons.[48] Importing a moral notion of fairness would be to acknowledge such norms independently of the agreement itself.

Still, in recent years one sees many feminist writers moving away from wholesale criticism of contractarian ethics, and, indeed, embracing a variety of contractarianism that is more amenable to feminist concerns. For example, Susan Moller Okin extends the Rawlsian project to include the family as a social institution. Okin revises the procedure in the original position by advocating a kind of empathic regard on the part of the agents in the original bargaining position: 'Rawls' theory of justice is itself centrally dependent upon the capacity of moral persons to be concerned about and to demonstrate care for others, especially others who are most different from themselves' (Okin 1989: 247). Jean Hampton (1993) offers a defence of the contractarian approach, arguing one can be a feminist and a contractarian: justice is a value that operates between friends and family members, as well as members of civil society. Contractarian ethics can speak to these concerns, even if the tradition might seem to have left them out.

5. VIRTUE ETHICS

Anscombe inspired widespread disaffection with standard ethical theories with her very influential article 'Modern Moral Philosophy' (1981). There she argued that abstract normative concepts such as "ought" or "moral obligation" make no sense outside a legislative context. Thus, given the absence of God in most accounts of

---

[47] See e.g. Pettit (1993, 1999); McGinn (1999). For a defence of Scanlon against this type of criticism, see Ridge (2001).

[48] For more on this problem for Gauthier's contractarianism, see Morris (1991).

what we morally ought to do, she holds that modern moral philosophy should just give it up and instead look to psychology for guidance. There should be greater focus on moral psychology and the virtues. Taking this seriously, many philosophers have come to favour a virtue-ethical approach to moral evaluation. After some disagreement about how exactly to define "virtue ethics", the field seems to have centred on the following claim: virtue ethics treats virtue evaluation as the "primary" mode of evaluation; thus, any account of right action that is virtue-ethical needs to define right action in terms of virtue (otherwise, the account of virtue is derivative of the account of right action).

Several writers have attempted to do this, most notably Rosalind Hursthouse and Michael Slote. Hursthouse defines "right action" in the following way:

An action is right iff it is what a virtuous agent would, characteristically, do in the circumstances, except for tragic dilemmas, in which a decision is right iff it is what such an agent would decide, but the action decided upon may be too terrible to be called 'right' or 'good.' (And a tragic dilemma is one from which a virtuous agent cannot emerge with her life unmarred.) (Hursthouse 1999: 79)

Leaving aside the issue of tragic dilemmas, the idea that Hursthouse is appealing to is that we use the virtuous agent as an exemplar of sorts.[49] However, her procedure is underdescribed in that it is not clear what circumstances we should consider in applying it. For example, suppose that Bill knows that he buckles under pressure— he is less than virtuous. He then finds himself in a situation in which some people in a burning building need help, and he is in a position to help them. The "virtuous" person would run into the burning building (assuming that the objective risk to the person is small). But Bill knows that once inside the building, confronted with flames and smoke, he would freeze and be unable to help. Should he then run into the burning building? If Hursthouse's procedure leads to an affirmative response, it is mistaken.[50] But if we are to build in imperfections, and ask what a person who was not virtuous would do, then the account appears incoherent.

Hursthouse's approach is neo-Aristotelian. Michael Slote has recently developed an account with Humean roots—one that advocates a form of sentimentalism.

Slote's account is distinctive in that it is a pure form of evaluational externalism. On Slote's view, the moral quality of an action depends on the agent's motives in that it must be an expression of the agent's virtuous motives. Thus, the standard of "rightness" will be a purely internal one. What is brought about by the action is irrelevant. Slote has a problem, which he is aware of, in that such an account can be charged with moral autism, or being too insular and self-absorbed. He counters this by claiming that a person who has a good motivational structure will care

---

[49] For a more detailed discussion of this condition in Hursthouse's account, see Driver (forthcoming).

[50] I have adapted this case from some of the cases one sees in the literature on actualism, which is a view that holds that the agent ought to consider what he will actually do in determining what he ought to do. For more on this issue, see Jackson and Pargetter (1986).

about what happens in the world; thus, the good agent is not entirely cut off from what actually happens. This manoeuvre has some success; however, it leaves open the possibility of a person performing a right action and exemplifying virtuous motivation, even though what he does is always a disaster. Such a moral klutz would nevertheless be acting rightly as long as he cared about others and tried to make his actions effective in the proper way. Actual failure to make his actions effective in this way does not affect the rightness of those actions, on Slote's account. The advantage of such an internal approach is that it provides great insulation against moral luck. As with Kant, what matters to the moral quality of what you do is your internal psychological states. What happens in the world is subject to all kinds of luck factors over which the agent ultimately has no control. And without control, there can be no responsibility. That being said, this approach seems problematic in that many persons, even those who are not consequentialists, will hold that consequences matter morally—it is just that they may not be the only thing that matters. Slote abandons this.

An additional worry has to do with how one can spell out what "expresses" a virtue without circularity. Slote has to argue that the right action is an expression of virtue and not simply caused by the virtue. This is because there may be particular occasions on which a benevolent person fails to actually act benevolently (Slote 2001: 17). So, the act must express the benevolence of the person in order to be the right act. Slote also needs to add this condition to rule out cases of neutral actions that might be caused by benevolent motives: it may be that benevolent persons eat red apples instead of green ones, but this doesn't count since eating a red apple is not an expression of benevolence. However, this puts a real burden on Slote to explain what exactly is meant by "expresses" benevolence. If he does this by noting that these actions must be benevolent ones, the circularity worry comes up.[51]

Another worry with internalist approaches in general is that, although they score points for insulating agents against moral luck, they also seem to cut the agent off from the world. Hursthouse's brand of virtue ethics avoids this problem since the virtues, while characterized by certain psychological states of the agent, must also somehow contribute to human flourishing, and in her case she ties the flourishing to that of the virtuous agent. Evidence for this, she thinks, is that parents tend to educate their children to be virtuous. And, presumably, parents are very concerned with the well-being of their children. Thus, there is some evidence that we hold the virtues to contribute to individual flourishing. Some will find Hursthouse's approach a bit more intuitively plausible in this regard than Slote's, though in my opinion Hursthouse's approach still has the problem of placing too many psychological requirements on virtue. Though she softens this requirement in her account, her account would still rule out what I have elsewhere (Driver 2001, ch. 2)

---

[51] I make this point in Driver (2003).

called 'the virtues of ignorance'—traits like modesty that seem, at least in some cases, to involve actual ignorance on the part of the virtuous agent.

6. FEMINIST ETHICS

Another strand has been inspired by the work of Carol Gilligan. Her book *In a Different Voice* (1982) raised the issue of gender differences in moral thinking. By attacking Lawrence Kohlberg's account of moral development in children, Gilligan pointed to the possibility of significant gender differences in ethical thought. This led, or fed into, at any rate, the challenge to "justice" or "rule"-based systems of morality. Female experience was said to be more particularistic, caring, and nurturing, commensurate with the sort of experiences most females have and the norms that tend to govern their relationships with others. Nel Noddings (1984) developed an "ethics of care" approach that incorporated these particularistic insights and portrayed the "justice" approach as rigid and cold, neglecting the emotional. Indeed, this has been a hallmark of early feminist ethics—the claim that a very masculine sense of "reason" and "rationality" has dominated ethical evaluation, at the expense and even denigration of emotion. The 'ethics of care' approach has developed its own following, particularly in health care ethics. Again, there is a connection to work being done in virtue ethics. Michael Slote views his virtue-ethical approach as one that develops an ethics of care that is responsive to many of the criticisms of standard ethics raised by feminist philosophers.

However, as Samantha Brennan has pointed out (1999), feminist ethics has come a long way from its early roots. Indeed, both Gilligan's work and Nel Noddings's development of the ethics of care have come under increasing critical scrutiny among feminist philosophers. For example, Alison Jaggar (1991) has suggested that, though the care approach has been an important development, particularly because of its criticism of the standard theories, it is also flawed because it is too narrow an approach to ethics. Elizabeth Spelman (1991) has pointed to the dangers of simply focusing on a contrast between "feminine" care and "masculine" justice, when the reality is more complex.[52]

Additionally, earlier feminist philosophers had suggested a radical approach to ethical theory. Since traditional ethical theory, and, it was thought, associated

---

[52] On Spelman's view, too much focus on the care perspective can lead people to ignore the various ways in which women have mistreated each other, and the significance of that to doing feminist moral theory.

concepts such as "rights", were skewed by only accounting for male experience, such concepts should be jettisoned. This claim is reminiscent of the sort of eliminativism one saw in virtue ethics, although the reasons for it are different. However, this eliminativism has been rejected by other feminist ethicists who, instead, try to develop feminist accounts of "rights" and "responsibilities". Rather than attacking the concepts themselves, they focus their attack on non-feminist understandings of the concepts, which are taken to be defective because of their individualism and their failure to incorporate relational factors. The challenge to this relational approach, however, is to avoid extreme relativism. While some would embrace relativism, many would not, since it would undercut the revisionist aspirations of many feminist ethical theorists. The relational approach seems inconsistent with the view that certain practices elsewhere are just plain wrong—practices that involve the subjection of women and other vulnerable groups. This is a serious problem for an approach motivated by a desire to see reforms implemented that would contribute to the equality and well-being of women. Along these lines, Alison Jaggar writes:

Against the relativist tendency in feminist ethics should be set feminism's concern that its moral critique of the practices (and theory) of the larger society—and perhaps even the practices (and theory) of other societies—should be objectively justified. Feminist ethics recognizes that we inhabit a painfully prefeminist world and takes itself to be contributing to the transformation of this world into one in which the basic moral commitments of feminism have become universally accepted. (Jaggar 1991: 94–5)

Feminist conceptions of moral theory cover a very wide range of different views with varying theoretical commitments. They are joined, however, in the belief that standard ethical theories have undervalued women's experience and concerns.

7. CONCLUSION

Normative ethical theory has undergone a transformation in the last generation. Challenges have been made to normative ethical theory—particularly to the commitment to impartiality and the view that there is a single moral principle sufficient to guide action. Greater focus on relationships, virtues, and less abstract issues has transformed the development of the major theories. Consequentialism, in particular, has shown great resilience in meeting the challenges posed by critics who are concerned about placing excessive weight on impartiality and oversimplification. However, a future challenge remains. Research in psychology may yield explanations for some of our intuitions that reveal *explanations* that call into question the justifying force of intuition. To the extent that all the theories we have considered here have, to some degree, felt compelled to conform to common-sense intuitions, they may be mistaken. It may well be that normative ethical theory should embrace reformist goals.

REFERENCES

Adams, Robert (1976). 'Motive Utilitarianism'. *Journal of Philosophy*, 73: 467–81.

Anscombe, G. E. M. (1981). 'Modern Moral Philosophy', in *The Collected Papers of G. E. M. Anscombe: Ethics, Religion and Politics*. Minneapolis: University of Minnesota Press.

Audi, Robert, and Sinnott-Armstrong, Walter (eds.) (2002). *Rationality, Rules, and Ideals*. Lanham, Md.: Rowman & Littlefield.

Bales, Eugene (1971). 'Act-Utilitarianism: Account of Right-Making Characteristics or Decision-Making Procedure?' *American Philosophical Quarterly*, 8: 257–65.

Baron, Marcia (1995). *Kantian Ethics Almost Without Apology*. Ithaca, NY: Cornell University Press.

Bentham, Jeremy (1823). *Introduction to the Principles of Morals and Legislation*. London: W. Pickering.

Brandt, Richard (1979). *A Theory of the Good and the Right*. Oxford: Clarendon Press.

Brennan, Samantha (1999). 'Recent Work in Feminist Ethics'. *Ethics*, 109: 858–93.

Brink, David (1989). *Moral Realism and the Foundations of Ethics*. Cambridge: Cambridge University Press.

Broome, John (1991). *Weighing Goods*. Oxford: Blackwell.

Carritt, E. F. (1947). *Ethical and Political Thinking*. Oxford: Clarendon Press.

Cummiskey, David (1996). *Kantian Consequentialism*. New York: Oxford University Press.

Dreier, James (ed.) (forthcoming). *Contemporary Debates Ethical Theory*. Malden, Mass.: Blackwell.

Driver, Julia (1992). 'Caesar's Wife: On the Moral Significance of Appearing Good'. *Journal of Philosophy*, 89: 331–43.

—— (2001). *Uneasy Virtue*. New York: Cambridge University Press.

—— (2003). Review of Michael Slote, *Morals from Motives*. *Journal of Ethics*, 7: 233–7.

—— (forthcoming). 'Virtue Theory', in James Dreier (ed.), *Contemporary Debates in Ethical Theory*. Malden, Mass.: Blackwell.

Dworkin, Ronald (1977). *Taking Rights Seriously*. Cambridge, Mass.: Harvard University Press.

Feldman, Fred (1997). *Utilitarianism, Hedonism, and Desert: Essays in Moral Philosophy*. Cambridge: Cambridge University Press.

Finnis, John (1980). *Natural Law and Natural Rights*. Oxford: Clarendon Press.

Foot, Philippa (1978). 'The Problem of Abortion and the Doctrine of Double Effect', in Foot, *Virtues and Vices and Other Essays*. Berkeley: University of California Press.

Gauthier, David (1986). *Morals by Agreement*. New York: Clarendon Press.

—— (1990). *Moral Dealing*. Ithaca, NY: Cornell University Press.

George, Robert (1993). *Making Men Moral*. Oxford: Clarendon Press.

Gert, Bernard (1998). *Morality*. New York: Oxford University Press.

Gilligan, Carol (1982). *In a Different Voice*. Cambridge, Mass.: Harvard University Press.

Hampton, Jean (1993). 'Feminist Contractarianism', in Louise Antony and Charlotte Witt (eds.), *A Mind of One's Own*. Boulder, Colo.: Westview Press.

Harman, Gilbert (1977). *The Nature of Morality*. New York: Oxford University Press.

Herman, Barbara (1993). *The Practice of Moral Judgment*. Cambridge, Mass.: Harvard University Press.

Hooker, Brad (2000). *Ideal Code, Real World: A Rule-Consequentialist Theory of Morality*. Oxford: Oxford University Press.

Horowitz, Tamara (1998). 'Philosophical Intuitions and Psychological Theory'. *Ethics*, 108: 367–85.

Hurka, Thomas (1993). *Perfectionism*. New York: Oxford University Press.

Hursthouse, Rosalind (1999). *On Virtue Ethics*. New York: Oxford University Press.

Jackson, Frank, and Pargetter, Robert (1986). 'Oughts, Options, and Actualism'. *Philosophical Review*, 95: 233–55.

Jaggar, Alison (1991). 'Feminist Ethics: Projects, Problems, Prospects', in Claudia Card (ed.), *Feminist Ethics*. Lawrence: University Press of Kansas.

Kagan, Shelley (1988). 'The Additive Fallacy'. *Ethics*, 99: 5–31.

—— (1989). *The Limits of Morality*. New York: Oxford University Press.

—— (1998). *Normative Ethics*. Boulder, Colo: Westview Press.

Kahneman, Daniel, and Tversky, Amos (1979). 'Prospect Theory: An Analysis of Decision Under Risk'. *Econometrica*, 47: 263–91.

Kamm, Frances (1998). 'Moral Intuitions, Cognitive Psychology, and the Harming-versus-Not-Aiding Distinction'. *Ethics*, 108: 463–88.

—— (2000). 'Nonconsequentialism', in *The Blackwell Guide to Ethical Theory*. Malden, Mass.: Blackwell.

Kant, Immanuel (1969). *Foundations of the Metaphysics of Morals*, trans. Lewis White Beck, with critical essays ed. Robert Paul Wolff. New York: Macmillan.

Kavka, Gregory (1983). 'The Toxin Puzzle'. *Analysis*, 43: 33–6.

Kittay, Eva (1999). *Love's Labor: Essays on Women, Equality, and Dependency*. London: Routledge.

Korsgaard, Christine (1983). 'Two Distinctions in Goodness'. *Philosophical Review*, 2: 169–95.

—— (1986). 'The Right to Lie: Kant on Dealing with Evil'. *Philosophy and Public Affairs*, 15: 325–49.

—— (1996). 'From Duty and for the Sake of the Noble: Kant and Aristotle on the Morally Good Action', in Stephen Engstrom and Jennifer Whiting (eds.), *Aristotle, Kant, and the Stoics*. Cambridge: Cambridge University Press.

Lockhart, Ted (2000). *Moral Uncertainty and its Consequences*. New York: Oxford University Press.

Lyons, David (1965). *The Forms and Limits of Utilitarianism*. Oxford: Oxford University Press.

McCloskey, H. J. (1957). ' "Two Concepts of Rules"—a Note'. *Philosophical Review*, 66: 466–85.

McGinn, Colin (1999). 'Reasons and Unreasons'. *New Republic*, 220: 34–8.

McIntyre, Alison (2001). 'Doing Away with Double Effect'. *Ethics*, 111: 219–55.

Malm, Heidi (1992). 'In Defense of the Contrast Strategy', in John Martin Fischer and Mark Ravizza (eds.), *Ethics: Problems and Principles*. Fort Worth, Tex.: Harcourt, Brace, Jovanovich.

Mintoff, Joe (1997). 'Rational Cooperation, Intention, and Reconsideration'. *Ethics*, 107: 612–43.

Moore, G. E. (1988). *Principia Ethica*. Amherst, NY: Prometheus Books.

Morris, Christopher (1991). 'Moral Standing and Rational-Choice Contractarianism', in Peter Vallentyne (ed.), *Contractarianism and Rational Choice*. New York: Cambridge University Press.

Mulgan, Tim (2001). *The Demands of Consequentialism*. Oxford: Clarendon Press.

Murphy, Liam (2000). *Moral Demands in Nonideal Theory*. New York: Oxford University Press.

Nagel, Thomas (1979). 'The Fragmentation of Value', in Nagel, *Mortal Questions*. New York: Cambridge University Press.

Noddings, Nel (1984). *Care: A Feminine Approach to Ethics and Moral Education*. Berkeley: University of California Press.

Nozick, Robert (1974). *Anarchy, State and Utopia*. New York: Basic Books.

Okin, Susan (1989). *Justice, Gender, and the Family*. New York: Basic Books.

O'Neill, Onora (1996). 'Kant's Virtues', in Roger Crisp (ed.), *How Should One Live?* Oxford: Clarendon Press.

Parfit, Derek (1984). *Reasons and Persons*. Oxford: Clarendon Press.

Pateman, Carole (1988). *The Sexual Contract*. Stanford, Calif.: Stanford University Press.

Pettit, Philip (1984). 'Satisficing Consequentialism', p. II. *Proceedings of the Aristotelian Society*, suppl. vol., 58: 165–76.

—— (1993). *The Common Mind*. New York: Oxford University Press.

—— (1997). 'The Consequentialist Perspective', in Marcia Baron, Philip Pettit, and Michael Slote, *Three Methods of Ethics: A Debate*. Malden, Mass.: Blackwell.

—— (1999). 'Doing Unto Others'. *Times Literary Supplement* (25 June), 7–8.

—— and Smith, Michael (2000). 'Global Consequentialism', in Brad Hooker, Elinor Mason, and Dale E. Miller (eds.), *Morality, Rules, and Consequences*. Lanham, Md.: Rowman & Littlefield.

Quinn, Warren (1993). 'Actions, Intentions, and Consequences: The Doctrine of Doing and Allowing', in Quinn, *Morality and Action*. Cambridge: Cambridge University Press.

Rachels, James (1975). 'Active and Passive Euthanasia'. *New England Journal of Medicine*, 292: 78–80.

Railton, Peter (1984). 'Alienation, Consequentialism, and the Demands of Morality'. *Philosophy and Public Affairs*, 13/2: 134–71. Repr. in Samuel Scheffler (ed.), *Consequentialism and its Critics*. Oxford: Oxford University Press, 1988.

—— (1989). 'Naturalism and Prescriptivity'. *Social Philosophy and Policy*, 7: 151–74.

Rawls, John (1955). 'Two Concepts of Rules'. *Philosophical Review*, 64: 3–13.

—— (1971). *A Theory of Justice*. Cambridge, Mass.: Belknap Press.

—— (1985). 'Justice as Fairness: Political not Metaphysical'. *Philosophy and Public Affairs*, 14: 223–51.

Richards, David (1971). *A Theory of Reasons for Action*. Oxford: Clarendon Press.

Ridge, Michael (2001). 'Saving Scanlon: Contractualism and Agent-Relativity'. *Journal of Political Philosophy*, 9: 472–81.

Ross, W. D. (1988). *The Right and the Good*. Indianapolis: Hackett.

Sandel, Michael (1982). *Liberalism and the Limits of Justice*. Cambridge: Cambridge University Press.

Scanlon, Thomas (1982). 'Contractualism and Utilitarianism', in Amartya Sen and Bernard Williams (eds.), *Utilitarianism and Beyond*. Cambridge: Cambridge University Press.

—— (1998). *What we Owe to Each Other*. Cambridge, Mass.: Harvard University Press.

Scheffler, Samuel (2000). *The Rejection of Consequentialism*. Oxford: Clarendon Press.

Singer, Peter (1972). 'Famine, Affluence, and Morality'. *Philosophy and Public Affairs*, 1: 229–43.

Sinnott-Armstrong, Walter (1988). *Moral Dilemmas*. Oxford: Blackwell.

Skorupski, John (1995). 'Agent-Neutrality, Consequentialism, Utilitarianism . . . A Terminological Note'. *Utilitas*, 7: 49–54.

Slote, Michael (1984). 'Satisficing Consequentialism', p. I. *Proceedings of the Aristotelian Society*, suppl. vol., 58: 139–63.

—— (2001). *Morals from Motives*. Oxford: Oxford University Press.

Smart, J. J. C., and Williams, Bernard (1973). *Utilitarianism: For and Against*. Cambridge: Cambridge University Press.

Smith, Michael (2001). 'Immodest Consequentialism and Character'. *Utilitas*, 13: 173–94.

Spelman, Elizabeth (1991). 'The Virtue of Feeling and the Feeling of Virtue', in Claudia Card (ed.), *Feminist Ethics*. Lawrence: University Press of Kansas.

Stocker, Michael (1976). 'The Schizophrenia of Modern Ethical Theories'. *Journal of Philosophy*, 73: 453–66.

—— (1990). 'Friendship and Duty: Some Difficult Relations', in Owen Flanagan and Amélie Oksenberg Rorty (eds.), *Identity, Character, and Morality: Essays in Moral Philosophy*. Cambridge, Mass.: MIT Press.

Thomson, Judith Jarvis (1976). 'Killing, Letting Die, and the Trolley Problem'. *The Monist*, 59: 204–17.

van Roojen, Mark (1999). 'Reflective Moral Equilibrium and Psychological Theory'. *Ethics*, 109: 846–57.

Watson, Gary (1998). 'Some Considerations in Favor of Contractualism', in Watson, *Rational Commitment and Morality*. Cambridge: Cambridge University Press.

Wolf, Susan (1982). 'Moral Saints'. *Journal of Philosophy*, 79: 419–39.

CHAPTER 3

MORAL EPISTEMOLOGY

KAREN JONES

1. INTRODUCTION

Meta-ethics comprises three branches: semantics, metaphysics, and epistemology. However, while epistemological concerns drive much of contemporary meta-ethical theorizing, epistemology tends to receive less explicit attention than semantics and metaphysics.[1] In part, this might be because of an assumption that only moral realists need provide us with an epistemology, for only if we suppose that there are moral properties and facts that are appropriately independent of our moral beliefs and attitudes will we need to tell a story about how we can come to know them.[2] Irrealist accounts might be thought to face considerably reduced epistemological burdens, or to escape them altogether. For example, non-cognitivism is typically taken to be a sceptical meta-ethical position that denies the possibility of moral

---

[1] For example, several of the most significant recent works in meta-ethics offer little explicit discussion of epistemological issues; see Gibbard (1990); Smith (1994); Blackburn (1998). An exception is Timmons (1999). Timmons's book is widely reviewed; however, these reviews focus exclusively on the semantics and metaphysics and overlook the epistemology (see Dreier 2002).

[2] For definitions of realism and irrealism, see Timmons (1999: 16).

knowledge.[3] Moral discourse, not being fact-stating, is not answerable to epistemic norms. Blackburn (1996: 82), however, denies this. The same moves that the non-cognitivist makes to accommodate the assertoric surface form of moral discourse enable the non-cognitivist to talk of truth (though not, of course, of correspondence truth). Once we can talk of moral truth, we can talk of moral knowledge and wonder whether we have it (Blackburn 1996: 86).

It turns out that the relationship between the three branches of meta-ethics is complex and mediated by broader philosophical assumptions, such as assumptions about the correct theory of truth. Moreover, some accounts of moral epistemology are compatible with a variety of different semantic and metaphysical positions, others are tailored to fit specific metaphysical pictures.[4] A full exploration of these interconnections is beyond the scope of this chapter, which focuses on epistemology; however, in Section 3 below I will say something about rival non-epistemological approaches to the question of theory acceptance in ethics.

General epistemology and philosophy of science has long recognized the importance of social factors—both contextual and institutional—in transmitting and justifying belief. I will argue that the best prospect for developing available positions in moral epistemology lies in paying greater attention to the sociality of moral knowledge. Thus, moral epistemology ought to be moving towards a more social epistemology. Social epistemology is not an epistemological theory as such, but rather a research project characterized by a commitment to understanding the role of social relations and institutions in the production of knowledge. Social epistemology is a normative and not merely a descriptive project inasmuch as it aims to evaluate and not merely describe our epistemic practices. It is this commitment to normative assessment and prescription that makes social epistemology distinct from the sociology of knowledge. Central questions in social epistemology include the justification of testimony, the role of epistemic divisions of labour and norms for cognitive authority, the role of social interests in inquiry, and the role of socially available background beliefs in justification. These questions can be addressed within a variety of epistemological frameworks. However, within moral epistemology, coherentist and contextualist accounts of justification are better equipped to recognize the role of social factors in the production of moral knowledge than are neo-intuitionist accounts, whether generalist or particularist.

---

[3] It is routine for non-cognitivism to be taxonomized as a species of scepticism; see e.g. Sayre-McCord (1996).

[4] For example, see Dreier (2002) for the claim that Timmons's contextualism is independent of his metaphysics and semantics; coherentist approaches have likewise been adopted by realists and constructivists about moral properties. Particularist versions of intuitionism, such as those advocated by McDowell and Dancy (discussed in Sect. 4 below), are, however, only plausible given certain assumptions about the nature of moral properties.

2. The Case for Asymmetrical Scepticism

All claims to empirical knowledge are vulnerable to challenge by global sceptical hypotheses: if we cannot rule out the possibility that we are being deceived by an evil demon or are brains in a vat, and if the principle of closure holds, then everyday claims to knowledge are undermined.

Global sceptical hypotheses can be used to motivate scepticism regarding claims to moral knowledge, but the most interesting forms of moral scepticism are local rather than global and are motivated by apparent disanalogies between ethics and paradigm kinds of inquiry, such as scientific inquiry, that common sense identifies as generating knowledge. The putative disanalogies that motivate scepticism about ethics without supporting general scepticism include the following:

1. Moral discourse, while having surface assertoric form, appears to have non-assertoric function: we use it to condemn and to praise, to recommend, require, and proscribe. Thus, moral discourse is action-guiding in a way that the fact-stating discourses of science and common sense are not (Ayer 1946; Hare 1952). There is, it might seem, a conceptual connection between sincerely accepting a moral proposition and being disposed to act.[5]

2. In ethics there appears to be persistent, rationally unresolvable disagreement. While disagreement itself does not rule out moral knowledge, rationally unresolvable disagreement does: if there is a fact of the matter under dispute, and if it is possible to come to know it, then, in the long run, one would expect inquirers to converge in their belief. In the sciences, where disagreement is present, there is good explanation for it and reason to suppose that convergence will eventually be reached. Mackie (1977: 36), for example, suggests that disagreement in science results from 'speculative inferences or explanatory hypotheses based on inadequate evidence'. Such explanations appear unavailable in ethics, where disagreement 'seems to reflect people's adherence to and participation in different ways of life' (Mackie 1977: 36).

3. An inference to the best explanation requires that we posit unobservable scientific entities to explain our scientific observations and beliefs. There is no similar inference to the best explanation requiring that we posit moral facts to explain what Harman (1977: 6) calls our moral observations; that is, our 'immediate judgement made in response to the situation without any conscious reasoning having taken place'. Putative explanations that appeal to moral facts to explain moral observations can be replaced, without loss of explanatory power, by explanations that refer exclusively to non-moral facts and facts about the observer's moral sensibility. The

---

[5] Positions that assert some such conceptual connection are labelled 'internalist'. For a discussion of a variety of different internalist theses, see Brink (1989, ch. 3) and Smith (1994, ch. 3).

concern that moral facts do not explain moral 'observations' is the epistemic face of a more general problem: moral properties might be thought to be explanatorily impotent and so fail a widely accepted test for reality. According to the explanatory test for reality, we need posit only such properties and entities as pull their weight in our best causal-explanatory theories of the world.[6]

4. Moral theorizing is typically taken to use the method of wide reflective equilibrium, a method which begins from a set of considered moral judgements, both particular and general, and seeks to bring these into coherence with each other and with other relevant beliefs, including but not limited to beliefs about psychology, sociology, economics, and biology. The coherence relation sought is richer than mere consistency and includes relations of explanation and justification, as when, for example, a general moral principle is shown to systematize a number of particular moral judgements. This method, it might be claimed, has no analogue in the methods used in the empirical sciences. Moreover, showing our moral beliefs are in reflective equilibrium, even *wide* reflective equilibrium, will do nothing to show that they are true or even likely to be true—unless, that is, we are constructivists about moral facts and suppose them to be just whatever emerges from the proper use of the method itself. If we are not constructivists, wide reflective equilibrium is a garbage-in/garbage-out method and cannot in itself confer justification on the beliefs that result from it. Thus wide reflective equilibrium might be thought to be both distinct from and *inferior to* the methods we use in paradigm forms of knowledge-seeking inquiry.[7]

5. Scepticism about moral knowledge can be motivated by an induction on the past history of claims to moral knowledge and of the ideological function of those claims in reinforcing relations of dominance and subordination—whether of class, race, or gender. This source of scepticism is not much discussed in the philosophical literature, though it has a long philosophical pedigree, from Thrasymachus (Plato 1974), to Marx (Miller 1984), to contemporary feminists (Redstockings Collective 1970: 601). It is, I suspect, the source of much ordinary scepticism about moral knowledge.

Points 2–5 combine to generate what seems to be a powerful argument for asymmetrical scepticism regarding scientific or common-sense claims to knowledge and claims to moral knowledge. If our moral sensibilities are all that is needed to explain our moral judgements and if those sensibilities are themselves to be explained by features of our upbringing, bringing those beliefs into reflective equilibrium will do nothing to bring them into contact with the world. Worse yet, if the features of our upbringing that explain our sensibilities are themselves to be explained by the ideological needs of prevailing social and economic relations, morality is revealed to be a sham. Thus the induction argument is a final turn of

---

[6] McDowell (1985) contains a critical discussion of the explanatory test.

[7] For a clear statement of this objection, to which my formulation is indebted, see Boyd (1988); these issues are first raised in Dworkin (1973).

the screw that simultaneously supports scepticism about moral knowledge and scepticism about our practical allegiance to morality.

Rejoinders to the argument for asymmetrical scepticism can be divided into two camps. Theorists in the first camp offer a 'straight' answer; that is, they reject each of the alleged sources of asymmetry between moral and scientific or common-sense claims to knowledge. Moral discourse is fact-stating, disagreement is neither more nor less rationally resolvable in science than in ethics, moral properties are explanatorily potent and sometimes explain our moral observations, the method of wide reflective equilibrium just is the method used in science, and, though vulnerable to ideological distortion, some claims to moral knowledge survive reflective scrutiny. Cornell-style moral realists exemplify this approach and are discussed in Section 5 below.

The second camp houses a more diverse group of theorists who reject the argument's sceptical conclusion while accepting that ethics is disanalogous to science in significant respects. Neo-intuitionists, whether generalist or particularist, fall into this group and are discussed in Section 4 below, as does Timmons, whose contextualism is discussed in Section 6. Following Darwall, Gibbard, and Railton's (1992) terminology, we can label theorists who offer a straight answer 'continuity theorists' since they stress the continuity between ethics and science. Those who accept one or more significant disanalogies between ethics and science count as discontinuity theorists. However, not all discontinuity theorists give an epistemic answer to the question of what justifies or underwrites our ethical beliefs; moreover, there are two quite different questions which we might want a theory of moral epistemology to answer (and they may receive different answers). Thus, before surveying the three current main contenders for a theory of moral epistemology, we need to get clearer about the question or questions that we might be asking and about the range of strategies available for answering them.

3. Theory Acceptance and Justified Belief

The central question in moral epistemology is the question of whether and if so under what conditions our moral beliefs are justified. There are, however, two quite different things that we might have in mind when we ask whether a belief is justified. Intuitively, these can be distinguished by noting the difference between 'when moral beliefs are justified and when people are justified in believing them' (Sinnott-Armstrong 1996: 37). More technically, the distinction is marked as the difference between doxastic justification and propositional justification (Timmons 1999: 179).[8] Doxastic justification concerns the justification of an individual's beliefs; that is, it applies to belief tokens. Propositional justification, in contrast, applies to belief types: a belief is propositionally justified on the basis of a body of evidence, argument, or the like, just in case that body of evidence or argument provides support for the propositional content of the belief (Timmons 1999: 179–80; Kvanvig 1992: 65).

Timmons (1999: 181) argues that certain common, though contestable, assumptions about the relationship between doxastic and propositional justification together with a picture of the structure of justification in ethics leads to the supposition that doxastic justification requires the agent to have propositional justification for a moral theory. Suppose that particular moral propositions are justified by being shown to be derivable from the general moral principles that constitute a moral theory. Suppose, further, that for a person to be justified in holding a particular moral belief, she must have propositional justification for the content of that belief (and believe it for the reasons that justify it). Then it will follow that to be justified in believing a particular moral proposition, an agent must accept a moral theory. But her acceptance of that theory must itself be justified, which, by the assumption that doxastic justification requires propositional justification, will require that she be propositionally justified in accepting that theory (and believe it for the reasons that justify it). The fundamental question in moral epistemology becomes the question of theory acceptance in ethics.

In areas of inquiry that readily acknowledge the sociality of knowledge, there is no temptation to conflate the question of theory acceptance and the question of the doxastic justification of belief. Lay persons are justified in believing scientific propositions on the basis of expert say-so. Experts might have to come to their beliefs the hard way through following appropriate methods governing theory acceptance, but a division of cognitive labour lets the lay person's belief be justified provided it meets norms for the testimonial transmission of belief, whatever we suppose them to be.[9]

Whether or not we accept Timmons's explanation for why meta-ethics projects tend to focus on the question of theory acceptance, it is unquestionably true both that this has been the focus and that the questions of theory acceptance and of justified belief are conceptually distinct and may require different kinds of answers. Indeed, an examination of some of the answers that have been offered by discontinuity theorists to the question of theory acceptance in ethics quickly reveals that our choices for strategies to address the question of theory acceptance are not limited

[8] Copp (1991) prefers the labels 'subjective justification' and 'objective justification', but these labels are already in multiple use.

[9] Daniels draws the analogy between his defence of the method of wide reflective equilibrium and accounts of theory acceptance offered by philosophers of science. He explicitly disavows any intention of speaking to the question of the conditions under which an individual is justified in believing a moral proposition (Daniels 1979: 257).

to the epistemic. Following Copp (1991: 217) we can distinguish between those approaches that attempt to show that we have reason to believe a moral theory to be true and those that attempt to show the rationality of accepting a theory, where such arguments might appeal to constraints inherent in practical reasoning (Gewirth 1978), to rational choice considerations (K. Baier 1958; Gauthier 1986), or to purposes assumed to be inescapable (Copp 1995). The former approaches are epistemic and take the question of theory acceptance to have the same basic structure in ethics and in science: both are to be addressed using the resources of theoretical rationality. The latter are practical reasoning theories and take as fundamental the notion of a reason for action rather than a reason for belief.[10]

If we construe moral epistemology very broadly, so that any answer to the question of what justifies acceptance of a moral theory counts as a moral epistemology, we risk not noticing the fundamental difference between epistemic and practical rationality approaches to this question. On the other hand, if we construe moral epistemology quite narrowly, as being only, or chiefly, about the conditions under which an individual's moral beliefs are justified, we risk overlooking epistemic answers to the question of theory acceptance; and, in particular, risk not fully appreciating the scope of coherentist moral epistemologies, which can be, and are, offered as an answer to both questions (Section 5).

There are additional reasons for wanting to keep separate the questions of theory acceptance and doxastic justification: if we conflate them and require that agents be justified in accepting a moral theory before they count as justified in their particular moral judgements, our epistemic standards for justified belief risk being very demanding (Timmons 1999: 182). Intuitionists, who are also generalists, offer their epistemology as an account both of theory acceptance in ethics and of when an individual's moral beliefs are justified, but they may escape a charge of over-demandingness since on their view we can have non-inferential justification for some moral beliefs (Section 4).[11] Particularist intuitionists reject the picture of the structure of justification in ethics that sees the justification of particular judgements as resting on subsuming them under general moral principles. We can have non-inferential knowledge of particular moral propositions (Section 4). Contextualism (Section 6) is offered exclusively as an account of when an individual is justified in believing a moral proposition.

Related to the objection that conflating the question of theory acceptance and justification of belief risks making the conditions for justified belief over-demanding, yet distinct from it, is the concern that if we overlook this distinction we build into our moral epistemology an assumption of cognitive individualism. The cognitive individualist is suspicious of all claims of cognitive authority, assigning to each

---

[10] For an excellent discussion of the general features of practical reasoning theories and a comprehensive survey of examples, see Darwall *et al.* (1992).

[11] Timmons (1999: 233) accuses Audi of developing an overly demanding version of intuitionism. See Sect. 6 for an argument that Timmons's own account is insufficiently demanding.

person the responsibility to examine the evidence in favour of a claim and to make up his or her own mind about it: testimony is ruled out as a possible source of justified moral belief. Perhaps there are good reasons for ruling out testimony as a source of justified *moral* belief, but it would take arguments to show this and it should not be merely assumed on account of failing to distinguish the epistemology of theory acceptance and the epistemology of belief in the domain of the moral.[12]

4. INTUITIONISM

After a period of being so out of fashion that Mackie (1977: 38) felt he could assert that 'it is easy to point out its implausibilities', intuitionism is undergoing a revival. Intuitionism as an epistemological position should be distinguished from intuitionism as a methodological doctrine (Williams 1995: 182). Because of the influence of Rawls (1971), the term 'intuitionism' has come to name the substantive moral position that there is a plurality of basic moral principles and no procedure for ranking them, as well as to name the epistemological position that some moral beliefs are immediately or non-inferentially justified.[13] Some pluralists such as Ross (1930) are also epistemological intuitionists, but it is important to keep the methodological and epistemological theses distinct, since either can be held independently of the other.

It is generally accepted that intuitionism in ethics is motivated by foundationalism together with a claim about the autonomy of ethics and the desire to avoid moral scepticism (Frazier 1998; Sinnott-Armstrong 1992; Sturgeon 2002: 190–1).[14] The argument begins with the familiar problem of the regress of justification. Inferential justification is *conditional*: If S believes that-p on the basis of an inference from q, then S is justified in believing that-p only if S is justified in believing that-q and the inference is legitimate. If the justification for q is itself inference-based, then a regress threatens. The foundationalist solves the regress problem by

---

[12] See Jones (1999) for a defence of testimony as a source of moral knowledge.

[13] Brink (1989: 116) assumes that intuitionists are committed to the existence of *self*-justifying beliefs; this, claims Brink, is tantamount to allowing the limit case of circular justification. However, this is an uncharitable reading of the intuitionist position, and not a definition of it, though it remains to be established whether the intuitionist can tell a plausible story about how such non-inferential justification is possible.

[14] A qualification is needed here: particularist variants of intuitionism, such as those advocated by Dancy (1993), McDowell (1985), and McNaughton (1988), seem to be motivated by rejecting the principlist picture of the structure of justification in ethics (Sect. 3) and by analogies with perception rather than by foundationalism.

positing non-inferentially justified beliefs (basic beliefs) that serve to anchor the chains of justification. The autonomy of ethics thesis claims that no moral proposition can be derived from a set of purely non-moral propositions; thus, the chain of inferential justification cannot be anchored entirely outside the domain of the ethical. Hence, either no moral beliefs are justified, or some must be non-inferentially justified.

The core claim of intuitionism—that some moral beliefs are non-inferentially justified—can be developed along different axes into distinct varieties of intuitionism depending on, among other things, the generality of the propositions belief in which it is claimed to be justified without inference (are they about high-level principles, mid-level principles, such as prima facie duties, or particular moral facts?), and the nature of the capacity for intuition (is it a rational capacity, analogous with the capacity for mathematical intuition, or is it more analogous with a perceptual capacity?). Two very different forms of intuitionism, diverging at both these junctures, claim recent attention. Audi offers a reworking of Ross's rationalist intuitionism, which focuses on the possibility of non-inferential knowledge of prima facie duties and is thus a version of generalist intuitionism.[15] Audi's work is influential because it strips intuitionism of accretions once assumed to be core components of the view. The result is a leaner and more plausible intuitionism that is better able to respond to objections. The second variant of intuitionism claims that we can have non-inferential justification for particular moral beliefs on account of having a kind of perceptual access to moral reality, an access made possible by our moral sensibilities.[16] This version of intuitionism is motivated by particularism or the thesis that moral properties are shapeless with respect to descriptive properties (Little 2000: 279). The particularist claims that whether a given consideration, such as 'it would be fun', is morally relevant, and if it is relevant what valence it has—whether it counts in favour or against a course of action or state of affairs—can depend on the other considerations that are present in the situation: 'the behavior of a reason . . . in a new case cannot be predicted from its behaviour elsewhere' (Dancy 1993: 60). Ethical perception is a matter of seeing the salience of considerations in a given context.

In what follows, I will focus on Audi's generalist intuitionism, which, though able to escape many of the familiar objections to intuitionism, has problems providing

---

[15] Audi's explication and defence of a Rossian notion of self-evidence is part of a broader project that includes defending the possibility of non-inferential knowledge of particular moral facts. However, I focus on Audi's re-evaluation of Ross, since this has been the most influential part of his project and has stimulated re-evaluations of other major intuitionists; see Stratton-Lake (2002).

[16] Some authors identify intuitionism with a specific view about the nature of our intuitive capacities; namely, that they are rational, rather than perceptual or affective (Stratton-Lake 2002: 7; Darwall 2002: 252–3). These authors thus deny that moral sense theorists and sensibility theorists, such as McDowell, are intuitionists. While this difference is of great significance, it seems to me that the shared core claim of non-inferential justification is sufficiently distinctive to provide the basis for grouping these positions together. In so doing, I side with Williams (1995).

a plausible theory of error. This is the most serious problem for particularist versions of intuitionism as well. The objections first.

Intuitionism has been variously charged with (1) requiring the existence of some mysterious faculty of moral intuition (Mackie 1977: 38); (2) promoting dogmatism (Nowell-Smith 1954: 46); (3) being inadequate to the phenomenology of moral deliberation (Mackie 1977: 38); (4) being unable to account for disagreement; (5) lacking a plausible theory of error (Gaut 2002: 144).[17]

The core move in Audi's lean intuitionism consists in providing an account of self-evidence that (i) makes plain the distinction between believing a proposition that is self-evident and believing of a proposition that it is self-evident; (ii) distinguishes between propositions that are immediately self-evident and propositions that are mediately self-evident; and (iii) recognizes epistemic overdetermination. Audi thinks it plausible that Rossian prima facie duties satisfy this account of self-evidence. According to Audi (1996: 114):

A self-evident proposition is (roughly) a truth such that the understanding of it is (a) sufficient for one's being justified in believing it (i.e., for having justification for believing it, whether one in fact believes it or not)—this is why such a truth is evident *in itself*—and (b) sufficient for knowing the proposition provided one believes it on the *basis* of understanding it.

One can fail to believe propositions that are self-evident since they need not be *obvious*, and might be graspable only on the basis of considerable reflection. Thus there can be disagreement about which propositions are self-evident, and propositions that someone takes to be self-evident need not be so. Moreover, nothing in the account of self-evidence rules out possessing inferential justification for propositions that are self-evident and believing them on inferential grounds as well as or instead of on the basis of reflection.

It is plain how the view that emerges addresses objections 1–4: the capacity for reflection is hardly mysterious; we should be fallibilists about our judgements of self-evidence; given it takes reflection to grasp a self-evident proposition, arriving at a moral judgement, even one that is claimed to be the object of intuition rather than inference, might require hard reflective work and is not something that we can achieve 'by just sitting down and having an ethical intuition' (Mackie 1977: 38). If the objection from disagreement is merely the complaint that disagreement should not be so much as possible according to an intuitionism that appeals to self-evidence, then it is answered by the distinction between immediate and mediately self-evident propositions. If, however, the objection from disagreement is that the intuitionist has no means of rational persuasion in the face of disagreement that survives all best attempts at reflection, then it is answered by recognizing the possibility of epistemic overdetermination: we might be able to convince someone of the truth of a self-evident proposition by offering an argument for that proposition.

---

[17] For a discussion of objections 1–2 and 4, see Stratton-Lake (2002: 1–28).

This answer, however, pushes the work of rational resolution from intuition to inference. If someone thinks long and hard about a moral proposition yet fails to see its putative self-evidence though persuaded of its truth, we are forced to attribute to them a failure properly to grasp the proposition in question even though they seem to meet all normal standards for adequate grasp of the proposition. If someone thinks long and hard about a proposition and remains unpersuaded of its truth by argument, then again we must say that they have failed to grasp the proposition. This diagnosis of the failure looks implausible on two counts: first, it seems implausible to say that those who fail to see the truth or the putative self-evidence of the proposition fail properly to grasp it; secondly, we have been offered no explanation as to why they should have failed to grasp it, while others apparently no better situated are able to do so. Thus, the outstanding problem for the intuitionist is to come up with a credible explanation for error (Gaut 2002: 144). Coherentism has more resources, at least, for offering such explanations since the coherentist can appeal to inferential failures and divergence in background beliefs (though how contentious these explanations are will become apparent in Section 5).

5. REALIST COHERENTISM

Coherentism in epistemology offers an alternative to foundationalist conceptions of the structure of justification; in particular it offers an alternative solution to the problem of the regress of justification. Recall that the foundationalist claims that the regress is stopped in a set of beliefs that are non-inferentially justified. A coherentist denies that there are any non-inferentially justified beliefs: all justification is inferential. In the standard coherentist account, regress is stopped by chains of justification looping back on themselves, but the circularity is not vicious, claims the coherentist, because a set of beliefs that is consistent and that has rich explanatory and justificatory relations among its members is mutually supporting.[18] According to coherentism, justification admits of degrees: S's belief that-p is fully justified when it is part of a maximally coherent set of beliefs and S's belief that-p is at least partly explained by the fact of p's so cohering (a basing requirement).

Coherentism in ethics can be motivated either by a global commitment to a coherentist epistemology, or by the observation that moral inquiry, whether philosophical or common-sense, takes the form of a search for reflective equilibrium.

---

[18] For a rival coherentist account, see Sayre-McCord (1996), who argues that the coherentist can allow that merely permissibly justified beliefs can provide positive support for other beliefs.

While it is possible to hold that the method of reflective equilibrium provides us with a useful heuristic for achieving moral beliefs that are justified without supposing that they are justified in virtue of satisfying the method, coherentism is typically thought to gain support from the philosophical and common-sense use of reflective equilibrium.[19]

Within moral epistemology, the chief defenders of coherentism are also advocates of a naturalist, non-reductive, version of moral realism. It is prima facie puzzling, however, why someone who supposes that there are moral properties and facts that are independent of our moral beliefs and attitudes would suppose that our moral beliefs are justified to the extent that they are in reflective equilibrium. How can such a presupposition-rich method be a method for coming to know about judgement-independent moral facts?

According to Brink, the trick to reconciling a coherence theory of justification with realism is to note that among the beliefs that we seek to bring into coherence—and that we *must* seek to bring into coherence if we are to have a comprehensive and explanatory belief system—are second-order beliefs, or beliefs about our beliefs and the reliability of the mechanisms that produced them. Those second-order beliefs lend justificatory support to first-order beliefs and are in turn supported by first-order beliefs and by other second-order beliefs. In this way, we come to form a picture of ourselves as inquirers and come to understand how it is that we can reliably detect certain features of the world (Brink 1989: 127). According to the realist coherentist, moral facts and properties are among those features of the world that we can reliably detect.

Coherentism in moral epistemology, like coherentism regarding ordinary empirical belief, faces an input objection: unless we have some reason to suppose that there is input from the world in generating a sufficient number of our beliefs, there will be no reason to suppose that seeking coherence among our beliefs will be truth-conducive. While justified beliefs might be false, it seems that any adequate account of justification must show how satisfying the conditions it identifies as constitutive of justification would be truth-conducive.[20] The garbage-in/garbage-out objection to the method of wide reflective equilibrium just is the input objection in its moral guise.

Recall that wide reflective equilibrium begins from a set of considered moral judgements that result from subjecting our moral judgements to an initial filtering.

[19] Sayre-McCord (1996) distinguishes between heuristic, practical, and epistemic uses of the method of reflective equilibrium. An error theorist about morality who denies that any of our moral beliefs are justified yet recognizes the need for us to continue with morality as a social practice will defend the method of wide reflective equilibrium on non-justificatory grounds. Being heirs to conflicting moral traditions we must seek coherence among our beliefs if we are to have an action-guiding moral practice. Such a practice serves a useful social function and therefore we need the method of reflective equilibrium. Thanks to Charles Pigden for discussion on this point.

[20] See Brink (1989: 106) and Timmons (1999: 202–4) for a discussion of truth-guaranteeing versus truth-conducive accounts of justification and a defence of the weaker truth-conduciveness requirement.

The input objection in moral epistemology targets the use of these considered moral judgements. An adequate answer to the input objection must do two things: (i) provide a plausible account of the filters that are needed in the move from initial moral judgements to considered moral judgements; (ii) give us reason to accord defeasible 'epistemic standing' (Darwall *et al.* 1992) to our considered moral judgements. It is important to see why the epistemic standing accorded to considered moral judgements need only be defeasible. The method of wide reflective equilibrium, though conceptually describable as a two-stage process, is dialectical rather than static: considered moral judgements can be revised in the light of the deeper theoretical understanding that emerges as the result of the use of the method; this deeper theoretical understanding can also lead to revisions in our conception of the filters needed in the move from initial to considered moral judgements.

Brink (1989: 132) recognizes the need to address the filtering problem, and offers the following as a solution:

To begin with, moral beliefs formed under conditions generally conducive to the formation of true belief will be more reliable than moral beliefs not formed under these conditions. A belief that is based on available (nonmoral) evidence and is thus well informed, that results from good inference patterns, that is not distorted by obvious forms of prejudice or self-interest, that is held with some confidence, that is relatively stable over time is formed under conditions conducive to truth...A yet more reliable class of moral beliefs is picked out by the addition of certain morally motivated conditions...The conditions for membership in the class of reliable moral beliefs can be morally motivated so long as that motivation has general plausibility, not peculiar to one the competitors [i.e. competitor theories under investigation].

Brink suggests that impartiality is just such a non-controversial additional constraint to add in selecting the inputs into wide reflective equilibrium. But it is not at all clear what is meant by impartiality and, on any more substantive reading than that 'like cases be treated alike' (Herman 1991: 776), impartiality is contested as a characterization of the moral point of view; some feminists, for example, argue that a commitment to impartiality is an expression of a typically male trajectory of moral development (Gilligan 1982). In a similar vein, Walker (1996: 267) charges that the use of 'our' considered judgements obscures the question of just whose these judgements are, masks the social location of the moral inquirer, and allows the moral theorist to claim an unearned authority. Concerns can also be raised about filtering 'obvious forms of prejudice'—charges of bias tend to stick most readily against those with passionate non-mainstream political agendas and thus 'prejudice' as a filtering device is readily co-opted for ideological purposes (Antony 2002). Other lists of filtering devices are similarly inadequate: Rawls, for example, suggests 'calmness', but sometimes indignation improves moral judgement and calmness shows we have not appreciated the morally significant features of a situation (Daniels 1979: 258).

An answer to the filtering problem must, on the one hand, avoid appeal to ethically substantive constraints that are contested by currently live competitor theories and, on the other hand, add filters additional to those provided by the common-sense understanding of good *general* doxastic practice, for without such additional filters the sanctioned start-up sets will potentially be very diverse, thus threatening convergence and raising doubts about the truth-conduciveness of the method. Coherentism has the resources for a richer answer to the filtering problem, but marshalling them requires closer attention to the role of social factors in the production of moral belief and in the distribution of moral credibility, as well as closer attention to the empirical study of the cognitive and affective capacities that support moral competence.

The coherentist should add such filters as are recommended by the anthropological, historical, psychological, and sociological study of moral belief. Sociology and history reveal the ideological function of many moral claims: we filter our input sets by subjecting them to ideology critique and by examining the plausibility of possible Nietzschean genealogies of those beliefs. Feminist scepticism about moral claims often takes the form of ideology critique and offers genealogies that simultaneously explain and debunk common moral beliefs. Ideology critique needs to be seen as a *fundamental* part of moral epistemology. As commonly practised, especially within applied ethics, the method of reflective equilibrium tends to be insensitive to ideology critique. However, there is no reason in principle why it should overlook the role of the social location of the moral inquirer in shaping his or her beliefs and every reason to think it is *only* by paying attention to such factors that the coherentist will be able to identify a rich and plausible set of filtering devices.

This suggestion regarding how to strengthen filters on the inputs into wide reflective equilibrium makes the selection of filters theory-dependent: we use history, sociology, and psychology, and, *crucially*, we also presuppose that we have some moral knowledge. We make judgements about which social or psychological mechanisms are distorting and which are not, on the basis of assumptions about which changes in moral judgement are improvements and which are not. For example, it is only on the assumption of the moral equality of men and women that we can see and filter the distorting influence of patriarchal assumptions on moral judgement. Similarly for the distorting influence of class on conceptions of human rights that construe those rights in merely negative terms. The selection of filtering mechanisms is necessarily dependent on moral presuppositions; as our substantive moral beliefs change, so too does our conception of good filtering devices.

Once we recognize that any conception of good filtering devices embeds substantive background moral beliefs, we can see that it will be no trivial matter to carry out the second stage of an adequate response to the input objection. We might have thought that, having given a plausible answer to the filtering problem and so defended the devices used in the move from initial judgements to considered judgements, we would have *thereby* defended according defeasible epistemic standing to our considered moral judgements. They are, after all, just those judgements that result from filtering according to our best conception of the conditions for the reliable formation of moral beliefs. But if that conception itself relies on moral beliefs, it seems we must have already assumed that some moral beliefs have epistemic standing, and this is so even if we allow that our conception of good filtering devices and our best moral theories exert ongoing dialectical pressure on each other.

The obvious move for the realist coherentist is to claim that all inquiry is presupposition-laden. We have no choice but to use such presupposition-laden methods of inquiry, whether in ethics or in science. If the theory-dependence of method supports scepticism, then we cannot be asymmetrical sceptics, but must be sceptics about science as well. Boyd argues that scientific method is theory-dependent in at least the following ways: in the construction of scientific instruments used in experimentation, in deciding which artefacts should be controlled for in good experimental design, and in the selection of the rival hypothesis to test a theory against. The puzzle of how such theory-dependent methods can yield knowledge of a belief-independent world is solved if we suppose that the background theories embedded in our methodology are sufficiently approximately true in *relevant* respects. If we start from reliable enough initial theories, then we will be able to use theory-dependent methods to generate more theoretical knowledge. That know-ledge then becomes embodied in new experimental design and practice (Boyd 1983, 1988). In the same way, having some true moral beliefs will enable a roughly ade-quate conception of filtering devices, which will improve the input into wide reflect-ive equilibrium, which will improve our moral understanding, which will in turn improve our conception of filtering devices, and so on.[21] Boyd (1988: 206–9) claims that the method of wide reflective equilibrium just is the method used in science.

Sturgeon's (1985) rejoinder to Harman's objection that moral facts and properties are not needed to explain our moral observations has a similar dialectical structure: if we are allowed to assume that we have some approximately true moral beliefs, we can construct perfectly good explanations for our moral beliefs (including our so-called moral observations) that appeal to moral properties and facts. If we are not allowed to assume any background beliefs in constructing and assessing such explanations, then neither should we be allowed to assume background beliefs in constructing and assessing scientific explanations. But if we cannot assume that our background beliefs are approximately true in assessing scientific explanations, we will be forced from asymmetrical scepticism to a more general scepticism.

The analogy between science and morality is not, however, quite so easily established. Perhaps what is motivating Harman is the thought that our sensibilities are themselves to be explained by facts about our upbringing (Harman 1977: 4), so that the possibility of their deliverances being massively false is to be taken seriously,

---

[21] Nothing in the method itself demands that this understanding should be capturable in the form of a relatively concise set of principles; though this has tended to be assumed by advocates of the method and by their anti-theory critics alike. See A. Baier (1985) and Walker (1998).

in a way it isn't to be taken seriously in the scientific case. If so, then the 'moral observations' objection is not distinct from Mackie's (1977: 36) argument from disagreement in one important respect: both challenge the notion that the deliverances of our moral sensibilities covary with moral facts by suggesting that they covary instead with 'people's adherence to and participation in different ways of life'.

The first line of defence for the realist coherentist again calls for recognizing the sociality of moral knowledge: it is unquestionably true that our moral beliefs vary with upbringing and it is true that, whatever ideology critique we engage in, we are going to bring to our moral reasoning background presuppositions of various kinds and that these presuppositions are going to be explained by social facts. However, we should not assume that when we offer a social explanation for a belief we debunk that belief. Social explanation is not incompatible with epistemic explanation. *Some* social explanations are debunking (the kinds of social explanations offered in ideology critique, for example); some social explanations are not debunking. A social explanation will be debunking just in case it points to social mechanisms and institutions that are likely to transmit false beliefs; non-debunking just in case it points to social institutions and mechanisms that are likely to transmit true beliefs and other needed cognitive skills. The social institution of postgraduate training that inducts a researcher into a research paradigm is capable of equipping her with a set of relevant background beliefs, inchoate intuitions, and ways of framing research questions that enable her to engage in knowledge-generating scientific practice (Boyd 1988: 193; Kuhn 1970). Recognizing that our moral sensibilities are social products does nothing, *of itself*, to show that they are unreliable. Recognizing the diversity of such sensibilities, might, however.

Morality and science might be thought to be disanalogous in a way that has significant repercussions for an adequate answer to the input objection: while there are good inductive grounds provided by the success of science to accord credibility to the background beliefs used in its presupposition-laden methods, there seems to be no parallel inductive argument to support assigning credibility to our background moral beliefs. Disagreement is rife and it is easy to see how someone with different considered moral judgements can claim that theirs, and not ours, are formed under conditions conducive to reliability. Recognizing that we can offer genealogies of many moral beliefs that were formerly widely held can promote epistemic humility; recognizing that genealogy is a game two can play can promote epistemic defeat. Thus, the argument from disagreement remains the greatest threat to realist coherentism. If asymmetrical scepticism can be supported, it will be on those grounds.[22]

---

[22] In this I concur with the assessment of Darwall *et al.* (1992) and Sturgeon (1985). For a rejoinder to the argument from disagreement, see Brink (1984). Moody-Adams (1997) contains a detailed examination of the use of anthropological work in meta-ethical argument, especially the use of such work in defending relativism.

6. CONTEXTUALISM

Contextualism is a recent arrival on the map of positions in moral epistemology (Timmons 1993, 1996, 1999). It is self-conscious in its recognition of the importance of social facts in determining whether an agent is justified in holding a belief. Social facts come in twice over: first, in determining what beliefs require justification, and secondly, in determining what standards and conditions an agent has to meet in order to have justification. Contextualism in moral epistemology is an outgrowth of contextualism in general epistemology, but, as Timmons defines the position— sometimes preferring to call it 'structural contextualism'—it is different from the position that has come to be called just plain 'contextualism' in general epistemology. 'Contextualism' in general epistemology names the thesis that the truth-value of a sentence expressing a knowledge ascription can vary with the context in which it is uttered.[23] Contextualism in general epistemology is compatible with either foundationalist or coherentist accounts of the structure of justification. 'Structural contextualism', or 'contextualism', as the term figures in moral epistemology, is intended as a rival to foundationalism and coherentism.

Recall that coherence theorists solve the regress problem by denying that justification is linear: chains of justification circle back on themselves, interconnect, and become webs of mutual support; foundationalists, in contrast, solve the regress problem by positing non-inferentially justified basic beliefs. Timmons (1999: 187) characterizes structural contextualism as follows:

> (SC) Regresses of justification may legitimately terminate with beliefs, which in the context in question are not in need of justification. Let us call these latter beliefs contextually basic beliefs.

Timmons introduces structural contextualism as a description of the structure of our actual moral justificatory practice, but defends it as a structure that survives reflective scrutiny (Timmons 1999: 213). He is motivated by an anti-sceptical assumption: according to our ordinary epistemic judgement, many of our moral beliefs are justified and, other things being equal, our theories of justification should preserve these ordinary assessments. Timmons thus seems to be giving short shrift to the argument for asymmetrical scepticism. In part, this is because he is not attempting to give a straight answer to it. According to Timmons, there are indeed significant asymmetries between scientific and moral discourse: though both are assertoric and truth-apt, moral discourse is evaluative rather than descriptive and there are no judgement-independent facts and properties to be truth-makers

---

[23] For this definition and excellent overviews of contextualism, see De Rose (1999) and Pryor (2001). The terminological difference is explained by the influence of Annis (1978) on Timmons's position. Annis presents his position as a rival to coherentism and foundationalism.

for moral sentences.[24] But in part, also, it is because the contextualist distinguishes ordinary justificatory contexts from philosophical contexts in which sceptical hypotheses are to be taken seriously: we don't have to be able to rule out sceptical hypotheses in order to have day-to-day justification for our moral beliefs. It seems, moreover, that contextualism is not tied to Timmons's particular brand of irrealism, and could be adopted by a realist as one plank in their 'straight' answer to the argument for asymmetrical scepticism, provided that they independently address the arguments from action-guidingness, disagreement, and explanatory impotence.

Timmons claims that, in ordinary contexts of engaged ethical thinking, certain mid-level moral generalizations serve as contextually basic and can be used in justifying other non-basic moral beliefs.[25] The first stage of the argument for the possibility of contextually basic moral beliefs consists in the defence of a norm of epistemic responsibility; the second, in showing that the use of mid-level moral generalizations as contextually basic is compatible with the norm of epistemic responsibility.

Timmons adopts the standard naturalist approach to the question of how to justify epistemic norms. According to that approach, a norm is defended by showing how, given the kind of finite cognitively limited creatures we are, following that norm helps us achieve our epistemic goals. Timmons (1999: 200) advances the following norm as contributing to the epistemic goal of truth:[26]

> (ER*) Normally, a person is epistemically responsible in believing some proposition p at time t only if S checks all of those obvious counterpossibilities whose seriousness is indicated by an adequate set of background beliefs at t.

On the one hand, given we are cognitively limited and have non-epistemic goals as well as epistemic ones, demanding that an inquirer check all counter-possibilities no matter how inferentially remote would be unreasonable. 'Obviousness' is relative to the standard capacities of human inquirers (Timmons 1999: 199). On the other hand, to demand an inquirer check only those counter-possibilities suggested by the background beliefs they actually hold would be insufficiently demanding and would let irresponsible inquirers with shabby background belief sets off the hook. (ER*) recognizes the role of social context: what constitutes an adequate set of background beliefs is a function of information that is socially available. Drawing on Sosa (1991: 27), Timmons claims that an epistemically responsible inquirer is required to be able to rule out alternative hypotheses that are taken seriously in the inquirer's epistemic community: that the hypotheses are taken seriously makes them relevant.

---

[24] For an excellent overview of his position, along with expressions of doubt about its stability, see Dreier (2002).

[25] As Timmons recognizes, particularists could develop rival contextualist accounts in which particular moral judgements are contextually basic; thus the Rossian account Timmons explores is intended as illustrative rather than definitive of contextualism (Timmons 1999: 213).

[26] For a naturalistic discussion of epistemic goals other than truth, see Goldman (1986, ch. 2).

The second stage of the argument for moral contextualism consists in showing that, in ordinary contexts, taking certain mid-level moral generalizations, such as lying is wrong, as basic does not violate this norm of epistemic responsibility. These mid-level generalizations are acquired as a result of our moral education, are constitutive of a particular moral outlook, and are accepted as regress-stoppers in ordinary contexts. They provide the terms in which we approach specific moral issues and structure our moral thinking (Timmons 1999: 218). Moreover, we have the second-order doxastic commitment to them that is characteristic of contextually basic beliefs: that is, we take them to be epistemically sound, though we need not have higher-order beliefs about the reliability of the processes that lead us to have them (Timmons 1999: 206).

Timmons (1999: 218) argues that taking such mid-level moral generalizations to be contextually basic in ordinary contexts violates no norm of epistemic responsibility:

such moral beliefs, in such contexts are taken for granted: no serious doubts or challenges are considered or taken seriously by the relevant community. Since a large part of being epistemically responsible is a matter of being able to detect and deal with 'relevant' challenges—and in the ordinary context of moral justification, challenges to mid-level moral generalizations are not relevant—one's holding such beliefs and basing other, non basic beliefs on them is not subject to epistemic criticism and so one is epistemically justified in holding them without having justifying reasons.

There are other contexts, of course, in which one is not justified in taking these beliefs as basic: philosophical contexts, for example, in which we are called on to defend the possibility of justified moral belief from sceptical challenge.

The argument for asymmetrical scepticism might lead us to wonder whether moral scepticism isn't relevant in day-to-day justificatory contexts; after all, ordinary folk *do* take moral scepticism seriously in a way that they do not take seriously scepticism about scientific knowledge; moreover, at least some people seem to take it seriously even in 'engaged' contexts such as when co-deliberating about a proposed professional code (Timmons 1999: 221). This raises the vexed question of when if ever one is epistemically required to enter a 'high standards' context. There is reason to think that this familiar problem for contextualism will be especially difficult for the moral contextualist, given that philosophical moral scepticism has deep roots in ordinary contemporary moral thinking and thus has a tendency to bleed into everyday contexts.

I want to focus on a different set of concerns, concerns that are internal to the project of contextualist moral epistemology. These concerns suggest that the best way of developing a contextualist moral epistemology is to afford a yet more nuanced recognition of the role of social facts in shaping and justifying moral belief. Timmons recognizes the role of social facts in shaping what beliefs are contextually basic and in determining what alternatives have to be ruled out when a belief is not contextually basic. Feminist contributions to the project of social epistemology establish that there is a *politics* to credibility. Any attempt to recognize the role of social facts in epistemic justification that fails to recognize the role of the *political* in the social is apt to set the bar for justification too low, and Timmons's account can be charged with doing just that.

If norms for epistemic responsibility are to recognize our finitude, they must not demand that we rule out all possible alternatives (there are infinitely many such alternatives), nor can they demand that we rule out any alternative that someone, somewhere has countenanced as relevant. We are allowed to ignore 'kooky' alternatives—hence Timmons's focus on those alternatives that are taken seriously within a community. However, in a given community, whose rival hypotheses are taken seriously and whose are not can be a function of relations of dominance and subordination as much as a function of epistemic merit. Moreover, which rival hypotheses get to be seriously countenanced, whether or not by anyone who is recognized as someone to be taken seriously, is partly determined by the ideological grip of dominant interests and by the openness of the community to outsiders. It might be easy to overlook the role of ideological forces in determining what beliefs count as contextually basic so long as one is focusing on generalizations such as 'Lying is wrong'. However, gender and social status have been accepted as regress-stopping reasons and many currently accepted mid-level generalizations such as 'Stealing is wrong' are open to ideological critique. The problem of whose rival hypotheses are to be taken seriously also arises in the context of justifying non-basic beliefs, since what counts as an adequate justification for a non-basic belief will be affected by the range of alternatives that must be taken seriously.

Timmons charges coherentism with setting the bar for justification too high in so far as it demands that the inquirer form second-order beliefs about the reliability of her first-order beliefs. In all probability, most of us are insufficiently reflective to meet this requirement and certainly insufficiently reflective to meet the further requirement that our second-order beliefs be themselves justified (Timmons 1999: 240). However, if coherentism sets the bar too high (and we might not concede this, since we can instead claim that justification admits of degrees), this form of contextualism, which requires only that we take our basic beliefs to be epistemically sound, seems to set it too low. In ordinary contexts, we require positive justification for our moral beliefs only when a challenge has been articulated and backed with sufficient authority to have it taken seriously within our community. We are not required to engage in ongoing reflective monitoring of our epistemic practices so that they are tuned to the possibility of ideological and other distortion in claims to moral knowledge.

Summarizing naturalist approaches in feminist epistemology, Walker (1996: 275) claims that 'Normative standards of epistemic practice will require self-reflexive strategies of criticism that are historically informed and politically sensitive...'. There are two ways of thinking about how these self-reflexive strategies should operate and, correspondingly, two different conceptions of the epistemic burden that they demand. On the first account, these self-reflexive strategies must always be actively engaged. They thus place a continuous positive epistemic burden on inquirers. Understood in this way, good epistemic practice will demand that we form higher-order beliefs about our belief-forming mechanisms and so the resulting position will not be distinguished from coherentism with respect to epistemic demandingness.

On the second account, the requirement for self-reflection on epistemic practice is satisfied if the inquirer has a dispositional sensitivity to the possibility of ideological and other distortions. Were it reasonable to distrust a belief, the responsible inquirer would actively engage historically informed and politically sensitive self-reflective strategies: no such beliefs will be treated as contextually basic, whether or not credible members of her community are challenging those beliefs. Satisfying this requirement, conceived dispositionally, will place burdens on moral inquirers: the responsible moral inquirer will have to engage in ideology critique, at least on occasion. She will have to form some beliefs about the reliability of her first-order moral beliefs, but she may not have to form the kind of comprehensive account of their reliability required by the coherentist.

This suggestion seems to me in keeping with the spirit of Timmons's contextualism, more demanding though it is. Many of the mid-level generalizations identified by Timmons probably would count as justified without requiring further critical reflection. But other mid-level generalizations that have been taken to be contextually basic, and some that are still taken to be contextually basic, probably will not. That's going to mean, I suspect, that our theory of justification will not have the result that much of our ordinary moral epistemic assessment is correct even when considered by the standards of day-to-day justification. So much the worse for our ordinary epistemic assessment. Justified moral beliefs aren't *that* easy to come by.

References

Annis, D. (1978). 'A Contextualist Theory of Epistemic Justification'. *American Philosophical Quarterly*, 15: 213–19.

Antony, L. (2002). 'Quine as Feminist: The Radical Import of Naturalized Epistemology', in L. Antony and C. Witt (eds.), *A Mind of One's Own: Feminist Essays on Reason and Epistemology*, 2nd edn. Boulder, Colo: Westview Press.

Audi, R. (1996). 'Intuitionism, Pluralism and the Foundations of Ethics', in W. Sinnott-Armstrong and M. Timmons (eds.), *Moral Knowledge? New Readings in Moral Epistemology*. Oxford: Oxford University Press.

Ayer, A. J. (1946). *Language, Truth and Logic*. New York: Dover.

Baier, A. (1985). 'What Do Women Want in a Moral Theory?' *Noûs*, 19: 53–63.

Baier, K. (1958). *The Moral Point of View*. Ithaca, NY: Cornell University Press.

Blackburn, S. (1996). 'Securing the Nots: Moral Epistemology for the Quasi-Realist', in W. Sinnott-Armstrong and M. Timmons (eds.), *Moral Knowledge? New Readings in Moral Epistemology*. Oxford: Oxford University Press.

Blackburn, S. (1998). *Ruling Passions: A Theory of Practical Reasoning*. Oxford: Clarendon Press.

Boyd, R. (1983). 'On the Current Status of the Issue of Scientific Realism'. *Erkenntnis*, 19: 45–90.

—— (1988). 'How to Be a Moral Realist', in G. Sayre-McCord (ed.), *Essays on Moral Realism*. Ithaca, NY: Cornell University Press.

Brink, D. (1984). 'Moral Realism and Skeptical Arguments from Disagreement and Queerness'. *Australasian Journal of Philosophy*, 62: 111–25.

—— (1989). *Moral Realism and the Foundations of Ethics*. Cambridge: Cambridge University Press.

Copp, D. (1991). 'Moral Skepticism'. *Philosophical Studies*, 62: 203–33.

—— (1995). *Morality, Normativity, and Society*. New York: Oxford University Press.

Dancy, J. (1993). *Moral Reasons*. Oxford: Blackwell.

Daniels, N. (1979). 'Wide Reflective Equilibrium and Theory Acceptance in Ethics'. *Journal of Philosophy*, 76: 256–82.

Darwall, S. (2002). 'Intuitionism and the Motivation Problem', in P. Stratton-Lake (ed.), *Ethical Intuitionism: Re-evaluations*. Oxford: Clarendon Press.

—— Gibbard, A., and Railton, P. (1992). 'Towards *Fin de Siècle* Ethics: Some Trends'. *Philosophical Review*, 101: 115–89.

De Rose, K. (1999). 'Contextualism: An Explanation and Defense', in J. Greco and E. Sosa (eds.), *The Blackwell Guide to Epistemology*. Oxford: Blackwell.

Dreier, J. (2002). 'Troubling Developments in Metaethics'. *Noûs*, 36: 152–68.

Dworkin, R. (1973). 'The Original Position'. *University of Chicago Law Review*, 40: 500–33.

Frazier, R. L. (1998). 'Intuitionism in Ethics', in E. Craig (ed.), *The Routledge Encyclopedia of Philosophy*. New York: Routledge.

Gaut, B. (2002). 'Justifying Moral Pluralism', in P. Stratton-Lake (ed.), *Ethical Intuitionism: Re-evaluations*. Oxford: Clarendon Press.

Gauthier, D. (1986). *Morals by Agreement*. Oxford: Clarendon Press.

Gewirth, A. (1978). *Reason and Morality*. Chicago: University of Chicago Press.

Gibbard, A. (1990). *Wise Choices, Apt Feelings: A Theory of Normative Judgment*. Cambridge, Mass.: Harvard University Press.

Gilligan, C. (1982). *In a Different Voice*. Cambridge, Mass.: Harvard University Press.

Goldman, A. (1986). *Epistemology and Cognition*. Cambridge, Mass.: Harvard University Press.

Hare, R. M. (1952). *The Language of Morals*. Oxford: Oxford University Press.

Harman, G. (1977). *The Nature of Morality: An Introduction to Ethics*. New York: Oxford University Press.

Herman, B. (1991). 'Agency, Attachment and Difference'. *Ethics*, 101: 775–97.

Jones, K. (1999). 'Second-Hand Moral Knowledge'. *Journal of Philosophy*, 96: 55–78.

Kuhn, T. (1970). *The Structure of Scientific Revolutions*. Chicago: University of Chicago Press.

Kvanvig, J. (1992). *The Intellectual Virtues and the Life of the Mind*. Lanham, Md.: Rowman & Littlefield.

Little, M. (2000). 'Moral Generalities Revisited', in B. Hooker and M. Little (eds.), *Moral Particularism*. Oxford: Clarendon Press.

McDowell, J. (1985). 'Values and Secondary Qualities', in T. Honderich (ed.), *Morality and Objectivity*. London: Routledge & Kegan Paul.

Mackie, J. L. (1977). *Ethics: Inventing Right and Wrong*. New York: Penguin.

McNaughton, D. (1988). *Moral Vision: An Introduction to Ethics*. Oxford: Blackwell.

Miller, R. (1984). *Analyzing Marx: Morality, Power and History*. Princeton: Princeton University Press.

Moody-Adams, M. (1997). *Fieldwork in Familiar Places: Morality, Culture and Philosophy*. Cambridge, Mass.: Harvard University Press.

Nowell-Smith, P. H. (1954). *Ethics*. New York: Penguin.

Plato (1974). *Plato's Republic*. Indianapolis: Hackett.

Pryor, J. (2001). 'Highlights of Recent Epistemology'. *British Journal of Philosophy of Science*, 52: 95–124.

Rawls, J. (1971). *A Theory of Justice*. Cambridge, Mass.: Harvard University Press.

Redstockings Collective (1970). 'Redstockings Manifesto', in R. Morgan (ed.), *Sisterhood Is Powerful*. New York: Vintage Books.

Ross, W. D. (1930). *The Right and the Good*. Oxford: Oxford University Press.

Sayre-McCord, G. (1996). 'Coherentist Epistemology and Moral Theory', in W. Sinnott-Armstrong and M. Timmons (eds.), *Moral Knowledge? New Readings in Moral Epistemology*. Oxford: Oxford University Press.

Sinnott-Armstrong, W. (1992). 'Intuitionism', in L. Becker (ed.), *The Encyclopedia of Ethics*. New York: Garland.

—— (1996). 'Moral Skepticism and Justification', in W. Sinnott-Armstrong and M. Timmons (eds.), *Moral Knowledge? New Readings in Moral Epistemology*. Oxford: Oxford University Press.

Smith, M. (1994). *The Moral Problem*. Oxford: Blackwell.

Sosa, E. (1991). 'How Do You Know?', in Sosa, *Knowledge in Perspective*. Cambridge: Cambridge University Press.

Stratton-Lake, P. (ed.) (2002). *Ethical Intuitionism: Re-evaluations*. Oxford: Clarendon Press.

Sturgeon, N. (1985). 'Moral Explanations', in D. Copp and D. Zimmerman (eds.), *Morality, Reason and Truth*. Totowa, NJ: Rowman & Allanheld.

—— (2002). 'Ethical Intuitionism and Ethical Naturalism', in P. Stratton-Lake (ed.), *Ethical Intuitionism: Re-evaluations*. Oxford: Clarendon Press.

Timmons, M. (1993). 'Moral Justification in Context'. *The Monist*, 76: 360–78.

—— (1996). 'Outline of a Contextualist Moral Epistemology', in W. Sinnott-Armstrong and M. Timmons (eds.), *Moral Knowledge? New Readings in Moral Epistemology*. Oxford: Oxford University Press.

—— (1999). *Morality without Foundations: A Defense of Ethical Contextualism*. Oxford: Oxford University Press.

Walker, M. (1996). 'Feminist Skepticism, Authority, and Transparency', in W. Sinnott-Armstrong and M. Timmons (eds.), *Moral Knowledge? New Readings in Moral Epistemology*. Oxford: Oxford University Press.

—— (1998). *Moral Understandings: A Feminist Study in Ethics*. New York: Routledge.

Williams, B. (1995). 'What Does Intuitionism Imply?', in Williams, *Making Sense of Humanity and Other Philosophical Papers, 1982–1993*. Cambridge: Cambridge University Press.

CHAPTER 4

MORAL PSYCHOLOGY

R. JAY WALLACE

1. INTRODUCTION

Moral psychology is the study of morality in its psychological dimensions. Its unity and interest as a subject derive from its connection to the larger subject of moral philosophy, conceived as the study of normative demands on action in general, and moral demands on action in particular. It is possible, to be sure, to study morality without paying any special attention to issues that might be called psychological. Traditionally, however, the normative questions at the centre of philosophical ethics have been understood to require a kind of treatment that is at least partly psychological. This is no doubt due to the fact that moral norms aim to govern action. When it succeeds relative to this aim, morality will of necessity leave psychological traces in the agents whose lives it governs—there will be distinctive patterns of motivation and emotional response that people are subject to who internalize and act on moral standards. If we wish to understand morality as a normative phenomenon, we must understand the psychological states and capacities that make it possible for it to regulate people's lives in the way it aspires to do.

More specifically, there seem to be two ways in which the connection between normativity and psychology can be approached. First, we can begin with some normative claim or aspiration, and ask about the psychological implications that it carries in its train. Thus, moral principles are normative if and to the extent that they provide people with reasons for action, considerations that count for or against prospective actions that people might perform. The standing of principles as normative reasons in this sense, however, seems potentially dependent on psychological facts about the agents to whom those principles apply. We need to ask about the powers and capacities that make it possible for people to comply with the demands of morality, and to consider whether such psychological factors condition morality's claim to our attention and concern. Secondly, we can take some psychological phenomenon, and explore its links to normative concepts and assumptions. Many of the emotions distinctive of moral life, for example, seem to be constituted in part by distinctively normative thoughts; to attain a realistic understanding of these emotions, we must therefore see them in relation to the forms of normative consciousness that they depend upon.

Moral psychology thus explores a variety of psychological phenomena through the unifying prism of a concern for normativity. It studies the psychological conditions for the possibility of binding norms of action; the ways in which moral and other such norms can be internalized and complied with in the lives of agents; and a range of psychological conditions and formations that have implications for the normative assessment of agents and their lives.

Contemporary moral philosophy has shown an intense interest in these questions at the nexus between psychology and normativity, questions that have traditionally helped to define philosophical ethics as a subject. These issues were pushed out of view by the style of meta-ethical discussion that dominated English-language moral philosophy during the middle part of the twentieth century. Debates between emotivists, prescriptivists, and descriptivists about the meaning of moral discourse, for example, were often conducted by philosophers who either agreed fundamentally in their conceptions of human agency and moral motivation, or whose disagreements in this area were relegated to an invisible place somewhere out of public philosophical view. The return of such disagreements to centre stage reflects a widespread conviction that many of the normative controversies in moral philosophy hinge on assumptions about moral psychology, which therefore need to be scrutinized directly by anyone with a serious interest in the subject.

In what follows I will try to illustrate the vitality of this area of research by discussing six clusters of issues that fall within the broad purview of moral psychology as defined above. They are motivation and desire; reasons and desires; moral motivation; identification, alienation, and autonomy; weakness and strength of will; and moral emotions.

2. MOTIVATION AND DESIRE

Morality is distinctively connected to reasons. It presents itself as a set of requirements on action that are normative, in so far as there are moral reasons for agents to act as the requirements prescribe. The fact that X would be wrong, or unkind, or unjust, for instance, would seem to be a reason at least for some agents not to do X, a consideration that recommends or counts against those agents X-ing. In this respect, morality is potentially a source of normative reasons for action. Morality equally seems to have an explanatory dimension, in so far as agents sometimes act for distinctively moral reasons. The reason why Peter chose to do Y rather than X, for instance, might be that X would have been wrong, or unkind, or unjust. In cases of this kind, morality is a source of explanatory or motivating reasons, a set of considerations relevant to explaining what people actually do. Both explanatory and normative reasons raise issues within moral psychology.

Start with explanatory reasons, which are reflected in an agent's motivations to action. There is a broadly Humean approach to issues in moral psychology that is built around a distinctive and controversial thesis about the role of desire in motivating persons to act. This is the thesis that motivation is essentially constituted by desire, so that cognitive or rational states are incapable by themselves of generating a motive.

Defenders of this Humean thesis appeal to the following two ideas (see, especially, Smith 1987). First, they suggest that motivating states are distinguished by a particular 'direction of fit' vis-à-vis the world; they are essentially states with which the world is to be brought into alignment, rather than states that aim to conform to the way the world (already) is. Secondly, they contend that to be in a state with this distinctive direction of fit is, in effect, to be in a state of desire. Hence the Humean conclusion that motivation is essentially constituted by desire.

The plausibility of this conclusion depends to a considerable degree on how the contrast between the rational and the non-rational is understood. For defenders of the Humean approach, the non-cognitive states essential to motivation are not desires in the distinctive sense familiar from such examples as appetite or yearning (in which, for instance, attention is focused on a particular object or possibility for action; Scanlon 1998: 37–41 refers to such states as desires in the 'directed-attention' sense. See also Schueler 1995), but rather pro-attitudes in the broadest possible sense. One question this raises is whether the very broad understanding of desire undermines the *explanatory* aspirations of the Humean approach to moral psychology. Traditionally, that approach has been thought to yield a certain schema for explaining intentional action, in terms of non-cognitive states to which the agent is subject, which (in concert with the agent's beliefs) both rationalize and cause the agent's behaviour (for a classic formulation of this schema, see Davidson 1980a). But if the non-cognitive states involved in motivation are merely pro-attitudes in the broadest sense, their presence might not tell us anything interesting about how intentional actions are ultimately to be explained. Thus from the fact that I chose to grade some papers this morning it follows that, in the pro-attitude sense, I 'wanted' to grade the papers. But this merely gives a characterization of what I was up to as I sat at my desk, revealing my intention in action (as it were); an intention of this kind is not itself typically a reason for action, but the kind of attitude that in favourable cases is formed in response to reasons, and in unfavourable cases may arise independently of my judgements about what I have reason to do. If this is right, then the possibility remains open that the reasons we cite to explain action may not themselves consist in desires, but rather may consist in beliefs of some kind or other (including, for instance, normative beliefs about what the agent has reason to do)—beliefs that render action intelligible *by* explaining the intentions that underlie it. So long as this possibility remains open, the desires that are ascribed in motivation will seem superficial from the explanatory point of view (this possibility is forcefully presented in Nagel 1978, ch. 5; see also Wallace 1990).

Both parties to this debate accept the assumption that explanatory reasons are constituted by psychological states of some kind; they differ as to whether the psychological states in question are desires or beliefs. But the assumption common to these different approaches has itself come under attack (see Dancy 2000; Bittner 2000; the version of the challenge sketched in this paragraph is due to Dancy). One point of departure for such an attack is the appealing thought that agents sometimes act for good reasons, so that the normative considerations that recommend or speak in favour of their acting in a particular way (say, doing X) are the very considerations that in fact lead them so to act. This is one version of what has been called 'internalism', the general thesis that there is a necessary connection between our normative reasons and our motivations. If explanatory reasons are constituted by psychological states, it seems that we can uphold internalism in this form only if normative reasons are themselves also constituted by psychological states. But the latter thesis seems implausible. At least in a wide range of cases, the considerations that recommend or speak in favour of the actions I have normative reason to perform would seem to be features of my circumstances and of the prospective actions open to me, not present psychological states of myself, or facts about the obtaining of such states. What speaks in favour of my going to the cinema tonight, for instance, is not the fact that I want to do so, nor the fact that I believe it might be good in some way to do so, but the different consideration that it would actually be good in some way to go to the cinema (because, for instance, I would enjoy the film that is showing, or because I promised my friend that I would meet her there) (cf. Quinn 1993). If this line of thought is correct, then the internalist connection between normative and explanatory reasons can be maintained only if we reject the assumption that explanatory reasons are constituted by psychological states of any kind, whether beliefs or desires.

This argument calls attention to an extremely important dimension of explanatory reasons, which is their connection to the normative considerations that cast actions in a favourable light, from the perspective of agency. When we deliberate about what to do, we reflect on the considerations that count for and against prospective courses of action, and our behaviour is informed by this distinctive point of view. An explanation in terms of reasons functions in part by enabling us to recover the deliberative perspective of agents, so that we understand the favourable light in which they saw what they were doing. At the same time, it seems to me equally important to acknowledge that the perspective from which actions are explained is not identical with the deliberative standpoint of the agent whose actions are in question. The deliberative point of view is defined by the normative question 'What should I do?'; this question is characteristically first-personal and prospective, posed by agents whose capacities for action enable them to determine for themselves what they are to do. The explanatory standpoint, by contrast, responds to the different question 'Why did A do X?' It is characteristically retrospective and third-personal, defined by the aim of understanding an action that has already been performed.

Once we are clear about the distinctive points of view within which normative and explanatory reasons have their place, it seems plausible that these two kinds of reason should systematically diverge. This remains true even if we accept the point that normative reasons do not themselves typically consist in beliefs and desires, and that explanatory reasons function by revealing the 'favourable light' in which agents saw their action. This favourable light is the light that is, so to speak, cast onto prospective actions in the deliberative perspective of agency, as the agent reflects directly on the considerations that recommend those actions. But when we pose the explanatory question, we abstract from the immediate deliberative horizon of the agent, and adopt a standpoint that brings the agent herself into view, as an object of reflection. Whereas the psychological states of an agent are typically transparent to the agent herself, when she is deliberating about what to do, they are very much in the picture when we pose the question to which explanatory reasons provide an answer. It thus seems perfectly natural that we should explain action by citing not the normative considerations that cast a favourable light on the action performed, but the fact that the agent saw what she was doing in the light of those considerations.[1] The motivating reason, in other words, admits of a psychological interpretation, whereas the normative reason does not (for a different response to the observation that desires are not salient in the deliberative horizon of the agent, see Pettit and Smith 1990).

3. Reasons and Desires

Let us now turn directly to normative reasons, the considerations that count for or against actions in the deliberative perspective of agency. If the argument considered

---

[1] In practice, of course, we often explain what people do without mentioning explicitly their psychological states: 'she left without saying goodbye because the store was about to close and there was something she needed to pick up'. In the explanatory context, however, statements of this kind are naturally taken as abbreviated ways of characterizing the agent's state of mind.

at the end of the preceding section is on the right lines, these do not themselves typically consist in beliefs or desires. When we deliberate about what to do, it is facts about our situation and the actions that are open to us that seem to have direct normative significance, not (facts about) our present states of desire and belief.

This conclusion can be reinforced by further reflection on what desires are. In the preceding section a distinction was drawn between desires in the philosopher's sense of generic pro-attitudes, and desires in the more specific sense that involves phenomenologically salient attraction to an object or option. Of these two senses of desire, it is the latter that might sometimes seem to possess normative signific-ance within the standpoint of deliberation—at least we sometimes say things that suggest that this is the case, such as 'I want to walk home today', in response to a colleague's offer of a ride. But how could the fact that one desires something in the directed-attention sense have direct deliberative significance?

There are two aspects of such desires that might seem important in this connec-tion. First, desires of this kind involve a kind of phenomenal attraction, an elusive sense of being drawn to an object or possibility for action. But it is difficult to see how phenomenal attraction of this kind might itself be significant in deliberative reflection about action. This becomes especially clear when we remind ourselves that phenomenal attraction can come apart from any assessment of the value of the object or action one feels attracted to—one might feel oneself strangely drawn to the prospect of stepping off a cliff, for example, without in any way thinking it would really be good to do so. In these cases, it would be odd to say that the fact of phenomenal attraction is a consideration that speaks in favour of the action one is attracted to; one's attraction is not a reason in favour of stepping off the cliff, that in the present case happens to be outweighed by the disadvantages of doing so, but a biographical consideration that is apparently without any direct deliberative significance at all (except perhaps as a tendency that one should try to overcome). If this is true of these extreme examples, the point would seem equally to apply to less extreme cases as well, in which the object of attraction is deemed by the agent to be valuable. One's present attraction might be indirectly significant in these delibera-tive contexts, if for instance it enhances the likelihood of prospective pleasure or enjoyment, but taken in itself it would not seem to count in favour of anything.

Similar remarks apply to a second dimension of phenomenal desire, which is its tendency to induce thoughts that are normatively coloured or structured. People in the grip of such desires do not merely feel drawn to the object of their desires; they also tend to think about those objects in a distinctive way, as things whose attain-ment would be good or desirable in some dimension or other. (Indeed, it is arguable that this second feature is connected to the first, i.e. that felt attraction is not independent of the tendency to normative cognition, but in fact to be made sense of partly in terms of this tendency—so that feeling drawn to an object just is, in part, thinking of that object in normative terms, as good or valuable in some way; see Wallace 2000.) Again, however, a mere tendency to entertain thoughts of this kind would not seem to be a consideration that itself recommends or speaks in favour of acting to bring about the object to which one is attracted. It is the concrete value of X-ing that speaks in favour of doing X, strictly speaking, not the agent's tendency to think of X-ing as desirable in some way or other. This becomes clear when we reflect on cases in which we are disposed to think of objects as good that are not good in fact, and that we do not ourselves *judge* to be good (as when, to take a mundane example, we are attracted to the prospect of remaining in bed when the alarm goes off on a work day, without really believing that that would be a good thing to do, in the circumstances). The mere fact that a prospective action *strikes* us as good in some way in such cases, in the manner characteristic of phenomenal desire, does not seem to be something that it would be correct to take into account deliberatively, as itself counting in favour of the action that is desired.

These remarks are not uncontroversial, of course (for a more positive treatment of the deliberative significance of desires, see Stampe 1987), but they seem to me to raise a serious doubt about the identification of normative reasons with desires. To accept this much, however, is not yet to establish that normative reasons are completely independent of desires. Even if we reject the idea that desires themselves have direct deliberative significance, it might still be the case that considerations can count as reasons for a given agent to act only if they stand in a suitable relation to that agent's present desires and dispositions. A position of this kind has influentially been defended by Bernard Williams (see 1981*a*, 1995*a,d*, 2001), who argues that one can have reason to do X only if there is some element in one's 'subjective motivational set'—some *desire*, in a suitably broad and formal sense—that would be served by so acting. Statements about an agent's reasons for action are thus 'internal', in the sense that their truth hinges on the shape of the agent's actual motivational profile. In defence of this conclusion, Williams appeals to a version of the thesis I referred to above as internalism, to the effect that normative reasons have a 'dimension of possible explanation'; specifically, if an agent A has reason to do X, then it must be possible for A to acquire a motivation to do X as a result of deliberating correctly. But, Williams contends, rational deliberation can give rise to a new motivation only by proceeding *from* some motivation to which the agent is already subject. It follows that A's reasons are constrained or conditioned by the elements already present in A's subjective motivational set.

This argument has sparked a wide-ranging and lively debate (see e.g. Cohen 1986; Hooker 1987; Korsgaard 1986; McDowell 1995; Milgram 1996; Parfit 1997; Scanlon 1998, app.; Smith 1995; Velleman 2000*c*; Wallace 1990). One point of controversy has been the version of internalism that Williams relies on, to the effect that A can have reason to do X only if it would be possible for A to acquire the motivation to do X through a rational deliberative process. If X is, say, objectively the right or best thing for A to do, then perhaps we should say that there is reason for A to do X even if A could only acquire the corresponding motivation by a non-deliberative process, such as conversion or habituation (this is essentially McDowell's 1995 suggestion). But even if we accept Williams's brand of internalism, there is room to question whether his conclusion about the connection between reasons and desires really follows from it. His argument rests on the assumption that deliberation can give rise to a new motivation only if it in some way begins from motivations to which the agent is already subject. But this assumption seems vulnerable to challenge: why should we think a priori that it is impossible for practical reflection to produce a certain kind of effect (i.e. motivation) if it is not appropriately grounded in the agent's subjective motivational set? (See e.g. Cohen 1986; Hooker 1987; Wallace 1990.) Furthermore, the fact that there is a sound deliberative route from a given agent's S to a new motivation does not guarantee that the agent will really be able to follow that deliberative route in practice: one could have a 'blind spot' even about means that are necessary relative to one's own acknowledged ends (cf. Scanlon's 'O'Brien' examples; 1998: 369–70). If this much is conceded, then the practical significance of the distinction between cases in which there is and cases in which there isn't a deliberative connection to the agent's existing motivations may become obscure.

A basic difficulty that is posed by Williams's position is that it is not entirely clear what it even means to say that rational deliberation must begin from an agent's existing subjective motivational set. Williams refers to the elements of such sets as 'desires', at least in a formal sense; but if the notion of a desire is construed sufficiently broadly, it becomes unclear whether his position would exclude any interesting possibilities. Thus, one might say that any agent who is actually moved to do X in a particular set of circumstances must have had a latent disposition to do X in circumstances of that kind, a disposition that was already part of the agent's subjective motivational set prior to action. But the claim that reasons depend on desires of this kind seems potentially vacuous, and so uninteresting (cf. Scanlon 1998: 368–9). On the other hand, attempts to give the claim that deliberation must begin from items in one's existing motivational profile more bite threaten to render that claim correspondingly implausible. Thus, one might suppose that deliberation begins from an agent's existing motivations when the agent expressly takes those motivations into account, reflecting on how the ends they supply may best be attained. If we construe deliberation in this way, however, then it seems we must attach to desires the kind of normative significance that was challenged above, holding that they are themselves considerations that recommend or speak in favour of actions in the deliberative point of view.

Perhaps the most promising alternative to Williams's position would maintain that normative reasons are based in the value of the actions that are open to a given agent (see Parfit 1997; compare Raz 1999a, and—in a different way—Scanlon 1998, app.). What gives a given agent reason to do X is the fact that X-ing would be good or worthwhile in some way or other. Some of the values that can be realized in action are, to be sure, such that they are conditioned by subjective features of the corresponding agent. The enjoyment that it would provide might be a reason for me to see a new movie by my favourite director; but that the movie would be enjoyable depends on subjective facts about my tastes, preferences, moods, and even desires in the directed-attention sense.[2] There is no reason to believe, however, that all of the values that can be realized in action are subjectively conditioned in this way. Consider, for instance, many of the values at the centre of moral concern, such as justice, kindness, consideration, and respect: that it would be, say, just to return the wallet I have found in the hallway to its owner does not depend on whether I find myself antecedently attracted to doing such a thing.

If we take this approach, however, then how are we to explain the 'internalist' connection between normative reasons and deliberated motivation? How can reflection on the potentially desire-independent values that provide us with reasons give rise to corresponding motivations to action? There are two ways in which philosophers have approached this question in recent work. The first approach emphasizes the continuities between practical and theoretical rationality, appealing to the same background dispositions that make possible rational belief revision to explain how reasoning can give rise to motivation. Thus, it has been suggested that a disposition to greater coherence in attitudes is what makes it possible for us to modify our beliefs in response to reasons, and that this same tendency might explain the capacity of practical reason to produce appropriate motivations to action (see Smith 1997, sects. 5–6). Alternatively, intentions have been characterized as instances of the broader class of 'judgement-sensitive attitudes', a class that includes beliefs, and that is distinguished by the intrinsic sensitivity of its members to the agent's judgements about reasons (see Scanlon 1998, ch. 1). If we follow this approach, then we will see no special problem about the capacity of practical reflection to give rise to motivation. Being moved to action in accordance with one's judgements about what one has reason to do will be made possible by the general dispositions and capacities, whatever they are, that are at work when we draw inferences in accordance with the principles of logic.[3]

A second approach would account for rational motivation by appealing to distinctively practical dispositions and capacities, beyond those at work in the

[2] It is important to distinguish here between the abstract property of being a reason, and the concrete evaluative property that provides or constitutes the reason. In the example discussed in the text it is a property of the latter rather than the former kind that is, strictly speaking, conditioned by the agent's desires. That enjoyment is a reason for seeing a movie is not a fact that in any way depends on the agent's desires; but whether a given film would prove enjoyable to a given agent may exhibit such dependence. This is presumably what leads Derek Parfit (1997: 128) to assert that all reasons are 'external': of no reason is it true that its status as a reason depends on the subjective motivational set of the agent.

[3] For a different take on the comparison between practical and theoretical reasoning, compare Blackburn (1995). Blackburn extracts from Lewis Carroll's discussion of the tortoise and Achilles the moral that our ability to revise our beliefs in accordance with such principles as *modus ponens* ultimately depends on a kind of orientation of the will, a non-cognitive attitude that cannot itself be represented as the acceptance of a premiss.

domain of theoretical rationality. Thus it might be suggested that it is constitutive of agency to have a disposition to do what one believes one ought to do, or to act for reasons, and that this disposition is what makes it possible for agents to form motivations that accord with their judgements about the balance of normative reasons for action (see e.g. Broome 1997; Velleman 2000a,d). In a different vein, it has been maintained that agents are distinctively equipped with a capacity for self-determining choice or decision, which is exercised when they form intentions to act that accord with their deliberative assessment of the normative landscape (Wallace 1999b). These approaches, too, can account for the internalist connection between normative reasons for action and motivation, without postulating that such reasons are necessarily conditioned by concrete elements in the agent's subjective motivational set. Whether we opt for an account that stresses continuities between practical and theoretical reason, or one that instead postulates distinctive capacities or dispositions in the two cases, may depend in turn on our understanding of the possibilities for irrationality in the two domains. Sometimes we fail to believe or to act in accordance with our assessment of the relevant reasons, and the background capacities and dispositions must be interpreted in a way that leaves room for this phenomenon. But I have argued (2001) that action is subject to more radical forms of irrationality than we manifest in the case of belief; if this is correct, it might suggest that the capacities that render possible the formation of rational attitudes must differ correspondingly in the two cases.

4. MORAL MOTIVATION

A traditional focus of concern for ethics has been to make sense of the distinctive forms of motivation that enable agents to internalize and respond effectively to moral standards. People who succeed in acting as morality requires, and whose behaviour is admirable from a moral point of view, have motivations that are different from those of the callous and the cruel. But how are we to understand these differences in motivational structures? A number of conflicting oppositions suggest themselves: between altruism and egoism; sympathy and indifference; rational principle and emotional warmth and spontaneity.

The issues canvassed in the preceding two sections cast this debate in a new light, however. If we understand morality as a distinctive domain of normative reasons for action, then it begins to seem that the motivations that render moral conduct possible might simply be those general capacities, whatever they are, that enable agents to understand what they have reason to do and to act accordingly. The idea that virtuous behaviour and conduct require *distinctive* motivations to action suggests that morality is a source of internal reasons in Williams's sense, reasons that are conditioned by the subjective motivations of the agent, requiring quite special forms of desire to be complied with. If we reject this picture, however, then the question arises whether there really is any special problem of moral motivation, beyond the more general issues that arise in trying to make sense of the human capacity to respond appropriately to judgements about what there is reason to believe and to do.

But this is not quite right, either. Even if we deny that moral requirements are conditioned by special forms of desire, there will be distinctive patterns that emerge in the intentions and motivations of those who are responsive to moral requirements and values. There will also be distinctive patterns of emotion and feeling that such agents are subject to, which reinforce their tendencies to moral behaviour in a variety of ways. It is an important task for moral psychology to characterize these patterns, and explore their implications for the lives of agents who strive to live well by morality's lights. One way to think about this task is as follows. If human agency involves essentially a responsiveness to normative requirements, then the motivations of moral agents will reflect their distinctive responsiveness to the norms at the heart of morality. The job of characterizing moral motivation, in other words, will go hand in hand with the job of character-izing the values or requirements that define the moral point of view; our access to what is distinctive about moral motivation will be by way of understanding what is distinctive about the values that structure morality as a unified domain of normat-ive considerations. This is in keeping with the general interpenetration of the normative and the psychological that is characteristic of the whole subject of moral psychology.

If these remarks are on the right lines, we can expect accounts of moral motivation to differ in a way that reflects divergent understandings of the normative structure of morality. Here are two kinds of approach that might be distinguished. Utilitarians see morality as unified around the idea of promoting welfare or happi-ness. The fundamental moral requirement is to maximize the impartial good, where this in turn is interpreted as a matter of satisfying the needs and preferences of humans and other animals. The normative status of this requirement, as a rea-son for action, derives from the idea that we each have reason to perform those actions whose consequences are impartially most valuable, as contributions to the well-being of sentient creatures. Agents who comply with this moral requirement structure their lives with the aim of promoting the well-being of the persons (and other animals) that they are in a position to affect. Their activities will in this way reflect a sympathetic concern for the interests of sentient creatures, and moral motivation can accordingly be understood as a generalization of the natural human tendency to identify sympathetically with the weal and woe of others (cf. Scanlon 1982; for a different way of developing the Humean idea that reflective sympathy is the basic moral motive, see Baier 1994).

A second approach treats moral requirements as principles that regulate the interactions of persons, defining the terms on which we can relate to one another with respect and mutual consideration. Morality, on this broadly Kantian interpretation of it, is organized around the value of mutual recognition, and the normative standing of moral requirements is thought to derive from their connection to this value. Virtuous agents acknowledge the normative significance of mutual recognition, and their activities are structured accordingly, in ways that express an appreciation of the importance of relating to other people on a basis of respect— they are manifestly concerned to conduct themselves in a manner that can be justified to anyone who might be affected by their behaviour (as a certain kind of contractualist might put the point; cf. Scanlon 1998).

Arrayed against these two traditional characterizations are a range of accounts that challenge the apparent distinctiveness of moral motivations. One such account, which we might call pluralistic, is distinguished by the claim that there is no substantive unity to morality as a normative domain (cf. Raz 1999b,c,d). Normative reasons stem from the values that can be achieved in human action, and these form a radically heterogeneous group. Morally admirable agents are people who exhibit a wide range of individual virtues in their personal activities and social interactions; but there is no master value or normative structure that such agents can be said to be distinctively responsive to. Philosophers who accept this pluralistic approach will tend to deny that there is any special issue that is raised by moral motivation in particular, beyond the general question of how people can be brought to understand and respond to *any* of the divers normative requirements that apply to them.[4]

A different and more radically sceptical approach holds that the psychic structures that enable agents to comply with moral requirements are not what they might seem to be on the surface. Conventional accounts treat moral motivation as a potentially rational response to basic values and normative requirements. But philosophers inspired by Nietzsche and Freud would deny this assumption, tracing the roots of moral motivation to more primitive and unconscious emotional and desiderative tendencies. Thus, the human ability to inhibit instinctual satisfaction in accordance with accepted social norms of conduct has been thought to require the harnessing of such antisocial mental forces as aggression and hostility, turning them back against their bearer in the service of self-control. The impetus to moral behaviour is not the rational mechanism whereby we respond to the values that bear on the assessment of our options for action, but psychic structures that are tied to our infantile needs and aims, and that have been moulded through socialization in ways that promote harmonious social life (an interesting example of this approach is Wollheim 1984, especially ch. 7).

---

[4] In this general vein, it is sometimes suggested that moral conduct must be made sense of by appeal to psychological tendencies that are, so far as possible, relevant to the explanation of other aspects of our lives, in which morality is not distinctively involved. For defences of this idea—associated with the theme of 'naturalism' about morality—see Wollheim (1993) and Williams (1995c).

I won't go into the prospects for this kind of unmasking approach to moral motivation, except to make two observations. First, whatever we think about the motivational structures that support morality in mature adult agents, it is important to register that these structures emerge developmentally from a primitive motivational economy driven by the infantile urges and needs that dominate the initial phases of human conscious life. An account of moral motivation must make it intelligible how the aims and concerns attributed to morally admirable adults might have developed from these more primitive beginnings. A large division in this area is between those who see moral education as having a genuinely transformative effect on the structure of human aims and desires (in the tradition of philosophers such as Aristotle and Rousseau), and the aforementioned unmaskers, who imagine that the primitive instincts of the infant are merely redirected rather than transformed through the process of socialization (the developmental moral psychology sketched in part 3 of Rawls 1971 is an influential example of the transformative approach). A second point to bear in mind is that morality itself can have a pathological aspect. The same psychic forces that make it possible for people to comply with central moral requirements also sometimes give rise to psychological formations that are disadvantageous, from the standpoint of individual well-being and good functioning. Examples include a tendency to be plagued by guilt feelings that one does not oneself really believe to be justified, or to dwell inordinately on the minor faults and peccadilloes of others, in a way that functions to reinforce one's sense of one's own superiority vis-à-vis one's fellows. Any account of moral motivation must leave room for these psychological possibilities, and for this purpose it is important to retain an awareness of the connection between the motivational tendencies operative in mature moral agents and the more primitive drives and yearnings out of which morality develops (cf. Deigh 1996; see also the suggestive account of 'authoritative motivation' in Scheffler 1992, ch. 5).

The general tendency of unmasking accounts is to emphasize the deleterious psychological costs that are imposed on people by the internalization of moral norms. Morality may be a condition of civilized social life, but the redirections of instinct that it requires leave deep scars on the psyches of those who are subject to its requirements. But even less sceptical accounts may raise questions about the compatibility of moral motivation with individual flourishing. Both utilitarian and Kantian approaches, for instance, have been thought to deliver interpretations of moral motivation that render it questionably compatible with the conditions of a meaningful human life. In particular, there are issues about whether the projects and personal relationships that give humans reason to go on in life could really be sustained in the presence of a thoroughgoing commitment to maximize the impartial good, or to act only in ways that can be justified by appeal to principles acceptable to all. Bernard Williams has argued (1973, 1981c), for instance, that these forms of impersonal moral motivation would have the effect of alienating moral agents from the partial concerns and attachments that form the real fabric of their individual lives. Defenders of both approaches have responded to this argument, pointing to a variety of ways in which a commitment to central moral values can be integrated into and thereby reconciled with the broader array of attachments that constitute an individual human character (see Herman 1993; Railton 1988; Scheffler 1992, ch. 3). I believe that these responses succeed in showing that there are forms of moral motivation that are not inherently inimical to the psychological conditions that make life worth living; but this important issue will no doubt continue to be a focus of future research in moral psychology.

5. Identification, Alienation, and Autonomy

It is an assumption of the preceding discussion that we can be motivated in ways that diverge from our more reflective or stable judgements about our actions and our lives (for defences of this assumption, see Stocker 1979 and Velleman 2000b). It seems that people sometimes fail to feel attracted to options that they judge to be worthwhile in some way or other (for instance, in moods of depression or distraction or boredom). Equally, they can be drawn to objects and activities that they do not really judge to be good on the whole—one might feel an urge to strike out at a child in a fit of anger or frustration, for example, or feel like staying in bed in the morning when one knows that an important meeting is coming up that one has to prepare for. In cases of this kind, it seems natural to say that agents are estranged in some way from motivating attitudes that are nevertheless in some sense their own. Such cases are to be contrasted with cases of what we might call autonomous agency, in which people are fully identified with the motivating attitudes to which they are subject. The connected phenomena of identification and estrangement have been a focus of intense discussion in recent philosophy.

A central question is how we are to account for identification. Harry Frankfurt, the philosopher who has done the most to put this set of topics on the agenda of contemporary philosophy, urges that identification can be made sense of only within a framework of a hierarchy of desires (see especially Frankfurt 1988a,b, 1999c). Persons are distinguished by the capacity for reflexive assessment of their own mental states, and they are identified fully with a given first-order attitude if the following condition is satisfied: they want unambivalently that the first-order desire should be effective in moving them to action, and this second-order attitude is itself one with which they are satisfied (this is the most recent version of his position, as explained in 1999c). An alternative approach, due to Gary Watson (see Watson 1982; cf. Raz 1999*e*; also Wallace 2000), is drawn in terms of a contrast between evaluation and motivation; the leading idea here is that we are identified with motivating attitudes to the extent that they reflect and accord with our judgements about what it would be good or worthwhile to do. Watson claims that Frankfurt's hierarchical approach attributes arbitrary significance and authority to desires of the second order, which are after all intrinsically indistinguishable from first-order desires of the sort that we can be alienated from. He sees the standpoint of the person as the standpoint of deliberative thought, issuing in reflective judgements about the value of actions. Frankfurt, for his part, asserts that persons can identify with attitudes that they do not endorse as good or valuable in any way; he suggests that the authority exhibited by second-order desires derives from their reflexivity, which expresses a necessary distinguishing characteristic of persons.

Ultimately the debate between proponents of these two accounts reflects a larger struggle, between cognitivist and non-cognitivist approaches to the fundamental dimensions of moral psychology (see Wallace 2000). Watson's account presupposes that the deliverances of deliberative reflection are genuine *judgements* (about one's normative reasons), to be contrasted with mere subjective inclinations or motivations, which can diverge from the agent's rational verdicts about what is to be done. Frankfurt, by contrast, treats the attitudes that are crucial for identification as non-cognitive states of pro-attitude; he is doubtful that we can really make sense of the idea that deliberation issues in rational judgements about what is the case, and believes that identification is anyway less a matter of rational assessment than of affective caring and concern. A third account, due to Michael Bratman (see 1999, 2002), combines elements of both approaches. Bratman takes identification to be a function neither of desire nor of evaluative judgement, but of agents' *policies*; in particular, he proposes that agents may be identified with those actions and states that accord with their policy of treating considerations as reason-giving. One can judge that a given motivational tendency (the desire for professional success, say) is reason-giving, without yet forming the higher-order policy of treating it as such; in this way, Bratman's account departs from Watson's suggestion that deliberative judgements are authoritative in thinking about the standpoint of the person. On the other hand, the higher-order attitudes that matter on his account are not mere desires, but policies; these distinctive kinds of states flow from the capacities for planning agency that set persons apart from creatures capable only of more rudimentary intentional activity.

A more radical alternative to the positions of Frankfurt and Watson questions whether we can really make sense of alienation from the kind of motivating attitudes that humans are typically subject to (see Scanlon 2002; Moran 2002). In the background here is the idea that phenomenal desires are not to be understood as sensations or brute motivational tendencies, but rather as attitudes that have a complex normative intentionality (e.g. as states in which it seems to one that certain considerations are normative reasons). If we understand phenomenal desire in this way, however, it becomes correspondingly difficult to accept the idea that agents might be estranged from attitudes of this kind. In virtue of their intentional content, phenomenal desires would seem to belong to the broader class of 'judgement-sensitive' attitudes that apparently define the point of view of the person; they are in this way expressions of who the person is, not merely things that happen to the person, and for this reason it seems appropriate to assess people partly on the basis of the desires to which they are subject. The set of attitudes with which we are actively identified expands, on this approach, to encompass all motivating states that involve forms of normative cognition.

The differences between these various approaches may reflect in part differences in interpretation of the notion of 'identification', which is far from being entirely perspicuous (for some sceptical remarks about the basic idea that there is a class of motivations with which we as agents are essentially identified, see Velleman 2002). In one sense, we are identified with those attitudes that reflect our thoughts about the way the world is and ought to be, and that form a potential basis for evaluative assessment of us. People who are self-absorbed, for example, consistently desire to put their own interests above those of other people, want to be the centre of attention, etc. Even if they succeed in resisting these desires, and judge them to be lamentable, the mere fact that they are subject to them has a significance for ethical reflection that is different from the significance of (say) a tendency to headaches or heartburn. The desires in question are linked to the way in which self-absorbed people tend to think about their relations to their fellows, and a susceptibility to them may therefore be considered an unattractive character trait, something that warrants certain kinds of moral criticism. On the other hand, if identification is traced to the more narrow forms of ethical assessment involved in moral blame and judgements of responsibility, then a more restrictive interpretation of the phenomenon may seem preferable. Many of the phenomenal desires to which we are subject resist our best efforts to criticize or control them, even when they involve a kind of normative intentionality. When this is the case, our phenomenal desires may not in fact be responsive to our reflective convictions about the balance of normative reasons, and this breakdown in our capacity to control them makes it questionable whether we are identified with them in the way that would undergird assessments of responsibility and blame (see Wallace 2002). A still different notion of identification is linked to the idea of autonomy, a condition attained when one's actions and feelings express one's most authoritative standpoint on the world, so that one stands completely behind them. This notion of identification as autonomy, which I believe to be most relevant to the original debate between Frankfurt and Watson, seems potentially to diverge both from the notion of ethical assessment and from that of moral responsibility.[5]

[5] Of course, autonomy is itself an extremely elusive ideal; on this point, see Arpaly (2003, ch. 5). A still different ideal of agency that has been proposed recently is that of orthonomy, or the capacity to govern oneself by the right; see Pettit and Smith (1993, 1996).

Some of the character traits with which we are most closely identified, however, may be so essential to who we are that we *cannot* effectively alienate ourselves from them. Thus it has recently been argued that our character as persons may be a source of volitional necessities, placing constraints on the things that it is so much as possible for us to will and to do. A volitional necessity is an incapacity to do something intentionally. Rogers Albritton (1985–6) has expressed doubts that there really are any genuine incapacities of this kind, contending that we cannot make sense of an internal obstacle to the mere act of willing (as opposed to a constraint on our capacity to achieve what we set out to do). Even if we agree that there can be such incapacities, however, it is important to acknowledge that not all of them are connected to our character as agents, or reflect anything interesting about who we essentially are. Thus one might be subject to a revulsion of eels so intense that one finds one cannot bring oneself to go into a body of water known to contain them, though one regrets this fact about oneself, and wishes one could overcome the revulsion (since the water actually seems rather pleasant for swimming). In the more interesting cases of volitional necessity, by contrast, the inability intentionally to do something is grounded in aspects of oneself that one is identified with, in at least one of the senses that are important to understanding personhood and character. When Luther announces, 'Here I stand, I can do no other', he is not merely reporting on some visceral revulsion that he finds that he is subject to, but telling us something more deeply revealing about who he is. How precisely the connection to identity and character is understood in such cases will depend in turn on the notion of identification one favours. On one plausible interpretation, volitional necessities are grounded in the deliberative point of view, and reflect one's inability to regard considerations of a certain kind as genuine reasons for action (see Williams 1981*d*, 1995*b*). A different interpretation would see the more significant volitional necessities as a manifestation of one's affective sense of what is important in life (Frankfurt 1988*c,d*, 1999*b*). It might well be that we are potentially subject to volitional necessities that are grounded in both of these aspects of ourselves, which can overlap and conflict in ways that frustrate any simple answer to the question of who we essentially are and how our identity is expressed in constraints on intentional action (for a subtle comparative discussion of the different conceptions of volitional necessity and their connection to conceptions of identification, see Watson 2002).

6. Weakness and Strength of Will

The issues of identification and alienation come to a head in reflection on the phenomenon of weakness of will (or *akrasia*). Agents who are weak-willed are not merely subject to inclinations that diverge from their authoritative verdicts about what it would be best to do; they act on those inclinations—freely and intentionally, and in full knowledge that they are going against their own convictions about how they ought to act. The classical philosophical problem of weakness of will is whether, and if so how, this phenomenon is so much as possible.

Weakness of will, in the striking form just characterized, appears to be a form of irrationality, a breakdown of the connections between authoritative judgement and appropriate response that apparently undergird rationality across the board, in both the theoretical and the practical spheres. This appearance has been challenged, however (see Arpaly 2003, ch. 2; McIntyre 1993; Frankfurt 1988c). There are cases in which attention to the broader range of attitudes to which agents are subject, and to the normative considerations relevant to the assessment of their actions, raises doubts about the assumption that weakness of will is always irrational. A classic example is Huckleberry Finn, who goes against the dictates of his conscience in refusing to hand over Jim: his action seems morally justifiable, and perhaps also rational, despite the fact that he himself does not exactly see it that way at the time of performance (see the discussion of this case in Bennett 1974). Cases of this kind occur when there is reason to question the justifiability of the practical judgement that the weak-willed agent goes against. That judgement may be dubious in the light of other things that the weak-willed agent already clearly accepts. One might for instance genuinely believe that one should watch less television, or get more exercise—one would assent fully to these propositions if reflecting on them clearly and calmly, say—and yet find oneself consistently thinking, when opportunities for television or exercise present themselves, that it would be best in the circumstances to watch another show, or skip the run for today. One would thereby fail to connect one's particular normative judgement to one's larger set of beliefs about what would be best. Alternatively, it might be (as in the example of Huck Finn) that there are objective considerations that speak against the better judgement, whose force the weak-willed agent does not yet fully appreciate at all.

Cases of these kinds are important, reminding us that *akrasia* occurs at only one node in a complex structure of traits and capacities whose broader function is to track value and to translate it into a suitable and sustained pattern of action (Rorty 1980). But it seems to me advisable to hang onto the idea that weakness of will is at least a local form of irrationality. That is, the failure to act in accordance with one's authoritative better judgement is, taken by itself, a breakdown in the processes that make rationality possible in thought and action; in exhibiting such a breakdown, one is *to that extent* irrational.[6] But it is compatible with this that one's local irrationality is embedded in a pattern of broader attitudes that is compensatory,

---

[6] This is of course not to say that one is simply stupid, or logically obtuse; but not all forms of irrationality need take those forms.

interacting with the local irrationality in a way conducive to one's overall capacity to discern the good and to act in the light of it. Thus, one's failure to abide by a local judgement about what it would be best to do in the immediate circumstances one confronts might cancel out a different and more significant failure to reason effectively in arriving at that local judgement in the first place. In akratically going for a run—for instance, as a way of avoiding grading the pile of student papers on one's desk—one might more effectively be advancing one's larger values than one would have been if one had adhered to the local judgement that it would be better not to. In the Huck Finn case, local *akrasia* might result from the operation of dispositions of spontaneous emotional sensitivity and response that enhance one's overall capacity to act on the deliberatively significant features of the situations one confronts (such as the humanity of Jim) (see McIntyre 1993).

The philosophical interest of *akrasia* lies in large measure in the pressure it brings to bear on our understanding of intention, desire, practical judgement, and their various contributions to action (for an overview of recent work on these traditional aspects of the problem, see Walker 1989; Mele 1987). Take the case of our practical judgements, about what it would be best to do in a given situation. There is a version of the thesis referred to above as internalism, according to which it is a condition of the genuineness of judgements of this kind that the person to whom they are ascribed be motivated accordingly. This condition finds clear expression in the following principle of Donald Davidson's (1980b; see also 1982): 'P2. If an agent judges that it would be better to do x than to do y, then he wants to do x more than he wants to do y'. But if practical judgement is linked with motivation in this direct way, there is an apparent difficulty in seeing how weakness of will can be so much as possible, at least on the natural assumption that intentional action always accords with one's strongest desires. In response to this difficulty, one might retain P2, but refine one's account of the practical judgements involved in cases of weakness, distinguishing (say) between the conditional judgements against which one acts and the unconditional judgements revealed in one's behaviour, to which P2 properly applies.[7] Alternatively (and perhaps also more straightforwardly), one might modify P2, contending that the connection between practical judgement and motivation is less direct than that principle would entail (this option is explored and defended in Audi 1979).

On the other side, there are common assumptions about the nature of intentional action that make it seem puzzling how actions of this kind can ever fail to correspond to one's own judgement about what it would be best to do. One such assumption is the Humean theory of motivation discussion in Section 2 above, to the effect that motivation always entails the presence of desire. This theory by itself

---

[7] This is Davidson's solution (1980b). Compare the account offered by Sarah Buss (1997), which distinguishes between the (hypothetical) practical judgements against which the *akrates* acts, and the (actual) practical judgements implicit in the *akrates*' behaviour.

does not render weakness of will problematic, but it can cause trouble in concert with other common assumptions about the nature of desire. Suppose, for instance, the following two theses are added to the Humean theory of motivation: (*a*) that desires always aim at what is believed to be valuable, and (*b*) that all values are ultimately commensurable, in some sense. With these theses in place, it becomes very hard to make sense of intentional actions that conflict with one's sincere judgement about what it would be best to do; from the agent's own point of view, there seems to be nothing in the weak-willed action capable of engaging one's desires, in the way necessary for intentional action. This is essentially the Socratic argument against weakness of will developed in Plato's *Protagoras*, an argument that can be resisted by weakening the connection between desires and beliefs about the good, or by challenging the assumption of the commensurability of values (for an influential defence of the latter response, see Wiggins 1991).

A different set of assumptions about intentional action that seem to leave no room for weakness of will is expressed in some versions of modern decision theory. According to this framework for thinking about rational action, value is ultimately a function of an agent's preferences over outcomes, where the strength of one's preferences is in turn understood causally. It follows that intentional action reflects one's strongest desires, together with one's beliefs about the probabilities of outcomes, in such a way that one always does what one believes will be 'best'—a position that apparently leaves no room for the striking form of weakness of will described above. Defenders of decision theory have argued that their approach to rational decision in fact has the resources to accommodate something like weakness of will (see Jackson 1984). The key is to attend to the *dynamics* of value, the ways in which one's preferences change over time in relation to one's evolving beliefs about the probability of outcomes. Weakness occurs when one's present strongest desire cannot be accounted for in terms of one's earlier desires together with one's new subjective probabilities. Against this, it has been maintained that not all changes in preference that satisfy these conditions are cases of genuine irrationality, and that even when such changes are irrational, they do not display the element of synchronic conflict between action and better judgement that is the hallmark of true weakness of will (see e.g. Cordner 1985). This raises the basic question whether the Humean approach, as elaborated in modern decision theory, is really adequate to account for the full range of phenomena to which a theory of rational action must apply.[8]

Traditionally weakness of will has been taken to be not only irrational, but also free or uncoerced. Thus it has seemed to many philosophers that weakness of will

---

[8] In response to this problem, it has been suggested that decision theory can be enriched to accommodate synchronic conflict by drawing on the kind of higher-order desires that figure in Frankfurt's hierarchical account of the structure of the will; see e.g. Bigelow *et al.* (1990). For critical discussion of both this strategy and Jackson's, see Kennett (1991).

can be distinguished from the different phenomenon of compulsion only if it is true that weak-willed agents are free to do what they believe to be best (on the importance of distinguishing weakness from compulsion in these terms, see Kennett 2001). But this assumption too has been challenged. Gary Watson, for instance, proposes that the distinction between weakness and compulsion properly turns on the question of whether the desires to which an agent gives in are ones that a normal and reasonable level of self-control would have enabled the agent to resist. If the answer to this question is yes, then we may speak of weakness rather than compulsion. It does not follow, however, that weak-willed agents are actually free to do what they believe best. Watson argues that we can *explain* the behaviour of such agents only if we assume that they are not free to act on their better judgement, on account of a failure to develop and maintain the normal capacities for self-control. This seems correct, but it raises the question why we should assume that human action is always fully explicable. What is to rule out the possibility that the behaviour of the weak-willed agent is ultimately inscrutable?

Watson's discussion draws attention to the important connections between weakness of will and self-control. Those who give in to the temptation to do something they believe to be bad either lack the normal powers of self-control, or fail to exercise them at the crucial juncture. Self-control, or strength of will, is thus the other side of the coin represented by weakness of will. Both weakness and strength of will can be understood either episodically (as when we refer to a single occasion on which one or the other of these phenomena occurred), or as traits of character, woven into the dispositions of the agent (as when we describe someone as having a high or low degree of will-power).[9] Episodic self-control can seem paradoxical: if the motivations grounded in one's better practical judgement are stronger than the temptation to which one is subject, there would seem to be no need for special measures of self-control; if by contrast the temptation is stronger than one's more authoritative motivations, self-control would seem to be impossible. But there are ways to avoid this apparent paradox. Self-control might result from a *combination* of motivational tendencies that together are sufficient to defeat a temptation strong enough to defeat any of them individually (see Kennett and Smith 1996). Alternatively, one's better desires, even if they are not strong enough to prevail against the temptation by themselves, might still be sufficient to initiate a mental process (focusing one's attention, for example) that brings about a change in one's motivational economy, such that one is eventually able to hold out against the wayward desire (cf. Mele 1987, chs. 4–5; 1995, ch. 3). The former approach represents episodic self-control as a synchronous phenomenon occurring at the sub-agential level, the latter as a diachronic process that is in some more robust sense initiated by

---

[9] Aristotle's discussion of *akrasia* in bk. 7 of the *Nicomachean Ethics* treats it primarily as a trait of character. For interesting recent discussions that follow Aristotle in this, see Hill (1991); Swanton (1992, ch. 10). For an interesting treatment of self-control as a trait of character, see Roberts (1984).

the agent (see the following debate: Mele 1997; Kennett and Smith 1997). They share a common—and to my mind questionable—assumption that the intentional activities of agents can be reconstructed as resulting from the causal force of desiderative forces to which the agent is subject at a given time. A less 'hydraulic' conception of agency might begin by rejecting the assumption that the pro-attitudes to which we are subject are all well understood on the model of vectors of causal force. Perhaps the human capacity to intend to do something is one that cannot be reconstructed in terms of the operation of desiderative forces to which the agent is subject at the time of action. In that case, both weakness and episodic strength of will may be rendered possible by a volitional capacity whose operations are not causally explicable in terms of the play of desiderative and cognitive forces to which the agent is subject (for some remarks in support of this general approach, see Wallace 1999*b*).

7. Moral Emotions

The moral emotions are a particular focus of concern within moral psychology. These may be understood as the emotions to which one is peculiarly susceptible in so far as one has a morally admirable character, and which accompany and reinforce one's acceptance of moral norms. The moral emotions in this sense include, perhaps most strikingly, the backward-looking emotions of shame, guilt, regret, and remorse, which are typically prompted by one's awareness that one has fallen short of one's own moral standards or ideals.

It can plausibly be argued that reactive emotions of these kinds are essential to our understanding of morality. Thus a natural way to understand morality is to see it as a set of norms that distinctively regulate these moral sentiments, defining the occasions when such emotions as resentment and guilt are called for. This assumption shows up in Allan Gibbard's (1990) expressivist proposal that moral judgements express the speaker's acceptance of norms that govern these reactive emotions. It is equally implicit in the idea, influentially articulated by P. F. Strawson (1982), that a susceptibility to the reactive moral sentiments fundamentally structures our interpersonal relations. Building on this idea, I have argued that moral accountability needs to be understood in relation to the reactive sentiments: we are responsible for what we do just in case it would be fair to respond to our actions with such emotions as resentment and indignation (Wallace 1994).

The plausibility of proposals such as these depends in part on how the reactive sentiments themselves are understood (recent general accounts of the emotions include Goldie 2000; Nussbaum 2001; Stocker with Hegeman 1996; Wollheim 1999). A good starting point for thinking about this issue is the observation that both

shame and guilt can be felt in response to a single event. An adequate characterization of these emotions must make clear how these two sorts of emotional response
differ from each other, even when they are directed at one and the same object. The
now standard approach solves this problem by emphasizing that shame and guilt
are propositional attitudes, in which an action or event is thought about in a distinctive way.[10] Guilty agents conceive of an action of theirs as a transgression or a
wrongdoing, whereas those subject to shame are responding to what they think of
as a failure or shortcoming on their part; guilt is thus connected to demands or
requirements that one accepts, while shame reflects a conception of what is valuable in one's life, as the potential basis of one's self-esteem. If we accept the idea
that these emotions are identified by their cognitive content,[11] we must interpret
that dimension of them in a way that allows for deviant or irrational manifesta-
tions of the emotions. Persons who are subject to survivor guilt, for instance, need
not really accept that they have done anything wrong in coming through a horrible
accident alive. To account for cases of this kind, we should perhaps see guilt as connected not with *beliefs* about wrongdoing in the fullest sense of the term, but rather
with our *thoughts*, which can structure our emotional experience even if we do not
really accept them as true (cf. Greenspan 1995, ch. 5).

   A different kind of issue concerns the rational assessment of the reactive
sentiments. A natural default position might be that feelings such as guilt, remorse,
or shame are appropriate and fitting when agents have voluntarily done something
that they acknowledge to be morally wrong or indefensible. In cases in which a
lamentable outcome is not the result of one's own voluntary activity, the rational
agent can feel only the kind of impersonal regret that is equally accessible to an
observer or uninvolved third party. This default position has been subjected to critical pressure from two directions. One line of objection, influentially articulated by
Bernard Williams (1981*b*), holds that it distorts both our emotional experience and
our understanding of our capacities for agency to ignore the space between personal guilt or remorse on the one hand, and impersonal regret on the other. It is
perfectly appropriate, Williams argues, for people to feel a kind of 'agent-regret'
that is not equally available to a third party about the unintended or involuntary
consequences of the things they do (his example is the lorry driver who, through
no particular fault of his own, runs over a child). On the other side, it has been
suggested that we would be better off if we could rid ourselves entirely of the

---

[10] See e.g. Rawls (1971, sects. 67, 73). For a subtle and qualified elaboration of this position, see
Taylor (1985). Williams (1993) argues against the 'progressivist' assumption that guilt represents a
higher stage of moral development than shame. A quite different take on shame and guilt may be
found in Wollheim (1999, lect. 3).

[11] Gibbard's account of moral judgement—which requires that the reactive sentiments should be
intelligible independently of moral judgement, hence that they cannot derive their content from such
judgements—suggests one possible basis for resisting this idea. His alternative account of the reactive
sentiments is in Gibbard (1990: 135–50).

tendency to feel regret about things that have happened in the past, *including* our own voluntary actions. This line of thought can be nourished by scepticism about freedom and responsibility, which might seem to deprive reactive sentiments, and the blame familiarly associated with them, of a normative basis. Or it might be supported by the Spinozistic thought that it is pointless to feel bad about things that have already happened, given that we can no longer do anything to change them (cf. Bittner 1992; for a defence of guilt in the face of increasing scepticism about it, both in the law and in society more generally, see Morris 1988). I myself believe that the default position remains defensible in the face of these objections. A susceptibility to the reactive sentiments seems virtually inevitable for those whose ongoing deliberations and social interactions are structured in terms of moral norms; furthermore, the capacities for agency that render the reactive sentiments fitting can be defended against sceptical attack (cf. Wallace 1994).

An altogether different emotion that has attracted interesting attention in recent years is love. This may not seem to be a moral emotion in the same way that the reactive sentiments clearly are; but it is, on any account, an emotion with great significance for morality. The things we love are among our defining priorities in life; they shape our deliberative horizon in ways that threaten to limit and relativize the claims of impartial morality (see Williams 1981c; compare Stocker 1981; Wolf 1992). As Harry Frankfurt (see 1999a,d) has argued, love makes things important that would otherwise be of no particular significance to us, subjecting us to distinctive volitional necessities that reflect our deepest sense of who we are. Frankfurt himself sees love not as a response to the independent value of its objects, but as a creative force, investing its objects with a value that they would not otherwise possess. This approach has a certain romantic appeal, but it is hard to reconcile with our sense that love, or at least some varieties of it, can be an inappropriate response to its object (consider romantic love of one's student, or of a child in one's care). An alternative approach, due to David Velleman (1999), treats love essentially as a response to reasons, an emotional openness to the value of the beloved as a rational agent. Since this is the very same value that underlies impartial morality, Velleman suggests that love is itself a moral emotion; it is not a threat to impartial morality, so much as a distinctive way of appreciating its central organizing value. But this ingenious theory seems to render love responsive to the wrong kind of reasons—reasons that are equally present in all rational agents, and that therefore do not distinguish one person from all the other candidates in the world who might be loved. An outstanding problem in this area is to devise an account of love that better accommodates the ways in which love is and ought to be responsive to reasons, while remaining true to our sense that it can be a capricious and creative force in our lives.[12]

---

[12] Kolodny (2003) presents an interesting response to this problem, turning on the idea that the reasons of love lie in the value of relationships.

REFERENCES

Albritton, Rogers (1985–6). 'Freedom of Will and Freedom of Action'. *Proceedings of the American Philosophical Association*, 59: 239–51.

Arpaly, Nomy (2003). *Unprincipled Virtue*. New York: Oxford University Press.

Audi, Robert (1979). 'Weakness of Will and Practical Judgment'. *Noûs*, 13: 173–96.

Baier, Annette (1994). 'Hume, the Women's Moral Theorist?' Repr. in Baier, *Moral Prejudices*. Cambridge, Mass.: Harvard University Press.

Bennett, Jonathan (1974). 'The Conscience of Huckleberry Finn'. *Philosophy*, 49: 123–34.

Bigelow, John, Dodds, Susan, and Pargetter, Robert (1990). 'Temptation and the Will'. *American Philosophical Quarterly*, 27: 39–49.

Bittner, Rüdiger (1992). 'Is it Reasonable to Regret Things One Did?' *Journal of Philosophy*, 89: 262–73.

—— (2000). *Doing Things for Reasons*. Oxford: Oxford University Press.

Blackburn, Simon (1995). 'Practical Tortoise Raising'. *Mind*, 104: 695–711.

Bratman, Michael (1999). 'Identification, Decision, and Treating as a Reason'. Repr. in Bratman, *Faces of Intention*. Cambridge: Cambridge University Press.

—— (2002). 'Hierarchy, Circularity, and Double Reduction', in Sarah Buss and Lee Overton (eds.), *Contours of Agency*. Cambridge, Mass.: MIT Press.

Broome, John (1997). 'Reasons and Motivation'. *Proceedings of the Aristotelian Society*, suppl. vol., 77: 131–46.

Buss, Sarah (1997). 'Weakness of Will'. *Pacific Philosophical Quarterly*, 78: 13–44.

Cohen, Rachel (1986). 'Are External Reasons Impossible?' *Ethics*, 96: 545–56.

Cordner, Christopher (1985). 'Jackson on Weakness of Will'. *Mind*, 94: 273–80.

Dancy, Jonathan (2000). *Practical Reality*. Oxford: Oxford University Press.

Davidson, Donald (1980a). 'Actions, Reasons and Causes'. Repr. in Davidson, *Essays on Actions and Events*. Oxford: Oxford University Press.

—— (1980b). 'How Is Weakness of Will Possible?' Repr. in Davidson, *Essays on Actions and Events*. Oxford: Oxford University Press.

—— (1982). 'Paradoxes of Irrationality', in Richard Wollheim and James Hopkins (eds.), *Philosophical Essays on Freud*. Cambridge: Cambridge University Press.

Deigh, John (1996). 'Love, Guilt, and the Sense of Justice'. Repr. in Deigh, *The Sources of Moral Agency*. Cambridge: Cambridge University Press.

Frankfurt, Harry (1988a). 'Freedom of the Will and the Concept of a Person'. Repr. in Frankfurt, *The Importance of What We Care About*. Cambridge: Cambridge University Press.

—— (1988b). 'Identification and Wholeheartedness'. Repr. in Frankfurt, *The Importance of What We Care About*. Cambridge: Cambridge University Press.

—— (1988c). 'Rationality and the Unthinkable'. Repr. in Frankfurt, *The Importance of What We Care About*. Cambridge: Cambridge University Press.

—— (1988d). 'The Importance of What We Care About'. Repr. in Frankfurt, *The Importance of What We Care About*. Cambridge: Cambridge University Press.

—— (1999a). 'Autonomy, Necessity, and Love'. Repr. in Frankfurt, *Necessity, Volition, and Love*. Cambridge: Cambridge University Press.

—— (1999b). 'Concerning the Freedom and Limits of the Will'. Repr. in Frankfurt, *Necessity, Volition, and Love*. Cambridge: Cambridge University Press.

—— (1999c). 'The Faintest Passion'. Repr. in Frankfurt, *Necessity, Volition, and Love*. Cambridge: Cambridge University Press.

—— (1999d). 'On Caring'. Repr. in Frankfurt, *Necessity, Volition, and Love*. Cambridge: Cambridge University Press.

Gibbard, Allan (1990). *Wise Choices, Apt Feelings*. Cambridge, Mass.: Harvard University Press.

Goldie, Peter (2000). *The Emotions*. Oxford: Oxford University Press.

Greenspan, P. S. (1995). *Practical Guilt*. New York: Oxford University Press.

Herman, Barbara (1993). 'Integrity and Impartiality'. Repr. in Herman, *The Practice of Moral Judgment*. Cambridge, Mass.: Harvard University Press.

Hill, Thomas E., Jr. (1991). 'Weakness of Will and Character'. Repr. in Hill, *Autonomy and Self-Respect*. Cambridge: Cambridge University Press.

Hooker, Brad (1987). 'Williams' Argument Against External Reasons'. *Analysis*, 47: 42–4.

Jackson, Frank (1984). 'Weakness of Will'. *Mind*, 93: 1–18.

Kennett, Jeanette (1991). 'Decision Theory and Weakness of Will'. *Pacific Philosophical Quarterly*, 72: 113–30.

—— (2001). *Agency and Responsibility*. Oxford: Oxford University Press.

—— and Smith, Michael (1996). 'Frog and Toad Lose Control'. *Analysis*, 56: 63–73.

—— —— (1997). 'Synchronic Self-Control Is Always Non-Actional'. *Analysis*, 57: 123–31.

Kolodny, Niko (2003). 'Love as Valuing a Relationship'. *Philosophical Review*, 112: 135–89.

Korsgaard, Christine (1986). 'Skepticism About Practical Reason'. *Journal of Philosophy*, 83: 5–25.

McDowell, John (1995). 'Might There Be External Reasons?', in J. E. J. Altham and Ross Harrison (eds.), *World, Mind, and Ethics*. Cambridge: Cambridge University Press.

McIntyre, Alison (1993). 'Is Akratic Action Always Irrational?', in Owen Flanagan and Amélie Oksenberg Rorty (eds.), *Identity, Character, and Morality*. Cambridge, Mass.: MIT Press.

Mele, Alfred R. (1987). *Irrationality*. New York: Oxford University Press.

—— (1995). *Autonomous Agents*. New York: Oxford University Press.

—— (1997). 'Understanding Self-Control: Kennett and Smith on Frog and Toad'. *Analysis*, 57: 119–23.

Milgram, Elijah (1996). 'Williams' Argument Against External Reasons'. *Noûs*, 30: 197–220.

Moran, Richard (2002). 'Frankfurt on Identification: Ambiguities of Activity in Mental Life', in Sarah Buss and Lee Overton (eds.), *Contours of Agency*. Cambridge, Mass.: MIT Press.

Morris, Herbert (1988). 'The Decline of Guilt'. *Ethics*, 99: 62–76.

Nagel, Thomas (1978). *The Possibility of Altruism*. Princeton: Princeton University Press.

Nussbaum, Martha (2001). *Upheavals of Thought*. Cambridge: Cambridge University Press.

Parfit, Derek (1997). 'Reasons and Motivation'. *Proceedings of the Aristotelian Society*, suppl. vol., 77: 99–130.

Pettit, Philip, and Smith, Michael (1990). 'Backgrounding Desire'. *Philosophical Review*, 99: 569–92.

—— —— (1993). 'Practical Unreason'. *Mind*, 102: 53–79.

—— —— (1996). 'Freedom in Belief and Desire'. *Journal of Philosophy*, 93: 429–49.

Quinn, Warren (1993). 'Putting Rationality in its Place'. Repr. in Quinn, *Morality and Action*. Cambridge: Cambridge University Press.

Railton, Peter (1988). 'Alienation, Consequentialism, and the Demands of Morality'. Repr. in Samuel Scheffler (ed.), *Consequentialism and its Critics*. Oxford: Oxford University Press.

Rawls, John (1971). *A Theory of Justice*. Cambridge, Mass.: Harvard University Press.

Raz, Joseph (1999a). 'Agency, Reason, and the Good'. Repr. in Raz, *Engaging Reason*. Oxford: Oxford University Press.

—— (1999b). 'On the Moral Point of View'. Repr. in Raz, *Engaging Reason*. Oxford: Oxford University Press.

—— (1999c). 'The Amoralist'. Repr. in Raz, *Engaging Reason*. Oxford: Oxford University Press.

—— (1999d). 'The Central Conflict: Morality and Self-Interest'. Repr. in Raz, *Engaging Reason*. Oxford: Oxford University Press.

—— (1999e). 'When We Are Ourselves: The Active and the Passive'. Repr. in Raz, *Engaging Reason*. Oxford: Oxford University Press.

Roberts, Robert C. (1984). 'Will Power and the Virtues'. *Philosophical Review*, 93: 227–47.

Rorty, Amélie Oksenberg (1980). 'Where Does the Akratic Break Take Place?' *Australasian Journal of Philosophy*, 58: 333–46.

Scanlon, T. M. (1982). 'Contractualism and Utilitarianism', in Amartya Sen and Bernard Williams (eds.), *Utilitarianism and Beyond*. Cambridge: Cambridge University Press.

—— (1998). *What We Owe to Each Other*. Cambridge, Mass.: Harvard University Press.

—— (2002). 'Reasons and Desires', in Sarah Buss and Lee Overton (eds.), *Contours of Agency*. Cambridge, Mass.: MIT Press.

Scheffler, Samuel (1992). *Human Morality*. New York: Oxford University Press.

Schueler, G. F. (1995). *Desire*. Cambridge, Mass.: MIT Press.

Smith, Michael (1987). 'The Humean Theory of Motivation'. *Mind*, 96: 3–61.

—— (1995). 'Internal Reasons'. *Philosophy and Phenomenological Research*, 55: 109–31.

—— (1997). 'In Defense of *The Moral Problem*: A Reply to Brink, Copp, and Sayre-McCord'. *Ethics*, 108: 84–119.

Stampe, Dennis (1987). 'The Authority of Desire'. *Philosophical Review*, 96: 335–81.

Stocker, Michael (1979). 'Desiring the Bad: An Essay in Moral Psychology'. *Journal of Philosophy*, 76: 738–53.

—— (1981). 'Values and Purposes: The Limits of Teleology and the Ends of Friendship'. *Journal of Philosophy*, 78: 747–65.

—— with Hegeman, Elizabeth (1996). *Valuing Emotions*. Cambridge: Cambridge University Press.

Strawson, P. F. (1982). 'Freedom and Resentment'. Repr. in Gary Watson (ed.), *Free Will*. Oxford: Oxford University Press.

Swanton, Christine (1992). *Freedom: A Coherence Theory*. Indianapolis: Hackett.

Taylor, Gabriele (1985). *Pride, Shame, and Guilt*. Oxford: Oxford University Press.

Velleman, J. David (1999). 'Love as a Moral Emotion'. *Ethics*, 109: 338–74.

—— (2000a). Introduction to *The Possibility of Practical Reason*. Oxford: Oxford University Press.

—— (2000b). 'The Guise of the Good'. Repr. in Velleman, *The Possibility of Practical Reason*. Oxford: Oxford University Press.

—— (2000c). 'The Possibility of Practical Reason'. Repr. in Velleman, *The Possibility of Practical Reason*. Oxford: Oxford University Press.

—— (2000d). 'What Happens When Someone Acts?' Repr. in Velleman, *The Possibility of Practical Reason*. Oxford: Oxford University Press.

—— (2002). 'Identification and Identity', in Sarah Buss and Lee Overton (eds.), *Contours of Agency*. Cambridge, Mass.: MIT Press.

Walker, Arthur F. (1989). 'The Problem of Weakness of Will'. *Noûs*, 23: 653–75.

Wallace, R. Jay (1990). 'How to Argue About Practical Reason'. *Mind*, 99: 355–85.

—— (1994). *Responsibility and the Moral Sentiments*. Cambridge, Mass.: Harvard University Press.

—— (1999*a*). 'Addiction as Defect of the Will: Some Philosophical Reflections'. *Law and Philosophy*, 18: 621–54.

—— (1999*b*). 'Three Conceptions of Rational Agency'. *Ethical Theory and Moral Practice*, 2: 217–42.

—— (2000). 'Caring, Reflexivity, and the Structure of Volition', in Monika Betzler and Barbara Guckes (eds.), *Autonomes Handeln*. Berlin: Akademie Verlag.

—— (2001). 'Normativity, Commitment, and Instrumental Reason'. *Philosophers' Imprint*, 1: 1–26.

—— (2002). 'Scanlon's Contractualism'. *Ethics*, 112: 429–70.

Watson, Gary (1982). 'Free Agency'. Repr. in Gary Watson (ed.), *Free Will*. Oxford: Oxford University Press.

—— (2002). 'Volitional Necessities', in Sarah Buss and Lee Overton (eds.), *Contours of Agency*. Cambridge, Mass.: MIT Press.

Wiggins, David (1991). 'Weakness of Will, Commensurability, and the Objects of Deliberation and Desire'. Repr. in Wiggins, *Needs, Values, Truth*, 2nd edn. Oxford: Blackwell.

Williams, Bernard (1973). 'A Critique of Utilitarianism', in J. J. C. Smart and Bernard Williams, *Utilitarianism: For and Against*. Cambridge: Cambridge University Press.

—— (1981*a*). 'Internal and External Reasons'. Repr. in Williams, *Moral Luck*. Cambridge: Cambridge University Press.

—— (1981*b*). 'Moral Luck'. Repr. in Williams, *Moral Luck*. Cambridge: Cambridge University Press.

—— (1981*c*). 'Persons, Character and Morality'. Repr. in Williams, *Moral Luck*. Cambridge: Cambridge University Press.

—— (1981*d*). 'Practical Necessity'. Repr. in Williams, *Moral Luck*. Cambridge: Cambridge University Press.

—— (1993). *Shame and Necessity*. Berkeley: University of California Press.

—— (1995*a*). 'Internal Reasons and the Obscurity of Blame'. Repr. in Williams, *Making Sense of Humanity*. Cambridge: Cambridge University Press.

—— (1995*b*). 'Moral Incapacity'. Repr. in Williams, *Making Sense of Humanity*. Cambridge: Cambridge University Press.

—— (1995*c*). 'Nietzsche's Minimalist Moral Psychology'. Repr. in Williams, *Making Sense of Humanity*. Cambridge: Cambridge University Press.

—— (1995*d*). 'Replies', in J. E. J. Altham and Ross Harrison (eds.), *World, Mind, and Ethics*. Cambridge: Cambridge University Press.

—— (2001). 'Postscript: Some Further Notes on Internal and External Reasons', in Elijah Milgram (ed.), *Varieties of Practical Reasoning*. Cambridge, Mass.: MIT Press.

Wolf, Susan (1992). 'Morality and Partiality'. *Philosophical Perspectives*, 6: 243–59.

Wollheim, Richard (1984). *The Thread of Life*. Cambridge, Mass.: Harvard University Press.

—— (1993). 'The Sheep and Ceremony'. Repr. in Wollheim, *The Mind and its Depths*. Cambridge, Mass.: Harvard University Press.

—— (1999). *On the Emotions*. New Haven: Yale University Press.

CHAPTER 5

AS A MATTER OF FACT: EMPIRICAL PERSPECTIVES ON ETHICS

JOHN M. DORIS AND STEPHEN P. STICH

Too many moral philosophers and commentators on moral philosophy . . . have been content to invent their psychology or anthropology from scratch. . . .

S. Darwall, A. Gibbard, and P. Railton (1997: 34–5)

1. INTRODUCTION

Regarding the assessment of Darwall and colleagues, we couldn't agree more: far too many moral philosophers have been content to *invent* the psychology or anthropology on which their theories depend, advancing or disputing empirical claims with little concern for empirical evidence. We also believe—and we expect Darwall, Gibbard, and Railton would agree—that this empirical complacency has impeded progress in ethical theory and discouraged investigators in the biological, behavioural, and social sciences from undertaking philosophically informed research on ethical issues.

We realize that some moral philosophers have taken there to be good reasons for shunning empirical inquiry. For much of the twentieth century, many working in analytic ethics—variously inspired by Hume's (1978: 469) pithy injunction against inferring *ought* from *is* and the seductive mysteries of Moore's (1903, esp. 10–17) 'Open Question Argument'—maintained that descriptive considerations of the sort adduced in the natural and social sciences cannot constrain ethical reflection without vitiating its prescriptive or normative character (e.g. Stevenson 1944: 108–10; R. M. Hare 1952: 79–93). The plausibility of such claims is both debated and debatable, but it is clear that they have helped engender suspicion regarding 'naturalism' in ethics, which we understand, broadly, as the view that *ethical theorizing should be an (in part) a posteriori inquiry richly informed by relevant empirical considerations.*[1] Relatedly, this anti-naturalist suspicion enables disciplinary xenophobia in philosophical ethics, a reluctance to engage research beyond the philosophical literature. The methodology we advocate here—a resolutely naturalistic approach to ethical theory squarely engaging the relevant biological, behavioural, and social sciences—flouts both of these anxieties.

Perhaps those lacking our equanimity suspect that approaches of the sort we endorse fail to heed Stevenson's (1963: 13) advice that 'Ethics must not be psychology', and thereby lapse into a noxious 'scientism' or 'eliminativism'. Notoriously, Quine (1969: 75) advocated eliminativism in his rendering of naturalized epistemology, urging philosophical 'surrender of the epistemological burden to psychology'. Quine was sharply rebuked for slighting the normative character of epistemology (e.g. Kim 1988; Stich 1993a), but we are not suggesting, in a rambunctiously Quinean spirit, 'surrender of the *ethical* burden to psychology'. And so far as we know, neither is anyone else. Ethics must not—indeed cannot—*be* psychology, but it does not follow that ethics should *ignore* psychology.

The most obvious, and most compelling, motivation for our perspective is simply this: It is not possible to step far into the ethics literature without stubbing one's toe on empirical claims. The thought that moral philosophy can proceed unencumbered by facts seems to us an unlikely one: there are just too many places where answers to important ethical questions require—and have very often presupposed—answers to empirical questions.

A small but growing number of philosophers, ourselves included, have become convinced that answers to these empirical questions should be informed by systematic

---

[1] Compare Railton's (1989: 155–6) 'methodological naturalism'.

empirical research.[2] This is not to say that relevant information is easy to come by: the science is not always packaged in forms that are easy on the philosophical digestion. As Darwall *et al.* (1997: 47 ff.) caution, one won't often find 'a well-developed literature in the social sciences simply awaiting philosophical discovery and exploitation'. Still, we are more optimistic than Darwall and colleagues about the help philosophers can expect from empirical literatures: science has produced much experimental and theoretical work that appears importantly relevant to ongoing debates in ethical theory, and some moral philosophers have lately begun to pursue empirical investigations. To explore the issues fully requires far more space than is available here; we must content ourselves with developing a few rather programmatic examples of how an empirically sensitive philosophical ethics might proceed.

Our point is not that reference to empirical literatures can be expected, by itself, to resolve debates in moral theory. Rather, we hope to convince the reader that these literatures are often deeply relevant to important debates, and it is therefore intellectually irresponsible to ignore them. Sometimes empirical findings seem to contradict what particular disputing parties assert or presuppose, while in other cases, they appear to reconfigure the philosophical topography, revealing that certain lines of argument must traverse empirically difficult terrain. Often, philosophers who follow these challenging routes will be forced to make additional empirical conjectures, and these conjectures, in their turn, must be subject to empirical scrutiny. The upshot, we conclude, is that an intellectually responsible philosophical ethics is one that continuously engages the relevant empirical literature.

2. CHARACTER

In the second half of the twentieth century the 'ethics of virtue' became an increasingly popular alternative to the Kantian and utilitarian theories that had for some time dominated normative ethics. In contrast to Kantianism and utilitarianism, which despite marked differences share an emphasis on identifying morally obligatory actions, virtue-centred approaches emphasize the psychological constitution, or character, of actors. The central question for virtue ethics, so the slogan goes, is not what sort of action to do, but what sort of person to be.[3] As Bernard Williams

---

[2] See Gibbard (1990: 58–61); Flanagan (1991); Goldman (1993); Johnson (1993); Stich (1993*b*); Railton (1995); Blackburn (1998: 36–7); Bok (1996); Doris (1996, 1998, 2002); Becker (1998); Campbell (1999); Harman (1999, 2000); Merritt (1999, 2000); Doris and Stich (2001); Woolfolk and Doris (2002).

[3] The notion that character is evaluatively independent of or prior to action is sometimes thought to be the distinctive emphasis of virtue ethics (see Louden 1984: 229; Watson 1990: 451–2). But this is

(1985: 1) has eloquently reminded us, the 'aims of moral philosophy, and any hopes it may have of being worth serious attention, are bound up with the fate of Socrates' question' How should one live?, and it has seemed to many philosophers, not least due to Williams's influence, that any prospects for a satisfying answer rest with the ethics of character. Allegedly, if ethical reflection is to help people understand and improve themselves and their relations to others, it must be reflection focused on the condition and cultivation of character (see Williams 1993: 91–5).

Virtue ethics, especially in the Aristotelian guises that dominate the field, typically presupposes a distinctive account of human psychology. Nussbaum (1999: 170), although she insists that the moniker 'virtue ethics' has been used to tag such a variety of projects that it represents a 'misleading category', observes that approaches so titled are concerned with the 'settled patterns of motive, emotion, and reasoning that lead us to call someone a person of a certain sort (courageous, generous, moderate, just, etc.)'. If this is a fair characterization—and we think it is—then virtue ethics is marked by a particular interest in moral psychology, an interest in the cognitive, affective, and emotional patterns that are associated with the attribution of character traits.[4] This interest looks to be an empirical interest, and it's natural to ask how successfully virtue ethics addresses it.

The central empirical issue concerns, to borrow Nussbaum's phrase, 'settled patterns' of functioning. According to Aristotle, genuinely virtuous action proceeds from 'firm and unchangeable character' rather than from transient motives (1984: 1105^{a}28–^{b}1); while the good person may suffer misfortune that impairs his activities and diminishes happiness, he 'will never (*oudepote*) do the acts that are hateful and mean' (1984: 1100^{b}32–4; cf. 1128^{b}29; cf. Cooper 1999: 299 ff.).[5] In an influential contemporary exposition, McDowell (1978: 26–7) argued that considerations favouring vicious behaviour are 'silenced' in the virtuous person; although such an individual may recognize inducements to vice, she will not count them as reasons for action. As we understand the tradition, virtues are supposed to be robust traits; if a person has a robust trait, she can be confidently (although perhaps not with absolute certainty) expected to display trait-relevant behaviour across a wide variety of

---

not plausibly understood to mean that virtue ethics is indifferent regarding questions of what to do; the question of conduct should be of substantial importance on both virtue- and action-centred approaches (see Sher 1998: 15–17).

⁴ Nussbaum (1999: 170) observes that Kantian and utilitarian approaches may share virtue ethics' interest in character. Space prohibits discussion, but if Nussbaum were right, our argument would have more sweeping implications than we contemplate here.

⁵ In Aristotle's view, the virtues are *hexeis* (1984: 1106^{a}10–12), and a *hexis* is a disposition that is 'permanent and hard to change' (1984: 8^{b}25–9^{a}9). This feature of Aristotle's account is emphasized by commentators: Sherman (1989: 1) says that for Aristotle (as well as for us) character traits explain why 'someone can be *counted on* to act in certain ways' (cf. Woods 1986: 149; Annas 1993: 51; Audi 1995: 451; Cooper 1999: 238).

trait-relevant situations, even where some or all of these situations are not optimally conducive to such behaviour (Doris 2002: 18).[6]

Additionally, some philosophers have supposed that character will be evaluatively integrated—traits with associated evaluative valences are expected to co-occur in personality (see Doris 2002: 22; Flanagan 1991: 283–90). As Aristotle (1984: 1144^{b}30–1145^{a}2; cf. Irwin 1988: 66–71) has it, the virtues are inseparable; given the qualities of practical reason sufficient for the possession of one virtue, one can expect to find the qualities of practical reason sufficient for them all.

While understandings of character and personality akin to those just described have been hotly contested in psychology departments at least since the critiques of Vernon (1964), Mischel (1968), and Peterson (1968), moral philosophers have not been especially quick in taking the matter up. Flanagan's (1991) careful discussion broached the issue in contemporary analytic ethics, while Doris (1998, 2002) and Harman (1999, 2000) have lately pressed the point less temperately: although they manifest some fraternal disagreements, Harman and Doris both insist that the conception of character presupposed by virtue ethics is empirically inadequate.

The evidence for this contention, often united under the theoretical heading of 'situationism', has been developed over a period of some seventy years, and includes some of the most striking research in the human sciences.

- Mathews and Canon (1975: 574–5) found subjects were five times more likely to help an apparently injured man who had dropped some books when ambient noise was at normal levels than when a power lawnmower was running nearby (80 per cent v. 15 per cent).
- Darley and Batson (1973: 105) report that passers-by not in a hurry were six times more likely to help an unfortunate who appeared to be in significant distress than were passers-by in a hurry (63 per cent v. 10 per cent).
- Isen and Levin (1972: 387) discovered that people who had just found a dime were twenty-two times more likely to help a woman who had dropped some papers than those who did not find a dime (88 per cent v. 4 per cent).
- Milgram (1974) found that subjects would repeatedly 'punish' a screaming 'victim' with realistic (but simulated) electric shocks at the polite request of an experimenter.
- Haney *et al.* (1973) describe how college students role-playing in a simulated prison rapidly descended to *Lord of the Flies* barbarism.

There apparently exists an alarming disproportion between situational input and morally disquieting output; it takes surprisingly little to get people behaving in

---

[6] This follows quite a standard theme in philosophical writings on virtue and character. For example, Blum (1994: 178–80) understands compassion as a trait of character typified by an altruistic attitude of 'strength and duration', which should be 'stable and consistent' in prompting beneficent action (cf. Brandt 1970: 27; Dent 1975: 328; McDowell 1979: 331–3; Larmore 1987: 12).

morally undesirable ways. The point is not that circumstances influence behaviour, or even that seemingly good people sometimes do lousy things. No need to stop the presses for that. Rather, the telling difficulty is just how insubstantial the situational influences effecting troubling moral failures seem to be; it is not that people fall short of ideals of virtue and fortitude, but that they can be *readily* induced to *radically* fail such ideals.

The argument suggested by this difficulty can be outlined as follows: a large body of research indicates that cognition and behaviour are extraordinarily sensitive to the situations in which people are embedded. The implication is that individuals— on the altogether plausible assumption that most people will be found in a range of situations involving widely disparate cognitive and behavioural demands—are typically highly variable in their behaviour, relative to the behavioural expectations associated with familiar trait categories such as honesty, compassion, courage, and the like. But if people's behaviour were typically structured by robust traits, one would expect quite the opposite: namely, behaviour consistent with a given trait—e.g. behaviour that is appropriately and reliably honest, compassionate, or courageous—across a diversity of situations. It follows, according to the argument, that behaviour is not typically structured by the robust traits that figure centrally in virtue-theoretic moral psychology. Analogous considerations are supposed to make trouble for notions of evaluative integration; the endemic lack of uniformity in behaviour adduced from the empirical literature undermines expectations of integrated character structures.

The situationist argument has sometimes been construed by philosophers as asserting that character traits 'do not exist' (Flanagan 1991: 302; Athanassoulis 2000: 219–20; Kupperman 2001: 250), but this is a misleading formulation of the issue.[7] In so far as to deny the existence of traits is to deny the existence of persisting dispositional differences among persons, the claim that traits do not exist seems unsustainable, and the exercise of refuting such a claim idle. (Indeed, it is a claim that even psychologists with strong situationist sympathies, e.g. Mischel 1968: 8–9, seem at pains to disavow.) The real issue dividing the virtue theorist and the situationist concerns the appropriate characterization of traits, not their existence or nonexistence. The situationist argument that needs to be taken seriously, and which to our mind stands unrefuted, holds that the Aristotelian conception of traits as robust dispositions—the sort which lead to trait-relevant behaviour across a wide variety of trait-relevant situations—is radically empirically undersupported. To

---

[7] Part of the reason for this error may be some spirited rhetoric of Harman's (e.g. the title of Harman 2000: 'The Nonexistence of Character Traits'). But Harman repeatedly offers qualifications that caution against it; he voices scepticism about the existence of 'ordinary character traits *of the sort people think there are*' (1999: 316) and 'character traits *as ordinarily conceived*' (2000: 223; our italics). This is to reject a particular conception of character traits, not to deny that character traits exist. For his part, Doris (1998: 507; 2002: 62–6) quite explicitly acknowledges the existence of traits, albeit traits with less generalized effects on behaviour than is often supposed.

put the ethical implications of this a bit aggressively, it looks as though attribution of robust traits like virtues may very well be unwarranted in most instances,[8] programmes of moral education aimed at inculcating virtues may very well be futile, and modes of ethical reflection focusing moral aspirations on the cultivation of virtue may very well be misguided.

At this point, the virtue theorist may offer one of two responses. She can accept the critics' interpretation of the empirical evidence while denying that her approach makes empirical commitments of the sort the evidence indicates is problematic. Or she can allow that her approach makes commitments in empirical psychology of the sort that would be problematic if the critics' interpretations of the evidence were sustainable, but deny that the critics have interpreted the evidence aright. The first option, we might say, is 'empirically modest' (see Doris 2002: 110–12): because such renderings make only minimal claims in empirical psychology, they are insulated from empirical threat. The second option, conversely, is 'empirically vulnerable' (see Railton 1995: 92–6): it makes empirical claims with enough substance to invite empirically motivated criticism.

We shall first discuss empirically modest rejoinders to the situationist critique. Numerous defenders of virtue ethics insist that virtue is not expected to be widely instantiated, but is found in only a few extraordinary individuals, and these writers further observe that this minimal empirical commitment is quite compatible with the disturbing, but not exceptionlessly disturbing, behaviour in experiments like Milgram's (see Athanassoulis 1999: 217–19; DePaul 1999; Kupperman 2001: 242–3). The critics are bound to concede the point, since the empirical evidence cannot show that the instantiation of virtue in actual human psychologies is impossible; no empirical evidence could secure so strong a result. But so construed, the aspirations of virtue ethics are not entirely clear; if virtue is *expected* to be rare, it is not obvious what role virtue theory could have in a (generally applicable) programme of moral education.[9] This rings a bit odd, given that moral education—construed as aiming for the development of the good character necessary for a good life—has traditionally been a distinctive emphasis in writing on virtue, from Aristotle (1984: 1099^b9–32, 1103^b3–26) to Bennett (1993: 11–16; cf. Williams 1985: 10). Of course, the rarity of virtue might be thought a contingent matter; given the appropriate modalities of moral education, the virtue ethicist might say, virtue can be widely inculcated. But philosophers, psychologists, and educators alike have tended to be a bit hazy regarding particulars of the requisite educational processes; theories of moral

---

[8] The difficulty is not limited to rival academic theories; there is a large body of empirical evidence indicating that everyday 'lay' habits of person perception seriously overestimate the impact of individual dispositional differences on behavioural outcomes. For summaries, see Jones (1990); Ross and Nisbett (1991: 119–44); Gilbert and Malone (1995); Doris (2002: 92–106).

[9] Of course, if the virtue theorist is an elitist, this need not trouble her. But while historical writers on the virtues have at times manifested elitist sympathies (Aristotle 1984: 1123^a6–10, 1124^a17–$^b32$; Hume 1975: 250–67), this is not a sensibility that is typically celebrated by contemporary philosophers.

education, and character education in particular, are typically not supported by large bodies of systematic research adducing behavioural differences corresponding to differing educational modalities (Leming 1997*a,b*; Hart and Killen 1999: 12; Doris 2002: 121–7).

It is tempting to put the situationist point a bit more sharply. It is true that the evidence does not show that the instantiation of virtue in actual human psychologies is impossible. But it also looks to be the case that the available systematic empirical evidence is compatible with virtue being psychologically impossible (or at least wildly improbable), and this suggests that the impossibility of virtue is an empirical possibility that has to be taken seriously. So while the evidence doesn't refute an empirically modest version of virtue ethics, it is plausibly taken to suggest that the burden of argument has importantly shifted: The advocate of virtue ethics can no longer simply assume that virtue is psychologically possible. If she can't offer compelling evidence—very preferably, more than anecdotal evidence—favouring the claim that virtue is psychologically possible, then she is in the awkward position of forwarding a view that would be undermined if an empirical claim which is not obviously false were to turn out to be true, without offering compelling reason to think that it won't turn out to be true.

Suppose the realization of virtue were acknowledged to be impossible: it might yet be insisted that talk of virtue articulates ethical ideals that are well suited—presumably better suited than alternatives, if virtue ethics is thought to have distinctive advantages—to facilitating ethically desirable conduct (see Blum 1994: 94–6). Asserting such a practical advantage for virtue ethics entails an empirical claim: reflection on the ideals of virtue can help actual people behave better. For example, it might be claimed that talk of virtue is more compelling, or has more motivational 'grip', than abstract axiological principles. We know of little systematic evidence favouring such claims, and we are unsure of what sort of experimental designs are fit to secure them, but the only point we need to insist on is that even this empirically modest rendering of virtue ethics may bear contentious empirical commitments. If virtue ethics is alleged to have practical implications, it cannot avoid empirical assertions regarding the cognitive and motivational equipment with which people navigate their moral world.

Even without an answer to such practical questions, it might be thought that virtue ethics is fit to address familiar conceptual problems in philosophical ethics, such as rendering an account of right action. In Hursthouse's (1999: 28; cf. 49–51) account of virtue ethics, 'An action is right iff it is what a virtuous agent would characteristically (i.e., acting in character) do in the circumstances.' Hursthouse (1999: 123–6, 136, 140) further insists that an action does not count as 'morally motivated' simply by dint of being the sort of thing a virtuous person does, done for reasons of the sort the virtuous person does it for; it must proceed 'from virtue', that is, 'from a settled state of good character'. If this requirement is juxtaposed with the observation that the relevant states of character are extremely rare, as an empirically modest rendering of virtue ethics maintains, we apparently get the result that 'morally motivated' actions are also extremely rare (a virtue-theoretic result, interestingly, with which Kant would have agreed). This need not trouble Hursthouse (1999: 141–60); she seems to allow that very often—perhaps always—one sees only approximations of moral motivation. It does trouble us. We think that less than virtuous people, even smashingly less than virtuous people, sometimes do the right thing for the right reasons, and these actions are fit to be honoured as 'morally motivated'. It may not happen as often as one would like, but morally motivated conduct seems to happen rather more frequently than one chances on perfect virtue. Oskar Schindler, the philandering war profiteer who rescued thousands of Jews from the Nazis, is a famous example of the two notions coming apart (see Kenneally 1982), but with a little attention to the history books, we can surely adduce many more. The burden of proof, it seems to us, is on those asserting that such widely revered actions are not morally motivated.

There are also serious questions about the competitive advantages enjoyed by empirically modest virtue ethics. It has seemed to many that a chief attraction of character-based approaches is the promise of a lifelike moral psychology—a less wooden depiction of moral affect, cognition, motivation, and education than that offered by competing approaches such as Kantianism and utilitarianism (Flanagan 1991: 182; Hursthouse 1999: 119–20). Proponents of virtue ethics, perhaps most prominently MacIntyre (1984) and Williams (1985, 1993), link their approach—as Anscombe (1958: 4–5) did in a paper widely regarded as the call to arms for contemporary virtue ethics—to prospects for more psychological realism and texture. We submit that this is where a large measure of virtue ethics' appeal has lain; if virtue ethicists had tended to describe their psychological project along the lines just imagined, as deploying a moral psychology only tenuously related to the contours of actual human psychologies, we rather doubt that the view would now be sweeping the field.

We contend that for virtue ethics to retain its competitive advantage in moral psychology it must court empirical danger by making empirical claims with enough substance to be seriously tested by the empirical evidence from psychology. For instance, the virtue theorist may insist that while perfect virtue is rare indeed, robust traits approximating perfect virtue—reliable courage, temperance, and the rest—may be widely inculcated, and perhaps similarly for robust vices—reliable cowardice, profligacy, and so on.[10] To defend such a position, the virtue theorist must somehow discredit the critic's empirical evidence. Various arguments might be thought to secure such a result: (i) The situationist experiments might be methodologically flawed; problems in experimental design or data analysis, for example, might undermine the results. (ii) The experiments might fail standards of ecological

---

[10] There is some question as to whether vices are expected to be robust in the way virtues are, but some philosophers seem to think so: Hill (1991: 130–2) apparently believes that calling someone weak-willed marks characteristic patterns of behaviour.

validity; the experimental contexts might be so distant from natural contexts as to preclude generalizations to the 'real world'. (iii) General conclusions from the experiments might be prohibited by limited samples; in particular, there appears to be a dearth of longitudinal behavioural studies that would help assess the role of character traits 'over the long haul'. (iv) The experiments may be conceptually irrelevant; for example, the conceptions of particular traits operationalized in the empirical work may not correspond to the related conceptions figuring in virtue ethics.

The thing to notice straight away is that motivating contentions like the four above require evaluating a great deal of psychological research; making a charge stick to one experiment or two, when there are hundreds, if not thousands, of relevant studies, is unlikely to effect a satisfying resolution of the controversy. The onus, of course, falls on both sides: just as undermining arguments directed at single experiments are of limited comfort to the virtue theorist, demonstrating the philosophical relevance of a lone study is not enough to make the critics' day. Newspaper science reporting notwithstanding, in science there is seldom, or never, a single decisive experiment or, for that matter, a decisive experimental failure. General conclusions about social science can legitimately be drawn only from encountering, in full detail, a body of research, and adducing patterns or trends. Doris (2002) has recently attempted to approximate this methodological standard in a book-length study, and he there concludes that major trends in empirical work support conclusions in the neighbourhood indicated by the more programmatic treatments of Doris (1998) and Harman (1999, 2000). Whether or not one is drawn to this conclusion, we think it clear that the most profitable discussion of the empirical literature will proceed with detailed discussion of the relevant empirical work. If an empirically vulnerable virtue ethics is to be shown empirically defensible, defenders must provide much fuller consideration of the psychology. To our knowledge, extant defences of virtue ethics in the face of empirical attack do not approximate the required breadth and depth.[11] Hopefully, future discussions will rectify this situation, to the edification of defenders and critics alike.

3. MORAL MOTIVATION

Suppose a person believes that she ought to do something: donate blood to the Red Cross, say, or send a significant contribution to an international relief agency. Does it follow that she will be moved actually to act on this belief? Ethical theorists use

---

[11] For example, Kupperman (2001) refers to nine items in the empirical literature in responding to Harman, and Athanassoulis (2000), three.

internalism to mark an important cluster of answers to this question, answers maintaining that the motivation to act on a moral judgement is a necessary or intrinsic concomitant of the judgement itself, or that the relevant motivation is inevitably generated by the very same mental faculty that produces the judgement.[12] One familiar version of internalism is broadly Kantian, emphasizing the role of rationality in ethics. As Deigh (1999: 289) characterizes the position, 'reason is both the pilot and the engine of moral agency. It not only guides one toward actions in conformity with one's duty, but it also produces the desire to do one's duty and can invest that desire with enough strength to overrule conflicting impulses of appetite and passion.' A notorious difficulty for internalism is suggested by Hume's (1975: 282–4) 'sensible knave', a person who recognizes that the unjust and dishonest acts he contemplates are wrong, but is completely unmoved by this realization. More recent writers (e.g. Nichols 2002) have suggested that the sensible knave (or, as philosophers often call him, 'the amoralist') is more than a philosophical fiction, since clinical psychologists and other mental health professionals have for some time noted the existence of sociopaths or psychopaths, who appear to *know* the difference between right and wrong but quite generally lack motivation to *do* what is right. If this understanding of the psychopath's moral psychology is accurate, internalism looks to be suffering empirical embarrassment.[13]

Internalists have adopted two quite different responses to this challenge, one conceptual and the other empirical. The first relies on conceptual analysis to argue that a person couldn't really believe that an act is wrong if he has no motivation to avoid performing it. For example, Michael Smith claims it is 'a conceptual truth that agents who make moral judgements are motivated accordingly, at least absent weakness of the will and the like' (Smith 1994: 66). Philosophers who adopt this strategy recognize that imaginary knaves and real psychopaths may *say* that something is 'morally required' or 'morally wrong' and that they may be expressing a judgement that they sincerely accept. But if psychopaths are not motivated in the appropriate way, their words do not mean what non-psychopaths mean by these words and the concepts they express with these words are not the ordinary moral concepts that non-psychopaths use. Therefore psychopaths 'do not *really* make moral judgements at all' (Smith 1994: 67).

This strategy only works if ordinary moral concepts require that people who *really* make moral judgements have the appropriate sort of motivation. But there is

---

[12] A stipulation: We refer to views in the neighbourhood of what Darwall (1983: 54) calls 'judgement internalism', the thesis that it is 'a necessary condition of a genuine instance of a certain sort of judgment that the person making the judgment be disposed to act in a way appropriate to it'. Space limitations force us to ignore myriad complications; for more detailed discussion, see Svavarsdóttir (1999).

[13] There is august precedent for supposing that the internalism debate has empirical elements. In his classic discussion, Frankena (1976: 73) observed that progress here requires reference to 'the psychology of human motivation'—'The battle, if war there be, cannot be contained; its field is the whole human world'. We hope that Frankena would have appreciated our way of joining the fight.

considerable disagreement in cognitive science about whether and how concepts are structured, and about how we are to determine when something is built into or entailed by a concept (Margolis and Laurence 1999). Indeed, one widely discussed approach maintains that concepts have no semantically relevant internal structure to be analysed—thus there are no conceptual entailments (Fodor 1998). Obviously, internalists who appeal to conceptual analysis must reject this account, and in so doing they must take a stand in the broadly empirical debate about the nature of concepts.

Smith is one moral theorist who has taken such a stand. Following Lewis (1970, 1972), Jackson (1994), and others, Smith proposes that a concept can be analysed by specifying the 'maximal consistent set of platitudes' in which the concept is invoked; it is by 'coming to treat those platitudes as platitudinous', Smith (1994: 31) maintains, that 'we come to have mastery of that concept'. If this is correct, the conceptual analysis defence of internalism requires that the maximally consistent set of platitudes invoking the notion of a moral judgement includes a claim to the effect that 'agents who make moral judgements are motivated accordingly'. Once again, this is an empirical claim. Smith appeals to his own intuitions in its support, but it is of course rather likely that opponents of internalism do not share Smith's intuitions, and it is difficult to say whose intuitions should trump.

In the interests of developing a non-partisan analysis, Nichols (2002) has been running a series of experiments in which philosophically unsophisticated undergraduates are presented with questions like these:

> John is a psychopathic criminal. He is an adult of normal intelligence, but he has no emotional reaction to hurting other people. John has hurt, and indeed killed, other people when he has wanted to steal their money. He says that he knows that hurting others is wrong, but that he just doesn't care if he does things that are wrong. Does John really understand that hurting others is morally wrong?

> Bill is a mathematician. He is an adult of normal intelligence, but he has no emotional reaction to hurting other people. Nonetheless, Bill never hurts other people simply because he thinks that it is irrational to hurt others. He thinks that any rational person would be like him and not hurt other people. Does Bill really understand that hurting others is morally wrong? (Nichols 2004: 74)

Nichols's preliminary results are exactly the opposite of what Smith would have one expect. An overwhelming majority of subjects maintained that John, the psychopath, did understand that hurting others is morally wrong, while a slight majority maintained that Bill, the rational mathematician, did not. The implication seems to be that the subjects' concept of moral judgement does not typically include a 'motivational platitude'. These results do not, of course, constitute a decisive refutation of Smith's conceptual analysis, since Smith can reply that responses like those Nichols reports would not be part of the maximally consistent set of platitudes that people would endorse after due reflection. But this too is an empirical claim; if Smith is to offer a compelling defence of it he should—with our enthusiastic encouragement—adduce some systematic empirical evidence.

A second internalist strategy for dealing with the problem posed by the amoralist is empirical: even if amoralists are conceptually possible, the internalist may insist, their existence is psychologically impossible. As a matter of psychological fact, this argument goes, people's moral judgements are accompanied by the appropriate sort of motivation.[14] A Kantian elaboration of this idea, on which we will focus, maintains that people's moral judgements are accompanied by the appropriate sort of motivation *unless their rational faculties are impaired*. (We'll shortly see that much turns on the fate of the italicized clause.) Recent papers by Roskies (2003) and Nichols (2002) set out important challenges to this strategy.

Roskies' argument relies on Damasio and colleagues' work with patients suffering injuries to the ventromedial (VM) cortex (Damasio *et al.* 1990; Saver and Damasio 1991; Bechara *et al.* 2000). On a wide range of standard psychological tests, including tests for intelligence and reasoning abilities, these patients appear quite normal. They also do as well as normal subjects on Kohlberg's tests of *moral* reasoning, and when presented with hypothetical situations they offer moral judgements that concur with those of normal subjects. However, these patients appear to have great difficulty acting in accordance with those judgements. As a result, although they often led exemplary lives prior to their injury, their post-trauma social lives are a shambles. They disregard social conventions, make disastrous business and personal decisions, and often engage in anti-social behaviour. Accordingly, Damasio and his colleagues describe the VM patients' condition as 'acquired sociopathy' (Saver and Damasio 1991).

Roskies maintains that VM patients do not act on their moral judgements because they suffer a *motivational* deficit. Moreover, the evidence indicates that these individuals do not have a *general* difficulty in acting on evaluative judgements; rather, Roskies (2003) maintains, action with respect to moral and social evaluation is differentially impaired. In addition to the behavioural evidence, this interpretation is supported by the anomalous pattern of skin-conductance responses (SCRs) that VM patients display.[15] Normal individuals produce an SCR when presented with emotionally charged or value-laden stimuli, while VM patients typically do not produce SCRs in response to such stimuli. SCRs are not entirely lacking in VM patients, however. SCRs are produced when VM patients are surprised or startled, for example, demonstrating that the physiological basis for these responses is intact. In addition, their presence is reliably correlated with cases in which patients' actions are consistent with their judgements about what to do, and their absence is reliably correlated with cases in which patients fail to act in accordance with their judgements. Thus, Roskies contends, the SCR is a reliable indicator of motivation.

---

[14] We prescind from questions as to whether the motivation need be overriding, although we suspect formulations not requiring overridingness are more plausible.

[15] SCR is a measure of physiological arousal, which is also sometimes called galvanic skin response, or GSR.

So the fact that VM patients, unlike normal subjects, do not exhibit SCRs in response to morally charged stimuli suggests that their failure to act in morally charged situations results from a motivational deficit.

On the face of it, acquired sociopathy confounds internalists maintaining that the moral judgements of rational people are, as a matter of psychological fact, always accompanied by appropriate motivation.[16] Testing indicates that the general reasoning abilities of these patients are not impaired, and even their moral reasoning seems to be quite normal. So none of the empirical evidence suggests the presence of a cognitive disability. An internalist might insist that these post-injury judgements are not *genuine* instances of moral judgements because VM patients no longer know the standard meaning of the moral words they use. But unless it is supported by an appeal to a conceptual analysis of the sort we criticized earlier, this is a rather implausible move; as Roskies notes, all tests of VM patients indicate that their language, their declarative knowledge structures, and their cognitive functioning are intact. There are, of course, many questions about acquired sociopathy that remain unanswered and much work is yet to be done. However these questions get answered, the literature on VM patients is one that moral philosophers embroiled in the internalism debate would be ill advised to ignore; once again, the outcome of a debate in ethical theory looks to be contingent on empirical issues.

The same point holds for other work on anti-social behaviour. Drawing on Blair's (1995) studies of psychopathic murderers imprisoned in Great Britain, Nichols (2002) has recently argued that the phenomenon of psychopathy poses a deep and complex challenge for internalism. Again, the general difficulty is that psychopaths seem to be living instantiations of Hume's sensible knave: although they appear to be rational and can be quite intelligent, psychopaths are manipulative, remorseless, and devoid of other-regarding concern. While psychopaths sometimes acknowledge that their treatment of other people is wrong, they are quite indifferent about the harm that they have caused; they seem to have no motivation to avoid hurting others (R. D. Hare 1993).

Blair's (1995) evidence complicates this familiar story. He found that psychopaths exhibit surprising deficits on various tasks where subjects are presented with descriptions of 'moral' transgressions like a child hitting another child and 'conventional' transgressions like a child leaving the classroom without the teacher's permission. From early childhood, normal children distinguish moral from conventional transgressions on a number of dimensions: they view moral transgressions as more serious, they explain why the acts are wrong by appeal to different factors (harm and fairness for moral transgressions, social acceptability for conventional transgressions), and they understand conventional transgressions, unlike moral transgressions, to be dependent on authority (Turiel *et al.* 1987; Nucci 1986).

---

[16] Roskies herself does not offer acquired sociopathy as a counter-example to the Kantian version of empirical internalism, but we believe the evidence *is* in tension with the Kantian view we describe.

For example, presented with a hypothetical case where a teacher says there is no rule about leaving the classroom without permission, children think it is OK to leave without permission. But presented with a hypothetical where a teacher says there is no rule against hitting other children, children do not judge that hitting is acceptable. Blair has shown that while autistic children, children with Down syndrome, and a control group of incarcerated non-psychopath murderers have relatively little trouble in drawing the moral–conventional distinction and classifying cases along these lines, incarcerated psychopaths are unable to do so.

This inability might be evidence for the hypothesis that psychopaths have a reasoning deficit, and therefore do not pose a problem for internalists who maintain that a properly functioning reasoning faculty reliably generates some motivation to do what one believes one ought to do. But, as Nichols (2002) has pointed out, the issue cannot be so easily resolved, because psychopaths have also been shown to have *affective* responses that are quite different from those of normal subjects. When shown distressing stimuli (like slides of people with dreadful injuries) and threatening stimuli (like slides of an angry man wielding a weapon), normal subjects exhibit much the same suite of physiological responses. Psychopaths, by contrast, exhibit normal physiological responses to threatening stimuli, but abnormally low physiological responses to distressing stimuli (Blair *et al.* 1997). Thus, Nichols argues, it may well be that the psychopath's deficit is not an abnormal reasoning system, but an abnormal affect system, and it is these affective abnormalities, rather than any rational disabilities, that are implicated in psychopaths' failure to draw the moral–conventional distinction.[17] If his interpretation is correct, it looks as though the existence of psychopaths does undermine the Kantian internalist's empirical generalization: contra the Kantian, there exists a substantial class of individuals *without rational disabilities* who are not motivated by their moral judgements.

We are sympathetic to Nichols's account, but as in the case of VM patients, the internalist is free to insist that a fuller understanding of psychopathy will reveal that the syndrome does indeed involve rational disabilities. Resolving this debate will require conceptual work on how to draw the boundary between reason and affect, and on what counts as an abnormality in each of these domains. But it will also require much more empirical work aimed at understanding exactly how psychopaths and non-psychopaths differ. The internalist—or at least the Kantian internalist—who wishes to diffuse the difficulty posed by psychopathy must proffer an empirically tenable account of the psychopath's cognitive architecture that locates the posited rational disability. We doubt that such an account is forthcoming. But— to instantiate once more our take-home message—our present point is that if internalists are to develop such an account, they must engage the empirical literature.

---

[17] Here Nichols offers support for the 'sentimentalist' tradition, which maintains that emotions (or 'sentiments') play a central role in moral judgement. For a helpful treatment of sentimentalism, see D'Arms and Jacobson (2000).

4. MORAL DISAGREEMENT

Numerous contemporary philosophers, including Brandt (1959), Harman (1977: 125–36), Railton (1986a,b), and Lewis (1989), have proposed dispositional theories of moral rightness or non-moral good, which 'make matters of value depend on the affective dispositions of agents' (see Darwall *et al.* 1997: 28–9).[18] The various versions differ in detail,[19] but a rendering by Brandt is particularly instructive. According to Brandt (1959: 241–70), ethical justification is a process whereby initial judgements about particular cases and general moral principles are revised by testing these judgements against the attitudes, feelings, or emotions that would emerge under appropriately idealized circumstances. Of special importance on Brandt's (1959: 249–51, 261–4) view are what he calls 'qualified attitudes'—the attitudes people would have if they were, *inter alia*, (1) impartial, (2) fully informed about and vividly aware of the relevant facts, and (3) free from any 'abnormal' states of mind, like insanity, fatigue, or depression.[20]

As Brandt (1959: 281–4) noted, much depends on whether all people would have the same attitudes in ideal circumstances—i.e. on whether their attitudes would *converge* in ideal circumstances. If they would, then certain moral judgements— those where the idealized convergence obtains—are justified for all people, and others—those where such convergence fails to obtain—are not so justified. But if people's attitudes generally fail to converge under idealized circumstances, qualified attitude theory apparently lapses into a version of relativism, since any given moral judgement may comport with the qualified attitudes of one person, and thus be justified for him, while an incompatible judgement may comport with the attitudes of another person, and thus be justified for her.[21]

Brandt, who was a pioneer in the effort to integrate ethical theory and the social sciences, looked primarily to anthropology to help determine whether moral attitudes can be expected to converge under idealized circumstances. It is of course

---

[18] These views reflect a venerable tradition linking moral judgement to the affective states that people would have under idealized conditions; it extends back to Hutcheson (1738), Hume (1975, 1978), and Adam Smith (2002).

[19] A particularly important difference concerns the envisaged link between moral claims and affective reactions. Firth (1952: 317–45) and Lewis (1989) see the link as a matter of meaning, Railton (1986b) as a synthetic identity, and Brandt (1959: 241–70) both as a matter of justification and, more tentatively, as a matter of meaning.

[20] Brandt was a prolific and self-critical thinker, and the 1959 statement may not represent his mature views, but it well illustrates how empirical issues can impact a familiar approach to ethical theory. For a helpful survey of Brandt's career, see Rosati (2000).

[21] On some readings, qualified attitude theories may end up a version of *scepticism* if attitudes don't converge under ideal circumstances. Suppose a theory holds 'an action is morally right (or morally wrong) iff all people in ideal conditions would judge that action is morally right (or morally wrong)'. Then if convergence fails to obtain in ideal conditions, this theory entails that there are no morally right (or morally wrong) actions.

well known that anthropology includes a substantial body of work, such as the classic studies of Westermarck (1906) and Sumner (1934), detailing the radically divergent moral outlooks found in cultures around the world. But as Brandt (1959: 283–4) recognized, typical ethnographies do not support confident inferences about the convergence of attitudes under *ideal* conditions, in large measure because they often give limited guidance regarding how much of the moral disagreement can be traced to disagreement about factual matters that are not moral in nature, such as those having to do with religious or cosmological views.

With this sort of difficulty in mind, Brandt (1954) undertook his own anthropological study of Hopi people in the American southwest, and found issues for which there appeared to be serious moral disagreement between typical Hopi and white American attitudes that could not plausibly be attributed to differences in belief about non-moral facts. A notable example is the Hopi attitude towards causing animals to suffer, an attitude that might be expected to disturb many non-Hopis: '[Hopi c]hildren sometimes catch birds and make "pets" of them. They may be tied to a string, to be taken out and "played" with. This play is rough, and birds seldom survive long. [According to one informant:] "Sometimes they get tired and die. Nobody objects to this" ' (Brandt 1954: 213).

Brandt (1959: 103) made a concerted effort to determine whether this difference in moral outlook could be traced to disagreement about non-moral facts, but he could find no plausible explanation of this kind; his Hopi informants didn't believe that animals lack the capacity to feel pain, for example, nor did they believe that animals are rewarded for martyrdom in the afterlife. According to Brandt (1954: 245), the Hopi do not regard animals as unconscious or insensitive; indeed, they apparently regard animals as 'closer to the human species than does the average white man'. The best explanation of the divergent moral judgements, Brandt (1954: 245) concluded, is a 'basic difference of attitude'. Accordingly, although he cautions that the uncertainties of ethnography make confident conclusions on this point difficult, Brandt (1959: 284) argues that accounts of moral justification like his qualified attitude theory *do* end in relativism, since 'groups do sometimes make divergent appraisals when they have identical beliefs about the objects'.

Of course, the observation that persistent moral disagreement appears to problematize moral argument and justification is not unique to Brandt. While the difficulty is long familiar, contemporary philosophical discussion was spurred by Mackie's (1977: 36–8) 'argument from relativity' or, as it is called by later writers, the 'argument from disagreement' (Brink 1989: 197; Loeb 1998). Such 'radical' differences in moral judgement as are frequently observed, Mackie (1977: 36) argued, 'make it difficult to treat those judgments as apprehensions of objective truths'. As we see it, the problem is not only that moral disagreement often persists, but also that for important instances of moral disagreement—such as the treatment of animals—it is obscure what sort of considerations, be they methodological or substantive, *could* settle the issues (see Sturgeon 1988: 229). Indeed, moral disagreement might be plausibly expected to continue even when the disputants are in methodological agreement concerning the appropriate standards for moral argument. One way of putting the point is to say that application of the same method may, for different individuals or cultures, yield divergent moral judgements that are equally acceptable by the lights of the method, even in reflective conditions that the method countenances as ideal.[22]

In contemporary ethical theory, an impressive group of philosophers are 'moral realists' (see Railton, 1986a,b; Boyd 1988; Sturgeon 1988; Brink 1989; M. Smith 1994). Adherents to a single philosophical creed often manifest doctrinal differences, and that is doubtless the case here, but it is probably fair to say that most moral realists mean to resist the argument from disagreement and reject its relativist conclusion. For instance, Smith's (1994: 9; cf. 13) moral realism requires the objectivity of moral judgement, where objectivity is construed as 'the idea that moral questions have correct answers, that the correct answers are made correct by objective moral facts, that moral facts are determined by circumstances, and that, by engaging in moral argument, we can discover what these objective moral facts are'. There's a lot of philosophy packed into this statement, but it looks as though Smith is committed to the thought, contra our relativist, that moral argument, or at least moral argument of the right sort, can settle moral disagreements. Indeed, for Smith (1994: 6), the notion of objectivity 'signifies the possibility of a convergence in moral views', so the prospects for his version of moral realism depend on the argument from disagreement not going through.[23] But can realists like Smith bank on the argument's failure?

Realists may argue that, in contrast to the impression one gets from the anthropological literature, there already exists substantial moral convergence. But while moral realists have often taken pretty optimistic positions on the extent of actual moral agreement (e.g. Sturgeon 1988: 229; M. Smith 1994: 188), there is no denying that there is an abundance of persistent moral disagreement. That is, on many moral issues—think of abortion and capital punishment—there is a striking failure of convergence even after protracted argument. The relativist has a ready explanation for this phenomenon: moral judgement is not objective in Smith's sense, and moral argument cannot be expected to accomplish what Smith and

---

[22] This way of putting the argument is at once uncontentious and contentious. It is uncontentious because it does not entail a radical methodological relativism of the sort, say, that insists there is nothing to choose between consulting an astrologer and the method of reflective equilibrium as an approach to moral inquiry (see Brandt 1959: 274–5). But precisely because of this, the empirical conjecture that moral judgements will not converge is highly contentious, since a background of methodological agreement would appear to make it more likely that moral argument could end in substantive moral agreement.

[23] Strictly speaking, a relativist need not be a 'non-factualist' about morality, since, for example, she can take it to be a moral fact that it is right for Hopi children to engage in their fatal play with small animals, and also take it to be a moral fact that it is wrong for American white children to do so. But the factualist–relativist will probably want to reject Smith's (1994: 13) characterization of moral facts as 'facts about the reasons that we all share'.

other realists think it can.[24] Conversely, the realist's task is to *explain away* failures of convergence; she must provide an explanation of the phenomena consistent with it being the case that moral judgement is objective and moral argument is rationally resolvable. For our purposes, what needs to be emphasized is that the relative merits of these competing explanations cannot be fairly determined without close discussion of actual cases. Indeed, as acute commentators with both realist (Sturgeon 1988: 230) and anti-realist (Loeb 1998: 284) sympathies have noted, the argument from disagreement cannot be evaluated by a priori philosophical means alone; what's needed, as Loeb observes, is 'a great deal of further empirical research into the circumstances and beliefs of various cultures'.

Brandt (1959: 101–2) lamented that the anthropological literature of his day did not always provide as much information on the exact contours and origins of moral attitudes and beliefs as philosophers wondering about the prospects for convergence might like. However, social psychology and cognitive science have recently produced research which promises to further discussion; the closing decades of the twentieth century witnessed an explosion of 'cultural psychology' investigating the cognitive and emotional processes of different cultures (Shweder and Bourne 1982; Markus and Kitayama 1991; Ellsworth 1994; Nisbett and Cohen 1996; Nisbett 1998; Kitayama and Markus 1999). A representative finding is that East Asians are more sensitive than Westerners to the field or context as opposed to the object or actor in their explanations of physical and social phenomena, a difference that may be reflected in their habits of ethical judgement. Here we will focus on some cultural differences found rather closer to home, differences discovered by Nisbett and his colleagues while investigating regional patterns of violence in the American North and South. We argue that these findings support Brandt's pessimistic conclusions regarding the possibility of convergence in moral judgement.

The Nisbett group's research can be seen as applying the tools of cognitive social psychology to the 'culture of honour', a phenomenon that anthropologists have documented in a variety of groups around the world. Although such peoples differ in many respects, they manifest important commonalties:

A key aspect of the culture of honor is the importance placed on the insult and the necessity to respond to it. An insult implies that the target is weak enough to be bullied. Since a reputation for strength is of the essence in the culture of honor, the individual who insults someone must be forced to retract; if the instigator refuses, he must be punished—with violence or even death. (Nisbett and Cohen 1996: 5)

According to Nisbett and Cohen (1996: 5–9), an important factor in the genesis of southern honour culture was the presence of a herding economy. Apparently, honour cultures are particularly likely to develop where resources are liable to theft, and

---

[24] See Williams (1985: 136): 'In a scientific inquiry there should ideally be convergence on an answer, where the best explanation of the convergence involves the idea that the answer represents how things are; in the area of the ethical, at least at high level of generality, there is no such coherent hope.'

where the state's coercive apparatus cannot be relied upon to prevent or punish thievery. These conditions often occur in relatively remote areas where herding is the main viable form of agriculture; the 'portability' of herd animals makes them prone to theft. In areas where farming rather than herding is the principal form of subsistence, cooperation among neighbours is more important, stronger government infrastructures are more common, and resources—like decidedly unportable farmland—are harder to steal. In such agrarian social economies, cultures of honour tend not to develop. The American South was originally settled primarily by peoples from remote areas of Britain. Since their homelands were generally unsuitable for farming, these peoples have historically been herders; when they emigrated from Britain to the South, they initially sought out remote regions suitable for herding, and in such regions, the culture of honour flourished.

In the contemporary South police and other government services are widely available and herding has all but disappeared as a way of life, but certain sorts of violence continue to be more common than they are in the North. Nisbett and Cohen (1996) maintain that patterns of violence in the South, as well as attitudes towards violence, insults, and affronts to honour, are best explained by the hypothesis that a culture of honour persists among contemporary white non-Hispanic southerners. In support of this hypothesis, they offer a compelling array of evidence, including:

- demographic data indicating that (1) among southern whites, homicides rates are higher in regions more suited to herding than agriculture, and (2) white males in the South are much more likely than white males in other regions to be involved in homicides resulting from arguments, although they are *not* more likely to be involved in homicides that occur in the course of a robbery or other felony (Nisbett and Cohen 1996, ch. 2);
- survey data indicating that white southerners are more likely than northerners to believe that violence would be 'extremely justified' in response to a variety of affronts, and that if a man failed to respond violently, he was 'not much of a man' (Nisbett and Cohen 1996, ch. 3);
- legal scholarship indicating that southern states 'give citizens more freedom to use violence in defending themselves, their homes, and their property' than do northern states (Nisbett and Cohen 1996: 63).

Two experimental studies—one in the field, the other in the laboratory—are especially striking.

In the field study (Nisbett and Cohen 1996: 73–5), letters of inquiry were sent to hundreds of employers around the United States. The letters purported to be from a hard-working 27-year-old Michigan man who had a single blemish on his otherwise solid record. In one version, the 'applicant' revealed that he had been convicted for manslaughter. The applicant explained that he had been in a fight with a man who confronted him in a bar and told onlookers that 'he and my fiancée were sleeping together. He laughed at me to my face and asked me to step outside if I was man enough.' According to the letter, the applicant's nemesis was killed in the ensuing fray. In the other version of the letter, the applicant revealed that he had been convicted of motor vehicle theft, perpetrated at a time when he needed money for his family. Nisbett and his colleagues assessed 112 letters of response, and found that southern employers were significantly more likely to be cooperative and sympathetic in response to the manslaughter letter than were northern employers, while no regional differences were found in responses to the theft letter. One southern employer responded to the manslaughter letter as follows (Nisbett and Cohen 1996: 75):

As for your problems of the past, anyone could probably be in the situation you were in. It was just an unfortunate incident that shouldn't be held against you. Your honesty shows that you are sincere. . . . I wish you the best of luck for your future. You have a positive attitude and a willingness to work. These are qualities that businesses look for in employees. Once you are settled, if you are near here, please stop in and see us.

No letters from northern employers were comparably sympathetic.

In the laboratory study (Nisbett and Cohen 1996: 45–8) subjects—white males from both northern and southern states attending the University of Michigan— were told that saliva samples would be collected to measure blood sugar as they performed various tasks. After an initial sample was collected, the unsuspecting subject walked down a narrow corridor where an experimental confederate was pretending to work on some filing. Feigning annoyance at the interruption, the confederate bumped the subject and called him an 'asshole'. A few minutes after the incident, saliva samples were collected and analysed to determine the level of cortisol—a hormone associated with high levels of stress, anxiety and arousal, and testosterone—a hormone associated with aggression and dominance behaviour. As Figure 5.1 indicates, southern subjects showed dramatic increases in cortisol and testosterone levels, while northerners exhibited much smaller changes.

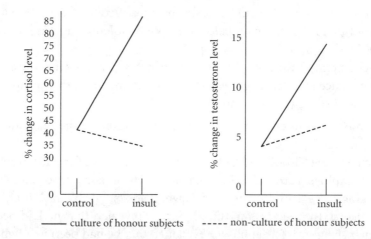

FIG. 5.1. The results of an experiment by Nisbett and Cohen in which levels of cortisol and testosterone increased much more substantially in culture of honour subjects who were insulted by a confederate

The two studies just described suggest that southerners respond more strongly to insult than northerners, and take a more sympathetic view of others who do so, manifesting just the sort of attitudes that are supposed to typify honour cultures. We think that the data assembled by Nisbett and his colleagues make a persuasive case that a culture of honour persists in the American South. Apparently, this culture affects people's judgements, attitudes, emotions, behaviour, and even their physiological responses. Additionally, there is evidence that child-rearing practices play a significant role in passing the culture of honour on from one generation to the next, and also that relatively permissive laws regarding gun-ownership, self-defence, and corporal punishment in the schools both reflect and reinforce southern honour culture (Nisbett and Cohen 1996: 60–3, 67–9). In short, it seems to us that the culture of honour is deeply entrenched in contemporary southern culture, despite the fact that many of the material and economic conditions giving rise to it no longer widely obtain.[25]

We believe that the North–South cultural differences adduced by Nisbett and colleagues support Brandt's conclusion that moral attitudes will often fail to converge, even under ideal conditions. The data should be especially troubling for the realist, for despite the differences that we have been recounting, contemporary northern and southern Americans might be expected to have rather more in common—from circumstance to language to belief to ideology—than do, say, Yanomamö and Parisians. So if there is little ground for expecting convergence under ideal conditions in the case at hand, there is probably little ground in a good many others. To develop our argument a bit further, let us revisit the idealization conditions mentioned at the beginning of this section: impartiality, full factual information, and normality.

Impartiality. One strategy favoured by moral realists concerned to explain away moral disagreement is to say that such disagreement stems from the distorting effects of individual interest (see Sturgeon 1988: 229–30); perhaps persistent disagreement doesn't so much betray deep features of moral argument and judgement as it does the doggedness with which individuals pursue their perceived advantage. For instance, seemingly moral disputes over the distribution of wealth may be due to perceptions—perhaps mostly inchoate—of individual and class interests rather than to principled disagreement about justice; persisting moral disagreement in such circumstances fails the impartiality condition, and is therefore untroubling to the moral realist.

But it is rather implausible to suggest that North–South disagreements over when violence is justified will fail the impartiality condition. There is no reason to

[25] The last clause is important, since realists (e.g. Brink 1989: 200) sometimes argue that apparent moral disagreement may result from cultures applying similar moral values to different economic conditions (e.g. differences in attitudes towards the sick and elderly between poor and rich cultures). But this explanation seems of dubious relevance to the described differences between contemporary northerners and southerners, who are plausibly interpreted as applying different values to similar economic conditions.

think that southerners would be unwilling to universalize their judgements across relevantly similar individuals in relevantly similar circumstances, as indeed Nisbett and Cohen's 'letter study' suggests. One can advocate a violent honour code without going in for special pleading.[26] We do not intend to denigrate southern values; our point is that while there may be good reasons for criticizing the honour-bound southerner, it is not obvious that the reason can be failure of impartiality, if impartiality is (roughly) to be understood along the lines of a willingness to universalize one's moral judgements.

Full and vivid awareness of relevant non-moral facts. Moral realists have argued that moral disagreements very often derive from disagreement about non-moral issues. According to Boyd (1988: 213; cf. Brink 1989: 202–3; Sturgeon 1988: 229), 'careful philosophical examination will reveal . . . that agreement on nonmoral issues would eliminate *almost all* disagreement about the sorts of moral issues which arise in ordinary moral practice'. Is this a plausible conjecture for the data we have just considered? We find it hard to imagine what agreement on non-moral facts could do the trick, for we can readily imagine that northerners and southerners might be in full agreement on the relevant non-moral facts in the cases described. Members of both groups would presumably agree that the job applicant was cuckolded, for example, or that calling someone an 'asshole' is an insult. We think it much more plausible to suppose that the disagreement resides in differing and deeply entrenched evaluative attitudes regarding appropriate responses to cuckolding, challenge, and insult.

Savvy philosophical readers will be quick to observe that terms like 'challenge' and 'insult' look like 'thick' ethical terms, where the evaluative and descriptive are commingled (see Williams 1985: 128–30); therefore, it is very difficult to say what the extent of the factual disagreement is. But this is of little help for the expedient under consideration, since the disagreement-in-non-moral-fact response apparently *requires* that one *can* disentangle factual and moral disagreement.

It is of course possible that full and vivid awareness of the non-moral facts might motivate the sort of change in southern attitudes envisaged by the (at least the northern) moral realist; were southerners to become vividly aware that their culture of honour was implicated in violence, they might be moved to change their moral outlook. (We take this way of putting the example to be the most natural one, but nothing philosophical turns on it. If you like, substitute the possibility of bloody-minded northerners endorsing honour values after exposure to the facts.) On the other hand, southerners might insist that the values of honour should be nurtured even at the cost of promoting violence; the motto 'Death before dishonour', after all, has a long and honourable history. The burden of argument, we think, lies with the

---

[26] The legal scholarship that Nisbett and Cohen (1996: 57–78) review makes it clear that southern legislatures are often willing to enact laws reflecting the culture of honour view of the circumstances under which violence is justified, which suggests there is at least some support among southerners for the idea that honour values should be universalizable.

realist who asserts—culture and history notwithstanding—that southerners would change their mind if vividly aware of the pertinent facts.

Freedom from abnormality. Realists may contend that much moral disagreement may result from failures of rationality on the part of discussants (Brink 1989: 199–200). Obviously, disagreement stemming from cognitive impairments is no embarrassment for moral realism; at the limit, that a disagreement persists when some or all disputing parties are quite insane shows nothing deep about morality. But it doesn't seem plausible that southerners' more lenient attitudes towards certain forms of violence are readily attributed to widespread cognitive disability. Of course, this is an empirical issue, and we don't know of any evidence suggesting that southerners suffer some cognitive impairment that prevents them from under-standing demographic and attitudinal factors in the genesis of violence, or any other matter of fact. What is needed to press home a charge of irrationality is evidence of cognitive impairment independent of the attitudinal differences, and further evid-ence that this impairment is implicated in adherence to the disputed values in the face of the (putatively) undisputed non-moral facts. In this instance, as in many others, we have difficulty seeing how charges of abnormality or irrationality can be made without one side begging the question against the other.

We are inclined to think that Nisbett and colleagues' work represents a potent counter-example to any theory maintaining that rational argument tends to con-vergence on important moral issues; the evidence suggests that the North–South differences in attitudes towards violence and honour might well persist even under the sort of ideal conditions we have considered. Admittedly, our conclusions must be tentative. On the philosophical side, we have not considered every plausible strategy for 'explaining away' moral disagreement and grounding expectations of convergence.[27] On the empirical side, we have reported on but a few studies, and those we do consider here, like any empirical work, might be criticized on either conceptual or methodological grounds.[28] Finally, we should make clear what we are *not* claiming: we do not take our conclusions here—even if fairly earned—to be a 'refutation' of moral realism, in as much as there may be versions of moral realism that do not require convergence. Rather, we hope to have given an idea of the empirical work philosophers must encounter if they are to make defensible conjec-tures regarding moral disagreement. Our theme recurs: Responsible treatment of the empirical issues requires reference to empirical science, whatever the science is ultimately taken to show.

[27] In addition to the expedients we have considered, realists may plausibly appeal to, *inter alia*, requirements for internal coherence and the different 'levels' of moral thought (theoretical versus popu-lar, abstract versus concrete, general versus particular) at which moral disagreement may or may not be manifested. Brink (1989: 197–210) and Loeb (1998) offer valuable discussions with considerably more detail than we offer here, Brink manifesting realist sympathies and Loeb tending towards anti-realism.

[28] We think Nisbett and Cohen will fare pretty well under such scrutiny. See Tetlock's (1999) favourable review.

5. THOUGHT EXPERIMENTS

Ethical reflection is often held to involve comparing general principles and responses to particular cases; commitment to a principle may compel the renunciation of a particular response, or commitment to a particular response may compel modification or renunciation of a general principle (Brandt 1959: 244–52; Rawls 1971: 20–1, 49). This emphasis on particular cases is not peculiar to ethics: 'intuition pumps' or 'thought experiments' have long been central elements of philosophical method (Dennett 1984: 17–18). In the instances we consider here, a thought experiment presents an example, typically a hypothetical example, in order to elicit some philosophically telling response; if a thought experiment is successful, it may be concluded that competing theories must account for the resulting response.[29] To extend the imagery of experimentation, responses to thought experiments are supposed to serve an evidential role in philosophical theory choice; the responses are data competing theories must accommodate.[30]

In ethics, one—we do not say the only—familiar rendering of the methodology is this: if an audience's ethical responses to a thought experiment can be expected to conflict with the response a theory prescribes for the case, the theory has suffered a counter-example. For instance, it is often claimed that utilitarian prescriptions for particular cases will conflict with the ethical responses many people have to those cases (e.g. Williams 1973: 99). The ethics literature is rife with claims to the effect that 'many of us' or 'we' would respond in a specified way to a given example, and such claims are often supposed to have philosophical teeth.[31] But who is this 'we'? And how do philosophers know what this 'we' thinks?

Initially, it doesn't look like 'we' should be interpreted as 'we philosophers'. The difficulty is not that this approach threatens a sampling error, although it is certainly true that philosophers form a small and peculiar group. Rather, the problem is that philosophers can be expected to respond to thought experiments in ways that reflect their theoretical predilections: utilitarians' responses to a thought

[29] There are substantive questions as to what sorts of responses to thought experiments may properly constrain philosophical theory choice. For example, what level of reflection or cognitive elaboration is required: are the responses of interest 'pre-theoretical intuitions' or 'considered judgements'? We will have something to say about this, but in terminology we will mostly favour the generic 'responses', which we mean to be neutral regarding issues such as cognitive elaboration.

[30] This analogy with science is not unique to our exposition. Singer (1974: 517; cf. 493) understands Rawls's (1971) method of reflective equilibrium as 'leading us to think of our particular moral judgments as data against which moral theories are to be tested'. As Singer (1974: 493 ff.) notes, in earlier treatments Rawls (1951) made the analogy with scientific theory choice explicit. We needn't hazard an interpretation of Rawls, but only observe that our analogy is not philosophically eccentric.

[31] For appeals of this kind, see Blum (1994: 179); G. Strawson (1986: 87–9); P. Strawson (1982: 68); Wallace (1994: 81–2); Williams (1973: 99–100; 1981: 22).

experiments might be expected to plump for maximizing welfare, integrity and loyalty be damned, while the responses of Aristotelians and Kantians might plump in the opposite direction. If so, the thought experiment can hardly be expected to *resolve* the debate, since philosophers' responses to the example are likely to *reflect* their position in the debate.

The audience of appeal often seems to be some variant of 'ordinary folk' (see Jackson 1998: 118, 129; Jackson and Pettit 1995: 22–9; Lewis 1989: 126–9). Of course, the relevant folk must possess such cognitive attainments as are required to understand the case at issue; very young children are probably not an ideal audience for thought experiments. Some philosophers may want to insist that the relevant responses are the 'considered judgements' or 'reflective intuitions' of people with the training required to see 'what is philosophically at stake'. But there is peril in insisting that the relevant cognitive attainments be some sort of 'philosophical sophistication'. Once again, if the responses are to help adjudicate between competing theories, the responders must be more or less theoretically neutral, but this sort of neutrality, we suspect, is rather likely to be vitiated by philosophical education. (Incredibly enough, informal surveys suggest that *our* students are overwhelmingly ethical naturalists!)

However exactly the philosophically relevant audience is specified, there are empirical questions that must be addressed in determining the philosophical potency of a thought experiment. In science, not all experiments produce data of evidentiary value; sampling errors and the failure of experimental designs to effectively isolate variables are two familiar ways in which experiments go wrong. Data resulting from such experiments is tainted, or without evidential value; analogously, in evaluating responses to a thought experiment, one needs to consider the possibility of taint. In particular, when deciding what philosophical weight to give a response to a thought experiment, philosophers need to determine the origins of the response. What features of the example are implicated in a response—are people responding to the substance of the case, or the style of exposition? What features of the audience are implicated in a response—do different demographic groups respond to an example differently? Such questions raise the following concern: ethical responses to thought experiments may be strongly influenced by ethically irrelevant characteristics of example and audience. Whether a characteristic is ethically relevant is a matter for philosophical discussion, but determining the status of a particular thought experiment also requires empirical investigation of its causally relevant characteristics; responsible philosophical discussion cannot rely on guesswork in this regard. We shall now give two examples illustrating our concerns about tainted origins, one corresponding to each of the two questions just asked.

Tversky and Kahneman presented subjects with the following problem:

> Imagine that the U.S. is preparing for the outbreak of an unusual Asian disease, which is expected to kill 600 people. Two alternative programs to combat the disease have been

proposed. Assume that the exact scientific estimate of the consequences of the programs are as follows:

If Program A is adopted, 200 people will be saved.

If Program B is adopted, there is a 1/3 probability that 600 people will be saved, and a 2/3 probability that no people will be saved.

A second group of subjects was given an identical problem, except that the programs were described as follows:

If Program C is adopted, 400 people will die.

If Program D is adopted, there is a 1/3 probability that nobody will die and a 2/3 probability that 600 people will die. (Tversky and Kahneman 1981: 453)

On the first version of the problem most subjects thought that Program A should be adopted. But on the second version most chose Program D, despite the fact that the outcome described in A is identical to the one described in C. The disconcerting implication of this study is that ethical responses may be strongly influenced by the manner in which cases are described or framed. Many effects of framing differences, such as that between 200 of 600 people being saved and 400 of 600 dying, we are strongly inclined to think, are ethically irrelevant influences on ethical responses (compare Horowitz 1998; Sinnott-Armstrong 2005). Unless this sort of possibility can be confidently eliminated, one should hesitate to rely on responses to a thought experiment for adjudicating theoretical controversies. Again, such possibilities can only be eliminated through systematic empirical work.[32]

Audience characteristics may also affect the outcome of thought experiments. Haidt and associates (1993: 613) presented stories about 'harmless yet offensive violations of strong social norms' to men and women of high and low socio-economic status (SES) in Philadelphia (USA), Porto Alegre, and Recife (both in Brazil). For example: 'A man goes to the supermarket once a week and buys a dead chicken. But before cooking the chicken, he has sexual intercourse with it. Then he cooks it and eats it' (Haidt et al. 1993: 617). Lower SES subjects tended to 'moralize' harmless and offensive behaviours like that in the chicken story: these subjects were more inclined than their privileged counterparts to say that the actor should be 'stopped or punished', and more inclined to deny that such behaviours would be 'OK' if customary in a given country (Haidt et al. 1993: 618–19). The point is not that lower SES subjects are mistaken in their moralization of such behaviours while the urbanity of higher SES subjects represents the most rationally defensible response. To recall our previous discussion of moral disagreement, the difficulty is deciding which of the conflicting responses to privilege, when both sorts of responses may be the function of more or less arbitrary cultural factors.

---

[32] Some authors—most notably Baron (1994)—have argued that the distorting influences of 'heuristics and biases' like those uncovered in the recent psychological literature on reasoning, judgement, and decision-making are widespread in everyday ethical reflection. For overviews of the relevant psychological literature, see Nisbett and Ross (1980); Kahneman et al. (1982); Baron (2001).

In presenting the Haidt group's work to philosophical audiences, our impression is that they typically decline to moralize the offensive behaviours, and we ourselves share their tolerant attitude. But of course philosophical audiences—by virtue of educational attainments if not stock portfolios—are overwhelmingly high SES. Haidt's work suggests that it is a mistake for a philosopher to say, as Jackson (1998: 32 ff.; cf. 37) does, that 'my intuitions reveal the folk conception in as much as I am reasonably entitled, as I usually am, to regard myself as typical'. The question is: Typical of what demographic? Are philosophers' ethical responses to thought experiments determined by the philosophical substance of the examples, or by cultural idiosyncrasies that are very plausibly thought to be ethically irrelevant? Once again, until such possibilities are ruled out by systematic empirical investigation, the philosophical heft of a thought experiment is open to question.[33]

The studies just described raise provocative questions about *how* responses to thought experiments are generated, but there may be equally provocative questions about *what* responses people actually have. And, to sound our now familiar theme, this question is one not credibly answered by guesswork. Indeed, we suspect that philosophical speculations about what responses to thought experiments are conventional may be wrong surprisingly often. We'll now report on one study conducive to such suspicions.

One of the most famous of philosophical conundrums, that of determinism and responsibility, can be derived—on one way of formulating the difficulty—from the juxtaposition of three claims that are individually quite plausible, but seem impossible to hold jointly:

(MRT) *Moral responsibility thesis*: Human beings are sometimes morally responsible for their behaviour.

(CT)   *Causal thesis*: All human behaviour is linked to antecedent events by deterministic causal laws. (See Scanlon 1988: 152.)

(PAP) *Principle of alternate possibilities*: A 'person is morally responsible for what he has done only if he could have done otherwise'. (See Frankfurt 1988: 1.)

Here's one way of putting it: If CT is true, it looks as though it is never the case that people could have done otherwise, but then, given PAP, MRT must be false.[34] There

---

[33] We applaud Jackson's (1998: 36–7) advocacy of 'doing serious public opinion polls on people's responses to various cases'. However, we expect this may be necessary more often than Jackson imagines. According to Jackson (1998: 37), 'Everyone who presents the Gettier cases [which are well-known epistemology thought experiments] to a class of students is doing their own bit of fieldwork, and we all know the answer they get in the vast majority of cases.' Yet Weinberg *et al.* (2002) found that responses to epistemology thought experiments like the Gettier cases varied with culture and SES; this suggests that philosophers need to be more systematic in their fieldwork.

[34] Our formulation is meant to be quite standard. Kane (2002a: 10) observes that statements of the difficulty in terms of alternative possibilities have dominated modern discussion. A recently prominent formulation proceeds not in terms of PAP, but by way of an 'ultimacy condition', which holds that an actor is responsible for her behaviour only if she is its 'ultimate source' (see McKenna 2001, esp.

are three standard responses to this trilemma. Two sorts of incompatibilists hold that MRT and CT cannot be held simultaneously: hard determinists (see Smart 1961: 303–6) reject MRT,[35] while libertarians (e.g. Kane 1996) insist that CT admits of exceptions in the case of human behaviour, and are thus able to maintain MRT. Compatibilists, on the other hand, assert that MRT and CT can be simultaneously maintained; one well-known expedient is to reject PAP, and insist that people may be legitimately held responsible even when they could not have done otherwise (see Frankfurt 1988: 1–12).

The literature is voluminous, and the proffered solutions range from controversial to deeply unsatisfying; indeed, there is heated disagreement as to what exactly the problem is (Dennett 1984: 1–19). Discretion being the best part of valour, we won't review the arguments here. Given our present concerns, we instead consider objections to the effect that compatibilism is in some sense badly counter-intuitive. One way of forming this complaint is to say that people's 'reactive attitudes'—ethical responses like anger, resentment, guilt, approbation, admiration, and the like—manifest a commitment to incompatibilism.[36] Here is Galen Strawson (1986: 88) on what he calls the 'incompatibilist intuition':

> The fact that the incompatibilist intuition has such power for us is as much a natural fact about cogitative beings like ourselves as is the fact of our quite unreflective commitment to the reactive attitudes. What is more, the roots of the incompatibilist intuition lie deep in the . . . reactive attitudes. . . . The reactive attitudes enshrine the incompatibilist intuition.[37]

Let's do a little unpacking. On Strawson's (1986: 31; cf. 2, 84–8) rendering, incompatibilism is the view that the falsity of determinism is a necessary condition for moral responsibility. To suggest that the 'incompatibilist intuition' is widespread, then, may be thought to imply that people's (possibly tacit) body of moral beliefs includes commitment to the claim that CT is incompatible with MRT.[38]

40–1). This does not impact the present discussion, however. First, notice that although some may maintain an ultimacy requirement and reject PAP, the two commitments need not be incompatible; Kane (1996, 2002b) holds them both. Secondly, as should become clear, the empirical work we describe below is relevant to both formulations.

[35] As Kane (2002a: 27–32) observes, relatively few philosophers have been unqualifiedly committed to hard determinism; Smart's (1961) views on responsibility, for example, are complex.

[36] Peter Strawson (1982) did the pioneering philosophical work on the reactive attitudes; he appears to reject the suggestion that such attitudes manifest a commitment to something in the spirit of incompatibilism.

[37] G. Strawson puts the point rather emphatically, but similar observations are commonplace. Cf. Nagel (1986: 113, 125); Kane (1996: 83–5).

[38] There is again a question about the scope of 'people'; Strawson's reference to 'natural facts' may suggest that he is making a boldly pancultural attribution, but he might be more modestly attributing the theory only to those people who embody something like the 'Western ethical tradition'. We will not attempt to decide the interpretative question, because the empirical work we describe troubles even the more modest claim.

This is an empirical claim. Moreover, it is an empirical claim that looks to entail predictions about people's moral responses. What are the responses in question?

Like many other philosophers making empirical claims about human cognition and behaviour, Strawson says relatively little about what predictions he thinks his claims entail. We won't put predictions in Strawson's mouth; instead, we'll consider one prediction that looks to follow from positing an incompatibilist intuition, at least on the familiar rendering of incompatibilism we've followed. Attributing a widespread commitment to an incompatibilist intuition is plausibly thought to involve the following prediction: for cases where the actor is judged unable to have done otherwise, people will not hold the actor responsible for what she has done.[39] In as much as this prediction is a good one, people should respond to thought experiments depicting an actor unable to do otherwise by abjuring attributions of responsibility and the associated reactive attitudes.

In a compatibilist spirit inspired by the work of Harry Frankfurt (1988), Woolfolk, Doris, and Darley (forthcoming) hypothesized that observers may hold actors responsible even when the observers judge that the actors could not have done otherwise, at least in cases where the actors appear to manifest 'identification'. Very roughly, the idea is that the actor is identified with a behaviour—and is therefore responsible for it—to the extent she 'embraces' the behaviour (or its motive), or performs it 'wholeheartedly'.[40] Woolfolk *et al.*'s suspicion was, in effect, that people's (possibly tacit) theory of responsibility is, contra Galen Strawson and others, compatibilist.

In one of the Woolfolk *et al.* studies, subjects read a story about two married couples vacationing together. According to the story, one of the vacationers has discovered that his wife is having an affair with his opposite number in the foursome; on the flight home, the vacationers' plane is hijacked, and armed hijackers order the cuckold to shoot the man who has been having an affair with his wife. In a 'low identification' variation, the story contained the following material:

Bill was horrified. At that moment Bill was certain about his feelings. He did *not* want to kill Frank, even though Frank was his wife's lover. But although he was appalled by the situation and beside himself with distress, he reluctantly placed the pistol at Frank's temple and proceeded to blow his friend's brains out.

Conversely, in a 'high identification' variation, the embittered cuckold embraces his opportunity:

Despite the desperate circumstances, Bill understood the situation. He had been presented with the opportunity to kill his wife's lover and get away with it. And at that moment Bill

---

[39] G. Strawson (1986: 25–31; 2002) may favour formulations in terms of ultimacy rather than PAP (see n. 33 above). This doesn't affect our argument, since the empirical work we recount below looks to trouble a prediction formulated in terms of ultimacy as well as the alternative possibilities formulation we favour.

[40] For some discussion, see Velleman (1992); Bratman (1996); Watson (1996); Doris (2002: 140–6).

was certain about his feelings. He wanted to kill Frank. Feeling no reluctance, he placed the pistol at Frank's temple and proceeded to blow his friend's brains out.

Consistent with Woolfolk and colleagues' hypothesis, the high-identification actor was judged more responsible, more appropriately blamed, and more properly subject to guilt than the low-identification actor.[41]

It is tempting to conclude that at least for the Woolfolk group's subjects (philosophy and psychology undergraduates at the University of California and Rutgers University), the incompatibilist intuition does not appear to be deeply entrenched. But at this point the incompatibilist will be quick to object: the above study may suggest that responsibility attributions are influenced by identification, but it says nothing about commitment to the incompatibilist intuition, because subjects may not have believed that the actor could not have done otherwise, and subjects therefore cannot be interpreted as attributing responsibility in violation of PAP. People may think that even when coerced, actors 'always have a choice'; in the classic 'your money or your life' scenario, the person faced with this unpleasant dilemma can always opt for her life. (We hasten to remind anyone tempted in such a bull-headed direction that the disjunct need not be exclusive!)

To address this objection, Woolfolk *et al.* attempted to elevate perceived constraint to the 'could not have done otherwise' threshold:

> The leader of the kidnappers injected Bill's arm with a 'compliance drug'—a designer drug similar to sodium pentathol, 'truth serum.' This drug makes individuals unable to resist the demands of powerful authorities. Its effects are similar to the impact of expertly administered hypnosis; it results in total compliance. To test the effects of the drug, the leader of the kidnappers shouted at Bill to slap himself. To his amazement, Bill observed his own right hand administering an open-handed blow to his own left cheek, although he had no sense of having willed his hand to move. The leader then handed Bill a pistol with one bullet in it. Bill was ordered to shoot Frank in the head. . . . when Bill's hand and arm moved again, placing the pistol at his friend's temple, Bill had no feeling that he had moved his arm to point the gun; it felt as though the gun had moved itself into position. Bill thought he noticed his finger moving on the trigger, but could not feel any sensations of movement. While he was observing these events, feeling like a puppet, passively observing his body moving in space, his hand closed on the pistol, discharging it and blowing Frank's brains out.

Strikingly, subjects appeared willing to attribute responsibility to the shooter even here: once again, a high-identification actor was judged more responsible, more appropriately blamed, and more properly subject to guilt than a low-identification actor. No doubt this is not the most 'naturalistic' scenario, but neither is it outlandish by philosophical standards. And it certainly looks to be a case where the actor would be perceived to fail the standard for responsibility set by PAP.[42] Indeed,

---

[41] Woolfolk *et al.* (forthcoming) obtained similar results for the prosocial behaviour of kidney donation: an identified actor was credited for making a donation even when heavily constrained.

[42] It also looks as though the actor fails an ultimacy condition (see nn. 34 and 39 above).

Woolfolk *et al.* found that subjects were markedly less likely to agree to statements asserting that the actor 'was free to behave other than he did', and 'could have behaved differently than he did', than they were in the case of simple coercion described above. These results look to caution against positing a widespread commitment to the incompatibilist intuition. Deciding empirical issues concerning habits of responsibility attribution will not, of course, decide the philosophical dispute between compatibilists and incompatibilists. Yet in so far as the incompatibilist is making claims to the effect that compatibilists cannot accommodate entrenched habits of moral response, the empirical evidence is entirely relevant.

Once more, some philosophers may insist that the responses of interest are not the relatively unschooled or intuitive responses of experimental subjects like the Woolfolk group's undergraduates, but the tutored judgements of philosophers. We've already given some reasons for regarding this strategy with suspicion, but it seems to us especially problematic for the particular case of responsibility. Philosophical arguments about responsibility, it seems to us, often lean heavily on speculation about everyday practice. For example, Peter Strawson's (1982: 64, 68) extremely influential exposition repeatedly stresses the importance of reactive attitudes in 'ordinary inter-personal relationships'. While it may not be too much of a stretch to imagine that philosophers sometimes indulge in such relationships, it *is* a stretch to suppose that they are the only folk who do so. It is very plausible to argue—as indeed those who have deployed something like the incompatibilist intuition have done—that the contours of the everyday practice of responsibility attribution serve as a (defeasible) constraint on philosophical theories of responsibility: if the theory cannot accommodate the practice, it owes, at a bare minimum, a debunking account of the practice. One might insist that philosophical theorizing about responsibility is not accountable to ordinary practice, but this is to make a substantial break with important elements of the tradition.

There are a couple of ways in which philosophers can avoid the sorts of empirical difficulties we have been considering. First, they can deny that responses to particular cases have evidential weight in ethical theory choice, as some utilitarians—unsurprisingly given the rather startling implications of their position—have been inclined to do (e.g. Kagan 1989: 10–15; Singer 2000, p. xviii). Alternatively, they can appeal to the results of thought experiments in an expository rather than an evidential role; for example, a thought experiment might be used by an author to elucidate her line of reasoning without appealing to the responses of an imagined audience like 'many of us'. To some philosophers, such solutions will seem rather methodologically draconian, threatening to isolate ethical theory from the experience of ethical life (see Williams 1985: 93–119, esp. 116–19). But our point here is less grand: many users of thought experiments in ethics apparently have been—and we strongly suspect will continue to be—in the business of forwarding an imagined consensus on their thought experiments as evidence in theory choice. For these philosophers we offer the following methodological prescription: a credible philosophical methodology of *thought* experiments must be supplemented by a cognitive science of thought experiments that involves systematic investigation with *actual* experiments. There are just too many unanswered questions regarding the responses people have, and the processes by which they come to have them. We've no stake in any particular answers to such questions. What we do have a stake in, as we have throughout, is the observation that responsible answers to such questions will be informed by systematic empirical investigation.

6. CONCLUSION

We needn't linger on goodbyes; the main contours of our exposition should by now be tolerably clear. We have surveyed four central topics in ethical theory where empirical claims are prominent: character, moral motivation, moral disagreement, and thought experiments. We have argued that consideration of work in the biological, behavioural, and social sciences promises substantive philosophical contributions to controversy surrounding such topics as virtue ethics, internalism, moral realism, and moral responsibility. If our arguments are successful, we have also erected a general methodological standard: philosophical ethics can, and indeed must, interface with the human sciences.[43]

REFERENCES

Annas, J. (1993). *The Morality of Happiness*. New York: Oxford University Press.
Anscombe, G. E. M. (1958). 'Modern Moral Philosophy'. *Philosophy*, 33: 1–19.
Aristotle (1984). *The Complete Works of Aristotle*, ed. J. Barnes. Princeton: Princeton University Press.
Athanassoulis, N. (2000). 'A Response to Harman: Virtue Ethics and Character Traits'. *Proceedings of the Aristotelian Society*, 100: 215–22.
Audi, R. (1995). 'Acting from Virtue'. *Mind*, 104: 449–71.
Baron, J. (1994). 'Nonconsequentialist Decisions'. *Behavioral and Brain Sciences*, 17: 1–42.

[43] For much valuable feedback, we are grateful to audiences at the Moral Psychology Symposium at the 2001 Society for Philosophy and Psychology meetings, the Empirical Perspectives on Ethics Symposium at the 2001 American Philosophical Association Pacific Division meetings, and a series of lectures on philosophy and cognitive science held at the Australian National University in July 2002—especially Louise Antony, Daniel Cohen, Frank Jackson, Michael Smith, and Valerie Tiberius. Thanks to Daniel Guevara, Jerry Neu, Alva Noë, and especially Don Loeb, Shaun Nichols, and Adina Roskies for comments on earlier drafts.

—— (2001). *Thinking and Deciding*, 3rd edn. Cambridge: Cambridge University Press.

Bechara, A., Damasio, H., and Damasio, A. R. (2000). 'Emotion, Decision Making and the Orbitofrontal Cortex'. *Cerebral Cortex*, 10: 295–307.

Becker, L. C. (1998). *A New Stoicism*. Princeton: Princeton University Press.

Bennett, W. J. (1993). *The Book of Virtues: A Treasury of Great Moral Stories*. New York: Simon & Schuster.

Blackburn, S. (1998). *Ruling Passions: A Theory of Practical Reasoning*. Oxford: Oxford University Press.

Blair, R. J. (1995). 'A Cognitive Developmental Approach to Morality: Investigating the Psychopath'. *Cognition*, 57: 1–29.

—— Jones, L., Clark, F., and Smith, M. (1997). 'The Psychopathic Individual: A Lack of Responsiveness to Distress Cues?' *Psychophysiology*, 34: 192–8.

Blum, L. A. (1994). *Moral Perception and Particularity*. Cambridge: Cambridge University Press.

Bok, H. (1996). 'Acting without Choosing'. *Noûs*, 30: 174–96.

Boyd, R. N. (1988). 'How to Be a Moral Realist', in G. Sayre-McCord (ed.), *Essays on Moral Realism*. Ithaca, NY: Cornell University Press.

Brandt, R. B. (1954). *Hopi Ethics: A Theoretical Analysis*. Chicago: University of Chicago Press.

—— (1959). *Ethical Theory: The Problems of Normative and Critical Ethics*. Englewood Cliff, NJ: Prentice-Hall.

—— (1970). 'Traits of Character: A Conceptual Analysis'. *American Philosophical Quarterly*, 7: 23–37.

Bratman, M. E. (1996). 'Identification, Decision, and Treating as a Reason'. *Philosophical Topics*, 24: 1–18.

Brink, D. O. (1989). *Moral Realism and the Foundations of Ethics*. Cambridge: Cambridge University Press.

Campbell, J. (1999). 'Can Philosophical Accounts of Altruism Accommodate Experimental Data on Helping Behaviour?' *Australasian Journal of Philosophy*, 77: 26–45.

Cooper, J. M. (1999). *Reason and Emotion: Essays on Ancient Moral Psychology and Ethical Theory*. Princeton: Princeton University Press.

Damasio, A. R., Tranel, D., and Damasio, H. (1990). 'Individuals with Sociopathic Behavior Caused by Frontal Damage Fail to Respond Autonomically to Social Stimuli'. *Behavioral Brain Research*, 41: 81–94.

Daniels, N. (1979). 'Wide Reflective Equilibrium and Theory Acceptance in Ethics'. *Journal of Philosophy*, 76: 256–84.

Darley, J. M., and Batson, C. D. (1973). 'From Jerusalem to Jericho: A Study of Situational and Dispositional Variables in Helping Behavior'. *Journal of Personality and Social Psychology*, 27: 100–8.

D'Arms, J., and Jacobson, D. (2000). 'Sentiment and Value'. *Ethics*, 110: 722–48.

Darwall, S. L. (1983). *Impartial Reason*. Ithaca, NY: Cornell University Press.

—— (1989). 'Moore to Stevenson', in Robert Cavalier, James Gouinlock, and James Sterba (eds.), *Ethics in the History of Philosophy*. London: Macmillan.

—— Gibbard, A., and Railton, P. (eds.) (1997). *Moral Discourse and Practice: Some Philosophical Approaches*. New York: Oxford University Press.

Deigh, J. (1999). 'Ethics', in R. Audi (ed.), *The Cambridge Dictionary of Philosophy*. Cambridge: Cambridge University Press.

Dennett, D. C. (1984). *Elbow Room: The Varieties of Free Will Worth Wanting*. Cambridge, Mass.: MIT Press.

Dent, N. J. H. (1975). 'Virtues and Actions'. *Philosophical Quarterly*, 25: 318–35.

DePaul, M. (1999). 'Character Traits, Virtues, and Vices: Are There None?', in *Proceedings of the 20th World Congress of Philosophy*, i. Bowling Green, Ohio: Philosophy Documentation Center.

Doris, J. M. (1996). 'People Like Us: Morality, Psychology, and the Fragmentation of Character'. Ph.D. diss., University of Michigan, Ann Arbor.

—— (1998). 'Persons, Situations, and Virtue Ethics'. *Noûs*, 32: 504–30.

—— (2002). *Lack of Character: Personality and Moral Behavior*. New York: Cambridge University Press.

—— and Stich, S. P. (2001). 'Ethics', in *The Encyclopedia of Cognitive Science*, philosophy ed. D. Chalmers. London: Macmillan Reference.

Ellsworth, P. C. (1994). 'Sense, Culture, and Sensibility', in H. Markus and S. Kitayama (eds.), *Emotion and Culture: Empirical Studies in Mutual Influence*. Washington: American Psychological Association.

Firth, R. (1952). 'Ethical Absolutism and the Ideal Observer Theory'. *Philosophy and Phenomenological Research*, 12: 317–45.

Flanagan, O. (1991). *Varieties of Moral Personality: Ethics and Psychological Realism*. Cambridge, Mass.: Harvard University Press.

Fodor, J. (1998). *Concepts: Where Cognitive Science Went Wrong*. Oxford: Oxford University Press.

Frankena, W. K. (1976). 'Obligation and Motivation in Recent Moral Philosophy', in K. E. Goodpaster (ed.), *Perspectives on Morality: Essays of William K. Frankena*. Notre Dame, Ind.: University of Notre Dame Press.

Frankfurt, Harry (1988). *The Importance of What we Care About: Philosophical Essays*. Cambridge: Cambridge University Press.

Gibbard, A. (1990). *Wise Choices, Apt Feelings: A Theory of Normative Judgment*. Cambridge, Mass.: Harvard University Press.

Gilbert, D. T., and Malone, P. S. (1995). 'The Correspondence Bias'. *Psychological Bulletin*, 117: 21–38.

Goldman, A. I. (1993). 'Ethics and Cognitive Science'. *Ethics*, 103: 337–60.

Haidt, J., Koller, S., and Dias, M. (1993). 'Affect, Culture, and Morality; or, Is it Wrong to Eat your Dog?'. *Journal of Personality and Social Psychology*, 65: 613–28.

Haney, C., Banks, W., and Zimbardo, P. (1973). 'Interpersonal Dynamics of a Simulated Prison'. *International Journal of Criminology and Penology*, 1: 69–97.

Hare, R. D. (1993). *Without Conscience: The Disturbing World of the Psychopaths Among Us*. New York: Pocket Books.

Hare, R. M. (1952). *The Language of Morals*. Oxford: Oxford University Press.

Harman, G. (1977). *The Nature of Morality*. New York: Oxford University Press.

—— (1999). 'Moral Philosophy Meets Social Psychology: Virtue Ethics and the Fundamental Attribution Error'. *Proceedings of the Aristotelian Society*, 99: 315–31.

—— (2000). 'The Nonexistence of Character Traits'. *Proceedings of the Aristotelian Society*, 100: 223–6.

Hart, D., and Killen, M. (1999). 'Introduction: Perspectives on Morality in Everyday Life', in M. Killen and D. Hart (eds.), *Morality in Everyday Life: Developmental Perspectives*, paperback edn. Cambridge: Cambridge University Press.

Hill, T. E. (1991). *Autonomy and Self-Respect*. Cambridge: Cambridge University Press.

Horowitz, T. (1998). 'Philosophical Intuitions and Psychological Theory', in M. DePaul and W. Ramsey (eds.), *Rethinking Intuition: The Psychology of Intuition and its Role in Philosophical Inquiry*. Lanham, Md.: Rowman & Littlefield.

Hume, D. (1975). *Enquiries Concerning Human Understanding and Concerning the Principles of Morals*, 3rd edn. Oxford: Oxford University Press.

—— (1978). *A Treatise of Human Nature*, 2nd edn. Oxford: Oxford University Press.

Hursthouse, R. (1999). *On Virtue Ethics*. Oxford: Oxford University Press.

Hutcheson, F. (1738). *An Enquiry into the Original of our Ideas of Beauty and Virtue, in Two Treatises*. London: D. Midwinter.

Irwin, T. H. (1988). 'Disunity in the Aristotelian Virtues'. *Oxford Studies in Ancient Philosophy*, supp. vol., 61–78.

Isen, A. M., and Levin, P. F. (1972). 'Effect of Feeling Good on Helping: Cookies and Kindness'. *Journal of Personality and Social Psychology*, 21: 384–8.

Jackson, F. (1994). 'Armchair Metaphysics', in J. O'Leary Hawthorne and M. Michael (eds.), *Philosophy in Mind*. Dordrecht: Kluwer.

—— (1998). *From Metaphysics to Ethics: A Defense of Conceptual Analysis*. New York: Oxford University Press.

—— and Pettit, P. (1995). 'Moral Functionalism and Moral Motivation'. *Philosophical Quarterly*, 45: 20–40.

Johnson, M. (1993). *Moral Imagination: Implications of Cognitive Science for Ethics*. Chicago: University of Chicago Press.

Jones, E. E. (1990). *Interpersonal Perception*. New York: W. H. Freeman.

Kagan, S. (1989). *The Limits of Morality*. Oxford: Oxford University Press.

Kahneman, D., Slovic, P., and Tversky, A. (1982). *Judgment under Uncertainty: Heuristics and Biases*. Cambridge: Cambridge University Press.

Kane, R. (1996). *The Significance of Free Will*. Oxford: Oxford University Press.

—— (2002a). 'Introduction: The Contours of Contemporary Free Will Debates', in R. Kane (ed.), *The Oxford Handbook of Free Will*. New York: Oxford University Press.

—— (2002b). 'Some Neglected Pathways in the Free Will Labyrinth', in R. Kane (ed.), *The Oxford Handbook of Free Will*. New York: Oxford University Press.

Keneally, T. (1982). *Schindler's List*. New York: Simon & Schuster.

Kim, J. (1988). 'What Is "Naturalized Epistemology"?', in J. Tomberlin (ed.), *Philosophical Perspectives, ii: Epistemology*. Atascadero, Calif.: Ridgeway.

Kitayama, S., and Markus, H. R. (1999). '*Yin* and *Yang* of the Japanese Self: The Cultural Psychology of Personality Coherence', in D. Cervone and Y. Shoda (eds.), *The Coherence of Personality: Social–Cognitive Bases of Consistency, Variability, and Organization*. New York: Guilford Press.

Kupperman, J. J. (2001). 'The Indispensability of Character'. *Philosophy*, 76: 239–50.

Larmore, C. E. (1987). *Patterns of Moral Complexity*. Cambridge: Cambridge University Press.

Leming, J. S. (1997a). 'Research and Practice in Character Education: A Historical Perspective', in A. Molnar (ed.), *The Construction of Children's Character: Ninety-Sixth Yearbook of the National Society for the Study of Education*, p. II. Chicago: University of Chicago Press.

—— (1997b). 'Whither Goes Character Education? Objectives, Pedagogy, and Research in Character Education Programs'. *Journal of Education*, 179: 11–34.

Lewis, D. (1970). 'How to Define Theoretical Terms'. *Journal of Philosophy*, 67: 427–46.

—— (1972). 'Psychophysical and Theoretical Identifications'. *Australasian Journal of Philosophy*, 50: 249–58.

—— (1989). 'Dispositional Theories of Value'. *Proceedings of the Aristotelian Society*, suppl. vol., 63: 113–37.

Loeb, D. (1998). 'Moral Realism and the Argument from Disagreement'. *Philosophical Studies*, 90: 281–303.

Louden, R. B. (1984). 'On Some Vices of Virtue Ethics'. *American Philosophical Quarterly*, 21: 227–36.

McDowell, J. (1978). 'Are Moral Requirements Hypothetical Imperatives?' *Proceedings of the Aristotelian Society*, suppl. vol., 52: 13–29.

—— (1979). 'Virtue and Reason'. *The Monist*, 62: 331–50.

—— (1987). *Projection and Truth in Ethics*. Lindley Lecture. Kansas: University of Kansas.

MacIntyre, A. (1984). *After Virtue*, 2nd edn. Notre Dame, Ind.: University of Notre Dame Press.

McKenna, M. (2001). 'Source Incompatibilism, Ultimacy, and the Transfer of Non-Responsibility'. *American Philosophical Quarterly*, 38: 37–51.

Mackie, J. L. (1977). *Ethics: Inventing Right and Wrong*. New York: Penguin.

Margolis, E., and Laurence, S. (1999). *Concepts*. Cambridge, Mass.: MIT Press.

Markus, H. R., and Kitayama, S. (1991). 'Culture and the Self: Implications for Cognition, Emotion, and Motivation'. *Psychological Review*, 98: 224–53.

Mathews, K. E., and Cannon, L. K. (1975). 'Environmental Noise Level as a Determinant of Helping Behavior'. *Journal of Personality and Social Psychology*, 32: 571–7.

Merritt, M. (1999). 'Virtue Ethics and the Social Psychology of Character'. Ph.D. diss., University of California, Berkeley.

—— (2000). 'Virtue Ethics and Situationist Personality Psychology'. *Ethical Theory and Moral Practice*, 3: 365–83.

Milgram, S. (1974). *Obedience to Authority*. New York: Harper & Row.

Mischel, W. (1968). *Personality and Assessment*. New York: Wiley.

Moore, G. E. (1903). *Principia Ethica*. Cambridge: Cambridge University Press.

Nagel, T. (1986). *The View from Nowhere*. New York: Oxford University Press.

Nichols, S. (2002). 'How Psychopaths Threaten Moral Rationalism; or, Is it Irrational to Be Amoral?' *The Monist*, 85: 285–304.

—— (2004). *Sentimental Rules: On the Natural Foundations of Moral Judgment*. Oxford: Oxford University Press.

Nisbett, R. E. (1998). 'Essence and Accident', in J. M. Darley and J. Cooper (eds.), *Attribution and Social Interaction: The Legacy of Edward E. Jones*. Washington: American Psychological Association.

—— and Cohen, D. (1996). *Culture of Honor: The Psychology of Violence in the South*. Boulder, Colo.: Westview Press.

—— and Ross, L. (1980). *Human Inference: Strategies and Shortcomings of Social Judgment*. Englewood Cliffs, NJ: Prentice-Hall.

Nucci, L. (1986). 'Children's Conceptions of Morality, Social Conventions and Religious Prescription', in C. Harding (ed.), *Moral Dilemmas: Philosophical and Psychological Reconsiderations of the Development of Moral Reasoning*. Chicago: Precedent Press.

Nussbaum, M. C. (1999). 'Virtue Ethics: A Misleading Category?' *Journal of Ethics*, 3: 163–201.

Peterson, D. R. (1968). *The Clinical Study of Social Behavior*. New York: Appleton-Century-Crofts.

Quine, W. v. O. (1969). 'Epistemology Naturalized', in Quine, *Ontological Relativity and Other Essays*. New York: Columbia University Press.

Railton, P. (1986a). 'Facts and Values'. *Philosophical Topics*, 14: 5–31.

—— (1986b). 'Moral Realism'. *Philosophical Review*, 95: 163–207.

—— (1989). 'Naturalism and Prescriptivity'. *Social Philosophy and Policy*, 7: 151–74.

—— (1995). 'Made in the Shade: Moral Compatibilism and the Aims of Moral Theory'. *Canadian Journal of Philosophy*, suppl. vol., 21: 79–106.

Rawls, J. (1951). 'Outline of a Decision Procedure for Ethics'. *Philosophical Review*, 60: 167–97.

—— (1971). *A Theory of Justice*. Cambridge, Mass.: Harvard University Press.

Rosati, C. S. (2000). 'Brandt's Notion of Therapeutic Agency'. *Ethics*, 110: 780–811.

Roskies, A. (2003). 'Are Ethical Judgments Intrinsically Motivational? Lessons from "Acquired Sociopathy"'. *Philosophical Psychology*, 16: 51–66.

Ross, L., and Nisbett, R. E. (1991). *The Person and the Situation: Perspectives of Social Psychology*. Philadelphia: Temple University Press.

Saver, J. L., and Damasio, A. R. (1991). 'Preserved Access and Processing of Social Knowledge in a Patient with Acquired Sociopathy Due to Ventromedial Frontal Damage'. *Neuropsychologia*, 29: 1241–9.

Scanlon, T. M. (1988). 'The Significance of Choice', in S. M. McMurrin (ed.), *The Tanner Lectures on Human Values*, viii. Salt Lake City: University of Utah Press.

Sher, G. (1998). 'Ethics, Character, and Action', in E. F. Paul, F. D. Miller, and J. Paul (eds.), *Virtue and Vice*. Cambridge: Cambridge University Press.

Sherman, N. (1989). *The Fabric of Character: Aristotle's Theory of Virtue*. New York: Oxford University Press.

Shweder, R. A., and Bourne, E. J. (1982). 'Does the Concept of the Person Vary Cross-Culturally?', in A. J. Marsella and G. M. White (eds.), *Cultural Conceptions of Mental Health and Therapy*. Boston, Mass.: Reidel.

Singer, P. (1974). 'Sidgwick and Reflective Equilibrium'. *The Monist*, 58: 490 517.

—— (2000). *Writings on an Ethical Life*. New York: HarperCollins.

Sinnott-Armstrong, W. P. (2005). 'Moral Intuitionism Meets Empirical Psychology', in T. Horgan and M. Timmons (eds.), *Metaethics After Moore*. New York: Oxford University Press.

Smart, J. J. C. (1961). 'Free-Will, Praise and Blame'. *Mind*, 70: 291–306.

Smith, Adam. (2002). *The Theory of Moral Sentiments*. New York: Cambridge University Press.

Smith, M. (1994). *The Moral Problem*. Oxford: Blackwell.

Stevenson, C. L. (1944). *Ethics and Language*. New Haven: Yale University Press.

—— (1963). *Facts and Values*. New Haven: Yale University Press.

Stich, S. (1993a). 'Naturalizing Epistemology: Quine, Simon and the Prospects for Pragmatism', in C. Hookway and D. Peterson (eds.), *Philosophy and Cognitive Science*, Royal Institute of Philosophy, suppl. 34. Cambridge: Cambridge University Press.

—— (1993b). 'Moral Philosophy and Mental Representation', in M. Hechter, L. Nadel, and R. E. Michod (eds.), *The Origin of Values*. New York: de Gruyter.

Strawson, G. (1986). *Freedom and Belief*. Oxford: Oxford University Press.

—— (2002). 'The Bounds of Freedom', in R. Kane (ed.), *The Oxford Handbook of Free Will*. New York: Oxford University Press.

Strawson, P. (1982). 'Freedom and Resentment', in G. Watson (ed.), *Free Will*. New York: Oxford University Press.

Sturgeon, N. L. (1988). 'Moral Explanations', in G. Sayre-McCord (ed.), *Essays on Moral Realism*. Ithaca, NY: Cornell University Press.

Sumner, W. G. (1934). *Folkways*. Boston: Ginn.

Svavarsdóttir, S. (1999). 'Moral Cognitivism and Motivation'. *Philosophical Review*, 108: 161–219.

Tetlock, P. E. (1999). 'Review of *Culture of Honor: The Psychology of Violence in the South*'. *Political Psychology*, 20: 211–13.

Turiel, E., Killen, M., and Helwig, C. (1987). 'Morality: Its Structure, Functions, and Vagaries', in J. Kagan and S. Lamb (eds.), *The Emergence of Morality in Young Children*. Chicago: University of Chicago Press.

Tversky, A., and Kahneman, D. (1981). 'The Framing of Decisions and the Psychology of Choice'. *Science*, 211: 453–63.

Velleman, J. D. (1992). 'What Happens When Someone Acts?' *Mind*, 101: 461–81.

Vernon, P. E. (1964). *Personality Assessment: A Critical Survey*. New York: Wiley.

Wallace, R. J. (1994). *Responsibility and the Moral Sentiments*. Cambridge, Mass.: Harvard University Press.

Watson, G. (1990). 'On the Primacy of Character', in Owen Flanagan and Amélie Oksenberg Rorty (eds.), *Identity, Character, and Morality: Essays in Moral Psychology*. Cambridge, Mass.: MIT Press.

—— (1996). 'Two Faces of Responsibility'. *Philosophical Topics*, 24: 227–48.

Weinberg, J., Nichols, S., and Stich, S. (2002). 'Normativity and Epistemic Intuitions'. *Philosophical Topics*, 29: 429–60.

Westermarck, E. (1906). *Origin and Development of the Moral Ideas*, 2 vols. New York: Macmillan.

Williams, B. A. O. (1973). 'A Critique of Utilitarianism', in J. J. C. Smart and B. A. O. Williams, *Utilitarianism: For and Against*. Cambridge: Cambridge University Press.

—— (1981). *Moral Luck: Philosophical Papers 1973–1980*. Cambridge: Cambridge University Press.

—— (1985). *Ethics and the Limits of Philosophy*. Cambridge, Mass.: Harvard University Press.

—— (1993). *Shame and Necessity*. Berkeley: University of California Press.

Woods, M. (1986). 'Intuition and Perception in Aristotle's Ethics'. *Oxford Studies in Ancient Philosophy*, 4: 145–66.

Woolfolk, R. L., Doris, J. M. (2002). 'Rationing Mental Health Care: Parity, Disparity, and Justice'. *Bioethics*, 16: 469–85.

—— —— and Darley, J. M. (forthcoming). 'Identification, Situational Constraint, and Social Cognition: Studies in the Attribution of Moral Responsibility.' *Cognition*.

PART II

SOCIAL AND POLITICAL PHILOSOPHY

CHAPTER 6

LIBERALISM AND DIVERSITY

LINDA BARCLAY

1. INTRODUCTION

According to its defenders, liberalism does better than merely accommodate diversity: it celebrates and promotes it. Its approach to diversity signals its most decisive advantage over its rivals such as Marxism and communitarianism and ensures it remains the only viable theory of justice for our increasingly diverse age. According to recent critics, liberalism, or popular versions of it, destroys diversity, particularly the differences among people that matter most to them. It imposes homogenizing values that have the potential to kill off unique ways of life, even whole societies.

Which of these views about liberalism is accurate turns on the kind of diversity at stake and whether diversity of that kind ought to be valued. Most contemporary liberals value diversity that arises from, or at least coheres with, individual choice, secured in two ways. First, equal opportunities understood as an absence of discrimination and a fair distribution of resources enable people to participate in the main institutions of society regardless of their race, ethnicity, sex, religion, and so on. Entrance to educational and political institutions, markets, trades, and professions depends on preference and ability rather than the colour of one's skin, one's religious affiliations, and the like. Secondly, extensive liberties enable people to make individual choices about the good life and to participate in the various civil groups and organizations of their choice, such as churches, sporting groups, and ethnic associations, without fear of penalty or persecution. As individuals are freed from the constraints of discrimination and circumstance, diversity in both public and private life is likely to flourish, limited only by the imperative to ensure that all individuals have similar opportunities, and, of course, the preferences of free and equal individuals: some activities and even ways of life will disappear, but for the wholly acceptable reason that they are no longer chosen.

Those who claim that liberalism fails to accommodate diversity generally attack one or both of these liberal ideals. It has been claimed that the liberal conception of equal opportunity does not go far enough to remove less obvious forms of discrimination or to nullify the ways in which ethnicity, religion, and gender prevent some people from genuine participation in society's main institutions. It has also been argued that the liberal understanding of liberty is insufficient to ensure genuine choice for religious and ethnic minorities and destroys just as many valuable "associations" as it helps to create. Anyone familiar with contemporary political philosophy will recognize these themes in both feminist and communitarian critiques of liberalism, but it is the rapidly burgeoning literature on what has become known as multiculturalism that is my main focus in this chapter.

This chapter will focus on the force of these criticisms when applied to individuals and groups. The next section will focus on whether liberalism can address less obvious forms of discrimination and bias that prevent *individuals* from exercising important choices and participating in society's main institutions. I will suggest that it can. The following section will consider whether liberalism can similarly answer the accusation that it is intolerant of some *groups* or associations. I will argue that while there is some scope for liberal accommodation in certain contexts, it is not possible for liberalism to meet many of the demands of those groups currently clamouring for special accommodation, because their demands are at odds with basic liberal principles. In the final section of the chapter I will offer a brief diagnosis of why some liberals nonetheless seem willing to betray liberal principles on their behalf.

My way of dividing up the issues is different from many other approaches, primarily because of my specific focus on liberalism. In particular, I wish to capture the significant moral distinction between forms of accommodation that enable individuals (albeit as members of groups) to do something for themselves, such as smoke a prohibited substance in a religious ceremony, from forms of accommodation that allow some members of a group to make decisions about other members of the group, such as the permission to withdraw children from school at an early age. Although the distinction will be blurred in hard cases, from the perspective of liberalism it is not the legal or political *form* (legal exemption, self-government powers, special funding) of multicultural accommodation that is primarily interesting, but what the legal or political accommodation *allows*.[1] My focus on liberalism also restricts the range of topics that are discussed. Interesting debates about

---

[1] For an extensive taxonomy of different forms of multicultural accommodation see Levy (1997).

school curricula or national symbols and a raft of other specific policy matters are omitted. Many of these conflicts raise real moral and political questions, but they are not specifically relevant, or vexing, for liberal political theory as such.

2. INDIVIDUALS

A standard understanding among defenders of multiculturalism is that removal of explicitly discriminatory laws is insufficient to secure genuine equality of opportunity. Will Kymlicka claims that to this limited extent defenders of multiculturalism have been victorious: 'few people continue to think that justice can simply be *defined* in terms of difference-blind rules and institutions' (Kymlicka 2002: 366). The requirement that students not display religious symbols in schools places Muslim girls at a disadvantage to Christian girls, as would a requirement by an employer that its workers not cover their heads. The requirement that police officers and military personnel wear a particular hat makes it very difficult for some Jews to seek employment in these areas. Sikhs are similarly disadvantaged by such policies as well as by the law that all construction workers wear protective helmets.

To defenders of multiculturalism, laws that disadvantage only some Jews, Muslims, or Sikhs, and not the Christian majority, are paradigmatic of discrimination. In contrast, Brian Barry argues that the fact that some laws are particularly burdensome only to people of a certain ethnic or religious persuasion is in itself no objection to them: *all* laws impact differently on different people just because the essence of laws is that they protect some interests and not others. Laws that prohibit rape prioritize the interests of potential rape victims over those who wish to rape, and paedophile laws prioritize the interests of children over paedophiles (Barry 2001: 34). One can similarly reject the claim that laws that differentially impact violate the liberal principle of neutrality. Most liberals who defend neutrality do not believe that the state's laws must be neutral in their *effects*. Liberals typically defend neutrality of justification: the state should not adopt a particular law simply for the reason that the (justice-respecting) way of life or activity it burdens is less worthy than those it does not burden (Kymlicka 1989*a*).

The doctrine of neutrality of justification highlights the limitations of Barry's argument. Laws against rape are adopted in order to impact detrimentally on rapists. If laws against rapists and paedophiles are analogous to dress code laws, then the multiculturalist is right to protest them for it would follow that they are adopted in order to discriminate against the interests of Sikhs and Jews. Whatever the merits of his choice of example, Barry would deny that most laws that differentially impact on certain religious or ethnic minorities are adopted in order to discriminate, something many multiculturalists would concede. Laws concerning dress codes are justified by the need for police and military personnel to be readily identifiable as well as to instil a degree of discipline and uniformity.

Although not adopted in order to discriminate, multiculturalists can still make two plausible objections to many burdensome laws. First, they can object that the law does not promote a particularly important end and thus should be removed, or, secondly, that the way it does promote an important end is unnecessarily framed to protect the interests of the religious and ethnic majority while ignoring the like interests of minorities. It is unthinkable in Western democracies to propose that police or military personnel not wear wedding rings, or that school students not be able to wear a cross around their necks. That Sundays, Easter, and Christmas are public holidays is hardly an accidental benefit to Christians.

These cases should bother liberals because, as Kymlicka argues, many are committed to something stronger than neutrality of justification when in comes to religion: they typically believe that the state shouldn't promote or play favourites with religion at all, including for purportedly neutral reasons (Kymlicka 2002: 344). For example, Barry claims that a just state is one that, among other things, treats religions fairly or equally. While in the main this will mean avoiding the promotion of any religion, it may allow for some favours, as long as those favours are extended equally to all religions: the funding of religious schools is an example (Barry 2001: 29).

Yet Barry's demand that the state treat religions equally is inconsistent with what he says about legal exemptions from general laws for members of religious minorities who are especially burdened by them. While accepting the multiculturalist's first objection that some burdensome laws can simply be removed, because the interests they promote are not important, Barry says of those laws that do protect important interests that the importance of the interests will nearly always rule out the legitimacy of exemptions. He suggests that animal protection laws that are inconsistent with the ritual slaughter required for halal and kosher meat, and head protection legislation that prevents Sikhs from riding motorcycles, fall into this category. Any concern about equality of opportunity or fairness is misplaced, for equal opportunity is satisfied if uniform rules create the same "choice sets" for everybody. People will make different choices from within uniform choice sets, depending on their preferences: 'the effect of some distinctive belief or preference is to bring about a certain pattern of choices from among the set of opportunities that are available to all who are similarly placed physically or financially' (Barry 2001: 36–7). Jews and Muslims, like everyone else, have the opportunity to eat meat but they choose not to avail themselves of it, just as Sikhs choose not to avail themselves of the opportunity to ride motorcycles. It is true that the choice set prohibits some people from doing what they want to do, but a person's just share of resources also prohibits her from living off champagne and caviar. A person who 'hankered for what is not permitted' (Barry 2001: 40) has an expensive taste that should not be compensated by extra resources or legal exemptions.

Using an equality of resources approach to distributive justice, Barry is defending a version of the difference-blind approach to justice that Kymlicka optimistically claims most people concede is inadequate, and one that is blind to the multiculturalist's second objection that some laws are avoidably framed to protect the interests of the majority. If the purpose and content of the laws that define the choice set favour the interests of, say, the Christian majority, then based on his own demand that liberals not play favourites, Barry is compelled to conclude that such laws are unfair quite irrespective of whether or not they are explicitly discriminatory. Barry's own attempt to deflate the worry that such laws may be unfair in this way is instructive. He argues that animal protection laws do not unfairly restrict the religious liberty of Jews and Muslims but only the ability to eat meat, something that is not demanded of Jews or Muslims. 'The law may condone the additional suffering of animals killed without prior stunning, but if it does we should be clear that what it is doing is accommodating the tastes of a subset of carnivores, not observing the demands of religious freedom' (Barry 2001: 45–6). Barry tells us of his (guilt-ridden) purchases of expensive organic meat because he believes that, on animal welfare grounds, the case against meat-eating cannot be answered. Indeed, laws that require humane slaughter address only a very small amount of the suffering endured by most animals raised for meat, something Barry must agree with. The reason there are not more laws is simple: the law defers heavily to the interests of carnivores, not only for the taste of flesh, but also for relatively inexpensive flesh. It seems more than reasonable for Jewish and Muslim carnivores to wonder why, if non-Jewish and non-Muslim majorities are so concerned about animal suffering, the only serious restrictions to meat production they are prepared to countenance are those that won't affect their interests. If considerable animal suffering is to be permitted so as to pander to the taste for inexpensive flesh, why is it not permitted to satisfy the same tastes of Jewish and Muslim minorities? Barry tells us that the state may not play favourites among religions: this is a case where it arguably does so. (Bhikhu Parekh 2000, ch. 8, provides a more general discussion of the complexities of determining what constitutes equal opportunities in these kinds of cases, as do Caney 2002; Kelly 2002; Miller 2002.)

Liberals have grounds to reject or modify laws which prevent individuals from exercising their choice to practise aspects of their religion or culture when the law does not pursue a legitimate end, or when the way it is framed unfairly favours the interests of one religion over another. But what of burdensome laws where the genuine end that the law promotes *unavoidably* conflicts with some practice that an individual may wish to engage in for religious or cultural purposes? Defenders of multicultural accommodation have argued that the importance of being able to practise one's religion or culture can create a justification for exempting certain individuals from observance of the law. The argument is not that there is unfairness, but that there is a clash between the interests that the general (and fair) law promotes, and the interest in being able to practise aspects of religion or culture.

Exemption from drug laws so as to enable the use of peyote in religious ceremonies may be an example, as well as exemption for Sikhs from head protection on construction sites.

Barry, like a number of sceptics before him, rejects the multiculturalist's belief that being able to practise aspects of one's religion or culture is as serious an interest (need?) as, for example, having a fair share of resources.[2] Others are also wary of accepting any kind of blanket exemption from general laws for religious practices (Gutmann 2000). On the other hand, a number of liberals, and certainly many within legal circles, believe that the interest in practising one's religion or aspects of one's culture can compete with and in some cases outweigh universal compliance with a fair law that promotes important ends, especially when the general law in question does not promote a so-called *compelling* government interest (e.g. McConnell 2000; Nussbaum 2000: 187–206; Swaine 2001: 312–14; Freeman 2002). One obvious challenge for such arguments is to show why specifically *religious* practices should be marked off for special protection in this way. The history of democratic countries shows a strong deference to religion in this regard, as does the history of liberal thought, although often for pragmatic and historical reasons pertaining to the destructive effects of religious conflict. Whatever the specific reasons for liberal deference to freedom of religion, most liberals are generally willing to concede exemptions from general laws in some cases, thus enhancing the capacity of members of religious minorities to participate in public institutions and to make (what they consider) important individual choices. What is generally at stake in these cases is whether the exempted practice really is central to religious worship, and whether the end the law promotes is compelling or not. It is rarely the case that liberal values themselves are in serious jeopardy, which is why the issue of limited legal exemptions for *individuals* has raised only minor liberal concern.

3. ASSOCIATIONS

Far more challenging from a liberal perspective are some of the demands made by groups, or their leaders, in the name of multicultural accommodation. The demands I focus on in this section primarily concern not what choices individuals can make for themselves, but what certain members of a group can be permitted to do to, or demand of, others within the group. Examples include: withdrawing

---

[2] Notably Barry is more sympathetic to exemptions when the interests competing with the interests the law promotes are *not* religious interests, especially those to do with promoting racial and religious harmony and avoiding social disruption (2001: 49–54).

children from school before the legal age; female genital mutilation; arranged (and enforced) marriages; different divorce and property arrangements for men and women; required participation in religious ceremonies; control over school curriculum including language of instruction; required use of a particular language within certain contexts. Accommodation of such practices can include any combination of legal exemptions from otherwise applicable laws, special financial assistance, or self-government powers.

While the distinction between individuals being able to choose to do something that concerns themselves and individuals being able to do something for or to others is relatively straightforward, it is frequently ignored in the multicultural literature. Thus, claims that liberalism favours 'individuals and groups leading their lives as they see fit' (Galston 2002: 3), or that group demand for accommodation 'is not simply the theological impulse to tyrannize over others . . . [but] the simple desire to be left alone' (Galston 1995: 520), pepper the literature, just as though there were no conceptual or moral distinctions between the freedom to govern oneself and the freedom to govern others. But of course there are such distinctions to be made, and the question is how liberals should make them.

3.1 Voluntary Associations

Liberals have always assumed that individuals will form associations, and have explicitly sought to enable this. The importance of liberty is to allow individuals to participate singly or with others in various pursuits—religious, political, artistic, and cultural—of their choosing. The point of neutrality is to ensure that the state scrupulously avoids favouring some of these pursuits on the grounds that they are more worthy than others: such value judgements are made by free and equal individuals, not government. It is a surprisingly common assumption within the multiculturalism literature that a liberal state cannot tolerate illiberal associations (Galston 2002: 21; Nussbaum 2000: 176). Yet one obvious option that liberty and neutrality enable is the formation of associations that do not themselves exemplify liberal values. Associations that are modelled by procedures and rules that restrict their members' freedom and violate norms of equality flourish in liberal democracies: the Catholic Church, Orthodox Judaism, even white supremacist and sado-masochistic groups are all permitted, even if some of their desired activities are not. Moreover, no special legal accommodation seems necessary for such groups to flourish: they do so just by the exercise of individual liberty rights and by governmental restraint. Why all the fuss in the recent multicultural literature?

The foregoing justification of illiberal groups is only compelling because it is taken for granted that illiberal associations are formed and sustained by free and equal people exercising their liberty. To put the point another way, what liberal principles seem to permit is the formation of illiberal *voluntary* associations. It is doubtful that liberalism can be as tolerant of illiberal religious and cultural groups because it is not plausible to suggest of many of these groups that they are voluntary associations, that is, chosen and sustained by free and equal individuals. More specifically, there are two aspects of most illiberal cultural and religious groups that strain their classification as voluntary associations: they are groups into which many of their members are born and they are all-encompassing. In short, they are groups that involve the rearing of children, including the attempt to inculcate in the young acceptance of a comprehensive way of life. Most voluntary associations in liberal democracies do not exhibit both of these features; many exhibit neither. A political organization or golf club is an association that one usually chooses to join as a well-informed adult. Nor are such associations all-encompassing: they don't usually require particular religious affiliations, modes of dress, sexual behaviour, and the like. Most members of the Catholic Church in Western democracies are born into the association, and membership may be somewhat more encompassing, with requirements (enforced or not) concerning sexual conduct and family life. Nonetheless, members are also likely to participate in many other organizations and institutions within the broader society and to have received a decent level of largely secular, liberal education. Under these conditions, membership will not be all-encompassing.

If encompassing groups into which people are born are to be conceived of as genuine voluntary associations, and thus defended by liberal principles of liberty and neutrality, they will be required to meet a raft of conditions that will render them more liberal. To put the point another way, given the nature of many religious and cultural groups, it is doubtful that they can in fact be both voluntary and markedly illiberal and thus defended by standard liberal principles of liberty and neutrality. That this is so is demonstrated by considering Chandran Kukathas's approach to group accommodation. He defends the right of associations to organize themselves in any way they see fit without state intervention (and without special state assistance). The argument is very straightforward: each individual is entitled to associate or dissociate freely as he or she pleases. If an individual no longer finds an association congenial he or she can dissociate: enforcing the right to dissociate is the only legitimate grounds for state intervention in associations. Preventing the dissatisfied from leaving is the only thing that associations must not do: denying education and life-saving medical treatment to children, arranged and enforced marriages, denying women the right to hold property or to divorce, clitoridectomy and ritual scarring without the consent of the victim, and life-threatening initiation ceremonies are all examples of practices which Kukathas argues associations should be left free to practise (Kukathas 1992: 126–7; 1997: 70).

Kukathas's view is a peculiar type of libertarianism: not just liberty from state interference over matters concerning oneself, but liberty to mutilate and kill one's children, for example (Barry 2001: 143). Conflating a man's dominion over himself with his dominion over others certainly has historical precedents: as we shall see, feminists have been quick to note its re-emergence in the multiculturalism literature. And, as Barry notes, matters are even worse for women and children than Kukathas's own examples would suggest (Barry 2001: 143–4). In his blanket rejection of state ("outside") interference in associations, there is nothing about *ritual* scarring, or clitoridectomy performed for specifically *religious* reasons, that is marked out for special protection. Scarring and genital mutilation performed for openly sadistic purposes, or just for fun, must also be permitted by the logic of Kukathas's argument. To allow mutilation for traditional or religious reasons, but not for fun, would be to do just what Kukathas rejects: to prevent people from freely associating according to their own conception of what makes life worthwhile.

Kukathas's theory has a superficial air of liberalism about it because of his claim that it is the voluntary acquiescence of individuals alone that gives associations their authority. He suggests that unhappy individuals can leave the group so long as there is 'an open market society to enter into' (Kukathas 1992: 134). Kymlicka is right to suggest that Kukathas's idea of what constitutes the ability to exit is 'bizarre' (Kymlicka 1992: 143). One can't get to the "open market society" if one is dead, or mutilated, or a small child, or completely lacking in the wherewithal to leave owing to a lack of education, systematic brainwashing, and a forced marriage at the age of 14 to a man three times one's age. As Susan Moller Okin argues, the effect, and very often the *raison d'être*, of most of the indignities that girls and women suffer within illiberal associations is to denude them of whatever resources might enable them to leave the group (Okin 2002). Kukathas's suggestion that an individual's "acquiescence" is evidence of her willing association appears to revive the discredited legal doctrine of implied consent: the state must not intervene in the marital relationship in the case of severe battery, because the battered wife's failure to leave implies consent (Shachar 2000: 80).

If encompassing groups into which people are born are to be defended by principles of liberty and freedom of association, as Kukathas wishes, then they need to meet a raft of conditions beyond the mere formal right of exit that he identifies. Most defenders of illiberal, encompassing associations concede, for example, that access to a decent level of education, awareness of alternatives, and an absence of brainwashing are necessary to realize the right of exit (Galston 2002: 123). The issue of education has been at the forefront in debates about liberalism and diversity, not only because education helps realize the right of exit, but because liberals correctly argue that the state has duties to protect the welfare of its vulnerable citizens and to ensure that they are properly educated to fulfil the requirements of liberal, democratic citizenship (Gutmann 1987, 1995; Macedo 2000). Yet it is often taken for granted in these debates that the potential clash between liberal education and diversity in associational life is a prima facie problem without addressing the question of why liberals should respect associational diversity in the first place. The argument here shows that if liberals should respect associational diversity because it is a product of individual liberty, then the reason for respecting diversity also justifies liberal education requirements. It follows that liberals simply shouldn't be bothered if educational requirements are inconsistent with the wishes of some illiberal groups because the kind of diversity they exemplify is not the kind that liberals respect. None of this is to deny that there will be ongoing debates about what level and type of education is required to realize the right of exit and to protect vulnerable citizens. Apart from educational requirements, it has also plausibly been argued that access to financial resources is necessary to realize the ability to leave a group, as the threat of destitution is sufficient to render ongoing participation involuntary (Barry 2001: 191–2; Rosenblum 1998: 101–3; Spinner-Halev 1999: 73–5).[3]

Educational and financial conditions for exit follow from the relatively weak requirement that individuals who no longer feel satisfied with their community be genuinely able to leave, thus rendering their ongoing participation properly voluntary. Even more liberalizing conditions are needed to meet the stronger requirement that individuals be able to reflect upon and critically assess whether their association truly fulfils their real interests. William Galston argues that true liberalism supports only the weak requirement: 'The politics of negative liberty seeks, first and foremost, to protect [a member's] ability to leave—although not necessarily to cultivate the awareness and reflective powers that may stimulate the desire to leave' (2002: 51). In contrast, Okin defends the stronger requirement and claims that pervasive female socialization which undercuts self-esteem and leads to an uncritical acceptance of female subordination can undermine the ability to exit as decisively as lack of education and poverty, as one is unable to reflect upon, or even imagine, alternatives (Okin 2002).

The upshot of Okin's argument is not modest: gendered associations (that is, those that assign specific and inferior roles to girls and women) are always suspiciously non-voluntary. In liberal countries feminists have won important victories in defeating the notion that the family, or any other voluntary association, is a special zone of privacy beyond legitimate state intervention. Most people (outside the multicultural debate) accept that battery, rape, and other crimes should be prohibited in any association. We have seen that basic education and access to financial resources is also demanded by the logic of voluntary association, even without the strong requirement of critical reflection. Despite these concrete measures, people will continue to form gendered associations, including family units, because women and men will choose to do so. Much further intervention to render such associations voluntary by Okin's standards would seem to jeopardize the meaningful ability to associate freely.

[3] An emphasis on material, social, and educational conditions for exit should not be taken to deny that exit may be exceedingly difficult because an individual's emotional attachment to her community renders her quite unable to imagine herself apart from it. Barry rightly argues that it is hardly appropriate for a *liberal* state to try to prevent individuals from becoming strongly attached to their associations in order to ensure that exit is always easy (2001: 164).

Yet many liberals are vulnerable to Okin's challenge, despite concerns about raising the standards of voluntariness too high. The importance of being able to assess and revise one's commitments is explicitly central to John Rawls's and Kymlicka's defence of individual rights, and Kymlicka argues that the liberal state acts to ensure that people have the genuine capacity to exercise those rights: 'a liberal state will want children to learn the cognitive and imaginative skills needed to evaluate different ways of life, and to survive outside their original community' (Kymlicka 2002: 237). Both Kymlicka and Rawls also argue that within the framework of a non-perfectionist state, how well associations do will depend on their own merits: worthwhile ways of life will be sustained by their ability to attract and retain members, less worthy ways of life will die out as members drift away. Liberal neutrality creates a marketplace of ideas within which, following Mill, the worth of different ways of life is to be proved practically (Rawls 1971: 331–2; Kymlicka 2002: 248). If Okin is right about the effects of female socialization in patriarchal associations, the endurance of a way of life may have little to do with its ability to compete in the cultural marketplace and more to do with its ability to raise new members unable to conceive of a better way of life.

Liberals who wish to maintain that legitimate diversity in association includes diversity in gender roles have two options. The first is to deny Okin's claim that gendered roles really do undermine women's capacity to assess and revise their attachments to patriarchal ways of life. Kymlicka (1991, 1999), for one, claims to have accepted Okin's argument about the destructive effects of gender socialization. Nancy Rosenblum (1998: 103–8), on the other hand, is sceptical whether we can so easily predict the effects of illiberal groups on individual psychology, as is Jeff Spinner-Halev (2001: 89). A second option is to accept Okin's claims about the effects of patriarchal association on some women's psychology, but to argue that practical attempts to prevent such association will be even more disastrous for freedom (not to mention political stability). Notably, Okin herself is unclear on what practical policy measures she thinks should follow from her argument.[4]

Issues concerning gender discrimination and freedom of association are vexing not only for questions of exit, but also for the liberal commitment to equality. Various private clubs refuse to extend membership to women; all religious groups wish to excommunicate unworthy members; some religious organizations refuse to extend certain forms of employment to women, or to those that do not conform, in their private lives, to the tenets of the faith. Some of these practices of discrimination can exacerbate the costs of exit for existing members—the threat of loss of employment can make it extremely difficult to leave a religious organization—but they also conflict with the general liberal prohibition on sexual and racial discrimination,

[4] In an earlier work Okin (1989) stressed the importance of fairer divorce laws, subsidized child care, and family-friendly work environments. Such measures enable people to avoid less gendered and hierarchical forms of family life if they wish, but they do nothing to prevent people from continuing to choose gendered associations, which is the problem being discussed here.

including by private associations. What complicates matters is that freedom of association will be exercised by some people to avoid others who are not of their preferred race, or ethnicity, or gender. Some liberals tend to weigh in favour of the freedom to practise (discriminatory) association (Rosenblum 1998, ch. 3), whereas others have little sympathy for the idea that freedom of association can justify discrimination that is otherwise illegal (Barry 2001: 165–76). Yet other liberals wish to balance, case by case, the importance of freedom of association against the government's interest in eliminating racial and sexual inequality, particularly in employment and access to wealth and positions of influence (Sunstein 1999: 85–94; Nussbaum 2000: 187–206). Just as individuals are more likely to win exemptions from otherwise applicable laws if their burdened practice has a religious basis, religious groups are usually treated more favourably by liberals than other associations, particularly if they can show that their discriminatory practices of exclusion go to the core of the faith, and, it seems, particularly if their discriminatory practices are sexist rather than racist in nature (Galston 2002: 112–13; Okin 2002: 212–14).

Notwithstanding unresolved tensions between freedom of association and equality, the upshot of the discussion so far is that encompassing associations cannot be exempt from numerous liberal requirements regarding education, the distribution of resources, and the physical and psychological treatment of their vulnerable members if they are to be properly classified as voluntary and thus defended on grounds of liberty and free association. One favoured strategy by defenders of illiberal associations who reject these liberalizing demands is to resist placing the question of accommodation within the framework of liberty and freedom of association. In particular, it is often claimed that membership in encompassing groups provides for some basic and important need, as opposed to a simple preference, and that that need cannot be satisfied if groups are forced to reform in ways that violate their central commitments. Avishai Margalit and Moshe Halbertal claim that each person has an overriding interest in preserving his 'personality identity', that is 'his way of life and the traits that are central identity components for him and the other members of his cultural group' (1994: 493–4). Claims about identity also pervade Galston's defence of illiberal groups: he claims that it is 'a matter of great importance for Jews to live in a society that permits them to live in accordance with their understanding of an identity that is given rather than chosen' (2002: 29). Well-known claims about identity and self-respect are also made by Margalit and Joseph Raz (1990) and Charles Taylor (1992).

I don't wish to dwell on the veracity of these claims, except to make three brief comments. First, everyone has an "identity" if that merely means traits that come from one's surrounding cultural structure and which are shared with others. Slaves have it, for example. That in itself tells us nothing about whether a given identity is valuable or as good as an alternative identity that might be acquired. Secondly, no plausible general claim about the importance of culture to any particular individual's identity and self-respect can be made without examining each individual's position and standing within the group (Okin 1998: 680). Precisely what is at stake in many critiques of multiculturalism is whether the self-respect of oppressed members of cultures is secured. Thirdly, the unjustified assumption of such arguments is that it is cultural, or ethnic, or religious association that provides the key to identity and self-esteem. But it has to be shown that these particular associations are more significant to each individual's identity and self-esteem than the myriad other associations she may belong to: the gay community, the philosophical community, the Democratic Party, and so on (Rosenblum 1998, ch. 9).

None of these comments deny that cultural, religious, and ethnic identity is extremely important to many people. It would be absurd to deny this. Nonetheless, the cultural, ethnic, or religious association into which many are born does cease to undergird their identity and self-esteem. It follows that legal exemptions and self-government measures that give leaders of groups illiberal power over their members can threaten as much as secure identity and self-esteem. In response to this, those who argue for accommodation based on identity and self-esteem are usually quick to emphasize that members who no longer identify with the group or feel any other kind of affinity with it must have a right of exit (Margalit and Halbertal 1994; Galston 2002). While the right of exit may go some way to answering the problems just raised, it also takes us directly back to specifying conditions needed to enable exit, which, in turn, will put serious strain on justifying the kind of self-government or legal exemptions that many illiberal groups have sought.

There is a further debate about whether voluntary cultural, ethnic, or religious associations are entitled to receive state funding. According to a resource approach to distributive justice, individuals should fund their activities out of their legitimate share of resources, and members' individual resources should fund groups. If individuals, singly or in groups, cannot fund their activities out of their fair share of resources, then they are required to revise their expensive preferences in light of what they can reasonably expect (Kymlicka 2002: 242). Part of the force of describing encompassing associations as fulfilling important identity needs is to challenge the claim that expensive "preferences" can always be so easily revised and that, therefore, one's legitimate expectations may sometimes exceed what might otherwise be regarded as one's general share of primary goods (Kymlicka 2002: 340; Cohen 1999).

Even setting aside contentious claims about identity and the difficulty of revision, prospects for special assistance to voluntary associations may not be as dim as this popular liberal view suggests. After all, not all liberal defenders of freedom reject state funding for various cultural pursuits: if such funding comes into conflict with the principle of neutrality, so much the worse for that principle (cf. Raz 1986). Moreover, a number of liberal neutralists argue that liberals can acknowledge the importance of protecting a cultural structure that provides complex and diverse opportunities for future generations without running afoul of neutrality: the purpose of state subsidy is to protect the cultural structure rather than particular cultural events (although of course the former is achieved via subsidies to many of the latter) (Dworkin 1985, ch. 11; Kymlicka 2002: 247–8). The interesting question is how we are to distinguish general support for a complex and diverse culture, on the one hand, from unjustly funding an expensive taste, on the other. By his examples (2002: 241–3), we can glean that Kymlicka believes funding otherwise unsustainable religious groups is funding an expensive taste whereas funding or providing tax exemptions for environmental activity or the preservation of historical artefacts is legitimate, culture-sustaining action. But what, precisely, is the principled distinction? Why can't the ultra-orthodox (who receive heavy state subsidy in Israel) claim state support for their endangered culture so as to ensure a complex and rich range of opportunities for future generations? There may be a principled distinction to make between these cases (although I doubt it); but neutralists have so far not made it. In an earlier defence of special assistance to certain ethnic groups, Kymlicka also tried to make much of a distinction between a cultural framework and specific activities within it (Kymlicka 1989*b*), with little success (Cohen 1999).

In any case, the claim that the anti-perfectionist state cannot justly fund voluntary associations like religious and cultural groups is hard to sustain in the light of real-world politics. Countries including Britain, the United States, and Australia offer substantial funding to artistic and cultural groups. Opera cannot be funded just out of patrons' resources, so it receives additional funding from the state. It seems only fair also to fund some of the festivals and activities central to the life of minority religious and cultural associations. Barry complains that funding minority cultural and religious activity diverts attention away from the more pressing worry of growing inequality of wealth (Barry 2001: 325–8). Little wonder that cultural and religious minorities believe they are treated unfairly if they are told to devote their energies exclusively to poverty matters while a tiny group of typically privileged white people are left free to enjoy their heavily state-sponsored opera (which Barry supports; 2001: 197). Barry argues that the justification for funding opera is that it is good. Quite apart from the questionable assumption that the reason for funding artistic projects is that they are "good" (for whom? at what?), it should strike anyone as too much of a coincidence that the art forms Barry considers excellent, and thus worthy of funding, are just those that are typically considered so by Western cultures (or, at least, some members of them).

While on grounds of fairness, and an openness to the possibility that excellence can be found in unfamiliar places, there may be good arguments for funding some minority cultural and religious activity, treating religious and cultural groups as voluntary associations is likely to win them relatively little accommodation in exerting power over their members: the reverse is more likely to be true. Encompassing groups that acquire the bulk of their members by birth will be required to honour all kinds of liberal demands regarding education, access to financial resources, and the physical and psychological treatment of their members in order to ensure that they are groups that people really can leave if they want to.

These conclusions are not tempered if such groups secure important identity and self-esteem needs for some of their members, as those who invoke the right of exit implicitly concede.

3.2 Non-Voluntary Associations

A number of high-profile liberal defenders of multicultural accommodation deny that exit is either a viable or desirable solution for disaffected members of certain kinds of ethnocultural groups. Appeal to the right of exit from these groups is flawed because it assumes that they should be treated as voluntary associations that members can join or at least abandon at will. Kymlicka argues that this is not true of groups that share a societal culture. A societal culture is a territorially concentrated culture centred on a shared language which pervades a range of institutions, from within which one can exercise one's freedom to make significant choices about one's life. On this view, it is misguided to treat ethnic, cultural, and religious groups as of a piece. Religious groups, for one, are not centred on a societal culture: roughly speaking, they offer one particular choice of association. In contrast, ethnocultural groups centred on a shared societal culture provide the framework from within which many choices, including choice of association, can be made. Many minority groups within the state provide their members with a societal culture—groups that Kymlicka dubs 'national minorities'. It is only groups that sustain societal cultures that he considers appropriate candidates for self-government rights (Kymlicka 1995, 2002).

I will focus on two problems with Kymlicka's attempted justification of self-government rights, both of which reveal the constraints faced by a specifically *liberal* defence of self-government rights for national minorities. The first problem is that very few groups will actually qualify for self-government rights given the liberal justification Kymlicka offers for those rights. The second problem is that the distinction between voluntary and non-voluntary associations that Kymlicka's argument relies on is difficult to sustain from a liberal perspective, with implications for the nature of self-government that Kymlicka defends. The combined upshot of these two problems is that while some national minorities plausibly qualify for special status or some protection, a liberal perspective gives us little reason to suppose that their special status distinguishes them all that much from voluntary associations in any case.

First, then, to the problem of how many groups qualify for self-government. Central to Kymlicka's justification of self-government is another crucial disanalogy between national minorities and encompassing religious groups (or voluntary associations in general): while the state can (and should) avoid interfering in the marketplace of voluntary associations, it does not, and cannot, avoid promoting one societal culture at the expense of others. The diffusion of a common language and common education is central to all modern nation-building activity. But whatever its merits, the promotion of a national societal culture can have devastating effects for the durability of minority cultures: one of the most important factors in determining whether a language survives, for example, is whether or not it is the language of government (Kymlicka 1995: 111).

Kymlicka (1995: 108–15; 2002: 343–52) suggests that it follows straightforwardly from this that the state should extend self-government privileges to minority national cultures as a way to rectify the disadvantages it imposes on them. The main problem with this apparently straightforward argument is that many liberals do *not* believe the state should exercise "benign neglect" towards language and culture, as perhaps it should with respect to voluntary associations, especially given that its favouritism need not violate neutrality of justification: it need not say that English is superior to an indigenous language, only that a shared language is essential for equal opportunity and the diffusion of a shared national identity from which we all benefit (cf. Barry 2001: 105–8). Such liberals need not, therefore, be at all embarrassed by state promotion of a particular societal culture and will suggest instead that the members of linguistic minorities integrate into the dominant societal culture.[5] While it is true enough that it is from within the framework of a societal culture that one makes choices, including choice of association, this in itself does not mean that one cannot change membership of societal cultures in much the same way as one can change membership of voluntary associations.

Kymlicka has more recently (2002: 343–8) claimed that it is unnecessary to show that people need access to their own societal culture, indeed, has suggested that the attempt to do so represents an earlier, defensive stage in the debate about self-government rights. Unfortunately, liberals cannot dispense with the question of whether or not people need access to their own societal culture as long as they remain divided over whether a shared societal culture is necessary and whether the expectation of integration is fair. While Kymlicka cannot avoid this debate, the evidence is on his side that people do cherish their own language highly, and resist and resent majority pressure to assimilate (1995: 84–90). Not only do many people tenaciously defend their ability to use their own language in public life, most efforts to integrate national minorities involuntarily have been nothing short of politically and socially disastrous.

The real problem for Kymlicka is that even conceding that people legitimately strive to retain their own societal culture in the presence of majority-imposed disadvantage does not justify self-government for as many groups as he supposes it does. He claims (2002: 346) that the societal culture that liberal nations can legitimately promote 'involves a common language and social institutions, rather than common religious beliefs, family customs, or personal lifestyles. Societal cultures within a

---

[5] Of course, liberals have nothing to say about what language people should use within the context of voluntary familial, ethnic, and cultural associations.

modern liberal democracy are inevitably pluralistic, containing Christians as well as Muslims, Jews, and atheists.' But if it is the burdens of the adoption and promotion of *language* that should be rectified, far fewer would-be self-governing groups than Kymlicka supposes will actually qualify. The Quebecois might, as for them the ability to use French in public life is at the heart of their self-government desires. On the other hand, it is hopelessly false to suppose that the main grievance of indigenous groups now is their inability to use their own language in public life. In Australia, for example, the hundreds of languages that existed before colonization have nearly all been destroyed, and many would-be self-governing indigenous communities primarily use English as their communal language. This is hardly to deny that state policies and laws have imposed particular burdens on indigenous communities: it's a ludicrous understatement to say so. But it is no longer primarily the diffusion of the English language that would-be self-governing indigenous communities wish to shield themselves from. It is the desire to protect their way of life, which is often centred on a fairly narrow religious or quasi-religious "lifestyle". Kymlicka also claims that one possible response to the disadvantages imposed by nation-building is withdrawal and isolation, for which he offers the Amish and the Hutterites as examples (2002: 348). But, again, it is plain silly to suggest that the Amish or Hutterites seek isolation because they wish to inure themselves from the diffusion of a common language. At the other end of the scale, Kymlicka's argument doesn't even explain the aspirations of the Scottish or the Irish, for whom language is no longer the motivating force behind their self-government aspirations (Barry 2001: 309–10).

The worry that very few groups will qualify for self-government rights arises from the liberal nature of Kymlicka's defence of those rights. Consider that a state might promote many things that would impact detrimentally on certain groups. It might promote Islamic religion and law for example, or secularism to the extent that the wearing of religious scarves and caps in workplaces and schools was prohibited. Such measures would certainly restrict the ability of various religious communities to live the life they wish. In these cases, the appropriate liberal response would not be to create a set of legal exemptions and self-government rights for burdened religious minorities: it would be for the state to stop promoting Islam and the repressive version of secularism. Unlike Islam or secularism, Kymlicka, like many other liberals, considers it legitimate for the liberal state to promote a shared societal culture as long as it is centred on shared language, and not religion and lifestyle. But if what is being promoted is largely just shared language, then the only disadvantage that requires rectification is damage to minority languages. It can be argued that "language" is being interpreted too narrowly here. Liberal states also celebrate particular historical events and use national symbols, some of which may be exclusionary in nature. It could be argued that the best rectification of exclusionary practices is simply to make them less exclusive: all Australian schoolchildren should learn about aboriginal cultures and their destruction and all Americans should celebrate the life of Martin Luther King. In any case, there is nothing amiss (or even unusual) about schooling and other state-funded services being tailored to some of the cultural and historical interests of a local population. In many cases this level of cultural tailoring can be achieved without the full raft of self-government rights that Kymlicka seems to have in mind.

The second problem for Kymlicka's defence of self-government rights—whether a convincing distinction between voluntary and non-voluntary groups can be made—is also intimately connected to liberal concerns. Kymlicka famously argues that it is precisely because self-governing groups are *not* like voluntary associations that they should be run in accordance with liberal principles. The claim, recall, is that members cannot abandon such groups at will: unlike voluntary associations, one cannot just leave if one no longer likes the rules. Moreover, once national minorities acquire a degree of self-government power, then they exercise political power and political power must be exercised liberally (Kymlicka 2002: 340–1; Barry 2001: 188–9). On these liberal premises, self-governing national minorities have even less latitude than voluntary associations to run themselves illiberally. The external protections that allow a national minority to protect itself from majority-imposed disadvantage are to ensure that members have ongoing access to the cultural framework that enables them to exercise choice: internal restrictions, which would enable the group to run itself illiberally by restricting the choice of its members, cannot be defended by these premises (Kymlicka 1995: 35–44; 2002: 340–3).

Numerous liberal critics have argued that it is not always possible to distinguish external protections from internal restrictions. Yael Tamir notes that land rights for indigenous collectives often mean that individuals have no private ownership of land, with substantial implications for their ability to make important choices (Tamir 1999: 163; Halley 1999: 102). More generally, Okin argues that a patriarchal societal culture can perpetuate the oppression of women and girls even while adhering to all formal liberal requirements to protect their civil and political rights (Okin 1999). She appears to suggest that patriarchal societal cultures should be denied any self-governing rights at all, even those that are clearly justified as external protections against majority-imposed disadvantage and that, in and of themselves, do not illiberally impact on individual members. The uglier undertones of this suggestion have been rightly criticized: minority cultures are threatened with extinction for their failures of gender equality, whereas the majority culture, despite all of its own failings in this regard, faces no such ultimatum (An-Na'im 1999: 61; Raz 1999: 96–7). A number of commentators have more plausibly argued that only self-government rights that are directly implicated in oppression should be withheld (Raz 1999: 97).

While critics have focused on the illiberal effects of apparently liberal self-government rights, I believe Kymlicka can equally be criticized for arguing that self-government power must be exercised strictly in accordance with liberal principles. The reason is simple: if a member of a national minority can exercise an effective right of exit, why should the liberal requirements be stricter for self-governing national minorities than for voluntary associations? Kymlicka's argument presupposes that life lived within one's original societal culture is too important to make its relinquishment either viable or desirable. He believes he needs that premiss to distinguish national minorities from voluntary associations and thus rebut the suggestion that national minorities can gradually integrate into the majority societal culture. But many indigenous people do not want to live life only within their native community: they want to move between their indigenous community and the broader society, accessing the benefits of both. Some indigenous people leave their communities altogether. Liberals would not defend laws designed to prevent them from doing so. But if a member of a national minority can exercise an effective right of exit, then she can just avoid the laws and rules she would otherwise be subject to, leaving us to question Kymlicka's (and Barry's) insistence that self-governing political power must be exercised strictly in accordance with liberal principles. Of course, if a member of the Pueblo can only access government-funded welfare, housing, and educational benefits through the Pueblo community, then she has no effective right of exit. If the traditional laws of the Pueblo are to be applied to her whether she accepts membership in the Pueblo or not, then membership in the Pueblo is substantially different from membership in the Amish, for example. My suggestion is that liberal philosophers would reject self-government rights that could be used to prevent members from moving into other parts of the country to enjoy their citizenship entitlements there, and nor would they wish to deny a person born into the Pueblo the later right to leave it. Many liberals would also want land and property rights to be devolved in a way that does not make it impossible for individuals to leave the community (Spinner-Halev 1999). While language issues can make exit difficult, few indigenous communities, and few Quebecois, want to be altogether denied some education in the dominant language. Most people find leaving their state terribly difficult, involving, as it does, leaving their family and friends, their work, and their language. Other individuals find leaving their state reasonably easy, even a relief. But there is one special attribute that makes states particularly difficult communities to leave: no liberal state prevents its members from leaving, but that imposes no obligation on any other state to take them in. This is not the case with members of smaller associations who, within liberal states, should have some ability to move about. This explains why the state is unequivocally required to organize itself in strict accordance with liberal principles yet smaller communities may be allowed a little more latitude.

The upshot is that there are no hard and fast distinctions to be made between voluntary and non-voluntary associations. Whether an association is voluntary or not is always a matter of the availability of exit, and the factors that affect whether exit is a viable option in any given case are enormously complex and multifarious. Reifying political power as marking the crucial distinction oversimplifies the force of that power when exercised by different types of polities. Indeed, Barry notes that Kymlicka is inconsistent in distinguishing self-governing national minorities from voluntary associations (Barry 2001: 163–5). Kymlicka not only claims that the Pueblo are required to guarantee freedom of religion for their members, he claims that the

Hutterites are required to do so as well. But, unlike the Pueblo, the Hutterites do not exercise political power and, like the Amish, they have never sought it. Kymlicka's demand that they allow their members choice of religion is like demanding the same of the Catholic Church. The reason he holds the Hutterites to liberal requirements can only be because he is impressed by the fact that it is hard for many members to leave a Hutterite community. But this concedes what I have just argued: that the boundary between voluntary and non-voluntary association cannot be demarcated by something as simple as whether or not a group exercises political power.

Nor can it be demarcated by any general claim about the importance of one kind of membership as opposed to another. Individuals may want to exercise an exit option from their societal culture, or at least the option to move back and forth between cultures, and given that those individuals are citizens of their countries they should be entitled to do so. The claim for self-government is not, after all, a claim for secession. There is no obvious reason why such groups should be required to reflect liberal principles more, or less, than a range of other encompassing associations. While dismissing the desirability of moving between societal cultures may be an effective strategy against the demand that national minorities integrate into the dominant culture, its illiberal implications need to be acknowledged. A member of Quebec may find it easier and a lot more desirable to move to Toronto than to abandon her Catholicism. No claims about identity and the importance of societal culture can ignore this common enough choice, and in a liberal state (of which Quebec is a part) no devolved self-governing political power should be able to prevent it. As with voluntary associations in general, any claim about the primary significance of one type of membership over another will always be vulnerable to the vagaries of individual preference and need. Liberals should be able to acknowledge the injustice of colonization and forced abandonment of one's societal culture without making implausible and potentially illiberal claims about its importance to each individual. If they can readily acknowledge the grave injustice of forced abandonment of one's religious community without denying that many individuals do willingly exit, they should be able to acknowledge the same of membership in a societal culture.

4. HISTORICAL JUSTICE AND COMMUNITARIANISM

Kymlicka is not alone among liberals in having more sympathy for the claims of indigenous people than for those of religious or other voluntary associations, despite the fact that his attempt to distinguish their claims from those of other

groups is somewhat overblown. Sympathy for their different historical circumstances, in particular colonization and the horrors that followed, appears decisive.
Kymlicka (1995: 116–20) explicitly denies that historical arguments can bear much
justificatory weight. Superficially at least, there appear to be good grounds for
liberal egalitarians to distance themselves from historic claims, both to avoid
Nozickian-type approaches to justice, and to avoid consent-based justifications for
political power, to both of which historical arguments may bear a resemblance. Yet
without reference to the significance of the historical status of national minorities,
Kymlicka's notion of societal culture cannot do the work he wants it to do. I have
already dwelt on the problem that fewer national minorities than he supposes,
including indigenous communities, will qualify according to his own argument.
There is also the reverse problem that some immigrant communities might do so:
after all, immigrant groups often share a language, a history, and various traditions.
Kymlicka argues (2001: 54) that it is not feasible for immigrant communities to
rebuild their original societal culture in their new country, and therefore integration is a better option for them. But issues of feasibility are quite normatively irrelevant. Even if immigrant communities could rebuild a functioning societal culture,
Kymlicka would deny them the self-governing privileges of colonized indigenous
people. In arguing that immigrants, unlike the colonized, *consented* to shift societal
cultures it is clear that historical principles are doing all the work (Kymlicka 1995:
95–6).[6] Liberals who have sympathy for the self-government claims of indigenous
people, and perhaps for cultures like Quebec, Ireland, and the like, need to confront, and defend, more explicitly the moral significance of historic injustice,
including the lack of consent to be governed. There has been a dearth of liberal
research in this area (although see Thompson 2002).

But it is the claims of communitarians that appear to be most decisively haunting
liberal sympathy for self-government protections. Although arguing that illiberal
national minorities are in breach of justice, Kymlicka notoriously claims that
liberal states should respond to them in much the same way they would to illiberal
sovereign states: except in cases of 'gross and systematic violation of human rights,
such as slavery or genocide or mass torture and expulsions' (Kymlicka 1995: 169),
dialogue and example should be favoured. But illiberal national minorities are not
like sovereign states. Their oppressed members are also citizens of the state and,
even worse, it may well be state-granted powers to such groups that facilitate
oppression. Both of these factors heavily implicate the state in the oppression of
members of illiberal self-governing communities. The state in no sense stands outside national minorities with whom it is historically, legally, and socially entwined.

---

6 Kymlicka also comes close to contradicting himself in making this argument. He claims to agree
with Rawls, who suggests that declining to exercise one's right to emigrate does not make political
authority voluntary (Kymlicka 1995: 86). Yet in the case of immigrants he appears to suggest
something almost contrary to that: that exercising the option to immigrate makes acceptance of the
dominant societal culture voluntary.

While some minorities regret the entanglement, as Jeremy Waldron says, 'here we all are' (Waldron 1995: 104). In any case, the type of intervention in foreign states that may be both feasible and justified may also be feasible and justified in the case of national minorities. We should generally avoid invading oppressive foreign states because it would be disastrous to life and health, among other things, to do so. So it would be in the case of a military invasion into a national minority: that's why no one has suggested it. But if it is acceptable to refuse to trade with an oppressive state, to deny it foreign aid and membership in international organizations, then similar strategies should be justifiable with respect to illiberal national minorities: a refusal to fund their illiberal schools, welfare organizations, and law courts, and disqualification from membership in national bodies, are examples. What deter-mines the matter is whether such strategies cause rioting, bloodshed, dissatisfac-tion, alienation and even greater internal oppression to an extent that the justice of adopting the strategies is outweighed by the harm they cause.

One version of the communitarian view that is especially popular in the multi-culturalism literature states that liberal principles concerning choice and equality are nothing more than another culturally specific view about the good life for com-munities, and it would be wrong to impose them on communities that do not share them. Indeed, imposing liberal values on illiberal communities is as bad as majority-imposed disadvantage with respect to language. Versions of this idea pervade not only self-consciously communitarian views (cf. Svensson 1979; van Dyke 1977) but many recent so-called liberal views of multiculturalism as well (Kukathas 1992; Galston 2002), just as though it were a new and startling discovery that the world is full of illiberal societies with unexpected implications for liberal principles. Despite Kymlicka's claims to the contrary, the communitarian view seems increasingly to affect his views as well. He has recently defended his liberal approach to multicul-turalism by arguing that its value is internal to liberalism itself: it helps liberals work out what they should say about multicultural accommodation given a consistent application of liberal principles. Far from suggesting that the value of his liberal arguments is that they help us to see what justice, in fact, requires, he asks, 'how can it be inappropriate for liberals to clear up their own thinking about minority rights? How can this be harmful to a dialogue with other groups? How can it be preferable for liberals to enter such a dialogue with vast misconceptions about the gulf between the liberal majority and ethnocultural minorities?' (Kymlicka 2001: 63). With liber-alism so explicitly reduced to a mere ethnoculturally relative (albeit majority) view of justice, communitarians appear to have achieved the decisive victory within the multiculturalism debate that evaded them earlier.

With respect to the power of groups over their members, liberalism should certainly not aspire to be neutral: liberalism cannot be all things to all people, and it is defined by its very non-neutral commitment to *some* notion of individual freedom. That commitment brings it directly into conflict with many illiberal groups and practices, and no amount of doctoring of liberal theory will eliminate the conflict.

There have been attempts to defend a liberal vision of political community without presupposing any controversial values, Rawls's being the most well developed (Rawls 1993). It is highly doubtful that Rawls's new formulation of his theory does achieve the desired independence from controversial liberal values: both the justi-fication of "political liberalism" and its concrete effects remain seriously unaccept-able to illiberal groups (cf. Gutmann 1995; Kymlicka 2002: 232–40). In a later article Kukathas attempts to defend a theory acceptable to all groups using the founda-tional value of toleration (Kukathas 1997). Apart from failing to sustain a coherent vision of political community, there can be no pretence that what is defended is any kind of liberal theory: not only is freedom accorded no value, the well-being of *individuals*—their freedom, basic welfare, and life—is explicitly accorded no sig-nificance either. Apparently without meaning to, Kukathas demonstrates as clearly as possible that a political theory hospitable to all groups has to give up on the importance of individuals. That can't possibly be a move a liberal can make.

In a liberal world where individuals can move in and out of ethnic, cultural, and religious communities if they wish, there will certainly be many losers. It is true enough that many people's identity and self-esteem is jeopardized if their commun-ities wither, something that will happen if large numbers of free members choose to leave. So too, many people's identity and self-esteem is severely jeopardized when their spouse leaves them, or when their disgruntled children refuse to associ-ate with them. Liberals don't need to deny that in cases like this there is obviously a clash of interests between those individuals wanting to exercise a choice of asso-ciation, and those who would wish to deny them this choice, but they do have to acknowledge that liberal principles side with the right to make choices about whom one associates with. Nor does liberalism need to deny that we each owe enormous debts to those from whom we have benefited: it only needs to point out, first, that there are ways to acknowledge one's debts without sacrificing the capacity to make important choices about one's life, and secondly, that our debts extend far beyond those we owe to local religious and ethnic communities (Levy 2000: 71; Waldron 1995). Within the debate about illiberal groups, communitarians have to argue that despite a person not choosing her membership in a group, despite it being one she feels no affinity with, despite its demands threatening her well-being, her values, and her sense of self, it is nonetheless acceptable for the group to exert over her power that can hinder her ability to leave. No wonder communitarians so often fail to explain what concrete political measures follow from their abstract claims about the self and community. It is testimony to the power if not the substance of com-munitarian rhetoric that it has inspired so much recent liberal backsliding. Time will tell how far liberals will allow their principles to be further eroded by ongoing communitarian claims within the multiculturalism debate.[7]

[7] I would like to thank Jakob Hohwy, Frank Jackson, Karen Jones, and Michael Smith for reading through an earlier draft.

References

An-Na'im, Abdullahi (1999). 'Promises We Should All Keep in Common Cause', in J. Cohen, M. Howard, and M. Nussbaum (eds.), *Is Multiculturalism Bad for Women?* Princeton: Princeton University Press.

Barry, Brian (2001). *Culture and Equality*. Cambridge: Polity Press.

Caney, Simon (2002). 'Equal Treatment, Exceptions and Cultural Diversity', in Paul Kelly (ed.), *Multiculturalism Reconsidered: Culture and Equality and its Critics*. Malden, Mass.: Polity Press.

Cohen, G.A. (1999). 'Expensive Tastes and Multiculturalism', in Rajeev Bhargava, Amiya Kumar Bagchi, and R. Sudarsham (eds.), *Multiculturalism, Liberalism and Democracy*. Oxford: Oxford University Press.

Dworkin, Ronald (1985). *A Matter of Principle*. Cambridge, Mass.: Harvard University Press.

Freeman, Samuel (2002). 'Liberalism and the Accommodation of Group Claims', in Paul Kelly (ed.), *Multiculturalism Reconsidered: Culture and Equality and its Critics*. Malden, Mass.: Polity Press.

Galston, William A. (1995). 'Two Concepts of Liberalism'. *Ethics*, 105: 516–34.

—— (2002). *Liberal Pluralism: The Implications of Value Pluralism for Political Theory and Practice*. Cambridge: Cambridge University Press.

Gutmann, Amy (1987). *Democratic Education*. Princeton: Princeton University Press.

—— (1995). 'Civic Education and Social Diversity'. *Ethics*, 105: 557–79.

—— (2000). 'Religion and State in the United States: A Defense of Two-Way Protection', in Nancy Rosenblum (ed.), *Obligations of Citizenship and the Demands of Faith: Religious Accommodation in Pluralist Democracies*. Princeton: Princeton University Press.

Halley, Janet E. (1999). 'Culture Constrains', in J. Cohen, M. Howard, and M. Nussbaum (eds.), *Is Multiculturalism Bad for Women?* Princeton: Princeton University Press.

Joppke, Christian, and Lukes, Steven (eds.) (1999). *Multicultural Questions*. Oxford: Oxford University Press.

Kelly, Paul (2002). 'Defending Some Dodos: Equality and/or Liberty?' in Paul Kelly (ed.), *Multiculturalism Reconsidered: Culture and Equality and its Critics*. Maiden, Mass.: Polity Press.

Kukathas, Chandran (1992). 'Are there Any Cultural Rights?' *Political Theory*, 20: 105–39.

—— (1997). 'Cultural Toleration', in I. Shapiro and W. Kymlicka (eds.), *Ethnicity and Group Rights*. New York: New York University Press.

Kymlicka, Will (1989a). 'Liberal Individualism and Liberal Neutrality'. *Ethics*, 99: 883–905.

—— (1989b). *Liberalism, Community, and Culture*. Oxford: Oxford University Press.

—— (1991). 'Rethinking the Family'. *Philosophy and Public Affairs*, 20: 77–97.

—— (1992). 'The Rights of Minority Cultures: Reply to Kukathas'. *Political Theory*, 20: 140–6.

—— (1995). *Multicultural Citizenship*. Oxford: Clarendon Press.

—— (1999). 'Liberal Complacencies', in J. Cohen, M. Howard, and M. Nussbaum (eds.), *Is Multiculturalism Bad for Women?* Princeton: Princeton University Press.

—— (2001). *Politics in the Vernacular: Nationalism, Multiculturalism and Citizenship*. Oxford: Oxford University Press.

—— (2002). *Contemporary Political Philosophy: An Introduction*, 2 edn. Oxford: Oxford University Press.

Levy, Jacob T. (1997). 'Classifying Cultural Rights', in I. Shapiro and W. Kymlicka (eds.), *Ethnicity and Group Rights*. New York: New York University Press.

—— (2000). *The Multiculturalism of Fear*. Oxford: Oxford University Press.

McConnell, Michael W. (2000). 'Believers as Equal Citizens', in N. Rosenblum (ed.), *Obligations of Citizenship and the Demands of Faith: Religious Accommodation in Pluralist Democracies*. Princeton: Princeton University Press.

Macedo, Stephen (2000). *Diversity and Distrust: Civic Education in a Multicultural Democracy*. Cambridge, Mass.: Harvard University Press.

Margalit, Avishai, and Halbertal, Moshe (1994). 'Liberalism and the Right to Culture'. *Social Research*, 64: 491–510.

—— and Raz, Joseph (1990). 'National Self Determination'. *Journal of Philosophy*, 87: 439–61.

Miller, David (2002). 'Liberalism, Equal Opportunities and Cultural Commitments', in Paul Kelly (ed.), *Multiculturalism Reconsidered: Culture and Equality and its Critics*. Malden, Mass.: Polity Press.

Nussbaum, Martha (2000). *Women and Human Development: The Capabilities Approach*. Cambridge: Cambridge University Press.

Okin, Susan Moller (1989). *Justice, Gender, and the Family*. New York: Basic Books.

—— (1998). 'Feminism and Multiculturalism: Some Tensions'. *Ethics*, 108: 661–84.

—— (1999). 'Is Multiculturalism Bad for Women?', in J. Cohen, M. Howard, and M. Nussbaum (eds.), *Is Multiculturalism Bad for Women?* Princeton: Princeton University Press.

—— (2002). '"Mistresses of their Own Destiny": Groups Rights, Gender, and Realistic Rights of Exit'. *Ethics*, 112: 205–30.

Parekh, Bhikhu (2000). *Rethinking Multiculturalism: Cultural Diversity and Political Theory*. Cambridge, Mass.: Harvard University Press.

Rawls, John (1971). *A Theory of Justice*. Oxford: Oxford University Press.

—— (1993). *Political Liberalism*. New York: Columbia University Press.

Raz, Joseph (1986). *The Morality of Freedom*. Oxford: Oxford University Press.

—— (1999). 'How Perfect Should One Be? And Who Is?', in J. Cohen, M. Howard, and M. Nussbaum (eds.), *Is Multiculturalism Bad for Women?* Princeton: Princeton University Press.

Rosenblum, Nancy (1998). *Membership and Morals: The Personal Uses of Pluralism in America*. Princeton: Princeton University Press.

—— (ed.) (2000). *Obligations of Citizenship and the Demands of Faith: Religious Accommodation in Pluralist Democracies*. Princeton: Princeton University Press.

Shachar, Ayelet (2000). 'On Citizenship and Multicultural Vulnerability'. *Political Theory*, 28: 64–89.

—— (2001). *Multicultural Jurisdictions: Cultural Differences and Women's Rights*. Cambridge: Cambridge University Press.

Shapiro, Ian, and Kymlicka, Will (eds.) (1997). *Ethnicity and Group Rights*. New York: New York University Press.

Spinner-Halev, Jeff (1999). 'Cultural Pluralism and Partial Citizenship', in Christian Joppke and Steven Lukes (eds.), *Multicultural Questions*. Oxford: Oxford University Press.

—— (2001). 'Feminism, Multiculturalism, Oppression, and the State'. *Ethics*, 112: 84–113.

Sunstein, Cass R. (1999). 'Should Sex Equality Law Apply to Religious Institutions?', in J. Cohen, M. Howard, and M. Nussbaum (eds.), *Is Multiculturalism Bad for Women?* Princeton: Princeton University Press.

Svensson, Frances (1979). 'Liberal Democracy and Group Rights: The Legacy of Individualism and its Impact on American Indian Tribes'. *Political Studies*, 27: 421–39.

Swaine, Lucas A. (2001). 'How Ought Liberal Democracies to Treat Theocratic Communities?' *Ethics*, 111: 302–43.

Tamir, Yael (1999). 'Against Collective Rights', in Christian Joppke and Steven Lukes (eds.), *Multicultural Questions*. Oxford: Oxford University Press.

Taylor, Charles (1992). 'The Politics of Recognition', in Amy Gutmann (ed.), *Multiculturalism and the 'Politics of Recognition'*. Princeton: Princeton University Press.

Thompson, Janna (2002). *Taking Responsibility for the Past: Reparation and Historical Injustice*. Cambridge: Polity Press.

van Dyke, Vernon (1977). 'The Individual, the State, and Ethnic Communities in Political Theory'. *World Politics*, 29: 343–69.

Waldron, Jeremy (1995). 'Minority Cultures and the Cosmopolitan Alternative', in Will Kymlicka (ed.), *The Rights of Minority Cultures*. Oxford: Oxford University Press.

CHAPTER 7

LAW

JEREMY WALDRON

1. THE IRRELEVANCE OF NATURAL LAW

Analytic legal philosophy addresses the nature of legal norms, their relation to moral and other reasons, and their interpretation and application by courts. Questions about the nature of law have long been dominated by the classic dispute between legal positivists and theorists of natural law. Positivists hold that whether a legal system exists in a given society, and if so what the answer is in that society to any particular legal question, are matters of fact about how power is exercised in that society. Natural lawyers believe that law is in the first instance a set of moral norms embodied in the way things are; they associate law with objective principles of justice and right, accessible to reason, which can be used as standards to judge the exercise of human power. So, according to natural law theory, we cannot say whether an edict enforced in a particular society has the status of *law* without considering whether it passes a certain threshold of objective right—*lex iniusta non est lex*—whereas according to legal positivism, the judgement that something is the law (of a particular jurisdiction) is a judgement of social fact which commits us to no such evaluation.

Today, with one or two exceptions,[1] legal philosophers are less interested in this large-scale issue than in some of the more technical questions that it generates. Some provisions of positive law seem to require us to make moral judgements about 'reasonableness' or 'appropriateness'. Can these be accommodated in a positivist theory?

---

[1] The best-known recent example of a mainstream natural law position is Finnis (1980).

Can questions about interpretation be settled without making value judgements? Even if some laws can be applied without evaluative judgement, are there not moral values implicit in our very ideal of the rule of law? Can these be entirely separated from our concept of law, so that the latter is subject to value-free analysis even if the former is not? Questions like these are stimulated by the work of theorists like Lon Fuller (1969) and Ronald Dworkin (1977, 1986; for his discussion of the 'natural law' label, see 1982: 165), who are sometimes labelled 'natural law' theorists simply because they criticize legal positivism (for Fuller's discussion of the 'natural law' label, see 1969: 96–106). But their jurisprudence does not convey the sort of strong commitment to transcendent natural law that one would find (say) in the work of Cicero or Aquinas. Instead they look more to values implicit in the way law is practised and the way courts do their work. Instead of obsessing about the natural law status of transcendent moral principles, they argue for a more sophisticated value-laden theory of what law *is*. Another way of putting this is to say that Fuller's and Dworkin's opposition to legal positivism does not really depend on moral realism (any more than the legal positivism of H. L. A. Hart depended on moral scepticism; see Hart 1994). No doubt, many modern opponents of positivism will defend moral realism if provoked; but it seems increasingly unnecessary for the issue to arise in modern analytical jurisprudence.[2]

2. THE NORMATIVITY OF CONVENTIONAL RULES

With the meta-ethics of natural law put aside, recent work has focused on a number of issues arising out of the leading statement of modern legal positivism, H. L. A. Hart's book *The Concept of Law*. According to Hart a legal system is a system of rules followed generally in a society, rules whose formation and application is governed by 'secondary' rules (rules about rules), practised among a powerful group that we may refer to as the officials of the society. Hart's two-layered account of legal rules—primary rules of conduct, and secondary rules identifying the primary rules, regulating their application, and constituting processes for legal change—has been enormously fruitful. Certainly it is an improvement on the older positivism of Jeremy Bentham and John Austin, which defined law as the command of a sovereign, with 'command' defined as the expression of a wish plus the threat of a sanction,

---

[2] Compare Dworkin (1996) with the more agnostic position in Dworkin (1986: 76–86). See also Waldron (1992: 158). But some natural law theorists do still insist that the issue of moral truth matters for law: see e.g. Moore (1982; 2003: 23).

and 'sovereign' defined as a powerful person or agency that the bulk of the members of a given society were in the habit of obeying (see Bentham 1970; Austin 1995). That older account exhibited a certain hard-headedness in its reliance on facts about power and obedience. But it left a whole lot of law unexplained, namely the law that actually constituted and regulated 'sovereigns' and other lawmakers. And it made the normativity of law mysterious: how can it be that people regard themselves as really bound, really obligated by law, if law is just a matter of commands and sanctions? The Bentham–Austin account had the advantage of enabling us to describe the (perhaps abominable) laws of other countries without committing ourselves to the norms that they embody. But it seems to misrepresent what Hart (1994: 56–7, 82–91) referred to as the 'internal aspect' of rules, i.e. their normativity for those who actually regard themselves as bound by them.

Now Hart claimed to have reconciled these two points of view, with what is known as the practice theory of rules. But it has proved difficult to state precisely and in a non-question-begging fashion what exactly the normativity of a practised rule consists in.

According to the practice conception, a rule exists when the behaviour of a group of people under certain circumstances converges and when they monitor their own and each other's behaviour in those circumstances in a way that can be captured in a normative proposition. Hart uses this conception to characterize both primary rules and secondary rules, and though he argues that in a mature legal system it is needed only for the characterization of the secondary rules, I am going to begin with a very simple example at the primary level.

It is a remarkable fact that cricket fans in England applaud not only the achievements of their own team, but also the achievements of the opposing team as well. They do this grudgingly, but they think it is something that for chivalric reasons they ought to do. Now, an American would never do this (at a baseball match), but the American can observe the English doing it. So what is the American to say about the normativity of the practice?[3] Should he say that the English have an obligation to applaud the opposition? I think he can report the English practice and the attitudes that inform it without saying anything like this. What he should say is that *the English* regard themselves and each other as obligated in this way. No doubt he needs a general sense of what it is like to regard oneself as obligated in order accurately to report this. But any claim the American makes about the English having an obligation to applaud will be a sort of *oratio obliqua*, which he may try and make explicit with various clumsy formulations like 'It is a rule *among them* to applaud the opposition'. This formulation is designed to indicate that he is not making *in his own voice* the normative statement that he thinks captures an accurate sense of their actions and attitudes. (And the English fans themselves may

---

[3] Let's assume he is watching this behaviour on television, so we are not distracted by the Americans' politely following local customs when they actually attend cricket games in England.

use this indirect formulation too, when they want to describe or reflect upon their normative commitment as opposed to acting on it or giving voice to it.)

Applauding the opposition is something the English fans do together, but one can imagine a solitary English gentleman doing it by himself (surrounded by an audience of uncouth teenagers who have abandoned the custom). But some practices make sense only on the assumption that others are participating. The English rule of driving on the left is like this. If most were to adopt the American practice of driving on the right, it would be irrational, even suicidal, for our English gentleman to persist with the old custom. The rule of driving on the left (or on the right) makes sense only as a convention solving a coordination problem; it has no independent merit.

Secondary rules may be like conventions in that sense. Since they are rules about the identification, enforcement, and amendment of rules which are to operate in a social context, they cannot be successfully practised unless a large body of people practise them together. Once again, we may use a simple example, though this time a fictional one.

An observer notices that the people of Freedonia assemble in the marketplace to make important social decisions and that they chide each other (and themselves) when they fail to turn up to the assembly. We can imagine an observer noting facts like this to build up his understanding of the secondary rules that constitute the Freedonian legal system. (As before, *he* would not chide a Freedonian who failed to attend the assembly; he detaches himself from the attitudes he is characterizing. And sometimes the Freedonians may also talk about their obligation in this detached fashion, for reflective or educational purposes.) Now, in reporting their attitudes, one of the things our observer notices is that the individual Freedonians themselves predicate their commitment to assembling regularly in the marketplace on the willingness of lots of other Freedonians to do so too. A Freedonian citizen would not think it worth turning up, nor would he chide himself for failing to turn up, if others didn't share his sense of obligation. This means that the behaviour of other Freedonians will figure among the reasons each Freedonian has for acting and for monitoring self and others in this way. Once again, this is something that our observer can notice and record without himself being committed to the collective enterprise; *the observer's* obligations are not conditioned by the behaviour of the other Freedonians in the way the individual Freedonians take their own obligations to be. Though it is true that, for the Freedonians, something normative is grounded on facts about what people generally think and do, there is still no move from 'is' to 'ought' that would require the observer also to acknowledge the existence of an obligation in anything other than an *oratio obliqua* sense. The reasons some Freedonians have for participating in assemblies are contingent on a sufficiently large number of others acting on these reasons as well. But the observer may have no reason for participating himself and no reason for saying (in his own voice) that the Freedonians should participate when others are ready to participate.

To understand the structure of what the Freedonians regard as their obligations, we have to view their practice of turning up in the marketplace as a convention that enables them to coordinate in an activity which they all have reason to regard as important. But it need not be *pure* coordination, like the rule of the road. The structure of the situation may be one of partial conflict. Though many Freedonians think it appropriate that collective decisions be made by regular assemblies in the marketplace, others may disagree and favour the election of representatives for this purpose. Still, even those who oppose the market assembly idea may think it better that all Freedonians settle on one mode of social decision-making even if it is not, according to them, the ideal mode. (And again, this is something our observer can note in their attitudes, without necessarily endorsing it himself.)

An account of the relation between conventions and disagreement along these lines helps deal with a criticism that Ronald Dworkin has made against Hart's theory. Dworkin cautions jurists against overuse of the idea of conventions in explicating the secondary rules which define a legal system. He argues that a constitutional practice—such as that the courts should defer to Parliament (in Westminster-style systems) or that a document drafted in 1787 should continue to be the leading point of reference for the American political system—is more like a consensus of independent political convictions (about democracy, for example, or about liberty) than like a convention such as the rule of the road (Dworkin 1986: 135–9). Part of what is going on here is that Dworkin wants to leave room for the possibility of substantive disagreement about the sources of law in an otherwise flourishing legal system. Someone in England who thinks courts should not always defer to Parliament ought not to be seen as an eccentric outlier in relation to an otherwise secure convention, like an Englishman driving on the left in America. On the contrary, Dworkin (1986: 37–43) believes that disagreements about what law is are part of a flourishing practice of debating how a society ought to be governed, and no account of how a legal system works will be adequate if it ignores or sidelines this essentially argumentative dimension. But my point about partial conflict coordination shows that the conventional practices which define the secondary rules of a legal system need not be conceived on the model of rule-of-the-road conventions. The convention among the Freedonians (and perhaps among the English about the relation between Parliament and the courts) is more like a settlement between people who have rival views about how best to spend the evening but most want to spend it together (these are sometimes referred to as 'battle-of-the-sexes' problems; see Luce and Raiffa 1957: 91. For the relevance of partial conflict coordination games to jurisprudence, see Waldron 1999: 103–4).

I suspect, too, that Dworkin exaggerates the determinacy of the conventions that are necessary for the positivist's conventionalist account to work. Absolute conformity of behaviour is not required: as Jules Coleman has argued (2001: 79 ff.), the convergence of behaviour associated with a given practice helps us identify the convention but it is not identical with it. What is important is that the behaviour and attitudes of most of the participants be such as to enable them to coordinate with others in a certain way—where the 'certain way' admits of tighter or looser specifications with room for substantial disagreement (2001: 96 ff., citing Bratman 1992: 327).

We may return to the Freedonian example to illustrate this point. Those who would ideally favour the election of representatives share with the more directly democratic Freedonians a commitment to participate in citizen assemblies because they all believe that a shared form of social decision-making is preferable to none at all. But the first group may hold this last belief only because they reckon it is possible for a citizen assembly to be governed by tight rules of procedure which make efficient decision-making possible. Now, those Freedonians who favoured citizen assemblies all along may or may not regard this issue of procedural efficiency as important: open-ended participation may be all that counts for them. But for better or worse, the former group and the latter group are committed to acting together in a way that will make the assembly system work. Room for disagreement arises because the structure of reasons that the one group has for upholding this commitment differs slightly from the structure of reasons that the other group has. So although the convention that defines the assembly is shared among *all* the participants, that sense of sharing also defines a site for argument, stemming out of political disagreement, as each participant in the convention uses the convention as a platform for trying to persuade the others to see the practice in a particular light.

3. INCORPORATIONISM AND THE SOURCES THESIS

Positivism is commonly associated with a view about the separability of legal judgment and moral judgement. Since, as Hart puts it (1994: 185–6), 'it is in no sense a necessary truth that laws reproduce or satisfy certain demands of morality', it ought to be possible, on the positivist account, to determine what the law of a given jurisdiction is on any given topic without making a moral judgement about that topic. Thus we can say that a law of a state provides capital punishment for murder or that it enforces contracts extracted by economic duress even while we condemn these outcomes or even while we are uncertain about how to respond to them morally. This distinction between moral judgement and legal judgment—the Separability Thesis—has been crucial to the self-image of positivism, and indeed it is partly definitive of the issue between positivism and natural law that I mentioned at the beginning of this chapter.

In modern jurisprudence, the Separability Thesis is often associated with another claim, which positivists call the Sources Thesis (Raz 1979: 37). The Sources

Thesis holds that systems of positive law depend for their operation on secondary rules of recognition which identify norms as law on the basis of institutional events associated with their enactment or on the basis of other aspects of their institutional pedigree (such as the holding of a court in a particular case). Source-based recognition is a practice which is likely to be particularly important for a pluralistic society—i.e. for a society where there is disagreement about what is morally right or just. In such a society, norms cannot be identified on the basis of shared moral criteria. Since moral judgement is a perpetual occasion of disagreement, there is no way to identify law except by reference to the sources specified in a secondary rule which associates the recognition of norms as law with their emergence from a certain institutional procedure (such as enactment in the Freedonian marketplace).

Plausible as this strong statement of the motivation behind legal positivism may be, it runs into the following difficulty. A lot of what we confidently identify as law seems to invite or even require exactly the sort of moral judgement that the positivist conception is supposed to exclude. This is true (by definition) of what jurists call standards, as opposed to rules—i.e. norms like 'Vehicles may not be driven at an unreasonable speed'. (Standards embody value predicates like 'reasonable', 'appropriate', or 'unconscionable' in their formulations, whereas rules use descriptive or even operationalized predicates like '... faster than 55 miles per hour'.) To find out what a standard requires of him, the citizen must make his *own* judgement about reasonableness (or whatever), which seems likely to lead to confusion and indeterminacy in a society that comprises people with differing senses of what is reasonable or people inclined to take different factors into account in making these determinations.

Now, the positivist may reply that we still use source-based criteria to recognize the norm; it is our source-based criteria, for example, that tell us that the legislature has laid down a standard for these cases, not a rule. But that is no comfort, for two reasons.

First, the characteristic we have noticed may be true not just of particular enacted provisions, but of the secondary rule—or perhaps we now should say 'the secondary *standard*'—of recognition itself. This is most evident in countries with a strong constitutional tradition, like the United States (see Waluchow 1994: 142–65). The US Constitution lays down a number of substantive norms that something must satisfy if it is to be recognized as valid legislation.[4] Some of these are rules but many of them are standards (e.g. '*Excessive* bail shall not be required, nor *excessive* fines imposed, nor *cruel* and unusual punishments inflicted'). Here the very criteria for identifying law are moral.[5] The conventions in which we (or our officials)

---

[4] For the distinction between constitutional provisions which are part of the criteria for the legal validity of legislation and constitutional criteria intended to work in a more regulative way, see Adler and Dorf (2003: 1105).

[5] Constitution of the United States, Eighth Amendment (my italics).

are supposed to be participating, which on Hart's account form the basis of secondary rules like the rule of recognition, cannot themselves be specified except in terms of the participants' agreeing to answer certain moral questions whenever an issue of recognizing something as law arises.

Secondly, a case can be made that the need for moral judgement is in fact pervasive in modern legal systems, and that it does not crop up only on the occasions when the legislature happens to have enacted a standard or where the constitution makes the validity of law turn on some moral issue. In following precedent, there is always a judgement that one case is 'relevantly like' another in some given respect, and that judgement of relevance may well involve moral considerations. The same is true, arguably, even for enacted rules: lawyers often argue that a literal interpretation of a statute should be rejected when it is absurd, and it would be idle to pretend that a judgement of absurdity does not involve the exercise of moral judgement. They say too that when two or more interpretations are possible, the one that has legal authority is the one that is the more reasonable or would appeal more to a reasonable legislator.[6] If this is true of legal reasoning generally, then it is impossible to say what the law is in a way that respects the distinction between source-based and moral considerations which is crucial for the positivist's Separation Thesis. Relevance, absurdity, and reasonableness do not refer to sources of law in the positivist sense: instead they require the judge to make controversial determinations of justice, value, right, and policy in his own voice.

Some of the most interesting recent debates in analytic jurisprudence are those that confront this difficulty. The hardline positivist response is called 'exclusive positivism', because it purports to exclude the possibility that law, as such, contains this moral element. It does so with several lines of argument. The first invites us to consider the possibility that the moral element in legislative and constitutional standards is not to be taken at face value: constitutional originalists, for example, sometimes say that 'cruel' in the Eighth Amendment means the same as 'what we [the Framers of the Eighth Amendment] think is cruel', thus inviting an historical not a moral judgement (by us, as we interpret the Amendment) (see e.g. Bork 1986: 823). As for the points about interpretation mentioned in the previous paragraph, it is sometimes said that if the text of a provision can be read as a rule it should be applied as such, and that the courts should not be in the business of making judgments about absurdity etc. (Occasionally, these two lines of argument diverge: textualists characteristically oppose appeals to original intent which seek to vary the interpretation of a provision when its text is clear.[7]) Whether this can be done for

---

[6] This is discussed further in Sect. 5 below.

[7] Cf. the condemnation of the decision in *Church of the Holy Trinity* v. *United States*, 143 U.S. 457 (1892) by Scalia (1997: 18–22). In *Holy Trinity*, the Supreme Court appealed to the intentions of the legislature to establish that the literal meaning of a text which prohibited encouraging aliens to come to the United States under a contract of employment should not apply to a church's paying the passage of an Englishman to be its minister.

interpretation generally is of course another question. Some would say there is inevitably an element of moral judgement even in applying descriptive or historical predicates (see Endicott 2001: 377).

Or the exclusive positivist can offer a different account, taking his cue from what courts do when they are faced with what appear to be standards. If the legislature says that vehicles must be driven at a reasonable speed, a court may hold in a particular case that driving faster than 50 mph is always unreasonable when it is snowing, and that will operate thereafter as a rule in a way that does not require subsequent judges to make moral judgements about this issue. Or if the Constitution forbids cruel punishment, the Supreme Court may rule that capital punishment is not per se cruel, in a way that removes the matter from moral judgement by subsequent judges. Taking his cue from this, the exclusive positivist may say that, in enacting a standard, the legislature or the framers of the constitution did not make a complete law; they made part of a law or an inchoate law and they left it up to the courts to complete it. Once the courts have finished the process of law-making, then we can identify the complete law by source-based criteria in the usual way, and the complete law we identify will be something to which authority can be attributed and which can operate in a context of moral disagreement in just the way that positivists have usually wanted.

But this line of argument, too, is open to criticism. To say that the Eighth Amendment or the statute saying that we should drive at a reasonable speed is not law as enacted is a highly counter-intuitive conclusion. Most of us would say that the court's decision converts one sort of law into another, not that it converts something non-legal into something legal. The proposition that judges when faced with standards should try to turn them into rules or that they should always announce and respond to precedents as though they were rules may or may not be a good idea (see Scalia 1989: 1175). But it is hardly an analytic point about law or the meaning of the norms in question.

On the other side there are those who believe there is no inconsistency between the core tenets of legal positivism and the existence of moral criteria for legality in general or for legal determinations in particular cases. Jules Coleman (1988: 3) once defined a weak form of the positivist thesis which denied nothing more than that there were necessarily moral criteria of legality: to sustain this position it would be enough that just one legal system could be imagined which would not require the use of moral criteria. Now, even this thesis may be hard enough to sustain in the light of the points about interpretation made earlier. But a more serious difficulty is the following. Inclusive positivists acknowledge that most actually existing legal systems do have moral criteria of legal validity, either in their constitutions or in the accepted practices of courts in interpreting laws and reaching particular legal conclusions. So now the burden is on them to explain how it is that the positivist orientation in jurisprudence continues to offer an illuminating characterization of such legal systems at a general level (for the suggestion that inclusive positivists now characterize legal positivism in a Ptolemaic way, with epicycles that move it far away from its original inspiration, see Dworkin 2002: 1165). The virtue of exclusive positivism, after all, is that it hooks up with some theory of what is necessary for law to operate in a modern society. We need legal judgment to be clearly separated from moral judgement under circumstances of moral dissensus (Waldron 1999: 39), or we need legal judgment to be clearly separated from moral judgement if law is to be in a position to claim authority (see Raz 1994). If law does not supersede first-order moral reasoning among those whose conduct it purports to govern, then it is difficult to see what function it can possibly serve. Exclusive legal positivism may offer a poor description of the laws and practices we actually have, but at least it is a motivated description. What is driving inclusive positivism? Why is it thought important to characterize what appears to be heavily moralized law in a positivist way?

Some inclusive positivists respond to this by saying that their legal theory is purely descriptive or conceptual: nothing is implied about the value or legitimacy of whatever answers to the concept of law as the (inclusive) positivist explicates it (Coleman 2001, ch. 12). But, whether they want to take that tack or not, they may also emphasize that it is substantively important to be able to characterize even moralized law in a positivist way, for the following reason. Provisions of the kind we are considering do not license all-purpose moral judgement in any or every legal context. In the case of enacted standards, whether they occur in legislation or in written constitutions, there is a positive-law specification of the kind of moral judgement that is to be made—and where exactly it is to be made—in the process of legal reasoning. Thus the Eighth Amendment does not license all-purpose review of the criminal justice system on moral grounds: it indicates that we are to make judgements about the character of the punishments that are imposed (as opposed, say, to judgements about what is defined as an offence) and that the judgements we are to make about the character of the punishments are to be judgements about their cruelty, not general judgements about their fairness or appropriateness. For all this, we have to refer to law as emanating from authoritative sources, for we know that the framing and specifying of particular contexts for moral judgement may differ from legal system to legal system.

Moreover, a positivist account points us in the right direction for understanding why there might be a moral element in a legal system's rule of recognition. I said, in Section 3, that a convention could be loose and contested and yet still operate as a solution to a partial conflict coordination problem. (If there had been insistence at the outset that the convention had to be watertight, the problem might not have been solved at all.) Similarly, we can imagine circumstances in which a partial conflict coordination problem might not be solved unless the convention incorporated a moral element. We might imagine that, for a particular population, a convention for recognizing and applying punitive norms would not be acceptable to some or all of those among whom it would have to be practised unless the convention had the effect of occasioning and facilitating a debate about cruelty. That is, some citizens might say to themselves: 'I will not accept a system of penal laws unless there is a guaranteed opportunity to debate whether particular punishments should be ruled out on account of their cruelty.' And they might add: 'I know there will be disagreement among us in our moral judgements about what is cruel. Still I would rather facilitate such a debate than participate in a penal system that afforded no such opportunity for airing our disagreements about cruelty.' And so they would make this a condition of their participation in any convention for recognizing rules of the relevant kind. Now, the emergence of a convention with this character, indeterminate though its outcomes might be, differs from a system whose rule of recognition involves no provision for substantive assessment of penal law at all and it differs from a system whose rule of recognition incorporates a more determinate convention (such as 'No capital punishment'). For general jurisprudence, then, the importance of the Sources Thesis survives the incorporation of moralistic law: we cannot tell what a particular legal system is like in this regard except by looking, in a positivist way, at the sources and conventions which define its fundamental criteria of validity.

4. Descriptive and Normative Jurisprudence

In the argument just given, I suggested that important social functions may be served by positive law's framing and facilitating certain moral debates. My aim was to expand our sense of the functions that positive law as such may perform, in order to rebut the view that the functionality of a legal provision depends on its offering guidance that supersedes first-order moral reasoning by those to whom the law is addressed.

This brings us to a general issue which has dominated modern legal philosophy. What is the appropriate methodology for general jurisprudence? When we try to answer to the question 'What is law?', should we think of ourselves as attempting to account for the value of certain institutions and practices, or should we confine ourselves to simply identifying the relevant institutions and practices, describing them in a general way that illuminates their main features but leaves it as a task for someone else (political philosophers, perhaps) to argue about the merits and demerits of this thing that we have described?

In the history of jurisprudence some of the best work has taken the former road. This is clearest in the case of natural law theories, which explicate the concept *law* rather as one would explicate concepts like *university* or *hospital*—in terms of their characteristic aspiration to promote certain values (justice, in the case of law; health and relief of suffering in the case of hospitals; education and the pursuit of knowledge in the case of universities) (the *loci classici* are Augustine 1950: 112–13 and Aquinas 1959: 59–65; see also Waldron 2001*a*: 759).

It is striking how much positivist jurisprudence has had this character as well. Thomas Hobbes and Jeremy Bentham certainly developed their legal theory in this spirit (see Hobbes 1996, ch. 26; Bentham 1970, chs. 1 and 14; 1931: 109–11). Their account of the nature of law was shaped and informed by their normative interest in the conditions necessary for peace and the general stability of expectations in people's dealings with one another. Their thesis was that this separability of legal judgment and moral judgement is a good thing, perhaps even indispensable (from a moral, social, or political point of view), and certainly something to be valued and encouraged. Many modern positivists, following the example of these writers, have therefore argued that positivism is best understood as itself a normative position (see Postema 1986: 328 ff.; MacCormick 1985: 1; Campbell 1996; Perry 1997: 129; Waldron 2001*b*: 411).

There is, of course, an air of paradox in attributing to legal positivism a view about the moral value of law, and no doubt a careful distinction of levels is necessary to prevent the values associated with such a positivist conception from leaking into the (amoral) process of identifying particular laws which that conception is supposed to privilege. And if we maintain such a distinction of levels, it might be argued that we can—once again—distinguish the conceptual or analytic claim about law made by legal positivism as such from the 'programmatic or normative interests certain positivists, especially Bentham, might have had' (Coleman 1988: 11). In other words, normative positivism seems to be a normative thesis *about* legal positivism: it still requires the analytic legal philosopher to do his work first, to establish the conceptual possibility of that which the normative theorist represents as desirable. Anyway, the accounts offered by normative positivists are implausible as general theories of law, the conceptual theorist will say. For even if modern positive law configures itself as it does for the sort of reasons Hobbes or Bentham thought important, it could nevertheless depart from these aims and, if it did, *it would still have to be regarded as law*. And in that case the task of explaining why it was bad law would fall to the political philosopher in the division of intellectual labour.

Those legal philosophers (positivist or not) who favour a normative jurisprudence sometimes accuse their opponents of offering nothing more than implausible semantic analysis of the word 'law', as though the only alternative to the normative enterprise were a linguistic one (see Dworkin's discussion of what he calls 'the semantic sting' in 1986, ch. 1). This accusation has been pretty well rebutted (see Coleman 2001: 179 ff.). But the issue between those who favour and those who oppose a normative method in jurisprudence remains open. I suspect it depends partly on what one thinks about the possibility of value-neutral conceptual analysis generally in the social sciences (see Waldron 2002: 378–80). H. L. A. Hart wrote at the beginning of *The Concept of Law* that he saw his enterprise as one of 'descriptive sociology', and he confirmed this in his posthumously published Postscript, where he wrote that his jurisprudence seeks a 'clarification' of what he calls 'the salient features of a modern municipal legal system' which may be attributed 'to any educated man' (Hart 1994, pp. v, 3, 240). The question is whether we can distinguish salient from non-salient features, or figure out what should count as a clarification, or attribute a distinctive shape to a set of social phenomena (the shape of the legal), without being guided by some sense of why the distinction between legal phenomena and other social phenomena matters (for a powerful argument to the effect that we cannot clarify law without some sense of why law is important, see Finnis 1980, ch. 1).

This can be developed generally as a point about fact–value separation (see e.g. McDowell 1981: 144), or it can be developed specifically with reference to legal phenomena. One way of pursuing the latter option is to consider the relation between the concept of law (and conceptual jurisprudence) and the political ideal of the Rule of Law. The impulse that has led some positivists to deny that their jurisprudence has a normative tendency has led them also to question whether it is a defining feature of a legal system that it serves the values associated with the Rule of Law. Joseph Raz (1983: 210), one of our leading theorists of the Rule of Law, indicates that he thinks the connection between the two is entirely contingent. Indeed he believes that the Rule of Law ideal is intended to correct many dangers of abuse that arise from law as such, which implies once again that law as such should not be defined by reference to that (or any) ideal. I think he is wrong about this. The Rule of Law ideal is intended to correct many dangers of abuse that arise from modern forms of governance, but to do so not by directly challenging the abuses (as oppressive or unfair etc.), but by insisting on a particular mode of governance which it is thought is more apt to protect us against abuse than (say) managerial governance or rule by decree. Now it is true that 'law' is not just a label we affix to whatever mode of governance turns out to have this salutary effect. The mode of governance we are interested in has developed to a certain extent under its own momentum and with its own self-understanding, and the emergence of the concept *law* is in part a matter of our fascination with such development. But only in part: the fascination with this mode of governance has also always involved some sense of the distinctive contribution and the importance of the contribution that it can make to social and political life. If we leave this latter element out of the picture, we will have an incomplete grasp of what law can offer but also of the concept of law and why it is shaped as it is.

5. INTERPRETATION

Besides the question 'What is law?', general jurisprudence directs us to some narrower issues about the interpretation of legal materials and the proper role of a judge. Law is a practical discipline. It exists in order to be applied to particular cases, and it is the judge who determines its formal application and who in that sense brings the law to life. I don't mean by this to associate myself with Bishop Hoadley's maxim 'whoever hath an absolute authority to interpret any written or spoken laws, it is He who is truly the Law Giver' (Benjamin Hoadley, Sermon Preached before the King, 1717, cited by Gray 1921: 102). We do not have to see judges as legislators to apprehend the role that they play in the legal system; and the nature of courts is such that the appropriate way for the judge to behave directly determines the appropriate way for counsel to argue, and so it also affects our general understanding of the specific nature of legal reasoning.

Interpretation can be approached from two directions. On one approach, interpretation refers to the way courts are supposed to deal with abstract, vague, ambiguous, or otherwise indeterminate legal provisions. We begin with a problem of meaning or application—the terms of some legal requirement are unclear (relative to the case in front of us or to a class of cases of which the case in front of us is an instance)—and 'interpretation' refers to a strategy for settling this difficulty, while in some sense keeping faith with the text of the requirement.[8] On the other approach, interpretation refers to the way in which the values, opinions, or inclinations of one legal agency (a judge, for example) are supposed to be related to the determinations of another legal agency (the legislature or perhaps the framers of the constitution). A judge is inclined to decide a particular case or class of cases in a certain way, and there is a question about the relation between this way of deciding the case and the way of deciding the case (or cases of this kind) set out in some legal provision that is supposed to be binding upon him. This second approach thinks of interpretation *politically*—in terms of authority and legitimacy—rather than linguistically.

Obviously the two approaches are connected. We may say that the less determinate the legal provision is, the greater the scope for the judge to pursue his own values, opinions, and inclinations in the matter before him while not appearing to depart from the provision that binds him. In other cases, though, the two approaches come apart. If the meaning of a provision is indeterminate, a judge may have no choice but to engage in 'interpretation', even though he has no particular wish to do this and no particular agenda of his own to follow. (What he most wants to do is apply the law.) Conversely, if a judge does have a substantive agenda of his own to follow—what he most wants to do is to do justice according to his own lights, or to promote the public good as he sees it—then he may strive to make it appear as though there is a problem with the meaning of the provision that is supposed to be binding upon him, even though this is not something that would

---

[8] We could just set the text aside when we found it to be indeterminate, and decide the case the best way we can, without it; I am assuming that that sort of pragmatic approach does not count as 'interpretation'.

strike anyone confronting the provision without such an agenda.[9] Admittedly there will come a point where the judge's pursuit of his own agenda departs so far from the text of the relevant provision as to make it implausible to describe what he is doing as interpretation. But opinions will differ as to where that point is, and the difference will be determined largely by competing theories of what the authority of the relevant provision is based on, competing accounts of what it is to be bound by such authority, and competing views of the rights and expectations that are founded upon it.

The first approach begins from the acknowledged indeterminacy of the language used in the law. Though legal texts may use terms of art, mostly the textuality of law draws on the resources of natural language and cannot expect to be any more determinate than those resources. Where natural language terms are vague, the binary demands of the legal enterprise—either defendant is guilty or not guilty, liable or not liable—are likely to give rise to problems in borderline cases (see Waldron 1994: 509). Where the meaning of a natural language term is best understood in a family resemblance way, puzzle cases may be differently disposed of depending on which paradigm set of resemblances one begins with. And where the meaning of a given term is associated, as Wittgenstein would say, with a form of life—where it is said of 'pornography', for example, that 'I know it when I see it' (Justice Potter Stewart in *Jacobellis* v. *Ohio*, 878 U.S. 184, 1964), or when it is said of sexual harassment that one either 'gets it' (i.e. understands the point of the concept) or one doesn't—in these cases legal problems will arise as we reach the edges of a given form of life or when we deal (as law has no choice but to deal) with the misunderstandings that arise when different forms of life come into contact with one another (see the discussion in Radin 1989 exploring the significance for law of the arguments about rule-following in Wittgenstein 1958; but see also Zapf and Moglen 1996: 485). These vicissitudes are reasonably well understood, and a number of theorists have argued that since they arise mainly around the margins of natural language use, and since natural languages seem to operate perfectly well for most ordinary purposes, it is not unreasonable to think that indeterminacy and the scope for interpretative controversy are quite limited (see Greenawalt 1992).

However, the second approach reminds us that the problem is not just linguistic and it is not enough to respond to charges of indeterminacy to point to the core of agreed meaning for most natural language terms (cf. Hart 1994 on the 'core' and 'penumbra' of the meaning of natural language terms). Litigants confront texts when they are already embroiled in disputes and looking to make legal provisions that apply to them disputable, if necessary disputable in a way that might seem counter-intuitive if the text were considered on its own. Or we can put the point less tendentiously: interpreting a legal provision is not just an exercise in construing the

---

[9] The case mentioned in n. 7 above—*Church of the Holy Trinity* v. *United States*, 143 U.S. 457 (1892)—provides a good example.

words; it involves relating them and their meaning to some sense of a purpose that might be served by making this particular form of words normative (cf. Fuller 1959: 666: 'the judicial process is something more than a cataloguing procedure').

Perhaps the most mundane source of interpretative controversy is when a legal provision prohibits actions that are A, and some particular action, x, strikes someone (a prosecutor or a litigant) as being so *like* things that are A that it is not inappropriate to raise the issue of whether it should be dealt with by the law in the very way that the law explicitly proposes to deal with things that are A, even though some would say that x really doesn't have feature A. The issue becomes one of interpretation when this is put forward for a whole class of cases (call them things that are B), or for x as a member of such a class, and put forward not as a proposal for legislative amendment—let's enact a prohibition on B to stand alongside the existing prohibition on A—but as an appropriate way of disposing of x in light of the prohibition on A. We may think, for example, that a prohibition on things that are A (excluding things like x) is seriously under-inclusive with regard to its purpose. It would be a better prohibition—there would be less of a 'gap' between the rule and its purpose—if it were enriched in the way that is proposed.[10] Of course it matters how exactly the purpose is specified. A ban on factory pollution and a ban on snowmobiles might both conserve the environment: but this would hardly be a basis for arguing that a ban on snowmobiles should be interpreted so as to include polluting factories as well. For the manoeuvre to look plausible *as an exercise in interpretation*, there must be a sense that prohibiting things that are B would not only serve the same general purpose as prohibiting things that are A, but serve exactly the same purpose in exactly the same way, giving rise to exactly the same issues, and so on.

All this assumes that we can make sense of the notion of *the purpose of a rule*. We assume that a rule serves a purpose (or that it embodies a principle: see Dworkin 1977: 90–100). Sometimes the purpose itself is mentioned in the legislation; often, however, it has to be inferred from or attributed to the provision by an interpreter. A common move is to associate the purpose of a rule with what was said in favour of the rule at the time it was first laid down. If a prohibition on A is in force because of the decision of some authoritative legal source L—a legislator, for example—then we may ask: 'How did L intend his prohibition to be understood? Did he intend it to apply also to acts of type B?'

The temptation to make the interpretative issue turn on this question of legislative intent is understandable (see e.g. Greenawalt 2000: 1609). As a general matter, people think that interpretation makes sense as an attempt to get at the true meaning of a statement and that the true meaning of a statement is either identical with

---

[10] A similar argument may be constructed for *over*-inclusive prohibitions, i.e. for excluding from the ambit of the prohibition on A some things that are indisputably A but whose prohibition doesn't serve the purpose of the prohibition on things that are A. For these differences, see Schauer (1991). See also Alexander and Sherwin (1994: 1191).

or a fairly straightforward function of the intentions of the person who uttered it.[11] When a person's statement is unclear, asking 'What did he mean?' is a way of finding out what he intended, and although we may not have direct access to this, we can gather evidence of it from what else he said at or around the time that he uttered the sentence whose meaning is now for some reason unclear. And in law this approach seems particularly appropriate. We defer to L's prohibition on A, not on account of our own belief that it is a good thing to prohibit A, but because L has the authority of a legislator. So if the meaning or point of the prohibition is unclear, it is natural to focus on L. Since what is authoritative for us is the rule he laid down in his performance of an intentional act,[12] any evidence of his intention can surely aid us in figuring out what it is to submit appropriately to his authority.

I have doubts, though, about justifying recourse to legislative history along these lines. Intentions are attributes of individuals. But in the enactment of legal rules, authority is usually attributed not to individuals per se but to individuals participating in processes under institutional auspices. The members of a legislature have authority, but they have authority only in regard to the legislative process. The point is particularly dramatic of course in the case of the large legislative assemblies one finds in most modern legal systems. They comprise many members and they have authority, not with regard to their individual intentions but with regard to their corporate power of action. We have methods of determining what acts a congress or a parliament has performed by reference to the proceedings, the texts that were made the focus of their proceedings, and the votes that were cast in the successive stages of that process (cf. Waldron 1999, chs. 4 and 6). But we have no way of according authority to anything else that is said in that process, which is deliberately made the focus of enactment in the same sort of way. It is true that what is accorded authority, as the result of such a process, is the production of a text conceived of—as in the case of all speech acts—as an intentional act. But the relevant intentions in this case are precisely those that are embodied in Gricean fashion in the ordinary meaningfulness of the words and sentences that the text uses (Grice 1957: 377). If they are unclear, then there is no other canonical element of intention that can help us.

What alternative is there? Abandoning the idea of legislator's intent need not involve abandoning the idea of legislative purpose (see Manning 2001: 5). We may attribute a purpose to a rule without regarding the expressed views of individual legislators as authoritative in such a dispute. They may carry evidentiary weight. Or we may want to adopt an altogether more forward-looking and constructivist approach to legislative purpose. Ronald Dworkin (1986, ch. 2) has suggested that

---

[11] Fish (1992: 300–1): 'there cannot be a distinction between interpreters who look to intention and interpreters who don't, only a distinction between the differing accounts of intention put forward by rival interpreters'.

[12] As Joseph Raz (1996: 264) points out, 'It makes no sense to give any person or body law-making power unless it is assumed that the law they make is the law they intended to make.'

interpreting a text is simply a matter of attributing value to it and then proceeding to resolve any difficulties with it in the light of that attribution. A good interpretation of something is thus an interpretation which shows it in its best light, which requires a judgment on the part of the interpreter which may or may not correspond with anything that the human authors of the rule had in mind when they voted for it. On Dworkin's account, this is also what artistic interpretation characteristically amounts to: a performer interprets the score of a Mozart sonata, choosing tempi, for example, when the score does not clearly indicate them, on a basis that makes the sonata (or his performance of the sonata) the best it can be. That Mozart himself would have played a passage at a given tempo may be relevant to the interpretative issue, but it cannot be conclusive if we are seeking to make the object of interpretation the best it can be in the circumstances of our present evaluation (including of course in the context inescapable sensibilities that have grown up since Mozart's time).

Some may object to this constructivist approach, along the following lines: If I govern my choice of tempi etc. by reference only to what sounds right or better *to me*, am I not giving up on the goal of fidelity to Mozart's composition? That may or may not be acceptable in music, but in law it rings alarm bells, because it sounds like a way of deviating from or evading the authority that we associate with the object of interpretation. A legal rule is supposed to prevail over against the particular values or political preferences of individual judges. For we disagree in our values and preferences, and one of the functions of legal texts is to settle on something that can stand in the face of that disagreement. But now if judges or officials are bringing their own values to the interpretation of the texts that are supposed to bind them, the idea of authority and the associated willingness to subordinate one's own values seem to have been abandoned.

The objection is surely valid against any attempt to vary or change the terms of the object which we are supposed to be interpreting. If I start substituting new notes in my performance that Mozart never wrote, on the ground that I think it would make his sonata sound better, that would not be an interpretation. Interpretation must have some fix on its object and aim to make *that* the best it can be; it must not just be seen as an occasion for the composer to make a statement of his own (before an audience who were expecting to hear Mozart) (see Dworkin 1986: 65–6 for the importance of this 'pre-interpretative' phase, at which we fix the identity of the object which is to undergo interpretation). But if the text is unclear anyway, there is no choice but to do *something* in the way of interpretation. And as we have already seen, the alternative approach in law—looking to legislative history for the appropriate values to guide our interpretation—also runs into difficulties about authority, inasmuch as authority attaches only to what has been enacted, not to what might have been in the minds of the enactors.

One final point, I think, makes the constructivist approach inescapable. Although we talk about the interpretation of particular legal provisions (the interpretation of this particular rule, or of that particular clause in the constitution), in fact the bearing of a legal provision on any given case is a function of its place in the law as *corpus iuris*, not a function of its meaning in isolation. Interpretation in law is necessarily holistic, and the meaning of a given provision P_n is the difference its presence makes to the bearing of the whole body of laws $W\{P_1, P_2, \ldots, P_n\}$ on particular cases. P_n might have been enacted by a conservative legislature, but it must now take its place in a set that includes some extant legal provisions enacted by liberals, some enacted by feminists, some by libertarians, and so on. Whatever we think about the original intentions behind P_n, the bearing of W on a particular case arguably cannot be dominated by values associated with just one of the provisions it contains. W itself may be the product of no one's intentions and there may be no coherent set of values associated canonically with W as such, and therefore available for the interpretation of W or any of its constituents. If nevertheless we face an inescapable issue of interpretation with regard to P_n, we may have no choice but to attribute a purpose to *the law* so far as the bearing (direct or indirect) of some aspect of it on a particular case is concerned. And it is arguable that that attribution can only be done constructively, which is not to say that any constructive attribution is beyond dispute, but rather that interpretative disputes about the law can only be disputes about what makes it better or best as a whole.

6. FOLLOWING PRECEDENT

There is a connected set of issues in adjudication having to do with the desire for stability and consistency in the law, even when the interpretation of authoritative texts is not the focus of legal argument. I refer to the doctrine of *stare decisis*—the principle that decisions by higher courts are binding on lower courts and perhaps even binding on coordinate courts addressing the same or a similar issue at a later time.

Suppose a court decides an individual case, *y*, in favour of the plaintiff, on the ground that *y* is C, and then in a later case, *z*, an argument is made that that case should be decided in the same way, because *z* is D and things that are D are like things that are C in some relevant sense. The issue is now slightly different from the case discussed in the previous section—interpreting a rule prohibiting A in regard to an individual case, *x*, which is B. In the situation we are now considering, there is no *textual* rule to interpret: there is just a decision in case *y*, made on certain grounds, and a following decision to be made in case *z*. To be sure, we can make it seem like an issue of interpretation by imagining that the court in case *y* laid down a rule, 'In any case which is C, the plaintiff is entitled to judgment'; that rule would then become the focus of interpretation; and following precedent would be a matter of interpreting the rule in *y* faithfully for subsequent cases. I think that would be a misleading way of stating the issue about precedent (see Dworkin 1977: 111 ff. for the 'gravitational force' (contrasted with the 'enactment force') of precedents). Individual cases generate something like common law rules (when they do) because of the way we follow precedent; following precedent is not a matter of an interpretative response to the rules which cases independently generate.

In common law adjudication, a decision is initially authoritative only *inter partes*, i.e. between the particular plaintiff and the particular defendant. But in subsequent similar cases, judges do not feel as unconstrained in their decision-making as we imagine the judge felt in the first of a series of cases of this kind. Why not? Why would it be wrong to decide the subsequent cases on their own merits, without reference to the earlier decisions? Any attempt to explain the importance of following precedent assumes a serious burden of proof. If judges were not constrained by precedent, they would be free to make the best decision they could in every case that came before them (this position is sometimes described as pragmatism: see Dworkin 1986: 151). (Of course, they would be constrained by authoritative texts like statutes and constitutions, but even in their interpretation of these they would be able to pursue their own best answers to the questions about interpretation we discussed in the previous section, unconstrained by earlier interpretative decisions.) Of course, the decision commanded by the precedent might be the best decision, and following it may be a matter of deferring to the wisdom of one's predecessors. But hard questions for precedent arise precisely in those cases where the judge has no reason except *stare decisis* for following an earlier decision he thinks may be wrong. No doubt judges will disagree about what it would be best to do in the absence of any constraint, and some will make decisions that others see as mistaken. But disagreement and accusations of mistake are associated with the practice of following precedent too. And as Ronald Dworkin (1986: 163) points out, in his acknowledgement of pragmatism as the default position which any defence of *stare decisis* must be able to displace, 'pragmatism claims to risk error at least about the right issue'.

Defences of *stare decisis* fall into two broad categories: arguments about the importance of consistency ('treating like cases alike') and arguments about the importance of predictability. The common association between following precedent and making the law predictable is surely important, up to a point. The need for a predictable social environment is one of the leading values associated with the Rule of Law (see Hayek 1960, chs. 9 and 10), and it might be thought that a practice of following established precedents that have already been made public serves this need better than a practice of allowing judges to decide cases in whatever way they think best. Unfortunately, this argument generates a case for following precedent only with regard to a precedent whose bearing on the case currently under consideration is clear and uncontroversial. But in fact, we take the doctrine of *stare decisis* much further than this: as actually practised, the doctrine requires a judge to address the question of which interpretation of a given precedent is better for the purpose of deciding the case in front of him, even though the case in front of him differs somewhat from the precedent, and even though the bearing of the precedent on the present case is unclear or controversial. The judge's resolution of that issue (which interpretation of the unclear precedent is best) may contribute little to social predictability—little more than if he directly engaged his own sense of justice or the social good in deciding the case in front of him. So the predictability argument does not explain our practice of wrestling with precedents to discover their bearing on cases that are not exactly similar, or to discern their gravitational force for cases that are quite remote (Dworkin 1986: 157–60).

The alternative most commonly cited in the literature is an argument about the moral importance of treating like cases alike. Now this is not just an argument about consistency in the sense of minimal rationality. Consistency in governmental decision-making is valued more in some areas than in others. As I write, the government of the United States stands accused of being inconsistent in its dealings with various 'rogue' states, as between Iraq and North Korea, for example; the argument is that the government should treat like situations alike. But the form of consistency important for law is narrower and more pressing than this. It is not merely that like situations should be treated alike: it is that individual persons are entitled to be treated even-handedly when their legal rights are at stake. To see this, we need to consider the individualist orientation of law.[13] In law the question is never just what the society, S, should do in regard to some situation: should S pursue policy Q or policy R? In law, the question is always what should be done (Q or R) as between the interests at stake of two individual members of the society, the two parties, i_1 versus i_2. And when the question is presented like that, it is not enough to get the choice right as between policy Q and policy R: we must get it right so far as its distinctive bearing on *these two litigants* is concerned. That's the focus in law, and everything we say about reason-giving—in our distinction between relevant and arbitrary reasons, for example—is focused at the level of the appropriate treatment of these two individuals, considered as persons and as right-bearers.[14]

The particular importance in law of treating like cases alike must be seen in this light, and that helps us understand why we might want to wrestle with a precedent long after the element of predictability has evaporated. If treating the present case in a way that is consistent with an earlier case is a matter of respect for persons,

[13] See Waldron (2001a: 759; 2003: 272–3, 293–4).

[14] Even in cases where society itself is a party—in a criminal prosecution ('*The People* v. *I*,' or '*United States* v. *I*,')—the structure of legal action always requires us not to consider only the broad array of reasons relevant to the society's interest (with the impact on poor old i_1 considered as a sort of incidental fallout). In criminal law, we foreground the impact on i_1 and we make prodigious efforts to check that there is nothing in i_1's circumstances to warrant withholding a burden or penalty that would otherwise be placed upon him.

then it cannot be a superficial concern that we abandon as soon as the analogies between the two cases become unclear. We owe it to the present litigant to try as hard as we can to figure out what treating him even-handedly (vis-à-vis earlier litigants) amounts to.

All this assumes, however, that even-handed treatment is actually an important aspect of respect for persons. But is it? Here again we must distinguish the lawyer's ideal of treating like cases alike from other moral or philosophical ideals. The sort of consistency that *stare decisis* upholds is not in itself a commitment to equality. We can see this if we consider a parent who believes at time t_1 that equal treatment of the children in her charge requires giving each of them one hour of undivided attention, but who comes to believe at a later time, t_2, that an allocation that generous will not leave enough time to go round, and that what equal treatment really requires is forty-five minutes of undivided attention for each person in her charge. Now, if the parent has dealt with one of her children on the basis of the view she held at t_1, on what basis should she decide the claim of the next child at t_2 when she has revised her view of what equality requires? Following precedent and treating her children equally pull in different directions in this case.

The most ambitious attempt to state an argument for treating like cases alike that goes beyond equality and also beyond mere logical consistency is that of Ronald Dworkin in *Law's Empire* (1986, ch. 6). Dworkin has argued that a determination to treat like cases alike (and to fathom what that principle requires of us even for unclear or controversial cases) is an aspect of our treating each other as members of a community, bound together to common standards that are developed in a principled way and not simply abandoned or replaced whenever there is a shift in the balance of power or the balance of moral reasons that happen to appeal to its judges or other officials. Dworkin's argument gives prominent place to the importance of community, but it is not itself a communitarian argument. The orientation remains individualist. A particular defendant, i_4, is required in a given case to accept a certain burden—for example, pay damages—in regard to a plaintiff, i_3; and there may be a question why he should put up with this when he (i_4) actually disagrees morally with the basis on which the court held him liable. The most persuasive answer to this sort of objection—which is really an issue about political obligation—rests on the principle of 'fair play': individual i_4 has lived and benefited under the principle that he is now required to bear the burden of (see Hart 1984: 85–6; Simmons 1979, ch. v). But of course this argument will only work if the principle remains in some sense constant as between the present case and some earlier case in which i_4 might have been the plaintiff (or from which i_4 might have enjoyed the indirect benefits of plaintiffs' profiting from this principle). Taken to an extreme, this argument might seem to require that the standards enforced in a community never change, that they always remain constant. Dworkin does not push to this extreme, and he is not defending *stare decisis* in any fanatical sense. Instead, his argument combines this notion of respect for individuals with the holistic sense, which we noticed at the end of Section 5, that the law bears on the members of a community as a whole rather than provision by provision. What we owe to a given individual, then, is not necessarily the benefit of a rigidly constant rule; but rather an unswerving determination to pay attention to principled consistency in the way that law as a whole bears on the situations of particular individuals like him over time.

7. SPECIAL JURISPRUDENCE

In this chapter I have focused mainly on philosophical issues as they arise in general jurisprudence. It would be wrong to end, however, without at least some mention of the philosophical issues that arise in special jurisprudence, i.e. that part of jurisprudence that concerns particular fields of law.

In recent years the philosophy of tort law has provided the most fertile ground for philosophical reflection (see e.g. Jules Coleman 1992; see also the papers collected in Owen 1996). One aspect of this concerns normative concepts used in law like *right* and *duty*. The leading principle of tort law is that a person who breaches what the law calls a duty of care to another, causing injury or damage, must compensate the other person for his loss. Now, should we understand this as simply a pragmatic strategy for burden-shifting, i.e. a strategy that seeks the most efficient allocation of the costs and benefits of economic activity in the community? Is causing damage or loss in this way something a person or a business should be free to do provided they are willing to pay damages when the cost of compensation to those affected would be less than the cost of avoiding the injury? If that is our understanding, we may wonder what work is done by the concepts of *duty* and *right* in our statement of the basic principle of tort doctrine: we say the plaintiff has a right not to be injured and right to compensation if he is; and we say the defendant had a duty to take care and has a duty to pay damages if he did not. On the other hand, if we take those moral concepts seriously, does that mean we have to treat the principle I cited as a moral principle of justice—corrective justice—which tort law recognizes and takes on board? Or is it a purely formal doctrine, giving us notions of the *legal* rights and *legal* duties (and their formal relations to one another) that can be comprehended without reference either to ideas of morality or to the goals of public policy?[15]

---

[15] For the pragmatic approach, see Posner (1995: 387–405); for corrective justice, see Coleman (1992); and for a purely formalist account of tort doctrine, see Weinrib (1988).

The way we answer these questions casts light not just on tort law but on legal principles generally. Law shares a vocabulary with moral discourse: rights, wrongs, duties, obligations, and so on. Some have argued that it would be better (less misleading) if 'every word of moral significance could be banished from the law ... and other words adopted which should convey legal ideas uncolored by anything outside the law' (Holmes 1897: 7). This, it is said, would leave us with prescriptions and threats of sanctions that could be grasped and followed as well by a bad man, who had no interest in morality, as by someone devoted to justice and the good of society. Others have argued that it is a misunderstanding to see 'right', 'duty', and 'obligation' as specifically moral concepts. They are normative concepts that legal systems share with systems of moral thought, but their function is to convey certain normative relations or certain relations between reasons for action, which can be operative in either sphere. On this account, right and duty may be indispensable in law—they cannot be replaced with a crude system of threats and prices of the sort that the bad man would recognize. But all that means is that law has its own normativity; it doesn't mean that law is necessarily entangled with morality.

We have already picked through some of the confusion that is apt to be generated here. In order to describe the norms of a legal system in a positivist way, we ourselves do not need to endorse the 'oughts' in terms of which its rules are phrased; we do not need to be parties to the conventions or subscribers to the principles which constitute the law we are characterizing (see above, Section 2). But that is not an argument in favour of the elimination of 'duty'-talk or of the language of morality generally from within the body of the law; nor is it an argument for reconstruing every legal ought simply as a prospect of sanctions; nor is it an argument for saying (or for denying) that law has its own normativity, distinct from that of morality. These positions are neither supported nor undermined by the positivist characterization of law in general; they must be argued for from within the law, on the grounds that a non-moral understanding (whether it is the understanding of a cynical economist or of a legal formalist) better represents what the members of the community whose law it is have committed themselves to when they adopt certain rules or pursue certain interpretations or wrestle with certain precedents. The same point can be made about the relation between law and moral disagreement within a community: the fact that it may be thought important, for roughly Hobbesian reasons, for members of a given community to be able to identify its law without having to make first-order moral judgements in their own voice is not a reason for denying the normativity or even the moral normativity of law: only, on this account moral normativity would be associated in the first instance not with the content of the law as such but with the moral importance of coordination, i.e. with the moral grounds of our determination to find norms that can stand among us even when we disagree about what those norms should (morally) be.

General jurisprudence has been my subject in this chapter, but the point of these final remarks is that general jurisprudence can take us only so far. When we descend to the level of special jurisprudence—the philosophy of tort or contract or crime—the most important contribution that the philosophy of law in general can make is to see that we are not distracted by the background importance of the positivist conception (whether its descriptive importance or its moral importance) from the detailed normative analysis that an understanding of particular areas of law requires.

REFERENCES

Adler, Matthew, and Dorf, Michael (2003). 'Constitutional Existence Conditions and Judicial Review'. *Virginia Law Review*, 89: 1105–1202.

Alexander, Larry, and Sherwin, Emily (1994). 'The Deceptive Nature of Rules'. *University of Pennsylvania Law Review*, 142: 1191–1225.

Aquinas, Thomas (1959). 'Summa Theologica, I–II', in A. P. d'Entrèves (ed.), *Aquinas: Selected Political Writings*. Oxford: Blackwell.

Augustine, St (1950). *On the City of God*. New York: Random House.

Austin, John (1995), *The Province of Jurisprudence Determined*, ed. Wilfrid E. Rumble. Cambridge: Cambridge University Press.

Bentham, Jeremy (1931). *The Theory of Legislation*, ed. C. K. Ogden. London: Kegan Paul.

—— (1970). *Of Laws in General*, ed. H. L. A. Hart. London: Athlone Press.

Bork, Robert (1986). 'The Constitution, Original Intent, and Economic Rights'. *San Diego Law Review*, 23: 823–32.

Bratman, Michael (1992). 'Shared Cooperative Activity'. *Philosophical Review*, 101: 327–41.

Campbell, Tom (1996). *The Legal Theory of Ethical Positivism*. Brookfield, Vt.: Dartmouth.

Coleman, Jules (1988). 'Negative and Positive Positivism', in Coleman, *Markets, Morals and the Law*. Cambridge: Cambridge University Press.

—— (1992). *Risks and Wrongs*. Cambridge: Cambridge University Press.

—— (2001). *The Practice of Principle*. Oxford: Oxford University Press.

Dworkin, Ronald (1977). *Taking Rights Seriously*, rev. edn. London: Duckworth.

—— (1982). ' "Natural" Law Revisited'. *University of Florida Law Review*, 34: 165–88.

—— (1986). *Law's Empire*. Cambridge, Mass.: Harvard University Press.

—— (1996). 'Objectivity and Truth: You'd Better Believe It'. *Philosophy and Public Affairs*, 25: 87–139.

—— (2002). 'Thirty Years On: Review of Jules Coleman, *The Practice of Principle*'. *Harvard Law Review*, 115: 1655–87.

Endicott, Timothy (2001). 'Law Is Necessarily Vague'. *Legal Theory*, 7: 377–83.

Finnis, John (1980). *Natural Law and Natural Rights*. Oxford: Clarendon Press.

Fish, Stanley (1992). 'Play of Surfaces: Theory and Law', in Gregory Leyh (ed.), *Legal Hermeneutics: History, Theory and Practice*. Berkeley: University of California Press.

Fuller, Lon L. (1959). 'Positivism and Fidelity to Law: A Reply to Hart'. *Harvard Law Review*, 71: 630–72.

—— (1969). *The Morality of Law*, rev. edn. New Haven: Yale University Press.

Gray, John Chipman (1921). *The Nature and Sources of Law*. New York: Macmillan.

Greenawalt, Kent (1992). *Law and Objectivity*. New York: Oxford University Press.

Greenawalt, Kent (2000). 'Are Mental States Relevant for Statutory and Constitutional Interpretation?' *Cornell Law Review*, 85: 1609–72.

Grice, H. P. (1957). 'Meaning'. *Philosophical Review*, 66: 377–88.

Hart, H. L. A. (1984). 'Are There Any Natural Rights?', in Jeremy Waldron (ed.), *Theories of Rights*. Oxford: Oxford University Press.

—— (1994). *The Concept of Law*, 2nd edn. Oxford: Clarendon Press.

Hayek, F. A. (1960). *The Constitution of Liberty*. London: Routledge & Kegan Paul.

Hobbes, Thomas (1996). *Leviathan*, rev. edn., ed. Richard Tuck. Cambridge: Cambridge University Press.

Holmes, Oliver Wendell (1897). 'The Path of the Law'. *Harvard Law Review*, 10: 457–78.

Luce, R. Duncan, and Raiffa, Howard (1957). *Games and Decisions*. New York: Wiley.

MacCormick, Neil (1985). 'A Moralistic Case for A-moralistic Law'. *Valparaiso Law Review*, 20: 3–41.

McDowell, John (1981). 'Non-Cognitivism and Rule-Following', in Steven Holtzman and Christopher Leich (eds.), *Wittgenstein: To Follow a Rule*. London: Routledge.

Manning, John (2001). 'Textualism and the Equity of the Statute'. *Columbia Law Review*, 1001: 1–127.

Moore, Michael (1982). 'Moral Reality'. *Wisconsin Law Review*, 82: 1063–1155.

—— (2003). 'The Plain Truth About Legal Truth'. *Harvard Journal of Law and Public Policy*, 26: 23–47.

Owen, David (ed.) (1996). *Philosophical Foundations of Tort Law*. Oxford: Oxford University Press.

Perry, Stephen (1997). 'Interpretation and Methodology in Legal Theory', in Andrei Marmor (ed.), *Law and Interpretation: Essays in Legal Philosophy*. Oxford: Clarendon Press.

Posner, Richard (1995). *Overcoming Law*. Cambridge, Mass.: Harvard University Press.

Postema, Gerald (1986). *Bentham and the Common Law Tradition*. Oxford: Clarendon Press.

Radin, Margaret Jane (1989). 'Reconsidering the Rule of Law'. *Boston University Law Review*, 69: 781–819.

Raz, Joseph (1979). 'Legal Positivism and the Sources of Law', in Raz, *The Authority of Law: Essays on Law and Morality*. Oxford: Clarendon Press.

—— (1983). 'The Rule of Law and its Virtue', in Raz, *The Authority of Law*. Oxford: Oxford University Press.

—— (1994). 'Authority, Law and Morality', in Raz, *Ethics in the Public Domain: Essays in the Morality of Law and Politics*. Oxford: Clarendon Press.

—— (1996). 'Intention in Interpretation', in Robert George (ed.), *The Autonomy of Law*. Oxford: Oxford University Press.

Scalia, Antonin (1989). 'The Rule of Law as a Law of Rules'. *University of Chicago Law Review*, 56: 1175–88.

—— (1997). *A Matter of Interpretation: Federal Courts and the Law*. Princeton: Princeton University Press.

Schauer, Frederic (1991). *Playing by the Rules: A Philosophical Examination of Rule-Based Decision-Making in Law and in Life*. Oxford: Clarendon Press.

Simmons, A. John (1979). *Moral Principles and Political Obligations*. Princeton: Princeton University Press.

Waldron, Jeremy (1992). 'The Irrelevance of Moral Objectivity', in Robert George (ed.), *Natural Law Theory: Contemporary Essays*. Oxford: Clarendon Press.

—— (1994). 'Vagueness in Law and Language—Some Philosophical Perspectives'. *California Law Review*, 82: 509–40.

—— (1999). *Law and Disagreement*. Oxford: Clarendon Press.

—— (2001*a*). 'Does Law Promise Justice?' *Georgia State University Law Review*, 17: 759–88.

—— (2001*b*). 'Normative (or Ethical) Positivism', in Jules Coleman (ed.), *Hart's Postscript: Essays on the Postscript to 'The Concept of Law'*. Oxford: Oxford University Press.

—— (2002). 'Legal and Political Philosophy', in Jules Coleman and Scott Shapiro (eds.), *Handbook on Jurisprudence and Political Philosophy*. Oxford: Oxford University Press.

—— (2003). 'The Primacy of Justice.' *Legal Theory*, 9: 269–94.

Waluchow, W. J. (1994). *Inclusive Legal Positivism*. Oxford: Clarendon Press.

Weinrib, Ernest J. (1988). 'Legal Formalism: On the Immanent Rationality of Law'. *Yale Law Journal*, 97: 949–1016.

Wittgenstein, Ludwig (1958). *Philosophical Investigations*, trans. G. E. M. Anscombe. Oxford: Blackwell.

Zapf, Christian, and Moglen, Eben (1996). 'Linguistic Indeterminacy and the Rule of Law: On the Perils of Misunderstanding Wittgenstein'. *Georgetown Law Journal*, 84: 485–520.

CHAPTER 8

DEMOCRATIC THEORY

DAVID ESTLUND

A man walks into a bar, orders a beer, and on tasting it cries, 'This is awful!'
'What do you mean?' asks the bartender. 'This beer is made with very shiny,
very quiet equipment. It's brewed in a beautiful part of the Black Forest in
Germany. The workers are very happy while they make it, and very well dressed
I might add. The aroma during brewing is exquisite. What's not to like?'
'But it tastes terrible,' says the man. 'Don't you care about your customers?'
'Of course I do,' the bartender replies, 'but they all like different beers, and this
is the only one that pleases them all equally, and we wanted to be fair.'
'You mean people actually like this swill?,' says the man.
'No,' says the bartender, proudly. 'Nobody likes it at all, and so no one likes it
more than anyone else.'
Finishing his beer, the man is impressed. 'In that case,' he says excitedly, 'pour
me another!'

1. INTRODUCTION

Democratic decisions, like beers, might be valuable because of the way they are
made, or they might be good decisions on independent grounds, apart from how
they were made. In the 1960s American voters elected politicians who perpetuated
a disastrous phase of the Vietnam War, a bad decision made by a fair procedure, at

least ostensibly. Of course, the procedure was probably not perfectly fair. In any case, the procedure's fairness or unfairness is a separate issue from whether perpetuating the war was wise or just. The value of the procedure and the value of the decision are two different things.

One of the fundamental philosophical issues in democratic theory is how important it is that political decisions are good decisions, and how important it is that they be made by good or appropriate procedures. The issue is interesting because these criteria can conflict. In principle, the procedure that would make the best decisions could be utterly elitist or authoritarian (suppose, for example, the masses are highly ignorant or bigoted). If Eugene McCarthy had somehow—say, peacefully but illegally—simply taken charge of US foreign policy in the mid-1960s, perhaps the lives of thousands of soldiers and civilians would have been spared. Because of our democratic principles, few of us think that he should have done so (even if it were possible). From a democratic point of view, the superior decision would have been made by a bad procedure.

If bad procedures might produce good decisions, and good procedures might produce bad decisions, then what are the relative roles of these two considerations in the best theoretical account of the importance of democratic political institutions? Are procedural values of overriding importance, so that, for example, fair or equal procedures are more important than good decisions even in matters of life and death, or grave threats to rights, justice, or well-being? Or are these standards for good decisions important enough that political procedures ought to be designed to promote them, apart from the superior intrinsic value other procedures might have? Is the modern approval of democracy based more on procedure, more on substance, or on some combination? The terms will turn out to be too vague as they stand, but they convey the general nature of the issue I will concentrate on.

My emphasis is narrow in this way, but it goes to the heart of a lot of recent democratic theory. In this chapter I will leave aside the aspects of democratic theory that revolve around empirical results and rational choice theorems.[1] Nor will I attempt a survey of issues in democratic theory. I want to concentrate on a very basic philosophical issue on which much recent normative democratic theory depends.[2] Careful attention to this issue is, I think, one of the most effective keys for unlocking the philosophical dimensions of competing theories of the value of democracy.

In Plato's dialogue *Euthyphro*, the question is raised whether something is pious because it is loved by the gods, or whether the gods love it because it is pious.

---

[1] For discussion of the latter, see Brennan and Pettit, Ch. 10 in this volume.

[2] I offer more coverage in Estlund (2002), and there is a large bibliography there. See also, Thomas Christiano's survey (Christiano 1990), and Dryzek (forthcoming). See additional surveys cited below in Sect. 5.

The 'Euthyphro question' has a form that crops up all over philosophy, and democratic theory is no exception. Many people today think that, at least under certain conditions, good political decisions are those that are democratically chosen. We don't have to accept the old slogan that *vox populi, vox dei* ('the voice of the people is the voice of God') to see the parallel to the Euthyphro question: are good (or just, or legitimate) democratic outcomes good because they are democratically chosen, or are they democratically chosen because they are good? I want to display and criticize the widespread sympathy in recent democratic theory for the former answer, the view (in its simplest form) that the value of democratic decisions is entirely a matter of their being democratic.

The two schools of thought that have exerted the most influence in normative democratic theory in the last quarter century or so are, as I will call them, *normative social choice theory* and *deep deliberative democracy*. Each is an important strand in a much broader theoretical movement: social choice theory and deliberative democracy, respectively.[3] I shall not be considering these broader movements nor holding them responsible for the characteristic views of the narrower strands that are my topic here, and which I will characterize more fully later. Normative social choice theory and deep deliberative democracy are antithetical on many matters, such as the power of reason in public political contexts, the nature of a citizen's duties in political participation, and the economic preconditions for legitimate democratic institutions. But they converge on a fundamental philosophical commitment: there is no normative standard (such as justice or the common good) by which collective political choices can appropriately be judged other than their being genuinely democratic.

I assume that the core of the idea of democracy is, or at least includes, the idea of citizens collectively authorizing laws by voting for them and/or for office-holders who make them.[4] We should normally understand someone, then, who rests some claim on the value of democracy to be resting it on the value of this procedural arrangement: the collective authorization of the laws by voting.[5] It isn't merely the emphasis on procedure, then, that is notable in recent democratic theory.

[3] Dryzek and List (2003) say social choice theory and deliberative democracy have dominated the theory of democracy in the past decade. Risse (2001) cites some literature showing the influence of social choice theory. Several surveys of the large literature on deliberative democracy are cited below in Sect. 5. The narrower approaches, normative social choice theory and deep deliberative democracy, are categories which I believe capture the most influential and central strands of the two larger theoretical movements in normative theory.

[4] Christiano (1990: 151) reaches for the most minimal definitional common ground with 'a society in which all or most of the population has the opportunity jointly to play an essential if not always very formative role in the determination of legislation and policy'. This leaves out explicit mention of voting, so my account of the core idea may be slightly less minimal, but Christiano's would do for my purposes. Richard Arneson (2001) offers, as uncontroversial, a gloss essentially equivalent to mine, including voting.   [5] I will discuss Joshua Cohen's apparent dissent from this proposition below.

The notable thing is the claim to explain the value of democratic procedures without appealing to any other (extra-democratic) values of democratic decisions, such as a tendency to be right or just or good on independent grounds.

It will help, first, to consider the idea of proceduralism in collective choice contexts in a general way. Then, before turning to a close and critical look at the two schools of thought, I briefly explicate the theory of democracy in the philosophy of John Rawls. This serves several purposes: first, Rawls's elaborate and well-known political philosophy incorporates, in one place or another, most of the uses of procedural reasoning I will identify, and so the numerous distinctions can be illustrated by being located in this more familiar context. Secondly, Rawls's theory of democratic legitimacy is not as well known or well understood as other parts of his view, and contrasts with the flight from substance I will explore and criticize.

My claims fall into a few main categories: (1) Certain influential strands in democratic theory claim to rely only on the values of democracy itself, and to eschew independent standards for deciding which political decisions are good. (2) These same strands of argument typically do not really live up to this proceduralist promise. (3) The normative plausibility of these theories depends on their departing from their official proceduralist ambitions, and accepting a role for procedure-independent standards of good outcomes.

2. Proceduralism in General

As it stands, the terminology of procedure and substance is too vague for our purposes. Roughly, of course, a substantive value in this context is one that is procedure-independent. One possible strong claim is that normative political theory should not appeal to any procedure-independent values at all—that the only available value is the value of democracy itself. The weaker, more limited claim on which I will focus is only that normative political theory should not appeal to any procedure-independent values *in the evaluation of political outcomes*—for this specific purpose only the value of democracy is available. This weaker view attempts to do without any standards of good political decisions (such as basic rights, or principles of justice, or the common good), except standards based on good ways of making decisions. It emphasizes procedural values in this way. But it might still appeal to non-procedural values. For example, it might assert the basic equality of persons without claiming that this value is itself based on or derived from the value of any decision procedure. It could be a substantive value in that sense. It might be appealed to as a basis for regarding certain equality-respecting decision procedures as valuable. Still, this is all compatible with the weaker way of avoiding substantive standards—the view that *political outcomes* are only evaluable in terms of the value of certain political decision procedures. It would be possible to hold that outcomes can only be evaluated in terms of the procedures that produced them (for examples, are they democratic?), and also hold that certain procedures are good ones because they respect certain substantive values (for example, equality of persons). The weaker view is still a flight from substance, but a more limited one. It holds that normative political theory should not evaluate political outcomes on any grounds other than whether they are democratic.

On this view the value of democratic procedures cannot ultimately be accounted for in terms of their promoting or aiming at independently good (just, right, etc.) outcomes. To see this more clearly requires a few distinctions.

A thing's instrumental value is its usefulness as a means to something else of value. I also want to use a slightly broader concept, that of *prospective* value: a thing's value as a means *or as an intended means* to something else of value. A screwdriver has prospective value for me if I use it with the purpose of achieving something else of value (removal of a screw). This kind of value does not depend on its actually being effective—on its having instrumental value.

There is another important kind of value which I will call *retrospective value*. A thing's retrospective value consists in its having been produced in a certain way, and apart from anything else about it. For example, when something, say a decision or a distribution, is praised as being fair or just, this sometimes means that there is something good about it by virtue of its having been produced by a fair or just procedure. It is being evaluated retrospectively in my sense, by looking back to how it was caused or produced.

When the procedure itself (not the outcome) is called fair or just (as in the previous paragraph) this could, I suppose, be yet another retrospective evaluation, a claim that the procedure was itself produced by a fair procedure. The law might be retrospectively fair or just as the outcome of a certain fair or just legislative procedure, and that procedure, in turn, might be fair merely in the retrospective sense of being the outcome of yet another fair procedure, say a constitutional procedure. But more normally, it means that the producing procedure was fair not in the retrospective sense, owing to its own procedural origin, but *intrinsically*: owing neither to its source nor to its uses.[6]

The view that political outcomes are not to be evaluated except on democratic procedural grounds entails a restriction on the kind of procedural grounds that are available: political procedures cannot be valued on prospective grounds, since that would involve the procedure-independent values being promoted or pursued. That

---

[6] The idea of intrinsic value is often construed as non-instrumental value. For present purposes, I narrow intrinsic value to the class of value that is neither prospective (roughly, derived from its uses), nor retrospective (roughly, derived from its source).

leaves retrospective and intrinsic grounds on which the procedures can be held to be valuable. But retrospective value cannot go back retrospectively forever; the retrospection must eventually find some intrinsic value, otherwise it is groundless—a wild-goose chase. So, certain political procedures must be held to be intrinsically valuable if political outcomes are only to be evaluated on procedural grounds. Here, then, is a serviceable name for the particular kind of flight from substance I will explore and criticize:

> *Intrinsic democratic proceduralism.* Only democratic political arrangements are legitimate, and the value of their being democratic does not depend on any qualities of democratic decisions other than whether they are democratic in two senses: (*a*) decisions must be made by democratic procedures, and (*b*) they must also not unduly undermine or threaten the possibility of democratic procedure in the future.

We should pause to note this second way in which a decision can be, or fail to be, democratic: according to whether it protects the conditions for decisions that are democratic in the first sense (retrospectively). For example, if a society with suitably democratic laws and practices votes to disfranchise women, the decision is undemocratic in this latter sense, undermining the possibility of democratic procedures, even if it were made by a perfectly democratic procedure. Intrinsic democratic proceduralism does not insist on using only retrospective standards for evaluating outcomes; it insists on evaluating outcomes only for whether they are democratic, and this question has both a retrospective and a prospective aspect. The distinguishing feature is that both aspects rely on the intrinsic value of democratic procedures. On this view democratic procedures are to be respected and promoted because of their intrinsic value.

The opposing view can be simply read off. Against the claim that appeals to substantive outcome standards (to use a compact phrase) are impermissible in normative democratic theory, the denial would say that such appeals are permissible. What makes this position interesting is the possibility that, in a stronger claim, normative democratic theory will be inadequate unless it avails itself of some standards for the evaluation of political outcomes beyond those that can be derived from the value of democratic procedure itself. I won't argue for this opposing view directly. Rather, I look closely at two influential versions of intrinsic democratic proceduralism, versions that I believe underlie quite a bit of contemporary normative democratic theory, in order to raise what I think are serious difficulties.

Before turning to that, however, it is worth looking at the structure of Rawls's account of democracy, partly to put this section's distinctions into a concrete and familiar setting, and partly to show that Rawls's view explicitly departs from the widespread view—intrinsic democratic proceduralism—that I have just sketched.

3. RAWLS ON DEMOCRACY

Rawls is not often treated as a theorist of democracy, but his book *A Theory of Justice* includes a distinctive approach to the relation between democratic procedures and substantive justice. Rawls (1999) aligns himself with 'deliberative democracy' in more recent work, but his account of democratic legitimacy, which I explain shortly, contrasts with what I call the deep deliberative democracy approach in ways that are often not sufficiently appreciated. It is easy to be misled by Rawls's emphasis on what he calls 'pure procedural justice' into thinking he eschews procedure-independent standards in political reasoning. In fact, however, Rawls is a direct opponent of the view that the only evaluative question about a political decision is whether it was produced by the right sort of procedure. This is clearest in the obvious application of his principles of justice to the outcomes of legislative processes.[7] For example, a legislated system of taxation might plainly undermine the social structure's tendency to promote the condition of the least well-off, contravening a principle of justice that Rawls calls the Difference Principle. Or, in a rather different case, a law might violate equal and broad liberties of political expression, violating the principle of justice guaranteeing this among other equal basic liberties, even if that law is produced by proper procedures.

Rawls (1971: 362) does say that a law's being unjust is not enough to deprive it of 'practical authority'. A law's justice can be distinguished from its practical authority, or, as Rawls later calls it 'legitimacy', since even unjust laws might be legitimate. (For example, perhaps taxes are unjustly high or low. Still, within a certain range they might yet be legitimate and binding law.) The idea of legitimacy retains a certain vagueness, but it generally connotes the moral permissibility of coercive enforcement of law and/or some strong and distinctively political moral reason for those addressed by the law to comply with it.[8] Rawls's view is that legitimacy does not require justice. This long-standing

[7] Rawls argues in *A Theory of Justice* (1971) that two principles for the justice of the basic structure of society are appropriate on the grounds that they would be acceptable to anyone in a certain 'original position' in which participants do not know, and so cannot exploit, any particular information about themselves such as their race, or intelligence, etc. In a brief statement incorporating certain later refinements, he states them this way: 'a. Each person has an equal right to a fully adequate scheme of equal basic liberties which is compatible with a similar scheme of liberties for all. b. Social and economic inequalities are to satisfy two conditions. First, they must be attached to offices and positions open to all under the conditions of fair equality of opportunity; and second, they must be to the greatest benefit of the least advantaged members of society' (1993: 291).

[8] For two recent discussions of the idea of legitimacy as compared with certain closely related ideas, see Simmons (1999) and Buchanan (2002).

feature of Rawls's view[9] is explained especially clearly in his 'Reply to Habermas'. He writes:

At some point, the injustice of the outcomes of a legitimate democratic procedure corrupts its legitimacy... But before this point is reached, the outcomes of a legitimate procedure are legitimate whatever they are. This gives us purely procedural democratic legitimacy and distinguishes it from justice, even granting that justice is not specified procedurally. Legitimacy allows for an indeterminate range of injustice that justice does not. (1995: 176)

Justice 'is not specified procedurally', and so even proper procedures can err. Still, the mere application of the procedure-independent principles of justice to laws is not enough to show that their legitimacy is thereby affected.

So, the legitimacy of outcomes is not determined by direct application of the standards of justice, at least within broad limits, and yet those standards have a definite role in the standard of legitimacy itself. On Rawls's view, the two principles of justice are recommended by virtue of their being agreeable in a certain hypothetical choice situation, the original position. Once these principles are determined, the question arises what the constitution of a just society ought to be like. Basic institutions, then, must not violate certain equal basic political liberties (such as freedom of expression, association, rights to vote, seek office, etc.), but they should also lead, so far as possible, to a future in which those liberties are likely to be well respected. Rawls argues that among the political institutions that will best ensure these things is a system of majority rule on many legislative matters, though constrained by judicial review (see 1971: 353, 356). Details aside, the decisions made by such institutions will sometimes be unjust, but they will yet be 'practically authoritative', or legitimate so long as the departures are within certain bounds.

The procedure-independent principles of justice, then, figure in several ways. In each case it is useful to put the point in terms of my distinctions between prospective, retrospective, and intrinsic procedural values.

(1) Outcomes are illegitimate if they violate certain basic liberties, specified in the principles of justice, which are constraints not themselves authorized by any democratic provenance, but some of which (what Rawls calls the 'political liberties'[10]) are based on the value of democratic procedures.

This is a prospective standard for evaluating outcomes of political procedures.

(2) Outcomes that are legitimate might yet be unjust by violating the two principles of justice, which are procedure-independent standards, in less serious ways.

<hr />

[9] See Rawls (1971: 350 ff.): 'The injustice of a law is not, in general, a sufficient reason for not adhering to it ...'

[10] Rawls means, roughly, equal rights to hold office and participate in political processes. For details, see Rawls (1971: 224–34, 277–9).

This is also a prospective consideration.

>   (3) Outcomes that are unjust but still legitimate owe their legitimacy to their being produced by certain fair or just procedures and not to their being correct in any further sense.

This is what I have called a retrospective procedural value.

>   (4) The legitimacy of laws produced by those procedures, even of some unjust laws, rests partly on the tendency (bound to be imperfect) of those procedures to produce laws that are just by the procedure-independent principles of justice.

This is yet another case of prospective evaluation of political procedures and their outcomes.

In many ways, Rawls's overall political philosophy avoids substantive matters in favour of thinner, or more formal, or more procedural values. The famous device of the original position illustrates this feature, by explicating the idea of substantive social justice in terms of a fair hypothetical choice procedure. Nevertheless, his account of democratic legitimacy has a central substantive element of a kind that both normative social choice theory and deep deliberative democratic theory hope and claim to avoid: the value of democratic institutions of political decision rests on an account of justice by which political outcomes can be directly evaluated, and which is logically independent of the value of democratic procedures, and is prior to them and authoritative over them in that sense.

I turn next to an approach that purports to be more proceduralist than this.

4. NORMATIVE SOCIAL CHOICE THEORY

Normative social choice theory is an influential approach to politics that derives its basic ideas from the mathematical field of 'positive' social choice theory pioneered by Kenneth Arrow and others.[11] Social choice theory studies mathematical functions or rules aggregating multiple individual preference rankings into a single collective preference ranking. For example, suppose that Joe ranks three social alternatives in this order: x, y, z. But Jane ranks them y, x, z. And others have their own rankings as well. By what rule should these individual rankings be brought together to determine a group ranking, in order to guide a group decision?

---

[11] See Arrow (1963); Sen (1970). Several collections of articles discussing social choice theory in the context of political philosophy include Barry and Hardin (1982); Elster and Hylland (1986); Sen's (1997) survey; Suzumura (2002).

Several leading results prove that no rule can jointly meet certain intuitively attractive conditions, which are supposed to ensure such things as fairness and responsiveness. Since those conditions are defended on normative grounds—on the basis of their being good or right—social choice theory always has this normative dimension.[12] Social choice theory mainly investigates more analytical questions such as which conditions logically preclude which rules. But I consider, more specifically, what I call normative social choice theory. The term is my own, and it refers to the widespread practice of drawing normative implications about democracy (such as whether it is a coherent ideal at all, or which voting rules should be employed) by appealing to formal results in social choice theory. Social choice theory is often said to show that the idea of democracy is incoherent,[13] or that it is no better than a random but peaceful way to change policies and officials (Riker 1982: 244). These interpretations of social choice theory depend, I think, on a confused idea of proceduralism. In this section I argue that social choice theory's subject matter is a certain conception of procedure-independent standards for evaluating social outcomes. It has nothing special to do with democratic procedures. Normative social choice theory really uses social choice theory's approaches to outcome evaluation in order to evaluate democratic procedures on *instrumental*, not procedural, grounds.

Social choice theory is often said to study social choice procedures, among them voting procedures, and so to study 'proceduralist' conceptions of democracy. Coleman and Ferejohn (1986: 7) are characteristic in their view that 'the modern theory of social choice contains a number of attempts to develop a defense of particular voting or collective-decision procedures by appeal to axioms aimed at characterizing one or another aspect of procedural fairness'. It is an 'essentially proceduralist project'.

Proceduralism as I have proposed to understand it avoids appeal to procedure-independent standards in the evaluation of outcomes. It avoids judging outcomes by such independent standards as Rawlsian principles of justice, for example. To see if normative social choice theory is proceduralist in that sense, we should look more closely at the pertinent idea of both procedure and independence. Consider independence first.

Coleman and Ferejohn suggest that what is distinctive about proceduralism is that the justification of the procedure relies on properties that are logically necessary to the procedure, implied by its definition, rather than contingent. For example,

---

[12] Arrow (1963: 31) says they 'express the doctrines of citizen sovereignty and rationality'. Suzumura (1996) interprets them as ensuring efficiency and democratic legitimacy. William Riker (1982) says they are conditions of fairness.

[13] Russell Hardin (1993: 170) writes that social choice theory shows that 'the democratic, majoritarian urge is . . . conceptually incoherent and, when defined in simple terms, practically infeasible'. Gerry Mackie (2003) cites a parade of authors drawing pessimistic conclusions about democracy from the literature of social choice theory.

social choice theory defines social choice procedures in terms of functions or aggregation rules from individual preference rankings to a social preference ranking. So, any two procedures that conform to the same aggregation rule are, from this standpoint, the same procedure. Since a given procedure conforms to a certain function by the procedure's very definition, social choice theory's approach would seem to count as a proceduralist kind of evaluation. By contrast, the *consequences* of using a certain procedure are, according to Coleman and Ferejohn, contingent rather than settled by definition, and so justifications of democratic procedures that rely on consequences are not proceduralist, but instrumentalist. This is a clear and significant distinction between theories, and I see no reason not to accept it.

But what if we ask what any of this has to do with democracy, conceived as putting certain matters up for a vote? Which are we to count as the 'procedure' that makes social choice theory proceduralist: the abstract aggregation rule from individual to social preferences (call this a *preference rule*), or the process of gathering and aggregating votes and, in a certain way, causally producing an outcome (call this a *voting process*)? One thing is clear: social choice theory of the axiomatic kind pioneered by Arrow[14] evaluates abstract aggregation functions or preference rules, rules that may or may not be obeyed by actual voting processes (since, for example, voters might not vote for their most preferred social alternative if voting for something else strategically serves their interests).

Normative social choice theory applies social choice theory's study of preference rules to the evaluation of voting processes, in which votes are cast, gathered, and counted. It judges them by their tendency to obey certain abstract aggregation rules: does the outcome lie at the top of an aggregate ranking which bears some certain logical relation to the individual rankings of the voters?

By Coleman and Ferejohn's useful definition of proceduralism (but contrary to their own claim) normative social choice theory is not employing a proceduralist kind of evaluation of voting processes, but an instrumentalist one. The reason is that actual voting processes are evaluated by their contingent tendency to produce outcomes that respect a certain abstract rule relating outcomes to individual preferences over the social alternatives—preferences that may or may not be accurately expressed in votes. If, instead, normative social choice theory simply evaluates abstract preference aggregation rules rather than voting processes, then it has no direct bearing on democratic procedures, and so couldn't count as a proceduralist account of democracy.[15]

[14] Arrow's own language may have encouraged the conflation of voting processes with preference rules. Arrow (1963: 23) wrote, 'By a social welfare function will be meant a *process or rule* which, for each set of individual orderings ... states a corresponding social ordering of alternative social states ...' (my italics). In a later essay (1979: 118), he says, '[a welfare judgement is] an evaluation of the consequences to all individuals based on their evaluations.... The process of formation of *welfare judgements* is logically equivalent to a social *decision process* or constitution' (my italics). And finally, 'We are seeking to model democracy' (Arrow 1982: 257).

[15] Tom Christiano (1993: 178–9) makes this point.

If this is the structure of normative social choice theory, then it does not really avoid using procedure-independent standards to evaluate outcomes of political procedures. It evaluates outcomes by an abstract relation to individual preferences, and then evaluates actual procedures on the basis of their instrumental value—their tendency to produce good outcomes.

This is not a bad thing. But normative social choice theory does not have some supposed advantage over instrumentalist theories of the value of democracy, by avoiding the controversial matter of what outcome standards are appropriate. Normative social choice theory is an instrumentalist account of the value of voting processes, and it asserts controversial outcome standards whenever it asserts a condition on preference rules.

Shoring up this claim of mine requires a look at a few natural replies meant to show that normative social choice theory is about voting processes after all. I consider three.

What if the preference rules are applied to actual preferences at actual times? Social choice theory conditions can be applied to the actual preferences of actual individuals at certain times, rather than concerning itself only with abstract possibilities and their logical properties. Would this be enough to show that normative social choice theory is evaluating voting processes themselves and not using preference rules to evaluate outcomes themselves? I don't think it would.

Suppose that the ruling dictatorial powers have decided that bicyclists shall be banned from all automobile roads. As it happens a 'vote' has also been taken on this matter out of idle curiosity, and the rule banning bikes received a majority. In this case, the law conforms to the abstract rule requiring that laws must be related to actual votes in a certain way: a majority of votes support the law. This is an abstract rule linking certain temporal individual inputs to certain social decisions by a mathematical relation. But intuitively, the decision to ban the bikers was not the outcome of any voting process that aggregated individual votes at all.

What if the inputs were not passive preferences, but acts of some kind? We might think that what's missing is actual acts and choices. But this won't be enough to capture the idea of retrospective evaluation[16]. The outcome of a fair bet is retrospectively fair only if the outcome is produced by the bet in the right way. Suppose my thieving uncle will take my watch whether I win the bet on which I have staked it or not. The bet will make no difference to the fate of my watch. As it turns out I lose the bet, though my uncle never actually bothers to discover this, and he takes the watch as he had planned in any case. His having the watch conforms to an abstract rule which takes our bets and certain facts as temporal inputs. But his having my watch is not retrospectively fair in the sense of being the outcome of a fair procedure. By analogy, the kind of conformity to preference rules that social choice theory studies does not, by itself, have any genuinely procedural element.

---

[16] Tom Christiano (1993: 182), for example, proposes to make the inputs actions rather than preferences.

Don't many social choice conditions imply the very sort of causal arrangement that constitutes a voting process? Perhaps what is missing is a certain causal relationship between people's preferences and the social outcome. When the dictator just happens to do what the people prefer, or my uncle just happens to take what the actual bet made his, it is a coincidence, and that seems to point to the lack of the right kind of causal relationships between events.

Some conditions or constraints on preference rules involve more than just a coincidence, and this forces us to go some extra distance in order to argue that, still, they are not about voting processes but about preference rules.

Social choice conditions sometimes require that the social ranking bear certain logical relations to sets of individual rankings that are merely possible but not actual. What matters is not some comparison of the social ranking to actual preferences (or choices, votes, etc.), but what the social ranking *would* have been if actual preferences had ('counterfactually') been otherwise. For example, consider the 'non-dictatorship' condition: There must be no person whose ranking of any pair of alternatives will be reflected in the social ranking regardless of anyone else's preferences (Arrow 1963: 30; Riker 1982: 118). This condition requires the consideration of more than just the actual cases in which individual preferences are aggregated into a social ranking. Even if Joe's preferences over A and B are always reflected in the actual outcome rankings, that would not show that the non-dictatorship condition is violated. There might yet be possible but non-actual profiles of individual preferences in which, according to the rule in question, Joe's preferences would be reversed in the social ranking. If there are these counterfactual possibilities, then the rule that always actually matches Joe's preferences does not violate non-dictatorship.

This counterfactual element of some choice conditions suggests a possible reply to my argument that social choice theory lacks the causal element that distinguishes voting processes from preference rules. It might fairly be asked, how could this sort of counterfactual condition be met unless there is some causal mechanism— some filter or device—in place that ensures that certain sets of preferences would, if actual, produce social rankings counter to Joe's? So perhaps (the objection goes) social choice theory is really about voting processes because it specifies certain causal relations, not just logical relations of actual inputs to outputs.

To rebut this we need to show that even such counterfactual conditions can be met while crucial elements of a voting process are missing. That is, even if counterfactual conditions guarantee that there is some causal relation between preferences and social rankings, more is required for voting processes. What more might be required?

The counterfactual element, we might say, requires that outcomes track preferences, not merely reflect them in actual instances.[17] But this is not enough to catch

---

[17] Philip Pettit explores the connections between counterfactual tracking of citizen interests, control, and democracy in Pettit (2001), and other writings of his cited there.

the idea of an outcome's retrospective procedural value as we ordinarily understand it. To see this, consider a revised version of the case of my thieving Uncle Joe. Suppose that his wife, my Aunt Molly, loves to see me win. When the coin flip goes my way, she cheers up and distracts my uncle with her amorous attentions, which keeps him from stealing my watch. So he only takes my watch, as it happens, when I lose the coin flip and his wife is being no fun. The outcome now tracks the outcome of the coin flip: it reflects the flip in actual instances, and also would have reflected the flip whatever it might have been. He would have taken the watch if he'd won the flip (but not for that reason), and left me the watch if he'd lost the flip (but not for that reason). Still, when my undistracted uncle takes my watch without regard for the outcome of the flip, he is stealing it. Even though the fair procedure (indirectly) caused him to take the watch, his having it is not the outcome of that fair procedure, since the procedure did not cause it in the right way. Retrospective procedural value or justification requires more than tracking the relevant procedural facts (even counterfactually and causally). This point is less arcane than it might sound. It's what lies behind the rather obvious proposition that a law is not justified as an outcome of democratic procedure just by varying (even counterfactually) with the majority of the preferences or votes expressed in such a procedure. There are lots of causal stories that might explain that relation other than democratic production, such as non-democratic links intervening in the causal chain.

We can apply these points to Riker's influential version of normative social choice theory (in Riker 1982). If social choice theory's aggregative rules are, as I claim, substantive standards for the evaluation of outcomes of temporal procedures, then in so far as Riker recommends certain social choice processes, such as certain voting schemes, he would be recommending them on instrumental grounds: their tendency to promote substantively good or just outcomes. Riker's 'fairness conditions' are conditions on an appropriate aggregative principle of substantive justice. We have just seen that they are not sufficient for procedural fairness in the retrospective sense, since meeting them does not require anything recognizable as a collective decision procedure and its outcome. Nor is meeting the usual social choice theory conditions necessary for a collective decision procedure. Citizens could evidently act jointly through a procedure of choosing officials or laws randomly from the set of options (plainly violating at least the Pareto condition).[18] Whether that would be a fair or good procedure is another matter. The point is that its being a collective choice procedure does not depend on its meeting standard social choice theory conditions. Those conditions apply procedure-independent standards of good outcomes.

[18] Henry Richardson's discussion of the idea of joint intentions in his account of democratic authority reflects (and cites much of) the contemporary literature on joint intention and action. The concerns bear little relation to the aggregation rules of social choice theory. See Richardson (2002).

Social choice theory is often held to limit itself to procedural values. But it does no such thing, as is clear once democratic procedures are distinguished from abstract aggregation rules, which are substantive standards for the evaluation of political outcomes. Even though the general social choice theory paradigm retains great interest and importance in many areas, most of the challenges familiar from traditional instrumental accounts of the value of democracy—which substantive standard shall be used, why we should think voting promotes a particular standard better than other arrangement, etc.—remain unaddressed by the application of social choice theory to democracy.[19]

5. Deep Deliberative Democracy

In general terms, deliberative democracy names the idea that political authority depends on a healthy application of practical intelligence in reasonably egalitarian public deliberation. It emphasizes the social processes that form individual attitudes, where social choice theory emphasizes rules for aggregating attitudes (i.e. preferences) that are, for purposes of analysis, taken as given. Deliberative democratic theory also distinctively understands practical rationality as including more than an individual's pursuit of her own aims. Certain claims by other agents are assumed to be unreasonable to ignore. There are these philosophical differences between the two schools as well as political differences. But central strands of both schools present themselves as 'proceduralist' theories, and I turn now to the critique of this claim in the case of deep deliberative democracy.

The popular turn to deliberative democracy was partly a reaction to the influence of the social choice model in normative contexts.[20] Social choice theory takes preferences as given, and does not ask whether they are wise, or ethically good, or

---

[19] Henry Richardson (2002) avoids relying on a supposed capacity of democratic procedures to promote good outcomes, but incorporates a prospective element nonetheless. (For a recent approach that asserts and defends such a capacity, see Goodin 2002.) On Richardson's view, the value of the procedure is still prospective, subordinate in a certain way to the procedure-independent values, the truths, at which it aims, whether or not it tends to get them right. If this gives Richardson's view an advantage over fair proceduralism, it stems from the fact that he does not restrict himself to intrinsic procedural values. His view, then, is on the right side of the division I am drawing. (It would be a separate matter whether his account of the importance of a political 'orientation to the truth' can succeed without any appeal to democracy's epistemic value.)

[20] For several overviews of the deliberative democracy movement, see Bohman and Rehg (1997, 1998) and Freeman (2000). The deliberative democracy literature and the normative social choice theory literature are brought into vigorous engagement in Dryzek (2000, ch. 2).

well considered. It can abstain from these matters and simply address the matter of aggregation of whatever set of preferences one wishes to aggregate: pre-deliberation, post-deliberation, it doesn't matter.

Critics of social choice theory's model of politics have often targeted the quality of individual preferences themselves, and called for more attention to how these preferences are formed.[21] The idea of aggregating individual preferences into a social choice seems misguided, many have thought, when the preferences themselves are the product of misinformation, manipulation, confusion, and ill will. More recently, others have responded to this point simply by arguing that the individual attitudes that should be consulted are those formed under more favourable conditions, such as edifying public political deliberation.

5.1 Habermas

For Jürgen Habermas, there are no standards that loom over the political process, policing its decisions, not even any standard of reason itself. 'We need not confront reason as an alien authority residing somewhere beyond political communication' (Habermas 1996: 285).[22] The only normative standards that apply to political decisions are non-instrumental evaluations of the procedures that produced them—in particular, standards of 'procedural rationality' (1996: 453) based on the power of reason in public political discourse. Any imposition (in theory or practice) of substantive—that is, procedure-independent—political standards would pre-empt the ultimately dialogical basis upon which Habermas thinks political normativity must rest.[23] Habermas claims to eschew procedure-independent standards as much as normative social choice theory does. The result is an approach to political theory in which social institutions are evaluated holistically: do they together constitute a rational process for forming public intentions for guidance of law and government?

On the other hand, Habermas believes, the proper political process cannot be understood independently of the guarantee of certain individual liberties, so it must operate so as to maintain these liberties. This allows a certain standard for directly evaluating outcomes after all: destruction of the relevant liberties would be illegitimate even if it had been decided by the proper procedure. Still, this standard is rooted in the non-instrumental value of a procedure of rational political communication—in a procedure's intrinsic value, not derived from the values it

---

[21] A good example is Sunstein (1991). Sunstein's discussion shows the influence of Elster (1983, 1986). The latter piece is explicitly under the influence of Habermas. Habermas (1996: 181) states this approach clearly.   [22] See also Cronin and De Greiff (1999, esp. 255–6).

[23] See Cronin and De Greiff (1999: 260).

produces or aims at. Habermas's account of proper procedures of rational political communication relies, of course, on what he famously calls the 'ideal speech situation', a hypothetical scenario in which participants are fully informed and unlimited by time, and where the course of deliberation is guided only by the force of reason, not by any other kind of power or influence.[24] Politics is not meant to resemble such an imaginary situation, but, evidently, it ought to have a tendency to produce the same decisions. On this view, then, outcomes are evaluated partly by standards that are independent of the actual instance or token procedure that produced them. This element of Habermas's view is not, then, a retrospective standard, referring back to actual instances of a decision process. It remains proceduralist only in a thinner sense: the prospective standard of protecting basic liberties is meant to be dictated entirely by a conception of political procedures that are to be promoted or maintained. Basic rights or liberties receive their status as constraints on political decisions only in this way, and so are still driven by procedural democratic values in this sense.

A theory could have this sort of constraint on political outcomes, but otherwise confine itself to retrospective evaluation of outcomes: did they arise from proper collective decision procedures? But Habermas's theory does not actually have this structure. It is not proceduralist in that way. The reason is that, according to Habermas, outcomes are legitimate when they *could* have been produced by ideal deliberative procedures.[25] The procedures that set the standard are hypothetical, imaginary. Whether a decision is legitimate or not is always logically independent of the actual procedure that produced it. It is a substantive, procedure-independent standard in this important sense.

The point here is similar to the one I pressed against normative social choice theory's claim to eschew substantive values in favour of intrinsic procedural values only. Recall that once we distinguished between a standard that calls for conformity to an abstract aggregative rule (preference rule) and a standard that calls for decisions to be causally produced by certain actual temporal procedures (voting processes), we saw that it is the former that normative social choice invokes. But then it becomes clear that conformity of outcomes to preference rules is just one among the contending standards by which outcomes might be directly evaluated. Whatever its comparative merits, it is a substantive standard of outcomes, logically independent of their procedural origins.

Deep deliberative democracy judges actual political processes by independent standards too. The reason is that the use of a hypothetical deliberative procedure as the standard for evaluating actual democratic decisions is just one way of holding outcomes to a standard that is logically independent of their actual procedural source. Granted, procedure figures in the ideal standard in a certain way. But it

---

[24] See discussion and citations in Baynes (1992: 112–15).
[25] See Habermas (1979: 186; 1996: 103–4); Elster and Hylland (1986: 31, 34, 259).

should have been antecedently clear that some standards of just outcomes will be, for example, contractualist, involving procedural ideas in that way. Rawls's two principles of justice, for example, are defended on certain grounds involving a hypothetical collective choice procedure: the original position. Nevertheless, they are standards by which outcomes can be evaluated quite apart from the outcomes' actual procedural source, as Rawls says (1995: 176): 'justice is not specified procedurally'. The tendency of democratic procedures to produce outcomes that meet these standards—the principles of justice—is an instrumental value of those procedures, not an intrinsic value, because the standard is logically independent of the actual procedural source.

Deep deliberative democracy, in effect, puts forward one or another contractualist standard for good political choices. Democratic values—values resting in actual democratic procedures—are not, in the end, fundamental and self-sufficient. Just as with normative social choice theory, a substantive outcome standard is often construed as an intrinsically procedural standard, and (non-democratic) substance such as justice or common good is thought to be avoided in a salutary way. Whatever the merits of social choice theory's aggregative substantive outcome standards, or deep deliberative democracy's different contractualist substantive outcome standards, they are substantive outcome standards and go beyond intrinsically procedural features of real democratic institutions.

5.2 Cohen

Joshua Cohen insists that democratic authority is free and self-determining. It is not under any other authority, not even the 'authority' of prior normative standards for better or worse choices. His debt to Habermas is explicit, and both seek to make democratic values the basis of normative political reasoning, not as one set of values among others, but as unrivalled—not in competition with or merely in the service of other, non-democratic values such as welfare, or the basic human rights familiar in the liberal tradition, or justice. Cohen constructs an ideal deliberative procedure, meant to 'highlight the properties that democratic institutions should embody, so far as possible'. The ideal is 'meant to provide a model for institutions to mirror' (Cohen 1997: 22), rather than merely a hypothetical construction in the manner of Rawls's original position. 'Ideal deliberation is *free* [partly] in that . . . the participants regard themselves as bound only by the results of their deliberation and by the preconditions for that deliberation. Their consideration of proposals is not constrained by the authority of prior norms or requirements' (1997: 22).

But there's a wrinkle. Cohen, like Habermas, complicates what looks at first like a clear reliance on the entirely procedural values of ideal democratic deliberation.

For Cohen the fundamental tenet of a deliberative account of democratic legitimacy is the principle that coercive political arrangements and decisions are morally illegitimate unless they can be justified in terms that can be accepted by citizens with the wide range of reasonable moral, religious, and philosophical views likely to emerge in any free society. Violations of this principle would leave some reasonable citizens without a justification in terms they could accept. Cohen argues that this is a violation of specifically democratic values. He writes, 'There are many ways to exclude individuals and groups from the people, but this surely is one' (1996: 103).

Cohen's central claim for our purposes is that this criterion of legitimacy is not some moral right imposed as a constraint on what democracies are morally allowed to do, but rather is itself part and parcel of the democratic ideal. According to Cohen, to impose restrictions on religious liberty under those conditions would be 'a failure of democracy';[26] not an instrumental failure—where proper democracy gets improper results—but a constitutive failure—a case of undemocratic politics. Partly to mark this claim, he calls the principle of legitimacy 'the principle of deliberative inclusion', putting a more democratic cast over the very same principle Rawls had introduced under the name 'the liberal principle of legitimacy' (1993: 137). This latter name, Cohen might seem to say, could misleadingly suggest that liberalism might be pitted against, or at least externally constrain, democracy. According to Cohen, democracy is constrained in no such way.

To defend a view of this kind it is necessary to explain what the value of democratic procedures consists in. It seems to hold that the procedures themselves are part of a society's justice or common good, constitutively rather than instrumentally. But then we need an account of why they should be thought to have such intrinsic value or importance. The intended account is still, overall, procedural rather than substantive in the following sense: once all the democratically motivated constraints are fully respected, the value of democratic procedures is held to be intrinsic in some way and not based on any tendency to promote other values such as justice or common good.

I doubt, in any case, that we should accept Cohen's construal of the Rawlsian criterion of legitimacy (could the arrangement be justified in terms acceptable to all reasonable citizens?) as a properly democratic consideration. It is too hypothetical, and so too independent of a decision's actual procedural source. The idea of democracy is being stretched too thin to be recognizable. If acceptability to all reasonable citizens is the core democratic requirement, then too many arguments count as democracy-based. A principle of democracy must surely assert something

---

[26] Cohen (1996: 103). Gutmann and Thompson (2002) suggest that while substantive principles are not to be avoided, they are also not to be treated as somehow outside of democratic theory properly conceived. Cohen's claim seems to me more ambitious: that the substantive principles that may be appealed to are themselves distinctively democratic values.

like inalienable popular sovereignty, the right of citizens actually to authorize their government, not merely to have a government that is justifiable from their point of view. Hobbes accepted a principle of individualized justifiability, which was surely not a democratic principle.[27] The Cohen–Rawls principle of individualized justifi ability is different from Hobbes's, and it is probably more supportive of a principle of democracy, but it is not inherently a more democratic principle. It is, rather, a certain liberal ideal of justification, one upon which the justification of the principle of democracy can be held to depend. I don't think this is any deficiency. The point is only that it would be misleading to deny it.[28]

As I defined intrinsic democratic proceduralism, then, Cohen does not accept it. He does not understand democracy as essentially procedural. Cohen stays within the value of democracy only by expanding the boundaries of that concept, not by con straining the menu of values to which he wishes to appeal. This is not an indifferent terminological matter, though. On his broader account of the idea of democracy, actual citizens turn out to be under the authority of standards for better or worse decisions (that is, are they justifiable in terms acceptable to all reasonable people?), and not 'free' in the more radical sense that Cohen, as quoted, seems to suggest. My verdict is the same for Cohen's view as it was for Habermas's: Cohen's view, as I understand it, depends for its plausibility on appealing to standards for evaluating political decisions on grounds going beyond whether they stem from or promote actual democratic procedures. His promising to stay entirely within the value of democracy itself could easily conceal this substantive element, though once it is made clear, it is merely terminological whether we should call his further standard of legitimacy a democratic value or not.

6. CONCLUSION

Normative social choice theory and deep deliberative democracy treat democracy as a kind of correspondence between outcomes and certain (reasonable or brute, actual or hypothetical) individual interests of the citizens. They have very different

[27] Hobbes, *Leviathan*; Kavka (1986).
[28] In a recent piece (2002), Cohen attributes this same view to Rawls, and defends it in new detail: laws or policies violating the liberal principle of legitimacy (acceptability to all reasonable citizens) can be criticized on the basis of distinctively democratic values, since there is no 'collective authorization' by the people if this principle is violated. But Cohen is happy to acknowledge that such a principle incorporates 'substantive' or procedure-independent standards. And he rightly denies that this alone would compromise political autonomy. And since he shows that Rawls's view is deeply democratic in two other ways—by requiring democratic political institutions, and by resting on a conception of

conceptions of this correspondence, but both argue for their own as an interpretation of the idea of democratic procedure—as if conformity to a certain pattern of interest satisfaction (or reasonable rejectibility, etc.) is a version of collective rule. I assume that democracy must, in some way, involve rule by the people, and that this is not the same as rule by others in accordance with proper utilitarian or contractualist principles of just outcomes. I do not oppose the appeal to these procedure-independent outcome standards. My point is to see them for what they are: values that go beyond the value of democracy, and values upon which the value of democracy itself probably depends. Normative democratic theory, then, cannot be *radically* democratic if this means that political decisions are to be evaluated entirely according to whether or not they are democratic.

The flight from procedure-independent normative substance that is attempted in normative social choice theory and deep deliberative democracy is, as it turns out, abortive, but the destination is not worthy in any case. Democratic deliberation, and so the democratic process considered as a whole, will probably have to be theoretically accounted for in a way that recognizes that it aims at some values outside itself. Of course, as is true for a philosophical theory of any kind, on any subject, there are significant challenges for a democratic theory of this more substantive sort as well.[29]

REFERENCES

Arneson, Richard (1993).'Democratic Rights at National and Workplace Levels', in D. Copp, J. Hampton, and J. Roemer (eds.), *The Idea of Democracy*. Cambridge: Cambridge University Press.

—— (2001). 'Defending the Purely Instrumental Account of Democratic Legitimacy'. *Journal of Political Philosophy*, 11: 122–32.

Arrow, Kenneth (1963). *Social Choice and Individual Values*, 2nd edn. New Haven: Yale University Press.

—— (1979). 'Values and Collective Decision Making', in Frank Hahn and Martin Hollis (eds.), *Philosophy and Economic Theory*. Oxford: Oxford University Press.

society as comprised of free equals—I fail to see what is gained by construing this principle of legitimacy, which says nothing about any actual acts of willing, or voting, or authorizing, as a conception democratic collective authorization. Stretching the idea of democracy in order to reach this view risks giving the impression that if the principle could not be accounted for democratically it would be incompatible with democracy, or in some other way inappropriate or unavailable. But Cohen's own discussion is ammunition against that conclusion.

[29] This research was supported by a sabbatical leave from Brown University and a Harsanyi Fellowship at the Social and Political Theory programme at the Research School for Social Sciences at Australian National University. I appreciate the discussions of these ideas I had with inhabitants (temporary and permanent) of the latter programme during my stay in 2001–2, especially John Dryzek, Bob Goodin, Gerry Mackie, Philip Pettit, and Michael Smith. Thanks also to Corey Brettschneider and John Tomasi for discussion of a late draft.

—— (1982). 'Current Development in the Theory of Social Choice', in Brian Barry and Russell Hardin (eds.), *Rational Man and Irrational Society?* Beverly Hills, Calif.: Sage.

—— Sen, Amartya, and Suzumura, Kotaro (eds.) (1996). *Social Choice Re-examined*, i. New York: St Martin's Press.

Barry, Brian, and Hardin, Russell (eds.) (1982). *Rational Man and Irrational Society?* Beverly Hills, Calif.: Sage.

Baynes, Kenneth (1992). *The Normative Grounds of Social Criticism*. New York: State University of New York Press.

Bohman, James, and Rehg, William (1997). Introduction to Bohman and Rehg (eds.), *Deliberative Democracy: Essays on Reason and Politics*. Cambridge, Mass.: MIT Press.

—— (1998). 'The Coming of Age of Deliberative Democracy'. *Journal of Political Philosophy*, 4: 418–44.

Buchanan, Allan (2002). 'Political Legitimacy and Democracy'. *Ethics*, 112: 689–719.

Christiano, Thomas (1990). 'Freedom, Consensus, and Equality in Collective Decision Making'. *Ethics*, 101: 151–81.

—— (1993). 'Social Choice and Democracy', in David Copp, Jean Hampton, and John Roemer (eds.), *The Idea of Democracy*. Cambridge: Cambridge University Press.

Cohen, Joshua (1996). 'Procedure and Substance in Democratic Theory', in Seyla Benhabib (ed.), *Democracy and Difference*. Princeton: Princeton University Press.

—— (1997). 'Deliberation and Democratic Legitimacy', in Alan Hamlin and Philip Pettit (eds.), *The Good Polity*. New York: Blackwell.

—— (2002). 'For a Democratic Society', in Samuel Freeman (ed.), *The Cambridge Companion to Rawls*. Cambridge: Cambridge University Press.

Coleman, Jules, and Ferejohn, John (1986). 'Democracy and Social Choice'. *Ethics*, 97: 6–25.

Cronin, Ciarin, and De Greiff, Pablo (eds.) (1999). *The Inclusion of the Other*. Cambridge, Mass.: MIT Press.

Dryzek, John (2000). *Deliberative Democracy and Beyond*. Oxford: Oxford University Press.

—— (forthcoming). 'Democratic Political Theory', in Gerald Gaus and Chandran Kukathas (eds.), *The Handbook of Political Theory*. Beverly Hills, Calif.: Sage.

—— and List, Christian (2003). 'Social Choice Theory and Deliberative Democracy: A Reconciliation'. *British Journal of Political Science*, 33: 1–2.

Elster, Jon (1983). *Sour Grapes: Studies in the Subversion of Rationality*. Cambridge: Cambridge University Press.

—— (1986). 'The Market and the Forum: Three Varieties of Political Theory', in J. Elster and A. Hylland (eds.), *Foundations of Social Choice Theory*. Cambridge: Cambridge University Press.

—— and Hylland, Aanund (eds.) (1986). *Foundations of Social Choice Theory*. New York: Cambridge University Press.

Estlund, David (2002). Introduction to Estlund (ed.), *Democracy*. London: Blackwell.

Freeman, Samuel (2000). 'Deliberative Democracy: A Sympathetic Comment'. *Philosophy and Public Affairs*, 29: 371–418.

Goodin, Robert (2002). *Reflective Democracy*. Oxford: Oxford University Press.

Gutmann, A., and Thompson, D. (2002). 'Deliberative Democracy Beyond Process'. *Journal of Philosophy*, 10: 153–74.

Habermas, Jurgen (1979). *Communication and the Evolution of Society*. Boston, Mass.: Beacon Press.

—— (1996). *Between Facts and Norms*. Cambridge, Mass.: MIT Press.

Hardin, Russell (1993). 'Public Choice vs. Democracy', in David Copp, Jean Hampton, and John Roemer (eds.), *The Idea of Democracy*. Cambridge: Cambridge University Press.

Hobbes, Thomas (1650). *Leviathan*.

Kavka, Gregory (1986). *Hobbesian Moral and Political Theory*. Princeton: Princeton University Press.

Mackie, Gerry (2003). *Democracy Defended*. Cambridge: Cambridge University Press.

Pettit, Philip (2001). *A Theory of Freedom*. Cambridge: Polity Press.

Rawls, John (1971). *A Theory of Justice*. Cambridge, Mass.: Harvard University Press.

—— (1993). *Political Liberalism*. New York: Columbia University Press.

—— (1995). 'Reply to Habermas'. *Journal of Philosophy*, 92: 132–80.

—— (1999). 'The Idea of Public Reason Revisited', in Rawis, *The Law of Peoples*. Cambridge, Mass.: Harvard University Press.

Richardson, Henry (2002). *Democratic Autonomy: Public Reasoning About the Ends of Policy*. Oxford: Oxford University Press.

Riker, William (1982). *Liberalism Against Populism*. San Francisco: W.H. Freeman.

Risse, Mathias (2001). 'Arrow's Theorem, Indeterminacy, and Multiplicity Reconsidered'. *Ethics*, 111: 706–34.

Sen, Amartya (1970). *Collective Choice and Social Welfare*. San Francisco: Holden-Day.

—— (1997). *Choice, Welfare and Measurement*. Cambridge, Mass.: Harvard University Press.

Simmons, A. John (1999). 'Justification and Legitimacy'. *Ethics*, 109: 739–71.

Sunstein, C. R. (1991). 'Preferences and Politics'. *Philosophy and Public Affairs*, 21: 3–38.

Suzumura, Kotaro (2002). 'Introduction', in K. J. Arrow, A. K. Sen, and K. Suzumura (eds.), Handbook of Social Choice and Welfare, i. Amsterdam: Elsevier.

CHAPTER 9

FEMINISM IN PHILOSOPHY

RAE LANGTON

INTRODUCTION

It has been said (at least once) that philosophy leaves everything as it is. Feminists, on the other hand, don't leave everything as it is; we are always wanting things to be different, and better. So what exactly have feminists to do with philosophy? The idea that philosophy leaves everything as it is conveys a picture of philosophy as somehow neutral, cut off from the action, unreceptive to change from, and unproductive of change to, the world beyond its walls. If philosophy is inert, feminists might as well leave it alone. But we don't. Why not?

In thinking about why not, it's worth noting that the slogan could suggest something else: not that philosophy is inert (as Wittgenstein may have meant; 1958, §124), but that it's conservative. Philosophy is not unreceptive to the world outside; everything does not, after all, leave philosophy as it is. Philosophy is open to influence, bears the marks of its makers, shows signs of the soil from which it has sprung. Philosophy is made in a social world, and a world that excludes women might leave signs of that exclusion in philosophy, and make philosophy an agent of that exclusion. Philosophy might act as an obstinate weight, a resistance to change, 'leaving everything as it is' as a dragging presence in the social world, not a walled-off absence from it. Then it would not be irrelevant to feminism. If philosophy were to manifest a political illness, and help perpetuate it, then feminist diagnosis and remedy might be called for—if remedy is possible. Pessimists might view philosophy's prognosis as bleak enough to rule out remedy, but such pessimism, I'll be assuming, is unwarranted.

I shall be asking how feminism might illuminate philosophy, and indeed vice versa. My aim is not so much to survey the immense continent of feminist philosophical research, as to display, and occasionally instantiate, some small parts of it. In thinking about how feminism has contributed to philosophy, it will be worth looking at two rather general ideas: the idea of *dualism*, and the idea of *androcentrism*. In thinking about how philosophy has contributed to feminism, it will be worth looking at one rather specific idea: the idea of *treating someone as an object*.

These limitations seem narrow enough, I expect, and in practice they will be even narrower than they antecedently seem. In considering dualism, I shall focus on one argument by Susan James, in the metaphysics of personal identity and survival. In considering anthropocentrism, I shall focus on one argument by Elizabeth Lloyd, in the philosophy of science, prompted by a debate in evolutionary biology about the origin of the female orgasm. In considering the idea of 'treating someone as an object', I shall focus on one elucidation of it by Martha Nussbaum, according to which someone can be 'treated as an object' by (among other things) having their autonomy denied. In a constructive spirit, I try to take her account further, looking particularly at that issue of autonomy denial. If the goal of the earlier sections is chiefly to display what I take to be some fruitful conversations between feminism and philosophy, the goal of this last section goes further, in a way that (I hope) more actively contributes to that ongoing conversation. I shall be interested in a question that at first sight looks a nonsense: whether someone might be 'treated as an object' not just by having their autonomy *denied*, but by having their autonomy *affirmed*. As it turns out, the question is not a nonsense, and we shall see that it matters to a number of concerns, both philosophical and feminist.

In the end we shall see that it isn't quite true that philosophy 'leaves everything as it is', in either of the senses mentioned at the outset. Philosophy is not inevitably walled off, and irrelevant; and even if it is sometimes a dragging, conservative presence, it needn't be. Feminism brings a radicalizing energy to philosophical inquiry, and philosophy returns the favour, in its own way.

Many philosophers have ascribed to philosophy a power of demolishing prejudice, destroying 'the habit of holding on to old opinions', as Descartes's meditator put it (Descartes 1641: 34); and there is no doubt that pioneer feminists found liberation in philosophy, even Descartes's philosophy. Cartesian method requires close scrutiny of prejudice. Cartesian dualism, whatever its defects, requires all of us, women included, to identify ourselves as essentially *thinking* beings—a significant attainment for creatures overly identified with their bodies. The emphasis on method and on mind are both evident in Mary Astell's work, as she probed that old opinion of the '*Natural Inferiority* of our Sex, which our Masters lay down as . . . Self-Evident and Fundamental'. She wrote:

Error, be it as antient as it may, [cannot] ever plead Prescription against Truth. And since the only way to remove all Doubts, to answer all Objections, and to give the Mind entire Satisfaction, is not by *Affirming*, but by *Proving*, so that every one may see with their own Eyes, and Judge according to the best of their own Understandings, [the author] hopes it is no presumption to insist on this Natural Right of Judging for her self . . . Allow us then as many Glasses as you please to help our Sight, and as many good Arguments as you can afford to Convince our Understandings: but don't exact of us we beseech you, to affirm that we see such things as are only the Discovery of Men who have quicker Senses; or that we understand and Know what we have by Hear-say only; for to be so excessively Complaisant is neither to see nor to understand. (Astell 1700: 9–10)

Astell advanced the cause of feminism through philosophical method, showing not just absence of proof but outright contradiction in many 'old opinions' about women. 'If *all Men are born free*,' she asked, 'how is it that all Women are born slaves'? (1700, p. 18.). And she drew from Cartesian dualism two feminist morals, a teleological and a practical. When a woman is a meditator, and discovers her nature as a thing that thinks, she discovers something about her purpose in life: 'a Rational Mind is too noble a Being to be Made for the Sake and Service of any Creature. The Service [a woman] at any time becomes oblig'd to pay to a Man, is only a Business by the Bye. Just as it may be any Man's Business and Duty to keep Hogs' (1700: 11).[1] *Hogs?* The humour is classic Astell, but it has a point. A man whose essence is to think may still owe duties to hogs, and a woman whose essence is to think may still owe duties to a man. But swineherdly duties and wifely duties are 'Business by the Bye', and not what human beings are made for. Her practical conclusion was radical, and at the time unthinkable for most of her readers. If women are creatures whose essence is to think, there should be institutions to foster and develop women's thinking: in short, colleges for women.

Astell did her philosophy as a feminist, and she did her feminism as a philosopher, finding no tension between her philosophy and her feminism. That doesn't mean there was no tension, of course. Feminists in recent times have found in Cartesian philosophy a vivid example of a philosophy implicitly hostile to women; and in thinking about how feminism can contribute to philosophy, dualism is our first port of call.

---

[1] The passage continues: 'he was not Made for this, but if he hires himself out to such an Employment, he ought conscientiously to perform it'. For more about Astell, see Perry (1986). On feminism and Cartesian rationalism, see Atherton (1993).

1. DUALISM

The problem signs are there, say feminist critics, even in the method: that strange fantasy of isolation, the lonely stove-heated room (but who is tending the fire?), the meditator doubting the existence of his hands and body (but who is bringing the meals?). The signs are there, they say, in the fantasy of autonomy, the denial of human relationship, the priority of the 'I', the epistemological ambition. Look, look, I can do it *all by myself*! My existence, my essence, my knowledge—I can do them all on my own! (With just a *little* help from God.) It is above all in the dualism that the signs are manifest: the denigration of the senses, the denigration of matter, the divorce of mind from matter. So feminist critique of Descartes has taken many forms, exploring his metaphors, putting the meditator on the analyst's couch, reading reasons as symptoms, reading arguments as the workings of subconscious and deeply misogynistic desire (see Irigaray 1985; Flax 1983).

Whatever the merits of this critique of Descartes himself, one might be tempted to think it anachronistic. How much investment do philosophers have in dualism these days? In contemporary philosophy of mind, dualism is the exception, not the rule. After all, it's not as if one needs a feminist agenda to suspect Descartes might be wrong. There are plenty of reasons beyond political reasons, beyond psychoanalytic reasons, for supposing Descartes mistaken, and it is no accident that dualists are fewer than they were. Yet feminists maintain a continuing interest in dualism, extending well beyond its most famous historical champion. Why?

Feminists have been bothered by a kind of dualistic thinking that informs many philosophical projects, Cartesian or not. Feminists have claimed that there is something gendered about oppositions between body and mind, between emotion and reason. Mind and reason, they say, have been associated with the masculine; body and emotion with the feminine; and these associations, overt in the work of past philosophers, continue covertly even in philosophy today. Faced with a gendered opposition between, say, mind and body, it is not enough to say that *women have minds too*, as Astell did eloquently enough. One needs also to question the division that makes mind so different from body, and valorizes mind at the body's expense. (*'Minds, yes'*, colleges for women, yes. But that doesn't have to mean *'Bodies, no'*.) So a feminist focus on Cartesian themes has contributed to a range of philosophical debates. A dubious strain of 'methodological solipsism' has been observed in political philosophy by a number of critics, including Alison Jaggar (1983): a dream of autonomy gone mad, with its assumption that something is only worth doing if you do it all by yourself. An analogous problem has been noted in moral epistemology by Karen Jones (1999)—an assumption that moral knowledge must be achieved *all by yourself*, not something that can be got 'second-hand', by way of testimony from others better situated than you are.

Doing justice to the range of feminist contributions on this topic is impossible, so keeping to the principle that it's better to display than survey, let us take a look at a recent, and representative, argument, in metaphysics. Susan James (2000) has tried to show how dualistic thinking is present even in supposedly anti-dualistic arguments, tracing it in contemporary analytic work on personal identity and survival.[2] On a traditional Cartesian way of thinking, a person at one time is identical with a person at a later time if and only if they are the very same mental substance. This Cartesian view has been opposed by Derek Parfit and others who say that what matters is not personal identity, but survival; and that a person may survive at a later time without being identical to what she was before. Survival, unlike identity, can come in degrees, so this on the face of things allows for a more flexible notion of the self. What interests James in this debate are the criteria philosophers use in thinking about survival. She observes how contributors to the debate have insisted upon a sharp distinction between two criteria, those of psychological continuity and physical continuity. To discover which of these is the relevant criterion for survival, we are asked to imagine the psychological continuity without physical continuity, and vice versa. To take the 'transplant' thought experiment: imagine that a person's memories and character are transplanted from one body into a different one. Where is the person now? The alleged intuitive answer is that the person is where the character and memories are, not where the previous body is. And so we are expected to conclude that the criterion for survival is psychological continuity, not physical continuity.

Now although this way of thinking is explicitly developed as an alternative to Cartesian dualism, its stark opposition between the physical and psychological makes it, in James's eyes, an immediate target of suspicion. The opposition helps to sustain a 'symbolically masculine' conception of personhood, says James. Transplant thought experiments tend to regard the body as an exchangeable container or receptacle for character or memory. Some philosophers acknowledge that this must be an oversimplification, that one cannot have body-swapping with just anybody, and still preserve psychological continuity: body-swapping between a man and a woman, between an emperor and a peasant, might fail to preserve all aspects of psychology. But James observes that those noting this problem tend to dismiss it. They say 'Let us forget this'; or they stipulate that the swapped bodies be extremely similar; or they simply assert that character can survive large and disastrous alterations to body-type—that someone can still be brave, say, even if they lose the physical capacity to do daring things. James is sceptical. Not all character traits are so readily maintainable, she says: courage, perhaps, but what of physical dexterity, or delight in one's sexuality? Changing the body might well change these

---

[2] In identifying this dualism, James is drawing upon the work of many other feminist theorists, most notably, perhaps, Genevieve Lloyd (1984). The reader is referred to James's first footnote (2000: 45) for other important references.

supposedly psychological traits. Furthermore, the assumption that continuity of memory can be had without continuity of body is at odds with the phenomenology of memory, she says: some memories, including memories of trauma and violence, are experienced at least partly *in the body*, or so survivors report (see e.g. Brison 1987). Applying the criterion of psychological continuity depends on a kind of laundering of memories and character traits, washing away all traces of body.

There are important questions, says James, about how body image, and recognition by others, can matter to who you are. According to some psychoanalytic theorists, a person's sense of their own body, as they take it to be represented by others (or as represented in mirror reflection), is a part or precondition of psychic integrity. And whether or not that is true, it may still be that body image and recognition by others both matter to one's sense of self—that who we are (or take ourselves to be?) can depend in part on who we are recognized and affirmed by others to be. Social recognition is mediated, at least in part, by perception of body. Suppose, says James, that the memories and character of a female fashion model are transplanted into the body of a male garage mechanic. What becomes of her body image now? Even on the assumption that friends and lovers believe her story, will they give her the kind of recognition and affirmation they did before? Some philosophers have insisted on the irrelevance of body to questions of this kind. Bodies are convenient tags for our recognition of other persons, and that's all. We use bodies, says Anthony Quinton, as

convenient recognition devices enabling us to locate the persisting characters and memory complexes...which we love or like. It would be upsetting if a complex with which we were emotionally involved came to have a monstrous or repulsive physical appearance...But that our concern and affection would follow the character and memory complex...is surely clear. (1975: 60)

James is again sceptical. That way of thinking fails to allow that a person's ability to sustain continuity might sometimes depend on other people recognizing and affirming them as embodied in a particular way.

When we imagine the memories and traits of a person being transplanted from one body to another, and imagine that as survival, we are imagining the person feeling much the same as before, committed, perhaps, to similar projects as before, committed to their own future just as before, and maintaining, perhaps, the very relationships they maintained before. But if the new body is sufficiently different, all that is surely up for grabs, says James. Many memories and traits will simply fail to survive the translation, the person may lose the recognition they enjoyed from others, may lose their projects, and lose emotional investment in the life they find themselves in. Some philosophers may insist there is still survival: but why go to such lengths to protect psychological continuity from the effects of the body and the rest of the world? Doesn't this begin to look just a little like Descartes's solipsistic meditator, so eager to wall off the world and the body, so eager to hold on to the mind as the real self? James concludes that when theorists of personal identity focus on psychological continuity as the stronghold of the self, 'they secure only a self which would in other circumstances be regarded as pathologically disturbed' (2000: 45): and in explaining why that could possibly seem attractive, we must go, she says, to the gendered structure of philosophical thinking.

2. ANDROCENTRISM

If ways of thinking are 'androcentric' when they reflect 'an orientation geared to specifically or typically male interests or male lives' (as Elizabeth Anderson 1995: 70 puts it[3]) then perhaps some kinds of dualistic thinking are androcentric. But if dualism is one possible manifestation of androcentrism, it is by no means the only one. One famous feminist contribution to ethics has been the charge of androcentrism brought by Carole Gilligan against the so-called 'Justice' perspective, a standard of moral maturity described by the developmental psychologist Lawrence Kohlberg. The capacity to assess moral situations in terms of impartial universal principles, reasons, and rights was described by Kohlberg as the pinnacle of moral development, and by this standard (itself identified through study of all-male samples) girls and women were found to be less morally mature than boys and men.

Gilligan accepted (controversially) that women's 'moral voice' is different, citing the following kind of example. Confronted with the question 'When responsibility to oneself and responsibility to others conflicts, how should one choose?', a male subject, Jake, responds, 'You go about one-fourth to the others and three-fourths to yourself'. Amy, on the other hand, responds,

Well, it really depends on the situation. If you have a responsibility with somebody else, then you should keep it to a certain extent, but to the extent that it is really going to hurt you or stop you from doing something that you really, really want, then I think maybe you should put yourself first. But if it is your responsibility to somebody really close to you, you've just got to decide in that situation which is more important, yourself, or that other person, and like I said, it really depends on what kind of person you are and how you feel about the other person or persons involved. (Gilligan 1982: 36–7)

Is Amy different? Yes. More long-winded? Hesitant? Perhaps. Immature? Decidedly not, according to Gilligan. Jake has a neat and crude rule, expressive of the 'Justice'

---

[3] See also Anderson's contributions on feminist epistemology in the *Stanford Encyclopedia of Philosophy*, <http://plato.stanford.edu> and Saul (2003: 256).

perspective. The voice of Amy expresses an ethic of 'Care' rather than justice, according to Gilligan (1982: 36–7), emphasizing responsibility, relationships, and the particularity of situation—a different voice, but by no means inferior.[4]

Androcentrism is as much at home in epistemology and philosophy of science as it is in ethics, and here again an example will have to serve to illustrate the point. Looking at a case study in evolutionary biology, Elisabeth Lloyd (1993) has shown how androcentrism can influence the pursuit of scientific knowledge: it can influence the framing of a question, and also the search for an answer to it.[5] The question she considers is one that is interesting and prima facie puzzling for evolutionary biologists, and indeed for anyone with an ounce of curiosity: namely, *why do women have orgasms?* In the context of evolutionary biology, the question is taken to imply a contrast, first between the situation of women and that of men; and second, between the situation of women and that of other female primates. Men have orgasms, but that presents no 'why' question for evolutionary biologists: it isn't hard to see why male orgasm might have 'adaptive value', as an obvious aid to reproducing one's genes, a powerful motivator for intercourse. But women don't need orgasms to reproduce. Moreover, the females of non-human primates get by well enough without them, or so it has been said. Hence the question: why do women have orgasms—given that women *do have* them (unlike other female primates), and *don't need* them (unlike men)?

In looking for answers, theorists looked for a link between orgasm and direct reproductive success, arguing that as a matter of fact women *do need* orgasms for reproductive success, or (more lamely) that at any rate orgasms can help.

Desmond Morris had one idea. Women walk upright, unlike other female primates, and that is why women have orgasms. As our hominid ancestors abandoned their knuckle-scraping ways and began to walk tall, they were faced with a new reproductive problem, posed by the simple force of gravity. The apes might take their post-coital promenade with impunity, precious sperm tucked safely inside; but for the biped human who too hastily arose for a stroll—alas, she risked losing all. Cue the female orgasm, as a helpful anti-gravity device:

If a female of our own species were so unmoved by the experience of copulation that she too was likely to get up and wander off immediately afterwards... [u]nder the simple influence of gravity the seminal fluid would flow back down the vaginal tract and much of it would be lost. There is therefore... a great advantage in any reaction that tends to keep the

---

[4] Discussed in Saul (2003: 208–9). Saul also reviews studies which suggest that most of the alleged differences disappear when adjustments are made for subjects' educational achievements. (I might add that, personally, I've never been quite sure why Jake's response is supposed to express Justice rather than, say, Egoism.)

[5] For extended development of the argument, see Lloyd (2005). Lloyd's example is also an important topic for Saul in her (2003, ch. 8: 'Feminism, Science and Bias'), where it receives an excellent discussion, and my description here is partly indebted to that of Saul. For discussion of a different kind of androcentrism in biology, with a focus on metaphors of control and agency in the gene, see Keller (1993).

female horizontal when the male ejaculates and stops copulation. The violent response of female orgasm, leaving the female sexually satiated and exhausted, has precisely this effect. (Morris 1967: 79)

According to Lloyd, Morris's theory was taken up by a number of later theorists including Gordon Gallup and Susan Suarez (1983), who said in its defence that 'the average individual requires about 5 minutes of repose before returning to a normal state after orgasm'.

There is a more widely accepted answer than Morris's anti-gravity theory, citing the adaptive role of orgasm in 'pair-bonding', which increases an organism's reproductive success. Offspring raised by heterosexually pair-bonded parents stand a greater chance of survival, as parents assist each other in child-rearing. Orgasm evolved for women because it supplied reward and motivation to engage in frequent intercourse, which in turn cemented the pair-bond, which in turn promoted reproductive success.

What, if anything, is androcentric about the shape of this question and its answers? To the extent that the question is supposed to be about why women, *unlike other primates*, have orgasms, it rests on a false presupposition. Unlike other primates? Female bonobos, pygmy chimpanzees, and stump-tailed macaques have wild sex lives: they scream with enjoyment as they practise what primatologists call 'genito-genital rubbing', they mount each other to stimulate themselves to orgasm. Such behaviour was for a considerable time not noticed as sexual at all, because it does not involve interaction with other males, does not correlate with hormonal oestrus, and is apparently of no reproductive significance. Instead such behaviour was seen as ' "greeting" behaviour, or "appeasement" behaviour, or "reassurance" behaviour, or "reconciliation" behaviour . . . or "food exchange" behaviour—almost anything, it seems, besides pleasurable sexual behaviour' (Begemihl 1999, quoted in Saul 2003: 235).[6] So androcentrism (among other biases) contributes to the shaping of a flawed question.[7]

What of the answers? If the question wrongly supposes that women are *unlike other primates* in experiencing orgasm at all, the answers wrongly suppose that women are *like men* in *how* they experience orgasm. The anti-gravity theory and the pair-bond theory both assume that women reliably achieve orgasm through penetrative heterosexual intercourse; the anti-gravity theory assumes in addition

---

[6] Lloyd likewise discusses the invisibility to theorists of most sexual activity among female primates (1993: 141–2); and, where visible, its devaluation, e.g. by a researcher of female orgasm among stump-tailed macaques, whose recording equipment was triggered by the *male's* increasing heart rate. When reminded that for this species the vast majority of orgasms occurred during sex among females alone, the reply was that he was only interested in the important orgasms.

[7] Other possible biases: the assumption that sex must be heterosexual (homosexual male behaviour may have been similarly ignored); and the adaptationist assumption that traits must themselves have adaptive advantage, rather than being, for example, side-effects of traits that have such advantage. These other biases are both discussed by Lloyd and Saul.

that women collapse, exhausted and appropriately horizontal, when they achieve it. Both sets of theorists blithely cited the then available clinical evidence: but that evidence flatly contradicts their assumptions, and on both counts, according to Lloyd.

The studies show that there is for women a significant 'orgasm–intercourse discrepancy', as Lloyd calls it. Only 20–35 per cent of women always (or almost always) experience orgasm with unassisted intercourse; around 30 per cent never do (Lloyd 1993: 144–5; she cites Hite 1976; Kinsey *et al.* 1953; and for cross-cultural comparison, Davenport 1977). *Not* to have an orgasm from unassisted intercourse is the experience of most women, most of the time, says Lloyd (1993: 144): 'not to put too fine a point on it, if orgasm is an adaptation which is a reward for engaging in frequent intercourse, it does not seem to work very well'. Lloyd allows that the orgasm–intercourse discrepancy is compatible with there being some selective advantage after all to female orgasm. But there is at the very least a prima facie problem that the anti-gravity and the pair-bonding theorists need to address; for if a trait is supposed to have evolved as an adaptation, yet is rarely used in its supposedly adaptive context, that calls for an explanation. Androcentrism manifests itself in the fact that it did not cross their minds to address it, notwithstanding their access to the relevant studies.

The anti-gravity theory of female orgasm attributes to women in addition a distinctive experience of orgasm's after-effects: the female is 'sexually satiated and exhausted', she needs to stay 'horizontal', she needs 'about 5 minutes' of 'repose'. Readers might not be wholly surprised to learn that the studies cited in support of these claims were studies of male sexual experience. (According to Lloyd 1993: 146, 148, Morris cites the Masters and Johnson 1966 studies of male sexual response; Gallup and Suarez cite the Kinsey *et al.* 1948 studies of male sexual response.) Not all women are satiated and exhausted after orgasm. On the contrary, 47 per cent in one survey did not feel that a single orgasm was always satisfying to them. Many women have (unlike men) the desire and capacity for more than one orgasm, without a significant break, sometimes (according to some studies) five or six within a matter of minutes, a capacity linked to the fact that all women tend, after orgasm, to return to the so-called 'plateau' phase of excitement, rather than the pre-aroused state (as men do) (for the 47 per cent figure, Lloyd cites Hite 1976: 417, and for the remainder Kinsey *et al.* 1953: 375–6 and Masters and Johnson 1966: 65).

It seems that androcentrism contributes to the shape of these flawed answers, then, as well as to the flawed question: for these explanatory hypotheses appear to reflect 'an orientation geared to specifically or typically male interests or male lives', as Anderson's phrase has it. We are left, though, with two questions, one for the philosopher of science, and one for the merely curious. I shall take a brief look at both.

If androcentrism can affect the practice of science at all these different levels, including the collecting of data, and the drawing up and evaluating of hypotheses, there is a question, first, about how philosophy of science should respond. Is there, or should there be, a distinctively feminist philosophy of science? Among feminists, various affirmative answers have been given, though all agree that the fact that women have been left out has hurt science (and hurt women); and the contribution of women can somehow help science (and help women). Feminist standpoint theory says that women can make a special contribution to knowledge: given their relative outsider-status and powerlessness, women occupy a relatively privileged epistemic position (comparable in certain respects to that of the workers, in Marxist theory)—a distinctive standpoint achievable, to a degree, by anyone willing to start their thought from women's lives (see e.g. Hartsock 1983; Harding 1993; Jaggar 1983). Helen Longino argues, however, that the issue is not so much the specialness of the standpoint, but rather the need for *diversity* in a scientific community. Scientific objectivity itself is not a property of an individual scientist or a particular theory, but of a scientific *community*: it results from the critical interactions of its diverse groups and members (including women), with all their different assumptions and different interests. Louise Antony responds that even individuals can learn to become more objective, so objectivity cannot just be a property of communities. Moreover, the goal is not to eliminate bias (for bias is inevitable and in her opinion sometimes healthy), but to discover which biases are good because they lead to truth, and which are bad because they lead to error. Feminism can contribute to a kind of naturalized epistemology by helping to discover, through study and experience, which biases lead to truth and which to error; and it will be particularly alert to androcentric biases leading to error in, for example, the work of evolutionary theorists of women's sexuality.

For the merely curious, there remains the original question, *why do women have orgasms?* Lloyd's own view is that the demand for an adaptationist answer to the 'why' question is misguided. There is no direct teleological answer. The female orgasm is an 'evolutionary freebie'. Women have orgasms because men need them to reproduce; and, from a developmental and embryological perspective, it is handy to make men and women somewhat alike. Men have nipples merely as a developmental side-effect of women's reproductive needs, but men don't need them. Women have orgasms merely as a developmental side-effect of men's reproductive needs, but women don't need them. Lloyd finds plausible this developmental hypothesis, which was initially proposed by Donald Symons (1979). Other feminists, though, have charged this hypothesis too with androcentrism. Look at that 'merely', they say. Surely that is being dismissive of female sexuality, denying the significance of female pleasure. Not necessarily, says Lloyd—indeed, not at all, unless you think (heaven forbid!) that significance is tied to reproductive advantage. The hypothesis is, on the contrary, emancipatory.

Think, after all, of our other evolutionary freebies. Take music, for instance: the ability we all have to make and enjoy music is 'merely' a happy by-product of cognitive abilities whose direct reproductive advantage lay elsewhere. But there's no real 'merely' about music: music is none the worse for its evolutionary by-product status, and some might say it is the better for it. Female sexuality would be none the worse either, and may be the better. As Lloyd says (1993: 149), 'the realm formerly belonging to the reproductive drive would now be open to much, much more'.[8] From this evolutionary perspective on orgasm, it may be the boys who want to make babies; but the girls just wanna have fun.

We have been thinking so far about how feminism might illuminate philosophy, focusing on two general ideas (and some particular applications) that have been central to feminist critique, namely the ideas of dualism, and of androcentrism. There is the converse question of how philosophy might illuminate feminism, a topic equally resistant to easy summary. But as we observed at the beginning, feminist philosophers seem to have had little trouble in putting together their feminism and their philosophy. Even Cartesian dualism could, in the hands of a Mary Astell, produce arguments for women's equality and women's education. More generally, feminist critiques that complain of dualism and androcentrism in philosophy very often draw upon other sorts of philosophy to serve their critique, and to construct better alternatives. Antony, as we just saw, finds a Quinean naturalized epistemology to be particularly congenial to a feminist philosophy of science, offering space for an empirical investigation into the biases that help or hinder.

Feminists have not hesitated to mine philosophy in their efforts to understand better the problems that bother them, as feminists. The idea of a speech act, for example, has been applied to topics that would not, in his wildest nightmares, have crossed J. L. Austin's own mind. The idea of speech that is not 'only words' (to borrow Catharine MacKinnon's phrase) has proved a fertile one for feminists keen to explore some hard and interesting questions. How is gender itself constructed? Judith Butler sees performativity in all social sayings and doings: beginning with that potent exclamation at birth—'It's a girl!'—our utterances never merely report gender, but actively construct it (see e.g. Butler 1990, 1997). There are some specific political questions: how might pornography subordinate women? If speech is a kind of act, and pornography is speech, there is a question about the kind of speech act pornography is. Perhaps it is speech that, as illocutionary act, subordinates women. Under what conditions does someone have freedom of speech? If speech is illocution, then in Austinian terms, it involves not just noises but uptake, a kind of recognition on the part of hearers: so freedom of speech might require not just the minimal conditions for uttering words, but the conditions for being appropriately heard.[9] Some feminists have used speech act theory to address a very basic question about language: what is the fundamental concept of linguistic meaning? Jennifer

---

[8] Feminists who criticize the developmental view: Hrdy (1999: 165); Caulfield (1985).

[9] These arguments are both developed in Langton (1993), drawing upon ideas implicit in work by Catharine MacKinnon. See also Mary Kate McGowan (2003). The idea that free speech might include freedom to perform illocutionary acts is also developed by Jennifer Hornsby, e.g. in Hornsby (1995) and Hornsby and Langton (1998).

Hornsby (2000) argues that the most basic idea is that of *saying something to someone*, and it involves hearers as well as speakers. These last two applications of Austinian ideas connect with a more general feminist opposition to atomism: one should not assume that we are self-sufficient speakers any more than that we are self-sufficient Cartesian knowers.

In considering more closely how philosophy might illuminate feminism, I want to home in now, by way of illustration and more, upon an idea from moral philosophy that has been taken up with great effect by feminists.

3. TREATING SOMEONE AS AN OBJECT

The thought that there might be something wrong with treating someone 'as an object' existed in philosophy long before feminism got hold of it, gaining one of its most famous expressions in Kant's work. For Kant, moral wrongdoing consists in the failure to treat humanity 'always ... as an end, never merely as a means', a failure to respect that humanity 'by virtue of [which] we are not for sale at any price' (Kant 1785: 429; 1797: 435). This historically Kantian idea has gained new impetus in recent applications by feminist thinkers, who have observed its relevance to oppression, and to the varied ways that women might have been treated as a means only, and sometimes put up for sale.[10] For feminists there is a focus on treatment encountered by women, and a claim that women's oppression (partly) consists in women's being treated 'as objects': Catharine MacKinnon says, 'To be sexually objectified means having a social meaning imposed on your being that defines you as to be sexually used ... and then using you that way' (1991: 122).

That notion of sexual 'use' echoes the Kantian stricture against treating a person as a mere means or instrument. Kant himself thought that sexual relationships presented special dangers about the 'use' of the other person, as Barbara Herman (1993) has emphasized, pointing out the common ground shared by Kant and certain feminists.

Martha Nussbaum draws together the Kantian and feminist ideas in an instructive study of what it might be to treat someone as an object. Objectification is a cluster

[10] The idea acquired its own self-contained verb, to 'objectify', and was taken up again by Marx, in his analysis of the oppression of the workers; and it has been used, in various forms, by continental philosophers, none of whom I know as well as I should, and few of whom had a particular interest in the situation of women. There is also an additional epistemological notion of objectification, in which projective belief plays a central role: for some feminist developments, see e.g. Haslanger (1993) and Langton (2004).

concept, on her way of thinking, in which the ideas of autonomy denial and instrumentality are at the core; but the cluster also includes related notions of inertness, fungibility, violability, ownership, and denial of subjectivity. Nussbaum's proposal deserves scrutiny, as an outstanding example of the kind of inquiry that is seamlessly feminist and philosophical; and I shall be wanting to ask whether the proposal does justice to the Kantian and feminist heritage Nussbaum claims for it, and if not, how it might best be augmented. I shall be drawing special attention to the idea of 'treating' in that notion of 'treating someone as an object'. And while Nussbaum places the *denial* of autonomy at centre stage, I shall also investigate a possibility that smacks of paradox: whether one might treat someone as an object through *affirming* their autonomy.

This latter question is of philosophical interest, and of practical interest to feminists as well. One feminist application of the idea of objectification has been to pornography, which has been thought to deny women's autonomy, in its depiction of women 'as objects, things or commodities'.[11] However, other pornography has been thought to affirm women's autonomy, representing women as not in the least object-like or subordinate, but as active sexual agents; and the suggestion has been that this, surely, is politically innocent. Joel Feinberg (1985: 144) describes with nostalgia some 'comic strip pamphlets' of the 1930s and 1940s, which 'portrayed . . . a kind of joyous feast of erotica in which the blessedly unrepressed cartoon figures shared with perfect equality. Rather than being humiliated or dominated, the women characters equalled the men in their sheer earthy gusto.'[12] The pornographic film *Deep Throat* was hailed for representing women as sexually autonomous, its heroine described as 'Liberated Woman in her most extreme form—taking life and sex on her own terms'.[13] Such descriptions aim to be vindications, aim to distinguish a liberating from a subordinating pornography. Indeed feminist anti-pornography legislation allows for just such a distinction, labelling non-subordinating pornography as 'erotica'. So in thinking about whether pornography might objectify women, it is tempting to think that the question must be about pornography that *denies* women autonomy—and not, surely, about pornography that *affirms* autonomy.

Well, the answer, as we shall see, is not so simple. Perhaps there really could be a liberating, autonomy-affirming pornography; certainly there are feminists who think the solution is not less pornography, but more—more pornography created by women, for women. Perhaps the 1930s and 1940s comic strips really were liberating;

---

[11] From the definition drafted by MacKinnon and Andrea Dworkin, see MacKinnon (1987: 176). Note that if pornography is defined as subordination, the possibility of non-subordinating pornography is ruled as a matter of terminology. I use a more vernacular sense of the term here.

[12] Feinberg adds, 'the episodes had no butt at all except prudes and hypocrites. Most of us consumers managed to survive with our moral characters intact'.

[13] The words of a commentator quoted in a documentary made by Mark Kermode and Russell Leven, *The Real Linda Lovelace*, first broadcast on Channel 4 in the UK, 26 Sept. 2002. At the time of writing, further details are available at Channel 4's website, <http://www.channel4.com/film/reviews/film.jsp?id=105584>.

for present purposes we might as well accept Feinberg's rosy evaluation. But while allowing this, one can also allow that it is not the whole story. The description of *Deep Throat* as representing 'Liberated Woman in her most extreme form' must in the end be resisted, not because its affirmation of autonomy is a sham, but because, as I shall argue, objectification sometimes *depends* on affirmation of autonomy. This may sound strange at first, but it turns out to be a natural enough consequence of the plurality of ways in which someone can be treated as object.

Nussbaum herself begins with a plurality, naming seven features that form the cluster concept of objectification, seven ways to 'treat an object as a thing':

1. *Instrumentality*: one treats it as a tool of one's own purposes.
2. *Denial of autonomy*: one treats it as lacking in autonomy and self-determination.
3. *Inertness*: one treats it as lacking in agency and activity.
4. *Fungibility*: one treats it as interchangeable (a) with other things of the same type, and/or (b) with things of other types.
5. *Violability*: one treats it as lacking in boundary-integrity, as something that it is permissible to break up, smash, break into.
6. *Ownership*: one treats it as something that is owned by another, can be bought or sold, etc.
7. *Denial of subjectivity*: one treats it as something whose experience and feelings (if any) need not be taken into account. (Nussbaum 1995: 257)

I take this to be a particularly helpful proposal about what 'object' amounts to, in the notion of 'treating as an object', and this is, in my view, at least half the story. The other half, as we shall see, rests not on what an 'object' is, but on what 'treating as' amounts to. Nussbaum's proposal gives content to the idea of objectification by teasing out a number of features associated with objecthood: an object lacks autonomy, lacks subjectivity, is inert, an appropriate candidate (sometimes) for using as a tool, exchange, destruction, possession.

While she observes that not all objects are candidates for 'objectifying' treatment (a painting is not violable, fungible, a mere instrument), it is in the application to persons that the idea of objectification gets its chief point. And in the case of persons, treatment relating to autonomy becomes central, she thinks, partly because of its implications for other modes of object-making. When you treat a person as autonomous, that seems to imply not treating them just as instrument; it seems to imply treating them as not simply inert, not owned, not something whose feelings need not be taken into account. In other words, instrumentality, inertness, ownership, and denial of subjectivity each imply denial of autonomy.[14] Instrumentality seems central too, but in a different way: many things are treated as lacking in

---

[14] She allows that treating as autonomous may be compatible with fungibility and boundary violation, factors perhaps salient for ideologies of gay male promiscuity, and practitioners of consensual sado-masochism.

autonomy which nonetheless ought not to be treated as mere means to one's ends—she mentions the examples of children, pets, and paintings. These examples suggest that while instrumentality may imply autonomy denial, the converse does not in general hold. Non-instrumental treatment is compatible with autonomy denial (young children), and with subjectivity denial (paintings). That said, when it comes to the treatment of adult human beings, the connections between instrumentality and autonomy denial are closer: non-instrumental treatment of adult human beings does imply treating them as autonomous. When it comes to adult human beings, she suggests that not treating someone as an instrument implies not denying their autonomy—and vice versa.[15]

She applies this idea to sexual objectification, attending to a variety of texts, from the relatively highbrow (D. H. Lawrence, James Joyce, Henry James) to the low (*Playboy*, and a sadistic sample from the work of one 'Laurence St Clair'); and she uses it to defend many aspects of the feminist understanding of women's subordination developed by Catharine MacKinnon and Andrea Dworkin, together with their associated critique of pornography. She develops at the same time a potentially surprising argument that some sorts of objectification, indeed some sorts of denial of autonomy, may be 'a wonderful part of sexual life'—surprising, if the initial thought was that objectification is a distinctive moral failure.[16]

If we are interested in whether Nussbaum's proposal does justice to the feminist philosophical understanding of 'treating someone as an object', it is worth asking whether there are aspects of the idea of an 'object' that are relevant to feminists, but absent from Nussbaum's proposal. With this in mind, the following could usefully be added to Nussbaum's list of seven:

8. *Reduction to body*: one treats it as identified with its body, or body parts.
This idea is absent from the official list, notwithstanding its prominence in Nussbaum's illustrative examples. It appears in a clause of the famous feminist

---

[15] There is an implicit biconditional: one treats an adult human being as mere means if and only if one denies their autonomy. One half of the biconditional is implied by Nussbaum's view that 'treating an item as autonomous seems to entail treating it as noninstrumental', i.e. (by contraposition) *instrumentality entails autonomy denial*. The other half of the biconditional is implied by her view that 'treating as autonomous [may] be a necessary feature of the noninstrumental use of adult human beings', i.e. non-instrumentality entails treating as autonomous, or (by contraposition) *autonomy denial entails instrumentality*, for adult persons (1995: 260, 261). This claim that instrumentality and autonomy denial are mutually entailing (for adult persons) is surely too strong. In terms of the distinctions made below, instrumentality entails autonomy denial construed as autonomy *violation*, it does not entail autonomy denial construed as *non-attribution* of autonomy. A liar or rapist may treat someone as a mere means, while attributing autonomy. In the other direction, there can be autonomy denial of either sort without instrumentality. A paternalistic doctor does not use the patient as a mere tool, or a means to his ends. When someone's autonomy is violated 'for their own good', this is not a *use* of the person. Nussbaum's examples suggest she wishes 'autonomy denial' to cover non-attribution *and* violation of autonomy, but neither of these have quite the intimate conceptual link with instrumentality she is after.

[16] She argues that, in a manner sensitive to context, in background conditions of equality, a mutual 'denial of autonomy' may be valuable, and she offers as an example the sexual self-surrender described by D. H. Lawrence in *The Rainbow*.

anti-pornography ordinance from which she takes inspiration, according to which (some) pornography treats women as 'dehumanized as sexual objects, things, or commodities... reduced to body parts'.

9. *Reduction to appearance*: one treats it primarily in terms of how it looks, or how it appears to the senses.

This is worth including for its importance, in different ways, to both Kantian and feminist thinking. It appears in Nussbaum's illustrative examples too, whether in the objectifying character of soft-core pornography, or in the relationship of a couple described by Henry James, who value each other in a purely aesthetic way, appropriate for fine paintings and antiques.

10. *Silencing*: one treats it as silent, lacking the capacity to speak.

Speech is a distinctive capacity of persons, just as distinctive perhaps as autonomy and subjectivity. Admittedly, this was not a particularly important idea for Kant, but it has been important to feminists, who hold that women's subordination is partly constituted by the fact that women have been silenced, for example, by pornography. 'Pornography makes [women's] speech impossible, and where possible, worthless. Pornography makes women into objects. Objects do not speak. When they do, they are by then regarded as objects, not as humans' (MacKinnon 1987: 182). Leaving aside the question of what exactly this silencing amounts to, the idea of silence has been central to feminist thinking about women's situation, and it is worth adding independently to Nussbaum's list.

With these inclusions, the relevant idea of an 'object' turns out to be of something lacking in subjectivity and autonomy, something inert, something that is an appropriate candidate for using as a tool, exchange, destruction, possession, all as Nussbaum suggested; and in addition it is something that is *silent*, something that is just an *appearance*, just a *body*.

Teasing out a plurality of features associated with objecthood is, I suggest, only half the task. In this idea of 'treating someone as an object', we need to look not only at the notion of an object, but also at the notion of *treatment*. Here too we confront a plurality, albeit a different one. 'Treat' is a wide-ranging verb that has been functioning as a dummy, standing in for a host of different attitudes and actions. 'Treating' may be a matter of attitude or act: it may be a matter of how one depicts or represents someone, or a matter of what one (more actively) does to someone. Supposing, for simplicity, we restrict our attention to treatment relating to autonomy; supposing, too, we agree with Nussbaum that lack of autonomy is a salient feature of objects, and that 'denying autonomy' is therefore an aspect of 'treating as an object': the question remains as to what denying autonomy amounts to.[17]

On Nussbaum's description, denial of autonomy takes place when one treats something 'as lacking in autonomy and self-determination' (Nussbaum 1995: 257).

---

[17] Supposing too that we had an uncontested vision of what autonomy might be! For some feminist debate about this, see e.g. Mackenzie and Stoljar (2000).

Here are some examples she uses to illustrate autonomy denial. One permissibly denies autonomy when one treats a pen, a painting, one's pets, one's small children, as non-autonomous. Ownership is by definition incompatible with autonomy, so slaves are denied autonomy: and 'once one treats as a tool and denies autonomy, it is difficult to say why rape or battery would be wrong, except in the sense of rendering the tool a less efficient tool of one's purposes'. Aspects of slavery anticipate the MacKinnon–Dworkin understanding of sexual objectification,

since [slavery] shows us how a certain sort of instrumental use of persons, negating the autonomy that is proper to them as persons, also leaves the human being so denuded of humanity, in the eyes of the objectifier, that he or she seems ripe for other abuses as well—for the refusal of imagination involved in the denial of subjectivity, for the denial of individuality involved in fungibility, and even for bodily and spiritual violation and abuse, if that should appear to be what best suits the will and purposes of the objectifier.

The relationship between the Brangwens, described by D. H. Lawrence, involves 'a mutual denial of autonomy', 'a kind of yielding abnegation of self-containment and self-sufficiency'. An example of hard-core sadistic pornography 'represents women as creatures whose autonomy and subjectivity don't matter at all', the woman's 'inertness, her lack of autonomy, her violability' is eroticized (Nussbaum 1995: 261, 264, 265, 273, 280).

Is autonomy denial a matter of attitude, or act, or both? Nussbaum's examples exploit a plurality of different ways of treating. An agent presumably *believes* the pen, the painting, the small child, are lacking in autonomy—that is why they then *act as if* they are lacking in autonomy—and act differently, depending on whether it is the child or the pen whose autonomy is 'denied'. In buying the slave, an agent thereby 'denies' autonomy: but in what sense? The act may presuppose an attitude, of failing to *regard* the slave as autonomous. The act of buying may be an act of autonomy denial that *violates* the slave's autonomy, preventing him from having any choice in the matter. Or perhaps slavery does something even worse to the slave's autonomy—*stifles* it, or *destroys* it.

To make a start, in considering autonomy denial, *non-attribution of autonomy* needs to be distinguished from *violation of autonomy*. I take it that non-attribution is primarily a matter of attitude, while autonomy violation is something more—a more active doing, perhaps one that prevents someone from doing what they choose. The distinction between non-attribution and violation is obscured, surely, by allowing 'autonomy denial' to label both. The two are independent: there can be autonomy denial *qua* non-attribution, without autonomy denial *qua* autonomy violation—and vice versa.[18] To illustrate the first possibility, there can be non-attribution of autonomy without violation of autonomy, in the 'objective' attitude

[18] For a related discussion of the relationship between using someone and failing to treat them as a person, see O'Neill (1990: 105): 'Making another into a tool or instrument in my project is one way of failing to treat that other as a person; but only one way.'

described so well by P. F. Strawson (1974: 9), the attitude of the doctor or social scientist: 'To adopt the objective attitude to another human being is to see him, perhaps, as an object of social policy; as a subject for what, in a wide range of sense, might be called treatment; as something...to be managed or handled or cured or trained.'[19] Someone denying autonomy in this attitudinal way need not deny autonomy in other ways. A doctor viewing his patient from the objective stance may act in ways that override his patient's choices, but he may not: perhaps institutional procedures of securing informed consent will prevent autonomy violation, notwithstanding the shortfall in the doctor's attribution of autonomy. To illustrate the second possibility, there can be autonomy violation without failure to attribute autonomy, as in the classic examples from Kant's *Groundwork*, where autonomy is attributed, *and* violated. Someone who makes a lying promise to repay his friend's money does not suppose his friend lacking in autonomy, but does violate his friend's autonomy, on the Kantian view. An example more relevant to feminists might be sadistic rape, i.e. rape where non-consent is actively sought, rather than disregarded or ignored. In this sort of case, it's not that he doesn't *listen* to her saying 'no', he *wants* her to say 'no'. Here there is violation of a woman's autonomy committed by someone who *affirms* her autonomy, attributes to her a capacity for choice—and desires precisely to overcome that choice, make her do what she chooses not to do.[20] In sadistic rape, someone is 'treated as an object' in part by attributing autonomy to them in one way—precisely so that autonomy can be denied a different way. Autonomy attribution is a necessary feature of this way of treating as an object.[21]

Reflection suggests that someone violating autonomy not only *can* at the same time affirm autonomy but must affirm it, when the violation is deliberate: autonomy violation is not just compatible with autonomy attribution, but requires it, the one autonomy denial (violation) depending on the absence of the other (non-attribution). Deliberate violation of someone's choice presupposes attribution of a capacity for choice. This underlines the distinctness of the two 'autonomy denials' of non-attribution and violation: it shows how an act may be autonomy-denying in one way, and not another; and further, that autonomy denial is not just compatible

---

[19] Strawson would not wish to reduce such attitudes to, for example, metaphysical beliefs about whether the person is free or autonomous.

[20] I assume there are other kinds of rape in which the woman's unwillingness is incidental, not included in the content of what is desired; or even, as in negligent rape, unnoticed.

[21] That means, incidentally, that there is an important difference between the latter sexual example and those typically described by Kant, which involve autonomy violation in the service of some other purpose (for example, gaining money), achievable innocently by other means. Sadistic rape violates autonomy, not in the service of some other purpose (for example, achieving sexual pleasure), but partly for its own sake: autonomy violation partly *constitutes* the agent's purpose. For a discussion of a related contrast in the social psychology literature, see Baumeister (1997, chs. 4: 'Greed, Lust, Ambition: Evil as a Means to an End', and 7: 'Can Evil Be Fun? The Joy of Hurting'), a psychological study of, roughly, a contrast between evil as means and as end.

with autonomy affirmation, but sometimes requires it. Here we have one way that objectification might actually *depend* on autonomy affirmation.

Non-attribution of autonomy, and autonomy violation, are two importantly different ways of denying autonomy: but still further possibilities are implicit in Nussbaum's discussion: for example, *self-surrender* of autonomy, and relatedly a *demand* for another's self-surrender of autonomy. These are features of Tom Brangwen's sexual experience, as described in *The Rainbow*, 'a kind of yielding abnegation of self-containment and self-sufficiency', offered by himself, and hoped for from his partner. This self-surrender, and the demand for it, are not failures to attribute autonomy, nor violations of autonomy. And while they are characterized as potentially 'wonderful' parts of sexual life, in conditions of mutuality and equality, an asymmetric version of the demand for surrender is less wonderful, being a feature of a different sadism, one that seeks surrender of autonomy, the 'abjuration' described unforgettably by Sartre (1943):

The spectacle which is offered to the sadist is that of a freedom which struggles against the expanding of the flesh, and which freely chooses to be submerged in the flesh. At the moment of abjuration…a freedom chooses to be wholly identified with this body; this distorted and heaving body is the very image of a broken and enslaved freedom.

The result sought by the sadist is that the other abjure herself, abjure her autonomy, freely choose to become thing-like. It misses something to place this demand for surrender under the generic label of 'autonomy denial', as if it were a version of what is going on when someone 'denies' autonomy to small children and inanimate objects.

Still further possibilities include the *destruction* or *stifling* of autonomy, perhaps implicit in the sexual slavery of *The Story of O*, described by Andrea Dworkin, and discussed by Nussbaum (1995: 269, quoting Dworkin 1974: 58). 'O is totally possessed. That means that she is an object, with no control over her own mobility, capable of no assertion of personality, her body is a body, in the same way that a pencil is a pencil, a bucket is a bucket.' This presents a deeper damage to autonomy, a snuffing out of the capacity for choice; or a stifling of that capacity, if it is prevented from growing in the first place.

We have been seeing how varied are the modes of 'treating', even when the aspect of 'objecthood', namely absence of autonomy, is held constant. This variation allows for the possibility of treatment that denies autonomy in one way, while affirming it in another. It allows for variation in moral significance: thinking of someone as lacking in autonomy is less invasive than violating or destroying their autonomy. Such variations are due not just to context-sensitivity (which Nussbaum rightly emphasizes), but to differences in what the agent is doing to autonomy itself: failing to attribute it, violating it, surrendering it, demanding that another surrender it, destroying it, stifling it.[22]

---

[22] More thought is needed about how these interact, the relevance of repetition and pervasiveness, and institutional support; whether repeated and widespread autonomy violations may, for example,

We can observe that this plurality of modes of treatment probably extends to other listed features of objecthood. Subjectivity denial, for instance, may be failure to attribute subjective mental states; systematically attributing the wrong subjective mental states; manipulating someone's subjective mental states; even perhaps invading, destroying, or stifling their subjectivity. Silencing may be failure to attribute a capacity to speak, preventing someone from speaking, destroying or stifling someone's capacity to speak. The diverse ways of *treating as* an object link up with the diverse aspects of *being* an object, creating combinatorial possibilities whose surface we have barely begun to scratch.

In applying this to the question of pornography, we can begin with Nussbaum's comment on a violent sexual tale in the work of 'Laurence St Clair', material which in her view would fall clearly in the scope of MacKinnon's definition. Nussbaum agrees with MacKinnon that such material is objectifying, notwithstanding an 'assuaging fiction' that this violating treatment 'is what she has asked for'—i.e. notwithstanding an 'assuaging fiction' that violation is *the woman's choice*. Nussbaum dismisses the affirmation of autonomy as, in this case, an 'assuaging fiction', but her remark brings us to the issue of pornography that 'affirms autonomy'.

Recall that *Deep Throat* was hailed as presenting 'Liberated Woman in her most extreme form, taking life and sex on her own terms'. Should that description be dismissed, as a mere 'assuaging fiction'? It is tempting to say yes, that the autonomy attribution is a sham: Linda Lovelace is hardly affirming her autonomy when she embarks on a life driven by nothing more than an insatiable desire for throat sex. That is a possible option, but it is not the only one. There is a clear sense in which it is not a sham: *Deep Throat* attributes genuine choices to its fictional heroine. There is also the real Linda to consider: and here too the film may have attributed real choices, affirming the autonomy of the *real* Linda. It claimed to be 'introducing Linda Lovelace as herself' (so the billing went), and in so doing, it depicted not only the fictional but the real Linda as acting autonomously. Extending further afield, there are women more generally to consider: and here again, if Linda is an iconic 'Liberated Woman', standing for all women, the film in a certain sense affirms the autonomy of women in the wider world.

Do these affirmations of autonomy (of the fictional Linda, the real Linda, or other women) settle the question of whether the film affirms autonomy *tout court*? No. There is scope for treatment that at once denies and affirms autonomy, as we have just seen. Paternalistic attitudes may deny autonomy through non-attribution, without denying autonomy through violation. Sadistic rape may affirm autonomy through attribution, while denying autonomy through violation. In general, autonomy affirmation is compatible with autonomy denial, once the plurality of possible modes of treatment is recognized. Even if *Deep Throat* were to affirm

destroy autonomy; how a one-off autonomy violation (e.g. being lied to once) is vastly different from a systematic pattern that requires institutional support (e.g. slavery).

women's autonomy in all the above ways, that would not settle whether it affirms autonomy *tout court.*

The film does not affirm autonomy *tout court.* First, the claim that the film affirmed the real Linda's autonomy, even if true, requires instant qualification: for the film also denied her autonomy, as documented in her own testimony, *Ordeal,* and as more or less admitted by her one-time husband and pimp, Charles Traynor. Autonomy was attributed to her in the film, but denied her in life. In a remarkable set of televised interviews, Traynor admitted the autonomy denial: 'She was pretty dumb. So everything she did, she had to be told how to do it, when to do it, and why she was doing it, and how to dress, and it just kinda rolled along like that, y'know... it was always a matter of telling her what to do.'[23] What she was told to do was (among other things) to *deny* that she was being told what to do. The message was 'Look as though it's your choice—or else'. Autonomy sells. Linda couldn't choose, but was more saleable if she looked like she could. She was a useful object, more useful if it looked like a subject. There is an odd sense in which her autonomy was *itself* commodified, thwarted in life but exaggerated, in fiction, for its cash value.

The film's autonomy attribution served autonomy violation. According to Linda's testimony in *Ordeal,* it took violence, rape, and death threats to make her play her role. Traynor admitted the violent relationship:

I was the dominant figure, she was a submissive figure, so if it reached the point where dominance had to take over, then dominance took over.... If you argue to a point and somebody keeps pushing you, you know, fists are bound to fly. I don't mind somebody putting in their two cents worth, but I don't want them to argue with me to the point where I get upset or violently upset, and... yeah, that happened, on occasion.... I think she didn't enjoy us getting in arguments with each other, but they say if you don't want me to get into an argument, don't argue with me.

Her interviews with the press, scripted by Traynor, convey not just violation of autonomy, but other kinds of autonomy denial, perhaps destruction or stifling of autonomy. Linda later said of those interviews:

I was just like a robot, I was told what to say and I said it, because if I didn't I was beaten, brutally.

Traynor admitted the scripting:

I schooled her on what to say. Always sound sexy. Always look cute. Wink at the camera. Wink at the interviewer... Always be titillating. You'd rather be having sex than doing anything. Y'know, it was just schooling, teaching her what to say, how to say it, and when to say it.

This is autonomy denial, and silencing too. What she was told to say was (among other things) to deny that she was being told what to say. Linda's own voice is

---

[23] This and the later quotations from Traynor and Marchiano are from interviews in the documentary made by Kermode and Leven, *The Real Linda Lovelace.*

silenced, in the scripted interviews, and silenced in a different way later on when her own testimony about abuse, in *Ordeal*, was sold as pornography.[24]

Finally, there is the autonomy of other women to think about. Linda is not just *a* woman, but *woman*, 'Liberated Woman in her most extreme form, taking life and sex on her own terms': there is autonomy attribution here, a vision of what autonomy is, not just for Linda, but for women in the wider world. But it can be argued that this autonomy affirmation serves autonomy denial, a false vision of autonomy being, after all, among the most potent enemies of autonomy. According to MacKinnon, and to testimony at the Minneapolis Hearings (see Minneapolis City Council 1988), the film legitimized a series of real-life autonomy violations, provoking an increase in throat rape (with associated suffocation), and an increase in unwanted and sometimes coercive attempts at throat sex. In affirming women's autonomy one way, and identifying that autonomy with sexual freedom, *Deep Throat*-style, it legitimized autonomy denial a different way, when the pornographer's image of women's choices was used to thwart real women's choices.

Some pornography, I conclude, might objectify even as it affirms autonomy: indeed, it might objectify through its autonomy affirmation, the way it objectifies depending on the distinctive way it affirms autonomy. The autonomy affirmation in *Deep Throat* (of a fictional Linda, a real Linda, or real women elsewhere) is one that serves autonomy denial (of a real Linda, and real women elsewhere). These denials of autonomy—the violations, silencings, or stiflings of autonomy—depend, substantially, on the affirmation of autonomy. That attribution of sexual autonomy to Linda was a structural feature of her oppressive circumstances, making abuse easier, hiding it, and hindering escape. That attribution of sexual autonomy to an iconic Liberated Woman, and thereby to other women, likewise facilitated violation of at least some other women's autonomy. Now whether *Deep Throat* is a typical or significant sample of autonomy-affirming pornography is a question I shall not, here, take time to address. But it is enough to suggest, I think, that pornography's way of affirming women's autonomy could, at least sometimes, be a way of denying women's autonomy; and there would be no paradox, at all, about that.

4. Concluding Regrets and Hopes

In arguing that feminism can illuminate philosophy and vice versa, it's best on the whole to try to show rather than tell—best, but also hardest, and I don't pretend to

---

[24] *Ordeal* was sold as pornography: this example of illocutionary disablement is discussed in Langton (1993), where a distinction is made between locutionary silencing due to threats (e.g. the scripted interviews) and illocutionary silencing (e.g. of *Ordeal*).

have succeeded in conveying much more than a glimmer. This chapter represents a very local and partial perspective on a vast and luxuriant continent, whose landscapes and borders it has barely begun to make visible, as its author is painfully aware. And daunted hopes aside, there is yet more trouble brewing, for we have ended up on dangerous ground. If feminist critique of philosophy has something to it, there are risks for feminist thinkers who value a two-way conversation, and who draw upon philosophy in trying to understand the very problems that bother them as feminists. Astell saw Cartesian philosophy as part of the solution to the problem she faced as a feminist: its method overturned prejudice, and its metaphysics cast women and men alike as essentially things that think. But if more recent feminist critique is right, dualism is not the solution, but the problem. Are all such feminist efforts fraught with danger? Audre Lorde (1984) famously said that 'the master's tools will never dismantle the master's house'—not quite true, as your average burglar or vandal could tell you, but the metaphor captures a methodological suspicion that is not easy to lay to rest.

Take that idea of 'treating someone as an object', for instance, initially elaborated by Kant, and developed by feminists wanting to understand the nature of women's oppression. For Kant himself, the idea rested on a dualism more profound than that of Descartes—an unfathomable division between the realm of determined phenomenal objects, and timeless, noumenally free selves. Treating someone as an object is failing to treat them as a subject, it is to make them, somehow, part of the determined phenomenal order. Most of us feel no need for such dizzying metaphysics. But those of us who more modestly suppose there is something wrong with treating people as things—with treating women as things—must face the kinds of questions Astell's work has faced, and that Parfit's work faced in James's discussion. Whence comes this deep conceptual division between subjects and objects, between persons and things? And whence comes the valorization of mentality and freedom, the denigration of the physical, implicit in the idea that there is something inherently wrong with denying someone's subjectivity, denying someone's autonomy, reducing someone to their body? In short: doesn't the charge of dualism apply as much to feminist work on objectification as it applies to anything else?

This is an uncomfortable place to end up, and little scope remains here for a proper answer. But there appears, at least, to be some possible room for give and take. One could accept the complaint in part. Kant's visceral horror at the prospect of any abandoning of autonomy is surely a mistake, and Nussbaum's positive evaluation of certain kinds of self-surrender (and thus of certain kinds of objectification?) is surely right. On the other hand, to have any bite, a charge of dualism had better be made with sensitivity, asking what exactly is so bad about this 'dualism', as manifested in this idea, in this way. Does the badness consist in the history, and how such dualism has been used against women in the past? Does the badness consist in what it does to women here and now? Or does it consist not so much in what it does, as in what it leaves out? I can't guess right now the answers to these questions; but my hunch is that it will take some careful philosophy to find them.

References

Anderson, Elizabeth (1995). 'Feminist Epistemology: An Interpretation and Defence'. *Hypatia*, 10: 50–84.

Astell, Mary (1700). *Reflections Upon Marriage*. London: John Nutt. Repr. in Patricia Springborg (ed.), *Astell's Political Writings*. Cambridge: Cambridge University Press, 1996.

Atherton, Margaret (1993). 'Cartesian Reason and Gendered Reason', in Louise Antony and Charlotte Witt (eds.), *A Mind of One's Own: Feminist Essays on Reason and Objectivity*. Boulder, Colo.: Westview Press.

Baumeister, Roy (1997). *Evil: Inside Human Violence and Cruelty*. New York: W. H. Freeman.

Begemihl, B. (1999). *Biological Exuberance: Animal Homosexuality and Natural Diversity*. London: Profile.

Brison, Susan (1987). 'Outliving Oneself: Trauma, Memory and Personal Identity', in Diana Tietjens Meyers (ed.), *Feminists Re-think the Self*. Boulder, Colo.: Westview Press.

Butler, Judith (1990). *Gender Trouble: Feminism and the Subversion of Identity*. London: Routledge.

—— (1997). *Excitable Speech: A Politics of the Performative*. London: Routledge.

Caulfield, Mina (1985). 'Sexuality in Human Evolution: What Is "Natural" in Sex?' *Feminist Studies*, 11: 343–63.

Davenport, W. (1977). 'Sex in Cross-Cultural Perspective', in F. Beach (ed.), *Human Sexuality in Four Perspectives*. Baltimore, Md.: Johns Hopkins University Press.

Descartes, René (1641). *Meditations on First Philosophy*, trans. John Cottingham. Cambridge: Cambridge University Press, 1986.

Dworkin, Andrea (1974). *Woman Hating*. New York: E. P. Dutton.

Feinberg, Joel (1985). *Offense to Others*. New York: Oxford University Press.

Flax, Jane (1983). 'Political Philosophy and the Patriarchal Unconscious', in Sandra Harding and Merrill Hintikka (eds.), *Discovering Reality*. Dordrecht: Reidel.

Gallup, Gordon, and Suarez, Susan (1983). 'Optimal Reproductive Strategies for Bipedalism'. *Journal of Human Evolution*, 12: 193–6.

Gilligan, C. (1982). *In a Different Voice*. Cambridge, Mass.: Harvard University Press.

Harding, Sandra (1993). 'Rethinking Standpoint Epistemology: What Is 'Strong Objectivity?', in L. Alcoff and E. Potter (eds.), *Feminist Epistemologies*. London: Routledge.

Hartsock, Nancy (1983). 'The Feminist Standpoint Theory: Developing the Ground for a Specifically Feminist Historical Materialism', in Sandra Harding and Meryl Hintikka (eds.), *Discovering Reality*. Dordrecht: Reidel.

Haslanger, Sally (1993). 'On Being Objective and Being Objectified', in Louise Antony and Charlotte Witt (eds.), *A Mind of One's Own: Feminist Essays on Reason and Objectivity*. Boulder, Colo.: Westview Press.

Herman, Barbara (1993). 'Could it Be Worth Thinking About Kant on Sex and Marriage?', in Louise Antony and Charlotte Witt (eds.), *A Mind of One's Own: Feminist Essays on Reason and Objectivity*. Boulder, Colo.: Westview Press.

Hite, S. (1976). *The Hite Report*. New York: Macmillan.

Hornsby, Jennifer (1995). 'Disempowered Speech'. *Philosophical Topics*, 23: 127–47.

—— (2000). 'Feminism in Philosophy of Language: Communicative Speech Acts', in Miranda Fricker and Jennifer Hornsby (eds.), *The Cambridge Companion to Feminism in Philosophy*. Cambridge: Cambridge University Press.

—— and Langton, Rae (1998). 'Free Speech and Illocution'. *Legal Theory*, 4: 21–37.

Hrdy, Sarah Blaffer (1999). *The Woman that Never Evolved*. Cambridge, Mass.: Harvard University Press.

Irigaray, Luce (1985). *Speculum of the Other Woman*, trans. Gillian Gill. Ithaca: Cornell University Press.

Jaggar, Alison (1983). *Feminist Politics and Human Nature*. Totowa, NJ: Rowman & Allanheld.

James, Susan (2000). 'Feminism in Philosophy of Mind: The Question of Personal Identity', in Miranda Fricker and Jennifer Hornsby (eds.), *The Cambridge Companion to Feminism in Philosophy*. Cambridge: Cambridge University Press.

Jones, Karen (1999). 'Second Hand Moral Knowledge'. *Journal of Philosophy*, 96: 55–78.

Kant, Immanuel (1797). *Groundwork of the Metaphysic of Morals*, trans. Mary Gregor. Cambridge: Cambridge University Press, 1997.

—— (1797). *Doctrine of Virtue*, trans. Mary Gregor. New York: Harper & Row, 1964.

Keller, Evelyn Fox (1993). *Refiguring Life: Metaphors of Twentieth-Century Biology*. New York: Columbia University Press.

Kinsey, A. C., Pomeroy, W. B., and Martin, C. E. (1948). *Sexual Behaviour in the Human Male*. Philadelphia: W. B. Saunders.

—— —— —— and Gebhard, P. H. (1953). *Sexual Behaviour in the Human Female*. Philadelphia: W. B. Saunders.

Langton, Rae (1993). 'Speech Acts and Unspeakable Acts'. *Philosophy and Public Affairs*, 22: 293–330.

—— (1995). 'Sexual Solipsism'. *Philosophical Topics*, 23: 149–87.

—— (2004). 'Projection and Objectification', in Brian Leiter (ed.), *The Future for Philosophy*. Oxford: Oxford University Press.

Lloyd, Elisabeth A. (1993). 'Pre-theoretical Assumptions in Evolutionary Explanations of Female Sexuality', *Philosophical Studies*, 69: 139–53.

—— (2005). *The Case of the Female Orgasm: Bias in the Science of Evolution*. Cambridge, Mass.: Harvard University Press.

Lloyd, Genevieve (1984). *The Man of Reason: 'Male' and 'Female' in Western Philosophy*. London: Methuen.

Lorde, Audre (1984). *Sister Outsider: Essays and Speeches*. Sydney: Crossing Press.

McGowan, Mary Kate (2003). 'Conversational Exercitives and the Force of Pornagraphy'. *Philosophy and Public Affairs*, 31: 155–89.

Mackenzie, Catriona, and Stoljar, Natalie (eds.) (2000). *Relational Autonomy: Feminist Perspectives on Autonomy, Agency and the Social Self*. Oxford: Oxford University Press.

MacKinnon, Catharine (1987). *Feminism Unmodified*. Cambridge, Mass.: Harvard University Press.

—— (1991). *Toward a Feminist Theory of the State*. Cambridge, Mass.: Harvard University Press.

Masters, W. H., and Johnson, V. (1966). *Human Sexual Response*. Boston, Mass.: Little, Brown.

Minneapolis City Council (1988). *Pornography and Sexual Violence: Evidence of the Links*. London: Everywoman. Transcript of *Public Hearings on Ordinances to Add Pornography as Discrimination Against Women*, Committee on Government Operations, 12–13 Dec. 1983.

Morris, Desmond (1967). *The Naked Ape*. London: Cape.

Nussbaum, Martha (1995). 'Objectification'. *Philosophy and Public Affairs*, 24: 249–91.

O'Neill, Onora (1990). 'Between Consenting Adults', in O'Neill, *Constructions of Reason*. Cambridge: Cambridge University Press.

Perry, Ruth (1986). *The Celebrated Mary Astell*. Chicago: University of Chicago Press.

Quinton, Anthony (1975). 'The Soul', in J. Perry (ed.), *Personal Identity*. Berkeley: University of California Press.

Sartre, Jean-Paul (1943). *Being and Nothingness*, trans. Hazel Barnes. London: Methuen.

Saul, Jennifer (2003). *Feminism: Issues and Arguments*. Oxford: Oxford University Press.

Strawson, P. F (1974). 'Freedom and Resentment', in *Freedom and Resentment and Other Essays*. London: Methuen.

Symons, Donald (1979). *The Evolution of Human Sexuality*. New York: Oxford University Press.

Wittgenstein, Ludwig (1958). *Philosophical Investigations*, trans. G. E. M. Anscombe. Oxford: Blackwell.

CHAPTER 10

THE FEASIBILITY ISSUE

GEOFFREY BRENNAN AND PHILIP PETTIT

1. INTRODUCTION

Much political philosophy seeks to identify those institutions that would be more desirable than alternatives under the ideal-theory assumption that whatever alternative is in place will command general compliance. This assumption means that the question of how likely it is that such institutions will engage prevailing incentives and command high levels of compliance is effectively assumed away. The failure to engage this question represents a potentially serious limitation on the relevance of political philosophy for real-world policy. It suggests that philosophy ought to seek something beyond the purely ideal sort of theory that is fashionable in many circles.

This chapter provides an overview of the case for such 'non-ideal' theory and of its prospects. In Section 2 we look at ideal theory in philosophy and at the problems it faces. In Section 3 we consider the emphasis on incentive-compatibility found among economists and sketch the possibility of developing that perspective within philosophy. In Sections 4 and 5 we examine two objections to the incentive-compatibility approach and show how they can be met. In the process of doing that, we outline a strategy for pursuing the approach that requires us to identify incentives that support virtue rather than driving it out. And then in Section 6 we look at one category of incentives—these are related to the desire for esteem—that seem to have this virtue-friendly character.

2. PHILOSOPHY AND IDEAL THEORY

The recent philosophical tradition in social and political theory distinguishes between analytical and normative theory. The analytical branch of the discipline is seen as an enterprise of modelling explanatory concepts like power and status, and evaluative concepts like freedom and justice and democracy. The normative branch involves an attempt to spell out the form that the state and related institutions would take were they fully to satisfy such evaluative concepts—were they to exemplify values like freedom or justice or democracy. In the earlier part of the twentieth century the analytical enterprise was dominant, at least in Anglo-Saxon circles; typical of the issues routinely debated was the question of whether freedom is best cast, in terms popularized by Isaiah Berlin (1958), as a negative or positive value.

This all changed, however, with the publication of John Rawls's *A Theory of Justice* (1971). That book served to shift the focus quite dramatically from the analytical to the normative. Often suggesting that issues of analysis or definition were of secondary interest, Rawls argued for returning to a concern with the assessment of social and political institutions of the kind that had been important to nineteenth-century utilitarians like Jeremy Bentham, John Stuart Mill, and Henry Sidgwick. Rawls held that justice is the primary virtue of institutions and presented the articulation of a theory of justice as the first task for normative theory. He maintained that the best way to articulate a theory of justice was to try, in a process of reflective equilibration, to identify institutional principles that would best satisfy, on the one hand, general ideas about the nature of justice and, on the other, considered judgements about the acceptability of their concrete implications. And he urged in defence of his own favoured principles that their claim to be just or fair was boosted by the fact that they would appeal to anyone who, ignorant of his or her own position in the society, was invited to choose the principles that would dictate its basic structure.

But apart from taking these noteworthy steps in the development of normative theory, Rawls introduced a style of theorizing that left an even deeper mark on contemporary philosophical thought. He suggested that in thinking about desirable institutions—for example, just or free or democratic arrangements—we should ask first about the institutions that would appeal in a world where everyone is disposed to internalize and comply with whatever principles of organization the theory favours. He persuaded the tradition that ideal theory, as he called it, is the sort of approach that political philosophy should take in the first instance and that we should look only as a secondary matter to the question of how to deal with problems of non-compliance.

Rawls himself, it is true, went some way towards arguing that his principles of justice would survive in the actual, non-ideal world. He devised the principles so that they did not require equality in the distribution of resources—they required only that the inequalities tolerated should have a positive impact among the worst-off—on the explicit grounds that otherwise economic incentive and initiative might be reduced. He urged that his principles were such that people raised under them would tend to develop a sense of justice, thereby making the dispensation stable. And he argued in his later book *Political Liberalism* (1993) that the principles would appeal even in a world where people maintain the sorts of doctrinal and religious disagreements that most of us would regard as understandable and reasonable: even in a world, therefore, where the principles are not endorsed out of a commitment to a comprehensive, liberal vision of society.[1]

But these gestures towards non-ideal or realistic normative theory did not involve acknowledging that, no matter how ideal the dispensation under which they live, some people are bound to prove resistant to the charms and the demands of that dispensation. Rawls never investigated the question of which institutions would best serve when the timber of humanity is crooked, to use Kant's phrase. Throughout his career, Rawls continued to exemplify and promote ideal-world rather than real-world normative theory. His vision may not have been entirely utopian—witness his line on equality of resources—but it did abstract from the problem that almost any set of principles for the organization of society, and certainly any principles of justice, are going to be burdensome for its members and so are not going to attract universal compliance.

How serious is this abstraction? Just how deep do compliance constraints in the design of appropriate institutional arrangements bite? We think that the abstraction is potentially very serious indeed—that compliance constraints in general bite very deeply. We shall not argue here that Rawls's own theory of justice is vitiated by the abstraction. That would be an interesting possibility to explore, but it is a task for another occasion. Our object here is to develop the more general claim that normative theory needs to take compliance constraints seriously and that failure to do so is capable in principle of undermining an entire normative enterprise.

We think this partly for reasons related to what economists describe as the theory of the second-best (Brennan 1993; Goodin 1995). Suppose it is accepted that a certain possible set of institutional arrangements is the most desirable system possible—the most just, the most democratic, or whatever—on the grounds that it best satisfies certain normative criteria. But suppose that that set of arrangements is not one that we could expect to be able to realize fully in the real world, since it requires a burdensome pattern of behaviour that people will not display in sufficient numbers or with sufficient reliability. Still, it may be tempting to think that, since this set of arrangements is the best possible under conditions of universal compliance,

---

[1] In the theory of justice between peoples, as distinct from justice within a given society, Rawls (1999) also considers the sort of non-ideal theory under which some states flout the principles of domestic justice—they deny their members important human rights—or are so burdened by poverty that they cannot live up to those principles: in particular, cannot support those rights.

then the best arrangements for a world of only partial compliance will be those that approximate the ideal set most closely, using some intuitive criteria of approximation. The ideal, so it might be thought, gives a pretty good fix on the best feasible. But that, according to the theory of the second-best, would be a serious mistake. Although the criteria are wholly satisfied under the ideal arrangements envisaged, they may be worse served by the real-world counterpart of those arrangements than by some available alternative that has quite a different character. The second-best option is often not the intuitively closest alternative to the first-best.

Consider an example from democratic theory. Thomas Christiano (1996) argues for an electoral-democratic vision of the polity on the grounds that the ideal democracy gives each individual the same political resources and guarantees that his or her interests will be equally well considered in governmental decision-making. But suppose, plausibly, that in the actual world that sort of regime is not going to attract general compliance. There are bound to be some in authority, let us say, who will not perform as the ideal requires of them; they may pay more attention to ensuring their re-election, for example, than the ideal would condone. Will the best real-world alternative still be the democratic system that most closely matches the visionary ideal? Will it be the alternative that does best by the considerations mentioned, allocating the same political resources to each and guaranteeing the equal consideration of their interests? Not necessarily.

Consider the alternative where those elected to parliament do not have ultimate power over the distribution of resources but make proposals that have to be approved by the members of an independent body—say, a body of experts appointed by a judicial elite—before they can be implemented. Although it departs from the democratic ideal, giving significant power to an unelected elite, such a system might do better in ensuring equal consideration of interests than any of the purer varieties of democracy available in the actual world. Under all of those varieties, it might be much more likely that people's interests would get to be considered, not on an equal basis, but only to the extent that they happen to belong to a lobby or a constituency that is electorally important to those in power or they happen to reside in a 'marginal electorate'.

The lesson should be clear. The danger of the ideal-theory abstraction is that it will lead philosophers to go for a soft, visionary focus in their normative thinking and to argue for an idealized system—an idealized democracy or an ideally just society—that is nowhere to be found and that might be counter-productive to try to establish. Consider those economic commentators who argue for the greater and greater expansion of the market on the assumption—the manifestly false assumption—that the expanded market will be the perfectly open, informed, and competitive arrangement that is described in their ideal models. Many philosophers observe, as will most professional economists, that this argument does not establish that the best real-world alternative, say in the provision of medical services, is to neglect real-world constraints and to go willy-nilly for market deregulation.

But as the observation tells against such simple-minded arguments for wholesale market deregulation, so analogous observations tell against the habits of ideal-world theorizing to which philosophers themselves are prone in their normative thinking.

The argument here generalizes to all forms of optimization in the face of all kinds of constraint. So consider a further example. Suppose that ideal theory stipulates that the ideal arrangement will fulfil certain conditions. Suppose that the world is such that all these conditions can't in general be fulfilled. This might be true of all possible worlds, as is the case revealed for example in Arrow's (1963) famous impossibility theorem, and the similar 'liberal paradox' exposed by Amartya Sen (1970). Or the conditions might be capable of being fulfilled in lots of possible worlds, but just not in our particular one or ones close to it—say, because of lack of resources. In all such cases, something will have to give. Not all the criteria can be fully met. Trade-offs between the desirable features the various criteria reflect will be necessary. And what final compromise is best will depend on the terms under which the various desirable features can be traded off. Different worlds will differ, in general, not only in relation to how much of each desirable feature can be secured, but also in relation to the terms of trade between those features.

So consider a further example. Martha Nussbaum (2002) has recently argued for an extension of the Rawlsian maximin principle to those incapable of entering into any form of social contract—the seriously handicapped, say. In her formulation, all of these persons should have their capabilities expanded to an appropriate threshold level. That, Nussbaum asserts, is just what Rawlsian conceptions of justice, properly interpreted, imply. But, of course, to do proper normative work the threshold level in question has to be set at a reasonably aspirational level: the Nussbaum modification would be rather uninteresting if the threshold were already met for pretty well all people, whatever their level of natural disadvantage. But in the world as we know it, that is not the case; and it is not likely to be the case under any really plausible world we can imagine. It is almost certain that there will remain seriously disadvantaged persons, whose capabilities lie below what we would think of as acceptable, under almost any imaginable arrangement. So how is the threshold formulation supposed to work in such a setting. Is it, for example, the case that we should aim to minimize the number of persons who fall below the threshold? That would certainly seem to be a plausible interpretation, but it has the unfortunate effect of mobilizing a practice of 'triage'. That is, individuals who are closest to the threshold should have the first call on limited resources precisely because the threshold is 'cheapest' to meet in their case. And equally, individuals who are furthest away—including specifically many of those groups whom Nussbaum specifically wants to include—will have to be left where they are, or conceivably 'even that which they have will (have to) be taken away'. Of course, minimizing the number of persons who fall below the threshold may not be the only rule of action the threshold approach allows. But it is surely a logical

THE FEASIBILITY ISSUE 263

interpretation of how we should perform the necessary rationing within the threshold approach. Perhaps the threshold idea is not intended to be taken too seriously. Perhaps its work is more to be thought of as motivating potential contributors than as providing a basis for operation among those doling out the support. The point here is that Nussbaum needs to provide some account of the work that thresholds are supposed to do in her scheme. But that is a requirement that the habits of 'ideal theory' serve to obscure. In a world of constraints, trade-offs are necessary and the manner in which those trade-offs are to be made is crucial for the outcomes that the theory recommends.

In the Nussbaum case (and lots of others like it) the constraint that applies is a resource constraint: there just isn't enough available to those assigned with the responsibility of action to get everyone up to the threshold level. But of course this resource constraint is just a motivational constraint in another guise. It is not the case that Nussbaum has set the threshold so high that the world GDP could not in principle cover the cost. It is rather that individuals—acting either as individual donors or as voters—are simply not prepared to act as the theory requires. Ideal theory in that sense just assumes away the problems with which alternative normative formulations must critically deal.

3. ECONOMICS AND INCENTIVE-COMPATIBILITY

A more general way of putting the point discussed in the last section is to say that normative thinking in social and political philosophy has concentrated on questions of desirability and not given sufficient attention to issues of feasibility. Philosophy has been prepared to consider feasibility to the extent of looking for arrangements that are going to fit with what Rawls (1971) describes as the circumstances of justice: that is, real-world situations where goods are in scarce if ready supply and people compete in pursuit of them. And equally philosophy has begun to take serious account of the inevitable fact, as Rawls (1993) conceives it to be, that people will have reasonable disagreements over how ideally they should behave and how their society should be organized (Waldron 1999). But as Rawls again illustrates, philosophical as distinct from economic approaches generally suppose that we should ask in the first place about what sociopolitical arrangement is most desirable, assuming full compliance with its demands, and only later inquire—if we inquire at all—into how problems of partial compliance should be dealt with.

The issue of feasibility that philosophers ignore is described among economists as the problem of incentive-compatibility. This is the problem of how to ensure that whatever arrangements are put in place—and whatever efforts of imagination and design may have been required to put them in place—they are arrangements that ordinary human beings are able in general to sustain. In particular, the arrangements are not motivationally too demanding; they are compatible with the incentives—the pedestrian or even the base incentives—that routinely and reliably affect what people do. Short of being pure conventions (Lewis 1969), socially beneficial institutions will almost all fail to attract full compliance but the degree of compliance forthcoming should be sufficient, at the very least, to keep the institutions in place and to enable them to promote the benefits for which they are designed.

It is worth mentioning that the problem of how to ensure such incentive-compatibility, and such intertemporal stability, though neglected in contemporary philosophy, was right at the centre of concerns in classical Greek and Roman ways of thinking. In that tradition, a prominent question was how to find a constitution that would be proof against corruption over time. Roman republicanism, which had such an influence on Renaissance and early modern political thought, was inspired, not just by the thought that it secured *libertas*, or freedom (Pettit 1997; Skinner 1998; Viroli 2002), but by the idea that the mixed constitution exemplified in the Roman republic offered the best hope of a stable political dispensation (Pocock 1975). This concern with finding institutions that were stable as well as desirable—in particular, stable in the presence of ordinary human motivation—remained central to the neo-Roman republicanism, inspiring later writers like Machiavelli, Harrington, and Montesquieu as well as the authors of the Federalist Papers.

But notwithstanding its classical lineage, the problem of incentive-compatibility has assumed a novel form since the rise of economics and of more economically shaped ways of thinking. This discipline has intruded two distinct sorts of assumptions about human beings that have shaped the debate about the issue. First, process-centred assumptions about the way in which desires or degrees of preference issue in action. And secondly, content-centred assumptions about the sorts of things that the agents desire: about which things they prefer and with what intensities. The one set of assumptions casts human beings as rational in a distinctive sense, the other as more or less egocentric or self-interested in the concerns they rationally pursue.

As far as process-based assumptions are concerned, the first thing to notice is that economists almost universally accept the weak claim that whenever people act, they do so as a result of their own desires or utility functions. They do not act on the basis of moral belief alone, for example; such belief issues in action, only if accompanied by a suitable desire. And they do not act just on the basis of perceiving what other people desire; the perception that someone desires something can lead to action only in the presence of a desire to satisfy that other person. Some thinkers toy with the possibility that agents may be capable of putting themselves under the control of something other than their own desires: for example, Mark Platts (1979) when he imagines that moral belief may motivate without the presence of desire; Amartya Sen (1982) when he speaks of the possibility of commitment; and Frederic Schick (1984) when he canvasses the notion of sociality. But the normal line is that all action is mediated via the desires of the agent.

How do people's desires lead to action, then, according to the economic way of thinking? The general assumption is that desires lead to actions via beliefs about the options available, about the likely consequences of those options, and so on. More specifically, the assumption is that they lead to actions that serve the desires well according to such beliefs; in other words, that they lead to subjectively rational actions. There are different theories as to what it is for an action or choice to serve an agent's desires well, according to his or her beliefs: about what it is for an action to be subjectively rational. But the family of theories available is well exemplified by the Bayesian claim that an action is rational just in case it maximizes the agent's expected utility (Eells 1982).

The Bayesian idea, roughly, is that every agent has a utility function that identifies a certain degree of utility, a certain intensity of preference, for every way the world may be—every prospect—and a probability function that determines, for each option and for each prospect, the probability that the choice of that option would lead to the realization of that prospect. An action will maximize the agent's expected utility just in case it has a higher expected utility than alternative options, where we determine the expected utility of an option as follows. We take the prospects with non-zero probability associated with the option; we multiply the utility of each prospect by the fraction representing the probability of its being realized in the event of the option's being chosen; and we add those products together.

So much for the assumptions that economists make about the way desires or preferences lead to action. What now of the assumptions that they make about the content of what human beings prefer or desire? The main question here is how far economists cast human beings as egocentric in their desires.

Many economists and economically minded philosophers endorse what is sometimes known as non-tuism. They hold that people's desires in regard to others are not affected by their perceptions of other people's desires: utility functions are independent (Gauthier 1986). Or they hold, more strongly still, that not only do people take no account of what others desire in forming their own desires in regard to others; any desires they have for what others should do, or for what should happen to others, are motivated ultimately by a self-centred desire for their own satisfaction (Gauthier 1986: 311). Economists endorse non-tuism to the extent that various economic models assume that any good I do you is, from my point of view, an externality for which ideally I would want to extract payment: an external benefit that I would ideally want to appropriate for myself—that is, 'internalize'

(Gauthier 1986: 87). But this seems to be a feature of particular models and not an assumption that is essentially built into the economic way of thinking. And it is a feature that affects only some of the standard results of the theories in question, not all of them (Sen 1982: 93).

But even if economics does not require people to be non-tuistic, even if it allows that they may have non-instrumental desires in relation to others—perhaps desires that are affected by their perception of what the others desire—still it does generally assume that there is something egocentric about the desires on which people generally act. This assumption is not an essential aspect of the rational choice theory they endorse but it is routinely deployed in the application of the theory. Whenever there is a conflict between what will satisfy me or mine and what will satisfy others, the assumption is that in general I will look for the more egocentric satisfaction. I may do so through neglecting your interests in my own efforts at self-promotion, or through helping my children at the expense of yours, or through jeopardizing a common good for the sake of personal advantage, or through taking the side of my country against that of others. The possibilities are endless. What unites them is that in each case I display a strong preference for what concerns me or mine, in particular a preference that is stronger than a countervailing preference for what concerns others.

The assumption that people are relatively self-regarding in their desires shows up in the fact that economists and rational choice theorists tend only to invoke relatively self-regarding desires in their explanations and predictions. They predict that as it costs more to help others, there will be less help given to others, that as it becomes personally more difficult to contribute to a common cause—more difficult, say, to take litter to the bin—there will be a lesser level of contribution to that cause, and so on. They offer invisible-hand explanations under which we are told how some collective good is attained just on the basis of their each pursuing their own advantage. And they specialize in prisoner's dilemma accounts that reveal how people come to be collectively worse off, through seeking each to get the best possible outcome for themselves.

The belief that people are relatively self-regarding may also be at the root of the Paretian or quasi-Paretian assumption of normative or welfare economics that it is uncontroversially a social benefit if things can be changed so that all preferences currently satisfied continue to be satisfied and if further preferences are satisfied as well. This assumption is plausible if the preferences envisaged are self-regarding, for only envy would seem to provide a reason for denying that it is a good if some people can get more of what they want for themselves without others getting less. But the assumption is not at all plausible if the preferences also include other-regarding preferences, for reasons to which Amartya Sen (1982, essay 2) has directed our attention.

Consider two boys, Nasty and Nice, and their preferences in regard to the distribution of two apples, Big and Small. Nasty prefers to get Big no matter who is in control of the distribution. Nice prefers to get Small if he is in control—this, because he is other-regarding and feels he should give Big away if he is in charge— but prefers to get Big if Nasty is in control: he is only human, after all. The Paretian assumption suggests—under the natural individuation of options—that it is better to have Nice control the distribution rather than Nasty. If we put Nice in control, then that satisfies Nasty—he gets Big—and it satisfies Nice as well: Nice's prefer- ence for having Big if Nasty is in control does not get engaged and Nice's preference for having Small—for giving Big away—if he is in control himself is satisfied. But this is clearly crazy: it means that we are punishing Nice for being nice, in particu- lar for having other-regarding preferences; and this, while apparently attempting just to increase preference satisfaction in an impartial manner. The lesson is that the Paretian assumption is not plausible once other-regarding preferences figure on the scene and so, if economists think that it is plausible—think indeed that it is uncontroversial—that suggests that they only have self-regarding preferences in view.

The assumption that human agents are rational, more or less self-regarding creatures has shaped a good deal of economic and related thought about how to make institutions incentive compatible. The idea has been to devise institutional arrangements that promise to survive and prosper—that promise to be stable—in a world where people are, as economics represents them, rational self-seekers. No matter how inherently desirable a scheme may seem to be—no matter how we would rejoice at the prospect of living in a world where it is implemented—the fact that it is not compatible with the *Homo oeconomicus* image of humankind means, according to this approach, that it is not deserving of serious attention except perhaps as an object of aesthetic appreciation.

This style of thinking, economically formulated though it is, fits well with the classical and modern tradition of political philosophy, as already suggested; what it breaks with is the recent, Rawlsian preference for ideal theory. We can represent support for the approach either as an argument for letting economic ways of thinking influence the philosophical exploration of normative political issues or as a plea for recalling political philosophy to the task of institutional design that bulked so large in an earlier era.

4. A PHILOSOPHICAL OBJECTION

We turn in this and the next section to consider two forms of objection to the incentive-compatibility approach. One is more philosophical in character, the other more empirical, but they turn out to have quite deep connections with one another.

The philosophical objection starts from the manifest fact, as we take it to be, that ordinary people do not conduct their lives in the relentless consideration of what is more likely to do well by them or theirs.[2] Rather, they orientate themselves in the run-of-the-mill situations in which most of their lives are led by reference to the lights provided by the cultural framing of those circumstances. They display the profile of *Homo sociologicus*, enacting now this role, now that, and generally living up to the expectations associated with those roles. This being so, the objection goes, how can it make sense to devise institutions with an eye to how well they serve more or less self-regarding incentives? Won't that amount to devising institutions for creatures who reason in a rather peculiar and untypical manner?

Consider the sorts of considerations that weigh with us, or seem to weigh with us, in a range of common-or-garden situations. We are apparently moved in our dealings with others by considerations that bear on their merits and their attractions, that highlight what is expected of us and what fair play or friendship requires, that direct attention to the good we can achieve together or the past that we share in common, and so on through a complex variety of deliberative themes. And not only are we apparently moved in this non-egocentric way. We clearly believe of one another—and take it, indeed, to be a matter of common belief—that we are generally and reliably responsive to claims that transcend and occasionally confound the calls of self-regard. That is why we feel free to ask each other for favours, to ground our projects in the expectation that others will be faithful to their past commitments, and to seek counsel from others in confidence that they will present us with a more or less impartial rendering of how things stand.

Suppose that people believed that they were each as self-regarding as economists appear to assume; suppose that this was a matter of common belief among them. In that case we would expect each of them to try to persuade others to act in a certain way by convincing them that it is in their personal interest to act in that way: this, in good part, by convincing them that they, the persuaders, will match such action appropriately, having corresponding reasons of personal advantage to do so. Under the economic supposition, there would be little room for anyone to call on anyone else in the name of any motive other than self-interest.

The economic supposition may be relevant in some areas of human exchange, most saliently in areas of market behaviour. But on the face of things it seems to apply much less across the broader range of human interaction. Within that broader range, people present each other with considerations that, putatively, they both recognize as relevant and potentially persuasive. I do not call on you in the name of what is just to your personal advantage; did I do so, that could be a serious insult. I call on you in the name of your commitment to certain ideals, your

---

[2] The discussion in this section follows the lines of Pettit (1995).

membership of certain groups, your attachment to certain people. I call on you, more generally, under the assumption that like me you understand and endorse the language of loyalty and fair play, kindness and politeness, honesty and straight talking. This language often has a moral ring but the terminology and concepts involved are not confined to the traditional limits of the moral; they extend to all the terms in which our culture allows us to make sense of ourselves, to make ourselves acceptably intelligible, to each other.

Consider how best an ethnographer might seek to make sense of the ways in which people conduct their lives and affairs. An ethnographer that came to the shores of a society like ours—a society like one of the developed democracies— would earn the ridicule of professional colleagues if they failed to take notice of the rich moral and quasi-moral language in which we ordinary folk explain ourselves to ourselves and to one another: the language, indeed, in which we take our bearings as we launch ourselves in action. But if it is essential for the understanding of how we ordinary folk behave that account is taken of that language, then this strongly suggests that economists must be mistaken—at least they must be overlooking some aspect of human life—when they assume that we are a relatively self-regarding lot.

The claim that ordinary folk are oriented towards a non-egocentric language of self-explanation and self-justification does not establish definitively, of course, that they are actually not self-regarding. We all recognize the possibilities of rationalization and deception that such a language leaves open. Still, it would surely be miraculous that that language succeeds as well as it does in defining a stable and smooth framework of expectation, if as a matter of fact people's sensibilities do not conform to its contours: if, as a matter of fact, people fall systematically short— systematically and not just occasionally short—of what it suggests may be taken for granted about them.

We are left, then, with a problem. The mind of *Homo oeconomicus* that is presupposed to the argument for making institutions incentive-compatible is that of a rational, relatively self-regarding creature. But the mind that people display towards one another in most social settings, the mind that is articulated in common conceptions of how ordinary folk are moved, is saturated with concerns that dramatically transcend the boundaries of the self. Doesn't this mean, then, that the incentive-compatibility approach is based on a falsehood and does not merit serious attention?

No, it does not. One response that is open to defenders of the approach is to argue that even if as a matter of fact people are not generally of the rational, self-regarding mentality described, still we should design our institutions for the worst-case scenario in which they are of such a mind (Brennan and Buchanan 1981). This may not appeal, of course, if catering for the worst-case scenario is likely to be a very bad strategy for more probable, better-case scenarios; and as we shall see in the next section, that may very well be so. But in any case there is another response available to theorists of incentive-compatibility. They may argue that despite appearances to the contrary, it is perfectly consistent to hold that people do

not normally think in terms of rational self-interest and yet to say that they conform to the economic picture; they are rational creatures whose behaviour serves
on the whole to promote their self-interest.

Suppose that people are generally content in non-market contexts, as the objection
says, to let their actions be dictated by the cultural framing of the situation in
which they find themselves. A friend asks for a routine level of help and, in the
absence of urgent business, the agent naturally complies with the request; it would
be unthinkable for someone who understands what friendship means to do anything else. There is an election in progress and, the humdrum of everyday life being
what it is, the agent spontaneously makes time for going to the polls; that is manifestly the thing to do, under ordinary canons of understanding, and the thing to do
without thinking about it. Someone has left a telephone message asking for a return
call about some matter and the agent doesn't hesitate to ring back; even if aware
that there is nothing useful they can tell the original caller, they shrink from the
impoliteness, in their culture, of ignoring the call. In the pedestrian patterns of
day-to-day life, the cultural framing of any situation will be absolutely salient to the
ordinary agent and the ordinary agent will more or less routinely respond. Or so at
least we are prepared to grant.

Suppose, however, that despite the hegemony of cultural framing in people's
everyday deliberations and decisions, there are certain alarm bells that make them
take thought to their own interests. People may proceed under more or less automatic, cultural pilot in most cases but at any point where a decision is liable to cost
them dearly in self-regarding terms, the alarm bells ring and prompt them to
consider personal advantage; and heeding considerations of personal advantage
leads people, generally if not invariably, to act so as to secure that advantage: they
are disposed to do the relatively more self-regarding thing.

Under these suppositions, self-regard will normally have no active presence in
dictating what people do; it will not be present in deliberation and will make no
impact on decision. But it will always be virtually present in deliberation, for there
are alarms that are ready to ring at any point where the agent's interests are likely
to be compromised and those alarms will call up self-regard and give it a more or
less controlling deliberative presence. People will run under cultural pilot, provided that that pilot does not carry them into terrain that is too dangerous from a
self-interested point of view. Let such terrain come into view, and they will quickly
return to manual; they will quickly begin to count the more personal losses and
benefits that are at stake in the decision on hand. This reflection may not invariably
lead to self-regarding action—there is such a thing as self-sacrifice, after all—but
the assumption is that it will do so fairly reliably.

If the suppositions I have described were realized, then it would be fair to say
that people are implicitly self-regarding: that they implicitly conform to the image
of the economic mind. The reason is that under the model of virtual self-regard, no
action is performed without self-regarding consideration unless it fails to ring

certain alarms: that is, unless it promises to do suitably well in self-regard terms. What it is to do suitably well may vary from individual to individual, of course, depending on their expectations as to what is feasible and depending on their self-regarding aspirations: depending on how much they want for themselves, and with what intensity. But the point is that regardless of such variations, the model of virtual self-regarding control does privilege self-regard in a manner that conforms to the image of the economic mind. Another way of putting this point is to say that under the model described, agents will generally be moved by certain considerations only if those considerations satisfy a certain negative, self-regarding condition: they do not lead towards a certain level of self-sacrifice. Let the considerations push an agent below the relevant self-regarding level of aspiration and the alarms bells will ring, causing the agent to rethink and probably reshape the project on hand.

The position that self-regard is given under the model of virtual self-regarding control is rather like that which it enjoys under Herbert Simon's (1978) model of satisficing as distinct from maximizing behaviour. People do pretty well in self-regarding terms, even if they do not do as well as possible. And it may even be that virtual self-regarding control enables them to do as well as possible in egocentric terms, for the absence of self-regarding calculation in most decisions represents a saving in time and trouble—these are virtues emphasized by Simon—and it may also secure other benefits: it may earn a greater degree of acceptance and affection, for example, than would a pattern of relentless calculation.

The picture of agents as rational and relatively self-regarding becomes perfectly plausible once it is taken to posit, not an active pattern of minute-by-minute calculation, but a pattern of just virtual control. The idea is that rational self-interest intrudes itself in human reasoning only on a need-to-intrude basis. Let things evolve under cultural framing so that there is no salient offence to an agent's self-interest, and rational calculation will stay off the scene. Let them cease to evolve in that way, however—in particular, let some signs of breakdown materialize—and it will more or less reliably make an appearance. Rational self-interest can have an important shaping effect on what people do and yet it may normally figure only as a standby cause that is waiting to be activated. It may generally stay out of the ratiocinative cockpit and still serve to determine where the pilot of reason and habit leads.

5. AN EMPIRICAL OBJECTION

As it is normally understood, the incentive-compatibility approach is associated with 'the knaves principle' that David Hume formulated as follows: in 'fixing the several checks and controls of the constitution, every man ought to be supposed a knave, and to have no other end in all his actions than private interest' (1875: 117–18). Bernard Mandeville had already endorsed that sort of principle when he said that the best sort of constitution is the one which 'remains unshaken though most men should prove knaves' (1731: 332).

The empirical objection to the incentive-compatibility approach is an objection, more specifically, to the use of the knaves principle in institutional design. The idea is that if we seek to design institutions fit to survive the presence of knaves, we may end up designing institutions that will not work very well among ordinary human beings. Ordinary human beings may be relatively self-regarding, as in the virtual model, but the suggestion is that they are not creatures whose only end is 'private interest'; and certainly they are not creatures, as the word 'knaves' suggest, who will stop at little or nothing to get their private way. The objection is that, this being so, the knaves principle—and, more generally, the emphasis on incentive-compatibility—may argue for the introduction of institutions that would actually be counter-productive.

This line of objection is supported by the work of a number of authors within the broad tradition of regulation and institutional design (Braithwaite 1989; Tyler 1990; Ayres and Braithwaite 1992; Le-Grand 1997). One of the most explicit critics of the knaves principle is the economist Bruno Frey, who charges that incentives designed to cope with the danger of knaves—the danger that there are some people who are not virtuously motivated to conform to certain socially beneficial arrangements—may have the effect of ensuring that those who previously had such virtue will lose it or fail to act on it (Frey 1997; Frey and Jegen 2001). Providing certain extra incentives for complying with the arrangements may 'crowd out' the incentives already there in many people and may have the effect of reducing the level of compliance overall.

Frey (1997: 16–17) argues, on the basis of his empirical research, that there are three conditions under which extra motivation may support virtuous, compliant motivation rather than supplanting it. First, the motivation provided does not suggest that the agent needs to be controlled from the outside. Secondly, it does not reduce the agent's self-esteem. And thirdly, it does not obscure the presence of virtuous motivation when the agent complies. These findings suggest that it might be crazy to design institutions on the Humean or Mandevillean model. For if we organize institutions around incentives that treat people as knaves—say, institutions that represent politicians as inevitably corrupt self-seekers—then we will often be putting in place incentives that meet these conditions. And so we have every reason to fear that the line we are taking is going to be a counter-productive one.

Nor is this the end of the story. Relying on knavish incentives to elicit more reliable compliance may activate other counter-productive factors besides those at which Frey gestures. For example, they may cause those to whom they are applied—say, certain officials in a political system—to resent the negative label implied, to become defiant in reaction to the pressure imposed, and to close ranks against outside judgement and criticism (Grabosky 1995; Pettit 1997, ch. 7).

And they may also have the effect of attracting into the domain in question those who are not particularly virtuous but who relish the opportunities provided by such incentives: say, penalties that may easily prove to be avoidable or, of course, high monetary rewards (Brennan 1996).

Is this objection a serious challenge for the project of non-ideal theory, as we have been describing it here? We do not think so. The reason is that non-ideal theory may take the issue of incentive-compatibility seriously without endorsing anything like the knaves principle. What the objection shows is that it would be a serious mistake to identify the project of institutional design that is embodied in the notion of non-ideal theory with that Humean principle.

The assumption behind the incentive-compatibility approach is not that people are ordinarily knavish but rather that virtuous motivation—the motivation to comply with whatever are accepted as socially beneficial institutions—is not necessarily going to be available at ideal levels. Not everybody is going to be virtuously motivated all of the time, even if most are well motivated most of the time. And so there is going to be a need to have institutions, so the idea goes, that guard against such failures of virtue, however temporary or local in character. Moreover, even those relatively rare individuals who are entirely uncorrupt and so disposed to act as political virtue requires may still be corruptible (Pettit 1997, ch. 7). Expose them to situations where they can satisfy selfish interests at very little risk of exposure—that is, to situations where personal incentives make a case for not complying with public institutions—and they may be likely to become corrupted. As Socrates in effect asked, who can say that they would remain uncorrupted if given the power of the ring of Gyges: the power of offending with the invisibility, and so the impunity, that that ring would confer?

This network of assumptions does not suggest that a concern for incentive-compatibility ought to lead us, necessarily, to apply the knaves principle in designing institutions. Given that virtue is in scarce or unassured supply—given that people will not always comply spontaneously or robustly with what their institutions require of them—the strategy that ought to appeal in the design of institutions is this. Don't rely on virtue alone to ensure compliance; but don't reduce the virtue that is already there in the population by resorting to motivating factors that crowd out virtue. Economize on virtue, by all means, but make sure that doing so does not erode the virtue on which you are economizing.

If we follow this more complex strategy, then what we must seek in institutional design is a pattern of incentives that serves on the one hand to support the virtue that is already there in the community but on the other to substitute for virtue in those cases where virtue fails. One way of following such a strategy would be to implement the following three-step procedure (Pettit 1997, ch. 7):

- First, try to arrange things so that people are recruited to institutional sites where their existing motivation is likely to support compliance with what is required there. Match opportunity to virtue.

- Secondly, try to ensure that the incentives available at different sites will support the survival of such virtuous motivation, not its erosion. Match incentive to virtue.
- Thirdly, try to ensure that those who fail to comply under such pressures—those who prove knavish—are exposed to suitable incentives: for example, penalties. Match incentive to vice.

We have emphasized throughout our discussion that the incentive-compatibility approach is consistent with traditional ways of thinking in political theory, even if it runs counter to the Rawlsian preference for ideal theory. It is worth mentioning that the complex strategy supported by the considerations about the danger of crowding out virtue is also to be found in the tradition. Mandeville and Hume may have gone for a knaves-principle version of the approach—and in doing so they may have had an important impact on the thinking of economists—but that was certainly not the version that predominated more generally in their century and before. James Madison (Madison *et al.* 1987: 343) articulates a version of the approach that is much more typical of the tradition when he writes in the Federalist Papers, No. 57: 'The aim of every political constitution is, or ought to be, first to obtain for rulers men who possess most wisdom to discern, and most virtue to pursue, the common good of the society; and in the next place, to take the most effectual precautions for keeping them virtuous whilst they continue to hold their public trust.'

One last observation. While the knaves principle represents a distortion of the incentive-compatibility approach, it does answer quite well to the image of that approach associated with orthodox economics. The paradigm of incentive-based regulation within economics is the competitive market in which an invisible hand ensures that so long as participants each seek to maximize their individual advantage—and so long as virtue therefore plays no necessary role—the social benefit of competitive pricing will inevitably materialize. The competitive market is not just incentive-compatible; it is compatible with the incentives of those knaves who, in Hume's words, have no other end than their private interest. This fact may explain why the knaves principle has often been taken as a straightforward articulation of the incentive-compatibility approach, not a serious distortion of it.

6. VIRTUE-FRIENDLY INCENTIVES

Perhaps the most telling demand on the strategy described in the previous section is to identify incentives that can support pre-existing virtue rather than crowding it out. We try to show in this final section that the demand can be met by providing a sketch of one category of motives that looks likely to satisfy it. These are motives associated with the desire to enjoy the good opinion of others, and to avoid their bad opinion, and we have explored them at length elsewhere (Brennan and Pettit 2004).

Our discussion in the previous section suggests that the ideal compliance-incentives which we might hope to put in place would have features like the following. They would operate better in the presence of virtue than in its absence, so that the habit of being influenced by those incentives would not erode virtue. They would operate in such a way that the fact that someone is virtuously motivated, if indeed they are so motivated, will not be hidden; thus their operation would not erode the person's image, including their self-image, as a virtuous person. And our exposing someone to those incentives, even doing so openly, would not suggest that we thought they were lacking in virtue; thus it would not elicit any resentment or defiance.

The problem with the ordinary run of rewards and penalties that we might think of introducing in institutional design is that they are likely to breach conditions of this kind. The monetary reward or penalty, for example, would operate in the absence of virtue. The manifest prospect of such a reward or penalty would conceal the presence of virtue, providing a more salient explanation for compliant behaviour. And our introducing such a sanction—say, as a manager might introduce it to motivate employees—would signal a belief that the people affected do not have the level of virtue that would guarantee compliance.

The economic tradition tends to think in terms of rewards and penalties of this kind, looking to the invisible hand of the market or the iron hand of management—including the management of the law—to ensure compliance with relevant institutions. But there is an older tradition of thinking—and one, ironically, to which Adam Smith (1982) was an ardent subscriber—according to which very different incentives routinely play the role of eliciting people's compliance with the institutions under which they live. The tradition suggests that in suitable circumstances people may be moved to do what is honourable and to avoid what is dishonourable—at least moved in part—because behaving in that manner will enable them to enjoy honour and escape dishonour.

Consider this passage from John Locke, writing in 1690:

For though Men uniting into Politick Societies, have resigned up to the public the disposing of all their Force, so that they cannot employ it against any Fellow-Citizen, any farther than the Law of the Country directs: yet they retain still the power of Thinking well or ill; approving or disapproving of the actions of those whom they live amongst, and converse with: And by this approbation and dislike they establish amongst themselves, what they will call Virtue and Vice. (Locke 1975: 353–4)

Locke is absolutely typical of his time, and of the broad tradition down to about the end of the eighteenth century, in emphasizing the role of what he called the law of opinion—or, as he might equally have said, the law of esteem and disesteem—in supporting the other laws established in society. This esteem-based dispensation prevails and has a powerful influence among people just so far as they each think well of good behaviour and think ill of bad or, more strictly, just so far as they are each seen or expected to think well and ill of such patterns of behaviour. The idea is that in conditions of mutual visibility people can provide one another with incentives to comply with the institutions that are established among them, at least so far as it is a matter of common belief that those institutions are socially benefi-cial and valuable. Those incentives will involve the reward of esteem in being seen to perform well, the penalty of disesteem or shame in being seen to perform badly.

Incentives of esteem and disesteem promise to meet the sorts of conditions mentioned above. They will operate more effectively to the extent that virtue is actually present, since the presence of virtue is the best predictor of being able to win esteem and avoid disesteem. That the motives are present means that people expect to be regarded as virtuous should they comply with the institutions under which they live. And that we introduce such motives, in the presumptive expecta-tion that they will be successful, argues that we think well of the agent involved, not badly; we take the agent to be the virtuous sort of person who will prove worthy of esteem.

This is not the place to expand on the potential importance of esteem motivation in institutional design and regulation. Our reason for drawing attention to it is to guard against any suggestion that the strategy described in the foregoing section is itself utopian, requiring the availability of incentives that are just not on offer in human life. As we think that the incentive-compatibility approach has to be distin-guished from the knaves principle, so we think that the habit of looking only to material sanctions in the design of institutions is also a mistake. Not only is there scope for deploying the invisible hand of the market—and, of course, the iron hand of management—in the design process. Crucially, there is also room for mobilizing what we describe as the intangible hand of esteem.

The intangible hand differs from the invisible hand in the following respect. The invisible hand shows how ordinary, not particularly virtuous actions can serve as input to a social process that makes for public good. The intangible shows how ordinary, not particularly virtuous motives can serve as input to a psychological process that equally makes for public good, supporting actions that produce such good. In the one case, unpromising behavioural material is turned to social benefit by a system for aggregating actions: paradigmatically, the market. In the other case, unpromising motivational material is turned to social benefit by a culture of shared valuation and a system of mutual visibility.

We mentioned earlier that the incentive-compatibility approach is often equated with applying the knaves principle to institutional design. Hand in hand with that mistake goes the equally common, and equally mistaken, assumption that the only reliable controls available for ensuring that people will act in a manner that conduces to the common good are the invisible hand of the market and the other the iron hand of law and administration—the iron hand of the state. The assump-tion that there are just two forms of social discipline shows up in the directions of government over the past decade or so. Governments have tried to market more and more of the services that used to be provided in the non-marketed sector of the economy—services in education, research, health, counselling, and the like. And, where marketing is impossible or problematic, they have sought to impose a tougher regime of monitoring and management: they have tried to subject those providing the services to ever more intrusive forms of surveillance and accounting.

We think that this dichotomous picture of regulatory possibilities is misconceived and that it distorts the search for incentive-compatible institutions. Not only should we look to what the motives exploited in those arrangements can do by way of supporting a given pattern of institutions. We should also consider what may be achieved by mobilizing the discipline of esteem and disesteem in support of the social and political institutions that we find desirable. It is worth noting, finally, that accepting the role of the desire for esteem in social life provides us with an explanation of why the effects of self-interest are often mobilized 'virtually'. Suppose that each individual is motivated by considerations of virtue, esteem, and interest in some (possibly widely varying) admixture. Recognize that to be seen to act from venal motives—or even in pursuit of esteem, in many cases—involves less esteem than to be seen to act out of considerations of virtue, or at least out of considerations that are unlikely to earn the actor disesteem. Then individuals will have reason to put themselves in the sway of estimable motives, to the extent that their motives are discernible by observers. So it will be no surprise that individuals seem to act from non-venal considerations most of the time. But equally it will be no surprise that if circumstances change in such a way that acting on the basis of such considerations starts to cost the actor a very great deal in interest terms, she will rethink her actions. There need be nothing particularly self-deceptive about this. The normal mode of reasoning in relation to action will genuinely be in terms other than self-interest. But self-interest will clock in to modify action, in cases where the actor comes to realize that the cost of failing to take interests explicitly into account has become too great. In this sense, including the desire for esteem as a motive helps explain the 'virtual' role that self-interest tends to play as well as directly providing possible resources for virtuous conduct.

7. CONCLUSION

Ideal theory runs the risk of leading us to recommend institutions that, for all we know, may be incapable of surviving in the world of motley human motivation. The institutions may be prone to collapse as a result of wholesale non-compliance and to leave the society worse off than if they had never been tried. The only possible response to this problem is to consider issues of incentive-compatibility as well as inherent desirability in assessing the merits of rival institutional arrangements. Political philosophy cannot ignore institutional design, leaving that project to more economic schools of thought. It has to give serious attention to the issues of stability that were at the centre of earlier concerns within the discipline but that have recently tended to disappear from the scene.

But the espousal of this non-ideal, real-world approach to political theory, so we saw, need not mean treating human beings as centres of relentless calculation about matters of self-interest; such matters may only have a virtual presence in people's minds. And it need not mean embracing the principle according to which institutions should be designed on the wholly pessimistic premiss that people may prove to be completely knavish. The project starts from the more modest, more realistic assumption that people vary in the extent and robustness of virtuous motivation and argues only for showing how that rule of virtue may be reinforced, and the institutions in question stabilized.

We illustrated the sort of recommendations to which the project may lead us by mentioning a strategy in which opportunity and incentive are matched to virtue before arrangements are made for dealing with those of a more vicious, non-compliant disposition. Central to this possibility was the prospect of finding incentives that would reinforce virtue, not undermine it. Without suggesting that they are the only incentives capable of meeting the bill, we called attention here to the esteem-based motives that figured importantly in traditional political theory. Such motives will operate better in the presence than in the absence of virtue and they will be effective only so far as virtue is imputed to those they move. One promising way of doing political theory in a non-ideal key is to insist that institutional assessments be supported with an analysis of how the institutions preferred may be expected to mobilize motives of esteem and disesteem, and to create a firmer infrastructure for their survival than unaided virtue would supply on its own.

REFERENCES

Arrow, K. (1963). *Social Choice and Individual Values*, 2nd edn. New York: Wiley.
Ayres, I., and Braithwaite, J. (1992). *Responsive Regulation*. New York: Oxford University Press.
Berlin, I. (1958). *Two Concepts of Liberty*. Oxford: Oxford University Press.
Braithwaite, J. (1989). *Crime, Shame and Reintegration*. Cambridge: Cambridge University Press.
Brennan, G. (1993). 'Economics', in R. E. Goodin and P. Pettit (eds.), *A Companion to Contemporary Political Philosophy*. Oxford: Blackwell.
—— (1996). 'Selection and the Currency of Reward', in R. E. Goodin (ed.), *The Theory of Institutional Design*. Cambridge: Cambridge University Press.
—— and Buchanan, J. (1981). 'The Normative Purpose of Economic "Science": Rediscovery of an Eighteenth Century Method'. *International Review of Law and Economics*, 1: 155–66.

—— and Pettit, P. (2004). *The Economy of Esteem: An Essay on Civil and Political Society*. Oxford: Oxford University Press.

Christiano, T. (1996). *The Rule of the Many: Fundamental Issues in Democratic Theory*. Boulder, Colo.: Westview Press.

Eells, E. (1982). *Rational Decision and Causality*. Cambridge: Cambridge University Press.

Frey, B. (1997). *Not Just for the Money: An Economic Theory of Personal Motivation*. Cheltenham: Edward Elgar.

—— and Jegen, R. (2001). 'Motivation Crowding Theory: A Survey'. *Journal of Economic Surveys*. 15: 589–611.

Gauthier, D. (1986). *Morals by Agreement*. Oxford: Oxford University Press.

Goodin, R. E. (1995). 'Political Ideals and Political Practice'. *British Journal of Political Science*, 44: 635–46.

Grabosky, P. N. (1995). 'Counterproductive Regulation'. *International Journal of the Sociology of Law*, 23: 347–69.

Hume, D. (1875). 'Of the Independence of Parliament', in T. H. Green and T. H. Grose (eds.), *Hume's Philosophical Works*, iii. London: Longmans.

Le-Grand, J. (1997). 'Knights, Knaves or Pawns? Human Behaviour and Social Policy'. *Journal of Social Policy*, 26: 149–69.

Lewis, D. (1969). *Convention*. Cambridge, Mass.: Harvard University Press.

Locke, J. (1975). *An Essay Concerning Human Understanding*. Oxford: Oxford University Press.

Madison, J., Hamilton, A., *et al.* (1987). *The Federalist Papers*. Harmondsworth: Penguin.

Mandeville, B. (1731). *Free Thoughts on Religion, the Church and National Happiness*. London: J. Roberts.

Nussbaum, M. (2002). *Beyond the Social Contract: Towards Global Justice*. Tanner Lectures in Human Values. Cambridge, Mass.: Harvard University Press.

Pettit, P. (1995). 'The Virtual Reality of Homo Economicus'. *The Monist*, 78: 308–29. Repr. with additions in Pettit, *Rules, Reasons, and Norms*. Oxford: Oxford University Press, 2002.

—— (1997). *Republicanism: A Theory of Freedom and Government*. Oxford: Oxford University Press.

Platts, M. (1979). *Ways of Meaning*. London: Routledge.

Pocock, J. (1975). *The Machiavellian Moment: Florentine Political Theory and the Atlantic Republican Tradition*. Princeton: Princeton University Press.

Rawls, J. (1971). *A Theory of Justice*. Oxford: Oxford University Press.

—— (1993). *Political Liberalism*. New York: Columbia University Press.

—— (1999). *The Law of Peoples*. Cambridge, Mass.: Harvard University Press.

Schick, F. (1984). *Having Reasons*. Princeton: Princeton University Press.

Sen, A. (1970). *Collective Choice and Social Welfare*. San Francisco: Holden-Day.

—— (1982). *Choice, Welfare and Measurement*. Oxford: Blackwell.

Simon, H. (1978). 'Rationality as Process and as Product of Thought'. *American Economic Review*, 68: 1–16.

Skinner, Q. (1998). *Liberty Before Liberalism*. Cambridge: Cambridge University Press.

Smith, A. (1982). *The Theory of the Moral Sentiments*. Indianapolis: Liberty Classics.

Tyler, T. R. (1990). *Why People Obey the Law*. New Haven: Yale University Press.

Viroli, M. (2002). *Republicanism*. New York: Hill & Wang.

Waldron, J. (1999). *Law and Disagreement*. Oxford: Oxford University Press.

PART III

PHILOSOPHY OF MIND AND ACTION

CHAPTER 11

INTENTIONALITY

GABRIEL SEGAL

1. INTRODUCTION

I shall begin with a sketchy historical introduction to the topic, which will help bring into focus some of the pressing issues for philosophy in the twenty-first century.

1.1 Brentano's Problem

'Intentionality' as it is typically used in analytic philosophy, meaning, roughly *representation* or "*aboutness*", derives from the work of Franz Brentano. Brentano (1874, quoted in Chisholm 1967) wrote:

Every mental phenomenon is characterised by what the scholastics of the Middle Ages called the intentional (and also mental) inexistence of an object, and what we would call, although not in entirely unambiguous terms, the reference to a content, a direction upon an object (by which we are not to understand a reality . . .), or an immanent objectivity. Each one includes something as an object in itself, although not always in the same way. In presentation something is presented, in judgement something is affirmed or denied, in love [something is] loved, in hate [something] is hated, in desire something is desired etc.

Thus for Brentano mental states are essentially related to certain kinds of objects or contents that have 'intentional inexistence' within the states. These came to be called 'intentional objects'. Brentano was particularly concerned with the problem of how we can represent things that don't exist outside of the mind, such as unicorns.

His original idea was that if one thinks about a unicorn, then one's thought has an intentional object that does exist. The object is not, however, a concrete inhabitant of external reality, but an ephemeral entity, existing in the mind only.

Brentano held that the objects of thought and experience were always such intentional entities. Thus if one is thinking about Paris, the immediate object of one's thought is an intentional object rather than a city. One's thought is true if there is a match of the right kind between the properties of the intentional object and those of the real object. An obvious problem with this view is that it offers no account of what determines the real object of thought (Paris), and hence leaves the nature of intentionality mysterious. Brentano himself came to realize this and abandoned the doctrine.[1]

Brentano's problem remains with us, and much of subsequent philosophy of mind is, in one or way another, concerned with it. When we think about a real object, such as Paris, it seems that the object of our thought is that real object, the city, with all its lights. Moreover, it seems that a mental state's capacity to relate in this way to real objects is important to the role that they play in the explanation of action. Suppose that Spike wants to go to Paris and believes that the best way of getting to Paris is by train. So Spike takes the train to Paris. It looks as though an important part of the explanation of why Spike ended up physically located in Paris is the fact that his desire and belief involved a concept that has that city as its object. So it looks as though intentionality must involve a real relation among real-world objects.

When we consider empty concepts, however, exactly the reverse conclusion seems tempting. Suppose that Angel hears of a fabulously wealthy city in South America called 'El Argentino'. He forms the desire to visit El Argentino and he comes to believe that the best way to get to El Argentino requires taking a ship to Mexico. He boards the ship and ends up in Mexico. It looks as though part of the explanation of why Angel acted as he did is that he had the specified desire and belief, featuring the concept that he associates with the expression 'El Argentino' (his 'El Argentino' concept). In this case, it looks as though the concept plays a role in explaining Angel's actions, even though it has no object. Moreover, it looks as though its possession or lack of a real-world object is irrelevant to that explanatory role. Angel would have acted as he did if El Argentino had existed and his beliefs had been true. Or so it would seem, at first blush.

I will return to Brentano's problem shortly. First I will introduce a second problem that is interwoven with it, a problem brought into focus by Gottlob Frege.

---

[1] Two of Brentano's students reacted to the problem by going to opposite extremes. Alexius Meinong (1904/1960) held there are such things as unicorns etc.: non-existent objects have a kind of being other than existence and so can be non-immanent objects of thought. Edmund Husserl held that mental states do not involve relations to objects at all, but rather are characterized by intrinsic properties: thinking of Paris might be understood along the lines of thinking Parisly (Husserl 1950). For a modern defence of non-existent objects, see Salmon (1998) and for a recent version of adverbialism, see Tye (1989).

1.2 Frege's Problem

Frege propounded a powerful and sophisticated theory of representation. His primary interest was in the development of formal languages for the purposes of mathematics and science, and his ideas about representation apply primarily to them. In his view, natural languages are flawed representational systems, not of much independent interest. However, his ideas remain central in current debates about representation.

The notion at the core of Frege's theory was that of reference. The reference of an expression is what it contributes to the truth-value of sentences in which it appears. Reference is a real relation between an expression and an object, the expression's referent. If a refers to b, then both a and b exist. The referent of a singular term is what one would ordinarily think the term stands for. For example, Venus is the referent of the term 'Venus' and also of 'Hesperus' and 'Phosphorus'. The referent of a sentence is its truth-value and predicative expressions refer to functions from objects to truth-values.

Since an expression's referent is what it contributes towards determining the truth-values of sentences, reference is governed by principle (P):

(P) Co-referring expressions may be intersubstituted in any sentence without altering the truth-value of that sentence.

For example, given that 'Hesperus' and 'Phosphorus' refer to the same thing, these terms ought to be intersubstitutable in any sentence without altering its truth-value. Linguistic contexts where (P) fails are typically called 'referentially opaque'.

(P) appears to be correct for many cases. But it appears to fail for propositional attitude reports (PARs), such as (1a) and (1b):

(1a) Spike believes that Hesperus is a planet.
(1b) Spike believes that Phosphorus is a planet.

It was in part to address this problem that Frege introduced another kind of content: sense. The sense of an expression is supposed to be a "mode of presentation" of its referent, a way the referent is presented in thought. Senses are objective, mind-independent objects. But our minds can grasp them. We understand an expression when we associate the right sense with it. Sense was also supposed to account for the cognitive properties of an expression: 'Hesperus is Hesperus' and 'Hesperus is Phosphorus' differ in their cognitive properties because they have different senses. Further, sense was supposed to contribute to the explanation of reference: an expression has its particular reference via its associated sense. And sense determines reference, in that if two expressions have the same sense, then they have the same reference.

Frege responded to the apparent violation of (P) by PARs by proposing that expressions in their content sentences (the p clauses in 'a believes/hopes...that p') refer to their senses, instead of their normal referents. Thus 'Phosphorus is a planet' in (1b) refers to its sense: the Fregean thought that Phosphorus is a planet. In line with this, Frege also held that the objects of propositional attitudes are themselves Fregean thoughts. To believe that Phosphorus is a planet is to stand in the appropriate doxastic relation to the thought that Phosphorus is a planet. In grasping the thought, one thinks about the planet.

It is natural to think that sense offers an appealing solution to Brentano's problem. Frege's own remarks on this topic, however, are somewhat cryptic. He certainly allowed that expressions can have sense and lack reference, for he explicitly claims this in various places, for example: 'The sentence "Odysseus was set ashore at Ithaca while sound asleep" obviously has a sense' (Frege 1892/1952: 62). Moreover, he held that the identity and nature of a term's sense was independent of the existence of its reference, since he goes on to say, 'The thought remains the same whether "Odysseus" means [i.e. refers to] something or not.'

However, whenever he discusses the matter, Frege focuses on fiction. And the kind of thoughts we have while indulging in fiction is of no relevance to Frege's concerns with the development of formal systems. If a term in a sentence lacks a referent, then, according to Frege, the whole sentence must lack a referent, hence cannot be true or false. But thoughts that are not true or false can play no role in serious theorizing. In Frege's view, logic could not apply to them.[2]

Frege's attitude to empty expressions occurring in serious uses, such as 'the least rapidly convergent series', is revealing. His view was that you must arbitrarily stipulate a referent for such expressions (Frege 1892/1952: 33). But this is very problematic. There are various referents one might choose that are all the same from a logical point of view. Whichever one you pick will have its own properties, and this will lead to sentences getting the wrong truth-values. Suppose, for example, that the chosen object is the empty set. 'There is no such thing as the least rapidly convergent series' then comes out false, rather than true. It is possible to stipulate semantic rules to avoid this sort of result. But these stipulations tend to be ad hoc and counter-intuitive, and it is far from clear that any adequate selection of them would be consistent with Frege's own philosophical views.

Notice further that the stipulated relation between 'the least rapidly convergent series' and the empty set doesn't enter into the right account of the semantic contribution of the empty expression to larger expressions. It evidently doesn't help provide a correct explanation of why 'There is no such thing as the least

---

[2] At a couple of points he calls such thoughts 'Scheingedanke', which was translated by Geach as 'Mock thoughts'. Gareth Evans (1982: 29) and John McDowell (1984) suggest that Frege did not think that Mock thoughts are thoughts at all. But this interpretation is inconsistent with Frege's repeated claims that sense without reference is possible. Moreover Frege says: 'Instead of "fiction", we could say "Mock Thought"' ('Statt "Dictung" koennten wir auch "Scheingedanke" sagen'). (1897/1983: 141). In the same work, he uses the term 'Scheineigenname' for an empty proper name. It is unlikely that he thought that a *Scheineigenname* isn't even a name. In view of this, it might be better to translate the somewhat technical terms 'Scheingedanke' and 'Scheineigenname' as 'Pretence thought' and 'Pretence name'. (Thanks to Mark Textor for help with Frege exegesis and German translation.) See also Makin (2000) and Sainsbury (2002) for discussion.

rapidly convergent series' is true. What is really doing the work in fixing the seman-tics of the expression must be something else, something other than a referent. Thus Frege's approach obscures Brentano's problem.

This point suggests that Evans is quite right when he refers to his treatment of empty expressions as 'the great fault-line in Frege's mature philosophy of language' (Evans 1982: 24). For it is difficult to see why Frege retained his insistence that every significant expression in serious discourse must have a referent. If the arbitrarily cho-sen referent of an empty expression does not reflect the expression's real semantics, then why bother with it? As Evans points out, it is quite possible to provide a logic that would be adequate for Frege's purposes and that does not require reference for all significant terms: a 'free' logic. One would simply specify rules for computing the values of complex expressions that correctly state the contribution of empty expres-sions. Perhaps Frege did not see this possibility, in which case there would have been a striking blind spot in the mind of the inventor of modern logic. Or perhaps he did see it, but rejected it for some unknown reason. Either way, there is evidence that very powerful intellectual currents are pulling Frege in different directions.

1.3 Russell's Solution

Bertrand Russell provided the obvious solution to the problem of 'the least rapidly convergent series', and other empty definite descriptions. Definite descriptions are complex expressions and their parts may be significant. It is obvious that the seman-tic features of definite descriptions are owed to those of their parts. So, as long as they all have reference, all should be well, even for a fundamentally reference-based seman-tics. All that is required is an account of how these referents combine to render significant the description as a whole. Russell's theory of descriptions achieves that.

Russell accounts for definite descriptions, in effect, by treating them as quantifiers. A sentence of the form 'the F is G' really means something that could be expressed as 'There is exactly one F and it is G'. Thus 'the F' can be significant even if it doesn't pick anything out. The theory of descriptions also offers an obvious explanation of why different co-referring descriptions have different cognitive value: 'the F = the G' can be informative, when true, because, in typical cases, it will not follow from the fact that just one thing is F that it (and it alone) is also G.

The quantificational treatment of definite descriptions occurring in technical discourse is very satisfactory. Whether it is correct for natural language is a matter of considerable controversy (for discussion, see Neale 1990; Larson and Segal 1995). But even if it is, there are many other types of expression that may be empty. For example, proper names ('Dracula') and general terms ('phlogiston', 'ghost').[3]

---

[3] Empty uses of demonstratives are also possible, of course. There are very important questions about demonstrative thoughts, which unfortunately I do not have space to discuss. See e.g. Evans (1981, 1982); Kaplan (1989, 1990); Peacocke (1981, 1983, 1993); Perry (1990); Segal (1989a).

Russell himself endeavoured to generalize the solution to all these cases. Thus 'Dracula' might be treated as equivalent to something like 'the greatest Transylvanian vampire', and 'phlogiston' as, say, 'the substance that, together with calx, composes metals'. These redeployments of the theory of descriptions are highly problematic, as we will see in subsequent sections.

2. Names and Name-Concepts

2.1 Kripke's Objection

The description theory of names is not very plausible, for reasons made clear by Saul Kripke (1972). If a name has the semantic content of an associated description, then the description must at least describe the name's bearer. And presumably speakers must associate the description with the name. But among the various descriptions that speakers associate with a name, which are the ones that provide its meaning, hence fix its reference? The theory might be intended as one about the meaning of a name in an individual's idiolect, in which case the descriptions would have to be known to the individual. Or it might be intended as one about the meaning of a name in the language of a community, in which case the descriptions might not all be known to all speakers.[4] But the same problems accrue to both choices. If we take the totality of associated descriptions, then, for many names that have a referent, the theory will predict that they do not, for there will be no individual satisfying all of the descriptions. And it seems unlikely that there is any non-arbitrary way of singling out a particular subset of the totality that will correctly and uniquely specify the name's referent. Indeed, in some cases, the description most closely associated with the name is false of the name's referent. Kripke points out that a description that many closely associate with 'Peano' might well be something like 'the man who discovered that certain axioms—the so-called "Peano's axioms"—characterize the natural numbers'. In fact, that description applies not to Peano, but to Dedekind. If that description is included in the relevant set, then 'Peano' refers either to Dedekind or to no one, if some of the other associated descriptions fail to apply to him.[5]

---

[4] Russell held a weak version, applying the theory to speakers at particular times. See Sainsbury (1993).

[5] One possibility for the description theorist would be to pick on metalinguistic descriptions, along the lines of 'the person called "Peano" in this linguistic community'. There is no space here to discuss the pros and cons of this proposal. A few people still defend versions of a descriptive view. See e.g. Bach (1994); Rosenberg (1994); Lewis (1997); Katz (2001).

Kripke offered a different picture of how a name gets its reference. In a broad range of cases, a person is baptized in a dubbing ceremony, and thereby comes to bear the name. Those present at the ceremony then go on to use the name with the intention of referring to the original subject of the baptism. Other speakers acquire the name from members of this group, and use it intending to refer to the same individual as that referred to by the speaker from whom they acquired the name. Thus reference is preserved by a chain of causal-intentional links between bearer and speaker.[6]

Kripke proposed a picture of the meaning of names that is radically different from both Russell's and Frege's, but rather goes back to John Stuart Mill (1843). On this picture, the meaning of a name is exhausted by its referent: empty names are meaningless, and co-referential names have the same meaning. The Millian view of names is closely associated with a particular view of PARs that emerged in the late part of the twentieth century and gained popularity by the turn of the twenty-first, a view I call 'neo-Russellianism'.

If the only content that names have is their referent, then, it would seem, prima facie, that that is all they can contribute to PARs. If that is right, then it looks as though PARs are not opaque and co-referential terms ought to be intersubstitutable, after all. Moreover, the content of a propositional attitude ascribed by a PAR whose content sentence contains a proper name should itself involve the name's referent. This suggests that attitude contents aren't Fregean thoughts. Rather they could be (so-called) Russellian propositions. A Russellian proposition is a structured abstract object containing real-world objects and properties. So, for example, to believe that Paris is beautiful would involve standing in a doxastic relation to a proposition that contains Paris itself, along with the property of beauty, something we might crudely represent by '$<<_{subject}$ Paris$>$, $<_{property}$ beauty$>>$'. Neo-Russellianism is the view that the contents of propositional attitudes are Russellian propositions.[7] It is our next topic.

2.2 The Neo-Russellian Problematic

Since apparently opaque PARs make up the canonical discourse of ordinary common-sense psychology, neo-Russellianism has consequences for our understanding of psychological explanation. Let us consider some of these.

---

[6] The "intentional" in "causal-intentional" is not in Brentano's sense.

[7] See Salmon (1986), Richard (1987), Soames (1987), Fodor (1994), Braun (2001a,b), and Millikan (2000) for versions of neo-Russellianism. The view is often just called 'Russellianism', but it differs sharply from Russell's own views precisely because it involves a commitment to a Millian treatment of proper names, rather than a descriptive one, so the term is misleading.

(2) is an example of a typical psychological explanation:

(2*a*) Willow wants to fly to Hesperus.
(2*b*) Willow believes that the USS *Evening Star* is about to depart for Hesperus.

so

(2*c*) Willow attempts to board the USS *Evening Star*.

If neo-Russellianism is correct, then (2) is semantically equivalent to (3):

(3*a*) Willow wants to fly to Hesperus.
(3*b*) Willow believes that the USS *Evening Star* is about to depart for Phosphorus.

so

(3*c*) Willow attempts to board the USS *Evening Star*.

On the face of it, (2) is a good explanation and (3) is not. If Willow doesn't believe that Hesperus is Phosphorus, then the psychological states cited in (3*a*) and (3*b*) would not explain (3*c*). Similarly, if we knew that (3*a*) and (3*b*) were true, we would not predict (3*c*), unless we thought that Willow believed that Hesperus is Phosphorus. Let's look at some of the responses available to the neo-Russellian.

According to Nathan Salmon (1986) and Mark Richard (1987) referentially equivalent PARs literally say the same things. PARs ascribe Russellian propositions as the objects of attitudes. The proposition that the USS *Evening Star* is about to depart for Hesperus is identical to the proposition that the USS *Evening Star* is about to depart for Phosphorus. We might represent it as either '$<<<_{subject}$ USS *Evening Star*>, $<_{object}$ Hesperus>> $<_{relation}$ is-about-to-depart-for>>' or, equivalently, '$<<<_{subject}$ USS *Evening Star*>, $<_{object}$ Phosphorus>> $<_{relation}$ is-about-to-depart-for>>'. So, if (2*b*) is true, then so is (3*b*). However, although belief itself is a binary relation between a person and a proposition, it entails the instantiation of a ternary relation between a believer, a proposition, and a "guise", where a guise is a way of thinking about a proposition.

According to this view, the use of different names in different PARs can pragmatically convey information about guises. (2) would typically convey that the guise featuring in Willow's desire to go to Hesperus is the same as that featuring in her belief that the ship is about to depart for Hesperus. Thus the picture of Willow's psychology conveyed by (2) is perfectly sensible. (3) might be taken to convey the reverse: that the belief and desire feature different guises corresponding to the different words used in the explanation.

This account of the semantics of PARs is certainly radical and interesting. However, it is consistent with a rather mainstream picture of psychological explanation. For it could allow that when somebody says something like (2), the explanatory work is done not by the utterances' literal meaning but rather by the meaning pragmatically conveyed. If guises were taken to be composed of descriptions, then psychological explanation would work as Russell himself had it.

David Braun (1998, 2001*a,b*) offers a version of neo-Russellianism that involves a more radical picture of psychological explanation. He does not appeal to pragmatics to differentiate (2) and (3). Rather, he argues that they are equally good, both citing particular events (of desiring and believing) that cause the action.

Braun's position might perhaps be strengthened if we were to add the claim that the descriptions of the causes offered in both explanations attribute to them properties that are relevant to the probability of their effect occurring. Thus someone who believes <<<$_{subject}$ USS *Evening Star*>, <$_{object}$ Hesperus>> <$_{relation}$ is-about-to-depart-for>>, and who would like <<<$_{subject}$ self>, <$_{object}$ Hesperus>> <$_{relation}$ goes-to>> to be true, is more likely to board the USS *Evening Star* than someone who lacks those attitudes. Such a person might think of the planet under the same guise in both cases, and so be able to deduce that they could satisfy their desire by boarding the spacecraft. Moreover, even if different guises are involved in the desire and the belief and these guises don't initially feature in an identity belief, there is still a fair chance that the person will end up boarding the spacecraft. They might, for example, make enquiries about which ships go to Hesperus, and be told about the USS *Evening Star*. Equally, they might come to hold the identity belief under the appropriate guises (see Fodor 1994, lect. 2, for a similar proposal and Segal, in preparation, for critical discussion).

It seems right that a psychological explanation framed in terms of Russellian propositions would be a genuine explanation. It is likely that if (3*a*) and (3*b*) are true, then the probability of (3*c*) is significantly higher than it would be if they were not.

There is room to doubt, however, that that is all that psychological explanations have to offer. Fodor (1987, ch. 1) points out that psychological explanations exploit relations among two kinds of properties of psychological states: causal and intentional. In (2), for example, we are told about the content of Willow's belief and desire. From this, we infer something about these states' causal powers; they are likely to cause Willow to act in a particular way. The way this type of explanation works is by predicting causal patterns from rational patterns among the contents. Boarding the USS *Evening Star* is the rational thing for Willow to do, given what she thinks and what she wants.

Someone with a more Fregean orientation than the neo-Russellians—a quasi-Fregean[8]—might argue that (3) fails as a psychological explanation because it fails to describe the explanans and explananda in a way that reveals a rational pattern. Of course, if Willow were to board the USS *Evening Star*, she would satisfy her desire. But obviously, if Willow herself doesn't think that Hesperus is Phosphorus, then she is not in a position to see this. For all she knows, if she boards the ship, she will end up somewhere other than where she wants. Hence, absent the identity belief, she would have no motive for boarding the ship.

[8] The term 'neo-Fregean' is sometimes used to pick out proponents of a particular blend of Russellian and Fregean views, inspired by Evans and McDowell. Hence my choice of 'quasi-Fregean' as a more general epithet for someone who believes that there is a kind of content other than reference.

Neo-Russellians have a natural line of response to this objection, which we will consider next.

2.2.1 *Rationality and Mental Syntax*

Sense was introduced to play certain explanatory roles: it was to explain cognitive value, referential opacity, reference, and, perhaps, the apparent significance of empty expressions. In each case, neo-Russellians must either motivate rejection of the apparent explanandum or find an alternative explanation. They typically avail themselves of a particular resource to make these moves, some analogue of mental words. Salmon has 'guises', Braun, 'ways of thinking', and Fodor, the 'Language of Thought'. Let us think of mental words ("Mentalese"), vaguely, as mental analogues of natural language words, probably physically realized by neural phenomena, that can be individuated independently of their semantic content and that have powers causally to influence one another and to move muscles.

Having a propositional attitude then involves having a mental sentence playing a particular causal role in one's head. If someone believes that vampires have no souls, then their mental sentence 'Vampires have no souls' will enter into the causal explanation of why they behave like someone who has that particular belief. To express this idea, I'll say that when someone believes that p, they 'believe*' a mental sentence which means that p.

A neo-Russellian might then distinguish two kinds of rationality: 'external' and 'internal' rationality. External rationality concerns patterns of thought and courses of action that are likely to succeed in the agent's actual environment. Patterns of external rationality can be accounted for in terms of Russellian propositions. Thus for someone who believes $<<<_{subject}$ USS *Evening Star*$>$, $<_{object}$ Hesperus$>>$ $<_{relation}$ is-about-to-depart-for$>>$ and who would like $<<<_{subject}$ self$>$, $<_{object}$ Hesperus$>>$ $<_{relation}$ goes-to$>>$ to be true, it would be externally rational to board the USS *Evening Star*. The explanations (2) and (3) both describe Willow in a way that entails that her action is externally rational, although (3) does so in a less helpful way, a way that would only be apparent to someone who knew that 'Hesperus' and 'Phosphorus' are co-referential.

Internal rationality, by contrast, is determined by logical relations among mental expressions, these relations being determined purely by the expressions' syntax. Suppose that someone believes* mental sentences like (4a) and (4b):

(4a) Anyone who wants to go to Hesperus should board the USS *Evening Star*.

(4b) I want to go to Hesperus.

They would be internally rational if they made an inference that caused them to believe* a sentence like (4c):

(4c) I should board the USS *Evening Star*.

Someone who believed* 'I want to go to Phosphorus', instead of (4b), and who failed to believe* 'Hesperus = Phosphorus' would not be internally rational to infer (4c), since the inference is invalid.

The view of psychology that this line leads to is one that involves two completely different levels of explanation. One concerns content, construed in terms of propositions. The second involves mental syntax.[9] Syntax, the level of psychological processing, usurps the place of Fregean sense as the locus of internal rationality.

A quasi-Fregean concern with this proposal would be that it fails to underwrite important pieces of psychology, ones that would be underwritten by the quasi-Fregean. In particular, the neo-Russellian apparatus fails to account for certain generalizations. The appropriate level of generality appears to require an additional level of content, something along the lines of sense.

For example, it would be reasonable for a historian of science to claim that ancient Babylonians argued over whether Hesperus is Phosphorus. But it is impossible to make sense of this claim with just the neo-Russellian apparatus. At the level of Russellian propositions, the claim is equivalent to saying that the astronomers argued over whether Hesperus was Hesperus, or whether Hesperus was the Evening Star. This fails to allow us to make any sense of what the historian would be saying. Russellian propositions are too coarse-grained to discriminate among a number of apparently quite different discussions that the historian might be attributing to the Babylonians.

But, the worry goes, mental syntax is too fine-grained. For it is unlikely that there will be any way of identifying the syntax of mental names in the minds or brains of different subjects. Suppose that a and b are two atomic expressions of one person's Mentalese and that c and d are two in another's. It is unlikely that if we consider only the syntax of these items, we will find any way of figuring out which corresponds to which.[10]

The quasi-Fregean view is that mental syntax and reference don't suffice as foundations for psychological explanation. We need also to recognize something along lines of sense. In particular, we need a kind of content that cuts fatter than mental syntax, that is relevant to opaque PARs, that cuts finer than reference, and that helps account for the rationalizing role of psychological explanation. I shall call such content 'quasi-sense'. One argument for the quasi-Fregean view arises in relation to Brentano's problem. We will consider this in the next subsection.

---

[9] See Field (1977) for an early articulation of this sort of view.

[10] In the case of natural language, there are ways of grouping phonological and orthographic tokens, determined by complex psychological, sociological, and historical factors which fix syntactic types in a way that allows for the same syntactic type to appear in different speakers' vocabularies (see Kaplan 1990 for discussion). Nothing analogous holds for Mentalese. A possible line of response for the neo-Russellian would be to propose that the syntax of Mentalese is parasitic on that of natural language: two individuals have the same Mentalese word if their Mentalese words are related in the right way to the same word of natural language.

2.2.2 *Empty Singular Concepts*

The neo-Russellian faces obvious problems with empty names. One might read (5) in a history book:

(5) The Egyptian Queen Hatchepsut believed that Ra requested her to build a great golden obelisk.

One might go on to read that Hatchepsut built an obelisk. But 'Ra' has no referent, and there is no suitable proposition to be the object of Hatchepsut's belief.

There are three options open to the neo-Russellian. The first would be to bite the bullet and say that the book is wrong about Hatchepsut—or perhaps that it fails to say anything about her, owing to its deployment of an empty name. The second would be to allow that one can adopt attitudes towards propositional fragments (see Segal 1989a and Braun 1993 for details). A propositional fragment is an incomplete proposition: a structured, abstract object with, as it were, a hole in it: fill the hole with an object, and the result is a proposition. Thus to believe that Ra is falcon-headed would be to believe a propositional fragment that might be crudely represented as '<<$_{subject}$ *x*>, <$_{property}$ falcon-headed>>', where '*x*' marks the hole. The third option would be to claim that 'Ra' refers to a mythical object (Salmon 1998). I will briefly consider these in turn.

The first option is very costly. There exists a good deal of apparently excellent history, anthropology, and psychology that ascribes propositional attitudes that apparently contain empty singular concepts. Simply to reject this work out of hand seems rash.

The second option runs into a special version of Frege's puzzle. All empty names now make the same contribution to PARs. The propositional fragment expressed by (6a) is the same as that expressed by any of (6b):

(6a) Ra asked me to build a great golden obelisk.
(6b) Buffy/Donald Duck/James T. Kirk asked me to build a great golden obelisk.

The problem is that these empty names don't seem to be intersubstitutable, even after special pleading. Many of us would accept that there is a sense in which if someone believes that Hesperus is a star, then it follows that they believe that Phosphorus is a star. And that's because it is true on the so-called 'de re' reading: if one believes of Hesperus that it is a star, then one believes of Phosphorus that it is a star (see Quine 1956 and Burge 1977 for discussion of the de re sense of 'believe'). But there can be no de re reading where there is no res. Hence it seems to be straightforwardly false that if someone believes something about Ra, then they believe the same thing about Buffy. Prospects for a psychology that simply regarded these as equivalent look dim. Something about Hatchepsut would be missed.

The third option at least holds out the prospect of preserving the truth of reports like (5). However, the option presents a strange picture of the role of reference in psychology. Recall that the reason for supposing that reference might matter in psychology was that it might involve relations between thinkers and objects that would be relevant to the explanation of interactions between them. Spike ends up in Paris partly because he has a concept with Paris as its referent. In this case, it is plausible that the referential relation between concept and city is based in part on a Kripkean causal–intentional chain between Spike and the city. And it is those very causal–intentional relations that we would expect to underwrite the explanatory role of reference. For they allow Spike to gather information about Paris, hence find his way there. Indeed, we might think of causal–intentional relations as providing the basis of a sort of information-bearing chain between concept and city: a set of conditions that allows Spike's dispositions to alter his 'Paris' beliefs to be appropriately conditioned by Paris's actual properties.

But it doesn't look as though anything analogous would work for relations to mythical objects. Ra's properties have no causal impact on Hatchepsut. It thus looks as though reference to mythical objects is not relevant to the psychological role of the concepts involved. The difference between the psychological roles of, for example, 'Buffy' and 'Ra' would have to be explained independently of their reference. But if it's possible to distinguish those concepts on psychological grounds that have nothing to do with reference, then one would expect the same to hold for 'Hesperus' and 'Phosphorus' concepts.

In the final analysis, there may not be a huge gap between quasi-Fregeans and neo-Russellians with respect to singular concepts. The real debate should probably be over whether non-singular concepts—e.g. concepts of red, relation, running, revolution, rarity, and rambunctiousness—possess some kind of sense-like content, or whether their mental syntax together with their association with properties, relations, or kinds accounts for their psychological role (see Fodor 1991a for a defence of the property view and Segal, in preparation, for criticism).

The following section offers a quasi-Fregean account that might be sufficiently far from Frege's Ur theory to alleviate neo-Russellian concerns (the account is largely drawn from Larson and Segal 1995). The account will also serve to introduce some ideas that will feature in what follows.

2.3 A Quasi-Fregean Theory of Name-Concepts

Let's suppose that a person's understanding of a proper name partly involves a concept of the name's bearer, a 'name-concept'. A concept is a mental particular, a component of thoughts. Let us further suppose that name-concepts are relatively permanent items in a thinker's repertoire. When you first encounter someone, you form a concept of them which you then retain as long as you remember them. It is also tempting to suppose that the concept owes its existence and nature to something like a mental dossier. In this dossier you collect descriptive information that you believe to be true of the individual. The content of the dossier determines the way in which you think of the individual and the way in which the concept behaves in thought.

We now have a possible quasi-Fregean account of the role of names in psychological explanation. A quasi-sense is a name-concept type. A token concept's quasi-sense is fixed by the information in its associated dossier. Two dossiers with the same descriptive contents will provide the same quasi-sense. Two dossiers with different descriptive contents will not provide exactly the same quasi-sense, but may perhaps provide very similar ones.

Quasi-senses can play some of the roles of Fregean senses. Thus they allow for significant empty concepts: one opens a mental dossier either falsely believing in the existence of an individual, or abstaining, or believing that it is fictional. Equally, one may have different concepts of the same individual.

We might suppose further that PARs are sensitive to quasi-senses. Since the dossiers that different people associate with the same name are likely to be different, we cannot help ourselves to the idea of "the" quasi-sense of, for example, 'Hesperus', and so we cannot say that when the term features in a PAR, it refers to its sense. But it is not implausible that our interpretation of PARs is sensitive to the contents of people's dossiers. Thus it is correct to characterize Hatchepsut's attitudes with the term 'Ra' (rather than 'Buffy') because there is an appropriate overlap of descriptions between Hatchepsut's dossier and ours.

What is the relation between quasi-sense and reference? Here the quasi-Fregean can side with the neo-Russellian. Quasi-sense neither explains nor determines reference. The reference of the concept is not fixed by the contents of the dossier, for the Kripkean reasons given above. Rather, something else must account for it. For a range of typical cases, perhaps the account would involve an information chain, as mentioned above. The idea would roughly be this: individual x has a name-concept, N, that refers to y, if x's dispositions to revise beliefs containing N are appropriately sensitive to y's properties. In typical cases, appropriate sensitivity is explained by an information chain. x and y are at opposite ends of the chain and other speakers provide the links. y's actual properties are causally relevant to the descriptions that go into people's dossiers, and to the things people tell each other when they use the name.

The difficulty would be to spell out the idea of appropriate sensitivity. For example, the chain need not endow x with only true beliefs about y. And infinitely many truths about y will always remain out of x's ken. Perhaps an account could be given in terms of the concept's endowing the possessor with some kind of general, although of course limited and fallible, capacity to discover truths about the object (for more on this, see Evans 1973, 1982).

In other cases, reference does not seem to have to do with information chains. Purely descriptive information can suffice to underwrite possession of a name-concept. For example, Tara might choose to adopt a name for the first male child born in the twenty-second century: say 'Manchile'. Tara might then try to make predictions about this child. She might create a dossier and proceed with her research. Such activity would seem to endow Tara with a concept that has a specific referent, even though the object doesn't yet exist. There is no information chain between the object and the concept, because that would require the object to be able to affect Tara's beliefs, and he can't do so yet. However, the description that fixes reference might play a somewhat similar role in conditioning Tara's 'Manchile' beliefs. If she is intelligent and well-informed, she might be able to learn quite a lot about Manchile. She might even be able to predict where and when he will be born, and might choose to go there and actually meet the baby.

One might then hope to develop an account of singular reference that would be of some use for psychological explanation, and one that would be constrained by it. We want to explain why I believe that Hatchepsut built a great golden obelisk, why Willow ended up on Venus, why Tara will be at a particular place at midnight on 31 December 2002. In each case, the subject's possession of a name-concept that refers to a particular object has a role to play in the explanation. Singular reference could fruitfully be thought of as whatever relation it is that plays that sort of role in those sorts of explanations.

We shall shortly look at non-singular concepts, with an eye to considering to what extent conclusions reached about name-concepts might apply to them. We will focus on natural kind concepts, and a view developed by Hilary Putnam (similar suggestions were also made by Kripke 1982). Before that I shall use the account of name-concepts to introduce some new ideas that will feature in the discussion of kind concepts.

2.4 Twin Earths, Extension-Independence, and Narrow Content

There are reasons to suppose that quasi-senses of names are reference-independent, in that their identity and existence don't essentially depend on their reference. The idea can be illustrated in terms of a philosophical device introduced by Hilary Putnam (1975): Twin Earths. Twin Earths are exact or nearly exact duplicates of Earth, atom for atom replicas, except for the occasional interesting difference. Let us imagine two Twin Earths, one being an exact duplicate of Earth, the other being as like Earth as possible, except that there, no Hatchepsut existed, although Twin Egyptologists thought that one did. I have Twins on these planets and they have 'Hatchepsut' concepts. For the purposes of this thought experiment, we can assume that we have exactly matching descriptions in our dossiers so that the quasi-senses of our concepts are the same. Thus they are reference-independent.[11]

---

[11] For a general defence of the reference-independence of the singular concepts, see Segal (1989a). For the other side, the "neo-Fregean" view, see McDowell (1977) and Evans (1982). The neo-Fregeans see senses as reference-dependent. No reference (normally) entails no sense: different reference entails difference of sense. For them, concepts are abstractions from concept possession, and possession of a

The idea of reference-independence is related to, but distinct from, an important notion introduced by Putnam in connection with Twin Earths, the notion of narrowness. A property is narrow if an object's possession of it does not essentially depend on any factors beyond the object's spatial boundaries. Narrow properties are intrinsic rather than relational. Thus Twins normally share their narrow properties, but may differ in their non-narrow (aka 'wide') ones. Correlatively, we have the notions of narrow and wide content: a content of a psychological state is narrow if a subject's being in a state with that content doesn't essentially depend on anything outside her skin. If a content is not narrow, then it is wide.

Narrowness is a stronger notion than reference-independence, since the latter requires independence from reference only and not from everything outside the skin. Quasi-senses are reference-independent, but they may not be narrow. A subject's possession of a concept with a particular quasi-sense may essentially depend on some feature of their environment other than the referent.

We will now move on to discuss a particular variety of non-singular concepts, so-called "natural kind" concepts, that have appeared to many to resemble singular concepts in important respects. We will consider to what extent that appearance is correct.

3. NATURAL KIND CONCEPTS

3.1 Putnam's Proposals

Putnam used a Twin Earth scenario to argue that the meaning of natural kind terms is wide. In so doing, he produced a model of these terms according to which they work much like names. Since his reasoning seems to apply more or less directly to the concepts we express by these terms, the model has important ramifications for philosophy of psychology. Here is Putnam's argument.

Putnam asked us to imagine a Twin of Earth in 1750, a time at which the chemical composition of water was not known. This Twin Earth is exactly like Earth in all superficially observable respects. The key difference is that the stuff that there fills the rivers and oceans and that Twin English-speaking people call 'water' is not composed of H_2O, but has a complicated composition that we can call 'XYZ'.

Putnam argued as follows. We intend to use our term 'water' to refer to the stuff we have actually been calling 'water' and to other samples of the same kind of liquid.

singular concept is understood in terms of relations to an object, such as information chains. You can relate to the same object in different ways, hence sense cuts finer than reference. But you can't relate to different objects in the same way. And you can't relate when there is no object to relate to.

Scientists tell us that the relevant kind is H_2O. XYZ is not H_2O and, chemically speaking, it constitutes a different kind of liquid. So our term 'water' is not true of Twin water. Moreover, the Earth term 'water' meant the same in 1750 as it does now: it is true of x if and only if x is a sample of H_2O. If a 1750 Earthman had come across a sample of XYZ and said 'That's water' he would have said something false. But the Twin Earth term 'water' extends over their local wet substance: it is true of XYZ and XYZ only.

Now let us consider a typical Earthman, Oscar, and his Twin Earth counterpart, Oscar$_T$ (ignoring the fact that humans are made out of water). By hypothesis, their narrow properties are the same. But the extensions[12] of their terms 'water' differ. So 'water' seems to be like the proper name 'Hatchepsut': its extension is not fixed by narrow properties of speakers.

Putnam sketched a two-factor account of natural kind terms that is somewhat similar to the two-factor account of names sketched above. One factor would include descriptive "markers" describing features useful for identifying the extension ('transparent, odourless, boils at 100 degrees C' etc.). The other would be the extension condition.

The descriptive content need not determine the extension. The account again is modelled on proper naming. According to Putnam, kind terms work roughly as if there had been a dubbing ceremony, along the following lines: someone pointed to some particular samples and said: 'The term "water" is to apply just to these samples and to anything else that is the same kind of liquid as them'. What counts as the same kind of liquid is to be determined by scientific investigation, which, if things go well, will tell us about nature's own joints.

Putnam's reasoning appears to carry over to the concepts we express by natural kind terms, although Putnam did not discuss the matter. Assuming that Oscar believes what he says, the belief he expresses when he says 'It is good to add water to whisky' differs in content from the belief that Oscar$_T$ expresses when he produces the same sounds. Oscar believes that it is good to add water to whisky. Oscar$_T$ believes, rather, that it is good to add Twin water to whisky.

According to the Putnamian picture, the extension conditions of natural kind concepts are determined in part by the actual nature of samples that are available in the local environment even when speakers are unaware of that nature. Putnam also argued that a second wide factor enters into determining extension: other people. He used the following illustration.

Putnam knows that elms and beeches are both deciduous trees, and he knows roughly what they look like. However, he cannot tell the difference between them. There is a Twin Earth very like this one, the only difference being that there, experts

[12] The term 'extension' is ambiguous. Usually it means the set of things a term is true of. But it is also used as short for 'extension condition', meaning the condition an object must meet if the term is to be true of it.

use the term 'elm' to refer to beeches and 'beech' to refer to elms. When Putnam uses the word 'elm' he means *elm*. By contrast, when Putnam$_T$ says 'elm' he intends to speak Twin English, and so he means *beech*.

Once again, the Putnamian picture portrays a similarity between proper names and natural kind terms. In both cases, speakers' intentions to defer to others are held to link the term to its extension. In the case of kind terms, it is a matter of deferring to experts to fix the extension of one's term. In both cases, the ordinary speaker uses the word with a meaning that others have provided for it.

Again, the conclusion appears to apply also to concepts: when Putnam says 'Elms are deciduous' he expresses his belief that elms are deciduous. When Putnam$_T$ makes the same noises, he expresses his belief that beeches are deciduous. So it appears as though the content of an individual's psychological states is partly fixed by the way other people use words.[13]

3.2 Internalism and Externalism

Putnam's arguments raise interesting questions about the content of psychological states. The conclusion of the arguments is that at least some of them have wide contents. Philosophers have reacted to the argument in a number of different ways. Under a crude categorization, these divide into two broad categories: internalism and externalism. An internalist believes that every psychological state has a narrow content. There are two subcategories of internalism. One view accepts the Twin Earth arguments, and allows for two kinds of content: wide and narrow. Thus, for example, the Oscars' 'water' concepts have different wide contents, but also have a shared narrow content. We might call this view 'two-factor internalism'. The other view (one-factor internalism) simply rejects the Twin Earth arguments and holds that the Oscars' 'water' concepts share a narrow content and have no additional wide content. Externalism is the denial of internalism and holds that at least some psychological states have wide contents and no narrow contents.[14]

Motivations for internalism are various. Many internalists have been motivated by the thought that narrow content is required in an account of psychological explanation. One idea, to put it very crudely, is that if content is going to do any real causal work in driving the body around, then it has to be narrow (Fodor 1987, 1991*b*). Another idea, put equally crudely, is that the role that Twins' counterpart psychological states play in their psychologies is sufficiently similar to warrant ascribing them the same contents (Fodor 1987; Noonan 1986; Segal 1989*a,b*, 2000).

---

[13] Tyler Burge has developed a detailed and highly influential defence of this kind of social externalism in a series of articles, the most important of which is Burge (1979).

[14] Little importance should be attached to the labels: 'internalism' and 'externalism' are used in different ways by different philosophers.

And there have been motivations for internalism of quite different sorts as well (Blackburn 1984; Segal 2000).

Externalists are sceptical that every concept has a narrow content. The scepticism has been partly motivated by the fact that it proves very hard to provide a decent account of it. What, for example, is the narrow content of the belief that the Oscars express when they say 'It is good to add water to whisky'?

It might seem tempting to propose that narrow content could be explained in terms of associated descriptions, much like the quasi-senses of proper names. Both Twins think of their local liquid as transparent, wet, tasteless, etc. The problem with this is that descriptive associations are just made up of more concepts. Unless these concepts have narrow contents—and so are not subject to externalist Twin Earth arguments—the problem remains. For the proposal to work, it would have to be that for every concept with a wide content, there is some set of descriptive associations whose contents are narrow and that suffices to account for the concept's cognitive role. But there is no obvious reason to suppose that that is the case. Someone impressed by social externalism, for example, would hold that most of our concepts have wide contents, and so would find the proposal implausible.

Other accounts of narrow content have been proposed. The majority of these have been offered by two-factor internalists. Wide content is understood in terms of extension conditions or something that determines extension conditions. And narrow content is something else, something divorced from extension (Fodor 1987; Block 1986). A common problem with such views is that if the content of psychological states is to appear like content, then it ought to be ascribed by PARs. But any content so ascribed seems to determine extension conditions. Oscar believes that it is good to add water to whisky. Oscar$_T$ doesn't: he believes that it is good to add Twin water to whisky. Here, the difference in extension of the Twins' concepts is reflected in the different PARs.

Shortly, I will outline a one-factor internalist alternative which allows that narrow content determines extension. The view involves rejecting the externalist interpretation of the Twin Earth experiments. It entails, for example, that Oscar does not believe that it is good to add water to whisky and Oscar$_T$ doesn't believe that it is good to add Twin water to whisky. What they both believe is that, let's say, it is good to add "dwater" to whisky, where dwater includes both XYZ and H_2O and anything suitably water-like: the hydroid motley.

3.3 Problems for Externalism

There are serious grounds for questioning externalism. I shall offer just a brief sketch of the main problem with social externalism, then discuss in more detail some problems with the externalist view of natural kind concepts.

3.3.1 *A Problem for Social Externalism*

The chief problem with social externalism is that it is in tension with any quasi-Fregean view of content. According to social externalism, when Putnam says 'elm', he expresses the same quasi-sense as an expert does when she uses the same term. This appears dubitable. Suppose that Putnam becomes friendly with a group of horticulturalists and happens to be present while they discuss the nature of *ulmi*. As he listens, Putnam learns enough to become expert in the use of '*ulmus*'. Were you to ask him what an *ulmus* is, he would give an expert response. However, it does not occur to him that '*ulmus*' is another name for elm, which in fact it is.[15] Hence he doesn't believe that *ulmi* are elms. This indicates that he associates different quasi-senses with the two terms. Presumably, it is the quasi-sense he expresses by '*ulmi*' that corresponds to the experts' concept, rather than the one he expresses by 'elm'. Hence Putnam and the experts mean different things by 'elm' after all (this style of argument is due to Loar 1988 and is elaborated and defended in detail in Segal 2000. Burge responds to it in Burge 1989 n. 13).

3.3.2 *Problems for Externalism About Kind Concepts*

A crucial premiss in Putnam's Oscar argument is the claim that 'water' in a 1750 speaker's mouth was already functioning as a natural kind term, in the sense that it was true of just H_2O. Putnam supported this claim with his model of the working of natural kind terms in lay vernacular: the dubbing-ceremony idea. The claim about the extension conditions of 'water' in 1750 and the model of kind terms are appealing and have won the support of many professional philosophers. However, there are good reasons to dispute them.

Putnam's model yields predictions about how the usage of a term should evolve as a community moves from pre-science to science. Suppose that in a pre-scientific community a term is typically applied to samples most of which fall within a natural kind. Suppose also that there are a few cases in which people apply the term to things that are only superficially like samples of the kind, or fail to apply it to samples of the kind which are superficially different. What happens when the science is done and the facts are discovered?

Putnam's model predicts that in standard cases, usage will adjust. Speakers will correct the under- or over-applications, in the light of their new knowledge. In fact, however, this often appears not to happen. Moreover, in cases where it does seem to happen, there are reasons to suspect that the meaning of the term has changed with the development of science, and that the new usage does not reflect the original meaning. Let us consider some examples.

---

[15] Presumably one can be an expert about *ulmi* without knowing that they happen to be called 'elms' in English.

'Whale' extends over large cetaceans, an order that includes porpoises and dolphins. Usage did not adapt to correct what would have seemed—if speakers were attempting to capture a natural kind—to be a case of under-application. The same applies to 'emerald' and 'aquamarine', both of which extend over beryl: the former green, the latter blue. Another example is 'cat', which extends over members of the family *Felidae*, but also over a few outsiders, such as civet cats (for more examples, see Wilson 1982; LaPorte 1996; Dupre 1999; Segal 2000).

Of course, there are cases where usage does alter with the development of science. For example, when people realized (by using telescopes) that Mars, Venus, etc. weren't self-luminous, they fairly soon ceased to call them 'stars'. But that does not show that prior to this change, people were wrong to call the planets 'stars'. Rather, the change in usage might have accompanied a change of meaning. Under this alternative, the term 'star' would originally have been true not just of stars, but of a motley of different kinds of heavenly bodies. When the important difference between planets and self-illuminating bodies was noticed, there was an adjustment of terminology that reflected this new knowledge and produced a more accurate classificatory scheme.

As a general model of the relation between lay and scientific usage, the idea has its attractions. For our classifications of natural phenomena serve many and various kinds of human concerns that often are not dominated by a passion for carving nature at its joints. And for most of our history we have had to do without science. There was certainly no science around while our distinctively human concept-forming mechanisms evolved, between (say) 4 million and 100,000 or 200,000 years ago. Given that, it's not so easy to see how lay words and concepts would have come to have natural kinds as their extensions. If Putnamian dubbing ceremonies actually occurred, then that might help explain it. But it is not easy to imagine our Cro-Magnon ancestors participating in them.

Our normal concepts for natural phenomena differ in very significant ways from our name-concepts of individuals (for the reverse view, see Millikan 2000). First, being able to reidentify particular individuals and being able to keep track of information about them are matters of importance to us in ordinary life. Keeping track of natural kinds, in the sense of being able to identify their instances, is less so. The fact that broccoli and cauliflower are con-subspecifics makes no difference to us when we want to know for how long they should be steamed. It doesn't matter to us that fish are genetically extremely diverse: they are similar enough from the human perspective all to be called 'fish'.

Secondly, we are good at reidentifying and keeping track of particular individuals, particularly with the help of other people and their capacity to use language to pass on information. We are relatively poor at reidentifying the same kind: superficial similarities prevent us from seeing deeper differences, and superficial differences prevent us from seeing deeper similarities. In the normal run of things, our cognitive relations to kinds are not grounded in an information chain, or a useful reference-fixing description, in the way our name-concepts are. Unsurprisingly, non-scientific people living in nature (such as tribespeople in Africa and Central and South America) don't have many classificatory schemes that correspond to scientific ones.

One important class of exceptions to the disparity between natural and scientific classifications lies in so-called "folk-biology": non-scientific understanding of animals and plants. There appears to be a high degree of convergence between science and the folk in the classification of what Scott Atran calls 'generic species' (Atran 1999). Classification by generic species, according to Atran, is a culturally universal method of folk-biological taxonomy of local flora and fauna. Generic species often correspond to scientific species or genera such as hummingbird, dog, and oak.

However, it is important to understand the nature of correspondence between lay generic–species concepts and scientific concepts. Their extensions are reasonably coincident in the actual world. But they are embedded in very different modes of thinking. The folk classification is not intended to be a first pass at limning the structure of the world, as that would be revealed by science.

There is evidence that the folk believe that species have essences and that these determine the individuation conditions of members of the species (Atran 1990; Gelman and Hirschfeld 1999). But this has nothing to do with science. The essences are provided by heaven, or other mystical powers (Pinker 1994: 425).

They appear not to think that genetic or kinship properties are definitive of membership of the category (Bailenson et al. 2002). They would probably regard a Twin robin as belonging to the same generic species as a robin, even after being told that its ancestry was completely unconnected with any robin on Earth.[16]

Thirdly, proper names are typically introduced by actual dubbing ceremonies or explicitly known conventions. And we explicitly understand the relation between the dubbing of an individual and the semantics of the name: for an object to be the extension of the name just is for it to be identical with the dubbed individual. By contrast, we are not normally aware of the origins of kind terms, nor do we have reliable and consistent intuitions about criteria for membership of the extension. We don't normally know, as lay speakers, what kind of kind the extension is supposed to be: whether it is a natural kind or a motley, if the former, at what level of generality it occurs (e.g. subspecies, species, genus . . .), etc.

Recall that an important part of the appeal of attributing wide content to name-concepts, from a psychological point of view, is that its referential relation might be relevant to the role of the concept in psychological explanation. The cognitive role of the concept is often sensitive to facts about the concept's referent, via associated beliefs (the contents of the dossier, on the suggested picture). Moreover, the referential relation between concept and object might enter into the explanation of real

---

[16] To adapt an analogy that Scott Atran used in a different context, one might wonder whether investigating human concepts of natural phenomena by studying city dwellers in a scientifically oriented society is like investigating human linguistic capacity by studying feral children.

interactions between the thinker and the object: Spike arrives in Paris partly because he has a concept that refers to Paris (see Williamson 2000 and Peacocke 1993 for discussion of the role of wide content in explanation).

Assuming that lay kind terms have natural kinds as their extensions offers little hope of such explanatory and predictive benefits. The suggested rival hypothesis that lay speakers deploy motley concepts does better. Consider Oscar. Under the natural kind hypothesis, his 'water' concept is true of just H_2O, while under the motley hypothesis it is true of dwater: H_2O and XYZ and anything suitably similar. 'Dwater' is our word for the motley, our translation of Oscar's term 'water', under the motley hypothesis. Since XYZ is superficially indistinguishable from water, a wide range of counterfactuals concerning Oscar's behaviour towards XYZ and water are going to be the same. For example, if Oscar were confronted with a glass containing some water or XYZ and was thirsty, then he would probably drink the contents of the glass. In these cases, attributing to him a dwater concept under-writes the counterfactuals more neatly than the alternative. He drinks the XYZ in the glass because it's dwater, and he believes that dwater is thirst-quenching. If we say instead that he believes that water is thirst-quenching, we have more explaining to do. We then have to point out that Oscar believes that the glass contains water, and that he does so because that's what it looks like to him.

It would not be to the point to object that to offer a complete explanation of Oscar's action, the motley hypothesis would also have to spell out auxiliary beliefs and perceptions of Oscar's; the belief that the glass contains dwater, caused by the fact that the sample looks like dwater to Oscar. For the whole point of invoking wide content was to allow us to appeal directly to real relations between subject and world in our explanations of interactions between the two: Spike arrives in Paris partly because he has a concept that refers to Paris. The information chain implicit in the concept allows the subject to acquire enough true beliefs to attain his goal. Wide content explanations are supposed to replace spellings-out of the psychological details with quantifications over them. Once we have to spell them out, no advantage is gained. But—ironically—when we do appeal in this direct way to the extension of a concept, we do better to attribute motleys than kinds.

Of course, if Oscar had the clear view that what he calls 'water' had a hidden real essence potentially discoverable by science, then that would provide at least some evidence for the kind hypothesis. But typically, outside scientific communities peo-ple don't seem to have such views. And even within them, people's intuitions are unstable. In the particular case of 'water', many people fairly explicitly now hold the view that it extends over H_2O only. But consider the following counterfactual. Suppose that friendly aliens had provided a taxi service between Earth and Twin Earth in the eighteenth century, and travel between the planets had become com-mon. People, unaware of any difference between the two hydroid substances, would have applied the term to both equally. When the differences were discovered, they would probably have said 'Oh, there are two kinds of water'.

Under the kind hypothesis, Earthmen would have been making a mistake when they first called XYZ 'water'. After sufficient interaction between Earth people and XYZ, there would have been an undetected shift in the extension of the concept. But these claims have no independent motivation. As I have emphasized, the reactions of the protagonists involved would not support that interpretation. Rather, they would leave the matter open. Suppose, for example, that when an Earth scientist first arrived on Twin Earth, he suspected for some reason that the watery substance there might be chemically different from Earth water. He might have said 'Hmm, I suspect this isn't really water'. But he might just as well have said 'Hmm, I suspect that this water might be interestingly different from water on Earth'.

4. CONCLUSION

Putnam (1975) wrote: 'Traditional philosophy of language...leaves out other people and the world; a better philosophy and a better science of language must encompass both.' It is worth considering the possibility that the role of other people and the world in determining the meanings of an individual's words and the concepts and thoughts that are available to her is very limited. With the exception of fixing the reference of singular concepts, maybe other people and the world can only make a difference to the contents of an individual's mind by the normal methods, that is, by having some causal impact on her.[17]

REFERENCES

Atran, S. (1990). *Cognitive Foundations of Natural History*. Cambridge: Cambridge University Press.

—— (1999). 'Itzaj Maya Folkbiological Taxonomy: Cognitive Universals and Cultural Particulars', in D. L. Medin and S. Atran (eds.), *Folkbiology*. Cambridge, Mass.: MIT Press.

Bach, K. (1994). *Thought and Reference*. Oxford: Oxford University Press.

Bailenson, Jeremy N., Shum, Michael S., Atran, Scott, Medin, Douglas L., and Coley, John D. (2002), 'A Bird's Eye View: Biological Categorization and Reasoning Within and Across Cultures'. *Cognition*, 84: 1–53.

Blackburn, S. (1984). *Spreading the Word*. Oxford: Oxford University Press.

[17] I am indebted to Scott Atran, David Bell, David Braun, Alex George, Richard Heck, Frank Jackson, Gideon Makin, John Milton, Mark Sainsbury, Susanna Siegel, Maja Spener, and Mark Textor for helpful comments and discussion.

Block, N. (1986). 'Advertisement for a Semantics for Psychology', in P. A. French, T. E. Vehling, and H.K. Wettstein (eds.), *Midwest Studies in Philosophy*, x: *Studies in Essentialism*. Minneapolis: University of Minnesota Press.

Braun, D. (1993). 'Empty Names'. *Noûs*, 27: 449–69.

—— (1998), 'Understanding Belief Reports'. *Philosophical Review*, 107: 555–95.

—— (2001*a*). 'Russellianism and Prediction'. *Philosophical Studies*, 105: 59–105.

—— (2001*b*). 'Russellianism and Explanation'. *Philosophical Perspectives*, 15: 251–89.

Brentano, F. (1874). *Psychology from an Empirical Standpoint*. Vienna.

Burge, T. (1977). 'Belief De Re'. *Journal of Philosophy*, 74: 338–62.

—— (1979). 'Individualism and the Mental', in P.A. French, T.E. Uehling, and H.K. Wettstein (eds.), *Midwest Studies in Philosophy*, iv: *Studies in Metophysics*. Minneapolis: University of Minnesota Press.

—— (1989). 'Wherein Is Language Social?', in A. George (ed.), *Reflections on Chomsky*. Oxford: Blackwell.

Chisholm, R. (1967). 'Intentionality', in P. Edwards (ed.), *The Macmillan Encyclopaedia of Philosophy*. New York: Macmillan.

Dupré, J. (1999). 'Are Whales Fish?', in D. L. Medin and S. Atran (eds.), *Folkbiology*. Cambridge, Mass.: MIT Press.

Evans, G. (1973). 'The Causal Theory of Names'. *Proceedings of the Aristotelian Society*, suppl vol., 47: 187–208.

—— (1981). 'Understanding Demonstratives', in H. Parret and J. Bouvaresse (eds.), *Meaning and Understanding*. Berlin: de Gruyter.

—— (1982). *The Varieties of Reference*. Oxford: Oxford University Press.

Field, H. (1977). 'Logic, Meaning and Conceptual Role'. *Journal of Philosophy*, 69: 379–409.

Fodor, J.A. (1987). *Psychosemantics*. Cambridge, Mass.: MIT Press.

—— (1991*a*). *A Theory of Content and Other Essays*. Cambridge, Mass.: MIT Press.

—— (1991*b*). 'A Modal Argument for Narrow Content'. *Journal of Philosophy*, 88: 5–26.

—— (1994). *The Elm and the Expert*. Cambridge, Mass.: MIT Press.

Frege, G. (1847). 'Logic'.

—— (1892/1952). 'Über Sinn und Bedeutung'. *Zeitschrift für Philosophie und Philosophische Kritik*, 100 (1892), 25–50. Repr. in *Translations from the Philosophical Writings of Gottlob Frege*, ed. P. Geach and M. Black. Totowa, NJ: Rowman & Littlefield, 1952.

—— (1897/1983). *Logick*, posthumously pub. In *Gottlob Frege. Nachgelassene Schriften*, ed. H. Hermes, F. Kambartel, and F. Kaulback, 2nd rev. edn. Hamburg: Felix Meiner Verlag.

Gelman, S., and Hirschfield, L. (1999). 'How Biological Is Essentialism?', in D. L. Medin and S. Atran (eds.), *Folkbiology*. Cambridge, Mass.: MIT Press.

Husserl, E. (1950). *Husserliana*. The Hague: Nijhoff.

Kaplan, D. (1989). 'Demonstratives', in J. Almog, J. Perry, and H. Wettstein (eds.), *Themes from Kaplan*. Cambridge: Cambridge University Press.

—— (1990). 'Thoughts on Demonstratives'. Repr. in P. Yourgrau (ed.), *Demonstratives*. Oxford: Oxford University Press.

—— (1990). 'Words'. *Proceedings of the Aristotelian Society*, suppl vol., 64: 93–119.

Katz, J. (2001). 'The End of Millianism'. *Journal of Philosophy*, 98: 137–66.

Kripke, S. (1972). 'Naming and Necessity', in D. Davidson and G. Harman (eds.), *Semantics of Natural Language*. Dordrecht: Reidel.

—— (1982). *Naming and Necessity*. Cambridge, Mass.: Harvard University Press.

LaPorte, J. (1996), 'Chemical Kind Term Reference and the Discovery of Essence'. *Noûs*, 30: 112–32.

Larson, R., and Segal, G. (1995), *Knowledge of Meaning: An Introduction to Semantic Theory*. Cambridge, Mass.: MIT Press.

Lewis, D. (1997). 'Naming the Colours'. *Australasian Journal of Philosophy*, 75: 325–42.

Loar, B. (1987). 'Social Content and Psychological Content', in R. Grimm and D. Merrill (eds.), *Contents of Thought: Proceedings of the 1985 Oberlin Colloquium in Philosophy*.

—— (1988). 'Social Content and Psychological Content', in R. H. Grimm and D. D. Merrill (eds.), *Contents of Thought*. Tucson: University of Arizona Press.

McDowell, J. (1977). 'The Sense and Reference of a Proper Name'. *Mind*, 86: 159–85.

—— (1984). 'De Re Senses', in C. Wright (ed.), *Frege: Tradition and Influence*. Oxford: Blackwell.

Makin, G. (2000). *The Metaphysicians of Meaning: Russell and Frege on Sense and Denotation*. London: Routledge.

Medin, D. L., and Atran, S. (eds.) (1999). *Folkbiology*. Cambridge, Mass.: MIT Press.

Meinong, A. (1904/1960). 'The Theory of Objects', in R. Chisholm (ed.), *Realism and the Background of Phenomenology*. Glencoe, Ill.: Free Press.

Mill, J. S. (1843). *A System of Logic*. New York: Harper Brothers.

Millikan, R. (2000). *On Clear and Confused Ideas*. Cambridge: Cambridge University Press.

Neale, S. (1990). *Descriptions*. Cambridge, Mass.: MIT Press.

Noonan, H. (1986). 'Russellian Thoughts and Methodological Solipsism', in J. Butterfield (ed.), *Language, Mind and Logic*. Cambridge: Cambridge University Press.

Peacocke, C. A. B. (1981). 'Demonstrative Thought and Psychological Explanation'. *Synthese*, 49: 187–217.

—— (1983). *Sense and Content*. Oxford: Oxford University Press.

—— (1993). 'Externalist Explanations'. *Proceedings of the Aristotelian Society*, 93: 203–30.

Perry, J. (1990). 'Frege on Demonstratives'. Repr. in P. Yourgau (ed.), *Demonstratives*. Oxford: Oxford University Press.

Pinker, S. (1994). *The Language Instinct: How the Mind Creates Language*. New York: HarperCollins.

Putnam, H. (1975). 'The Meaning of "Meaning"', in K. Gunderson (ed.), *Language, Mind and Knowledge*, Minnesota Studies in the Philosophy of Science. Minneapolis: University of Michigan Press.

Quine, W. v. O. (1956). 'Quantifiers and Propositional Attitudes'. *Journal of Philosophy*, 53: 177–87.

Richard, M. (1987). 'Attitude Ascriptions, Semantic Theory, and Pragmatic Evidence'. *Proceedings of the Aristotelian Society*, 87: 243–62.

Rosenberg, J. (1994). *Beyond Formalism*. Philadelphia: Temple University Press.

Russell, B. (1905). 'On Denoting'. *Mind*, 14: 479–93.

Sainsbury, R. M. (1993). 'Russell on Names and Communication', in Andrew Irvine and Gary Wedeking (eds.), *Russell and Analytic Philosophy*. Toronto: University of Toronto Press.

—— (2002). 'Departing from Frege', in Sainsbury, *Departing from Frege: Essays in Philosophy of Language*. London: Routledge.

Salmon, N. (1986). *Frege's Puzzle*. Cambridge, Mass.: MIT Press.

—— (1998). 'Non-Existence'. *Noûs*, 32: 277–319.

Segal, G. (1989a). 'The Return of the Individual'. *Mind*, 98: 35–57.

—— (1989*b*). 'Seeing What Is Not There'. *Philosophical Review*, 98: 189–21.

—— (2000). *A Slim Book About Narrow Content*. Cambridge, Mass.: MIT Press.

—— (in preparation). 'Keep Making Sense', in T. Crane (ed.), *Contemporary Philosophers in Focus: Jerry Fodor*. Cambridge: Cambridge University Press.

Soames, S. (1987). 'Direct Reference, Propositional Attitudes and Semantic Content'. *Philosophical Topics*, 15: 47–87.

Tye, M. (1989). *The Metaphysics of Mind*. Cambridge: Cambridge University Press.

Williamson, T. (2000). *Knowledge and its Limits*. Oxford: Oxford University Press.

Wilson, M. (1982). 'Predicate Meets Property'. *Philosophical Review*, 91: 549–89.

Wright, C. (ed.) (1984). *Frege: Tradition and Influence*. Oxford: Blackwell.

Yourgrau, P. (ed.) (1990). *Demonstratives*. Oxford: Oxford University Press.

CHAPTER 12

CONSCIOUSNESS

FRANK JACKSON

1. INTRODUCTION

There is a difference between being conscious and being unconscious. Our subject
is that difference. Since the rise of interest in materialist or physicalist theories of
mind, theorizing about consciousness has been largely driven by the debate over
whether it can be accommodated within materialism.[1] This is because it is widely
agreed by materialists and anti-materialists alike that consciousness is the great
challenge to materialist theories of mind. This debate will be our starting point for
a journey through recent philosophizing about consciousness.

2. ON BEING A MATERIALIST

The physical sciences—physics, chemistry, biology—tell us a great deal about what
our world is like. In addition, they tell us a great deal about what we are like. They

---

[1] I'll speak indifferently of materialism and physicalism. I take it readers know the kind of view
intended but I give a rough characterization below. In the literature there is a tendency to use 'physicalism' when it is important to highlight the rejection of 'spooky' *properties* in one's theory of mind
along with 'spooky' stuff.

tell us what our bodies are made of, the chemical reactions necessary for life, how our ears extract location information from sound waves, the evolutionary account of how various bits of us are as they are, what causes our bodies to move through the physical environment as they do, and so on. We can think of the true, complete physical account of us as an aggregation of all there is to say about us that can be constructed from the materials to be found in the various physical sciences. This account tells the story of us as revealed by the physical sciences.

Two questions have dominated recent philosophy of mind. One is whether or not, somewhere in this story, in some good sense or other, is to be found consciousness, as physicalists hold, or whether consciousness is a separate, additional ingredient, as dualist theories of minds and persons (and sentient animals in general) hold. Here is a way of thinking about the issue. Some cars have powerful engines. But the full account of the car's bits, how they fit together, and the way their arrangement affects the car's capacities and what it does when the accelerator is pressed will not (or need not) include words like 'powerful', and will not say explicitly that the car is powerful. However, the car's being powerful is not something extra that outruns what we include in the full, detailed account about the parts and their interactions. Someone who thought that the assembly line for powerful cars has a final stage, after all the bits are assembled, where power is injected, would have the wrong idea about motor cars. Materialists say the same about persons and consciousness. Mental states, and consciousness in particular, are not something that needs to be added to the physical account of persons, albeit they do not appear as such in the physical account of us.

The second question is, if consciousness is included in the full physical account of us, where is the section of that account that is about consciousness though not under that name? Is it the section on the neuroscience of certain parts of the brain, the section on information processing and how it underpins various functional abilities, the section on the evolution of representational states, or...? Or perhaps this is the wrong kind of question to be asking. Consciousness is neither an extra that needs to be added to the physical account—dualism is wrong; but nor is it something to be 'found' in the physical account of us—that's to ask a confused question.

3. Realism About Mental States and Consciousness

Everyone (almost) is a realist about mental states and consciousness in the sense that they grant that people on occasion really are in mental states and really are conscious. It *is* the case that we feel pain, believe in the special theory of relativity, see red, have our blood 'run cold', rehearse an argument in our heads, suffer pangs of jealousy, and so on. But most of us are realists in the stronger sense that we take mental states, including conscious ones, to play causal roles. Bodily damage causes pain, and pain in turn causes us to do something about that damage, and that's an important part of the evolutionary role of pain. And a similar story applies to mental states in general. They are elements in causal networks. True, behaviourists resist common sense on this point. They urge that explanations of behaviour in terms of being intelligent or desiring beer are nothing more than claims about patterns in behaviour.[2] But their resistance to the obvious position that intelligence and desire for beer are part of the cause of these patterns in behaviour, and so distinct from the patterns, is based on a curious hostility (as it now seems with the 20–20 vision of hindsight) to hypothesizing underlying causes—a methodology that has proved itself time and again in modern science, two obvious examples being molecular biology and the atomic theory of valency. The philosophically appealing and commonsensical position on mental states is a realism that avows that we are sometimes in one or another mental state *and* that these states are part of the causal nexus.[3]

If realism in this stronger sense is correct—as we assume from here on—there is no confusion in asking after the location of consciousness; it is located where the relevant cause is located. And if materialism is true, the location in question is to be found somewhere in the account of what we are like given in physical terms. But it helps to ask first about consciousness's location among the mental states *qua* mental states. The final step is then to locate those mental states, the ones that pertain most especially to consciousness, in the physical account of our nature. Near the end I will give a *rough* indication of where that might be, as I see matters.

4. WHERE DOES CONSCIOUSNESS FIT INTO THE INVENTORY OF MENTAL STATES?

It appears in two places, and this is in part an account of what we folk understand by consciousness and in part a piece of philosophical ground-marking.

We can distinguish the phenomenal mental states from the non-phenomenal ones. Phenomenal mental states have positions in similarity spaces: perceived

[2] Most famously, B. F. Skinner, see e.g. (1974), but Daniel Dennett writes at times in ways that invite a similar interpretation, see Dennett (1991, 'Appendix A (for Philosophers)').

[3] There is an understanding of realism about mental states that ties it to the view that which mental state a subject is in is quite separate from which mental state some interpreter of that subject judges or would judge that subject to be in. In that sense, realism is by definition opposed to interpretationist

colours are more or less alike; mild pain can shade into discomfort; an increase in felt heat slips over into pain; and so on. Thus the intuitive appeal of talking of phenomenal mental states as ones for which there is something it is like to be in them, in the famous phrase (see Nagel 1974). They have a phenomenology. In one established sense, the conscious mental states are those with a phenomenology—pain, pangs of hunger, and all the rest—and the phenomenon of consciousness resides in the fact that there are mental states with phenomenal character.

However, there is a separate distinction: that between being in a mental state *simpliciter* and that between, for example, reflecting on, being aware of, or making inferences from some mental state you are in. As you make your way across a crowded floor, you will have many perceptual experiences concerning where the objects and people around you are located—which is how you make it across the room safely—but only some will be perceptual experiences you are conscious of in the sense of reflecting on them or their grabbing your attention. And there is considerable plausibility in the view that you are conscious in the fullest sense when you are aware of being in a state which exhibits phenomenal character (see e.g. Armstrong 1999, ch. 10). When philosophers talk about the problem of consciousness, they typically mean to cover both the 'what it is like' property of some mental states, and that which is distinctive of being actively aware of some mental state one is in (see Block 2002 and Lycan 1996, ch. 1, for detail on this and related issues).

Our focus will be on the problem posed by mental states with a phenomenology. It is these mental states that have been seen as the biggest challenge to materialism and are why consciousness is so often cited as materialism's biggest challenge. A common assumption (sometimes somewhat hidden) has been that if we can solve that part of the problem of consciousness, then the part that deals with awareness of mental states will be a relatively easy coda. Our task now is to see why phenomenal mental states are such a challenge to materialism.

5. Why the Physical Story Seems to Leave Out the Phenomenal Side of Mental Life

We noted earlier that phenomenal states are similar and different, one to another, in distinctive ways. Various experiences of seeing red are alike in a highly distinctive

views of mind to be found in some writings of Daniel Dennett, see e.g. Dennett (1987) and Davidson (1974). We will not be concerned with this issue.

way missing from experiences of seeing green. Pains are alike in one way and itches in another; there is a similarity between various feelings of hunger that is lacking in the case of thirst, and so on. The core argument for holding that the physical story about us leaves out consciousness, in the sense of the mental states with a phenomenology, is that the distinctive similarities and differences between phenomenal mental states do not appear to correspond to those between physical states and their physical properties. Consider two pains. There is a highly distinct-ive commonality between them, one familiar to all who have suffered pain. But, runs the argument, this commonality differs from any to be found in the physical story about pain. The physical story will mention neuro-scientific properties, information processing ones, functional ones, evolutionary ones, and so on. These properties are all ways in which the various physical states and those in them may be alike (or different). But none, it seems, are the very commonality that we know and fear. The physical account will tell us, as it might be, that two physical states are alike in being typically caused by bodily damage and causing limb withdrawal from the source of the damage, but where is the *hurting* as such that causes the limb withdrawal? The same argument can be made for the perception of colour. We know the kinds of properties mentioned when physical scientists discuss colour: being caused by light with such and such wave length or reflectance properties, carrying information about the ripeness of food, enabling discriminations with survival value, prompting the word 'red' in our mouths, and so on. Such properties will underpin many similarities and differences, but none, it seems, corresponds to the 'redness' of seeing red.

There are many ways of sharpening the line of thought just outlined. One way appeals to the idea of a zombie (or imitation person) (for a simple but powerful presentation of this argument, see Campbell 1970: 99ff.; an extended, widely discussed presentation is part ii of Chalmers 1996). It is logically possible that I have a twin who is exactly like me in every physical respect: weighs what I weigh, is disposed to act in any given circumstance exactly as I do, has a brain whose neurophysiology is exactly like mine, and so on. It would be impossible for a third person to tell us apart; we'd be *identical* identical twins. However, despite our identity in physical nature, it seems logically possible that my twin be a zombie in that 'it' lacks consciousness in the sense of phenomenal experiences. It writhes as I do when stomach cramp strikes but it is *just* writhing. But then the phenomenal aspect of my mental life is a feature of me that outruns my physical nature. For I am physically identical to my zombie twin and, in consequence, what I have that it lacks is not part of my physical nature, just as dualists say.

However, the most discussed and intuitively powerful way of sharpening the line of thought is the knowledge argument, to which I now turn. It focuses on making the anti-physicalist case for our experience of colour.

6. THE KNOWLEDGE ARGUMENT AGAINST PHYSICALISM

Suppose that we have a brilliant physical scientist, Mary, who is confined in a room which is painted black and white throughout—walls, windows, chairs, and Mary herself.[4] Her information about the world and its workings comes from books without coloured pictures and from black-and-white television. However, the lectures delivered over the black-and-white television are amazing feats of exposition in physics, chemistry, biology, and cognitive science, and the same goes for the books. In addition, she has extraordinary powers of comprehension and retention. In consequence, she is extraordinarily knowledgeable about the physical nature of our world, the neurophysiology of human beings and sentient creatures in general, the functional and informational roles of their neurological states, and how these roles explain the way humans navigate the world and use colour words when confronted with flowers and fruit in daylight.

Can she deduce from this vast array of physical information what it is like to see yellow? It seems that she cannot. She knows that buttercups prompt the word 'yellow' in English speakers in daylight, and she knows the neuroscience and optical science of why this is so. She knows all about the kinds of light typically reflected by various objects and how they interact with human eyes and brains to cause the behaviours they do. Despite all this, it very much seems that there is something about our world, and especially persons' colour experiences, she is ignorant of. And her lack does not seem to be a matter of detail, something she might rectify by reading another black-and-white book, or being more attentive to what can be concluded from this or that body of information couched in physical terms. There seems to be a whole subject matter that escapes her.

This conclusion is reinforced by reflecting on what would happen should she be released from her room. Assuming there is nothing wrong with her colour vision despite its lack of exercise during her imprisonment, she would, it seems, learn something very striking about the nature of our world, including especially the nature of the colour experiences of her fellow humans. There is a striking similarity between the mental states of those persons on the occasions when they produce the colour words of which she was ignorant until her release. But *ex hypothesi*

---

[4] There are many statements of the knowledge argument, or of arguments close to the knowledge argument in one way or another. The statement below is closest to those in Jackson (1982, 1986). I no longer support the argument; see e.g. Jackson (1998). The argument has appealed to non-philosophers as well as philosophers, see e.g. Dunne (1927: 13–14). Over the years I have lost track of the many discussions I have had with supporters and opponents of the knowledge argument but I know that I have many debts.

she did know all there was to know physically. Therefore, there is more to know than all there is to know physically. Physicalism is false.

7. Why Resist?

On the face of it, the argument is compelling. Why not grant the conclusion? After all, even without the argument, the idea that consciousness is different in kind from anything that appears in the physical story is appealing, as we implicitly granted when we identified consciousness as materialism and physicalism's greatest challenge.

The reason for resisting is that our knowledge of the sensory side of psychology has a causal source. Seeing yellow and feeling pain impact on us, leaving a memory trace which sustains our knowledge of what it is like to see yellow and feel pain on the many occasions where we are neither seeing yellow nor feeling pain. This is why it is a mistake to say that someone could not know what seeing yellow and feeling pain is like unless they had actually experienced them: false 'memory' traces are enough. (The knowledge argument could have been developed by urging that Mary would learn something as a result of the induction of false memories of seeing colour despite already knowing all there is to know physically.) This places a constraint on our best opinion about the nature of our sensory states: we had better not have opinions about their nature which cannot be justified by what we know about the causal origin of those opinions. Now the precise connection between causal origin and rational opinion is complex, but for present purposes the following rough maxim will serve: do not have opinions that outrun what is required by the best theory of these opinions' causal origins (for something less rough, see Jackson and Pargetter 1985). Often it will be uncertain what the best theory is, or the question of what it is will be too close to the question under discussion for the maxim to be of much use. But in the case of sensory states, the maxim has obvious bite. We know that our knowledge of what it is like to see yellow and feel pain have purely physical causes. We know, for example, that Mary's transition from not knowing what it is like to see yellow to knowing what it is like to see yellow will have a causal explanation in purely physical terms. It follows, by the maxim, that what she learns had better not outrun how things are physically.

Despite having championed the knowledge argument in the past, I now think for these kinds of reasons that the right attitude to take to the argument is that it *must* go wrong—but where? We will now review some of the many suggestions as to where the wheels fall off.

8. OBJECTIONS TO THE KNOWLEDGE ARGUMENT

One line of objection draws on the phenomenon of egocentric knowledge.[5] In addition to knowledge directed towards what the world we live in is like, there is knowledge directed towards *who* and *where* one is, and *when* it is, and one can have complete knowledge of the first kind while being seriously deficient in knowledge of the second, egocentric kind. Here is a simple example. Suppose that some high-powered physics demonstrates that our world divides neatly into two, widely separated in space parts with nothing in between; one part is made of matter and the other is made of antimatter. Moreover, they are identical modulo their 'sign'. That is, if you take one of the parts and reverse the 'signs' on each item in it leaving everything else the same, you get an exact duplicate of the other part. In that case, we could not know which part we were in. There would be no way to tell the difference between being in the matter part and the antimatter part. Our surroundings and our bodies, for example, would be indistinguishable whether we were in the matter part or the antimatter part. In particular, Mary could not know which part she is in. What is more, she will not know who she is. Given her encyclopedic knowledge, she will no doubt know that there are two exactly alike, except for the sign reversal, people called 'Mary' in black-and-white rooms, but she will not know if she is Mary or anti-Mary.

The moral is that complete knowledge of what our world is like does not necessarily deliver knowledge of where one is or who one is. And other examples tell us that the same goes for *when* it is. If, for example, the fancy physics had told us that our world divides into two identical temporal halves, a first half and a second half, we and Mary would not know which half we lived in even if we knew all there is to know about what our world is like including that there are these two identical halves. We would each know that we live after the Second World War but would not know which of the two Second World Wars our lives follow. So the idea that physicalism is committed to complete knowledge of the physical delivering complete knowledge *simpliciter* is a mistake. There is more to knowledge than knowing what our world is like.

This point about the inadequacy of knowledge of what our world is like to necessarily deliver knowledge of who, where, and when we are is important and widely accepted. But it is far from clear that it goes to the heart of the knowledge argument. Mary's lack of knowledge seems, at least in large part, to concern what

---

[5] Perry (2001) contains a detailed discussion of a nuanced form of this objection. A useful entry into the extensive debate over the knowledge argument and consciousness more generally is Chalmers (2002, sect. 2). A collection dedicated to papers for and against the knowledge argument and with a detailed introduction by the editors is Stoljar and Nagasawa (2004).

her world is like, not her or anyone's identity, or spatial or temporal location in it. She is ignorant before her release, it seems, of what certain experiences are *like* in the sense of how they are similar and different, one to another (as we said above). That's the crux of the argument, and the apparent lack is quite different from a lack of egocentric knowledge.

A second objection starts from the point that the very same things, facts, and events can be known under many guises. The police may know Robinson under the guise of the main suspect in a bank raid; you may know him as your tennis partner; I may know him as the person who has just bought the house next door. The same happening may be Robinson's arrest; what stymied tennis today; the event that means the house is unoccupied. This suggests that we could grant that Mary's knowledge of what her world is like is incomplete without being forced to the conclusion that what is not known is non-physical. Her ignorance is a matter of there being features or categorizations of certain happenings in the world, especially those involving colour experience, that elude her while she is inside the room. All the same, the happenings in question are purely physical ones. When Mary leaves the room, she acquires knowledge but entirely through knowing about the very same physical things, facts, and events under different guises or under different categorizations. She gets new ways of categorizing happenings around her and thereby acquires new knowledge, but it is, all the same, knowledge of the purely physical and in consequence no threat to physicalism. The many ways of thinking of Robinson do not imply that there are many Robinsons.

The interest of this suggestion is clear but again it seems that the knowledge argument survives. For the guises, ways of categorizing, must all be consistent with physicalism if physicalism is true. This is because something falls under a guise inasmuch as it is itself the appropriate way: guises supervene on nature, as we say. But then, it seems, Mary could know about their applicability when inside the room. It is hard to see how, given physicalism, there could be ways of grouping things into categories that are, in principle, unavailable to her while in the room. Although there is one Robinson, for each guise that applies to him, there is a separate feature: it is a feature of Robinson that he is a suspect, that he is a tennis partner, and that he is the buyer of a house, and each of these features are distinct.

Of course, the ways of grouping may not be easy ones to latch onto. Consider, for example, someone who knows the Cartesian coordinates of a series of points that in fact lie on a circle without realizing that the points lie on a circle. It is not until they graph the points, or do the calculations that reveal that the points satisfy the relevant equation, that they make the discovery. They will then learn something, but it is plausible that they do not learn about a new feature—the circularity was 'there' in what they knew from the beginning—the learning was a matter of its becoming revealed when they saw that the points could be categorized in a certain way. Although it can be hard to spot the fact that a series of points given by their Cartesian coordinates lie on a circle, and it can be much harder to spot the relevant shape in more complex cases, it should be possible in principle to spot the relevant commonality if only one is smart enough and can put the data together aright. However, no amount of cleverness in assembling data and spotting patterns will in itself tell Mary in the black-and-white room what it is like to see red, or so it seems.

The point about ways of grouping phenomena together also bears on the common objection to the knowledge argument that what happens to Mary when she leaves the room is that she acquires new concepts and that's no reason to admit new properties; the objection is that the knowledge argument fallaciously slides from the acquisition of new concepts to knowing about new properties.[6] However, the sense in which Mary would seem to acquire a new concept is precisely that she learns of a new way of grouping experiences together. Think, for instance, of someone who acquires the concept of *inertial mass* and learns that it applies to certain items. What they learn is a new way in which the items resemble each other, and that *is* both to learn of a new property, the relevant unifier, and that it is instantiated in our world. In the same way, Mary's new concept seems to correspond to a new way for experiences to be alike, one that nowhere appears in the physicalists' picture. If this is right, there are properties that fail to appear in that picture, namely, those corresponding to her newly enlarged understanding of the respects of similarity which obtain on occasion between certain states of sentient creatures.

The next objection can be introduced by reference to the example of hard-to-spot patterns that is discussed above. The difference between, on the one hand, being in a situation where patterns in data are very hard to grasp although available in principle and, on the other hand, being in a situation where it is literally impossible to make the classifications is not always transparent. In consequence, runs this objection, we can and should insist that Mary can know what it is like to see yellow while in the room (I think this is Dan Dennett's objection to the knowledge argument; see Dennett 1991: 399; see also Churchland 1985). The strong intuition to the contrary is the result of the fact that it would be *extremely* hard for her to spot the relevant patterns, along with wrongly conflating the extremely hard with the impossible. This reply is sometimes coupled with the view that the way our brains enable us to see colour goes via the way our brains and optical systems pick up on very unobvious patterns in the effects coloured objects have on light (see e.g. Hilbert 1987). Mary's practical problem inside the room will be that her pattern detector, her optical system, is not being allowed to do its job of making sense of data that look, on the face of it, to be a complete mess. But if we suppose, as we should when evaluating the knowledge argument, that Mary has worked out *everything*, then she could know in principle on the basis of her vast data-bank of physical

---

[6] As Ned Block (2003) says, 'I accept the familiar refutation of this argument along the lines of: Mary learns a new concept of something she already knew. She acquires a phenomenal concept of a physical fact that she was already acquainted with via a physical concept.' Perhaps the best-known version of this reply is Loar (1990).

information, what it is like to see yellow, for she will have grasped the relevant similarities. In consequence, she will not learn what it is like to see yellow on her release; she will already know. True, runs this reply to the knowledge argument, when we imaginatively put ourselves in Mary's shoes as she emerges from the black-and-white room, we get the strong intuition that she would learn something about what the world is like, but this is only because we cannot, no matter how hard we try, imagine Mary having *that* much knowledge in the sense of being able to make suitably patterned sense of the huge aggregation of the disparate bits of information one gets from the pages of (black-and-white) books, lectures, and monitor screens.

I think this is the best reply to the knowledge argument but it needs bolstering by two considerations. One relates to what it is like to acquire certain abilities or know-how (as opposed to knowledge-that); the other relates to *where*, as we might put it, the qualities of phenomenal experience, *qua* the kind of experience it is, reside. (The first is prominent in discussions of the knowledge argument by Nemirow 1980, 1990 and Lewis 1990. The second is prominent in Jackson 2003a.)

The first point can be made fairly quickly; the second calls for a separate section.

People vary in their capacities to recognize patterns. People who are unusually good at learning a new language pick up the pattern that constitutes a sentence in a given language's being grammatical much faster than most of us. At the learning stage where we are still labouring with the grammar book to check, they can simply 'see' whether or not a sentence in the new language is grammatical. Good chess players can often recognize winning positions while the rest of us have to 'work it out'. Most of us can recognize that some object is moving but the motion-blind have to derive the fact from their observation that a single object is at different places at different times.

There is a distinctive 'what it is like' nature integral to the exercise of such recognitional capacities. We who have the ability to recognize that a sentence in language L is grammatical have a different kind of experience when presented with a given sentence in L from those who have to work it out; the grammatical sentences 'look' right, the ungrammatical sentences 'look' wrong. All the same, there is no difference in knowledge-that. Our knowledge-that is nothing more or less than that the given sentence is or is not grammatical in L. The same goes for the difference between most of us and the motion-blind. What we and they know may be the very same—that some object is or is not moving—but we who can recognize motion have a very different kind of experience. I think we should say much the same about Mary. The distinctive nature of the experience of seeing yellow that she has when she leaves the black-and-white room derives from the fact that she is exercising a recognitional capacity with respect to a commonality between, for example, buttercups and lemons, and it is one that she could in principle have worked out from the huge raft of physical data in her possession before leaving the room. What she knows about how things are has, therefore, not expanded; the difference is in her ability to recognize a pattern simply by looking, an ability she is able to exercise when and only when she is outside the room.

Why do we need to say more than this? The reason is that supporters of the knowledge argument can and do respond by saying that when Mary exercises the ability, she has a new kind of experience and it is this new kind that outruns the physical way things are. The exercising of the ability itself involves a new kind of experience that Mary cannot know about while in the room.

As far as I can see, the only way to blunt this response is to expose and reject an implicit assumption about the properties of experience *qua* experience that under-pins it. This is precisely what intentionalism about sensory experience does. It undermines the way of thinking about the qualities of phenomenal experience that lies behind the knowledge argument, the way encapsulated in the intuition that Mary learns about new ways for things to be alike. First I will discuss intentionalism and then we'll see how it undermines the knowledge argument.

9. INTENTIONALISM ABOUT SENSORY EXPERIENCE: DIAPHANOUSNESS

The predicates we use to describe things in our world also figure in our descriptions of sensory experience. We describe objects as round, yellow, and 2 metres away. We describe our experiences as of something yellow, 2 metres away, and round. Indeed, when we describe how things seem to us visually, we describe how *things* seem. There is no difference between describing a yellow experience and describing an experience putatively *of* some yellow thing.

This is the famous diaphanousness of experience. G. E. Moore (1922) is perhaps the best-known advocate of diaphanousness, but recent discussions have been especially influenced by Gilbert Harman's presentation. In a much quoted passage, he says:

When Eloise sees a tree before her, the colors she experiences are all experienced as features of the tree and its surroundings. None of them are experienced as intrinsic features of her experience. Nor does she experience any features of anything as intrinsic features of her experiences. And that is true of you too... Look at a tree and try to turn your attention to intrinsic features of your visual experience. I predict that you will find that the only features there to turn your attention to will be features of the tree... (Harman 1998: 667)

I think that diaphanousness is very plausible and I am going to assume it here. Our focus will be on the connection between diaphanousness and intentionalism.

Diaphanousness is often thought to be an argument in itself for intentionalism (Harman seems to be of this opinion), but in fact the path from the first to the second needs a good deal of argument.[7]

Diaphanousness is the thesis that the qualities of experience are qualities of the object of experience. Intentionalism is the thesis that the qualities of experience are properties of an intentional object in the sense that they are properties of the way things are being represented to be; the yellowness or squareness of a sensory experience resides in its representing that something is yellow or square. Both doctrines say that the properties are properties of the object of experience but intentionalism *adds* that that object is an intentional object. Intentionalism is, that is, a version of diaphanousness, and it is no small matter to show that we should adopt the version in question. This is clear when we look more closely at Harman's argument. What, exactly, is the object that is claimed to have the 'features' in the passage quoted? If it is the tree, we do not have a generally acceptable account of what makes an experience the kind of experience it is. We know that the very same experience can be had in the absence of any physical object including trees.[8] That is to say, the claim that 'the only features there to turn your attention to will be features of the tree' is not in general correct. What is plausible in general is that whenever we try to 'catch' the properties of an experience *qua* kind of experience that it is, all we seem to find are properties of *an* object whose nature determines the nature of the experience. But the nature of this object is a separate matter. Moreover, if one went by phenomenology—which is, after all, the basis for the claim that experience is diaphanous—the initially plausible view is that the object is an object in space-time and not an intentional object. That is why so many were beguiled by sense data for so long—those non-intentional objects tailor-made to be the objects of experience, to be the non-intentional objects that possess the properties that make an experience the kind of experience it is.[9]

In order to show that the object of experience is an intentional one, we must, I think, first distinguish some varieties of *representationalism* about experience and then use representationalism to argue from diaphanousness to intentionalism. There is no direct path from diaphanousness to intentionalism; we need to go via representationalism.

---

[7] As Tye (2000, ch. 3) argues, though not for my reasons.

[8] I'm assuming (with the majority) the falsity of certain 'there is no common element' views about experience defended in, for example, Hinton (1973). For a recent critique of no common element views, see Foster (2000).

[9] I was beguiled, see Jackson (1977, chs. 3 and 4).

10. Varieties of Representationalism

Minimal representationalism, as we might call it, holds that experience is *essentially* representational while being silent on whether an experience's representing that things are thus and so, for some suitable thus and so, exhausts its nature in the sense of settling it without remainder. Strong representationalism adds the exhaustion claim to minimal representationalism. We can call versions of minimal representationalism that hold that experience is essentially representational, but not exhaustively so, weak representationalism.

Strong representationalism is not the view that the *content* of an intentional state determines its nature *qua* mental state without remainder. Different intentional states may have the very same content—I may both believe and desire that it will rain. Strong representationalism is the doctrine that it is the content of an experience *plus* the fact that the experience represents that that content obtains *in the way distinctive of perceptual representation* that determines the experience's nature without remainder.[10]

I take it that strong representationalism is the doctrine with bite: enough philosophers take it for granted that experience is essentially representational, that a perceptual experience by its very nature points to things being a certain way, for minimal representationalism to count as orthodoxy. Of course, how to analyse the relevant notion of representation is controversial. What I am saying is orthodoxy is the core idea that a perceptual experience, by its very nature, invites its subject to believe that things are a certain way.[11] We may decline the invitation. We may indeed have no inclination to accept it.[12] All the same, if asked, is there a way things are that one is being directed to as something the experience makes belief-worthy, absent defeaters? It is very plausible that, necessarily, for every experience, there is such a way. After all, as I remarked earlier, the words we use to describe experience *qua* experience are the very words we use to describe the world and the things in it, and we take an experience we describe using those words to be in itself, albeit defeasibly, a reason for believing that how things are is that there are things in the world having the properties we use those words for.

There are dissenters to the kind of minimal representationalism I've tendentiously called orthodoxy, but I cannot think of an *argument* to persuade them to change

---

[10] Tye (2000: 45) describes and endorses a thesis he calls 'strong or pure representationalism'. It is similar to the thesis I am calling strong representationalism but differs in that it affirms that 'phenomenal character is one and the same as representational content that meets certain further conditions'. The job we give to kind of representation plus content of representation in strong representationalism he gives to a distinction between kinds of content. For my reservations about giving a distinction between kinds of content that kind of role, see Jackson (forthcoming).

[11] I borrow the 'invitation to believe' way of saying it from Foster (2000: 37 ff.).

[12] As many have urged when objecting to Armstrong's (1961) analysis. See e.g. Jackson (1977).

their minds. Such an argument would need to have premises more plausible than that perceptual experiences are, by their very nature, representational, and that, we representationalists insist, is not to be found. The live issue, or so it seems to me, is whether the only viable form of minimal representationalism is the strong kind, and there are a number of considerations that suggest that it is.

According to minimal representationalism, it is impossible to have a perceptual experience without thereby being in a state that represents that things are thus and so in the world. Here 'in the world' does not necessarily mean outside of the subject. Some experiences represent how your stomach is, for example. But although this concerns how things inside you are, it concerns how the world is in the sense of concerning how things are with something distinct from the experience itself. Strong representationalism goes further in maintaining that how an experience represents things as being exhausts its experiential nature. According to strong representationalism, the wrong way to think about an experience's nature is as partly constituted by how it represents things to be and partly by something else. How it represents things to be does the complete job.

There are two reasons for denying the 'composite' picture of an experience's nature once you have embraced the idea that experience is essentially representational. One is that it is hard to make sense of a phenomenal 'overflow' from the representational content. Such an overflow would appear to be something with feel but without representational content, but once we have feel, we have, it seems, representation. The phenomenology of visual experience is inextricably tied into putative colour somewhere, and that automatically gives it the content of representing something about how things are at the 'somewhere'. The experiences one has when one scrunches one's eyes shut or pushes one's eyeballs in are sometimes mentioned as a counter-example to this claim (or as a possible counter-example, see Block 1996). But although the putative locations, shapes, and colours are highly indeterminate and hard to pin down in such cases, they exist all the same. The representational content concerns how things of highly indeterminate, changing shapes and colours, and at some indeterminate distance in front of one are. Secondly, if experience consisted of a representational bit and a non-representational extra, we should be able to vary the 'extra' while leaving the representational content unchanged. This would mean that an experience's nature could vary without any change in how it represents things to be. And this, according to strong representationalism, is what cannot happen. Change an experience *qua* kind of experience it is and you *ipso facto* change how it represents things to be. A change in kind of experience is inevitably a change in how things are being represented to be.

I think this last claim is very plausible. It has, though, been challenged. A number of cases have been advanced which are argued to be ones where there is a difference in experience in the absence of a difference in how things are being represented to be. I think that there are good replies to these examples, but I won't argue that here. I don't have much to add to what others have said (see e.g. Tye 2000, ch. 4, and Lycan 1996, chs. 6 and 7, for detailed critical discussions of the alleged counter-examples from the representationalist standpoint). I will, however, discuss one case which seems to me especially interesting and challenging, and which often escapes discussion. I discuss it in the spirit of 'If this one doesn't work, none do'.

The example is a variation of one presented by Christopher Peacocke (2002). Consider a rectangular array of dots made up of four equally spaced rows and columns each containing four dots. When you look at it, your experience will represent that things are as diagrammed below (assuming nothing goes wrong).

Consistently with this, runs the objection, you may, as it might be, see it as four equally spaced rows, or as four equally spaced columns. In these two cases the experience is different but there is no difference in how things are being represented to be. If you had to diagram how things are being represented to be, the diagram would be the same in each case (and would be a diagram very like the one above). It follows, concludes the objection, that what an experience is like outruns how it represents things to be.

This objection overlooks the fact that how things are being represented to be is typically indeterminate to one degree or another. When you see the array as a set of rows, the 'fudge factor' for the positions of the columns is greater than that for the rows—the rows 'stand out' precisely because their positions are being more precisely represented; when you see the array as a set of columns, it is the other way around. This means that it isn't true that there is one diagram that equally captures how things are being represented to be in either case. In each case we need a *set* of diagrams, varying slightly, one from another, depending on the extent of the indeterminacies. In the case where you see the array as a set of rows, the variations in the location of the columns will be bigger than that of the rows, and when you see the array as a set of columns, it will be the other way around. If this treatment of the example is correct, a God-like creature whose representation of the array was wholly determinate would have a completely symmetrical experience on looking at the array. I think this consequence is the intuitively correct one. We see the array as a set of, say, rows only by 'letting' the columns go a bit 'fuzzy'.

It should, though, be noted that strong representationalism is not plausible for sensory mental states in general, including some that figure prominently in discussions of conscious mental states, namely bodily sensations and feelings. It is plausible that pain, for example, by its very nature represents. It represents that things are awry at the place where the pain is felt to be. But it does so along with a desire that this representational state cease, and this is part of the phenomenology. How much you want a pain to go away is plausibly part of how much it hurts. All the same, it is plausible that the case can be handled in a way strong representationalists find congenial. Desire is a representational state. In consequence, it is not a departure from the spirit of strong representationalism to hold that the feel of pain is a combination of how things are being represented to be in some part of one's body combined with the extent to which it is desired that this first-order representation cease forthwith.[13] We will, however, stay with the case of perceptual experiences that represent how things are without essential involvement with pro or con attitudes.

11. From Diaphanousness via Representationalism to Intentionalism

The issue before us now is how representationalism takes us from diaphanousness to intentionalism. The simplest route uses strong representationalism.

Diaphanousness says that the qualities of experience are nothing more than certain qualities of an object. There are three possibilities. One is that the qualities in question are the qualities of an intentional object and not of a non-intentional object. A second possibility is that the qualities are qualities of a non-intentional object and not of an intentional object. The final possibility is that the qualities are properties of both an intentional and a non-intentional object. The first is strong representationalism given diaphanousness, as it implies that the properties of an intentional object exhaust phenomenal nature. The second contradicts strong representationalism, as it says that the nature of experience is not determined by the qualities of an intentional object. The third contradicts strong representationalism as it implies that more than the qualities of an intentional object make up the nature of an experience (the more being the qualities of the non-intentional object). It follows that the only way diaphanousness and strong representationalism can be true together is if the qualities of experience are nothing more than certain qualities of an intentional object, the first possibility; but that is to say that intentionalism follows from diaphanousness plus strong representationalism.

However, interestingly, minimal representationalism—the thesis that experiences are essentially representational—also takes us from diaphanousness to intentionalism, as we will now see. Minimal representationalism says that an experience essentially represents that things are thus and so in the sense that what the experience is like

---

[13] One of the earliest treatments of bodily sensations and feelings along representational lines, though not put in quite these terms, is Armstrong (1962). For recent treatments, see Lycan (1996); Tye (1995).

entails that it represents that things are thus and so. How could this be? How could the properties the experience has that make it the kind of experience it is, in turn make it the case that it represents that things are thus and so. Let P be the relevant property of some experience E which both makes it the case that E is the kind of experience it is and that E represents that the way things are has property Q. We will review various possibilities for how P relates to Q and argue that the only viable ones, given diaphanousness, entail intentionalism about experience, the view that the properties of experience are properties of an intentional object.

By diaphanousness, P is a property of the object of E. Is this object an object in space-time—a non-intentional object, presumably some kind of constituent of E—or is it an intentional object, presumably the very way that things might be which is represented as being Q? Suppose the first, and further that P = Q. Then we face the puzzle of how an object in space-time's being Q essentially represents that Q is a property of how things are. We can understand how an object's being Q might essentially represent that it itself is Q, but the suggestion now under discussion is that an object's being Q essentially represents that something *else* is Q. As we noted earlier, minimal representationalism holds that experience essentially represents that the *world* is thus and so, where the reference to the world signifies that the representational content is directed to something other than the experience itself, and one thing's being thus and so does not, in and of itself, represent that something else is thus and so.

Some think in terms of projection when they address the issue of how experience speaks to the nature of the world. The idea seems to be that when we have an experience which is P, for suitable P, we project some property connected to P, the one we are calling Q, which may or may not be P itself, onto the world.[14] The experience represents that the world is Q by virtue of the combination of being P and the act of projection. This, however, would not help with the problem raised in the previous paragraph. For, first, is the act of projection part of what makes the experience the experience it is? If it is, we have a violation of diaphanousness. According to diaphanousness, it is the properties of the object of experience that settle the nature of experience, and projection is not a property of the object but instead is something done to certain properties of it. If, alternatively, the act of projection is not part of what makes the experience the experience it is, we have a violation of minimal representationalism. According to minimal representationalism, the experience's representing as it does is an essential part of its being the experience it is. It is not an 'extra' consequent upon an act of projection conceived as distinct from what makes the experience the experience it is. Secondly, how can projecting properties from one thing to another be a matter of necessity, even if we have qualifiers

[14] When P = Q, we have the view called literal projectivism by Sydney Shoemaker (1994). He is not endorsing it, but his reservations are different from mine and are advanced from the perspective of an opponent of the kind of representationalism being suggested here. This paper contains a helpful inventory of kinds of projectivism.

like that the projection be prima facie or *protanto* or...? Perhaps the projection is posited as something we find very natural, but we can resist the natural. So a projection account is incompatible with experiences, of *necessity*, pointing towards things being thus and so.

Now suppose that P is a property of a non-intentional object but is a property distinct from Q. There are two possibilities to survey. One is that P is the property of representing that Q, a property which is of course distinct from Q itself. But this *is* intentionalism. It comes to saying that what makes an experience the kind of experience it is—property P, as we are calling it—its representing that Q, which is another way of saying that the experience's nature is given by the nature of an intentional object. The second possibility is that P is distinct from representing that Q (and from Q). But then the problems raised above for the case where P = Q arise. Making P distinct from Q does not help with understanding how one thing's being P can *of necessity* represent some other thing's being Q, except in the special case where P is representing that Q.

It is time to see how intentionalism undermines the knowledge argument.

12. INTENTIONALISM AND THE KNOWLEDGE ARGUMENT

We noted that the core intuition fuelling the knowledge argument is that Mary learns about a new kind of similarity holding between experiences. The intuition is that the 'yellowness' of seeing butter is a previously unknown-to-Mary property that she realizes, on leaving the room, unites the experiences typically caused by seeing butter. The ability reply to the knowledge argument points out that there is a distinctive 'what it is like' nature integral to the exercise of recognitional capacities with respect to commonalities like being grammatical and moving, but, all the same, the commonalities being recognized are not new ones; they are old ones newly recognized. The gap in this reply, as we noted above, is that it invites the response that 'the exercising of the ability itself is a new kind of experience that Mary cannot know about while in the room'. We can now fill in the gap.

What unites how things have to be for the representations to be correct is not that which unites the items that share the content. Intentionalism tells us that what makes an experience the kind of experience it is is how it represents things to be; it is a property of an intentional object. This amounts to saying that the beguiling picture of the nature of experience that goes along with introspecting an experience and wondering how to find the 'yellowness' in the physical story about wavelengths, neural states, and functional roles is confused. The yellowness is not a property instance; it is how things are being represented to be. There is of course a new kind of experience, but its newness resides in its being a new kind of representational state; indeed, as the ability reply to the knowledge argument says, its newness is the exercise of a newly acquired recognitional and representational ability.

Here is a way to make the point via the traditional argument from illusion, an argument that few take seriously nowadays (I here draw on material in Jackson, forthcoming).

(1) When a straight stick immersed in water looks bent to some degree, its looking bent to that degree involves an instance of being bent to that degree.
(2) Nothing physical is or need be bent to that degree.

Therefore, physicalism's inventory of which properties are instantiated is incomplete; there is at least one instance of being bent to a certain degree that physicalism fails to account for.

Intentionalism says that this argument goes wrong because the first premiss is false. Looking bent to the degree in question is to be understood in terms of there needing to be something bent to that degree in order for the visual experience to represent correctly, not in terms that require that something be in fact bent to that degree.

13. SOME OUTSTANDING ISSUES

It will be obvious that I think that an intentionalism based on the claim that experience is essentially representational is the key to understanding consciousness. But there are many outstanding issues that any approach of this kind must address.

1. One concerns the relevant sense of representation. Many familiar cases of representation cited by philosophers involve causal covariance. Obvious examples are the way the number of tree rings represents the age of a tree, and the way the position of a pointer represents the level of petrol remaining in the tank. However, the sense in which mental states represent is not tied to normal causal covariation. Desires are representational states; they represent how subjects would like things to be. But, as we know only too well, there is no normal causal covariation between desiring something and its satisfaction. However, the core notion of representation—the notion whose varieties correspond to the differences between the way tree rings represent the age of trees, the way desires represent what is desired, the way three different scripts may represent three different possible endings for a film, the way a discarded architect's drawing might represent how one's house would have been

had you followed her first suggestion, and so on—is that of a systematic corre-spondence between the states that do the representing and how things are being represented to be. This gives us a handle on the question we started with: the chal-lenge to physicalism of finding the place of consciousness in the physical account of our world. For there is no special difficulty about giving an account of represen-tation in physical terms (see e.g. Stalnaker 1984). Given that representation is some kind of systematic correspondence between what does the representing and what is represented, this can be realized in a purely physical system, as the examples of petrol gauges and architects' drawings remind us. If our representationalist-cum-intentionalist position on consciousness is right, consciousness is to be found in the physical states that stand in the right kinds of correspondences to how things are being represented to be in order to constitute the distinctive way sensory states represent how things are.

2. There is a 'feeliness' about sensory experience. It surfaces in the persistent intuition that no matter how strong the arguments for a representationalist-cum-intentionalist approach to phenomenal mental states may be in the abstract, they will never be really satisfying. There is an *occurrent* something or other, not some-thing understandable in terms of a way things are being represented to be, that has to be fitted into any satisfying picture of conscious experience. Indeed, philosophers have found it necessary to coin a word, 'qualia' (singular 'quale'), for this feature of the mental. And as someone once in the grip of this intuition, I know its force.

Dennett has probably written more words attacking this intuition than any other philosopher, including papers with the evocative titles 'Quining *Qualia*' (1988) and 'Wondering Where the Yellow Went' (1981). I don't have much to add to what Dennett says and to what is said above about the case for representationalism-cum-intentionalism but let me risk the paragraph that follows.

We noted earlier the attraction of seeing the relevant variety of representation as constituting a standing invitation to believe, one we may or may not accept. What would it be like to be in receipt of a *standing* invitation to believe that there is something yellow and round in front of one; an invitation that remains while one's inclination to accept it—that is, to proceed to believe that there is in fact a yellow round object in front of one—waxes and wanes? Wouldn't it seem awfully like standing a relation to something yellow and round in front of one, something occurrent? Little wonder that the intuition is so strong.

3. The third outstanding issue is the debate over conceptual versus non-conceptual content (see Tye 1995, ch. 5). Many hold that the content of belief is conceptual whereas perceptual, and sensory content more generally, is non-conceptual.

Sometimes the idea seems to be that the content of belief itself contains concepts: the belief that there are two objects in front of me has as its content a structured entity containing *inter alia* the concept *two*. However, the sense of con-tent in play in this chapter is how things are being represented to be, and the belief that there are two objects in front of me represents how things are in front of me, not something to do with concepts. We may deploy concepts in capturing how thing are being represented to be, but our beliefs are not themselves about concepts (unless we are dealing with a belief like that the concept *two* is one children grasp very early in life).

More often the idea is that the content of belief is conceptual in the sense that, for example, in order to believe that there are two objects in front of one, you have to have the concept *two*. By contrast, it is possible to perceptually represent that there are two objects in front of one without having the concept *two*. However, the argument most often advanced for this contention is puzzling (or anyway it puzzles me). The argument is that you would not count as believing that there are two objects in front of one if one did not have the concept *two*, whereas a very young child may perceptually represent that there are two objects in front of her even if she lacks the concept *two*. This claim turns on what it is to have a concept, a controversial matter and one that may in the end be a matter of decision—that is, of deciding what it would be good to mean by 'having the concept *blah*'. But the puzzle does not relate to the controversy over what it is to possess a concept. It relates to the fact that the consideration advanced is a thesis about belief versus perceptual experience, not a thesis about content. The claim concerns what is required to have a certain belief and how it exceeds what is required in order to be in a certain perceptual state, and, be the claim correct or not, that is something about belief versus perceptual experience and not about their contents. We have at best an argument that belief is a conceptual state and that experience is a non-conceptual state. Perhaps that was always the intended conclusion, in which case the puzzle is over why the matter is not described as such.

4. The final issue I will mention concerns the sense in which we should be externalists about the relevant sense of representation. It is obvious that the relevant sense of representation is external in the sense that how experience represents things as being pertains, typically but not invariably, to how things are outside the subject. But should we be externalists in the sense of holding that how things are being represented to be may vary with variation in subjects' surroundings and history, in the absence of variation in the subjects' themselves—that is, in the absence of any variation in surroundings and history *impacting* on them from the skin in?

We do not worry about bursts of radiation behind thick sheets of lead precisely because they cannot affect us. We dodge bullets because doing so leaves us intact from the skin in. We take it that we are able to register differences in sensory experience by differences in intrinsically characterized behaviour: one nod for sensing red, two for green, as it might be. The principle cases like these suggest is that if how one is from the skin in is unchanged, one's experience is unchanged. (Differences in intrinsically characterized behaviour require differences from the skin in; the same is not true for relationally characterized behaviour obviously.) But if experiential character is tied to representation, this principle will require that we characterize the relevant sense of representation in a way that means that changes in representational content can only occur when there are changes from the skin in. Doppelgängers represent alike; or, as it is often put, representational content is narrow, not wide.

There is a large literature around this issue.[15] Many insist that the relevant sense of representation can only be a wide one, and use this as an argument against the representationalist-cum-intentionalist approach I have been supporting (see e.g. Block 1990). For they take it as obvious that doppelgängers are alike in mental phenomenology, and see representationalism as committed to denying this obvious fact. Others bite the bullet and deny that doppelgängers need have the same mental phenomenology (Lycan 1996). Finally, there are those who deny that the relevant sense of representation is wide (Jackson 2003b).

References

Armstrong, D. M. (1961). *Perception and the Physical World*. London: Routledge & Kegan Paul.
—— (1962). *Bodily Sensations*. London: Routledge & Kegan Paul.
—— (1999). *The Mind–Body Problem*. Boulder, Colo.: Westview Press.
Block, Ned (1990). 'Inverted Earth', in James Tomberlin (ed.), *Philosophical Perspectives*, 4: Action Theory and Philosophy of Mind. Atascadero, Calif.: Ridgeview.
—— (1996). 'Mental Paint and Mental Latex', in E. Villeneuva (ed.), *Philosophical Issues*, vii. Northridge, Calif.: Ridgeview.
—— (2002). 'Concepts of Consciousness', in David Chalmers (ed.), *Philosophy of Mind: Classical and Contemporary Readings*. New York: Oxford University Press.
—— (2003). 'Mental Paint', in Martin Hahn and Bjorn Ramberg (eds.), *Reflections and Replies: Essays on the Philosophy of Tyler Burge*. Cambridge, Mass.: MIT Press.
—— Flanagan, Owen, and Güzeldere, Güven (eds.) (1998). *The Nature of Consciousness*. Cambridge, Mass.: MIT Press.
Braddon-Mitchell, David, and Jackson, Frank (1996). *Philosophy of Mind and Cognition*. Oxford: Blackwell.
Campbell, Keith (1970). *Body and Mind*. London: Macmillan.
Chalmers, David (1996). *The Conscious Mind*. New York: Oxford University Press.
—— (ed.) (2002). *Philosophy of Mind: Classical and Contemporary Readings*. New York: Oxford University Press.
Churchland, Paul (1985). 'Reduction, Qualia, and the Direct Introspection of Brain States'. *Journal of Philosophy*, 82: 8–28.
Davidson, Donald (1974). 'Belief and the Basis of Meaning'. Repr. in Davidson, *Inquiries into Truth and Interpretation*. Oxford: Clarendon Press, 1984.
Dennett, Daniel (1981). 'Wondering Where the Yellow Went'. *The Monist*, 64: 102–8.
—— (1987). *The Intentional Stance*. Cambridge, Mass.: MIT Press.
—— (1988). 'Quining *Qualia*', in A. Marcel and E. Bisiach (eds.), *Consciousness in Contemporary Science*. New York: Oxford University Press.

---

[15] See e.g. Braddon-Mitchell and Jackson (1996, ch. 12) for an approach more sympathetic to narrow content than is usual currently; see e.g. Lycan (1996, ch. 6) for a discussion from the perspective of a strong supporter of the position that the relevant notion of content is wide.

—— (1991). *Consciousness Explained*. Boston, Mass.: Little, Brown.

Dunne, J. W. (1927). *An Experiment with Time*. London: Faber & Faber.

Foster, John (2000). *The Nature of Perception*. Oxford: Oxford University Press.

Harman, Gilbert (1998). 'The Intrinsic Quality of Experience', (1990), in James Tomberlin (ed.), *Philosophical Perspectives*, 4: *Action Theory and Philosophy of Mind*. Atascadero, Calif.: Ridgeview. Repr. in Ned Block, Owen Flanagan, and Güven Güzeldere (eds.), *The Nature of Consciousness*. Cambridge, Mass.: MIT Press.

Hilbert, David (1987). *Color and Color Perception*. Stanford, Calif.: CSLI.

Hinton, J. M. (1973). *Experiences*. Oxford: Clarendon Press.

Jackson, Frank (1977). *Perception*. Cambridge: Cambridge University Press.

—— (1982). 'Epiphenomenal Qualia'. *Philosophical Quarterly*, 32: 127–36.

—— (1986). 'What Mary Didn't Know'. *Journal of Philosophy*, 83: 291–5.

—— (1998). 'Postscript on Qualia', in Jackson, *Mind, Method, and Conditionals: Selected Papers*. International Library of Philosophy. London: Routledge.

—— (2003*a*). 'Mind and Illusion', in Anthony O'Hear (ed.), *Minds and Persons*. Royal Institute of Philosophy suppl. 53. Cambridge: Cambridge University Press.

—— (2003*b*). 'Narrow Content and Representationalism—or Twin Earth Revisited'. *Proceedings of the American Philosophical Association*, 77: 55–71.

—— (2004). 'Representation and Experience', in H. Clapin, P. Slezack, and P. Staines (eds.), *Representation in Mind: New Approaches to Mental Representation*. Oxford: Elsevier.

—— (forthcoming). 'The Knowledge Argument, Diaphanousness, and Representationalism', in Torin Alter and Sven Walter (eds.), *Phenomenal Concepts and Phenomenal Knowledge: New Essays on Consciousness and Physicalism*. Oxford: Oxford University Press.

—— and Pargetter, Robert (1985). 'Causal Origin and Evidence'. *Theoria*, 51: 65–76.

Lewis, David (1990). 'What Experience Teaches', in W. G. Lycan (ed.), *Mind and Cognition*. Oxford: Blackwell.

Loar, Brian (1990). 'Phenomenal States', in James Tomberlin (ed.), *Philosophical Perspectives*, 4: *Action Theory and Philosophy of Mind*. Atascadero, Calif.: Ridgeview.

Lycan, W. G. (1996). *Consciousness and Experience*. Cambridge, Mass.: MIT Press.

Moore, G. E. (1922). 'The Refutation of Idealism', in Moore, *Philosophical Studies*. London: Routledge & Kegan Paul.

Nagel, Thomas (1974). 'What Is It Like to Be a Bat?' *Philosophical Review*, 83: 435–50.

Nemirow, Laurence (1980). Review of T. Nagel, *Mortal Questions*. *Philosophical Review*, 89: 475–6.

—— (1990). 'Physicalism and the Cognitive Role of Acquaintance', in W. G. Lycan (ed.), *Mind and Cognition*. Oxford: Blackwell.

Peacocke, Christopher (2002). 'Sensation and the Content of Experience: A Distinction', in David Chalmers (ed.), *The Philosophy of Mind*. New York: Oxford University Press.

Perry, John (2001). *Knowledge, Possibility, and Consciousness*. Cambridge, Mass.: MIT Press.

Shoemaker, Sydney (1994). 'Self-Knowledge and "Inner Sense", Lecture III: The Phenomenal Character of Experience'. *Philosophical and Phenomenological Research*, 54: 291–314.

Skinner, B. F. (1974). *About Behaviourism*. London: Jonathan Cape.

Stalnaker, Robert (1984). *Inquiry*. Cambridge, Mass.: MIT Press.

Stoljar, Daniel, and Nagasawa, Yujin (eds.) (2004). *There's Something About Mary: Essays on Frank Jackson's Knowledge Argument*. Cambridge, Mass.: MIT Press.

Tye, Michael (1995). *Ten Problems of Consciousness*. Cambridge, Mass.: MIT Press.

—— (2000). *Consciousness, Color, and Content*. Cambridge, Mass.: MIT Press.

CHAPTER 13

ACTION

ALFRED R. MELE

1. INTRODUCTION

What are actions? And how are actions to be explained? These two central questions of the philosophy of action call, respectively, for a theory of the nature of action and a theory of the explanation of actions. Many ordinary explanations of actions are offered in terms of such mental states as beliefs, desires, and intentions, and some also appeal to traits of character and emotions. Traditionally, philosophers have used and refined this vocabulary in producing theories of the explanation of intentional actions. An underlying presupposition is that common-sense explanations expressed in these terms have proved very useful. People understand their own and others' actions well enough to coordinate and sustain complicated, cooperative activities integral to normal human life, and that understanding is expressed largely in a common-sense psychological vocabulary. Even if the viability of this general approach to explaining actions were taken for granted, however, theorists would face important questions about actions and their explanation. For example, we would want to know what actions are, what it is to act intentionally, and whether proper explanations of actions are causal explanations or explanations of another kind. These issues are the focus of this chapter.

2. CAUSALISM: BACKGROUND

A popular approach to understanding both the nature of action and the explanation of actions emphasizes causation. The conjunction of the following two theses may be termed *standard causalism*:[1] (1) An event's being an action depends on how it was caused. (2) Proper explanations of actions are causal explanations.

Familiar causal theories of action feature as causes such mental items as beliefs, desires, intentions, and related events (e.g. acquiring a proximal intention to A: in the basic case, an intention to A straightaway).[2] On an attractive theory of action, actions are analogous to money in a noteworthy respect. The piece of paper with which I just purchased a drink is a genuine US dollar bill partly in virtue of its having been produced (in the right way) by the US Treasury Department. A duplicate bill produced with plates and paper stolen from the Treasury Department is a counterfeit dollar bill, not a genuine one. Similarly, according to one kind of causal theory of action, a certain event is my buying a drink—an action—partly in virtue of its having been produced 'in the right way' by certain mental items (Davidson 1980; Brand 1984).[3] An event someone else covertly produces by remote control—one including visually indistinguishable bodily motions not appropriately produced by mental states of mine—is not a purchasing of a drink by me, even if it feels to me as though I am in charge.[4]

The question 'What are actions?' directly raises two sub-questions. How are actions different from non-actions? How do actions differ from one another? I have just provided a crude sketch (to be developed in Section 3) of one answer to the first sub-question. By the end of the 1970s a lively debate over the second sub-question—the question of action-individuation—had produced a collection of relatively precise alternatives.[5] In this chapter I proceed in a neutral way

[1] I borrow the term 'causalism' from Wilson (1989). (Wilson is a non-causalist.)

[2] Proximal intentions also include intentions to A beginning straight away, and intentions to continue doing something one is already doing.

[3] Alternative conceptions of action include an 'internalist' view according to which actions differ experientially from other events in a way that is essentially independent of how, or whether, they are caused (Ginet 1990); a conception of actions as composites of non-actional mental events or states (e.g. intentions) and pertinent non-actional effects (e.g. an arm's rising) (Mill 1961; Searle 1983); and views identifying an action with the causing of a suitable non-actional product by appropriate non-actional mental items (Dretske 1988)—or, instead, by an agent (Bishop 1989; O'Connor 2000).

[4] This view does not identify actions with *non-actional* events caused in the right way. That would be analogous to identifying genuine US dollar bills with pieces of printed paper that are not genuine US dollar bills and are produced in the right way by the US Treasury Department, and so identifying genuine US dollar bills would be absurd.

[5] Consider an example of Davidson's: 'I flip the switch, turn on the light, and illuminate the room. Unbeknownst to me I also alert a prowler to the fact that I am home' (1980: 4). How many actions does the agent, Don, perform? Davidson's *coarse-grained* answer is one action 'of which four descriptions have been given' (p. 4; cf. Anscombe 1957). A *fine-grained* alternative treats A and B as different actions if, in performing them, the agent exemplifies different act-properties (Goldman 1970). On this view, Don performs at least four actions, since the act-properties at issue are distinct. An agent may exemplify any of these act-properties without exemplifying any of the others. One may even turn on a light in a room without illuminating the room: the light may be painted black. Another alternative, a *componential* view, represents Don's illuminating the room as an action having various components, including (but not limited to) his moving his arm, his flipping the switch, and the light's going on (Ginet 1990; Thalberg 1977; Thomson 1977). Where proponents of the coarse-grained and fine-grained

regarding the leading contending theories of individuation (described in note 5). Readers may read my action variable "A" in accordance their preferred theory of action-individuation. The same goes for the term "action".

Causalism typically is embraced as part of a naturalistic stand on agency according to which mental items featured in causal explanations of the actions of physical beings in some way depend on or are realized in physical states and events. In principle, causalists can welcome any viable solution to the mind–body problem that supports an important place for 'the mental' in causal explanations of actions, including viable solutions according to which what does the causal work (in physical agents) is physical states and events that realize beliefs, desires, intentions, events of intention acquisition, and the like. Arguably, a mental item that figures in a genuine causal explanation of an action need not itself *be* a cause; its place in such an explanation may be secured partly by its relation to a physical cause that realizes it (see Mele 1992a, ch. 2). Causalism also is non-restrictive about free will. Although some causalists endorse compatibilism (the thesis that free action is compatible with determinism), that is optional for them.[6] Provided that causation is not essentially deterministic, causalists can embrace libertarianism, the conjunction of incompatibilism and the thesis that there are free actions.[7] Some non-causalists are incompatibilists, but there is no entailment here. Harry Frankfurt, a compatibilist (1988, chs. 1–2), rejects causalism (1988, ch. 6).

The idea that actions are to be explained, causally, in terms of mental states or events is at least as old as Aristotle: 'the origin of action—its efficient, not its final cause—is choice, and that of choice is desire and reasoning with a view to an end' (*Nicomachean Ethics* 1139[a]31–2). This idea continues to have a considerable following (including Bishop 1989; Brand 1984; Davidson 1980; Goldman 1970; Mele 1992a, 2003a; Velleman 1989, 2000). Owing partly to the influence of Wittgenstein and Ryle, causalism fell into disfavour for a time. The first major source of its revival is Donald Davidson's 'Actions, Reasons, and Causes' (1963; 1980, ch. 1).

There, in addition to rebutting familiar arguments against causalism and developing a positive causalist view, Davidson presents non-causalists with a difficult challenge. Addressed to philosophers who hold that when we act intentionally we act for reasons, the challenge is to provide an account of the reasons *for which* we in fact act that does not treat (our having) those reasons as figuring in the causation of the relevant behaviour (or, one might add, as realized in physical

theories find, respectively, a single action under different descriptions and a collection of intimately related actions, advocates of the various componential views locate a larger action having smaller actions among its parts.

[6] Determinism may be succinctly defined as 'the thesis that there is at any instant exactly one physically possible future' (van Inwagen 1983: 3).

[7] In Mele (1995) I develop three positions on free will, each of which relies on causalism: a libertarian position, a compatibilist position, and a position that is agnostic about compatibilism while advocating the existence of free will.

causes of the behaviour). The challenge is particularly acute when an agent has two
or more reasons for A-ing but A-s only for only one of them. Here is an illustration:

Al has a pair of reasons for mowing his lawn this morning. First, he wants to mow it this
week and he believes that this morning is the most convenient time. Second, Al has an urge
to repay his neighbor for the rude awakening he suffered recently when she turned on her
mower at the crack of dawn and he believes that his mowing his lawn this morning would
constitute suitable repayment. As it happens, Al mows his lawn this morning only for one
of these reasons. In virtue of what is it true that he mowed his lawn for this reason, and not
the other, if not that this reason (or his having it), and not the other, played a suitable causal
role in his mowing his lawn? (Mele 1997a: 240)

In Mele (2003a, ch. 2) I review detailed attempts to answer this challenge (Ginet
1990; Sehon 1994; Wallace 1999; Wilson 1989) and argue that they fail. Space
constraints preclude discussing the issue here.

A comment on reasons for action is in order. According to Davidson's influential
view, such reasons are complexes of beliefs and desires. It sometimes is claimed that
Davidsonian reasons for action really are not reasons at all. T. M. Scanlon, for
example, argues that 'desires almost never provide reasons for action in the way
described by [this] model' (1998: 43). Philosophical work on reasons for action
tends to be guided primarily either by a concern with the *explanation* of actions or
by a concern with the *evaluation* of actions or their agents. In work dominated by
the former concern, reasons for action tend to be understood as states of mind,
along broadly Davidsonian lines. Philosophers with the latter concern may be
sympathetic or unsympathetic to this construal, depending on their views about
standards for evaluating actions or agents. For example, a theorist whose evaluative
concern is with *rational* action and who holds that the pertinent notion of
rationality is subjective—in the sense that a proper verdict about the rationality or
irrationality of an agent's action is to be made from the perspective of the agent's
own desires, beliefs, principles, and the like, rather than from some external, or
partly external, perspective—may be happy to understand reasons for action as
states of mind. A theorist with a more objective conception of rational action or
rational agency also is likely to have a more objective conception of reasons
for action. Such a theorist may find it natural to insist that many or all reasons for
action are facts about the agent-external world.

Michael Woods remarks that 'the concept of a reason for action stands at the
point of intersection...between the theory of the explanation of actions and
the theory of their justification' (1972: 189). If there are agent-external justificatory
reasons for action, it may be that intentional actions are to be relatively directly
explained at least partly in terms of Davidsonian reasons and that when external
justificatory reasons contribute to explanations of intentional actions, they do so
less directly, by way of a causal contribution made by an agent's apprehending such
a reason to his acquiring a Davidsonian reason. An exploration of the possibility of
external justificatory reasons and of their compatibility with the existence of

Davidsonian reasons quickly takes one well beyond the philosophy of action into moral philosophy and value theory. For discussion of these possibilities, see Mele (2003a, chs. 3–6).

3. THREE ALLEGED PROBLEMS FOR CAUSALISM

Standard causalism, as I have characterized it, is a view about what actions are and how actions are to be explained. Thus, it offers answers to what I identified as the two central questions of the philosophy of action. In this section I discuss three alleged problems for causalism.

3.1 Causal Deviance

Deviant causal chains raise difficulties for causal analyses of action and of doing something intentionally. The alleged problem is that whatever causes are deemed both necessary and sufficient for a resultant event's being an action or for an action's being intentional, cases can be described in which, owing to a deviant causal connection between the favoured causes (e.g. events of intention acquisition) and a resultant event, that event is not an action or a pertinent resultant action is not done intentionally.

The most common examples of deviance divide into two types.[8] Cases of *primary deviance* raise a problem about a relatively direct connection between mental antecedents and resultant bodily motion. Cases of *secondary deviance* focus on behavioural consequences of intentional actions and on the connection between these actions and their consequences. The following are, respectively, representative instances of the two types of case:

A climber might want to rid himself of the weight and danger of holding another man on a rope, and he might know that by loosening his hold on the rope he could rid himself of the weight and danger. This belief and want [or, one might suppose, his *intention* to let go of the rope] might so unnerve him as to cause him to loosen his hold [unintentionally]. (Davidson 1980: 79)

A man may try to kill someone by shooting at him. Suppose the killer misses his victim by a mile, but the shot stampedes a herd of wild pigs that trample the intended victim to death. (Davidson 1980: 78)

---

[8] For a third type, see Mele (1992a: 207–10).

The second case can be handled by some version of the familiar suggestion that an action's being intentional depends on its fitting the agent's conception or representation of the manner in which it will be performed. Of course, how close the fit must be requires attention (see Mele and Moser 1997). Cases of primary deviance are more challenging.

Some causal theorists who assess cases of primary deviance as putative counter-examples to a causal account of what it is for an action to be intentional dismiss them on the grounds that they are not cases of action at all (Brand 1984: 18; Thalberg 1984). If this diagnosis is correct, primary deviance raises a question for attempted causal analyses of action. Can causalists identify something of a causal nature in virtue of which it is false that the climber performed the action of loosening his grip on the rope?

In a discussion of primary deviance, Alvin Goldman remarks: 'A complete explanation of how wants and beliefs lead to intentional acts would require extensive neurophysiological information, and I do not think it is fair to demand of a philosophical analysis that it provide this information. . . . A detailed delineation of the causal process that is characteristic of intentional action is a problem mainly for the special sciences' (1970: 62; cf. 166–9). Goldman's remark strikes some readers as evasive (Bishop 1989: 143–4; McCann 1974: 462–3), but he does have a point. A deviant causal connection between an x and a y is deviant relative to normal causal routes from xs to ys. Moreover, what counts as *normal* here is perspective-relative. From the point of view of physics, for example, there is nothing abnormal about Davidson's examples of deviance. And, for beings of a particular kind, the normal route from intention to action may be best articulated partly in neurophysiological terms.

One way around the problem posed by our neuroscientific ignorance is to design (in imagination, of course) an agent's motor control system. Knowing the biological being's design, we have a partial basis for distinguishing causal chains associated with overt action (i.e. action essentially involving peripheral bodily motion) from deviant motion-producing chains. If we can distinguish deviant from non-deviant causal chains in agents we design—that is, chains not appropriate to action from action-producing chains—then perhaps we would be able to do the same for normal human beings if we were to know a lot more than we do about the human body. I pursue this line of thought in Mele (2003a, ch. 2). Here I summarize that discussion, starting with some highlights of the design of my agents. I will call them M agents. The 'M' stands for mythical, since my account of their design took the form of a myth.

In M agents, the acquisition of a proximal intention initiates the sending of a 'command signal' to the motor cortex. The signal specifies the kind of action to be performed straight away and is transformed in the motor cortex into 'motor signals'—specific fine-grained executive signals to specific muscles and joints, which signals have the function of producing muscular motions. For example, the acquisition of a proximal intention gently to touch the tip of one's nose with the tip of one's right index finger initiates the sending of an appropriate command signal to the motor cortex, where it is transformed into specific motor signals to the appropriate muscles and joints. The motor signals 'command' the muscles and joints to move in certain ways. In the case of intentions that are for movements and not also for what may be termed 'agent-external results' (e.g. raising one's right hand, as opposed to touching a branch—or one's nose—with one's right hand), the signals command the muscles and joints to move in such ways that the completion of the movement would ensure satisfaction of the intention. When intentions include agent-external results, the signals command the relevant muscles and joints to move in ways appropriate to the satisfaction of the intention.

M agents are so designed that they engage in overt action *only if* the acquisition of a proximal intention plays this initiating role. Their neural architecture is such that the motor cortex produces motor signals by, and only by, transforming command signals initiated by acquisitions of proximal intentions. In the absence of motor signals produced by the motor cortex, M agents cannot act overtly. Their biological design includes no alternative route to overt action.

The *persistence* of a proximal intention also plays a role in M agents. Such persistence causally sustains the signalling process, and, hence, the relevant bodily motions, until the agent comes to believe either that achievement of the (final) goal represented in his intention is ensured or that continuing his present course of action is not worth the trouble.[9] The design of M agents also ensures that the dissolution of a proximal intention terminates associated action, unless the action has gone too far to be halted, as in cases of what I call 'direct ballistic continuation'. In a simple example of such continuation, an agent embarking on a conventional right-handed finger-snapping with his palm facing up presses his thumb and middle finger firmly together and then, maintaining the pressure, simultaneously slides the thumb to the right and the finger downward. After a certain point, the agent is no longer in control of the process. The finger whips downward, thumping into his palm next to his thumb, and the thumb slides off to the right. Here there is direct ballistic continuation of motions that had been guided. These ballistic motions may be regarded as part of the agent's action of snapping his fingers. What one may call 'agents' contributions' to their overt actions end with the termination of their *guided* bodily motions.

In M agents, intentions figure in the causal *guidance* of action sustained by a persisting intention.[10] Intentions are executive attitudes towards plans (Mele 1992a). These plans—the representational contents of intentions—range from simple representations of 'basic' actions to complex strategies for achieving remote goals.[11]

---

[9] On sustaining roles of persisting intentions, see Bishop (1989: 167–71); Brand (1984: 175); Mele (1992a: 130–1, 180–4, 192–4); and Thalberg (1984).

[10] On the guiding role of intentions, see Bishop (1989: 167–72); Brand (1984, part IV); Mele (1992a: 136–7, 220–3); and Thalberg (1984: 257–9).

[11] Roughly speaking, *basic* actions differ from non-basic actions in not being performed by way of performing another action.

When such a plan has more than a single node, receipt of feedback indicating that one's body is, moving according to plan and that one's bodily motions are getting one closer to one's goal promotes the occurrence of motions called for by the next portion of one's plan. Feedback indicating that things are veering off course fosters corrections of bodily motions, the standard for corrections being provided by the plan in the agent's persisting intention.[12] Even in the case of relatively simple actions like unclenching a fist, persisting intentions play a guiding role in M agents. Within a few milliseconds of acquiring a proximal intention to unclench his fist, an agent begins exhibiting motions called for by his intention, and he stops exhibiting such motions upon receiving feedback indicating that the fist is unclenched. The design of M agents is such that their 'directing' their ongoing bodily motions requires that persisting intentions of theirs be playing a guiding role.

The content of M agents' intentions is limited to representations accessible to consciousness. Supporting low-level motor schemata, which also are representational, are housed separately. Some are activated by the acquisition of a proximal intention, others by a combination of the persistence of such an intention and feedback about progress towards the intended goal.[13] A match between representations of this kind and feedback promotes execution of the next step in the intention-imbedded plan. Radical mismatches sometimes produce serious confusion, but many mismatches foster useful minor adjustments.

Scott Sehon (1997) contends that reflection on causal deviance in cases like Davidson's climber justifies the rejection of causalism (cf. Wilson 1989, ch. 9). As it happens, this climber is an M agent named Mel. Can causalists identify something of a causal nature in virtue of which it is false that Mel performed the action of loosening his grip on the rope? Since Davidson's case is sketchy, several versions need to be considered.

Version 1. Mel's acquiring the intention, N, to rid himself of the danger of holding his climbing partner on his rope by loosening his hold does not result in motor signals being sent. Instead it unnerves Mel, with the result that he loses control over his hands. His grip loosens and the rope slips from his hands.

Here, Mel does not perform the action of loosening his grip; for M agents are so designed that they can perform overt actions only in cases in which the acquisition of a proximal intention results in motor signals being sent to appropriate muscles. It might be claimed that there is no difference between *motor signals* that initiate bodily motions and *nervousness* that does this. In M agents, this is false. Their motor signals carry instructions to muscles and joints whereas their nervousness

---

[12] On differences between 'error-correcting' and 'predictive' kinds of feedback control, see Jordan (1996: 78–87).

[13] If action begins in the brain (Brand 1984: 20; Mele 1992*a*: 201–2), the functioning of motor schemata in the production of a bodily motion, including schemata proximately activated by the acquisition of a proximal intention, may be a *constituent* of an action.

contains no such instructions. Moreover, in M agents, the 'motor control system'—a biological system constituted by the motor cortex and associated areas of the central nervous system—plays an indispensable role in the production of overt action whereas bodily motion directly produced by nervousness is produced independently of this system. In M agents, direct causation of bodily motion by nervousness is very different from direct causation of bodily motion by motor signals.

Version 2. Mel's acquiring intention N results in appropriate motor signals being sent, and the intention is quickly extinguished. The motor signals do not reach his muscles or joints. Instead, they unnerve him, with the result that he loses both his grip on the rope and his intention.

Given that Mel is an M agent, he performs the action of loosening his grip on the rope only if a relevant intention of his sustains the pertinent motions of his body. Because the relevant intention is extinguished before the pertinent bodily motions occur, Mel does not perform the action of loosening his grip.

Version 3. Again, Mel's acquiring intention N results in appropriate motor signals being sent, which signals do not reach his muscles or joints. Again, the signals unnerve Mel, with the result that he loses his grip on the rope. However, intention N is not extinguished. In fact, its persistence causally sustains the nervousness that results in Mel's temporary loss of control over his hands (cf. Mele 1992a: 202–3).

As an M agent, Mel's acting with his hands requires a relevant intention of his to play a guiding role in the production of his hand motions. But no intention is playing this role; Mel's nervousness prevents that by temporarily depriving him of control over his hands. So, once again, Mel is not performing the action of loosening his grip.

Version 4. Mel's acquiring intention N results in appropriate motor signals being sent. This time, those signals reach their targeted muscles and joints, and he begins to loosen his grip on the rope. His fingers start moving. This unnerves him, with the result that he loses his grip on the rope (cf. Mele 1992a: 202–3; Sehon 1997: 201–2). In beginning to loosen his grip, he does not yet loosen it sufficiently for the rope to unravel from his hand; the nervousness that results in his losing his grip plays an intervening causal role. And the continued presence of intention N causally sustains the nervousness that results in Mel's temporary loss of control over his hands.

Although there was a time at which Mel was beginning to loosen his hold on the rope, he does not perform the action of dropping his partner, nor the action of loosening his hold enough to drop his partner. Given his construction as an M agent, Mel is incapable of contributing to the continuation of an overt action of his once his relevant bodily motions are not being guided by an intention of his. This itself does not entail that, after becoming unnerved, Mel is no longer performing the action of loosening his hold; for, in some cases, direct ballistic continuations of motions that had been guided may be parts of actions, as in the finger-snapping example. However, the nervousness-produced motions of Mel's hands are not direct ballistic continuations of his previous motions. After all, they are produced by the nervousness that his beginning to loosen his grip causes. Even if they are, in some sense, continuations of earlier motions, they are not direct ballistic continuations. So, in short, Mel's performance of the action of loosening his hold ends too soon for him to have performed the action of dropping his partner, or the action of loosening his hold enough to drop his partner.

Now, my design myth is a myth. One feature of the neural architecture of M agents is that the motor cortex produces motor signals only by transforming command signals initiated by the acquisition of a proximal intention. My description of M agents leaves it open that this is a magical feature. One might imagine that there is no way to avoid the possibility that a counterfeit of such a command signal—e.g. a counterfeit signal produced by direct electronic stimulation of the brain and not by the acquisition of a proximal intention—is transformed into motor signals. Then again, M agents may be so designed that such intervention shuts down the motor control system. In any case, my crucial claim in this connection is that the design of M agents is such that they can perform overt actions only if their acquiring a proximal intention initiates the sending of motor signals to appropriate muscles. The possibility of counterfeit command signals undermines this claim only if there are cases in which such a signal, and not the acquisition of a proximal intention, initiates an overt *action*. Are there such cases?

Imagine that a neuroscientist stimulates an M agent's brain in a way that sends a 'command' signal to the motor cortex and he does not produce the signal by producing an intention. The signal is translated into motor signals that directly cause bodily motions. An intuitive reaction is that the being does not act. Rather, he is manipulated in such a way that his body mimics action. The being is the locus of bodily motion rather than the performer of an action. (Wilder Penfield reports: 'When I have caused a conscious patient to move his hand by applying an electrode to the motor cortex of one hemisphere I have often asked him about it. Invariably his response was: "I didn't do that. You did." When I caused him to vocalize, he said, "I didn't make that sound. You pulled it out of me"; 1975: 76. The patients' reactions are natural and plausible.)

Imagine now that an M agent has just acquired a proximal intention to take a pear from a tree and, owing to neurological blockage, his acquiring the intention does not send a command signal. A kindly neuroscientist sends a counterfeit of such a signal and things proceed as in the preceding case. Here again an intuitive judgement is that the being does not act and his body mimics action. The same intuition, I submit, will emerge in response to any example of either of the two styles at issue.[14]

---

[14] Three points about predictable intuitions should be made. First, if the scientist were to equip a being suffering from neurological blockage with a device that rapidly produces appropriate command signals in response to acquisitions of intentions, intuitions would shift. But notice that in such cases intention acquisition triggers the machinery. Secondly, a significantly weaker shift in the same direction may or may not occur on the supposition that the scientist regularly stands in for the device: the M being acquires or forms intentions and the scientist sends appropriate 'command' signals in response. The scientist's himself *acting* in producing the signals complicates matters. A natural reaction

344 ALFRED R. MELE

Suppose that a neuroscientist produces a proximal *intention* in an M agent by directly stimulating the agent's brain and the acquisition of this intention leads to appropriate bodily movement in the normal way, which includes the intention's playing the initiating, sustaining, and guiding roles I described. The agent certainly has been manipulated, but I see no good reason to deny that he has been manipulated into performing an action. There is a difference between (1) Mr X causing Mr Y's body to move without causing Y to move Y's body and (2) Mr X causing Y to move Y's body. The two cases featuring the production of counterfeit command signals are instances of (1), I have suggested. An intuitive reaction to the case of intention induction is that it is an instance of (2).

Consider a pair of cases. In the first, a hypnotist manipulates Daphne in such a way that her hearing the word 'duck' will straight away cause her to acquire a proximal intention to quack like a duck for five seconds. Daphne hears the word, acquires the intention, and executes it. The quacking is initiated, sustained, and guided by her intention. It is natural to hold that Daphne performs the action of quacking. Seemingly, she intentionally quacks. (To be sure, Daphne may wonder what has come over her.)

Now imagine a counterpart case in which, in the absence of any relevant intention, Daphne emits quacking sounds because a neuroscientist produced a command signal that was transformed in the motor cortex into motor signals that caused motions that in turn caused the sounds. Apparently, Daphne did not perform the action of quacking. In producing the sounds via a route that does not involve intention, the process at work does not involve Daphne as an agent. She may wonder what has come over her, but such puzzlement is not ensured by the details of the case. Suppose that the quacking sounds were produced in the way just described *and* the hypnotist produced in Daphne a proximal intention to quack, which intention played no role in the production of the sounds, owing to the neuroscientist's manipulation. If Daphne thinks she is performing a quacking action, she is wrong.

There is evidence that when sighted people move their hands towards targets, vision of the hand and arm helps calibrate proprioceptive signals (Ghez *et al.* 2000: 505). 'The nervous system must also transform the intended direction and extent [of hand movement] into feedforward control signals distributed to motor neurons and muscles. For the resulting movement trajectory to conform to the one that was

is that the M being sets a goal and the scientist has a greater claim to be the person who moves the being's body accordingly than the being himself does. By contrast, in the former case, seemingly, the M being moves his body and his doing so is a process that involves the device. The difference between him and a normal M agent is that the normal agent's moving his body involves only natural, biological machinery. Thirdly, if the neuroscientist were merely to *enable* a being's acquiring an intention to send an appropriate command signal—e.g. by removing a blockage that is in place at the time—intuitions would strongly favour the being's acting. One way to block various irksome questions would be to stipulate that M agents are so designed that all alien intervention simply shuts these beings down, but attention to such questions is useful.

intended, feedforward commands need to anticipate the effects of both environmental forces and of forces arising within the musculoskeletal system itself' (Ghez *et al.* 2000: 505–6). This is a feature of M agents too. Obviously, there is, in principle, room for monkey business here—e.g. for alien interveners—and in processes for the guidance of action in general. However, the design of M agents is such that any alien intervention into normal processes of guidance simply shuts down the motor control system. Some alien intervention may be capable of assisting agents in acting, but the design of M agents precludes such assistance.

I asked whether causalists can identify something of a causal nature in virtue of which it is false (in versions of the case in which this *is* false) that Mel, an M agent, performed the action of loosening his grip on the rope. The answer certainly seems to be yes. As far as I can tell, my myth, stripped of its magical feature, is coherent. And even though the story is relatively simple, it provides the basis for a causal diagnosis of ways in which primary causal deviance blocks action in an agent of a certain kind. The mix of causal initiation, sustaining, and guiding that I have been describing seems to do the trick in an M agent.

Anti-causalists will wish to develop counter-examples to the claim that the involvement of this mix in the production of bodily motion is conceptually sufficient, in an M agent, for action. I see no way of conclusively proving this sufficiency, and I welcome attempted counter-examples. If they fail, or instead motivate useful refinement of the mix, I obviously would regard that as good news. A counter-example that showed that *no* story about how particular motions of a particular M being are caused can provide conceptually sufficient conditions for action would be bad news for causalists, but I doubt that one is forthcoming. And if there are conceptually sufficient conditions of a causal nature for action in M agents, there is good reason to believe that the same is true of human beings.

3.2 Negative Actions

Alleged examples of negative actions include not moving one's body and not voting in an election, when it is intentional on one's part, or 'for a reason', that one does not do these things.[15] In so far as "intentional" and "for a reason" apply in this way to a not-doing, it is claimed that not-doing is an action, a negative one. So-called negative actions pose an apparent problem for causalism. In particular, if they—or some of them—are uncaused actions (Frankfurt 1988, ch. 6), causalism is false. Such actions also pose an apparent problem for part of my own causalist package, my account (Mele 2003*a*, ch. 6) of what it is for an attitude essentially to encompass motivation to A. Very roughly, on my account, an attitude *x* of an agent S essentially encompasses motivation in S to A if and only if, necessarily, if *x* were to function

[15] On 'it was intentional on [S's] part that [S] did not [A]', see Davidson (1985: 219).

non-deviantly and effectively, x would be a cause of its own satisfaction that contributes to this by inducing an appropriate trying in S. The worry is that although a desire or intention for a negative action, A, essentially encompasses motivation to A, non-deviant, effective functioning of such a desire does not involve its inducing the agent to *try* anything, since there is nothing—including trying to A, and trying anything else—that the agent *does* in A-ing.

I will sketch arguments for two theses:

(1) Some alleged negative actions are successful tryings, in which case they are not negative in a way that is problematic for causalism or for the account just sketched.

(2) No alleged desired or intended negative actions that do not involve trying are actions.

Trying, as I understand it, does not require a special effort. When I intentionally type the word "type", I try to type it even if I encounter no special resistance. Although people may often reserve attributions of trying for instances in which an agent makes a special effort, this is a matter of conversational implicature and does not mark a conceptual truth about trying (see Adams and Mele 1992: 325; Armstrong 1980: 71; McCann 1975: 425–7; and McGinn 1982: 86–7). Any alleged negative A-ing that does involve trying to A, as I will explain, can be handled by causalists is just the way they handle typical intentional 'positive' A-ings.

Ann wants to do her part in a passive resistance protest. She wants to remain utterly limp as the police drag her away from the courthouse doorway where she had been lying, even though the dragging is painful. While she is being dragged, Ann works hard to master urges to move her body in ways that would minimize pain; she works hard to see to it that she does not move her body. Ann actively uses cognitive control techniques that, as she knows, send signals to muscles to remain relaxed, and she succeeds in keeping her body limp. "Tries" can smoothly replace "works" here. Ann tries hard to see to it that she does not move her body; she tries to do this by using the mental self-control techniques.

If 'Ann's not moving her body' describes an action (one perhaps more fully described as 'Ann's seeing to it that she does not move her body'), it is plausible that it describes her successful attempt to keep her body limp. In this, Ann's seemingly negative action is comparable to her positive action of stretching her limbs when she is released. That action is a successful attempt to stretch her limbs (see Adams and Mele 1992).

Wittgenstein asks (1953: 621): 'What is left over if I subtract the fact that my arm goes up from the fact that I raise my arm?' Frederick Adams and I argue that the answer is the agent's trying to raise it (Adams and Mele 1992). Consider a similar question: What is left over if the fact that Ann's body remains limp is subtracted from the fact that she sees to it that her body remains limp? A plausible answer is her trying to keep her body limp.

If Ann's seemingly negative action is comparable, in the ways just mentioned, to the positive actions of her stretching her limbs and Wittgenstein's raising his arm, it is nicely accommodated by a causal theory of what actions are and of how actions are explained. Ann has a reason for seeing to it that she does not move her body: she wants to do her part in the protest and believes that this requires keeping herself from moving her body while she is being dragged. It is natural to say that it is *for this reason* that she sees to it that she does not move her body. Suppose that the reason figures non-deviantly in the production of an intention to see to it that she does not move her body by exercising certain self-control techniques and the intention plays a normal causal role in the production of the successful effort Ann makes to keep her body limp. If 'Ann's not moving her body' describes an action, namely, her successful attempt to keep her body limp, a causal approach to analysing action is well suited to it.

For the sake of argument, I have supposed that 'Ann's not moving her body' describes an action. My own view is that it does not (though, for example, 'Ann's seeing to it that she does not move her body' does). I will motivate my view partly by examining a trio of twists on Ann's scenario. In the first, Al, Ann's protesting companion, wants not to move his body should he be dragged away. Because he doubts that he has enough will-power to use techniques like Ann's, he is carrying an instant-unconsciousness pill. The pill, Al knows, induces complete unconsciousness for ten minutes. When Al sees the police draw near, he swallows the pill. Unconsciousness instantly sets in. His body goes limp and remains that way while he is being dragged away, as planned. Al does not move his body, and he successfully tries to bring it about that he does not move it. However, his attempt, unlike Ann's, ends before the police take hold of him, and 'his not moving his body' plainly does not describe an action. Instead, it describes an intended non-actional consequence of his pill-taking action. While he is unconscious, Al has no control at all over his body, and agents who have no control over their bodies at a time are not performing bodily actions at that time.

Here is a second twist. This time, the pill is an instant-paralysis pill. Al remains conscious after taking it, but complete paralysis instantly sets in for ten minutes. His body goes limp and remains that way while the police drag him away. Here again, 'Al's not moving his body' does not describe an action and instead describes a desired consequence of an action. As in the preceding case, Al has no control over his body while he is being dragged away. By taking the pill, Al brings it about that he does not move his body. 'Al's taking the pill' and 'Al's bringing it about that he does not move his body' do describe actions.

In a third twist, Al has learned a mental trick for self-paralysis. He thinks a magic word to paralyse his body and continuously thinks it to keep his body paralysed as he is being dragged away. Does 'Al's not moving his body while he is being dragged away' describe an action, or does it instead describe a non-actional consequence of the pertinent mental actions? Seemingly, the latter. Al brings it about that he does not move his body over the interval at issue, and his bringing this about is an action composed of a series of effective mental actions. The mental actions keep him completely paralysed, and his paralysis ensures that he does not move his body. But his not moving his body is not an action. So, at least, I claim. It is not an action because the entire time he is not moving it he is completely paralysed, and completely paralysed agents lack the bodily control required for bodily actions.

Critics may resist on the grounds that it is intentional on Al's part that he does not move his body and it is for a reason that he does not move it. I discuss these matters shortly. But it is worth pointing out now that the 'intentional' and 'for a reason' claims are no less true in the first two twists; and in those scenarios, not moving his body is not an action Al performs. Critics may also encourage me to imagine that Al sometimes *moves* his body by thinking words, or that Al is a special agent whose effective plans for moving his body always feature his thinking words. The imagined Al might be put together in such a way that, as he knows, in order to get his arms to rise, and to rise in the way he intends, he must think a certain word. His thoughts of words are translated into motor signals, and onlookers believe that Al raises his arms in just the way we normally do. My imagined critics may ask whether, when things go according to plan, Al raises his arms. Other things being equal, I say yes. The normal route from intention to bodily motion in Al is different from the normal route in us, but it is a route and it does involve appropriate trying. Al's trying to raise his arms encompasses thinking a certain word; our trying to raise ours does not. Am I being inconsistent in claiming that Al raises his arms, an action, while also claiming that his not moving his body is not an action, even though he uses magic words in both connections? Not at all. What Al does by thinking the magic word in the alleged 'negative action' scenario is to prevent himself from moving his body—that is, from engaging in action of a certain kind—by keeping himself paralysed. If by 'Al performs the negative action of not moving his body' my critics mean no more than that Al performs actions that prevent him from moving his body, I have nothing more to object to than their choice of words.

Return to Ann. Given the way her self-control techniques work, she seemingly does more than simply to prevent herself from moving her body. Ann's successful attempt to keep her body limp has a more direct connection to her body's remaining limp. The former is related to the latter in the way that an ordinary agent's successful ordinary attempt to raise his arms is related to his arms' rising. Ordinarily, agents who try to raise their arms do not so try by trying to prevent their arms from remaining unraised; and Ann, who tries to keep her body limp (which limpness entails her not moving her body), does not so try by trying to prevent herself from moving it. Rather, she tries to prevent herself from moving it—and tries to keep it limp—by trying to keep her muscles relaxed, and she tries to do the latter by employing cognitive control techniques that send relaxing signals to her muscles. By means of her employment of these techniques, Ann prevents herself from moving her body. Should it be said, then, that 'Ann's not moving her body' describes an action? I see no need to say that. As with Al in the trio of twists, Ann's not moving her body is plausibly regarded as a non-actional consequence of actions of hers. And there are perfectly fine 'positive' action-descriptions of what she does: for example, Ann keeps her body limp by employing cognitive control techniques that send relaxing signals to muscles, and she keeps herself from moving her body by employing these techniques.

Alleged negative actions of another kind—negative intentional A-ings that do *not* involve trying to A—also require attention. Compare the following case with Ann's. Bob works the midnight shift. On the night before election day he decides not to vote. Because Bob dislikes the candidates, he has been considering various modes of protest. He decides on the passive mode of not voting. Bob gets home from work before the polls open. As is his practice, he sets his alarm for 7 p.m. and crawls into bed. Since he has decided not to vote, he sees no reason to depart from his daily routine. When the alarm wakes Bob, the polls are closed.

Suppose that it is intentional on Bob's part that he does not vote. That certainly does not entail that he performed the intentional (negative) action of not voting. Bob was sound asleep and not acting at all while the polls were open. So he was not during that time intentionally not voting, if intentionally not voting is supposed to be an action. (Nor was he unintentionally not voting, if that is supposed to be an action—an unintentional one.) How, then, is it intentional on Bob's part that he does not vote? Well, Bob intentionally prepared himself to fall asleep, owing partly, in a quite ordinary way, to his intention not to vote, and in the knowledge that, if things go according to plan, he will not vote; and things went according to plan. That may be enough.

The sentence 'Bob did not vote for a reason' is ambiguous. 'It was for a reason that Bob did not vote' captures the intended meaning in the present case. The truth of this assertion does not entail that Bob, who was asleep the entire time the polls were open, performed an action of not voting. So in virtue of what might the assertion be true? Suppose that the reason, R, for which Bob did not vote is a Davidsonian one constituted by his desire to protest and a belief that not voting is a fine way of protesting. Obviously, if Bob did not perform an action of not voting, R is not a cause of such an action. But R presumably is a rationalizing cause of Bob's intention not to vote, which intention plays an important role in the account offered in the preceding paragraph of its being intentional on Bob's part that he did not vote. I suggest that the combination of R's relation to this intention and the process described in the preceding paragraph that begins with Bob's acquiring this intention and ends when he wakes is sufficient for its being true that, for reason R, Bob did not vote.

The following case differs significantly from both Ann's and Bob's. Like Bob, Cyd has decided to protest against the slate of candidates by not voting in the election. Unlike Bob, she works the morning shift. On election day, she goes about her business as usual. She drives to work, performs various tasks there, and so on.

By the time she leaves work, the polls are closed. Although Bob is not acting at all while the polls are open, Cyd is performing all sorts of actions then. Is not voting among them?

Consideration of the following pair of cases will help in answering this question. On the evening before the election, Don is worried that he will acquire a compulsive desire to vote tomorrow. He wants to protest by not voting. So he takes a pill that will ensure that he sleeps through the election. Edna is in the same boat; she has a similar worry and a similar desire. However, she has no pills. She locks herself in a cell and throws away the key so that she will not succumb to her anticipated desire to vote. Edna is right about acquiring a powerful desire to vote. While the polls are open, she spends all of her time trying—vigorously but unsuccessfully—to break out of her cell.

Don intentionally brings it about that he does not vote. In so far as this is so, it is intentional on his part that he does not vote. But not voting is not an intentional action that Don performs. Like Bob, he is not acting at all while the polls are open. Edna, too, intentionally brings it about that she does not vote. Unlike Don and Bob, she is acting while the polls are open. However, not voting is not among the actions that she is intentionally performing then. Indeed, her intentional actions at the time are aimed at enabling her to get to the polls to vote.

Edna is reminiscent of Odysseus. Wanting to hear the Sirens' song and believing that the normal consequence is leaping to one's death, Odysseus has himself tied to his ship's mast. He intentionally brings it about that he does not leap into the sea, and in so far as that is true, it is, in a very real sense, intentional on his part that he does not leap. But *while* he is lashed to the mast, listening to the song and struggling against the ropes so that he can swim towards the Sirens, is it intentional on his part that he does not leap? That is, is it intentional on his part *at this time* that he does not leap. Opinions may diverge. However, neither a yes nor a no answer entails that his not leaping is an action. If the answer is yes, the intentionality derives from an intentional action that Odysseus performed earlier, as in Bob's and Don's cases; and while the polls were open they were not performing an action of not voting. If the answer is no, there is little to recommend the thesis that his not leaping is an action. The same is true of Edna's not voting.

Return to Cyd. Unlike Edna, she is not trying to bring it about that she votes. Nor, however, while the polls are open is she trying not to vote. She is simply going about her business as usual, as planned. Her plan was to protest by not voting and to go about her business instead of voting. It is intentional on Cyd's part that she does not vote, and she intentionally makes it true that she does not vote by intentionally going about her business as usual in executing a plan for the day that includes not voting. But none of this entails that not voting is among the actions she performs. I have explained how a not-doing can be intentional on one's part, how one can intentionally make it true that one does not A, and how it can be for a reason that one does not A without one's performing an action of not A-ing.

My explanation cancels what is supposed to support the intuition that there are not-doings—non-events like Cyd's not voting whose negative status entails that they do not encompass trying—that are actions while leaving in place another common intuition: namely, that all actions are events.

My admittedly limited survey of various types of alleged negative actions has consistently turned up either non-actions or positive actions misdiagnosed as negative ones. Elsewhere (Mele 2003a, ch. 6, sect. 4), I conclude from a broader investigation of this kind that so-called negative actions do not pose an evident threat to causalism.

3.3 Vanishing Agents

Some philosophers claim that causalism is inconsistent with there being any actions at all, that it makes agents *vanish*. A. I. Melden writes:

It is futile to attempt to explain conduct through the causal efficacy of desire—all *that* can explain is further happenings, not actions performed by agents.... There is no place in this picture... even for the conduct that was to have been explained. (1961: 128–9)

Thomas Nagel voices a similar worry:

The essential source of the problem is a view of persons and their actions as part of the order of nature, causally determined or not. That conception, if pressed, leads to the feeling that we are not agents at all.... *my doing* of an act—or the doing of an act by someone else—seems to disappear when we think of the world objectively. There seems no room for agency in [such] a world... there is only what happens. (1986: 110–11)

On a straightforward interpretation, Nagel's worry is not very worrisome. Tigers and bears presumably are part of the natural order. Setting aside the mind–body problem and radical sceptical hypotheses (it is all a dream, the only biological entities are brains in vats, and the like), it seems clear that such animals act. Tigers and bears fight, run, eat, and so on. When they do these things they are acting. The same is true of us, even if we are part of the natural order. And what is it *not* to be part of the natural order? Supernatural beings—e.g. gods and ghosts—are not part of the natural order. That a being needs to be supernatural in order to act is an interesting proposition, but I will not worry about trying to falsify it until I see an argument for it that commands respect. Another way not to be part of the natural order is to be abstract in the way that numbers and propositions are. Human beings are not abstract in that way.

David Velleman voices a variant of Nagel's worry. He contends (1) that standard causal accounts of action and its explanation do not capture what 'distinguishes human action from other animal behavior' and do not accommodate 'human action *par excellence*' (1992: 462; cf. 2000, ch. 1). He also reports (2) that his objection to what he calls 'the standard story of human action' (1992: 461), a causal story, 'is not that it mentions mental occurrences in the agent instead of the agent himself [but] that the occurrences it mentions in the agent are no more than occurrences in him, because their involvement in an action does not add up to the agent's being involved' (p. 463). Velleman says that this problem would remain even if the mind–body problem were to be solved (pp. 468–9), and, like Nagel (1986: 110–11), he regards the problem as 'distinct from the problem of free-will' (1992: 465 n. 13).

Here, Velleman runs together two separate issues. Human agents may be involved in some of their actions in ways that chimps, bears, and wombats are involved in many of their actions. Human agents do not vanish in such actions. Scenarios in which human agents vanish are one thing; scenarios in which actions of human agents do not come up to the level of human action par excellence, whatever that may be, are another.

Causalists are entitled to complain that Velleman has been unfair to them. In his description of 'the standard story' (1992: 461), he apparently has in mind the sort of thing found in the work of causalists looking for what is common to all (overt) intentional actions, or all (overt) actions done for reasons, and for what distinguishes actions of these broad kinds from everything else. If some non-human animals act intentionally and for reasons, a story with this topic *should* apply to them. Also, human action par excellence may be intentional action, or action done for a reason, in virtue of its having the properties identified in a standard causal analysis of these things. That the analysis does not provide sufficient conditions for, or a story about, human action par excellence is not a flaw in the analysis, given its target. If Velleman were to believe that causalism lacks the resources for accommodating human action par excellence, he might attack 'the standard story' on that front, arguing that it cannot be extended to handle such action. But Velleman himself is a causalist. Moreover, causalists have offered accounts of kinds of action—e.g. free or autonomous action and action exhibiting self-control (the contrary of weakness of will)—that exceed minimal requirements for intentional action or action done for a reason.[16] It is not as though their story about minimally sufficient conditions for action of the latter kinds is their entire story about human actions.

Locating interesting differences between some human actions and the actions of non-human animals is an important project. Good work on it will continue to emerge, including work exploring potential roles for higher-order attitudes and other relatively sophisticated attitudes in understanding philosophically interesting differences (see Bratman 1999; Frankfurt 1988, 1999; Mele 2003a, ch. 10; Velleman 1992, 2000). That work will be more useful and less likely to mislead if its claims are consistent with the theses that to be a human agent is to be a human being who acts and that many non-human animals act.

---

[16] Many compatibilists are causalists about action. For a causalist account of self-control, see Mele (1995).

4. INTENTIONAL ACTION: TARGETS
OF ANALYSIS

Intentional action is of primary importance in the philosophy of action. If there were no intentional actions, actions would attract little interest at best and perhaps there would be no actions at all.[17] In discussions of freedom of action, intentional action occupies centre stage: we are much less concerned with conditions for the freedom of non-intentional actions. And although we are morally accountable for some unintentional actions, as in cases of negligence, moral assessment of actions is focused primarily on intentional actions. An impressive body of literature is devoted to the project of analysing intentional action. I have reviewed some of it elsewhere (Mele 1992b, 1997b). This section identifies a source of disagreement about the nature of intentional action that requires attention in future work on the topic.

Michael Bratman argues that to do justice both to 'our concern with responsibil-ity' and to regularities of a kind required if intentions are to play explanatory roles plausibly attributed to them, 'we need to allow our concern with responsibility to shape what is done intentionally without similarly shaping what is intended' (1987: 125). He adds: 'To the extent to which our scheme for determining what is intended is shaped by our concern, not only with explanation of action but with the assignment of responsibility, it will be harder to find such regularities. Such a concern would tend to lead to the ascription of intentions which do not play their normal roles in motiva-tion and practical reasoning.' Stephen Sverdlik and I defend the opposing view that although Bratman is right in holding that correct attributions of intentions have no special sensitivity to moral considerations, correct judgements about what is done intentionally also are not sensitive to such considerations (Mele and Sverdlik 1996).

This disagreement raises an important question. When philosophers offer analyses of 'S intentionally A-ed' what should their goal be? One answer is that it should be to analyse the folk concept of intentional action as reflected in folk judgements about actions. But there are other possibilities. A theorist whose primary concern with intentional action is understanding its aetiology may feel comfortable about setting aside widely shared folk judgements about what is done intentionally that are strongly influenced by factors having little or no bearing on the production of action. Such a theorist may not have the goal I identified, and that may be fine.

I will explain this last remark shortly, after I identify a related disagreement. Suppose that 'in firing his gun', a sniper who is trying to kill a soldier 'knowingly alerts the enemy to his presence' (Harman 1997: 151). Gilbert Harman claims that although the sniper 'does not intend to alert the enemy', he *intentionally* alerts the

---

[17] Davidson argues that every action is intentional under some description (1980, ch. 3); cf. Hornsby (1980).

enemy, 'thinking that the gain is worth the possible cost' (p. 151). Bratman makes a similar claim about a runner who reluctantly wears down some heirloom shoes (1987: 123; cf. Ginet 1990: 75–6).

In Mele and Sverdlik (1996) there are arguments for an opposing view of 'side-effect actions' such as these. To be sure, Harman's sniper and Bratman's runner do not unknowingly or accidentally perform the actions at issue. So many readers will deny that the sniper *unintentionally* alerted the enemy and that the runner *unintentionally* wore down his shoes. But that denial does not obviously commit one to holding that these actions are *intentional*. There may be a middle ground between intentional and unintentional action. Arguably, actions that an agent in no way aims at performing and are not parts of anything he is aiming at but also are not performed unknowingly or accidentally are properly located on that middle ground. They may be *non*-intentional, as opposed to *un*intentional (Lowe 1978; Mele and Sverdlik 1996: 274).

Joshua Knobe produces weighty evidence for the proposition that common-sense judgements about what is done intentionally are strongly influenced by moral considerations. For example, subjects responded very differently to the following two cases:

(1) Jake desperately wants to win the rifle contest. He knows that he will only win the contest if he hits the bull's-eye. He raises the rifle, gets the bull's-eye in his sights, and presses the trigger. But Jake is not very good at using his rifle. His hand slips on the barrel of the gun, and the shot goes wild.... Nonetheless, the bullet lands directly on the bull's-eye. Jake wins the contest.

(2) Jake desperately wants to have more money. He knows that he will inherit a lot of money when his aunt dies. One day, he sees his aunt walking by the window. He raises his rifle, gets her in his sights, and presses the trigger. But Jake is not very good at using his rifle. His hand slips on the barrel of the gun, and the shot goes wild.... Nonetheless, the bullet hits her directly in the heart. She dies instantly. (2003: 313)

Knobe reports that 28 per cent of the respondents to case 1 and 76 per cent of the respondents to case 2 'said the behavior was intentional' (pp. 313–14). Obviously, the main difference between the cases is a moral one. A subsequent experiment in which it was first made salient to subjects that people can properly be blamed for behaviour that is not intentional (e.g. a drunk driver's accidentally killing a pedestrian) had a very similar result (pp. 316–18).

Perhaps Socratic questioning would bring folk judgements about case 2 into line with folk judgements about case 1 (see Mele 2001), and perhaps not. However this may be, it is worth exploring the possibility that the folk concept of intentional action is layered in such a way that when its moral layer is removed, something very useful—arguably, *more* useful—for action-theoretic purposes remains. That remainder may be what some philosophers in the business of providing analyses of intentional action have tried to analyse. It also is possible that there is a non-moral layer that grounds Harman's and Bratman's judgements about the sniper and the runner and that stripping it away would uncover precisely what theorists who count no side-effect actions as intentional (e.g. Mele and Sverdlik 1996; Mele and Moser 1997) have attempted to analyse. Some of the disagreements in the literature on the nature of intentional action may have their source in the disputants' having different targets of analysis. This matter requires attention in future work on the topic. We philosophers who take on the project of analysing intentional action should say what our target is and why we selected it (see Mele 2003b).

In this chapter I have limited the discussion to issues concerning which the philosophy of action is largely autonomous. Even within those boundaries, I have set aside many important matters, including deciding, ability, 'subintentional action' (O'Shaughnessy 1980, ch. 10; cf. Hamlyn 1990, ch. 7), basic action, and group action. However, given the centrality of action explanation and the nature of action and intentional action to the philosophy of action, it made good sense to organize my discussion around these topics. In so far as I have advocated a positive major thesis here, it is that causalism is true. Offering an adequate defence of that thesis in a single chapter is impossible. As I see it, given the nature of the philosophical issues, the best way to defend causalism is to develop a detailed causal theory of action and its explanation that one shows to be immune to the objections that have been raised against causalism and to be clearly superior to competing extant theories. I would like to think that, jointly, Mele (1992a) and (2003a) come close to doing this.[18]

References

Adams, F., and Mele, A. (1992). 'The Intention/Volition Debate'. *Canadian Journal of Philosophy*, 22: 323–38.

Anscombe, G. (1957). *Intention*, 2nd edn. Ithaca, NY: Cornell University Press.

Aristotle (1915) *Nicomachean Ethics*, in *The Works of Aristotle*, ed. W. Ross, ix. London: Oxford University Press.

Armstrong, D. (1980). 'Acting and Trying', in D. Armstrong, *The Nature of Mind*. Ithaca, NY: Cornell University Press.

Bishop, J. (1989). *Natural Agency*. Cambridge: Cambridge University Press.

Brand, M. (1984). *Intending and Acting*. Cambridge, Mass.: MIT Press.

Bratman, M. (1987). *Intention, Plans, and Practical Reason*. Cambridge, Mass.: Harvard University Press.

—— (1999). *Faces of Intention*. Cambridge: Cambridge University Press.

Davidson, D. (1963). 'Actions, Reasons, and Causes'. *Journal of Philosophy*, 60: 685–700. Repr. in Davidson, *Essays on Actions and Events*. Oxford: Clarendon Press, 1980.

—— (1980). *Essays on Actions and Events*. Oxford: Clarendon Press.

[18] Parts of this chapter derive from Mele (1992b, 1997a,b, and 2003a). I am grateful to the editors for comments on a draft of this chapter.

Davidson, D. (1985). 'Replies to Essays I–IX', in B. Vermazen and M. Hintikka (eds.), *Essays on Davidson*. Oxford: Clarendon Press.

Dretske, F. (1988). *Explaining Behavior*. Cambridge, Mass.: MIT Press.

Frankfurt, H. (1988). *The Importance of What We Care About*. Cambridge: Cambridge University Press.

—— (1999). *Necessity, Volition, and Love*. Cambridge: Cambridge University Press.

Ghez, Claude, Krakauer, J., Sainburg, R., and Ghilardi, M. (2000). 'Spatial Representations and Internal Models of Limb Dynamics in Motor Learning', in M. Gazzaniga (ed.), *The New Cognitive Neurosciences*. Cambridge, Mass.: MIT Press.

Ginet, C. (1990). *On Action*. Cambridge: Cambridge University Press.

Goldman, A. (1970). *A Theory of Human Action*. Englewood Cliffs, NJ: Prentice-Hall.

Hamlyn, D. (1990). *In and Out of the Black Box*. Oxford: Blackwell.

Harman, G. (1997). 'Practical Reasoning', in A. Mele (ed.), *The Philosophy of Action*. Oxford: Oxford University Press.

Hornsby, J. (1980). *Actions*. London: Routledge & Kegan Paul.

Jordan, M. (1996). 'Computational Aspects of Motor Control and Motor Learning', in H. Heuer and S. Keele (eds.), *Handbook of Perception and Action*, ii. London: Academic Press.

Knobe, Joshua (2003). 'Intentional Action in Folk Psychology: An Experimental Investigation'. *Philosophical Psychology*, 16: 309–24.

Lowe, E. J. (1978). 'Neither Intentional nor Unintentional'. *Analysis*, 38: 117–18.

McCann, H. (1974). 'Volition and Basic Action'. *Philosophical Review*, 83: 451–73.

—— (1975). 'Trying, Paralysis, and Volition'. *Review of Metaphysics*, 28: 423–42.

McGinn, C. (1982). *The Character of Mind*. Oxford: Oxford University Press.

Melden, A. (1961). *Free Action*. London: Routledge & Kegan Paul.

Mele, A. (1992*a*). *Springs of Action*. New York: Oxford University Press.

—— (1992*b*). 'Recent Work on Intentional Action'. *American Philosophical Quarterly*, 29: 199–217.

—— (1995). *Autonomous Agents*. New York: Oxford University Press.

—— (1997*a*). 'Agency and Mental Action'. *Philosophical Perspectives*, 11: 231–49.

—— (1997*b*). Introduction to A. Mele (ed.), *The Philosophy of Action*. Oxford: Oxford University Press.

—— (2001). 'Acting Intentionally: Probing Folk Notions', in B. Malle, L. Moses, and D. Baldwin (eds.), *Intentions and Intentionality: Foundations of Social Cognition*. Cambridge, Mass.: MIT Press.

—— (2003*a*). *Motivation and Agency*. New York: Oxford University Press.

—— (2003*b*). 'Intentional Action: Controversies, Data, and Core Hypotheses'. *Philosophical Psychology*, 16: 325–40.

—— and Moser, P. (1997). 'Intentional Action', in A. Mele (ed.), *The Philosophy of Action*. Oxford: Oxford University Press.

—— and Sverdlik, S. (1996). 'Intention, Intentional Action, and Moral Responsibility'. *Philosophical Studies*, 82: 265–87.

Mill, J. S. (1961). *A System of Logic*, 8th edn. London: Longmans, Green.

Nagel, T. (1986). *The View from Nowhere*. New York: Oxford University Press.

O'Connor, T. (2000). *Persons and Causes*. New York: Oxford University Press.

O'Shaughnessy, B. (1980). *The Will*. Cambridge: Cambridge University Press.

Penfield, W. (1975). *The Mystery of the Mind*. Princeton: Princeton University Press.

Scanlon, T. (1998). *What We Owe to Each Other*. Cambridge, Mass.: Harvard University Press.

Searle, J. (1983). *Intentionality*. Cambridge: Cambridge University Press.

Schon, S. (1994). 'Teleology and the Nature of Mental States'. *American Philosophical Quarterly*, 31: 63–72.

—— (1997). 'Deviant Causal Chains and the Irreducibility of Teleological Explanation'. *Pacific Philosophical Quarterly*, 78: 195–213.

Thalberg, I. (1977). *Perception, Emotion, and Action*. Oxford: Blackwell.

—— (1984). 'Do our Intentions Cause our Intentional Actions?' *American Philosophical Quarterly*, 21: 249–60.

Thomson, J. (1977). *Acts and Other Events*. Ithaca, NY: Cornell University Press.

van Inwagen, P. (1983). *An Essay on Free Will*. Oxford: Clarendon Press.

Velleman, J. D. (1989). *Practical Reflection*. Princeton: Princeton University Press.

—— (1992). 'What Happens When Someone Acts'. *Mind*, 101: 461–81.

—— (2000). *The Possibility of Practical Reason*. Oxford: Clarendon Press.

Wallace, R. J. (1999). 'Three Conceptions of Rational Agency'. *Ethical Theory and Moral Practice*, 2: 217–42.

Wilson, G. (1989). *The Intentionality of Human Action*. Stanford, Calif.: Stanford University Press.

Wittgenstein, L. (1953). *Philosophical Investigations*. New York: Macmillan.

Woods, M. (1972). 'Reasons for Action and Desire'. *Proceedings of the Aristotelian Society*, suppl. vol., 46: 189–201.

CHAPTER 14

COGNITIVE SCIENCE

MARTIN DAVIES

1. INTRODUCTION

A century ago, psychology was in the process of separating from philosophy and becoming an experimental science, while also distinguishing itself from physiology. From 1879, when Wilhelm Wundt began conducting experiments in a laboratory in Leipzig, the emerging discipline of experimental psychology was to be the science of the conscious mind. But by the 1920s, and especially in the United States, this conception of psychology had given way to the behaviourism of J. B. Watson and later B. F. Skinner. According to many accounts of the history of psychology, the restoration of the mind as the proper subject matter of the discipline came in the 1950s and amounted to a revolutionary end to the behaviourist era.

The so-called 'cognitive revolution' (Gardner 1985) in American psychology owed much to developments in adjacent disciplines, especially theoretical linguistics and computer science. Indeed, the cognitive revolution brought forth not only a change in the conception of psychology, but also an interdisciplinary approach to understanding the mind, involving philosophy, anthropology, and neuroscience along with computer science, linguistics, and psychology. Many commentators agree in dating the conception of this interdisciplinary approach, cognitive science, to 11 September 1956, the second day of a symposium on information theory held at MIT (Miller 2003). Over the next twenty years or so, cognitive science developed an institutional presence through research centres, conferences, journals, and a substantial infusion of funds from the Alfred P. Sloan Foundation.

2. PERSONAL AND SUBPERSONAL
LEVELS OF DESCRIPTION

From 1956 and through the 1960s discussion in analytic philosophy of mind concerned competing theses about the metaphysics of mind: behaviourism, central state materialism, and functionalism. The 1960s also saw the publication of books by three of the most major figures in the philosophy of cognitive science. Noam Chomsky's *Aspects of the Theory of Syntax* was published in 1965, with its striking claim about cognitive states that are inaccessible to consciousness, states of tacit knowledge of syntactic rules (1965: 8): 'Obviously, every speaker of a language has mastered and internalized a generative grammar that expresses his knowledge of his language. This is not to say that he is aware of the rules of the grammar or even that he can become aware of them.' In 1968 Jerry Fodor published his first book, *Psychological Explanation: An Introduction to the Philosophy of Psychology*. And Daniel Dennett's *Content and Consciousness*, with its distinction between personal and subpersonal levels of description, appeared in 1969.

2.1 Dennett's Distinction

We may say that 'a person pulled his hand away from the stove...because it hurt' (Dennett 1969: 91). But, Dennett says, we cannot, at this *personal* level of description, elaborate an account of the processes that led the person to remove his hand. This is because (p. 94): 'The only sort of explanation in which "pain" belongs is non-mechanistic.'

The general picture is that, at the personal level, we talk about persons as such— as experiencing, thinking subjects and agents. We describe what people feel and what people do, and we explain what people do in terms of their sensations, desires, beliefs, and intentions. These personal-level explanations are of a distinctive, not straightforwardly causal, kind and they do not work by elaborating accounts of mental processes. Still less do they work by postulating physical mechanisms underpinning the activities of persons. An account of the physical mechanisms that are involved when a person withdraws his hand from a hot stove belongs at a quite different level of description and explanation. We abandon 'the explanatory level of people and their sensations and activities' and shift to 'the *sub-personal* level of brains and events in the nervous system' (p. 93). At this subpersonal level of description and explanation, the kinds of occurrences that are described receive causal explanations in purely mechanistic terms.

2.2 Intentional Systems: An Apparent Tension and Two Ways to Resolve It

Descriptions of persons in terms of beliefs and desires—*intentional* descriptions—exhibit the logical property of intensionality; descriptions that figure in the physical sciences are, in contrast, extensional. When Dennett asks (p. 40), 'Could there be a system of internal states or events, the extensional description of which could be upgraded into an Intentional description?', we might expect that he would answer in the negative. That is what the distinction between personal and subpersonal levels of description might seem to suggest. But in fact Dennett says (p. 40): 'The answer to this question is not at all obvious, but there are some promising hints that the answer is Yes.'

His strategy for developing these hints makes use of the notion of an intentional system and the related notion of the *intentional stance*. These notions are central in Dennett's later work in philosophy of mind. But the character of the strategy for attributing intentionality to physical phenomena is already apparent in *Content and Consciousness* (pp. 78, 80):

the relation between Intentional descriptions of events, states or structures (as signals that carry certain messages or memory traces with certain contents) and extensional descriptions of them is one of *further interpretation*. . . . The ideal picture, then, is of content being ascribed to structures, events and states in the brain on the basis of a determination of origins in stimulation and eventual appropriate behavioural effects, such ascriptions being essentially a heuristic overlay on the extensional theory.

There appears to be a tension in Dennett's position here. The interpretative strategy of 'heuristic overlay' could be adopted towards a system that is not a person. Yet intentional descriptions were supposed to belong at the personal level, which is the level of 'people and their sensations and activities'.

To the extent that this apparent tension is genuine, there seem to be two ways to resolve it. One way would be to hold hard to what is distinctive of persons and to deny that personal-level intentionality can be literally attributed to subpersonal-level systems. The other way would be to take a more relaxed view of the distinction between the personal and subpersonal levels of description and to allow that personal-level intentionality is the product of adopting a stance that can just as well be adopted towards subpersonal-level systems. This second, broadly reductionist, approach to intentionality and representation has, in fact, been dominant in recent philosophy of mind and cognitive science.

The first way of resolving the apparent tension in Dennett's position is apt to lead to a worry about the theoretical foundations of cognitive science. For it may seem that the appeal to unconscious representations and tacitly known rules involves a kind of category mistake in which distinctively personal-level notions, such as representation and rule, are applied at a subpersonal level of description. We shall consider responses to this worry in the next section.

3. Intentionality and the Foundations of Cognitive Science

In 'Artificial Intelligence as Philosophy and as Psychology', Dennett's concern is with an apparent problem posed by the fact that the notion of a representation goes along with that of an interpreter (1978: 122): 'something is a representation only *for* or *to* someone'. So cognitive science's appeal to internal representations requires an appeal, also, to internal interpreters of those representations—that is, to homunculi. And this looks like the beginning of a regress. Whether or not the threat of regress is genuine, Dennett's account seems to offer a way of moving the notion of representation to a subpersonal level of description without committing a category mistake. For it involves populating the subpersonal level with little persons.

3.1 Homunculi, and 'As If' Intentionality

Dennett's solution to the problem of the regress begins from the thought that the performance of a cognitive task can be secured by having subsystems perform parts of the task. These subsystems are to be thought of initially as intelligent homunculi whose functions are in turn discharged by sub-subsystems and so on. But the crucial point is that these are ever less intelligent homunculi with ever simpler tasks to perform. So, in the end, the simplest tasks can be performed by mere mechanical devices, the homunculi are discharged, and the threat of an infinite regress is avoided (see also Block 1995*a*).

In this account, talk about internal representations goes along with talk about little people, just as we should expect of a personal-level notion. But, of course, the talk of homunculi is metaphor. There are no little people there, just little mechanisms. And, once the homunculi are discharged, the whole story can be retold, this time literally rather than metaphorically, without any talk of intentionality, representations, or rules. Personal-level notions enter the subpersonal-level account only as a metaphorical staging post en route to the non-metaphorical neurophysiological truth.

The overall picture that emerges is this. When we stress what is distinctive about persons, we make literal use of personal-level notions. Literal application of those same notions to pieces of cognitive machinery would be illegitimate, just as the foundational worry suggests. But the metaphorical use of personal-level notions in subpersonal-level psychological descriptions is conceptually unproblematic as, of course, is the purely biological description of neural mechanisms. So the personal level is distinguished from two legitimate subpersonal levels, one making use of 'as if' intentional descriptions and the other making use of literal biological descriptions.

Treating subpersonal-level talk about representations and rules as 'as if' personal-level talk is, then, one way of avoiding the worry about the theoretical foundations of cognitive science. But it is not the only way.

3.2 Indicator Aboutness and Subdoxastic Aboutness

We sometimes say that the spots on a child mean or indicate that the child has measles or that the clouds in the sky mean or indicate that it will rain. The notion of meaning that is in play here is not conceptually dependent on the notion of linguistic meaning, nor on the idea of what someone believes. As Fred Dretske puts it (1986: 18): 'Naturally occurring signs mean something, and they do so without any assistance from us.' This *indicator aboutness* is closely related to the notion of a signal carrying information. It can be explicated in terms of reliable causal covariation between events of two types—for example, between occurrences of a certain kind of cloud formation and occurrences of rain.

Some notion in the vicinity of indicator aboutness seems to lie at the heart of much research in cognitive science and cognitive neuroscience. For example, when a pattern of neuronal activity is found to be reliably correlated with the instantiation of a particular property by objects presented to an animal, that pattern is taken to be the animal's brain's way of representing that property. But, for at least two reasons, indicator aboutness itself is not satisfactory as a kind of representation. First, it does not allow for the possibility of misrepresentation. Secondly, it is too cheap; too many things reliably causally covary with each other. So something must be added and, at this point, many of the theories that have been advanced to account for the representational nature of physical states appeal to some notion of teleological function. The basic idea is that what a type of event (such as a pattern of neuronal activity) represents is not the worldly condition that events of that type actually covary with, but rather the condition that those events are supposed to covary with.

In some cases, a type of event has a function because of the intentions of a designer. Thus, consider the familiar example of a fuel gauge. If the states of the fuel gauge reliably covary with the states of the fuel tank, then the position of the needle, towards the bottom of the scale, indicates that the tank is nearly empty. Since the fuel gauge it doing what it was designed to do, the needle's position not only indicates, but also represents, the tank's being nearly empty. But now suppose that the fuel gauge starts to malfunction, the covariation becomes unreliable, and the needle takes up a position towards the bottom of the scale even when the tank is full. Then the position of the needle no longer indicates that the tank is nearly empty. But it does still represent—it misrepresents—the tank as being nearly empty, since this is what the position of the needle is supposed to indicate. Adding a teleological component seems to allow for the possibility of misrepresentation; and it makes representation less ubiquitous than indication. Of course, if teleological function were always to depend on the intentions of a designer, then the resulting notion of representation would be derivative from the intentionality of the designer's thoughts. But we can move towards a notion of representation that is not conceptually dependent on personal-level mental notions, such as belief and intention, if we consider teleological functions that are the products of natural, rather than intentional, selection.

Stephen Stich proposes that the unconscious representational states that are invoked in cognitive science—states that 'play a role in the proximate causal history of beliefs, though they are not beliefs themselves' (1978: 499)—should be called 'subdoxastic states'. Let us extend that terminology and label the putative representationality of those states *subdoxastic aboutness*. If personal-level intentionality cannot be literally attributed to subpersonal-level systems, then subdoxastic aboutness is different from the aboutness of propositional attitudes like beliefs and intentions. But it does not follow that an attribution of subdoxastic aboutness is really a metaphorical attribution of attitude aboutness.

3.3 Personal-Level Intentionality and Subpersonal-Level Representation

At the end of Section 2, I distinguished two ways of resolving an apparent tension in Dennett's position. In this section I have explored the consequences of resolving the tension in the first way. If we stress what is distinctive about persons and accept that personal-level intentionality cannot be literally attributed to subpersonal-level systems, then what are we to make of subpersonal-level representation? The overall picture that emerged from Dennett's appeal to, and ultimate discharge of, homunculi had the personal level of description distinguished from two subpersonal levels. At one of these, the level of information-processing psychology, we use 'as if' personal-level intentional descriptions; at the other, the level of neuroscience, we use literal biological descriptions. But now we see that an alternative picture is available, in which information-processing psychology makes use of descriptions that are literal rather than metaphorical. For it is plausible that a notion of subdoxastic aboutness can be elucidated in terms of causal covariation plus evolutionary function, natural meaning plus natural selection.

Those who adopt the second way of resolving the apparent tension in Dennett's position take a more relaxed view of the distinction between the personal and subpersonal levels of description. They regard the intentionality of people's conscious mental states as of a piece with the representational properties of the states of neural and cognitive systems. So their hope is that attitude aboutness itself can be elucidated in terms of causal covariation and evolutionary function. As I mentioned earlier, this broadly reductionist approach to intentionality and representation has been the dominant one in both philosophy of mind and cognitive science (Stich and Warfield 1994).

It would be fair to say, however, that none of the theories proposed within this dominant approach has been accepted as providing a fully satisfying account of the intentionality of ordinary conscious mental states like beliefs. A critic of the approach, looking for a pattern in the failure, might suggest that the inadequacy of the reductionist approach results from its severing the connection between intentionality and distinctive features of a person's mental life such as consciousness (Searle 1990). So there might seem to be some pressure towards rejecting the reductionist approach and assigning to cognitive scientific descriptions a metaphorical status at best. But we have been arguing that an intermediate or hybrid position is available. The broadly reductionist programme may be adequate to account for subpersonal-level representation even if it does not provide a fully satisfying account of personal-level intentionality.

3.4 Philosophy and Cognitive Science

I have described a position that is intermediate between two extremes. Towards one end of the spectrum there is a broadly reductionist view about intentionality. Towards the other end of the spectrum there is a negative view about cognitive science. When we consider the relationship between philosophy of mind and cognitive science more generally, we find a similar pattern. Towards one end of the spectrum there is cognitive scientism—the view that the proper business of the philosophy of mind is simply to hand the substantive questions over to cognitive science. Towards the other end of the spectrum there is philosophical isolationism—the view that, even if cognitive science is not built on a category mistake, it still has little or nothing to contribute to the philosopher's project of plotting the contours of our conceptual scheme. An intermediate position has it that, contrary to cognitive scientism, philosophy makes a distinctive theoretical contribution using a methodology different from that of the empirical sciences while, contrary to philosophical isolationism, philosophical theory cannot be insulated from the findings of empirical research.

These views about the interdisciplinary relationship go along naturally with views about the relationship between the personal-level descriptions that are of primary interest to philosophy of mind and the subpersonal-level descriptions that figure in cognitive scientific theorizing. Cognitive scientism goes with a broadly reductionist view of personal-level descriptions. Philosophical isolationism goes with the view that the relationship between personal-level and subpersonal-level descriptions is one of relative independence.

Once again, an intermediate position is available. As against the reductionist view, cognitive science may well not provide fully satisfying explanatory accounts of personal-level phenomena such as free agency or the intentionality of thoughts. This first aspect of the intermediate position is a generalization of the familiar idea that cognitive scientific accounts of conscious experience leave an explanatory gap. But as against the claim of independence, philosophical theorizing may itself reveal that personal-level descriptions, cast in terms of experience, thought, and agency, impose subpersonal-level requirements. When philosophical theorizing system-atizes our conception of ourselves as persons, that conception may turn out to have built into it commitments about what the underpinning information-processing machinery must be like.

4. TACIT KNOWLEDGE CHALLENGED AND DEFENDED

Chomsky's claim that ordinary speakers possess tacit knowledge of a generative grammar for their language stands as the canonical example of cognitive science's appeal to unconscious representational states.

4.1 Chomsky's Project

A grammar is, in the first instance, something abstract; it is a collection of rules that generate a set of structural descriptions of sentences. But a specification of a grammar may be put forward as a partial account of what a particular language user (tacitly) knows; that is, as a partial psychological description of that language user. Thus, in recent versions, statements of a grammar are said to be about I-language (internalized language) conceived as the attained state of the language faculty (Chomsky 1986: 22–3; 1995: 18).

The aim of the theoretical linguist is to provide a correct account of the body of specifically linguistic tacit knowledge possessed by a language user. This body of knowledge is the speaker's *competence*, and linguistic competence is contrasted with linguistic *performance*, which is the actual use of language—and so of this body of knowledge—in concrete situations. Performance includes using a sentence to say something, interpreting someone else's utterance, or silently thinking in words. It also includes making judgements about whether a sentence is grammatical, whether a sentence is ambiguous, and so on. In language use, linguistic knowledge is drawn on by cognitive processes whose operation is subject to all the usual constraints of time and space and to the possibility of malfunction. Also, language use draws on knowledge that falls outside the domain of theoretical linguistics, including knowledge about people's beliefs and other mental states, knowledge about conversational practices, and—as the interpretation of metaphors illustrates—an open-ended mass of knowledge about the workings of the non-linguistic world. So the relationship between competence and performance may be relatively indirect consistently with the idea that competence is somehow drawn on in performance.

Whether a sentence is grammatical is a question about competence. It is a question about which structural descriptions are generated by a tacitly known collection of rules. But whether a sentence is judged by language users to be grammatical or acceptable, or to sound right, is a question about performance. Clearly, there could be countless reasons why a sentence that is grammatical might be judged—reflectively or unreflectively—to be unacceptable. There could be countless reasons why a sentence that is ambiguous might be judged to have just one meaning or why a sentence that literally means one thing might be interpreted as meaning something quite different. It would involve multiple misreadings of Chomsky to think that the aim of the theoretical linguist is to produce a smoothed out systematization of unreflective judgements by language users.

If a grammar provides a correct description of a language user's tacit knowledge, then the grammar is said to be *descriptively adequate*. So, the aim of the theoretical linguist is to specify descriptively adequate grammars; that is, true accounts of the I-language—the attained state of the language faculty—of individual speakers. But there is then a pressing question how the attained state of tacit knowledge is arrived at. Chomsky's view here is that it is not possible to explain this attainment without postulating a substantial body of tacit knowledge as an innate endowment; that is, as the initial state of the language faculty.

In early versions of the theory, the innate endowment was supposed to be a body of knowledge about the forms that rules, and so grammars, could take; it was an innate linguistic theory. Any particular hypothesis about this innate linguistic theory was subject to two kinds of constraint. It was constrained from above, so to speak, by the formal requirement that the linguistic theory, together with information available in the environment of the young child learning a language, should correctly determine a single grammar as the grammar of which the child would acquire tacit knowledge. A linguistic theory meeting this formal requirement was said to be *explanatorily adequate*. But, in addition to the requirement of 'adequacy-in-principle', there was also a constraint from below; namely that the processes required to effect the transition from innate endowment to attained state should be 'feasible' given the 'constraints of time and access', as Chomsky (1965: 54) puts it.

There are disputes in cognitive science about whether we need to attribute tacit knowledge of linguistic rules to language users and especially about the claim that a substantial body of linguistic knowledge must be regarded as innate. But, within cognitive science, it is not denied that the notion of tacit knowledge is a legitimate one. Even someone who claims that there is no need to appeal to tacit knowledge of linguistic rules in order to account for sentence-processing, or no need to appeal to innate knowledge in order to account for language acquisition, allows that the notion of tacit knowledge makes sense. But within philosophy the attitude towards tacit knowledge has been much more critical. We shall consider two kinds of criticism that go beyond general resistance to the idea of the cognitive unconscious.

4.2 Wittgensteinian Worries and Quine's Challenge

There are criticisms of Chomsky's project that arise from the later philosophy of Ludwig Wittgenstein. For example, a worry about the appeal to tacit knowledge might be based on the thought that the notion of a rule of language belongs with the idea of a normative practice. Rules determine (logically rather than causally) what is correct or incorrect and participants in the practice advert to rules to justify, criticize, or excuse their actions. The proper response to this worry is to distinguish the notion of a tacitly known rule from the notion of a rule that figures in a normative practice. Ordinary language users do not, of course, advert to tacitly known rules to justify their judgements about sentences. Rules of language as Chomsky conceives them 'are not normative in this sense' (2000: 98).

In a wide-ranging Wittgensteinian critique of Chomsky's project, Gordon Baker and Peter Hacker (1984) anticipate the response on behalf of Chomsky that tacit knowledge of a rule is constituted by the presence of a mechanism that ensures conformity to the rule. About this idea they raise two important questions. One is the question how, given this kind of account of tacit knowledge, we can distinguish between tacit *guidance* by a rule and mere *conformity* to the rule (Baker and Hacker 1984: 298). This, in essence, is the challenge that W. V. Quine (1972) posed. We shall review Quine's challenge now and return to Baker and Hacker's second question later.

A subject can behave in a way that conforms to a rule without using the rule to guide his behaviour for, as Quine uses the notion of guidance, it requires explicit verbalizable knowledge. Chomsky's tacit knowledge is supposed to be an intermediate notion. While it requires less than explicit knowledge, it cannot be equated with mere conformity. For there will always be alternative sets of rules that require just the same behaviour for conformity—that are 'extensionally equivalent' in Quine's terminology. And it is part of the idea of tacit knowledge that a speaker's actual behaviour might, in principle, be correctly explained in terms of tacit knowledge of one set of rules rather than tacit knowledge of another extensionally equivalent set of rules.

It is at this point that Quine poses his challenge (1972: 444): 'If it is to make sense to say that a native was implicitly guided by one system of rules and not by another extensionally equivalent system, this sense must link up somehow with the native's dispositions to behave in observable ways in observable circumstances.' He insists that, if an attribution of tacit knowledge is an empirical claim that goes beyond a summary of conforming behaviour, then it should be possible to indicate what kinds of evidence would count in favour of or against that empirical claim. More fundamental, however, than the question of what evidence would support an attribution of tacit knowledge is the question what the correctness of such an attribution would consist in.

4.3 Evans's Response and an Account of Tacit Knowledge

While Chomsky himself focuses on tacit knowledge of syntax, much of the philosophical literature considers tacit knowledge of semantic theories such as truth-conditional theories of meaning. Responding to Quine's challenge adapted to this case, Gareth Evans proposed a constitutive account of tacit knowledge in terms of dispositions (1981: 328): 'I suggest that we construe the claim that someone tacitly knows a theory of meaning as ascribing to that person a set of dispositions— one corresponding to each of the expressions for which the theory provides a distinct axiom.' For this purpose, it is vital that attributing a disposition to a person is not just describing a regularity in that person's behaviour.

Thus, consider a semantic theory that includes an axiom saying that a particular name 'a' refers to the dog Fido and another axiom saying that a particular predicate 'F' is satisfied by things that bark. Tacit knowledge of this semantic theory requires having a disposition corresponding to 'a', and a disposition corresponding to 'F', and so on for each of the other expressions for which the theory includes an axiom. But having these dispositions is not just a matter of treating each sentence containing 'a' as meaning something about Fido and treating each sentence containing 'F' as meaning something about barking. For someone might exhibit those regularities as a result of learning the meanings of a large number of complete sentences from a phrasebook, yet without having any sensitivity to the way in which the sentences are built up from expressions like 'a' and 'F'. Rather, says Evans (pp. 329–30), an attribution of tacit knowledge of the semantic theory 'involves the claim that there is a single state of the subject which figures in a causal explanation of why he reacts in this regular way to all the sentences containing the expression'. Tacit knowledge of the semantic theory requires that all the instances of the regularity involving sentences containing 'a' should have a common causal explanation, all the instances of the regularity involving sentences containing 'F' should have a common causal explanation, and so on. This requirement would *not* be met in the case of someone who had acquired only phrasebook knowledge.

Quine's challenge highlights the fact that evidence from patterns in performance may not itself help us decide between competing attributions of tacit knowledge. As the example of phrasebook knowledge illustrates, a pattern of performance on the task of assigning meanings to sentences might be shared by one subject who possesses, and another subject who lacks, tacit knowledge of a semantic theory with separate axioms for 'a', 'F', and so on. But given the kind of constitutive account just sketched, we can readily imagine empirical evidence that would confirm, and other evidence that would disconfirm, an attribution of tacit knowledge of one or another syntactic or semantic theory. So we can go some way towards meeting Quine's challenge, even on its own terms.

The coherence of Evans's account strongly suggests that there is nothing conceptually wrong with Chomsky's invocation of tacit knowledge in linguistic theory. But we should not leave the issue without returning to Baker and Hacker's critique and, in particular, to the second of the two questions that they raise about accounts of tacit knowledge cast in terms of mechanisms whose presence causally explains conformity to a rule. Although tacitly known rules do not play a justificatory role, the body of tacit knowledge (competence) determines grammaticality. But language users make mistakes and mechanisms malfunction. So competence is not perfectly reflected in performance; for example, grammaticality is not perfectly reflected in judgements of acceptability. The worry, then, is that, to give an account of tacit knowledge in terms of a mechanism's explanation of a pattern in performance, we need some account of what would constitute an error in the operation of the mechanism. For otherwise, every feature of performance will have to be reflected in the rules that are tacitly known.

Here, with an apparent threat to the distinction between something's seeming right and being right (Wittgenstein 1953, §202), we are in the vicinity of Wittgenstein's rule-following considerations, especially as they are developed by Saul Kripke (1982). A fully satisfying account of tacit knowledge must make room for the fact that there is a gap between seeming right and being right—that performance is an imperfect guide to competence.

5. The Language of Thought Hypothesis

As we understand it here, Fodor's language of thought hypothesis is a hypothesis about internal representational states that figure in subpersonal-level psychological structures and processes. Many of these representational states are clear examples of subdoxastic states and of the cognitive unconscious. But the language of thought hypothesis is, of course, also supposed to apply to states of thinking and, in particular, to occurrent thoughts—states or events that are neither subdoxastic nor unconscious. It may be tempting to suppose that, when it is thoughts that are at issue, the hypothesis is an answer to the question whether people think 'in language'—whether, in conscious thinking, sentences of one's natural language come silently before the mind. But, in fact, the language of thought hypothesis does not concern the phenomenology of conscious thinking and so is quite distinct from the 'thinking in natural language' hypothesis (Carruthers 1996).

5.1 Intentional Realism and Syntactic Properties

We can begin from the assumption that personal-level events of conscious thought are underpinned by occurrences of physical configurations belonging to types that figure in the science of information-processing psychology. These physical configurations can be assigned the contents of the thoughts that they underpin. So we assume that, if a person consciously or occurrently thinks that p, then there is a state that has the representational content that p and is of a type that can figure in subpersonal-level psychological structures and processes. This assumption is what Fodor (1987) calls *intentional realism*. We do not assume that the properties of these underpinning states, other than their representational contents, are evident to the thinking subject's introspection. Then the language of thought hypothesis says, first, that these states that underpin thoughts have *syntactic properties* and, secondly, that the same goes for other states in the domain of information-processing psychology.

Fodor (1987: 16–21) imposes three conditions on syntactic properties. First, a syntactic property is a physical property (though this is not intended to require that a syntactic property should be a property that figures in fundamental physics). Secondly, a syntactic property is correlated with a semantic property. Thirdly, a syntactic property is a determinant of causal powers and so of causal consequences. Fodor says that shape, which is an intrinsic property, is the right sort of property to be a syntactic property. So we can take it that the three conditions are intended to have the consequence that a syntactic property is an intrinsic property of a representation. This helps to explain why semantic or representational properties themselves do not qualify as syntactic properties. For accounts of the semantic properties of representations typically appeal to causal relational properties, on both the input side and the output side; and these are certainly not intrinsic properties.

Clearly, the language of thought hypothesis is very far from being trivially true. In principle, a physical configuration with the representational content that Fido barks might be syntactically unstructured. It might not have two causally potent physical properties, one correlated with the semantic property of being about Fido and the other correlated with the semantic property of being about barking.

5.2 Compositionality and Inference to the Best Explanation

Whether the language of thought hypothesis is true is a substantive empirical claim that cannot be settled by introspection alone. In *The Language of Thought* (1975), Fodor's argument in favour of the hypothesis begins from the idea that the best cognitive psychological theories postulate internal representations and processes that manipulate those representations. This is surely enough to motivate the claim that there are internal states with both semantic properties and intrinsic causally potent properties. But why should the intrinsic causal properties be syntactic properties? Why should they be correlated with the semantic properties?

Here, Fodor takes over from philosophy of language the notion of *compositionality*: the meanings of whole sentences depend on the meanings of their parts. Compositionality provides an explanation of semantic *productivity*. For where a sentence's constituent parts—or, more generally, its intrinsic properties—are correlated with semantic properties, the recombination of these parts or properties allows the construction of further sentences with different but related semantic properties. For example, the syntactic structure in 'Fido barks' and in 'Fiona sings' guarantees that we can recombine constituent parts in order to express the thoughts (both false, let us suppose) that Fido sings and that Fiona barks. In contrast, where intrinsic properties are not correlated with semantic properties there is no reason to expect semantic productivity. A language might contain two syntactically unstructured sentences, one meaning that Fido barks and the other that Fiona sings, but not provide for the expression of any other thoughts at all.

Where we find semantic productivity, we naturally postulate compositionality as its explanation; and that involves postulating representations with syntactic properties. So Fodor can construct an argument in support of the language of thought hypothesis—an inference to the best explanation—by showing that the schemes of representation postulated by cognitive psychological theories exhibit a measure of semantic productivity. He does this (1975, ch. 1) by pointing to examples in which a cognitive process needs to range over representations of states of affairs drawn from an open-ended domain.

Not all the cognitive processes that operate, according to this line of argument, over syntactically structured representations are thought processes. But when we consider the case of thoughts the line of argument seems particularly compelling. For semantic productivity seems to be at the very heart of thinking. If someone is able to frame the thought that Fido barks and the thought that Fiona sings, then that person is in a position to frame (even if not to believe) the thought that Fido sings and the thought that Fiona barks.

5.3 Tacit Knowledge of Rules and Syntactically Structured Representations

Semantic productivity provides one line of argument in support of the language of thought hypothesis; but there is also a quite general connection between tacit knowledge of rules and syntactic properties of representations. We can illustrate this connection with a very simple example.

Consider the task of assigning pronunciations to letter strings. In particular, consider the 125 three-letter strings that can be built from a set of five possible onset consonants, five possible vowels, and five possible coda consonants; and suppose that these strings have pronunciations that conform to regular letter–sound rules. If an information-processing system assigns pronunciations correctly, then there are fifteen patterns in its input–output relation, of which one example would be this: Whenever the input represents a letter string whose onset consonant is 'B', the output represents a pronunciation that begins with the sound /B/.

According to the account of tacit knowledge sketched earlier (Section 4.3), tacit knowledge of rules requires the presence of a battery of causal-explanatory states, one state corresponding to each rule. In the present example, each such state would function as a causal common factor in explaining the twenty-five instances of one input–output pattern. Suppose that this requirement is met by having a processing mechanism corresponding to each rule, and consider the twenty-five input configurations that represent strings beginning with the letter 'B'. These physical configurations need to share some property that will engage or activate the 'B'-to-/B/ processing mechanism. This property, which we may suppose to be physical and intrinsic, will be a determinant of causal consequences and it will be correlated with the semantic property of representing a string beginning with the letter 'B'. In short, this property will meet Fodor's conditions for being a syntactic property. But the information-processing system also embodies tacit knowledge of fourteen other letter–sound rules including, for example, the 'I'-to-/I/ rule for a vowel and the 'N'-to-/N/ rule for a coda consonant. So, by the same argument, the input representation of the three-letter string 'BIN' must have three syntactic properties correlated with the three semantic properties of representing a string beginning with 'B', representing a string with 'I' in the middle, and representing a string ending in 'N'.

The general connection between tacit knowledge of rules and syntactic properties of representations is thus that processing systems that embody tacit knowledge of rules need to have syntactically structured input representations. There is compositionality here. The representational content of an input configuration is determined by the semantic properties correlated with the three syntactic properties that it instantiates. But, whereas the earlier argument in support of the language of thought hypothesis (Section 5.2) was an abductive argument for compositionality as the explanation of semantic productivity, the argument just outlined is a more nearly deductive argument from the involvement of tacit knowledge in cognitive processes.

5.4 Concept Possession and the Language of Thought Hypothesis

Just as the argument from semantic productivity seems particularly compelling in the case of thoughts, so also it is plausible that we have tacit knowledge of rules involving thoughts, namely, rules of inference. The reason is that possessing particular concepts involves a thinker in commitments to particular *forms* of inference. Commitment to a form of inference is not just commitment to each of a number of inferences that happen to instantiate that form. Rather, the commitment is to accept or perform those inferences 'in virtue of their form' (Peacocke 1992: 6). The form of the inferences should figure, somehow, in the causal explanation of the thinker's performing those inferences. It is not obvious what this requirement comes to (Peacocke 1992: 183–4). But a kind of inference to the best philosophical explanation suggests that performing inferences in virtue of their form involves meeting the conditions for tacit knowledge of the corresponding rule of inference.

Now consider a thinker who thinks a thought in whose content the concept C is a constituent, and suppose that R is a tacitly known rule of inference in whose premiss the concept C figures. We have assumed that such a personal-level event of conscious thought is underpinned by the occurrence of a physical configuration to which we can assign the same content. So, just as a physical configuration that represents a letter string beginning with 'B' needs to have a syntactic property that engages the 'B'-to-/B/ processing mechanism, so also a physical configuration whose content involves the concept C needs to have a syntactic property that engages the R processing mechanism. And, just as a physical configuration that represents the three-letter string 'BIN' must have three recombinable syntactic properties corresponding to its three semantic properties, so also the physical configuration that underpins a thought whose content has several concepts as constituents must have several recombinable syntactic properties encoding those concepts. For we assume that, for each concept that a thinker possesses, there is at least one form of inference to which the thinker is committed.

If the initial idea about tacit knowledge of rules of inference is correct, then the general connection between tacit knowledge and syntactically structured representations provides a relatively straightforward philosophical argument in support of the language of thought hypothesis (Davies 1991). It would surely be overly ambitious to suppose that philosophy, unaided by detailed empirical investigation, could settle the question whether or not the language of thought hypothesis is true of the information-processing that takes place inside the heads of human beings. But it is not overly ambitious to suppose that philosophical theory may uncover, within our ordinary conception of ourselves as conscious thinking subjects and agents, commitments to particular kinds of cognitive structures and processes.

6. COMPUTATIONAL PSYCHOLOGY AND LEVELS OF EXPLANATION

Although the argument for a general connection between tacit knowledge of rules and syntactically structured representations establishes only a one-way dependence, it is clear that syntactic structure and tacit knowledge are made for each other. In typical cases where they go together, the rules that are tacitly known are cast in terms of items in some task domain and the properties of those items—for example, in terms of letter strings and their orthographic and phonological properties. Cognitive processes operate over input representations to generate output representations in ways that are dictated by the rules. And this can be done mechanically because the semantic properties of representations—for example, what letter string is being represented—are encoded by syntactic properties and these, being intrinsic and causally potent, are the sorts of properties (unlike semantic properties) that can engage mechanisms.

6.1 The Computational Theory of Mind

Putting syntactically structured representations and tacitly known rules together yields the computational theory of mind. Representational mental states have, or are underpinned by states that have, syntactic properties; and cognitive processes are computational processes that operate over those representations in virtue of their syntactic properties.

It may seem that the very fact that it is syntactic properties, rather than representational properties, that do the causal work presents a problem for the computational theory of mind. For it is part of our everyday conception of the mind that the representational properties of mental events are crucial to the causal consequences of those events. It is because my belief has the specific content that it does that it has the specific causal consequences that it does. The postulation of syntactic properties was supposed to help explain how causal-explanatory claims about thoughts, conceived as representational states, could be true. But now it may seem that the syntactic properties make the representational properties causally irrelevant.

One way of responding to this concern about the computational theory of mind is to draw a distinction between a more inclusive class of causally *explanatory* properties and a narrower class of causally *efficacious* properties. As Frank Jackson and Philip Pettit say (1988: 392): 'Features which causally explain need not cause.' Jackson and Pettit argue that representational properties are not causally efficacious properties because of the highly relational nature of content. But a representational property could still be a causally explanatory property. It could figure in causal explanations and in causal laws. So the prospects seem to be good for defending the computational theory of mind by saying that it is because syntactic properties are causally efficacious that representational properties are causally explanatory.

6.2 Levels of Explanation in Computational Psychology

At the beginning of his book on the computational processes involved in human vision, David Marr (1982) sets out an approach that has been influential within cognitive science and much discussed by philosophical commentators. Marr describes in some detail the grounds for his conviction that, in neurophysiological investigations of vision in the 1970s, 'something was going wrong' (p. 14) and 'something important was missing' (p. 15). This culminates in the following striking claim (p. 19): 'There must exist an additional level of understanding at which the character of the information-processing tasks carried out during perception are analyzed and understood in a way that is independent of the particular mechanisms and structures that implement them in our heads.' Thus Marr was led to propose that information-processing mechanisms have to be understood at three levels. The first is the level of the computational theory that tells us what is being computed, why—given the requirements imposed by the task—this is being computed, and how in principle this might be computed—'what is the logic of the strategy by which it can be carried out' (p. 25). The second level of understanding involves the specification of a scheme or format of representation and an algorithm by which the computation is to be carried out. And the third level is the level of physical realization.

In general, experimental research in cognitive psychology is directed towards understanding at the second level. The aim is to develop theories about the representational structures and the computational processes that are actually implicated in performance of an information-processing task. Different algorithms and different representational formats lead to different predictions about the performance of subjects—different predictions about reaction times, for example. But any such theory about cognitive structures and processes is constrained *from above* by the first-level abstract theory of the task and, at least in principle, *from below* by the third-level theory about physical realization. Marr (p. 27) is explicit that it is the constraint from above that is more crucial and, in this sense, he recommends a top-down, rather than a bottom-up, approach to cognitive scientific research.

7. Informational Encapsulation and the Modularity of Mind

The generic idea of modularity is familiar from everyday life. For example, furniture and stereo systems are 'modular'. They are built from components, each of which makes a relatively independent contribution to the functionality or the performance of the system as a whole. If it is the generic idea of modularity that is in play, then it is relatively uncontroversial that the mind, conceived as an information-processing system, is modular. But Fodor's modularity thesis goes beyond this uncontroversial claim.

The background to the thesis is provided by a taxonomy of cognitive mechanisms. First, there are transducers, whose outputs are the representations from which mental information-processing begins. What is represented at this initial stage is something proximal—typically, the pattern of stimulation at a sensory surface. Secondly, there are input systems that perform inference-like transitions from these initial representations of the proximal stimulus to representations of the properties and distribution of distal objects. The processing in these systems is computational and the function of these systems is 'to so represent the world as to make it accessible to thought' (Fodor 1983: 40). The outputs of the input systems are representations of worldly objects, properties, events, and states of affairs. Thirdly, there are central cognitive systems that subserve thinking, problem-solving, planning, and the fixation of belief. Given this background, Fodor's modularity thesis says that input systems share theoretically important properties that are different from the properties of central systems. Input systems typically exhibit the marks of modularity; central systems do not.

7.1 The Essence of Fodorian Modularity

Fodor lists nine marks of modularity of which six are relatively straightforward. Modules are domain-specific; that is, they are specialized for tasks like the analysis of spoken words and sentences or the perception of faces. The operation of modules is mandatory and fast. Modules are associated with fixed neural architecture, they exhibit characteristic and specific patterns of breakdown, and their ontogeny exhibits a characteristic pace and sequencing. The remaining three marks require more comment.

First, there is only limited central access to the mental representations that modules compute. That is, the information at the various intermediate stages of a module's computation is not generally available to the subject; the states of affairs represented at those stages are not thereby accessible to thought. Secondly, the final outputs of modules, which are available to central systems, are 'shallow' (1983: 86). What Fodor means by this is that the interface between modules and central systems comes relatively early. In the case of sentence-processing, for example, the output of the module might specify which sentence was uttered and it might specify the literal meaning of that sentence. But it would not specify whether the sentence was intended ironically or metaphorically—nor, more generally, what overall message the speaker was trying to communicate. The final mark is the one that Fodor describes as 'perhaps the most important aspect of modularity' (p. 37) and even as its 'essence' (p. 71). Modules are *informationally encapsulated*; that is, the information that is available within a module is considerably less than all the relevant information that is represented within the organism. In particular, the processes in a module do not draw on all that the subject knows or believes. The canonical illustration of informational encapsulation is provided by visual illusions. In the Müller-Lyer illusion, even though I know perfectly well that the two lines are the same length, perception still presents one line as longer.

Fodor's modularity thesis has a positive part and a negative part. Input systems exhibit the marks of modularity; central systems do not. Arguments about the positive part mainly concern the claim that input systems are informationally encapsulated. Defence of that claim is facilitated by the idea that the outputs of an input system are shallow, so that the interface between input systems and central systems comes relatively early. It is more challenging when we bring other ideas to the foreground. Thus, for example, it was part of the initial picture that input systems represent worldly states of affairs so as to make them accessible to thought. Indeed, Fodor says (1983: 136 n. 31): 'It seems to me that we want a notion of perceptual process that makes the deliverances of perception available as the premises of *conscious* decisions and inferences.' These ideas favour the assignment of more, rather than less, processing to input systems, with the interface between input systems and central systems coming correspondingly later.

So long as the negative part of Fodor's modularity thesis is not called into question, arguments about the positive part can be regarded as revealing conflicting pressures on the location of the interface between modules—conceived as informationally encapsulated input systems—and central systems. But, in fact, the negative part of the thesis has been called into question.

7.2 Central Systems and the Limits of Modularity

One of the marks of modularity is domain specificity, and it is natural to think of modules as solving problems of specific types: What kind of object is this? Whose face is this? What word is this? What sentence, with what structural description, is this? If a type of problem is solved by a module, then there is a mechanical procedure—an algorithm—for solving problems of that type. More accurately, there is an empirically feasible mechanical procedure for solving problems of that type tolerably well (no less well than the module solves them). The other side of the modularity coin is that, if there is no empirically feasible mechanical procedure for solving problems of some particular type, then problems of that type must be solved by the central systems if they are solved at all.

Fodor suggests that we think about fixation of beliefs by analogy with the process of confirmation of hypotheses in science and he points to two features of hypothesis confirmation. First, confirmation is *isotropic* (1983: 105): 'the facts relevant to the confirmation of a scientific hypothesis may be drawn from anywhere in the field of previously established empirical (or, of course, demonstrative) truths'. Secondly, confirmation is *Quinean* (p. 107): 'the degree of confirmation assigned to any given hypothesis is sensitive to properties of the entire belief system'. If Fodor is right about the analogy between belief fixation in individual thinkers and hypothesis confirmation in science, then it seems clear that the processes of belief fixation cannot be informationally encapsulated and that there is no mechanical procedure for deciding what to believe.

If belief fixation cannot be the business of a module, then, given the taxonomy of cognitive mechanisms that is the background to Fodor's modularity thesis, solving the problem of what to believe must be done by the central systems. But the same features that make belief fixation ill-suited to modularity also make it extremely difficult to understand and, in particular, difficult to understand in terms of the computational theory of mind. More generally, according to Fodor, the prospects for an empirically feasible computational theory of central cognitive processes are dim (1983: 107): 'the more global (e.g. the more isotropic) a cognitive process is, the less anybody understands it. *Very* global processes, like analogical reasoning, aren't understood at all.'

The overall situation appears to be this. The arguments for syntactically structured representations are particularly compelling in the case of thoughts (Section 5). Syntactic structure and tacit knowledge of rules are made for each other and the computational theory of mind is the result of bringing them together (Section 6). Yet the application of the computational theory of mind in the domain of thought is problematic. *Modus ponens* inferences fit the computational theory well enough; but inference to the best explanation fits the theory less well, perhaps even to the point of intractability.

The limitations of the computational theory of mind have been a recurrent theme in Fodor's work, at least since the final chapter of *The Language of Thought*, where he says (1975: 200): 'There seem to be some glaring facts about mentation which set a bound to our ambitions.' But someone might hope to bring central cognitive processes within the scope of the computational theory of mind by rejecting the negative part of Fodor's modularity thesis and maintaining instead that the mind is modular through and through—*massively modular* (Sperber 2002). The idea would be that central cognitive processes, like input processes, are subserved by modules; not one module for thinking, one for problem-solving, one for planning, and one for belief fixation, but a host of modules, each dedicated to the solution of a particular, and perhaps quite idiosyncratic, type of problem. The task for someone wanting to make use of this idea is, of course, to show how the features of human thought that seem problematic for the computational theory of mind could emerge from a massively modular cognitive architecture.

The massive modularity hypothesis draws some support from evolutionary psychology, from examples of domain specificity in cognitive development, and from dissociations between impairments in the performance of central cognitive tasks. Fodor argues against it in *The Mind Doesn't Work That Way* (2000). I cannot review that debate here, but perhaps it is enough to note that there are serious open questions about the scope and limits of the approach to cognitive science that I have been describing.

8. MODULES AND COGNITIVE NEUROPSYCHOLOGY

Research in cognitive neuropsychology has two complementary aims. One is to use theories about normal cognitive processes to help understand disorders of cognition that result from stroke or head injury. The other is to use data from people with acquired disorders to test and further develop theories of normal cognition. This programme of research is based on a number of assumptions of which the first is that the mind is modular in the sense that there are relatively independent processing and storage components that can be selectively damaged. The second assumption is that the modular structure, or *functional architecture*, of the mind as a whole, and of the systems responsible for the performance of particular tasks, is the same for all normal (neurologically intact) subjects. Alfonso Caramazza (1986: 49) calls this the assumption of *universality*. The third assumption is that, when one component is damaged, this does not bring about massive reorganization of the prior modular structure. Rather, the undamaged components continue to operate as before, so far as this is compatible with the impaired operation of the damaged component. Caramazza (p. 52) calls this the assumption of *transparency*.

When we study normal subjects, the assumption of universality licenses the averaging of data across groups of subjects in order to assess hypotheses about the normal information-processing system. But when we study brain-damaged subjects, we cannot antecedently assume that the information-processing systems of different patients have been damaged in identical ways—even if the patients have been given the same clinical diagnosis. Rather, we reach hypotheses about damage to the normal system as putative explanations of specific patterns of impaired performance. So cognitive neuropsychology typically proceeds by the study of single cases. A series of single-case studies yields, via the assumption of transparency, multiple constraints on theories about the normal functional architecture.

8.1 The Dual-Route Theory of Reading Aloud

To see the methodology of cognitive neuropsychology at work, consider the task of reading single words aloud (Coltheart 1985). So far as this is an information-processing task, it calls for transitions from representations of orthography to representations of phonology. One way of carrying out the task would involve, for each orthographic input representation, a direct mapping to a phonological output representation, drawing on *lexical* information about the orthography and phonology of a single word. Another way would involve, for each orthographic input representation, the assembly of a phonological output representation, drawing on *non-lexical* information about regular letter–sound correspondences. The *dual-route* theory of the processes involved in mature reading aloud of single words starts from the idea of a lexical route and a non-lexical route from print to speech. In the case of regular words, both routes would deliver the same correct pronunciation. In the case of irregular words like 'PINT' or 'YACHT', the lexical route would be vital for a correct pronunciation, while in the case of pronounceable non-word letter strings like 'SLINT' or 'VIB', only the non-lexical route would deliver a pronunciation.

Since the dual-route theory of reading aloud involves two relatively autonomous processing systems, we can consider predictions about the consequences of selective damage to one route or the other. If the lexical route were damaged while the non-lexical route continued to operate unimpaired, then the predicted pattern of performance would be preserved reading of regular words and non-words but regularization errors on irregular words (for example, 'PINT' pronounced to rhyme with 'MINT'). If the non-lexical route were damaged while the lexical route continued to operate unimpaired, then the predicted pattern of performance would be preserved reading of both regular and irregular words but impaired pronunciation of non-words.

In fact, each of these patterns of performance is found in patients with acquired disorders of reading. The first is surface dyslexia; the second is phonological dyslexia. So the dual-route theory of normal reading promises to help us understand these acquired disorders. We can explain them in terms of selective damage to some components of the normal reading system while other components continue to operate as before. To the extent that these are not just good explanations of surface dyslexia and phonological dyslexia but the best explanations, the dual-route theory of reading is supported and competing theories are disconfirmed.

8.2 Double Dissociation Arguments

People with surface dyslexia and people with phonological dyslexia instantiate a *double dissociation* of reading impairments. People with surface dyslexia show impaired reading of irregular words but intact reading of non-words while people with phonological dyslexia show the reverse pattern—impaired reading of non-words but intact reading of irregular words. The dual-route theory accounts for this double dissociation of impairments in terms of damage to separate component systems or processing modules that are implicated in reading irregular words (the lexical route) and in reading non-words (the non-lexical route).

The general pattern here is that a double dissociation between impairments in the performance of two tasks supports theories that postulate separate processing modules that are responsible for, or at least distinctively implicated in, performance of those two tasks (Shallice 1988, pt. 3). Thus, for example, suppose that we find people with impaired recognition of faces but intact recognition of visually presented objects and other people with impaired recognition of visually presented objects but intact recognition of faces. This double dissociation of impairments would support theories that postulate separate modules implicated in face-processing and in visual object-processing.

Double dissociation arguments occupy a central position in the practice of cognitive neuropsychology and it is sometimes said that evidence of associations or of one-way dissociations is of less value than evidence of double dissociations. First, evidence of associations is said to be of less value than evidence of dissociations because associations of impairments might just reflect facts about neuro-anatomy. Even if separate modules are responsible for two tasks, the locations of the neural regions that subserve the tasks might make it virtually impossible for one module to be damaged while the other is spared. Secondly, evidence of one-way dissociations is said to be of less value than evidence of double dissociations because, even if two tasks are performed by a single module, damage to that system may result in performance of the more difficult task being impaired while performance of the easier task remains intact.

It is correct that arguments from associations to shared modules, or from one-way dissociations to separate modules, must address the possibility of alternative explanations of the data. And it is correct that these particular kinds of alternative explanation are not clearly available in the case of double dissociations. But none of this should be allowed to obscure the fact that double dissociation arguments, like arguments throughout normal science, are abductive. They work by inference to the best explanation (Coltheart and Davies 2003).

9. The Challenge from Connectionism

While the basic ideas behind connectionist models of cognitive processes have a long history, contemporary research on connectionist, parallel distributed processing, or neural network models owes much to the appearance in 1986 of two major volumes by David Rumelhart, Jay McClelland, and the PDP Research Group.

Connectionist modelling of cognitive processes has captured the imagination of both cognitive scientists and philosophers at least in part because it seems to support many different challenges to the dominant classical approach to cognitive science. Because connectionist networks are 'brainlike', they seem to enjoy an advantage of plausibility over classical information-processing systems. Because networks are said to work without syntactically structured representations or tacitly known rules, connectionism seems to favour an alternative to the computational theory of mind. Because networks 'learn', connectionism seems to offer support to those who reject nativism. Because networks without modular architectures are said to show double dissociations of impairments after damage, connectionism seems to undermine the methodology of cognitive neuropsychology.

9.1 Units, Connections, and the Brain

The formal or numerical description of a connectionist network speaks of units and of connections between units. Each unit has a level of activation between zero and one; each connection has a weight that can be any real number, positive or negative. The level of activation of an individual unit is determined by an activation function given the input that the unit receives as a result of activation at units that are connected to it and the weights on those connections. In most connectionist networks, units are organized into layers: a layer of input units and a layer of output units with one or more layers of hidden units in between. Suppose that we impose a pattern of activation on the input units of a layered network. Given the activation function and the weights on the connections, this determines a pattern of activation over the hidden units and that in turn determines a pattern of activation over the output units.

The basic ideas of connectionism are neurally inspired, with units and their activation levels, connections and their weights being simplified analogues of neurons and their firing rates, synapses and their strengths. It is sometimes suggested that, for this reason, connectionist cognitive science enjoys an advantage of plausibility over the classical approach to information-processing. But here we need to consider two kinds of case. First, some connectionist networks are offered as models of the operation of real populations of neurons—for example, in the hippocampus (Rolls 1989) or in the parietal cortex (Pouget and Sejnowski 2001). There is a great deal of important and illuminating work here at the neurobiological level, where there is an intimate relationship between representation and algorithm, on the one hand, and physical realization, on the other.

But, secondly, in the case of many connectionist models of cognitive processes there is no suggestion that the units and connections in the models correspond to real neurons and synapses (Smolensky 1988: 3). These models belong at a level of description that presumably supervenes on the neurobiological and, ultimately, on the fundamental physical. But it is not clear why, as putative descriptions of cognitive processes, they should be reckoned more plausible for being 'brainlike'.

9.2 Representations, Rules, and Learning

In connectionist networks, patterns of activation over units are the vehicles of representation. For any given pattern of activation considered as a representation, the property of containing a particular sub-pattern of activation is an intrinsic and causally potent property. But is it a syntactic property?

Consider, for example, patterns of activation that represent three-letter strings (Section 5.3). If each three-letter string is represented by an entirely separate pattern of activation, then these patterns are syntactically unstructured representations even if they are distributed over several units. If each three-letter string is represented by a pattern of activation made up of separate sub-patterns representing the onset, vowel, and coda, then the patterns are syntactically structured representations with a compositional semantics. But, in between these extremes, there is a third possibility. The patterns of activation representing three-letter strings beginning with 'B', for example, might not have a sub-pattern strictly in common, yet might still be similar. In this case, it can be at most approximately true that the representations of three-letter strings are syntactically structured (Smolensky 1988: 16–17).

Rumelhart and McClelland (1986: 218) suggest that connectionist networks 'may provide a mechanism sufficient to capture lawful behavior, without requiring the postulation of explicit but inaccessible rules'. The intended contrast here is with tacitly known rules that are inaccessible to consciousness but are *explicit* in the sense that they are represented in a format with syntactic structure and stored in a way that requires additional processes of search and access before the knowledge can be used. In the case of connectionist networks, rules are not explicit in this sense, for knowledge is stored in the weights on connections.

Now, it is true that classical cognitive science does, at least sometimes, postulate rules that are explicit in the sense that is relevant here. But the notion of tacit knowledge explained earlier (Section 4.3) does not require explicitness. It allows that tacit knowledge of a rule might be directly embodied in a processing mechanism. So far, then, there is no reason why a connectionist network should not embody tacit knowledge of rules. But the general connection between tacit knowledge of rules and syntactically structured input representations ensures that, if it is at most approximately true that the input representations are syntactically structured, then it can be at most approximately true that the network embodies tacit knowledge of rules.

Paul Smolensky (1988: 11) says that the reason for the departure from syntactic structure is a 'dimensional shift' between the concepts used in a classical task analysis and the semantics of individual units in the network. But there is nothing about connectionist modelling as such that requires schemes of input representations that are so obliquely related to a classical description of the task domain. And, where there is no dimensional shift, there is no reason of principle why a network should not embody tacit knowledge of rules that are cast in the same terms that figure in a classical task analysis. Thus suppose that a connectionist model of reading aloud makes use of input representations with syntactic properties (sub-patterns of activation) that are correlated with representation of individual letters. Then we can intelligibly ask whether the model generates pronunciations of regular words and pronounceable non-words by drawing on regular letter–sound rules, and the fact that the model is a connectionist one does not, by itself, rule out the possibility that the answer to the question might be affirmative.

In connectionist networks, patterns of activation over units are relatively transitory vehicles of input and output representations. More abiding knowledge about the task domain is embodied in weights on the connections. Networks are said to 'learn' in the sense that there are algorithms for adjusting the weights on connections in order to bring input–output performance more closely into conformity with a training set of input–output pairs. A network's progress through the epochs of a training regime is sometimes taken as a model of a process of cognitive development (Rumelhart and McClelland 1986). But the idea of algorithms for extracting from a training set information about patterns or regularities is not exclusive to connectionism. There is a body of classical cognitive scientific research on rule induction and there are studies comparing the performance of classical algorithms and algorithms used for training connectionist networks (McLaughlin and

Warfield 1994). Connectionism does not offer any special support to those who reject nativism.

9.3 Modularity and Dissociations in Networks

Connectionist cognitive science is not opposed to the generic idea of modularity. But the way in which knowledge is stored in the weights on connections opens up the possibility that there may be less modularity in a network than we might expect given a classical analysis of the task.

In an influential paper William Ramsey, Stephen Stich, and Joseph Garon (1990) investigate the way in which a simple feedforward network might depart from *propositional modularity*, which is the claim that (p. 504) 'propositional attitudes are *functionally discrete, semantically interpretable*, states that play a *causal role* in the production of other attitudes, and ultimately in the production of behavior'. A network was trained by back-propagation of error to generate as output the correct verdict ('yes' or 'no') on each of sixteen propositions, such as 'Dogs have fur' and 'Cats have gills', that were encoded by patterns of activation across the input units. Knowledge of the verdicts on all sixteen propositions was embodied in the weights on the connections in the network. But there were not sixteen separate processing mechanisms responsible for the sixteen input–output transitions.

In a similar way, there are connectionist models of reading aloud that do not incorporate the modularity to which the dual-route theory is committed. In these models, there are not two separate processing mechanisms corresponding to the lexical route and the non-lexical route. Rather, after the network has been trained on about 3,000 monosyllabic words, the weights on the connections are responsible for producing pronunciations for regular words, irregular words, and pronounceable non-words (Plaut *et al.* 1996).

Because connectionist models often exhibit less modularity than their classical counterparts, it is natural to suppose that they may face special challenges from evidence of double dissociations. So, when a network performs two cognitive tasks without containing two separate processing mechanisms, it is important to investigate whether damaging (or 'lesioning') the network can result in a double dissociation of impairments.

One possibility is that, while there are not two component modules or two routes from input to output, the performance of one task depends more heavily on one aspect of the network while the performance of the other task depends more heavily on some other aspect. In such a case, it may be that a double dissociation of impairments can be produced by damaging the network in two different ways; for example, damage to some connections versus damage to other connections (Plaut 1995).

Suppose, however, that there is no principled way of damaging the network so as to produce a double dissociation and that the typical result of damage is impaired performance of both tasks. Then—a second possibility—there may still be sufficient variability in the exact levels of performance of the two tasks so that, if the network is damaged many thousands of times, particular patterns of impairment and sparing that instantiate a double dissociation may occur (Juola and Plunkett 2000).

In these ways and others, connectionist cognitive science may offer putative explanations of double dissociations of impairments without postulating separate processing mechanisms that are distinctively implicated in normal performance of the two tasks. These alternative explanations are candidates for being the best explanation and they confront the totality of relevant evidence alongside the putative explanation that appeals to separate modules. But it does not follow that connectionism has somehow revealed that 'double dissociations don't mean much' (Juola and Plunkett 2000). No evidence ever constitutes a logical guarantee of the truth of the theory that correctly explains it (Coltheart and Davies 2003).

In a review of work on the cognitive neuropsychology of language, Mark Seidenberg says (1988: 405): 'One of the main characteristics of the cognitive neuropsychological approach as it has evolved over the past few years . . . is that very little attention is devoted to specifying the kinds of knowledge representations and processing mechanisms involved.' Seidenberg's complaint here is that many models of cognitive processes are presented as box-and-arrow diagrams, with very little detail about either algorithm or representational format. Such models are not explicit enough to be implemented as computer programs and in this respect they compare unfavourably with connectionist models.

But clearly, explicitness and implementation need not be exclusively associated with connectionist cognitive science. Max Coltheart and his colleagues have developed an implemented version of the classical dual-route model of reading aloud, and they list twenty-seven effects, observed in experiments with normal and brain-damaged subjects, that the model simulates (Coltheart et al. 2001). Their claim is that no other presently implemented computational model of reading aloud can match this level of success. David Plaut and his colleagues (1996) also claim advantages for their connectionist model and, of course, there are other models as well, classical, connectionist, and hybrid.

The issue between these models of reading aloud will not be settled simply by appeal to the ostensible benefits of connectionism, such as neural plausibility, departures from syntactic structure and tacitly known rules, learning, and the simulation of dissociations. Rather, to the extent that the issue is settled at all, this will be by the normal method of extended comparison of competing research programmes as they face evidence from a multitude of sources. The same goes, more generally, for the issue between classical and connectionist approaches to cognitive science.

10. Prospects for the Philosophy of Cognitive Science

This chapter has focused on foundational issues (Sections 2 and 3) and then on one approach to cognitive science, the classical computational approach involving tacitly known rules and syntactically structured representations. These are certainly important elements in analytic philosophy of cognitive science. But other elements, also important, have been neglected.

First, the classical approach to cognitive science faces challenges, not only from connectionism (Section 9), but also from neuroscientific reductionism and from approaches that draw on evolutionary psychology (Barkow *et al.* 1992), robotics (Brooks 1991), dynamic systems theory (Port and van Gelder 1995), and artificial life (Boden 1996), and, more generally, from approaches that stress the idea that cognition as we know it is an activity of minds that are both *embodied* and *embedded* in a worldly environment (Clark 1997).

Secondly, according to the view of the relationship between philosophy and cognitive science that was suggested earlier (Section 3.4), philosophical theory may reveal that our conception of ourselves as persons has built into it commitments to particular kinds of cognitive structures and processes. Empirical research in cognitive science reveals whether those commitments are met. If they are met, then we learn how an aspect of our personhood is possible (Peacocke 1992, ch. 7). If they are not met, then we are obliged to revise our philosophical theory or our conception of ourselves.

Given this general view of the interdisciplinary relationship, we should expect that a host of relatively detailed empirical findings from specific programmes of research in cognitive science would impact on philosophical theory to enrich, refine, or even cast doubt on, aspects of our conception of ourselves as experiencing, thinking subjects and agents. Thus consider, for example, the Kantian line of thought explored by Peter Strawson (1959, ch. 2) and subsequently by Evans (1980). Our conception of the world as a world of objective particulars that exist independently of our experience of them is a conception of a spatial world. We conceive of ourselves as moving through that world so that our experience is explained jointly by the properties of objects and our location. The cognitive science of *spatial representation* helps to explain how this objective conception is possible (Eilan *et al.* 1993).

Perhaps the cognitive scientific finding that has been most discussed in philosophy is that some patients with damage to primary visual cortex (area V1), who consequently have a blind region in their visual field and who report no visual experience when stimuli are presented in that blind region, are nevertheless able to discriminate stimulus properties when they are asked to guess. This is the phenomenon of *blindsight*: 'visual capacity in a field defect in the absence of acknowledged awareness' (Weiskrantz 1986: 166). Under forced-choice conditions, a blindsight subject may be able to discriminate shape properties between X and O, movement properties between horizontal and vertical, wavelength properties between red and green (Stoerig and Cowey 1992), and even affective properties between happy and fearful faces (de Gelder *et al.* 1999).

People with *prosopagnosia* are unable to recognize and identify familiar faces. If, for example, a patient is asked to classify photographs as being of familiar or unfamiliar faces, he or she may perform at chance levels. Yet the patient's skin conductance responses may discriminate between the familiar and the unfamiliar faces. This is a kind of 'covert recognition'. A patient with prosopagnosia may be unable to classify the faces of famous people according to their occupation (for example, politician or television personality) although he can, of course, correctly assign occupations to the *names* of these people. But, in some cases, presenting the face of a television personality alongside the name of a politician or vice versa interferes with the patient's performance when asked to assign an occupation to the name, just as it does in normal subjects (Young 1998). Information about the occupation of the person whose face is presented affects performance even though it is not available for verbal report.

These neuropsychological phenomena and thought experiments based on them are important for both empirical and philosophical theories about perception and consciousness. The blindsight patient reports no visual experience of the stimulus and, despite being able reliably to guess some of its properties, is not able to make normal use of this information for reporting, reasoning, and planning. Ned Block (1995*b*) suggests that, in part because of the absence of both *phenomenal consciousness* and *access consciousness* in such cases, the two notions of consciousness are liable to be confused. But he argues that they are at least conceptually dissociable and, in particular, that we can make sense of a hypothetical 'super-blindsight' patient who is able to make free use of information about stimuli in the blind region for reporting, reasoning, and planning, yet still does not have any visual experience of those stimuli. If this is right, then, even if a satisfying explanation of access consciousness could be given in information-processing terms, this would still not be an explanation of phenomenal consciousness.

These neuropsychological phenomena also raise questions about the extent to which normal subjects are authoritative about the workings of their own minds. A normal subject would probably find it compelling to suppose that, when he sees the face of a television personality, his conscious recognition of the face interferes with his classification of a simultaneously presented name as that of a politician. Although this is likely to be correct, the fact that the same pattern of interference is found in patients who are unable to recognize faces raises an alternative possibility. It is at least conceivable that, contrary to what it is so compelling to suppose, the interference is produced in normal subjects in the same way as in people with prosopagnosia, by a process of which the subject is quite unaware (Stone and Davies 1993).

David Milner and Melvyn Goodale (1995) argue that vision has two functions, representation of the world in *perception* and control of our *action* on the world. They also argue that these two functions are subserved by different neural pathways, the *ventral* and the *dorsal* streams (see also Jacob and Jeannerod 2003). While the two visual pathways diverge from primary visual cortex, they are not affected in the same way by damage to area V1. The ventral stream (vision for perception) depends almost totally on V1 for its inputs and so a patient with damage to V1 has a perceptual deficit. But cortical sites along the dorsal stream (vision for action) continue to receive visual information from subcortical structures and so some visual control of action may be preserved even in the absence of visual perception. Milner and Goodale suggest that the blindsight patient's responses may be explained in terms of cues that are provided by activity in mechanisms of visuo-motor control. On this account, blindsight is not perception without awareness but action without perception.

Impairments to the two functions of vision dissociate in both directions in patients with damage to one or the other visual pathway. But a mismatch between visual perception and visually controlled action can also be found in normal subjects who experience visual *illusions* that relate to the relative sizes of objects. It can happen, for example, that two objects are really the same size, one looks larger, yet a subject reaches towards and grasps the objects in just the same way, with a grip aperture that is appropriate to the real size of the objects. It can also happen that two objects are really different sizes, they look the same, yet a subject reaches differently—once again, with a grip aperture that is appropriate to the real size. This finding places some constraints on philosophical theories about representation and, particularly, about the non-conceptualized representational content of perceptual experiences (Peacocke 2001). It is not obvious how to construct a theory of perceptual representation that is adequate to cases in which how the object really is (on the input side) and how the object is acted on (on the output side) are in harmony with each other, but there is a mismatch between both and the way that the object is perceived to be (Clark 2001).

People with *unilateral visual neglect* fail to report visually presented stimuli on one side of space (usually the left side of space, following damage to the right hemisphere of the brain). When John Marshall and Peter Halligan (1988) asked a neglect patient to classify pairs of line drawings as same or different, she said that two drawings of a house, in one of which the left side of the house was on fire, were identical. But when, under forced-choice conditions, she was asked which house she would rather live in, she reliably chose the house that was not burning. Here there is a pattern similar to that in blindsight and in prosopagnosia with covert recognition. There is evidence that information is affecting the subject's performance even though the subject is unable to use that information normally for reporting, reasoning, and planning. For this reason, blindsight and neglect are sometimes run together in philosophical discussion.

But unilateral neglect patients are not blind. Their problem is not primarily visual but, at least in part, *attentional* (Vallar 1998; Aimola Davies 2004). Their deficit is not so much in perception as in exploration. The difference between unilateral neglect and blindsight becomes vivid when we consider another experiment using pictures. When neglect patients are asked to copy line drawings, they typically produce a picture that is incomplete on the left side. When neglect patients are asked to identify and copy a drawing of a house with flames coming from the left side they identify the drawing as simply of a house and produce a picture from which left-side details, including the flames, are omitted. But when they are shown a picture of an object that can only be identified by the information on the left (e.g. a toothbrush or a garden rake with its head towards the left) at least some of the patients identify the object correctly and produce a picture with all the left-side details intact (Maguire 2000).

Some people with unilateral neglect also have bizarrely false beliefs. Some deny ownership of a limb on the neglected side. Some claim to be able to move a limb that, in reality, is paralysed as a result of their brain damage. These are *delusions*: false beliefs that are firmly maintained despite their massive implausibility in the light of evidence that is available to the subject (Stone and Young 1997; Davies *et al.* 2001). Although there are countless further points at which cognitive scientific research impacts on philosophical theory, this will be my final example. The points of contact in this case include the relationship between experience and belief and the idea that attribution of beliefs is subject to some kind of rationality constraint.

Delusions occur, not only in neglect patients, but also in other cases of brain damage and in people with schizophrenia. The delusion that is most familiar in the philosophical literature is the *Capgras delusion*, in which the subject maintains that a close relative (often the spouse) has been replaced by an impostor. Hadyn Ellis and Andy Young (1990) suggest that the Capgras delusion can be explained, at least in part, in terms of a neuropsychological impairment that is the mirror image of prosopagnosia with covert recognition. The subject recognizes the presented face as looking just like the face of the spouse, but the affective response, and so the skin conductance response, that would usually accompany perception of a familiar face is absent, and so something seems wrong. The delusional belief is an attempt to make sense of this conflict. The problem with this explanation of the delusion is, of course, that there are much more plausible ways for the subject to make sense of this anomalous experience of the spouse's face. So it seems that we need to appeal to some *second factor* in the aetiology of the delusion—some impairment in the systems responsible for adopting and revising beliefs. But it is difficult to say anything illuminating about the cognitive or computational nature of this second factor—and this is hardly surprising if we do not understand the processes of normal belief fixation (Section 7.2).

References

Aimola Davies, A. M. (2004). 'Disorders of Spatial Orientation and Awareness', in J. Ponsford (ed.), *Cognitive and Behavioral Rehabilitation: From Neurobiology to Clinical Practice*. New York: Guilford Press.

Baker, G. P., and Hacker, P. M. S. (1984). *Language, Sense and Nonsense: A Critical Investigation into Modern Theories of Language*. Oxford: Blackwell.

Barkow, J. H., Cosmides, L., and Tooby, J. (eds.) (1992). *The Adapted Mind: Evolutionary Psychology and the Generation of Culture*. Oxford: Oxford University Press.

Block, N. (1995*a*). 'The Mind as the Software of the Brain', in E. E. Smith and D. N. Osherson (eds.), *An Invitation to Cognitive Science*, iii: *Thinking*, 2nd edn. Cambridge, Mass.: MIT Press.

—— (1995*b*). 'On a Confusion About a Function of Consciousness'. *Behavioral and Brain Sciences*, 18: 227–47.

Boden, M. (ed.) (1996). *The Philosophy of Artificial Life*. Oxford: Oxford University Press.

Brooks, R. A. (1991). 'Intelligence without Representation'. *Artificial Intelligence Journal*, 47: 139–59.

Caramazza, A. (1986). 'On Drawing Inferences About the Structure of Normal Cognitive Systems from the Analysis of Patterns of Impaired Performance: The Case for Single-Patient Studies'. *Brain and Cognition*, 5: 41–66.

Carruthers, P. (1996). *Language, Thought and Consciousness*. Cambridge: Cambridge University Press.

Chomsky, N. (1965). *Aspects of the Theory of Syntax*. Cambridge, Mass.: MIT Press.

—— (1986). *Knowledge of Language: Its Nature, Origin, and Use*. New York: Praeger.

—— (1995). *The Minimalist Program*. Cambridge, Mass.: MIT Press.

—— (2000). *New Horizons in the Study of Language and Mind*. Cambridge: Cambridge University Press.

Clark, A. (1997). *Being There: Putting Brain, Body, and World Together Again*. Cambridge, Mass.: MIT Press.

—— (2001). 'Visual Experience and Motor Action: Are the Bonds too Tight?' *Philosophical Review*, 110: 495–519.

Coltheart, M. (1985). 'Cognitive Neuropsychology and the Study of Reading', in M. I. Posner and O. S. M. Marin (eds.), *Attention and Performance XI*. Hillsdale, NJ: Lawrence Erlbaum Associates.

—— and Davies, M. (2003). 'Inference and Explanation in Cognitive Neuropsychology'. *Cortex*, 39: 188–91.

—— Rastle, K., Perry, C., Langdon, R., and Ziegler, J. (2000). 'DRC: A Dual Route Cascaded Model of Visual Word Recognition and Reading Aloud'. *Psychological Review*, 108: 204–56.

Davies, M. (1991). 'Concepts, Connectionism, and the Language of Thought', in W. Ramsey, S. Stich, and D. Rumelhart (eds.), *Philosophy and Connectionist Theory*. Hillsdale, NJ: Lawrence Erlbaum Associates.

—— Coltheart, M., Langdon, R., and Breen, N. (2001). 'Monothematic Delusions: Towards a Two-Factor Account'. *Philosophy, Psychiatry and Psychology*, 8: 133–58.

de Gelder, B., Vroomen, J., Pourtois, G., and Weiskrantz, L. (1999). 'Non-Conscious Recognition of Affect in the Absence of Striate Cortex'. *NeuroReport*, 10: 3759–63.

Dennett, D. C. (1969). *Content and Consciousness*. London: Routledge & Kegan Paul.

Dennett, D. C. (1978). 'Artificial Intelligence as Philosophy and as Psychology', in Dennett, *Brainstorms: Philosophical Essays on Mind and Psychology*. Brighton: Harvester Press.

Dretske, F. (1986). 'Misrepresentation', in R. J. Bogdan (ed.), *Belief: Form, Content and Function*. Oxford: Oxford University Press.

Eilan, N., McCarthy, R., and Brewer, B. (eds.) (1993). *Spatial Representation: Problems in Philosophy and Psychology*. Oxford: Blackwell.

Ellis, H. D., and Young, A. W. (1990). 'Accounting for Delusional Misidentifications'. *British Journal of Psychiatry*, 157: 239–48.

Evans, G. (1980). 'Things without the Mind: A Commentary upon Chapter Two of Strawson's *Individuals*', in Z. van Straaten (ed.), *Philosophical Subjects*. Oxford: Oxford University Press. Repr. in Evans, *Collected Papers*. Oxford: Oxford University Press, 1985.

—— (1981). 'Semantic Theory and Tacit Knowledge', in S. Holtzmann and C. Leich (eds.), *Wittgenstein: To Follow a Rule*. London: Routledge & Kegan Paul. Repr. in Evans, *Collected Papers*. Oxford: Oxford University Press, 1985.

Fodor, J. A. (1968). *Psychological Explanation: An Introduction to the Philosophy of Psychology*. New York: Random House.

—— (1975). *The Language of Thought*. New York: Crowell.

—— (1983). *The Modularity of Mind*. Cambridge, Mass.: MIT Press.

—— (1987). *Psychosemantics: The Problem of Meaning in the Philosophy of Mind*. Cambridge, Mass.: MIT Press.

—— (2000). *The Mind Doesn't Work That Way*. Cambridge, Mass.: MIT Press.

Gardner, H. (1985). *The Mind's New Science: A History of the Cognitive Revolution*. New York: Basic Books.

Jackson, F., and Pettit, P. (1988). 'Functionalism and Broad Content'. *Mind*, 97: 381–400.

Jacob, P., and Jeannerod, M. (2003). *Ways of Seeing: The Scope and Limits of Visual Cognition*. Oxford: Oxford University Press.

Juola, P., and Plunkett, K. (2000). 'Why Double Dissociations Don't Mean Much', in G. Cohen, R. A. Johnston, and K. Plunkett (eds.), *Exploring Cognition: Damaged Brains and Neural Networks: Readings in Cognitive Neuropsychology and Connectionist Modelling*. Hove: Psychology Press.

Kripke, S. A. (1982). *Wittgenstein on Rules and Private Language*. Oxford: Blackwell.

McClelland, J. L., Rumelhart, D. E., and the PDP Research Group (1986). *Parallel Distributed Processing: Explorations in the Microstructure of Cognition*, ii: *Psychological and Biological Models*. Cambridge, Mass.: MIT Press.

McLaughlin, B. P., and Warfield, T. A. (1994). 'The Allure of Connectionism Reexamined'. *Synthese*, 101: 365–400.

Maguire, A. M. (2000). 'Reducing Neglect by Introducing Ipsilesional Global Cues'. *Brain and Cognition*, 43: 328–32.

Marr, D. (1982). *Vision*. New York: W. H. Freeman.

Marshall, J. C., and Halligan, P. W. (1988). 'Blindsight and Insight in Visuo-Spatial Neglect'. *Nature*, 336: 766–7.

Miller, G. A. (2003). 'The Cognitive Revolution: A Historical Perspective'. *Trends in Cognitive Sciences*, 7: 141–4.

Milner, A. D., and Goodale, M. A. (1995). *The Visual Brain in Action*. Oxford: Oxford University Press.

Peacocke, C. (1992). *A Study of Concepts*. Cambridge, Mass.: MIT Press.

—— (2001). 'Does Perception Have a Nonconceptual Content?' *Journal of Philosophy*, 98: 239–64.

Plaut, D. C. (1995). 'Double Dissociation without Modularity: Evidence from Connectionist Neuropsychology'. *Journal of Clinical and Experimental Neuropsychology*, 17: 291–321.

—— McClelland, J. L., Seidenberg, M. S., and Patterson, K. (1996). 'Understanding Normal and Impaired Word Reading: Computational Principles in Quasi-Regular Domains'. *Psychological Review*, 103: 56–115.

Port, R. F., and van Gelder, T. (eds.) (1995). *Mind as Motion: Explorations in the Dynamics of Cognition*. Cambridge, Mass.: MIT Press.

Pouget, A., and Sejnowski, T. J. (2001). 'Simulating a Lesion in a Basis Function Model of Spatial Representations: Comparison with Hemineglect'. *Psychological Review*, 108: 653–73.

Quine, W.V. (1972). 'Methodological Reflections on Current Linguistic Theory', in D. Davidson and G. Harman (eds.), *Semantics of Natural Language*. Dordrecht: Reidel. Repr. in G. Harman (ed.), *On Noam Chomsky: Critical Essays*. New York: Anchor Press and Doubleday, 1974.

Ramsey, W., Stich, S., and Garon, J. (1990). 'Connectionism, Eliminativism and the Future of Folk Psychology', in J. E. Tomberlin (ed.), *Philosophical Perspectives*, 4: *Action Theory and Philosophy of Mind*. Atascadero, Calif.: Ridgeview.

Rolls, E. T. (1989). 'Parallel Distributed Processing in the Brain: Implications of the Functional Architecture of Neuronal Networks in the Hippocampus', in R. G. M. Morris (ed.), *Parallel Distributed Processing: Implications for Psychology and Neurobiology*. Oxford: Oxford University Press.

Rumelhart, D. E., and McClelland, J. L. (1986). 'On Learning the Past Tenses of English Verbs', in D. E. Rumelhart, J. L. McClelland, and the PDP Research Group, *Parallel Distributed Processing: Explorations in the Microstructure of Cognition*, i: *Foundations*. Cambridge, Mass.: MIT Press.

—— —— and the PDP Research Group (1986). *Parallel Distributed Processing: Explorations in the Microstructure of Cognition*, i: *Foundations*. Cambridge, Mass.: MIT Press.

Searle, J. R. (1990). 'Consciousness, Explanatory Inversion, and Cognitive Science'. *Behavioral and Brain Sciences*, 13: 585–96.

Seidenberg, M. S. (1988). 'Cognitive Neuropsychology and Language: The State of the Art'. *Cognitive Neuropsychology*, 5: 403–26.

Shallice, T. (1988). *From Neuropsychology to Mental Structure*. Cambridge: Cambridge University Press.

Smolensky, P. (1988). 'On the Proper Treatment of Connectionism'. *Behavioral and Brain Sciences*, 11: 1–23.

Sperber, D. (2002). 'In Defense of Massive Modularity', in I. Dupoux (ed.), *Language, Brain and Cognitive Development: Essays in Honor of Jacques Mehler*. Cambridge, Mass.: MIT Press.

Stich, S. (1978). 'Beliefs and Subdoxastic States'. *Philosophy of Science*, 45: 499–518.

—— and Warfield, T. A. (eds.) (1994). *Mental Representation: A Reader*. Oxford: Blackwell.

Stoerig, P., and Cowey, A. (1992). 'Wavelength Sensitivity in Blindsight'. *Brain*, 115: 425–44.

Stone, T., and Davies, M. (1993). 'Cognitive Neuropsychology and the Philosophy of Mind'. *British Journal for the Philosophy of Science*, 44: 589–622.

—— and Young, A. W. (1997). 'Delusions and Brain Injury: The Philosophy and Psychology of Belief'. *Mind and Language*, 12: 327–64.

Strawson, P. F. (1959). *Individuals: An Essay in Descriptive Metaphysics*. London: Methuen.

Vallar, G. (1998). 'Spatial Hemineglect in Humans'. *Trends in Cognitive Sciences*, 2: 87–97.

Weiskrantz, L. (1986). *Blindsight: A Case Study and Implications*. Oxford: Oxford University Press.

Wittgenstein, L. (1953). *Philosophical Investigations*. Oxford: Blackwell.

Young, A. W. (1998). *Face and Mind*. Oxford: Oxford University Press.

PART IV

PHILOSOPHY OF LANGUAGE

CHAPTER 15

REFERENCE AND DESCRIPTION

SCOTT SOAMES

1. THE REVOLT AGAINST DESCRIPTIVISM

1.1 Names

The modern discussion of reference begins with a revolt, led by Saul Kripke, against theories of the meaning and reference of proper names inspired by Gottlob Frege (1970) and Bertrand Russell (1905). In 'Naming and Necessity' (1980) Kripke attacked both the view that the meanings (semantic contents) of names are given by descriptions associated with them by speakers, and the view that their referents are determined (as a matter of linguistic rule) to be the objects that satisfy such descriptions. The view about reference is taken to follow from the view about meaning, but not vice versa. Thus, all of Kripke's arguments against descriptive theories of reference are also arguments against descriptive theories of meaning, but some arguments against the latter do not apply to the former.

We begin with these arguments. Let n be a proper name, D be a description or family of descriptions associated with n by speakers, and ... D^* ... be a sentence that arises from ... n ... by replacing one or more occurrences of n with D^*. When D is a description we let $D^* = D$, when D is a family of descriptions $D_1 ... D_k$, we let D^* be the complex description *the thing of which most, or a sufficient number, of the claims: it is D_1 ... it is D_k are true*. Kripke attacks the following corollaries of descriptivism about the meanings of names.

C. Since the semantic content of (proposition expressed by)...*n*...(as used by s in context C) is the semantic content of (proposition expressed by)...*D**...(as used by s in C),

   M. ...*n*...is true w.r.t. s, C, and a possible world-state w iff...*D**...is true w.r.t. C, and w. Since

   (i) *If D* exists, then D* is D**

      is a necessary truth,

   (ii) *If n exists, then n is D**

      is also necessary;

E. anyone who knows/believes the proposition expressed by...*n*... (w.r.t. C) knows/believes the proposition expressed by...*D**...(w.r.t. C), and the ascriptions **Ralph knows/believes that n is F** and **Ralph knows/believes that D* is F** (as used by s in C) agree in truth-value. Since the proposition expressed by (ii) is the same as the proposition expressed by (i), it is knowable a priori, and the claim, **It is knowable a priori that if n exists, then n is D*** is true.

Kripke's argument against M is known as *the modal argument*. Here is a particular version of it. Consider the name *Aristotle*, and the descriptions *the greatest student of Plato*, *the founder of formal logic*, and *the teacher of Alexander the Great* that many of us associate with it. Although Aristotle satisfies these descriptions,

(1) *If Aristotle existed, then Aristotle was D**

is not a necessary truth, where D^* is either any description in this family, or the complicated description *the individual of whom most, or a sufficient number, of the claims:...are true* constructed from the family. On the contrary, Aristotle could have existed without doing any of the things for which he is known; he could have moved to another city as a child, failed to go into philosophy, and never been heard from again. When evaluated at such a possible scenario the antecedent of (1) is true, while the consequent is false. Since (1) is false in this scenario, it is not necessary truth, which means that this family of descriptions doesn't give the meaning of *Aristotle*. According to Kripke, this is no accident; there is, he suggests, no family D_A of descriptions such that (i) the referent of *Aristotle* is the unique individual who satisfies most, or a sufficient number, of the descriptions in D_A, (ii) ordinary speakers associate D_A with *Aristotle*, believing its referent to be the unique individual who satisfies most, or a sufficient number, of D_A's members, and (iii) (1) expresses a necessary truth when D^* is the complicated description constructed from D_A. If this is right, then M is false, and names are not synonymous with descriptions associated with them by speakers.

The key point in the argument is Kripke's conviction that there was an individual x (Aristotle) such that a sentence *Aristotle was F* is true at an arbitrary world-state w iff at w, x had the property expressed by F. Otherwise put, there was a unique individual x such that for any predicate F and world-state w, the proposition we actually use **Aristotle was F** to express would have been true if the world were in w iff were the world in w, x would have had the property (actually) expressed by F. This is the basis of his doctrine that *Aristotle* is a **rigid designator**.

> *Definition of rigidity.* A singular term t is a rigid designator of an object o iff t designates o in all worlds in which o exists, and t never designates anything else.

> *Intuitive test for rigidity.* A singular term t is a rigid designator iff **the individual who is t could not have existed without being t, and no one who is not the individual who is t could have been t** is true; otherwise t is non-rigid.

Using the notion of rigidity, we can state the general form of the modal argument.

The general version of the modal argument
  (i) Proper names are rigid designators.
 (ii) If a description D gives the meaning (content) of a term t, then D is rigid iff t is.
(iii) So, the meanings or contents of proper names are not given by non-rigid descriptions.

Since the descriptions we have been considering are non-rigid, the meaning of *Aristotle* is not given by them. In *Naming and Necessity,* Kripke leaves the modal argument there, concluding that there are no meaning-giving descriptions associated with names by speakers. In so doing, he appears, tacitly, to assume that the only candidates for being meaning-giving descriptions are non-rigid. Though understandable, this assumption is not beyond question, and will be revisited later. Kripke's epistemological argument against E may be reconstructed as follows:

The epistemological argument

  (i) When D* is a description concerning well-known characteristics of the referent of an ordinary name n, it is not the case (i) that one knows or believes the proposition expressed by **n is F** iff one knows or believes the proposition expressed by **D* is F**, (ii) that **Ralph knows/believes that n is F** and **Ralph knows/believes that D* is F** invariably agree in truth-value, (iii) that the proposition expressed by **If n exists, then n is D*** is knowable a priori, or (iv) that **It is knowable a priori that if n exists, then n is D*** is true.
 (ii) So, descriptions concerning well-known characteristics of the referents of ordinary names do not give their meanings (semantic contents).
(iii) Since these are the descriptions standardly associated with names by speakers, E is false, and the meanings of names are not given by descriptions speakers associate with them.

Two features of the argument stand out. First, it tacitly assumes that if n meant the same as D*, then **Ralph believes, knows, or knows a priori that n is F** would have the same truth-value as **Ralph believes, knows, or knows a priori that D* is F**. Although a case can be made that Kripke did tacitly assume this, the theoretical basis for this assumption goes beyond what he explicitly stated. Secondly, the argument form is general, and need not be limited to claims about a priori knowledge, or even to claims about knowledge and belief, as opposed to other attitudes. The point is to show that the proposition expressed by **n is F** is different from the proposition expressed by **D is F**. This is done by showing that a person can bear a certain attitude to one of these propositions without bearing it to the other. Although the relation one bears to a proposition when one knows it a priori is useful for making this point, it is not the only such relation to which one might appeal.

We now turn to Kripke's reason for accepting premiss (i). His text is replete with thought experiments supporting it, one of them being the famous Gödel–Schmidt example, concerning the origins of Gödel's famous incompleteness theorem (Kripke 1980: 83–4). Kripke imagines our belief that Gödel discovered the incompleteness theorem being proven false by historical scholarship that reveals that he stole it from Schmidt. Of course, Kripke is not saying that any such thing really happened, or even that we don't know that it didn't. The point is that we don't know this a priori. By contrast, we do know a priori that the discoverer of the incompleteness of arithmetic discovered the incompleteness of arithmetic (if anyone did). So, the proposition expressed by *Gödel discovered the incompleteness of arithmetic (if anyone did)* is not the same as the proposition expressed by *The discoverer of the incompleteness of arithmetic discovered the incompleteness of arithmetic (if anyone did)*, and the description does not give the meaning of the name *Gödel* for us—no matter how central attribution of the theorem to Gödel is to our beliefs about him. Kripke takes this point to extend to other descriptions speakers may associate with *Gödel*, and to proper names generally. He concludes that the meanings of proper names are not given by any descriptions that pick out an individual in terms of famous achievements, or important characteristics. Given this, one is hard-pressed to see how they could be given by any descriptions at all. Kripke therefore concludes that E is false, and that names are not synonymous with descriptions.

He is, however, careful to distinguish this conclusion from one that holds that the referents of proper names are not determined, as a matter of linguistic rule, to be whatever objects satisfy the descriptions associated with them by speakers. According to this weakened version of descriptivism, descriptions associated with a name semantically fix its referent at the actual world-state, without giving its meaning. Once its referent is determined there, it is stipulated to retain that referent with respect to all other world-states; thus it is a rigid designator. Several corollaries are taken to follow. (i) The speaker has a description, or family of descriptions, D associated with n that he takes to be uniquely satisfied by some object or other.

(ii) An object o is the referent of n iff o uniquely satisfies D (or a sufficient number of the descriptions in D, if D is a family). (iii) Since the speaker knows this on the basis of semantic knowledge alone, the speaker knows on that basis that the sentence *If n exists, then n is D** expresses a truth. In sum, when D semantically fixes the reference of n, understanding n requires knowing that its reference is fixed by D. This holds even though D does not give the meaning of n.

Kripke's arguments against this version of descriptivism are known as *the semantic arguments*, which are designed to constitute counter-examples to each of its corollaries. The Gödel–Schmidt scenario is taken to provide a counter-example to both (ii) and (iii). It is a counter-example to (iii) because we don't know, simply on the basis of our linguistic competence, that the sentence *If Gödel existed, then Gödel was D** is true, when D is a description, or family of descriptions encompassing our most important knowledge of Gödel. It is a counter-example to (ii) because when one imagines a state of the world just like ours except that, unknown to speakers, Kripke's fantasy about Gödel's plagiarism is true, we take those speakers to be referring to Gödel, not Schmidt, when they use the name *Gödel*. Thus, the referent of *Gödel*, as used by those speakers, is not the individual that satisfies the descriptions they associate with it. If these arguments are correct, then description theories of the referents of names are incorrect.

There is, however, a distinction to be made. Although Kripke suggests that the meanings of names are never given by descriptions that speakers associate with them, he does allow that in rare cases the referent of a name may be semantically fixed by a description. In most normal cases, however, proper names are seen as having their referents fixed by a historical chain of reference transmission. Typically, the chain begins with an ostensive baptism in which an individual is stipulated to the bearer of a name n. Later, when n is used in conversation, new speakers encounter it for the first time and form the intention to use it with the same reference as their sources. Different speakers may, of course, come to associate different descriptions with n, but in the usual case this doesn't affect reference transmission. As a result, speakers further down the historical chain may use n to refer to its original referent o, whether or not they associate descriptions with n that uniquely denote o.

So Kripke has an alternative to descriptivist theories of reference determination. What about meaning? On his account, it would seem that the only semantic function of a name is to refer, in which case one would expect ordinary proper names to be regarded as Russellian logically proper names (without Russell's epistemological restrictions on their bearers) (for discussion of Russell's doctrine of logically proper names, see Soames 2003a, ch. 5). However, Kripke does not draw this, or any other, positive conclusion about the meanings of names, or the propositions semantically expressed by sentences containing them. Along with nearly everyone else, he recognizes that one can understand different co-referential names without knowing that they are co-referential, and certainly without judging them to have the same meaning. However, this doesn't show that they don't mean the same thing, unless one accepts the questionable principle that anyone who understands a pair of synonymous expressions must recognize them to be synonymous (or at least coextensive)—something Kripke never does. In *Naming and Necessity*, he does argue that Hesperus is Phosphorus is not knowable a priori, whereas the triviality that Hesperus is Hesperus is (for explication and criticism of Kripke's argument, see Soames 2003*b*, ch. 15). This view, together with natural assumptions about meaning, compositionality, propositions, and propositional attitude ascriptions, could be used to argue that *Hesperus* and *Phosphorus* differ in meaning, despite being co-referential. However, Kripke neither gives such an argument, nor draws such a conclusion. Moreover, he has no account of what, over and above their referents, the meanings of names might be. Finally, in 'A Puzzle About Belief' (1979) he maintains that no definite conclusions can be drawn about the meanings of names from apparent failures of substitution of co-referential names in belief ascriptions. On his view, these puzzles arise from principles of belief attribution that transcend any doctrine about the meaning of names. Hence, he resists drawing any positive conclusion about their meaning, or about the propositions semantically expressed by sentences containing them.

1.2 Natural Kind Terms

The challenge to descriptivism is not limited to proper names, having been pressed by Kripke (1980, lect. 3) and Hilary Putnam (1970, 1973, 1975) against descriptive analyses of natural kind terms like *gold, tiger, water, heat, colour, and red*. Kripke argues that, like proper names, these terms are not synonymous with descriptions associated with them by speakers; and, like names, they acquire reference in two ways. One way involves direct presentation of samples, together with the stipulation that the term is to apply to all and only instances of the unique natural kind (of a certain sort) of which nearly all members of the sample are instances; the other involves the use of a description to pick out a kind by some, usually contingent, properties. Later, when the term is passed from speaker to speaker, the way in which the reference was initially established normally doesn't matter—just as with names. As a result, speakers further down the linguistic chain may use the term to apply to instances of the kind, whether or not the descriptive properties they associate with the term really pick out its members. In addition, scientific investigation may lead to the discovery of properties that are necessary and/or sufficient for membership in the kind. According to Kripke, these discoveries are expressed in theoretical identification sentences like those in (2), which are necessary, but knowable only a posteriori.

(2*a*) Water is H_2O.
(2*b*) Lightning is electricity.

1.3 Indexicals, Quantification, and Direct Reference

Starting with lectures given by David Kaplan in 1971, and continuing with published work of Kaplan (1979, 1989) and John Perry (1977, 1979), a further challenge to descriptivism was mounted, focusing on the role of context in understanding indexicals like *I, now, today, here, actually, you, she,* and *that.* Although the referents of these terms vary from one context of utterance to another, their meanings do not. For example, to know the meanings of *I, today,* and *she* is, roughly, to know the rules in (3).

(3a) One who uses *I*—e.g. in a sentence ***I am F***—refers to oneself, and says of oneself that one 'is F'.

(3b) One who uses *today*—e.g. in a sentence ***Today is F***—refers to the day the utterance takes place, and says of that day that it 'is F'.

(3c) One who uses *she*—e.g. in a sentence ***She is F***—refers to a contextually salient female, and says of her that she 'is F'.

These rules provide two kinds of information: they tell us how the referents of indexicals depend on aspects of contexts in which they are used; and they implicitly identify the semantic contents of these terms with their referents in contexts.

In order to understand this talk of content, one must grasp Kaplan's intuitive semantic framework. Sentences express propositions, which are their semantic contents; those containing indexicals express different propositions, and so have different contents, in different contexts. Nevertheless, the meaning of a sentence is constant; it is a function from contexts to contents. Kaplan's word for this is *character.* The picture is recapitulated for subsentential expressions. For example, the character of *I* is a function that maps an arbitrary context C onto the agent (speaker) of C, which is the semantic content of *I* relative to C.

There are two anti-descriptivist implications here. First, the referents of at least some indexicals are not determined by descriptions speakers associate with them. One example from Perry (1977: 487) is Rip Van Winkle, who awakes on 20 October 1823 after sleeping for twenty years, and says, not realizing what happened, *Today is 20 October 1803.* In so doing, he speaks falsely because his use of *today* refers to the day of the context, no matter what description he may have in mind. Another example involves Kaplan's identical twins Castor and Pollux, raised in qualitatively identical environments to be molecule for molecule identical and so, presumably, to associate the same purely qualitative descriptions with the same terms (Kaplan 1989: 531). Despite this, each refers to himself, and not the other, when he uses *I.* These examples show that the referents of indexicals are not always determined by purely qualitative descriptions that speakers associate with them. Although this leaves open the possibility that some indexicals may have their referents semantically fixed by descriptions containing other indexicals, it precludes the possibility that all indexical reference is determined in this way.

The second anti-descriptivist implication is that since the semantic content of an indexical in a context is its referent, its content is not that of any description. In order to make this point, one must move beyond the formal system developed in 'On the Logic of Demonstratives' (Kaplan 1979), to the conception of structured contents that Kaplan characterizes in 'Demonstratives' (1989: 496–7) as the intuitive philosophical picture underlying his approach. On this picture, the proposition expressed by S in C is a complex encoding the syntactic structure of S, the constituents of which are (or encode) the semantic contents in C of the words and phrases in S. For example, the proposition expressed in C by a sentence *i is F* is a complex in which the property expressed by F is predicated of the referent o of the indexical i; this is the same as the singular proposition expressed by *x is F*, relative to an assignment of o to the variable "x". By contrast, the proposition expressed by ***The D is F*** in C is a complex consisting of the property expressed by F plus a complex consisting of (or encoding) the content of *the* together with the structured complex which is the semantic content in C of the descriptive phrase D. On one natural analysis, this proposition ascribes the higher-order property of being instantiated by whatever uniquely instantiates the property expressed by D to the property expressed by F.

The claim that the semantic content of an indexical relative to a context is not the same as that of any description is supported by commonplace observations about propositional attitudes. Suppose, to adapt Russell's famous example, that on some occasion in which George IV spied Walter Scott, he gave voice to his new-found conviction, saying *He [gesturing at Scott] isn't the author of Waverley*. Had this occurred, each of the following ascriptions would have been true.

(4a) The author of *Waverley*, namely Scott, is such that George IV said that he wasn't the author of *Waverley*.

(4b) George IV said that you weren't the author of *Waverley*. (said addressing Scott)

(4c) George IV said that I wasn't the author of *Waverley*. (said by Scott)

(4d) George IV said that he [pointing at Scott] wasn't the author of *Waverley*. (said by a third party in another context)

On Kaplan's picture, these reports are true because the semantic content of the sentence George IV uttered (in his context), and so the proposition he asserted, is the same as the content of the complement clauses in the reports of what he said. Whatever descriptions speakers who utter (4b,c,d) may associate with the indexicals are irrelevant to the semantic contents of the reports.

We are now ready to define the notion of a directly referential term, and contrast it with a relativized notion of rigid designation.

> *Direct reference.* A term t is directly referential iff for all contexts C and assignments A, the referent of t with respect to C and A = the content of t with respect to C and A.

Relativized rigid designation. A singular term t is a rigid designator iff for all contexts C, assignments A, world-states w, and objects o, if t refers to o with respect to C, A, and w, then t refers to o with respect to C, A, and w in all world-states w in which o exists, and t never refers to anything else with respect to C, A, and any world-state w*.

With this understanding, all directly referential singular terms are rigid designators, but not vice versa (e.g. *the square root of 25* is rigid but not directly referential). According to Kaplan, indexicals and variables are directly referential. Salmon (1986) and Soames (2002) extend this view to proper names.

Before leaving Kaplan's framework it is important to consider two indexical operators used to construct rigidified descriptions out of non-rigid descriptions. One, *dthat*, combines with a description D to form a directly referential singular term **dthat [D]** the content of which, relative to C and A, is the unique object denoted by D relative to C and A. The other, *actually,* stands for the world-state C_w of the context in a manner analogous to the way in which *now* stands for the time C_t, and *I* stands for the agent C_A, of the context. *Actually* combines with a sentence S to form a complex sentence **Actually S** the content of which in C is a proposition that predicates of C_w the property of being a world-state in which the proposition expressed by S in C is true; hence **Actually S** is true with respect to C and world-state w iff S is true with respect to C and C_w, and whenever S is true in C_w, **Actually S** is a necessary truth. The corresponding fact about descriptions is that whenever **the x: Fx** denotes a unique individual o in C_w, **the x: actually Fx** denotes o with respect to C and all possible world-states in which o exists, and never denotes anything else. Hence *actually* is a rigidifier; however, the resulting rigidified descriptions are not directly referential.

1.4 Philosophical Implications

Although it seems evident that the propositions expressed by (5) are knowable only a posteriori, it appears to be a consequence of the non-descriptive semantics of names, natural kind terms, and the actuality operator that each of these sentences expresses a necessary truth, if it is true at all.

- (5*a*) Saul Kripke ≠ David Kaplan.
- (5*b*) Lightning is electricity.
- (5*c*) If Thomas Jefferson existed, then the person who actually wrote the Declaration of Independence was Thomas Jefferson.

Since we know that (5*a*) − (5*c*) are true, it follows that they are examples of the necessary a posteriori. The best examples of the contingent a priori are sentences like (6).

(6) If someone wrote the Declaration of Independence, then the person who actually wrote the Declaration of Independence wrote something.

It follows from the semantics of *actually* plus the fact that Thomas Jefferson wrote the Declaration of Independence that (6) is false in a world-state in which Thomas Jefferson wrote nothing and someone else wrote the Declaration of Independence. Assuming that the world could have been in such a state, we conclude that (6) expresses a contingent truth. However, this truth can be known without doing empirical research. Since anyone in the actual world-state can know it to be true simply by understanding it, it would seem to be knowable a priori. On this view, then, not all necessary truths are a priori, and not all a priori truths are necessary.

2. AN ATTEMPT TO REVIVE DESCRIPTIVISM

2.1 Motivations

Despite the attack on descriptivism, some believe that the anti-descriptivists' conclusions are too extreme, and that properly modified descriptive analyses are capable of withstanding their arguments. This view is fuelled by three main factors. First is the conviction that anti-descriptivists have not adequately addressed Frege's puzzle about substitution of co-referential terms in attitude ascriptions and Russell's problem of negative existentials. There is still a widespread belief that these problems show that names cannot be directly referential. Although Kripke never asserted that they were, it is hard to see how, if his doctrines are correct, they could be anything else. According to him, the meaning of a name is never the same as that of any description, and the vast majority of names do not even have their referents semantically fixed by descriptions. If these names are so thoroughly non-descriptional, it is not clear how their meanings could be other than their referents. Consequently, one who takes that view to have been refuted by Frege and Russell will suspect that the power of Kripke's arguments must have been exaggerated, and will be motivated to find a way of modifying descriptivism that can withstand them.

The second factor motivating descriptivists is their conviction that critics like Kripke have focused on the wrong descriptions. To be sure, it will be admitted, for many speakers s and proper names or natural kind terms n, the descriptions most likely to be volunteered by s in answer to the question *To what, or to whom, do you refer when you use n?* neither give the meaning of n, nor semantically fix its reference. Often s will respond by citing what s takes to be the most well-known and important characteristics of the putative referent(s), about which s may be mistaken. However, the referents of these terms must be determined in some way, and surely, whatever way it is can be described. Thus, for each name or natural kind term n, there must be some description D that correctly picks out its referent(s)— perhaps one encapsulating Kripke's own causal-historical picture of reference transmission.

Is there any reason to believe that speakers associate D with n? Some descriptivists think so. In fact, the very success of Kripke and others in eliciting uncontroversial judgements about what names would refer to if used in various counterfactual situations has been taken to show that speakers must be implicitly guided by a descriptive theory that determines reference. For example, Frank Jackson (1998*b*: 212) argues that

if speakers can say what refers to what when various possible worlds are described to them, description theorists can identify the property associated in their minds with, for example, the word 'water': it is the disjunction of the properties that guide the speakers in each particular possible world when they say which stuff, if any, in each world counts as water. This disjunction is in their minds in the sense that they can deliver the answer for each possible world when it is described in sufficient detail, but it is implicit in the sense that the pattern that brings the various disjuncts together as part of the, possibly highly complex, disjunction may be one they cannot state.

This is a remarkable defence. If correct, it would mean that descriptive theories of reference are virtually guaranteed, a priori, to be irrefutable, since any refutation would require a clear, uncontroversial description of a possible scenario in which n referred to something o not satisfying a description putatively associated with n by speakers—whereas the very judgement that n does refer to o in this scenario would be taken by Jackson to demonstrate the existence of an implicit description in our minds that successfully determines reference, whether or not we can articulate it.

The third factor motivating a descriptivist revival involves the inability of some to see how any single proposition could be either both necessary and a posteriori, or both contingent and a priori, as anti-descriptivists maintain. How, these philosophers ask, can evidence about the actual world-state be required to establish p, if p is true in every possible state in which the world could be (including states in which no such evidence exists)? Or again, if q is contingent, then there are states that the world could be in, such that were the world in them, q would be false. But how could one possibly know without appeal to evidence that the world is not in such a state? The former worry casts doubt on the necessary a posteriori, the latter on the contingent a priori.

In addition to endorsing these sceptical worries, some descriptivists—e.g. Frank Jackson, David Chalmers, and David Lewis—adhere to antecedent philosophical commitments that make the existence of propositions that are both necessary and knowable only a posteriori impossible. One of these commitments is to metaphysical possibility as the only kind of possibility. Although these theorists recognize different metaphysically possible ways that the world could be, they reject the idea that, in addition to these, there are epistemologically possible ways that the world might be—states which, though metaphysically impossible, cannot be known by us a priori not to obtain (Chalmers 1996: 136–8; Jackson 1998a: 67–74). This restriction of epistemic possibility to metaphysical possibility renders the necessary a posteriori problematic from the start—since it precludes explaining it by citing metaphysically necessary propositions for which empirical evidence is needed to rule out metaphysically impossible, but epistemologically possible, world-states in which they are false (for an explanation along these lines, see Soames 2005b, and forthcoming). When one adds to this Lewis's (1996: 422) analysis of knowing p as having evidence that rules out all possible ways of p's being untrue, one has, in effect, defined propositions that are both necessary and knowable only a posteriori out of existence. Since, when p is a necessary truth, there are no metaphysically possible ways of its being untrue, it follows that there are no possible ways of p's being untrue at all, and hence that knowledge of p never requires empirical evidence. So, the necessary a posteriori is impossible. A different philosophical commitment that leads to the same conclusion identifies propositions with sets of metaphysically possible world-states (or functions from world-states to truth-values). On this view, there is only one necessary proposition—which is known a priori (see Stalnaker 1978, 1984; Lewis 1996: 422–3; Jackson 1998a: 71–4, 75–8). But if that is right, then the anti-descriptivist semantics that leads to the conclusion that there are necessary a posteriori propositions must be mistaken.

2.2 Strategy

The main strategy for constructing descriptive analyses of names and natural kind terms combines attempts (i) to find reference-fixing descriptions capable of withstanding Kripke's semantic arguments, (ii) to avoid the modal argument, either by rigidifying these descriptions, or by insisting that they take wide scope over modal operators in the same sentence, and (iii) to use two-dimensional semantics to avoid the epistemological argument, and explain away putative examples of the necessary a posteriori and the contingent a priori. The most popular strategy for finding reference-fixing descriptions is *causal descriptivism*, which involves extracting a description from Kripke's causal–historical account of reference transmission. Details aside, the general idea is clear enough, as is illustrated by the following passage from David Lewis:

Did not Kripke and his allies refute the description theory of reference, at least for names of people and places? Then why should we expect descriptivism to work any better for names of colors and color experiences? . . . .I disagree. What was well and truly refuted was a version of descriptivism in which the descriptive senses were supposed to be a matter of famous deeds and other distinctive peculiarities. A better version survives the attack: *causal descriptivism*. The descriptive sense associated with a name might for instance be *the place I have heard of under the name 'Taromeo'*, or may be *the causal source of this token: 'Taromeo'*, and for an account of the relation being invoked here, just consult the writings of causal theorists of reference. (Lewis 1997, n. 22; see also 1984; Kroon 1987; Searle 1983, ch. 9; Chalmers 2002)

The second part of the descriptivists' strategy is the attempt to avoid Kripke's modal argument. The simplest way of doing this, once one has what one takes to be a reference-fixing description, is to rigidify it using *actually* or *dthat* (this strategy is advocated by Frank Jackson (e.g. 1998*b*: 213–14)). An alternative method is to analyse names as meaning the same as non-rigid descriptions that are required to take large scope over modal operators (and modal predicates) in the same sentence, while taking small scope when embedded under verbs of propositional attitude (this strategy originated with Michael Dummett 1973). Although the details can be complicated, the guiding idea is simple. Descriptivists want to explain apparent instances of substitution failure involving co-referential proper names in attitude ascriptions by appealing to descriptive semantic contents of names occurring in the complement clauses; however, they also want to guarantee substitution success when one co-referential name is substituted for another in modal constructions. The different strategies of dealing with Kripke's modal argument are designed to do that.

The final weapon in the descriptivists' strategic arsenal is (ambitious) two-dimensionalism. To illustrate, we begin with a pair of contingently co-designative descriptions that have been rigidified.

(7) If there is a unique object that is actually F and a unique object that is actually G, then the x: actually Fx = the y: actually Gy.

Since the descriptions are co-designative, (7) is a necessary truth. But if asked, *What does one need to know in order for (9) to be true of one?*, it is natural to answer that it is necessary and sufficient that one know that which is expressed by (8).

(8) If there is a unique object that is F and a unique object that is G, then the x: Fx = the x: Gx.
(9) x knows that if there is a unique object that is actually F and a unique object that is actually G, then the x: actually Fx = the x: actually Gx.

Since (8) is knowable only a posteriori, the two-dimensionalist concludes that (7) is an example of the necessary a posteriori.

A similar story can be told about the contingent a priori. Let **the x: Fx** be a non-rigid description which designates some individual o in the actual world-state, but which designates other individuals with respect to other possible world-states. (10) is then a contingent truth that is false with respect to world-states in which **the x: Fx** designates some individual other than o.

(10) If there is a unique F, then the x: actually Fx = the x: Fx.

But if one asks *What does one need to know in order for (12) to be true of one?*, the natural answer is that for this to be true, it is sufficient that one know that which is expressed by (11).

(11) If there is a unique F, then the x: Fx = the x: Fx.

(12) x knows that if there is a unique F, then the x: actually Fx = the x: Fx.

Since (11) is knowable a priori, the two-dimensionalist concludes that (10) is an example of the contingent a priori.

There are two different, and competing, lessons a two-dimensionalist might draw from these examples. One is that although the proposition expressed by (7) is genuinely both necessary and knowable only a posteriori, the reason it is a posteriori is that it has the peculiarity that it can be known only by virtue of knowing a different, related proposition (expressed by (8)); similarly, although the proposition expressed by (10) is genuinely both contingent and knowable a priori, the reason it is a priori is that it can be known by virtue of knowing the distinct proposition expressed by (11). This, as we shall see, leads to a view I call *weak two-dimensionalism*. A different possible two-dimensionalist lesson is that what is required by the truth of (9) and (12) is not that the agent know the propositions expressed by (7) and (10) at all, but simply that the agent know the propositions expressed by (8) and (11). Although the necessary proposition expressed by (7) is, on this view, knowable a priori, this is compatible with the fact that the knowledge reported by (9) is (and can only be) a posteriori. Similarly, although the contingent proposition expressed by (10) is knowable only a posteriori, this is compatible with the fact that the knowledge reported by (12) is a priori. This way of looking at things is characteristic of *classic*, or *strong*, *two-dimensionalism*.

Although both versions of two-dimensionalism allow the descriptivist to maintain that he has accounted for examples of the necessary a posteriori and the contingent a priori, strong two-dimensionalism has greatest appeal for theorists like Lewis, Jackson, and Chalmers. In addition to smoothly accommodating their antecedent philosophical commitments, strong two-dimensionalism fits better than weak two-dimensionalism does with the causal-descriptive analyses of names and natural kind terms. If, in order to avoid Kripke's semantic arguments, one is going to analyse n along the lines of Lewis's *the x: actually x is the thing I have heard of under the name n*, then one will not want the result that whenever r reports the knowledge of an agent using an ascription, *a knows that n is so and so*, r's report can be true only if the agent knows that whatever individual the reporter r has actually heard of under the name n 'is so and so'. Strong two-dimensionalism avoids this absurdity by analysing attitude ascriptions as reporting relations between the agent and certain propositions distinct from the propositions semantically expressed by their complement clauses. Since this is not true of weak two-dimensionalism, strong two-dimensionalism is, initially, the more attractive choice.

2.3 Strong Two-Dimensionalism

Although contemporary two-dimensionalism is often cast as a proposal for a systematic semantic theory of natural language, often what is provided is more of a theory sketch than a theory. The best-known formal two-dimensionalist model, given by Martin Davies and Lloyd Humberstone in 'Two Notions of Necessity' (1980), provides explicit semantics for a very simple language—a modal version of the propositional calculus with a normal necessity operator, an actuality operator, and a new operator that takes one outside the usual modal model in a certain way. Such models are triples—consisting of a set W of world-states (called 'worlds'), a designated actual world-state @, and a valuation function that assigns intensions (functions from world-states to extensions) to the non-logical vocabulary. The basic operators are:

> **Necessarily S** is true in a model M w.r.t. w iff S is true in M w.r.t. all worlds in W.
>
> **AS** is true in M w.r.t. w iff S is true in M w.r.t. @.
>
> **FS** is true in M w.r.t. w iff for all models M′ that differ from M at most regarding which world @′ is designated as actual, S is true in M′ w.r.t. w.

A further operator, *FA*, is definable in terms of the last two.

> **FAS** is true in M w.r.t. w iff for all models M′ that differ from M at most regarding which world @′ is designated as *actual*, S is true in M′ w.r.t. @′.

According to Davies and Humberstone (1980: 3), '*FA*α says: whichever world had been actual, α would have been true at that world considered as actual'—not the most edifying formulation. A clearer explanation is that *FA*α says that α (understood as we actually understand it) expresses a truth in any context, no matter what the designated world-state of the context. They use this operator to capture Gareth Evans's (1979) distinction between *deep* and *superficial necessity*, which are translated into their system as follows:

> A true sentence S is superficially contingent iff **Necessarily S** is false.
> A true sentence S is deeply contingent iff **FAS** is false.
>
> S is superficially necessary iff **Necessarily S** is true.
> S is deeply necessary iff **FAS** is true.

Davies and Humberstone support Evans's idea that all examples of the contingent a priori are sentences that are superficially contingent, but deeply necessary, and that this provides an explanation of their status. But what, precisely, is the explanation? How is it that *It is a necessary truth that S* may be false when *It is knowable a priori that S* is true? Since Davies and Humberstone do not offer any fully precise theory about this, we need to supplement their account with explicit semantics for *it is knowable a priori* ____. Think of an *indexical model* as a family of Davies–Humberstone models, each of which differ from the others only in the world-state designated as *actual*. Call these designated world-states *contexts*. Then *FA* is an operator on Kaplan-style characters, and the proposition expressed by *FAS* is the set of all contexts/world-states iff for every context C, the character of S assigns to C a proposition true at C; otherwise *FAS* expresses the empty set of contexts/world-states. The characteristic two-dimensionalist claim about the a priori is that S is a priori iff *FAS* is true.

One way to think about this would be to characterize *it is knowable a priori* ____ as operating on the character of S—even as being synonymous with *FA*.[1] Though this is a possible alternative, it is not, by itself, very revealing, since surely we understand the operator on the basis of understanding the two-place predicate ____ *knows a priori* ____ the second argument of which is the same as the second argument of ____ *knows* ____. Regarding these predicates, the Davies–Humberstone picture allows two natural variations—to treat *knows* as a two-place predicate of an agent and the character of its complement sentence, or to treat it as a two-place predicate of an agent and the proposition which is the set of contexts/world-states to which the character of its complement sentence assigns the value truth. The latter, having the advantage of making the object of knowledge a proposition, has proven to be the more popular.

We can now give the desired strong two-dimensionalist explanation of the contingent a priori. For any sentence S, the *primary intension* of S is the proposition that its character expresses a truth—i.e. the set of contexts/world-states C to which the character of S assigns a proposition true at C. The proposition expressed by S at C is the *secondary intension* of S at C. Although the primary and secondary intensions of some sentences will be the same, in many cases in which S contains the actuality operator—e.g. (7) and (10)—they will be different. **It is a necessary truth that S** is true in C iff the secondary intension of S in C is true in all possible world-states; **It is knowable a priori that S** is true in C iff the primary intension of S is knowable a priori. Davies and Humberstone suggest that in every genuine case of the contingent a priori the two intensions/propositions are different. (10) is a case of the contingent a priori, since its secondary intension is contingent while its primary intension—which is the secondary intension of (11)—is both necessary and a priori. There is no puzzle about how any one proposition can be both contingent and a priori, since none is.

The account easily extends to examples like (7). Although its secondary intension is necessary, its primary intension is identical with the contingent, a posteriori truth that is the secondary intension of (8). As before, there is no puzzle about the necessary a posteriori status of (7), since the proposition that is necessary is not the one that is knowable only a posteriori. Of course, we have so far considered only examples of the contingent a priori and the necessary a posteriori containing the actuality operator. To extend the view to all Kripkean instances of these two categories, the

---

[1] Stalnaker (1978: 83) calls what is essentially this operator 'the apriori truth operator.'

two-dimensionalist must analyse all names and natural kind terms as rigidified descriptions (not containing any unanalysed names or natural kind terms).[2] This, in a nutshell, is descriptive strong two-dimensionalism. According to it, the necessary a posteriori and the contingent a priori are, in effect, linguistic illusions, born of equivocation between primary and secondary intension.

3. Critique of the Descriptivist Revival

3.1 Problems with Strong Two-Dimensionalism

The first difficulty with this attempt to revive descriptivism is that strong two-dimensionalism faces powerful counter-arguments (additional arguments of the same sort, plus arguments against other forms of two-dimensionalism, can be found in Soames 2005b, forthcoming).

Argument 1

(1) According to strong two-dimensionalism, epistemic attitude ascriptions *a knows/believes that S* report that the agent bears the knowledge/belief relation to the primary intension of S.

(2) Let *the F* and *the G* be two contingently co-designative, non-rigid descriptions. Since for every context C, the character of *the F = the G* expresses a truth with respect to C iff the character of *the actual F = the actual G* does too, the two primary intensions are identical. Thus, the ascriptions *a knows/believes that the actual F = the actual G* and *a knows/believes that the F = the G* are necessarily equivalent.

(3) Hence, the truth-value of

> *Necessarily [if the actual F = the actual G and Mary believes that the actual F = the actual G, then Mary believes something true]*

is the same as the truth-value of

> *Necessarily [if the actual F = the actual G and Mary believes that the F = the G, then Mary believes something true]*.

Since the latter modal sentence is false, so is the former.

---

[2] Davies and Humberstone express a healthy degree of scepticism about this part of the project. As a result, they cannot be seen as definitively embracing full-fledged strong, descriptive two-dimensionalism. Nevertheless, they provided the semantic basis for the later development of this view. For a full account of the details and nuances of their paper see Soames 2005b, ch. 6.

(4) Similarly, the truth-value of

> *Necessarily [if Mary believes that the actual F = the actual G, and if that belief is true, then the actual F = the actual G].*

is the same as the truth-value of

> *Necessarily [if Mary believes that the F = the G, and if that belief is true, then the actual F = the actual G].*

Since the latter modal sentence is false, so is the former.

(5) Since, in fact, the initial modal sentences in (3) and (4) are true, strong two-dimensionalism is false; modal and epistemic operators in English do not take systematically different objects.

Argument 2

(1) According to strong two-dimensionalism, names are synonymous with rigidified descriptions. Let o be an object uniquely denoted, in our present context, by the non-rigid description *the D*, let n be a name of o, and let the strong two-dimensionalist analysis of n be *the actual D*.

(2) Then, according to strong two-dimensionalism, *John believes that n is the D* will be true (as used in our present context) relative to an arbitrary counterfactual world-state w iff *John believes that the D is the D* is true with respect to w. (I here assume (1) and (2) of argument 1.)

(3) This means that in counterfactual world-states with respect to which *the D* doesn't denote o, and hence in which *the actual D = the D*, and *n = the D*, are false, *John believes that n is the D* will count as reporting the same belief, with the same truth-value, as *John believes that the D is the D*. But surely, beliefs which are not about the referent of n can't correctly be described by sentences of the form *John believes that n...*

(4) In general, for any agent a and any counterfactual world-state w, if a name n denotes an object o in our present context C, then (i) *John believes that n is F* (as used in C) is true when evaluated at w only if (ii) *John believes that y is F* is true at w with respect to an assignment of o to the variable "y". Strong two-dimensionalism is false, since it wrongly allows (i) to be true at w when (ii) is false at w.

Further arguments against strong two-dimensionalism make crucial use of indexicals like *I* and *now* the referents of which are not fixed by descriptions. In order to integrate these expressions into the two-dimensionalist framework, one must expand contexts to include designated agents and times, in addition to designated world-states. This has an immediate formal consequence. In the original Davies–Humberstone system, the meaning of S was a function from world-states, to propositions expressed by S relative to those world-states, and the primary intension of S was a proposition true when evaluated at w iff the meaning of S assigns w a proposition that is true at w. Cleaving to the standard, strong two-dimensionalist identification of propositions with sets of world-states we may identify the primary intension of S with the set of world-states w, such that the meaning of S assigns to w a set of world-states containing w. Hence, the primary intension of S and the secondary intension of S (relative to a context) are both propositions (sets of world-states), and the roles of being a context in which sentences expresses propositions, and of being a counterfactual circumstance in which propositions are evaluated, are two different dimensions of the same thing—a world-state.

This changes when contexts (but not circumstances of evaluation) are expanded to include designated agents and times. Although the secondary intension of S relative to C remains a set of world-states, which we may call an *ordinary proposition*, the primary intension of S is now identified with the set of contexts to which the meaning of S assigns ordinary propositions that are true in (contain) the world-states of the contexts. Call these *pseudo-propositions*. We no longer have one thing which plays the roles of both context and circumstance of evaluation, and we no longer have one kind of thing that occurs as arguments to both modal operators and *it is knowable a priori* ____. Instead, we have contexts and world-states in the first case, and ordinary propositions and pseudo-propositions in the second.

What is it to believe or know something which is not an ordinary proposition? Perhaps examples will help.

(13a) I am here now.
(13b) I am not Saul Kripke.

If I were to assertively utter (13a) now I would express the (ordinary) proposition that SS is in Princeton at 11.30 a.m. on 22 August 2002. Although this proposition is contingent, the meaning of (13a) generates a truth in every context; so strong two-dimensionalism classifies it as a case of the contingent a priori. The situation is just the reverse with (13b), which is classified as necessary and a posteriori. Although these characterizations are defensible, they raise a question. What do I know in these cases, and what do I report myself as knowing, when, in the same context, I assertively utter (14a) and (14b)?

(14a) I know that I am here now.
(14b) I know that I am not Saul Kripke.

The natural answer is that what I know, and report myself as knowing, is the same as what I (truly) report Gideon as knowing when I assertively utter (15a) and (15b) and our new graduate student, Harold, as not knowing when I assertively utter (16a) and (16b).

(15a) Gideon knows that I am here now.
(15b) Gideon knows that I am not Saul Kripke.

(16a) Harold doesn't know that I am here now.
(16b) Harold doesn't know that I am not Saul Kripke.

What is that? Not the primary intensions of (13a) and (13b). Each of us accepts (in his own context) the meanings of (13a) and (13b) which in turn generate these primary intensions. (Each would sincerely say 'I am here now' and 'I am not Saul Kripke'.) However, although each of us bears the same relation to these primary intensions, Harold doesn't know what Gideon and I do, and Gideon's knowledge, unlike mine in the case of (13a), is not a priori. The other likely option is that what is known, and reported to be known, in these cases are the ordinary propositions which are the secondary intensions of (13a) and (13b) in my contexts. It might be maintained that Gideon and I know these propositions in virtue of accepting, and being justified in accepting, different meanings (characters) which assign our respective contexts the same propositions; whereas Harold fails to know these propositions because there is no meaning that he accepts (and is justified in accepting) which assigns these propositions to a context with him as agent. On this view, the reason my knowledge reported in (14a) arguably counts as a priori is that the meaning I accept requires no empirical justification for accepting; the reason Gideon's (reported in (15a)) doesn't is that his does require such justification.

Although this is not unreasonable, it contradicts rather than vindicates strong two-dimensionalism. In the case of the (a) sentences, the thing known by Gideon and me (but not Harold) is a single proposition that is both contingent and known a priori by me; thus there are propositions that are both contingent and knowable a priori. In the case of the (b) sentences, the thing known by Gideon and me is a single proposition that is both necessary and knowable only a posteriori. Moreover, since Harold fails to know it despite its necessity, propositions cannot be sets of possible world-states after all.

What, then, is to become of two-dimensionalism, as a semantic framework within which to attempt a descriptivist revival? As I see it, the most plausible option is to modify it by (i) identifying secondary intensions of sentences with structured propositions, and meanings of sentences with functions from contexts to structured propositions, (ii) recasting 'primary intensions' of sentences as meanings (i.e. characters) rather than propositions determined by them, (iii) analysing the relevant attitude ascriptions *x v's that S*—as ambiguous between (a) a standard reading in which the ascription is true relative to a context C iff the agent accepts some meaning M which assigns to the agent's context the structured proposition p which is the proposition semantically expressed by S relative to C, and (b) a de se reading in which it is true relative to C iff the agent accepts the meaning of S (see Lewis 1979; Perry 1977). According to this, weakened version of two-dimensionalism, a proposition p is both necessary and knowable only a posteriori iff (i) p is necessary, (ii) p is knowable in virtue of one's justifiably accepting some meaning M (and knowing that it expresses a truth), where M is such that (a) it assigns p to one's context, (b) it assigns a false proposition to some other context, and (c) one's justification for accepting M (and believing it to express a truth) requires one to possess empirical evidence, and (iii) p is knowable only in this way. Similarly, p is both contingently true and knowable a priori iff in addition to being contingently true, p is knowable in virtue of one's justifiably accepting some meaning M (and knowing that it expresses a truth), where M is such that (*a*) it assigns p to one's context, (*b*) it assigns a true proposition to every context, and (*c*) one's justification for accepting M (and believing it to express a truth) does not require one to possess empirical evidence.

This system—*weak two-dimensionalism*—gives a two-dimensionalist account of (7) and (10), without being falsified by our arguments against strong two-dimensionalism. But can it be used to vindicate descriptivism, and avoid Kripke's arguments about names and natural kind terms? To be successful, descriptivists must find reference-fixing descriptions that escape his semantic arguments; they must rigidify those descriptions (or give them wide scope) in a way that avoids his modal and epistemological arguments; and they must show that this can be done without sacrificing the (alleged) virtues of standard descriptivist solutions to the puzzles of Frege and Russell.

3.2 Why One Should Not Expect to Find Reference-Fixing Descriptions

Recall Jackson's a priori defence of descriptivism. He argued, in effect, that the claim that the referents of expressions are semantically fixed by descriptions is irrefutable, since any refutation requires clear intuitions about what refers to what in different situations, and these can only be explained as arising from reference-fixing descriptions semantically associated with expressions by speakers. I disagree. First, there are clear cases in which we have no trouble identifying the referent of a term t, even though it is clear that there is no reference-fixing description associated with t by speakers. Kaplan's example of the identical twins Castor and Pollux, discussed earlier, is a case in point. We have no trouble identifying Castor as the referent of his use of *I*, and Pollux as the referent of his, just as we have no trouble recognizing ourselves as referents of our own uses. This is so despite the fact that the referent of *I* is not semantically fixed, for any of us, by descriptions we semantically associate with it. If this is true of *I*, it is surely also true of *now*, and may be true of other expressions as well. Secondly, even in cases in which there may be descriptions picking out the referent of a term that are, in some sense, associated with it by speakers, it remains to be shown these descriptions play any role in its semantics. One can describe possible scenarios in which our intuitions tell us that speakers use the word *and* to mean disjunction, the material conditional, the property of being a necessary truth, or the property of being a philosopher. Even if one were to grant the assumption that these intuitions arise from some internalized theory T that unconsciously guides us, it would not follow that the meaning of *and*—its character in Kaplan's sense—is one that yields as content in a context whatever satisfies the relevant description extractable from T. Surely not every word is a descriptive indexical in Kaplan's sense. To miss this point is to miss the distinction between (i) semantic facts about what an expression means, or what its referent or content is in a context, and (ii) pre-semantic facts in virtue of which the expression has the meaning, and hence the referents and contents in different contexts, that it does. Whereas the descriptivist needs reference-fixing descriptions to be involved in (i), Jackson's argument can't exclude the possibility that their only role is in (ii). Finally, the claim that our ability to categorize cases in certain ways presupposes the sort of underlying knowledge required by the description theory is tendentious in something like the way that Plato's attribution of a priori knowledge of mathematics to the slave boy in the *Meno* is tendentious. There are other ways to explain the recognition of new facts.

For these reasons, it is an error to assume that descriptions semantically fixing the referents of names and natural kind terms must be available. Instead of looking for some a priori guarantee, one must consider candidate descriptions case by case. When one does this, the results are not promising. An often noted fact about names is the enormous variability in the descriptive information associated with the same name by different speakers. Although most speakers who have enough familiarity with a name to be able to use it possess some descriptive information about its referent, little, if any, of this information is common to all of them—certainly not enough to identify the referent uniquely. What is more, many speakers would not be able to articulate any uniquely identifying description. The same point applies to natural kind terms like *water*, for which Jackson suggests the reference-fixing description 'something like: belonging to the kind which most of the clear, potable samples, acquaintance with which lead [led?] to the introduction of the word "water" in our language [belong to]' (1998*b*: 212). This clearly won't do. First, in order to understand *water*, an ordinary speaker doesn't have to have a view about what led to its introduction into our language. Secondly, one doesn't have to know that samples of water are standardly clear and potable. Imagine an unusually unfortunate English speaker, brought up in dismal and restricted circumstances, who never drank water, never imagined that anyone else did, and whose only acquaintance with it was with a cloudy stream of water spilling out of a drainpipe from a laundry. This person might correctly use *water* to refer to water, and might say and know, just as we do, that water is used for washing, but not know that water is often clear and potable. Since such a speaker may well understand the word, and use it to designate instances of the same kind that we do, without associating it with Jackson's proposed description, that description is not part of its meaning, and does not qualify as semantically fixing its referent.

As indicated earlier, examples like these have led several descriptivists to embrace causal descriptivism, according to which the reference-fixing description for a name (or kind term) n is something like ***the thing I have heard of under the name "n"*** or, perhaps, ***the causal source of this token of "n"***, where, David Lewis reminds us, to find 'an account of the relation being invoked here, just consult the writings of causal theorists of reference'. There are three problems with this view. First, I might use *Zaza* to refer to a certain dog in the neighbourhood, having forgotten that I introduced the name myself, and wrongly thinking that I picked it up from someone else. Since in such a case I use the name to refer to the dog, though I may never have heard it used by anyone else, there is some difficulty with Lewis's first description. The second problem is common to both descriptions, and to certain versions of the casual–historical theory of reference from which they are extracted. As Jonathan McKeown-Green (2002) has pointed out, not all cases in which a speaker successfully uses a name n to refer are cases in which he has either introduced n himself, or acquired n from someone else with the intention of preserving the reference of his source. Suppose, for example, that one knows of a certain region in Ireland in which the residents of different towns see to it that there is always exactly one person bearing the name *Patrick O'Grady*. Learning of this curious fact, I set out to visit the region to interview the different men bearing that name. On entering a pub in a new town, I announce 'I am looking for Patrick O'Grady, whom I am willing to pay for an interview for my new book'. In so doing I successfully use the name to refer to the man, and say something about him—not because I have acquired the name through a causal–historical chain of reference transmission, but because I am able to speak the language of the community in which the referent of the name has already been established.

This brings us to the third, and most fundamental, problem with the attempt to appropriate causal–historical theories of reference transmission for the purposes of descriptivism. Egocentric, metalinguistic descriptions associated with names are no more parts of their meanings than similar egocentric, metalinguistic descriptions are parts of the meanings of other words in the language. Standardly, when a speaker uses any word—*magenta, abode, osteopath, alphabetize, necessarily*, etc.— he intends to use it in accord with the linguistic conventions of the community. He intends to use it to refer to, or express, whatever other competent members of the community do. In the case of proper names, it is recognized both that a given name may be used by only a subpart of the community, and that different members of the relevant subcommunity (who use the name to refer to the same individual) may associate it with very different descriptive information without the name meaning something different for each of them. Thus, the general intention that one's use of words conform with the linguistic conventions of one's community translates, in the case of most names, into the intention to use them to refer to whomever or whatever other relevant members of the community use them to refer to. Some such intention is a standard condition on normal language use, not a part of meaning.

There is a larger lesson here involving historical chains of reference transmission. On the picture one often gets, a name isn't part of my language at all until I either introduce it myself, or encounter someone else using it, and form the reference-fixing intention that in my idiolect it will refer to whatever it refers to in the idiolects of those from whom I acquire it. This picture is misleading. The language I speak is a common language, of which the name is part before I ever encounter it. As a speaker, I need not know all the linguistic properties of the words in my language; my knowledge is partial, just as my knowledge of other social institutions of which I am a part is partial. Nevertheless, since I am a competent member of the linguistic community, I can appropriate a word that may be new to me, and use it with the meaning and reference it has already acquired. In the case of a name, the word probably entered the language via the stipulation of some authorities—say the parents of a newborn child. It is retained in the language by a practice of various speakers using it to refer to that individual; and speakers normally encounter it for the first time by hearing others use it—everyone intending to use it with the meaning or reference it already attained. If this picture is right, then historical chains, though they exist, are not themselves reference-determining mechanisms. (This conception of the proper way to view historical chains of reference transmission is developed in McKeown-Green 2002, ch. 9). Thus, no metalinguistic descriptions invoking them are going to play the role of semantically fixing the reference of names (or natural kind terms).

3.3 Why the Modal and Epistemological Arguments Can't Be Avoided

In this section we put aside problems about finding reference-fixing descriptions in order to focus on the problems that would confront the descriptivist, even if such descriptions could be found. In order to avoid Kripke's modal argument, such descriptions must either be rigidified or stipulated to take wide scope over modal operators. There are overwhelming difficulties with each of these options.

First, consider *actually* rigidified descriptions. Suppose (i) that *Saul Kripke ≠ David Kaplan* is an example of the necessary a posteriori, (ii) that **the x: SKx** and **the x: DKx** are descriptions that semantically fix the referents of the two names, (iii) that **the x: SKx ≠ the x: DKx** is contingent because there are world-states in which the two descriptions denote the same person, and (iv) that the contents of the two names are given by **the x: actually SKx** and **the x: actually DKx**. On these assumptions *Saul Kripke ≠ David Kaplan* conforms to the theses of weak two-dimensionalism. However, the analysis is incorrect, because (iv) is incorrect. The problem with it is based on the fact that actual believers share many beliefs with merely possible believers. I, along with others, believe that Saul Kripke ≠ David Kaplan; and it is not unreasonable to suppose that we also believe of the actual world-state @ that it is a world-state with respect to which it is true that Saul Kripke ≠ David Kaplan. A similar point holds for merely possible believers. In some possible world-states w, various agents believe that Saul Kripke ≠ David Kaplan; in addition, they believe of w that it is a world-state with respect to which it is true that Saul Kripke ≠ David Kaplan. However, they need not have any beliefs about @. Supposing they don't, I would be wrong if I were now to say, *In w, they believe that the x: actually SKx ≠ the x: actually Dkx*. Thus, if (iv) is correct, I must have been wrong in saying *In w, they believe that Saul Kripke ≠ David Kaplan*. Since I wasn't wrong; (iv) isn't correct (this argument is presented and defended in detail in Soames 2002: 39–49).

When spelled out in detail, this argument makes use of the weak two-dimensionalist assumption that, on a standard reading of *x believes that S*, the ascription is true with respect to a context C and world-state w iff in w the agent believes the proposition expressed by S in C—an assumption traditional descriptivists often employ when using Frege's puzzle and Russell's problem of negative existentials to 'refute' non-descriptive analyses. What the argument shows is that if the content of a name n is given by an *actually*-rigidified description, then, on this reading, a belief ascription containing n in the complement clause is true of an agent x with respect to a merely possible world-state w only if in w x believes certain things about (not w) but the world C_w of the context used to report x's belief. Since there is no such reading of English belief ascriptions, the descriptivist proponent of weak two-dimensionalism cannot take the contents of names to be given by *actually*-rigidified descriptions.

The problem gets worse when one realizes (i) that the only plausible reference-fixing descriptions to which the actuality operator might be attached contain indexicals referring to the speaker and/or his utterance and time of utterance[3] and (ii) that the only remotely plausible candidates for such descriptions are variants of those put forward by Lewis and other causal descriptivists. For example, consider Lewis's *thing I have heard of under the name "Venus"* or *causal source of this token of "Venus"*. Under the reading of belief ascriptions just indicated, my utterance of

(17) The ancient Babylonians believed that Venus was a star

is true only if the ancients had views about me and which things I have heard of under which names, or about the causal sources of specific utterances of mine. Obviously, this is absurd; these ascriptions have no such readings. Nor do they have

---

[3] Both me and my Twin Earth duplicate associate the same purely qualitative descriptions with n, while using it to refer to different things. If this is to be accounted for by reference-fixing descriptions, they will have to contain indexicals referring to particular contextual parameters.

the second, de se reading that the two-dimensionalist sometimes alleges them to have—namely, one in which (17) is true only if the ancient Babylonians accepted the character of the complement of (17), which, on the Lewis causal-descriptivist analysis, they would do only if they took themselves to have heard of some object under the name "Venus". In fact, my utterance of (17) is true, even though they were not familiar with the name "Venus", and so would not have accepted this character. Finally, the absurdity of combining this analysis of names with the de se reading of belief ascriptions posited by some two-dimensionalist is brought out by (18).

> (18a) My friends in Mexico City believe Henry has been badmouthing me.
> (18b) My friends in Mexico City believe that the x: actually I have heard of x under the name "Henry" has been badmouthing me.

On this analysis, (18a) is analysed as (18b), and hence is predicted to be true iff each friend in Mexico City accepts the character of the complement sentence, and so believes that someone he has heard of under the name "Henry" has been badmouthing him. This cannot be.

The lesson to be drawn is that even if the causal descriptivist could provide reference-fixing descriptions for names and natural kind terms, the semantic contents of these terms could not be given by rigidifying these descriptions using the actuality operator. What about using *dthat*? Although this would avoid some of the absurdities involving *actually*, others would remain, and one new problem would surface. The difficulties that remain concern the second, de se reading of attitude ascriptions posited by the two-dimensionalist. If the purportedly reference-fixing descriptions to which *dthat* is attached are—as they must be—egocentric, metalinguistic descriptions of the sort provided by causal descriptivist, then the absurdities just discussed involving ascriptions like (17) and (18) carry over to analyses employing *dthat* rather than *actually*. When one considers the standard reading in which attitude ascriptions report relations between agents and the propositions semantically expressed by their complement clauses, the situation changes. If names are taken to be *dthat*-rigidified descriptions, we get the desired result that it is possible to believe that Saul Kripke ≠ David Kaplan without believing anything about the actual world-state, or other contextual parameters; but we also get the result that the semantic content of a name, relative to a context C, is just its referent in C, and so (i) co-referential names are substitutable without change in content or truth-value in attitude ascriptions, and (ii) negative existentials involving so-called empty names are predicted either not to express propositions at all, or to express propositions with gaps in them. In short, this version of descriptivism faces Frege's puzzle and Russell's problem in essentially the same way that anti-descriptivist theories do. In effect, this version of descriptivism is equivalent to direct-reference theories of names to which one has added (*a*) dubious claims about descriptions semantically fixing the referents of names, and (*b*) the postulation of an extra reading of belief ascriptions containing names that they do not have. For these reasons, appealing to *dthat*-rigidified descriptions is problematic for the descriptivist.

The only remaining descriptivist alternative for dealing with the modal argument involves analysing names as (non-rigid) descriptions that are required to take wide scope over modal operators, while retaining small scope when they occur embedded under verbs of propositional attitude. To adopt this strategy is, in effect, to give up appealing to a two-dimensionalist framework, since the alleged difference between the behaviour of a sentence containing a name when embedded under a modal operator and its behaviour when embedded under an epistemic operator (verb of propositional attitude) is now attributed simply to scope. As before, the strategy can scarcely get off the ground because the only remotely plausible reference-fixing descriptions contain indexicals referring to the speaker and/or his utterance and utterance time; and the content of such a description is never what a name n contributes to the proposition expressed by *x believes that n is F*. Thus, this approach cannot plausibly account for elementary examples like (17). In addition, the strategy of assigning different scopes to the alleged descriptive contents of names embedded in modal and epistemic constructions leads to absurdities similar to those revealed by the arguments given above against strong two-dimensionalism (Soames 2002: 25–39).

4. Prospects of Non-Descriptivism

Having raised difficulties for descriptivism, I close by pointing the reader to leading attempts to address the concerns that have motivated descriptivism, without embracing descriptive semantic analyses. The first concern involves the necessary a posteriori and the contingent a priori. Although some philosophers have found it difficult to understand how a single proposition can be both necessary and knowable only a posteriori, Kripke provided the needed clue at the very outset. Some properties—e.g. the property of being made of molecules, the property of being a human being, and the property of being not identical with me—are essential to anything that has them. We know this a priori about many properties, even though we can know of a particular that it has one of these properties only a posteriori. If P expresses such a property and o is an object that has it, then the proposition expressed by *If x exists, then x is P* relative to an assignment of o to "x" will be necessary, but knowable only a posteriori. Although there is no real mystery here, working this view out in appropriate generality and using it to put to rest objections to the necessary a posteriori is a subtle and sometimes tricky matter. However, it can be done (see Soames 2004, 2005*b*). The connection between the contingent a priori and non-descriptivist semantics is more troublesome. Although there are genuine examples, like (10), that are both contingent and knowable a priori, it is (contra Kripke) doubtful that any such examples involve proper names or natural kind terms (see Salmon 1987–88; also Soames 2003*b*, ch. 16; 2005*b*).

The final set of concerns facing non-descriptive analyses of names are those posed by the puzzles of Frege and Russell. Among the semantically non-descriptive strategies for dealing with Frege's puzzle are those developed by Nathan Salmon (1986), David Braun (1998, 2002), Mark Richard (1990), Richard Larson and Peter Ludlow (1993), Mark Crimmins (1992), and me (2002, 2005*a*). In addition, Salmon has made substantial progress on Russell's problem of negative existentials (1987, 1998). So, although the traditional problems for directly referential accounts of names have not gone away, progress on them continues to be made.[4]

REFERENCES

Braun, David (1998). 'Understanding Belief Reports'. *Philosophical Review*, 107: 555–95.
—— (2002). 'Cognitive Significance, Attitude Ascriptions, and Ways of Believing Propositions'. *Philosophical Studies*, 108: 65–81.
Chalmers, David (1996). *The Conscious Mind*. New York: Oxford University Press.
—— (2002). 'On Sense and Intension', in J. E. Tomberlin (ed.), *Philosophical Perspectives*, 16: *Language and Mind*. Oxford: Blackwell.
Crimmins, Mark (1992). *Talk About Beliefs*. Cambridge, Mass.: MIT Press.
Davies, Martin, and Humberstone, Lloyd (1980). 'Two Notions of Necessity'. *Philosophical Studies*, 38: 1–30.
Dummett, Michael (1973). *Frege: Philosophy of Language*. New York: Harper & Row.
Evans, Gareth (1979). 'Reference and Contingency'. *The Monist*, 62: 161–89.
Frege, Gottlob (1970). 'On Sense and Reference', in *Translations from the Philosophical Writings of Gottlob Frege*, ed. Peter Geach and Max Black. Oxford: Blackwell.
Jackson, Frank (1998*a*). *From Metaphysics to Ethics*. Oxford: Oxford University Press.
—— (1998*b*). 'Reference and Description Revisited', in J. E.Tomberlin (ed.), *Philosophical Perspectives*, 12: *Language, Mind and Ontology*. Oxford: Blackwell.
Kaplan, David (1979). 'On the Logic of Demonstratives'. *Journal of Philosophical Logic*, 8: 81–98.
—— (1989). 'Demonstratives', in J. Almog, J. Perry, and H. Wettstein (eds.), *Themes from Kaplan*. New York: Oxford University Press.

[4] Thanks to Jim Pryor and Ali Kazmi for helpful comments on an earlier draft. For a more thorough treatment of many of the issues discussed in this chapter, see Soames (2005*b*).

Kripke, Saul (1979). 'A Puzzle About Belief'. Repr. in Peter Ludlow (ed.), *Readings in the Philosophy of Language.* Cambridge, Mass.: MIT Press, 1997.

—— (1980). *Naming and Necessity.* Cambridge, Mass.: Harvard University Press.

Kroon, Fred (1987). 'Causal Descriptivism'. *Australasian Journal of Philosophy*, 65: 1–17.

Larson, Richard, and Ludlow, Peter (1993). 'Interpreted Logical Forms'. *Synthese*, 95: 305–56.

Lewis, David (1979). 'Attitudes *De Dicto* and *De Se*'. Repr. in Lewis, *Philosophical Papers.* New York: Oxford University Press, 1983.

—— (1984). 'Putnam's Paradox'. Repr. in Lewis, *Papers in Metaphysics and Epistemology.* Cambridge: Cambridge University Press, 1999.

—— (1996). 'Elusive Knowledge'. Repr. in Lewis, *Papers in Metaphysics and Epistemology.* Cambridge: Cambridge University Press, 1999.

—— (1997). 'Naming the Colours'. Repr. in Lewis, *Papers in Metaphysics and Epistemology.* Cambridge: Cambridge University Press, 1999.

Ludlow, Peter, and Larson, Richard (1990). 'Interpreted Logical Forms'. *Synthese*, 95: 305–56.

McKeown-Green, Jonathan (2002). The Primacy of Public Language. Ph. D. diss., Princeton University.

Perry, John (1977). 'Frege on Demonstratives'. *Philosophical Review*, 86: 474–97.

—— (1979). 'The Problem of the Essential Indexical'. *Noûs*, 13: 3–21.

Putnam, Hilary (1970). 'Is Semantics Possible?' Repr. in Putnam, *Philosophical Papers*, ii. Cambridge: Cambridge University Press.

—— (1973). 'Explanation and Reference'. Repr. in Putnam, *Philosophical Papers*, ii. Cambridge: Cambridge University Press.

—— (1975). 'The Meaning of "Meaning" '. Repr. in Putnam, *Philosophical Papers*, ii. Cambridge: Cambridge University Press.

Richard, Mark (1990). *Propositional Attitudes.* Cambridge: Cambridge University Press.

Russell, Bertrand (1905). 'On Denoting'. *Mind*, 14: 479–493.

Salmon, Nathan (1986). *Frege's Puzzle.* Cambridge, Mass.: MIT Press.

—— (1987). 'Existence', in J. E. Tomberlin (ed.), *Philosophical Perspectives*, 1: *Metaphysics*. Atascadero, Calif.: Ridgeview.

—— (1987–8). 'How to Measure the Standard Metre'. *Proceedings of the Aristotelian Society*, 88: 193–217.

—— (1998). 'Nonexistence'. *Noûs*, 32: 277–319.

Searle, John (1983). *Intentionality.* Cambridge: Cambridge University Press.

Soames, Scott (2002). *Beyond Rigidity.* New York: Oxford University Press.

—— (2003a). *Philosophical Analysis in the Twentieth Century*, i. Princeton: Princeton University Press.

—— (2003b). *Philosophical Analysis in the Twentieth Century*, ii. Princeton: Princeton University Press.

—— (2004). 'Knowledge of Manifest Kinds'. *Facta Philosophica*, 6: 159–81.

—— (2005a). 'Naming and Asserting', in Z. Szabó(ed.), *Semantics vs. Pragmatics*. Oxford: Oxford University Press.

—— (2005b). *Reference and Description: The Case against Two-Dimensionalism.* Princeton: Princeton University Press.

Soames, Scott (forthcoming). 'Kripke, the Necessary Aposteriori, and the Two-Dimensionalist Heresy', in M. Garcia-Carpintero and J. Macia (eds.), *The Two-Dimensionalist Framework: Foundations and Applications*. Oxford: Oxford University Press.

Stalnaker, Robert (1978). 'Assertion'. Repr. in Stalnaker, *Context and Content*. Oxford: Oxford University Press, 1999.

—— (1984). *Inquiry*. Cambridge, Mass.: MIT Press.

CHAPTER 16

MEANING AND UNDERSTANDING

IAN RUMFITT

We cannot hope to understand language as a theorist hopes to understand it unless we understand speech. We cannot hope to understand speech unless we take account of the aim of communication.

(P. F. Strawson, 'Meaning and Context')

1. INTRODUCTION

Something that a theorist of language may hope to understand—or to understand better as the result of his theorizing—is the notion of meaning, at least as it applies to sentences, words, and other linguistic expressions. As we try to attain such an improved understanding, Strawson's warning is salutary. As he says, we cannot hope to understand the notion of an expression's meaning unless we enjoy at least a basic understanding of the nature of human speech (and writing). For our sentences and words have meaning only in so far as they could be used in speech or writing. He is also right to say that we cannot hope to understand speech unless we take account of the aim of communication. Some speech, of course, has no communicative purpose. Soliloquy may be a rather grand term for our private mutterings;

but the term means no more than talking when alone, and this is something we all do on occasion. When we do it, moreover, our words are likely to bear their ordinary meanings. Most speech and writing, however, is an attempt at communication, and our words and sentences are shaped so as to serve our communicative purposes. We cannot hope to construct a general theory of meaning without understanding those purposes and knowing how our words and sentences serve them.

In writing this assessment of the current state of philosophical theorizing about meaning, I have taken Strawson's warning to heart. In so theorizing, we need to take equal account of the speaker who utters meaningful sentences and words, and the listener who hears them. Some philosophers have doubted whether the notion of meaning is one that we need. For reasons that will emerge, I think that we do need it. We need it, though, as one concept among the many that are needed to describe instances of successful communication. The mark of successful communication is that the hearer will not only have heard the speaker's message, but will also have understood it. That is why I have yoked understanding with meaning as the topic for this chapter.

2. GRICE ON MEANING

We may begin, though, with some remarks about meaning per se. I shall broach the topic by considering some of the ideas of the philosopher who made the most interesting attempt to analyse this notion in what he took to be more primitive terms.

The English verb 'mean' is used in many different ways. The applications of most interest to a theorist of language are those in which it is used to specify the significance of a linguistic expression. Thus we have statements like "The German sentence 'Schnee ist weiss' means that snow is white"; "The German word 'Schnee' means snow". One question for the philosophy of language is what such statements come to. Another, and perhaps prior, question, however, concerns the relation between these statements and those in which the subject of "mean" stands for a person rather than a linguistic expression. For in addition to statements like "The German word 'Schnee' means snow", we have "By the word 'snow', Tom meant cocaine". In addition to "The French sentence 'Vous avez goûté un ver entier' means that you have tasted a whole worm", we have: "When he said 'You have tasted a whole worm', Dr Spooner meant that you have wasted a whole term". As the last example makes clear, what so-and-so meant is often distinct from what he actually said, or indeed from anything that could easily be recovered from the ordinary meanings of the words he uttered.

A basic question for the theory of meaning is whether one of these uses of "mean" may be analysed in terms of the other. There should be no presumption in favour of an affirmative answer. In many languages unrelated verbs are used to translate "So-and-so means..." and "This expression means...". (In German, for example, the former would be translated *meint* and the latter *bedeutet*.) All the same, in his William James lectures of 1967 (Grice 1989, pt. 1: 'Logic and Conversation'; see esp. lect. 6: 'Utterer's Meaning, Sentence-Meaning, and Word-Meaning'), H. P. Grice sketched an ambitious analytical programme whereby all members of the first family of uses were eventually to be explicated in terms of the second notion of meaning, a notion that he called 'utterer's meaning'. Earlier (1957), he had attempted to analyse the notion of utterer's meaning in terms of the speaker's intention to induce certain responses in his audience. Thus, where *u* is what Grice liked to call an indicative type (or declarative) utterance, he analysed

> By uttering *u*, the speaker *U* meant that *P*

as meaning

> For some audience *A*, *U* intended his utterance *u* to induce in *A* the belief that *P*, by means of *A*'s recognition of that intention.

Or—to employ a useful abbreviation that Grice introduced in the William James lectures—for some audience *A*, *U* M-intended his utterance *u* to induce in *A* the belief that *P*. Grice's account of the relation between utterer's meaning and sentence-meaning needs to be understood in the light of this analysis of utterer's meaning. As the analysis makes clear, Grice conceived of meaning something by a declarative utterance as a matter of intending to induce a belief in an audience. To have command of an idiolect, he then claimed, is to have certain procedures in one's repertoire by whose implementation one may hope to induce beliefs. In the special case where *S* is a declarative type sentence, then, he analysed

> Sentence *S* means that *P* in *U*'s idiolect

as meaning

> *U* has in his repertoire the following procedure: to utter a token of *S* if *U* intends (wants) *A* to believe that *P*.

The sentence *S* is said to mean that *P* among members of a group (as opposed to having that meaning in an idiolect) if some members of the group have the relevant procedure in their repertoire, 'the retention of this procedure being for them conditional on the assumption that at least some (other) members of the group have, or have had, this procedure in their repertoires' (1989: 127).

Grice confessed that he was 'not certain that a general form of definition can be provided' to extend this explication from sentence-meaning to word-meaning (p. 131). But in the cases of word-meaning he attempted to treat, the idea was to explicate a word's meaning in terms of the meanings of a favoured range of declarative sentences in which the word figures. Adjectives are the one verbal category for which Grice developed this idea in any detail, and for an adjective the range of favoured declarative sentences comprises all simple predications in which the adjective is used. In Grice's mouth, the adjective "shaggy" means hairy-coated. It does so, he thinks, by virtue of his repertoire's including the following procedure: to utter a simple predication containing "shaggy" when, for some audience A, U wants A to believe the subject of that predication to be hairy-coated.

We need not speculate whether this account might eventually extend to explicate assignments of meaning to words of other kinds. For even when confined to sentence-meanings, it limps so badly that any discussion of whether it could go the full distance to a general theory of linguistic meaning is moot.

As I remarked, Grice's own way of developing his account of the relation between sentence-meaning and utterer's meaning presupposes that meaning something by a declarative utterance involves intending to induce a belief in an audience. That presupposition, however, is already a mistake. If it were correct, then one requirement for the successful performance of an act of meaning something by a declarative utterance would be the fulfilment of this intention; that is, the audience would have to acquire the belief that the speaker had intended to induce in him. But this is not a requirement for meaning something. I may succeed in saying something, and mean what I say, even though my audience does not believe what I say. Moreover, I may say something, and mean it, without intending that my audience should believe it. I may be morally certain that they will not believe what I say; if so, I cannot be said to intend to induce them to believe what I say. Or again, I may say it without caring whether my audience believes what I say. For all that, it may be important to say it. It may be important to place it on the record, and I may say it (and mean it) for that end alone.

Although he always held that meaning something by a declarative utterance involves intending to induce a belief in an audience, Grice vacillated over what the relevant belief was. In his 1957 article, he took it that meaning that P involves intending to get one's audience to believe that P. In the William James lectures, however, he offered an emended account. There, he discusses the case of 'the counter-suggestible man':

A regards U as being, in certain areas, almost invariably mistaken, or as being someone with whom he cannot bear to be in agreement. U knows this. U says 'My mother thinks very highly of you' with the intention that A should (on the strength of what U says) think that U's mother has a low opinion of him. Here there is some inclination to say that, despite U's intention that A should think U's mother thinks ill of him, what U *meant* was that U's mother thinks well of A. (1989: 107)

If what we have some inclination to say about this case is true, then the 1957 analysis of meaning stands refuted. As Grice observes (1989: 111), however, even in this case, *A* is intended to think that *U thinks* that *U*'s mother has a high opinion of *A*. For this reason among others, Grice emended his original account of utterer's meaning for declarative utterances in the William James lectures. "By uttering *u*, the speaker *U* meant that *P*" is now analysed as "For some audience *A*, *U* *M*-intended his utterance *u* to induce in *A* a belief that *U* believes that *P*".

This emendation, though, does not help. First, as many commentators have observed, it deprives Grice's overall theory of meaning of much of its initial plausibility. In Dummett's words (1993: 171), 'language is certainly used primarily as contributing to our transactions with the world, rather than as conveying how it is with us in our thinking parts'. For this reason, I have suppressed the emendation in expounding Grice's account of the relation between utterer's meaning and sentence-meaning. Secondly, while the emendation may perhaps deal with the example of the counter-suggestible man, it fails to address some of the other cases which appear to show that intending to induce a belief is not necessary for meaning something by a declarative utterance. A speaker, we noted earlier, may say that *P* and mean it without caring whether his audience comes to believe that *P*. Equally, though, he may say that *P* and mean it without caring whether his audience comes to believe that he (the speaker) believes that *P*. Again, under the emended analysis, a necessary condition for successfully performing the act of producing an utterance and thereby meaning that *P* will be that the audience should come to believe that the speaker believes that *P*. But inducing this belief is no more necessary for the successful performance of that act than is inducing the belief that *P*. I have given elsewhere the example of the Birmingham Six, each of whom protested to their police interrogators 'We did not plant the bombs'. Their audience did not believe that they had not planted the bombs. But neither did they believe that any of the Six believed that they had not planted the bombs. For all that, in uttering those words, each of the Six succeeded both in saying and in meaning that they had not planted the bombs. They could truly claim that they had protested their innocence throughout.

What this brings out is a basic mistake in Grice's account of utterer's meaning. On his analysis, meaning something by a declarative utterance is a matter of intending to induce a belief in an audience. If this analysis were correct, then a requirement for successfully performing such a speech act would be the induction of the appropriate belief. On neither of his specifications of the relevant belief, however, is this necessary for the successful performance of the speech act. In order to say something and mean it, it is not necessary that one's audience should accept what one says, nor is it necessary that they should accept that one is sincere in speaking as one does. To be sure, in order to tell someone something, some response or "uptake" is required on the audience's part. Even with telling, however, the required response is not acceptance of one's message, or of one's sincerity. There is no contradiction in saying "I told you so; but you didn't believe me; and you didn't even believe that I believed what I was telling you". Rather, the sort of uptake required for someone to be told something is that the audience should understand, or grasp, what he has been told.

John Searle (1969: 47) once put the present objection to Grice as follows. 'The characteristic intended effect of meaning is understanding, but understanding is not the sort of effect that is included in Grice's examples of effects. It is not a per-locutionary effect.' One might wonder whether understanding is always the intended effect of meaning something. One can, after all, say something and mean it in soliloquy, where there is no audience who could possibly fail to understand what one means. Understanding, however, does seem to be the characteristic intended effect of a whole range of relational speech acts—such as telling someone something, asking him a question, asking (or ordering) him to do something. Or, better, it is the primary requirement for the successful performance of one of these speech acts. In asking someone a question, you may or may not be hoping for an answer. (Perhaps you are obliged to ask him a question whose answer you would rather not hear.) But whether or not you get an answer, you will have succeeded in asking him the question so long as he understands it. In ordering someone to do something, you may or may not intend that he should obey. (Perhaps you issue the order knowing that he will be unable to obey it, and your intention in issuing it is to earn the right to punish him for disobedience.) But whether or not he obeys, you will have succeeded in ordering him to do it so long as he understands the order.

If these observations are to lead anywhere, we shall need to investigate what is involved in understanding what one has been told, or told to do, or asked. Before embarking on that investigation, however, it is worth considering where our observations leave Grice's project of first analysing utterer's meaning and then explicating sentence-meaning in its terms. With regard to the first enterprise, Searle (1969: 47) is surely right to deny that we can 'amend Grice's account so that meaning is analysed in terms of understanding [rather than in terms of the induction of belief]. That would be too circular, for one feels that meaning and understanding are too closely tied for the latter to be the basis for an analysis of the former.' But even if we take as given the notion of an utterer's meaning something, along with a correlative notion of understanding, we shall not be able to reinstate anything like Grice's account of sentence-meaning. It would be no good to analyse "Sentence S means that P in U's idiolect" as meaning

> U has in his repertoire the following procedure: to utter a token of S if U intends (wants) A to understand that P.

For in this context, "understand" means "accept", and this variety of understanding is not correlative to meaning. One might instead try

> U has in his repertoire the following procedure: to utter a token of S if U intends (wants) A to understand him as having said that P.

But while this formula may be equivalent to "Sentence *S* means that *P* in *U*'s idiolect", it hardly constitutes an analysis. It comes to no more than "*U* uses the sentence *S* to say that *P*", which does not advance the discussion without an account of saying. In particular, it is quite unclear whether saying can be explicated without invoking the notion of sentence-meaning. If it cannot, then the impression the formula gives of having advanced the discussion is spurious.

3. UPTAKE IN COMMUNICATION

Negative as my conclusions so far have been, they point the way towards a more promising approach to the topic of meaning than Grice's programme of trying to reduce the notion to ostensibly more primitive terms. As we saw, there is a range of relational speech acts whose successful performance consists in the audience's "tak ing up" the utterance in the right way. One feature of Grice's treatment of sentence-meaning that seems to be correct is this: a sentence's meaning must somehow relate to the way people use it to communicate with one another. By looking in more detail at what communicative uptake involves, we may hope to attain a better understanding of meaning.

I take the term *uptake* from J. L. Austin, who introduced it in the course of his discussion of three different sorts of thing that we do when we say something. Saying something, Austin (1975: 109) tells us, always involves performing 'a *locutionary* act, which is roughly equivalent to uttering a certain sentence with a certain sense and reference'. It also involves performing '*illocutionary* acts such as informing, ordering, warning, undertaking, &c.' In addition, it may (though it need not) involve performing '*perlocutionary* acts: what we bring about or achieve *by* saying something, such as convincing, persuading, deterring, and even, say, surprising or misleading'. These various things done are related: it is by performing a locutionary act that I shall perform an illocutionary one; and it is by performing an illocutionary act that I may perform a perlocutionary one. Thus I can warn you that there is a bull in a certain field by uttering the words "There is a bull in that field" with a certain sense and reference. And by giving you that warning, I may deter you from entering the field.

A speaker may say something when soliloquizing, with no communicative intent. So given our intended focus on communication, we shall need a correspondingly general notion of saying something *to* someone, which is understood to cover all the more specific communicative speech acts of telling someone something, asking him something, ordering him to do something, etc. We may then ask how the hearer must respond if a speaker is to succeed in saying something to him.

"Uptake" is Austin's general term for the needed response, but his account of locutionary, illocutionary, and perlocutionary acts needs to be refined before it can be applied to communicative speech acts. 'To say something', Austin observes,

is always to perform the act of uttering certain vocables or words, i.e. noises of certain types belonging to and as belonging to a certain vocabulary, in a certain construction, i.e. conforming to and as conforming to a certain grammar, with a certain intonation, &c. This act we may call a 'phatic' act, and the utterance which it is the act of uttering a 'pheme'. (1975: 92)[1].

The term "pheme" is useful. But saying something *to* someone—as it might be, telling him something, asking him something, ordering him to do something—involves more than merely uttering a pheme. Indeed, it involves more than getting one's audience to hear one uttering a pheme. Knowing your penchant for eavesdropping, I may contrive matters so that you overhear me saying to someone else "Smith is a twit". You will have heard me utter a pheme; but this sort of hearing is no basis for my telling you anything. Telling someone something, asking him something, etc., involve performing a particular kind of relational phatic act which I shall call *directing* a pheme at an audience. Performing an act of this kind involves, at the very least, catching the attention of one's intended audience and getting him to recognize that he is the intended audience. It is true that we say "I told you so, but you were not listening". But such instances are not successful cases of telling. The speaker's communicative purposes have not been achieved. What more is involved in the successful direction of a pheme is the next question we must address.

If I am to succeed in telling you that there is a bull in that field, then your "taking up" my remark must in normal circumstances involve at least this:

(*a*) You must know which Austinian pheme I have directed at you. In the case of the warning about the bull, you must know that the pheme I directed at you was the English sentence "There is a bull in that field".

But what exactly is involved in knowing which pheme I have directed at you?
Searle once observed that

human communication has some extraordinary properties, not shared by most other kinds of human behaviour. One of the most extraordinary is this [α]: If I am trying to tell someone something, then (assuming certain conditions are satisfied) as soon as he recognizes that I am trying to tell him something and exactly what it is that I am trying to tell him, I have succeeded in telling it to him. Furthermore [β], unless he recognizes that I am trying to tell him something and what I am trying to tell him, I do not fully succeed in telling it to him. In the case of illocutionary acts we succeed in doing what we are trying to do by getting our audience to recognize what we are trying to do. (1969: 47)

---

[1] In a footnote on that page, Austin explains that he uses '"utterance" only as equivalent to *utteratum*', i.e. to "what is uttered". (Appending a Latin suffix to an Old Dutch stem was no doubt his idea of a joke.) I do not follow him in this. As I use the term, an utterance is a particular, datable, episode of speech. I shall, however, appropriate his useful terms "pheme" and "rheme" for some of the things that are uttered when someone says something.

As features of interpersonal acts, properties α and β are indeed unusual. Suppose that we are playing tennis. Then, if I am to pass you on the backhand, it is certainly not necessary that you should recognize my intention to do so. Indeed, so far from constituting my success, your recognition of my intention to pass you is likely to contribute to my failure. And in fact none of Austin's examples of perlocutionary relational speech acts exhibits either Searlean property. This is evident in the case of misleading someone. If I am to succeed in misleading you, it will in general be necessary that you should not recognize that I intend to do so. But the point also holds for the case of persuasion. Recognizing that you intend to persuade me that such-and-such (or to do such-and-such) is not sufficient for my being so persuaded. Your intention to persuade me may be all too evident without my being at all persuaded. Neither is my recognition of your intention necessary if you are to persuade me. On the contrary; an apparently disinterested statement of a case is often more persuasive than a hard sell.

As we have seen, telling someone something involves more than merely uttering a pheme. It involves, as I put it, *directing* a pheme at the audience. Do these acts of direction have either of Searle's extraordinary properties? Will I have succeeded in directing a pheme at you if you recognize that I am trying to direct a pheme at you and you know which pheme I am trying to direct at you (property α)? In the sense of "direct" that is of most interest to the theory of communication, I think that the answer is yes. Manifesting an intention to utter certain words does not, of course, guarantee success. Our tongues and pens can slip, and such slips sometimes matter, notably in the more or less ritualized forms of speech that first caught Austin's attention. In ordinary communication, however, the first thing that matters is that the speaker should make his phatic intentions manifest to the intended audience. Even if he has mispronounced them, we take a speaker to have uttered certain words if we recognize his intention to utter them. Ordinary communication, indeed, could scarcely get under way if we denied ourselves such latitude. Austin describes words as being noises of certain types; but if the typology were to be strictly according to the canons of the International Phonetic Alphabet, then people with speech impediments would fail to utter phemes when they speak. Similarly, if the typology of manuscript words were to be strictly in accordance with the norms of copperplate, then those of us with poor handwriting would fail to inscribe phemes when we write. In so far as the utterance or inscription of phemes is supposed to be necessary for communication, such conclusions are absurd; and they are absurd because the first thing that matters in communication is that the hearer (or reader) should discern the speaker's phatic intentions. If those intentions are discerned, a certain basic level of communication will have been achieved; and we may say that the speaker has succeeded in directing the relevant pheme at his audience even if he has not pronounced (or written) that pheme correctly. Acts of direction, then, should be understood as possessing the first of Searle's extraordinary properties.

What of the second such property (labelled β above)? Can I succeed in directing a pheme at you if you do not recognize that that is what I am intending to do? As the case of the eavesdropper shows, I can certainly say something, with you as my intended audience, without your recognizing that that is what I intend. Such a case, however, would not be an instance of my telling you something, or my asking you something, or my telling you to do something. So if direction is to serve as the relational phatic act that underpins the acts we called saying something *to* someone, it should be understood as exhibiting property β too. It should be noted, though, that in many cases of communication, the speaker's identification of his audience will be by description. If you are reading this chapter, then I shall have succeeded in directing many phemes at you. In performing those acts of direction, I shall have fulfilled various communicative intentions. Those intentions, however, must be specified using a description. My intention is to direct the phemes in question at whoever may read the chapter.

The last two paragraphs give, I hope, some idea of what is involved in knowing which pheme has been directed at one. But knowing so much clearly falls far short of what is necessary for a full understanding of the utterance. What more is required? 'To say something', Austin observed,

is, generally, to perform the act of using that pheme or its constituents with a more or less definite 'sense' and a more or less definite 'reference' (which together are equivalent to 'meaning'). This act we may call a 'rhetic' act and the utterance which it is the act of uttering a 'rheme'.

Austin's invocation of the Fregean categories of sense and reference is rather casual. But it is natural to employ these notions in characterizing the next noteworthy level of understanding, or uptake, which goes beyond knowing what pheme has been directed at one. For if the utterance in question contains some referring expressions, a hearer who fully takes it up must know to which object or objects the speaker is referring by way of those expressions. Having ascertained that, he will also need to know what the speaker is saying about those objects, or what he is asking about them, or what he is ordering or requesting his audience to do with or to those objects. Following Austin, we may say that a hearer who knows so much possesses a *rhetic* understanding of the relevant utterance. Our next task is to investigate what such understanding involves.

What, in the first place, is involved in knowing to which object, or objects, a speaker is referring? The answer depends, I think, on the character of the referring expression that the speaker uses to effect the reference. In some cases, the expression in question will have a conventional meaning which uniquely determines a referent, given information about the context of utterance. In such a case it suffices, in order to know to which object the speaker is referring, that one should: (*a*) know that the referring expression in question is indeed used with the relevant conventional meaning; and (*b*) apprehend the relevant information about the context of utterance. A clear example of a referring expression of this first kind is the (singular) first-person pronoun. Once

I have recognized that a word is being used as such a pronoun, then I will know that in using it the speaker is referring to himself. In knowing so much, I may not (as we say) 'know who the speaker is'. But that just means: I may lack a means of identifying the speaker that is independent of his being the speaker. Thus, I may be said not to know who the speaker is if I cannot see who is speaking in a crowded room, or if I do not know the speaker's proper name. In these cases, what I lack is knowledge that would enable me to identify the speaker after he finishes speaking.

Words like "I", however, are unusual among referring expressions in having their referents determined by a simple convention of this kind. Other paradigms among referring expressions are proper names and demonstratives, but the linguistic conventions constraining the use of these expressions do not in general determine their reference on a given occasion of use. A speaker who used the English name "Henry" to refer to a woman would, I suppose, be flouting a convention, but knowing that there is such a convention does not take one very far in knowing to whom a speaker who says "Henry is getting on" is referring. (Or knowing to what he is referring: he may be talking about his car.) Again, there is a convention that "that man" should be used to refer to a man who is in some way salient to both speaker and hearer. But this demonstrative expression may be used successfully to make a singular reference even in circumstances in which more than one man is salient.

For names and demonstratives, then, our question remains. What is involved in knowing to which object a speaker who uses such an expression is referring? As with the level of phatic understanding, I think that what is crucial is discerning the speaker's referential intentions. That discerning these intentions plays some role in ascertaining reference is beyond doubt. If someone says "This case is closed", a necessary first step in ascertaining what he is referring to will be discovering whether, in using the word "case", he intends to be speaking of a piece of luggage or a legal action. I suggest, though, that they play a more central role than this. A hearer who is trying to understand what the user of a referring expression is saying will be concerned to find out to which object the speaker intends to refer in using that expression. And having found that out, he will take him as having referred to that object, even if there is no established convention of referring to the object in that way, and even if he would not himself refer to the object in that fashion. Irritated in the course of a philosophical discussion, I might expostulate: "Big Nose here asserts that all truth is relative. But he can offer no coherent account of why in that case we should accept any of his assertions." This may be the first and last time the gentleman in question is referred to as "Big Nose". But the improvised nature of my referring expression need not prevent my audience from knowing to whom I am referring when I use it, and thereby my communicating with them successfully. In most cases, indeed, referring to something, in the course of telling or asking someone something about it, exhibits both of Searle's extraordinary properties. If I am trying to refer to something (as part of a communicative act) then as soon as my audience recognizes that I am trying to refer to something, and recognizes what it is that I am trying to refer to, then communication will have been effected, at least as far as the reference goes. Conversely, unless he recognizes that I am trying to refer to something, and recognizes what I am trying to refer to, my attempt at communication will not have fully succeeded. To say so much is not to deny the importance, for certain theoretical purposes, of notions of conventional or semantic reference. But those purposes lie at some distance from our present task of delineating the conditions for successful communication—of describing what it takes for a speaker's message to get across to his audience.

Knowing what a speaker is referring to does not itself suffice for a rhetic understanding of an utterance. One also needs to know what he is saying, or asking, about the objects he refers to, or what commands or requests he is making about those objects. "Saying", "asking", and "commanding" are to be taken here in senses that are perhaps artificially thin. As Austin uses the term, a hearer may enjoy a rhetic understanding of an utterance even if he does not know with what illocutionary force it has been issued. "Saying" in the present context, then, does not mean "asserting" (which is a species of illocutionary force). Rather, to know what a speaker has said is to know what proposition a speaker has expressed, or what properties he has attributed to the object or objects to which he refers. (The intended sense of "say", then, is that of the German verb *aussagen*, rather than *behaupten*.) Thus a hearer will enjoy a rhetic understanding of the remark "John's recent behaviour has been that of a perfect gentleman" if he knows to whom the speaker is referring, and knows what sort of behaviour is being attributed to him, even if he is in doubt whether the attribution constitutes an actual assertion or whether it is an ironical comment on John's latest outrages. Of course this rather thin sense of "say", and the correspondingly thin senses of "ask" and "command", need further explication, which I aim to provide in the next section[2].

The relevant notion of saying is perhaps clear enough, though, to ask what is involved in attaining this level of understanding. In this respect too, I suggest, attaining rhetic understanding is a matter of discerning the relevant communicative intentions. A cooperative hearer who recognizes my intention that he should take my utterance as saying that such-and-such will so take it (Searle's property α). Furthermore, he will not so take it unless he recognizes that I intend him to take it in that way (property β). In many cases, of course, the sense in which a pheme is manifestly intended to be taken is not one that is generally or authoritatively recognized to be a "correct" sense. Many people misuse words and forms of sentence construction. But even though a hearer may protest in such a circumstance that the

---

[2] In some cases, there may be no simple answer to the question what the speaker is saying about the objects to which he refers. A poet, for example, may deliberately choose an ambiguous pheme, so that the most one can say about the rhetic act he performs is that his words could be taken as saying one thing, but could also be taken as saying another. In achieving such an effect, he is clearly exploiting the linguistic resources of the relevant language just as adroitly as someone who takes care to speak unambiguously. But I shall suppress the complications that such cases generate.

pheme does not really have the sense the speaker is attaching to it, he will still take it in that sense. Or at least, he will so take it if he is prepared to give to the speaker the grain of salt that communication so often requires. The manifestly intended sense of a word is not always one that has been recognized by the dictionary.

Some may fear that this conception of the right sense opens the gates to a semantic free-for-all, whereby anything—or almost anything—can be the sense of any word or any construction. But I do not think that it does. To qualify as the sense of an utterance, a sense must be the one that the speaker *manifestly* intends. The speaker, in other words, must enable the hearer to *recognize* that he intends his utterance to be understood as saying that such-and-such. This is a substantial constraint, which prevents any old sense from qualifying as the content of an utterance. When a speaker is using a word in one of its customary senses, we shall usually be able to recognize this (using the dictionary if we have to). And we shall usually be able to recognize the sense that a speaker intends to assign to a word when he makes a well-entrenched misuse of it. For example, we have no difficulty in under-standing someone who complains that some of his neighbours have been flaunting the law, however much we may deplore his misuse of the verb "to flaunt". Again, a gifted writer may coin a neologism (or assign a new sense to an old word) without needing to give an explicit definition: he may be able to convey the intended use of the word more obliquely. In many cases, however, a speaker who strays from the beaten semantic tracks will simply fail to enable his hearers to recognize the sense he intends to convey; he will then fail to communicate. There was once an Oxford philosopher who was prone to respond to (the not infrequent) demonstrations that his claims had absurd consequences by saying "I did not mean my words to bear any sense under which they would have that implication". In many cases, however, his hearers could attach no sense to his words which would fail to sustain the implication. It is no achievement to escape, or to evade, refutation by failing to communicate anything at all.

A speaker who enjoys a rhetic understanding of an utterance, then

(b) will know what the speaker has said (or asked, or commanded) in produc-
    ing the utterance or inscription. In our leading example, he will know to
    which field the speaker has referred, and he will know that the speaker has
    said that that field contains a bull, i.e. an uncastrated male ox.

There are further levels of uptake that a hearer may attain. A hearer may enjoy a rhetic understanding of an utterance without knowing with what force it was issued. Thus, a hearer who fully apprehends the illocutionary act performed by the speaker

(c) will also know what force the utterance has. In our example, he will know
    that the utterance has the force of a warning, and is not merely a comment
    on the passing scene, or an encouragement to enter the field and antagonize
    the bull.

While a hearer will often know what force an utterance has by virtue of knowing which rheme has been expressed to him, and he will often know which rheme has been expressed to him by virtue of knowing which pheme has been directed at him, understanding is not always so ordered. For example, I may know that the speaker is describing the field in question as containing a male ox, rather than a papal edict, only because I recognize that his words have the force of a warning. Again, if a word in a manuscript has been partially obliterated, I may be able to ascertain which word it is (and thereby reconstruct the pheme inscribed) only because I know what the whole sentence was intended to say. It remains the case, however, that it is *by* directing a certain pheme at his audience that a speaker (or writer) will have expressed a certain rheme to him, and will have expressed it with a certain illocutionary force. Moreover, it is by doing these things that the speaker may also perform certain perlocutionary acts—such as dissuading his interlocutor from entering the field.

4. RHETIC UNDERSTANDING AND TRUTH

Let us now focus more closely on level (*b*) of our analysis of uptake. In Austin's example, this is the level of understanding that you will enjoy if you know that I have said that there is a bull in the field (though you may not know whether my words were a warning or had some other illocutionary force). Many philosophers have supposed that enjoying this level of understanding of a declarative utterance is a matter of knowing under what conditions the utterance is true. Thus in the *Tractatus*, Wittgenstein wrote that 'to understand a declarative sentence in use means to know what is the case if it is true' (4.024). Cognate formulae may be used to explicate the cognate level of understanding for non-declarative utterances. Thus: to understand a command (or a request) is to know what will be the case if it is obeyed (or complied with). To understand an optative utterance (such as "Would that he were here now") is to know what is the case if it is gratified. To understand a yes–no question is to know what is the case if it may be truly answered in the affirmative. (Or, perhaps, it is to know that and to know what is the case if it may be truly answered negatively.) Wittgenstein's formula extends less naturally to the case of WH-questions. But even they may be brought within the fold. To a first approximation, the utterance of a WH-question may be understood as an utterance of an incomplete expression, together with a request to supply something of which the incomplete expression is true. Thus an utterance of "Who killed Cock Robin?" may be understood as an utterance of the predicative expression "ξ killed Cock Robin", together with a request to name or describe something of which that incomplete expression is true. Understanding the WH-question, then, will involve understanding the component incomplete expression, and a variant of Wittgenstein's formula specifies the relevant kind of understanding. For to understand "ξ killed Cock Robin", it may be suggested, is to know how it is with an object—to know what that object is like—if the incomplete expression is true of it.

There is, I think, something basically right about Wittgenstein's formula as an explication of the level of understanding on which we are now focusing. But in order to see what is right about it, and where refinements are needed, it helps first to stand back and ask why we might have an interest in the sort of understanding of utterances that is marked out at level (b). In expounding my account, I shall focus on what I call *sayings*: utterances which say something, whether or not they are assertions. I shall indicate in passing, though, how the treatment might extend to other sorts of utterance.

We often have reason to believe that a speaker is telling the truth about some matter even though we have no antecedent reason to believe what he is telling us—antecedent, I mean, to hearing him speak. Hartmut is a leading authority on modern German history, who does not make assertions unless he is pretty certain that they are true. He is also rather serious-minded, and is not given to joking about historical matters. So whenever I hear him say something about modern German history, I have reason to take his utterance to be true. In particular, then, when I hear him say "In März 1890, hat Bismarck das Kanzleramt niederlegt", I shall have reason to take this utterance to be true. By itself, however, having reason to do that gives me no reason to believe anything about the course of German history. In particular, I may have reason to take this utterance to be true without having any reason to believe that Bismarck resigned the chancellorship in March 1890. For I might have no idea that this is what the utterance says. If, on the other hand, I understand Hartmut's utterance as saying so much, then the reason that I have to take his utterance to be true will extend to provide reason to believe that Bismarck resigned the chancellorship in that month. More generally, if I understand an utterance u as saying that P, then any reason that I may have for taking u to be true will extend to provide reason to believe that P. One mark of understanding, then, is that reasons for believing an utterance to be true spread over to reasons for believing whatever it is that the utterance says. This dimension of understanding is clearly important. It is important because we often need to find out something where the easiest way to find it out—perhaps the only way—is to ask someone whom we take to be authoritative and trustworthy. I suggest that it is this dimension of understanding that we are trying to capture when we speak of understanding what an utterance says.

Understanding what an utterance says also allows reasons for believing what it says to spread back to provide reasons for taking it to be true. Suppose that I have reason to believe that Bismarck resigned the German chancellorship in March 1890. By itself, this gives me no reason to mark as true an examination candidate's inscription of the words "In März 1890, hat Bismarck das Kanzleramt niederlegt".

But if I understand his inscription as saying that Bismarck resigned the chancellorship in that month, then I shall have reason to mark it as true. More generally, if I understand an utterance *u* as saying that *P*, then any reason that I may have for believing that *P* will extend to provide reason for taking *u* to be true. This mark of understanding is also important. It is important because we often need to assess utterances or inscriptions for truth. Assessments of this kind made with reason may be expected to be better than those made without.

Understanding what an utterance says also allows reasons for disbelieving, or denying, what it says to spread back to provide reasons for taking it to be false. Suppose that I have reason to deny that Bismarck resigned the German chancellorship in March 1890. By itself, this gives me no reason to mark as false an examination candidate's inscription of the words "In März 1890, hat Bismarck das Kanzleramt niederlegt". But if I understand his inscription as saying that Bismarck resigned the chancellorship in that month, then I shall have reason to mark it as false. More generally, if I understand an utterance *u* as saying that *P*, then a reason that I may have for denying that *P* will extend to provide reason for taking *u* to be false. This mark of understanding is also important, and for much the same reason as before. We often need to assess utterances or inscriptions for falsehood as well as truth.

Finally, understanding what an utterance says allows reasons for taking it to be false to spread to provide reasons for denying or disbelieving what it says. If I have reason to suppose that Hartmut is out to mislead me when he says "In März 1890, hat Bismarck das Kanzleramt niederlegt", then I shall have reason to take this utterance to be false. By itself, having reason to take this utterance to be false gives me no reason to deny that Bismarck resigned the chancellorship in March 1890. For I might have no idea that this is what Hartmut's utterance says. If, on the other hand, I understand Hartmut's utterance as saying so much, then the reason that I have to take that utterance to be false will extend to provide reason to deny that Bismarck resigned the chancellorship during that month. More generally, if I understand an utterance *u* as saying that *P*, then any reason that I may have for taking *u* to be false will extend to provide reason to deny or disbelieve that *P*. This feature of understanding is less important than any of the others, for we rarely find ourselves with reason to take utterances to be false which are antecedent to reasons to deny what they say. All the same, it is a feature of understanding what an utterance says.

My understanding an utterance *u* as saying that *P*, then, is a state which has the following four characteristics:

(*a*) it gives me reason to believe that *P*, in the event of my having reason to take *u* to be true;

(*b*) it gives me reason to take *u* to be true, in the event of my having reason to believe that *P*;

(*c*) it gives me reason to believe that not *P*, in the event of my having reason to take *u* to be false; and (*d*) it gives me reason to take *u* to be false, in the event of my having reason to believe that not *P*.

What goes for reasons for belief also goes, *pari passu*, for knowledge. My understanding an utterance *u* as saying that *P* puts me in a position

(*a*) to know that *P*, in the event of my coming to know that *u* is true;
(*b*) to know that *u* is true, in the event of my coming to know that *P*;
(*c*) to know that *u* is false, in the event of my coming to know that not *P*; and
(*d*) to know that not *P*, in the event of my coming to know that *u* is false.

Understanding a saying, in other words, allows knowledge to spread back and forth between the saying's content and attributions of truth to it, and between that content's negation and attributions of falsity to the saying.

A hearer who knows what is commanded by an imperative utterance has a similar ability to move from a semantic evaluation of the utterance to a conclusion about what has happened *in rebus*. For suppose that I know what John has been told to do, when I hear him being told "Close the window". In that case, I shall have reason to believe (or know) that he has closed the window, in the event that I have reason to believe (or know) that the utterance has been obeyed. Again, I shall have reason to believe (or know) that he has not closed the window, in the event that I have reason to believe (or know) that the utterance has been disobeyed. More generally, if I understand the utterance *u* as an order, directed to *x*, to φ, I shall

(*a*) have reason to believe that *x* has φ'd, in the event that I have reason to believe that *u* has been obeyed; and
(*b*) have reason to believe that *x* has not φ'd, in the event that I have reason to believe that *u* has been disobeyed.

As before, there is a corresponding point about knowledge. My understanding *u* as ordering *x* to φ puts me in a position

(*a*   to know that *x* has φ'd, in the event of my coming to know that *u* has been obeyed; and
(*b*) to know that *x* has not φ'd, in the event of my coming to know that *u* has been disobeyed.

There is nothing, though, in the understanding of an order which corresponds to clauses (*b*) and (*c*) in our account of the rhetic understanding of a saying. Knowing that John has closed the window gives me no reason to suppose that he has obeyed an order to do so. Before anyone can obey an order, he must at least be aware that it has been issued. But John may have closed the window in ignorance of any order to do so.

The capacity to move from an appropriate semantic assessment of an utterance (such as that it is true, or that it has been obeyed) to a conclusion about how things stand (or how they have been changed) in the world is central to our command of language. Accordingly, I suggest that we should take a person's possessing such a capacity as constituting his enjoying a rhetic understanding of an utterance. On the view that I am recommending, then, a state of rhetic understanding is a way of gaining new knowledge (or new reasons for belief) from old. The old knowledge, and the old reasons for belief, concern certain basic semantic attributes of the various kinds of utterance: that this saying is true, that that order has been disobeyed. The new knowledge, and the beliefs for which one has newly acquired reasons, concern various facts about the world: that Bismarck resigned the chancellorship in such-and-such a month; that John has closed the window. In the case of sayings—although not of orders—a state of rhetic understanding also provides for the reverse sort of acquisition, whereby knowledge of the world grounds knowledge of the truth and falsity of sayings. In either case, rhetic understanding may be classified as a second-order cognitive capacity: one who possesses it is in a position to gain new knowledge from old.

It may be worth making some observations about this account of rhetic understanding—and, more particularly, about this account of what is involved in the rhetic understanding of a saying:

1. Some philosophers agree with me that understanding is a cognitive matter. But they hold that understanding a saying is a matter of knowing a proposition—a proposition which states the saying's truth conditions, or perhaps its conditions of warranted assertibility. There is no reason, however, to suppose that possessing a second-order cognitive capacity of the kind I have described is equivalent to knowing any proposition. Indeed no proposition presents itself, knowledge of which is equivalent to possessing the cognitive state described.

Some who deny that rhetic understanding is propositional knowledge take it to be a kind of practical knowledge instead. They understand understanding to be a matter of knowing how to use an expression, rather than any kind of knowledge-that. But this description does not seem right. It makes sense to describe someone as knowing how to use a word or a sentence, but this variety of practical knowledge does not always amount to the sort of understanding that we are trying to capture. A man may be said to know how to use the sentence "Quod erat demonstrandum" if he has been taught to use it to signal the end of a proof. But in knowing so much he may not know what an inscription of those words says. Our account explains why not. In having been taught to write those words at the end of a proof, he may not know that a reason to take an inscription of them to be true provides reason to believe that the proof's conclusion has, indeed, been demonstrated.

A better analogy for the sort of second-order capacity that I take rhetic understanding to be is with an inferential capacity. A thinker who is capable of making inferences involving disjunction (for example) is in a position to know that Stephen is in Paris, in the event of his coming to know both that Stephen is either in London or in Paris, and also that he is not in London. More generally, such a thinker is in a position to know that Q, in the event of his coming to know that P or Q, and that not P. The analogy with a state of rhetic understanding is not perfect. For one thing, making inferences from premises which one has reason to accept (even making such inferences correctly or validly) does not always give one reason for accepting the conclusion. I may have reason to believe that P or Q, and reason to believe that not P, and yet no reason to believe that Q. For the proposition that Q may be patently absurd, so that the only thing to do on realizing that it follows from two premises that I accept is to go back and reconsider my grounds for accepting them. All the same, the analogy is suggestive. Logicians have the notion of deriving rules of inference from more primitive rules. Clearly, not all the "rules" that correspond to the rhetic understanding of complete sayings can be primitive; perhaps none of them is. The relation between derived and primitive rules in a logical system may be a helpful model as we describe how our rhetic understanding of complete sayings depends upon our understanding of their parts.

2. Our analysis enables us to separate the wheat from the chaff in Wittgenstein's thesis 'To understand a declarative sentence in use means to know what is the case if it is true' or, as we may now put it, 'To enjoy a rhetic understanding of a saying is to know what is the case if it is true'. In this formula, the word "what" is an interrogative pronoun. A thinker will possess the knowledge that Wittgenstein says constitutes rhetic understanding if he knows something which answers the question "What is the case if the saying is true?" The occurrence of "if" here has the force of a biconditional. Since two's being prime is something that is always the case, it is something that is the case if any saying you care to choose is true. Appreciating that triviality, however, does not give one a rhetic understanding of every saying. The claim must be, then, that enjoying a rhetic understanding of a saying consists in knowing something which answers the question "What is the case if, but only if, the saying is true?" This claim may initially seem plausible. Where the saying in question is Hartmut's utterance of the words "In März 1890, hat Bismarck das Kanzleramt niederlegt", a true answer is: "His saying is true if, but only if, Bismarck resigned the chancellorship in March 1890". Knowing so much may seem both necessary and sufficient for understanding Hartmut's saying.

Having such knowledge is surely necessary for understanding a saying. If I understand u as saying that P, then I shall know, after minimal reflection, that u is true if and only if P. So I shall know something which answers the question "What is the case if, but only if, u is true?" There are, however, notorious problems with the claim that having such knowledge suffices for understanding a saying. One correct answer to the question "What is the case if, but only if, Hartmut's saying is true?" is: "It is true if and only if Bismarck resigned the chancellorship in March 1890". But if that answer is correct then (barring an eccentric logic for "if") so must be the following: "His saying is true if and only if Bismarck resigned the chancellorship in March 1890 and arithmetic is incomplete". A man may know an answer to the question about Hartmut's saying, then, by virtue of knowing that the saying is true if and only if Bismarck resigned the chancellorship in March 1890 and arithmetic is incomplete. (Perhaps he comes to know this through being told it.) But he will certainly not understand the saying if he thinks that it says that Bismarck resigned the chancellorship in March 1890 and arithmetic is incomplete. Neither will he understand it if he is in doubt which of the true answers to the question gives the content of the saying. So a thinker can, in the specified sense, know what is the case if a saying is true without understanding it.

Ideas of James Higginbotham's (1992: 5) suggest a variant of Wittgenstein's thesis which evades the present difficulty.

To a first approximation, [he writes] the meaning of an expression is what you are expected, simply as a speaker, to know about its reference. As a speaker of English, you are expected, for example, to know that 'snow is white' is true if and only if snow is white; to know that 'snow' refers to snow, and that 'is white' is true of just the white things; and to know quite generally that the result of combining a singular term noun phrase with a predicate in the form of an intransitive adjective is true just in case the predicate is true of the reference of the term. If, and only if, you know these things do you know that the sentence 'snow is white' means that snow is white.

This explication of meaning may be true; for certain purposes, moreover, it may be useful. But I do not think that it advances our quest. In the formula 'the meaning of an expression is what you are expected, simply as a speaker, to know about its reference', the parenthetical qualifier 'simply as a speaker' is essential. Someone who knows what snow is at all may be expected to know that it is white. In particular, an ordinary speaker of English may be expected to know this. Since, as Higginbotham says, he may also be expected to know that "snow is white" is true if and only if snow is white, he may further be expected to know that "snow is white" is true. But it is surely not part of the meaning of "snow is white" that it is true. This observation is not, of course, intended as an objection to Higginbotham. The point is simply that we cannot delete the qualifier 'simply as a speaker' from his proposal.

Given, though, that this qualifier is essential, what exactly does it mean? A natural gloss would be: 'simply by virtue of understanding the relevant expression'. Higginbotham's thesis would then say: 'the meaning of an expression is what you are expected, simply by virtue of understanding it, to know about its reference'. That formula nicely encapsulates the idea that I have been developing: namely, that the notions of meaning and understanding are coeval, and have to be understood in relation to one another. The formula does not, however, help to determine more exactly what is involved in possessing a rhetic understanding of a saying, or of any other kind of utterance. One could say: 'To possess a rhetic understanding of a saying is to know what one is expected to know, simply by virtue of understanding it, about its conditions of truth and falsity'. But while that claim is surely true, it throws little light on the nature of rhetic understanding. For it leaves quite unspecified what is the basis for expecting someone to know something, simply by virtue of enjoying a rhetic understanding of it. Our account supplies what is missing.

What one expects someone to know, by virtue of enjoying such an understanding of an expression, is something which, when combined with cognate knowledge about the other expressions in a saying, will enable him to convert reasons for deeming the saying to be true (or false) into reasons for beliefs about the world, and vice versa. Our account explains, indeed, why a speaker who takes Hartmut's utterance to say that Bismarck resigned the chancellorship in March 1890 and arithmetic is incomplete is labouring under a misunderstanding. What Hartmut says, and the proposition that Bismarck resigned the chancellorship in March 1890 and arithmetic is incomplete, necessarily coincide in truth-value. For all that, a hearer who acquires reason to believe that Hartmut's saying is true acquires no reason to believe that arithmetic is incomplete. A fortiori, he acquires no reason to believe that Bismarck resigned the chancellorship in March 1890 and arithmetic is incomplete.

3. It may still be puzzling why knowing (or having reason to believe) that Hartmut's saying is true if and only if Bismarck resigned the chancellorship in March 1890 is not sufficient for understanding it. After all, it may be argued, the four inferences

P if and only if Q; P; so Q
P if and only if Q; Q; so P
P if and only if Q; not P; so not Q
P if and only if Q; not Q; so not P

are one and all valid. It seems, then, that if a subject knows that P if and only if Q, he will be in a cognitive state which gives him reason to believe that Q, in the event of his acquiring reason to believe that P; and which gives him reason to believe that P, in the event of his acquiring reason to believe that Q; etc. That cognitive state, moreover, will put him in a position to know that Q, in the event of his coming to know that P; and to know that P, in the event of his coming to know that Q; etc. Applied to the present case, then, a subject who knows that Hartmut's saying is true if and only if Bismarck resigned the chancellorship in March 1890 seems to be perfectly placed to make the transitions that I have suggested are constitutive of a rhetic understanding of the saying. So why should we not say that enjoying that understanding is simply a matter of knowing that the saying is true if and only if Bismarck resigned the chancellorship in March 1890?

The answer depends on how the biconditional connective is understood. If it is taken materially, then "P if and only if Q" is strictly equivalent to "(Either not P or Q) and (either P or not Q)". So a thinker who knows that P, and that Q, and who is minimally competent with disjunctions, will know that P if and only if Q (with "if and only if" read materially). Suppose then that I know that Hartmut's saying is true (perhaps through being told that it is), and that I also know that Bismarck resigned the chancellorship in March 1890. Suppose also that I am minimally competent with disjunctions. In that case, I shall know that Hartmut's saying is true if and only if Bismarck resigned the chancellorship in March 1890. It is clear, however, that I may know so much without having any idea of what Hartmut was saying. In particular, I may know so much without my having any reason to believe that Bismarck did not resign the chancellorship in March 1890, in the event of my acquiring reason to take Hartmut's saying to be false, and without my having any reason to take Hartmut's saying to be false, in the event of my acquiring reason to believe that Bismarck did not then resign the chancellorship.

This shows that knowledge of our material biconditional does not suffice to sustain the reason-providing transitions in which, as I take it, a rhetic understanding of Hartmut's saying consists. Can we do better if we read the biconditional connective differently? According to Gilbert Ryle, the conditional statement "If P then Q" is best understood as an "inference warrant": a licence to perform the inferences from "P" to "Q", from "not Q" to "not P", and so forth. As he explains

knowing 'If P, then Q', is rather like being in possession of a railway ticket. It is having a licence or warrant to make a journey from London to Oxford ... As a person can have a ticket without actually travelling with it and without ever being in London or getting to Oxford, so a person can have an inference warrant without actually making any inferences and even without ever acquiring the premisses from which to make them. (1971: 239–40)

As a description of the conditional construction in English, Ryle's account clearly will not do. To take an example of John Skorupski's, I have good reason to believe that if Mrs Thatcher is a master criminal, we shall never know that she is. In certain circumstances, indeed, I may know this: suppose, for example, that I know that she had the opportunity to destroy any evidence there may be of her criminality, and that I know that she would not let such an opportunity slip. That knowledge, however, does not consist in my readiness to infer that we shall never know that she is a master criminal in the event of my 'acquiring the premiss' that she is one. On the contrary. Acquiring the premiss presumably means coming to know it. And in the event that I do come to know that she is a master criminal, I shall certainly not infer that we shall never know that she is one.

All the same, one could (I suppose) understand the conditional construction in the way that Ryle describes: his description, indeed, generalizes the use of it that is made by intuitionistic mathematicians. And if it is so understood, one could say that understanding u as saying that P is a matter of knowing that u is true if and only if P. I do not recommend saying this, though. As we have seen, the knowledge in question is not knowledge of the corresponding material conditional; there is indeed no reason to take it to be propositional knowledge at all. Accordingly, representing it in an apparently propositional form is at best potentially misleading. To the extent, however, that Ryle's account approximates to the correct account of the English conditional, we may explain the enduring attractiveness of the idea that understanding a saying as saying that P is a matter of knowing that it is true if and only if P.

4. It would, I suggested earlier, be less misleading to represent a subject's state of rhetic understanding of a saying as a quartet of quasi-inference rules in the form

> From the premiss or hypothesis that u is true, infer that P, and vice versa

and

> From the premiss or hypothesis that u is false, infer that it is not the case that P, and vice versa.

A preoccupation of philosophers concerned with meaning has been to explain how—or at least to sketch a possible explanation of how—a hearer may come to understand a saying which is of type that he has not hitherto heard.[3] On the view that I am recommending, such an explanation will be provided by explaining how a hearer comes to go by certain quasi-inference rules when he has not been expressly trained in the use of type sentence the rule concerns.

As I suggested above, one model for such an explanation is the way certain rules of a formal system may be derived from more primitive rules. Our analysis of WH-questions has already brought out how quasi-inference rules apply to utterances of predicates as well as complete sayings. Thus a speaker who enjoys a rhetic understanding of an utterance v of the predicate "there is a bull in . . ." will be in a cognitive state which may be characterized by the following quartet of quasi-inference rules:

> From the premiss or hypothesis that v is true of x, infer that there is a bull in x, and vice versa

and

> From the premiss or hypothesis that v is false of x, infer that there is no bull in x, and vice versa.

He will also know that if an utterance u is the result of combining the incomplete utterance v with an utterance that makes a reference to a particular field, f, then

> From the premiss or hypothesis that u is true, we may infer that v is true of f, and vice versa.

and

> From the premiss or hypothesis that u is false, we may infer that v is false of f, and vice versa.

---

[3] See especially Davidson (1984a, b). It would take all the space at my disposal properly to expound the subtle holism of Davidson's approach to meaning. The reader is instead referred to David Wiggins's admirable (1997), which traces the descent of Davidson's approach from the Tractarian idea in which my own account of rhetic understanding originates.

If, then, he hears an utterance u which is of the words "There is a bull in that field", and which is such that the component utterance of the referring expression "that field" refers to f, then these rules will combine to yield the derived rules:

> From the premiss or hypothesis that u is true, infer that there is a bull in field f, and vice versa

and

> From the premiss or hypothesis that u is false, infer that there is no bull in field f, and vice versa.

We may, in this way, explain how it is that the hearer comes to be in the second-order cognitive state that we took to constitute rhetic understanding of the saying u.

Many philosophers who have aimed to explain our ability to understand novel sayings have tried to do so by attributing propositional knowledge to the relevant hearer—knowledge which could account for his knowing another proposition, namely, the T-theorem for the relevant saying. And in the example just given, the derivation of the pertinent rule mimics the derivation of the T-theorem for the saying. It is important to note, however, that the approach in terms of derived rules allows a welcome new flexibility. For alongside rules of inference (or quasi-inference) a formal system may contain rules of proof: rules for deriving new rules from old. Rules of proof are particularly well adapted to describing the capacities that characterize a hearer who understands certain iterable linguistic devices, whose significance cannot be captured by an axiom. A clear example of such a device is the sentence-forming operator on sentences "It is necessarily the case that". If one took Davidson's own truth-theoretical axioms as a model for capturing the significance of this operator, one would suppose that the axiom governing it was as follows:

> $\ulcorner$It is necessarily the case that $S\urcorner$ is true as potentially uttered by person p at time t if and only if it is necessarily the case that S is true as potentially uttered by person p at time t.

An instance of this axiom, however, is

> "It is necessarily the case that two is a prime number" is true as potentially uttered by me now if and only if it is necessarily the case that "Two is a prime number" is true as potentially uttered by me now,

which is false. The left-hand side of this biconditional is true, while the right-hand side is false, for it is not necessary that the words "Two is a prime number", as they are potentially uttered by me now, should express a necessary truth. Of course, the failure of this simple suggestion does not show that there is no way of capturing the rhetic contribution of "It is necessarily the case that" by way of a truth-theoretical axiom, though I have explained elsewhere why other natural suggestions also fail (see Rumfitt 2001). But in any case it is striking that the rhetic contribution this operator makes may be captured simply using a rule of proof. For we may posit a rule of proof which says that where u is an utterance of a sentence S for which we already have the rules:

From the premiss or hypothesis that u is true, infer that P, and vice versa

and

From the premiss or hypothesis that u is false, infer that it is not the case that P, and vice versa

we may further extend the derivation of rules so that where v is an utterance of the sentence ⌜It is necessarily the case that S⌝, we also have the rules:

From the premiss or hypothesis that v is true, infer that it is necessarily the case that P, and vice versa

and

From the premiss or hypothesis that v is false, infer that it is not necessarily the case that P, and vice versa.

5. Meaning Revisited

Where, finally, do these investigations leave the notion of meaning itself? We started from the idea that an expression's meaning was best understood in terms of communicative speech. Having delineated the conditions for successful communication—however provisionally and sketchily—how are we to elucidate the notion of meaning?

I should elucidate it as follows. Attaining a rhetic understanding of an utterance, I suggested, is largely a matter of ascertaining what the speaker intends to say, or to ask, or to order one to do. Sometimes, the circumstances will enable one to do that even when unfamiliar words, or unfamiliar constructions, are being used. In general, however, ascertaining what rhetic act the speaker is performing will only be possible when speaker and hearer have undergone a similar habituation in the words and the constructions that are employed. That habituation will result in knowledge—common knowledge—of some features of the words and constructions that help to explain how it is that a hearer can apprehend the rhetic intentions of the speaker. And such features of the word or construction in question may be deemed to be part of its meaning. An expression's meaning, we might say, comprises whatever is commonly known about it which helps to explain how those who use it can make their rhetic intentions manifest.

This elucidation is highly schematic. Elaborating it for particular classes of words and constructions is a matter for empirical investigation into the languages which contain the relevant words and constructions. But even the most cursory look at the data inspires a few cautionary remarks. In the first place, there is far less scope for novelty and innovation with the meanings of particular forms of sentence construction than there is with words. A speaker who tries to use the familiar combination of noun phrase followed by verb phrase to raise a WH-question is likely to be met with total incomprehension. We may expect, then, that a satisfactory semantic theory for a language will associate each form of sentence construction with a small, finite number of rhetic acts that may be performed by uttering sentences of that form, as when one says that an instance of the construction simply comprising noun phrase and intransitive adjective will be such that knowledge of its truth (or falsity) extends to knowledge that the object referred to by the noun phrase does (or does not) possess the attribute expressed by the adjective. With the lexicon, however, matters stand very differently. As we had occasion to remark, there are expressions—such as the pronoun "I"—whose referents (in a given context of utterance) are uniquely determined by a simple convention or rule. And our elucidation of the notion of meaning entails—what one might in any case expect—that a statement of the relevant rule gives the meaning of the expression. As we also had occasion to remark, however, such expressions are unusual, and in other cases there is nothing in one's training with a word which yields a rule which can settle the reference given information about some small number of contextual parameters, identifiable in advance. It is true that empirical investigation has revealed more system and structure in some items of the lexicon than a casual observer might expect. But those investigations do not support the view that words bear a small, finite number of senses which determine a reference, given values for a small number of contextual parameters. A word like "I" belongs at one extreme of a spectrum within the lexicon; it is not a paradigm or an exemplar. Philosophers sometimes write as though a sentence's meaning were constructed out of rigid, preformed lexical meanings in something like the way a three-dimensional figure may be constructed out of pieces of Meccano. The use we make of sentences in communication, however, is far more fungible than this picture would allow. And it is wholly unclear what use we might have for a notion of meaning that is divorced from explaining successful communication when it occurs.

References

Austin, J. L. (1975). *How to Do Things with Words*, 2nd edn. Oxford: Clarendon Press.
Davidson, Donald (1984a). 'Theories of Meaning and Learnable Languages'. Repr. in Davidson, *Inquiries into Truth and Interpretation*. Oxford: Clarendon Press.
—— (1984b). 'Truth and Meaning'. Repr. in Davidson, *Inquiries into Truth and Interpretation*. Oxford: Clarendon Press.

Dummett, Michael (1993). 'Language and Communication', in Dummett, *The Seas of Language*. Oxford: Clarendon Press.

Grice, H. P. (1957). 'Meaning'. *Philosophical Review*, 66: 377–88.

—— (1989). *Studies in the Ways of Words*. Cambridge, Mass.: Harvard University Press.

Higginbotham, James (1992). 'Truth and Understanding'. *Philosophical Studies*, 65: 3–16.

Rumfitt, Ian (2001). 'Semantic Theory and Necessary Truth'. *Synthese*, 126: 283–324.

Ryle, Gilbert (1971). ' "If", "So", and "Because" ', in Ryle, *Collected Papers*, ii. London: Hutchinson.

Searle, J. R. (1969). *Speech Acts*. Cambridge: Cambridge University Press.

Strawson, P. F. (1997). 'Meaning and Context', in Strawson, *Entity and Identity and Other Essays*. Oxford: Clarendon Press.

Wiggins, David (1997). 'Meaning and Truth Conditions: From Frege's Grand Design to Davidson's', in Bob Hale and Crispin Wright (eds.), *A Companion to the Philosophy of Language*. Oxford: Blackwell.

CHAPTER 17

TRUTH

PAUL HORWICH

There is an aura of peculiar depth and obscurity surrounding our concept of truth, and philosophy abounds with theories designed to illuminate it, to say what it is for beliefs and statements to possess that special quality. The most important trend of the last fifteen years in this area has been away from traditional approaches, which have taken for granted that truth is some sort of 'substantive' property (i.e. a property with a hidden nature calling for theoretical articulation), and towards the development of so-called *deflationary* theories in which that assumption is rejected. Therefore, I shall focus in this review on the differences between these two general perspectives, on the reasons for favouring the deflationary point of view, and on the relative merits of the alternative accounts of this type. I will argue that the best of the deflationary proposals is the one known as "minimalism", according to which our possession of the concept of truth derives from our regarding each proposition as equivalent to the proposition that it is true.

What defines 'deflationism' in the present context is a cluster of four interlocking ideas about the truth predicate: one at the level of pragmatics, concerning its function; another at the level of philosophical import, concerning the alleged theoretical profundity of the notion it expresses; a third at the level of semantics, concerning the way in which its meaning is fixed; and a fourth at the level of metaphysics, concerning what sort of property, if any, the truth predicate stands for, and what the fundamental facts are concerning that property. More specifically, the four-pronged deflationary position is as follows:

1. Our word "true" has an idiosyncratic conceptual function, an unusual kind of utility. What exactly that function is supposed to be varies from one deflationary

account to another: the truth predicate is said to be a device of *emphasis*, or *concession*, or *generalization*, or *anaphora*. But there is agreement that we must distinguish its *raison d'être* from that of other terms, and that we must especially beware against assimilating it to empirical predicates—such as "red", "tree", and "magnetic"—whose utility resides in their role in prediction and causal explanation.

2. In light of the first point, truth is not, as often assumed, a *deep* concept and should not be given a pivotal role in philosophical theorizing (e.g. as a basic element in the explanation of meaning, or as the key to our conception of reality). Its actual philosophical significance is somewhat back-handed—lying in the fact that so many problems are exacerbated by our failure to appreciate its rather mundane function and the peculiar principle of use which enables this function to be fulfilled.

3. The non-predictive non-explanatory role of the truth predicate implies that its meaning is not *empirical*—i.e. its deployment is not based on a rule that instructs us to accept

$$x \text{ is true} \leftrightarrow x \text{ is F},$$

where "F" articulates some observable characteristic (or fuzzy cluster of empirical characteristics). Nor does "true" abbreviate a complex *non*-empirical expression (in which case, what is postulated to explain its usage would nonetheless be an explicit definition). Rather, the central principle governing our overall deployment of the truth predicate is, very roughly speaking, that each statement articulates the conditions that are necessary and sufficient for its own truth. In other words, we are required to accept that the statement made by "Dogs bark" is true just in case dogs bark, and so on. It is some such basic rule of use that provides the truth predicate with its distinctive meaning and which (as we shall see) equips it to perform its distinctive function.

4. In so far as "true" does not have the role, and the meaning-constituting use, of an empirical predicate, we can appreciate a priori that there will be no reductive analysis of truth to empirical (i.e. naturalistic) properties. Similarly, we can see that the fundamental facts about truth will not be laws relating it to empirical phenomena. As in the case of *logical* notions—or, as one might well put it, our *other* logical notions—the most that can be expected, by way of theory, is a systematization of the superficial facts to which we are committed by the meaning of the truth predicate—for example, the fact that if dogs bark then it is true that they do, and so on.[1] This is what is meant by saying that the property of truth is not 'substantive'.[2]

---

[1] For arguments in support of this claim, see Horwich (1998: 50–1).

[2] Recent philosophical literature is replete with conflicting proposals about the right way to distinguish between 'deflationary' and 'non-deflationary' theories. However, just because the term at issue

Judged by this cluster of criteria, the following well-known accounts of truth cannot qualify as deflationary:

The correspondence theory, whereby "*x* is true" means "*x* corresponds to a fact". (Or, alternatively, whereby the truth of statements is explained in terms of the referents of their constituents, and reference is then defined in terms of some causal correspondence relation).[3]

The proof theory, whereby "*x* is true" means "*x* is provable".[4] Note that if coherence amongst beliefs is taken to provide empirical proof, then the proof theory of truth subsumes the coherence theory.[5]

The pragmatic theory, whereby "*x* is true" means "*x* is useful to believe".[6]

Davidson's theory, whereby truth is indefinable but plays a vital role in the causal explanation of verbal behaviour.[7]

None of these accounts attributes any peculiar non-predictive, non-explanatory role to the truth predicate. None insists on its theoretical unimportance. None of them supposes its meaning to be captured by something more or less tantamount to a disquotational schema. And none regards it as unreasonable to look for a theory of the truth-facts that goes significantly beneath such trivialities. Thus, they are each the product of overgeneralization—tending to assimilate truth to more familiar (i.e. empirical) properties. Consequently, they should never have been expected to hold, and the emergence of specific disqualifying defects in them can hardly be surprising.

here is a piece of jargon whose meaning is to be stipulated, that does not put the alternative proposals beyond the possibility of rational assessment. On the contrary, the merits of each candidate may be determined by reference to two considerations: first, whether the proposed basis of classification is deep and interesting; and secondly, whether "deflationism" would be an apt label for that basis. On the first point, I believe it is indicative of the theoretical depth of the proposal advanced here that its four criteria correlate so well with one another. And on the second point, the word "deflationism" nicely captures the idea that truth is less profound and potent that has traditionally been assumed, and (as a consequence) that it does not require the sort of theoretical characterization that has traditionally been sought. I am not claiming that these considerations amount to a demonstration that my way of drawing the deflationism–inflationism distinction is best. Indeed, given the vagueness of the terms (such as "interesting" and "appropriate") in which this matter is to be judged, there are likely to be other reasonable definitions. However, it must be stressed that this issue is of very minor importance compared to that of providing the best account of truth, and is independent of that problem. Even if some other characterization of 'deflationism' turns out to be preferable to mine, that could not bear on the intrinsic merits of the specific ('minimalist') account of truth that I advocate here, but merely on the appropriateness of categorizing it as 'deflationary'.

[3] Wittgenstein (1922); Austin (1950); Alston (1996); Field (1972). Some philosophers (e.g. Armstrong 2004) advocate a 'truthmaker principle'—"For every true proposition there is something whose existence implies the truth of that proposition"—and take this to be a form of correspondence theory. However, I follow Lewis (2001) in regarding a commitment to truthmakers, not as a theory of truth, but as a generalization of specific metaphysical claims (e.g. "There is something whose existence implies that dogs bark") that have nothing to do with the property of truth.

[4] Peirce (1932–3); Dummett (1978); Putnam (1981).

[5] Bradley (1914); Blanchard (1939; see esp. 260–79); Walker (1989).

[6] James (1909); Papineau (1991).   [7] Davidson (1990).

For example, a decent correspondence theory would require accounts of 'correspondence' and of 'fact'—accounts that no one has been able to supply. Indeed it can be argued that the conceptual order that it would propose is precisely the wrong way around, and "facts" should be really defined as "truths".[8] The best non-deflationary response to these difficulties has been to explain truth in terms of reference, as Tarski suggested (see below), but then to diverge from Tarski and offer a definition of reference in terms of causation.[9] But this plan has never been realized in a decent concrete proposal. And one good reason for thinking that it never could be is the phenomenon of reference to abstract (i.e. *non*-causal) objects, such as numbers, universals, and fictional characters.

Equally serious difficulties plague the proof theory. In the first place, our powers of discovery are limited. Consequently, many statements are true despite our having no actual proof of them (and not even any *possibility* of proving them). Note that 'powerful evidence' cannot be taken to constitute 'proof' (in the sense required by this account), since we surely cannot conclude, in light of what is *certainly* powerful evidence for some claim, that we are *certain* of its truth. In the second place, it is doubtful whether an adequate notion of "*can* be proved" is available. The problem is, for example, that something's actually being red is quite consistent with the existence of a metaphysically possible world in which it is observed (i.e. proved) to be green. And in the third place, there appears to be nothing incoherent in supposing that even though we have what we regard as a proof of some proposition—even though our being certain of its truth is fully justified— the proposition happens nonetheless to be false.

So the proof theory exaggerates the admittedly significant correlation between what is true and what we have established (or will or could establish). Similarly, the pragmatic theory begins with an important insight—namely, that deliberations and decisions based on true beliefs tend to be more successful than those based on false ones. But it also goes too far in attempting to transform this observation into a strict definition. For it is obvious that actions deriving from correct assumptions (e.g. "The operation has a 99 per cent success rate") will sometimes be disastrous, and that false assumptions (e.g. Newtonian mechanics) can be extremely useful.

Finally, a word on Davidson's theory, which diverges from deflationism in attributing a *causal* role to truth and in denying that anything like 'disquotation' can suffice to capture our conception of it. These divergences result from Davidson's scepticism about *meaning*. For once meaning is discarded, then its causal–explanatory job (in helping to account for linguistic behaviour) will have to be done by something else—and the alternative that Davidson latched onto was the *truth* condition of a sentence. Thus truth is saddled with meaning's causal–explanatory

---

[8] Moore (1927). Similar objections can be made against the supposition that truth may be defined by means of the *identity* of true propositions with facts, as suggested by Jennifer Hornsby (1997).

[9] This idea was sketched by Hartry Field (1972).

function and therefore becomes too substantive to be defined merely by a trivial disquotational equivalence.

But Davidson's meaning-scepticism (like all other forms of philosophical scepticism) is based on highly dubious assumptions. Specifically, he dismisses (as insufficiently explanatory) the naive Fregean picture, in which the meanings of complex expressions are the values of applying the meanings of certain terms (functions) to the meanings of others (arguments). And this is what leads him to conclude that full-blooded meaning-entities could not accommodate the phenomenon of compositionality—the dependence of sentence meanings on the meanings of their parts—and therefore that no such entities should be taken to exist. But if, as I would suggest, the explanatory demands on meaning-entities that are imposed by Davidson are inflated and illegitimate, and our superficial, Fregean picture of compositionality is acceptable after all, then his sceptical conclusion is undermined; so there will be no need to press the property of truth into the sort of explanatory service that would call for anything more than a deflationary account of what it is.[10]

Partly as a reaction against all the troubles that come from taking for granted that truth is a 'substantive' property like most others,[11] the radically different, 'deflationary' perspective has recently gained in popularity. Among accounts of this latter sort, the most prominent and promising are:

> *The redundancy theory*, whereby "The proposition *that p* is true" means the same as "*p*".[12]

> *The minimalist theory*, whereby we mean what we do by the truth predicate in virtue of our underived acceptance of the material equivalence schema "The proposition *that p* is true $\leftrightarrow p$".[13]

> *Tarski's theory*, whereby truth, for the sentences of a given language, is defined in terms of reference within that language, which is in turn defined by a mere list of what its words refer to. Note that Tarski is quite clear that the meaning of the expression "true in English" is implicitly fixed by the disquotation schema. The purpose of his further theorizing is to put this idea into the form of a 'respectable' (i.e. explicit) definition.[14]

> *The sentence-variable analysis*, whereby "*x* is true" means the same as "$(\exists p)(x = \,<p> \;\&\; p)$".[15]

> *The prosentential theory*, whereby "it is true" is a kind of dummy sentence, or sentence variable, whose relation to other sentences is similar to the relationship between pronouns and other singular terms.[16]

---

[10] See Davidson (1984). For details of my criticism, see Horwich (2005).

[11] For further discussion of these problems, see Kirkham (1992); Engel (2002); Kuenne (2003).

[12] Strawson (1950).   [13] See Horwich (1998).   [14] Tarski (1943–4, 1958).

[15] Ramsey (1927, 1991); Hill (2002); Kuenne (2003). Note that "$<p>$" is an abbreviation of "the proposition *that p*".   [16] Grover *et al.* (1975); Brandom (1994, esp. ch. 5).

The disquotation theory, whereby our concept of truth for sentences (at least for the context-*in*sensitive part of our *own* language) is captured by the strong equivalence of " '*p*' is true" and "*p*".[17]

These accounts meet my four conditions for being deflationary. First, their advocates typically stress some distinctive, mundane function of our truth predicate. Secondly, the theoretical work that is given to it is confined by this view of its function. Thirdly, they each take the fundamental (meaning-constituting) use of the word to be (very roughly speaking, and each in its own way) the assumption that every statement articulates its own truth condition. And fourthly, these theories concur in denying that the property of truth has any naturalistic reductive analysis, and in denying that its character may be captured by principles relating it to empirical phenomena.

So much for the intension and extension of the expression "deflationary view of truth". Let me now compare and contrast the various accounts that fall under it, and explain why I think that minimalism is the most attractive of them. I'll proceed by considering its competitors one at a time, briefly stating what I take their relative disadvantages to be.

According to the redundancy theory, "*p*" and "It is true that *p*" and "The proposition *that p* is true" say exactly the same thing. No meaning is added either by "It is true that..." or by "The proposition that...is true"; so they are redundant. This implies that the logical form of, for example

The proposition *that Fido is a dog* is true

is simply

Dog[Fido],

which in turn implies that the English truth predicate is not a *logical* predicate.

But in that case we are unable to explain the validity of the following inference schema, whose deployment is vital to our use of the term

X is true	Ed's claim is true
X = <*p*>	Ed's claim is that Fido is a dog
∴ <*p*> is true	∴ That Fido is a dog is true
∴ *p*	∴ Fido is a dog

For in order that the first part hold (as an instance of Leibniz's Law), it is necessary that "is true" be a logical predicate.

Suppose, in order to rectify this crippling defect, we make a small adjustment to the redundancy theory—continuing to claim that the concept of truth is captured by the equivalence of "<*p*> is true" and "*p*", but deploying a weaker notion of

---

[17] Quine (1990); Leeds (1978); Field (1994).

equivalence—no longer *synonymy*, but merely an a priori known and metaphysically necessary *material* equivalence. We thereby arrive at minimalism. More precisely, the minimalist contention is that our meaning what we do by "true" is grounded in the fact that the word's overall use stems from our acceptance of the schema "<p> is true ↔ p" (a fact from which the necessity and apriority of its instances may be inferred).[18] Given this modification of the redundancy theory, the word "true" *can* be treated as a logical predicate; and so the sorts of inference that are essential (if there is going to be any point in having a truth predicate) will be evidently valid.

Now suppose that someone, while fully sympathizing with this line of thought, nonetheless aspires to provide an *explicit definition* of truth. Is there some way of reformulating the content of minimalism so that it will take that desired form?

This was Tarski's problematic, and his answer was yes. He recognized that it will not do simply to say

$$x \text{ is true} \equiv [x = <\text{dogs bark}> \text{ and dogs bark; or}$$
$$x = <\text{pigs fly}> \text{ and pigs fly; or}$$
$$\dots \text{ and so on}]$$

since this would be an ill-formed attempt at an infinitely long statement. And he saw that he would therefore have to focus on the truth of the *sentences* of specific languages; because only for such a notion—i.e. "true in L"—might it be feasible to derive each of the infinitely many conditions for its application from a finite base (namely, of principles concerning the finitely many words in L). It would not have been an option for Tarski to offer an account of how the truth-values of *propositions* depend on the referents of their components, because there are infinitely many such components (i.e. possible basic concepts) whose referents would each require specification. Rather, his only reasonable strategy was to offer a separate account for each language—an account whose base lists the referents of each of its words and gives the principles determining how the referents (and truth-values) of complex expressions depend on them. Such a base could then, with a certain logical ingenuity, be rejigged into the form of an explicit definition.

This is an elegant result; but the costs are heavy. In the first place, we don't get an account of the notion that initially puzzled us: namely, *truth* as applied to what we believe, to the things our utterances express. In the second place, although one might decide to aim instead at an account of *sentential* truth—i.e. aim to capture what we mean by "expresses a truth of L"—the Tarskian approach to that problem is clearly deficient. For various features of our *actual* understanding of this expression will not be captured by a Tarskian definition: (*a*) that our actual understanding

---

[18] It can be argued that our acceptance of this schema, although sufficient, is not *necessary* for us to mean what we do by "true". For someone may not be convinced that there *is* a single property whose possession by any proposition is equivalent to that proposition. But he will nonetheless understand the word "true" as we do, as long as he acknowledges that *if* such a property exists, it is the property of *truth*. For further discussion, see Horwich (2005, ch. 6).

is based, compositionally, on what we mean by "expresses", "true", "in L", etc., and on the way these terms are combined; (*b*) that it does not presuppose a prior understanding of *every* one of L's words; and (*c*) that in so far as any notion of reference is presupposed by it, that notion will not be definable by a mere list of what each word of L happens to refer to. And in the third place, it's only for a limited range of formal languages that Tarski-style explanations of truth in terms of word-reference can be supplied. There are notorious difficulties in giving such a treatment of attributive adjectives, belief attributions, conditionals, and many other natural language constructions.[19]

Supposing, for these reasons, that we judge Tarski's account not to be good enough. Is there any *alternative* explicit definition that will capture his insight that the essence of the matter is the equivalence of "<*p*> is true" and "*p*"?

Well there is the view that I called the sentence-variable analysis—first articulated by Frank Ramsey and urged these days by Christopher Hill and Wolfgang Kuenne:

$$x \text{ is true} \equiv (\exists p)(x = <p> \ \& \ p).$$

Evidently, the variable '*p*' and quantifier '∃*p*' that are deployed on the right-hand side are non-standard. Unlike the normal existential quantifier, which binds variables that occur in *singular-term* positions and which formalizes the word "something", this one binds variables that occur in *sentence* positions and does not appear to correspond to any of the expressions of a natural language.

So one cause for concern is whether these notions are coherent. We might well be troubled by an inability to say what the variables range over, and by the licence to quantify into opaque 'that'-clauses. And there is no easy escape from these difficulties in simply supposing that the new variables and quantifiers are *substitutional*; since substitutional quantifiers are standardly explained in terms of truth—"{∃*p*}(...*p*...)" means "The result of substituting a sentence for '*p*' in '...*p*...' is true"—and therefore cannot be used to explain what truth is.

But even if we set aside questions of coherence, there is the further objection that our *actual* understanding of the truth predicate cannot be built on notions that we don't yet have. And there are two reasons for thinking that sentential quantifiers and variables don't already exist either in natural languages or in languages of thought. In the first place, it is hard to find any clear cases. For example, it would be implausible to suppose that when we say

For any way things might be, either they are that way or they are not,

what we are actually thinking is

$$(p)(p \lor -p),$$

---

[19] For more on Tarski's proposal—including a discussion of the 'liar' paradoxes—see Horwich (2006).

since this would miss a great deal of the original's structure. A better account is given by the straightforwardly faithful

$(x)(y)[(x$ is an n-tuple of things & y is an n-adic property$) \rightarrow (x$ has $y \vee x$ does not have $y)]$.

And in the second place, if we did have such variables and quantifiers, then our actual deployment of the truth predicate would be highly surprising. For some of the generalizations that it enables us to formulate (e.g. "Everything of the form '$p \vee -p$' is true") could be articulated more directly in terms of our sentential variables. Why would there not be a natural language way of saying "$(p)(p \vee -p)$"?

This is not to deny that one might now decide to introduce the new apparatus, and then proceed to formulate a definition of "true" in terms of it. But it can hardly be supposed that such a definition would constitute our *present* understanding of the truth predicate, since we don't yet have the terms and notions that are needed for it.

Against this point it might be protested that it is not really a requirement on a definition that it be psychologically accurate—that it fully capture our pre-existing basis for using the word. Consider, for example, Frege's innovative definitions of the numerals in terms of sets, or his definition of the ancestral relation in terms of predicate logic.

However, the moral here is that we must distinguish *two* conceptions of 'definition', corresponding to two things that we might be trying to do with it: one kind is *descriptive*, the other *revisionary*; one attempts to articulate what is already meant, the other specifies and recommends a new meaning. In these terms, my primary objection to the sentence-variable analysis of truth was that it does not do the first job—it is not descriptively accurate.

But, in addition, it has no evident value as a suggestion about what we *ought* to mean by "true". In order to justify such a revision, we would need to identify some defect in our present notion—a defect that would be remedied by replacing it with the proposed new one. Or else we would have to have some independent rationale for introducing the new forms of variable and quantifier in terms of which an equally useful, new notion of truth could easily be defined. But no such case has been made. And, even if it were to be made, we should not forget that the suggested revision would inevitably bypass our main original problem, which was to demystify truth as we actually conceive of it.

Suppose then, in light of the failure of either Tarski's account or the sentence-variable analysis to provide a plausible definition that is both explicit and deflationary, we face the fact that there was never any reason in the first place to expect the truth predicate's meaning to be fixed by an explicit definition.[20] Where

---

[20] It is argued by some philosophers (following Tarski 1958; Gupta 1993) that an explicit definition may be needed in order to explain our acceptance of *generalizations* about truth (such as "Every instance of 'If p, then p' is true"). I attempt to rebut this argument in Horwich (1998: 137–8; 2006).

does that leave us? Well, as we have seen, one possibility is to embrace minimalism, whereby the truth predicate applies to propositions, and its meaning is constituted, not by any explicit definition, but by our commitment to the equivalence schema. However, perhaps something better than minimalism can be found?

For example, there is the prosentential point of view (initially proposed by Grover, Camp, and Belnap 1975), whereby the word "true" is a meaningless part of the unstructured dummy sentence "it-is-true", which, like a pro*noun*, gets its reference from something in the context of utterance. Thus the "He" in "He was Austrian" can be used to refer to Wittgenstein; and the "it" in "If a triangle has equal sides, then it has equal angles" is a bound variable—formally, "$(x)(ESx \rightarrow EAx)$". And, allegedly, the function of "it-is-true" is analogous: it can be used to have the same reference as (i.e. to have the same truth-value as) someone's preceding remark that dogs bark. Moreover, the "it-is-true" in "Everything is such that if Mary stated that it-is-true, then it-is-true" is a bound variable—formally, "$(p)(\text{Mary stated that } p \rightarrow p)$".

This point of view clearly has a close affinity with the just-mentioned sentence-variable analysis. But instead of supposing that the word "true" is a genuine logical predicate, explicitly *definable* in terms of sentential variables and quantifiers, the prosententialist says that the English word "true" is *not* a genuine logical predicate, since it is an undetachable part of a sentence variable. As we have just seen, the underlying logical form of "Everything Mary said is true" is supposed to be "$(p)(\text{Mary said that } p \rightarrow p)$", which contains no predicate corresponding to the word "true": its role was merely to help us to construct the prosentence "it-is-true", represented formally by the letter "p".

Thus the prosententialist is denying the claim I made, in objecting to the sentence-variable analysis, that we don't already deploy the needed variable and quantifier notions. His view is that we are in fact deploying them via our use of the truth predicate. But of course, this response cannot vindicate that analysis. For the sentence variables that it invokes are *composed* from the word "true", and therefore cannot qualify as a suitable basis in terms of which to define it. Thus prosententialism is a quite distinct point of view.[21]

But a serious difficulty with the orthodox version of it (as developed mainly by Dorothy Grover 1992) is that most of our uses of the truth predicate do not occur in the context of the supposedly canonical phrase "it-is-true". Consider, for example,

(*a*) Goldbach's Conjecture is true

and

(*b*) All Mary's statements are true.

---

[21] One might be tempted to combine the two accounts and to maintain that our truth *predicate* is defined, along the following lines, in terms of the *prosentential component*: "x is true $\leftrightarrow$ something is such that x is the proposition that it-is-true, and it-is-true". But it would be hard to defend the implication that "true", in current English, is ambiguous (in that particular way).

In order for orthodox prosententialism to handle such cases they must first be transformed into sentences in which all the occurrences of the truth predicate *do* occur in the context of "it-is-true". For example:

(*a**) Something is such that Goldbach's Conjecture is the proposition that *it-is-true*, and *it-is-true*

(*b**) Everything is such that if Mary stated that *it-is-true*, then *it-is-true*.

But one might well wonder what the grounds could be for regarding the original sentences and their alleged underlying versions as equivalent to each other. *If* the word "true" could be treated as a logical predicate, then the sentence-pairs in question would be semi-formalizable by

(*A*)   True (Goldbach's Conjecture)
(*A**) $(\exists x)[(\text{Goldbach's Conjecture} = <\text{true}(x)>) \text{ \& true}(x)]$

(*B*) $(x)[\text{Mary stated}(x) \rightarrow \text{true}(x)]$
(*B**) $(x)[\text{Mary stated}(<\text{true}(x)>) \rightarrow \text{true}(x)),$

which (given classical logic and the T-schema) are indeed equivalent. But the reasoning that establishes their equivalence relies on an assumption which the prosententialist insists is mistaken: namely, that the word "true" is a logical predicate. To accept that assumption is to deny prosententialism; but to reject it is to prevent prosententialism from being able to cover most of the constructions in which the word "true" actually appears.

These difficulties are avoided by Robert Brandom's alternative version of prosententialism, which he calls "the anaphoric theory of truth".[22] For on this view "It is true" is far from the only prosentence. Rather, any instance of "X is true" is a prosentence. In particular, when the "X" is a singular term, it does not in that context have its normal referential function—namely, to identify X as the object of predication— but serves instead to indicate the reference (=truth-value) of the entire prosentence: namely, that its truth value is the same as X's. For example, on this view, the sentence "Goldbach's Conjecture is true" does not, as one might naively think, pick out a certain arithmetical proposition and predicate truth of it. Rather, it is a prosentence that is stipulated to have the same reference as Goldbach's Conjecture—i.e. the same truth-value as the proposition that every even number is the sum of two primes.

However, Brandom's modification of prosententialism ought to be seen as a considerable retreat from the initial idea. For, in the first place, the crucial analogy with pronouns has been lost; since there is no such thing as a complex pronoun of which one component specifies the referent of the whole. In the second place, the substance of Brandom's central proposal is that

X and <X is true> are stipulated to have the same truth-value,

---

[22] See Brandom (1994, 2002).

which is trivially tantamount to the minimalist claim: namely, that we accept, underived, instances of the schema

$<p>$ is true $\leftrightarrow p$.

And in the third place, there are various cases in which the truth predicate is attached to something other than a singular term: for example, "Every proposition of the form '$p \vee -p$' is true" and "Something John said was true". Therefore, further rules (and hence additional and undesirable complications) are going to be necessary in order to tell us what the anaphoric antecedent is in each such case.

So the bottom line on prosententialism, it seems to me, is that the process of rescuing it from glaring inadequacies pushes it more and more in the direction of minimalism.

Finally, we must consider the disquotational approach, suggested by Quine and championed these days by Hartry Field. The advantage of this approach, according to its proponents, is that it has no need for certain 'creatures of darkness'—namely, propositions. For the truth predicate is applied to *sentences* and its core meaning is given (for context-insensitive sentences of one's home language) by the equivalence of " 'p' is true" and "p".

But precisely this alleged advantage is, in my opinion, a disadvantage. For the ordinary truth predicate is primarily applied to such things as 'what John believes', 'what we are supposing for the sake of argument', 'what Mary was attempting to express', and so on: that is, not to sentences, but to propositions. Therefore, in so far as we want to demystify *our* concept of truth—to clarify the meaning of *our* truth predicate—the disquotational approach is simply a non-starter.

Not only that; but once we take into account how the approach will have to be developed if it is to be adequate even as a treatment of *sentential* truth, then its initial promise of dispensing with 'creatures of darkness' pretty much disappears. For the pure disquotational schema holds only in so far as the two "p" 's are replaced by sentences *with the same meaning*. Moreover, in order to account for applications of the truth predicate to utterances made in contexts that differ from one's own, or that are couched in foreign languages, then disquotationalism needs a 'projection' principle, along the lines of

Utterance u has the same meaning as my "p" $\rightarrow$ (u is true $\leftrightarrow$ "p" is true),

which, when combined with the pure disquotation schema, yields

u has the same meaning as my "p" $\rightarrow$ (u is true $\leftrightarrow p$).

So it turns out that disquotationalism cannot, in the end, avoid entanglement with the notion of meaning. Granted, we haven't yet shown that it needs to go all the way to an ontology of propositions. But given the possibility of introducing these entities by means of the schema

u has the same meaning as my "p" $\rightarrow$ (u expresses the proposition that p), that further step is small and innocuous. For assuming that our disquotationalist is already prepared to countenance *some* abstract objects (e.g. numbers, or sets, or word types), then the *abstractness* of propositions cannot be what bothers him. The only reasonable worry could be over the prospect of supplying coherent identity conditions for them. But, as we have just seen, his disquotational theory can be adequate only in so far as sense *can* be made of the locution "*u* has the same meaning as 'p'"—i.e. only in so far as there *is* a coherent statement of such conditions.[23] Thus the alleged benefit—the conceptual economy—that was supposed to compensate for the abandonment of our current concept of truth turns out to be non-existent.

Well, that's the end of my brazenly self-interested comparative survey of deflationary views. Perhaps the best way of establishing a theory is to derive it from uncontroversial premises. And another good strategy is to defend it against objections. But a third approach is to criticize alternative theories—and that is what I've been engaged with here, in support of minimalism. I'm not of course suggesting that competition-bashing is all that needs to be done. In fact I would concede that the other two modes of support are in the end more important.[24] But the present approach does, I think, have a certain priority. For, by placing minimalism in opposition to its alternatives, we help clarify what it is not, and therefore what it is—which is essential if we are eventually going to be able to devise positive arguments in favour of it and respond adequately to objections levelled against it. Moreover, as Holmes said to Watson, 'When you have eliminated the impossible, whatever remains, however improbable, must be the truth.'[25]

REFERENCES

Alston, W. P. (1996). *A Realist Conception of Truth*. Ithaca, NY: Cornell University Press.
Armstrong, D. A. (2004). *Truth and Truthmakers*. Cambridge: Cambridge University Press.
Austin, J. L. (1950). 'Truth'. *Proceedings of the Aristotelian Society*, suppl. vol., 24: 111–28.
Blanchard, B. (1939). *The Nature of Thought*. London: Allen & Unwin. Pages 260–79 repr. in
    M. Lynch (ed.), *The Nature of Truth*, ed. M. Lynch. Cambridge, Mass.: MIT Press, 2001.
Bradley, F. H. (1914). *Essays on Truth and Reality*. Oxford: Clarendon Press.
Brandom, R. (1994). *Making it Explicit*. Cambridge, Mass.: Harvard University Press.
—— (2002). 'Explanatory vs. Expressive Deflationism About Truth', in R. Schantz (ed.),
    What Is Truth? Berlin: de Gruyter.

[23] This is not to deny that it will sometimes (perhaps often) be *indeterminate* whether or not a given foreign utterance, *u*, has the same meaning as a given local sentence. But that would not count at all against the idea that *some* proposition is expressed by *u*. The implication would merely be that there is an indeterminacy in which one it is—an indeterminacy in whether it is the proposition expressed by our "*p*", or the one expressed by our "*q*", etc.

[24] See Horwich (1998, 2000).

[25] A. Conan Doyle, *The Sign of Four*. I would like to thank Frank Jackson, John MacFarlane, and Stephen Neale for their helpful comments on an earlier draft of this chapter.

Davidson, D. (1984). 'Truth and Meaning', in Davidson, *Truth and Interpretation*. Oxford: Clarendon Press.

—— (1990). 'The Structure and Content of Truth'. *Journal of Philosophy*, 87/6: 279–328.

Dummett, M. (1978). *Truth and Other Enigmas*. Cambridge, Mass.: Harvard University Press.

Engel, P. (2002). *Truth*. Chesham: Acumen.

Field, H. (1972). 'Tarski's Theory of Truth'. *Journal of Philosophy*, 69: 347–75.

—— (1994). 'Deflationist Views of Meaning and Content'. *Mind*, 94/3: 249–85.

Grover, D. (1992). *A Prosentential Theory of Truth*. Princeton: Princeton University Press.

—— Camp, J., and Belnap, N. (1975). 'A Prosentential Theory of Truth'. *Philosophical Studies*, 27: 73–125.

Gupta, A. (1993). 'A Critique of Deflationism'. *Philosophical Topics*, 21: 57–81.

Hill, C. S. (2002). *Thought and World*. Cambridge: Cambridge University Press.

Hornsby, J. (1997). 'Truth: The Identity Theory'. *Proceedings of the Aristotelian Society*, 97: 1–24.

Horwich, P. (1998). *Truth*, 2nd edn. Oxford: Oxford University Press.

—— (2005). 'Deflating Compositionality', in Horwich, *Reflections on Meaning*. Oxford: Oxford University Press. Also in E. Borg (ed.), *Meaning and Representation*. Oxford: Blackwell, 2002.

—— (2006). 'A Minimalist Critique of Tarski on Truth', in B. Armour-Garb and J. C. Beale (eds.), *Deflationism and Paradox*. Oxford: Oxford University Press.

James, W. (1909). *The Meaning of Truth*. New York: Longman, Green.

Kirkham, R. L. (1992). *Theories of Truth*. Cambridge, Mass.: MIT Press.

Kuenne, W. (2003). *Conceptions of Truth*. Oxford: Oxford University Press.

Leeds, S. (1978). 'Theories of Reference and Truth'. *Erkenntnis*, 13: 111–29.

Lewis, D. (2001). 'Forget About the "Correspondence Theory of Truth"'. *Analysis*, 61/4: 275–80.

Moore, G. E. (1927). 'Facts and Propositions'. *Proceedings of the Aristotelian Society*, suppl. vol., 7: 171–206.

Papineau, D. (1991). 'Truth and Teleology', in D. Knowles (ed.), *Explanation and its Limits*. Cambridge: Cambridge University Press.

Peirce, C. S. (1932–3). *Collected Papers*, vols. ii–iv. Cambridge, Mass.: Harvard University Press.

Putnam, H. (1981). *Reason, Truth and History*. Cambridge: Cambridge University Press.

Quine, W. v. O. (1990). *Pursuit of Truth*. Cambridge, Mass.: Harvard University Press.

Ramsey, F. (1927). 'Facts and Propositions'. *Proceedings of the Aristotelian Society*, suppl. vol., 7: 153–70.

—— (1991). 'The Nature of Truth', *Episteme*, 16: 6–16. Repr. in *Truth: Original Manuscript Materials (1927–1929) from the Ramsey Collection at the University of Pittsburgh*, ed. N. Rescher and U. Majer. Pittsburgh: University of Pittsburgh.

Strawson, P. (1950). 'Truth'. *Proceedings of the Aristotelian Society*, suppl. vol., 24: 129–56.

Tarski, A. (1943–4). 'The Semantic Conception of Truth'. *Philosophy and Phenomenological Research*, 14: 341–75.

—— (1958). 'The Concept of Truth in Formalized Languages', in Tarski, *Logic, Semantics, Metamathematics: Papers from 1923 to 1938*. Oxford: Oxford University Press.

Walker, R. C. S. (1989). *The Coherence Theory of Truth*. London: Routledge.

Wittgenstein, L. (1922). *Tractatus Logico-Philosophicus*. London: Routledge & Kegan Paul.

CHAPTER 18

....

PRAGMATICS

....

DAN SPERBER AND DEIRDRE WILSON

1. INTRODUCTION

....

Pragmatics is often described as the study of language use, and contrasted with the study of language structure. In this broad sense, it covers a range of loosely related research programmes from formal studies of deictic expressions to sociological studies of ethnic verbal stereotypes. In a more focused sense (the one we will use here), pragmatics contrasts with semantics, the study of linguistic meaning, and is the study of how contextual factors interact with linguistic meaning in the interpretation of utterances. Here we will briefly highlight a range of closely related, fairly central pragmatic issues and approaches that have been of interest to linguists and philosophers of language in the past thirty years or so. Pragmatics, as we will describe it, is an empirical science, but one with philosophical origins and philosophical import.

References to pragmatics are found in philosophy since the work of Charles Morris (1938), who defined it as the study of the relations between signs and their interpreters; however, it was the philosopher Paul Grice's William James lectures at Harvard in 1967 that led to the real development of the field. Grice introduced new conceptual tools—in particular the notion of IMPLICATURE—in an attempt to reconcile the concerns of the two then dominant approaches to the philosophy of language, Ideal Language Philosophy and Ordinary Language Philosophy (on the philosophical origins of pragmatics, see Recanati 1987, 1998, 2004a,b). Ideal language philosophers in the tradition of Frege, Russell, Carnap, and Tarski were studying language as a formal system. Ordinary language philosophers in the tradition of the later Wittgenstein, Austin, and Strawson were studying actual linguistic usage, highlighting in descriptive terms the complexity and subtlety of meanings and the variety of forms of verbal communication. For ordinary language philosophers, there was an unbridgeable gap between the semantics of formal and natural languages. Grice showed that the gap could at least be reduced by sharply distinguishing sentence meaning from speaker's meaning, and explaining how relatively simple and schematic linguistic meanings could be used in context to convey richer and fuzzier speaker's meanings, made up not only of WHAT WAS SAID, but also of what was implicated. This became the foundation for most of modern pragmatics.

Grice (1967: 47) proposed a rather vague general principle (Modified Occam's Razor) for deciding whether some aspect of interpretation is semantic or pragmatic: *Senses are not to be multiplied beyond necessity*. However, judgements about what is "necessary" have too often been affected by disciplinary parochialism and opportunistic considerations. When the work of Montague and Davidson suggested that natural language semantics could be directly studied as a formal system, Gricean pragmatics offered a rationale for dismissing a variety of hard-to-handle intuitions as irrelevant to semantics. A good example of this is Nathan Salmon's claim that failure of substitutivity in belief contexts is only apparent, and can be explained away in terms of Gricean implicatures (Salmon 1986). However, when formal semanticists feel they have the tools to handle some specific regularity in interpretation, they tend to treat it as *ipso facto* semantic, and to see a pragmatic account as inferior and unnecessary. Thus, the treatment of natural language conditionals has proved a rich field for formal elaboration (e.g. Jackson 1991), while the Gricean pragmatic approach to conditionals has been neglected. By the same token, pragmatists tend to assume that whatever they feel capable of accounting for is automatically pragmatic, on the ground that pragmatic explanations are more general, albeit vaguer. A more principled and generally accepted division of labour between semantics and pragmatics will involve more collaborative work. The recent development of formal pragmatics (Stalnaker 1999; Kadmon 2001; Blutner and Zeevat 2003; Asher and Lascarides 2003) is to be welcomed in this context.

2. THREE APPROACHES TO PRAGMATICS

The approaches to pragmatics we will consider here all accept as foundational two ideas defended by Grice (Grice 1989, chs. 1–7, 14, 18) (for representative collections, see Davis 1991; Kasher 1998; Horn and Ward 2004). The first is that sentence meaning is a vehicle for conveying a SPEAKER'S MEANING, and that a speaker's meaning is an overtly expressed intention which is fulfilled by being recognized.[1] In developing this idea, Grice opened the way for an inferential alternative to the classical code model of communication. According to the classical view, utterances are signals encoding the messages that speakers intend to convey, and comprehension is achieved by decoding the signals to obtain the associated messages. On the inferential view, utterances are not signals but pieces of evidence about the speaker's meaning, and comprehension is achieved by inferring this meaning from evidence provided not only by the utterance but also by the context. An utterance is, of course, a linguistically coded piece of evidence, so that comprehension involves an element of decoding. How far does linguistic decoding take the hearer towards an interpretation of the speaker's meaning? Implicitly for Grice and explicitly for John Searle (1969: 43), the output of decoding is normally a sense that is close to being fully propositional, so that only reference assignment is needed to determine what is said, and the main role of inference in comprehension is to recover what is implicated. Following Recanati (2004a), we will call this a LITERALIST approach to semantics. However, a major development in pragmatics over the past thirty years (going much further than Grice envisaged) has been to show that the explicit content of an utterance, like the implicit content, is largely underdetermined by the linguistically encoded meaning, and its recovery involves a substantial element of pragmatic inference. Following Recanati (2004a), we will call this a CONTEXTUALIST approach.

The second foundational idea defended by Grice is that, in inferring the speaker's meaning, the hearer is guided by the expectation that utterances should meet some specific standards. The standards Grice proposed were based on the assumption that conversation is a rational, cooperative activity. In formulating their utterances, speakers are expected to follow a Cooperative Principle, backed by maxims of Quantity (informativeness), Quality (truthfulness), Relation (relevance), and Manner (clarity) which are such that 'in paradigmatic cases, their observance promotes and their violation dispromotes conversational rationality' (Grice 1989: 370):

Cooperative Principle (Grice 1967: 26–7)

Make your contribution such as is required, at the stage at which it occurs, by the accepted purpose or direction of the talk exchange in which you are engaged.

Quantity maxims

(1) Make your contribution as informative as is required (for the current purposes of the exchange).
(2) Do not make your contribution more informative than is required.

---

[1] In Grice's original formulation, ' "[Speaker] meant something by x" is (roughly) equivalent to "[Speaker] intended the utterance of x to produce some effect in an audience by means of the recognition of this intention" ' (Grice 1957: 220). For discussion and reformulation, see Strawson

Quality maxims

Supermaxim. Try to make your contribution one that is true.
(1) Do not say what you believe to be false.
(2) Do not say that for which you lack adequate evidence.

Maxim of Relation

Be relevant.

Manner maxims

Supermaxim. Be perspicuous.
(1) Avoid obscurity of expression.
(2) Avoid ambiguity.
(3) Be brief (avoid unnecessary prolixity).[2]
(4) Be orderly.

When an utterance has several linguistically possible interpretations, the best hypo-thesis for the hearer to choose is the one that best satisfies the Cooperative Principle and maxims. Sometimes, in order to explain why a maxim has been (genuinely or apparently) violated, the hearer has to assume that the speaker believes, and was trying to communicate, more than was explicitly said. Such implicitly communicated propositions, or implicatures, are widely seen (along with presuppositions and illocutionary force) as the main subject matter of pragmatics.[3]

Most current pragmatic theories share Grice's view that inferential comprehension is governed by expectations about the behaviour of speakers, but differ as to what these expectations are. Neo-Griceans such as Atlas (2005), Gazdar (1979), Horn (1984, 1989, 1992, 2000, 2004, 2005), and Levinson (1983, 1987, 2000) stay relatively close to Grice's maxims. For instance, Levinson (2000) proposes the following principles, based on Grice's Quantity and Manner maxims (and given here in abridged form):

Q-Principle (Levinson 2000: 76). Do not provide a statement that is informationally weaker than your knowledge of the world allows.

I-Principle (Levinson 2000: 114). Produce the minimal linguistic information sufficient to achieve your communicational ends.

M-Principle (Levinson 2000: 136). Indicate an abnormal, non-stereotypical situation by using marked expressions that contrast with those you would use to describe the corresponding normal, stereotypical situations.

(1964); Searle (1969, 1983); Schiffer (1972); Recanati (1986, 1987); Grice (1982); Sperber and Wilson (1986); Bach (1987); Neale (1992).

2 The wording of this maxim (and perhaps of the supermaxim of Manner) is a nice illustration of Grice's playfulness.

3 In this chapter, we will focus on the recovery of explicit truth-conditional content and implicatures; for brief comments on the treatment of presupposition and illocutionary force, see Sec. 6 and n. 15.

Each principle has a corollary for the audience (e.g. "Take it that the speaker made the strongest statement consistent with what he knows") which provides a heuristic for hearers to use in identifying the speaker's meaning.

For many philosophers and linguists, an attraction of the neo-Gricean programme is its attempt to combine an inferential account of communication with a view of language strongly influenced by formal semantics and generative grammar. The aim is to solve specifically linguistic problems by modelling pragmatics as closely as possible on formal semantics, assigning interpretations to sentence–context pairs without worrying too much about the psychological mechanisms involved. The following comment from Gazdar (1979: 49) gives a flavour of this approach:

> The tactic adopted here is to examine some of the data that would, or should, be covered by Grice's quantity maxim and then propose a relatively simple formal solution to the problem of describing the behaviour of that data. This solution may be seen as a special case of Grice's quantity maxim, or as an alternative to it, or as merely a conventional rule for assigning one class of conversational meanings to one class of utterances.

Accordingly, neo-Griceans have tended to focus on GENERALIZED conversational implicatures, which are 'normally (in the absence of special circumstances)' carried by use of a certain form of words (Grice 1967: 37), and are therefore codifiable to some degree. For example, the utterance in (1a) would normally convey a generalized implicature of the form in (1b):[4]

(1a) Some of my friends are philosophers.
(1b) Not all of my friends are philosophers.

Levinson (2000) treats generalized implicatures as assigned by default to all utterances of this type, and contextually cancelled only in special circumstances. PARTICULARIZED implicatures, by contrast, depend on 'special features of the context' (Grice 1967: 37), and cannot be assigned by default. For example, the speaker of (2a) would not normally implicate (2b), but this implicature might be conveyed if (2a) were uttered (in England) in response to the question 'Are the pubs open?':

(2a) It's midnight.
(2b) The pubs are closed.

Neo-Griceans, and formal pragmatists in general, have little to say about particularized implicatures.[5] The result is a significant narrowing in the domain of

---

[4] On generalized implicatures and the neo-Gricean approach, see Horn (1984, 1992, 2004, 2005); Levinson (1983, 1987, 2000); Hirschberg (1991); Carston (1995, 1998); Green (1995); Matsumoto (1995); Sperber and Wilson (1995).

[5] Grice himself does not seem to have seen the distinction between generalized and particularized implicatures as theoretically significant. For discussion, see Carston (1995, 1998, 2002); Sperber and Wilson (1995); for experimental evidence on default inference, see Noveck (2001); Chierchia et al. (2001); Bezuidenhout and Morris (2004); Papafragou and Musolino (2003); Breheny et al. (2004); Sperber and Noveck (2004).

pragmatic research, which has yielded valuable descriptions of data from this domain, but is driven largely by methodological considerations.

Relevance theory (Sperber and Wilson 1986; Carston 2002; Wilson and Sperber 2002, 2004), while still based on Grice's two foundational ideas, departs from his framework in two important respects. First, while Grice was mainly concerned with the role of pragmatic inference in implicit communication, relevance theorists have consistently argued that the explicit side of communication is just as inferential and worthy of pragmatic attention as the implicit side (Wilson and Sperber 1981). This has implications not only for the nature of explicit communication but also for semantics. As noted above, Grice and others (e.g. Searle and Lewis) who have contributed to the development of an inferential approach to communication have tended to minimize the gap between sentence meaning and speaker's meaning. They treat sentences as encoding something as close as possible to full propositions, and explicit communication as governed by a maxim or convention of truthfulness, so that the inference from sentence meaning to speaker's meaning is simply a matter of assigning referents to referring expressions, and perhaps of deriving implicatures. Relevance theorists have argued that relevance-oriented inferential processes are efficient enough to allow for a much greater slack between sentence meaning and speaker's meaning, with sentence meaning typically being quite fragmentary and incomplete, and speaker's explicit meaning going well beyond the minimal proposition arrived at by disambiguation and reference assignment.

Relevance theory also departs substantially from Grice's account of the expectations that guide the comprehension process. For Griceans and neo-Griceans, these expectations derive from principles and maxims: that is, rules of behaviour that speakers are expected to obey but may, on occasion, violate (e.g. because of a clash of maxims, or in order to indicate an implicature, as in Grice's account of tropes). For relevance theorists, the very act of communicating raises precise and predictable expectations of relevance, which are enough on their own to guide the hearer towards the speaker's meaning. Speakers may fail to be relevant, but they can not, if they are genuinely communicating (as opposed, say, to rehearsing a speech), produce utterances that do not convey a presumption of their own relevance.

Relevance theory starts from a detailed account of relevance and its role in cognition. RELEVANCE is defined as a property of inputs to cognitive processes (whether external stimuli, which can be perceived and attended to, or internal representations, which can be stored, recalled, or used as premises in inference). An input is relevant to an individual when it combines with available contextual assumptions to yield POSITIVE COGNITIVE EFFECTS: for example, true contextual implications, or warranted strengthenings or revisions of existing assumptions. Everything else being equal, the greater the positive cognitive effects achieved, and the smaller the mental effort required (to represent the input, access a context, and derive these cognitive effects), the greater the relevance of the input to the individual at that time.

Relevance theory is based on two general claims about the role of relevance in cognition and communication:

Cognitive Principle of Relevance. Human cognition tends to be geared to the maximization of relevance.

Communicative Principle of Relevance. Every act of overt communication conveys a presumption of its own optimal relevance.

As noted above, these principles are descriptive rather than normative. The First, or Cognitive, Principle of Relevance yields a variety of predictions about human cognitive processes. It predicts that our perceptual mechanisms tend spontaneously to pick out potentially relevant stimuli, our retrieval mechanisms tend spontaneously to activate potentially relevant assumptions, and our inferential mechanisms tend spontaneously to process them in the most productive way. This principle has essential implications for human communication. In order to communicate, the communicator needs her audience's attention. If attention tends automatically to go to what is most relevant at the time, then the success of communication depends on the audience taking the utterance to be relevant enough to be worthy of attention. Wanting her communication to succeed, the communicator, by the very act of communicating, indicates that she wants the audience to see her utterance as relevant, and this is what the Communicative Principle of Relevance states.

According to relevance theory, the PRESUMPTION OF OPTIMAL RELEVANCE conveyed by every utterance is precise enough to ground a specific comprehension heuristic that hearers may use in interpreting the speaker's meaning:

Presumption of optimal relevance

(*a*) The utterance is relevant enough to be worth processing.
(*b*) It is the most relevant one compatible with the communicator's abilities and preferences.

Relevance-guided comprehension heuristic

(*a*) Follow a path of least effort in constructing an interpretation of the utterance (and in particular in resolving ambiguities and referential indeterminacies, in going beyond linguistic meaning, in supplying contextual assumptions, computing implicatures, etc.).
(*b*) Stop when your expectations of relevance are satisfied.

A hearer using the relevance-theoretic comprehension heuristic during online comprehension should proceed in the following way. The aim is to find an interpretation of the speaker's meaning that satisfies the presumption of optimal relevance. To achieve this aim, the hearer must enrich the decoded sentence meaning at the explicit level, and complement it at the implicit level by supplying contextual assumptions which will combine with it to yield enough conclusions (or other cognitive effects) to make the utterance relevant in the expected way. What route should he follow in disambiguating, assigning reference, constructing a context, deriving conclusions, etc.? According to the relevance-theoretic comprehension heuristic, he should follow a path of least effort, and stop at the first overall interpretation that satisfies his expectations of relevance. This is the key to relevance-theoretic pragmatics.

The Gricean, neo-Gricean, and relevance-theoretic approaches are not the only theoretical approaches to pragmatics (even in the restricted sense of "pragmatics" we are using here). Important contributors to pragmatic theorizing with original points of view include Anscombre and Ducrot (1983); Asher and Lascarides (1995, 1998, 2003); Bach (1987, 1994, 1999, 2001, 2004); Bach and Harnish (1979); Blutner and Zeevat (2003); Clark (1977, 1993, 1996); Dascal (1981); Ducrot (1984); Fauconnier (1975, 1985, 1997); Harnish (1976, 1994); Hobbs (1979, 1985, 2004); Hobbs et al. (1993); Kasher (1976, 1982, 1984, 1998); Katz (1977); Lewis (1979, 1983); Neale (1990, 1992, 2004, forthcoming); Recanati (1987, 1995, 2002, 2004a); Searle (1969, 1975, 1979); Stalnaker (1974, 1999); Sweetser (1990); Travis (1975, 2001); van der Auwera (1981, 1985, 1997); van Rooy (1999); Vanderveken (1990–1). However, the approaches outlined above are arguably the dominant ones.

In the rest of this chapter we will briefly consider four main issues of current interest to linguists and philosophers of language: literalism versus contextualism in semantics (Section 3), the nature of explicit truth-conditional content and the borderline between explicit and implicit communication (Section 4), lexical pragmatics and the analysis of metaphor, approximation, and narrowing (Section 5), and the communication of illocutionary force and other non-truth-conditional aspects of meaning (Section 6). We will end with some comments on the prospects for future collaboration between philosophy and pragmatics.

3. LITERALISM AND CONTEXTUALISM IN SEMANTICS

Grice's distinction between saying and implicating is a natural starting point for examining the semantics–pragmatics distinction.[6] One of Grice's aims was to show that his notion of speaker's meaning could be used to ground traditional semantic notions such as sentence meaning and word meaning (Grice 1967, ch. 6). In his framework, a speaker's meaning is made up of what is said and (optionally) what is implicated, and Grice sees sentence meaning as contributing to both. What a speaker *says* is determined by truth-conditional aspects of linguistic meaning, plus

[6] On the saying–implicating distinction, see Carston (2002, ch. 2.2); Wilson and Sperber (2002, sec. 7); Recanati (2004a, ch. 1). For representative collections on the semantics–pragmatics distinction, see Turner (1999); Szabó (2005).

disambiguation, plus reference assignment. Thus, identifying what the speaker of (3) has said would involve decoding the truth-conditional meaning of the sentence uttered, disambiguating the ambiguous word "pupil", and assigning reference to the indexicals "I" and "now":

(3) *I* have two *pupils now.*

The resulting proposition is sometimes called the LITERAL MEANING of the utterance, or the PROPOSITION EXPRESSED. Grice saw the truth-value of a declarative utterance like (3) as depending on whether this proposition is true or false. By contrast, the meanings of non-truth-conditional expressions such as "but", "moreover", or "so" are seen as contributing to what is CONVENTIONALLY IMPLICATED rather than what is said; in Grice's terms, conventional implicatures involve the performance of 'higher-order' speech acts such as contrasting, adding and explaining, which are parasitic on the 'central, basic' speech act of saying (Grice 1989: 359–68).[7] For Grice, the semantics–pragmatics distinction therefore cross-cuts the saying–implicating distinction, with semantics contributing both to what is said and to what is implicated.

However, although he allows for semantic contributions to implicit content, and although his Quality maxims ("Do not say what you believe to be false", "Have adequate evidence for what you say") are presented as applying at the level of what is said, Grice seems not to have noticed, or at least not to have pursued the idea, that pragmatic inference might contribute to explicit content apart (perhaps) from helping with disambiguation or reference assignment. It therefore seemed quite feasible to many (apparently including Grice himself) to combine a literalist approach to semantics with a Gricean approach to pragmatics.[8] The result was a division of labour in which pragmatists concentrated on implicatures, semanticists concentrated on literal meaning, and neither paid sufficient attention to potential pragmatic contributions to the proposition expressed.

As noted above, literalist approaches to semantics treat sentences as encoding something close to full propositions. Extreme forms of literalism, found in early versions of formal semantics, were adopted by neo-Griceans such as Gazdar (1979), whose slogan *Pragmatics = meaning minus truth conditions* was very influential. On an extreme literalist approach, the sense and reference of (3) are seen as determined by purely linguistic rules or conventions, whose output would generally coincide with the intended sense and reference, but might override them in the case of a clash. More moderate literalists see the output of semantics as a logical form with variables for indexicals and other referential expressions, needing only reference assignment to yield a fully propositional form.

---

[7] Karttunen and Peters (1979) extend Grice's notion to other non-truth-conditional items such as "even". Blakemore (1987, 2002) and Bach (1999) criticize the notion of conventional implicature and offer alternative accounts; on non-truth-conditional meaning, see Sect. 6.

[8] Hedges are necessary because Grice does occasionally suggest that what is said may go beyond the literal meaning. See his comments on 'dictiveness without formality' in Grice (1989: 361).

On a contextualist approach to semantics, by contrast, sentence meaning is seen as typically quite fragmentary and incomplete, and as falling far short of determining a complete proposition even after disambiguation and reference assignment have taken place. A considerable body of work in semantics and pragmatics over the last thirty years suggests strongly that the gap between sentence meaning and proposition expressed is considerably wider than Grice thought, and is unlikely to be bridged simply by assigning values to referential expressions. Thus, consider (4):

(4a) The sea is *too cold*.
(4b) That book is *difficult*.

Even after disambiguation and reference assignment, sentences (4a) and (4b) are semantically incomplete: in order to derive a complete, truth-evaluable proposition, the hearer of (4a) must decide what the speaker is claiming the sea is too cold for, and the hearer of (4b) must decide whether the speaker is describing the book as difficult to read, understand, write, review, sell, find, etc., and by comparison to what. It is quite implausible that these aspects of truth-conditional content are determined by purely linguistic rules or conventions, and fairly implausible that they are determined merely by assigning values to linguistically specified variables. Given an inferential system rich enough to disambiguate, assign reference, and compute implicatures, it is more natural (and parsimonious) to treat the output of semantics as a highly schematic logical form, which is fleshed out into fully propositional form by pragmatic inferences that go well beyond what is envisaged on a literalist approach. The result is a division of labour in which semanticists deal with decoded meaning, pragmatists deal with inferred meaning, and pragmatic inference makes a substantial contribution to truth-conditional content.

In fact, the contribution of pragmatic inference to the truth-conditional content of utterances goes much further than examples (3)–(4) would suggest. Consider (5):

(5a) I'll bring a *bottle* to the party.
(5b) I'm *going to* sneeze.
(5c) If you leave your window open and a burglar *gets in*, you have no right to *compensation*.

Whereas in (4) inferential enrichment is needed to complete a fragmentary sentence meaning into a fully propositional form, in (5) inferential enrichment of a fully propositional form is needed to yield a truth-conditional content that satisfies pragmatic expectations (e.g. the Presumption of Optimal Relevance from Section 2). Thus, the speaker of (5a) would normally be understood as asserting not merely that she will bring some bottle or other, but that she will bring a *full* bottle of *alcohol*; the speaker of (5b) would normally be understood as asserting not merely that she is going to sneeze at some time in the future, but that she is going to sneeze *very soon*; and the speaker of (5c) would normally be understood as asserting that if a burglar gets in *through the window as a result of* its being left open by the hearer, the hearer has no right to compensation *for any consequent loss*. Enrichments of this type are surely driven by pragmatic rather than semantic considerations. They argue for a contextualist approach to semantics, combined with an inferential pragmatics which makes a substantial contribution to the proposition expressed.

From a radical literalist perspective, on which the semantics–pragmatics borderline should coincide with the borderline between saying and implicating, examples such as (4)–(5) show unexpected 'intrusions' of pragmatic inference into the domain of semantics. As Levinson (2000: 195) puts it, 'there is no consistent way of cutting up the semiotic pie such that "what is said" excludes "what is implicated"'. Literalists see this as a problem. Levinson's solution is to abandon Grice's view that saying and implicating are mutually exclusive. From a contextualist perspective, on which the semantics–pragmatics distinction coincides with the borderline between decoding and inference, examples such as (4)–(5) come as no surprise. An obvious way of handling these cases is to analyse the assignment of truth conditions to utterances in two phases. In one phase of analysis, natural language sentences would be seen as decoded into schematic logical forms, which are inferentially elaborated into fully propositional forms by pragmatic processes geared to the identification of speakers' meanings.[9] These propositional forms would be the primary bearers of truth conditions, and might themselves provide input, in a second phase of analysis, to a semantics of conceptual representations (what Fodor calls 'real semantics') which maps them onto the states of affairs they represent. On this approach, there is no pragmatic 'intrusion' into a homogeneous truth-conditional semantics. Rather, there are two distinct types of semantics—linguistic semantics and the semantics of conceptual representations—of which the first, at least, is contextualist rather than literalist.[10]

4. Explicit and Implicit Communication

In much of contemporary philosophy of language and linguistics, the notions of saying and literal meaning are seen as doing double duty, characterizing, on the one hand, the

---

[9] Decoding and inferential elaboration actually overlap in time as online comprehension proceeds, with components of the sentence providing input to elaboration as soon as they are decoded. Moreover, disambiguation, i.e. the selection of one of several decoding hypotheses, is typically affected by pragmatic elaboration.

[10] For accounts along these lines, see Sperber and Wilson (1986, 1998a); Carston (1988, 2002); Recanati (1989, 2004a); Wilson and Sperber (2002); Neale (2004, forthcoming). Alternative, more literalist accounts, have been defended in Stanley (2000, 2002); Stanley and Szabó (2000).

(minimally enriched) output of semantics, and, on the other, what is explicitly communicated by an utterance. We have already argued that the traditional notions of saying and literal meaning are inadequate for semantic purposes: sentence meaning is much more schematic than literalist approaches to semantics suggest. We now want to argue that they are also inadequate for pragmatic purposes: what is explicitly communicated by an utterance typically goes well beyond what is said or literally meant, and may be vaguer and less determinate than is generally assumed.

In analysing the notion of speaker's meaning, Grice introduced the terms "implicate" and "implicature" to refer to what is implicitly communicated, but rather than use the symmetrical "explicate" and "explicature", or just talk of what is explicitly communicated, he chose to contrast what is implicated with the ordinary language notion "what is said". This terminological choice reflected both a presupposition and a goal. The presupposition was that "what is said" is an intuitively clear, common-sense notion. The goal was to argue against a view of meaning that ordinary language philosophers were defending at the time. As noted in Section 1, to achieve this goal, Grice wanted to show that what is said is best described by a relatively parsimonious semantics, while much of the complexity and subtlety of utterance interpretation should be seen as falling on the implicit side. We share Grice's desire to relieve the semantics of natural language of whatever can be best explained at the pragmatic level, but we take a rather different view of how this pragmatic explanation should go.

We suggested in Section 3 that the intuitive truth-conditional content of an utterance—what the speaker would normally be taken to assert—may go well beyond the minimal proposition obtained by decoding, disambiguation, and reference assignment. We will develop this claim in more detail by considering an example in which Lisa drops by her neighbours, the Joneses, one evening as they are sitting down to supper, and the following exchange takes place:

(6a) ALAN JONES. Do you want to join us for supper?
(6b) LISA. No thanks. I've eaten.

On a standard Gricean account, what Lisa has said in uttering (6b) is that she has eaten something or other at some time or other. However, what she would normally be understood as asserting is something stronger: namely, that she has eaten *supper* on the *evening of utterance*. Inferential elaborations of this type, which seem to be performed automatically and unconsciously during comprehension, are ruled out by Grice's account of what is said.

The term "explicature" was introduced into relevance theory, on the model of Grice's "implicature", to characterize the speaker's explicit meaning in a way that allows for richer elaboration than Grice's notion of "what is said":

> *Explicature* (Sperber and Wilson 1986: 182). A proposition communicated by an utterance is an EXPLICATURE if and only if it is a development of a logical form encoded by the utterance.

The process of DEVELOPING a logical form may involve not only reference assignment but other types of pragmatic enrichment illustrated in (4)–(6). The implicatures of an utterance are all the other propositions that make up the speaker's meaning:

> *Implicature* (Sperber and Wilson 1986: 182). A proposition communicated by an utterance, but not explicitly, is an IMPLICATURE.

Thus, Lisa's meaning in (6b) might include the explicature that she has eaten supper on the evening of utterance[11] and the implicature that she doesn't want to eat with the Joneses because she's already had supper that evening.

Explicatures are recovered by a combination of decoding and inference. Different utterances may convey the same explicature in different ways, with different proportions of decoding and inference involved. Compare Lisa's answer in (6b) (repeated below) with the three alternative versions in (6c)–(6e):

(6a) ALAN. Do you want to join us for supper?
(6b) LISA. No thanks. I've eaten.
(6c) LISA. No, thanks. I've already eaten supper.
(6d) LISA. No, thanks. I've already eaten tonight.
(6e) LISA. No, thanks. I've already eaten supper tonight.

All four answers communicate not only the same overall meaning but also the same explicature and implicatures. If this is not immediately obvious, there is a standard test for deciding whether some aspect of the speaker's meaning is part of the explicit truth-conditional content of the utterance or merely an implicature. The test involves checking whether the item falls within the scope of logical operators when embedded into a negative or conditional sentence: explicit truth-conditional content falls within the scope of negation and other logical operators, while implicatures do not (Carston 2002, ch. 2.6.3). Thus, consider the hypothesis that the explicature of (6b) is simply the trivial truth that Lisa has eaten something at some point before the time of utterance, and that she is merely *implicating* that she has eaten that evening. The standard embedding test suggests that this hypothesis is false. If Lisa had replied "I haven't eaten", she would clearly not have been asserting that she has never eaten in her life, but merely denying that she has eaten supper that very evening. So in replying "I've eaten", Lisa is explicitly communicating that she has eaten supper that very evening.

Although all four answers in (6b)–(6e) convey the same explicature, there is a clear sense in which Lisa's meaning is least explicit in (6b) and most explicit in (6e), with (6c) and (6d) falling in between. These differences in DEGREE OF EXPLICITNESS are analysable in terms of the relative proportions of decoding and inference involved:

> *Degrees of explicitness* (Sperber and Wilson 1986: 182). The greater the relative contribution of decoding, and the smaller the relative contribution of pragmatic inference, the more explicit an explicature will be (and inversely).

---

[11] We are considering here only what we call basic or first-level explicatures. We also claim that there are higher-level explicatures incorporating speech act or propositional attitude information; for comments, see Sect. 6.

When the speaker's meaning is quite explicit, as in (6e), and in particular when each word in an utterance is used to convey one of its encoded meanings, what we are calling the explicature is close to what might be commonsensically described as the explicit content, or what is said, or the literal meaning of the utterance. The less explicit the meaning, the more responsibility the hearer must take for the interpretation he constructs: in relevance-theoretic terms, explicatures may be STRONGER or WEAKER, depending on the degree of indeterminacy introduced by the inferential aspect of comprehension. Whether the explicature is strong or weak, the notion of explicature applies straightforwardly. However, the same is not true of the notions of literal meaning and what is said. When asked what Lisa has *said* by uttering (6b) ("I've eaten") with a relatively weak explicature, people's intuitions typically waver. The weaker the explicature, the harder it is to paraphrase what the speaker was saying except by transposing it into an indirect quotation ("She said she had eaten"), which is always possible, but does not really help to specify the content of what was communicated. In such cases, the notions of explicature and degrees of explicitness have clear advantages over the traditional notions of literal meaning and what is said.[12]

According to our account, the recovery of both explicit and implicit content may involve a substantial element of pragmatic inference. This raises questions about how explicatures and implicatures are identified, and where the borderline between them is drawn. We have argued that the linguistically encoded meaning of an utterance gives no more than a schematic indication of the speaker's meaning. The hearer's task is to use this indication, together with background knowledge, to construct an interpretation of the speaker's meaning, guided by expectations of relevance raised by the utterance itself. This overall task can be broken down into a number of sub-tasks:

Sub-tasks in the overall comprehension process

(a) Constructing an appropriate hypothesis about explicatures by developing the linguistically encoded logical form.

(b) Constructing an appropriate hypothesis about the intended contextual assumptions (IMPLICATED PREMISES).

(c) Constructing an appropriate hypothesis about the intended contextual implications (IMPLICATED CONCLUSIONS).

---

[12] For discussion of the relevance-theoretic account of explicatures and alternative views on the explicit–implicit distinction, see Bach (1994, 2004); Levinson (2000: 186–98); Horn (2004, 2005); Stanley (2000, 2002); see also Carston (2002, ch. 2.5); Recanati (2004a). Bach introduces a notion of "impliciture", distinct from implicature, to cover those aspects of what is said that are not linguistically encoded. He rejects the notion of explicature on the ground that pragmatic inferences are cancellable and nothing cancellable can be explicit. By this criterion (on which the explicit–implicit distinction essentially reduces to the coding–inference or semantics–pragmatics distinction), not even disambiguation and reference assignment can contribute to explicit content, and the resulting notion falls well short of Grice's notion of what is said.

These sub-tasks should not be thought of as sequentially ordered. The hearer does not *first* decode the sentence meaning, *then* construct an explicature and identify an appropriate context, and *then* derive a range of implicated conclusions. Comprehension is an online process, and hypotheses about explicatures, implicated premises, and implicated conclusions are developed in parallel, against a background of expectations which may be revised or elaborated as the utterance unfolds. In particular, the hearer may bring to the comprehension process not only a general presumption of relevance, but more specific expectations about how the utterance will be relevant to him (what implicated conclusions he is intended to derive), and these may contribute, via backwards inference, to the identification of explicatures and implicated premises. The overall process is guided by the relevance-theoretic comprehension heuristic presented in Section 2 ("Follow a path of least effort in constructing an interpretation that satisfies your expectations of relevance").

A crucial point about the relation between explicatures and implicatures is that implicated conclusions must be deducible from explicatures together with an appropriate set of contextual assumptions. A hearer using the relevance-theoretic comprehension heuristic is therefore entitled to follow a path of least effort in developing the encoded schematic sentence meaning to a point where it combines with available contextual assumptions to warrant the derivation of enough conclusions to make the utterance relevant in the expected way. This is what happens in Lisa's utterance (6*b*) (repeated below):

(6*a*) ALAN JONES. Do you want to join us for supper?
(6*b*) LISA. No thanks. I've eaten.

Lisa's utterance "No thanks" should raise a doubt in Alan's mind about why she is refusing his invitation, and he can reasonably expect the next part of her utterance to settle this doubt by offering an explanation of her refusal. From encyclopedic information associated with the concept EATING, he should find it relatively easy to supply the contextual assumptions in (7):

(7*a*) People don't normally want to eat supper twice in one evening.
(7*b*) The fact that one has already eaten supper on a given evening is a good reason for refusing an invitation to supper that evening.

These would suggest an explanation of Lisa's refusal, provided that the encoded meaning of her utterance is enriched to yield an explicature along the lines in (8):

(8) Lisa has already eaten supper on the evening of utterance.

By combining (7) and (8), Alan can derive the implicated conclusion that Lisa is refusing his invitation because she has already had supper that evening (which may in turn lead on to further implications), thus satisfying his expectations of relevance.

On this approach, explicatures and implicatures are constructed by mutually adjusting tentative hypotheses about explicatures, implicated premises and implicated conclusions in order to satisfy the expectations of relevance raised by the utterance itself.[13]

The mutual adjustment process suggests an account of how implicated premises may be 'accommodated' in the course of comprehension (Lewis 1979). Consider the exchange in (9):

(9a) BILL. I hear you've moved from Manhattan to Brooklyn.
(9b) SUE. The rent is lower.

In interpreting Sue's utterance in (9b), Bill will expect it to be relevant to his preceding remark, for instance by disputing it, elaborating on it, or answering a question it raises (e.g. "Why did you move?"). In ordinary circumstances, the easiest way to arrive at a sufficiently relevant interpretation (and hence at the interpretation favoured by the relevance-theoretic comprehension heuristic) would involve interpreting "the rent" to mean *the rent in Brooklyn*, and "cheaper" to mean *cheaper than in Manhattan*.[14] (9b), so understood and combined with an assumption such as (10), provides the answer to an implicit question raised by Bill:

(10) A lower rent is a reason to move.

Of course, not everyone would be prepared to move in order to get a lower rent, and Bill may not have known in advance whether Sue would or not; in Lewis's terms, in interpreting her utterance he may have to ACCOMMODATE an assumption such as (10). In the relevance-theoretic framework, what Lewis calls accommodation involves adding a new (i.e. previously unevidenced or under-evidenced) premiss to the context in the course of the mutual adjustment process geared to satisfying the hearer's expectations of relevance. Which premises are added will depend on the order in which they can be constructed, via a combination of backward inference from expected conclusions and forward inference from information available in memory. By encouraging the hearer to supply some such premises in the search for relevance, the speaker takes some responsibility for their truth.[15]

---

[13] On the explicit–implicit distinction in relevance theory, see Sperber and Wilson (1986, chs. 4.2, 4.4); Carston (2002, ch. 2.3); Wilson and Sperber (2004). For a more detailed analysis of the mutual adjustment process for (6b), see Wilson and Sperber (2002, table 1).

[14] Definite descriptions such as "the rent" in (9b) have been treated in the pragmatic literature as cases of "bridging implicature" (Clark 1977) and analysed using relevance theory by Matsui (2000); Wilson and Matsui (2000); Sperber and Noveck (2004).

[15] To the extent that pragmatic "presuppositions" can be analysed as implicated (or accommodated) premises (cf. Grice 1981; Atlas 2004), the mutual adjustment process also sheds light on their derivation. On other types of "presuppositional" effect, see Sperber and Wilson (1986, ch. 4, sect. 5) and Sect. 6 below.

Implicatures, like explicatures, may be stronger or weaker, depending on the degree of indeterminacy introduced by the inferential element of comprehension. When the hearer's expectations of relevance can be satisfied by deriving any one of a range of roughly similar conclusions, at roughly comparable cost, from a range of roughly similar premises, the hearer also has to take some responsibility for the particular premisses he supplies and the conclusions he derives from them. In interpreting Sue's utterance in (9b), for example, Bill might have supplied any of the premises in (11) or many others of a similar tenor:

(11a) A substantially lower rent for an otherwise comparable residence is a good reason to move.
(11b) Sue could not afford her Manhattan rent.
(11c) Sue would rather spend as little as possible on rent.
(11d) The relative benefit of living in Manhattan rather than Brooklyn was not worth the high rent Sue was paying.

The implicated conclusion that Bill will derive from Sue's utterance depends on the particular implicated premiss he supplies. Still, it is clearly part of Sue's intention that Bill should provide some such premiss and derive some such conclusion. In other words, Sue's overall meaning has a clear gist, but not an exact paraphrase. The greater the range of alternatives, the WEAKER the implicatures, and the more responsibility the hearer has to take for the particular choices he makes. Much of human communication is weak in this sense, a fact that a pragmatic theory should explain rather than idealize away.

Grice (1967: 39–40) comments in passing on the indeterminacy of implicatures:

Since to calculate a conversational implicature is to calculate what has to be supposed in order to preserve the supposition that the Cooperative Principle is being observed, and since there may be various possible specific explanations, a list of which may be open, the conversational implicatum [implicature] in such cases will be a disjunction of such specific explanations; and if the list of these is open, the implicatum will have just the kind of indeterminacy that many actual implicata [implicatures] do in fact seem to possess.

However, he did not pursue the idea, or suggest how the indeterminacy of implicatures might be compatible with their calculability, which he also regarded as an essential feature. In the Gricean and neo-Gricean literature, this problem is generally idealized away:

Because indeterminacy is hard to handle formally, I shall mostly ignore it in the discussion that follows. A fuller treatment of implicatures would not be guilty of this omission, which is really only defensible on formal grounds. (Gazdar 1979: 40)

Relevance theory argues that indeterminacy is quite pervasive at both explicit and implicit levels, and provides an analysis that fits well with Grice's intuitive description.

5. LEXICAL PRAGMATICS: METAPHOR, APPROXIMATION, AND NARROWING

The claim that an utterance does not encode the speaker's meaning but is merely a piece of evidence for it has implications at the lexical level. Metaphors and other tropes are the most obvious cases where the meaning conveyed by use of a word goes beyond the linguistically encoded sense. Relevance theory gives a quite different account of these lexical pragmatic phenomena from the standard Gricean one. Gricean pragmatics is often seen as having shed new light on the distinction between literal and figurative meaning. The distinction goes back to classical rhetoric, where it was assumed that (in modern terms):

(a) Linguistic expressions have a literal meaning.
(b) They are normally used to convey this literal meaning.
(c) Literal meanings are primary; figurative meanings are produced by systematic departures from literal meaning along dimensions such as similarity (in the case of metaphor), part–whole relationships (in the case of synecdoche), contradiction (in the case of irony), and so on.
(d) Figurative meanings are paraphrasable in literal terms, and can therefore be literally conveyed.
(e) When a meaning is conveyed figuratively rather than literally, it is in order to please or impress the audience.

Much of contemporary philosophy of language shares these assumptions, from which it follows that only literal meaning matters to the study of meaning. Metaphor, irony, and other tropes are seen as more relevant to aesthetics and the study of literature than to philosophy of language.

The classical view of figurative meaning was challenged by the Romantics. Against the view of figures as mere ornaments, they claimed that tropes have no literal paraphrases and that language is figurative through and through. The Romantic rejection of the literal–figurative distinction has had more influence on literary studies and continental philosophy than on analytic philosophy. However, recent work in cognitive psychology and pragmatics (e.g. Lakoff 1987; Gibbs 1994; Glucksberg 2001) also challenges the classical view in a variety of ways, some of which should have philosophical relevance.

Grice's account of tropes is closer to the classical than the Romantic approach. Suppose that the speaker of (12) or (13) manifestly could not have intended to commit herself to the truth of the propositions literally expressed: it is common knowledge that she knows that John is not a computer, or that she thinks it is bad weather:

(12) John is a computer.
(13) It's lovely weather.

She is therefore overtly violating Grice's first maxim of Quality ("Do not say what you believe to be false"). According to Grice, such overt violation or FLOUTING of a maxim indicates a speaker's intention: the speaker intends the hearer to retrieve an implicature which brings the full interpretation of the utterance (i.e. what is said plus what is implicated) as close as possible to satisfying the Cooperative Principle and maxims. In the case of tropes, the required implicature is related to what is said in one of several possible ways, each characteristic of a different trope. With metaphor, the implicature is a simile based on what is said; with irony, it is the opposite of what is said; with hyperbole, it is a weaker proposition, and with understatement, a stronger one.[16] Thus, Grice might analyse (12) as implicating (14) below, and (13) as implicating (15):

(14) John processes information like a computer.
(15) The weather is bad.

As in the classical rhetorical approach, literal meanings are primary, and figurative meanings are associated with literal meanings in simple and systematic ways. What Grice adds is the idea that figurative meanings are derived in the pragmatic process of utterance comprehension and that this derivation is triggered by the fact that the literal interpretation is an overt departure from conversational maxims.

However, there is a problem with explaining the interpretation of tropes in terms of standard Gricean implicatures. In general, the recovery of an implicature is meant to restore the assumption that the maxims have been observed, or that their violation was justified in the circumstances (as when a speaker is justified by her ignorance in providing less information than required)(Grice 1989: 370). In the case of tropes, the first maxim of Quality seems to be irretrievably violated, and the implicature provides no circumstantial justification whatsoever: what justification could there be for implicitly conveying something true by saying something blatantly false, when one could have spoken truthfully in the first place? In fact, there is some textual evidence to suggest that Grice had in mind a slightly different treatment, on which the speaker in metaphor or irony does not actually *say*, but merely 'makes as if to say' what the sentence she utters literally means (Grice 1967: 34). But in that case, since nothing is genuinely said, the first Quality maxim is not violated at all, and an account in terms of overt violation does not go through.

A Gricean way to go (although Grice himself did not take this route) would be to argue that what is violated is not the first maxim of Quality but the first maxim of Quantity ("Make your contribution as informative as is required"), since if nothing is said, no information is provided. The implicature could then be seen as part of an overall interpretation that satisfies this maxim. However, this creates a

---

[16] Here we will consider metaphor and related phenomena. For analyses of irony and understatement, see Sperber and Wilson (1981; 1986, chs. 4.7, 4.9; 1990; 1998*b*); Wilson and Sperber (1992).

further problem, since the resulting interpretations of figurative utterances would irretrievably violate the Manner maxims. In classical rhetoric, where a metaphor such as (12) or an irony such as (13) is merely an indirect and decorative way of communicating the propositions in (14) or (15), this ornamental value might help to explain the use of tropes (in so far as classical rhetoricians were interested in explanation at all). Quite sensibly, Grice does not appeal to ornamental value. His supermaxim of Manner is not "Be fancy" but "Be perspicuous". However, he does assume, in accordance with classical rhetoric, that figurative meanings, like literal meanings, are fully propositional, and paraphrasable in literal terms. Which raises the following question: isn't a direct and literal expression of what you mean *always* more perspicuous (and in particular less obscure and less ambiguous, cf. the first and second Manner maxims) than an indirect figurative expression?

There are deeper problems with any attempt (either classical or Gricean) to treat language use as governed by a norm of literalness, and figurative utterances as overt departures from the norm. Apart from creative literary metaphors and aggressive forms of irony, which are indeed meant to be noticed, ordinary language use is full of tropes that are understood without attracting any more attention than strictly literal utterances. This familiar observation has now been experimentally confirmed: reaction-time studies show that most metaphors take no longer to understand than their literal counterparts (Gibbs 1994; Glucksberg 2001; see also Noveck *et al.* 2001). This does not square with the view that the hearer of a metaphor first considers its literal interpretation, then rejects it as blatantly false or incongruous, and then constructs a figurative interpretation.

Moreover, while there is room for argument about which metaphors are noticed as such and which are not, ordinary discourse is full of utterances which would violate the first maxim of Quality if literally understood, but are not perceived as violations by ordinary language users. We are thinking here of approximations and loose uses of language such as those in (16)–(19) (discussed in greater detail in Wilson and Sperber 2002):

(16) The lecture starts *at five o'clock*.
(17) Holland is *flat*.
(18) SUE. I must *run* to the bank before it closes.
(19) JANE. I have a terrible cold. I need a *Kleenex*.

If the italicized expressions in (16)–(19) are literally understood, these utterances are not strictly true: lectures rarely start at exactly the appointed time, Holland is not a plane surface, Sue must hurry to the bank but not necessarily run there, and other brands of disposable tissue would do just as well for Jane. Despite the fact that hearers do not normally perceive them as literally false, such loose uses of language are not misleading. This raises a serious issue for any philosophy of language based on a maxim or convention of truthfulness. In some cases, it could be argued that the words are in fact ambiguous, with a strict sense and a more general sense, both known to competent language users. For instance, the word "Kleenex", originally a brand name, may also have come to mean, more generally, a disposable tissue. However, such ambiguities ultimately derive from repeated instances in which the original brand name is loosely used. If "Kleenex" now has TISSUE as one of its lexical senses, it is because the word was often loosely used to convey this broader meaning before it became lexicalized.

Approximations such as (16) and (17) are generally treated in philosophy of language under the heading of VAGUENESS. Vagueness can itself be analysed in semantic or pragmatic terms. There are certainly words with vague linguistic senses—"old" or "ovoid", for instance—and vagueness is therefore at least partly a semantic phenomenon. With other expressions, such as "five o'clock", "hexagonal", or "flat", it seems more appropriate to assign a precise semantics and propose a pragmatic explanation of why they are frequently understood as approximations. David Lewis argues that in such cases, 'the standards of precision in force are different from one conversation to another, and may change in the course of a single conversation. Austin's "France is hexagonal" is a good example of a sentence that is true enough for many contexts but not true enough for many others' (1979: 245).

Both standard semantic and pragmatic treatments of vagueness presuppose that there is a continuum or a fine-grained series of cases between narrower and broader interpretations. This may indeed be true of semantically vague terms such as "old" or "ovoid", and of terms such as "flat", "hexagonal", or "five o'clock", which are often understood as approximations (Gross 2001). However, with "run" in (18) and "Kleenex" in (19), no such continuum exists. There is a sharp discontinuity, for instance, between running (where both feet leave the ground at each step) and walking (where there is always at least one foot on the ground). Typically (though not necessarily), running is faster than walking, so that "run" may be loosely used, as in (18), to indicate the activity of going on foot (whether walking or running) at a speed more typical of running. But walking at different speeds is not equivalent to running relative to different standards of precision. "Run", "Kleenex", and many other words have sharp conceptual boundaries, frequent loose interpretations, and no ordered series of successively broader extensions which might be picked out by raising or lowering some standard of precision. Such cases of loose use seem to call for a special kind of pragmatic treatment, since they are non-literal, but neither the Gricean account of figurative interpretation nor the standard pragmatic treatment of vagueness applies to them.

Do we need four different kinds of analysis for literal, vague, loose, and figurative meanings? Relevance theory is unique in proposing a unified account of all these cases. From the general claim that an utterance is a piece of evidence about the speaker's meaning, it follows, at the lexical level, that the function of words in an utterance is not to encode but merely to indicate the concepts that are constituents of the speaker's meaning. We are not denying that words do encode concepts (or at least semantic features), and that they are (at least partly) decoded during the comprehension process; however, we are claiming that the output of decoding is merely a point of departure for identifying the concepts intended by the speaker. The presence in an utterance of an expression with a given sense licenses a variety of (typically non-demonstrative) inferences. Some of these inferences contribute to satisfying the hearer's expectations of relevance, and are therefore drawn. Others don't, and aren't. In the process, there is a mutual adjustment between explicatures and implicatures. The decoded content helps to identify the inferences that make the utterance relevant as expected, and is readjusted so as to warrant just those inferences that contribute to the relevance of the utterance as a whole. In particular, the constituent concepts of the explicature are constructed ad hoc, starting from the linguistically encoded concepts, but quite often departing from them so as to optimize the relevance of the overall interpretation (Carston 1997; 2002, ch. 5; Sperber and Wilson 1998a; Wilson and Sperber 2002; Wilson 2003).

Suppose, for instance, you have a lecture one afternoon, but don't know exactly when it is due to start. You are told, "The lecture starts at five o'clock". From this utterance, and in particular from the phrase "at five o'clock", together with contextual premises, you can draw a number of inferences that make the utterance relevant to you: that you will not be free to do other things between five and seven o'clock, that you should leave the library no later than 4.45, that it will be too late to go shopping after the lecture, and so on. None of these inferences depends on "five o' clock" being strictly understood. There are inferences that depend on a strict interpretation (for instance, that the lecture will have begun by 5.01), but they don't contribute to the relevance of the utterance, and you don't draw them. According to the relevance-theoretic approach, you then take the speaker to be committed to the truth of a proposition that warrants just the implications you did derive, a proposition which might be paraphrased, say, as "The lecture starts between five o'clock and ten past", but which you, the hearer, would have no need to try and formulate exactly in your mind. Note that if the speaker had uttered the more accurate "between five o'clock and ten past" instead of the approximation "at five o'clock", the overall effort required for comprehension would have been increased rather than reduced, since you would have had to process a longer sentence and a more complex meaning without any saving on the inferential level. Note, too, that we cannot explain how this approximation is understood by assuming that the standard of precision in force allows for, say, a variation of ten minutes around the stated time. If the lecture might start ten minutes *earlier* than five o'clock, then the inferences worth drawing would not be the same.

This process of ad hoc concept construction via mutual adjustment of explicatures and implicatures is quite general. It works in the same way with metaphors. Consider the metaphor "John is a computer" in two different exchanges:

(20a) PETER. Is John a good accountant?
(20b) MARY. John is a computer.

(21a) PETER. How good a friend is John?

(21b) MARY. John is a computer.

In each case, the encoded sense of "computer" draws the hearer's attention to some features of computers that they may share with some human beings. Like the best accountants, computers can process large amounts of numerical information and never make mistakes, and so on. Unlike good friends, computers lack emotions, and so on. In each case, Peter builds an ad hoc concept indicated, though not encoded, by the word "computer", such that John's falling under this concept has implications that answer the question in (20a) or (21a). Note that Mary need not have in mind the precise implications that Peter will derive, as long as her utterance encourages him to derive the kind of implications that answer his question along the intended lines. So the Romantics were right to argue that the figurative meaning of a live metaphor cannot be properly paraphrased. However, this is not because the meaning is some non-truth-conditional set of associations or "connotations". It is because it consists of an ad hoc concept that is characterized by its inferential role and not by a definition, and moreover this inferential role, to a much greater extent than in the case of mere approximations, is left to the hearer to elaborate. Metaphorical communication is relatively weak communication.

In the case of approximations or metaphors, concept construction results in a broadening of the encoded concept; in other cases, as in (5a) ("I'll bring a bottle") and (6b) above, it results in a narrowing. Recall that in (6), Lisa has dropped by her neighbours, the Joneses, who have just sat down to supper:

(6a) ALAN JONES. Do you want to join us for supper?

(6b) LISA. No, thanks. I've eaten.

As noted above, in order to produce a relevant interpretation of Lisa's answer "I've eaten", some enrichment of the encoded sentence meaning must take place. In particular, the time span indicated by the perfect "have eaten" must be narrowed down to the evening of utterance, and "eaten" must be understood as conveying the ad hoc concept EAT SUPPER. If Lisa has eaten supper on the previous day, or eaten an olive that evening, she would literally *have eaten*, but not in a relevant sense. In still other cases, the result of the same process of meaning construction is that the concept indicated by use of the word "eaten" as a constituent of the intended meaning is the very one it encodes. If Lisa is supposed to follow a religious fast and says "I've eaten", then the concept EAT that is part of her meaning is just the linguistically encoded one: a single olive is enough to break a fast.

The comprehension process itself does not involve classifying interpretations as *literal, approximate, loose, metaphorical*, and so on. These classifications belong to linguistic theories, including folk and philosophical theories, and play a role in metalinguistic arguments. However, a pragmatic approach suggests that these notions may denote regions on a continuum rather than sharply distinct categories, and may play no role in a proper theory of language use.

6. Procedural Meaning:
Speech Acts, Presuppositions,
and Indexicals

We have tried to show that a contextualist approach to semantics combined with a relevance-oriented approach to pragmatics can yield appropriate accounts of speaker's meaning. Starting with the strongest candidates for literalist treatment—constructions which are plausibly analysed as encoding concepts that contribute to explicit truth-conditional content—we have argued that even with these strongest candidates the case for literalism does not go through. Many aspects of explicit truth-conditional content are not encoded at all, and utterances do not always communicate the concepts they encode. Moreover, a wide range of linguistic constructions contribute to other aspects of speaker's meaning than explicit truth-conditional content, or encode aspects of meaning that are not plausibly analysed in conceptual terms. Examples include illocutionary force indicators, presupposition triggers, indexicals and demonstratives, focusing devices, parentheticals, discourse connectives, argumentative operators, prosody, interjections, and so on. Because these constructions fall outside the scope of standard literalist approaches, their linguistic meaning is sometimes characterized as "pragmatic" rather than semantic (although the proposed analyses have rarely shown much concern for how they might contribute to a properly inferential pragmatics). We see these items as providing strong evidence for a contextualist approach to semantics combined with a relevance-oriented pragmatics, and will end by briefly considering how they might be approached within the framework we have outlined.

Speech act theorists such as Austin, Searle, Katz, and Bach and Harnish underlined the fact that a speaker's meaning should be seen not merely as a set of (asserted) propositions, but as a set of propositions each with a recommended propositional attitude or illocutionary force. The treatment of illocutionary and attitudinal meaning has developed in parallel to the treatment of explicit truth-conditional content, with early literalist accounts replaced by more contextualist accounts in which the role of speakers' intentions and pragmatic inference is increasingly recognized.[17] In relevance theory, these non-truth-conditional aspects of speaker's meaning are analysed as HIGHER-LEVEL explicatures constructed (like the basic explicatures considered in Section 4) by development of encoded schematic sentence meanings. In uttering (22), for example, Mary might convey not only the

---

[17] See e.g. Strawson (1964); Searle (1969, 1975); Katz (1977); Recanati (1987); Tsohatzidis (1994); Sadock (2004).

basic explicature in (23*a*), which constitutes the explicit truth-conditional content of her utterance, but a range of higher-level explicatures such as (23*b*)–(23*d*) (any of which might contribute to overall relevance):

(22) Confidentially, I didn't enjoy the meal.
(23*a*) Mary didn't enjoy the meal.
(23*b*) Mary is telling Peter confidentially that she didn't enjoy the meal.
(23*c*) Mary is admitting confidentially to Peter that she didn't enjoy the meal.
(23*d*) Mary believes she didn't enjoy the meal.

As this example shows, higher-level explicatures, like basic explicatures, are recovered through a combination of decoding and inference, and may be more or less explicit. Thus, Mary could have made her meaning more explicit by uttering (24), and left it less explicit by merely indicating through her behaviour or tone of voice that she was speaking to Peter in confidence:

(24) I tell you confidentially, I didn't enjoy the meal.

Speech act theorists distinguish DESCRIBING from INDICATING. Descriptive expressions may be seen as encoding concepts in the regular way (although we have argued that the encoded concept gives no more than a schematic indication of the speaker's meaning). Indicators are seen as carrying other types of information, which contribute to speaker's meaning in other ways than by encoding regular concepts. As illustrated by (22)–(24)("Confidentially, I didn't enjoy the meal", "I tell you confidentially, I didn't enjoy the meal"), higher-level explicatures may be conveyed by a mixture of describing and indicating. While illocutionary adverbials and parentheticals such as "confidentially", "I tell you confidentially", "I tell you in total and utter confidence" clearly have descriptive content, mood indicators such as declarative or interrogative word order, imperative, indicative, or subjunctive verb morphology, and exclamatory or interrogative intonation fall on the indicating side. How is their encoded meaning to be analysed, if not in conceptual terms? We would like to suggest that their semantic function is to guide the hearer in the inferential construction of higher-level explicatures by narrowing the search space, increasing the salience of certain candidates, and diminishing the salience of others. In some cases, the search space may be reduced to a single plausible candidate, while in others, there may be several, so that the resulting explicatures may be stronger or weaker. As expected, conceptual encoding leads to stronger communication than linguistic indication (Wilson and Sperber 1988, 1993; Sperber and Wilson 1986, ch. 4.10; Ifantidou 2001).

As noted at the beginning of this section, languages have a rich variety of indicators, which contribute to other aspects of speaker's meaning than illocutionary force; in the framework we have outlined, these would be analysed on similar lines to mood indicators, as contributing to relevance by guiding the hearer towards the intended explicit content, context, or conclusions. Consider, for instance, the contribution of the indexical or demonstrative "here" to the explicit truth-conditional content of (25):

(25) I have been *here* for two hours.

The semantic function of "here" is simultaneously to indicate that a referent is required and to restrict the search space to a certain class of candidates, some of which may be made more salient by gesture, direction of gaze, or discourse context (and will therefore be more accessible to the relevance-theoretic comprehension heuristic). Even when all these clues are taken into account, they may not determine a unique interpretation. For example, (25) may be true (and relevant) if "here" is understood to mean "in this library", but false if understood to mean "in this room" or "on this spot". The encoded meaning of "here" is only a clue to the speaker's meaning, which is recovered, as always, by mutual adjustment of explicatures and implicatures in the search for optimal relevance.

Finally, a range of items such as "even", "still", "but", "indeed", "also", and "after all", which have been seen as encoding information about "presuppositions", conventional implicatures, or argumentative orientation instead of (or as well as) descriptive information,[18] may be analysed as restricting the search space for implicated premises and conclusions, or as indicating what type of inferential process the hearer is intended to go through in establishing relevance. To give just one illustration, compare (26a) and (26b):

(26a) John is a philosopher and he enjoys detective stories.
(26b) John is a philosopher but he enjoys detective stories.

As these examples show, although "and" and "but" are descriptively equivalent, they orient the hearer towards different types of interpretation (Ducrot 1984; Blakemore 1987, 2002; Hall 2004). The use of "and" in (26a), for example, is compatible with an interpretation in which the fact that John enjoys detective stories is unsurprising given that he is a philosopher, while the use of "but" in (26b) suggests an interpretation in which the fact that John is a philosopher makes it surprising that he enjoys detective stories. The effect of "but" is to narrow the search space for inferential comprehension by facilitating access to certain types of context or conclusion: it may therefore be seen, like mood indicators and indexicals, as indicating a rather abstract property of the speaker's meaning: the direction in which relevance is to be sought.[19]

The few attempts that have been made to provide a unified account of indicators have been based on the speech act distinction between conditions on USE and conditions on TRUTH (Recanati 2004b). However, as noted above, not all indicators

---

[18] See e.g. Stalnaker (1974); Wilson (1975); Gazdar (1979); Karttunen and Peters (1979); Grice (1981); Anscombre and Ducrot (1983); Sperber and Wilson (1986, ch. 4.5); Blakemore (1987, 2002); Wilson and Sperber (1993); Bruxelles *et al.* (1995); Horn (1996); Kadmon (2001); Atlas (2004); Hall (2004); Iten (forthcoming).

[19] For an account of interjections within this framework, see Wharton (2003).

are analysable in speech act terms, and the distinction between conditions on truth and conditions on use runs the risk of becoming trivial or non-explanatory when removed from the speech act framework. While it is clear why certain acts have felicity conditions (e.g. only someone with the appropriate authority can give an order, perform a baptism, and so on), it is not clear why linguistic expressions such as "it" and "that", or "even" and "also", which have no obvious analysis in speech act terms, should have conditions on their appropriate use. By contrast, if the function of indicators is to contribute to inferential comprehension by guiding the hearer towards the speaker's meaning, the conditions on their use fall out as a natural consequence. More generally, from a radical literalist perspective, it is surprising to find any items at all that contribute to meaning without encoding concepts. From the perspective outlined in this chapter, there is no presumption that all linguistic meaning should be either conceptual or truth-conditional: the only requirement on linguistic meaning is that it guide the hearer towards the speaker's meaning by indicating the direction in which relevance is to be sought.

7. CONCLUSION

When pragmatics emerged as a distinct discipline at the end of the 1960s, analytic philosophy was dominated by philosophy of language, and the cognitive sciences were still in their infancy. Since then, as the cognitive sciences have matured and expanded, priority in philosophy has shifted from philosophy of language to philosophy of mind. The development of pragmatics reflects this shift. Part of Grice's originality was to approach meaning as a primarily psychological phenomenon and only derivatively a linguistic one. By underlining the gap between sentence meaning and speaker's meaning, he made it possible, of course, for ideal language philosophers to ignore many context-dependent features of speaker's meaning that ordinary language philosophers had used as evidence against formal approaches. However, far from claiming that linguistic meaning was the only type of meaning amenable to scientific treatment and worthy of philosophical attention, he suggested that speaker's meaning was relevant to philosophy and could be properly studied in its own right. As pragmatics has developed, it has become increasingly clear that the gap between sentence meaning and speaker's meaning is wider than Grice himself thought, and that pragmatic inference contributes not only to implicit content but also to truth-conditional aspects of explicit content. While the effect may be to remove from linguistic semantics more phenomena than some semanticists might be willing to relinquish, it does not make the field any less challenging: in fact, the semantics–pragmatics interface becomes an interesting interdisciplinary area of research in its own right. However, as the gap between sentence meaning and speaker's meaning widens, it increasingly brings into question a basic assumption of much philosophy of language, that the semantics of sentences provides straightforward, direct access to the structure of human thoughts. We have argued that linguistic meanings are mental representations that play a role at an intermediate stage in the comprehension process. Unlike speaker's meanings (which they resemble in the way a skeleton resembles a body), linguistic meanings are not consciously entertained. In other words, whereas speakers' meanings are salient objects in personal psychology, linguistic meanings only play a role in sub-personal cognition.

Within pragmatics itself, there is a tension between more linguistically oriented and more cognitively oriented approaches. By idealizing away from properties of the context that are hard to formalize, and focusing on aspects of interpretation (e.g. "presuppositions" or "generalized implicatures") which exhibit a kind of code-like regularity, it is possible to extend the methods of formal semantics to a sub-part of the pragmatic domain (assuming that these phenomena are genuinely pragmatic, which is in some cases contentious) (Kadmon 2001; Blutner and Zeevat 2003). Good or bad, the resulting analyses are unlikely to generalize to the whole domain of pragmatics. The cognitive approach, and in particular relevance theory (on which we have focused here), approaches verbal comprehension as a psychological process. The challenge is precisely to explain how the closed formal system of language provides effective pieces of evidence which, combined with further evidence from an open and dynamic context, enable hearers to infer speakers' meanings. The methods to be used are those of cognitive psychology, including modelling of cognitive processes, experimental tests, studies of communication pathologies (e.g. autism), and evolutionary insights. Pragmatics so conceived is relevant to linguistics because of the light it throws on the semantics–pragmatics interface. Its main relevance is to cognitive psychology, and in particular to the study of mind-reading and inference mechanisms. Its implications for the philosophy of language are largely cautionary and deflationary, amounting mainly to downplaying the philosophical significance of linguistic meanings. Its main philosophical relevance is to philosophy of mind. In particular, by describing comprehension, a very common, easy, everyday process, as a form of richly context-dependent inference, pragmatics provides an illustration of how to approach central cognitive processes, which, precisely because of their context-dependence, have been treated by Fodor as a major mystery for cognitive psychology and philosophy of mind.

References

Anscombre, Jean-Claude, and Ducrot, Oswald (1983). *L'Argumentation dans la langue*. Brussels: Mardaga.

Asher, Nicholas, and Lascarides, Alex (1995). 'Lexical Disambiguation in a Discourse Context'. *Journal of Semantics*, 12: 69–108.

——— (1998). 'The Semantics and Pragmatics of Presupposition'. *Journal of Semantics*, 15: 239–300.

——— (2003). *Logics of Conversation*. Cambridge: Cambridge University Press.

Atlas, Jay (2004). 'Presupposition', in Laurence Horn and Gregory Ward (eds.), *The Handbook of Pragmatics*. Oxford: Blackwell.

—— (2005). *Logic, Meaning, and Conversation: Semantical Underdeterminacy, Implicature, and their Interface*. Oxford: Oxford University Press.

Bach, Kent (1987). 'On Communicative Intentions: A Reply to Recanati'. *Mind and Language*, 2: 141–54.

—— (1994). 'Conversational Impliciture'. *Mind and Language*, 9: 124–62.

—— (1999). 'The Myth of Conventional Implicature'. *Linguistics and Philosophy*, 22: 327–66.

—— (2001). 'You Don't Say?' *Synthese*, 127: 11–31.

—— (2004). 'Pragmatics and the Philosophy of Language', in Laurence Horn and Gregory Ward (eds.), *The Handbook of Pragmatics*. Oxford: Blackwell.

—— and Harnish, Robert Michael (1979). *Linguistic Communication and Speech Acts*. Cambridge, Mass.: MIT Press.

Bezuidenhout, Anne, and Morris, Robin (2004). 'Implicature, Relevance and Default Inferences', in Dan Sperber and Ira Noveck (eds.), *Experimental Pragmatics*. London: Palgrave.

Blakemore, Diane (1987). *Semantic Constraints on Relevance*. Oxford: Blackwell.

—— (2002). *Linguistic Meaning and Relevance: The Semantics and Pragmatics of Discourse Markers*. Cambridge: Cambridge University Press.

Blutner, Reinhard, and Zeevat, Henk (2003). *Optimality Theory and Pragmatics*. London: Palgrave.

Breheny, Richard, Katsos, Napoleon, and Williams, John (2004). 'An Online Investigation into Defaultness in Implicature Generation'. Cambridge: RCEAL. (submitted)

Bruxelles, Sylvie, Ducrot, Oswald, and Raccah, Pierre-Yves. (1995). 'Argumentation and the Lexical Topical Fields'. *Journal of Pragmatics*. 24: 99–114.

Carston, Robyn (1988). 'Implicature, Explicature and Truth-Theoretic Semantics', in Ruth Kempson (ed.), *Mental Representation: The Interface Between Language and Reality*. Cambridge: Cambridge University Press. Repr. in Steven Davis (ed.), *Pragmatics: A Reader*. Oxford: Oxford University Press, 1991; Asa Kasher (ed.), *Pragmatics: Critical Concepts*, iv. London: Routledge, 1998.

—— (1995). 'Quantity Maxims and Generalised Implicature'. *Lingua*, 96: 213–44.

—— (1997). 'Enrichment and Loosening: Complementary Processes in Deriving the Proposition Expressed?' *Linguistische Berichte*, 8: 103–27.

—— (1998). 'Informativeness, Relevance and Scalar Implicature', in Robyn Carston and Seiji Uchida (eds.), *Relevance Theory: Applications and Implications*. Amsterdam: John Benjamins.

—— (2000). 'Explicature and Semantics'. *UCL Working Papers in Linguistics*, 12: 1–44. Repr. in Stephen Davis and Brad Gillon (eds.), *Semantics: A Reader*. Oxford: Oxford University Press, forthcoming.

—— (2002). *Thoughts and Utterances: The Pragmatics of Explicit Communication*. Oxford: Blackwell.

Chierchia, Gennaro, Crain, Stephen, Guasti, Maria Teresa, Gualmini, Andrea, and Meroni, Luisa (2001). 'The Acquisition of Disjunction: Evidence for a Grammatical View of Scalar Implicatures', in *BUCLD 25 Proceedings*. Somerville, Mass.: Cascadilla Press.

Clark, Herbert H. (1977). 'Bridging', in Philip Johnson-Laird and Peter Wason (eds.), *Thinking: Readings in Cognitive Science*. Cambridge: Cambridge University Press.

—— (1993). *Arenas of Language Use*. Stanford, Calif: CSLI.

—— (1996). *Using Language*. Cambridge: Cambridge University Press.

Dascal, Marcelo (1981). 'Contextualism', in Herman Parret, Marina Sbisà, and Jef Verschueren, (eds.), *Possibilities and Limitations of Pragmatics*. Amsterdam: John Benjamins.

Davis, Steven (ed.) (1991). *Pragmatics: A Reader*. Oxford: Oxford University Press.

Ducrot, Oswald (1984). *Le Dire et le dit*. Paris: Minuit.

Fauconnier, Gilles (1975). 'Pragmatic Scales and Logical Structure'. *Linguistic Inquiry*, 6: 353–75.

—— (1985). *Mental Spaces: Aspects of Meaning Construction in Natural Language*. Cambridge, Mass.: MIT Press and Bradford Books.

—— (1997). *Mappings in Thought and Language*. Cambridge: Cambridge University Press.

Gazdar, Gerald (1979). *Pragmatics: Implicature, Presupposition and Logical Form*. London: Academic Press.

Gibbs, Ray (1994). *The Poetics of Mind: Figurative Thought, Language and Understanding*. Cambridge: Cambridge University Press.

Glucksberg, Sam (2001). *Understanding Figurative Language*. Oxford: Oxford University Press.

Green, Mitchell (1995). 'Quantity, Volubility, and Some Varieties of Discourse'. *Linguistics and Philosophy*, 19: 83–112.

Grice, H. Paul (1957). 'Meaning'. *philosophocal Review*, 66: 377–88. Repr. in Grice, *Studies in the Way of Words*. Cambridge, Mass.: Harvard University Press, 1989.

—— (1967). *Logic and Conversation*. Repr. in Grice, *Studies in the Way of Words*. Cambridge, Mass.: Harvard University Press, 1989. Page References are to the 1989 edn.

—— (1981). 'Presupposition and Conversational Implicature', in Peter Cole (ed.), *Radical Pragmatics*. New York: Academic Press. Repr. in Grice, *Studies in the Way of Words*. Cambridge, Mass.: Harvard University Press, 1989.

—— (1982). 'Meaning Revisited', in Neil Smith (ed.), *Mutual Knowledge*. London: Academic Press. Repr. in Grice, *Studies in the Way of Words*. Cambridge, Mass.: Harvard University Press, 1989.

—— (1989). *Studies in the Way of Words*. Cambridge, Mass.: Harvard University Press.

Gross, Steven (2001). *Essays on Linguistic Context-Sensitivity and its Philosophical Significance*. London: Routledge.

Hall, Alison (2004). 'The Meaning of "But": A Procedural Reanalysis'. *UCL Working Papers in Linguistics*, 16: 199–236.

Harnish, Robert Michael (1976). 'Logical Form and Implicature', in T. Bever, J. Katz, and D. T. Langendoen (eds.), *An Integrated Theory of Linguistic Ability*. New York: Crowell. Repr. in Steven Davis (ed.) (1991). *Pragmatics: A Reader*. Oxford: Oxford University Press.

—— (1994). 'Mood, Meaning and Speech Acts', in Savas Tsohatzidis (ed.), *Foundations of Speech-Act Theory: Philosophical and Linguistic Perspectives*. London: Routledge.

Hirschberg, Julia (1991). *A Theory of Scalar Implicature*. New York: Garland.

Hobbs, Jerry (1979). 'Coherence and Coreference'. *Cognitive Science*, 3: 27–90.

—— (1985). *On the Coherence and Structure of Discourse*, CSLI Report 85–37. Menlo Park, Calif.: CSLI.

—— (2004). 'Abduction in Natural Language Understanding', in Laurence Horn and Gregory Ward (eds.), *The Handbook of Pragmatics*. Oxford: Blackwell.

Hobbs, Jerry, Stickel, Mark, Appelt, Douglas, and Martin, Paul (1993). 'Interpretation as Abduction'. *Artificial Intelligence*, 63: 69–142.

Horn, Laurence (1984). 'Towards a New Taxonomy for Pragmatic Inference: Q- and R-Based Implicature', in D. Schiffrin (ed.), *Meaning, Form, and Use in Context*. Washington: Georgetown University Press.

——(1989). *A Natural History of Negation*. Chicago: University of Chicago Press.

——(1992). 'The Said and the Unsaid', in *SALT II: Proceedings of the Second Conference on Semantics and Linguistic Theory*. Columbus: Ohio State University Linguistics Department.

——(1996). 'Presupposition and Implicature', in Shalom Lappin (ed.), *The Handbook of Contemporary Semantic Theory*. Oxford: Blackwell.

——(2000). 'From IF to IFF: Conditional Perfection as Pragmatic Strengthening'. *Journal of Pragmatics*, 32: 289–326.

——(2004). 'Implicature', in Laurence Horn and Gregory Ward (eds.), *The Handbook of Pragmatics*. Oxford: Blackwell.

——(2005). 'The Border Wars: A Neo-Gricean Perspective', in Ken Turner and Klaus von Heusinger (eds.), *Where Semantics Meets Pragmatics*. Amsterdam: Elsevier.

——and Ward, Gregory (eds.) (2004). *The Handbook of Pragmatics*. Oxford: Blackwell.

Ifantidou, Elly (2001). *Evidentials and Relevance*. Amsterdam: John Benjamins.

Iten, Corinne (forthcoming). *Linguistic Meaning, Truth Conditions and Relevance*. London: Palgrave.

Jackson, Frank (ed.) (1991). *Conditionals*. Oxford: Oxford University Press.

Kadmon, Nirit (2001). *Formal Pragmatics: Semantics, Pragmatics, Presupposition and Focus*. Oxford: Blackwell.

Karttunen, Lauri, and Peters, Stanley (1979). 'Conventional Implicature', in Choon-Yu Oh and David Dineen (eds.), *Syntax and Semantics*, xi: *Presupposition*. New York: Academic Press.

Kasher, Asa (1976). 'Conversational Maxims and Rationality', in Kasher (ed.), *Language in Focus: Foundations, Methods and Systems*. Dordrecht: Reidel. Repr. in Kasher (ed.), *Pragmatics: Critical Concepts*, iv. London: Routledge, 1998.

——(1982). 'Gricean Inference Revisited'. *Philosophica*, 29: 25–44.

——(1984). 'Pragmatics and the Modularity of Mind'. *Journal of Pragmatics*, 8: 539–57. Rev. repr. in Steven Davis (ed.), *Pragmatics: A Reader*. Oxford: Oxford University Press, 1991.

——(ed.) (1998). *Pragmatics: Critical Concepts*, i–iv. London: Routledge.

Katz, Jerrold (1977). *Propositional Structure and Illocutionary Force*. New York: Crowell.

Lakoff, George (1987). *Women, Fire and Dangerous Things*. Chicago: University of Chicago Press.

Levinson, Stephen (1983). *Pragmatics*. Cambridge: Cambridge University Press.

——(1987). 'Minimization and Conversational Inference', in Jef Verschueren and Marcella Bertuccelli-Papi (eds.), *The Pragmatic Perspective*. Amsterdam: John Benjamins.

——(2000). *Presumptive Meanings: The Theory of Generalized Conversational Implicature*. Cambridge, Mass.: MIT Press.

Lewis, David (1979). 'Scorekeeping in a Language Game'. Repr. in Lewis, *Philosophical Papers*, i. New York: Oxford University Press, 1983.

——(1983). *Philosophical Papers*, i. New York: Oxford University Press.

Matsui, Tomoko (2000). *Bridging and Relevance*. Amsterdam: John Benjamins.

Matsumoto, Yo (1995). 'The Conversational Condition on Horn Scales'. *Linguistics and Philosophy*, 18: 21–60.

Morris, Charles (1938). *Foundations of the Theory of Signs*. Chicago: University of Chicago Press.

Neale, Stephen (1990). *Descriptions*. Cambridge, Mass: MIT Press.

—— (1992). 'Paul Grice and the Philosophy of Language'. *Linguistics and Philosophy*, 15: 509–59.

—— (2004). 'This, That and the Other', in Anne Bezuidenhout and Marga Reimer (eds.), *Descriptions and Beyond: An Interdisciplinary Collection of Essays on Definite and Indefinite Descriptions and Other Related Phenomena*. Oxford: Oxford University Press.

—— (forthcoming). *Linguistic Pragmatism*. Oxford: Oxford University Press.

Noveck, Ira (2001). 'When Children Are More Logical Than Adults: Investigations of Scalar Implicature'. *Cognition*, 78: 165–88.

—— Bianco, Maryse, and Castry, Alain (2001). 'The Costs and Benefits of Metaphor'. *Metaphor and Symbol*, 16: 109–21.

Papafragou, Anna, and Musolino, Julien (2003). 'Scalar Implicatures: Experiments at the Semantics–Pragmatics Interface'. *Cognition*, 86: 253–82.

Recanati, François (1986). 'On Defining Communicative Intentions'. *Mind and Language*, 1: 213–42.

—— (1987). *Meaning and Force*. Cambridge: Cambridge University Press.

—— (1989). 'The Pragmatics of What Is Said'. *Mind and Language*, 4: 295–329. Repr. in Steven Davis (ed.), *Pragmatics: A Reader*. Oxford: Oxford University Press, 1991.

—— (1995). 'The Alleged Priority of Literal Interpretation'. *Cognitive Science*, 19: 207–32.

—— (1998). 'Pragmatics', in Edward Craig (ed.), *Routledge Encyclopaedia of Philosophy*, vii. London: Routledge.

—— (2002). 'Unarticulated Constituents'. *Linguistics and Philosophy*, 25: 299–345.

—— (2004a). *Literal Meaning*. Cambridge: Cambridge University Press.

—— (2004b). 'Semantics and Pragmatics', in Laurence Horn and Gregory Ward (eds.), *The Handbook of Pragmatics*. Oxford: Blackwell.

Sadock, Jerry (2004). 'Speech Acts', in Laurence Horn and Gregory Ward (eds.), *The Handbook of Pragmatics*. Oxford: Blackwell.

Salmon, Nathan (1986). *Frege's Puzzle*. Cambridge, Mass.: MIT Press.

Schiffer, Stephen (1972). *Meaning*. Oxford: Clarendon Press.

Searle, John (1969). *Speech Acts*. Cambridge: Cambridge University Press.

—— (1975). 'Indirect Speech Acts', in Peter Cole and Jerry Morgan (eds.), *Syntax and Semantics*, iii: *Speech Acts*. New York: Academic Press.

—— (1979). *Expression and Meaning*. Cambridge: Cambridge University Press.

—— (1983). *Intentionality*. Cambridge: Cambridge University Press.

Sperber, Dan, and Noveck, Ira (eds.) (2004). *Experimental Pragmatics*. London: Palgrave.

—— and Wilson, Deirdre (1981). 'Irony and the Use–Mention Distinction', in Peter Cole (ed.), *Radical Pragmatics*. New York: Academic Press. Repr. in Steven Davis (ed.), *Pragmatics: A Reader*. Oxford: Oxford University Press, 1991.

—— —— (1986). *Relevance: Communication and Cognition*. Oxford: Blackwell; Cambridge, Mass.: Harvard University Press.

—— —— (1990). 'Rhetoric and Relevance', in John Bender and David Wellbery (eds.), *The Ends of Rhetoric: History, Theory, Practice*. Stanford Calif.: Stanford University Press.

—— —— (1995). 'Postface' to the 2nd edn. of Sperber and Wilson, *Relevance: Communication and Cognition*. Oxford: Blackwell.

Sperber, Dan, and Wilson, Deirdre (1998a). 'The Mapping Between the Mental and the Public Lexicon', in Peter Carruthers and Jill Boucher (eds.), *Language and Thought: Interdisciplinary Themes*. Cambridge: Cambridge University Press.

——— (1998b). 'Irony and Relevance: A Reply to Seto, Hamamoto and Yamanashi', in Robyn Carston and Seiji Uchida (eds.), *Relevance Theory: Applications and Implications*. Amsterdam: John Benjamins.

Stalnaker, Robert (1974). 'Pragmatic Presuppositions', in Milton Munitz and Peter Unger (eds.), *Semantics and Philosophy*. New York: New York University Press. Repr. in Stalnaker, *Context and Content: Essays on Intentionality in Speech and Thought*. Oxford: Oxford University Press.

——— (1999). *Context and Content: Essays on Intentionality in Speech and Thought*. Oxford: Oxford University Press.

Stanley, Jason (2000). 'Context and Logical Form'. *Linguistics and Philosophy*, 23: 391–434.

——— (2002). 'Making it Articulated'. *Mind and Language*, 17: 49–68.

——— and Szabó, Zoltán (2000). 'On Quantifier Domain Restriction'. *Mind and Language*, 15: 219–61.

Strawson, Peter (1964). 'Intention and Convention in Speech Acts'. *Philosophical Review*, 73: 439–60. Repr. in John Searle (ed.), *The Philosophy of Language*. Oxford: Oxford University Press, 1971.

Sweetser, Eve (1990). *From Etymology to Pragmatics: Metaphorical and Cultural Aspects of Semantic Structure*. Cambridge: Cambridge University Press.

Szabó, Zoltán (ed.) (2005). *Semantics vs Pragmatics*. Oxford: Oxford University Press.

Travis, Charles (1975). *Saying and Understanding*. Oxford: Blackwell.

——— (2001). *Unshadowed Thought: Representation in Thought and Language*. Cambridge, Mass.: Harvard University Press.

Tsohatzidis, Savas (ed.) (1994). *Foundations of Speech Act Theory: Philosophical and Linguistic Perspectives*. London: Routledge.

Turner, Kenneth (ed.) (1999). *The Semantics–Pragmatics Interface from Different Points of View*. Oxford: Elsevier Science.

van der Auwera, Johan (1981). *What Do We Talk About When We Talk? Speculative Grammar and the Semantics and Pragmatics of Focus*. Amsterdam: John Benjamins.

——— (1985). *Language and Logic: A Speculative and Condition-Theoretic Study*. Amsterdam: John Benjamins.

——— (1997). 'Conditional Perfection', in A. Athanasiadou and R. Dirven (eds.), *On Conditionals Again*. Amsterdam: John Benjamins.

Vanderveken, Daniel (1990–1). *Meaning and Speech Acts*, 2 vols. Cambridge: Cambridge University Press.

Van Rooy, Robert (1999). 'Questioning to Resolve Decision Problems', in P. Dekker (ed.), *Proceedings of the Twelfth Amsterdam Colloquium*. Amsterdam: ILLC.

Wharton, Tim (2003). 'Interjections, Language and the "Showing/Saying" Continuum'. *Pragmatics and Cognition*, 11: 39–91.

Wilson, Deirdre (1975). *Presuppositions and Non-Truth-Conditional Semantics*. London: Academic Press. Repr. Aldershot: Gregg Revivals, 1991.

——— (2003). 'Relevance and Lexical Pragmatics'. *Italian Journal of Linguistics/Rivista di Linguistica*, 15: 273–91.

——— and Matsui, Tomoko (2000). 'Recent Approaches to Bridging: Truth, Coherence, Relevance', in J. de Bustos Tovar, P. Charaudeau, J. Alconchel, S. Iglesias Recuero, and C. Lopez Alonso (eds.), *Lengua, Discurso, Texto*, i. Madrid: Visor Libros.

—— and Sperber, Dan (1981). 'On Grice's Theory of Conversation', in P. Werth (ed.), *Conversation and Discourse*. London: Croom Helm. Repr. in Asa Kasher (ed.), *Pragmatics: Critical Concepts*, iv. London: Routledge, 1998.

———— (1988). 'Mood and the Analysis of Non-Declarative Sentences', in Jonathan Dancy, Julius Moravcsik, and Christopher Taylor (eds.), *Human Agency: Language, Duty and Value*. Stanford, Calif.: Stanford University Press. Repr. in Asa Kasher (ed.), *Pragmatics: Critical Concepts*, iv. London: Routledge, 1998.

———— (1992). 'On Verbal Irony'. *Lingua*, 87: 53–76.

———— (1993). 'Linguistic Form and Relevance'. *Lingua*, 90: 1–25.

———— (2002). 'Truthfulness and Relevance'. *Mind*, 111: 583–632.

———— (2004). 'Relevance Theory', in Laurence Horn and Gregory Ward (eds.), *The Handbook of Pragmatics*. Oxford: Blackwell.

PART V

METAPHYSICS

CHAPTER 19

CAUSATION

NED HALL

1. INTRODUCTION

Let's start with a sampling of philosophical accounts of causation. Famously, Hume (1748, sect. VII) took causation to consist in constant conjunction: an event of type E has an immediately preceding event of type C as its cause just in case C-events are always followed by E-events. Fastforwarding about 200 years, the core idea that causation consists in the instantiation of lawful regularities received an update from Davidson (1967), who argued that the regularity or law in question need not be explicit: the truth conditions for a claim of the form 'event C caused event E' are simply that there be some feature of C and some feature of E such that the two events are 'covered' by a causal law relating events with these features. Mackie (1965) took the regularity approach in a slightly different direction, arguing that C is a cause of E just in case it is an essential part of a condition lawfully sufficient in the circumstances for E. Lewis (1973a) developed a very different idea suggested by Hume, drawing on successes in the clarification of the semantics of counterfactual conditionals in order to analyse causation by means of them: event E counterfactually depends on event C just in case if C had not occurred, E would not have; causation itself Lewis took to be the ancestral of counterfactual dependence. More recently (2004a), Lewis modified this approach to incorporate a different kind of counterfactual relation. On the updated view, C can also cause E if, roughly, had the manner of C's occurrence differed in any of a large number of ways, the manner of E's occurrence would have correspondingly differed.

In the last twenty-five years or so, Lewis's approach has eclipsed the Mackie–Davidson approaches as a source of inspiration for work in the philosophy of causation: the literature houses dozens of variations on the counterfactual analysis of causation, whereas regularity accounts seem to have fallen into disuse. Meanwhile, a number of quite different approaches have taken root. Several authors (see e.g. Good 1961, 1962; Suppes 1970; Salmon 1980; Eells 1991; Mellor 1995; Kvart 2004) have looked to *probabilistic* relations as the key to understanding causation, trying to build on the core key idea that causes should render their effects more probable. Strikingly different yet again is the approach of those who see causation as fundamentally a matter of a *physical connection* between cause and effect, typically involving the transfer of some quantity. Several writers (Fair 1979; Salmon 1994; Dowe 2000) look to physics for guidance as to what these quantities are: thus, Fair takes the crucial quantity to be energy; Dowe lets it be any quantity that, according to fundamental physics, is conserved. Ehring (1997) by contrast takes this approach in a more metaphysical direction, arguing that causation essentially involves the transfer of a trope, a particularized property.

However disparate, these approaches share a common reductionist commitment: for they are all at the very least compatible with the view that facts about what causes what reduce to some more basic set of facts—e.g. the totality of non-modal facts about the world, together perhaps with the facts about the fundamental laws that govern the world. Others (Tooley 1987, 1990; Armstrong 2004) argue instead that causal relations are themselves part of the fundamental ontology of the world, and facts about their instantiation do not even supervene on—let alone reduce to—more metaphysically basic facts. (Intimations of a view like this can be found in Anscombe 1971.)

That will do for now. As is evident from even so brisk a tour, philosophy of causation sprawls across a heterogeneous landscape of positions. The extent of the sprawl would be hard to convey even in a leisurely survey, given how deep run the differences in approach, aims, and methodology. One might see such pluralism as a sign of health. Unfortunately, a more accurate assessment warrants less optimism, for philosophers working within different paradigms tend to engage very little with one another. This state of affairs is all the more unfortunate, given what has been, in recent years, a remarkable upsurge of interest in causation among psychologists, computer scientists, statisticians, and other non-philosophers (see e.g. Pearl 2000). A minor intellectual renaissance is brewing, and philosophers ought to, but do not yet, occupy the forefront of it.

An overview like this is going to require a heavy investment in taxonomy; in providing one I will try to highlight those areas where philosophical disagreement about causation can most fruitfully be joined. Let's start, though, with a rare but important area of agreement.

2. PRIMARY VERSUS SECONDARY CAUSAL LOCUTIONS

English employs a wide variety of causal locations. Suzy throws a rock at a window, breaking it. Consequently,

(1*a*) *Suzy* causes the window to break.
(1*b*) Her *rock* causes the window to break.
(1*c*) Her rock's *momentum* (as opposed to its colour) causes the window to break.
(1*d*) Her *throw* causes the window to break.
(1*e*) The *fact that she throws* the rock causes the window to break.
(1*f*) Billy is standing nearby; his *failure to stop her* causes the window to break.

Already, we have evidence that causes can be people, things, property instances, events, facts, and omissions. Similar examples suggest that effects can also be highly disparate—although, curiously, perhaps not *quite* as disparate as causes (try coming up with a natural English sentence which describes a *thing* as an effect: it can be done, but only with some strain). Nor does the disparity end here, as witness examples like the following:

(1*g*) Suzy's throw caused the window to break in part *because* the window was so fragile.
(1*h*) Suzy's throw was *the* cause of the window's breaking.

There is a widespread consensus that the right way to handle such profusion is to single out a narrow class of locutions as the most important ones, the ones that an account absolutely has to get right. Dealing with the remainder is typically seen as a kind of mopping up action. This decision about which locutions to consider primary and which secondary typically goes hand in hand with some metaphysical claim to the effect that certain items are the *fundamental* causal relata; the cash value of this claim is that causal facts about other sorts of items are to be explained by means of, or somehow reduced to, causal facts involving the fundamental relata. Thus, I might take statements of the form 'Event C causes event E' to be primary, and announce that on my account events are the fundamental causal relata; that takes care of (1*d*) automatically, and perhaps (1*e*), if I can argue that it is merely elliptical for (1*d*). I might then say that what makes *Suzy* a cause of the window's breaking is, roughly, that Suzy participates in an event—her throw—that causes the window's breaking; likewise for her rock. Sentences like (1*h*) call for a different strategy, since it will hardly do to hold that the window's breaking has but *one* cause; I might therefore hold, as many do, that the definite article singles out not the *only* cause, but rather the cause most *salient* in the context.

3. The Causal Relata: Events versus Facts

I'm not done: (1c), (1f), and (1g) still need treatment, and the question of which treatment is best leads straight into controversy. We will touch on that controversy in Section 7; for the moment, let us take on board the utility of this distinction between primary and secondary locutions, between more and less fundamental causal facts. Now comes our first major area of dispute: how should this distinction be drawn? The two serious candidates are these:

Events. The primary locution is 'Event C causes event E'; the fundamental causal relata are thus events.

Facts. The primary locution is 'The fact that P causes it to be the case that Q'; the fundamental causal relata are thus facts.

In the literature, Events seems to be the odds-on favourite. Regrettably, that literature fails to provide any particularly compelling reasons why this should be so. Often, one encounters the opinion that Facts does not even merit refutation, since, obviously, facts are abstract in a way that automatically renders them unsuitable to be causes or effects. But this opinion does not withstand scrutiny, as Bennett (1988) and especially McGrath (2002) have shown. Davidson (1967) offers a famous but fallacious argument that the logical form of causal claims militates against Facts; again, see Bennett for a rebuttal. What's more, the insistence that facts cannot be causes or effects has consequences whose awkwardness goes under-appreciated. We'll review these issues in Section 7. Until then—and only to make the discussion less cumbersome—we will proceed under the assumption that Events is correct.

4. Reductionism versus Non-Reductionism

The second major source of disagreement will require a bit of setting up. Begin with the assumption that there is some fundamental ontological structure to the world, some set of truths about the world that serve as a basis to which all other truths about the world reduce (we need 'reduce' here, and not the clearer 'supervene'; for the latter notion does not build in the asymmetry of the former). Add that these fundamental facts divide into non-modal or categorical facts—e.g. about what objects there are, and what purely non-modal properties and relations they have at what times—together with facts about the laws of nature. Taking our inspiration from physics, let's go a bit further, construing the fundamental non-modal facts about our world to be the facts about what its complete physical state is at every moment, and construing 'laws of nature' to be the fundamental physical laws that govern how these states evolve over time. (If we're going to be completely up to date, we should add to this inventory facts about the geometrical structure of space-time, and remark that instantaneous physical states are to be understood as instantaneous states along some foliation of the space-time.) Causal facts, then, will somehow reduce to these facts.

There are two broad classes of approach in the philosophy of causation that agree with this basic reductionist premiss, and two broad classes of approach that dispute it. Let's take them in turn.

One way to be a reductionist is to look for what I call a 'nomological entailment relation' that can hold between events, and then identify causation with that relation. The label is intended to be more evocative than tight-fitting, and rather than try to give some precise characterization I will begin with examples:

Crude sufficient condition account. C causes E iff C and E both occur, and from the fact that C occurs, together with the laws, it follows that E occurs.

Crude necessary condition account. C causes E iff C and E both occur, and from the fact that E occurs, together with the laws, it follows that C occurs.

Crude probabilistic account. C causes E iff C and E both occur, and the probability that E occurs, given that C occurs, is greater than the probability that E occurs, given that C does not occur.

Mackie-style regularity account. C causes E iff C and E both occur, and from the fact that C occurs, together with some suitable auxiliary premisses describing contingent facts about the circumstances in which C occurs, together with the laws, it follows that E occurs; but this fact does *not* follow from the auxiliary premisses and the laws alone.

Simple counterfactual account. C causes E iff C and E both occur, and had C not occurred, E would not have occurred.

Lewis-style counterfactual account. C causes E iff C and E both occur, and there is a (possibly empty) set of events $\{D_1, D_2, \ldots, D_n\}$ such that if C had not occurred, D_1 would not have occurred; and if D_1 had not occurred, D_2 would not have occurred; ... and if D_n had not occurred, E would not have occurred.

In each case, the analysis displays something that we might, speaking loosely, call an *entailment* relation between the fact that the cause occurs and the fact that the effect occurs—where that relation is, crucially, mediated by the fundamental laws. (In the case of counterfactual analyses, this mediation is behind the scenes, and happens in virtue of the role that the fundamental laws play in fixing the truth-values of the counterfactuals; see, for example, Lewis 1973b.)

The physical connection views sketched earlier illustrate a second, different way to be a reductionist. The essential feature of these views is that causation consists (at least partly) in the transfer of something from cause to effect; the differences concern what that something is. Strikingly different from nomological entailment accounts though they are, such views clearly count as reductionist, at least on the plausible assumption that what gets transferred to what reduces to basic non-modal facts, together with the facts about what the fundamental laws are.

Anti-reductionism likewise comes in two flavours. One of these, for which I take as inspiration Shoemaker (1980) and Cartwright (1999), holds that the items that populate our world possess, as a matter of primitive, not-further-explicable meta-physical fact, certain causal powers: there is no interesting sense to be made of a totality of 'non-modal' facts about the world to which causal facts (partly) reduce. What's more, on one very natural way of developing this view, laws are not some *additional* feature of reality, but rather serve as mere summaries—more less accurate—of the causal powers objects possess.

An example, to try to make the contrast clear: Both the reductionist and this kind of non-reductionist will agree that two negatively charged particles will exert a repulsive force on each other. (To keep things simple, pretend that these are Newtonian particles.) Here, crudely, is how the reductionist understands this claim: the two particles each possess a certain property, and there is, in addition, a fundamental law of nature which describes the total force on each particle partly as a function of its distance from the other particle and these properties. While it is certainly correct to say, on this view, that the particles possess a *causal power* to repel like-charged particles, that fact is, as it were, only *derivative* on the facts just mentioned. (Perhaps it reduces to a certain kind of counterfactual detailing what would happen, were the particles placed in proximity to each other, and were no other sources of force present.) The non-reductionist we are considering sees things differently. She holds that part of what it is for the particles to be negatively charged is for them to have the causal power to repel each other. In the order of being, as it were, this fact is primary.

To finish our survey, let us consider a very different way to be a non-reductionist. Here, Tooley (1990) and Armstrong (2004) are exemplars. Thus Armstrong, commenting on Lewis's work, writes:

In the course of these discussions Lewis introduces his justly celebrated 'neuron diagrams'. These involve imaginary systems of neurons that are hooked up according to certain often quite complex causal patterns of firings and inhibitions of firing. They are then used to illustrate such situations as epiphenomenal events, preemptive causation, causal redundancy and so on.

When we look at these diagrams, we can immediately see that they are possible causal patterns, in most cases empirically possible patterns (you could construct such a circuit). Counterfactual theories of causation (and, it may be added, Regularity theories and Probability-raising theories of causation) struggle with these diagrams. Wittgenstein spoke of an open door that we had only to see and go through to escape philosophical confusion.... The solution that I recommend to the problems posed by the neuron diagrams is very simple. Where there is an arrow in a diagram showing that one neuron brings it about that another neuron fires, or is rendered incapable of firing, take it that here there is *a genuine two-term relation of singular causation* holding between cause and effect. Where there is no such arrow, deny that there is any such relation. This is the open door. (Armstrong 2004: 446; my italics)

The surrounding context makes clear that Armstrong does not mean to be offering a theory of neuron-causation, but a theory of causation quite generally. Moreover, his talk of a 'genuine two-term relation' is meant to signal that causal relations are part of the *fundamental ontology* of the world (on his preferred view, causation is a *universal*). There is no problem, on this view, with including in one's fundamental ontology an interesting, rich range of non-modal facts, nor with introducing fundamental laws to govern what non-modally happens. It is just that facts about what causes what need to be introduced as an *additional* ingredient of reality, not to be reduced—by counterfactual or any other means—to the remaining ingredients.

Let me now try to encapsulate the differences between the four types of philosophical account of causation. Imagine that you are a god, setting out to construct a possible world. According to the reductionist, all you need to do is to lay down what, non-modally speaking, happens, and lay down the fundamental laws that govern what happens; you will thereby automatically have generated all the facts about what causes what. Nomological entailment approaches say that you will have done so because you will have generated all the facts about the relevant sort of nomological entailment (counterfactual dependence, probability-raising, or whatever). Physical connection approaches say that you will have done so because you will have laid down all the facts about which of the relevant quantities get transferred from where to where. By contrast, a non-reductionist of the second type thinks that your job is not done yet: you still need to specify which events instantiate the causal relation. And a non-reductionist of the first type thinks that what you have done has simply been misdescribed: there is no way for you to lay down a totality of facts about what, non-modally speaking, happens. You can introduce objects into the world and endow them with properties—but you *thereby* introduce causal powers into the world. Furthermore, having done so, there is no need for you to introduce laws; what laws there are is already automatically fixed by what sorts of things there are, and what sorts of properties—and therefore causal powers—they possess.

5. METHODOLOGICAL ISSUES

Can any considerations make one of these four approaches appear more compelling than the others? I think so. But to bring them out we will need to focus on two methodological questions: What is the proper *aim* of a philosophical account of causation? And what are the proper methods of investigation for achieving this aim?

The first question seems to have an obvious answer: the aim is to explain what causation *is*. Perhaps. But this answer sounds a lot better coming from a non-reductionist, especially one of the Tooley–Armstrong variety, than it does coming from a reductionist. The former sort of philosopher can offer up his account as part of a description and explication of the fundamental ontological structure of the world, and to be sure, no one with a taste for metaphysics would doubt the significance of such an enterprise. But matters are otherwise for the reductionist. By her own lights, her account of causation will add nothing whatsoever to a description or explication of the fundamental ontological structure of the world. That does not mean that her project is unimportant. It is just that its true significance will be masked by the glib claim that she is simply trying to explain what causation is.

Here is a comparison that might be helpful. Imagine that we are trying to figure out what life is—what the distinction is between living and non-living entities. Now, someone with vitalist sympathies will see this project as immensely important, for this is a distinction that, by his lights, carves nature at its joints. But from the standpoint of modern biology the significance of this enterprise lies elsewhere, and hinges entirely on the *utility* (for the discipline of *biology*, presumably) possessed by whatever distinction one comes up with. Similarly, I suggest that the most honest way for the reductionist about *causation* to advertise her project is as follows: in 'analysing' causation, she is trying to come up with a precise account of a distinction (or set of distinctions) that will serve some useful theoretical purposes (most obviously, in other areas of philosophical inquiry). The significance of this difference in methodological orientation between the reductionist and the non-reductionist will, I hope, become clearer as we proceed, and in particular, as we review the standard techniques that philosophers have used to support their views.

Turn now to the second question raised above, and consider the sorts of 'data' that a philosopher has to rely on, when giving an account of causation. The data, not surprisingly, take the form of intuitions, which come in three varieties:

1. There are intuitions about the causal structures of specific hypothetical cases: one describes such a case, and then elicits intuitive judgements—ideally, firmly held, widely agreed upon intuitive judgements—about what causes what. Here is an example that will come in for a lot of discussion later on:

   Suzy First: Suzy throws a rock at a window. It flies through the air, strikes the window, and breaks it. Suzy's friend Billy throws a rock at the window, too. He's slower, so her rock gets there first; but if she hadn't thrown it, the window would have shattered all the same, thanks to his throw.

The intuitive judgement that Suzy's throw is a cause of the window's breaking, and Billy's is not, fits the bill: it is extremely firmly held and widely shared. As we will see later on, it is also a very important intuition, for a number of attempts to give a reductionist account of causation founder on this case.

2. There are intuitions about cases that are harder to classify, but that are called upon not so much to refute some specific proposal but to establish some sweeping claim about causation. Here I have in mind the cases that Tooley in particular relies on to motivate his variety of non-reductionism. A clear instance is the following (Tooley 1990). I'll henceforth call this the 'Tooley-case':

Given [the assumption that there is nothing incoherent in the idea of an uncaused event], one can consider a world where objects sometimes acquire property Q without there being any cause of their doing so, and similarly for property R, and where, in addition, the following two statements are true:

(1) It is a law that, for any object x, x's having property P for a temporal interval of length Δt either causes x to acquire property Q, or else causes x to acquire property R;
(2) It can never be the case, for any object x, that x's having property P for a temporal interval of length Δt causes x to acquire both property Q and property R.

Suppose, finally, that an object a in such a world, having had property P for the appropriate interval, acquires both Q and R. In view of the law described in statement (1), either the acquisition of Q was caused by the possession of P for the relevant interval, or else the acquisition of R was so caused. But, given statement (2), it cannot be the case that the possession of P for the relevant interval caused both the acquisition of Q and the acquisition of R. So once again, it must be the case that one of two causal states of affairs obtains, but the totality of facts concerning, first, the non-causal properties of, and relations between, events, secondly, what laws there are, and thirdly, the direction of causation in all potential causal processes, does not suffice to fix which causal state of affairs obtains.

Grant the cogency of the case (a mistake, as I'll argue later), and Tooley's brand of non-reductionism follows at once.

3. There are intuitions about the general principles that govern the causal relation. Here are some examples (to which both Events and Facts could be added):

Transitivity. Causation is transitive; if C is a cause of D and D of E, then C is thereby a cause of E.

Intrinsicness. The causal structure of a process is intrinsic to that process.

Locality. Causes are connected to their effects via temporally (stronger: spatio-temporally) continuous chains of intermediate causes.

Omissions. Absences—failures of events to occur—can be causes and effects.

Dependence. Counterfactual dependence suffices for causation: if distinct events C and E both occur, but E would not have if C had not, then C is thereby a cause of E.

Three comments about such principles are in order. First, it should not be thought that their intuitive appeal, such as it is, provides decisive grounds for endorsing them. This is partly because of the possibility of outright counter-examples. (For example, several cases in the literature purport to refute Transitivity.) But it is also partly because an insistence on them may carry severe theoretical costs: consider, for example, the difficulty in wedding Events to Omissions. Secondly, these principles can receive independent support on the basis of theoretical considerations. For example, one reason for *endorsing* transitivity—even in the face of the alleged counter-examples—is that unless one does so one cannot construct an account that will get some clear and obvious cases right (see Lewis 1973a). Thirdly, tensions may arise between various of these principles; for example, it is probably impossible to maintain both Locality and Dependence (see Hall 2002).

Obviously, one overarching aim for a philosophical account of causation is to accord as much as possible with the sorts of intuitions just canvassed. But there is bloody warfare about their relative priority. Tooley, unsurprisingly, leans great weight on the Tooley-case and others like it, whereas reductionists like myself are inclined to dismiss them out of hand. Again, Lewis takes it as a non-negotiable datum that facts cannot be causes or effects; Bennett sees this position as involving a crude mistake. Even when it comes to intuitions about the causal characteristics of hypothetical cases, opinions vary. Some philosophers, for example, see the purported counter-examples to transitivity as decisive, whereas others see them as merely misleading. (Compare, in this regard, McDermott 1995 with Lewis 2004a.) Comparatively rare are examples such as Suzy First, which, on the one hand, have a great deal of probative value, and, on the other hand, command intuitive verdicts so firm that virtually no philosophers would care to reverse them. So a philosopher of causation who wants to get beyond a foot-stamping defence of some position has her work cut out for her. In what follows, I will outline one plan for navigating the competing demands of the various intuitions just sketched.

6. THE CASE FOR NOMOLOGICAL ENTAILMENT ACCOUNTS

The first step will be to argue the merits of a nomological entailment approach. Let's begin by reviewing three further constraints on an account of causation, independent of the constraint of 'intuitive fit'.

First, it would be desirable to have an account that applies across a wide range of possible worlds, especially worlds with different laws from our own. Causation is to a good extent 'topic-neutral'—at least when the topic is the fundamental laws of nature. We will see that this desideratum spells trouble for physical connection accounts.

Secondly, and more importantly, an account of causation needs to be 'level-neutral': it needs to respect the insight that causal relations obtain at and across a wide variety of levels of description. I drink some coffee, and perk up as a result. There is causation at the level of my body: drinking the coffee causes me to perk up. There is causation at the biochemical level, involving the interaction of caffeine molecules with other molecules in my body. There is causation at the atomic and subatomic levels as well. And causation can cross levels: in suitable circumstances, the decay of a radioactive atom can bring about the birth of a child (by way of a romantic story involving two nuclear chemists, as it might be).

It is not enough merely to recognize the existence of causal relations at and across different levels. For these relations are not independent of one another: When I perk up as a result of drinking the coffee, for example, this body-level causal fact is not somehow completely metaphysically separate from and independent of the bio-chemical causal facts involving the behaviour of the caffeine in my bloodstream. Now, the nature of this dependence is an intricate and subtle matter. All the same, an account of causation should not render it a complete mystery, and as we will see, a Tooley–Armstrong-style non-reductionism founders on this requirement. (We will also see trouble for physical connection accounts in even recognizing the existence of causal facts at any level other than the most microphysical.)

Finally, as noted above, we should hope for an account that does some useful theoretical work. Again, this desideratum is particularly important for reductionists.

Let's turn to a more detailed look at the four broad classes of account, starting with Shoemaker–Cartwright-style non-reductionism.

For our purposes, the significant part of this position is the claim that there is no content to the notion of 'non-modal fact'—or at any rate, not enough to meet the reductionist's needs. Why not? Because, so the story goes, to specify a thing's prop-erties or relations to other things is—with metaphysical necessity—to at least par-tially specify its causal powers. (Even in the case of its spatio-temporal relations? Never mind.) Recall our electrons, exerting a repulsive force on each other in virtue of their negative charge. Could those electrons have existed in a world in which they possessed exactly the intrinsic physical properties that they in fact possess, but *attracted* each other? One might think not; one might think that to the extent that we have a grip on what it is for something to possess such-and-such a negative charge, it is inconceivable that two things could possess this property and not repel each other. That is, it is *essential* to this property that a thing possessing it have the causal power to repel other things possessing it. And once such a connection is rec-ognized between fundamental physical properties and associated causal powers, it seems unlikely that this connection could be limited to the micro level. It is much more likely that it will percolate on up to the most macro of levels, so that even the possession of ordinary properties will be necessarily connected to the possession of certain causal powers. (Thus, Shoemaker contends that a knife's property of being knife-shaped is necessarily connected to its power to cut.)

But no harm will come to the reductionist from simply conceding the point. What she needs is some reasonably clear conception of the sorts of fundamental facts to which all other facts, and in particular causal facts, reduce. We have already provided such a conception: fundamental facts are facts about the geometry of space-time, about the instantaneous physical states the world occupies, and about the fundamental laws that govern their evolution. She might wish to claim, in addition, that this package of ingredients has a purely non-modal component (instantaneous states, plus space-time geometry), and a modal component (the fundamental laws). The Shoemaker–Cartwright position, if correct, shows that she can't, by showing in essence that there is no way to specify a complete instantaneous physical state of the world without placing substantial constraints on the fundamental laws. So what? The additional claim is an optional extra, and abandoning it leaves untouched what is central to the reductionist picture.

That is an important result. Certainly, the Shoemaker–Cartwright view is *compatible* with a kind of primitivism about causation that stands in direct opposition to reductionism—namely, the kind that holds that all that can be said about causation is that objects in the world possess various causal powers that are manifested on various occasions, with no prospect for an informative general theory of how these powers are constituted, and likewise no prospect for an informative general theory of the causal relation. This view strikes me as pointlessly defeatist: at best it is a position to end up with, after all other avenues have been thoroughly and exhaustively investigated. It is crucial to see, then, that it gains no support from what may well be an attractive position about the metaphysics of properties.

Before proceeding to the second, Tooley–Armstrong variety of non-reductionism, it will be helpful to review a well-known and important distinction between two conceptions of properties and relations. On the first, 'non-discriminating' conception, properties are cheap: it is not merely that for every (suitably non-pathological) predicate, there is a property or relation that is its extension, it is that for every function mapping possible worlds to sets of n-tuples of objects that exist in them, there is an n-place relation. Roughly, any way of classifying yields up a property or relation, and thus there is no sense in which properties and relations help carve nature at its joints.

On the second, 'sparse' conception, what counts as a property or relation is vastly more restricted. In my view, the guiding intuition for this conception is the following: what properties and relations there are at a world is limited by the requirement that there be just those properties and relations that are needed to specify exactly what is true at that world, and no more. (See Lewis 1983 for additional characterizations.) Thus, if there is the property of being F, and the property of being G, then there is no such property as the property of being either F or G; for the pattern of instantiation of F-ness and G-ness will automatically fix the pattern of instantiation of this other 'property', and so its addition to the list of properties would be redundant in a way that disqualifies it.

Two points, by way of clarification. First, the guiding intuition is only that, since the foregoing requirement can obviously be met by distinct families of properties and relations. Secondly, a combination of physicalism with a modest brand of scientific realism yields the view that one of the aims of science—fundamental physics in particular—is to provide us with an inventory of the properties and relations, sparsely conceived, that are instantiated in our world.

The Tooley–Armstrong view is a thesis about properties and relations, sparsely conceived. It is the thesis that the list of such properties and relations includes causation as one of its members. That is clearly their intent, and at any rate to understand their position as having in mind the non-sparse conception would render it utterly trivial, since everyone agrees that on that conception, causation is one of the relations that exist. (Even those who think that there is no such thing as causation: for they will simply take it to be the empty relation.)

One significant motivation for this view comes from a certain kind of thought experiment, of which the Tooley-case is an instance. If successful, these thought experiments would appear to establish that facts about what causes what do not even supervene on, let alone reduce to, facts about the fundamental laws, together with the facts about the pattern of instantiation of fundamental properties and relations. The most natural response? Insist that causation simply needs to be included on this list of fundamental properties and relations.

But the value of these thought experiments is doubtful. First, the cases tend to be described in ways that are question-begging, at least if the opponent is the reductionist. Notice that it was crucial to Tooley's example that the statement of the laws explicitly involved the notion of causation. To see this, try running through the example with 'causes' replaced by 'is followed by'. Do that, and the case can no longer be described consistently, for we are told that it is a law that being F is followed by exactly one of being G and being H, and also that it is compatible with this law that being F can be followed by both being G and being H. So, specifying the content of the law in the way that he did was crucial for the success of Tooley's example.

But a sober-minded reductionist should not accept that the fundamental laws to which she thinks the causal facts in part reduce are ever specified in such terms. To be sure, laws of the special sciences might need to be specified in part by appeal to the notion of causation; for example, it is a law of metallurgy that, in the absence of interfering factors, heating a metal bar causes it to expand. But the fundamental laws are different. Our best models for them, after all, come from fundamental physics, where these laws are typically captured in the form of differential equations, or in the form of recipes for constructing differential equations (e.g. Hamilton's equations in classical mechanics, or the Schrödinger equation in non-relativistic quantum mechanics). And the content of these laws is exactly that such-and-such complete physical states are followed (with nomological necessity, if you like) by such-and-such other complete physical states.

Secondly, even if Tooley succeeds in showing that our ordinary concept of causation carries with it non-reductionist commitments, the reductionist is well within her rights simply to respond, 'So much the worse for our ordinary concept'. Compare the case of 'life': you can tell an understandable, conceptually coherent story according to which a rock is alive, even though it has the internal physical structure of, well, a rock. But no concept of life as articulated by biologists or philosophers of biology will allow that this is a genuine metaphysical possibility. It is laughable to suggest that this points up some deep flaw in the work of those biologists and philosophers of biology. Rather, what it shows is that to the extent that we want a precisely articulated concept of life that will serve some useful purpose, the structure of our ordinary intuitions about the word 'life' are at best an imperfect guide to the structure that concept should have. A reductionist can and should say the same thing about the concept of causation.

So much for one of the main motivations for the Tooley–Armstrong view. What other motivations are there? As far as I can see, the only important remaining one consists in despair at the prospects for any other, more illuminating account of causation (cf. the passage from Armstrong quoted earlier). In response, I do not think that the full range of resources available to reductionists has yet been appreciated, let alone exhausted; Section 7 will indicate why.

So much for the reasons in favour of non-reductionism. On the other side of the balance sheet lie two very serious problems. The first concerns the requirement of level-neutrality—the requirement that an account of causation should respect the existence of causal relations at all levels from the most microphysical to the most macrophysical. Now, it is not that the non-reductionist cannot respect the existence of such relations; for example, when I drink the coffee there is, on his view, a two-place singular relation of causation that obtains between the event of my drinking and the event of my perking up, and likewise a multitude of instances of this relation at the biochemical level (between events involving caffeine and the cells of my body). What is a complete mystery is why there should be any relations whatsoever of metaphysical dependence between the patterns of instantiation of causation at these different levels. Minimally, it seems that we should have this much: if in any world the pattern of events in my body is exactly as it actually is, and the pattern of instantiation of causal relations at the biochemical level is exactly as it actually is, then so too the events of my drinking the coffee and my perking up instantiate the causal relation. But if all we say about the causal relation is that it is one of the fundamental relations instantiated in our world, then our view provides no resources for explaining why this relation of metaphysical dependence should hold.

Compare a simple counterfactual analysis. It is rather plausible that from the claim that the events in my body are exactly as they actually are, and the claim that the patterns of counterfactual dependence at the biochemical level are exactly as they actually are, it will follow (bracketing pre-emption: see Section 7) that my perking up counterfactually depends on my drinking the coffee. By contrast, the

Tooley–Armstrong view leaves the connections between causation at different levels unacceptably mysterious.

The second problem is epistemological. What, on the non-reductionist account, could possibly be the evidence for any causal claim? This problem famously dates back to Hume, who argued that neither perception nor introspection acquaints us with any instance of a 'necessary connection'. Now, one might doubt Hume's sweeping claim, and think, for example, that in the case of the impacts of various objects on one's body one directly perceives causal relations. But that possibility is a red herring, as witness the fact that in a wide variety and perhaps the vast majority of cases, our knowledge of or justified beliefs about causal relations are inferential. You flip a switch, and a light goes on. You flip the switch back to its original position, and the light goes off. You repeat the experiment a hundred times, and the same correlation obtains. You infer that flipping the switch (say, the first time) *caused* the light to go on. You did not perceive this causal relation. All the same, your inference certainly seems reliable. But it is a mystery why, on the non-reductionist view, it should be.

Isn't such underdetermination of theory by data everyone's problem? No: not underdetermination of *this* variety. Compare garden-variety underdetermination of the kind that yields to a familiar application of inference to the best explanation: we believe that there are atoms, for example, because of the stunning success of a worked out atomic hypothesis at explaining a vast range of observable phenomena. Whatever you think of this style of inference, you can at least agree that we do not have a *best* explanation unless we have *an* explanation. Well, what observable phenomena does the non-reductionist *explain* by means of the hypothesis that events (e.g. the flipping of the switch and the light's going on) instantiate some fundamental, two-term relation? None, as far as I can see. Calling this relation 'causation' only helps hide this failure from view.

Let's turn now to physical connection accounts. A common motivation for them is that they allegedly make the investigation of causation properly empirical (see, for example, Fair 1979). The thought, apparently, is that 'cause' is a natural kind term, and what is needed in order to give an account of causation is some empirical hypothesis about what relation causation is. But this claim seems to involve a basic confusion about the semantics of causal terms. Here I am content to follow Schaffer's excellent discussion (2004). He points out that our semantic intuitions about hypothetical cases involving laws quite different from the actual laws show that 'cause' and other related terms do not function in anything like the same way that terms like 'water', 'gold', etc. do. This observation reveals, in addition, an important limitation on physical connection accounts, which is their failure to generalize across a wide range of other possible laws. It is not merely that specific such accounts (e.g. that causation involves transfer of momentum) are hostage to physics as we currently conceive it, but that causal relations can, apparently, obtain even in worlds whose laws do not pick out any quantity as one that might plausibly be 'transferred' in all and only causal interactions.

It is sometimes thought that physical connection accounts gain support from pre-emption cases like Suzy First. For, allegedly, the only thing that distinguishes Suzy's throw from Billy's is that there is a momentum-carrying process connecting her throw to the shattering which, at the moment of the shattering, results in a transfer of momentum from the rock to the window—whereas there is no such process connecting Billy's throw to the shattering. (Ehring leans heavily on cases such as this to motivate his account.) But this motivation is misguided, and seeing why points out another serious problem with physical connection accounts. Add some detail to the case: Billy's rock, as it moves through the air, pushes air molecules ahead of it, and those bump into other air molecules, etc. And let us suppose that some of the air molecules thus moved strike the window at the exact moment that Suzy's rock strikes it, transferring some small quantity of momentum to the window. According to physical connection accounts, the revelation of these extra details ought to reverse the original judgement, turning this into a case of symmetric overdetermination: *both* Suzy's and Billy's throws count as causes of the window's breaking, since both are connected to it by the transfer of some appropriate quantity. But that is plainly false. Transfer of some quantity is thus not enough for causation; the account needs to be supplemented by some story about what counts as a *relevant* transfer of the quantity. What's more, in a world as chock full of stuff—e.g. photons and other tiny, fast-moving particle—as ours, to say that transfer of some quantity is *required* for causation is to say virtually nothing at all, for, plausibly, every event will be connected in such a way to every other event in its future light cone. It thus seems that all of the work will be done by the account of 'relevant transfer'. On the face of it, the most plausible way in which to develop such an account is by appeal to counterfactuals or perhaps probabilities—exactly the tools that a nomological entailment account will wheel out.

The problem just raised arises even at the most microphysical level: imagine a situation, for instance, in which particles A and B simultaneously collide with particle C, and particle C reacts in some way—but given the distinct physical characteristics of A and B, it is only the collision with A that *causes* this reaction. But even if this problem is somehow solved at the microphysical level, it won't go away at the macrophysical level. To make this clear, let's pretend that the microphysics is as congenial as possible to a physical connection account: all that happens at the microphysical level is that tiny, perfectly rigid billiard balls collide with each other in perfectly elastic collisions. The physical connectionist can thus say that at the microphysical level, causation consists in the carrying or transfer of momentum. Meanwhile, here at the macrophysical level I am alternately sipping coffee and orange juice, and a bit later perk up. It was sipping *coffee* that caused me to perk up, not sipping orange juice (my blood sugar was fine, I just needed a caffeine dose). But there is, patently, no way to account for this causal difference in terms of transfer of momentum: both the events result, by complicated routes, in the transfer of momentum to the particles that make up my brain, for example. Nor, to further dramatize the point, would one be able to account for the fact that is the *caffeine* in the coffee that perks me up, not (for example) the coffee temperature—even though, in virtue of the temperature, a bit more momentum gets transferred into the particles of my body than would have been the case if the coffee had been cool. The upshot of this sort of example should be obvious: even if a physical connection account works at the microphysical level, there is no plausible way to extend it into an account of causation at any other level. The requirement of level neutrality is thus violated in a rather stark manner.

Time to consider one final view, before turning triumphantly to nomological entailment accounts. This view, for reasons that will emerge shortly, is hard to characterize with respect to the reductionism–non-reductionism distinction. The following passages from Menzies will serve as an introduction:

The first step in providing a ... definition of the causal relation is to set down the central tenets of our folk theory of causation—the platitudes about causation which are common knowledge among us. There are many such platitudes: for example, it typically coincides with a temporal ordering of events so that causes precede effects; it typically coincides with the means–end relation so that if an effect is an end, its causes are means to it; causes explain their effects. The *postulate of the folk theory of causation* will consist of a conjunction of all such platitudes; or better, a long disjunction of all conjunctions of most of the platitudes. The most important platitudes—the ones which are crucial to the concept of causation—will be elements in all the conjunctions in this long disjunction. In the subsequent discussion I concentrate on a simple formulation of the postulate of the folk theory of causation, a formulation which takes the postulate to be a conjunction of three crucial platitudes. ... These three crucial platitudes, then, will be taken to form the basis of the postulate of the folk theory of causation. On the basis of this postulate, we can frame an explicit definition of the causal relation: The definition runs: the *causal relation is the intrinsic relation that typically holds between two distinct events when one increases the chance of the other event*. (The notion of increase in chance, used here, is to be understood in the counterfactual manner elucidated in Lewis's theory . . .) (Menzies 1996: 97, 101)

(The platitudes are that causation is a two-place relation between distinct events, that it is intrinsic to its relata, and that it is connected in the way indicated to counterfactual chance-raising.)

Consider the abstract form of the proposal (drawn, as Menzies makes clear, from the treatment of theoretical terms in Lewis 1970): We focus on some domain of relations. We exhibit a set of characteristics, drawn from the 'folk theory of causation', that relations in the domain might or might not possess. We identify causation as the unique relation in the domain possessing these characteristics. Why proceed in this way?

Menzies' principal reason is that he is impressed by what looks to be the utter failure of reductionist accounts to handle cases such as Suzy First, and probabilistic variants thereof. The strategy of taking 'causation' to be a theoretical term, amenable to the kind of treatment just sketched, seems a promising alternative: what distinguishes Suzy's throw from Billy's as a cause of the window's breaking is that the pair <Suzy's throw, breaking> instantiates the unique relation which plays the role picked out by our folk theory of causation, whereas the pair <Billy's throw, breaking> does not.

But there is less here than meets the eye. First, a minor problem: in all likelihood *nothing* will fit Menzies' definition, because of the unfortunate requirement that causation be intrinsic to its relata. This fuse is lit; a bit later that bomb explodes. Suppose the first event causes the second. That it does so is surely partly determined by features of the situation *extrinsic* to the lighting and the explosion—e.g. that this fuse is *connected to* that bomb.

Set this problem aside—perhaps by removing or suitably amending the requirement of intrinsicness. A more serious problem remains. Zero in on the first step: what, exactly, is the domain of relations over which we should quantify?

Perhaps it is the domain of fundamental relations, that is, relations understood in accordance with the *sparse* conception of properties and relations. But then the proposal turns into Tooley–Armstrong-style non-reductionism, with extra bells and whistles that add nothing of value.

Perhaps, then, it is the domain of relations, understood in accordance with the *non-discriminating* conception of properties and relations. But then a dilemma arises. On the one hand, the definition offered might be so demanding that no relation can fit it. On the other hand, if any relation fits it, then the account will become trivial, since the definition will pick out this relation *too directly*. Let me explain, by way of a simple illustration.

Suppose Menzies drops the intrinsicness requirement, so that the causal relation is, now, defined to be the relation that typically holds between two distinct events when one increases the chance of the other event. Now it is indeed possible for a relation to fit this definition. In fact, here is one relation—a relation in, remember, the non-discriminating sense—that fits it as well as could be desired: it is the relation that holds between two distinct events when one increases the chance of the other event. But *this* relation cannot be what Menzies has in mind: for if it is, then we have made no progress on the pre-emption problem that originally motivated his approach. Making the definition more sophisticated won't help in the slightest: for again, if it can be met by any relation, it can be met by that relation that holds between distinct events exactly when . . . , with the blanks filled in by the definition itself. In short, we can see that the use of the word 'typically', and indeed of the whole apparatus of theoretical definition, is doing *no work*: if the account succeeds, it succeeds because the definition in fact *constitutes a successful analysis of causation* of the kind Menzies thinks is unattainable.

Might there be a middle way? That is, might there be a way to specify boundaries on the relations being quantified over that are broad enough to distinguish Menzies' approach from the Tooley–Armstrong view, but narrow enough to avoid the foregoing trivialization? Perhaps. Menzies, for example, tries to appeal to a criterion of 'naturalness'. But what is unnatural about the relation of chance-raising?

Again, one might restrict the domain to relations that can be described, simply, using the resources of fundamental physics. But then the account runs afoul of the problems that beset physical connection accounts. My own suspicion is that the project is misconceived: the idea that we get any illumination into the nature of causation by conjoining the central platitudes involving the concept, and defining causation as that relation which satisfies them, is misguided. Of course we will gain illumination by *figuring out* what the central platitudes are. But we gain nothing further by trying to leverage them in the way Menzies does into a definition of causation. Better, I think, to return to the honest toil of trying to come up with an explicit, reductive analysis of this notion.

The next sections will consider the most promising options for such an analysis, and some of the most striking obstacles they still need to overcome. But let us first review some of their principal strengths. I will do so by considering, purely by way of illustration, the simplest counterfactual account, according to which event C is a cause of distinct event E just in case, if C had not occurred, E would not have occurred (the lessons generalize straightforwardly to more sophisticated accounts).

The account is intuitively attractive, not only because it works for a very wide range of cases, but also because its seems to get those cases right for the right reasons. What's more, it cleanly meets our desideratum that a theory of causation should be neutral as to the precise content of the laws: all the account requires of the laws is that, together with the actual facts, they fix truth-values for the needed counterfactuals, and standard semantics for counterfactuals (see Lewis 1973b) shows how this can be done provided only that the laws draw a distinction between those worlds that are nomologically possible and those that are not. Finally, level-neutrality poses no problem whatsoever, since it is routine that macrophysical events such as my perking up can counterfactually depend on other macrophysical events such as my drinking the coffee. And, as we've already seen, there is no deep mystery why there should be interesting relations of metaphysical dependence between causal facts at different levels. None of this is to say that the counterfactual account is correct, for it's not. It is rather that before one complains too bitterly about the problems that beset it and other reductionist nomological entailment accounts, one should keep vividly in mind how deep and systemic are the problems that beset the major rivals.

There is, finally, a very different but important reason for thinking that the philosopher interested in understanding causation would best spend her efforts by investigating the prospects for some nomological entailment account. And that is because even if she fails to come up with such an account, the lessons learned along the way—about such topics as varied as the nature of the causal relata, the varieties of causal pre-emption, tensions between basic theses involving causation such as Transitivity, Intrinsicness, and Dependence, the relation between ordinary causation and causation involving omissions, and much more—are rich enough to repay these efforts many times over. To put the point another way, some failures are more interesting than other failures; the problem with the rivals to nomological entailment accounts is not merely that they fail so disastrously, but that they do so in a boring fashion. One learns little of value from their demise. What follows, though regrettably brief, will try to point out some of the most important ways in which matters are otherwise, for nomological entailment accounts.

7. Nomological Entailment Accounts and the Crucial Examples: Pre-emption, Omissions, and Transitivity

First we need to narrow drastically the scope of discussion. As anyone with even a passing acquaintance with the literature in this area knows, it is heavily driven by examples, and by now they are legion. We will consider just a handful of those examples that have the most to teach about the proper form of a theory of causation: certain kinds of pre-emption, certain examples involving omissions, and certain purported counter-examples to Transitivity. (For a much more thorough survey, see Hall and Paul forthcoming.)

A theory of causation needs a guiding idea, and two seem most worth taking seriously. The first is that the occurrence of the cause *makes a difference to* the occurrence of the effect. The second is that what distinguishes the causes of some effect is that they collectively *suffice* for that effect. Each of these ideas can be developed in a number of different ways, but to fix ideas—and, again, to keep the discussion manageable—let us assume that the development of the first identifies causation with some sort of counterfactual dependence: given some event E, its causes at some earlier time t are to be those t-events on which it depends (leaving open whether this is simple counterfactual dependence, or some more complicated variety). As to the second, we should understand it as building in some requirement of non-redundancy, so that what distinguishes a set of causes is not merely that the elements collectively suffice for the given effect, but that no proper subset of them does. So: given some event E, its causes at some earlier time t are those t-events collectively minimally sufficient for t (leaving open exactly how 'sufficient' is to be defined). Let us henceforth label these approaches the *dependency* approach and the *sufficiency* approach.

Are causes and effects here *events* or *facts*? We should leave that for theory to decide, resisting the widespread assumption that the 'abstractness' of facts offends against taking them to be causal relata. For this bias is utterly without justification. Observe, first, that as soon as you attempt to construct a nomological entailment account of causation, facts are already implicated, even if only facts of the form 'the fact that event C occurred'. After all, when we talk, for example, of counterfactual dependence of event E on event C, that is really derivative: in the first instance, counterfactual dependence is a relation between the fact that event C occurred and the fact that event E occurred. Secondly, the automatic removal of this option from the table makes for trouble when we consider causation involving omissions.

Granted, matters are otherwise for Tooley–Armstrong non-reductionism, or for physical connectionist reductionism. Non-reductionism treats causal relations as part of the fundamental ontology of the world; plausibly, relations of this sort need certain sorts of relata. For example, if one is convinced (with Armstrong) that relations of this sort are universals, then they need particulars as relata, and we might grant that facts are not particulars. Again, if one thinks of causation as involving the transfer of something from cause to effect, then cause and effect need to be the sorts of things that can transfer and receive stuff. Perhaps events can do so, but facts can't. However, once those two approaches have been abandoned, and we have turned instead to approaches that see causation as, at heart, involving some relatively abstract relation of some sort of nomological entailment, then the ontological scruples that the two abandoned positions motivate should likewise be abandoned. Continued concern over the 'abstractness' of facts makes no sense.

Concern of another sort *does* make sense, at least if one adopts the sufficiency approach. For unless we restrict which sorts of facts are allowed to be causes and effects, the existence of purely logical relations among facts will make it impossible to discern when facts stand in the proper relations of sufficiency. Kim (1971) makes this point very effectively against Mackie, and it is worth reviewing here. Consider a case where Suzy throws a rock at a window, breaking it, and at the same time Billy throws a rock at a different window, breaking it as well. We want it to come out that the fact that Billy threw his rock causes it to be the case that his window broke. Let P be the fact that he threw his rock, and Q the fact that his window broke; then we need to find some set which includes P and is minimally sufficient for Q. Suppose we have done so. Then, regardless of how we analyse 'sufficient', it would seem that we can construct another set, as follows: let R be the fact that Suzy threw her rock, and simply replace P by the pair (R, either not-R or P). The resulting set will like-wise be minimally sufficient for Q: so the fact that Suzy threw her rock causes it to be the case that Billy's window broke. That is a disaster, and one way to circumvent it is to insist that facts can count as causal relata only when tied to particular events—that is, they must be facts of the form 'the fact that event C occurred'. The fan of Events would be well within her rights to complain that there is little difference between this position and the position that it is events that are the fundamental causal relata.

Still, this is only one move in a debate that really needs to be allowed to run its course. First, it is curiously difficult to advance a similar argument against the combination of Facts with a dependency approach. Secondly, similar problems will plague the fan of Events, unless she is equipped with a theory of events that will enable her to distinguish causal from non-causal relations between them (cf. Kim 1973; for a response, see Lewis 1986c). Finally, troubles of a different sort arise for the fan of Events when she insists on forcing certain sorts of causal locutions involving omissions into her preferred mould.

Of this more shortly. For ease of exposition, we will pretend, until we can no longer do so, that causes and effects are events. Time now to turn to the examples.

Begin with cases of redundant causation, which feature the presence of back-up processes poised to bring about the given effect. Such cases come in a number of distinct flavours (see Hall and Paul 2003 for a comprehensive survey). Here I will consider just one variety, sometimes called 'late pre-emption', and exhibited in Suzy First. One causal process brings about some event E (in this case, the window's breaking), and by doing so, prevents the back-up process (initiated by Billy's throw) from itself bringing about this event. (Contrast cases of 'early pre-emption', where some stage of the main process itself cuts short the back-up process. For example, it might be that Billy, when he sees Suzy winding up to throw, decides not to throw himself.)

Cases of late pre-emption are utterly mundane, evoke rock-solid intuitions (Suzy's throw is a cause of the window's breaking; Billy's is not), and are extraordinarily difficult to handle, for the simple reason that for a very wide range of nomological entailment relations, the genuine cause and the idle back-up will be symmetric with respect to that relation. Thus, both Suzy's throw and Billy's throw are elements of sets of events minimally sufficient for the window's breaking, the window's breaking counterfactually depends on neither, etc.

Rather than go through an exhaustive list of the various attempts that have been made to break this symmetry, let me simply fastforward to what I think are by far the two most plausible approaches. The first is a dependency approach, recently developed by Yablo (2002) and Hitchcock (2001), as well as others. It aims to show that the effect *does* differentially depend on the cause, provided one is careful to specify the right form of dependence (which, following Yablo, I will call 'de facto dependence'). The guiding idea is that, *holding fixed* how certain aspects of the situation actually play out, the effect depends upon the cause, but does not depend upon the idle back-up. In Suzy First, for example, the counterfactual that bears witness to the causal status of Suzy's throw is something like the following: if Suzy had not thrown, and if (as actually happens) Billy's rock had still not struck the window, then the window would not have broken. The idea is that there is no similar way to construct a counterfactual that will bear witness to the causal status of Billy's throw—since, as it actually happens, Suzy's rock *does* strike the window. I think this idea is attractive enough to deserve serious exploration, although it has yet to be developed in a fully adequate form. Part of the reason is that we need a rigorous recipe for picking out what, in the actual situation, should be held fixed as one moves to the counterfactual situation in which the candidate cause C does not occur. (Both Yablo and Hitchcock go some way towards providing such a recipe, but more work needs to be done.) Secondly, we need clear truth conditions for the sorts of counterfactual used in this account, since it is not at all obvious how to evaluate what goes on in a world in which Suzy does not throw, Billy does throw (for that fact is, all agree, to be held fixed), but Billy's rock somehow fails to strike the window.

The second strategy for handling cases of late pre-emption tries to build on the thesis that, roughly, the causal structure of a process is intrinsic to it. The idea, in outline, and illustrated by way of example, is as follows: Consider a case where Suzy is all by herself, and throws a rock at the window, breaking it. One could reasonably expect that an account could get the causal structure of *that* situation right. But in Suzy First there is a structure of events connecting her throw to the window's breaking that is *intrinsically just like* the process that unfolds in this simpler case. So if an analysis can get the causal structure of such simpler cases right, then perhaps it can discern the causal structure of more complicated cases by finding in them intrinsic matches of what goes on in the simpler cases. But here too there is work to be done. For example, in Suzy First there is also a structure of events connecting Billy's throw to the shattering that is intrinsically at least somewhat like what goes on in a situation where Billy alone throws. So the strategy, if it is going to work, needs to develop a notion of intrinsic similarity *in relevant respects*. (See Hall 2003 for an attempt to do so.)

Let us turn now to cases involving omissions. These come in at least three varieties; the following case illustrates all of them:

> *The Trip.* Joey, seeing Suzy about to throw a rock at a window, runs towards her to try to stop her. Unfortunately, he trips over a tree root, and consequently doesn't reach her in time. She throws. The window breaks. If he hadn't tripped, he would have stopped Suzy, and the window would not have broken.

Here we have causation *by* omission: Joey's failure to stop Suzy is a cause of the window's breaking. And causation *of* omission: the trip prevents Joey from stopping Suzy (i.e. causes his failure to do so). And, finally, causation *by way of* omission (aka causation by *double-prevention*): Joey's trip is a cause of the window's breaking by way of his failure to stop her (his trip prevented him from stopping her; had he done so, the window would not have broken).

A clean treatment of these varieties of causation that merely extends some treatment that works for more ordinary cases has proved enormously difficult to come by. There are a number of reasons.

First, our judgements involving causation by omission in particular seem peculiarly sensitive to *normative* considerations. Example (from Sarah McGrath): Suzy goes away on vacation, leaving her favourite plant in the hands of Billy, who has promised to water it. Billy fails to do so. The plant dies—but would not have, had Billy watered it. So Billy's failure to water the plant caused its death. But Vladimir Putin also failed to water Suzy's plant. And, had he done so, it would not have died. So why do we not *also* count his omission as a cause of the plant's death? Because, unlike Billy, he made no promise to water it. But what does such a normative consideration have to do with *causation*? A natural response is: nothing—the causal structure of the example is what it is quite independently of who promised what to whom, or indeed of any other normative consideration. But then our ordinary judgements involving causation by omission commit deep and systematic errors. The literature, when it notices this problem, tends to badly underestimate its difficulty. (See Beebee 2004 and especially McGrath 2002 for notable exceptions.)

Secondly, an approach that insists that causation relates *events* will, confronted with omission-involving causation, lead to a badly distorted ontology. That is because omissions are not, in any decent sense, a species of event, and treating them as such yields only confusion. Ordinary events can be located in space and time, involve particular objects as constituents, have other ordinary events as parts, possess detailed intrinsic natures. None of this holds for omissions. Granted, you might think that x's failure to F is located wherever x is, at the relevant time (e.g. Billy's failure to water Suzy's plants takes place wherever he is, at the time that he should have been watering the plants). But there may be no 'relevant' time. (McGrath again: Billy never runs a triathlon. When does *that* happen?) And there may be no 'x'. Billy, let us imagine, dies in a tragic accident, and so fails to meet Suzy for lunch the next day. Where does this omission take place (granting, for the sake of argument, that it takes place during lunchtime)? Where Billy is? But he isn't. You could, perhaps, make up an answer. But if so, you ought in good conscience to recognize that that is all you are doing.

Better to treat causation involving omissions as causation involving a certain kind of *fact*—namely, a fact to the effect that no event of such-and-such type occurs. This approach gains confirmation from the way we support claims of causation by omission. We typically do so by way of an appeal to a counterfactual of the form 'If an event of type C had happened, event E would not have happened'. From such a claim one can straight away infer (modulo the worries about normative considerations) that the failure of an event of type C to occur caused E to occur. What we *don't* do is to pick out some particular event C, and say that if only *it* had occurred, then E would not have. The friend of Facts has a distinct edge, here.

More interesting results begin to emerge when we consider how a sufficiency approach might be extended to cover causation involving omissions. The problems seem dire, and come quite clearly into view if we adopt a natural analysis of 'sufficient': say that a set of time t events S is sufficient for later event E iff, had only the events in S occurred at t, E would (still) have occurred. If so, can a set of events be minimally sufficient for some omission? No: for the *empty* set will itself be sufficient. Can a set of events minimally sufficient for E *include* an omission? No: for even if we treat it as an event, its removal from S will not, on the given analysis, affect the set's sufficiency for E. Finally, consider a set S sufficient for E that includes a 'double-preventer': an event C that prevents something that would in turn have prevented E. Then removing C will not affect sufficiency, since the test for sufficiency asks us to consider a situation in which the prevented threat to E is *also* absent. Should we blame the analysis of sufficiency? I don't think so: other attempts to flesh out this notion either remain hopelessly vague (cf. Mackie 1965) or run into worse problems (for discussion, see Hall, forthcoming).

Things look bad for a sufficiency approach. But there might be a way out: distinguish causation involving omissions from 'normal' causation, and insist that a sufficiency approach is well suited to the latter, a dependency approach to the former. (Hall 2004 adopts this approach; Lewis 2004b disputes it.) That's not crazy: causation involving omission typically fails, for example, to enter into the causal patterns of pre-emption and overdetermination that are so easy to construct when one is dealing with garden-variety causal processes, and that is some reason for thinking it needs a distinct kind of treatment. More importantly, evidence in favour of such a bifurcation emerges when we consider the alternative: adopt a dependency approach across the board. Now, the problem is not with accommodating the varieties of causation involving omission. It is rather that the dependency approach does so in a way which (i) directly conflicts with Transitivity; (ii) undercuts the strategies sketched above for handling late pre-emption.

The Trip neatly illustrates the first of these problems. If Joey had not seen Suzy, he would not have run towards her. If he had not run towards her, he would not have tripped. If he had not tripped, the window would not have broken. A dependency approach will see a causal link at each step. If causation is transitive, it will follow that Joey's seeing Suzy is a cause of the window's breaking. Examples like this are embarrassingly easy to construct: the presence of some threat to E causes a response which prevents that threat, thus ensuring E's occurrence; but it ought not to follow that the presence of the threat was *among the causes* of E. (Observe that a fan of bifurcation has a natural response: Transitivity is correct, but only for garden-variety causation, *not* for causation involving omissions.)

Examples like this have led some authors to deny transitivity (see e.g. McDermott 1995). But doing so won't help with the second problem. Recall that there were two strategies for coping with late pre-emption that looked at all promising: the intrinsicness strategy and the de facto dependence strategy. But the kind of intrinsicness thesis needed to underwrite the first of these strategies is systematically violated in cases of causation involving omissions. This is perhaps clearest in cases of double-prevention: Event E depends on event C only because C blocks some threat to E. So this dependence is secured by virtue of facts *extrinsic to* the 'process' (such as it is) connecting C to E: namely, the *existence of the threat*. For if there is no threat, there is no dependence of E on C, and certainly no causation of E by C. That fact directly conflicts with the claim that the causal structure of a process is intrinsic to it (even when the claim is spelled out with proper precision: see Hall 2003). The bifurcationist can say that Intrinsicness holds only of one *kind* of causation—the kind exhibited in, for example, cases of late pre-emption. She can therefore avail herself of the intrinsicness strategy for handling such cases. The unificationist cannot.

What of the other strategy: say that in cases of late pre-emption (as elsewhere), the cause is distinguished as that on which the effect de facto depends? Well, consider once again cases of threat-cancelling. Event C occurs, initiating a threat to E, by way of intermediate event D. But C also triggers a response to this threat. C is not thereby a cause of E. But E *does* de facto depend on C: for, *holding fixed that D occurs*, if C had not occurred, then no response to the threat from D would have occurred, and so E would not have occurred. We get the same unacceptable result we saw two paragraphs ago. (As a nice corollary, we can see that it was hasty of McDermott *et al.* to blame *transitivity* for these results.)

So the state of play seems to be this: A sufficiency approach must distinguish two kinds of causation, and content itself with providing a theory of just one of them: namely, garden-variety causation that does not involve omissions. Its prospects for handling the most difficult examples—cases of late pre-emption—seem to me to be good; in doing so, it will necessarily place the Intrinsicness thesis at centre stage. A dependency approach need not distinguish two kinds of causation, but cannot appeal to Intrinsicness in order to handle late pre-emption, and may be able to pursue the alternative de facto dependence strategy only at the cost of awkward verdicts about cases of threat-cancelling.

8. The Value of Further Work

It's a tangled dialectical thicket, and it only gets worse once one starts to consider other varieties of pre-emption, symmetric overdetermination, different challenges to transitivity, issues involving the asymmetry of causation... What's more, one needs to remember that, in the face of some horribly unintuitive consequence (e.g. that cancelled threats turn out to be causes), it is open to a theorist to bite the bullet, and remind us all that the theoretical utility of the account may well pay for its lack of fit with intuition. It's safe to say that *a lot* of work remains to be done before we will be able to command a clear view of the best possible accounts, let alone of their distinctive theoretical virtues. I'll close by quickly considering one specific pay-off that such work ought, in my view, to aim for.

I noted, in the introduction, that there has been in the last decade or so an upsurge of interest in causation *outside* of philosophy. One important strand of research focuses on how statistical data can be used to draw inferences about causal structures. Central to this approach are 'causal models', intended to represent systems of 'variables' connected by 'mechanisms'. (These terms are all drawn from Pearl 2000, a very important recent book on the subject.) By careful appeal to and analysis of such causal models, it is possible to develop subtle ways of empirically testing causal hypotheses in light of statistical data. But to my mind two serious problems as yet prevent this approach from attaining the kind of scientific rigour it ought to have. Both are foundational. First, crucial notions—most notably, the notion of a 'mechanism'—are left almost wholly obscure, in a way which makes it impossible to say anything general or informative about what makes any given situation apt for description by one causal model rather than another. Secondly, the way causal models are typically used draws no distinction whatsoever between ordinary causal processes and causal connections involving omissions—so, for example, no distinction whatsoever is drawn between the way in which Suzy's throw causes the window to break, and the way in which Joey's trip causes the window to break. That seems to me a serious mistake. Earlier, in Section 6, I spent a lot of time shoring up nomological entailment accounts by criticizing their rivals. But I think a more inspiring reason for continuing to pursue them is that no other approach has, as far as I can see, a prayer of providing the kind of account of causation that can set this important area of research on a sound conceptual footing. Every once in a while the boundaries between philosophy and some other scientific discipline blur, in a way that offers up to philosophers the chance to make a genuine contribution to their non-philosophical colleagues. Now is such a time.

REFERENCES

Anscombe, G. E. M. (1971). *Causality and Determination: An Inaugural Lecture*. Cambridge: Cambridge University Press.

Armstrong, D. M. (2004). 'Going Through the Open Door Again: Counterfactual vs. Singularist Theories of Causation', in John Collins, Ned Hall, and L. A. Paul (eds.), *Causation and Counterfactuals*. Cambridge, Mass.: MIT Press. Earlier version in Howard Sankey (ed.), *Causation and Laws of Nature*. Dordrecht: Kluwer, 1999.

Beebee, Helen (2004). 'Causing and Nothingness', in John Collins, Ned Hall, and L. A. Paul (eds.), *Causation and Counterfactuals*. Cambridge, Mass.: MIT Press.

Bennett, Jonathan (1988). *Events and their Names*. Indianapolis: Hackett.

Cartwright, Nancy (1999). *The Dappled World*. Oxford: Oxford University Press.

Collins, John, Hall, Ned, and Paul, L. A. (eds.) (2004). *Causation and Counterfactuals*. Cambridge, Mass.: MIT Press.

Davidson, Donald (1967). 'Causal Relations'. *Journal of Philosophy*, 64: 691–703.

Dowe, Phil (2000). *Physical Causation*. New York: Cambridge University Press.

Eells, Ellery (1991). *Probabilistic Causality*. Cambridge: Cambridge University Press.

Ehring, Douglas (1997). *Causation and Persistence*. New York: Oxford University Press.

Fair, David (1979). 'Causation and the Flow of Energy'. *Erkenntnis*, 14: 219–50.

Good, I. J. (1961). 'A Causal Calculus I'. *British Journal for the Philosophy of Science*, 11: 305–18.

—— (1962). 'A Causal Calculus II'. *British Journal for the Philosophy of Science*, 12: 43–51.

Hall, Ned (2002). 'Non-Locality on the Cheap? A New Problem for Counterfactual Analyses of Causation'. *Noûs*, 36: 276–94.

—— (2003). 'The Intrinsic Character of Causation', in Dean Zimmerman (ed.), *The Metaphysics Annual*. Oxford: Oxford University Press.

—— (2004). 'Two Concepts of Causation', in John Collins, Ned Hall, and L. A. Paul (eds.), *Causation and Counterfactuals*. Cambridge, Mass.: MIT Press.

—— forthcoming. *Causation*. Oxford: Oxford University Press.

—— and Paul, L. A. (2003). 'Causation and Preemption', in P. Clark and K. Hawley (eds.), *Philosophy of Science Today*. Oxford: Oxford University Press.

—— (forthcoming). *Causation and the Counterexamples: A Traveler's Guide*. Oxford: Oxford University Press.

Hitchcock, C. (2001). 'The Intransitivity of Causation Revealed in Equations and Graphs'. *Journal of Philosophy*, 98: 273–99.

—— (ed.) (2004). *Contemporary Debates in Philosophy of Science*. Malden, Mass.: Blackwell.

Hume, David (1748). *An Enquiry Concerning Human Understanding*.

Kim, Jaegwon (1971). 'Causes and Events: Mackie on Causation'. *Journal of Philosophy*, 68: 426–41.

—— (1973). 'Causes and Counterfactuals'. *Journal of Philosophy*, 70: 570–2.

Kvart, Igal (2004). 'Causation: Probabilistic and Counterfactual Analyses', in John Collins, Ned Hall, and L. A. Paul (eds.), *Causation and Counterfactuals*. Cambridge, Mass.: MIT Press.

Lewis, David (1970). 'How to Define Theoretical Terms'. *Journal of Philosophy*, 67: 427–46. Repr. in Lewis, *Philosophical Papers*. Oxford: Oxford University Press, 1983.

—— (1973a). 'Causation'. *Journal of Philosophy*, 70: 556–67. Repr. with postscripts in Lewis, *Philosophical Papers*, ii. Oxford: Oxford University Press, 1986.

—— (1973b). *Counterfactuals*. Cambridge, Mass.: Harvard University Press.

—— (1983). 'New Work for a Theory of Universals'. *Australasian Journal of Philosophy*, 61: 343–77. Repr. in Lewis, *Papers in Metaphysics and Epistemology*. Cambridge: Cambridge University Press, 1999.

—— (1986a). *Philosophical Papers*, ii. Oxford: Oxford University Press.

—— (1986b). Postscripts of 'Causation', in Lewis, *Philosophical Papers*, ii. Oxford: Oxford University Press.

—— (1986c). 'Events', in Lewis, *Philosophical Papers*, ii. Oxford: Oxford University Press.

—— (1999). *Papers in Metaphysics and Epistemology*. Cambridge: Cambridge University Press.

—— (2004a). 'Causation as Influence', in John Collins, Ned Hall, and L. A. Paul (eds.), *Causation and Counterfactuals*. Cambridge, Mass.: MIT Press. Abbreviated version in *Journal of Philosophy*, 97: 182–97.

—— (2004b). 'Void and Object', in John Collins, Ned Hall, and L. A. Paul (eds.), *Causation and Counterfactuals*. Cambridge, Mass.: MIT Press.

McDermott, Michael (1995). 'Redundant Causation'. *British Journal for the Philosophy of Science*, (46): 523–44.

McGrath, Sarah (2002). 'Causation by Omission', in McGrath, 'Causation in Metaphysics and Moral Theory'. Ph.D. diss., MIT.

Mackie, J. L. (1965). 'Causes and Conditions'. *American Philosophical Quarterly*, 2: 245–64.

Mellor, D. H. (1995). *The Facts of Causation*. London: Routledge.

Menzies, Peter (1996). 'Probabilistic Causation and the Pre-Emption Problem'. *Mind*, 105: 85–117.

Pearl, Judea (2000). *Causality: Models, Reasoning and Inference*. Cambridge: Cambridge University Press.

Salmon, Wesley (1980). 'Probabilistic Causality'. *Pacific Philosophical Quarterly*, 61: 50–74.

—— (1994). 'Causality without Counterfactuals'. *Philosophy of Science*, 61: 297–312.

Sankey, Howard (ed.) (1999). *Causation and Laws of Nature*. Dordrecht: Kluwer.

Schaffer, Jonathan (2004). 'Causes Need Not Be Physically Connected to their Effects:The Case for Negative Causation', in C. Hitchcock (ed.), *Contemporary Debates in Philosophy of Science*. Malden, Mass.: Blackwell.

Shoemaker, S. (1980). 'Causality and Properties', in Peter van Inwagen (ed.), *Time and Cause*. Dordrecht: Reidel.

Suppes, Patrick (1970). *A Probabilistic Theory of Causality*. Amsterdam: North-Holland.

Thomson, Judith (2003). 'Causation: Omissions'. *Philosophy and Phenomenological Research*, (66): (81)–103.

Tooley, Michael (1987). *Causation: A Realist Approach*. New York: Oxford University Press.

—— (1990). 'Causation: Reductionism versus Realism'. *Philosophy and Phenomenological Research*, suppl. vol., 50: 215–36.

van Inwagen, Peter (ed.) (1980). *Time and Cause*. Dordrecht: Reidel.

Yablo, Stephen (2002). 'De Facto Dependence'. *Journal of Philosophy*, 99: 130–48.

CHAPTER 20

MODALITY

LLOYD HUMBERSTONE

Modality is not an alluring theme. I should be glad to plead the fragmentary
nature of the present work as an excuse for passing it by in silence.

(F. H. Bradley, *The Principles of Logic*)

1. INTRODUCTION

What follows is an attempt to move the heart of any reader whose initial inclination
is to share Bradley's evaluation of the subject. It may be too much to hope that such
readers are wholly won over to the present author's opinion on this matter, namely,
that philosophy departments of a broadly analytical stripe—or at least their graduate
schools—would do well to post an inscription resembling that said to have greeted
those at the gates of Plato's Academy: 'Let no one who is ignorant of modal logic
enter here.' Although one might expect the philosophical interest of modal logic to lie
mainly in the area of modal predicate logic, what follows mostly concerns propositional modal logic, which will already provide ample food for thought—even though
many issues of interest will for that reason not get discussed (essentialism, transworld
identity and predication, *de re* versus *de dicto*, various supervenience doctrines, etc.).
While there will be plenty to say about various modal notions—in particular over
their logical behaviour—there will be no attempt to address the question of whether

such notions and the judgements in which they figure are in some way philosophically problematic. It is a well-attested fact that from time to time in the history of thought, this or that class of statements has come to seem contentious. Disjunctions were regarded by Russell as problematic in not corresponding to anything in reality (Russell 1918: 1940). Modal statements—though those sharing these qualms might think of 'statements' here as a misnomer—have often aroused suspicion on broadly empiricist grounds: when φ is not itself true, in virtue of what could 'It is possible that φ' be true? Again: what does the claim that *it is necessary that* φ add to the claim that φ? And so on. (Blackburn 1986 gives such questions an eloquent airing.) We will not be pausing over the question whether modality should give rise to any greater concern than disjunction—or even negation (cf. Price 1994)—though some reactions to a response to one aspect of this concern (discomfort with intensionality), namely possible worlds semantics, will occupy us briefly at the conclusion of this survey (the end of Section 6, and Section 7).

2. MODAL CONSTRUCTIONS AND THE SQUARE OF OPPOSITION

In the 1950s and 1960s several philosophers became aware of the structural similarities between the sets of relationships between quantificational constructions charted by the traditional Square of Opposition (of Aristotelian syllogistic) and the sets of relationships obtaining between various notions expressed by certain one-place sentence operators. The seminal source here is von Wright (1951) (paper 1 in Montague 1974, originally published in 1960 and presented orally five years before that, also deserves mention). If we think of $\Box\varphi$ as representing 'Necessarily φ'[1] (or 'It is necessarily the case that φ') and $\Diamond\varphi$ as representing 'Possibly φ' ('It is possible that φ'), then we may chart such relationships in the Modal Square of Opposition (Fig. 20.1). The top right-hand corner of this diagram then houses the statement that it is impossible that φ, for which reason we don't need a special primitive impossibility operator. The parenthetical representation is presumed to be equivalent to what it appears beside, and similarly in the bottom right-hand corner. Indeed, with the quantificational analogy in mind, we do not even need both $\Box$ and $\Diamond$ as primitive, since we could regard either as abbreviating the result of flanking the other with negations signs ($\neg$). (This interdefinability would not be plausible—for

---

[1] We use 'φ', 'ψ', . . . as schematic letters for (declarative) sentences of English in informal discussion and for formulas of the language of (usually propositional) modal logic in formal discussion.

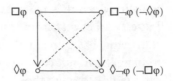

FIG. 20.1. The Modal Square of Opposition

the same reason as in the case of the universal and existential quantifiers—if we took our underlying non-modal logic to be given by intuitionistic rather than classical logic: circumnegation does not in that setting give duality.) In what follows, especially for the purposes of Section 4, $\Box$ will be taken as primitive and $\Diamond$ as defined in the manner indicated. The Modal Square is to be read in the same manner as its syllogistic prototype (annotated with a–e–o–i,[2] reading clockwise from upper left): the top horizontal line connects contraries, the bottom horizontal line, subcontraries, while the diagonals link contradictories, and the vertical lines indicate a superaltern-to-subaltern relationship holding in the direction shown by the arrows.

Among the many alternative readings for $\Box$ and $\Diamond$ aside from taking them as representing notions of necessity and possibility—called *alethic* interpretations—are the *epistemic* and *doxastic* interpretations: read $\Box\varphi$ as 'Such-and-such a subject knows that φ' and 'So-and-so believes that φ', respectively, with $\Diamond\varphi$ as 'It is compatible with the given subject's knowledge (respectively: belief) that φ'. Then we have *deontic* readings, both normative and reportive, with $\Box\varphi$ as 'It ought to/should be the case that φ'—with 'must' instead in an apparently stronger construction (both normative), or 'It is obligatory/required that φ' (reportive)—and correlatively $\Diamond\varphi$ as 'It is morally permissible that φ' (or—reportive version—'permitted that φ'). In this last case what occupies the position of impossibility is impermissibility or wrongness (or forbiddenness, to use the reportive style). Often a more suggestive special-purpose notation is used for the $\Box$ operator in studies of these areas: thus 'O' (for 'obligatory' or 'ought') in the deontic case, 'K' and 'B' for the epistemic and doxastic cases—as in Hintikka (1962), and so on. (In Sections 3 and 4 we use 'O' not in the deontic sense just mentioned but as a schematic letter for any one-place sentence operator.) All of these candidate readings for $\Box$ (and $\Diamond$) are described as modal notions—in the broad sense, we might add, since sometimes "modal" is understood more narrowly as pertaining to the alethic interpretation. Or, rather, alethic interpretations: for we have not singled out logical necessity from, for example, nomic (or "natural") necessity (and

---

[2] For general terms S and P, SaP, SeP, SoP and SiP are read 'Every S is P', 'No S is P', 'Some S is not P', and 'Some S is P' respectively. We say 'general terms' rather than 'predicates' because in discussions of Aristotelian logic the word 'predicate' is usually reserved for the second argument of (what we may regard as) the binary quantifiers a, e, i, and o—that represented by 'P' in the schemas just listed (with 'S' being similarly mnemonic for 'subject term'). There is also, by contrast with post-Fregean predicate logic, a standing background presumption that each of the general terms involved in the square of opposition relations is true of at least one thing.

possibility), or more narrowly still, for example, physical necessity (and possibility), or the time-dependent notion of inevitability or now-unpreventability (Prior 1967: 177 ff.). And even "logical necessity" has been used in broader and narrower senses, depending on whether metaphysical necessity is intended or just, as people say, strictly logical necessity. Further afield semantically from all of the above notions but reasonably describable as modal in the broad sense are the tensed notions of pastness and futurity ('$\Box\varphi$' as 'It will always be the case that φ', for example), and, in connection with the theory of vagueness, the notion of being determinately true (cf. Fine 1975; Pelletier 1984; Burgess 1997). In view of these many interpretations of the symbolism, outside of the context of any one application of modal logic, the safest mental pronunciation of '$\Box$' and '$\Diamond$' is as *box* and *diamond*, respectively.

One of the most useful aspects of the Modal Square is the contrast it draws attention to between the upper and lower right-hand corners, which differ in respect of the relative scope of '$\Box$' and '$\neg$'. The following remarks on this distinction, as it bears on the deontic interpretation of '$\Box$' and its expression in English, are hard to improve on; they come from Robinson (1971: 199 ff.):

Ought and *ought not* are not contradictories. Given that it is false that you ought to visit John, it does not follow that you ought not to visit John. Perhaps you are free to visit him or not visit him, as you wish. . . . Hence it is quite difficult to deny an *ought* proposition correctly and unmistakably without saying more than the mere denial. If someone tells you that you ought to visit John, you cannot safely contradict him by saying 'No, I ought not'; for that tends to imply that you have a duty to keep away from John. You must say something elaborate like 'No, it is not the case that I ought to visit John', or else employ another verb altogether, like 'No, I need not'. . . . The defect is not confined to *ought*. It exists in other moral words, *should* and *must*.

For understanding modal talk in general, then, it is helpful to bear in mind the distinction—stressed here by Robinson for the deontic case—between cases in which the syntactically simplest way of negating a claim produces a contrary rather than a contradictory claim. Accordingly we shall expend considerable energy in clarifying the contrary–contradictory distinction later on in the present section (as well as in Appendices 20.1 and 20.2). Although our interest for the topic of modal logic should indeed be on the various modal auxiliaries, it is hard to resist quoting Robinson's further comment that a

related defect occurs in the words *right* and *wrong*. They too often have the result of dividing the moral possibilities into two, whereas they are three.[3] The wrong is merely the forbidden; but the right is the commanded and the permitted, poorly distinguished from each other.

Though the sentiment is just what is called for, 'commanded' and 'permitted' aren't quite the right words, conflating the reportive and normative: 'obligatory'

---

[3] The trichotomy Robinson has in mind is represented by the three corners of the downward-pointing triangle in Fig.20.3 below.

and 'permissible' are what is needed here, though they do have an admittedly stilted sound to them. We can put the point in terms of 'wrong' (= 'impermissible' in the stilted vocabulary): talk of what it is right to do invites confusion between what it is wrong not to, on the one hand, and what it is not wrong to do, on the other.

The reportive–normative distinction just invoked is alive and well in the English system of modal auxiliaries (understood loosely, as to including constructions with 'to' rather than just a bare infinitive), as Robin Lakoff observed with the case of saying 'Anna has to stay home on Sundays'—merely reporting a parental decree—as opposed to 'Anna must stay home on Sundays'—endorsing such a decree (Lakoff 1972: 240). (There is a similar distinction between deontic *may* and *can*, the former used only for giving permission, the latter both for giving and for reporting permission.) One might take exception to the description of 'should' and 'must', at the end of the first quotation from Robinson above, as *moral* words. In the 1970s especially, considerable efforts were made to provide unified accounts of the semantics of the modal auxiliaries—conspicuously in Wertheimer (1972, ch. 3) and in Kratzer (1977)[4]—so as to rebut widely current but arguably profligate ambiguity claims: that as well as the deontic or moral sense of 'should' (and 'ought to') there is an epistemic or probabilistic sense ('Since he left at noon, he should have arrived by now'), that as well as the deontic 'must' and 'may' we have an epistemic and perhaps also a logical 'must' and 'may', etc.[5] (A similar attempt at a unified treatment, with telling examples and suggestive commentary, though without explicit analysis at any stage, is to be found in White 1975. White has subjected this talk of epistemic *may, must*, etc., to strong criticism, though the precise ground of his complaint eluded this reader.[6] Accordingly we continue with the terminology. The current epistemic *must* is to be distinguished from the epistemic interpretation of □ mentioned above, and the distinction is similar to that between the normative and

---

[4] Bolinger (1989) surveys a number of similar proposals, mostly from later publications. By contrast Groenendijk and Stokhof (1975) maintain the ambiguity claims for the central modal auxiliaries. An especially interesting account of these matters appears in Sweetser (1990, ch. 3).

[5] Rivière (1981) notes that for the epistemically interpreted modal auxiliaries, English observes a hierarchy of increasing certainty—*might, may, should, must*—but that the difference between the last two items is not simply one of relative certainty: 'Since you know Albert Smith, the poet, you must read a lot' versus *'Since you know Albert Smith, the poet, you should read a lot'. (These examples are adapted from those of Rivière 1981: 181, which have 'So' for 'since'—making both ungrammatical unless repunctuated. The asterisk indicates only the unavailability of the epistemic reading.)

[6] It is certainly not the same complaint as is aired in Groenendijk and Stokhof, to the effect that the (interpretations of the) modal auxiliaries labelled epistemic should instead be regarded as conversational—indicating consistency or inconsistency with what is presumed in the conversational background. (In fact the authors go further and distinguish the truth conditions from the more pragmatic notion of conversational correctness—roughly, assertibility—but we cannot go into such details here.) What we are calling epistemic *may* has an interesting non-epistemic treatment in terms of speech acts in Hare (1971: 37 ff.), as paraphrasing a putatively "negated performative"—'I do not say that not φ', and paralleling Hare's account of deontic *may*—something of a unificatory move, then—as 'I do not command that not φ'.

reportive readings of deontic □: we could say that the Hintikka-style epistemic □ is reportive since it is used to report that the subject in question knows something, while the 'must' currently under consideration is *expressive*, purportedly expressing the speaker's epistemic state. Of course any such choice of terminology is contentious and buys into debates in the philosophy of language better skirted here.) As it happens, the particular phenomenon Robinson is discussing in the first quotation above—the interpretation of syntactical negation—is something of a thorn in the side of these well-intentioned unificatory accounts, a point which is clearest in the case of 'must': why is it while in the deontic case, 'We must leave' and 'We mustn't let them down' have '□' and '□¬' readings, for the (we continue perhaps loosely to call it) epistemic case, '(In view of the amount of blood on the walls), she must be dead' has a '□' reading, we cannot get the corresponding '□¬' with 'mustn't' here, and need instead to say (for example) 'She can't still be alive'?[7] Similarly, 'may not' with epistemic *may* has the interpretation ◊¬; with deontic *may* this phrase has the preferred interpretation ¬◊, the alternative interpretation being available for this case only given marked intonation. (Cf. 'can not' versus 'cannot'; the semantic significance of intonation and vowel reduction for constructions like these is one theme in Bolinger 1989. The different effects of a succeeding *not* on *may* are described in the following section in terms of pre-negation and post-negation.) Epistemic possibility indicators feature in a construction which, in view of the analogy alluded to in Section 1 between suspicions about disjunction and suspicions about modality, deserves to be mentioned here. In an appendix, entitled 'Dyirbal Logic', Dixon (1972) speaks of open and closed alternations, the latter being what is usually understood by disjunction, the former allowing the disjoining of several alternatives without the presumption that they are exhaustive. He tells us that while *or* in English is generally used for (not necessarily binary) closed disjunctions, there is no corresponding lexical item in Dyirbal, and open disjunctions are expressed, not with the aid of a similarly functioning sentence connective, but with a modal construction amounting (for alternatives φ, ψ) to 'It might be that φ, (and) it might be that ψ'.[8] While this will naturally raise an eyebrow— consider the embeddability prospects for the two constructions, for example—in anyone especially keen to defend a pragmatics–semantics boundary, we should not miss out on the interest of Dixon's discussion on this score, especially as that

---

[7] In Wertheimer (1972: 105) the issue is raised (and further taken up in pp. 107–9) of the apparent distinction to be drawn between 'must not' and 'cannot', both seeming to express impossibility, though also seeming to be far from synonymous in English. See also Lakoff (1972: 245). Somewhat marginal counter-examples to the current claim may be found in Bolinger (1989, examples (86)–(89)).

[8] Dixon (1972: 363) gives the following as the direct English translation of a Dyirbal passage: 'I saw a fish, what was it down there?—it might have been a barramundi, or it might have been a red bream'. The inclusion of *or* here rather spoils the point he is making, though, for which reason we give the form above as 'It might be that φ, (and) it might be that ψ'. The appearance of an 'or' in cases like this will be touched on below. However, I do not discuss the *may–might* distinction, referring the reader to the items in the References list cited in this section apropos of the semantics of modal auxiliaries.

boundary is itself not something set in stone. (It is in any case far from clear what the truth conditions—as opposed to assertibility conditions—of "open" disjunctions are.)

It is not only in the deontic area that the formal symbolism helps to clear us of some traps—highlighted in the quoted passages from Robinson—set by English as to the relative scopes of negation and a modal operator. A similar issue arises in doxastic logic, as was noted in Hintikka (1962: 15), for the construction '*a* doesn't believe that φ', with the ambiguity between a $\Box \neg \ \varphi$ reading and a $\neg \Box \varphi$ reading. The point was treated in the heyday of transformational grammar in terms of a rule of "*Neg*-Raising" which lifted the negation out of the lower clause and into the higher, to obtain the former reading. (See items 8 and 9 in Seuren 1974.) This ambiguity has many well-known repercussions for philosophical topics (e.g. J. Williams 1979), and affects several other propositional attitude verbs—such as 'want' (though "boulomaic logic", to use Kenny's term for this application of modal logic, has not been included in this quick overview: see note 31). While 'know' escapes this particular phenomenon, caution is needed over '*a* doesn't know that φ' for a different reason, often described in terms of *presupposition*—already noted in Hintikka (1962: 12–14). While on the *neg*-raised interpretation of '*a* doesn't believe that φ', the logical form is $\Box \neg \varphi$, on the presuppositional interpretation of '*a* doesn't know that φ', the form is $\varphi \wedge \neg \Box \ \varphi$: so in neither case do we have the contradictory of $\Box \varphi$ ($= \neg \Box \ \varphi$) as the English syntax might lead us to expect.

Next, we need to concede that while it is pedagogically convenient to assume—as our exposition just has—that epistemic *must* behaves like the $\Box$ operator of the familiar alethic modal logics, this assumption turns out in retrospect to be a gross oversimplification. On this score, it was Karttunen (1972) who set the cat among the pigeons, though it has taken a long time for the point to sink in among some of the pigeons. Karttunen's observation was that, whereas according to the familiar epistemic and alethic modal logics (including among their theorems the formula **T** given in Section 4, which may here be considered as the schema $\Box \varphi \rightarrow \varphi$), $\Box \varphi$ is a stronger statement than φ, this is not how the word 'must' behaves in English, in which, by contrast, 'She must be dead' is a weaker statement, not a stronger statement, than 'She is dead'.[9] Roughly, the former statement would be made by someone in possession of overwhelming indirect evidence that the party in question is dead, and the latter by someone in possession of direct evidence to that effect or else on the presumption that it is an established fact that she is dead. By way of further illustration: according to a television documentary on the 1966 Chicago murders attributed to Richard Speck, although Speck—claiming to have no memory of the incident—had conceded on the basis of the (fingerprint and

---

[9] While we are at it, we should recall a complementary puzzle: deontic 'must' is supposedly not subject to the principle **T**, so what explains the oddity of saying—something which is fine with 'should' or 'ought to' for 'must'—'He must go, but he won't'? (See Lyons 1977: 846 and references there cited.)

eyewitness) evidence the police confronted him with that he must have been the one who killed the eight nurses, this was not regarded by the police as a confession.[10]

What—one would like to know in more detail—*is* this direct–indirect evidence distinction? Does it bear on truth conditions or only on the conditions of appropriate assertion? One attempt at doing formal justice to Karttunen's observation may be found in Veltman (1981), which develops a semantic framework in which the entities with respect to which statements are evaluated are not to be thought of—as on the semantics reviewed in Section 5 below—as possible worlds, but as possible states of information about the world, and the resulting logic has a very different flavour from that of the normal modal logics (in a sense of "normal" given in Section 4)—though a translation, itself exhibiting some unusual features, can be found which embeds Veltman's logic into one of the latter (van Benthem 1986a; Barba Escriba 1989). The present state of play would appear to be that we have yet to obtain a clear view of the logical and semantic behaviour of the modal auxiliaries. One promising suggestion is that at least some of them should be thought of as analogous to the evidential particles and affixes famously found in certain Amerindian languages—a suggestion made for the case of 'must' in at least two of the contributions to Chafe (1986).[11] Nor do we have a clear view of the interactions between the modal auxiliaries and the familiar binary connectives, in particular 'or'. When someone says 'Either you have to pay the fare or you have to get off the tram', the logician's reaction is likely to be that the speaker is confused, meaning to say something of the form $\Box(\varphi \vee \psi)$ but coming out with something of the form $\Box\varphi \vee \Box\psi$ by mistake. This reaction itself may be where the confusion lies, however, as with the allegation once current that speakers of "negative concord" dialects of English betrayed a logical confusion in saying—with an utterance of 'I didn't see nothing' something of the form '$\neg\neg\exists x.\varphi(x)$' where they should have had '$\neg\exists x.\varphi(x)$'. Even better known are the problematic interactions of 'or' with $\Diamond$-type modalities. When people say 'I might come with you or I might stay home' to indicate that *both* possibilities are open, is it a confusion—'or' for 'and'—or are there coherent accounts of the meaning of 'might' and of 'or' which when combined predict exactly such a construction? (I have not hesitated to employ this construction in the present chapter, as in the final sentence of this section.)

[10] The Speck case is treated in the BBC television series, available under the name *Great Crimes and Trials of the Twentieth Century: Bizarre Murders* (1994), available on video, in which the point about Speck's concession not being a confession is made. The genuineness of Speck's claimed amnesia is attested to in many places in Altman and Ziporyn (1967), in which the 'must' construction is also much in evidence, as in his words quoted on p. 14: 'Everybody says I did it. Must be so. If they say I did it, I did it.' Note that Speck firmly believed that he was guilty, and that since he had killed the nurses, he deserved to die, so the 'must' signals the indirectness of the evidence rather than its inconclusiveness. (See also the following note.)

[11] See (Chafe 1986, chs. 16 and 17). It seems that this 'must' heralds the introduction of inferred data into a conversation, rather than having to be repeated every time such information is subsequently invoked. (It is not clear that Veltman's account reflects this.) Further discussion of epistemic modality and evidentiality is provided in Palmer (1986, ch. 2).

A related topic goes under the name of "Free Choice Permission", where again something looking disjunctive seems to mean something conjunctive. This time there is one occurrence of the ◊-type modality in the disjunctive formulation, with an 'or' in its apparent scope: 'You may take it or leave it', seeming to mean 'You may take it and you may leave it'. Suggestive (if not always pellucid) discussion of these issues may be found in Jennings (1994). The interaction of the modal notions with *if___then*... has proved even more troublesome than their interaction with *or*, and the less said above it here, the better. Let us turn back from all such issues to the more solid ground provided by the (Modal) Square of Opposition.

We could enlarge our picture—Figure 20.1—by taking up a suggestion of Robert Blanché, and add points at the top and bottom, representing respectively the disjunction of the two forms in the current top corners and the conjunction of those in the bottom corners (see Blanché 1953; 1966, ch. 4; and further references to be found in Sauriol 1969; the idea appears independently in Gottschalk 1953). To annotate the new Hexagon of Opposition, we add lines connecting the new top point to the old top points, with arrows going *towards* the new point, and lines connecting the new bottom point to the old bottom points, with arrows going *away from* the new point. (The reader might care to draw this diagram now, for later reference; its internally inscribed hexagram appears as Figure 20.3 below.) If we were reading □ as expressing necessity (and correlatively ◊ as possibility) then the new base point represents contingency and the new apex, non-contingency. The diagonals of the Hexagon continue, then, to link contradictories. Some work has been done on the modal logic of (non-)contingency and its non-alethic analogues. Kuhn (1995) gives an elegant treatment as well as some further references to the literature, in which literature 'It is non-contingent whether φ' and 'It is contingent whether φ' frequently appear—and I shall follow suit—in the notation $\Delta \varphi$, $\nabla \varphi$, respectively. (Note that the appropriate complementizer for '(non-)contingent' here is *whether*, rather than *that*: talk of its being contingent that φ is talk of its being contingently true that φ, i.e. contingent whether φ and also true that φ.[12]

---

[12] *Pace*, among others, Montgomery and Routley (1966: 318) or Kneale and Kneale (1962: 86); the latter work is, however, a good source of information on the Modal Square of Opposition and on Aristotle's somewhat garbled attempts to codify modal inference. (Further information may be gathered from Horn 1989, §1.1), which has the advantage, over the Kneales' discussion, of supplying references to the work of Cajetan, the medieval discoverer of the Modal Square in the form we are discussing it.) A bizarre attempt to depict the Epistemic Square of Opposition appears in Alexandrescu (1983: 20), in which the lower left and right corners are glossed 'x does not know whether p is false' and 'x does not know whether p is true', presumably because of the author's linguistic difficulties with the *whether–that* distinction—though working purely with modal formulas, on the following page the author writes (adapting the notation somewhat, with K and B for the epistemic and doxastic □'s) that '$\neg Kp$ implies rather the disjunction $Bp \vee B\neg p$', a mistake it is hard to explain in any such terms. The *whether–that* confusion has caused trouble in the logic of vagueness too: see the diagnostic remarks in Pelletier (1984). (Unfortunately a trace of this very confusion survives in Pelletier's own glosses: on p. 416, while it is conceded that $\Delta\varphi$ is equivalent to the negation of $\nabla \varphi$, and the latter is glossed as 'it is indeterminate whether φ', the former is glossed as 'it is determinate that φ'!)

This notion does not appear at any of the vertices of the Hexagon or the Octagon we shall be seeing mentioned below; its logical location is not given until Figure 20.A1.) For example, the deontic analogue of contingency is sometimes called "indifference", it being morally indifferent whether φ when it is neither obligatory nor forbidden that φ (see von Wright 1957: 58–74). Of course this interpretation of the phrase 'morally indifferent' is somewhat contentious, since—to mention only one kind of consideration—it might be held that supererogatory acts are neither required nor prohibited by the moral code expressed in so classifying them, without being morally indifferent (according to that code) since they are on the contrary of great moral worth (following Chisholm 1963: 2, where some interesting historical information on the deontic incarnation of the Modal Square of Opposition may also be found). Indeed, as this way of putting the point shows, the whole question of the analogy between deontic logic and alethic modal logic has been perennially subject to challenge: perhaps we should be dealing in the former case with predicates of acts or act types rather than with sentential operators. See von Wright (1957) on this issue—not further taken up here—and for further discussion of some of matters arising, Hintikka (1971) Makinson (1981, 1983). A partial compromise frequently explored has been the introduction of agent-relativized deontic operators, with $\Box_a \varphi(a)$ recording the existence of an obligation on the agent a to the effect that it be the case that $\varphi(a)$ (cf. Hilpinen 1969; Horty 2001; as well as Humberstone 1991 and references therein cited; to which Lakoff 1972—see the discussion in pp. 236–9—should be added, as well as Lewis 1968, sect. v). This is in any case how the knowledge and belief operators of epistemic and deontic logic are generally understood—as tacitly involving reference to the knowing or believing subject (though there are some special interpretations where this is not so, as with common knowledge and impersonal knowledge). And one can envisage similar relativizations for alethically interpreted operators, along the lines of 'It is possible for a that——', which may or may not be connected with the attribution of *abilities* to individuals.[13]

3. Contrariety and Subcontrariety

Returning to the Modal Square of Opposition itself, for any given choice of $\Box$ operator for the top left-hand corner, it is worth noting that to obtain the corresponding (perhaps complex) operator occurring at any of the corners we can apply either of

---

[13] Probably for this case a richer logical vocabulary is needed, though; see Brown (1988, 1990).

∘	ι	ν	π	δ
ι	ι	ν	π	δ
ν	ν	ι	δ	π
π	π	δ	ι	ν
δ	δ	π	ν	ι

FIG. 20.2. How operator-transformations compose

two transformations to it, to be called *post-negation*[14]—transforming any 1-ary operator O into O¬ and 'pre-negation'—alias (near enough) sentential negation—obtaining ¬O. If we denote these transformations by π and ν, we observe that we could apply one after the other, getting the same result (the circumnegation '¬O¬') regardless of the order in which they are applied. Keeping up the use of Greek letters, we denote this by δ (mnemonic for 'dual'). And of course we could apply neither, giving the identity transformation ι.[15] As Wiseman (1970) observes (cf. also Gottschalk 1953, with Brown 1984 a highly pertinent further discussion, as well as van Benthem 1986*b*, ch. 6), the result is that we have a four-element group—traditionally called the Klein 4-group—with the Cayley table shown as Figure 20.2 when the group operation is composition of transformations (here symbolized by ∘). (Figure 20.2 appears, differently notated, as van Benthem 1986*b*: 110, fig. 25.)

This apparatus tells us little about the logical relationships between the modal notions at the four corners of the Modal Square of Opposition. ν swaps the diagonals, while δ and π effect respectively a vertical and a horizontal interchange, but nothing in the picture tells us that the □ is logically stronger than, rather than weaker than, δ (□) (=◊), as is indicated by the downward arrows on the sides of the Square in its traditional orientation (Figure 20.1). It does, however, allow us to raise conceptual questions well worth asking, such as the following. Let us say that

---

[14] No connection with what is sometimes (after Emil Post) called 'Post negation', a certain function definable for many-valued logics with finite matrices with linearly ordered sets of elements. Pre-negation and post-negation are sometimes (e.g. Horn 1989: 217, 237) called, respectively, *outer* and *inner* negation. Cf. also Simons (1993), in which a more elaborate treatment may be found than is encapsulated in our figure.

[15] O is here presumed 1-ary, of course. But suppose we want a similar treatment for *n*-ary O. Then as well as ι and ν, we should recognize *n* distinct post-negations, $\pi_1, \ldots, \pi_n$, with $\pi_i(O)$ applied to $\varphi_1, \ldots, \varphi_n$ being what results from applying O to $\varphi_1, \ldots, \varphi_{i-1}, \neg\varphi_i, \varphi_{i1}, \ldots, \varphi_n$. What is normally called the dual of such an O is then the result of applying ν and all the π_j ($j = 1, \ldots, n$) to O (in any order). For the full story we need to add transformations corresponding to permuted argument positions also, such as that which when applied to ternary O gives an operation whose result as applied to $\varphi_1, \varphi_2, \varphi_3$ in that order is what result from applying the result of applying O to $\varphi_2, \varphi_3, \varphi_1$, in that order. Some details for the binary case may be found in Bender (1966), though presented with the misleading suggestion that the transformations involved here are operations on propositions, rather than on propositional operators, and without specifically isolating the transformations π_j. (A propositional operator can be regarded as a sentence connective which is congruential in the sense introduced below.)

a transformation τ on (singulary) operators O corresponds to a singulary connective # when for all O, $[\tau(O)](\varphi)$—the result of applying $\tau(O)$ to an arbitrary sentence φ—is always equivalent to #($O\varphi$).[16] We know because of the way it was introduced in the first place, that corresponding, in this sense, to the transformation ν on operators there is the sentence connective $\neg$. Indeed, one might object that we should really say that it is ν that corresponds to $\neg$, since well-known processes of categorial grammar reveal that any operator from sentences to sentences induces a uniquely appropriate operator from sentence operators to sentence operators.[17] On the other hand, it is not hard to see that there is in the case of π, for instance, no corresponding connective. Such a claim must be understood relative to a logic since we asking about the existing of # with #($O\varphi$) equivalent to $[\pi(O)](\varphi)$ and this means 'logically equivalent', thereby making it sensitive to choice of logic—to say nothing of the tacit understanding that we require such an equivalence for all operators O and all formulas φ available in the language of the logic in question. In fact let us assume that we are considering only logics in which any substitution instance of an accepted principle is itself accepted, so that instead of universally quantifying over φ here, we can simply replace the schematic letter 'φ' with a propositional variable (or "sentence letter"), p, say. So let us fix on **S4** as a representative example with respect to which to illustrate the point about post-negation. (An explanation as to which logic **S4** is follows in due course.) Any other logic according to which

(i) $\Box\Box p$ and $\Box p$ are equivalent, while
(ii) $\Box\neg\Box p$ and $\Box\neg p$ are not equivalent

would serve as well. From (i), and the hypothetical #, we conclude

(iii) #$\Box\Box p$ and #$\Box p$ are equivalent.

But then by the supposed equivalence for any φ, of #($O\varphi$) and $[\pi(O)](\varphi)$

(iv) $[\pi(\Box)]\Box p$ and $[\pi(\Box)]p$ are equivalent,

---

[16] In '$[\tau(O)](\varphi)$', the parentheses around 'φ' (usually omitted) as well as those around 'O', are marking the position of the *argument* to some function, while the square brackets around '$\tau(O)$' are simply grouping devices to clarify which function is being applied: to show that we are applying $\tau(O)$ to φ, and not—say—τ to O and φ. We generally dispense with as much of this punctuation as can be dropped without risk, in the context, of confusion. Since this note is appended to a sentence in which we speak both of operators and of connectives, it should be remarked here that no official distinction (between an n-ary sentence operator and an n-ary connective) is intended and the choice of vocabulary is merely a matter of evoking appropriate connotations. In particular, certainly not to be excluded is the case of 1-ary (or "singulary") connectives just on the grounds that no two things are being "connected" in this case.

[17] Indeed the process is more general than this, explaining also why quantifiers, for instance, can be negated or indeed conjoined. See Geach (1972), or the index entries under 'Geach Rule' in van Benthem (1991). An especially helpful quick summary is provided by van Benthem (1989: 231): 'For instance, the Geach Rule allows constituent structures in which a function combines not just with its "completed" arguments, but also with "parametrized" versions thereof.' This is why I described pre-negation as 'near enough' to be being ordinary (sentential) negation above.

which contradicts (ii). (The interested reader is invited to verify that ι is like ν in having a corresponding sentence operator whereas δ is like π in lacking one.) Note that this argument subsumes the observation that a proposition—understood as what is in common to any logically equivalent statements—does not have a unique contrary (Geach 1969); 'subsumes' because while post-negation gives contraries for $\square$ and $\square\neg$, it gives subcontraries for $\lozenge$ and $\lozenge\neg$. This point is already familiar from syllogistic logic, with the example of *SeP* and its contrary *SaP*, since *SeP* expresses the same proposition as *PeS*, with "canonical" contrary *PaS*, by no means equivalent to *SaP*: would the real contrary of the proposition expressed indifferently by *SeP, PeS*, please stand up? (This question is adapted from a question asked about negation in Dunn 1986: 214.) We return to this issue below (and to this particular example in Appendix 20.2).

Of course there is an unspoken further assumption used in the above argument concerning the connective #, namely that this connective is *congruential* in the sense of not being sensitive to the replacement of one statement (or formula) in its scope by another (logically) equivalent statement (formula). For the transition from (i) to (iii) involves just such a replacement and the argument only works if we may take the results of the replacement to be themselves logically equivalent. In fact I have already, earlier, tacitly assumed that only congruential operators are at issue. For instance, Figure 20.2 tells us that $\delta \circ \delta = \iota$, i.e. that for any operator O, $(\delta\delta)p$ and Op are equivalent.[18] Let us work through this. δO is $\neg$O$\neg$, so $\delta\delta$O is $\neg\neg$O$\neg\neg$, and our claim amounts to one of the equivalence of $\neg\neg$O$\neg\neg p$ with Op. Since we are assuming classical behaviour on the part of the non-modal vocabulary, the initial pair of negations in $\neg\neg$O$\neg\neg p$ can certainly be dropped. But this assumption gives us only the equivalence of O$\neg\neg p$ with $(\delta\delta$O$)p$, and for the equivalence of either of these with Op, and we need a separate congruentiality assumption allowing the interchange of equivalent formulas within the scope of O.

With this assumption of congruentiality in force, we can make the following observation about the defined operators of non-contingency (Δ) and contingency (∇, which is $\nu(\Delta)$) mentioned above, which contrasts in this respect with $\square$ and $\lozenge$: $\pi(\Delta) = \Delta$ and $\pi(\nabla) = \nabla$ (from which it follows also that $\delta(\Delta) = \nu(\Delta)$, and

---

[18] The fact that $\delta \downharpoonleft \delta = \iota$ means that δ is its own inverse in the group depicted in Fig. 20.2, whereas π and ν are each other's inverses. Note that this is a different matter from the existence of a (two-sided) inverse for a sentence operator O, meaning by that an operator O' for which each of O'Op and OO'p is equivalent to p. An exploration of the existence of such inverses for the operators $\square$ of normal modal logics (a phrase defined below) may be found in Humberstone and Williamson (1997). Left inverses to $\square$ (discussed in that paper), which is to say operators L, for which $L\square p$ and p are equivalent, bear on our current topic in the following way: any logic either possessing such an L or conservatively extendable to a logic possessing one already has, or can be conservatively extended so as to have, a sentential analogue # of π of the type shown above not to exist in the case of S4: for we may define #$\varphi = \square\neg L\varphi$, which gives the equivalence of #$\square\neg p$ with $[\pi(\square)](\neg p)$. (Note that, so defined, # is a sentence operator which corresponds to π as applied, specifically, to $\square$: to obtain the effect of post-negating $\lozenge$ we need $\lozenge L\neg\, \varphi$.)

likewise for ∇). In fact it is easy to see that the same holds for any singulary operator $O_\#$ defined in terms of a commutative binary connective # and a given operator $\square$ by:

$$O_\#\varphi = O\varphi \# O\neg\varphi.$$

In the case of $O = \square$ or $O = \lozenge$, we get $O_\#\varphi$ as Δ or as ∇ by taking #, respectively, as $\vee$ or $\wedge$. (Alternatively, we obtain ∇ by keeping O as $\square$ and choosing # as *nor* (negated disjunction).) Whether we take O as $\square$ or as $\lozenge$, $O\varphi \leftrightarrow O\neg\varphi$ turns out to be equivalent, in any normal modal logic (as defined in the following section) to $\nabla\varphi \vee \square\bot$, which is in turn equivalent in **KD** (a rather weak such logic, defined in Section 4 below) to the first disjunct. In this example, our binary commutative # was $\leftrightarrow$. *Exercise*: What happens if we take # as exclusive disjunction (and O as $\square$ or $\lozenge$)? (This paragraph was inspired by remarks in Khamara 2001; Appendix 20.1 makes use of its results.[19])

Although the ideas of contingency and non-contingency present no great obstacle to understanding, we should pause to notice their novelty by contrast with anything available in (classical) non-modal propositional logic. Let $\varphi(p, r_1, \ldots, r_n)$ be any formula constructed from the exhibited propositional variables by means of the Boolean connectives ($\wedge, \neg, \rightarrow$, etc.). When we write '$\varphi(\psi, r_1, \ldots, r_n)$' we understand this to denote the result of substituting the formula ψ uniformly for all occurrences of p in $\varphi(p, r_1, \ldots, r_n)$. Here we use '$\vdash$' for the relation of tautological consequence: to say that what appears on its right follows from what appears on its left by truth-functional logic. A key point to observe about this relation is that for any formula $\varphi(p, r_1, \ldots, r_n)$ as above, we have

$$\varphi(p, r_1, \ldots, r_n) \leftrightarrow \varphi(\neg p, r_1, \ldots, r_n) \vdash \varphi(p, r_1, \ldots, r_n) \leftrightarrow \varphi(q, r_1, \ldots, r_n).$$

The reason behind this is that any truth-value assignment (respecting the intended meanings of the connectives) which verifies the left-hand formula must assign the same truth-values to the formulas flanking the '$\leftrightarrow$'. Thus the $(n + 1)$-ary truth-function associated with the context φ gives the same value when its first argument is replaced by the opposite truth-value (T for F or vice versa). In that case, the formulas on the right of the '$\vdash$' must also have the same truth-value, since q has either the same truth-value as p on the assignment in question or else the opposite truth-value, to which difference, as we have just noted, the truth-function associated with

---

[19] Elaborating an idea of Ackrill (1963: 151), Khamara calls a modality O *two-sided* when (as we would put it) $O = \pi(O)$, and diagnoses some illicit moves in Aristotle's discussion as involving a conflation of the one-sided notions of necessity and possibility ($\square$ and $\lozenge$) with their two-sided cousins (Δ and ∇). To avoid such confusions, it is preferable to use "non-contingent" rather than "necessary" when the two-sided notion is at issue. Corresponding confusions abound in closely related areas. For example, the logical positivists (among others) tended to define analyticity as truth in virtue of meaning and then talk as though every statement was either analytic or synthetic, though for the latter to be so we should have to take "analytic" in a two-sided Δ-style sense rather than the Δ-style sense officially defined. This observation may be found in Robinson (1958: 277).

φ is indifferent. Thus the biconditional on the right must also be true on the assignment in question. Having established the correctness of the $\vdash$-statement inset above, we note that therefore if the formula on the left is itself a truth-functional tautology (a $\vdash$-consequence of the empty set), then so is that on the left. Recall that any variable occurring in a formula which does not occur in every formula logically equivalent to that formula is said to occur *inessentially* in the formula, this means that whenever a formula—here represented by $\varphi(p, r, \ldots, r_n)$—of truth-functional logic is logically equivalent to the result of replacing one of it variables (p in our case) by its negation, that variable occurs inessentially in the formula, since the formula is equivalent to the result of replacing that formula by any other (q in this presentation). In particular, then, to connect with the above discussion, putting $n = 0$, whenever $\varphi(p)$ is equivalent to $\varphi(\neg p)$, p occurs inessentially in $\varphi(p)$, this formula being equivalent to $\varphi(q)$. (It further follows that either $\varphi(p)$ or its negation is a tautology, though this is not an aspect of the situation in focus here.) This of course is very different from the situation in modal logic, as the case of Δ and ∇ illustrates. Δp and $\Delta \neg p$ are logically equivalent (on the account provided by any plausible modal logic) even though p occurs essentially in Δp, and the latter is by no means equivalent to Δq: from the non-contingency of p, the non-contingency of q does not follow. The reason for this disanalogy may roughly be put down to the fact that, as it would be expressed from the perspective of the possible worlds semantics for modal logic (Section 5 below), the language of modal logic provides for non-truth-functional contexts. A more accurate diagnosis of the present point, however, would direct our attention not so much to the fact that Δ and ∇ are not truth-functional as to the fact that these operators are, more specifically, not extensional. (The distinction involved here is explained in Section 6, where a more careful formulation will be found. The point on which this bears is the justification of the inset $\vdash$ claim above in terms of what happens with the truth-function associated with φ.) The present point is simply that these operators, in being equivalent to their own post-negations while still depending on their arguments, present us with something undreamt of in the realm of non-modal classical propositional logic.

Blanché (1953 and elsewhere) not only extended the Square of Opposition (modal or syllogistic) to the Hexagon described above and diagrammed by the cooperative reader—he made some further striking observations about the relations to be found on that diagram. To avoid a cluttered diagram here, Figure 20.3 appears without the perimeter on which the various implicatons would be indicated. The full diagram, including the perimeter and numerous informative annotations, may be found in Blanché (1953: 105).[20] It appears there with the vertices

---

[20] A nice version of this diagram appears in Geerts and Melis (1976: III). Blanché's Hexagon has been rediscovered by several writers since, perhaps most recently appearing in Simons (1993: III)—with no reference to Blanché himself.

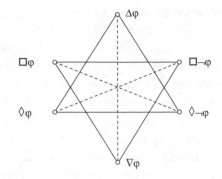

Fig. 20.3. Blanché's Hexagram

labelled in terms of the syllogistic square rather than the modal square, with the top and bottom points labelled *u* and *y*. (Think of *SuP* as meaning all or no *S*'s are *P*'s and *SyP* as meaning that some *S*'s but not all *S*'s are *P*'s. Blanché in fact uses capital letters for *a, e, i, o, u,* and *y*.) The edges of the upward-pointing triangle in the inscribed hexagram appearing here as Figure 20.3 connect pairs that are subcontraries, while the edges of the downward-pointing triangle connect contraries—at least as the notions of contrariety and subcontrariety are defined in what I call the Simple Semantic Account, below (see further Horn 1989: 218 and surrounding discussion). It is these aspects of the full picture on which I concentrate here. I begin by backing up a little and addressing the concepts of contrariety and subcontrariety.

Two considerations work in tandem to drive us towards thinking of contrariety and subcontrariety, at least in the first instance, as relations between sentence operators or (perhaps, as for the syllogistic case, binary) quantifiers, rather than between propositions—alternatively put, between statements but subject to invariance under logical equivalence of statements. One is a point already touched on: it would be nice to preserve the propriety of talking of *the* (sub)contrary of whatever it is that has a (sub)contrary, but as remarked above, this is not possible if we take the relata to be propositions. The second point is what we might call the 'say more' consideration. Forgetting about the previous point for a moment and working with (sub)contrariety as relating statements or propositions, we can put the thought like this. While it is no doubt handy for many purposes to employ "minimal" notions of (sub)contrariety, asking only that contraries be incapable of joint truth and subcontraries incapable of joint falsity,[21] the traditional account says more. It says that for two statements to be contraries, we need not only that it is impossible for both to be true together, but also that it *is* possible for them both to be false together, while for subcontraries, we need not only that it is impossible for both to be false together, but also that it *is* possible for them both to be true together. It is well known that for suitable choices of *S* and *P*, we can arrive at cases

---

[21] This is what is called the 'say less' treatment in Humberstone (2003).

in which *SaP* and *SeP*, traditionally regarded as syllogistic contraries, are not capable of joint falsity (see Sanford 1968; Humberstone 2003 shows that Sanford's positive suggestions as to how to respond to this situation are not adequate). On certain not implausible assumptions about necessity and possibility there will be at least some statements φ for which it is non-contingent whether necessarily φ: for example, all normal modal logics (as defined in the following section) have formulas φ for which $\Box\Delta\varphi$ is provable. But the latter is equivalent precisely to a denial of the claim that it is possible for $\Box\varphi$ and $\Box\neg\varphi$ both to be true, so such a pair will not be contraries if we follow the traditional account and 'say more'. Now, if instead of thinking of contrariety (and similarly for subcontrariety) as a relation between statements, we think of it as relating operators (or quantifiers), then we can say that necessity and impossibility are contraries and mean by it that (i) for any φ, $\Box\varphi$ and $\Box\neg\varphi$ are incompatible, (ii) it is not the case that for all φ at least one of $\Box\varphi$ and $\Box\neg\varphi$ must be true. In other words we can after all 'say more' (namely (ii)). We can express this succinctly as a condition on singulary sentence operators if we add constant operators **1** and **0** with defining characteristic that for φ, $\mathbf{1}(\Box\varphi)$ and $\mathbf{0}(\varphi)$ are logically equivalent respectively to $\top$ and $\bot$, and binary operator modifiers $\wedge$ and $\vee$ defined parametrically in terms of their sentence connective namesakes (thus $O_1 \wedge O_2$ applied to φ is equivalent to $O_1\varphi \wedge O_2\varphi$ and similarly for $\vee$). Then we offer as what we call the *Simple Semantic Account* of (sub)contrariety:

> O_1 and O_2 are *contraries* iff (i) $O_1 \wedge O_2 = \mathbf{0}$ and (ii) $O_1 \vee O_2 \neq \mathbf{1}$.
> O_1 and O_2 are *subcontraries* iff (i) $O_1 \vee O_2 = \mathbf{1}$ and (ii) $O_1 \wedge O_2 \neq \mathbf{0}$.

Having introduced the Simple Semantic Account in order to do justice to the 'say more' consideration, we note that there has been some advance in respect of the first consideration also, in weeding out some cases of non-uniqueness. This is seen most easily with the syllogistic example, for which we envisage an analogous account, the binary quantifiers *a* and *e* being contraries because (i) for any *S*, *P*, their application to *S* and *P* (in that order) yields statements not both of which can be true, while (ii) the same cannot be said with the word 'true' replaced by 'false'. Before reviewing the status of a modal example given earlier, a word should be said about the use of '=' in the above formulation of the Simple Semantic Account of (sub)contrariety. Strictly speaking, having introduced $O_1 \wedge O_2$ as a certain sentence operator and **0** as another, we should not be saying for example that $O_1 \wedge O_2 = \mathbf{0}$, since '=' should be flanked by singular terms (or individual variables) and not by sentence operators. What is meant of course is that given the congruentiality assumption in force throughout this discussion, we can think of the flanking expressions here as denoting certain functions from propositions, conceived of as equivalence classes of sentences (or statements), to propositions, and the equality means that the same such function is represented by the flanking expressions. This said, we can return to the earlier example in which we assumed that **S4** was the correct alethic modal logic and showed that in the sense there explained there was no sentence operator corresponding to post-negation. Recycling the example for present purposes, we have that $\square\neg\square$ is a contrary of $\square\square$ ($=\square$) and so is $\square\square\neg$ ($=\square\neg$). (We need **S4** as the right logic here because in **S5**, for instance, clause (ii) of the definition of contrariety would not be satisfied for the former claim; clause (i) is all right for both **S4** and **S5**. More on these two logics, and others, appears in Section 4; in neither of them are the prefixes $\square\neg\square$ and $\square\neg$ equivalent.) What Blanché noticed, however, was that quite independently of such arguably recherché matters as hang on particular decisions about the logical powers of iterated modal operators, the Simple Semantic Account of contrariety—to focus on that case—inevitably faces another uniqueness problem.

In essence, the point is that although contrariety is a binary relation, contraries always come in threes. Once we have two statements which cannot both be true but can both be false, we have a third statement to the effect that they *are* both false. This cannot be true together with either of the first two, but it can be false along with either of them—namely whenever the other of them is true. Such a triad is represented in Figure 20.3 by the downward-pointing triangle. It is easy to check that on the Simple Semantic Account of contrariety, this makes $\square$ and ∇ contraries, just as surely as it makes $\square$ and $\square\neg$ (alias $\pi(\square)$) contraries, and this not only for alethically interpreted $\square$ but for any $\square$ whose logical behaviour is as described by the Modal Square. Similarly, the upward-pointing triangle has at its vertices operators any two of which are subcontraries. We concentrate on the case of contrariety. Blanché's attitude to this situation seems to have been one of acceptance—indeed delight (at the novel contraries disclosed). Still, it would be of some interest to see if something closer to the intuitive idea that while the notions of necessity and impossibility are contraries (to stick with the alethic interpretation for illustrative purposes), the notions of necessity and contingency are not. While the issue may seem entirely terminological, it is not quite that. For there remains the question of whether there is any relation, whatever one chooses to call it, which can be objectively isolated, holding between necessity and impossibility (or obligatoriness and wrongness) but not between, say, necessity and contingency (or obligatoriness and moral indifference). The word 'objectively' here is meant to exclude a dependence of the way the relation is specified on the particular linguistic expression given to the relata. A more discriminating account than the Simple Semantic Account should only be taken seriously if, when it rules that O_1 and O_2 are contraries, a different ruling would not have arisen as a result of privileging at any stage one statement over a logically equivalent statement, or as a result of considering one language rather than another expressively equivalent language with different primitive expressions. According to the spirit behind the search for such an alternative account, the different Squares of Opposition which Blanché is happy to abstract from his Master Hexagon represent spurious substitutes for the real thing in that the top line of the square does not connect genuine contraries. Figure 20.4 depicts two such squares, with the top left-hand corner and the top right-hand

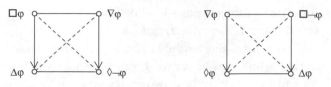

FIG. 20.4. Two spurious Modal Squares?

corner of the square of Figure 20.1 left *in situ* in the two cases (respectively) but with new neighbours.

Exactly as in the traditional Modal Square (depicted in Figure 20.1), the relations of implication and (in)compatibility obtain between the corresponding corners of these new squares. But, the ruling of the Simple Semantic Account notwithstanding, there remains an intuitive sense in which necessity and contingency are not contraries, and nor are non-contingency and non-necessity subcontraries even though they are linked by horizontal lines in the first square in Figure 20.4.[22] Nor do contingency and impossibility seem in the tightest imaginable sense contraries, though occupying different top corners in the second square—and similarly for its bottom corners and the subcontrariety relation. Here is an expression of this sentiment from Simons (1993: 115); the reference to 'three things' is to Blanché's observation summarized by saying that contraries (according to the Simple Semantic Account), come in threes:[23]

> merely having three things or a ternary division does not exhaust all we feel to belong to the square in its traditional logical applications, even though all the requisite relations and functions are definable algebraically. In the traditional cases we can likewise define six different squares if we wish, but usually only one has the right 'feel' about which element is in the A position and which in the E position.

But what refinement of the Simple Semantic Account might be available?

To the question just posed we offer as an answer: one merely adds a third condition to (i) and (ii) in the Simple Semantic Account of (sub)contrariety, and that third condition—in both cases—is that O_1 and O_2 should be each other's post-negations. (It is enough to say that O_2 is the post-negation of O_1, since this relation

---

[22] The intuitive sense in which necessity and impossibility are genuine contraries while necessity and contingency are not may be connected to the notion of polar (or scalar) contrariety for predicates (general terms), as explained in Horn (1989: 39), and similarly for the syllogistic quantifiers, illustrating the point here: *e* and *a* are contraries in marking opposite ends of a scale which goes from 0 per cent ('of *S*'s are *P*'s') to 100 per cent, whereas the same cannot be said for *y* and either of *a*, *e*.

[23] In fact there is no reference to Blanché's work in Simons (1993). Nor would there have been any mention of Simons here had I not accidentally stumbled on the anthology in which it appears, between completing the first draft of this survey and revising it for publication. All references to Simons have been incorporated at this later stage. Not only does Simons share the same intuitive hostility to these various spurious squares (though he is not especially concerned with the Modal Square), but his suggested solution as to how to exclude them is essentially that defended here—though put slightly differently (in terms of "obversion" rather than post-negation).

is symmetric.) For the syllogistic case, with which we shall not be concerned further, the analogue of post-negation would be negation-of-the-predicate, so, still using the 'π' notation in the case of $q \in \{a, e, i, o, u, y\}$ for any S, P, $S\pi(q)P$ is $Sq\,\bar{P}$, in which we use overlining for negating a general term. This means that the uniqueness desideratum is satisfied for (sub)contrariety on this "Refined Account" (as we may call it), by contrast with the Simple Semantic Account, since an operator O has a unique post-negation. The issue naturally arises as to whether introducing post-negation in this way perhaps stops the account from being appropriately language-independent and, as it was put above, objective. Two grounds for scepticism on this score will be raised and dismissed, the first here and the second in Appendix 20.1 below.

The first objection simply dresses up in an attractive way the point that the logical relations between the statements schematically represented at the points of Blanché's Hexagon provide for the deviant squares of Figure 20.4 as no less legitimate than the prototype depicted in Figure 20.1. We can usefully begin with a change in our style of diagram. These various exotically annotated squares and hexagons resemble more closely the accoutrements of some cabbalistic ritual than the serious diagrams one expects from systematic work in logic. So let us repackage, in Figure 20.5, the information in the annotated hexagon as the Hasse diagram of the Boolean algebra of equivalence classes of formulas at the vertices of the hexagon, with top and bottom elements added, and one formula following from another just in case one can trace an *upward* path from the latter to the former using the lines on the diagram.

We need at once to correct the oversimplified description of what is represented by the nodes of this diagram. Although, in replacing the schematic 'φ' of earlier diagrams by a concrete formula, the propositional variable q, the real intention is not to label the nodes with formulas, even taken as representatives of their (logical) equivalence classes, but to have the labels be operators. The top and bottom elements, **1** and **0**, I have already introduced as such operators. We could just write '$\Box\neg$', 'Δ', etc. for the operators, but here what we are dealing with is abbreviations for longer expressions which are more suited to the extraction of such operators from arbitrary formulas (or statements). Or rather, not extraction so much as abstraction—λ-abstraction. Appendix 20.1 will exploit the greater flexibility of this λ notation. (This usage is not uncommon in discussions, for example, of fragments of the language of intuitionistic logic, e.g. in de Lavalette 1981.) The idea is that a λ expression $\lambda\,p_i.\psi$ where ψ is any formula, is a functor that can be applied to a formula φ to yield the result of replacing all occurrences of the propositional variable p_i in ψ by the formula φ. For a rigorous presentation, one should say 'free occurrences' here, but the only use of this apparatus I make avoids λ expressions inside λ expressions, and we never need more than one variable "bound" by a λ. I adopt the convention of using q as that variable. Finally, labels such as '$\Box\neg q$' in Figure 20.5 are really abbreviations of the corresponding λ expressions (here, $\lambda q.\Box\neg q$). We

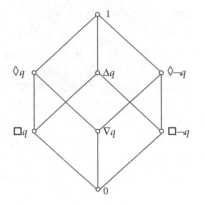

FIG. 20.5. A nice respectable Boolean algebra

have to rethink what it is for elements X, Y, of the Boolean algebra there depicted to be such that $X \leq Y$; I said that this meant that Y followed from X, but now X and Y are operators and not formulas (or equivalence classes thereof). Clearly what is meant is given by a parametric interpretation: $X \leq Y$ just in case, for all φ, $Y(\varphi)$ follows from $X(\varphi)$; it is perfectly reasonable to call this a logical relation between X and Y. This said, we can now formulate the first objection. All the logical relations between the operators of the hexagon are displayed in Figure 20.5, including those employed in the Simple Semantic Account of (sub)contrariety, the ∧ and ∨ of that account being the meet and join operations in this Boolean algebra. But there is nothing in Figure 20.5 that tells us what is the post-negation of what! If we wanted to indicate this, we would have to do so with some superadded notation, such as arcs linking the □q node to the □¬q node, with a loop from the Δq node to itself. These non-straight lines connect an operator with its post-negation. (Similarly for the nodes on the next 'layer' up, with loops also on the 1 and 0.) They cannot be recovered from the Boolean algebraic structure of Figure 20.5. □q stands in exactly the same logical relations to Δq as it does to □¬q, since there is an automorphism of the Boolean algebra of Figure 20.5 that keeps □q fixed while interchanging Δq and □¬q. Thus, the envisaged objection concludes, the idea that there is a special ('objective') logical relation of post-negation is simply a mirage.

The reply to this objection is that although the whole story about the logical properties of and relationships between statements (or formulas) is told by the Boolean algebra, the same cannot be said for the case of operators. Figure 20.5 tells us only about such relations between O_1 and O_2 as can be read off from the relations between $O_1\varphi$ and $O_2\varphi$ for an arbitrary *but fixed* φ. The concept of post-negation involved a relationship (namely equivalence) between $O_1\varphi$ and $O_2\psi$ where φ and ψ are different (in particular, where ψ is the negation of φ). A simpler example of this phenomenon arises with the concept of a *monotone* operator, by which is meant an operator O such that whenever ψ follows from φ, Oψ follows from Oφ. (This is a stronger property than congruentiality, mentioned above.) This is surely as objective a logical property of any operator possessing it, but it is given no recognition in the Boolean algebra of Figure 20.5, since there is nothing special about the monotone $\Box$ that sets it apart from the non-monotone Δ or $\Box\neg$: these are just the three atoms of the Boolean algebra (elements with nothing between them and $\mathbf{0}$), and any two can be exchanged by a Boolean automorphism. Again, the key point is that being monotone is not a matter of the logical relations between the results of attaching operators to a fixed statement, being defined in terms of attaching them to arbitrary pairs φ and ψ. This concludes our dismissal of the first objection to the objectivity of the Refined Account of (sub)contrariety. Consideration of the second objection is deferred to Appendix 20.1. Appendix 20.4 exhibits a Boolean algebra incorporating the (equivalence classes of) formulas which involve occurrences of q not in the scope of a modal operator; the present algebra is a sub-algebra of that algebra, which appears as Figure 20. A1.

4. MODAL LOGICS

It is useful to become a bit more explicit about the notions of congruentiality and monotony deployed above and to relate them to some other conditions, to reveal what the Modal Square of Opposition does and does not display about the different modal theatres to which we have seen that it applies (alethic, deontic, etc.). To this end, let us for simplicity identify logics with certain sets of formulas in a language with some functionally complete set of Boolean connectives and any further connectives,[24] in terms of which well-formedness is defined as usual on the basis of a countable set of propositional variables. The sets of formulas counting as logics will be those which are closed under Uniform Substitution (of arbitrary formulas for propositional variables) and under the consequence relation of classical propositional logic.[25] We often refer to the formulas in a logic as "provable" in the logic, and write '⊢', subscripted by a name of the logic, to indicate that this is the status of

---

[24] By "functionally complete", we mean to require functional completeness in the strong sense that every n-ary truth-function can be obtained by composition from those associated with the primitive connectives, including the case of $n = 0$, so we assume that one or both of the 0-place connectives $\top$, $\bot$ (truth and falsity constants respectively) are primitive. This will gives us formulas—called 'pure formulas' below—constructed with the aid of no propositional variables. For definiteness, let us assume that this language has countably many such variables (also called 'sentence letters'), $p_1, \ldots, p_n, \ldots$ the first two of which we usually write as p, q.

[25] Another way of expressing this second condition is to say that the set contains all truth-functional tautologies and is closed under *modus ponens*. (The functional completeness condition means that even if $\rightarrow$ is not primitive, it is definable, so the reference to *modus ponens* does make sense.)

the formula following. (One could of course treat the logics themselves as consequence relations, but avoid doing so simply for the sake of continuity with the
bulk of the literature on modal logic.[26] Indeed many more exotic conceptions have
been offered of what a logic should in this context be taken to be: various examples
appear in Humberstone 1988; Blamey and Humberstone 1991; Wansing 1994, 1996,
1998*a*, *b*.) We are now in a position to offer formal logic-relative definitions of congruentiality, monotony and some related notions (the following terms are taken
from writings of David Makinson, Krister, Segerberg, and B. F. Chellas; see Chellas
1980, ch. 8, for explanation of and practice with, terminology differing only slightly
from that used here). Let **S** be a logic and O be a primitive or defined singulary
connective in the language of **S**. Then we say that

O is *congruential* according to **S** when for all formulas φ, ψ, if $\vdash_S \varphi \leftrightarrow \psi$ then
$\vdash_S O\varphi \leftrightarrow O\psi$.

If we replace the occurrences of '$\leftrightarrow$' here by '$\rightarrow$', then we get the definition of 'O is
monotone according to **S**'. When we employed this terminology earlier, noting the
non-monotony of ∇, what was meant was that according to any logic plausibly for-
malizing the notion of contingency, the (congruential) operator symbolizing non-
contingency would not be monotone. It is very common to see over-hasty verdicts
in this respect. For example, Linsky (1967) includes an argument against Russell's
theory of descriptions which relies on the assumption that the (complex) operator
'*a* wished to know whether ____' was monotone.[27] Once this assumption is made
explicit, as here, its falsity is obvious. (Even idealizing to the extent of taking '*a* wishes
that' and '*a* knows that' to be monotone, the tell-tale *whether*-construction—cf.

---

[26] If one wishes to explore modal logic without the assumption of a functionally complete stock of
Boolean connectives available—a project which throws up some surprises—something like the identification of logics with consequence relations becomes inevitable. Examples of such explorations may
be found in Humberstone (1990) and Dunn (1995). It should be emphasized, and will become abun-
dantly clear from our discussion in Sect. 5 of the preservation characteristics of various formula-to-
formula rules, that there are in fact many natural but distinct consequence relations associated with a
single modal logic in the "set of formulas" sense. The consequence relation that is relevant here is what
amounts, for a logic determined by a class of frames, to preservation of truth at an arbitrary point in
an arbitrary model on a frame in the class, as we pass from the left to the '$\vdash$'.

[27] In Linsky (1967: 71 ff.) we read: 'Asked whether he wants to know whether one, and only one,
individual wrote *Waverley* and is identical with Scott, George IV might answer that this is not what he
wishes to know, since he *already* knows that one, and only one, individual wrote *Waverley*; what he
does not know is whether the author of *Waverley* is Scott.' But clearly I might want to know whether
both my children are safe at home, even if I already (take myself to) know that one of them is—even,
indeed, if I know that specifically that, say, the younger one is at home, I may still wonder whether it's
the case that both are. Similarly, I can bring it about that both are home when I march one in from the
street, when the other is already at home through no intervention on my part. Since I can thus bring
it about that $\varphi \wedge \psi$ without both bringing it about that φ and bringing it about that ψ, a sentence
operator treatment of '*a* brings it about that____' should not render this as monotone—let alone normal (*pace* Pörn 1970). Several approaches to the logic of bringing about are discussed in Segerberg
(1992), which also includes the relevant Modal Square, as extracted from the writings of St Anselm by
D. P. Henry; see also the discussion of work by Belnap and others in Horty (2001, ch. 2).

the case of ∇ and Δ—gives the game away.) For a second example, consider the following observation—made in Perry (1986: 99) as part of a campaign for a more general semantic framework than possible worlds semantics (outlined briefly below):

Suppose the bed's collapsing made it the case that Cicero lost sleep. It seems that...it does not follow that the bed's falling made it the case that $7 + 5 = 12$.

Since the sum of 7 and 5 would have been 12 whatever had happened with Cicero's bed, one must agree that any account on which this equation is made to be true by the bed's collapsing is faulty. The use of a possible worlds semantics brings with it (on pain of considerable artificiality) the congruentiality of all operators interpreted with its aid, so from 'The bed's collapsing made it the case that Cicero lost sleep', the inference to 'The bed's collapsing made it the case that (Cicero lost sleep and $7 + 5 = 12$)' will be legitimate. Perry may well object to this already, but it is simply not correct to think that the possible worlds apparatus commits us to the legitimacy of an inference from this interim conclusion to the further conclusion 'The bed's collapsing made it the case that $7 + 5 = 12$', at least if the latter is interpreted as implying that if the bed had not collapsed then it would not have been the case that $7 + 5 = 12$. As has already been remarked, congruentiality does not imply the property of monotony defined above, though it is implied by it and this has been the basis of an objection to assuming the even stronger property of normality for a range of applications of modal logic—in particular to the case in which propositional attitudes are involved such as the epistemic and doxastic cases. The 'problem of logical omniscience' involved here has been much discussed in the literature: see Hintikka (1962), Lenzen (1978, ch. 3), and Stalnaker (1999, chs. 12–14).

As already mentioned, if O is monotone according to **S**, it follows that O is congruential, though not conversely; further, if O is congruential according to **S**, O is monotone according to **S** if and only if for all φ, ψ, we have

(Mono) $\vdash_S O(\varphi \wedge \psi) \rightarrow O\varphi$.

This is equivalent to the result of putting '$O\varphi \wedge O\psi$' in the consequent, giving one half of what is often meant by saying that (according to the logic in question) O distributes over conjunction. The other half, which does not follow from (Mono), we state separately as:

(Reg) $\vdash_S (O\varphi \wedge O\psi) \rightarrow O(\varphi \wedge \psi)$.

O is *regular* according to **S** if O is monotone according to **S** and (Reg) is satisfied; alternatively put: if O is congruential according to **S** and the strengthening of (Reg) to a biconditional is satisfied (for all φ, ψ).[28] This biconditional is what is meant by saying that O distributes over conjunction. It is not hard to see that when this is

[28] Warning: the term 'regular' is used in an unrelated sense in Hughes and Cresswell (1968).

provable in **S**, then so is the result of replacing O by $\delta(\text{O})$ and $\wedge$ by $\vee$; $\delta(\text{O})$, in other words, distributes over disjunction (according to **S**). Finally, O is *normal* according to **S** if O is regular according to **S** and in addition, $\vdash_{\textbf{S}} \text{O}\top$. Another way of packaging these definitions is in terms of the following:

> *Normality Rule.* From $\vdash(\varphi_1 \wedge \ldots \wedge \varphi_n) \to \psi$ to $\vdash(\text{O}\,\varphi_1 \wedge \ldots \wedge \text{O}\varphi_n) \to \text{O}\psi$.

Then O is monotone according to **S** if **S** is closed under the special $n = 1$ case of the above rule, regular according to **S** if **S** is closed under the $n = 2$ case of the rule (which implies the $n = 1$ case since we may take $\varphi_1 = \varphi_2$), and is normal according to **S** if **S** is closed under the rule for arbitrary $n \geq 0$. This is equivalent to requiring closure under just the $n = 0$ and $n = 2$ cases of the Normality Rule. When O is written as $\square$, the $n = 0$ case, in which the implications displayed reduce to their consequents, is called the rule of Necessitation. Another very common (equivalent) characterization of normality according to **S** (a logic in the above sense) proceeds by requiring closure under the rule of Necessitation and also adding to the condition that **S** should prove the formula

> **K**$_{\text{O}}$ $\text{O}(p \to q) \to (\text{O}p \to \text{O}q)$.

The analogy between the various candidates for top left-hand corner in Modal Square of Opposition can be put in these terms: according to a suitable logical treatment of these notions—making some oversimplifications to be corrected presently—they deserve to emerge as normal operators. Naturally there have been several objections to such a treatment. For example, Regularity has been questioned for the deontic interpretation: if φ and ψ are incompatible, could it not be nonetheless that each ought (for different reasons perhaps) to be true—presenting a moral dilemma in the case in which O is understood as an agent-implicating 'ought' operator—without it being so that their impossible conjunction ought to be true. So one reads in, for example, Schotch and Jennings (1981a), where (Reg) is called 'Aggregation', and where one may find a modification of the Kripke semantics—see the following section—designed to invalidate this principle. (Cf. also B. Williams 1972, where the principle in question is labelled 'Agglomeration'. Specifically Schotch and Jennings object to the principle given as **D** below, though they have no objections to something equivalent to it given regularity, namely $\neg\text{O}(p \wedge \neg p)$; we write **D** with '$\square$' rather than 'O', when we come to it, remarking here only that it is more natural to object to this principle when the operator in question—however it is written—is given an 'ought' reading than when it is read as a deontic 'must'.) Even monotony has been queried for this operator in some quarters, e.g. in Jackson (1985), Jackson and Pargetter (1986), though we cannot go into the objections here. (For some discussion, see Humberstone 1991: 154–6, 162; rather different grounds for objection arise from the well-known "paradoxes" of deontic logic, three of which are conveniently listed in Jones and Pörn 1985: 276.)

Various aspects of normality have played a crucial role in arguments for the main "negative" claims of traditional philosophy: scepticism and incompatibilism. In the former case, one argues that a subject has no knowledge of something commonly taken to be known about (e.g. the immediately surrounding physical environment) because such knowledge would imply the existence of further knowledge (e.g. that there is no powerful demon, mad scientist, etc., controlling all sensory inputs) the subject clearly does not possess. In the latter case one argues that an agent has no freedom to act in other than the way in which that agent will in fact act because such a freedom would imply a further freedom (to make antecedent circumstances other than the way they were) the agent clearly does not possess. The "further implications" alluded to here are appeals to the monotone nature of the operators 'a knows that' and 'a can bring it about that'. (We have already queried this property for the apparently simpler 'a brings it about that' in note 27.) In the latter case, we may thinking of this as a consequence of the fact that $\delta(O)$ is monotone for any monotone O, with the O in the latter case being the operator 'It is now unpreventably-for-a the case that', presumed normal. There is an extra complication in the second case because either the presumption of duality just made or else the claim that this operator is indeed normal is threatened by examples circulated in the 1970s by Anthony Kenny and Asa Kasher seeming to show that 'a can bring it about that' does not distribute over disjunction (see Kenny 1975: 137; Gallois 1977: 101), which bears on the version of the argument for incompatibilism defended especially by van Inwagen (1975, 1983), in the following way. Rather than saying, as in the crude summary above, that for someone about to, for example, drive to the shops, the ability not to drive to the shops would imply an ability 'to make antecedent circumstances other than the way they (in fact) were', we should really say that incompatibilism gives only the conclusion that they have the power to make it the case either that the laws of nature were different or that the antecedent circumstances were different. Instead of resting content with the claim that this disjunctive power is something no ordinary agent possesses, van Inwagen pursues the matter further, claiming that such a disjunctive power would imply the more evidently unpossessed power either to make the laws different or to make the past different—whence the interest in distribution over disjunction in this case. (The Kenny–Kasher examples alluded to above motivated the work referred to in note 13.[29]) In the epistemic case, there was a noticeable tendency to react by proposing analyses of knowledge which revealed 'a knows that' to be non-monotone (an approach pioneered by Fred Dretske and popularized by Robert

[29] The interested reader is directed to Huemer (2000) and Widerker (2002) for more recent evaluations—respectively unfavourable—of the argument for incompatibilism here under consideration. It should be added that van Inwagen's argument actually involves two notions of necessity, logical necessity and unavoidability/now-unpreventability, a feature our oversimplified discussion ignores.

Nozick—for references, see Dancy 1985 or any other epistemology text[30]) and to defend epistemic logics in which the operator was accorded a non-monotone treatment (Schotch and Jennings 1981*b*; Schotch 2000).

So far we have allowed any number of non-Boolean ('additional') connectives in our conception of what a logic is, but if we have just a single such additional primitive connective, of arity 1, namely $\Box$ (in terms of which we take $\Diamond$ to be defined as in Section 2) arriving at the mid-twentieth-century notion of a *modal logic*, then we apply all the terminology to modal logics by transferring it across from the behaviour of $\Box$ according to the logic in question. (These are what would more informatively be called monomodal logics. In general, for an '*n*-modal' logic, we should have *n* primitive operators $\Box_1, \ldots, \Box_n$. Several applications alluded to above are naturally pursued as bimodal logics—i.e. $n = 2$: tense logic, for instance, with past as well as future tense taken into consideration, or combined epistemic and doxastic logic. We are also ignoring many "broadly modal" operators which are *k*-ary for $k > 1$, such as the counterfactual conditional connective(s) of Lewis 1973.[31]) Thus a modal logic **S** is *congruential, monotone, regular,* or *normal,* depending as $\Box$ is respectively congruential, monotone, regular, or normal according to **S**.[32] (Recall from the preceding paragraph in any logic in which $\Box$ is monotone—and hence in any normal modal logic—$\Diamond$ is also monotone. Regularity, however, is not inherited from O to $\delta(O)$: it would be disastrous if it were, since we do not want to be committed to claiming that the conjunction of any two things which are possible, permissible, etc., is itself possible, permissible, ...) Although the most popular systematization of the alethic, deontic, modalities have been as normal modal logics, this is not by any means built into the Square of Opposition itself, which instead makes a different demand: that $\Box\varphi$ should provably imply $\Diamond\varphi$. If, as is customary, we call the smallest normal modal logic **K**, then the point is that the formula

D $\Box p \to \Diamond p$

---

[30] There is a tendency for non-logical work in epistemology to talk vaguely about "closure" without making it clear whether monotony, regularity, or full normality is at issue:all are reasonable articulations of the idea that what is known by a fixed subject is closed under deduction. (To reduce the element of idealization, such conditions are sometimes stated with an added rider to the effect that—to give the "normality" formulation—the subject *knows that* ψ follows from $\varphi_1, \ldots, \varphi_n$.)

[31] See also the references there (1973, ch. 5) to conditional obligation in deontic logic, and 'since' and 'until' in tense logic. Von Wright's 'A New System of Modal Logic' (1957: 89–126) features primitive dyadic necessity and possibility operators with an intended alethic interpretation, on which there seems to have been no—e.g. semantical—research done, at least none published in English. (I once encountered a German publication on the subject but lost the reference before taking steps to procure a translation.) We do not include strict implication in this list because although it can be taken as primitive, it can instead—and usually is—taken as defined (by $\Box(\varphi \to \psi)$) in terms of Boolean connectives and singulary non-Boolean connectives.

[32] Sometimes—e.g. Chellas and Segerberg (1994)—normal modal logics are defined as here but without the requirement of closure under Uniform Substitution. An interesting 'non-substitution-invariant' bimodal logic with intended doxastic–epistemic application appears in Halpern (1996). It is sometimes felt that without an insistence on closure under Uniform Substitution for logics, we are in

is not provable in **K**, and the smallest normal modal logic in which it is accordingly a proper extension of **K**, called **KD**. So the Square of Opposition demands in this respect something more than normality. In another respect, it demands less. If we give $\Box\varphi$ the reading 'It is probable that φ', meaning more likely than not that φ, then we can see that **D** would be an acceptable principle, but the appropriate modal logic (explored in Hamblin 1959[33]) would not be normal, since the regularity condition (Reg) would fail on this interpretation.

While we are recalling standard names (mostly from Lemmon and Scott 1977) for various modal principles, we should add **T**, **U**, **4**, and **5** to the list:

T $\Box p \to p$
U $\Box(\Box p \to p)$
4 $\Box p \to \Box\Box p$
5 $\Diamond p \to \Box\Diamond p$.

Names for normal modal logics containing these formulas are obtained by concatenating 'K' with the labels subject to the further convention that 'KT' before a numeral is abbreviated to 'S'. (But we use 'S' *tout court* as a variable for modal logics— and not just for normal extensions of **KT**.) Thus in particular the logic **S4** mentioned earlier is **KT4**, while **S5**, the other most widely known modal logic for the alethic interpretation(s) of '$\Box$', is **KT5**. (The earlier items in C. I. Lewis's sequence of logics, S1, S2, and S3—whose names do not appear reproduced in bold-face since they are not formed in accordance with the above conventions—are non-normal modal logics with mainly a cult following today.) We could have said that **S5** is **KT45**, but it less confusing to avoid labels involving redundancy like this, since **4** is provable in **KT5**. (On the other hand, '**KDB4**' is an irredundant label for this same logic, where **B** is $p \to \Box\Diamond p$.) This is slightly surprising since if we rewrite **5** as having '$\neg\Box p$' for its antecedent and '$\Box\neg\Box p$' for its consequent, we obviously get something yielding the same normal modal logics, and now we can compare **4** and **5** in the following way: whereas **4** says (roughly) that nothing can be contingently necessary, **5** says that nothing can be contingently non-necessary. Thus together they say that anything has whatever modal status it has non-contingently. It comes as a surprise to learn that, as additions to **KT**, one can entertain the former

danger of losing the distinction between logics and theories, but this is not correct since even those logics (such as Halpern's) which are not closed under Uniform Substitution are closed under variable-for-variable substitutions (unlike arbitrary theories). I should acknowledge that even with unrestricted substitution, some have argued that modal logics do not deserve to be called logics. Examples include Harman (1972); Kuhn (1981).

[33] For corrections to Hamblin's discussion, see Burgess (1969: 272). In several editions (in the 1980s) of his text, *Primary Logic*, used by first-year logic students at Monash University, Aubrey Townsend gave a quantificational analogue of this example: a Square of Opposition with 'Most S are P' and 'Few S are P' in the top left and top right corners of the square, respectively. The analogue for this case of the failure of regularity is the invalidity of the inference from 'Most S are P_1' and 'Most S are P_2' to 'Most S are P_1 and P_2' (by contrast with the case of 'Every S is P').

hypothesis (embodied in **S4**) without the latter but not conversely, so that what they amount to 'together' is already given just by **5**. (The relevant deduction establishing this claim may be found in Hughes and Cresswell 1968: 49 or 1996: 58.) On the other hand, as is remarked in Montgomery and Routley (1966), in a formulation with non-contingency primitive, we can extend **KT** to **S4** by adding the first of these, and extend **KT** to **S5** by adding the second:

$$\Delta p \to \Delta\Delta p \qquad \Delta\Delta p$$

which gives us a pair of axioms whose comparative strength is clearer. The following characterization of **S5** comes from C. I. Lewis:

> In my opinion the principal logical significance of the system S5 consists in the fact that it divides all propositions into two mutually exclusive classes: the intensional or modal, and the extensional or contingent. According to the principles of this system, all intensional or modal propositions are either necessarily true or necessarily false. . . . For extensional or contingent propositions, however, possibility, truth, and necessity remain distinct. (Lewis and Langford 1959: 501)

Let us say that formulas φ, ψ, are *S-equivalent* for a modal logic **S** when $\vdash_S \varphi \leftrightarrow \psi$. We take Lewis to be claiming, quite correctly, that the following classes partition the set of formulas:

> *Class I*: containing all formulas φ for which $\vdash_{s5} \Delta\varphi$.
> *Class II*: containing all formulas φ for which no two of $\Diamond\varphi$, φ, $\Box\varphi$ are **S5**-equivalent.

Let us imagine the references to **S5** replaced by a reference to an unspecified modal logic **S**. The claim that this division for **S** is a partition of the set of formulas amounts to the claim that an arbitrary φ lies in Class I if and only if it does not lie in Class II, and for any **S** extending **KT**, not belonging to Class II is equivalent to the following disjunction:

$$(\alpha) \ \vdash_S \Diamond\varphi \to \varphi \ or \ (\beta) \ \vdash_S \varphi \to \Box\varphi \ or \ (\gamma) \ \vdash_S \Diamond\varphi \to \Box\varphi,$$

whose third disjunct is a rewriting of the condition for φ's membership in Class I (understood relative to **S**). So Class I and Class II are mutually exclusive for any **S** $\supseteq$ **KT** (in fact for any **S** $\supseteq$ **KD**). The claim that these classes are jointly exhaustive is more demanding, requiring that (α) should imply (γ) and that (β) should imply (γ). It is not hard to see that the implication from (α) to (γ) holds for all formulas φ if and only if the implication from (β) to (γ) does, and that neither holds when **S** = **S4**, **S5** being the least extension of **S4** for which these implications do hold. (The implication from (α) to (γ) delivers **5** from $\Diamond\Diamond p \to \Diamond p$, an "inverted" variant of **4**. Here we are taking φ as $\Diamond p$.) Thus Class I and Class II are jointly exhaustive for **S5** but not for **S4**. We should add that the implication, for arbitrary φ, from (α) to (β), is also equivalent to the implication, for arbitrary φ, from (β) to (α), as is noted in Chellas and Segerberg (1994), where this transition is studied under the name the 'MacIntosh Rule'. Again, **S5** but not **S4** is closed under the rule, meaning that a famous version of the Modal Ontological Argument (for the existence of God) is supported by the former though not the latter logic, one of the few cases— perhaps the only historically attested case—in which a decision on the correct alethic modal logic bears on an issue not indigenous to modal metaphysics or the philosophy of logic. (See the opening paragraph of Chellas and Segerberg 1994, and the reference to J. J. MacIntosh there given.) Here is a 'horizontalized' version of the transition from (β) to (α) in the form of the schema

$$\Box(\varphi \to \Box\varphi) \to \Box(\Diamond\varphi \to \varphi)$$

or more simply, since any formula $\Box\psi \to \Box\chi$ belongs to **S4** (or any extension thereof) if and only if the simpler $\Box\psi \to \chi$ does (see Prior 1962: 201 for this version of the Modal Ontological Argument, and Oppy 1995: 65–84, 248–59, for a discussion of others, as well as supplementary references):

$$\Box(\varphi \to \Box\varphi) \to (\Diamond\varphi \to \varphi).$$

Again, this schema is derivable in **S5** though not in **S4**, and taken as an additional axiom(-schema), converts **S4** into **S5** (consider φ as $\Box p$). The Modal Ontological Argument takes as premises the two antecedents of an instantiation of this schema with φ replaced by 'God exists'. The first premise supposedly reflects an aspect of the concept of God—that nothing falling under this concept could exist contin- gently; and the second premise is meant to be something the average atheist should be prepared to accept—that even if this possibility is not realized, it is at least a 'broadly logical' possibility that God should exist. So the conclusion, to the effect that this possibility is indeed realized after all, will come as a surprise to such an atheist. We are not concerned here with the acceptability of the premises of this argument, so much as with its validity, which, as remarked, is uncharacteristically sensitive to the choice of modal logic. Where we expect such differences to mani- fest themselves is in theorizing about the relative merits of these logics as formal- izations of the notion of (broadly logical) necessity and possibility themselves, or alternatively in more liberal-minded suggestions that there is no such unique notion to be formalized, but two, one of which is captured in **S4** and the other by **S5**. Let us use the ambiguous phrase 'conception of necessity' to cover both (i) an account of the supposedly single notion of (logical) necessity and (ii) a *concept* of necessity, for the liberal proposal according to which two such concepts are in play. Then we can say that a recurrent theme in this vein (Lemmon 1959; Halldén 1963; Skyrms 1978; J. P. Burgess 1999) has been that **S4** deals well with a conception of necessity as demonstrability or provability,[34] while **S5** deals well with a conception

---

[34] Informal provability, that is. The modal logic of provability in formal theories providing their own provability predicates (whose behaviour is simulated by the $\Box$ operator of modal provability logic) is quite a different matter, treated in Boolos (1993) and elsewhere. There are some comparative remarks on these two subjects in the final section of Skyrms (1978).

of necessity as validity or logical truth (model-theoretically construed). Given the emphasis on the distinction between *a priori* knowability on the one hand and necessity on the other in Kripke (1980), it is far from clear that the former deserves to be considered under the heading of (any kind of) necessity at all, but let us leave that to one side. (In fact, for the main examples Kripke considers, apriority can be treated as "deep necessity", in the sense of Evans 1979. In any case, 'It is *a priori* knowable that' is certainly a candidate for treatment as the $\Box$ of a normal modal logic, whether or not the $\Box$ concerned deserves to be read as 'necessarily'.[35]) The key contrast is over the unacceptability of 5 on the former conception: while on that demonstrability conception the assumption that $\Box\varphi$ allows the conclusion that $\Box\Box\varphi$, since we can exhibit the assumed demonstration of φ and check its status as such (thereby justifying 4) there is not in general anything to exhibit, on the assumption that $\neg\Box\varphi$, which would allow us to conclude that $\Box\neg\Box\varphi$ (thereby calling into question 5). Here is a counter-proposal on this score, from J. R. Lucas (1982: 29), which begins with a summary of the upshot of 5:

> If it is not disproved, then it is proved that it is not disproved. After all, if a disproof were offered we could check it over and be sure that it was a disproof, and conversely if it is not a disproof, we can check it over and prove that it is not a disproof. Underlying this argument is the assumption that every proof and every disproof is recognisable for what it is.

(The original has a paragraph break after the first sentence and has the word 'presented' between 'is' and 'recognisable' in the final sentence.) This justification fails because the relevant hypothesis is that there is no proof of a certain statement, not that a particular putative proof fails to constitute a genuine proof. The fact that the latter can be demonstrated by inspection of the would-be proof does not show that no alternative correct proof is available. It may be that—perhaps with a tacit restriction to a particular area of knowable fact—a better argument can be found for the conclusion that the two conceptions of necessity coincide, i.e. that whatever is necessary in the demonstrability sense is necessary in the validity sense, and vice versa. Would this show that the logics governing these notions were one and the same, and in particular, could not be, as envisaged above, **S4** in the one case and **S5** in the other? Surprisingly, perhaps, the answer is that it would *not* show this; the subtle fallacy involved here is diagnosed and discussed in Williamson (1998).

Before leaving the Lewis-inspired distinction between Classes I and II too far behind, we should note how our characterization of the formulas in the former class—the provably non-contingent formulas—is related to another class of formulas, which again should be defined in a logic-relative way. Adapting the terminology of Anderson and Belnap (1975), we say that a formula φ is *necessitative* according to **S**, just in case there exists some formula ψ; for which **S** $\varphi \leftrightarrow \Box\psi$;.[36] Then

---

[35] Some logical preliminaries here may be found in Anderson (1993); for qualms about regularity ('agglomeration') in this case, see Sorensen (2001, ch. 6).

[36] In Anderson and Belnap (1975: 36) the actual term introduced is 'necessitive', so we are restoring the lost 'ta' the analogy with conjunction–conjunctive, negation–negative, etc., requires, given that the

a point of contrast between **S4** and **S5** is that for the latter logic but not the former, the classes of provably non-contingent and of necessitative formulas coincide. A counter-example in the case of **S4** is obtained by putting $\varphi = \Box\neg p$, a formula which is necessitative according to any modal logic but whose non-contingency amounts to the formula $\Diamond\Diamond p \rightarrow \Box\Diamond p$, a formula **S4**-equivalent to **5**. (We could equally well have chosen φ as $\Box p$. Rewriting the last implicational formula as $\Box\neg\Diamond p \vee \Box\Diamond p$, alias $\Delta\Diamond p$, we see that in **S5** a formula can be provably non-contingent without being provably necessary or provably impossible, since neither of the disjuncts here is **S5**-provable; such cases never arise for **S4** because the latter logic satisfies something called the Rule of Disjunction in Lemmon and Scott 1977, q.v. for details.) On the other hand, for both logics, as for all extensions of **KT**—cf. the earlier discussion of Classes I and II—the provably non-contingent formulas are all necessitative, since if φ is provably non-contingent, we make take the required ψ as φ itself.

Informal discussions of modality frequently confuse the necessary with the necessitative. Kneale (1947) notes the extreme oddity of the question set for the symposium to which that paper is a contribution: 'Are necessary truths true by convention?' His point was that whatever 'true by convention' might mean, it at least implies that whatever has this status might not have been true (conventions settling only what could have been settled differently by a different convention), which is blatantly inconsistent with being a necessary truth. Probably what the theme-setter had in mind was, rather, 'Are necessitative truths true by convention?', i.e. are necessitative statements, when true, true by convention? (Here we understand 'necessitative' not in the above logic-relative sense, but as meaning that the statement in question is one to the effect that some statement is necessarily true.) An equivalent question about necessary truths themselves would ask not whether they were *true* by convention, but whether they were *necessary* by convention, and a negative answer to this question would amount to rejecting **4** as embodying a correct modal principle. The same issue arises for the question as to whether the necessary truths are true as a result of a choice on the part of God, which on pain of deserving a very abrupt negative answer, should have 'necessary' replaced by 'necessitative', or else 'true' by 'necessary'.[37] A confusion between these two concepts is evident in writers who announce, for example, that the general form of a law of nature is $\Box\forall x(\varphi(x) \rightarrow \psi(x))$, where the $\Box$ represents some kind of nomic or causal necessity.[38]

---

corresponding noun here is 'necessitation'. The term 'apodeictic' is sometimes used to mean *necessitative*, especially in historical discussions, but we avoid it here because it has acquired through such discussions connotations connecting it with the (extraneous) idea of certainty.

[37] A very informative discussion of this question, as answered affirmatively by Descartes, may be found in McFetridge (1990, essay IX), the distinction of current interest coming to the fore especially in pp. 177–9 thereof.

[38] Traces of such a confusion may be found in Burks (1951), for example, and Ayer (1963), as witness the following remarks from p. 229 of the latter work: 'To say that generalizations of law cover possible as well as actual cases is to say that they entail subjunctive conditionals. If it is a law of nature that the planets move in elliptical orbits, then it must not only be true that the actual planets move in elliptical orbits; it must also be true that if anything were a planet it would move in an elliptical orbit . . .'.

The distinction between necessity and necessitativity has also been brought to bear on the fallacious principle that necessary conclusions never follow validly from contingent premises, whose fallaciousness as well as whose widespread endorsement was so well demonstrated in Routley and Routley (1969). With 'necessary' and 'contingent' interchanged, we have a perfectly correct principle, following immediately from the normality rule for $\Box$

$$\vdash (\varphi_1 \wedge \ldots \wedge \varphi_n) \to \psi \text{ implies } \vdash (\Box\varphi_1 \wedge \ldots \wedge \Box\varphi_n) \to \Box\psi.$$

The first $\vdash$-statement here represents the hypothesis that ψ follows from the premises φ_i, and the second that if those premises are all necessary, so is ψ. The principle just described as correct simply weakens the final conclusion that from '$\Box\psi$' to '$\Delta\psi$'. J. Alberto Coffa once pointed out that some of the counter-examples to the incorrect form of the principle suggest a reformulation: that no necessitative conclusions follow validly from premises none of which are themselves necessitative. The reformulation needs considerable refinement (supplied by Coffa in Anderson and Belnap 1975, §21.1.2) and is in any case tailored to the relevant logic $\mathbf{E}$ rather than to anything counting as a modal logic in the sense defined above. A version of the $\Box$ of normal modal logics is definable by taking $\Box\varphi$ as an abbreviation of $(\varphi \to \varphi) \to \varphi$ where the arrow symbolizes not material implication but the entailment connective of $\mathbf{E}$. An example of the idea of changing from necessity to necessitativity is that whereas $\vdash_\mathbf{E} p \to (p \vee \neg p)$, we do not have $\vdash_\mathbf{E} p \to \Box(p \vee \neg p)$. So although an arbitrary statement entails a necessary statement ($\Box(p \vee \neg p)$ being provable in $\mathbf{E}$), the corresponding necessitative statement is not entailed. Such a move is, however, of no help in the context of normal modal logics, in any of which a formula φ provably implies any provable ψ (including, as in the present case, $\psi = \Box(\varphi \vee \neg\varphi)$). A suggestion of a different kind which may turn out to be more useful for normal modal logics is tentatively developed in Humberstone (1982), for the special case of $\mathbf{S5}$.[39]

Advocates of conventionalist and "divine command" theories of necessity often end up endorsing the claim that nothing is necessarily necessary (and a non-normal modal logic in which $\Diamond\Diamond p$ is provable (such as the system S7 mentioned in Hughes and Cresswell 1968: 269)), rather than the claim that whatever is necessary is necessarily so (and the logic $\mathbf{S4}$), though it is unclear why the conventions or divine decisions that supposedly confer necessity on propositions should not do so

---

The first sentence here says that the content of a law entails certain subjunctive conditionals, which is not substantiated by the second sentence, according to which it is rather the content of the claim that something *is* a law that entails the conditionals in question.

[39] The notion of globality, or more specifically the corresponding "one-sided" property of being globally true in that paper seems close to the proposed explication of necessity in Nozick (2001: 129) not as truth in all accessible worlds but of "indigenous" truth in all accessible worlds. (On the other hand, it may be that the best treatment of Nozick's ideas lies in the framework of two-dimensional modal logic—something not within the ambit of the present survey.)

for propositions that are already necessitative. It should also be noted that conventionalist arguments against the existence of truths of the form $\Box\Box p$ typically involve giving a different interpretation to the two $\Box$-substatements (for a fuller discussion, see Pap 1958, ch. 5, §.D), suggesting that perhaps the serious contenders here are **S4** and some non-normal alternative in which not only $\Diamond\Diamond p$ but $\Diamond p$ itself is provable (Mortensen 1989).[40] Salmon (1986, 1989) has objections to **S4** which seem to have more to do with the Sorites Paradox than with anything distinctly modal—for a fuller expression of which reaction, see Forbes (1992). And finally, we add that C. I. Lewis himself felt that **S4** was too strong, objecting even to the weaker (non-normal) logic S3 on the grounds that, symbolizing strict implication here by means of '$\rightarrow$' (i.e. writing $\varphi \rightarrow \psi$ for $\Box(\varphi \rightarrow \psi)$), the suffixing principle

$$(p \rightarrow q) \rightarrow ((q \rightarrow r) \rightarrow (p \rightarrow r))$$

these logics endorse was implausible for an construal of $\rightarrow$ as representing entailment. This objection, which may be found in Lewis and Langford (1959: 496), is clearly of a piece with the 'ultra-relevantist' considerations of Routley *et al.* (1982), in pp. 269–78 of which the objection is elaborated. Clearly, the point has nothing to do with the merits of (S3 or) **S4** as an alethic modal logic, and concerns the correct formalization of an entailment-expressing connective. (Recall, from any historical account of modal logic, that Lewis was only interested in necessity and possibility for their role in the definition of strict implication, his favoured candidate for such a connective.)

The status of **S4** and **S5** as serious contenders for the logic of alethic modality is not mirrored by their status as suitable epistemic logics. For this interpretation of $\Box$, the principle **5** has little to commend in (see especially Lenzen 1978: 179),[41] and even **4** (though, by contrast with **5**, defended in Hintikka 1962) has come in for serious criticism (e.g. in Lemmon 1967; Williamson 1992). If we are prepared to make such idealizations as seem involved in regarding epistemic logic as a normal modal logic at all—setting worries about logical omniscience aside, then—the status of **T** is not in question, so we have at least **KT**. But for the doxastic and deontic interpretations, we must clearly jettison this principle, and **D** and **U** have been proposed as suitable weakenings—both being provable in **KT**, with **T** not provable in **KD** or **KU** (or indeed **KDU**). For the deontic case, we remark that on pain of having to construe the negation signs differently before and after the $\Box$ in the consequent of **D** (which consequent appears, recall, in primitive notation, as '$\neg\Box\neg p$'), it is best to take $\Box$ in this application as a sentence operator rather than a predicate of act

---

[40] Likewise Nozick (2001: 120): 'I shall maintain that there are no interesting and important metaphysical necessities. Moreover, I attempt to formulate a position according to which even logical and mathematical truths are not, at the most basic level, ontological necessities.'

[41] For a contrasting view, see Halpern (1996, sect. 1).

types; how the latter approach (favoured in von Wright's early work) would cope with **U** at all is far from clear.[42] For the doxastic interpretation, **D** amounts to a consistency assumption on the believing subject. (One might wish to distinguish the seriously inconsistent believer who believes, for some φ, the internally inconsistent $\varphi \wedge \neg \varphi$, from the moderately inconsistent subject believing nothing of this form but believes φ and also believes $\neg\varphi$. Because of the regularity of normal modal logics, this distinction cannot be sustained in the setting of doxastic logics as normal—making room for complaints analogous to those of Schotch and Jennings 1981a, mentioned above, for the deontic case.)

Returning to a theme from Sections 2 and 3, let us note that for normal modal logics extending **KT**, we can usefully extend Blanché's Hexagon to an Octagon, interposing a new point between that occupied by $\Box\varphi$ and that occupied by $\Diamond\varphi$ on the left-hand side, to be occupied by φ *simpliciter*, with a similar interpolating point on the right-hand side for $\neg\varphi$. Thus again, diagonals link contradictories; arrows run downward on the left and right sides of this octagon. (A quite different octagon of opposition will be considered in Appendix 20.2.) To apply the transformations of Figure 20.2, we can think of φ as represented by the application of the identity truth-function, represented, say, by 'It is the case that————'. As with the top and bottom points added in extending Figure 20.1 to a hexagon, a degenerate situation arises for those transformations here. While in that case we saw that π coincided with ι (and thus also δ with ν), in the present instance π coincides with ν (and thus δ with ι). One may be inclined to read the current additions as 'Actually φ' and 'Actually $\neg\varphi$', so as to have a modally flavoured sentence adverb interposed between 'Necessarily' and 'Possibly', but a discussion of the logical behaviour of this particular adverb—which may seem, like 'it is the case that', to be a mere redundancy until one considers its effect within the scope of a $\Box$ or $\Diamond$—would take us too far afield (into the realm of 'two-dimensional modal logic') to justify its inclusion in the present survey (see Forbes 1985, ch. 4, §5; 1989, ch. 2, §3; Humberstone 2004

---

[42] Concerning **U** as a deontic principle, Prior (1962: 229), writes that 'it was originally suggested to me by Mrs. J. F. Bennett (in 1953 or 1954) as an example of a synthetic *a priori* proposition.' As a doxastic principle, **U** may seem to ignore the lessons of the preface paradox (Makinson 1965); a discussion of this issue would perhaps be the better for the introduction of propositional quantifiers—not undertaken here—so that we could distinguish between $\forall p\Box(\Box p \rightarrow p)$ and $\Box\forall(p(\Box p \rightarrow p)$. A similar distinction is made in Kenny (1966) apropos of what he calls the boulomaic application modal logic—reading '$\Box$' as 'the subject desires that . . . '. Such quantifiers are not part of our official formal language but we shall have occasion to make informal use of them from time to time. Naturally one has to be careful about their scope. For example, in Hughes and Cresswell (1996: 139) we read a purported explanation of the presence of the principle (= **W**) $\Box(\Box p \rightarrow p) \rightarrow \Box p$ in the modal logic of (formal) provability as follows: 'One way of interpreting one of Gödel's incompleteness theorems is that if you could prove the consistency of arithmetic, which might be described by saying that you could prove that whatever is provable is true, i.e., $\Box(\Box p \rightarrow p)$, then you could prove anything, $\Box p$.' But what this gloss would bear on is at best $\forall p\Box(\Box p \rightarrow p) \rightarrow \forall p\Box p$ or $\Box\forall p (\Box p \rightarrow p) \rightarrow \forall p\Box p$, whereas what **W** with explicit quantification requires is rather $\forall p(\Box(\Box p \rightarrow p) \rightarrow \Box p)$. (Cresswell's notation altered in the quotation to match our own.)

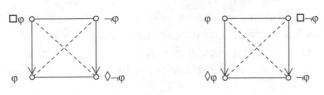

FIG. 20.6. Further spurious squares

surveys some applications of special interest to the author; references to further work may be found in all these sources). We should note that if the original Square of Opposition—rather than Blanché's Hexagon—is extended by such additional points, then we get another Hexagon of Opposition, whose syllogistic incarnation was unveiled in Czeżowski (1955).[43] Like Blanché, Czeżowski claims that two further perfectly legitimate squares of opposition (aside from the traditional square) may be extracted from this hexagon: see Figure 20.6.

As in Figure 20.4, the first square depicted in Figure 20.6 keeps the upper left and lower right positions (*a* and *o*) of Figure 20.1 (the traditional version) intact, varying the other two positions, while the second square retains the upper right and lower left (*e* and *i*) positions while hiring out the remaining two positions to new occupants. Czeżowski gives a syllogistic–quantificational version of these squares, as does Simons (1993: 116) for the first of them, who, unlike Czeżowski and Blanché, shares the view urged above that despite the verdict of the Simple Semantic Account of (sub)contrariety, the imputation of spuriousness is correct. It seems preferable, as already remarked, to replace this account with something more demanding, and the discussion above (as well as below, in Appendices 20.1 and 20.2) aimed at making such replacement seem attractive applies no less in the present case, *mutatis mutandis*.

The first time people started talking about 'normal' modal logics, that appellation did not have its current sense. The term is used only for normal (in the current sense) extensions of **KT** in Kripke (1963), rather than for all normal logics, thus excluding not only, for example, **KD**, but also **K** itself—named after Kripke because it is the weakest logic to which the (simplest form of the) Kripke semantics for modal logic applies. (A brief review of this semantics follows shortly.) The ability of this semantics to arrange for the validation of **T**, although the latter may appear to be a fundamental modal principle, turns out to be a matter of imposing a condition on the accessibility relations of the models this semantic framework supplies, whereas such aspects of $\Box$ as its distributing over conjunction are ineradicably built into that framework. Even more unwisely, some early writers on modal logic (see Lemmon 1959; Anderson 1958, 1966) demanded of a normal modal logic that converse of **T** should *not* be provable. It is much more convenient to avoid any

---

[43] We are not here concerned with the details of Czeżowski's proposals for syllogistic; see Mackie (1958).

such "negative" conditions, so that for any set of formulas there is always such a thing as the smallest normal modal logic containing all formulas in the set. (For example, this means that the normal modal logics form a lattice under inclusion: with conditions requiring unprovability, the required lattice joins need not exist.)

5. KRIPKE SEMANTICS

The ideas underlying the use in the pre-Kripkean period of modal logic of algebraic and matrix methods for showing the unprovability of this or that formula in this or that logic were pretty clearly those made explicit by Kripke in presenting his model-theoretic semantics in the late 1950s and early 1960s. (See Kripke 1967 and the reference there to the work of Jónsson and Tarski. Historical information about the development of possible worlds semantics may be found in Bull and Segerberg 1984, pt. I; 2001; and Copeland 1996, 1999, 2002; as well as Simons 2001. The essential reconceptualization of the matrix elements—from being thought of as generalized truth-values to being thought of as distributions of ordinary truth-values over a space of possibilities, is evident in Prior 1955. A more technical history of the subject, including the relationship of algebraic and model-theoretic semantics, is provided by Goldblatt 2003.) Most people were delighted—Fleischer (1984) providing a striking exception—at the readily visualizable models that emerged, and the connection between antecedently familiar conditions on binary relations and various historically significant modal logics. The relations in question are the second ingredients in the notion of a model $\mathcal{M}$ as a triple $\langle U, R, V \rangle$ in which U is a non-empty set on which R is a binary relation (the 'accessibility relation' of the model) and V is a function assigning to each propositional variable a subset of U. The latter can be thought of as a stipulation on the part of $\mathcal{M}$ as to the set of elements of U—themselves to be thought of as possible worlds or perhaps instead, with the tense-logical interpretation of $\square$ in mind, as moments of time—verifying a given variable. In the interests of neutrality between these and yet further informal glosses, the elements of U will be referred to simply as points. The general notion of truth for an arbitrary formula φ at $u \in U$ relative to the model $\mathcal{M} = \langle U, R, V \rangle$ (notated '$\mathcal{M}\vDash$) φ' is then defined inductively by setting this to hold in the case of $\varphi = p_i$ just in case $u \in V(p_i)$, for $\varphi = \top$ (always (i.e. regardless of u), for $\varphi = \bot$, never, and for Boolean compounds by following the usual truth-table recipe, i.e. $\mathcal{M} \vDash_u \varphi_1 \vee \varphi_2$ just in case $\mathcal{M} \vDash_u \varphi_1$ or $\mathcal{M} \vDash_u \varphi_2$, etc. The parameter u comes to life with the inductive clause for $\square$ (i.e. the case in which φ is $\square \psi$, for some formula ψ), for which we require $\mathcal{M} \vDash_u \square \psi$ just in case for all $v \in U$ such that Ruv, we have $\mathcal{M} \vDash_v \psi$. (Given the way we defined $\Diamond$, a similar clause follows for the case of $\Diamond\psi$, with 'some' replacing 'all'.) Thus if we are thinking of □ as representing, for example, nomic necessity, *Ruv* can be thought of as holding when no natural laws of *u* are violated in *v*, and so be read as saying that *v* is nomically possible relative to *u*; if we have the tense-logical interpretation of □ mentioned above in mind (□φ as 'It will always be that φ'), then *Ruv* amounts to: the moment *u* is earlier than the moment *v*; and so on. The general idea is simply that while we want to interpret □, when considering the truth-value of a formula □φ at *u*, as demanding the truth of φ at each of a set of points, we want to allow this set to vary with the choice of *u*, so we need a function *f* to assign to each *u* a set of points *f(u)*, φ's truth at each of which is necessary and sufficient for the truth of □φ. But such functions are informationally equivalent to binary relations, since given *f* we may define *Ruv* iff $v \in f(u)$, and given *R* we may define $f(u) = \{v|Ruv\}$. In fact, to avoid a proliferation of new letters, we shall sometimes denote the latter set by *R(u)*.

A modal logic **S** is *sound* with respect to a class of models when every formula provable in the logic is true throughout (= at every point in) every model in the class, *complete* w.r.t. a class of models when every formula true throughout every model in the class is provable in the logic, and *determined by* a class of models when it is sound and complete w.r.t. that class. Then it turns out that every consistent normal modal logic is determined by some class of models, and indeed—*inter alia*—by some class containing just one model, making that model a *characteristic* model for the logic. (The canonical models for consistent normal modal logics, as explained in any modal logic text published after 1970, are such characteristic models. A brief and pleasant introduction to this topic may be found in the survey article Cresswell 2001 §7.1.3.) More interestingly formulated results speak of a large class of models, and include the fact that **K** is determined by the class of all models, **KT** by the class of all models with reflexive accessibility relations, **K4** by the class of all models with transitive accessibility relations, **S4** by the class of all models with transitive reflexive accessibility relations, and **S5** by the class of all models whose accessibility relations are equivalence relations, as well as by the following proper subclass thereof: the class of models $\langle U, R, V \rangle$ in which *R* is the universal relation on *U*.[44] This last variation is included for the sake of those wanting to see □ in terms of truth at all possible worlds, without the encumbrance of an accessibility relation (since for this last class of models, the 'such that *Ruv*' condition, being vacuously satisfied, can be ignored). At the end of the preceding paragraph, I mentioned that for every point *u*, the truth of any formula □φ at *u* depends on the truth of φ throughout a certain set of points temporarily denoted there by *f(u)*. The idea of doing without an accessibility relation

---

[44] While the accessibility relation of the canonical model for **S5** is an equivalence relation, it is not universal, so further work (a consideration of 'generated submodels') is required to extract this further completeness result. For the cases cited earlier, the canonical model construction suffices. Similarly in the case of the axioms listed earlier: the provability of **B, D, 5**, and **U** in a (consistent) normal modal logic guarantees that its accessibility relation is, respectively, symmetric, serial (i.e. satisfies: $\forall u$ $\exists v(Ruv)$), Euclidean (satisfying: $\forall u,v,w(Ruv \rightarrow (Ruw \rightarrow Rvw))$, that is), and enjoys the following weakening of reflexivity: $\forall u,v$ $(Ruv \rightarrow Rvv)$.

amounts to taking f as a constant function returning U as its value. A slight weakening of this idea would amount to requiring f to be a constant function, without the further demand that its value should be U. In this case models can be recast as having the form $\langle U, U_0, V \rangle$ with $U_0 \subseteq U$, with the clause for $\Box$ in the truth definition now saying that $\Box\varphi$ is true at an arbitrary $u \in U$ just in case φ is true at each $v \in U_0$. The logic determined by the class of these models is **K45**—or **KD45**, if we add the further condition that $U_0 \neq \varnothing$.

Results of the type sampled above speak of classes of models—and here we revert to the standard notion of a model as of the form $\langle U, R, V \rangle$—satisfying various conditions, but these conditions never address the V component of the models concerned, so it is natural to reformulate them so as to address not models but instead frames, where the *frame* of the model $\langle U, R, V \rangle$ is simply the pair $\langle U, R \rangle$. Frames give the structural aspects of models, abstracting away from the vicissitudes of the assignment of truth-sets to (in the first instance) the propositional variables. A formula φ is *valid* on a frame $\langle U, R \rangle$ when it is true throughout every model $\langle U, R, V \rangle$ on that frame; we sometimes say that $\langle U, R \rangle$ *validates* φ in this case. (We use 'true' when a fixed V is at issue and 'valid' whenever the notion concerned quantifies over all V—including below, when we consider a local version of validity 'at a point'. This principle is not followed by all. Hughes and Cresswell 1968, 1996, use the phrase 'valid in a model' for 'true throughout a model', and van Benthem 1985 uses 'true' when talking about frames.) Then given a class $\mathbb{C}$ of frames, we say that a modal logic **S** is *sound* w.r.t. $\mathbb{C}$ when every formula provable in **S** is valid on each frame in $\mathbb{C}$, *complete* w.r.t. $\mathbb{C}$ when every formula valid on each frame in $\mathbb{C}$ is provable in **S**, and *determined by* $\mathbb{C}$ when **S** is both sound and complete w.r.t. $\mathbb{C}$ For any class $\mathbb{C}$ of frames the modal logic determined by $\mathbb{C}$ is a normal modal logic. (This is not so for classes of models, since we required closure under Uniform Substitution in our definition of normality.) In this terminology, we can reformulate the completeness results of the previous paragraph, saying, for example, that **KT**, **S4**, and **S5** are determined by the classes of reflexive frames, reflexive transitive frames, and equivalence relational frames respectively, and in the case of **S5** by the class of universal frames. (A frame $\langle U, R \rangle$ is reflexive if R is reflexive, and similarly for transitivity and other properties of binary relations.) But the automatic guarantee of such a result for any consistent normal modal logic is now no longer forthcoming: there are normal modal logics which are not determined by any class of frames. Such Kripke-incomplete logics, as they are called, were first discovered by S. K. Thomason and K. Fine in the 1970s—see Thomason (1972)—since which time many further examples have been described, some of them much simpler (in the sense of having axiomatizations with a few relatively short axioms).[45]

[45] See van Benthem (1979a)—or van Benthem (1985: 72 ff.)—for such an example, further discussed in Hughes and Cresswell (1984: 57–62). A more general discussion of incompleteness may be found in Chagrov and Zakharyaschev (1997, ch. 6). The existence of incomplete logics—indeed logics which are incomplete relative to a much more general possible worlds semantics than the Kripke

A modification, usually going by the name of *general frame*, of the notion of a frame, which incorporates an aspect of the earlier algebraic semantics was introduced to overcome this limitation in the Kripke semantics—every normal modal logic being determined by a class of general frames—but the latter notion is not defined here; for present purposes it suffices to say that general frames come equipped with a set of subsets of U (answering to certain closure conditions corresponding to the various connectives) and are deemed to validate formulas which are true throughout every model in which the propositional variables are restricted to having these distinguished subsets as their truth-sets. (It is these subsets—the candidates for expressible propositions, we might say—that correspond to the elements of the modal algebras.) The focus on (Kripke) frames themselves led to new questions such as the following: calling a class $\mathbb{C}$ of frames *modally definable* when there is a set of modal formulas such that $\mathbb{C}$ is precisely the class of frames on which all formulas in the set are valid, we can ask which classes of frames are modally definable. The class of transitive frames, for example, is modally definable, since a frame is transitive if and only if it validates **4** or, equivalently, if and only if it validates every theorem of **K4**. (Thus we can take either {**4**} or **K4** as a set of formulas which 'modally defines' this class.) I noted above that **S5** is determined by the class of all equivalence relational frames as well as by the class of universal frames. It modally defines the former class, the latter not being modally definable at all.[46]

The distinction between truth throughout a model and validity on a frame is a distinction between notions which both involve all the points of the frame concerned, as opposed to a single point taken by itself. In the terminology of van Benthem (1985), they are *global* as opposed to *local* notions, but as is pointed out there, we also have a corresponding distinction—depending on whether a single valuation V is concerned or all such valuations—at the local level. In the former case, we have the fundamental notion (in terms of which all the rest are defined) of truth at a point in a model. In the latter case we have the notion of the *validity of a formula φ at a point $u \in U$ in the frame* $\langle U, R \rangle$—writing this as '$\langle U, R \rangle \vDash_u \varphi$',

---

semantics under discussion here—lends added interest to completeness results: witness the title (as well as the content) of van Benthem (1984). The apparently contradictory tone conveyed by the title of Routley and Meyer (1976) is explained by the deployment there of a version of the notion of *general frame* mentioned in the following sentence of the text.

[46] Whenever we have two classes of frames determining a single modal logic, the classes cannot both be modally definable. For suppose that **S** is determined by $\mathbb{C}_1$ as well as by a distinct class $\mathbb{C}_2$, and that sets of formulas Γ_1, Γ_2 respectively define these two classes. Then, since every frame in $\mathbb{C}_1$ validates (all formulas in) Γ_1, by the completeness of **S** w.r.t. $\mathbb{C}_1$, $\Gamma_1 \subseteq \mathbf{S}$. Now consider any frame $\langle U, R \rangle \in \mathbb{C}_2$. Since **S** is sound w.r.t. $\mathbb{C}_2$, all theorems of **S**, and thus in particular the formulas Γ_1, are valid on $\langle U, R \rangle$. But since all frames validating Γ_1 lie in $\mathbb{C}_1$, we have $\langle U, R \rangle \in \mathbb{C}_1$. Since $\langle U, R \rangle$ was an arbitrary element of $\mathbb{C}_2$, this shows that $\mathbb{C}_2 \subseteq \mathbb{C}_1$. A similar argument gives the converse inclusion, showing that $\mathbb{C}_1$ and $\mathbb{C}_2$ are not distinct after all. For another application of this 'double determination implies undefinability' point, we may cite **K** as determined by the class of all frames as well as by the class of all irreflexive frames; since the former class is modally definable (by any $\Gamma \subseteq \mathbf{K}$), the latter is not. Much further information about modal definability may be found in van Benthem (1985).

meaning by this that $\langle U, R, V \rangle \vDash_u \varphi$ for all V (i.e. for all V such that $\langle U, R, V \rangle$ is a model). In such a case φ owes its truth at u in a model not at all to the vagaries of point-relative truth-value assignments (supplied by V) but to u's structural position in the frame. For example, in a frame $\langle U, R \rangle$, $\Box p \leftrightarrow p$ is valid at all those points u for which $R(u) = \{u\}$, and $\Diamond\Box\bot$ at all those u for which there exists v with Ruv and $R(v) = \varnothing$. In both cases, the 'all those' can be strengthened to 'all and only those', revealing room for a localized version of the earlier notion of modal definability. (An extensive discussion of the two versions is provided by van Benthem 1985.) The second of the examples just given is a case of a formula which can be valid at a point in a frame but cannot be valid on a frame, since the promised "end-point" v cannot itself satisfy the condition—bearing R to an end-point—imposed on u. This formula is one disjunct of a disjunction, the other being $\Box\bot$ true at exactly the end-points, the disjunction itself giving the tense logic of "ending time", i.e. the logic determined by the class of frames in which each point is either an end-point or bears R to (sc.'is earlier than') some end-point (Prior 1967, ch. 4, §6). (One may of course wish to add this disjunction as an axiom to others already securing completeness w.r.t. the class of strict linear orders.) I have slipped into speaking of $\Box\bot$ as being true at the end-points, rather than valid at them. Call any formula which contains no propositional variables (and thus is built up from $\top$ and $\bot$ by means of the Boolean connectives and $\Box$) a *pure* formula. Clearly for such formulas, the distinction between truth at a point in a model and validity at that point in the frame of the model comes to nothing (since V makes no contribution to settling the formula's truth-value). We use the notion introduced in Section 4 of the **S**-equivalence of formulas φ, ψ (holding when $\vdash_S \varphi, \leftrightarrow \psi$), and we shall say that φ has the *local truth-to-validity property* when for all models $\langle U, R, V \rangle$, and all $u \in U, \langle U, R, V \rangle \vDash_u \varphi$ implies $\langle U, R \rangle \vDash_u \varphi$. Then what has just been said gives the 'if' direction of the following, which is a minor variation on Theorem 1.14.5 in Goldblatt (1993: 55).

> *Observation* 1. A formula φ has the local truth-to-validity property if and only if φ is **K**-equivalent to some pure formula.

A proof of (the 'only if' half of) Observation 1 may be found in Appendix 20.3 below. That proof reveals that any φ with the local truth-to-validity property is **K**-equivalent to the result—itself a pure formula—of substituting any pure formulas for the propositional variables in φ. To illustrate this, consider the formula $\Box p \to \Diamond p$ (alias **D**). By rewriting this as $\Diamond \neg p \lor \Diamond p$ and then back-distributing the $\Diamond$, we obtain $\Diamond(\neg p \lor p)$ and thus evidently the pure formula $\Diamond\top$. This equivalent may be obtained by the methods of substitutions just indicated by substituting either $\top$ or $\bot$ for p in **D**. In the former case, we get $\Box\top \to \Diamond\top$ with a **K**-provable, and thus detachable, antecedent, while in the latter we obtain $\Box\bot \to \Diamond\bot$ with a **K**-refutable consequent and thus with $\neg\Box\bot$ as a truth-functional consequence, again rewritable as $\Diamond\top$. More exotic substitutions, e.g. $\Diamond\Box\bot$ for p, are all **K**-equivalent to this; for the case just mentioned we get $\Box\Diamond\Box\bot \to \Diamond\Diamond\Box\bot$, for which case we invite the reader to check the claimed equivalence.

The set of all formulas valid at a given point $u \in U$ in a frame $\langle U, R \rangle$ is a modal logic, since it includes all tautologies and is closed under *modus ponens*—this rule preserving truth at a point in a model and so *a fortiori* validity at a point in a frame—as well as Uniform Substitution (this being a rule which preserves validity at a point but not truth at a point). Indeed, such a set of formulas includes not only all truth-functional tautologies but also all the theorems of **K**, though it is in general not a normal modal logic since there is no guarantee of closure under Necessitation. (The validity of φ at u does not secure the validity of $\Box\varphi$, since the latter requires that φ be valid at each $v \in R(u)$. A trap for the unwary lurks here: while $\Box\varphi$ is valid at a point just in case φ is valid at each of that point's R-successors, it is *not* the case for arbitrary φ that $\Diamond\varphi$ is valid at a point just in case φ is valid at at least one of that point's R-successors. See note 50 for a counter-example.)

There is an additional property of considerable significance possessed by the modal logics **S** comprising the formulas valid at a given point in a frame, namely their *Halldén-completeness*, by which is meant that for all formulas φ, ψ with no propositional variable in common, whenever $\vdash_S \varphi \vee \psi$, we have $\vdash_S \varphi$ or $\vdash_S \psi$. Thus the (normal modal) logic determined by a frame $\langle U, R \rangle$ (i.e. strictly speaking, by $\{\langle U, R \rangle\}$) is "homogeneous" in the sense that the same formulas are valid at each $u \in U$, must be Halldén-complete. This sufficient condition is not necessary, however, so for a more informative statement we introduce the following concept. A frame $\langle U, R \rangle$ is *strongly heterogeneous* if there exist U_1, U_2 with $U = U_1 \cup U_2$, and formulas φ_1, φ_2, with φ_1 valid (in $\langle U, R \rangle$) at each point in U_1 though not at each point in U_2, and φ_2 valid at each point in U_2 though not at each point in U_1. (I add 'strongly' because this is stronger than a mere failure of homogeneity in the sense just introduced. The 'though not at' parts of the definition impose the further requirement that neither U_1 nor U_2 is empty.) The 'ending time' frames described above, for instance, provide U_1 and U_2 as the set of non-end-points and the set of end-points, with φ_1, φ_2, as respectively $\Diamond\Box\bot$ and $\Box\bot$. In this case, we have $U_1 \cap U_2 \neq \varnothing$, though that is not required by the general definition. The same division into U_1 and U_2 described here works for any frame containing points with and points without R-successors, though only the weaker formula $\Diamond\top$ (rather than the $\Diamond\Box\bot$ just used) is in general guaranteed to play the φ_1 role. (Thus **K**, being determined by a frame—e.g. the frame of its canonical model—meeting this condition, is also Halldén-incomplete.) In general, there is no guarantee that $\varphi1$ and φ_2 are pure formulas,[47] so from the existence of a strongly heterogeneous frame determining **S**, to obtain a disjunction $\varphi \vee \psi$ witnessing the Halldén-incompleteness of **S**, we take

---

[47] A ready supply of cases in which the disjuncts are not equivalent to pure formulas can be obtained from the observation that where M_1 and M_2 are any distinct strings of occurrences of $\Box$ and $\Diamond$, the smallest normal modal logic in which $(M_1 p \wedge M_2 p) \rightarrow p$ is provable proves the disjunction $(M_1 p \rightarrow p) \vee (M_2 q \rightarrow q)$, often without proving either disjunct—thus making for Halldén-incompleteness. Examples and variations on this theme may be found in Humberstone (1985).

φ as φ_1 and ψ as the result of substituting new variables for those in φ_2 which have occurrences in φ. This is as much as needs to be said for the proof of

> *Observation* 2. If a normal modal logic **S** is determined by a frame $\langle U, R \rangle$, then **S** is Halldén-incomplete if and only if $\langle U, R \rangle$ is strongly heterogeneous.

Observation 2 pertains only to normal modal logics, whereas Halldén's original discussion (Halldén 1951) attempted to cast doubt on the semantic tractability especially of certain non-normal logics. A further restriction is that it also addresses only the Kripke-complete normal modal logics. But what may seem to be a tighter restriction yet—namely that, from among the logics determined by classes of frames, only those determined by at least one such class of cardinality 1 are considered—is not an additional restriction: if **S** is determined by any class of frames $\mathbb{C}$, then **S** is determined by a single frame. To obtain this from $\mathbb{C}$, simply take for each non-theorem of **S**, a copy—different copies for different non-theorems—of one frame in $\mathbb{C}$ invalidating that formula, and then consider the union, in the obvious sense, of these (at most countably many) frames as a single frame in its own right (this is Lemma 6.5 in van Benthem 1985). This ('disjoint union' as it is called) construction is important for our present theme in another respect too, since, intuitively, failures of homogeneity may arise not only within a frame (from point to point) but also between frames. For example, one might be convinced that moments of time are either all arranged like the integers (with $<$) or like the real numbers (with $<$), but not sure which. Each of these frames is homogeneous, but each frame validates a formula not valid on the other, so the logic determined by the pair is Halldén-incomplete. But this case does fall under the ambit of Observation 2 after all, since the disjoint union of the two frames, though not a natural object of interest in its own right, determines the same logic and is strongly heterogeneous. More information on the intriguing topic of Halldén-completeness may be gathered from Hughes and Cresswell (1968: 268– 72), Schumm (1993), and Chagrov and Zakharyaschev (1997, ch. 15), all of which supply copious references to earlier discussions.

Observation 1 addressed what we called the local truth-to-validity property. We could consider also a corresponding *global truth-to-validity property*, possessed by a formula φ just in case for all models $\langle U, R, V \rangle$, $\langle U, R, V \rangle \vDash \varphi$ implies $\langle U, R \rangle \vDash \varphi$. Here the two notations respectively mean that φ is true throughout the model in question and that φ is valid on the frame of that model. The analogue of Observation 1 would fail in this case, in particular in its 'only if' direction. To see this, recall that we gave (the pure formula) $\Diamond\Box\bot$ as an example of a formula which can be valid at a point in a frame but which cannot be valid on any frame. In view of our Observation, we can equally well see this as an example of a formula which can be true at a point in a model but cannot be true throughout a model. But other examples of the latter phenomenon fail to qualify as examples of the former, a well-known case being that of the formula $p \wedge \neg\Box p$. Since this formula can never be true throughout a model, it vacuously possesses the global truth-to-validity property: but it is not hard to see that no formula in which p does not occur can be **K**-equivalent to this formula, and in particular, no pure formula can be; thus 'local' cannot be replaced by 'global' in the above Observation. This is hardly surprising, however, since the notion of **K**-equivalence deployed there is itself a local notion, holding between two formulas when they are true at precisely the same points in an arbitrary model. The global analogue of this relation is that holding between two formulas when they are true throughout the same models, which can be given a syntactic formulation, using the following concept. Let us say that ψ is $\Box$-*derivable* from φ in **S** if there exist $k_1, \ldots, k_m$ $(k_i \geq 0)$ for which:

$$\vdash_S (\Box^{k_1} \varphi \wedge \ldots \wedge \Box^{k_m} \varphi) \rightarrow \psi.$$

(Here the superscript in '$\Box^k$' indicates k occurrences of '$\Box$'.) If each of φ, ψ, is $\Box$-derivable from the other in **S**, we call these formulas $\Box$-*interderivable* in **S**.

> *Observation* 3. A formula φ has the global truth-to-validity property if and only if φ is $\Box$-interderivable in **K** with some pure formula.

A proof of Observation 3 can be obtained from that supplied in Appendix 20.3 for Observation 1, supplemented by a verification that formulas $\Box$-interderivable in **K** are true throughout the same models. (The technical literature on modal logic also contains discussions of formulas whose validity on a general frame meeting this or that further condition guarantees its validity on the underlying Kripke frame—e.g. Goldblatt 1993: 53 ff., 73 ff. on "d-persistent" and "r-persistent" formulas.)

Our recent example, $p \wedge \neg\Box p$, of a formula which can be true at a point (though, unlike the earlier example of $\Diamond\Box\bot$, it cannot be valid at a point) but cannot be true throughout a model provides us with an opportunity to supplement the remarks above about the preservation characteristics of some fundamental rules. Just as *modus ponens* preserves truth at a point in a model and Uniform Substitution preserves validity at a point in a frame, so Necessitation preserves truth-throughout-a-model. (We hyphenate to avert a potential ambiguity.) As with the first two rules, we can add for Necessitation 'and *a fortiori* preserves validity on a frame'. The (stronger) claim made here for Necessitation, that any model throughout which φ is true is a model throughout which $\Box\varphi$ is also true, implies that no formula of the form $\varphi \wedge \neg\Box\varphi$ is true throughout any model, since this would mean that its first conjunct was, and hence that the Necessitation of that conjunct was, which contradicts the second conjunct. (However, one should not go away with the idea that whenever no model verifies $\varphi \wedge \neg\psi$, for a particular choice of φ, ψ, then every model verifying φ verifies ψ. For a counter-example, vary the earlier case of $p \wedge \neg\Box p$ by putting $\varphi = \neg\Box p$ and $\psi = \neg p$.) We can make a more 'localized' version of the claim that Necessitation preserves truth throughout a model $\langle U, R, V \rangle$ by saying that for each point $u \in U$, this rule preserves truth throughout the *environment* of u, where this is defined to be $R(u) \cup \{u\}$. Now a formula ψ is true throughout u's environment precisely when $\psi \wedge \Box\psi$ is true at u. Thus we can recycle the earlier observation that no formula of the form $\varphi \wedge \neg\Box\varphi$ can be true throughout a model—reformulated now in terms of truth throughout an arbitrarily selected point's environment—to give: no formula $\psi \wedge \Box\psi$ can be true at a point when ψ itself has the form $\varphi \wedge \neg\Box\varphi$. Of course this is easily seen syntactically, and it needs only that $\Box$ is monotone according to the background logic (so it could be replaced by $\Diamond$ in a normal modal logic, and the semantic gloss just given would no longer be apposite): for $\psi \wedge \Box\psi$ in the case envisaged is $(\varphi \wedge \neg\Box\varphi) \wedge \Box(\varphi \wedge \neg\Box\varphi)$, giving a contradiction when we conjoin the $\neg\Box\varphi$ of the first conjunct with the $\Box\varphi$ provided, thanks to monotony, by the second. Simple as this consideration is, it underlies a considerable number of philosophical problems, as was shown in Sorensen (1988). For example, with a doxastic interpretation of $\Box$ we have a diagnosis of Moore's Paradox—$\varphi \wedge \neg\Box\varphi$ cannot be both true and believed (by the subject in question) to be true—while with an epistemic reading, Fitch's Paradox[48] is the relevant application: the conjunction cannot be known (we need not say: be both true and known, assuming **T** for this reading[49]). For the latter application we have in mind the impersonal notion 'it is known by someone or other that', so the point about monotony is relevant: regularity fails for this interpretation.

The rule of Uniform Substitution, which, as mentioned above, preserves validity on a frame because it preserves, for an arbitrary point in a frame, validity at that point, is familiar from non-modal (propositional) logic, but in the latter setting, the rule admits of a generalization not available for normal modal logics. Since the failure of this generalized rule in modal logic (in the sense that not all normal modal logics are closed under the rule) lends many issues in a modal logic a distinctive flavour, the generalization seems worth giving here. (It does not seem to have found its way into the literature.) We say that a logic (in some propositional language, including $\wedge$ among its connectives) **S** is *closed under Internal Uniform Substitution* when the following condition is satisfied for all m. For any formulas $\chi_1, \ldots, \chi_m$ of the language of **S** and any $\varphi \in \mathbf{S}$ with a subformula ψ (possibly occurring several times) such that some propositional variable p_i whose only occurrences in φ lie within ψ, we have $\varphi(\psi') \in \mathbf{S}$, where $\varphi(\psi')$ is the result of replacing occurrences of ψ in φ by ψ', the latter being $\psi(\chi_1) \wedge \ldots \wedge \psi(\chi_m)$, $\psi(\chi_j)$ being the result of substituting χ_j for p_i uniformly in ψ. The term 'internal' is used here to emphasize that ψ can be a proper subformula of φ. For the case in which ψ just is φ, then $\varphi(\psi')$ is the conjunction of various substitution instances of φ, and so we have this

---

[48]   This is discussed in Sorensen (1988). An especially informative treatment is provided by Rabinowicz and Segerberg (1994). Note that Fitch's Paradox is essentially a bimodal matter, involving knowledge and (logical) possibility. For the formal points as they bear on Moore's Paradox, see Smiley (1963: 132). (We have in mind the "standard" interpretation of Moore's Paradox here—cf. Williams 1979.)

[49]   Indeed for the doxastic reading, given a suitably strong logic $\Box(\varphi \wedge \neg\Box \varphi)$ will already be inconsistent, without the need for the other conjunct, $\varphi \wedge \neg\Box\varphi$; any monotone logic proving $\Box p \rightarrow \Diamond\Box p$ will do.

special case whenever **S** is closed under both Uniform Substitution (as standardly understood) and the formation of conjunctions. The 'Internal' version of Uniform Substitution allows for the replacement even of subformulas (e.g. in the scope of ¬) by such a conjunction, provided that all occurrences of the variable substituted for are confined to the subformula in question.

> *Observation* 4. Classical propositional logic is closed under Internal Uniform Substitution, while in general normal modal logics are not.

The first half of the claim is proved in Appendix 20.3, and **KT** can be pressed into service to illustrate its second half here. Take as our counter-example the case in which $m = 2, \chi_1 = p \ (= p_1), \chi_2 = q \ (= p_2), \varphi = \Diamond p \rightarrow \Box p)$. This formula is provable in **KT**, as one may see using Kripke models or alternatively by a syntactic transformation (reformulate the implication as a disjunction and distribute the $\Diamond$ across). Indeed, we have already entertained the relevant considerations in the discussion after Observation 3: no formula of the "Moorean" $\varphi \wedge \neg \Box \varphi$ form, including in particular $p \wedge \neg \Box p$, can be true throughout a point's environment. But in a reflexive frame the environment of u, defined as $R(u) \cup \{u\}$, coincides with $R(u)$, so $\Box(p \wedge \neg \Box p)$ is false throughout any model on such a frame, and its negation—which we can rewrite as $\Diamond(p \rightarrow \Box p)$—is accordingly **KT**-provable. Closure under Internal Substitution then requires, when ψ is the subformula $p \rightarrow \Box p$, and the i of our characterization of this requirement above is taken as 1, that $\Diamond((p \rightarrow \Box p) \wedge (q \rightarrow \Box q))$ should be provable in **KT**. But the latter formula is not even **S5**-provable, as is revealed by taking a model with two points accessible to themselves and each other with p true at one and q at the other.[50] There is, incidentally, a feature of this example—setting to one side the issues about Internal Uniform Substitution—that might be misunderstood by those unfamiliar with modal logic. One might think that there is no reason to expect the formula

$$\Diamond((p \rightarrow \Box p) \wedge (q \rightarrow \Box q))$$

to be provable simply because each of $\Diamond(p \rightarrow \Box p)$ and $\Diamond(q \rightarrow \Box q)$ is provable, for the same reason that in general $\Diamond(\varphi \wedge \psi)$ does not follow from $\Diamond \varphi$ and $\Diamond \psi$: the existence of separately φ-verifying and ψ-verifying accessible worlds does not imply the existence of a single $(\varphi \wedge \psi)$-verifying such world. The confusion in this reaction is buried in the phrase 'follow from'. The justification given pertains to the local-preservation-of-truth understanding of this phrase, whereas our transition needs

---

[50] The example just given is closely related to the discussion in Lemmon and Scott (1977: 74–6), though the authors do not there highlight any connections with a possible generalization of the Uniform Substitution rule. This example also shows—not unrelatedly—how the validity of a formula $\Diamond \varphi$ at a point in a frame does not imply the validity of φ at some accessible point, since taking φ as $p \rightarrow \Box p$ we have $\Diamond \varphi$ valid at all points in a reflexive frame, even when no points in the frame validate φ (since for a point u to validate φ it is necessary and sufficient that $R(u) \subseteq \{u\}$—a condition we can easily violate in a reflexive frame).

only something more global: preservation of truth throughout any characteristic model for the logic under consideration. In terms introduced in Smiley (1963), we are considering the passage from $\Diamond\varphi$ and $\Diamond\psi$ to $\Diamond(\varphi \wedge \psi)$ as a rule of *proof*, not as a rule of *inference*. (The rule may be found in Bull 1967 to give an extension of **S4**; the conditional

$$\Diamond p \rightarrow (\Diamond q \rightarrow \Diamond(p \wedge q))$$

is certainly not provable in this extension.) In this respect its status would be like that of the rule of Necessitation itself, rather than like the rule *modus ponens*: designed to deliver theorems from theorems, not conclusions from arbitrary assumed premisses. Rules of inference—an informal notion only, given the way we have set matters up—should preserve truth at an arbitrary point in any model in a class of models determining the logic, but the semantic status of rules of proof cries out for articulation against a more sophisticated background than we have made available.[51]

6. REFLECTIONS ON THE SEMANTICS

Is there any significance in the fact that the main examples given above to illustrate the local and global notions of validity were motivated by the tense-logical interpretation of '$\Box$', rather than what would more traditionally be regarded as a

---

[51] Since we have identified modal logics with (certain) sets of formulas, the most that can be asked of a rule of proof is that it should be admissible for a given logic, i.e. that the class of theorems should be closed under the rule. But if, more refinedly, we said that two axiomatizations are axiomatizations of the same modal logic not just when the provable formulas are the same, but also the derivable rules, then we can make the further demand that a certain rule of proof should actually be derivable in the logic in question (cf. Porte 1981). If we take **K** as axiomatized with schemata rather than a rule of Uniform Substitution, but otherwise as described above, then we find that its derivable rules are exactly those that preserve truth throughout $\mathcal{M}$ for each model $\mathcal{M}$. If we add the converse of the rule of Necessitation ("Denecessitation") as a primitive rule, then we get a different logic, on the refined conception, since this rule is admissible but not derivable in **K** as just described. (For admissibility, use Lemmon and Scott 1977, Theorem 3.5, putting $n = 1$; for underivability, observe—e.g. by semantic methods—that **T** is not a theorem of **KU**.) This different logic would be determined in the usual sense by the class of all models but would not be (shall we say?) rule-determined by this class, a failure of "rule-soundness" w.r.t. the class, since Denecessitation does not preserve truth throughout each model. These considerations suggest a modification of the criticism in Schurz (1994) of J. Perzanowski's attempt to argue that what is usually called the modal fallacy (of inferring $\Box\psi$ from $\Box(\varphi{\rightarrow}\psi)$ and φ) is not after all fallacious: it is not so much that necessitation is a merely admissible—i.e. admissible but not derivable—rule, so much as that it is a rule of proof, not a rule of inference.

genuinely modal (which is not to say specifically alethic) interpretation? The following words are taken from Gabbay (1976: 61):

In modal logic we are given the syntactical system that formalizes some notion…and we try to find a convenient class of structures for which the system is complete. In tense logics we are interested in the class of structures and ask, is there a logic X (or a set of axioms) that 'characterizes' this class?

Historically, this is a rough description of the direction of curiosity, though the second question is perhaps better formulated as one of how to axiomatize the logic determined by the given structures.[52] We still have the issue of how to interpret the talk of structures, whether as models or—more naturally no doubt—as frames. A hypothesis about the structure of time is pursued tense-logically by concentrating on a class of frames, perhaps containing only a single frame, and asking what logic is determined by this class. (This represents the hypothesis as being to the effect that instants are related by the earlier–later relation as they are in some frame in the class, the logic determined being correct under that hypothesis.) In certain cases, though, the focus of tense-logical exploration is a hypothesis not in this sense about the structure of time but about its interaction with the course of events, a notable example in this genre being the investigation by Prior (1968) of the issue of whether the passage of time requires the occurrence of change—the latter being essentially a notion at the level of models rather than frames, since we are concerned with the change in the truth-values of statements or formulas from one point to another. Prior suggested that the answer to this question was negative on the grounds that if we consider the normal extension of **K** by the following 'end-of-change' principle:

End-of-Change $\Diamond(\Box p \lor \Box \neg p) \lor \Box \bot$

then we find that the following formula, mentioned above as an axiom for ending time,

End-of-Time $\Diamond \Box \bot \lor \Box \bot$

is not provable in the resulting logic. The simple argument for this unprovability claim is that the result of erasing all tense operators in End-of-Change gives a truth-functional tautology while the result of a similar erasure in End-of-Time does not, from which it follows that the rules defining the class of normal modal logics do not suffice for the deduction of the latter from the former.[53] (Alternatively

---

[52] Here we assume Gabbay means what we mean by 'determines' when he says 'characterizes', rather than 'modally defines', for parity with the modal task—in his description of which 'complete' means 'sound and complete'.

[53] Does this argument involve any confusion as to whether End-of-Change (for example) is the formula $\Diamond(\Box p \lor \Box \neg p) \lor \Box \bot$ or instead the "erased" version $(p \lor \neg p) \lor \bot$? Certainly not—*pace* S. G. Williams (1986, second sentence of §iv). (Williams is actually discussing an earlier version of Prior's argument, involving an error corrected in Prior 1968, though not an error affecting the methodological points made in our discussion or by Williams.)

put: the former is valid on the one-point reflexive Kripke frame while the latter is not, while the rules alluded to preserve validity on an arbitrary frame.) For reasons best not entered into here, End-of-Change involves a considerable complexity, because of its first disjunct (the notoriously troublesome "McKinsey axiom"), so let us consider a much simplified version of the argument, with starting point (a) and terminus (b):

   (a) $\Box p \vee \Box \neg p$
   (b) $\Box\Box\bot$.

(a) says—very roughly—that there will be no changes,[54] while (b) says that an end-point is at most one step of the earlier–later relation away. By the preceding erasure argument, (b) is not derivable from (a), even together with the theorems of **K4**. So by Prior's lights, this would be held to show that even if there are no changes to come, it does not follow that an "end-of-time" is in the offing. However, anyone inclined, for whatever reason, to the view that there can be no (passage of) time without change would not be satisfied with the very liberal notion of a model based on a frame, since this allows models $\langle U, R, V \rangle$ in which although Ruv (for u, $v \in U$) no formula changes in truth-value in the passage from u to v. Let us define an *Aristotelian model* to be one in which this possibility is ruled out. Then whenever a formula $\Diamond\varphi$ is true at a point, there is some formula ψ for which $\neg\psi \wedge \Diamond(\varphi \wedge \psi)$ is true at that same point. (If the formula you first thought of that changed in truth-value from u verifying $\Diamond\varphi$ to the later v verifying φ went from being true to being false rather than vice versa, take ψ as its negation.) Any point verifying $\Diamond\Diamond\varphi$ in an Aristotelian model, then, verifies, for some formulas ψ_0, ψ_1:

   $\neg\psi_0 \wedge \Diamond\psi_0 \wedge \neg\psi_1 \wedge \Diamond(\varphi \wedge \psi_1))$.

Thus, throwing away the first conjunct and some of the rest of the formula, the point verifies

   $\Diamond(\neg\psi_1 \wedge \Diamond\psi_1)$

so if we were dealing with an Aristotelian model on a transitive frame, the point in question verifies

   $\Diamond\neg\psi_1 \wedge \Diamond\psi_1$.

In particular, taking φ as $\top$, our point verifies

   $\Diamond\Diamond\top \rightarrow (\Diamond\neg\psi_1 \wedge \Diamond\psi_1)$.

---

[54] Less roughly: if all substitution instances of (a) are true at a point in a model then at no accessible ("later") point can a formula change its truth-value. With McKinsey's axiom—(a) preceded by $\Diamond$—there is the further question of a distinction *à la* note 58 above between a '$\forall p\Diamond$' and a '$\Diamond\forall p$' reading, as well as the possibility of passing from truth to validity, provided it is validity on a general frame, on which see Thomason (1972, §4).

But the substitution instance of (*a*) which puts ψ_1 for *p* is the negation of the consequent here, giving us the negation of the conclusion, which is **K**-equivalent to (*b*). No one should be talked out of believing that time cannot pass without the occurrence of change on the basis of Prior's argument, then. (Of course, we have not really shown how to implement the strategy of "Aristotelian model theory" deductively. One way would be to add propositional quantification to the object language and the axiom schema $\Diamond\varphi \rightarrow \exists q(\neg q \wedge \Diamond(\varphi \wedge q))$, *q* not occurring in φ.[55] Another might involve instead keeping the language the same but adding what are called 'Gabbay-style rules' after the treatment of Gabbay 1981.[56] We return to the issue of tense-logic versus modal logic ('proper') raised by the above quotation from Gabbay 1976 below.)

While for the most part Gabbay's remarks, quoted above, about modal logic starting with logics and looking for determining classes of structures—by which let us now understand *frames*—by contrast with tense logic starting with classes of structures and looking for the logics determined is borne out by the history of the subject(s), it is worth drawing attention to the interesting exception provided by Pargetter (1984), in which, by contrast with the usual pattern, Pargetter seeks enlightenment as to the appropriate modal logic for $\square$ as nomic necessity, starting with a certain metaphysical conviction which finds expression as a condition on frames. The metaphysical condition is that every possible world has a 'Hume copy' agreeing with it on matters of particular fact but having no natural laws.[57] (Thus one version of Humean inductive scepticism starts with the claim that, however law-governed and non-accidental we might believe the world to be, we are in possession of no evidence that tells us we are in such a world as opposed to its Hume copy—or one of its Hume copies, should we wish to allow for the possibility that there are several; the informal use of the functional notation '$h(u)$' below should not be taken as ruling out this possibility.) At such lawless worlds, the only things that are nomically necessary are the things that are logically necessary: every world is accessible, by the nomic accessibility relation, to the Hume copy, $h(u)$, say, of a world u.[58] And since the course of history in $h(u)$ is as in u, this means that no law

[55] What would be closer to our intentions here would be something involving not only propositional quantification, but another device we are eschewing, namely the back-reference 'actuality' operator A (temporal reading: 'Now'), with whose aid we could write $\square\exists q(q \wedge \neg Aq)$, intending the propositional quantifier to be read substitutionally, say with a substitution class comprising the quantifier-free $\square$-free formulas. The schema in the text says that if φ is true at some later time, then something now false is true alongside φ at some later time—which does not force this to be the *same* later time. Note that we are assuming the accessibility relations for these temporal applications to be irreflexive.

[56] As a matter of historical interest, such a rule appears already in Saito (1966, 1968), figuring non-redundantly in an axiomatization of **K**.

[57] A refinement of this discussion appears in Bigelow and Pargetter (1990: 248 ff.), in which something called a Heimson world replaces the Hume world, but this does not affect the formal developments and will be ignored here.

[58] Note that the logical necessities are included, on this usage, as a special and generally uninteresting case of the nomic necessities. One could, if one wished, take as a primitive operator, an O for which

of u is violated in $h(u)$, since that would mean a law of u was violated in u—something assumed in this discussion to be out of the question. (That is, we assume the axiom **T** for nomic necessity, and correspondingly, that the accessibility relation is reflexive.[59]) This means that to every world u there is nomically accessible a world, $h(u)$, from which all worlds are accessible. Accordingly we call a frame $\langle U, R \rangle$ a *Pargetter frame* when it satisfies the condition which we shall here write as an explicit first-order sentence in the language of such frames (so quantifiers range over U, and we do not distinguish notationally between the relation R and a two-place predicate with that relation as its interpretation):

Par $\forall v \exists w (Rvw \wedge \forall x(Rwx))$.

Thus an appropriate modal logic for nomic necessity will be that determined by the class of reflexive Pargetter frames: we have the research situation Gabbay noted was characteristic of tense logic, starting with a class of structures and looking for (an axiomatization of) the logic determined thereby.[60] We use the notation $R^k xy$ to mean that y can be reached from x in k steps by the relation R (taking this to amount to $x = y$ when $k = 0$), and by a *point-generated* frame mean a frame $\langle U, R \rangle$ with $u \in U$ such that for any $v \in U$, $R^k uv$ for some k. Clearly, the point-generated frames satisfying Par are exactly those satisfying the (in general, less restrictive) condition, for all $i, j \in \mathbb{N}$:

$Par_{i,j}$ $\forall u \forall v (R^i uv \rightarrow \exists w (Rvw \wedge \forall x(R^j ux \rightarrow Rwx)))$.

A simple canonical model argument shows, where **KPar** is the smallest normal modal logic containing, for every $m, n, k_1, \ldots, k_n \in \mathbb{N}$, the formula:

Par $\Diamond^m \Box (\Box^{k_1} p_1 \vee \ldots \vee \Box^{k_n} p_n) \rightarrow (\Box^{k_1} p_1 \vee \ldots \vee \Box^{k_n} p_n)$,

that **KPar** is determined by the class of Pargetter frames. (The point-generated subframes of the canonical frame for this logic satisfy—for all i, j—$Par_{i,j}$, which suffices for the completeness half of this claim, whose soundness half is easily checked.) By standard methods, we get the result that **KTPar** is determined by the class of reflexive Pargetter frames, and is therefore a plausible candidate for the

---

'$O\varphi$' meant that it is nomically but not logically necessary that φ: see Bacon (1981) for this particular exercise in logical gymnastics. One might even hold that it is part of the meaning of such phrases as "nomically necessary"—as opposed to a mere conversational implicature of their use—that the logically necessary be excluded. A similar thought for deontic logic finds expression in Jones and Pörn (1985). (The authors attempt to apply the apparatus developed there to the distinction between *ought* and *must* in Jones and Pörn 1986, but the proposal seems more like a stipulation than a serious analysis of the distinction.)

[59] Montague (1974: 82) rejects **T** for nomic necessity because he is thinking of the laws of some fixed world as determining once and for all what is nomically possible, rather than letting nomic possibility at w depend on the laws of w.

[60] Note that the class of frames satisfying Par is not modally definable, not being closed under disjoint unions.

appropriate logic of nomic necessity. In fact, in the presence of **T**, we can reduce the complexity of the axiom schema **Par**, trading it in for one axiom and a simpler schema:

(1) $\Diamond \Box \Box p \rightarrow \Box \Box p$

(2) $(\Diamond\Diamond p_1 \wedge \ldots \Diamond\Diamond p_n) \rightarrow \Diamond(\Diamond p_1 \wedge \ldots \wedge \Diamond p_n)$

which can be proved in **KPar**, and from which **Par** can be proved when they are added to **KT**. It is this axiomatization of **KTPar** which is mentioned in Pargetter (1984), where G. E. Hughes is credited with having supplied the completeness proof.

Although the above material has been included for the sake of an example running counter to Gabbay's generalization about tense logic and modal logic, we should not leave it without mentioning a further aspect of the situation given prominence in Pargetter (1984) and Bigelow and Pargetter (1990). On the assumption that broadly logical necessity should be interpreted by universal quantification over all worlds, the point of interest is that *Par* has the consequence that any frame satisfying this condition is what Kuhn (1989) calls *two connected*: any world x can be reached from any world v by R^2: by two steps of the relation R, that is. In the present instance, this is because we can get by R from v to a Hume copy $h(v)$—represented in the formal rendering of *Par* by the existentially quantified variable 'w'—and thence by R to x. Thus in terms of our nomically interpreted $\Box$ we have a ready-made representation of broadly logical necessity in the shape of $\Box^2$. For reasons which are not entirely clear, Pargetter (1984) and Bigelow and Pargetter (1990) are happy to say that this provides a reductive analysis of logical necessity in terms of nomic necessity, but unhappy to say that it provides a definition of the former in terms of the latter.[61] Be that as it may, we should observe that two-connectedness is strictly weaker than the condition *Par* above, being obtainable from it by an $\exists\forall$ to $\forall\exists$ move, as is evident from these formulations:

Par $\forall v \exists w \forall x (Rvw \wedge Rwx)$.

Two-Connectedness $\forall v \forall x \exists w (Rvw \wedge Rwx)$.

The class of frames studied in Kuhn (1989) satisfies the weaker two-connectedness condition but not Pargetter's condition, but in models on these frames $\Box^2$ still acts

---

[61] When they speak of a reduction of logical to nomic necessity Bigelow and Pargetter seem to have in mind reduction in the sense of the philosophy of science tradition (reduction of heat to kinetic energy, etc.), and thus not an *a priori* matter, for which reason talk of definition may be out of place. They do say (1990: 249) that the reduction 'requires a metaphysical lemma, namely the accessibility of a Hume or Heimson world corresponding to each lawful world' and is accordingly not 'a purely logical or definitional matter'. But on the previous page the authors have argued it to be a merit of their account that because of the reduction it affords of logical to nomic modality, 'the theory is not committed to a multiplicity of independent, primitive modal concepts, only to the acceptance of a single core modality'. But according to the previously quoted sentiment, the nomic and logical modal concepts do remain definitionally independent.

as a universal quantifier over all points; however, since these points are themselves to be thought of as ordered pairs of possible worlds, rather than as single possible worlds, one should not conclude that this composite operator is construable as representing broadly logical necessity, even if one were antecedently convinced that the appropriate accessibility relation for the latter was the universal relation on any given (point-generated) frame. □ itself is intended to represent a somewhat technical notion of absolute necessity, absolute in the sense of that to which other modal notions (such as nomic accessibility or the obligatoriness of deontic logic) can be treated as relative notions of necessity, as explained in Smiley (1963). Because we are not here covering two-dimensional modal logic—the source of the ordered pairs just mentioned—we leave the interested reader to consult Kuhn (1989) where a complete axiomatization of the logic of absolute necessity may be found.[62] As for the matter of nomic versus broadly logical (alias metaphysical) necessity raised in Pargetter's discussion, it needs to be remarked that while this at one time seemed a very clear distinction, it has become problematic since (especially) Kripke's *Naming and Necessity*, published in 1972 first (Kripke 1980), with a spate of cases of what were previously assumed to be nomically necessary but metaphysically contingent being proposed for reclassification as among the *a posteriori* (metaphysical) necessities whose existence was argued in that work (see Elder 1994 and the works listed in note 1 thereof, for some examples, as well as Shoemaker 1998).

Sometimes what may first present itself as a condition on *models*, making apparently essential reference to the valuation component V thereof, turns out to be equivalent to a condition on *frames*, in the sense that the logic determined by the class of models meeting the former condition is determined by the class of frames meeting the latter. For example, we may be interested in those models in which any two points agree on the truth-values of all □-formulas. The logic determined by this class of models is **K45**, already mentioned above as the logic determined by the class of all (models on) transitive Euclidean frames. (Observation 5(ii) below gives another example.) As well as being complete w.r.t. this class, there is also a more motivationally salient determining class of frames (cf. our earlier discussion), obtained by taking point-generated subframes therefrom: the class of frames $\langle U, R \rangle$ in which $R(u) = R(v)$ for all $u, v \in U$. More interesting conditions involve *conditional* agreement requirements, for example to the effect that if u and v agree on all □-free formulas, they agree on all □-formulas. We can formulate this as a supervenience condition on models, and it appears here as (3) in a list of such conditions. We may wish to require that any model should respect the supervenience

(1) of identity of points on the truth of formulas, or
(2) of identity of points on the truth of atomic formulas, or
(3) of the truth of arbitrary formulas on the truth of atomic formulas.

---

[62] Hale (1996) discusses a different—though somewhat similarly motivated—notion under the name of absolute necessity, picking up a theme from McFetridge (1990, essay VIII).

By (1) and (2) we understand the conditions that $u = v$ whenever points u and v in a model verify the same formulas, or, respectively, the same atomic formulas, and by (3) that points verifying the same atomic formulas verify precisely the same formulas.[63] Since points verifying the same formulas in any given class of formulas automatically verify the same Boolean compounds of such formulas, this formulation is equivalent to that given above, to the effect that agreement on □-free formulas implies agreement on all formulas. And while (2) implies (1), though not (in general) conversely, clearly (1) taken together with (3) has (2) as a consequence. Since any consistent normal modal logic is determined by its canonical model and the points in a canonical model are just sets of formulas which formulas, moreover, are true (in that model) at exactly those points having them as elements, all such logics are determined by a class of models satisfying (1). Let us say that a logic has the *countable model property* when each of its non-theorems is false at some point in a model with countably (= finitely or denumerably) many points. While many normal modal logics lack the (correspondingly understood) finite model property, all such logics have the countable model property, by the construction in Makinson (1966).[64] For these, we can show determination by a class of models satisfying (2), since we can use all the countably many propositional variables not occurring in a non-theorem φ, and change the V of a counter-model to φ so that each of those variables is true at exactly one of the points, without jeopardy to the falsity of φ (at the point in which it was false in the model thus changed).[65] Restricting attention to the class of Aristotelian models we distinguished above involves a step in the direction of requiring distinct points to differ as to what was true at them, but note that we were not advocating such a restriction—only pointing out that it would be a natural restriction to impose for someone who believed that the passage of time required the presence of change.

In fact, most who have commented on this issue see here a radical difference between moments of time and possible worlds, with such a restriction being implausible for the former case and plausible for the latter. For example, Fine (1977: 158) writes

What goes on in a possible world necessarily goes on in that world; indeed the identity of a world is determined by its content. But what goes on at an instant is purely, or largely,

---

[63] The atomic formulas are the nullary connectives ⊤ and ⊥ and the propositional variables p_i.

[64] Note that we are not saying that all normal modal logics have the countable *frame* property, meaning that every non-theorem is invalid on some countable frame for the logic (i.e. frame validating all theorems of the logic). This is far from being the case: see Kracht (1999). (This issue is complicated by the fact that Kracht sometimes uses the term 'model' meaning a *frame for* a particular logic. A similar usage may be found in Thomason 1972.)

[65] We are considering what is sometimes called weak as opposed to strong completeness, throughout. In the latter case, the procedure described here may not be available since there may be no propositional variables 'left over': see Dunn (1973, §3). Dunn is discussing a supervenience condition like that being considered here, under the name 'Supposition that there are no irreducible modal facts', against the background of a variant of the Kripke semantics developed by himself and L. F. Goble.

accidental; the identity of an instant is determined, if at all, by its position in the temporal structure.

This sentiment is endorsed by McGinn (1981: 152);[66] the point is put by Forbes (1985: 77 ff.) in the following terms (à propos of the 'logical space' metaphor):

However, crucial features of places and times which appear to underpin the plausibility of realism about these entities have no parallel in the logical space of possible worlds. For places and times, there is a distinction between the item and its occupier, a material object in the case of a place, and an event in the case of a time.... However, this conception is quite inapplicable to logical space; given a world, one cannot distinguish a location and a content contingently located there, no matter which component one identifies with the world itself.

While there seems to be an intuitive disanalogy roughly along the lines sketched by these writers, there is also an obvious difficulty articulating it clearly. The adverbs 'necessarily' and 'accidentally' in Fine's formulation, and 'contingently' in Forbes's, are (alethic-)modal in force and would need to be replaced by their temporal analogues in the case of times. This spoils the disanalogy, since, to adapt Fine, it is equally true (to the extent—no different from the modal case—that it is intelligible) to say that 'what goes on at an instant always goes on at that instant', and, adapting Forbes, that 'given a time one cannot distinguish a location and a content temporarily located there'. Whatever the correct articulation of the disanalogy may be, one consequence of the existence in the temporal case and the non-existence in the modal case of a distinction, as Forbes puts it, between the item and its occupier is that while we have no difficulty in making sense of the idea of several distinct times at which precisely the same things are the case (one special case of which is the idea of time without change), we have great difficulty in making sense of the idea of there being several distinct worlds at which precisely the same things are the case. Hence the motivation for considering supervenience conditions such as (1) and (2). However, in view of the ease with which it was shown above that restricting attention to models satisfying those conditions makes no difference to the logic determined, we should probably conclude that an appropriate formal rendering has yet to be found of the idea that possible worlds are not to be thought of, like moments of time, as vehicles for what goes on in them.

The condition (3) which played a merely ancillary role in the above discussion is susceptible of several variations that are not without logical repercussions. Of two that come to mind, demanding respectively the supervenience

(3′) of the truth of arbitrary formulas on the truth of their atomic subformulas, or
(3″) of the truth of modal formulas $\Box\varphi$ on their immediate subformulas φ,

---

[66] A different disanalogy—one we cannot go into here—between quantification over times and worlds for the explication of tensed and modal discourse is alleged in McGinn (2000: 73 ff.); this work also picks up the supervenience issue (pp. 84–6).

we shall consider the second. More explicitly, the relevant condition is that for any formula φ and any model $\mathcal{M} = \langle U, R, V \rangle$, if v, w agree on φ (i.e. $\mathcal{M} \vDash_v \varphi$ iff $\mathcal{M} \vDash_w \varphi$), then v and w agree on $\Box\varphi$. This generalizes the condition mentioned in connection with **K45** that any two points agree on all $\Box$-formulas, by making such agreement conditional on agreement in respect of the immediate subformula of any given $\Box$-formula. We can again consider models on point-generated frames, which leads to the schemas (schematic—as with **Par** above—in that we are summarizing collectively all the results of making a particular choice of m, $n \geq 0$):

(*) $(\Diamond^m(p \wedge \Box p) \to \Box^n(p \to \Box p)$.
(**) $(\Diamond^m(\neg p \wedge \Box p) \to \Box^n(\neg p \to \Box p)$.

Since we are thinking here primarily of alethic modal logic, we would no doubt be led to add these to **KT** rather than to **K**, in which case (**) would be redundant, since it is already provable (having a **KT**-refutable antecedent; the first conjunct in the antecedent of (*) could also be dropped as redundant in this setting). For the moment, however, it is worth considering them as addenda to **K**, since this allows us to make a point of some interest in greater generality. The issue pertains to variations on the theme of truth-functionality, so we need to introduce some functional notation for truth-values. Given a model $\mathcal{M} = <U, R, V>$ with $u \in U$, we use the notation $V_u(\varphi)$ for the truth-value of φ at u in $\mathcal{M}$. That is $V_u(\varphi) = \mathrm{T}$ if $\mathcal{M} \vDash_u \varphi$, and $V_u(\varphi) = \mathrm{F}$ otherwise. Then to say that a (perhaps defined) singulary operator O is *truth-functional* in $\mathcal{M}$ is to say the following, in which 'f' ranges over singulary truth-functions, and 'φ' and 'u' over formulas and elements of U respectively:

Truth-functionality $\exists f \forall \varphi \forall u. \ V_u(O\varphi) = f(V_u(\varphi))$.

Since this condition—set out in formal quantifier notation to make the fact vivid—has two universal quantifiers in the scope of an existential quantifier, we can weaken it in either of two ways, moving one or the other universal quantifier to the left of the existential:

First weakening $\forall \varphi \exists f \forall u. \ V_u(O\varphi) = f(V_u(\varphi))$.
Second weakening $\forall u \exists f \forall \varphi. \ V_u(O\varphi) = f(V_u(\varphi))$.

We could of course move both universal quantifiers to the front, but the result is then a condition that is automatically satisfied. The second weakening corresponds to what in a minor adaptation of the terminology of Humberstone (1986) would be called the *pseudo-truth-functionality* of O in $\mathcal{M}$. To cite an example from that paper, in the canonical model for **K**, the operator O defined by $O\varphi = \varphi \leftrightarrow \Box\bot$ is pseudo-truth-functional but not truth-functional. The syntactic counterpart of this semantic fact is that this O is *extensional* according to **K**, in the sense that for all φ, ψ,

$\vdash_K (\varphi \leftrightarrow \psi) \to (O\varphi \leftrightarrow O\psi)$, even though—attesting to a failure of truth-functionality—there is no Boolean compound $\varphi(p)$ of p for which

$$\vdash_K Op \leftrightarrow \varphi(p).$$

Łukasiewicz once proposed as a plausible alethic modal logic one according to which $\Box$ itself was extensional in the sense just described, though this has found few defenders (for description and criticism, see Hughes and Cresswell 1968: 307–10), and we note that the smallest normal modal logic with $\Box$ extensional is K + $(p \rightarrow \Box p)$. Our current concern, however, is with the first weakening rather than the second, since it is this that is equivalent to (3″), for the case of O = $\Box$. To see this, suppose that, as (3″) demands, in a model $\mathcal{M} = \langle U, R, V \rangle$ in which any points agreeing on φ agree on $\Box\varphi$;. This means that for any given φ; we can construct a truth-function f thus: if there is any point verifying (in $\mathcal{M}$ φ) and also $\Box\varphi$, put $f(T) = T$ and if there is any point verifying φ but not $\Box\varphi$, put $f(T) = F$. We can never be forced to make both of these assignments because that would mean a violation of (3″): points agreeing on φ but differing on $\Box\varphi$. Similarly, if there is any point not verifying φ while verifying $\Box\varphi$, put $f(F) = T$ and if there is a point not verifying either φ or $\Box\varphi$, put $f(F) = F$. For the same reason as before, one never has to make both assignments. Of course it may happen that, for example, there is no point verifying (respectively, falsifying φ), in which case our recipe yields no value for $f(T)$ (resp. $f(F)$), in which case these values may be chosen arbitrarily. (The '$\exists f$ in the first weakening of Truth-functionality, as elsewhere, does not say that there is a *unique* function f.) Clearly f as here specified meets the condition laid down by the first weakening. And if that condition is satisfied, it is obvious that we have (3″) since the truth-value of $\Box\varphi$ at points agreeing on the truth-value of φ is fixed by the result of applying the (or rather 'any') f promised by the first weakening to that truth-value. Readers experienced in the canonical model method of completeness proofs will have no difficulty supplying (via a consideration of point-generated submodels) the proof of Observation 5 here, whose second part gives a characterization in terms of first-order conditions on frames:

> *Observation* 5(*i*). The logic determined by the class of all models satisfying the supervenience condition (3″) is the normal extension of K by (*) and (**).

> *Observation* 5(*ii*). The logic mentioned under (i) is determined by the class of all frames $\langle U, R \rangle$ satisfying: $\forall v \forall w \forall x (Rwx \rightarrow (x = w \vee x = v \vee Rvx))$ and $\forall v \forall w \forall x (Rwx \rightarrow (Rvv \vee Rvw \vee Rvx))$.

The two first-order conditions cited under (ii) correspond to the (*) and (**) respectively, in the sense that the claim made would be correct if only one of (*), (**), was used to obtain the logic and the corresponding condition retained in the specification of the class of frames determining it. It may be possible to simplify the axiomatic basis given for the extension of K described here. After all, parallel reasoning would lead to the conclusion that the normal extension of **K** by (for all $m, n \geq 0$)

(***) $\Diamond^m \Box p \to \Box^n \Box p$

gives the logic determined by the class of frames $\langle U, R \rangle$ satisfying

$\forall v \forall w \forall x (Rwx \to Rvx)$,

which is to say the frames in which $R(\bullet)$ is a constant function, which class we have already remarked determines **K45**: thus in this case the infinite bundle of axioms (***) can be replaced by two, that obtained by taking $m = 0$ and $n = 1$ (alias **4**) and that obtained by taking $m = 1$ and $n = 0$ (an "inverted" variant of **5**). While on the subject of axiomatics, it is worth raising a query. Hasn't half of the story of supervenience-on-subformulas been left out: shouldn't (*) and (**) be supplemented by (*′) and (**″) here?

(*′) $\Diamond^m (p \wedge \neg \Box p) \to \Box^n (p \to \neg \Box p)$.
(**′) $\Diamond^m (\neg p \wedge \neg \Box p) \to \Box^n (\neg p \to \neg \Box p)$.

The answer is that these have not been left out after all, (*′) following from (*)—and likewise (**′) from (**)—by contraposition (and relettering m and n).

While a semantic characterization in terms of frames, as in part (ii) of Observation 5, seems informative, there are perhaps some issues concerning the propriety of the apparatus abstracting frames from models for those sympathetic to the view cited above from Fine, McGinn, and Forbes, to the effect that possible worlds, unlike moments of time, are individuated by what goes on at them. The idea of different models on the same frame seems to flout this conception, though the tension may be reduced by a disclaimer to the effect that frames in the relevant sense are to be taken as isomorphism classes of frames in the objector's sense. A presumably related worry, which can be put in terms of models or frames (here we choose the former), and which again reflects a felt disanalogy for many between the Kripke model theory for tense logic on the one hand and modal logic (narrowly construed) on the other, is the problematic nature of the idea of an *intended* model. According to widespread opinion, while there are times other than the present time, there are no worlds other than the actual world. As Lewis (1986: 20, for example) has emphasized, this seems to leave the apparently interesting deliverances of possible world semantics without application, whereas on his own view one particular example of the 'set of points W' of a Kripke model is provided by the real modal universe comprising the actual world and all the other possible worlds, no less real for not being actual (i.e. for not being ours). This view of Lewis's has come to be known as modal realism, and in the form defended by him, is associated with various supplementary doctrines, such as the proposal that a possible world is simply a spatio-temporally maximal part of reality; this particular supplement thereby makes available a reductive account of modal notions, roughly as follows: what is possible is what is true in at least one such maximal region, what is necessary is what is true in all of them. Most of those who discuss this "possible worlds realism" do so to object to it, on a variety of grounds: it is ontologically extravagant, it renders the truth of modal claims unknowable to us by placing what makes them true beyond our epistemic grasp since we enter into no causal relations with non-actual worlds (McGinn 1981; Peacocke 1999, ch. 4), it makes it puzzling why we should care about modal claims if their subject matter is as the account would have it (Blackburn 1984: 214),[67] it inappropriately rules out what seems to be a genuine possibility—that a single possible world, the actual world, for instance, might have non-spatio-temporally related parts (van Inwagen 1986; Bigelow and Pargetter 1987; or Bigelow and Pargetter 1990: 189–93), and so on.[68] Readers interested in these issues will find many of the protagonists' papers anthologized in Tooley (1999) and subjected to a comparative and critical treatment in Chihara (1998). Although Chihara concentrates his attention on (David) Lewis, Plantinga, and Forbes, he also includes a survey of the considerable literature on modal fictionalism sparked by the appearance of Rosen (1990) in which this view is given a sympathetic airing. We conclude our discussion with a few points on this position.

7. ONE PHILOSOPHICAL REACTION TO THE SEMANTICS

It is common to hear the suggestion that the apparatus of possible worlds semantics is a heuristically helpful *façon de parler*, a useful fiction. One might expect an articulation of this view to run along the following lines, where *PW* is the possible worlds account (the hypothesis of possible worlds, as Rosen 1990 often calls it—this being the fiction in question) and *P** is the modal realist's non-modal paraphrase, in the language of possible worlds, of a modal statement *P*:[69]

(1) According to *PW*: *P* if and only if *P**.

The modal realist asserts this without the initial 'According to *PW*' prefix. Rosen's idea is somewhat different. Instead, his modal fictionalism asserts (Rosen 1990: 335)

(2) *P* iff according to *PW*, *P**.

---

[67] This point has been taken up in McFetridge (1990: 145) and Rosen (1990, §9).

[68] There are also what might be thought of as "technical" difficulties for the possible worlds framework, such as that raised in Kaplan (1995).

[69] Here we follow the literature on fictionalism cited in this section in using notations such as '*P*', as well as in conducting the discussion at a considerably more informal level than in earlier sections.

It should also be mentioned that *PW* for purposes of (2) includes not only the general non-modal principles of modal realism in so far as these pertain to the plurality of universes, the principle of recombination etc., as articulated in Lewis's *On the Plurality of Worlds* (1986), but also an "encyclopedia" which lists all the non-modal truths about the intrinsic character of our universe. (Quite a bit of non-fiction in the *PW* fiction, then.) Rosen illustrates this with the case in which *P* is the statement that there might have been blue swans, which the fictionalist biconditional (2) above says is equivalent to

(3) According to *PW*, there is a universe containing blue swans.

There may not seem to be much wrong with this particular instantiation of (2). But trouble for the position has come from other cases, such as the following. Brock (1993) (cf. also Rosen 1993) remarks that the modal realist will want to say not only that 'There is a plurality of worlds' is true, but that it is necessarily true—true at all worlds—which gives a problem when we consider a special case of (2):

(4) It is necessary that many worlds exist if and only if, according to *PW*, it is true at every world that many worlds exist.

(The word 'many' has been inserted here to make it clear that we are concerned with more than one world.) Brock then argues that since, according to *PW*, it is true at every world that many worlds exist, the modal fictionalist is committed to the left-hand side of this biconditional, and thus, via the inference from $\Box\varphi$ to φ,[70] to the claim that many worlds exist: precisely the claim that it was the point of modal fictionalism to avoid making.[71] A useful observation from Noonan (1994) is that, understood as an informal gloss on the official *PW*-paraphrases in Lewis (1968), it is not correct that according to *PW*, it is true at every world that many worlds exist: it is true at every world, rather, that only that world exists. Let us set that observation aside to note the logical interest of a suggestion explored in Brock (1995: 56)—also reported in Menzies and Pettit (1994: 36)[72]—on the assumption that the original objection is correct. Brock's proposal is that the fictionalist treatment provided above for 'Necessarily *P*', which is given in (5), should be replaced by that summarized in (6):

(5) According to *PW*, in all worlds, *P**.
(6) [According to *PW*, in all worlds, *P**] and *P*.

---

[70] Since this discussion takes necessity as truth at all worlds, the appropriate logical principles are those of **S5**, so this appeal to **T** is not controversial.

[71] Brock mentions but finds unattractive the possibility of restricting the range of the '*P*' in the general fictionalist biconditional (2) above so as to exempt statements about possible worlds; Rosen (1993) also mentions this possibility, and has the same reaction—that any such restriction seems artificial.

[72] In Brock's own favoured account, 'According to *PW*...' is replaced by 'If *PW* were true then ...', but this is independent of the present point.

This would dispose of the earlier problem, raised by (4), since instead of the right-hand side of (4), as the proposed fictionalist paraphrase of 'Necessarily, many worlds exist' we have a conjunction, one of whose conjuncts is the right-hand side of (4) (the part after 'and only if') and the other of which is 'many worlds exist'. Thus, on Brock's solution, the fictionalist need not be committed to the truth of the left-hand side of (4), now that some of the proposed paraphrase has been excluded from the scope of the 'According to PW' prefix. This is a little inelegant in that it destroys the formerly uniform pattern of providing fictionalist paraphrases by prefixing 'According to PW' to the recursively specified translation ( )*. It also appears vulnerable to a Gettier-style objection, as we can see by considering (7):

(7) Necessarily, either there are many worlds or some swans are white.

Presumably the fictionalist—and in particular the fictionalist committed to the non-existence of non-actual worlds, as opposed to one agnostic on this score—would not wish to be committed to (7). Weakening by the addition of the first disjunct does not undermine the contingency of the fact that some swans are white: if all swans had been blue then 'There are many worlds or some swans are white' would have been false. But the new procedure—instantiating (6)—ties the truth of (7) to that of a conjunction whose conjuncts are (8) and (9), both of which are true:

(8) According to PW, in all worlds: there are many worlds or some swans are white.
(9) There are many worlds or some swans are white.

(8) is true because according to PW the first disjunct of the embedded disjunction, and hence the disjunction itself, is true, while (9) is true because its second disjunct is true.

Whether this criticism is taken as fatal to the modified version of fictionalism, the comment about (8) just made helps to show something about it as well as the original version, namely, that we need to take the prefix 'According to PW' as a monotone operator. Indeed, for the view to work out at all, we need to go further, and assume that in its logical behaviour this prefix functions as a normal operator. Otherwise there will be no account of the validity of the ('regularity') inference

(10) Necessarily P; necessarily Q; *therefore* necessarily (P and Q).

Possible worlds semantics explains the validity of this inference, and the invalidity of the inference (11) below, by reducing it to the fact that the universal quantifier distributes over conjunction but the existential quantifier does not:

(11) Possibly P; possibly Q; *therefore* possibly (P and Q).

One central theme in Forbes (1985) was the challenge facing someone who does not accept modal realism but finds the corresponding facts about the universal and existential quantifier irresistibly explanatory of the distribution of validity across the modal cases (10) and (11). Forbes's response to this challenge will not occupy us here,[73] but should mention that while the Kripke semantics involves a universal quantifier in giving the world-relative truth conditions of □-formulas, the same is true of a number of different semantical approaches which for reasons of space it has not been possible to go into. In the same general area, a semantics to be found in Garson (1972) and van Fraassen (1971: 151–3) treats the truth of □φ at a point in a model u by universal quantification over functions from points to points, as well as giving an interesting informal gloss on why this is a reasonable thing to be doing. Again in the same general area, we could quantify over (non-empty) *regions* of logical space rather than *points* therein, even going so far as to refuse to think of the regions as sets of points at all. (This semantics is reviewed in Forbes 1985: 18–22 (for modal propositional logic) and 43–7 (for quantified modal logic); it is the analogue of a semantics for tense logic with truth evaluated over intervals rather than at instants. Further information may be found in Humberstone 1988: 418, with an interesting application of similar semantic ideas appearing in Cresswell 2004.) Very differently inspired is McKinsey's 'substitutional semantics' for modal logic—dating from a 1945 paper but most conveniently explained in Anderson and Belnap 1975: 122–3)—which treats the modal operators as quantifiers over certain syntactic substitutions. In all these cases, □ and ◊ are interpreted by means of universal and existential quantification, and the validity and invalidity of—suitably formalized versions of—(10) and (11) respectively flow from this fact.[74] What becomes of (10) in the fictionalist treatment? Using the unmodified form for simplicity, the paraphrase gives

(12)   According to *PW*, in all worlds P^*; according to *PW*, in all worlds Q^*; *therefore* according to *PW*, in all worlds (P^* and Q^*).

For this we need not only that the prefix 'in all worlds' is regular, but that the same holds of the prefix 'According to *PW*' itself. So the phenomenon of explanation by reduction to the familiar (taking quantifiers as more familiar than non-truthfunctional sentence operators) so characteristic of possible worlds semantics goes

---

[73] Some criticisms may be found in Chihara (1998: 142–61). A distinction we are not going into here, between "modalism" and "actualism", two strands of opposition to Lewis-style modal realism, is also covered by Chihara. The idea that possible worlds semantics is explanatory also arises at another level (roughly: globally rather than locally), as we may illustrate by the question, 'Why are **4** and **B** provable in **KT5**?' and the answer: because every reflexive Euclidean frame is transitive and symmetric. (Such explanations may sometimes predict a non-existent explanandum, in view of the phenomenon of Kripke-completeness.)

[74] The title of Kuhn (1980) speaks of 'quantifiers as modal operators', suggesting an explanatory reduction in the reverse direction. But this is intended to evoke Montague's work cited in note 1 above, in which the model-theoretic semantics of quantifiers is tailored to resemble that to which we are accustomed in the case of modal operators: in both cases the metalinguistic work is done not modally by operators but by quantification. (Kuhn updates Montague's treatment so that accessibility relations within a model—rather than relations between models—are used. Those interested in this way of working out the analogy will find it further developed in van Benthem 1994.) Indeed it is far from clear whether one could expect a converse direction of reduction. Even the use of a modal metalanguage in which to present accounts of validity for a modal object language is problematic; some first steps down this path may be found in Humberstone (1996).

missing in the fictionalist substitute: the vital fictionalist prefix exhibits logical behaviour not explainable in terms of the logic of the quantifiers.[75]

APPENDIX 20.1 A SECOND WORRY ABOUT POST-NEGATION

The "Refined Account" of contrariety and subcontrariety offered in Section 3 supplemented the Simple Semantic Account with the condition that the operators standing in these relations should be each other's post-negations. This raised the worry that the post-negation relation was not implicit in the Boolean algebra of logical relations among the operators, perhaps casting doubt on its legitimacy. The reply to this objection, broached with the aid of Figure 20.5 in our discussion, was that the reason for this lay in that fact that the Boolean algebra in question revealed only the logical relations between operators which derive from corresponding relations between the results of applying those operators to an arbitrary but fixed statement, whereas post-negation, as well as other more familiar logical matters (such as monotony), essentially concerned the application of operators to different statements, and should not therefore be expected to emerge from such an algebraic representation. Here I address a second kind of worry about the legitimacy of post-negation.

We may, the objector begins, regard the post-negation of O as saying about (the proposition expressed by) φ as saying what O says about $\neg\varphi$. This way of putting matters is designed as a reminder of the idea that, for example, what the sentence Fa says about a, Fb says about b. Here F is a one-place predicate and a and b are names, so strictly the phrase 'about a' should be interpreted as 'about the denotation of a', and similarly with 'b'. To get a closer analogy across the part-of-speech changes involved here (an operator being something that takes a sentence to make a sentence rather than something that takes a name to make a sentence), we should replace the 'b' by a term involving application of a function symbol (by analogy with the role of $\neg$), such as '$f(a)$'. But, the objection continues, it is well known that there is no objective language-independent notion corresponding to such phrases as 'What Fa says about a' (Humberstone 2000 provides a discussion of some of the issues involved here). Rather there are many non-equivalent predicates that may be applied to a which happen to yield statements logically equivalent to Fa. To take three examples, presented with the aid of the λ notation, we have $\lambda x.Fx$, $\lambda x.x = a \to Fx$, and $\lambda x.x = a \wedge Fx$. Although these give equivalent results when predicated of a, they give non-equivalent results when predicated of an arbitrary individual. So also in the case of current concern, there is no one thing that $O\varphi$ says about φ. With the propositional abstraction use of λ introduced after Figure 20.5, we have, for example,

(1) $\lambda q.Oq$.
(2) $\lambda q.((q \to \varphi) \to O\varphi)$.
(3) $\lambda q.((\varphi \to q) \to O\varphi)$.
(4) $\lambda q.((q \leftrightarrow \varphi) \to O\varphi)$.

---

[75] Rosen (1990) stressed that the fictionalism there described did not avoid primitive modality, but reduced the number of primitive modal notions to one—that represented by the story prefix. The present point is intended to be different: the explanation of aspects of the logical behaviour of □ now appeals to the possible worlds apparatus as well as to corresponding aspects of that very behaviour on the part of the new prefix.

(5) $\lambda q.((q \to \varphi) \to Oq)$.
(6) $\lambda q.((\varphi \to q) \to Oq)$.
(7) $\lambda q.((q \leftrightarrow \varphi) \to Oq)$.
(8) $\lambda q.(O(q \to \varphi) \leftrightarrow Oq)$.

When any of these λ-expressions is applied to the particular formula φ the result is equivalent to $O\varphi$. But the results of applying them to $\neg\varphi$ vary. (1) gives the ('preferred') post-negation $O\neg\varphi$. In the case of (2) we have $[\lambda q.((q \to \varphi) \to O\varphi)](\neg\varphi)$ reducing to $(\neg\varphi \to \varphi) \to O\varphi$, this being equivalent to $\varphi \to O\varphi$, while for (3)–(7), we end up with $\varphi \vee O\varphi, \alpha, \varphi \to O\neg\varphi$, and $\varphi \vee O\neg\varphi$, and α again, respectively. Since these are the results of substituting $\neg\varphi$ for q in (2)–(7), we can equally regard them as resulting from applying the λ-expressions differing from those listed in having q uniformly replaced by $\neg q$. Now, the objection proceeds, any of these (2)⁻–(7)⁻ (let's call them) has as good a claim as (1)⁻ $(= \lambda q.O\neg q)$ to being the post-negation of O. Finally, when we come to (8), and making the further assumption, to record which we shall rewrite O as $\Box$, that O is a normal modal operator, we find that while, as in the other cases, $[\lambda q.(O(q \to \varphi) \leftrightarrow Oq)](\varphi)$ is equivalent to $O\varphi$, i.e. $\Box\varphi$,[76] $[\lambda q.(O(q \to \varphi) \leftrightarrow Oq)](\neg\varphi)$ reduces to $O(\neg\varphi \to \varphi) \leftrightarrow O\neg\varphi$, and thus to $\Box\varphi \leftrightarrow \Box\neg\varphi$. Now as long as $\Box$ has a logic at least as strong as **KD**, as we noted in discussion (in Section 3) of the general identity $O_{\#}\varphi = O\varphi \# O\neg\varphi$ for commutative binary #, $O\varphi \leftrightarrow \Box\neg\varphi$ is in turn equivalent to $\nabla\varphi$. Concluding the objection, then, not only is there no privileged post-negation of a given operator O, but when O is taken as the $\Box$ of Figure 20.5, the 'post-negation' condition (with which we hoped to refine the Simple Semantic Account) is satisfied by taking as a post-negation of $\Box$, (8)⁻ (i.e. $\lambda q.(O(\neg q \to \varphi) \leftrightarrow O\neg q)$: thus that refinement does not have the claimed effect of revealing a special relation $\Box$ stands in to $\Box\neg$ that it does not stand in to ∇. The superadded loops and arcs we envisaged supplementing Figure 20.5 to bring out the real (sub)contrariety relationships not implicit in that diagram are revealed as arbitrarily favouring one rather than another post-negation of $\Box$.

The reply to this argument against the objectivity of the envisaged supplementation is that the argument commits the very fallacy it begins by drawing attention to: that there is some one thing that $O\varphi$ can be regarded as saying about φ. The 'post-negation' terminology was first introduced above by (in effect) defining the post-negation of O as $\lambda q.O\neg q$ $(=(1)⁻)$. The fact that as applied to φ, this gives $O\neg\varphi$, does not mean that, for any other O' with O'φ equivalent to $O\varphi$, the post-negation $\lambda q.O'\neg q$ of O' will also count as a post-negation of O, precisely because there is no route back from (the equivalence class of) $O\varphi$ to a single operator—which 'says about φ what $O\varphi$ says about φ'. The operators listed under (1)–(8) are non-equivalent despite the equivalence of the results of applying them to the particular formula φ, and the fact that they have different post-negations (given by (1)⁻–(8)⁻) does not mean that somehow each of them has all of the latter among its own post-negations.

Appendix 20.2 Yet More Contraries? Keynes and Hacker's Octagon of Opposition

In our first discussion of the (non-)uniqueness of contraries, mention was made of the fact that *SeP* has *SaP* as a contrary, but also, since *SeP* expresses the same proposition as *PeS*, the

---

[76] The aspect of normality used here is that $\Box(\varphi \to \varphi) \leftrightarrow \Box\varphi$ is equivalent to $\Box\varphi$.

further contrary—from, as it were, a different square of opposition (based on P, S, rather than S, P)—in the shape of PaS, something not equivalent to SaP. Edward Hacker has produced an elegant diagram in which the traditional logical relations between all a, e, i, and o statements constructed from a given S, P and their "term-negations", $\overline{S}$, $\overline{P}$. This extremely informative diagram appears in Hacker (1978: 353) as well as in Parry and Hacker (1991: 248), the latter source explaining the traditional syllogistic moves needed to navigate around it and among the different labels for its eight nodes (Conversion, Obversion, and Contraposition). Interestingly enough, apparently unbeknownst to Hacker, essentially the same diagram—though with some of the relations less explicitly indicated—and under the same name ('Octagon of Opposition'), may found in Keynes (1906: 144). Each node with a contrary has two contraries, and likewise for subcontraries. We concentrate on contraries, as above, for expository convenience. For the moves just mentioned to yield equivalents, then because of the subaltern implications from SaP to SiP and SeP to SoP, we have to assume that not only S but also P is true of at least one thing, and also that each is false of at least one thing. (Since SeP is presumed equivalent by conversion to PeS and the latter implies PoS, SeP requires for its truth that P is true of something; since SaP is presumed equivalent by contraposition to $\overline{P}a\overline{S}$ and the latter implies that $\overline{P}$ is true of something, so does the former.) We put this briefly by saying that each of S, P, is required to be neither empty nor universal. The "traditional" contrary of SaP (suggested by expressing it that way), namely SeP, is incompatible with SaP because if both were true, S would have to be empty; the "new contrary" of SaP, namely $\overline{S}aP$, is incompatible with it because if both were true, P would have to be universal. Here we are thinking of contrariety as a relation between propositions, so equivalent statements have the same contraries, and each proposition has numerous linguistic representations. In fact in Hacker's scheme, each has four such representations. In particular, the proposition expressed by SaP is expressed by any of:

$$SaP,\ Se\,\overline{P},\ \overline{S}\,eP,\ \overline{P}\,a\overline{S},$$

while $\overline{S}\,aP$'s equivalence class comprises

$$\overline{S}\,aP,\ \overline{P}\,aS,\ \overline{S}\,e\overline{P},\ \overline{P}\,e\overline{S}.$$

In fact, we find it more convenient to distinguish the eight statements constructible from S, P—in either order—in a formalism which takes them, specifically, in that order. This leads us to increase the number of constructional devices (binary quantifiers, that is). Because of its historical use in connection with relational converses, we add a 'cup' diacritic to the two syllogistic quantifiers, a and o, which do not allow conversion, getting $\breve{a}$ and $\breve{o}$, to be used for the 'converse' quantifiers; that is:

Given any general terms X, Y: $X\breve{a}Y$ is to be equivalent to YaX; and $X\breve{o}Y$ to YoX.

At this point we have run out of vowels (especially since we do not want a clash with the earlier Blanché-derived usage of u and y) and will write XjY for $\overline{X}aY$ and XkY for the negation (contradictory) of this. We use 'j' as mnemonic for 'jointly exhaustive', since that is how the classes of X's and Y's must be for XjY to be true, and 'k' simply because it is the next letter of the alphabet. Now we can list the eight S, P statements in a uniform manner—i.e. with the same arguments in the same order—as:

$$SaP,\ SeP,\ SiP,\ SoP,\ S\breve{a}P,\ S\breve{o}P,\ SjP,\ \text{and}\ SkP.^{77}$$

---

[77] In fact, Keynes (1906: 141) also has a uniform notation for the eight quantifiers; where q is one of a, e, i, o, Keynes uses '$\overline{q}$' for the quantifier which maps S and P to what q maps the complementary general terms to.

Re-expressed with the aid of this notation, Keynes–Hacker's Octagon of Opposition displays (i) *SeP* and *SjP* as the two contraries of *SaP*, (ii) *SeP* and *SjP* (again) as the two contraries of *SăP*; (iii) *SaP* and *SăP* as the two contraries of *SeP*, and (iv) *SaP* and *SăP* (again) as the two contraries of *SjP*. We pause to note the structural contrast with Blanché's account, in which any one of *SaP*, *SeP*, and *SyP* (= Some but not every *S* is *P*) has each of the other two as contraries. And while Blanché's trio of contraries here are pairwise mutually exclusive though not in general (i.e. for arbitrary *S*, *P*) pairwise jointly exhaustive, but jointly exhaustive as a trio, there is no analogue to this last feature in the scheme of Keynes and Hacker (for example, in the case of (i), *SeP*, *SjP*, and *SaP* can all be false). These contrasts are respects in which the accounts of Blanché and Keynes–Hacker differ but not of course respects in which they conflict, since we could if we wished to produce an account combining the observations of both. Though we dealt with the modal version of Blanché's novel contraries in the text and (implicitly) in Appendix 20.1, it is clear that an analogous treatment of the syllogistic version is available, and that there is a similar point to be made apropos of Keynes–Hacker's new contraries.

I expressed a preference for a notion of contrariety as applying to quantifiers or operators rather than to statements or propositions, and in particular for an explication of this notion as our "Refined Account", supplementing the Simple Semantic Account with the condition that the contrary operator or quantifier should be the post-negation of the given operator or quantifier, understanding by post-negation in the case of binary quantifiers the operation which keeps the quantifier the same and negates its second argument (the 'predicate' in traditional parlance). The contrary of *a* is *e*, and conversely, and Blanché's *y* does not enter the story, despite its passing the test set by the Simple Semantic Account. The post-negation of *y* is (to within equivalence) *y* itself, so since *SyP* and *Sπ(y)P* are not in general incompatible, expressing equivalent propositions, *SyP* has no contrary, any more than *SiP* has. The same remarks on *a* and *e* apply in response to the more elaborate scheme presented by Keynes and Hacker, and about the illustrative case of what might be thought to be claimed as a new candidate contrary to *a*, namely *j*, something should be said. (In fact, since both authors are discussing contrariety among propositions rather than binary quantifiers, no such claim is explicitly being made by them.) After addressing this issue, we turn to the application of the Octagon to modal notions.

The quantifier *j* applied to *X* and *Y* in that order yields a proposition true just in case *X* and *Y* jointly exhaust the domain of discourse. So, by the general principle that $X\pi(q)Y$ is to be equivalent to $Xq\,\overline{Y}$, $\pi(j)$ applied to *X* and *Y* in that order yields a proposition true just in case *X* and $\overline{Y}$ jointly exhaust that domain, which is the proposition (expressed by) *XăY*; therefore the post-negation of *j* is *ă*. (It will be clear now why we introduced the order-uniform notation above.) Since the other conditions of the Simple Semantic Account of contrariety are satisfied in this case too, the 'genuine' contraries are *a* and *e* on the one hand, and *j* and *ă* on the other. One may be worried by the start of this little story, which speaks of the application of *j* to *X* and *Y* 'in that order'. Since *XjY* and *YjX* are equivalent, what is this talk of a particular order doing? Viewed as a binary operation, *j* is commutative. (Of course, once can equally well regard binary quantifiers semantically as binary relations—as we did above in thinking of *ă* as the converse of *a*—in which case we would be saying that *j* is symmetric. But the operational perspective is more helpful for the sake of the arithmetical analogy to be given below.) The worry would be that our definition of the post-negation—and hence of 'the' contrary—of a given quantifier has traded illicitly on favouring one way over another of expressing a proposition, by taking the general terms in a particular order when the same proposition is equally well expressed by choosing the converse order. This is a mistake, however, in that we are precisely trying to define the post-negation (or the contrary) not of a proposition, but of a binary quantifier. Of course, had we been trying to define π as mapping the proposition expressed by XqY to that expressed by $Xq\bar{Y}$, we should not have succeeded in defining a function at all, for precisely the point just noted: the value of the function would depend on the representative statement chosen to express its propositional argument, rather than on the proposition expressed. (In terms of our main discussion, this would be a failure of congruentiality.) Let us try to rearticulate the worry without directing it at this misformulated position. The thought would have to be that since j is commutative, it should not matter whether we apply $\pi(j)$ to X, Y, in that order, or to Y, X in that order. This amounts to saying that π should preserve commutativity, and there is no reason to expect or demand this. Suppose that we were thinking of arithmetical operations instead, and defined a mapping f from one binary operation $\circ$ to another $f(\circ)$ by the stipulation that the value of $f(\circ)$ for the arguments x, y in that order is to be $x \circ 2y$. (Note that whereas in Section 3, '$\circ$' symbolized functional composition, here it stands for an arbitrary binary operation.) Clearly f is well defined by this stipulation: a unique value—a certain binary operation on numbers—has been supplied for any $\circ$. We use "prefix" notation for (some) operations here in the interests of clarity. Taking as a candidate $\circ$ the (commutative) operation of addition, we have:

(i) $+(1, 3) = +(3, 1)$.

Let us calculate the results of replacing $+$ by $f(+)$: $[f(+)](1, 3) = +(1, 2 \times 3) = +(1, 6) = 7$. That is what the replacement does to the left-hand side. For the right-hand side: $[f(+)](3, 1) = +(3, 1 \times 2) = +(3, 2) = 5$. Since $7 \neq 5$, we have

(ii) $[f(+)](1, 3) \neq [f(+)](3, 1)$.

In view of (ii), f does not preserve commutativity. Have we somehow obtained a contradiction? Are (i) and (ii) inconsistent, with an untoward dependence of f on the way its argument happened to be written—as $+(1, 3)$ or as $+(3, 1)$. No, because that number, variously denoted, was not the argument of the function f. (Just as the proposition expressed by XaY is not an argument of π.) Of course, there would have been trouble if the two sides of (ii) were the results of applying some function to each side of (i). That would have happened if we had tried to define a function, g, say, from numbers to numbers by the stipulation—here reverting to the customary infix notation—that $g(x + y)$ was to be $x + 2y$. The arguments of f as we defined it were not numbers but binary operations on numbers. Likewise, *mutatis mutandis*, in the case of π, propositions and quantifiers.

What becomes of the (current) Octagon of Opposition when we turn from syllogistic to modal logic? We need to back up a little before addressing this question directly. We have given several tense-logical examples concentrating on the future tense, though in general tense logic is concerned with bimodal frames $\langle U, R_1, R_2 \rangle$ in which R_1 and R_2 are each other's converses (and various other conditions of interest are also satisfied, varying from logic to logic). Then we can interpret a future-tense operator $\square_1$ ('G' in traditional tense-logical notation) by quantification over R_1-related points alongside a past-tense operator $\square_2$ ('H') by means of R_2. Consider instead bimodal frames $\langle U, R_1, R_2 \rangle$ in which (perhaps among other things) R_1 and R_2 are each other's complements (relative to $U \times U$). Note that if $\langle U, R_1 \rangle$ is a strict linear order, then the results of expansion-by-converses and expansion-by-complements are quite similar, the latter relation being the reflexive closure of the former. In general, the two are very different, and while the class of frames in which R_2 is the converse of R_1 is modally definable,[78] the

---

[78] By $\{p \to \square_1 \lozenge_2 p, p \to \square_2 \lozenge_1 p\}$. Adding these two formulas as axioms to the smallest normal bimodal logic (i.e. logic according to which each of $\square_1$, $\square_2$, is normal) gives the fundamental tense logic K_t.

class of frames in which R_2 is the complement of R_1 is not (since it is not closed under disjoint unions, for example). There is nothing to stop us from seeking the logics determined by various class of 'relation + complement' frames of interest, however.[79] We envisage such an interest arising from a given area of modal logic (in the broad sense) with regard to which we are already thinking of a particular relation (in any given frame) as the accessibility relation, for which reason, taking this as the R_1 of our new frames, we speak of R_2 as the relation of *inaccessibility*. And instead of writing '$\Box_1$,' and '$\Box_2$,', we write '$\Box$' and '$\blacksquare$' (with '$\blacklozenge$' for $\delta(\blacksquare)$). If we assume the **D** axiom not only for $\Box$ but also for $\blacksquare$—so, semantically, restricting attention to frames in which every point has some point accessible to it and some point inaccessible to it— then we have the subaltern implications in each of two (modal) squares of opposition, one based on the one operator and the other on the other. The eight vertices of these two squares taken together correspond to the eight vertices of the Hacker Octagon, using the analogy of 'Every S is P' with 'Every accessible point verifies p'. (That is, fix an arbitrary $u \in U$ in a model on one of the current frames, and interpret S as true of precisely the points in $R(u)$.) Thus just as $\Box p$ corresponds to SaP, $\Diamond p$ to SiP, etc., from the familiar squares, so $\blacksquare p$ corresponds to $\bar{S}aP$, or SjP in the uniform notation suggested above, and $\blacklozenge p$, $\blacksquare\neg p$, $\blacklozenge\neg p$ respectively to (in the uniform notation) $S\breve{o}P$, $S\breve{a}P$, and SkP. However, the logical relations displayed in Hacker's Octagon between the various corners of these two squares cannot plausibly be expected to survive in the present setting. To take only one example, unlike a and j, $\Box$ and $\blacksquare$ are not even contraries on the Simple Semantic Account of contrariety. It is not open to us to prevent each formula φ from being true throughout both $R(u)$ $(=R_1(u))$ and its complement, since even imposing such a restriction for the propositional variables, we should still be stuck with this as the fate of, for example, $\top, p \to p$, etc. The source of this disanalogy is that we can no longer impose the neither-empty-nor-universal requirement in the 'predicate' position, on which the obversion, conversion, and (in particular) contraposition moves depend in arriving at the full panoply of octagonal relationships.

APPENDIX 20.3 PROOFS OF OBSERVATIONS 1 AND 4

These proofs justify some claims from Section 5, beginning with:

> *Observation* 1. A formula φ has the local truth-to-validity property if and only if φ is **K**-equivalent to some pure formula.

---

[79] See Humberstone (1983, 1987) for such inquiries; this apparatus may be seen at work in, for example, Goranko (1990), Kracht (1999), and references cited therein. The idea also appears in an interesting epistemic application in Levesque (1990). An application to deontic logic may be found in Bailhache (1977, 1980) and van Benthem (1979b); the authors are trying to formalize a notion of free choice permission (mentioned in our earlier discussion), P, say, with $P(p \lor q)$ equivalent to $Pp \land Pq$, and note that this holds if we put: $P\varphi$ true at u iff all φ-verifying points are accessible to u. (Alternatively: all points inaccessible to u verify $\neg\varphi$.) This has the untoward consequence that Pp implies $P(p \land q)$, since if all p-verifying points are accessible to u, then certainly so are all $(p \land q)$-verifying points. It is hard to see that there is any notion of permissibility for which such an implication holds. Yet, regardless of the semantic details, it is easily seen to be a consequence of taking free choice permission seriously to the extent of having the operator P for which the above equivalence is satisfied be congruential. We simply substitute $(p \land q)$ for q in the equivalence, and the left-hand side is, by congruentiality, equivalent to p, while the right-hand side has $p \land q$ as a conjunct (and hence as a consequence). Perhaps we should not take free choice permission so seriously, after all.

We need the following lemma for the proof. We use the following notation: $\varphi(p)$ for a formula φ in which p occurs, and $\varphi(\psi)$ for the result of substituting the formula ψ for all occurrences of p in φ.

LEMMA. *For any formula* $\varphi(p)$, *if*

(*) *For all models* $\mathcal{M}_1 = <U, R, V_1>$, $\mathcal{M}_2 = <U, R, V_2>$ *on the same frame, and all* $u \in U$, *we have* $\mathcal{M}_1 \vDash_u \varphi \Leftrightarrow \mathcal{M}_2 \vDash_u \varphi$,

then

(**) *For any formula* ψ, $\varphi(p)$ *is* **K***-equivalent to* $\varphi(\psi)$.

Proof. Suppose (*), but not (**). Thus for some formula ψ, we have either (a) $\nvdash_K \varphi(p) \to \varphi(\psi)$ or (b) $\nvdash_K \varphi(\psi) \to \varphi(p)$. In case (a), since **K** is determined by the class of all models, we have some model $\mathcal{M}_1 = <U, R, V_1>$ with $u \in U$ and $\mathcal{M}_1 \vDash_u \varphi(p)$ while $\mathcal{M}_1 \nvDash_u \varphi(\psi)$. Then putting $V_2(p) = \{v \in U \mid \mathcal{M}_1 \vDash_v \psi\}$ gives a model $\mathcal{M}_2 = <U, R, V_2>$ with $\mathcal{M}_2 \nvDash_u \varphi(p)$, which contradicts (*) since $\mathcal{M}_1 \vDash_u \varphi(p)$. The case of (b) is similar.

As to the proof of Observation 1, taking the 'if' direction being clear, we proceed to the 'only if' direction. Suppose that φ has the local truth-to-validity property. This is equivalent to (*) of the Lemma, so using that result, we may successively replace the propositional variables in φ by any pure formulas (as the ψ of (**)), thereby obtaining a pure formula **K**-equivalent to φ.

We turn to Observation 4, according to which classical propositional logic is closed under what we called Internal Uniform Substitution, whereas in general normal modal logics are not. The latter point was illustrated in the main discussion, so here we restrict attention to establishing the positive claim. Recall that what this means is that

(†) If $\vdash \varphi$, and φ has a subformula ψ to which all φ's occurrences of p_i are confined, then $\vdash \varphi(\psi')$, where $\varphi(\psi')$ has ψ throughout φ replaced by any conjunction ψ' of substitution instances of ψ got by substituting formulas $\chi_1, \ldots, \chi_m$ for p_i.

In (†) the symbol '$\vdash$' is used to indicate provability, but to establish the correctness of this claim for the case of provability in classical (propositional) logic, it is most convenient to use this same symbol to stand for an arbitrary consequence relation. (In Section 2 this notation was used specifically for the consequence relation associated with classical logic.) Such a relation, we shall say, is *determined by* a class $\mathcal{V}$ of (bivalent) valuations—meaning by this functions assigning to each formula (of the language of the consequence relation) one of the values T, F—when for any set Γ of formulas and any formula φ, we have $\Gamma \vdash \varphi$ if and only if every valuation in $\mathcal{V}$ assignings the value T to all formulas in Γ also assigns the value T to φ. A k-ary truth-function (i.e. function from $\{T,F\}^k$ to $\{T,F\}$) is idempotent if whenever each of its k arguments is the same element of $\{T,F\}$, its value is that same element. Finally, by way of terminology, we say that a k-ary truth-function f is associated on a valuation v with a k-ary (not necessarily primitive) connective $*$ when for all formulas $\varphi_1, \ldots, \varphi_k$,

$$v(*(\varphi_1, \ldots, \varphi_k)) = f(v(\varphi_1), \ldots, v(\varphi_k)).^{80}$$

---

[80] There will be no danger of confusing this use of 'v' with its use in the main body of our discussion, as a variable over points in a Kripke model. In our discussion of truth-functionality versus extensionality in Sect. 6, we used the notation 'V_u' for the valuation induced by a point u in such a model, and the

LEMMA. *Suppose ⊢ is a consequence relation determined by some class of valuations on each of which an $(n + 1)$-ary connective # is associated with some truth-function and on each of which an m-ary connective ∗ is associated with an idempotent truth-function. Then for all formulas $\alpha_1, \ldots, \alpha_m, \beta_1, \ldots, \beta_n$, in the language of ⊢ we have*

$$\#(\alpha_1, \beta_1, \ldots, \beta_n), \ldots, \#(\alpha_m, \beta_1, \ldots, \beta_n) \vdash \#(\ast(\alpha_1, \ldots, \alpha_m), \beta_1, \ldots, \beta_n).$$

Proof. If the above ⊢-statement does not hold, then there is some valuation v in the class the lemma supposes ⊢ to be determined by, which assigns T to each formula on the left of the '⊢' and F to that on the right. Thus $v(\#(\ast(\alpha_1, \ldots, \alpha_m), \beta_1, \ldots, \beta_n)) = f_\#(v(\ast(\alpha_1, \ldots, \alpha_m)), v(\beta_1), \ldots, v(\beta_n))) = F$, where $f_\#$ is the truth-function associated with # on v, while $f_\#(v(\alpha_1), v(\beta_1), \ldots, v(\beta_n)) = \ldots = f_\#(v(\alpha_m), v(\beta_1), \ldots, v(\beta_n)) = T$. Suppose not all of $v(\alpha_1), \ldots, v(\alpha_m)$ are equal. In that case $m \geq 2$, and so since there are only the two truth-values, T and F, one of the $v(\alpha_i)$ must coincide with $v(\ast(\alpha_1, \ldots, \alpha_m))$, contradicting the fact that $f_\#(v(\ast(\alpha_1, \ldots, \alpha_m)), v(\beta_1), \ldots, v(\beta_n)) = F$. Suppose then that all of $v(\alpha_1), \ldots, v(\alpha_m)$ are equal. Then since the truth-function $f_\ast$ associated with ∗ on v is by hypothesis idempotent, $v(\ast(\alpha_1, \ldots, \alpha_m)) = f_\ast(v(\alpha_1), \ldots, v(\alpha_m))$ has the same value as the α_i have, again contradicting the fact that $f_\#(v(\ast(\alpha_1, \ldots, \alpha_m)), v(\beta_1), \ldots, v(\beta_n))) = F$.

Although we do not need it for present purposes, for the benefit of those familiar with "generalized" or "multiple-conclusion" consequence relations, under the conditions given in the Lemma, the ⊢ claim it promises under those conditions also holds in dual form (i.e. with the left- and right-hand sides reversed), as the above proof shows, given some interchanges of 'T' and 'F'. In proving the second half of Observation 4 below as a corollary to the Theorem appearing presently, we make use of the fact that every (not necessarily primitive) # in (non-modal) classical propositional logic satisfies the above condition that the consequence relation of the latter logic is determined by a class of valuations on each of which # is associated with a truth-function. As a technical aside, we note that this is not the case for intuitionistic propositional logic, so one might consider the fate, in that setting, of a suitably modified version of the above Lemma, understanding (m-ary) ∗ to be idempotent according to ⊢ when $\ast(\alpha_1, \ldots, \alpha_m) \dashv\vdash \alpha$ if $\alpha_1 = \ldots = \alpha_m = \alpha$. The natural question to ask is whether for any $(n + 1)$-ary connective # and m-ary ∗ idempotent according to the intuitionistic consequence relation, we have for this choice of ⊢, the following:

for all $\alpha_1, \ldots, \alpha_m, \beta_1, \ldots, \beta_n$: $\#(\alpha_1, \beta_1, \ldots, \beta_n), \ldots, \#(\alpha_m, \beta_1, \ldots, \beta_n) \vdash \#(\ast(\alpha_1, \ldots, \alpha_m), \beta_1, \ldots, \beta_n).$

The answer to this question is no, as we may see by taking $\#(\varphi, \psi)$ as $\varphi \to \psi$ and $\ast(\varphi, \psi)$ as the idempotent $(\varphi \to \psi) \to \psi$, since, with $n = 1$ and $\beta_1 = \alpha_1 = p$ and $\alpha_2 = \beta \bot$, an affirmative answer would require:

$$p \to p, \bot \to p \vdash ((p \to \bot) \to \bot) \to p,$$

whose left-hand formulas are intuitionistically provable but whose right-hand formula is not. (Note that the general pattern here is given by $\alpha_1 \to \beta, \alpha_2 \to \vdash \#(\alpha_1, \alpha_2) \to \beta$, so the

natural generalization of that distinction relativizing these notions to an arbitrary class of valuations would have us count n-ary ∗ as extensional w.r.t. the class when there is some for each valuation in the class there is some truth-function f associated with ∗ on that valuation, and truth-functional w.r.t. the class when there is some truth-function associated with ∗ on every valuation in the class.

present point also illustrates a failure of 'or-elimination' for the somewhat disjunction-like $\#(\alpha_1, \alpha_2) = (\alpha_1 \to \alpha_2) \to \alpha_2$, classically but not intuitionistically equivalent to $\alpha_1 \lor \alpha_2$.) Indeed, in intuitionistic logic we can even give such counter-examples when the idempotent $\ast$ is taken as $\wedge$ (though I have not been able to transform such cases into counter-examples to the claim that intuitionistic propositional logic enjoys closure under internal substitution, leaving the correctness of that claim as an open question).

A consequence relation, no less than a logic in the 'set of formulas' sense, can be closed under Uniform Substitution, meaning by this that whenever $\Gamma \vdash \varphi$, we have $\{s(\psi) \mid \psi \in \Gamma\}$ $\vdash s(\varphi)$, for any substitution s. (However, all we need for the proof below is that the 'formula logic' comprising the consequences by $\vdash$ of the empty set is closed under Uniform Substitution.)

THEOREM. *Suppose $\vdash$ is a consequence relation closed under Uniform Substitution and satisfying the conditions of the Lemma for $\#$ and $\ast$ and that $\psi, \beta_1, \ldots, \beta_n$, are formulas of which the only one in which the variable p_i occurs is ψ. Then if $\vdash \#(\psi, \beta_1, \ldots, \beta_n)$, we have for all substitutions $s_1, \ldots, s_m$ which act as the identity substitution on all variables other than p_i: $\vdash \#(\ast(s_1(\psi), \ldots, s_m(\psi)), \beta_1, \ldots, \beta_n)$.*

Proof. If $\vdash \#(\psi, \beta_1, \ldots, \beta_n)$, then by Uniform Substitution we get $\vdash s_i(\#(\psi, \beta_1, \ldots, \beta_n))$ for $i = 1, \ldots, m$. Since these substitutions only change formulas constructed with p_i, this means that we have $\vdash (\#(s_1(\psi), \beta_1, \ldots, \beta_n)), \ldots, \vdash (\#(s_m(\psi), \beta_1, \ldots, \beta_n))$, and hence, by the Lemma, taking α_i as $s_i(\psi)$, we conclude that $\vdash \#(\ast(s_1(\psi), \ldots, s_m(\psi)), \beta_1, \ldots, \beta_n)$.

As a corollary, we obtain the result—set down above in (†)—that the consequence relation of classical propositional logic, $\vdash$ in what follows, is closed under Internal Uniform Substitution, as Observation 4 claims. For suppose $\vdash \varphi$, with φ having a subformula ψ to which occurrences of p_i in φ are confined. Then we can write φ in the form $\#(\psi, \beta_1, \ldots, \beta_n)$, for a suitable choice of $\#$ (and in fact we can also require that the β_i all be propositional variables). Our formulation (†) requires that $\vdash \varphi(\psi')$, where $\varphi(\psi')$ has ψ throughout φ replaced by any conjunction ψ' of substitution instances of ψ got by substituting formulas $\chi_1, \ldots, \chi_m$ for p_i. In the current notation ψ' is $\ast(s_1(\psi), \ldots, s_m(\psi)) = s_1(\psi) \wedge \ldots \wedge s_m(\psi)$, and the Theorem tells us that $\vdash \varphi(\psi')$, since the conditions it imposes on $\vdash$, $\#$, and $\ast$ are all satisfied.[81] Notice that we could equally well have obtained as a corollary a variant result by taking $\ast(s_1(\psi), \ldots, s_m(\psi))$ as $s_1(\psi) \lor \ldots \lor s_m(\psi)$, though the conjunctive formulation used in the definition of internal (uniform) substitution is what is relevant to the example,[82] discussed at the appearance of Observation 4 in Section 5, of how such normal modal logics as **KT, S4**, and **S5** fail to be closed under internal substitution: provability of $\Diamond(p \to \Box p)$ contrasted with unprovability of $\Diamond((p \to \Box p) \wedge (q \to \Box q))$. Note that in this example $n = 0$: there are no "side-formulas" $\beta_1, \ldots, \beta_n$.

---

[81]   Here we have in mind the class of all Boolean valuations as the determining class for $\vdash$, i.e. those valuations that associate the expected truth-functions with such primitive connectives as are present. Thus whereas all the Theorem requires is that every valuation in the determining class associates a truth-function (an idempotent truth-function) associated with $\#$ (with $\ast$), in the present instance we have the stronger $\exists \forall$ forms of these $\forall \exists$ requirements—see the preceding note.

[82]   In view of the availability of the disjunctive version just noted, a more explicit terminology might in other contexts be desirable, in which the current idea of internal substitution was referred to as 'conjunctively internal' substitution.

Appendix 20.4 A Slightly Bigger Picture

Here, for brevity, we write $\bar{q}$ for $\neg q$ and put $X(q) = \Box q \lor (\bar{q} \land \nabla q)$. Thus $X(\bar{q})$ is $\Box \bar{q} \lor (q \land \nabla \bar{q})$, which is equivalent to $\Box \bar{q} \lor (q \land \nabla q)$. See Figure 20. A1. The sixteen equivalence classes of modal formulas in a single variable shown in Figure 20.A1 are listed in Carnap (1946: 48), but it seems worthwhile to display their logical relations in a Hasse diagram, as here, to fill out the picture provided by Figure 20.5 from our Section 3, which can be seen sitting inside the current Boolean algebra as a subalgebra. Carnap was concerned with enumerating the one-variable formulas—to within equivalence—arising in **S5**, but the picture is the same for any normal modal logic from **KT** to **S5** (and indeed considerably beyond: the intrepid reader is invited to construct similar diagrams for **KD** and— larger still—for **K**; there are 2^6 and 2^8 elements, respectively, in these two cases, compared with our modest 2^4). Of course there is a certain arbitrariness in deciding which formula to write down from each equivalence class. For example, instead of '$\bar{q} \lor \Delta q$', we could have used '$\bar{q} \lor \Box q$', and instead of '$\bar{q} \land \nabla q$', '$\bar{q} \land \Diamond q$' (to say nothing of "Blanché-style" alternatives, such as '$q \lor \nabla q$' for '$\Diamond(q$', or forms in which negation occurs other than pre-atomically . . .).

  If someone is asked to list quickly and without repetitions representatives of the equivalence classes of formulas of **KT** that can be written without a modal operator in the scope of a modal operator, there is a good chance that only fourteen of the above sixteen candidates will be recorded, with—in my experience—those most likely to go missing being what I have called $X(q)$ and $X(\bar{q})$, which latter I shall revert to writing as $X\neg(q)$. A glance at Figure 20.A1 shows that these two are each other's complements: they have **1** as their least upper bound and **0** as their greatest lower bound. Thus, treating the labels as labels for the equivalence classes involved, $X\neg(q) = \neg X(q)$, or, reformulating the point, with $X = \lambda q.X(q)$, pre-negating and post-negating X give the same result, or again: X is self-dual ($X = \delta(X)$, in the notation of Section 3). It seems surprising to find such an unusual modality, or indeed anything at all, lurking, alongside truth (i.e. alongside

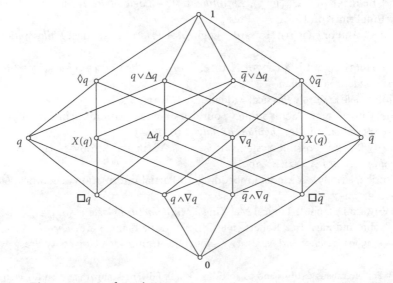

Fig 20. A1. Figure 20.5 and environs

$\lambda q.q$), between necessity and possibility in this one-variable fragment. What was abbreviated to $X(q)$ was $\Box q \lor (\overline{q} \land \nabla q)$: an ungainly, disjunctive mouthful, as is an obvious equivalent: $\Box q \lor (\overline{q} \land \Diamond q)$. We should recall, however, that even $\Diamond q$ itself has the disjunctive representation $q \lor \nabla q$, in which again the disjuncts are completely independent (logically), though we do not think of the claim that it is possible that q as suffering from any such cobbled together disjunctivity, and it takes some cognitive effort to see that these two representations are indeed equivalent. (One might regard Δq as itself artificially disjunctive: but think of it as saying that any two accessible worlds agree on the truth-value of q.) So perhaps something as simply graspable as the idea of possibility can be found in the case of $X(q)$, as defined. An alternative representation of $X(q)$ is available in the form of $(q \rightarrow \Box q) \land \Diamond q$, though this—or more accurately the result of preceding this with 'λq'—still seems hard to grasp as expressing a unitary concept. In our current state of understanding, however, such hyperintensional considerations have a somewhat speculative ring to them, it being hard to say in precise terms even what is meant by talk of expressing a unitary concept here.[83]

REFERENCES

Ackrill, J. L. (1963). *Aristotle's Categories and De Interpretatione*. Oxford: Clarendon Press.

Alexandrescu, Sorin (1983). 'Saying and (Dis)believing', in Herman Parret (ed.), *On Believing: Epistemological and Semiotic Approaches*. Berlin: De Gruyter.

Altman, Jack, and Ziporyn, Marvin (1967). *Born to Raise Hell: The Untold Story of Richard Speck*. New York: Grove Press.

Anderson, Alan Ross (1958). 'A Reduction of Deontic Logic to Alethic Modal Logic'. *Mind*, 67: 100–3.

—— (1966). 'The Formal Analysis of Normative Systems', in N. Rescher (ed.), *The Logic of Decision and Action*. Pittsburgh: University of Pittsburgh Press.

—— and Belnap, Nuel D. (1975). *Entailment: The Logic of Relevance and Necessity*, I. Princeton: Princeton University Press.

Anderson, C. Anthony (1993). 'Toward a Logic of *A Priori* Knowledge'. *Philosophical Topics*, 21: 1–20.

Ayer, A. J. (1963). 'What Is a Law of Nature?', in Ayer, *The Concept of a Person, and Other Essays*. London: Macmillan.

Bacon, John (1981). 'Purely Physical Modalities'. *Theoria*, 47:134–41.

Bailhache, Patrice (1977). 'Sémantiques pour des systèmes déontiques intégrant permission faible et permission forte'. *Logique et Analyse*, 20: 286–316.

—— (1980). 'Several Possible Systems of Deontic Weak and Strong Norms'. *Notre Dame Journal of Formal Logic*, 21: 89–100.

Barba Escriba, J. (1989). 'A Modal Embedding for Partial Information Semantics'. *Logique et Analyse*, 32: 131–7.

Bender, Edward D. (1966). 'Logical Mappings'. *Mathematical Gazette*, 50: 132–3.

Bigelow, John, and Pargetter, Robert (1987). 'Beyond the Blank Stare'. *Theoria*, 53: 97–119.

—— —— (1990). *Science and Necessity*. Cambridge: Cambridge University Press.

---

[83] For several suggestions and corrections I thank Edward Khamara and Su Rogerson.

Blackburn, Simon (1984). *Spreading the Word*. Oxford: Clarendon Press.

—— (1986). 'Morals and Modals', in Graham Macdonald and Crispin Wright (eds.), *Fact, Science and Morality*. Oxford: Blackwell.

Blamey, Stephen, and Humberstone, Lloyd (1991). 'A Perspective on Modal Sequent Logic'. *Publications of the Research Institute for Mathematical Sciences, Kyoto University*, 27: 763–82.

Blanché, Robert (1953). 'Sur l'opposition des concepts'. *Theoria*, 19: 89–130.

—— (1966). *Structures intellectuelles*. Paris: Librairie Philosophique J. Vrin.

Bolinger, Dwight (1989). 'Extrinsic Possibility and Intrinsic Potentiality: 7 on May and Can + 1'. *Journal of Pragmatics*, 13: 1–23.

Boolos, George (1993). *The Logic of Provability*. Cambridge: Cambridge University Press.

Bradley, F. H. (1883). *The Principles of Logic*, i. Oxford: Oxford University Press.

Brock, Stuart (1993). 'Modal Fictionalism: A Response to Rosen'. *Mind*, 102: 147–50.

—— (1995). *'Paradise for Nothing? A Critique of Modal Fictionalism'*. Master's thesis, Australian National University.

Brown, Mark A. (1984). 'Generalized Quantifiers and the Square of Opposition'. *Notre Dame Journal of Formal Logic*, 25: 303–22.

—— (1988). 'On the Logic of Ability'. *Journal of Philosophical Logic*, 17: 1–26.

—— (1990). 'Action and Ability'. *Journal of Philosophical Logic*, 19: 95–114.

Bull, Robert A. (1967). 'On the Extension of S4 with *CLMpMLp*'. *Notre Dame Journal of Formal Logic*, 8: 325–9.

—— and Segerberg, Krister (1984). 'Basic Modal Logic', in D. M. Gabbay and F. Guenthner (eds.), *Handbook of Philosophical Logic*, ii: *Extensions of Classical Logic*. Dordrecht: Reidel.

—— —— (2001). 'Basic Modal Logic', in D. M. Gabbay and F. Guenther (eds.), *Handbook of Philosophical Logic*, 2nd edn., iii. Dordrecht: Kluwer.

Burgess, John A. (1997). 'Supervaluations and the Propositional Attitude Constraint'. *Journal of Philosophical Logic*, 26: 103–19.

Burgess, John P. (1969). 'Probability Logic'. *Journal of Symbolic Logic*, 34: 264–74.

—— (1999). 'Which Modal Logic Is the Right One?' *Notre Dame Journal of Formal Logic*, 40: 81–93.

Burks, A. W. (1951). 'The Logic of Causal Propositions'. *Mind*, 60: 363–82.

Carnap, Rudolf (1946). 'Modalities and Quantification'. *Journal of Symbolic Logic*, 2: 33–64.

Chafe, Wallace, and Nichols, Johanna (eds.) (1986). *Evidentiality: The Linguistic Coding of Epistemology*. Norwood, NJ: Ablex Publishing.

Chagrov, A. V., and Zakharyaschev, M. (1997). *Modal Logic*. Oxford: Clarendon Press.

Chellas, B. F. (1975). 'Basic Conditional Logic'. *Journal of Philosophical Logic*, 4: 133–53.

—— (1980). *Modal Logic: An Introduction*. Cambridge: Cambridge University Press.

—— and Segerberg, K. (1994). 'Modal Logics with the MacIntosh Rule'. *Journal of Philosophical Logic*, 23: 67–86.

Chihara, Charles (1998). *The Worlds of Possibility*. Oxford: Clarendon Press.

Chisholm, Roderick M. (1963). 'Supererogation and Offence: A Conceptual Scheme for Ethics'. *Ratio*, 5: 1–14.

Copeland, B. J. (1996). 'Prior's Life and Legacy', in Copeland (ed.), *Logic and Reality: Essays on the Legacy of Arthur Prior*. Oxford: Clarendon Press.

—— (1999). 'Notes Toward a History of Possible Worlds Semantics', in Krister Segerberg (ed.), *The Goldblatt Variations*. Uppsala University Department of Philosophy Preprints Series.

Copeland, B. J. (2002). 'The Genesis of Possible Worlds Semantics'. *Journal of Philosophical Logic*, 31: 99–137.

Cresswell, M. J. (2001). 'Modal Logic', in Lou Goble (ed.), *The Blackwell Guide to Philosophical Logic*. Oxford: Blackwell.

—— (2004). 'Possibility Semantics for Intuitionistic Logic'. *Australasian Journal of Logic*, 2: 11–29.

Czeżowski, Tadeusz (1955). 'On Certain Peculiarities of Singular Propositions'. *Mind*, 64: 392–5.

Dancy, Jonathan (1985). *An Introduction to Contemporary Epistemology*. Oxford: Blackwell.

de Lavalette, G. R. Renardel (1981). 'The Interpolation Theorem in Fragments of Logics'. *Indagationes Mathematicae*, 43: 71–86.

Dixon, R. M. W. (1972). *The Dyirbal Language of North Queensland*. Cambridge: Cambridge University Press.

Dunn, J. Michael (1973). 'A Truth Value Semantics for Modal Logic', in H. Leblanc (ed.), *Truth, Syntax and Modality*. Amsterdam: North-Holland.

—— (1986). 'Relevance Logic and Entailment', in D. M. Gabbay and F. Guenthner (eds.), *Handbook of Philosophical Logic*, iii: *Alternatives to Classical Logic*. Dordrecht: Reidel.

—— (1995). 'Positive Modal Logic'. *Studia Logica*, 55: 301–17.

Elder, Crawford L. (1994). 'Laws, Natures, and Contingent Necessities'. *Philosophy and Phenomenological Research*, 54: 649–67.

Evans, Gareth (1979). 'Reference and Contingency'. *The Monist*, 62: 161–89.

Fine, Kit (1975). 'Vagueness, Truth, and Logic'. *Synthese*, 30: 265–300.

—— (1977). Postscript to A. N. Prior and K. Fine, *Worlds, Times and Selves*. London: Duckworth.

Fleischer, Isidore (1984). ' "Kripke Semantics" = Algebra + Poetry'. *Logique et Analyse*, 27: 283–95.

Forbes, Graeme (1985). *The Metaphysics of Modality*. Oxford: Clarendon Press.

—— (1989). *Languages of Possibility: An Essay in Philosophical Logic*. Oxford: Blackwell.

—— (1992). 'Worlds and States of Affairs: How Similar Can they Be?', in K. Mulligan (ed.), *Language, Truth and Ontology*. Dordrecht: Kluwer.

Gabbay, Dov M. (1976). *Investigations in Modal and Tense Logics with Applications to Problems in Philosophy and Linguistics*. Dordrecht: Reidel.

—— (1981). 'An Irreflexivity Lemma with Applications to Axiomatizations of Conditions on Tense Frames', in Uwe Mönnich (ed.), *Aspects of Philosophical Logic*. Dordrecht: Reidel.

Gallois, André (1977). 'Van Inwagen on Free Will and Determinism'. *Philosophical Studies*, 32: 99–105.

Garson, James W. (1972). 'Two New Interpretations of Modality'. *Logique et Analyse*, 15: 443–59.

Geach, P. T. (1969). 'Contradictories and Contraries'. *Analysis*, 29: 187–90.

—— (1972). 'A Program for Syntax', in D. Davidson and G. Harman (eds.), *Semantics of Natural Language*. Dordrecht: Reidel.

Geerts, W., and Melis, L. (1976). 'Remarques sur le traitement de modalités en linguistique'. *Langages*, 43: 108–23.

Goble, Lou (ed.) (2001). *The Blackwell Guide to Philosophical Logic*. Oxford: Blackwell.

Goldblatt, Robert (1993). *Mathematics of Modality*. Stanford, Calif.: CSLI.

—— (2003). 'Mathematical Modal Logic: A View of its Evolution'. *Journal of Applied Logic*, 1: 309–92.

Goranko, Valentin (1990). 'Modal Definability in Enriched Languages'. *Notre Dame Journal of Formal Logic*, 31: 81–105.

Gottschalk, W. H. (1953). 'The Theory of Quaternality'. *Journal of Symbolic Logic*, 18: 193–6.

Groenendijk, Jeroen, and Stokof, Martin (1975). 'Modality and Conversational Information'. *Theoretical Linguistics*, 2: 61–112.

Hacker, Edward A. (1978). 'The Octagon of Opposition'. *Notre Dame Journal of Formal Logic*, 16: 252–3.

Hale, Bob (1996). 'Absolute Necessities'. *Philosophical Perspectives*, 10: 93–117.

Halldén, Sören (1951). 'On the Semantic Non-Completeness of Certain Lewis Calculi'. *Journal of Symbolic Logic*, 16: 127–9.

—— (1963). 'A Pragmatic Approach to Modal Theory'. *Acta Philosophica Fennica*, 16: 53–64.

Halpern, Joseph Y. (1996). 'Should Knowledge Entail Belief?' *Journal of Philosophical Logic*, 25: 483–94.

Hamblin, C. L. (1959). 'The Modal "Probably"'. *Mind*, 68: 234–40.

Hare, R. M. (1971). *Practical Inferences*. London: Macmillan.

Harman, Gilbert (1972). 'Is Modal Logic Logic?' *Philosophia*, 2: 75–84.

Hilpinen, Risto (1969). 'An Analysis of Relativized Modalities', in J. W. Davis, D. J. Hockney, and W. K. Wilson (eds.), *Philosophical Logic*. Dordrecht: Reidel.

Hintikka, Jaakko (1962). *Knowledge and Belief: An Introduction to the Logic of the Two Notions*. Ithaca, NY: Cornell University Press.

—— (1971). 'Some Main Problems of Deontic Logic', in R. Hilpinen (ed.), *Deontic Logic: Introductory and Systematic Readings*. Dordrecht: Reidel.

Horn, Laurence R. (1989). *A Natural History of Negation*. Chicago: University of Chicago Press.

Horty, John F. (2001). *Agency and Deontic Logic*. Oxford: Oxford University Press.

Huemer, Michael (2000). 'Van Inwagen's Consequence Argument'. *Philosophical Review*, 109: 525–44.

Hughes, G. E., and Cresswell, M. J. (1968). *An Introduction to Modal Logic*. London: Methuen.

—— —— (1984). *A Companion to Modal Logic*. London: Methuen.

—— —— (1996). *A New Introduction to Modal Logic*. London: Routledge.

Humberstone, Lloyd (1982). 'Necessary Conclusions'. *Philosophical Studies*, 41: 321–35.

—— (1983). 'Inaccessible Worlds'. *Notre Dame Journal of Formal Logic*, 24: 346–52.

—— (1985). 'The Formalities of Collective Omniscience'. *Philosophical Studies*, 48: 401–23.

—— (1988). 'Extensionality in Sentence Position'. *Journal of Philosophical Logic*, 15: 27–54. Corrections, *Journal of Philosophical Logic*, 17: 221–3.

—— (1987). 'The Modal Logic of "All and Only"'. *Notre Dame Journal of Formal Logic*, 28: 177–88.

—— (1988). 'Heterogeneous Logic'. *Erkenntnis*, 29: 395–435.

—— (1990). 'Expressive Power and Semantic Completeness: Boolean Connectives in Modal Logic'. *Studia Logica*, 49: 197–214.

—— (1991). 'Two Kinds of Agent-Relativity'. *Philosophical Quarterly*, 41: 144–66.

—— (1996). 'Homophony, Validity, Modality', in B. J. Copeland (ed.), *Logic and Reality: Essays on the Legacy of A. N. Prior*. Oxford: Clarendon Press.

—— (2000). 'What *Fa* Says About *a*'. *Dialectica*, 54: 1–28.

—— (2003). 'Note on Contraries and Subcontraries'. *Noûs*, 37: 690–705.

—— (2004). 'Two-Dimensional Adventures'. *Philosophical Studies*, 118: 17–65.

—— and Williamson, Timothy (1997). 'Inverses for Normal Modal Operators'. *Studia Logica*, 59: 33–64.

Jackson, Frank (1985). 'On the Semantics and Logic of Obligation'. *Mind*, 94: 177–95.

Jackson, Frank, and Pargetter, Robert (1986). 'Oughts, Options, and Actualism'. *Philosophical Review*, 95: 233–55.

Jennings, R. E. (1994). *The Genealogy of Disjunction*. New York: Oxford University Press.

Jones, Andrew J. I., and Pörn, Ingmar (1985). 'Ideality, Sub-Ideality and Deontic Logic'. *Synthese*, 65: 275–90.

—— (1986). ' "Ought" and "Must" '. *Synthese*, 66: 89–93.

Kaplan, David (1995). 'A Problem in Possible-World Semantics', in W. Sinnott-Armstrong, D. Raffman, and N. Asher (eds.), *Modality, Morality, and Belief: Essays in Honor of Ruth Barcan Marcus*. Cambridge: Cambridge University Press.

Karttunen, Lauri (1972). 'Possible and Must', in J. P. Kimball (ed.), *Syntax and Semantics*, i. New York: Seminar Press.

Kenny, Anthony (1966). 'Happiness'. *Proceedings of the Aristotelian Society*, 66: 93–102.

—— (1975). *Will, Freedom, and Power*. Oxford: Blackwell.

Keynes, J. N. (1906). *Studies and Exercises in Formal Logic*, 4th edn. London: Macmillan.

Khamara, E. J. (2001). 'Modality in Aristotle's *De Interpretatione*', in preparation.

Kneale, William (1947). 'Are Necessary Truths True by Convention?' *Proceedings of the Aristotelian Society*, suppl. vol., 21: 119–33.

—— and Kneale, Martha (1962). *The Development of Logic*. Oxford: Clarendon Press.

Kracht, Marcus (1999). 'Modal Logics that Need Very Large Frames'. *Notre Dame Journal of Formal Logic*, 40: 141–73.

Kratzer, Angelika (1977). 'What "Must" and "Can" Must and Can Mean'. *Linguistics and Philosophy*, 1: 337–55.

Kripke, Saul A. (1963). 'Semantical Considerations on Modal Logic'. *Acta Philosophica Fennica*, 16: 83–94.

—— (1967). 'Reviews (##5660, 5661) of E. J. Lemmon, "Algebraic Semantics for Modal Logics. I and II" '. *Mathematical Reviews*, 34: 1021–2.

—— (1980). *Naming and Necessity*. Oxford: Blackwell.

Kuhn, Steven T. (1980). 'Quantifiers as Modal Operators'. *Studia Logica*, 39: 145–58.

—— (1981). 'Logical Expressions, Constants, and Operator Logic'. *Journal of Philosophy*, 78: 487–99.

—— (1989). 'The Domino Relation: Flattening a Two-Dimensional Logic'. *Journal of Philosophical Logic*, 18: 173–95.

—— (1995). 'Minimal Non-Contingency Logic'. *Notre Dame Journal of Formal Logic*, 36: 230–4.

Lakoff, Robin (1972). 'The Pragmatics of Modality'. *Chicago Linguistics Society*, 8: 229–46.

Lemmon, E. J. (1959). 'Is there Only One Correct System of Modal Logic?' *Proceedings of the Aristotelian Society*, suppl. vol., 33: 23–40.

—— (1967). 'If I Know, Do I Know that I Know?', in A. Stroll (ed.), *Epistemology: New Essays in the Theory of Knowledge*. New York: Harper & Row.

—— with Scott, D. S. (1977). *An Introduction to Modal Logic*, ed. K. Segerberg. Oxford: Blackwell.

Lenzen, Wolfgang (1978). *Recent Work in Epistemic Logic*, Acta Philosophica Fennica, 30.

Levesque, Hector J. (1990). 'All I Know: A Study in Autoepistemic Logic'. *Artificial Intelligence*, 42: 263–309.

Lewis, C. I., and Langford, C. H. (1959). *Symbolic Logic*, 2nd edn. New York: Dover.

Lewis, David (1968). 'Counterpart Theory and Quantified Modal Logic'. *Journal of Philosophy*, 65: 113–26.

—— (1973). *Counterfactuals*. Oxford: Blackwell.

—— (1986). *On the Plurality of Worlds*. Oxford: Blackwell.

Linsky, Leonard (1967). *Referring*. London: Routledge & Kegan Paul.

Lucas, J. R. (1982). 'Moods and Tenses'. Merton College Hilary Term Lectures, Oxford.

Lyons, John (1977). *Semantics*, ii. Cambridge: Cambridge University Press.

McFetridge, Ian (1990). *Logical Necessity and Other Essays*, ed. J. Haldane and R. Scruton. London: Aristotelian Society.

McGinn, Colin (1981). 'Modal Reality', in R. Healey (ed.), *Reduction, Time and Reality*. Cambridge: Cambridge University Press.

—— (2000). *Logical Properties*. Oxford: Clarendon Press.

Mackie, J. L. (1958). ' "This" as a Singular Quantifier'. *Mind*, 67: 522–6.

Makinson, David (1965). 'The Paradox of the Preface'. *Analysis*, 25: 205–7.

—— (1966). 'On Some Completeness Theorems in Modal Logic'. *Zeitschrift für mathematische Logik und Grundlagen der Mathematik*, 12: 379–84.

—— (1981). 'Quantificational Reefs in Deontic Waters', in R. Hilpinen (ed.), *New Studies in Deontic Logic*. Dordrecht: Reidel.

—— (1983). 'Individual Actions Are Very Seldom Obligatory'. *Journal of Non-Classical Logic*, 2: 7–13.

Menzies, Peter, and Pettit, Philip (1994). 'In Defence of Fictionalism About Possible Worlds'. *Analysis*, 54: 27–36.

Montague, Richard (1974). *Formal Philosophy*, ed. R. H. Thomason. London: Yale University Press.

Montgomery, H., and Routley, R. (1966). 'Contingency and Non-Contingency Bases for Normal Modal Logics'. *Logique et Analyse*, 9: 318–28.

Mortensen, Chris (1989). 'Anything Is Possible'. *Erkenntnis*, 30: 319–37.

Noonan, Harold W. (1994). 'In Defence of the Letter of Fictionalism'. *Analysis*, 54: 133–9.

Nozick, Robert (2001). *Invariances: The Structure of the Objective World*. Cambridge, Mass.: Harvard University Press.

Oppy, Graham (1995). *Ontological Arguments and Belief in God*. Cambridge: Cambridge University Press.

Palmer, F. R. (1986). *Mood and Modality*. Cambridge: Cambridge University Press.

Pap, Arthur (1958). *Semantics and Necessary Truth*. New Haven: Yale University Press.

Pargetter, Robert (1984). 'Laws and Modal Realism'. *Philosophical Studies*, 46: 335–47.

Parry, William T., and Hacker, Edward A. (1991). *Aristotelian Logic*. Albany, NY: State University of New York Press.

Pcacocke, Christopher (1999). *Being Known*. Oxford: Clarendon Press.

Pelletier, F. J. (1984). 'The Not-So-Strange Modal Logic of Indeterminacy'. *Logique et Analyse*, 27: 415–22.

Perry, John (1986). 'From Worlds to Situations'. *Journal of Philosophical Logic*, 15: 83–107.

Pörn, Ingmar (1970). *The Logic of Power*. Oxford: Blackwell.

Porte, Jean (1981). 'The Deducibilities of S5'. *Journal of Philosophical Logic*, 10: 409–22.

Price, Huw (1994). 'Semantic Minimalism and the Frege Point', in S. L. Tsohatzidis (ed.), *Foundations of Speech Act Theory*. London: Routledge.

Prior, A. N. (1955). 'Many-Valued and Modal Systems: An Intuitive Approach'. *Philosophical Review*, 64: 626–30.

—— (1962). *Formal Logic*, 2nd edn. Oxford: Clarendon Press.

—— (1967). *Past, Present and Future*. Oxford: Clarendon Press.

Prior, A. N. (1968). 'Time and Change'. *Ratio*, 10: 173–7.

Rabinowicz, W., and Segerberg, K. (1994). 'Actual Truth, Possible Knowledge'. *Topoi*, 13: 101–15.

Rivière, Claude (1981). 'Is *Should* a Weaker *Must*?' *Journal of Linguistics*, 17: 179–95.

Robinson, Richard (1958). 'Necessary Propositions'. *Mind*, 67: 289–304.

—— (1971). 'Ought and Ought Not'. *Philosophy*, 46: 193–202.

Rosen, Gideon (1990). 'Modal Fictionalism'. *Mind*, 99: 327–54.

—— (1993). 'A Problem for Fictionalism About Possible Worlds'. *Analysis*, 53: 71–81.

Routley, Richard, and Meyer, Robert K. (1976). 'Every Sentential Logic Has a Two-Valued Worlds Semantics'. *Logique et Analyse*, 19: 345–65.

——Plumwood, V., Meyer, R. K., and Brady, R. T. (1982). *Relevant Logics and their Rivals*. Atascadero, Calif.: Ridgeview.

——and Routley, Valerie (1969). 'A Fallacy of Modality'. *Noûs*, 3: 129–53.

Russell, Bertrand (1986). 'The Philosophy of Logical Atomism', in John G. Slater (ed.), *The Philosophy of Logical Atomism and Other Essays 1914–19: The Collected Papers of Bertrand Russell*, vii. London: Allen & Unwin.

—— (1940). *An Inquiry into Meaning and Truth*. London: Allen & Unwin.

Saito, Setsuo (1966). 'On the Completeness of the Leibnizian Modal System with a Reduction'. *Proceedings of the Japan Academy*, 42: 198–200.

—— (1968). 'On the Leibnizian Modal System'. *Notre Dame Journal of Formal Logic*, 9: 92–6.

Salmon, Nathan (1986). 'Modal Paradox: Parts and Counterparts, Points and Counterpoints', in P. A. French, T. E. Uehling, and H. K. Wettstein (eds.), *Midwest Studies in Philosophy*, xi: *Studies in Essentialism*. Minneapolis: University of Minnesota Press.

—— (1989). 'The Logic of What Might Have Been'. *Philosophical Review*, 98: 3–34.

Sanford, D. H. (1968). 'Contraries and Subcontraries'. *Noûs*, 2: 95–6.

Sauriol, Pierre (1969). 'Remarques sur le théorie de l'hexagone logique de Blanché'. *Dialogue*, 7: 374–90.

Schotch, P. K. (2000). 'Skepticism and Epistemic Logic'. *Studia Logica* 65: 187–98.

——and Jennings, R. E. (1981a). 'Non-Kripkean Deontic Logic', in R. Hilpinen (ed.), *New Studies in Deontic Logic*. Dordrecht: Reidel.

—— (1981b). 'Epistemic Logic, Skepticism, and Non-Normal Modal Logic'. *Philosophical Studies*, 40: 47–67.

Schumm, George F. (1993). 'Why Does Halldén-Completeness Matter?' *Theoria*, 59: 192–206.

Schurz, Gerhard (1994). 'Admissible versus Valid Rules: A Case Study of the Modal Fallacy'. *The Monist*, 77: 376–88.

Segerberg, Krister (1992). 'Getting Started: Beginnings in the Logic of Action'. *Studia Logica*, 51: 347–78.

Seuren, Pieter. (ed.) (1974). *Semantic Syntax*. London: Oxford University Press.

Shoemaker, Sydney (1998). 'Causal and Metaphysical Necessity'. *Pacific Philosophical Quarterly*, 79: 59–77.

Simons, Peter (1993). 'Opposition, Obversion, and Duality', in R. Poli (ed.), *Consciousness, Knowledge and Truth*. Dordrecht: Kluwer.

—— (2001). 'A Precarious Relationship: Modal and Many-Valued Logic, 1900–1955', in Werner Stelzner and Manfred Stöckler (eds.), *Zwischen traditioneller und moderner Logik*. Paderborn: Mentis.

Sinnott-Armstrong, W., Raffman, D., and Asher, N. (eds.) (1995). *Modality, Morality, and Belief: Essays in Honor of Ruth Barcan Marcus*. Cambridge: Cambridge University Press.

Skyrms, Brian (1978). 'An Immaculate Conception of Modality; or, How to Confuse Use and Mention'. *Journal of Philosophy*, 75: 368–87.

Smiley, T. J. (1961). 'On Łukasiewicz's Ł-Modal System'. *Notre Dame Journal of Formal Logic*, 2: 149–53.

—— (1963). 'Relative Necessity'. *Journal of Symbolic Logic*, 28: 113–34.

Sorensen, Roy (1988). *Blindspots*. Oxford: Clarendon Press.

—— (2001). *Vagueness and Contradiction*. Oxford: Clarendon Press.

Stalnaker, Robert C. (1999). *Context and Content*. Oxford: Oxford University Press.

Sweetser, Eve (1990). *From Etymology to Pragmatics*. Cambridge: Cambridge University Press.

Thomason, S. K. (1972). 'Semantic Analysis of Tense Logics'. *Journal of Symbolic Logic*, 37: 150–8.

Tooley, Michael (ed.) (1999). *Necessity and Possibility: The Metaphysics of Modality*. New York: Garland.

van Benthem, Johan (1979a). 'Syntactic Aspects of Modal Incompleteness Theorems'. *Theoria*, 45: 63–77.

—— (1979b). 'Minimal Deontic Logics' (Abstract). *Bulletin of the Section of Logic*, 8: 36–42.

—— (1984). 'Possible Worlds Semantics: A Research Program that Cannot Fail?' *Studia Logica*, 43: 379–93.

—— (1985). *Modal Logic and Classical Logic*. Naples: Bibliopolis.

—— (1986a). 'Partiality and Nonmonotonicity in Classical Logic'. *Logique et Analyse*, 29: 225–46.

—— (1986b). *Essays in Logical Semantics*. Dordrecht: Reidel.

—— (1989). 'Syntactic Type-Change and Syntactic Recognition', in G. Chierchia, B. H. Partee, and R. Turner (eds.), *Properties, Types and Meaning*, i: Dordrecht: Kluwer.

—— (1991). *Language in Action: Categories, Lambdas and Dynamic Logic*. Amsterdam: North-Holland.

—— (1994). 'A New World Underneath Standard Logic: Cylindric Algebra, Modality and Quantification', in Krzystof Apt, Lex Schrijver, and Nico Temme (eds.), *From Universal Morphisms to Megabytes: A Baayen Space Odyssey*. Amsterdam: Stichting Mathematisch Centrum.

van Fraassen, Bas C. (1971). *Formal Semantics and Logic*. London: Macmillan.

van Inwagen, Peter (1975). 'The Incompatibility of Free Will and Determinism'. *Philosophical Studies*, 27: 185–99.

—— (1983). *An Essay on Free Will*. Oxford: Clarendon Press.

—— (1986). 'Two Concepts of Possible Worlds', in P. A. French, T. E. Uehling, and H. K. Wettstein (eds.), *Midwest Studies in Philosophy*, xi: *Studies in Essentialism*. Minnesota: University of Minneapolis Press.

Veltman, Frank (1981). 'Data Semantics', in J. A. G. Groenendijk, T. M. V. Janssen, and M. B. J. Stokhof (eds.), *Formal Methods in the Study of Language*, pt. 2. Amsterdam: Stichting Mathematisch Centrum.

von Wright, G. H. (1951). *An Essay in Modal Logic*. Amsterdam: North-Holland.

—— (1957). *Logical Studies*. London: Routledge & Kegan Paul.

Wansing, Heinrich (1994). 'Sequent Calculi for Normal Modal Logics'. *Journal of Logic and Computation*, 4: 125–42.

—— (ed.) (1996). *Proof Theory of Modal Logic*. Dordrecht: Kluwer.

Wansing, Heinrich (1998a). 'Translation of Hypersequents into Display Sequents'. *Logic Journal of the IGPL*, 6: 719–33.

——— (1998b). *Displaying Modal Logic*. Dordrecht: Kluwer.

Wertheimer, Roger (1972). *The Significance of Sense*. Ithaca, NY: Cornell University Press.

White, Alan R. (1975). *Modal Thinking*. Oxford: Blackwell.

Widerker, David (2002). 'Farewell to the Direct Argument'. *Journal of Philosophy*, 99: 316–24.

Williams, Bernard (1972). 'Ethical Consistency', in Williams, *Problems of the Self*. Cambridge: Cambridge University Press.

Williams, John N. (1979). 'Moore's Paradox—One or Two?' *Analysis*, 39: 141–2.

Williams, S. G. (1986). 'On the Logical Possibility of Time without Change'. *Analysis*, 46: 122–5.

Williamson, Timothy (1992). 'Inexact Knowledge'. *Mind*, 101: 217–42.

——— (1998). 'Iterated Attitudes'. *Proceedings of the British Academy*, 93: 85–133.

Wiseman, C. (1970). 'The Theory of Modal Groups'. *Journal of Philosophy*, 67: 367–76.

CHAPTER 21

TIME

D. H. MELLOR

1. Space, Time, and Relativity

Many scientists, and some philosophers, still accept the canard that there is no such thing as progress in philosophy. There is no better way to scotch this canard than to see how far the philosophy of time has come in the last hundred years. The advance started with two developments at the start of the last century, one in physics and one in metaphysics, Einstein's 1905 special theory of relativity (Einstein *et al.* 1923), and McTaggart's (1908) *A*- and *B*-series theory of time and change. They revealed unexpected problems with two basic assumptions about time: that it is independent of space, and that it flows. These revelations, and later work in other areas of physics and philosophy, have greatly changed our ideas about time, and still inform the best work on its philosophy.

First, Einstein. Special relativity does not, as some have thought, assert a new unity of time and space. It should never have been news that time and the dimensions of space resemble each other more than they resemble any other way of ordering things, e.g. by their temperatures. To see this, consider first that, at any one time, space is or embodies an array of possible ways (namely, spatial points) by which things can be in contact, and so can interact immediately (at those points). What makes this array (and hence space itself) three-dimensional is the fact that there are only three independent ways in which two things *a* and *b* can fail to be in contact at any one time, e.g. by *a*'s being north-or-south, east-or-west, or above-or-below *b*.

This fact about space provides the extended sense in which any array of possibilities may be called a 'space'. It is in this sense that time combines with space to constitute the 'space' we call 'space-time' (Smart 1955). For whatever else time is, it too is a way in which *a* and *b* can fail to be in contact when in the same place, by being there at different times. And this is the only non-spatial way in which contact can fail. For whenever *a* and *b* (or their surfaces) share any spatial location, they are then and there in contact, and able thereby to interact immediately (if at all), however much they may differ in other ways.

Adding time to space thus completes a four-dimensional array of possible ways (space-time points) by which things can be in contact. This is what marks off time and space from everything else: the fact that people and things can—literally—contact each other by, and only by, being in the same place at the same time. The most important part of the answer to the question 'What is time?', which tells us how it differs from everything but space, is that it is one of the four dimensions of space-time. That is as true in Newtonian as it is in relativistic physics.

But time's being a dimension of spacetime does not make it spatial. Compare, for example, the 'colour space' shown in Figure 21.1, which represents the array of possible ways (single colours) by which things can match in colour. This space is three-dimensional, because there are just three independent ways in which two things can fail to match in colour: namely, by differing in hue, brightness, or saturation. Yet no one thinks that hue's being a dimension of colour space makes it spatial, let alone that using a spatial dimension to represent it, as Figure 21.1 does, makes it so. Nor would anyone infer from the fact that hue, brightness, and saturation are dimensions of colour space that they must be alike in any other respect, which they obviously are not. And it is, as Reichenbach noted in his (1928, §16), no more sensible to draw such inferences from diagrams like Figure 21.2, which use a spatial dimension to represent time as a dimension of space-time. Neither the form nor the content of this diagram shows that time is as spatial as space-time's

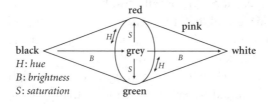

FIG. 21.1. 2-D spatial representation of 3-D colour space

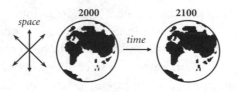

FIG. 21.2. 2-D spatial representation of 4-D colour space

other dimensions; and relativity does not say that it is. It does indeed link time to space in a new and striking way, but not (*pace* Quine 1960, §36) in a way that spatializes time. But as some may still think it does, it is worth saying again why it does not.

Note first that relativity uses the speed of light to give spatial and temporal distances a common measure, as when stars and galaxies are said to be N light years away. That in itself is nothing: any useful speed can provide a temporal measure of spatial distance, as when a hotel claims to be five minutes' walk from the sea. But in relativity the speed of light, c, does more than this: it provides a fixed exchange rate between spatial and temporal components s and t of a fixed space-time separation d of any two events e and f, given by

(1) $d^2 = s^2 - (c\,t)^2,$

where s and t vary from one 'reference frame' to another, and a frame may be defined by crediting any object, that is not accelerating, with a specific velocity (which may be zero).

Now let e and f be events that are some time t apart at (say) the North Pole, so that, taking the earth to be at rest, $s = 0$. So as t is positive, say t_0, $d^2 = -(c\,t_0)^2$ must be negative. (This, as s cannot be negative, stops t being zero in any frame, which is why intervals with negative d^2 are called 'timelike', and intervals with positive d^2, where s cannot be zero, 'spacelike'.) Next, take a reference frame in which the earth is moving, thus making s positive, say s_1. Then as d is a constant, t^2 in this frame, t_1^2, must equal $t_0^2 + (s_1/c)^2$. And similarly for all other pairs of frames: to keep d constant, s^2 and t^2 must differ by amounts Δs^2 and Δt^2 such that

(2) $\Delta s^2 = c^2\Delta t^2.$

This is what I mean by calling c an exchange rate between s and t for any e and f: its square is the ratio of the differences in their squares between any two reference frames.

The fact that (2) states an exchange rate, not an identity, is not always so obvious, especially when t is measured in years and s in light years. For then, as $c = 1$, (2) reduces to $\Delta t^2 = \Delta s^2$, which can look like an identity statement implying that t is as spatial as s. The quickest way to see that this is not so, and that (2), and hence (1), do not make t spatial, is to relate s to its components in any three orthogonal directions, e.g. the north-south, east-west, and up-down distances x, y, and z between e and f. Using that relation,

(3) $s^2 = x^2 + y^2 + z^2,$

to expand (1) into

(4) $d^2 = x^2 + y^2 + z^2 - (c\,t)^2$

shows how differently special relativity treats the spatial and temporal components of space-time separations.

2. COSMOLOGY AND THE PRESENT

If relativity does not make time like space, it does link their ontologies. The Leibniz–Clarke correspondence (1717), about whether time and space are entities, or kinds of relations between events and things, treats these questions about time and space separately. But even special relativity's limited interchangeability of spatial and temporal distances shows that there is really only one question: is there more to space-time than the spatio-temporal relations of events? That question is still open (Earman 1989; Nerlich 1994, pt. 2) and all I can say here is that general relativity, by making matter affect the curvature of space-time, which then affects matter's inertial properties, makes space-time look to me like an entity (Redhead 1998).

Besides relativity's implications for the ontology of space-time, it also poses problems for some accounts of how time differs from space. To see these we need our other innovation in the philosophy of time, McTaggart's two ways of ordering times into A- and B-series. The latter orders times by the *earlier* relation (or its converse, the later relation), while the former does it by their pastness, presence, or futurity. Either way, 'the varied simultaneous contents of a single [time] form an event . . . a compound substance consisting of simultaneous events' (McTaggart 1927, §306). So in both series the order of times fixes the time order of the universe-wide events E, F, . . . that are their contents, and hence that of all the local events which E, F, . . . contain. Both series thus require a simultaneity relation, to collect local events into the universe-wide ones from whose order they inherit their own.

The relevance of relativity to this is that it makes simultaneity at a distance relative to a reference frame. Take Polaris (the Pole star), reportedly about 390 light years away. If it is, a light signal that left earth in 2000 and was reflected back from near Polaris would return in 2780. But the earthly year of its reflection, r, is not thereby fixed, but varies with our choice of reference frame, i.e. (in effect) with how fast, if at all, we take the earth to be moving through space. In the earth's 'rest frame' r occurs in 2390, but other equally good frames place r in any year between 2000 and 2780. Different frames will thus combine different local events into the universe-wide events of McTaggart's time series. For while our rest frame combines r with events here in 2390, others will combine it with much earlier or later ones. In short, different frames produce different A- and B-series. Does this matter?

McTaggart considers the possibility of 'several real and independent time series' (oddly enough without mentioning the theory that implies them) and says that 'if there could be any A-series at all, and there were any reason to suppose that there were several distinct B-series, there would be no additional difficulty in supposing that there should be a distinct A-series for each B-series' (1927, §§322–3). And nor there would for him, since he takes all events and times to be equally real, wherever they are in his A- and B-series.

The theories for which relativity poses a problem are those that confine reality to the present (Prior 1970), or to the past and present (Broad 1923, pt. I, ch. II), so that to become present is to come to exist. Now whether something far off exists can hardly depend on a factually unconstrained choice of reference frame; yet if distant simultaneity does so, then so does what is present at a distance, since to be present there is to be simultaneous with what is present here.

Such theories therefore need a suitably privileged frame to define absolute simultaneity. This may be generated by inferring from our inability to measure a one-way (rather than a round trip) speed of light that its having one, the same in all directions (as my Polaris tale assumes), is not a fact but a convention (Salmon 1975, ch. 4). If it is, then we could, without denying any facts, give our reflection r the earthly date 2390 in all frames by taking light to travel out and back at one-way speeds which, by convention, we take to vary appropriately from frame to frame, and to differ from each other in nearly all frames other than ours.

This, however, will not do. For first, it is obviously not a convention but a fact that light has a one-way speed, the same in all directions and in all frames (Nerlich 1994, ch. 4). And if it was a mere convention, then whether something exists at a distance could no more credibly depend on it than on a factually free choice of reference frame. This is why few of those who take existence to depend on presence now rely on this verificationist reading of special relativity. Instead, they either deny that its non-spatial dimension is time (Q. Smith 1993, ch. 7), modify the theory to yield a suitably privileged reference frame (Tooley 1997, ch. 11), or look to other physics, especially cosmology, to remedy its deficiencies (Swinburne 1981, ch. 11). Of these responses, the first two seem to me to need better grounds for rejecting relativity as it stands, and as the theory of space-time it purports to be, than they have; while I deny that modern cosmology enables remote existence to depend on temporal presence, for the following reasons.

The relevant facts are these. On a large enough scale (that of clusters of galaxies), the universe looks much the same in all directions, and seems to be expanding uniformly from every point P within it. Its expansion takes remote clusters of galaxies away from P at speeds, proportional to their distances from P, given by the Hubble constant (0.037 metres per second per light year). This fact lets us define a rest frame at P (the one that makes the Hubble constant the same in all directions) which gives P a unique universe-wide simultaneity relation. But as the universe *is* expanding, anything at rest at P will be moving in the rest frames of all points with a spacelike separation from P. Thus in Polaris's frame, 390 light years to our north, anything at rest in our frame will be moving south at $390 \times 0.037 = 14.5$ metres per second. So our rest frame and Polaris's will give the reflection r (and all other remote events) different earthly dates, as will all other remote rest frames. And nothing in cosmology makes any of these frames, or the simultaneity they define, better than any other.

To this Swinburne and others reply with another definition of simultaneity made possible by the universe's uniform expansion. For suppose identical clocks here and

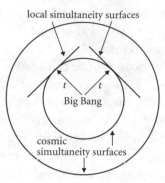

FIG. 21.3. Cosmic and local simultaneity relations

on Polaris had stayed at rest in their local rest frames ever since the Big Bang. Then we can define simultaneity between here and Polaris as the same time since the Big Bang as measured by such clocks, and similarly for all other remote locations. And while the simultaneity relation given by this 'cosmic time' differs from that given by any local rest frame, as Figure 21.3 shows, it is a very credible way of picking out what is happening *now* anywhere else in the universe.

The credibility of this way of defining temporal presence does not, however, extend to the idea that remote existence depends on it. For the continuing uniqueness of the present so defined depends on a permanent universe-wide large-scale isotropy, i.e. on the size, shape, and contents of the whole of space-time. But this makes the present depend on what exists elsewhere in space-time rather than the other way round. Cosmic time, far from rescuing the idea of existence depending on temporal presence, if anything raises the stakes against it.

3. TIME AND CHANGE

The existence of many equally good pairs of A- and B-series may make it hard to deny reality to parts of them; but it is, as McTaggart sees, no objection to the series themselves. Nor does it vitiate his claim that, for the non-spatial dimension of space-time to be temporal, it must be the dimension of change.

Change here I take to be temporal variation in the properties of things. By this I mean that changes are things having, at different times, incompatible properties, i.e. properties that no one thing could have at the same time. There are of course many families of properties whose members are incompatible in this sense, like mass, temperature, size, and shape. And by properties here I mean *intrinsic* properties, not the relational properties whose variations McTaggart also called changes but we do not, since we think things can gain or lose them without changing at all, as when a sibling's birth makes one lose the relational property of being an only child. Whether we should limit real changes to intrinsic properties—and what makes properties intrinsic (Langton and Lewis 1998)—may indeed be debated; but not here. All we need here are undeniable instances of change, which temporal variations of mass, temperature, size, and shape certainly are.

Time is certainly the dimension of change in this sense: variations must be temporal to be changes. But why is spatial variation not change? Admittedly, some properties, like size and shape, cannot vary spatially across an object. But some can, yet their spatial variations—like a poker's being hot at one end and cold at the other—are still not changes. Why not? It is not enough to say that temporal variation is what 'change' *means*, since that does not explain why we limit its meaning in this way. So why do we, and what light can our doing so shed on how time differs from space?

Note first that what stops a difference between different things, like one poker's being hot and another cold, being a change is that here there is no one thing that changes. But if this is all that stops differences being changes, a poker's temperature varying along its length should also be a change. And if it is not because this too is only a difference between different parts of it, such as its two ends, then why is not a poker's cooling also just such a difference, between different temporal parts of it?

Whether objects extended in both space and time have temporal as well as spatial parts is a moot point (Armstrong 1980; Simons 1987, ch. 5; Mellor 1998a, ch. 8.2). But settling it will not tell us what makes time and space differ. For it obviously will not if pokers do have temporal as well as spatial parts; while if they do not, this difference between time and space must surely follow from, rather than explain, a more basic one. What might that be?

McTaggart's answer invokes the apparent flow of time. First, he argues that change needs more than temporal variation. For if a poker is hot at one B-time t and cold at another, t', then it always was and always will be hot and cold at those times: those B-facts never change. The only facts that change are A-facts, like the poker's being hot *now*, which is a fact when t is the present time and not when t' is. This is why McTaggart thinks that only the A-series, whose continuous changes constitute the flow of time, can make time the one and only dimension of change that we all agree it is.

But is he right? The A-series does after all have spatial analogues. Imagine yourself in York, on the London–Edinburgh railway line. Then York is *here* (the analogue of *now*), Edinburgh is about 200 miles *north of here* (analogous to *later than now*), and London about 200 miles *south of here* (*earlier than now*). And just as only at t is t the present time, so only in York is York the (spatially) present place. In Edinburgh, York is not here but 200 miles south of here, while in London,

London is here and York is 200 miles north of here. And similarly in all other spatial directions.

This, however, no more makes space like time than relativity makes time like space. The mere description of a spatial A-series does not entail its reality, i.e. that on top of facts about how far north or south of each other London, York, and Edinburgh are, there are also facts about which of them (if any) is here, and about how far from here, and in which directions, the others are (Williams 1992). So what distinguishes time from space may be precisely that the temporal A-series is real and its spatial analogues are not. For since, as we have seen, time's being one dimension of space-time does not stop it differing from the others, this could be just what the difference is. It could be a primitive and inexplicable fact that one of space-time's dimensions has a real A-series, this being what makes it the dimension of change that we call time.

4. The Ontology of the A-Series

This, however, is a poor theory, since it raises serious questions that it can neither answer nor show to be unanswerable. For example: Why has space-time only one dimension with a real A-series (and what would the world be like if it had more)? Why is this the dimension picked out by relativity? And so on. If time does differ from space in this way, the difference (like that between temporal and spatial parts) must surely follow from something more basic.

But perhaps there is no difference here, for perhaps not even time has a real A-series. So McTaggart argues, which is why he says that time is unreal. For if time entails change, and that entails an A-series, then no A-series means no change and so no time. But then, if the temporal terms like 'earlier' that define the B-series have no application, there is no B-series either. There is merely McTaggart's (1927, §347) 'C-series': a real dimension of what we call space-time, but not one that deserves to be called time.

Put like this, McTaggart's denial of time is less incredible. For not only, as he notes, is it Kant's view (1781, A33); in his sense he shares it with all those who, like Quine (1960, §36), think time is spacelike. Still, credible or not, the question here, since no one denies that space-time *has* a non-spatial dimension that we all call time, is how this dimension differs from the other three. But then, *pace* McTaggart and Q. Smith (1993, ch. 7: see Section 2 above), it is better to keep calling the dimension 'time' than to drop that question just because it fails McTaggart's test for being the dimension of change.

But does it fail that test? Many philosophers still think not (Oaklander and Smith 1994, pt. 2), and McTaggart's (1927, §329–32) argument that it does, sound though I think it is, is too famous and contentious to be restated yet again in his way. It does, however, have a non-spatial analogue that may sway agnostic minds. This starts with the personal analogue of *now* and *here*, namely *me*, and consequent analogues of the A- and B-series. The former relates people to *me*, as in *my* cousin, neighbours, employer, etc. The latter relates them not to me but to each other, as in Mike's cousin, Jill's neighbours, Jack's employer, etc. How are such pairs of 'series' related?

First, these personal A-series are parasitic on their B-series counterparts. For the latter are definable by who is related to whom, regardless of which of them, if any, is me; and those B-relations then fix all their corresponding A-relations. Thus if Hugh is Mike's cousin and I am Hugh, I must be Mike's cousin; and similarly in all other cases. So these personal A- and B-series can only differ if there is in reality more to *my* being Mike's cousin than to *Hugh's* being Mike's cousin; which will be so only if my being Hugh is itself a substantial part or aspect of reality.

Yet it cannot be, as an analogue of McTaggart's argument shows. Of course, when Hugh says 'I am Hugh', that A-statement is true, and when Mike says 'I am Mike', that is true too. The question, however, is what facts, if any, make these statements true; and before I can answer that I must say what I mean here by 'facts'. I cannot mean facts in any sense which makes it trivially true that

'I am Hugh' is true if and only if it's a fact that I am Hugh,

since that sense is obviously too weak to tell us what, if anything, *makes* it true, and hence a fact, that I am Hugh. For in this sense it is also trivially true that

'Murder is wrong' is true if and only if it's a fact that murder is wrong.

But this truth cannot show that, for murder to be wrong, the world must contain objective values: expressivist and subjectivist theories of value which deny this are not so easily refuted. What we want to know is whether, in a more serious sense of 'fact', 'Murder is wrong' is *made* true by facts containing objective values. That is the question, and it is a serious question about the ontology of value, not a trivial question in the theory of truth.

This is the serious truth-making sense of 'fact' in which I say that the A-fact that I am Hugh cannot be what makes Hugh's A-statement 'I am Hugh' true. For as Hugh and Mike cannot both be me, that fact would make Mike's A-statement 'I am Mike' false, which it is not. Likewise, the A-fact that I am Mike cannot be what makes Mike's statement true, since that would make Hugh's statement false. In other words, taking these A-statements to be made true by corresponding A-facts only generates contradictions, by requiring the A-fact that I am Hugh both to exist, to make Hugh's 'I am Hugh' statement true, and not to exist, to enable Mike's 'I am Mike' statement also to be true.

But if these A-facts cannot make these A-statements true, B-facts clearly can. Statements of the forms 'I am *x*' and '*x* is my cousin' (where '*x*' is a term like 'Hugh', not one like 'me') can be made true respectively by being said by *x* and a cousin of *x*. And similarly for all other personal A-statements: they can all be made true by facts about which B-people say what, and how they are related to whom, regardless of which of them is me. And only by taking such B-facts to be what make all personal A statements true can we, without contradiction, say what does so.

Similarly with temporal A-truths like 'It is now noon' said at noon and 'It is now midnight' said at midnight. The first statement cannot be made true by its now being noon, for that would make the second statement false. Nor can the second be made true by its now being midnight, for it would make the first statement false. Here too, taking these A-statements to be made true by corresponding A-facts only generates contradictions, by requiring the fact that it is now noon both to exist, to make the noon 'It is now noon' statement true, and not to exist, to enable the midnight 'It is now midnight' statement also to be true.

That, in substance, is McTaggart's argument. To reject it, one must say that, at noon, the midnight statement 'It is now midnight' is false (cf. Q. Smith 1993, ch. 4.3). But this is like Hugh saying that Mike's statement 'I am Mike' is false, which is absurd. Of course 'It is now midnight' *would* be false if said at noon, just as 'I am Mike' would be false if said by Hugh. But said when and by whom they *are* said, these statements are as plainly true at all times and for all people as (to give a spatial example) a north-pointing 'York 200 miles' sign in London is at all places.

And then it is as plain in the temporal as in the personal case what makes A-statements true. Being said at noon is what makes 'It is now noon' true, and similarly for A-statements about the past and future. Any statement of the form '*e* is (N days) past' is made true by being made (N days) later than *e*; just as any statement of the form '*e* is (N days) future' is made true by being made (N days) earlier than *e*. The facts that make A-statements true are all B-facts.

5. The Semantics of the A-Series

Or are they? Is it really just a B-fact that *e* is earlier than another event *f*? Not for McTaggart, for whom B-facts need A-facts to make them temporal, and so something more than C-facts. In other words, the temporal meaning of 'earlier', which defines the B-series, depends on the meanings of 'past', 'present', and 'future' that define the A-series; and this remains a common view (Gale 1968, pt. II).

Yet it is not true. We saw in Section 2 how A- and B-series share the same concept of simultaneity; and they also share the same concept of being *earlier*. For the link between the two series is undeniable: the past is earlier than the present, and the present earlier than the future, in the very same sense in which e is earlier than f. And then, as in the personal case of Section 4, the B-series must come first, since that depends only on what is earlier than what, regardless of where anything is in the A-series. So, for example, e is earlier than f independently of their ever-changing A-locations; but not conversely, since e's being earlier than f makes e always less future or more past than f. And this will be so even on the A-theory that e is made earlier than f by becoming present earlier than f: for that too is an unchanging B-fact about which of two events (e's becoming present, f's becoming present) is the earlier.

The fact is that temporal, personal, and spatial A-concepts all depend on their corresponding B-concepts, not the other way round. Indeed it is only their B-concepts—of the properties and relations that distinguish different people, places, and times—that distinguish these three sets of A-concepts. For given the former, the difference between the latter reduces to that between *me*, *here*, and *now*: since any A-statement, however complex, is equivalent to a B-statement plus one or more A-statements saying who *I* am, where *here* is, and/or which B-time is *now*. And what differentiates these basic A-concepts, by making them refer respectively to whomever has them, and to where and when they do so, is the kind of B-belief that the A-beliefs they occur in combine to yield.

Take, for example, my A-beliefs that I am Hugh, and that I am male, which yield the B-belief that Hugh is male. I say (Mellor 1998*b*) that the fact that the B-belief they yield is personal is what makes these A-beliefs personal rather than temporal or spatial, i.e. makes them refer to me, rather than to the place or time I hold them at. Similarly for spatial and temporal A-beliefs, like my beliefs that today is 16 August and fine: what makes those A-beliefs temporal is that the B-belief they yield, that 16 August is fine, is temporal. But if combining to yield temporal B-beliefs is what makes A-beliefs temporal, then the latter must get their content from the former. And so they do: our A-concepts of past, present, and future are defined by our B-concept of being earlier: all events located at any B-time t are automatically present at t, past at all earlier times, and future at all later ones.

How then do we get our *earlier* concept, and differentiate it from spatial concepts like being above, or to the left? The answer is that we learn to recognize its instances, as when we see that '1' appears earlier than '2' on a digital clock, and to distinguish them from (for example) seeing '1' to the left of '2' on a clock with hands. What makes our temporal and spatial concepts differ is that we can tell the difference between temporal and spatial B-relations—the very difference we have yet to explain.

However, before explaining that difference, we must meet two well-known objections to this B-account of temporal concepts. The first is that we see things as temporally present, but not as spatially present. Thus while I can see that my clock's hands are moving at some spatial distance from here, I can never see them as moving at a temporal distance from now: whatever we see, we see as present. Is this not a basic difference between the temporal and spatial concepts that experience gives us: the former being *A*-concepts, the latter not?

No: the idea that we see events as present comes from confusing what we see with the experience of seeing it, which is indeed always present. But that is a mere tautology, a consequence of the fact that the experiences we think are present are those we have while we are thinking that. While as for *what* we see, that never *looks* present—or past, or future. We cannot, for example, see which of two celestial events is the earlier by seeing which looks more past. If we could, cosmology would be far easier than it is, since we could *see* how long ago what we see in telescopes happened, which of course we cannot. We cannot even refute people who claim to see the future in a crystal ball by pointing to the visible pastness of what they see, for there is no such thing (Mellor 1998*a*, chs. 1.5, 4.3).

Why then do we mostly take what we see to be temporally present? The reason is that the light which shows us nearby events travels far faster than we usually need to react to it (Butterfield 1984). This is especially true of events, like the approach of predators, partners, or food, on our timely reaction to which we depend for survival. If we let our eyes tell us that these events were future, we would not act on them in time; and if we let them tell us that they were very past, we would not act on them at all; and either way we would die out. It is in order to survive that we need the default habit of believing that what we see is present, which is why evolution has bred this habit into us.

This brings me to the other objection to a *B*-theory of *A*-concepts, its apparent implication that an *A*-belief is just a kind of *B*-belief, e.g. that a predator is approaching when I believe it is. Yet thinking at *t* that something is happening *now* is never the same as thinking it is happening at *t*. Take Prior's (1959) example of my thanking goodness at *t* that an unpleasant experience is over. As Prior says, to realize that it is over is not to realize that it ended before *t*, a fact I could have known (and thanked goodness for) in advance. Perry (1979) makes a related point about personal *A*-beliefs: to vary his example, no *B*-belief of mine that Hugh Mellor, the author of *Real Time II*, the occupant of 25 Orchard Street, etc., is due to finish this chapter this week will make me do so unless I believe *I* am due to do so. Similarly for spatial beliefs: the *B*-belief that I am to leave a train at Cambridge will not make me do so until I acquire the *A*-belief that Cambridge is *here*.

This is a general phenomenon. Apart from beliefs about (for example) what always was, is, and will be, few if any *A*-beliefs can be *B*-beliefs, since they affect our actions differently. So no *B*-theory that identifies *A*- with *B*-beliefs, by giving *B*-translations of *A*-statements, can be right. The realization that *B*-theories not only cannot but need not do this (Smart 1980) planted the seed of the so-called 'new theory of time', whose growing influence is variously assessed in Oaklander and Smith's (1994) collection of that title.

The chief problem facing the new theory is this. If what makes any token utterance *k* of (for example) 'It's fine now' true is its being made when the weather's fine, how can that B-truth-condition not be what k means? The best-known answer (Kaplan 1989) is to divide the meaning of 'It's fine now' into a *content* (its B-truth-condition), which varies with t, and a *character* (the function from t to this content), which does not. Then at t, while 'It's fine now' has the same content as 'It's fine at t', it has a different character, and that is how their meanings differ.

I think this is wrong, and that 'It's fine now' only means its 'character', the function from t to its truth condition at t. Kaplan only makes its 'content' (that function's value at t) part of what it means in order to preserve the thesis that 'If what we say differs in truth-value . . . , that is enough to show that we say different things.' But this begs the question against A-theorists, for whom 'It's fine now' does always say the same thing (that it's fine *now*), even if what it says is not always true. While even B-theorists may jib at making 'It's fine now' say at t what 'It's fine at t' says: for this implies that (i) it says something different every instant and (ii) only those who know *when* they are saying 'It's fine now' know what they are saying.

This is why I take all temporal A-sentences to mean the functions from any B-time t to their B-truth-conditions at t (Mellor 1998a, ch. 7). Similarly, I take 'Cambridge is here' to mean the function from any B-place s to its truth condition at s, namely that s is at or within Cambridge; 'I am male' to mean the function from any B-person x to its truth condition when said or thought by x, namely that x is male; and so on. This is how I take A-sentences to differ in meaning from the B-sentences that say what B-facts would make them true: their B-truth-conditions, the values of the functions that I say are their meanings, vary from time to time, place to place, or person to person, while the functions themselves, which are what the B-sentences state, do not. This also shows, as Kaplan cannot, how at any time t we can know what 'It's fine now' means, and believe it, without knowing what t is. For we need not know that in order to know what this function of t is, or to believe it, i.e. to believe that, whatever the truth condition is that is this function's value for the relevant t, it holds.

But whether these functions exhaust the meanings of A-sentences or not, they certainly give them the right truth-values, e.g. making 'It's fine now' true when and only when it is said in fine weather. That is enough to show why these A-sentences are untranslatable by B-sentences. For whether or not the same thing can be said truly at one time and falsely at another, no two sentences can mean the same if one is true and the other false at the same time (and place, and for the same person). And while B-sentences are true, if at all, at all times, and for everyone, most A-sentences are at best true only at some times and for some people. That is why they cannot be translated even by the B-sentences that say when, where, and for whom they are true, and therefore why no B-theorist need claim that they can.

So far, so good for the new theory of time. But not good enough for its opponents, who deny that all true A-sentences can be made true by B-facts (Q. Smith 1993, ch. 3). Imagine a time t when, as no one has written or is thinking or saying anything, there are no mental or physical tokens of any sentence, and in particular not of

'There are no tokens now'.

So although this is true at t, it cannot be made true by B-facts about true tokens of it, since no tokens of it can be true. This certainly refutes the so-called token-reflexive theory, that what makes a sentence true at any time (and place and for any person) is whatever would make its tokens true at that time and place and for that person. But if that is not what makes sentences true, what does?

The answer here is obvious enough: what makes 'There are no tokens now' true at any t is the fact that there are no tokens at t. But it is also problematic: for if there are no tokens at t, *what* is made true at t, and by what? To the first question my answer is of course this function, which I say is what 'There are no tokens now' means, and is true at any t if and only if its value there, the truth condition that there be no tokens at t, holds. To the second question, my answer is simply the absence of tokens at t. Both answers raise further questions—such as how absences can be truth-makers—that I cannot discuss here, but on whose answers the content and prospects of the new theory of time will depend.

6. WHAT A-BELIEFS DO FOR US

Suppose, however, if only for argument's sake, that the new theory of time is true: that most A-sentences are untranslatable by B-sentences and yet are made true, when they are true, by B-facts. Why then do we use such sentences? If it cannot be to state facts, there being no A-facts to state, what do we use them for?

The most important thing that the A-beliefs A-sentences express do for us we saw in Section 5: they enable us to act when and where we need to do so. Only *my* A-belief that Cambridge is *here*, and here *now*, will get me off the late train from London, and similarly in other cases. Whenever we need or want to act at particular times and/or places, we need A-beliefs to make us do so. Why is this?

I say (Mellor 1998a, ch. 7.3) that the reason we need A-beliefs is that we are *agents*, most of whose actions depend on our beliefs, and depend for their success on when we do them. It is of course no news that our beliefs affect what we do, since we mostly do what we believe will get us what we want. When I go out to shop, or take a coat to keep warm, my actions are caused not only by what I want but by what I believe: that the shops are open, that it is cold outside, and so on. This much is obvious, the only question being why some of these beliefs must be A-beliefs, as they evidently must: that the shops are open *now*, that it is cold outside *here*, and so on.

To see why this is, consider how I catch the late train to Cambridge from London. I leave a London pub in time to get to King's Cross station just before 11.15, because I believe the train I want to catch leaves there then. But it takes more than this to make me leave the pub when I do, since I have wanted to catch this train, and believed that it leaves King's Cross at 11.15, for hours. To make me leave the pub, I must also get the A-belief that the time to do so—say 10.45—is *now*. And when I do get that belief, I will leave the pub whether or not it is true, i.e. whether or not I get the belief at 10.45. Here as elsewhere, the truth-values of my beliefs are irrelevant to how and when they make me act.

What they are relevant to is whether my actions succeed. Only if the beliefs that make me leave my pub (that King's Cross is just under thirty minutes away and it is now 10.45) are true will I succeed in getting to the station just before 11.15. This link too is general, since truth is the property of beliefs which ensures the success of the actions they combine with our desire to cause, i.e. ensures that those actions will do what we wanted them to do (Whyte 1990). Thus if, as I believe, the shops are open when I go out, I will get to shop, and if not, not. If, as I believe, it is cold outside, the coat I put on to keep me warm will do so, and if not, not (since I would be warm anyway). And so on. This is not of course to say that we cannot act successfully on false beliefs, when their falsity cancels out, as when I leave the pub late but catch my train anyway because King's Cross is closer than I thought. But luck like this is too rare to refute the rule that, generally, the truth conditions of our beliefs are those in which the actions they help to cause succeed.

The relevance of this rule is that, as my examples show, the success of our actions almost always depends on when and where they are done. I must leave for the station in time to catch the train; shop hours and outdoor temperatures vary from time to time and place to place; and so on. So for our actions to succeed, they need to be caused by beliefs that are indeed true when and where we have them, but are not true always and everywhere. So true B-beliefs, just because they *are* true always and everywhere, are not enough. We also need A-beliefs, precisely because *their* truth-values, and hence B-truth-conditions, can vary across time and space. Without these we could not time or place the myriad actions which, if they are to get us what we want, must be done at the right B-time and the right B-place. That is why, even in a world with no A-facts, agents will always need A-beliefs.

But to be capable of timely action, it is not enough to have A-beliefs: we must have them when they are true. And so, on the whole, we do. We make mistakes, naturally: not all our A-beliefs are true, any more than all our B-beliefs are; but many are. But as, unlike B-beliefs, A-beliefs are not always true, we must keep changing them, at intervals ranging from several times a second for beliefs about what I am now seeing, to once a decade or more for beliefs about where I live or whether so-and-so is still alive.

Still, however stable some of our A-beliefs are, we have so many that we are always having to change some of them—from future to present to past—to try and keep them true. These changes, when conscious, are what we interpret, rightly or wrongly, as the flow or passage of time. So that is another thing our ever-changing *A*-beliefs will do for us, even in a *B*-world. They will give us an experience of time flowing that is as real as their changes and even, when they change at the right time, true in the sense of giving us true *A*-beliefs. This is the truth in Grünbaum's (1964: 324) view that, if physics needs only *B*-facts, 'the becoming [present] of an event, as distinct from its merely being, is…no more than the entry of its effect(s) into the immediate awareness of a sentient organism'. But then this must not be read as saying that there are mental *A*-facts which put the mental beyond the reach of a *B*-physics. For if a *B*-physics can explain belief at all, it can certainly explain *B*-facts about what *A*-beliefs we have, how we get them, how they make us act, and what *B*-facts make them true.

7. Time and Causation

In calling temporal variations in our *A*-beliefs 'changes', I have again assumed that time is the dimension of change. But I have still not said what makes it so if time does not flow. What then, if not the flow of time, distinguishes time from space, and makes it the dimension of change?

The obvious answer to the first question is causation. It is after all a striking fact that most causes and effects are separated in time as they need not be in space. Many effects are where their causes are, as when heating water causes it to boil. And those that are not may be in any spatial direction from their causes, as when fires throw out heat all round, whereas none are known to precede them. Hence the theory of Robb (1914) and Reichenbach (1928, §21) that time is the dimension of causation and that what distinguishes *earlier* from *later* is the fact that causes precede their effects.

Whether this theory will do depends on what we mean by causation. It will not do if, with Hume (1748, §60), we define a cause as 'an object, *followed* by another', since this uses time and its direction to define causation. Nor will it do if, like Mackie (1974, ch. 7), we think effects are 'fixed' by their causes becoming present, for then causation gets its direction and efficacy from the flow of time. Others, however, like Lewis (1973), who do not use time to distinguish causes from effects, can without circularity use causation to give time a direction (Le Poidevin 1991, ch. 7). Thus while Tooley (1997, ch. 4) links causation to the flow of time, as Mackie does, he uses the former to define the latter and, by denying that the future exists, enables causes not merely to 'fix' their effects by making them present but to bring them into existence.

Causal theories may thus be held without circularity by *A*- or *B*-theorists. But they face other objections (Smart 1969; Sklar 1985, chs. 9–10), such as the causal independence of many temporally ordered pairs of events, and the apparent simultaneity of much causation, as in Kant's (1781, A203) ball causing a hollow in the cushion it rests on, or a train whose rigidity requires its engine to set it moving all at once. These two objections can be met, for example by making causation link fields at all temporally ordered space-time points, and by denying that anything can be *perfectly* rigid (Mellor 1998a, ch. 10.3–4). But as none of these defences is unassailable, they need bolstering by positive reasons for adopting a causal theory of time order.

One reason is that the theory can explain the difference between relativity's timelike and spacelike intervals (see Section 1) by making light the fastest transmitter of causation, thereby explaining why causation never links events whose separation is spacelike. (Non-locality in quantum physics, which looks like unmediated causation at a spatial distance, only really threatens the weaker 'sense of locality that requires that correlation between spacelike separated events always be factorable out by a common cause'; Skyrms 1980: 127.)

Another reason is that the theory lets B-theorists explain why we can perceive but not affect the past, and affect but not perceive the future. There is of course really only one thing to explain here, since perception is as causal a process as action: what stops our senses showing us the future is what stops our actions affecting the past, namely the fact that causes precede their effects. This fact, however, is explained very differently on different theories of time and causation: of those mentioned above, Mackie explains it by the 'fixity' of the past, Tooley by the non-existence of the future. But for those who put all times on a modal and ontological par, a causal theory of time order gives by far the best explanation of these striking differences between past and future.

Better still, a causal theory can explain Kant's (1781, B50) famous definition of time as 'the form of inner sense', i.e. of our experiences, whose order must therefore be temporal. This fact, however, does not explain why causes precede their effects; whereas a causal theory can explain how we perceive the time order of our own experiences, as follows (Mellor 1998a, ch. 10.5).

Suppose I perceive the time order of two events, *e* and *f*, by first seeing *e* and then seeing *f*. The time order of these perceptions fixes the time order I thereby perceive: the event I see first will be the event I see to *be* first. But what, if not unconscious visual processing (Dennett 1991, ch. 6.3), makes this so? Something must, since I could see *e* and *f* without seeing their time order at all; but what? The answer is causal: my perception of *e* so affects my perception of *f* that the latter also tells me that *e* precedes *f*. So the time order that these perceptions make me perceive is fixed by their causal order: if my perception of *f* had affected my perception of *e* in the same way, I would have seen *f* precede *e*. That is why, if the causal order of my perceptions fixes *their* time order, what I see first is what I thereby see to *be* first.

Of course my perceiving *e* precede *f* will not in general entail that *e* in fact precedes *f*, as when I perceive lightning to precede a simultaneous thunder clap because light travels faster than sound. But if whatever links e and f to my perceptions of them takes the same time to do so, their time order *will* be what I perceive it to be. So if, in particular, e and f are not external events but internal experiences, all of which take a similarly short time to intimate themselves to me, they are bound to have the time order I perceive them to have. That is how causation gives us the almost infallible knowledge of the time order of our own experiences that makes Kant's definition of time so appealing: the real form of his inner sense is causation.

Last, and best of all, a causal theory can explain why time is the dimension of change (Le Poidevin 1991, ch. 8; Mellor 1998a, ch. 10.6; 2001). In my view, it does so by supplying the necessary condition for change, noted in Section 3, that there be a single thing that changes. For a thing cannot keep its identity unless it also keeps some of its properties. Some of mine, for example, like being an animal, may be essential to me, i.e. such that I could not lose them, since nothing that lacked them could be me (Wiggins 1980, chs. 2–3; Olson 1997). But even if no property of mine is essential in this sense, so that I could change by sufficiently numerous stages into a pillar of salt, no one thinks I could survive the simultaneous loss of *all* my intrinsic properties. So while any one property of mine *is* changing, I must, in order to preserve my identity through that change, keep enough other properties of mine *un*changed.

Now what keeps properties unchanged over time is the same as what makes them change: causation. My present height, temperature, views of time, and other fairly constant properties of mine are what they are now because, since nothing has happened to change them, that is what they were a minute ago. The causation of stasis may be less obvious than that of change, but it is no less real, and no less necessary to secure the identity that is needed to make a difference a change.

This is why spatial variation in a thing's properties, for example from the hot to the cold end of a poker, is never a change. Because causation cannot link facts across spacelike intervals, no poker can have any property at one end just because it has the same property at the other end at the same time. That is what stops a poker's two ends being not just two parts of a single thing, but a single thing in two places at once, thereby stopping any difference of properties between them being not just a difference but a change in the poker as a whole. And that is why, if time is the dimension of causation, only temporal variation can be change.

8. Epilogue

These are my reasons for agreeing with Robb, Reichenbach, and their followers that time is the causal dimension of space-time. I agree with them because I think no other view of time explains as much and faces fewer objections. However, until there is more consensus about what (or even whether) causation is, this view must remain both provisional and vague. There is still much to do in the philosophy of time.

Still, as we have seen, it has already been transformed in the last hundred years by developments in several areas. Einstein changed our ideas of how time differs from space and how it relates to causation, just as McTaggart changed our notion of the flow of time. In the philosophy of language, theories of meaning have shown how what A- and B-statements mean depends on what makes them true (Davidson 1967). Semantic theories of indexicals like 'now', 'here', and 'I' have shed new light on McTaggart and shown how A-truths can be made true by B-facts while differing from B-truths. While new theories of the mind (defining beliefs and desires by how they make us act; P. Smith and Jones 1986, chs. 10–13) and of truth (as what makes the actions beliefs cause succeed) have combined to show why our A-beliefs are as indispensable as they are irreducible.

This is just some of the twentieth-century work that has advanced our understanding of the aspects of time dealt with above. Then there are the many issues I have had no space to discuss: how the direction of time relates to cosmology, radiation, thermodynamics, statistical mechanics, quantum theory, and decision-making; whether space-time is an entity or a set of space-time relations; whether time must be linear; the source of space-time's metric and whether it is intrinsic or conventional; whether space-time is discrete, dense, or continuous; Zeno's paradoxes of motion; whether time travel, backward causation, or cyclical time is possible; modal and tense logic, and the sense in which the past is necessary and alternative futures are possible; how to understand time in fiction; time and eternity, and whether God or anything else can be outside time.

On these issues too much progress has been made, and there is clearly more to come, as the literature shows. For examples, besides works already referred to, see Friedman (1983), Flood and Lockwood (1986), Horwich (1987), Le Poidevin and Macbeath (1993), Price (1996), Le Poidevin (1998), and Butterfield (2000), and 'Time', 'Continuants', 'Eternity', 'Zeno of Elea', and related articles in Craig (1998).[1]

References

Armstrong, D. M. (1980), 'Identity through Time', in P. van Inwagen (ed.), *Time and Cause: Essays Presented to Richard Taylor*. Dordrecht: Reidel.

Broad, C. D. (1923), *Scientific Thought*. London: Kegan Paul.

Butterfield, J. (1984). 'Seeing the Present'. Repr. in R. Le Poidevin (ed.), *Questions of Time and Tense*. Oxford: Clarendon Press, 1998.

[1] This chapter has drawn on material in Mellor (1998a, 2001) by permission of the former's publisher and the latter's editor. If asked to justify my choice of topics, I can only say that I cannot, as Oscar Wilde once put it, 'accept all schools of art with the grand catholicity of an auctioneer', since I am not an auctioneer.

Butterfield, J. (ed.) (2000), *The Arguments of Time*. Oxford: Oxford University Press.

Craig, E. J. (ed.) (1998). *Routledge Encyclopedia of Philosophy*. London: Routledge.

Davidson, D. (1967). 'Truth and Meaning'. *Synthese*, 17: 304–23.

Dennett, D. C. (1991). *Consciousness Explained*. London: Penguin.

Earman, J. (1989). *World Enough and Space-Time*. Cambridge, Mass.: MIT Press.

Einstein, A., *et al.* (1923). *The Principle of Relativity*. London: Methuen.

Flood, R., and Lockwood, M. (eds.) (1986). *The Nature of Time: Problems in the Philosophy of Science*. Oxford: Blackwell.

Friedman, M. (1983). *Foundations of Space-Time Physics: Relativistic Physics and Philosophy of Science*. Princeton: Princeton University Press.

Gale, R. M. (1968). *The Language of Time*. London: Routledge & Kegan Paul.

Grünbaum, A. (1964). *Philosophical Problems of Space and Time*. London: Routledge & Kegan Paul.

Horwich, P. (1987). *Asymmetries in Time: Problems in the Philosophy of Science*. Cambridge, Mass.: MIT Press.

Hume, D. (1748). *An Enquiry Concerning Human Understanding*. Repr. in Hume, *Enquiries Concerning the Human Understanding and Concerning the Principles of Morals*, ed. L. A. Selby-Bigge. Oxford: Clarendon Press, 1902.

Kant, I. (1781). *Critique of Pure Reason*. Repr. trans. N. Kemp Smith. London: Macmillan, 1933.

Kaplan, D. (1989). 'Demonstratives', in J. Almog, J. Perry, and H. Wettstein (eds.), *Themes from Kaplan*. New York: Oxford University Press.

Langton, R., and Lewis, D. K. (1998). 'Defining "Intrinsic"'. *Philosophy and Phenomenological Research*, 58: 333–45.

Leibniz, G. W., and Clarke, S. (1717). *The Leibniz–Clarke Correspondence*. Repr. ed. H. G. Alexander. Manchester: Manchester University Press, 1956.

Le Poidevin, R. (1991). *Change, Cause and Contradiction: A Defence of the Tenseless Theory of Time*. New York: St Martin's Press.

—— (ed.) (1998). *Questions of Time and Tense*. Oxford: Clarendon Press.

—— and Macbeath, M. (eds.) (1993). *The Philosophy of Time*. Oxford: Oxford University Press.

Lewis, D. K. (1973). 'Causation', in Lewis, *Philosophical Papers*, ii. Oxford: Oxford University Press, 1986.

Mackie, J. L. (1974). *The Cement of the Universe*. Oxford: Clarendon Press.

McTaggart, J. M. E. (1908). 'The Unreality of Time'. *Mind*, 18: 457–84.

—— (1927). *The Nature of Existence*. Cambridge: Cambridge University Press.

Mellor, D. H. (1998*a*). *Real Time II*. London: Routledge.

—— (1998*b*). 'Transcendental Tense I'. *Aristotelian Society Supplementary Volume*, 72: 29–43.

—— (2001). 'The Time of our Lives', in A. O'Hear (ed.), *Philosophy at the New Millennium*. Cambridge: Cambridge University Press.

Nerlich, G. (1994). *What Spacetime Explains: Metaphysical Essays on Space and Time*. Cambridge: Cambridge University Press.

Oaklander, L. N., and Smith, Q. (eds.) (1994). *The New Theory of Time*. New Haven: Yale University Press.

Olson, E. T. (1997). *The Human Animal: Personal Identity without Psychology*. Oxford: Oxford University Press.

Perry, J. (1979). 'The Problem of the Essential Indexical'. *Noûs*, 13: 3–21.

Price, H. (1996). *Time's Arrow and Archimedes' Point*. New York: Oxford University Press.

Prior, A. N. (1959). 'Thank Goodness that's Over'. *Philosophy*, 34: 12–17.

—— (1970). 'The Notion of the Present'. *Studium Generale*, 23: 245–8.

Quine, W. v. O. (1960). *Word and Object*. Cambridge, Mass.: MIT Press.

Redhead, M. L. G. (1998). 'Relativity Theory, Philosophical Significance of', in E. J. Craig (ed.), *Routledge Encyclopedia of Philosophy*. London: Routledge.

Reichenbach, H. (1928). *The Philosophy of Space and Time*. Repr. trans. M. Reichenbach and J. Freund. New York: Dover, 1957.

Robb, A. A. (1914). *A Theory of Time and Space*. Cambridge: Cambridge University Press.

Salmon, W. C. (1975). *Space, Time, and Motion: A Philosophical Introduction*. Encino, Calif.: Dickenson.

Simons, P. (1987). *Parts: A Study in Ontology*. Oxford: Clarendon Press.

Sklar, L. (1985). *Philosophy and Spacetime Physics*. Berkeley: University of California Press.

Skyrms, B. (1980). *Causal Necessity*. New Haven: Yale University Press.

Smart, J. J. C. (1955). 'Spatialising Time', *Mind*, 64: 239–41.

—— (1969). 'Causal Theories of Time'. Repr. in Smart, *Essays Metaphysical and Moral*. Oxford: Blackwell, 1987.

—— (1980). 'Time and Becoming', in P. van Inwagen (ed.), *Time and Cause: Essays Presented to Richard Taylor*. Dordrecht: Reidel.

Smith, P., and Jones, O. R. (1986). *The Philosophy of Mind: An Introduction*. Cambridge: Cambridge University Press.

Smith, Q. (1993). *Language and Time*. Oxford: Oxford University Press.

Swinburne, R. G. (1981). *Space and Time*, 2nd edn. London: Macmillan.

Tooley, M. (1997). *Time, Tense, and Causation*. Oxford: Clarendon Press.

Whyte, J. T. (1990). 'Success Semantics'. *Analysis*, 50: 149–57.

Wiggins, D. (1980). *Sameness and Substance*. Cambridge, Mass.: Harvard University Press.

Williams, C. E. (1992). 'The Date Analysis of Tensed Sentences'. Repr. in L. N. Oaklander and Q. Smith (eds.), *The New Theory of Time*. New Haven: Yale University Press, 1994.

CHAPTER 22

CONSTITUTION

MARK JOHNSTON

Constitution, at first glance, the relation between an item and its components or parts, is a topic-neutral relation of vast generality, applying wherever the notion of complexity gets a foothold. Accordingly, it is a great mistake to restrict prematurely the scope of one's account of constitution to a few categories such as material objects and arbitrary aggregates. For one then runs the risk of misplaced generality, of mistaking idiosyncratic features of a specific category or kind of item for general principles governing the relation of constitution itself.

1. About eighty years ago Stanisław Leśniewski presented a formal theory of the part–whole relation, a theory that came to be called 'mereology'. It was taken up by Henry Leonard and Nelson Goodman (1940), and has been put to a great deal of work in generating supposed results in ontology. For example, mereology has proved crucial in motivating and implementing the account of persistence as perdurance. And its credentials seemed so secure that David Lewis (1991) was prompted to try to reduce set theory to mereology plus the theory of the singleton.

One way to introduce mereology is to start with the notion of a part and then introduce two definitions, thus

(D1) x and y *overlap* just in case they have a common part. Otherwise they are entirely *distinct*.

(D2) An item is a *fusion* of some other items just in case it has all of them as parts and has no part that is distinct from each of those items.

The characteristic axioms of mereology are then stated as follows:

That parthood is transitive, i.e. a part of a part of an item is also a part of that item.

That there is no restriction on the formation of wholes, i.e. given any items there is some item that is their fusion.

That the wholes so formed are unique, i.e. given any items there is just one item that is their fusion.

From these three axioms a fourth crucial postulate concerning parthood follows, namely

That parthood is reflexive, i.e. every item is a part of itself.

Here is a telling example of misplaced generality. As we shall see, at least three of these four postulates are false. However, there is another way of interpreting mereology: not as a general but quite false theory of constitution, but rather as a specific account of the parts of an idiosyncratic and rather tedious kind of item, the mereological sum.

So reinterpreted the four crucial postulates will be:

That a part of a part of a mereological sum is also part of that sum.

That there is no restriction on the formation of mereological sums, i.e. given any items there is some mereological sum that is their fusion.

That the mereological sums so formed are unique, i.e. given any items there is just one mereological sum that is their fusion.

That every mereological sum is a part of itself.

As we shall see, whether there really are mereological sums will depend on whether there are wholes which are utterly undemanding and unstructured: utterly undemanding in that they ask no more of their parts than that they exist at some time or other, and unstructured in that they confer on their parts no distinctive structure of their own.

If mereology is at best the account of the parts of an idiosyncratic kind of item then we shall have to rethink the many quite general ontological results that have been derived from it. For so reinterpreted, mereology could no more be the ground of those results than Mariology (the theology of the Virgin) could be the ground of the central claims of Christian theology. Mereology will be at best a tributary, maybe only a backwater, of ontology.

2. Of any item in any category, be it a state, event, process, material object, arte-fact, organism, person, quantity of stuff, property, state of affairs, set, or mereological sum, we may inquire whether it is simple or complex, in the sense of having parts. Of anything that is complex we may inquire as to what principle unifies those parts into the whole that is the complex item. The principle had better not be merely another part, for the question would remain: Consider that part along with the

other parts, what condition is such that its holding of *all* these parts gives us the whole? And that would be the principle we really seek.

So glue may hold together parts of a model airplane; but glue is another part and it counts as a part along with the wings, the tail, and the fuselage because of a pattern of bonding holding among it and the other parts. The pattern of bonding is not another part, but rather a way of realizing a principle of unity that must hold among the parts if they are to be parts of the model airplane. Roughly, they must hang together in the modelled shape of an airplane in such a way as to resist (but alas not always to prevent) separation in the face of the range of forces to which we usually subject such models.

We may make a distinction between a complex item's parts, its principle or principles of unity, and its origin, or more generally its placement in a pattern of generative operations. All three factors may enter into the account of what it is for a specific item to exist, but in what follows we shall prescind from origins, and concentrate on parts and principles.

A principle of unity for a given item is a relational condition holding of some other items, such that (origins aside) what it is for the given item to exist is for the condition to hold among those items. Each real kind of complex item has associated with it a characteristic principle of unity. Here is a useful example: the principle of unity for the molecules characteristic of hydrochloric acid (HCl molecules) is the holding of the following relational condition: covalent bonding between a hydrogen ion (H^+) and a chlorine ion (Cl^-). The principle of unity holds of the ions and is the essential condition for existence of the molecule. It is simply a proposition of chemistry that what it is for a given HCl molecule to exist is for there to be a hydrogen ion covalently bonded to a chlorine ion. Using our terminology, it is therefore a consequence of a proposition of chemistry that covalent bonding between a hydrogen ion and a chlorine ion is a principle of unity for HCl molecules.

Despite the usefulness of this example, it does not seem to be essential to the notion of a part that the parts of an item are in any way joined or bonded to make up the item. Abstract items can have parts or components. So sets might be taken to have their members as parts, without any requirement of bonding or attachment being relevant. Conjunctive properties have their conjuncts as parts but nothing besides conjunction is required for the parts to make up the relevant whole. And the debate over whether propositions contain individuals and properties as parts rather than senses or modes of presentation of individuals and properties is not menaced by any odd supposition that any analogue of material bonding holds among the components of the proposition. In each of these cases there are indeed different principles of unity in play, but it does not follow that there are different notions of part in play. There is a semantic question as to whether the notion of part in play is entirely univocal across all subject matters, as Leśniewski, Goodman, and Leonard appear to have supposed, or represents a 'focal meaning' that is further elaborated within a subject matter, or even from context to context (for an extensive examination of this semantic question, see Moltmann 1995). But this is a question best addressed at the end of an investigation that tries to get as far as possible on the assumption of univocity.

In a full account of these matters, and certainly in any treatment of the identity over time of those items that exist in time, it would be helpful to distinguish two aspects of a principle of unity, the synchronic and the diachronic. In what follows, I will elide this distinction, and talk of the principles of unity of items existing in time as incorporating both aspects.

3. As to the parts of any item, since they in their turn are items in some category or other, we may inquire as to whether they are simple or complex. If they are complex, we may inquire as to their principles of unity and their parts. And so on, either without end or terminating in simples.

We might thus foresee a hierarchical conception of items, parts, and principles of unity, a conception that could do duty in a fundamental ontology. For, first, the principles and (possibly variable) parts that pertain to any real kind of item have the best claim to be central to the account of what it essentially is to be that kind of item, which means that they must figure in the real definition of the kind of item. Secondly, we may hope to get some constraints of the identity and difference of real kinds and the categories that subsume them by noticing the characteristic principles of unity that govern items in this or that kind. Thirdly, by 'decomposing' an item downward through the various parts and principles that pertain to it we may further articulate the essence of the item. Fourthly, descent in the hierarchy of items, parts, and principles may give content to the idea of some items being *ontologically more fundamental* than the items out of which they are composed, with the simples or basic items, if any, being the most ontologically fundamental. And fifthly, we may hope to find some regularity in a coherent set of principles and basic (or relatively more basic) items in certain categories and thereby discharge the task of ontology, namely providing a comprehensive account of what there is and how it hangs together.

Of course, thanks to its vast distance from empirical detail, any such fundamental ontology will have a laughable impracticality compared with the results of the special sciences. But some of the interest of fundamental ontology will lie in the way it clarifies the stringent conditions of ontological reduction and so exposes as unworkable the popular 'naturalistic' ambition to turn some special science into a fundamental ontology.

4. A fundamental, although oft-neglected, distinction in the theory of parts and wholes is the distinction between *a principle of unity* for any given composite item and a mere *principle of division* for that item. This generates a distinction between the parts of an item unified by a principle of unity for that item and the parts of the item only disclosed by a mere principle of division for that item. For short, let us call these 'u-parts' and 'd-parts'. It will transpire that items can have the same simplest parts, the same 'atomic' parts if you will, and yet be distinct in virtue of having different u-parts

and d-parts. One consequence of this is that spatio-temporal coincidence of distinct items is more much common than is widely supposed.

A statement of a principle of unity for the item can take the following canonical form:

> *What it is for* ... (the specific item is specified here) ... *to exist is for these parts* ... (some parts are specified here) ... *to* ... (the principle of unity is specified here).[1]

As in: *What it is for* this HCl molecule *to exist is for* this positive hydrogen ion and this negative chlorine ion *to* be covalently bonded together.

Or in: *What it is* for this spoon *to exist is for* a stem and a shallow bowl *to* satisfy the following condition: the stem is to be attached to the bowl in such as way as to facilitate the transport of food and liquids into the mouth.

More formally, a principle of unity for an item of a given kind K is a 'generative condition' $R(x, \ldots)$; that is, a condition such that it lies in the essence of $R(x, \ldots)$ that if $R(a, \ldots)$ there exists a K with $a, \ldots$ as its immediate parts. A generative condition can be variably polyadic, e.g. the condition: ... coexist at some time or other, which is the unity condition for mere aggregates. Or this condition: ... are taken up in a life, which is the only unity condition that Peter van Inwagen (1990) recognizes in the domain of material particulars.

5. What then of d-parts, parts disclosed *only* by a *mere* principle of division for the item? The account of what it is for a certain item to exist may centrally involve a second item, a whole, of which the first is a part. So it is with, say, the lower half of a person's flesh, understood as a varying organic item that remains as the person grows and acquires or loses weight. What it is for the (variable) lower half of a person's flesh to exist is for the person's flesh to exist and for it to have a lower half.

---

[1] This formulation may seem to be insufficiently general for a full theory of items. We may want to recognize complexity in items that do not, and even could not, exist; items such as the Meinongian round square. A more general idiom may be introduced in this way. Consider two versions of the notion of *what it would take for an item to be*; namely, one that concerns the contingent antecedent conditions required for the item to come into being, and another that concerns what those conditions would result in, i.e. *what it would it be for the item to be.*

The idiom 'what it would be for the item to be' leaves open the possibility that the item in question need not exist. So there are different accounts of what it would be for the round square to exist and for the four-sided triangle to exist. Thus room is made for the idea that an item need not exist in order to have an essence, for example the round square has a different essence from the four-sided triangle. What it would be for the round square to exist involves roundness and squareness being combined in a way that guarantees that no such item exists. What it would be for the round square to exist is too demanding for the round square to exist. Likewise for the four-sided triangle.

When it comes to items that exist, the main concern of this chapter, then we may use this more restricted idiom: What it is for this item to be? And this question is answered by giving the essence of the item in question. When the item in question is complex, the account of the essence of the item—the real definition of the item—may be given by way of its constituents and principle of unity.

What unites this part with the upper half of the same person's flesh? As the adolescent's bones elongate, entirely different organic structures may lie at the demarcation between the top half and the lower half of his flesh. There is no general and non-arbitrary account of what unites the upper and lower halves of a person's flesh. Instead of there being a principle of unity holding of the two halves, there is a principle of spatial *division* which when applied to a person's flesh at any given time distinguishes two 'parcels' of flesh as the upper and lower halves.

So also with the second half of Walt Disney's life, which was twenty-five years in extent when he was 50, forty-three years in extent at his death, and which would increase further if he is ever revived from his cryogenic sleep. What it is for the (variable) second half of Disney's life to exist is for Disney's life to have a certain extent and for it to have a second half. Given Disney's life up to a certain time, there is a principle of temporal division that distinguishes two periods as the first and second halves of his life. Those parts are d-parts in the sense that they arise 'as a result of' applying a principle of division to an item already conceived of as a whole.

The analysis of the distinction between principles of unity and principles of division is a matter of some importance and delicacy. Certainly the analysis is not merely formal. Whereas a principle of unity can be thought of as associated with a function from given items to an item that those items make up, a principle of division is associated with a function from a given item to items that make up the given item. If that were all there was to the matter then we could take the inverse of any function that was characteristic of a principle of division and have a function characteristic of a principle of unity. But there is, in general, no guarantee that the inverse of a function associated with a principle of division will be a natural or non-arbitrary function appropriate for a principle of unity. For given an item of a certain kind, an arbitrary division of that item may disclose parts which are related only in ways that can also be found among items which do not make up a whole of the kind in question.

In the case of the upper half of a person's flesh the principle of division is: Consider a person's flesh at a particular time, then horizontally divide it into upper and lower portions so that each contains equal amounts of flesh. The fact that this principle of division is applicable to a person's flesh at a given time guarantees the holding of something like the following relational condition between portions of flesh at the time in question: being seamlessly stacked, equal portions of flesh. Why isn't this a principle of unity for the person's flesh, at least at the time in question?

Well, a principle of unity for a given item is a relational condition holding of some other items—its immediate parts—such that what it is for the item to exist is for the parts to stand in the relation. It is not the case that what it is for a person's flesh at a time to exist is for there to be equal portions of flesh that are seamlessly stacked. For if we stacked two equally fleshy twins so that their touching flesh merged seamlessly there would not be a third person whose flesh was the flesh of both twins. So what it is for a person's flesh to exist is not for there to be equal portions of flesh seamlessly stacked. Thus, being seamlessly stacked, equal portions of flesh is not a principle of unity for a person's flesh at a time or over time. What it is for an item to be a person's flesh over time is not for there to be seamlessly stacked, equal portions of flesh.

So the top and bottom halves of a person's flesh are parts of that flesh disclosed *only* by a *mere* principle of division of the person's flesh (and so not also by a principle of unity of a person's flesh). They are thus d-parts. And given our definitions of d-parts and u-parts, no d-part is a u-part, or vice versa. This exclusive distinction between u-parts and d-parts will serve to develop the basic idea of this chapter, namely that complex items, both abstract and concrete, typically have significant partitional structure. In this regard, mereological sums represent a notable exception, an exception that has unfortunately come to dominate our thinking about constitution.

We can now give a simple characterization of immediate constitution in general and of immediate material constitution in particular. x is an immediate constituent of y just in case x is a u-part of y. x is an immediate material constituent of y just in case x is a material u-part of y. The d-parts of an item are parts all right; but they are not, in this targeted sense, immediate constituents of the item. They are not the parts that the item is constituted out of; they need not be mentioned in an account of what it is to be the item. It is the u-parts of an item that are the genuinely constitutive parts of that item.

6. Reductionist theses with respect to items of a given sort can now be seen to admit of differing degrees of reductive ambition. There is a reductionism of parts: a claim to the effect that all u-parts of the items in some interesting category (say, all items ostensibly in space-time) lie in some other interesting category, such as the mental or the physical. And there is a reductionism of principles, a claim that all the principles of unity of items in some interesting category are reductive and invoke properties that lie in some *other* interesting category.

Neither of these reductionist theses involve claims about *identity*, a happy result since reduction is an asymmetric relation and identity is a symmetric relation. The default construal of someone who asserts the identity of a pain with a brain process should be that he is an anti-reductionist, one who believes that brain processes have interesting mental properties. Reduction is 'nothing-but'-ery; whereas identification affirms the equal standing of the identificands. The fact that identification affirms the equal standing of the identificands is often obscured by the reflex treatment of genuinely reductive statements such as 'Water is H_2O' or 'Lightning is electrical discharge' as involving the 'is' of identity rather than the 'is' of constitution. By being told that every case of lightning is materially constituted by some electrical discharge, we are told something genuinely reductive about lightning (for more on this, see Johnston 1997).

Once that observation is made, things look deeply unpromising for such familiar reductive materialist claims as 'Pain is the firing of C-fibres' or 'Pain is bodily disorder'. Pain fills regions, be they areas or volumes, of living bodies. It fills such regions dissectively, in the sense that every sub-region of a region of a body that is filled with pain is filled with pain. But neither firings of C-fibres nor conditions of bodily disorder dissectively occupy the regions they occupy. A d-part of a C-fibre firing, a part marked off by an arbitrary spatial division of the region occupied by the C-fibre firing, need not be a C-fibre firing. So also with a damaged, pressured, or otherwise disordered region of the body. Not every sub-region of this region will contain a damaged, pressured, or otherwise disordered region of the body. So pains are neither identical with, nor constituted by, the firing of C-fibres. And they are neither identical with, nor constituted by, bodily disorder.

One strong form of materialism is a materialism of items; the thesis that all the independent parts and principles of unity exhibited by the particulars in space-time are material or topic-neutral. Besides the dissective occupancy of regions of the body by bodily sensations, another obstacle to a materialism of items is the phenomenology of inner experience, which is experience seemingly of a *subject* of experience, or a self; a whole with an apparently mental principle of unity. Or, at least, a whole with no apparent physical principle of unity.

A schematic picture of how in the spatio-temporal realm there could come to be non-material items is now more clearly in view. Thanks to complexity in the material properties had by some material items, non-material properties might emerge and hold of or among such items. They could then form the basis of a non-material principle of unity for a spatio-temporal item, even if that item had only material parts. This still leaves the mystery of the emergence of non-material properties, but it does show how a dualism of particulars could have its origin in a dualism of properties, and without requiring ectoplasmic or immaterial stuff. It is a commonplace that we don't need abstract parts to have an abstract entity; it suffices for the set of Socrates and Plato to be abstract that its principle of unity does not itself involve causal or spatio-temporal relations holding among Socrates and Plato. So also, we don't need non-material parts to have non-material items in the spatio-temporal realm. It is enough that the relevant principle of unity is not exhausted by physical relations.

So, for example, I have argued elsewhere (Johnston 2004) that an act of seeing is the disclosure of part of the visible nature of an item to a subject. For all that this says about seeing, the item seen could be a material object and the subject could be an animal. Both are items that rightly or wrongly have been held to pose no special problems for materialism. Yet there remains the constitutive relation of the act of seeing, the disclosure of something of the visible nature of some item. And there remains the principle of unity of the act, namely that the relation hold of the items, i.e. the animal does have disclosed to it something of the visible nature of the material object. The relation that is both a constituent and cited in the principle of unity, the relation of disclosure, is not itself a causal relation, even if some part of the animal's body, i.e. its visual system, must come under the causal influence of the material object for the relation of disclosure to hold between the material object and the animal. One way of seeing that the relation in question is not itself a causal relation is that the animal is not in any relevant sense a cause or an effect in this transaction. Nor is disclosure a mere spatio-temporal relation. Nor is disclosure the kind of relation or some compound out of the relations—attraction, repulsion, physical exclusion, etc.—described in a science of matter. But that means that an act of seeing is not a material item; its principle of unity is not a relation, nor a compound of relations, properly countenanced in any science of matter.

7. The distinction among u-parts and d-parts means that there are at least two relevant notions of a simple. A simple could be something with no parts, neither u-parts or d-parts. Or a simple could be something with no u-parts. It counts as a simple because it has no parts united by a principle of unity. Still, it could have d-parts, parts disclosed by a mere principle of division. So there could be material simples with a left half and a right half, and so extended in space. Material simples do not have to be point particles. They just have to lack u-parts, *constitutive* parts.

8. Given the distinction between u-parts and d-parts we may now begin to consider how the supposedly axiomatic claims about parts fare when variously interpreted as applying to either kind of part.

Most arbitrary temporal slices or segments of a given activity will be merely d-parts of that activity. We may allow that there is such a thing as last night's dinner party between 9.00 and 9.01 p.m., but there need be no relation between that slice of the dinner party and the minute-long slices before and after it, such that the relation is properly cited in a unity condition for dinner parties. There may have been an embarrassing hiatus between 8.59 and 9.01, during which nothing really happened at the dinner party. Suppose the guests and the hosts literally 'froze' at that point. Even so, that period does get included in the dinner party just because it is enveloped by sub-activities characteristic of dinner parties. They froze *during* the dinner party. Those moments were the most embarrassing *part* of the dinner party. Yet the relation between the two slices that occupy the successive minutes of the freeze need exhibit nothing of those features properly cited in a unity condition for dinner parties.

While arbitrary temporal slices or segments need not correspond to any u-parts of an activity, it is still the case that what it is to be the activity is to be a sequence of certain temporally extended events united in a certain way. So a dinner party may really consist of the following sequence of independent, temporally extended event parts:

> the greeting of the guests,
> the downing of drinks,
> the pre-dinner chatting,

the serving and consuming of the soup,
the serving and consuming of the main course,
the serving and consuming of the dessert,
the host's disconcerting party piece,
and then the hurried farewells.

These temporally extended event-parts might constitute a dinner party that happens to last for three hours and seventeen minutes. But they constitute that dinner party in a way in which the dinner party is *not* constituted out of the first seventeen-minute temporal slice of the party and the last three-hour temporal slice of the party. The first series of temporally extended events is a series of parts united by a principle of unity for such dinner parties. That will be something like this: occupying a position in a sequence of events each effected either by the hosts or by the guests for the intended outcome of their mutual feeding and entertainment. They are the parts and that is the principle that would have to be mentioned in an adequate account of what it is for the dinner party to exist.

By contrast, the party's last three-hour slice need not be one in a sequence of events effected either by the hosts or by the guests for the intended outcome of their mutual feeding and entertainment. So also with an arbitrary one-minute segment of the u-part that is the party piece. Therefore the d-parts of the u-parts of an item need not be u-parts of the item.

Nor need it be the case that u-parts of u-parts of an item are themselves u-parts of that item. Oliver Letwin, a former graduate student in the Princeton Philosophy Department, is part of the present shadow Cabinet of Britain. Arguably he is a u-part, properly mentioned in an account of what it is to be that group. His kidneys are part of him; again, arguably, u-parts of him. But his kidneys are not u-parts of the shadow Cabinet. Therefore u-parthood is not transitive.

My father was a part of the Normandy invasion, thanks to his playing a role in the execution of the invasion. His earlobes were parts of him, but neither earlobe was a u-part, a constitutive part, of the Normandy invasion. Perhaps activities like invasions can be thought of as certain sorts of complex events. Perhaps events can be thought of as having individuals, properties, and regions among their constituent parts. But my father's earlobes are none of these. Neither is an individual that played, in any relevant sense, a role in the execution of the invasion. Neither is one of the constituent properties which might be invoked in an account of the invasion. And neither is a space-time region in which the invasion occurred.

Were my father's earlobes d-parts of the Normandy invasion? The Normandy invasion was a complex activity. The d-parts of an activity will be its arbitrary temporal and spatial slices. My father's left earlobe was not a temporal slice of the Normandy invasion. Nor was it an arbitrary spatial slice of the battle or of any of its arbitrary temporal slices. These are such things as the invasion in (arbitrary) region R, or the invasion in (arbitrary) region R at time *t*. There are indeed items *associated* with my father's left earlobe at particular times that do count as d-parts of the Normandy invasion. So over time my father's left earlobe swept out a spatio-temporal worm. That worm itself was not a d-part of the Normandy invasion. For it has spatio-temporal parts that exist before the Normandy invasion, spatio-temporal parts that are therefore not ever parts of the Normandy invasion. But if we consider the restrictions of that worm to spatio-temporal regions in which the Normandy invasion occurred, then we might have items which could be counted as d-parts of the Normandy invasion. But none of these items is an earlobe of myfather. Thus my father's earlobes are not themselves d-parts of the Normandy invasion.

So my father's earlobes, while parts of a part of the Normandy invasion, were neither u-parts nor d-parts of the invasion. Nor did they lie somewhere in the ancestral chains of u-parts and d-parts of the invasion. It follows that his earlobes were not parts of the invasion at all. But they were parts of him and he was a part of the invasion. Therefore parthood is not transitive.[2]

Nor is it in general true that a d-part of a d-part of an item is a d-part of that item. An animal's outer quarter-inch—its outermost quarter-inch thick surrounding part—is a d-part of the animal, and that odd slice of protoplasm contains as a sub-slice, or d-part within it, the animal's skin. But the animal's skin is an organ that might be cited in its principle of unity. This d-part of a d-part of the animal would then be a u-part of the animal. Thus d-parthood is not transitive.

The spurious appeal of the transitivity of parthood depends on being blind to the variety of principles of unity. A restricted diet of mereological sums may be the source of such spurious appeal, for the constraint placed on the parts of a given sum by its principle of unity is utterly undemanding. All that is required is that the parts of the sum exist at some time or other. Now it will always be the case that the further parts of the parts that make up a sum exist at some time or other. So there is no obstacle to transitivity holding for the parts of a sum. But this is a special case; special because the condition which the principle of unity of a sum places on the parts of that sum is so undemanding that it automatically holds of a part of a part of any sum.

---

[2] Peter Simons (1987) responds to another version of this kind of problem by suggesting that in such cases 'non-transitivity arises by narrowing or specifying some basic broad part-relation, the specifications introducing concepts themselves intrinsic to part–whole theory, such as function, causal contribution and lines of command. The existence of such examples does not in any way entail that there are not more basic senses of "part" which are transitive' (p. 108). The suggestion that the concept of a principle of unity and its correlate concept of a u-part are extrinsic to 'part–whole theory' is clearly untenable. Moreover, the idea that the transitive notion is 'more basic' really does run foul of the observation that being a u-part of and being a d-part of are determinates of the determinable of being a part of. In fact, a determinate is more basic than its determinable, in the sense that the determinable is ontologically dependent on its determinates.

Likewise for reflexivity. It will not in general be true that the principle of unity that holds of the (distinct) parts of an item also holds of those parts and the item itself. However, when the principle of unity merely requires that the parts of the whole exist at some time or other, there will be no obstacle to including the whole itself as a non-dependent part. But again, this is a special feature of mereological sums, one that does not apply to complex items quite generally. So an item is not, in general, a u-part of itself.

Since one way of being a part of a whole is being a u-part of that whole, and with respect to this way of being a part a whole is not part of itself, it follows that the relation of being a part of is not reflexive. For there are determinate versions of this determinable relation that are not reflexive.

In discussions of parthood inspired by mereology, this observation is usually sidelined by pointing out that mereologists can certainly define a notion of *proper* parthood that is not reflexive (for example, Casati and Varsi 1999: 33–4). The definition is obvious: x is to be a proper part of y just when x is a part of y and x is not identical with y. However, this allegedly 'definitional' manoeuvre itself serves to highlight the fact that the mereologist really has a disjunctive notion of parthood. In some cases a whole will count as u-part of itself, e.g. when the whole is a sum. In most other cases not. So there are determinate versions of the determinable relation of being a part of that are not reflexive. So the determinable relation of being a part of is not reflexive. Nonetheless, the disjunctive relation of *being a part of an item or being identical with that item* is always reflexive, thanks to the reflexivity of identity. Focusing thus on a disjunctive target for ontological analysis or real definition might be a marginally acceptable way to proceed if we could rely on the view that identity of items is just a matter of their having just the same parts. Then our disjunctive analysandum would not simply yoke together two quite different topics. For identity would just be the extreme case of part-sharing.[3] But we should not rely on the view that identity of items is a matter of their having just the same parts. That view is false, as we shall see below. The disjunctive analysandum *being a part of an item or being identical with that item* does yoke together two quite different topics.

Accordingly, we should not fudge nor flinch on reflexivity of parthood. The determinable relation of being a part of is not reflexive, for it has determinates, such as the relation of being a u-part of, which are not reflexive.

A further cautionary remark is this: A u-part may not have a unique position in the downward chain of u-parts of u-parts of u-parts and so on. . . . So, the next room may be filled with ordnance. The ordnance in the next room is a collection of weapons and can serve as an item in our extended sense. Its principle of unity may be no more than being weapons in the next room. So in the room there are

---

[3] This is just what Casati and Varsi (1999: 34) assert, following Lewis.

rocket launchers, shotguns, machine guns, pistols, knives, and tomahawks. Among the machine guns is an M16*, a machine gun so designated because it is an M16 with a small shotgun attached to the underside of its barrel. The M16* is a u-part of the ordnance. The attached shotgun is a u-part of the M16*. But the attached shotgun is also—directly as it were—a u-part of the ordnance. It would be properly counted among the shotguns in the ordnance in the next room.

So u-parthood, while not transitive, is not anti-transitive either.

9. Before turning to the familiar problems of material constitution, it may be helpful to subdivide principles of unity. A principle of unity may be *self-sustaining*, in that the causal explanation of its holding of some parts will appeal to its *having* held of those parts. So consider again the HCl molecule: what it is to be such a molecule is to be a positive hydrogen ion and a negative chlorine ion bonded together in a covalent bond. The bonding pattern is the principle and the ions are the parts. But notice that thanks to the bonding and consequent electron transfer the ions are *kept* proximate and bonded together. In such a case the principle of unity sustains its own holding. Similarly with the bonding of carbon atoms making up a diamond. The inter-atomic tetrahedral bonding is self-sustaining in that it provides for a hardness, toughness, and rigidity that preserves that very pattern of inter-atomic bonding.

A principle of unity may be *static*, in that its holding of certain parts requires that the parts it holds of remain as they are and remain ordered as they are. So consider a word token, certain token letters arranged in such a way as to spell the type of word in question. Changing or rearranging the letters typically will not preserve the identity of the word token.

A principle of unity may instead be *dynamic*, in that its holding of certain parts may allow or require that the parts it holds of vary over time, either by those very parts undergoing intrinsic change, or by their being replaced with parts of the same kind, or by their being shed without replacement. A paradigm case is a living thing whose organic matter is unified into an organism by a minimal categorical basis of a multi-track disposition to such life functions as ingestion, assimilation, excretion, growth, metabolic repair, and so on and so forth. In this case, the principle of unity—some parts providing the categorical basis of such a disposition to life functions—is a complex structure of biochemical relations whose holding of the organic matter of the living thing *requires* the matter to be exchanged over time. Once again, the model of a mereological sum of different quantities of matter existing at different times would radically misrepresent the principle of unity of a living thing. Even though the sum 'changes' its matter over time, and so may at each time consist of just the same matter as a given organism, what it is for a quantity of matter to be part of the sum at a given time is just for it to exist at that time. But what it is for a quantity of matter to be part of the organism at a given time is for it to stand in the complex structure of biochemical relations that is the categorical basis of the disposition to various life functions. Thus to identify a living thing with a cross-time sum of quantities of organic matter would be among the crudest of category mistakes.

Many physical systems are like organisms in that they have principles of unity that are self-sustaining and dynamic. Stars may be taken as an illustrative case. For some matter to be matter of a star is for it to be involved in a 'breathing' cycle of nuclear explosive expansions and gravitational contractions, expansions and contractions that make up the stable oscillation in size that is characteristic of a 'healthy' star. Expansions of a star's gaseous matter lower the internal temperature and pressure, which in turn means the force of gravity temporarily wins out. Conversely, contraction of the gaseous matter increases the internal temperature and pressure and a new cycle of expansion begins. A star 'dies' by gravitational collapse. Gravity overwhelms the expansive forces, so that the principle of unity that guaranteed the stable oscillation holds no more of the matter. (So whence the invidious distinction between organisms and stars on the score of being real items?)

10. Of the many kinds that items fall under, some kinds are such that the items that exemplify them exemplify them contingently, while others are such that the items that exemplify them do so necessarily. And there are kinds that admit of both sorts of exemplification. We, it seems, are briefly, and so contingently, fluid-dwellers, while krill is permanently and necessarily so.

In the face of this apparent disorder, the following explanatory strategy suggests itself. Assign items to so-called 'real kinds', kinds such that

(a) the members of each such kind share a fully determinate essence,
(b) the full analysis or real definition of the conditions on membership in the kind would exhaust the essence of its members, and
(c) the patterns of necessary exemplification of kinds by items are entailed by their assignment to real kinds; that is, entailed by their essences.

Perhaps in carrying out such an explanatory enterprise some of the initial data will have to be reconstrued. But in any event, this explanatory ambition should be taken as fixing the notion of a real kind.

Of course, in this explanatory endeavour we might find that there is no good account of what it is to be some of the items that we initially recognize, no real definition or account of their essence, and hence no real kind under which they fall. One such example might be *mere* intentional objects, 'objects' such as the thing that Ponce de León was searching for according to the story that he searched for the Fountain of Youth. It may well be that the Fountain of Youth is not an item in some arcane category such as the merely possible or the non-existent. 'It' may not be an item at all. Perhaps mere artefacts may have to be assimilated to mere intentional objects, where the psychological states in question are group-based conventions of treating and using physical systems as thus and so. But such conclusions, if drawn at all, should be drawn late in the day. At the beginning of a theory of parts, no ostensible item should be spurned. Otherwise we risk ignoring distinctions which may illuminate even the ultimate residuum of real as opposed to merely nominal items, i.e. items needed only to make smooth the ways of referential semantics.

Now if as we said the principle of unity of a complex item is part of the essence of the item, then items will be of a given real kind only if they each have the very same principle of unity. Against that background the following question will seem less than ideally posed:

> What general condition do some (material) items have to satisfy in order to constitute a further item?

A further (material) item of what real kind? Unity conditions are kind-relative and mischief can be worked by arguments that neglect this. An example of an argument which looks badly insensitive to the kind-relativity of principles of unity might be the following. You supposedly get a model airplane by gluing the parts together, but (as many believe) you don't get a further thing by gluing two people together, so whatever happens as a result of gluing cannot be sufficient for some things to make up a whole! That sort of argument has had too much of a run in the theory of constitution. Principles of unity are kind-relative.

11. We have seen that generalizing the account of an idiosyncratic kind of item, the mereological sum, so as to arrive at a general theory of constitution arguably goes wrong with respect to the reflexivity and transitivity of parthood. And this is because sums have utterly undemanding principles of unity.

Sums not only have undemanding principles of unity; they lack any *distinguished* principles of unity. If S, the sum of a and b, is summed with S', the sum of c and d, then of the resultant sum S* it is equally correct to say:

> What it is for S* to exist is for S and S' to exist at some time or other and for them to exhaust a sum.

> What it is for S* to exist is for S, c, and d to exist at some time or other and for them to exhaust a sum.

> What it is for S* to exist is for a, b, and S to exist at some time or other and for them to exhaust a sum.

> And so on, for any divisions of a, b, c, d. For any principle of division of the sum we have something which corresponds to a principle of unity for the sum.

Contrast the set $\{\{a,b\}, \{c,d\}\}$, for which the distinguished unity condition is stated by saying that what it is for the set $\{\{a,b\}, \{c,d\}\}$ to exist is for $\{a,b\}$ and $\{c,d\}$ to exist and for them to exhaust the members of a set.

In the case of a sum, any principle of division will have as its inverse something that is a principle of unity for the sum. So a sum has only u-parts. Any division of the sum, however arbitrary, will be a division into parts that exist at some time or other and so satisfy a condition of unity for the sum.

Accordingly, a sum, unlike a set of sets or almost every other kind of item, has no articulated structure, at least none that does not derive from the individual structures of the items that are its parts. And here is another route to the conclusion that parties, molecules, stars, organisms, word tokens, and so on and so forth are not sums. They have a distinguished structure of u-parts determined by demanding principles of unity.

This bears on the ground of the principle of uniqueness of mereological summation, and on why uniqueness fails once we allow other sorts of items. Just because mereological sums have no articulated structure, there is no basis for distinction among mereological sums with just the same parts. But a structure-inducing principle of unity can be such a basis. Magnetic letters that spell out the word "ton" can be rearranged to spell out the word "not". The first word token and the second word token are different wholes. They have the very same parts, but different principles of unity. The parts have to be differently arranged to get the one word token rather than the other.

12. This means that if there wholes other than mereological sums then it is certainly the case that two or more items can be in the same place at the same time, even though they share a decomposition into the same ultimate parts. Consider a word token, say "ton". What it is for that word token to exist is for certain letters to exist and for them to be arranged in a certain order. We can also decompose the token into its material atomic parts. The sum of those atomic parts will be in the same place as the word token.

Pretend for the moment that the atoms of chemistry are simples, in the sense of having no parts at all. Does it follow from the fact that the word token and the sum share a decomposition into the same atomic parts that they have the very same parts? That is provable in Leśniewski's mereology, which works with the undiscriminating disjunctive notion of being a part *sans phrase* of an item or being identical with that item. However, any such 'proof' of the claim that if two items decompose into the same atoms then they have the very same parts will depend upon working within a framework that abstracts away from significant partitional structure.

Letting the different styles of bracketing indicate different principles of unity, consider Aleph, the following item:

[$<a, b>$, $<c, d>$], where a, b, c, and d are atoms.

Now all the parts of a sum of atoms are themselves atoms or sums of atoms. But $<a, b>$ is not an atom, nor a sum of atoms. Neither is $<c, d>$. So Aleph has parts, u-parts, which are not parts of the sum of a, b, c, and d. Yet Aleph and this sum decompose into the same atoms.

We are now in a position to see just how to find both a sum and a different complex item with just the same atomic parts. The general principle is that a complex item whose u-parts are not atoms but are composed of atoms can share just the same atomic parts with the sum of those atoms.

We also have a general result about co-occupancy. So long as we suspend a certain subtlety about the potential difference in grain of the material boundaries of material items in different categories, and hence a potential difference in location among different material items made of the same atoms, summing will provide a host of cases of two material items in the same place at the same time. For example, the word token "atom" and the sum of its letters will consist of the same atoms and so be in the same place at the same time.

13. Still, our marginalizing of sums may now make this kind of co-occupancy seem irrelevant to what was really being denied by those who insisted that you cannot have two material items in the same place at the same time. To the extent that sums have utterly undemanding and non-structuring principles of unity, they may seem to be degenerate sorts of material items.

So sums of material things aside, can there be two or more distinct material items in the same place at the same time?

Consider the story of Leatherskin and Rindmaiden. Leatherskin is a Brazilian beach addict. Over many years he has come to be covered with a thick layer of leathery dead skin. Suppose the dead skin is now an inactive coating, and does nothing to help sustain his basic life functions.

Let us then inquire as to the extent of Leatherskin's organism, the extent of a certain organic whole, which we understood earlier as organic material parts unified by the principle that they together provide a minimal categorical basis for dispositions to various life functions. On the hypothesis that Leatherskin's dead coating does nothing to help sustain any life functions, the coating can be omitted from the list of organic material parts that together provide a categorical basis for dispositions to Leatherskin's life functions. On this view, his leathery skin is like a tight-fitting, total body suit. It is not part of his body. Perhaps it attaches to his body by bonding forces, so that there may be a compact bonded system that is slightly larger than his body and includes the leathery skin along with the members of some set of exhaustive parts of his body, as it might be the cells or the organic molecules. Even so, Leatherskin does not exhibit two distinct systems, the organic whole and the bonded unit, with just the same material parts. All we have is a case of an organic system being contained within a bonded unit. Yet the case of Leatherskin does serve to bring out this point: organic molecules, or living and dead cells, can be bonded together in two interestingly different ways. The first way is exhibited at the interface between Leatherskin's organism and his leathery coating. The second way is exhibited within Leatherskin's organism. The second, but not the first, provides a minimal categorical basis for a disposition to various life functions.

Now consider Rindmaiden, who lives in the very cold north, and has a useful way of fighting off its icy depredations. She has a very thick skin, hard and dead, a rind, if you will. Her rind is an insulating layer that keeps her body temperature within the range required for her to continue to live. As with Leatherskin, we find here a bonded unit that includes her outer skin. If we now apply our criterion for determining the extent of an organism we get an interesting result. We ask: Which are the organic material parts that hold together in such a way as to provide a minimal categorical basis for dispositions to various life functions? By this criterion, the Rindmaiden's dead skin is part of her organism. (Compare a necrotic organ that still crucially supports the organs around it.) Her organism is coextensive with the bonded unit of cells that make up her body. Here we have two physical systems consisting of the same simplest parts or 'atoms', differently organized.

So we have two physical systems in the same place at the same time.

Indeed, now that we have laboured through the cases of Leatherskin and Rindmaiden we can see that what is true of Rindmaiden is true of us. Coextensive with our organisms are bonded units made of the same simplest parts, but different u-parts.

14. Attention to principles of unity shows that contrary to the dogmas of the day there is no general obstacle to two or more distinct items having the very same parts, be they u-parts or d-parts, *throughout their entire careers.*

Suppose we have a happy case of unremitting reciprocated love, as with the Father and the Son. We then have two states of affairs: the Son loving the Father and the Father loving the Son. These are distinct states of affairs, coexistent in time. But they have the same constituents, the Father, the Son, and the relation of loving.

That may not seem obvious, especially now that we have emphasized the significance of layered internal structure. We can countenance the arbitrary formation of relational properties by saturating all but one argument place of a relation. And relational properties then can be among the immediate constituents of states of affairs. So why shouldn't the immediate constituents of the state of affairs of the Father loving the Son be the Father and the relational property of Loving the Son; while the immediate constituents of the state of affairs of the Son loving the Father would be the Son and the relational property of Loving the Father? The basic constituents of the state of affairs would be the same; but this would not show that the constituents are the same. After all, the sets $\{a, \{b,c\}\}$ and $\{c, \{b,a\}\}$ have different constituents, despite sharing just the same 'atoms'.

However, what holds for sets may make for more distinctions among states of affairs than we are prepared to countenance. The Father's loving Himself; that is a single state of affairs. But if we allow that the intermediate formation of relational properties from relations and individuals adds significant intermediate structure to states of affairs then we can distinguish two states of affairs, the one consisting of the Father and the relational property of Being loved by the Father, the other consisting of the Father and the relational property of Loving the Father. Obviously, this is a distinction without a difference; which suggests that the intermediate formation of relational properties from relations and individuals does not add significant structure to states of affairs.

So the case of reciprocated, coeval love between the Father and the Son does show that there can be two distinct states of affairs having the very same u-parts throughout their entire careers.

Well, maybe this is so for states of affairs. But could there be distinct *physical systems or material objects* (middle-sized, relatively compact, non-living physical systems) with the very same parts throughout their entire career?

Some suppose that such a case is the case of the copper statue and the piece of copper that wholly constitutes it, at least when the statue and the piece are cast and destroyed together. The favoured argument for distinctness of the statue and the piece has always been a modal argument; for example, that the piece could survive certain deformations which the statue could not. Such arguments produce a stand-off, since they can apparently be met by a counterpart theorist or by anyone who is prepared to assert that there is a systematic sort of opacity in the subject positions of modal predications.

However, armed with a more sophisticated conception of parts that is allowed for by mereology, we are now in a position to see that there is a non-modal argument for distinctness of the copper statue and the piece of copper.

The thing to notice is that although the copper statue and the piece of copper are made of just the same copper atoms, *they have different material parts*. For they have different principles of unity, different enough to guarantee different u-parts. For example, suppose the statue is of a bull; then its u-parts will include, say, the bull's head, its torso, and its tail. These parts have to hang together in a certain bull-ish way for the statue to exist. These parts will also correspond to parts of the piece of copper, but not necessarily to *u-parts* of the piece of copper. Typically the u-parts of the piece of copper are smaller, perhaps articulated, but undetached, pieces of the copper. These parts have to hang together in a different way for the piece (as opposed to the statue) to exist. There is no reason to suppose that quite generally the same parts have to hang together in the same way for the copper statue and the piece of copper to exist.

For suppose the construction of the statue involves eleven still-articulated copper cables wrapped around each other in the form of a bull. Then the piece of copper has eleven u-parts. We unwind the copper cable that makes up the bull's head and then wind it seamlessly into the bull's torso. The piece of copper has survived; indeed it has not lost a part. The statue of the bull survives but it has lost a part, namely its head. Therefore, the statue had a part which the piece of copper did not have. Therefore, they were, and are, distinct though coincident items.

Notice also that the emphasis on principles of unity allows us to explain an important difference between the copper statue and the piece of copper. The unwinding of the copper cable that makes up the bull's head *deforms* the statue. It does not *deform* the piece of copper. That is to say that the unwinding violates certain ideal formal conditions found in the principle of unity of the statue, conditions not to be found in the principle of unity of the piece of copper.

Perhaps some will deny that there is a piece of copper made up of the copper cables. They will say that there are just eleven copper cables wound around each other and no piece that they constitute, and so no material object distinct from but coextensive with the statue of the bull.

But here is no great matter. For the same points can be made by considering a copper statue formed by winding a single long copper cable around itself in a certain way. (Think of a doll made from a single piece of string.) The copper cable *is* a material object, a long one indeed, but none the worse for that. The cable may be homogeneous copper throughout, in which case its u-part will be a certain quantity of copper, or it may consist of strands of copper wire twisted to make it up, in which case its u-parts are the strands. Surely when we unwind the first part of the long cable that makes up the bull's head the unwound d-part of the cable does not cease to exist. Nor is the cable deformed. But the bull's head is no more, and the statue of the bull is deformed. Though the cable and the statue are in the same place at the same time, they have different principles of unity and different u-parts.

A helpful objector might now respond as follows. 'Look, the d-part of the cable that makes up the bull's head just is the bull's head and so just is the u-part of the statue in question. Here we have the "is" of contingent predication. This d-part of the cable, say the first six feet of the cable, was temporarily shaped as a bull's head and then it was straightened out. While it was shaped as a bull's head it was an u-part of the statue of the bull.'

This is an initially appealing suggestion, but one that leads to another, less appealing suggestion. If the bull's head is just the first six feet of the cable with the contingent property of being twisted into the shape of a bull's head, how can we resist supposing that the statue of the bull itself is the whole sixty feet of cable with the contingent property of being twisted into the shape of a bull?

As I understand it, Judith Jarvis Thomson (1998) takes precisely this view, at least as applied to 'doubled' artefacts such as cables made into statues (a more general and radical version of this view is found in O'Leary-Hawthorne and Cortens 1995).

What then is wrong with such a view, a view on which the head is identical with the first six feet of cable and the statue is identical with the whole sixty feet of cable? Well, suppose we unwind the statue of the bull by unwinding the cable. We stop when half the cable is unwound. If the statue of the bull is constructed so that half of the cable is used to make up the densely wound head, then after unwinding the head we may be halfway through unwinding the cable, while only beginning on unwinding the statue. So unwinding the statue is a distinct event from unwinding the cable. Yet apart from the statue and the cable these events share the very same constituents. They involve the same property, unwinding, and they occur at the same place and the same time. Moreover, they occupy the same 'location' in the causal network. They have the same causes and effects. Although the two events are both unwindings, they are distinct unwindings because distinct items, the statue and the cable, are being unwound. It is because these items are distinct that their distinct unwindings can occur at different rates.

Here, as elsewhere, the Thomson view deprives us of the required distinct subjects of predication. On her view, there is no distinct statue to be unwound, so we must treat talk of the statue being unwound as equivalent to talk about the cable being unwound, while it is contingently arranged as a statue. But it isn't equivalent. For while the cable is still arranged as a statue, I may have unwound half of the cable and only *one-sixth* of the statue.

The same defect—depriving us of required subjects of predication—is found in more radical positions such as Peter van Inwagen's (1990), which has it that in the material world there are only simples arranged thus and so, and living things. The simples arranged cable-wise and the simples arranged statue-wise are the very same items. So where are we to find the item that is half unwound and the item that is not yet half unwound?

Indeed, we do not think of simples as the kind of things that can be unwound at all. So on van Inwagen's approach there is nothing there to be unwound. This is one of many cases in which he cannot claim even Berkeley's dubious distinction of "speaking with the vulgar". Here and elsewhere, what the vulgar mean to say is not able to be said of simples.

As against this, suppose for the moment that you can make sense of simples being unwound *qua items arranged thus and so.*[4] One might then say that the simples *qua* arranged cable-wise are half-unwound, while the simples *qua* arranged statue-wise are not. Notice that this way of responding is not favourable for van Inwagen's ultimate position. His whole argument for the existence of living things is that he himself thinks and is not a simple, and that a mere plurality (not his favoured expression) of some simples cannot think. Once one allows "*qua*"-talk to mediate predication of what otherwise cannot be directly predicated of some simples, van Inwagen's crucial positive argument for the existence of organic wholes is in jeopardy. This the argument that mere 'pluralities' of simples cannot think, so we need organisms as subjects of thought. If simples *qua* arranged cable-wise can be unwound even though simples cannot be unwound *simpliciter*, why can't simples *qua* arranged organically think even though a mere 'plurality' of simples *simpliciter* cannot think? What is then left of the argument that we still need to recognize organic wholes beyond the simples?

In any case, all this "*qua*"-talk seems ill-founded; you might say it has feet of *qua*. (This is one reason to prefer the pronunciation of "*qua*" as *kwey*.) For it does seem that the items that are unwound are unwound *simpliciter*, rather than *qua* this or that kind of thing. The predicate "... is half unwound" and its ilk are not referentially opaque. When considering an item that might satisfy the predicate, one does

---

[4] If this is to be even apparently helpful to van Inwagen, we must not understand the semantics of *qua*-predication to involve *qua*-objects which satisfy the *qua*-ed predicate essentially.

not need to clarify whether we are considering the item *qua*-this or *qua*-that. One simply looks to the parts of the item to determine how much of it is unwound. The same with painting. Because they have different parts, you could paint half of the outside of the cable red, without painting half of the outside of the statue red. Is "... is painted" referentially opaque? Is "half of. . ."? Is "outside of. . ."?

The philosophical intelligence is idly employed when one simply asserts referential opacity, and then goes on to observe that given the assertion, the conclusion of distinctness can then be resisted in a principled way. The burden is on the defender of referential opacity to explain its source in the non-extensionality of the predicates involved. And it is worthwhile investigating how far the defender of referential opacity would have to go to do this quite generally. Let us say that a given part of a material object is an *outermost part* in a given direction from its centre of mass if there is no part continuous with the given part further away from the centre of mass in that direction. When an item is folded on itself, its outermost parts touch, in the sense that no three-dimensional item can fit between them.

I take it that the predicates "... is a part of...", "... is the centre of mass of...", "... in the direction of...", "... continuous with..." "... is three-dimensional" and "... is between..." introduce no referential opacity. And the quantifiers involved in the definitions of *outermost part* and *touching* introduce no referential opacity.

Now suppose the cable is folded or twisted upon itself very near its centre of mass. Then the cable will have outermost parts that touch in the defined sense. This may occur at a place *inside* the statue. But it does not occur inside the cable. Inside the cable, there are copper atoms in an atomic array, surrounded by more of the same; so inside the cable we will not find outermost parts. Is "... is inside..." referentially opaque, so that an item x can be inside and item y only under the description d of y? Apart from the programme of identifying co-occupants, one would never have thought so. The insides of items would be whatever they are even if there had been no thoughts or descriptions of such items.

So, the précis of the case of the copper statue of the bull and the copper cable is as follows. They have the same atomic parts. So subtleties of boundaries aside, they can be in the same places throughout their entire careers. But they are distinct, since they have different u-parts. Their distinctness can make for distinct events involving the very same property, time, place, and location in the causal network, distinct events such as the unwinding of the statue and the unwinding of the cable.

The dominance of mereology, with the resultant pictures of material objects as either sums of atoms or sums of temporal parts, has helped obscure the ubiquity of complete material co-occupancy. This in its turn has distorted the study of constitution, where many have taken the ban on co-occupancy to have the status of an axiom.

15. To return to our deeper question: Could there be distinct physical systems or material objects with the very same parts throughout their entire career? We can now see that this is indeed possible. It just requires distinct principles of unity that happen to hold of the very same parts for the very same period of time.

That might happen this way. There could be super-dense spheres which when placed in a magnetic field of a certain intensity come to attract each other with massive electrostatic forces so as to bind together to form a tetrahedron. As the ambient magnetic field massively increases, the electrostatic forces reverse and the whole system blasts apart into its constituent spheres. The short-lived tetrahedron represents a physical system; its parts are the spheres and its principle of unity is that they should be bound together in a tetrahedron by electrostatic forces. But coexisting with this electrostatic system is a gravitational system; one with the same spheres as parts and a different principle of unity, namely that the spheres should be bound together in a tetrahedron by gravitational forces.

To confirm that these are indeed distinct physical systems, we need to have a clear case in which one could exist without the other. Suppose then that if the magnetic field were to massively drop, the electrostatic forces that hold between the spheres would diminish to zero. The electrostatic system is no more, but the gravitational system remains intact, and the spheres continue to be bound together in the tetrahedron by gravitational forces.

Nor should we say that talk of such physical systems is really talk of some items during a phase, such as while they are magnetically bound together, or while they are electrostatically bound together. At least we should not do this without being prepared to take the same view about all material objects. For a material object is just a middle-sized, relatively compact, non-living physical system.

16. Are there other cases, besides the imagined tetrahedrons, where two wholes have the very same u-parts and d-parts?

Consider sporks, a camper's implement that combines the functions of a spoon and a fork. You can make a spork in several ways. You can take a metal fork and hammer down the non-working end and then fashion it into a bowl that will serve to spoon up food and liquids. Or you can take a metal spoon and cut thin rectangles out of its non-working end so as to create the tines that will serve to *spear* food. (We are camping, remember.) Or you can cast the item outright. By whatever route, the result is arguably a fork and a spoon and a spork, all in the same place at the same time.

I say this with full consciousness of the fact that in some quarters the case of the spork, the spoon, and the fork will excite the temptation to treat these supposedly distinct items as only some one underlying item arranged spoon-wise and fork-wise, and hence spork-wise. The most plausible underlying item will be a variable physical system or structure. But this temptation, like other temptations, is inherently general. It involves a readiness to treat like cases alike. That would mean that we are to treat all artefacts as phases on underlying physical systems. The objection to that general strategy is the objection to Thomson and van Inwagen canvassed earlier: we lose required subjects of predication.

Let us restrict ourselves to sporks made in the third way, by being cast outright. Consider one such, and its coextensive spoon and the fork. They came into being at the same time and they have common parts. The common parts of the spork, the spoon, and the fork are the bowl, the stem, and the tines. The bowl is an unusual design feature of the fork, while the tines are unusual design features of the spoon. The bowl is a contingent part of the fork: it could be hammered back into a more familiar, non-working end and the fork (but not the spoon) would survive the change. The tines are contingent parts of the spoon: they could be snipped off and the spoon (but not the fork) would be truncated but survive the change. So the spoon and the fork are distinct items, since one could exist without the other. Yet we can imagine a case where they always have the same parts: the tines, the stem, and the bowl.

Notice how the idea of a principle of unity helps explain this case: a case of two things–the fork and the spoon—with common parts, but with different parts playing the role of essential and accidental parts. The spoon is the stem, the bowl, and the tines united by a dynamic principle of unity: roughly the principle that these parts or most of them or functional replacements of most of them should be arranged in such a way as to be able to function as a spoon. So although the principle holds of the tines, its holding of them depends not at all on their being tines as opposed to something that can be grasped in order to spoon up food or liquid. The fork is the stem, the bowl, and the tines united by a different dynamic principle of unity: roughly the principle that these parts or most of them or functional replacements of most of them should be arranged in such a way as to be able to function as a fork. So although the principle holds of the bowl, its holding of the bowl depends not at all on its being a bowl as opposed to something that can be grasped in order to mash and spear and scoop up food.

By thus filling out the principle of unity for an item we can come to understand how it is that the item has some of its parts (or some of its part types) accidentally, and others essentially.

There is another sort of contingent part-sharing, one in which there are two things with the same parts, although one of these things could grow or acquire an extra part that would count as part of it, but not of the other thing with which it formerly shared all its parts. To modify an example of Saul Kripke's, in the Australian desert there is a particular kind of rootless tumbleweed which will only flower after a flooding rain. Many die without ever being graced by a flower. For their whole lives they consist simply of a spherical stem structure. But even such a tumbleweed is not identical with the stem structure which happens to exhaust its parts. For if the tumbleweed were to flower, the flower would be part of the tumbleweed but not part of the stem. What is happening here?

I say that there are two similar but distinct principles of unity in play, the one governing the stem structure and the other governing the tumbleweed. Botanists could tell us more about these similar but distinct principles of unity, operating at different levels of organization within the organism. But we can still understand the part-sharing arrangement between the stem structure and the tumbleweed without these details.

Suppose the stem structure has jointed parts branching off each other. They count as parts of the stem because they are organically unified in a way appropriate to making up a stem. But they also count as part of the tumbleweed because they are organically unified in a way appropriate to making up a tumbleweed. That is why the parts of the tumbleweed are parts of the stem structure and vice versa. Yet if the tumbleweed were to flower, the flower and the jointed parts of the stem would then be organically unified in a way appropriate to making up a tumbleweed. However, the flower and the jointed parts of the stem would not be organically unified in a way appropriate to making up a stem structure.

Again, the fundamental ground for the distinctness of the tumbleweed and the stem structure is not modal. It lies in their distinct principles of unity. Here, as elsewhere, modality is consequential upon essence and accident.

17. John Locke (1690) wrote 'We never finding, nor conceiving it possible, that two things of the same kind should exist in the same place at the same time, we rightly conclude that, whatever exists anywhere at any time excludes all of the same kind, and is there itself alone.' Following Locke, David Wiggins (1968) claimed that although there could be several material objects in the same place at the same time, there could not be two material objects of *the very same substance kind* in the same place at the same time. If we think of a material object as a middle-sized, relatively compact, non-living physical system then, like all physical systems, material objects will only have material parts. So it will be interesting to inquire whether there could be two material objects of the very same substance kind and with the very same material parts throughout their coextensive careers.

This question, like Locke's claim and the Wiggins thesis, is systematically ambiguous thanks to the ambiguity of "very same kind". For that phrase can admit of a variety of restrictions. Aren't poodles all of the very same kind? Well, there is the standard poodle and the miniature poodle. But is that a difference in kind? Well, the difference between the English racing greyhound and the whippet is a difference in kinds of breeding (the whippet is related to both the English greyhound and the terrier) and hence a difference in breed. Isn't that a difference in kind?

Notice that these are all substance kinds in Wiggins's sense. That is, they are each such that members of the kind cannot migrate out of the kind. Once a poodle, always a poodle. But as to what makes for a difference in kind or even in substance kind, we still don't know, because as yet there is nothing definite to be known. We need to specify what we mean by a kind.

A worthwhile form of the question about same parts and same kinds focuses on real kinds in the sense specified earlier. Things are of a real kind if they have just the same determinate essence, hence just the same principle of unity, and at the most specific level of sameness. (A real kind is thus an *infima species*.)

Could there then be two material objects of the very same real kind with the very same material parts throughout their coextensive careers? What would make them distinct? Their principles of unity would be the same and their parts would be the same. Moreover, since by hypothesis they are coextensive in space and time, they presumably came into being from the same material origins.

Nevertheless, if we allow ever so little determinability in the kind in question, and hence some difference in the principles of unity in question, then we can find two material objects of the very same kind with just the same parts (and in the very same place) throughout their entire careers.

18. Consider road signs, which I take to be both artefacts and material objects. Their parts, namely 'signage' and word tokens, are material, even though their principles of unity involve intentional conditions. What a road sign can reasonably be expected to convey to passers-by enters into the identity of the sign: it is part of what it is to be the sign in question. So if the same physical piece of signage first says 'Roadwork Ahead' and then is repainted to say 'Eat at Joe's' we have two different signs made of the same piece of signage and different word tokens. They also differ in what the signage and the tokens can be reasonably expected to convey. It is not a contingent feature of a sign (as opposed to a piece of signage) that it warns rather than exhorts.

Nevertheless, the principle of unity for a sign seems to be dynamic, in that the same sign can survive some change in the word tokens displayed upon it. So if we begin with a piece of signage that says 'Eat at Joes' and the sign-maker later feels the need to correct his spelling by adding the apostrophe to indicate the possessive, so that the sign now reads 'Eat at Joe's' then this is the same sign, now corrected.

A sign can survive augmentation of its constitutive word tokens, as well as their correction. Having corrected the spelling in the sign, the sign-maker may feel that 'Eat at Joe's' is just too unemphatic, and may add an exclamation mark to compensate. So it is the same sign that first says 'Eat at Joes' then 'Eat at Joe's' and finally 'Eat at Joe's!' Each of the three sequences of tokens can be reasonably expected to convey the same message to the passer-by.

So what it is for a road sign exhorting passers-by to eat at Joe's to exist at a certain place along a highway is for there to be at that place some signage visibly displaying (possibly varying) word tokens that may reasonably be taken to convey to passers-by that they should eat at Joe's.

Now consider the (fictional) story of the Begin Highway. Between Haifa and Tel Aviv a highway is to be built in the generic American style with all the usual entries, exits, crossovers, landscaped banks, and, of course, the ubiquitous green and white signage in English. The friends of Menachem Begin wish to memorialize Begin by naming the highway after him. So they pay a Mr Janus, who is in the business of building and maintaining signs, to put up a green-and-white sign naming the highway the Begin Highway.

It so happens that Janus is the very same man contracted by the highway builders to put up the usual signage around the highway. And this calls for, among other things, a green-and-white sign indicating the start of the highway, a sign saying, as they do, 'Begin Highway'.

Janus thinks it will be frustrating to many motorists to see one English sign naming the highway the Begin Highway as well as another indicating where the highway begins. He thinks that some motorists will say 'Enough already with all this Begin stuff!' while others will be thoroughly confused as to where the highway really begins. So Janus forms the plan to use the very same piece of signage and the very same word tokens both to name the highway after Begin and to indicate where the highway begins. He thus produces two signs in the same place at the same time, and there they remain throughout their careers. The one sign, the 'Begin Highway' sign, names the highway and so carries out the communicative intentions of the friends of Begin. The other sign, the 'Begin Highway' sign, indicates where the highway begins and so carries out the communicative intentions of the builders of the highway. The friends of Begin drive by and only see the first sign. Most other motorists only see the second. I mean they all see the signage and the word tokens, but only some see it as naming the highway.

The friends of Menachem Begin eventually come to realize what has happened, and they are furious with Janus. They say 'The highway company paid you to put a sign there and we paid you to put up a sign there, but there is only one sign there'. Janus demurs. He argues as follows:

> There must be two signs there. For I could make either one cease to exist by augmenting the other. I could prefix the first word token on the piece of signage with 'M.' and then since the signage would now read 'M. Begin Highway' it could not be reasonably taken to indicate where the highway begins. By changing the signage in this way I would have augmented the sign that names the highway and caused the other sign to cease to exist. Now you can't augment something that doesn't already exist. So the sign that names, the sign you paid me for, has been there all along.
>
> Notice that I could instead interpolate 'The' between the word tokens on the piece of signage and then since the signage would now read 'Begin The Highway' it could not be reasonably taken to name the highway after Begin. By changing the signage in this way I would have augmented the sign that indicates where the highway begins and caused the other sign to cease to exist. Again, you can't augment something that doesn't already exist. So the sign that indicates, the sign they paid me for, has been there all along.
>
> So there have been two signs there all along.
>
> Signs, you may take it from me, are individuated by their signage, their possibly varying word tokens, *and* what they can be reasonably expected to communicate.

Although I think Janus is right about the identity of road signs, my point is not to insist that there are two signs there as opposed to one sign doing double communicative duty. The point is instead a conditional one. To the extent that we think that there is more than one sign we must think that the principle of unity for the sign that names is different from the principle of unity of the sign that indicates. It cannot be that what unites the word tokens and the piece of signage into a road sign is just that the former is painted on a visible part of the latter. It must rather be that the tokens should be painted on the signage with the reasonable expectation that they convey to passers-by that the highway is named after Begin, or alternatively, with the reasonable expectation that they convey to passers-by that the highway begins near the sign. Absent something like this more demanding principle of unity for signs, there is no distinguishing the signs.

For given a single utterly specific principle of unity and just the same material parts at the same times, there is no discerning two material objects with that principle and those parts. So there is no discerning two material objects of the very same real kind with the very same material parts throughout their coextensive careers. But if the location of a material object is wholly determined by its principle of unity and where its material parts are located, then a version of the Wiggins thesis follows. There is no discerning two material objects of *the very same real kind* in the very same place throughout their entire careers.

Kit Fine (2000) has a similar example: two distinct letters consisting of the very same orthographic tokens on the very same paper. One letter is in English and the other is in code. The two missives achieve different communicative effects. Fine takes this to be at odds with the Locke–Wiggins thesis. As we have seen, it is and it isn't at odds with the Locke–Wiggins thesis. Everything depends on how we construe "same kind" as it figures in the Locke–Wiggins thesis. What is clear is that a missive in English and a missive in code will likely have a different principle of unity governing the same orthographic tokens. The spirit of the Locke–Wiggins thesis, as well as the ambiguous letter of the Locke–Wiggins thesis, is certainly compatible with that.

19. Throughout, we have found no reason to respect the general claim of uniqueness of composition, the 'axiom' that distinct wholes must have distinct parts. This is because distinct principles of unity can be another source of distinct wholes.

However, a theorist might try to save the 'axiom' of uniqueness of composition by treating a principle of unity as another sort of part, a property part conceived of in the fashion of an immanent universal. So consider what we called a bonded unit. On the theorist's conception, the parts of the bonded unit would be the cells (or the molecules) *and* the variably polyadic relational property of being bonded together. The property part would be what distinguishes this bonded unit from other wholes with just the same ordinary parts.

The conception takes some getting used to. We ordinarily think that all the parts of a material object lie on or within the surface of the object. If we extend this requirement to property parts, then we will get the absurd result that relations like being bonded together can get closer to themselves. (Imagine two bonded units approaching each other.) No, the friend of property parts will have to get comfortable with the idea that property parts are not within the material objects they are part of. Indeed, they had better not be in space-time at all. For one can't make sense of other things getting further away or closer to from some property. Properties, relations among them, are unapproachable.

On this conception of relations as property parts, each material object will share parts with some states of affairs. So, if what it is for a certain cross to exist is for one plank to be attached to another at right angles, then on the conception in question the cross consists of the planks and the relation of being attached at right angles. But those same constituents will be u-parts of the state of affairs of the planks being attached together at right angles.

This illustrates the central difficulty with the conception. The principle of unity for the state of affairs is distinct from the constituent relation of the state of affairs; the principle of unity in question requires that the constituent relation *holds* of the constituent planks. But on the conception of objects as having as property parts the very relations that are their own principles of unity, it will often be true—and this is fatal to the conception—that the principle of unity will not hold of itself and the other parts of the object. So it is with being attached together at right angles. This is a relation that could not possibly hold of three things, one of which is a relation.

So also with bonding, a principle of unity for bonded units such as molecules. What is it for this property part, bonding, along with the ordinary parts, to make up a genuine whole, the whole that is the molecule or the bonded unit? The holding among the ordinary parts of a principle of unity, being bonded together, was supposed to account for why the ordinary parts made up the whole that is a bonded unit. But it does not account for why the ordinary parts and the property parts make up such a whole. For being bonded together does not hold of them.

Suppose some other relational property R held of the property parts and the ordinary parts, and it was in virtue of the holding of that relational property of all these parts that all these parts formed a genuine whole. Well then, it is R and not being bonded together that is the principle of unity that we seek. So if R is the principle of unity, the present conception will count it as another part, alongside the ordinary parts.

The obvious problem is that there will be no general guarantee that R holds of all the parts *and itself*. Unless R is such as to hold among all the parts and itself, it cannot be the principle of unity that we seek. For since it is itself supposed to be a part, then it should hold of all the other parts and itself. Otherwise there would be no account of what in virtue of which *all* the supposed parts form a whole. It is hard to see how there will be such 'partly autological' relational properties for all of the various kinds of complex objects that there are. If R is the variably polyadic property of this, that, and the other parts existing at some time or other, then R will hold of itself. Once again, this feature disappears as soon as we move beyond sums and begin to consider wholes with more demanding principles of unity.

This is the crux of the difficulty with the idea that principles of unity are further parts of the objects they govern. The relational properties that are the plausible uniters of ordinary parts into complex objects will not in general hold of the ordinary parts and themselves. There is therefore no basis for including them as parts along with the ordinary parts in some putative object.

So there seems to be no way round the rejection of the 'axiom' that distinct wholes must have distinct parts.

20. There is one crucial postulate of mereology left standing, namely:

> That there is no restriction on the formation of wholes, i.e. given any items there is some item that is their fusion.

This will be true if the corresponding postulate governing mereological sums is true, namely:

> That there is no restriction on the formation of mereological sums, i.e. given any items there is a sum that is their fusion.

For if there are sums, and this postulate holds of them, then the sums are the very items that 'fuse', or unite, any arbitrarily chosen items. The very idea of a sum is the idea of a whole that 'arises' from arbitrary aggregation of other items, a whole that exists just on the condition that those items exist at some time or other. So it seems that the postulate must hold if there are sums.

But are there sums?

Let us go back to the idea of a principle of division of a whole whose converse is not a principle of unity for that whole. Such a *mere* principle of division is a way of dividing a whole which will yield at least some d-parts. A paradigm of a mere principle of division is arbitrary spatial or temporal segmentation. You take a spatially extended item, say a material object, and divide it into as many fine-grained spatial slices as you like. These arbitrary undetached spatial parts of the material object typically will be d-parts. Or you take a temporally extended item, such as an activity, divide it into as many fine-grained temporal slices as you like. These arbitrary undetached temporal parts typically will be mere d-parts.

It is very natural to think of arbitrary aggregation as reversing the effect of arbitrary segmentation, in the sense that taking the sum or aggregate of the parts 'produced' by segmentation gives you back the item that was segmented. Arbitrary aggregation or mereological summation seems to put Humpty-Dumpty back together again, at least from his merely d-parts.

Yet if the idea of reversal is correct and if there is arbitrary segmentation, then there is no arbitrary aggregation or mereological summation!

That can be seen by returning to the dinner party. It consists of the following u-parts: the greeting of the guests, the downing of drinks, the pre-dinner chatting, the serving and consuming of the soup, then of the main course, and then of the dessert, followed by the host's disconcerting party piece and then the hurried farewells. These temporally extended event-parts of the dinner party are united by a principle of unity appropriate to such dinner parties. This will be something like: occupying a position in a sequence of events each effected either by the hosts or by the guests for the intended outcome of their mutual feeding and entertainment. They are the parts and that is the principle that would have to be mentioned in an adequate account of what it is to be the dinner party.

The dinner party also admits of segmentation into arbitrary temporal slices or temporal parts; it may be segmented, for example, into one-minute parts. Take those one-minute parts and sum them. Then, by reversal, we recover the dinner party as the result of summing.

But as a matter of fact, we do *not* recover the dinner party by summing all the one-minute parts of the dinner party. The result of summing is a mereological sum of parts. And the dinner party is not a mereological sum of parts. One consideration is this: all the temporal parts of a sum of temporal parts will be essential to it, while many of those parts will not be essential parts of the dinner party. The host's interminable party piece could have been very much shorter in length. Although I take this to be a sound objection to identifying parties with sums, it has produced a famous stalemate with the friends of counterpart theory.

Attention to different sorts of parts provides another consideration, which is not met by counterpart theory. All the parts of the mereological sum will be u-parts of the sum, but most of those parts will be d-parts of the dinner party. So the dinner party is not the sum.

The friend of arbitrary aggregation or mereological summation must therefore deny either arbitrary segmentation or reversal. But arbitrary aggregation and arbitrary segmentation seem to stand or fall together. (Given either one, you can mount a plausible defence of the other.) And given arbitrary aggregation and arbitrary segmentation, reversal seems very plausible. Arbitrary segmentation is sometimes introduced as what would reverse arbitrary aggregation.

Perhaps reversal can be consistently denied, but perhaps also enough has been done to suggest that the theory of parts should be and can be thoroughly reconceived.

21. We have seen that once the idea of a principle of unity is in place, the ban on material co-occupancy emerges as entirely unwarranted. For allowing principles as well as parts to define wholes implies that there could be two wholes with the same material parts and hence the same location. Unfortunately, several theorists have written as if the study of constitution should be conditioned by a ban on material co-occupancy. Among the most striking theories developed in this spirit is that of Michael Burke (1992, 1994a,b, 1997). It may be instructive to see where he thinks the ban leads.

Burke takes the view that statues are essentially statues, and that non-statues such as mere pieces of copper are essentially non-statues. It follows that when a piece of copper is moulded into a statue, there is no room for the identity of the statue and the original piece of copper. Given the ban on co-occupancy, there is also no room for two things, the original piece of copper and the newly created statue, in the same place at the same time. Burke discerns a third option: the original piece of copper has ceased to exist and a statue has come into being. When his opponents insist that surely something has persisted through the change that began with the mere piece and ended with the statue, Burke's reply is that there is indeed something that persists through the change. It is the copper, either a mere quantity of matter or a mere plurality of atoms. In neither case do we have another material object there, along with the statue. So we do not have a case of two material objects in the same place at the same time.

Burke intends to generalize the morals he draws from the statue and the piece of copper to every case of ostensible material co-occupancy. To do so he introduces the notion of a dominant (substance) sortal. Burke suggests that one sortal dominates another when satisfying the first implies having a wider range of properties than is implied by satisfying the second. So he supposes that Copper Statue dominates Piece of Copper, since if we have a copper statue before us, it follows that we have something which weighs a certain amount, is made of copper, has a size and a shape, *and is a statue*. In order to determine what we have before us we should find the dominant sortal, a sortal which dominates any other ostensible sort of thing there before us. Those ostensible things will not themselves be genuine material objects. At best, there will be pluralities or quantities instead.

We are not told why only *dominant* sortals and their corresponding principles of unity make for genuine material objects. What is the ontological connection between implying more (varieties of) properties and not allowing for a material co-occupant which implies fewer (varieties of) properties?

In the absence of a clear connection, another hypothesis suggests itself: In so far as the notion of a dominant sortal can be made clear, it plays a role not in ontology but in the statement of the constraints on conversational cooperativeness. In describing what there is before us we are under the default but defeasible constraint of conveying relevant information as efficiently as we can. Deploying a description which implies more properties is a canonical way of doing that. But on this view it is not that there is no piece of copper there, cohabiting with the statue. It is just that, *ceteris paribus*, it is less helpful to cite the piece rather than the statue. For if we cite the statue it will follow that we have there something with the properties of the piece. But not vice versa.

In any case, this is not Burke's view. Instead, he takes the existence of an instance of a dominant sortal to exclude the coexistence in the same place of an instance of a dominated sortal.

To see if it does, recall spoons and sporks, camper implements that combine the functions of a spoon and a fork. The sortal Spork seems to dominate the sortal Spoon. From the fact that we have an (intact) spork before us it follows that we also have before us something with the properties of a spoon. But not vice versa. On a natural construal, Burke's view implies that when in the presence of a spork we are not also in the presence of a cohabiting spoon.

(There is another construal of Burke's view of sortal dominance, one that places weight on 'sorts' of properties. Perhaps both spoons and sporks have the same range of sorts of properties, they are artefacts, implements, material objects, etc. But this would mean that neither sortal dominates, so there is then no reason to suppose that when in the presence of a spork we are not also in the presence of a spoon. Let us put that aside, and see if the assumption of sortal dominance can help us in this case.)

As we said, a spork can be made in several ways. You can cast the item outright. You can take a metal fork and hammer down the non-working end and then fashion it into a bowl that will serve to spoon up food and liquids. Or you can take a metal spoon and cut thin rectangles out of its non-working end so as to create the tines that will serve to pick up food.

Focus on this third way. Burke must say of it that it leads to the destruction of the original spoon. And that seems wrong. Why should a spoon cease to exist when the design of its non-working end is modified?

Aficionados of the history of cutlery may speak to us of spoons with all sorts of elaborate design features on their non-working ends. And some of these design features may also be functional. So, some noble spoons may have round holes in their non-working ends, holes that were intended to support the spoons on hooks for storage purposes.

So even if the notion of a dominant sortal gets a foothold in the case of the spork, we nonetheless seem to have a case of co-occupancy whenever we have a spork.

Then there are cases of putative co-occupancy where Burke's notion of a dominant sortal has no relevant application. The case of the Begin Highway is one such case, where the relevant sortals, if distinct, are clearly not such that one 'dominates' the other.

A different kind of problem arises for Burke when we examine his decisive move of allowing *only* mere quantities or pluralities to persist through certain changes. According to Burke, when the piece of copper is shaped into a statue, the piece ceases to exist as the statue comes into being. He recognizes this is initially surprising, but some of the surprise is dissipated by finding something that persists, namely a plurality of copper atoms: a 'many' and not another one cohabiting with the statue. What is not clear is whether this strategy has sufficiently general application to make Burke's account viable.

Recall the Australian tumbleweed, which consists for most of its career of a stem structure, flowering as it does very rarely. When the tumbleweed flowers, it consists of a flower and a stem structure, *numerically the same stem structure that was there before the flowering*. Given the ban on co-occupancy, and the relevant claim that a non-plant (i.e. the stem structure) is essentially a non-plant, Burke will have to deny this and find something else that persists and continues to constitute the flowering tumbleweed. Otherwise, we should have to recognize before the flowering two things, the tumbleweed and the stem-structure, there in the same place at the same time. Could what persists be a mere 'many', a plurality or collection of plant cells, for instance? One problem is that stem structures and tumbleweeds are paradigm matter-exchangers—they have dynamic principles of unity that allow total change in constituent cells over time. So we may imagine two roughly contemporaneous changes in the tumbleweed over time: it changes its constituent cells and it flowers. No mere plurality of cells survives this period. Yet something stem-like survived. What is it then, if it is not the original stem structure? Burke's only relevant option is to say that it is the tumbleweed that survived, and that the stem structure came into being as a result of the tumbleweed's flowering. After the flowering, the stem structure is a genuine part of the tumbleweed, along with the flower. But it did not exist before the flowering. It came into existence with the flowering! Before the flowering there was a tumbleweed and a plurality of cells. With the flowering, there came to be a stem structure constituted by a (possibly different) plurality of plant cells.

We can make this last consequence worse. For the tumbleweed might flower twice during a particularly friendly spring. It flowers, those flowers are shed, and a few days later it flowers again. Whereas a botanist would trace the same stem structure throughout the two episodes of flowering, Burke might say that there are two distinct stem structures, one coming into being at the first flowering, and the other coming into being at the second flowering, which seems at odds with botany. Or he might say that there is one stem structure that exists intermittently. This would be a single stem structure that comes into existence after the first flowering, ceases to exist after the flowers fall off, and then 'returns' from ontic limbo with the second flowering. There may be cases in which an item intermittently exists, but they are all cases of disassembly or some other radical intrinsic change in the relation among the item's parts. Neither applies in the case of the tumbleweed and the stem structure.

Perhaps Burke may just deny that stem structures exist at all, not even as parts of plants that have flowered. However, the same worry about intermittent existence without disassembly or the like arises with his own example of the piece of copper and the statue. Surely we can use the same piece of copper to make successively a statue of a baseball and then of a cricket ball. (We smooth out the pattern of the seam and then create a different seam pattern.) Burke must say that the piece of copper exists intermittently. A repugnant consequence.

So it seems that it is not the case that an instance of an object of one sort excludes an instance of an object of a different sort in the same place at the same time. This fact is best explained by recognizing that the distinct principles of unity which are associated with the sorts Piece of Copper and Statue can be definitive of different wholes.

Again, in so far as the notion of a dominant sortal can be made clear, it seems to play a role not in ontology but in the statement of the constraints on conversational cooperativeness. Asked 'What is over there?' we are under a prima facie obligation to try to avoid citing an instance of a dominated sortal, as when we say that there is a piece of copper over there, while knowingly referring to the location of a statue. In knowingly citing an instance of a dominated sortal, we are being uncooperative by conveying less relevant information than we could, even using roughly the same number of words. Since the common cases appear to be ones in which there is a dominant sortal that is instanced in a given region, we may acquire the habit of thinking that there is, commonly or always, just one right answer to the question 'What is over there?' This itself can encourage the bias against co-occupancy. But here we simply have a habit of thought produced by a conversational convention.

22. Our simple characterization of immediate constitution in general and of immediate material constitution in particular, namely

> x immediately constitutes y just in case x is a u-part of y. x immediately materially constitutes y just in case x is a material u-part of y,

may not seem to go far enough.

For it does not provide an account of constitution *sans phrase*, the notion about which there is so much unresolved, and perhaps irresolvable, controversy. Is this really a defect?

One hypothesis that would explain why the many, very canny, people who have attempted to define constitution *sans phrase* have not fallen into agreement about how to proceed is that there are just too many ways to proceed. Once we divide an item into its u-parts, the question of whether we should count all their parts, and parts of parts, and so on as further "constituting" parts, as opposed to say only the sub-parts that are u-parts of the immediate u-parts, may be merely a matter of taste. Certainly English is too tolerant a master to force us to use "constitution" for one as opposed to another extension of the notion of immediate constitution.

In contrast with the controversy over constitution *sans phrase*, the distinction between u-parts and d-parts is not a verbal matter. It is an ontological distinction of great generality, a distinction that would obtain even if there were no speakers of languages at all.

Even if this or that proposal to extend the notion of constitution beyond the case of immediate constitution may be something of a matter of taste, it still remains that one can open oneself to significant counter-example in following this or that tasteful rule.

The notion of *material* constitution is something of a philosopher's invention, one answering to disparate constraints. One source of the idea is that material constitution is to be something of a surrogate for identity, at least in the sense that when one thing wholly materially constitutes another, then the massive similarity in properties between the two things is to be explained by the one wholly constituting the other. Another source of the idea is that if something is a material part of a material object it is among the material constitutors of that object. Still others suppose that the material stuff of which a material item is made materially constitutes that thing, even if we think of this stuff as 'atomless gunk', i.e. as never resolving into a plurality of items. (Though it may now be becoming standard to reserve the term 'composition' for the relation between a material item and the stuff that makes it up.)

There are several quite different questions in play here. One related question which has attracted some attention concerns the analysis of the relation of *wholly constituting*, a relation that might hold between the piece of copper and the statue or between an organism and the human being whose organism it is.

23. Lynne Rudder Baker takes this relation as her target for analysis in her recent book *Persons and their Bodies* and in a follow-up paper, 'On Making Things Up', which revises her original analysis (Baker 2002).

By way of a preliminary clarification of her analysandum, Baker specifies the relevant relation of constitution as asymmetric, irreflexive, and non-transitive.

A central notion deployed in her analysis is that of a 'primary kind', where an item's primary kind is specified by the answer to the question 'What most fundamentally is this item?' Baker adds that items have their primary-kind properties essentially, so primary kinds seem to be akin to the substance sortals of David Wiggins. They do not, however, seem to exhibit the full specificity of real kinds. For Baker tells us, 'Michelangelo's *David* was most fundamentally a statue. Trigger was most fundamentally a horse.'

Baker's final analysis (Baker 2002: 41–2) is set out as follows:

Let F and G be primary kinds. An F constitutes a G only in certain circumstances—different circumstances for different primary kinds. Call the circumstances in which an F constitutes a G, 'G-favorable' circumstances. Only in certain circumstances with certain laws and conventions in force does a piece of plastic constitute a driver's licence; only in circumstances including an organismic environment and perhaps even evolutionary history does a conglomerate of cells constitute a human heart. G-favorable circumstances are the milieu in which something can be a G. The G-favorable circumstances are those necessary but not sufficient for something to be a G. Then when a suitable F is in G-favorable circumstances, then it comes to constitute a G. When a piece of marble is in statue favorable conditions, then it comes to constitute a statue. . . . Now we can define 'constitution'.

x (wholly) constitutes y at t $=_{df}$ There are distinct primary-kind properties F and G and G-favorable circumstances such that:

(1) x has F as its primary-kind property and y has G as its primary-kind property;
(2) x and y are spatially coincident at t;
(3) x is in G-favorable circumstances at t;
(4) $(\Box\forall z\forall t[(z$ has F as its primary-kind property and z is in G-favorable circumstances at t$) \rightarrow \exists u(u$ has G as its primary-kind property and u is spatially coincident with z at t$)]$;

(5) $\Diamond\exists t[x$ exists at t & $\sim\exists w(w$ has G as its primary-kind property and w is spatially coincident with x at t)]; and

(6) If y is immaterial, then x is also immaterial.

There are three striking features of this analysis; its complexity, its avoidance of the notion of a part, and its crucial reliance on undischarged modal notions. Those who think that the clearest case of constitution is the relation between an item and its u-parts will find those three features individually suspect and collectively inadequate. The relation between an item and its u-parts seems to be relatively simple, and it also is a relation whose holding might have different modal consequences depending on the sorts of principles of unity governing the different wholes that we might consider. We should see the modal consequences of constitution not as something brute, and as a matter of fact definitive of constitution, but rather as flowing from the nature of the relation of constitution and from the wholes and parts it might hold among. This point will become more obvious when we descend to cases.

Before we do, it should be said that Baker is quite adamant about avoiding reliance on the notion of a part. Unfortunately, that is largely because she takes mereology to be the last word on parts.

To see how the modal consequences of constitution might differ, depending on the wholes and parts we consider, focus on Baker's fifth clause. Is it in general true that the consitutor only contingently constitutes and is coincident with the constituted item?

Certainly that is not the case for Socrates and the singleton of Socrates. Socrates constitutes his singleton, he is a u-part of his singleton, but there is no situation in which Socrates exists and a singleton (in fact the singleton of him) does not. Baker will probably disallow this case as a counter-example either because she does not take Socrates to wholly constitute his singleton or because she will not grant that the singleton is spatially located where Socrates is.

Still, the fact that constitution can hold necessarily between parts and an item, in the sense that it is necessary given the parts that the constituted item exists, will not go away. A collection of items and its sum are such that the items constitute the sum, and do so necessarily, in the sense that necessarily if they exist then the sum exists and has them as parts. Furthermore, the sum is where the collection is. So again we have non-contingent constitution and cohabitation.

We can also imagine examples in the organic world that make the same point.

Death is a substantial change. The living body has an organic remnant, a corpse, which may for a while occupy roughly the same space as the living body it replaced. But the remnant, the dead body, is a numerically different item from the living body. (As John Cleese famously said, a dead parrot is an ex-parrot.) So also with organic parts. The organic relics of the saints are not numerically the same items as those parts that were once living parts of their bodies. They are the mere remains of those parts.

Consider then a variant on the tumbleweed and the stem structure. (In what follows, I always mean the living stem structure, the item that ceases to exist and is replaced by an organic remnant when the tumbleweed dies.) It could be that some tumbleweed undergoes random genetic variation of a sort that prevents it from flowering. This confers a comparative advantage on the tumbleweed's offspring: they use less energy on display and they are less attractive to dingoes. Thus a new species of tumbleweed—the non-flowering Australian tumbleweed—develops. (It may remain true that throughout the genus consisting of the old and new species, stem structures are parts of tumbleweeds, as they are parts of any plants that have stem structures.) The stem structure of a tumbleweed of the new species wholly constitutes and is always coincident with the tumbleweed. But contrary to condition (5) in Baker's analysis, it is not contingent that the stem structure of a tumbleweed of the non-flowering species is always coincident with a tumbleweed of the non-flowering species.

As well as cases where Baker's crucial modal conditions are not satisfied because of the sorts of wholes in question, there are cases in which certain sorts of wholes happen to satisfy those conditions without the one whole constituting the other. Kit Fine and Judith Thomson, among others, have drawn our attention to two distinct kinds of wholes; in Fine's (1995) terminology "aggregates" and "compounds". An aggregate of some items exists only when one or another of its constituents exists, whereas a compound exists only when all its constituent items exist. An aggregate need not be the product of *arbitrary* aggregation; in that sense it need not be a mereological sum.

Consider the aggregate of Plato and Socrates and the compound of Plato and Socrates. Take one of those fortunate moments when Plato and Socrates both existed. The aggregate and the compound, though different items with different unity conditions, will be spatially coextensive at such a time. And the kinds Aggregate and Compound look to be primary kinds; for they are properly invoked in the answer to the respective questions about what the aggregate of Plato and Socrates and the compound of Plato and Socrates *fundamentally are*. Moreover, it seems that an aggregate can be in a compound-favourable condition, to use Baker's terminology. That is to say, all the items in the aggregate can in fact coexist. It is necessary that in such a favourable condition there is a compound that is spatially coincident with the aggregate. Moreover, it is contingent that when the aggregate of Plato and Socrates exists there is a compound that is spatially coincident with it. Nor is the one immaterial and the other not.

Yet for all that, we do not want to say that in the compound-favourable conditions the aggregate of Plato and Socrates constitutes the compound of Plato and Socrates. We do not want to say that because the aggregate is not a u-part of the compound. It is not a part at all. It is just that the aggregate and the compound share the same decomposition into parts. Only those who remain in the thrall of mereology would now suppose that it follows from the existence of a common decomposition that one is part of the other.

In the case of the aggregate and the compound, the same parts are indeed constituting different wholes; but even this along with all of Baker's conditions does not mean that one of the wholes constitutes the other. Instead the two distinct wholes are ontologically on a par.

Nor will it suffice for Baker to sweep aside all complexes and aggregates, say on the grounds that they are not genuine kinds of material items. For the same issue of two distinct wholes satisfying Baker's requirements without a relation of constitution holding between them arises in several of the cases of material items already discussed.

The cohabiting electromagnetic and gravitational systems provide one such a case. Recall the super-dense spheres. When placed in a magnetic field of a certain intensity they come to attract each other with massive electrostatic forces so as to bind together to form a tetrahedron. As the ambient magnetic field massively increases, the electrostatic forces reverse and the whole system blasts apart into its constituent spheres. The short-lived tetrahedron represents a physical system; its parts are the spheres and its principle of unity is that they should be bound together in a tetrahedron by electrostatic forces. But coexisting with this electrostatic system is a gravitational system—a system with the same spheres as its parts, yet having a different principle of unity, namely that the spheres should be bound together in a tetrahedron by gravitational forces.

To satisfy Baker's requirements, suppose that if the magnetic field were to massively drop, then the electrostatic forces that hold between the spheres would diminish to zero. The electrostatic system would be no more, but the gravitational system would remain intact, and the spheres would continue to be bound together in the tetrahedron by gravitational forces.

So now: The gravitational system and the electromagnetic system exhibit distinct primary kinds, and there is a time at which they are coincident in space. At that time, the gravitational system is in a condition of being governed by certain laws in the right ambient magnetic field, a condition 'favourable' for an electrostatic system. Necessarily, the laws and the field together guarantee that there is an electromagnetic system spatially coincident with the gravitational system. But it is contingent that there is any such sort of co-occupancy, since the unity condition of the electromagnetic system holds contingently of the parts of that system. And neither the gravitational system nor the electrostatic system is immaterial. Baker's requirements for the gravitational system constituting the electromagnetic system are thus satisfied.

Yet for all that, we do not want to say that in the favourable conditions the gravitational system constitutes the electromagnetic system. We do not want to say this because the gravitational system is not a u-part of the electromagnetic system. It is not a part at all. It is just that the gravitational and the electromagnetic system share the same decomposition into parts. (Again, it does not follow from the existence of a common decomposition that each whole is part of the other.) The same parts are constituting two distinct wholes, but even this along with all of Baker's requirements does not mean that one of the wholes constitutes the other. Instead, the two distinct wholes are ontologically on a par.

Mutatis mutandis for a spoon and a fork that make up a spork. Suppose you take a metal spoon and cut thin rectangles out of its non-working end so as to create the tines that will serve to transport food. You now have a spoon and a fork, made of the same material parts and coextensive in space. The common parts of the spoon and the fork are the bowl, the stem, and the tines. The bowl is an unusual design feature of the fork: while the tines are unusual design features of the spoon. The bowl is a contingent part of the fork, it could be hammered back into a more familiar, non-working end and the fork (but not the spoon) would survive the change. The tines are contingent parts of the spoon: they could be snipped off and the spoon (but not the fork) would be truncated but survive the change. So the spoon and the fork are distinct items, since one could exist without the other. Again, this modal difference is grounded in a non-modal difference. It is because they have distinct principles of unity, which require different things of their respective ends, that the spoon and the fork have different conditions of existence.

Without going through the details once again, it should be clear that, in such a case, Baker's analysis, combined with the right choice of favourable conditions, implies that the spoon constitutes the fork. But it does not: it is simply that the spoon shares its parts with the fork. In such a case, Baker's analysis will also imply that the fork constitutes the spoon. But it does not: it is simply that the fork shares its immediate parts with the spoon. We have two wholes, ontologically on a par, sharing parts. The spoon does not constitute the fork, nor does the fork constitute the spoon.

It is important not to mislocate this objection as simply the objection that Baker, in intending to analyse an asymmetric relation, has instead provided a set of conditions that can be symmetrically satisfied. That is *another* objection that follows from the case of the spoon and the fork. The prior objection is that in the case of the spoon and the fork the analysis gets things wrong twice over. It has the spoon constituting the fork, and it has the fork constituting the spoon. The same objection would emerge from a "symmetric" replaying of the electrostatic and the gravitational physical systems.

This objection and the objection from asymmetry both might be handled by adding a seventh condition. The obvious seventh condition would be to stipulate asymmetry by requiring that the first six conditions do not hold between y and x as well as between x and y. But now the seven conditions can hardly be taken as analysing constitution, as opposed merely to providing an adventitious corralling of some preferred examples. For we now know too much about why we should add such a condition guaranteeing asymmetry: the relation of being a u-part of, otherwise known as the relation of immediately constituting, is an asymmetric relation. After all the struggle not to mention parts, it is in fact insight into the parthood relation that is conditioning the amendments to the struggling analysis.

Dean Zimmerman and Ted Sider have offered a different type of counter-example to Baker's analysis, a counter-example that involves material items that can interpenetrate and so co-occupy. Sider has us imagine a possible world in which the laws of nature allow two material things of the same primary kind in the same place at the same time. He observes that from Baker's analysis it follows that in such a world when some item x constitutes another item y it will also constitute any third item of the same primary kind as y that just happens to share the same spatial location with y. And this is manifestly the wrong result when the third item shares no parts in common with x.

Zimmerman insists that the way around such cases is finally, after all, to appeal to the relation of parthood. He proposes that Baker replace clause (6) in the analysis with his own:

(6*) x and y share at least one complete decomposition.

(Where S is a complete decomposition of x just in case every member of S is a part of x, no members of S have any parts in common, and every part of x not in S has a part in common with some member of S.)

This amounts to requiring that at some level of decomposition x and y are made of the same parts.

However Zimmerman's amendment also gives many wrong results. The gravitational and the electromagnetic systems share a decomposition into parts, the spheres for instance. The same parts, the spheres, are constituting two distinct wholes. But even this along with all of Baker's requirements does not mean that one of the wholes constitutes the other. Instead, the two wholes are ontologically on a par. So it is with the compound and the aggregate, the spoon and the fork, Janus's two signs, and so on and so forth. Each of these pairs of items share a decomposition into parts, but in no pair does either item constitute the other.

The basic problem is that in none of these cases do we have one item being a u-part of the other. That is why, contrary to the analyses of Zimmerman and Baker, we do not have in these cases constitution of either item by the other.

By now it should be obvious where all this is going. We do need the notion of parthood to 'analyse' constitution, for immediate constitution is the relation of u-parthood. Yet as we try to go further and attempt to analyse constitution without qualification we seem to be getting little or no return on our investment.

Nor need we go further. Of any given item at any ontological level we may inquire what its immediate constitution is. The answer is given by citing its u-parts. We may then inquire as to the immediate constitution of each of these parts, thus arriving at their u-parts. And so on and so forth. There is no further useful work that a 'full-blown' analysis of constitution would do.[5]

---

[5] Special thanks to Mark Greenberg, Gilbert Harman, Sarah-Jane Leslie, James Pryor, and Gideon Rosen for their help with this chapter.

REFERENCES

Baker, Lynne Rudder 2002. 'On Making Things Up: Constitution and its Critics'. *Philosophical Topics: Identity and Individuation*, 30: 31–51.

Burke, Michael (1992). 'Copper Statues and Pieces of Copper: A Challenge to the Standard Account'. *Analysis*, 52: 12–17.

——(1994a). 'Dion and Theon:An Essentialist Solution to an Ancient Puzzle'. *Journal of Philosophy*, 91: 129–39.

——(1994b). 'Preserving the Principle of One Object to a Place'. *Philosophy and Phenomenological Research*, 54: 591–624.

——(1997). 'Preserving the Principle of One Object to a Place', in M. Rea (ed.), *Material Constitution*. Lanham, Md.: Rowman & Littlefield.

Casati, Robert, and Varsi, Achille (1999). *Parts and Places*. Cambridge, Mass.: MIT Press.

Fine, Kit (1995). 'Compounds and Aggregates'. *Noûs*, 28: 137–58.

——(2000). 'A Counterexample to Locke's Thesis'. *The Monist*, 83: 357–61.

Johnston, Mark (1997). 'Manifest Kinds'. *Journal of Philosophy*, 94: 564–83.

——(2004). 'The Obscure Object of Hallucination'. *Philosophical Studies*, 120: 113–83.

Leonard, Henry, and Goodman, Nelson (1940). 'The Calculus of Individuals and its Uses'. *Journal of Symbolic Logic*, 5: 45–55.

Lewis, David (1991). *Parts of Classes*. Oxford: Blackwell.

Locke, John (1690). *An Essay Concerning Human Understanding*.

Moltmann, Frederika (1995). *Parts and Wholes in Semantics*. Oxford: Oxford University Press.

O'Leary-Hawthorne, John, and Cortens, Andrew (1995). 'Towards Ontological Nihilism'. *Philosophical Studies*, 54: 143–65.

Sider, Ted (2002). Review of Lynne Rudder Baker, *Persons and Bodies*, *Journal of Philosophy*, 99: 45–8.

Simons, Peter (1987). *Parts: A Study in Ontology*. Oxford: Clarendon Press.

Thomson, Judith Jarvis (1998). 'The Statue and the Clay'. *Noûs*, 32: 149–73.

van Inwagen, Peter (1990). *Material Beings*. Ithaca, NY: Cornell University Press.

Wiggins , David (1968). 'On Being in the Same Place at the Same Time'. *Philosophical Review*, 77: 90–5.

Zimmerman, Den (2002). 'Persons and Bodies: Constitution without Mereology?' *Philosophy and Phenomenological Research*, 64/3: 599–606.

PART VI

EPISTEMOLOGY

CHAPTER 23

KNOWLEDGE AND SCEPTICISM

TIMOTHY WILLIAMSON

Scepticism is a disease in which healthy mental processes run pathologically unchecked. Our cognitive immunity system, designed to protect our conception of the world from harmful errors, turns destructively on that conception itself. Since we have false beliefs, we benefit from the ability to detect our mistakes; removing our errors tends to do us good. Our cognitive immunity system should be able to destroy bad old beliefs, not just prevent the influx of bad new ones. But that ability sometimes becomes indiscriminate, and destroys good beliefs too. That can happen in several ways. I start by considering two of them.

(I) Sometimes we can detect an error in ourselves by suspending belief in the proposition at issue, while we assess its truth or falsity on the basis of our remaining beliefs and any new ones that we may form in the process of investigation. For example, someone may test his belief that Toronto is the capital of Canada by consulting an encyclopedia, as a result of which he forms the belief that it says that Ottawa is the capital of Canada, which he combines with his independent belief that whatever the encyclopedia says about such matters is true to conclude that Ottawa rather than Toronto is the capital of Canada. If he cannot find the encyclopedia, he may find himself unable to decide on the basis of what is left whether Toronto is the capital, but still abandon his old belief on the grounds that it was unwarranted. The original belief survives the test only if it can be recovered, starting from what is left when it is suspended.

Since belief is not a purely voluntary matter, we cannot just abandon a belief at will, but we can still avoid reliance on it in a particular inquiry. The phrase 'suspend belief' will be applied to that case too. In this sense, suspending belief in p is consistent with believing p. The suspension test often takes a dialectical form. One tries to convince an opponent who does not already accept the belief; one needs a starting point that the opponent will accept (in order not to "beg the question"). Even when we have no opponent, we can imagine one.

The test works properly only if we also suspend belief in various propositions closely related to the original one: for example, that Toronto is the large capital (which entails the original proposition that it is the capital), that one knows that Toronto is the capital (which also entails the original proposition), that either it is snowing or Toronto is the capital (which is entailed by the original proposition), and that the work of reference will say that Toronto is the capital (which is logically independent of the original proposition). One's opponent could not be expected to accept such propositions; one's belief in them depends on one's belief in the original proposition. If we were allowed to use them in answering the question, the test would be too easy to be useful.

As we become more reflective, we apply the test to more abstract and general beliefs, to beliefs ever more central to our whole system of beliefs. We test our old belief that we have souls, or that what looks bent is bent, or that no proposition entails its own negation. To apply the test properly to such beliefs, we must suspend increasingly large numbers of related beliefs, thereby leaving a decreasing proportion of our original belief system unsuspended. Moreover, once we start testing our beliefs in the reliability of our usual methods of belief acquisition, we must also suspend our use of those methods, for otherwise our beliefs in their reliability would pass the test too easily. To test your belief that someone is trustworthy, it is not enough to ask him whether he is trustworthy. How much is left when we apply the test to our belief that we perceive an external world?

Sooner or later we arrive at beliefs so central that their suspension would leave us too cognitively impoverished to accomplish anything useful. For example, if we test the belief that there are good reasons, we must suspend any belief that something is a good reason, so we cannot acknowledge anything as a good reason to assert or to deny that there are good reasons, or even to leave the question unanswered. Beyond some point, applying the test does more harm than good to our belief system. But our disposition to apply the test to any proposition in which we are seriously interested has no absolute internal inhibiting mechanism. The test evolved under conditions of less than maximal reflectiveness. In most practical contexts, the propositions in which we are seriously interested are peripheral enough to our belief system to make the test harmless or beneficial. In philosophy, by contrast, we are interested in propositions so central to our belief system that the test has devastating results when properly applied: it leaves us with virtually nothing. We realize that, yet still feel that it would be blinkered and dogmatic to refuse to test our most cherished beliefs in the way in which we are accustomed to test less cherished beliefs, especially when a real or imagined opponent challenges us to do so.

One form of scepticism exploits our vulnerability to the suspension test. The sceptic drives us to apply the test to ever more central beliefs, with predictable consequences. In so far as we are willing and able to abide by the results of the test, we are forced step by step to abandon our whole system of beliefs. In effect, the sceptic's challenges force us down a regress of justifications.

(II) Sometimes, without suspending my belief in any proposition, I reach a conclusion about the objective correlation, or lack of it, between the conditions under which I believe some proposition and those under which it is true. A sufficiently poor correlation indicates that the proposition is not known to be true, for some kind of reliability is a necessary (if insufficient) condition for knowledge. Suppose, for example, that my review of my past performance indicates this: my believing one day that it will rain the next day provides no evidence at all for rain the next day. My weather predictions do no better than chance. Then my belief that it will rain tomorrow hardly constitutes knowledge that it will rain tomorrow.

We can be slightly more precise by speaking in probabilistic terms. Let us say that a proposition q is *evidence for* a proposition p if and only if the conditional probability of p on q is higher than the unconditional probability of p ($\text{Prob}(p \mid q) >$ $\text{Prob}(p)$): that is, q raises the probability of p.[1] Thus if the conditional probability that it will rain given that I believe that it will rain is no higher than the unconditional probability that it will rain, then that I believe that it will rain is not evidence that it will rain, and the status of the belief as knowledge is endangered. More generally, where Bp is the proposition that one believes p, if $\text{Prob}(p \mid Bp) \leq$ $\text{Prob}(p)$, then Bp is not evidence for p, and the epistemic status of belief in p is under threat.

A special case of the apparent undermining occurs when p is certain conditional on the assumption that it is *not* believed, for it follows that Bp is not evidence for p. In symbols, if $\text{Prob}(p \mid {\sim}Bp) = 1$ then $\text{Prob}(p \mid Bp) \leq \text{Prob}(p)$.[2] Roughly: since all ${\sim}p$ possibilities are Bp possibilities, adding the information Bp cannot reduce the

---

[1] The conditional probability $\text{Prob}(p \mid q)$ may be defined in terms of unconditional probabilities as $\text{Prob}(p \& q)/\text{Prob}(q)$ when $\text{Prob}(q)$ is non-zero. Note that, in the sense defined in the text, q may be evidence for p even if q itself is unknown or even false: the relation between p and q is a purely conditional one.

[2] Proof: If $\text{Prob}(p \mid {\sim}Bp) = 1$ then $\text{Prob}(p \mid Bp) = \text{Prob}(Bp)\text{Prob}(p \mid Bp) + (1{-}\text{Prob}(Bp))\text{Prob}(p \mid Bp) \leq \text{Prob}(Bp)\text{Prob}(p \mid Bp) + \text{Prob}({\sim}Bp)\text{Prob}(p \mid {\sim}Bp) = \text{Prob}(p)$. The result holds even on the weaker assumption that $\text{Prob}(p \mid Bp) \leq \text{Prob}(p \mid {\sim}Bp)$.

proportion of $\sim p$ possibilities among unexcluded possibilities. Although this case might seem too special to matter, it is crucial to many sceptical arguments.

The sceptic makes me imagine a scenario in which, although my experience and beliefs are relevantly similar to my actual experience and beliefs, I am dreaming, or being manipulated by an evil demon, or floating as a brain in a vat, so that very many of my beliefs are false.[3] Since I actually believe that I am not in the sceptical scenario, in the sceptical scenario I also believe that I am not in the sceptical scenario; in no possible situation am I in it without believing that I am not in it.[4] Thus I am certainly not in it, conditional on my not believing that I am not in it. Symbolically, if s is the proposition that I am in the sceptical scenario, $\mathrm{Prob}(\sim s \mid \sim B\sim s) = 1$. Consequently, $\mathrm{Prob}(\sim s \mid B\sim s) \leq \mathrm{Prob}(\sim s)$. In other words, that I believe that I am not in the sceptical scenario is not evidence that I am not in the sceptical scenario, for it does not raise the probability that I am not in it. This casts doubt on my supposed knowledge that I am not in the sceptical scenario.

Of course, sceptics rarely formulate their arguments in terms of the probability calculus. Nevertheless, such calculations provide a convenient way of capturing the widespread intuition that one's belief that one is not in the sceptical scenario is unreliable.[5]

So far nothing has been said about the kind of probabilities at issue. They are not pure subjective probabilities (degrees of belief), for I may be certain that I believe p: but if $\mathrm{Prob}(Bp) = 1$ then automatically $\mathrm{Prob}(p \mid Bp) = \mathrm{Prob}(p)$, so Bp would not be evidence for p whatever the epistemic status of belief in p.[6] Rather, we need probabilities that give some weight to possibilities in which p is not believed, in

---

[3] The description 'the sceptical scenario' is not being defined, circularly, in terms of the condition 'I believe that I am not in the sceptical scenario'. That in the sceptical scenario I believe that I am not in it is a consequence, not a part, of the definition.

[4] In a much-discussed application of semantic externalism, Putnam (1981: 1–21) argued that causal constraints on reference ensure that the brain in the vat cannot entertain the proposition that it is not a brain in a vat. However, even if the argument works for some sceptical scenarios, it seems to fail for others, such as that of a recently envatted brain (Smith 1984). For a recent exchange on semantic externalist replies to scepticism and further references, see DeRose (2000) and Williamson (2000b).

[5] The poor correlation between $\sim s$ and $B\sim s$ is more usually articulated by means of the counterfactual conditional $\square\rightarrow$: $s \square\rightarrow B\sim s$ is true (if I were in the sceptical scenario, I would believe that I was not in it). Nozick's influential counterfactual analysis of knowledge makes the truth of $\sim p \square\rightarrow \sim Bp$ (or a complex variant thereof) necessary for knowing p, so the falsity of $s \square\rightarrow \sim B\sim s$ precludes knowing $\sim s$ (1981: 172–288). Nozick's analysis is subject to counter-examples (see the essays in Luper-Foy 1987; Williamson 2000a: 147–63 and references therein). The use of conditional probabilities shows that a similar problem for knowing $\sim s$ can be articulated without counterfactuals. One advantage of the condition $\mathrm{Prob}(p \mid Bp) \leq \mathrm{Prob}(p)$ over $\sim p \square\rightarrow \sim Bp$ is that the former holds while the latter fails in cases involving a correct judgement of quantity with a large margin for error by a largely reliable subject who nevertheless has a systematic tendency to very slight misjudgements; intuitively, that tendency does not justify a sceptical verdict in such cases (Williamson 2000a).

[6] The point is close to the problem of old evidence in Bayesian epistemology: if $\mathrm{Prob}(e) = 1$ then $\mathrm{Prob}(h \mid e) = \mathrm{Prob}(h)$, where e is the evidence and h a hypothesis. See Earman (1992: 119–35); Howson and Urbach (1993: 403–8); Maher (1996); Williamson (2000a: 220–1).

order to isolate the effect of the information that it is believed. They are possible in the sense that they could have obtained, even if we are sure or know that they do not obtain. We need not treat the probabilities as purely a priori, for we can investigate empirical correlations between our belief states and states of the world a posteriori, perhaps in the spirit of Quine's naturalized epistemology.[7] The results of such investigations might nevertheless shake our claims to knowledge from within, as with my beliefs about tomorrow's weather. The argument can use such empirical probabilities; it is independent of their exact values.

Given the kind of probability at issue, we may assume that the proposition that I believe that I am not in the sceptical scenario has probability less than one ($\text{Prob}(B{\sim}s) < 1$), because I could have been convinced by the sceptic to abandon my belief that I am not in the sceptical scenario. We may further assume that, conditional on my believing that I am not in the sceptical scenario, it is not certain that I am not in it ($\text{Prob}({\sim}s \mid B{\sim}s) < 1$), because I could have been in it and would then have believed that I was not in it. Given these two plausible extra assumptions, the information that I believe that I am not in the sceptical scenario actually *lowers* the probability that I am not in it, and therefore raises the probability that I am in it ($\text{Prob}({\sim}s \mid B{\sim}s) < \text{Prob}({\sim}s)$, so $\text{Prob}(s) < \text{Prob}(s \mid B{\sim}s)$). That I believe that I am not in the sceptical scenario is evidence that I *am* in it.

Call belief in p *truth-indicative* if one's belief in p is evidence for its truth ($\text{Prob}(p \mid Bp) > \text{Prob}(p)$), and *falsity-indicative* if one's belief in p is evidence for its falsity ($\text{Prob}(p \mid Bp) < \text{Prob}(p)$). Belief that one is not in a sceptical scenario is not just not truth-indicative; it is falsity-indicative. Such a belief looks to be in bad shape. Falsity-indicativeness is a better criticism than lack of truth-indicativeness. After all, if p is a tautology, the probability calculus guarantees that $\text{Prob}(p) = \text{Prob}(p \mid Bp) = 1$, so belief in p is neither truth-indicative nor falsity-indicative; that does not show that one cannot know p. The absence of falsity-indicativeness looks more plausible as a necessary condition for knowledge than truth-indicativeness.

Could one respond to the problem by sacrificing the recherché philosophical belief that one is not in the sceptical scenario, while retaining the familiar beliefs with which one negotiates the everyday business of life? Very many of my everyday beliefs entail that I am not in the sceptical scenario. I am watching television only if I am not a brain in a vat. We tend to regard deduction as a paradigmatic way of extending our knowledge. If I know that I am watching television, I can come to know that I am watching something by competently deducing the conclusion that I am watching something from the premiss that I am watching television. Similarly, if I know that I am watching television, why cannot I come to know that I am not in the sceptical scenario by competently deducing that I am not in it from the

---

[7] See Quine (1969); Kornblith (1994).

premiss that I am watching television? I have no difficulty in performing the deduction itself. Contrapositively, if I cannot know that I am not in the sceptical scenario, how can I know that I am watching television? We thus appear to lose most of the knowledge that we ordinarily take ourselves to have.

The problem for an everyday proposition p is not that Bp lowers the probability of p. That I believe that I am watching television surely raises the probability that I am watching television. The problem is less direct. We have a compelling principle something like this:

CLOSURE(K)   If one knows $p_1, \ldots, p_n$ and believes q in the light of competent deduction of q from $p_1, \ldots, p_n$ then one knows q.

The phrase 'in the light of competent deduction' here is intended to apply both when one's belief in q originates in the deduction and when it originated otherwise but is now sustained by that deduction and perhaps by many others. Now if p entails q, belief in p may be truth-indicative even if belief in q is falsity-indicative. But if a necessary condition for knowing p is that belief in p not be falsity-indicative, then the effect of CLOSURE(K) is to strengthen that necessary condition: one knows p only if belief in no proposition q that p entails is falsity-indicative (given that there is no problem about believing q in the light of competent deduction from p). It is this stronger putatively necessary condition for knowing that everyday propositions flout, because they entail that one is not in a sceptical scenario.[8] A similar argument can be given with the proposition that one is not in a specified sceptical scenario replaced by the bare proposition that one does not falsely believe p ($\sim(\sim p\ \&\ Bp)$), which is also a logical consequence of p.

If the problem only concerned knowledge, some philosophers might respond by abandoning claims to knowledge and retreating to claims of justified true belief instead.[9] Knowing q is not necessary for having a justified true belief in q, for Gettier (1963) showed that having a justified true belief in q is not sufficient for knowing q. Since false premises entail some true conclusions, one can believe a true proposition q on the basis of competent deduction of q from a false proposition p; if one's belief in p is justified, so too is one's belief in q; thus one has a justified true belief in q, but does not know q, because one's belief in q depends on a false premiss. The idea of conceding scepticism about knowledge while resisting it about justified true belief assumes that one can have a justified belief in a proposition q without knowing anything else to justify q. For the sake of argument,

---

[8] Dretske (1970) and Nozick (1981) contain scepticism by rejecting the closure principle. On Nozick's analysis, one can even know $p\ \&\ q$ without knowing p. Non-closure is currently unpopular. Contextualists (see below) typically argue that closure holds in any given context, but may appear to fail if the context changes in the course of the argument (DeRose 1995).

[9] For examples of this marginalization of knowledge, see Craig (1990: 272); Earman (1993: 37); Kaplan (1985); Wright (1991: 88).

let us grant that dubious assumption.[10] The argument in the Gettier case assumed a closure principle for justified belief rather than knowledge, like this:

CLOSURE(JB) If one has justified belief in $p_1, \ldots, p_n$ and believes q in the light of competent deduction of q from $p_1, \ldots, p_n$ then one has justified belief in q.[11]

Since deduction preserves truth, CLOSURE(JB) entails that if one has justified true belief in $p_1, \ldots, p_n$ and believes q in the light of competent deduction of q from $p_1, \ldots, p_n$ then one has justified true belief in q. But the sceptic might argue that if one has a justified belief that belief in p is falsity-indicative, one does not also have a justified belief in p. In particular, if I have a justified belief that belief that I am not in the sceptical scenario is falsity-indicative, then I do not have a justified belief that I am not in the sceptical scenario. But since my belief that belief that I am not in the sceptical scenario is falsity-indicative is justified (or no less justified than my belief that I am not in the sceptical scenario), my belief that I am not in the sceptical scenario is not justified. Given CLOSURE(JB), this conclusion is the thin end of the wedge for a general scepticism about justified belief, just as, given CLOSURE(K), the conclusion that I do not know that I am not in the sceptical scenario is the thin end of the wedge for a general scepticism about knowledge. For I can believe that I am not in the sceptical scenario in the light of competent deduction from an everyday belief; by CLOSURE(JB), if the everyday belief were justified, so would be my belief that I am not in the sceptical scenario. By hypothesis, the latter belief is not justified.

---

[10] Unger (1975: 197–249) and Williamson (2000a: 184–208) argue that justification depends on knowledge.

[11] Some hold that a belief is justified if and only if it has a probability greater than some threshold constant c less than 1 (for example, 90 per cent), on some appropriate probability distribution. They will object to CLOSURE(JB) that sometimes p_1 and p_2 each have probabilities greater than c while their conjunction p_1 & p_2 has probability less than c. On their view, someone who both believes the conjuncts and believes the conjunction on the basis of competent deduction from the conjuncts has justified belief in the conjuncts but not in the conjunction (see Kyburg 1970). Consequently, they would restrict CLOSURE(JB) to single-premiss deductions (if q is a logical consequence of p, the probability of q is at least as high as the probability of p). This restriction does not affect the applications of CLOSURE(JB) in the text, which are to single-premiss deductions, in both the Gettier case and the sceptical argument. Of course, the probabilistic standard for justified belief has highly questionable consequences: one may have justified belief in each member of an obviously inconsistent set of propositions: for example, 'Ticket number n will not win the lottery' for each natural number $n < 1,000,000$ and 'For some natural number $n < 1,000,000$, ticket number n will win the lottery'. Another putative objection to CLOSURE(JB) is that one might be justified in believing various complex propositions (perhaps on the basis of testimony) but then competently deduce a contradiction from them and somehow get oneself to believe it on that basis (perhaps aided by a paraconsistent logician) without having a justified belief in the contradiction. But this objection misreads CLOSURE(JB) as a diachronic principle. Its intended reading is synchronic: if at time t one has justified belief in $p_1, \ldots, p_n$ and at t one believes q on the basis of competent deduction of q from $p_1, \ldots, p_n$ then at t one has justified belief in q. Once one has deduced the contradiction, one no longer has justified belief in all the premisses (modulo the issue raised in the first objection). For difficulties in formulating logical constraints on rationality, see Harman (1986).

Therefore, my everyday belief is also not justified. Thus, even if the justification of belief does not depend on knowledge, sacrificing knowledge of everyday truths is not enough to appease the sceptic's style of argument, for it devours justified belief in those truths as well.

(I) and (II) represent quite distinct routes into scepticism. Unlike (I), (II) does not depend on the suspension of belief. Even if one is certain that one is not in the sceptical scenario, and reasons accordingly, one must still concede that the belief is falsity-indicative. But the differences between (I) and (II) do not preclude mixed strategies for testing one's beliefs by a combination of the two methods. For example, one might use testing by strategy (I) to undermine the belief that one is not in the sceptical scenario of strategy (II). In practice, mixing often takes the form of opportunistic switching between the two strategies: the sceptic employs whichever is not under current examination. Still, less disreputable mixed strategies also exist. But many sceptics prefer one strategy to the other. Sceptics motivated by internalist concerns about justification may find strategy (I) more compelling than strategy (II). Sceptics motivated by externalist concerns about reliability may find strategy (II) more compelling than strategy (I).

Is scepticism of one kind or another irresistible? Of course, we can laugh off the sceptical arguments, refusing to take them seriously and continuing to believe what we always believed. But that sounds like a mere refusal to do one's job as a philosopher, or one's duty as a reflective person. A more interesting suggestion is that although sceptics speak truly, they do so by creating special contexts of utterance in which their words express truths: by making sceptical scenarios discursively salient they drive up the contextually relevant standards for the correct application of the term 'know' to a point at which they apply to virtually nothing, even though they have wide application as used in everyday contexts. Thus in a conversation about travel someone says truly 'Mary knows that the train leaves at noon', while simultaneously in an epistemology class someone else is saying of the same person, equally truly, 'Mary does not know that the train leaves at noon', for sceptical scenarios are relevant only in the latter context. According to *contextualism*, sentences involving 'know' express different propositions with different truth-values as used in different contexts, because the reference of 'know' varies with the context of utterance, even if the reference of every other constituent is held fixed.[12] A similar contextualist line might be taken about other epistemic terms, such as 'justified'.

---

[12] Unger (1986), Cohen (1988), DeRose (1995, 1999), and Lewis (1996) propose versions of contextualism; Schiffer (1996) offers criticism. For two recent exchanges, see Feldman (2001), Cohen (2001), Williams (2001), and Williamson (2001). See Pryor (2001) for a brief survey of different forms of contextualism. The view that the application of 'know' depends on the context in which the subject of the ascription (rather than the ascriber) is thinking or speaking (Williams 1996) is not contextualism in the present sense. Although the subject and the ascriber are identical in first-person ascriptions, the two roles are still distinct. Contextualism has predecessors in accounts on which knowing p is a matter of ruling out (in some sense to be explained) relevant alternatives in which p is false (Goldman 1976; Dretske 1981).

Once sceptics have manipulated the context, in the epistemology seminar, contextualists are apt to console themselves with the thought that although most denials of "knowledge" in that context of scepticism are correct, in everyday contexts many assertions of "knowledge" are also correct. For example, although 'I do not know that there is a whiteboard in the room' expresses a truth as uttered in the seminar, 'He knows that there is a whiteboard in the room' expresses a truth as uttered simultaneously outside the seminar about the same person. But that thought underestimates the gravity of the situation in which the sceptic has put contextualists, on their own analysis. For since 'know' is a factive verb, the truth of 'He knows that there is a whiteboard in the room', as uttered outside the seminar, requires the truth of 'There is a whiteboard in the room' as uttered outside the seminar and therefore as uttered inside the seminar too (since no context-dependence in the latter sentence is relevant here). Thus the consoling thought commits them to claims such as 'There is a whiteboard in the room', while their contextualism commits them to claims such as 'I do not know that there is a whiteboard in the room'. Consequently, in the seminar, they are committed to this:

(MK) There is a whiteboard in the room and I do not know that there is a whiteboard in the room.

But (MK) is Moore-paradoxical: although (MK) could be true, it is somehow self-defeating to assert (MK). Thus contextualists are not entitled to the consoling thought. In the seminar, they should not say that 'He knows that there is a whiteboard in the room' expresses a truth outside the seminar. They might say 'I do not know that the sentence "He knows that there is a whiteboard in the room" does not express a truth outside the seminar'. But since they must also admit 'I do not know that the sentence "He knows that there is a whiteboard in the room" expresses a truth outside the seminar', they are not identifying some positive feature of the everyday situation; they are simply confessing ignorance of its status. A similar argument applies to contextualism about justification. At least in the seminar, contextualists are at the sceptic's mercy and cannot look outside for help.[13]

Should we surrender as much as contextualists do to the sceptic's arguments? Let us first investigate how radical those arguments are. They are often assumed not to touch beliefs about one's own mental states. For example, if I feel dizzy, I know that I feel dizzy, even if I do not know that there is a whiteboard in the room. It is the status of one's beliefs about the world external to one's present state of mind that is supposed to be in question. But it is not obvious that the sceptic's styles of argument are so limited.

Using strategy (I), I start by testing my belief that I feel dizzy. I suspend it, and others relevantly related to it, but then immediately recover them by my usual methods for forming beliefs about my current mental states. Then, however,

---

[13] See also Williamson (2001).

I decide to test my belief that my methods for forming beliefs about my current mental states are reliable. Once I have suspended that belief, and others relevantly related to it, and the use of the methods themselves, can I really recover them from what remains? *Perhaps* I can, by some clever philosophical argument. But then I decide to test my belief that my methods of abstract argument are reliable. After all, it is not as though most clever philosophical arguments turn out to be sound. Once I have suspended my belief that my methods of abstract argument are reliable, and others relevantly related to it, and the use of the methods themselves, how can I recover them from what remains? Not by a clever philosophical argument, for the use of such an argument is not part of what remains, on pain of begging the question. Thus strategy (I) has no internal limitation that would protect my belief that I am feeling dizzy. If moderate sceptics apply strategy (I) to beliefs about the external world but not to beliefs of the kinds just discussed, they seem to be using a method of argument when they like its conclusions and avoiding it when they do not. Such opportunism is less intellectually impressive than the willingness of extreme sceptics to deny that I know, or even have a justified true belief, that I am feeling dizzy.

With strategy (II), my belief that I feel dizzy looks at first sight better off, for how could one construct a sceptical scenario in which I appear to myself to feel dizzy without actually feeling dizzy? However, let SS be a sceptical scenario in which I am a brain in a vat but appear to myself to be walking on a sandy beach; in SS, I neither feel dizzy nor appear to myself to feel dizzy nor believe myself to feel dizzy; in SS, I believe that I am not in SS. How things appear to me in SS is utterly different from how they actually appear to me. In actuality, as well as in SS, I believe that I am not in SS. Both in actuality and in SS, my belief that I am not in SS is falsity-indicative, for exactly the same reason that applies to any other belief that one is not in a sceptical scenario. My belief that I am not in SS lowers the probability that I am not in SS. The crucial point for strategy (II) is that I believe in the sceptical scenario that I am not in it, whatever my actual mental state.[14] Thus if not being falsity-indicative is necessary for a belief to constitute knowledge, I do not know that I am not in SS. Similarly, if not being falsity-indicative is necessary for a belief to be justified, my belief that I am not in SS is not justified. But that I feel dizzy entails that I am not in SS. I believe that I am not in SS in the light of that competent deduction. Consequently, by CLOSURE(K) and CLOSURE(JB), I neither know nor have a justified belief that I feel dizzy. Thus my belief that I feel dizzy is vulnerable to strategy (II).

Moderate sceptics will protest that they have been misinterpreted. In effect, they concede that a falsity-indicative belief *can* constitute knowledge, or be justified. So even for a sceptical scenario that matches one's actual situation in its appearance to one, they cannot claim that its agreed feature, that in it one believes that one is not

---

[14] Schiffer (1996) uses a related example.

in it, by itself prevents one from knowing or having a justified true belief that one is not in it. If such knowledge or justified true belief is blocked, it must be for a more specific reason.

A natural thought is that I can *discriminate* between the actual situation and SS, but cannot discriminate between the actual situation and a sceptical scenario SS* in which I am a brain in a vat but the world appears to me just as it actually does. For example, both in the actual situation and in SS* I feel dizzy; in SS I do not feel at all dizzy. Of course, if my mental state in the actual situation differed from my mental state in SS only in some respect that was concealed from me, that would not enable me to discriminate between the actual situation and SS. The point is that I am aware of whether I feel dizzy. Both in the actual situation and in SS*, I know that I feel dizzy. In SS, I know that I do not feel dizzy. Even if I did not know in SS that I did not feel dizzy, knowing in the actual situation that I feel dizzy enables me to know that I am not in SS, for I know by definition of 'SS' that in SS I do not feel dizzy, and from the premises that I feel dizzy and that in SS I do not feel dizzy I can competently deduce the conclusion that I am not in SS. Given that I make the deduction in my actual situation, by CLOSURE(K) I know that I am not in SS.

By parallel reasoning, if I do know in the actual situation that I have hands, that enables me to know that I am not in SS*, for I know by definition of 'SS*' that in SS* I lack hands, and from the premises that I have hands and that in SS* I lack hands I competently deduce the conclusion that I am not in SS*. By CLOSURE(K), I know that I am not in SS*.[15] But the moderate sceptic who allows that I know that I feel dizzy does not allow that I know that I have hands. Why is my belief that I feel dizzy supposed to be epistemically better off than my belief that I have hands? The salient difference between them is that we have been given a possible situation in which I falsely believe that I have hands but no possible situation in which I falsely believe that I feel dizzy. If the sceptic is assuming that the mere possibility of error precludes knowledge, why should we accept that premiss?

We should not take for granted that even beliefs about one's current mental state are infallible. Someone feels dizzy, is aware of doing so, and complains about it to others, who react with concern. Gradually the dizzy feeling wears off, but he is enjoying all the attention too much to notice; he needs to believe that it is deserved. If he now asks himself whether he feels dizzy, he still answers sincerely that he does; he believes falsely that he feels dizzy. The story contains no impossibility. Of course, if one believes truly that one feels dizzy, then no sceptical scenario is possible in which one is in exactly the same mental state but believes falsely that one feels dizzy, for feeling dizzy is an aspect of one's mental state. But if one's own current mental state is not perfectly transparent to one, then sceptical scenarios are relevant in which one is in a slightly different mental state and falsely believes that one feels dizzy. Confirmation of this lack of transparency comes from the non-transitivity of

---

[15] See Klein (1995) for related discussion.

indiscriminability. When my mental state changes only gradually, I go through a long series of mental states $M_0, M_1, M_2, \ldots, M_n$, such that for no i can I discriminate between M_i and M_{i+1} (as presented to me at those times): I notice no change from one state to the next. Nevertheless, I can easily discriminate between M_0 and M_n; they are manifestly different. It follows that M_i and M_{i+1} are qualitatively distinct for at least some i: for since qualitative identity is a transitive relation, if M_i and M_{i+1} were qualitatively identical for every i then M_0 and M_n would be qualitatively identical too, which they are not. Therefore, at least two mental states are qualitatively distinct but indiscriminable (as presented to the subject at the relevant times). Thus there are unnoticeable differences between mental states.[16]

Why are sceptics often reluctant to apply their arguments to knowledge of one's own current mental states? Start from the notion of rationality, as a criterion of praise and blame. A central requirement of rationality is that one should proportion one's belief to the evidence. It is praiseworthy to do so, blameworthy to do otherwise. Rational and irrational agents are responsible to the standard of rationality. But if agents are not in a position to know whether they are conforming to a given standard, it seems unfair to hold them responsible to that standard.[17] Thus it is natural to suppose that people are in a position to know whether they are conforming to the standard of rationality. In sceptical scenarios, subjects are still culpable for their irrationality (if any), even though they are blameless for their ignorance. In particular, they should be in a position to know whether they are proportioning their belief to their evidence, and therefore in a position to know what their evidence is, even in a sceptical scenario. Consequently, their evidence cannot be what would count as evidence in a normal scientific or legal context— the result of an experiment, the testimony of a witness—for one can be blamelessly deceived about such matters in a sceptical scenario. Only one's current mental states seem to have a chance to survive this filtering process. Thus they come to occupy a privileged role as all that is left to count as evidence. They are what other beliefs are measured against. Once the evidence base is attenuated that far, it is hardly surprising that external world scepticism should look plausible. But not even one's own current mental states really meet the exacting condition. For reasons of the kind noted above, one is not always in a position to know whether one is in a given mental state, for example, whether one feels dizzy.

Should we conclude that we have no evidence at all? A more plausible alternative is to be less purist about praise and blame: we can be responsible to a standard even if we are sometimes not in a position to know whether we are conforming to it. Thus we need not always be in a position to know what our evidence is; that is consistent with the claim that p is part of one's evidence only if one knows p, for one is not always in a position to know what one's knowledge is. What would count as

[16] The argument is developed more rigorously in Williamson (2000a: 93–134).
[17] Compare BonJour (1985).

evidence in a scientific or legal context may therefore count as genuine evidence after all. We refuse to be stampeded by sceptical scenarios into attenuating our evidence base according to the sceptic's demands.[18]

The proposed view is inconsistent with various forms of internalism, which guarantee us infallible epistemic access to our own states with respect to specified matters of justification. Whatever those states are, we are not always in a position to know whether we are in them. But the argument does not refute weaker internalist theses, according to which we are *typically* in a position to know whether we are in the relevant states, and the knowledge may be of a special non-observational kind. Nor does the argument show that justified belief is not necessary for knowledge.[19]

The terminology of 'internalism' and 'externalism' suggests a Cartesian picture, on which the mind forms an inner world, to which it has direct access, while access to the external world is at best indirect. Given that picture, one can debate whether matters of justification belong wholly to the inner world. But the prior question is whether the picture is correct. On an alternative picture, paradigmatic mental states include cognitive and conative relations to independently existing objects in one's environment: loving honey, seeking honey, seeing honey, tasting honey, remembering honey. Since mental states have non-mental constituents (such as honey), they do not constitute an inner world in any useful sense. Believing that there is honey in the hive is a mental state that involves a relation to one's environment, for one's belief to be about honey; knowing that there is honey in the hive is a mental state that involves a further relation to the environment, since one can be in it only if there is honey in the hive. Like belief states, knowledge states can play an essential role in causal explanations of action.[20] Although one is not always in a position to know whether one knows, for virtually no mental state is one always in a position to know whether one is in it. On this view, one should not concede to the sceptic that one could be in one's current total mental state even if most of one's beliefs were false, for if one knows p and knowing p is a mental state, one could not be in one's current total mental state without knowing p.

When sceptics try to *argue* that one does not know (or does not have a justified belief) that one is not in a sceptical scenario, they tacitly assume deeply problematic epistemological principles. Scepticism's great strength is that sometimes we ourselves cannot see how honestly to dissent. It can feel like mere empty bravado to insist that one does know, or have a justified true belief, that one is not in the sceptical scenario. However firmly one wishes to resist the sceptics, one may be

[18] See Williamson (2000*a*: 164–208) for this view, and Fumerton (2000) for a critique.

[19] For versions of internalism, see BonJour (1985) and Fumerton (1995). A recent critique is Goldman (1999).

[20] See Williamson (2000*a*: 21–92) on knowing as a mental state. McDowell (1995) and Gibbons (2001) defend similar views. The idea is widespread that the contents of propositional attitudes depend constitutively on the subject's environment (Burge 1979; compare Putnam 1973). The proposed view of knowing extends the environmental dependence to the attitudes to those contents.

betrayed from within by one's own intuitions. Of course, at other points in the dialectic sceptics will insist that mere intuitions have no rational force. But no inconsistency in sceptics' treatment of intuitions shows anti-sceptics how to live with the sceptical tendency of their own intuitions. Sceptics are troublemakers who can disrupt our position without having a coherent position of their own, by presenting us with considerations to which we cannot find a response that we find satisfying.[21] If they are sick, they infect us with their sickness. Although some people have more natural immunity than others, probably few epistemologists feel no conflict at all within themselves between sceptical and anti-sceptical tendencies.

What should our attitude be to our sceptical intuitions, if we have them? It may help to consider other cases in which intuitions conflict. What should someone do in a practical dilemma? Presenting the case with one emphasis elicits the strong intuition that she should ϕ; presenting the same case with another emphasis elicits the strong intuition that it is not the case that she should ϕ. A contextualist might say that the sentence 'She should ϕ' expresses a true proposition as uttered in the context of the first presentation but a different and false proposition as uttered in the context of the second presentation. Yet that attempted resolution of the conflict feels quite unconvincing. In the context of the first presentation, it is intuitive that the sentence 'She should ϕ' expresses a true proposition *even as uttered in the context of the second presentation*; in the context of the second presentation, it is intuitive that the same sentence expresses a false proposition *even as uttered in the context of the first presentation*. The agent must choose between ϕ ing and not ϕ ing. The practical question is whether the proposition $s\,\phi$ that 'I should ϕ' expresses in her context is true. A speaker in another context who uses 'She should ϕ' to express a proposition that does not match $s\,\phi$ in truth-value thereby loses touch with the practical question. For that question, the agent's context has primacy. To focus on the practical question, one lets 'She should ϕ' express a proposition materially equivalent to $s\,\phi$. Consequently, in different contexts with a focus on the practical question 'She should ϕ' expresses propositions materially equivalent to each other, and the relevant form of contextualism fails.

One might suppose that 'know', unlike 'should', has no practical aspect. Arguably, however, the question 'Do I know p?' is closely related to the practical questions 'Should I assert p?' and 'Should I believe p?' (Williamson 2000a). Perhaps this practical aspect of 'know' gives primacy to the subject's context: if third-person or past-tense 'knowledge' ascriptions must express propositions materially equivalent to that expressed by the first-person present-tense 'I know p' as uttered by the subject, then they must express propositions materially equivalent to each other, and again the relevant form of contextualism fails.

Contextualism supplies a perfectly general strategy for resolving any apparent disagreement whatsoever. Since some disagreements are genuine, we should not

---

[21] Compare Feyerabend (1978: 143).

always follow that strategy. The conflict of intuitions does not always disappear on further reflection. At least some intuitions are mistaken.[22] Moreover, they are explicably, not blankly, mistaken. Whether the agent should φ depends on the balance between many complex, unquantifiable, subtly interacting considerations, some genuinely weighing one way, others genuinely weighing the other way. The concept of what should be done provides no algorithm for weighing all these factors against each other or integrating them into a final verdict. It is no surprise that one can make each verdict intuitive by highlighting considerations that favour it; what else would one expect? The cases need not even be borderline. For even if the considerations on one side heavily outweigh those on the other, a skilled presenter can still present the outweighed considerations so strikingly that they appear to outweigh the others.

Surely the same phenomenon can occur for epistemic concepts too. Whether one knows (or one's belief is epistemically justified) also depends on the balance between many complex, unquantifiable, subtly interacting considerations. In many realistic cases, some weigh one way, others the other way. The concept of knowledge or of epistemic justification provides no algorithm for weighing all these factors against each other or integrating them into a final verdict. No wonder that the skilled sceptic can present the considerations that favour a negative verdict so vividly that they intuitively appear to outweigh the considerations on the other side. It does not follow that the sceptic is right, even in the context of the epistemology seminar; the case may not even be borderline. Nor does it follow that the sceptic is wrong, even in the everyday context. As before, the intuitions that predominate in one context spill over to judgements about the truth-values of sentences as uttered in the other context. In the everyday context, it is intuitive that someone in the epistemology class who says 'Mary does not know that the train leaves at noon' is overestimating her epistemic difficulties. In the epistemology class, it is intuitive that someone in the everyday context who says 'Mary knows that the train leaves at noon' is underestimating her epistemic difficulties. Although such data are not decisive against contextualism, they tend to support the non-contextualist explanation.

If we are sensitive to many complex considerations when we assess matters of knowledge or justification, does it follow that our concept of knowledge or our concept of justification is analysable in terms of our concepts of those complex considerations? No. Suppose that we grasped the concept of knowledge or of justification simply by means of examples of situations in which someone knows or is justified and of the opposite. When we assessed matters of knowledge or justification, we should therefore compare the case at hand with our paradigms of knowledge or justification and of ignorance or lack of justification. The comparative similarity would depend on many complex considerations, to which we should

[22] I ignore various forms of relativism.

need to be sensitive, but our concept of knowledge or of justification would not be analysable in terms of our concepts of those complex considerations. The very act of comparison might cause us to notice similarities and differences that we had not previously conceptualized. If recognizing a face does not require conceptual analysis, why should recognizing knowledge or justification do so?

No doubt a purely paradigmatic account of epistemic concepts is too simple. For example, it seems essential to grasping the concept of knowledge that one appreciate the entailment from *S knows that P* to *P*. Nevertheless, paradigms involving perception, memory, testimony, and deduction may play a large role in our grasp of the concept of knowledge. That is not to say that the concepts of perception, memory, testimony, and deduction are in any sense prior to the concept of knowledge: without some grasp of epistemic considerations, one would be unable to appreciate the difference between the successful, knowledge-providing cases of perception, memory, testimony, and deduction and the failures. If all that sounds messy, it may be the normal position for empirically applicable abstract concepts such as *time, causation, body, mind, meaning, society, intention, choice,* and *government.*

When Gettier showed that knowledge is more than justified true belief, many epistemologists reacted by trying to construct an alternative analysis of the concept of knowledge. Since knowledge implies true belief, but not vice versa, they sought whatever it is that, added to true belief, makes knowledge. Some proposed further constraints additional to justification: for example, that the premises as well as the conclusion of the justifying argument should be true. Others proposed more external constraints on the relation between the belief state and the truth of the belief: for example, a causal, reliable, lawlike, or counterfactual connection. Each particular analysis is generally agreed by a majority of epistemologists to be refuted by counter-examples; it does not even give necessary and sufficient conditions for knowledge. Some continue to seek. This was the usual fate of programmes for the analysis of concepts in twentieth-century philosophy, which is somewhat surprising on the assumption that we grasp such analyses in grasping the concepts. But why accept that assumption? The regress of analysis must stop somewhere, presumably; why should it not stop with concepts like the concept of knowledge? There need be no concept that, added to the concept of true belief, makes the concept of knowledge. Quite generally, if the concept C applies only where the concept C* applies, and not vice versa, it does not follow that the concept C is analysable in terms of the concept C* and other concepts. *Same person* applies only where *weighs the same* applies, and not vice versa, but the concept of personal identity is not to be analysed in terms of the concept of identity of weight and other concepts. Although nobody has proved that the concept of knowledge is not a complex combination of simpler concepts, we have no good reason to think that it is such a combination.[23]

---

[23] Shope (1983) surveys earlier post-Gettier attempts to analyse knowing.

Suppose that we do apply the concept of knowledge on the basis of something more like a fallible recognitional capacity than a conceptual analysis. Our susceptibility to both sceptical and anti-sceptical intuitions demonstrates that our willingness to apply the term 'know' varies strongly with context. Contextualists try to reconcile the intuitions by postulating that what relation we use the term to refer to varies accordingly; we have seen reason to doubt their account. A more pessimistic interpretation is that the term 'know' expresses no coherent concept: there is no relation that the associated "recognitional capacity" is a capacity to recognize. We "recognize" that we know the truth of various everyday propositions, we "recognize" that we do not know that we are not in a sceptical scenario in which those propositions are false, and we "recognize" that knowledge is closed under competent deduction. The constraints are all built into the concept of knowledge, but no relation could satisfy them all. The pessimist could argue on similar grounds that even the epistemic term 'justification' expresses no coherent concept.[24]

The pessimist seems to rely on an over-simple view of how recognitional capacities determine reference. For example, our most primitive forms of reference to some spatial properties and relations of shape, size, and distance are presumably determined by our corresponding perceptual recognitional capacities, even though, notoriously, the structure of our visual system renders us susceptible to various spatial illusions and paradoxes. No assignment of reference would make all the perceptual appearances veridical, but we are not tempted by the conclusion that our most primitive spatial terms do not express coherent concepts. Some spatial properties and relations play a sufficiently large role in the explanation of the perceptual appearances for us to count as referring to them, even though they falsify some of those appearances; the structure of our perceptual systems can take up the explanatory slack. Analogously, the relation of knowing may play a sufficiently large role in the explanation of our epistemic intuitions for us to count as referring to it, even though it falsifies some of those intuitions; perhaps the structure of the mechanisms underlying our epistemic judgements can take up the explanatory slack. The intuition that one cannot know that one is not in a sceptical scenario may thus be a conceptual illusion. Of course, we want a good reason to blame that as the conceptual illusion, rather than blaming the intuition that many ordinary people know the truth of many ordinary propositions, or the intuition that knowledge is closed under competent deduction. But the reason might be that classifying the sceptical intuitions as illusions involves postulating far less extensive illusions than would be involved in classifying the anti- or non-sceptical intuitions as illusions.[25]

We might go further by conjecturing a constraint on an assignment of reference: that in normal circumstances it should tend to make our perceptual beliefs (those in which we take perceptual appearances at face value) count as knowledge

---

[24] Schiffer (1996) proposes a form of pessimism.
[25] On the epistemology of intuition, see Bealer (1999) and DePaul and Ramsey (1998).

(not just as true). Such a constraint does not amount to a cast-iron guarantee that our perceptual beliefs are not massively false; a coin with the tendency to land heads and tails equally often may happen to land heads every time it is tossed. We lack perceptual knowledge only if we are very unlucky; the sceptic was still wrong to argue that we could not have had perceptual knowledge. Analogously, we may conjecture, a constraint on an assignment of reference is that in normal circumstances it should tend to make our intuitive beliefs (those in which we take conceptual appearances at face value) count as knowledge. In particular, it should tend to make our intuitive epistemological beliefs count as epistemological knowledge. They cannot all count, but the exceptions should as far as possible be minimized.[26] The sceptic was wrong to argue that we could not have known that we had perceptual knowledge. Although general constraints on interpretation do not explain how we know in any particular case, they do suggest that the odds are stacked against the sceptic.[27]

References

Bealer, G. (1999). 'The A Priori', in J. Greco and E. Sosa (eds.), *The Blackwell Guide to Epistemology*. Oxford: Blackwell.

BonJour, L. (1985). *The Structure of Empirical Knowledge*. Cambridge, Mass.: Harvard University Press.

Burge, T. (1979). 'Individualism and the Mental', in P. French, T. Uehling, and H. Wettstein (eds.), *Midwest Studies in Philosophy*, iv: *Studies in Metaphysics*. Minneapolis: University of Minnesota Press.

Cohen, S. (1988). 'How To Be a Fallibilist'. *Philosophical Perspectives*, 2: 91–123.

—— (2001). 'Contextualism Defended: Comments on Richard Feldman's "Skeptical Problems, Contextualist Solutions" '. *Philosophical Studies*, 103: 61–85.

Craig, E. (1990). 'Three New Leaves to Turn Over'. *Proceedings of the British Academy*, (76): (265)–81.

Davidson, D. (1986). 'A Coherence Theory of Truth and Knowledge', in E. Lepore (ed.), *Truth and Interpretation*. Oxford: Blackwell.

DePaul, M., and Ramsey, W. (eds.) (1998). *Rethinking Intuition: The Psychology of Intuition and its Role in Philosophical Inquiry*. Lanham, Md.: Rowman & Littlefield.

DeRose, K. (1995). 'Solving the Skeptical Problem'. *Philosophical Review*, 104: 1–52.

---

[26] Compare Davidson (1986). The idea that belief aspires to the condition of knowledge (not just of truth) is sketched in Williamson (2000*a*: 41–8).

[27] This chapter (written in 2001) shamelessly favours my own prejudices and interests. Attempting nothing like a comprehensive survey of contemporary epistemology, I have left much significant work unmentioned. For a sense of the variety of contemporary epistemology, see Greco and Sosa (1999). A compact survey is Pryor (2001). For most of the current approaches to the problem of scepticism, see DeRose and Warfield (1999). Thanks to Alexander Bird and Nico Silins for comments on an earlier draft. Exchanges with Keith DeRose and John Hawthorne have also been very helpful.

—— (1999). 'Contextualism: An Explanation and Defense', in J. Greco and E. Sosa (eds.), *The Blackwell Guide to Epistemology*. Oxford: Blackwell.

—— (2000). 'How Can We Know that We're Not Brains in Vats?' *Southern Journal of Philosophy*, suppl. vol., 38: 121–48.

—— and Warfield, T. (1999). *Skepticism: A Contemporary Reader*. Oxford: Oxford University Press.

Dretske, F. (1970). 'Epistemic Operators'. *Journal of Philosophy*, 67: 1007–23.

—— (1981). 'The Pragmatic Dimensions of Knowledge'. *Philosophical Studies*, 40: 363–78.

Earman, J. (1992). *Bayes or Bust?* Cambridge, Mass.: MIT Press.

—— (1993). 'Underdetermination, Realism and Reason', in P. French, T. Uehling, and H. Wettstein (eds.), *Midwest Studies in Philosophy*, xviii: *Philosophy of Science*. Notre Dame, Ind.: University of Notre Dame Press.

Feldman, R. (2001). 'Skeptical Problems, Contextualist Solutions'. *Philosophical Studies*, 103: 87–98.

Feyerabend, P. (1978). *Science in a Free Society*. London: NLB.

Fumerton, R. (1995). *Metaepistemology and Skepticism*. Lanham, Md.: Rowman & Littlefield.

—— (2000). 'Williamson on Skepticism and Evidence'. *Philosophy and Phenomenological Research*, 60: 629–35.

Gettier, E. (1963). 'Is Justified True Belief Knowledge?' *Analysis*, 23: 121–3.

Gibbons, J. (2001). 'Knowledge in Action'. *Philosophy and Phenomenological Research*, 62: 579–600.

Goldman, A. (1976). 'Discrimination and Perceptual Knowledge'. *Journal of Philosophy*, 73: 771–91.

—— (1999). 'Internalism Exposed'. *Journal of Philosophy*, 96: 271–93.

Greco, J., and Sosa, E. (eds.) (1999). *The Blackwell Guide to Epistemology*. Oxford: Blackwell.

Harman, G. (1986). *Change in View: Principles of Reasoning*. Cambridge, Mass.: MIT Press.

Howson, C., and Urbach, P. (1993). *Scientific Reasoning: The Bayesian Approach*, 2nd edn. Chicago: Open Court.

Kaplan, M. (1985). 'It's Not What You Know That Counts'. *Journal of Philosophy*, 82: 350–63.

Klein, P. (1995). 'Skepticism and Closure: Why the Evil Genius Argument Fails'. *Philosophical Topics*, 23: 213–36.

Kornblith, H. (ed.) (1994). *Naturalizing Epistemology*, 2nd edn. Cambridge, Mass.: MIT Press.

Kyburg, H. (1970). 'Conjunctivitis', in M. Swain (ed.), *Induction, Acceptance, and Rational Belief*. Dordrecht: Reidel.

Lewis, D. (1996). 'Elusive Knowledge'. *Australasian Journal of Philosophy*, 74: 549–67.

Luper-Foy, S. (1987). *The Possibility of Knowledge: Nozick and his Critics*. Totowa, NJ: Rowman & Littlefield.

McDowell, J. (1995). 'Knowledge and the Internal'. *Philosophy and Phenomenological Research*, 55: 877–93.

Maher, P. (1996). 'Subjective and Objective Confirmation'. *Philosophy of Science*, 63: 149–74.

Nozick, R. (1981). *Philosophical Explanations*. Oxford: Oxford University Press.

Pryor, J. (2001). 'Highlights of Recent Epistemology'. *British Journal for the Philosophy of Science*, 52: 95–124.

Putnam, H. (1973). 'Meaning and Reference'. *Journal of Philosophy*, 70: 699–711.

—— (1981). *Reason, Truth and History*. Cambridge: Cambridge University Press.

Quine, W. (1969). 'Epistemology Naturalized', in Quine, *Ontological Relativity and Other Essays*. New York: Columbia University Press.

Schiffer, S. (1996). 'Contextualist Solutions to Scepticism'. *Proceedings of the Aristotelian Society*, 96: 317–33.

Shope, R. (1983). *The Analysis of Knowing: A Decade of Research*. Princeton: Princeton University Press.

Smith, P. (1984). 'Could We Be Brains in a Vat?' *Canadian Journal of Philosophy*, 14: 115–23.

Unger, P. (1975). *Ignorance: A Case for Scepticism*. Oxford: Oxford University Press.

—— (1986). 'The Cone Model of Knowledge'. *Philosophical Topics*, 14: 125–78.

Williams, M. (1996). *Unnatural Doubts*. Princeton: Princeton University Press.

—— (2001). 'Contextualism, Externalism and Epistemic Standards'. *Philosophical Studies*, 103: 1–23.

Williamson, T. (2000*a*). *Knowledge and its Limits*. Oxford: Oxford University Press.

—— (2000*b*). 'Skepticism, Semantic Externalism, and Keith's Mom'. *Southern Journal of Philosophy*, suppl. vol., 38: 149–58.

—— (2001). 'Comments on Michael Williams' "Contextualism, Externalism and Epistemic Standards"'. *Philosophical Studies*, 103: 25–33.

Wright, C. (1991). 'Scepticism and Dreaming: Imploding the Demon'. *Mind*, 100: 87–116.

CHAPTER 24

PERCEPTION

M.G.F. MARTIN

1. INTRODUCTION

Different views about perception are commonly distinguished by the claims they make about the direct or immediate objects of perception. Direct realists affirm that we directly or immediately perceive physical objects and that these objects are mind-independent. Indirect realists accept that there are such mind-independent objects and that we refer to them and have knowledge of them, but suppose us only to have indirect or mediated contact with them. Phenomenalists have commonly insisted that the objects of sense must be immediately or directly apprehended, and consequently have questioned whether there are mind-independent objects for us to think about in the first place. What, though, is it to claim that sensory awareness of some item is indirect rather direct? And what is the significance of the divide?

Presumably many readers know that Warsaw is the capital of Poland. Few of those who do know this will be aware of quite how they know it. They may dimly remember learning geographical facts at school, without recalling exactly the occasion on which they learnt this. They may know how to go and check the fact if their knowledge is challenged, and they might even know how to justify themselves in terms of general evidence about the organization of Europe. Still, neither of these is quite being able to identify the actual means by which they came to know or persist in knowing the fact in question. On the other hand, all readers of this page can discover that the first letter on the page is a 'P'. But in this case, it should be clear how you can come to know this fact: you can just see that that's the case.

It may well not be true of most of our knowledge of the world that we have any access to exactly how we know these things, but in the case of many trivial particular matters of fact we often do know that our current perception puts us in a position to know these things. Correspondingly, the fact that some object is now perceptually salient to you is often a reason for you to single it out and think about it, or try to discover further facts about it. While not all of our perceptions need be conscious, our conscious awareness of the world typically is perceptual, and in reflecting on this we come to be aware of the objects and facts we have perceptual access to.

Now one might think that this picture of how perception, awareness, and knowledge fit together presupposes that perception of the world around us is direct: that what perception gives us directly is the ordinary objects of perception about which we form so many opinions. The importance of the question about direct perception, then, may lie in the role that our conception of how we perceptually relate to things affects our conception of how we come to think about and know about many aspects of the world around us.

Typically philosophers who have thought that there is a distinction to be drawn between direct and indirect perception have thought it also obvious that we cannot directly perceive the objects around us which we suppose ourselves to know about through perception even if we do not perceive mere representatives of them in the form of sense-data, impressions, or percepts. For it has been common to suppose that if we perceive solid objects, we do so through perceiving only proper parts of them, their surfaces.

In the first section of the chapter I focus on the grounds for supposing this to be so and one radical strategy for resisting it. In the second section I turn to the persisting reasons for supposing that we cannot perceptually be directly in contact with the world around us. Whether the argument is successful depends in part on what we take perceptual awareness of ordinary objects to involve. There are at least two possible ways of holding on to the idea that we have direct awareness of the mind-independent world—one an intentional or representational approach to perception, the other a disjunctivist approach to perception—and it is not clear whether we do have a determinate conception of what direct awareness must involve that will decide between these two approaches, or so I suggest in the closing section.

2. Seeing One Thing in Virtue of Seeing Another

Frank Jackson identifies a number of different threads in defenders of the immediate–mediate or direct–indirect distinction:[1] one invoking the presence or

---

[1] (Jackson 1977, ch. 1). Although this work is a defence of a sense-datum theory of vision, Jackson more recently defends a form of intentionalism or representationalism about perception.

absence of inference;[2] that what is immediately perceived is that which is entirely known through perception;[3] or that what is immediately perceived is that which is entirely perceived at a time.[4] Jackson replaces these with a clear account of the contrast, an account applicable directly to the perception of objects rather than facts, and one that does not presuppose that there are sense-data or other non-physical intermediaries in perception:

... x is a *mediate object of (visual) perception* (for S at t) iff S sees x at t, and there is a y such that $(x \neq y$ and) S sees x in virtue of seeing y. An *immediate object of perception* is one that is not mediate; and we can define the relation of *immediately perceiving* thus: S immediately perceives x at t iff x is an immediate object of perception for S at t... (Jackson 1977: 19–20)

Jackson explains that the connective 'in virtue of' here is not to be treated as a paraphrase of a causal connective, as when one says 'He is angry in virtue of the lack of service in this restaurant'. It is, rather, used in the sense of showing some analytic or definitional relation between the two facts introduced by antecedent and consequent. The appeal to definition here could be loosened, perhaps by taking on Thomas Baldwin's suggestion that ' "p in virtue of q" is true where the fact that q explains why p obtains' (1990: 240). We need to restrict this, though, in line with Jackson, to those uses of 'explains' in non-causal contexts.[5]

Moore and Broad assume that visual perception of physical objects is at least mediated by visual perception of their surfaces. Further argument or reflection may then show that such perception is mediated by non-physical sense-data (or in Broad's terms 'sensa') as well. Jackson, in common with this tradition, supposes that our seeing the surfaces of objects mediates our seeing the objects themselves:

We commonly see things in virtue of seeing *other* things: I see the aircraft flying overhead in virtue of seeing its underside (and the aircraft is not identical with its underside); I see the table I am writing on in virtue of seeing its top; I first see England on the cross-channel ferry in virtue of seeing the white cliffs of Dover... (Jackson 1977: 19)

Jackson gives us a brief piece of reasoning to this conclusion in the next paragraph. We cannot define perception of a part of an object in terms of perception of the whole object, because one could have seen the part without seeing the object (had the part been part of another object, for example), and one could have seen the

---

[2] This he draws from Armstrong (1961), attempting to elucidate Berkeley. Cf. also Pitcher's interpretation of Berkeley on vision in Pitcher (1977: 9–13).

[3] This he attaches to Price's discussion of the tomato. See the last two chapters for an alternative treatment of this passage. He also finds this in Don Locke's thought that immediate perception 'does not go beyond what is perceived at the particular moment' (Locke 1967: 171).

[4] This he draws from Broad (1956) and Moore (1922).

[5] So one might think that explanation is not really more basic here than our grip on 'in virtue of'. For one can as easily explain to someone that there are non-causal explanations by giving them cases in which they recognize that one thing holds in virtue of another but in which there can be no causal connection.

object without seeing this part of it. So seeing the object can be neither necessary nor sufficient for seeing the part, and hence cannot be that in virtue of which one sees the part. This, of course, does not establish Jackson's point: even if we grant that one does not see the table top in virtue of seeing the table, it does not follow that one sees the table in virtue of seeing the top; one might just see both the table and the top, and neither seeing need be in virtue of the other. So Jackson relies tacitly on the assumption that there must be some constitutive link between the two facts. Why suppose that?

Jackson presents the problem about immediate perception as parallel to certain other cases in which one fact holds in virtue of another. For example, that one object touches another through one part of it touching a part of the other; that one is located in a country in virtue of being located in a city in that country; that an object is coloured in virtue of some part being coloured. In each example we have one fact involving a relation holding in virtue of another fact containing the same relation. So we might try to answer the question we just raised by generalizing the problem: what does one say back to a sceptic in relation to one of these other domains when he or she denies that there is any constitutive link between the facts at issue? For example, what could one say to someone who accepted that someone, Fred, is located in the United States and also accepts that Fred is located in Carson City but denies that Fred is located in the United States in virtue of being located in Carson City?

One might suggest that it is part of our semantic competence in talk of the location of such concrete objects as people that the one locative fact has to hold in virtue of the other. Hence the sceptic must be revealing some kind of misunderstanding of what is said, or at least of how things can come to be the case. Is there any way we can highlight what has gone wrong on the sceptic's part? As in the case of seeing, it is not appropriate to assume that one is located in one place in virtue of being located in another, and then determine that one of these facts must obtain in virtue of the other. For someone sceptical about the idea that one occupies some locations in virtue of occupying others may just deny that facts about an individual's location in one place need hold in virtue of the individual's location in any other place.

There are some things for us to add to the story. There is not simply one way of occupying a region of space. In general, we have a conception of the ways in which objects such as tables or chairs, or human beings, can occupy particular regions of space. So, for example, a human being will generally displace other solid objects from a region of space occupied by him or her. We can, thereby, make sense of the minimum region of space that such an object occupies through excluding from that region any solid entity entirely distinct from it. It is this sense of location that most concerns us when we wish to fill a Mini with students, or determine the number of items a passenger can place in an aeroplane locker. In turn, our understanding of what it takes for an object to occupy a region of space in its entirety intersects with our understanding of topology and the ways in which sub-regions of a space can be entirely enclosed within that space; and our understanding of geography and politics, which allows certain regions of land thereby to be included as parts of other regions.

In terms of these further claims, we can have some sense of truths that obtain independently of ascertaining the truth of Fred's being in the United States which seem to suffice, given our normal understanding, for Fred so being located once we grant that the region in which he completely excludes other physical bodies is in a certain space within Carson City. The sceptic's lack of competence would then seem to be revealed in an ability to make the move from this set of uncontested truths to the claim that Fred is located in the United States. Or, alternatively, given that the sceptic does not deny that Fred is in the United States, the lack of competence may be revealed in a failure to grasp how one thing can be so in virtue of another.[6]

In Jackson's presentation of the account of seeing, immediately seeing an object is taken as primitive, and what it is for an object to look some way to one is explained in terms of either immediately seeing it and it being the way it looks, or immediately seeing some other thing which is in fact the way that the first object looks to be (and hence in virtue of seeing which one sees the first). The ambition would therefore seem to be to explain the other perceptual vocabulary of 'looks' in terms of 'sees', and hence to presuppose that we can explain the distinction between 'immediately sees' and 'mediately sees' before understanding what it is for something to look some way. If one adopts this strategy, there would seem to be no parallel story for seeing to the one sketched above for the case of location. Hence we would seem to have no purchase on showing what aspect of our concept of seeing the sceptic would be getting wrong.

If we gave up Jackson's explanatory ambition, we might instead attempt to illuminate immediate perception by taking seeing objects and objects looking some way to one as equally primitive notions through which we understand the other. The analogy with location would then be restored. The basic idea is that just as a material object occupies a region through excluding other concrete items from it, an object is immediately seen where it thereby looks some way to one, and occupies in part the visually experienced scene.

Note that this is not to claim that we can reduce or entirely explain what it is to see an object in terms of how it contributes to how things look to one when one is seeing. That would be a hopeless task. First, not all cases of things looking some way to one need be cases of perceiving, or even of perceiving objects: one can be hallucinating for example, or one may be seeing but not seeing any particular thing. Even where one does see some object and things look a certain way to one, still one

---

[6] Whether one should suppose that this really is an aspect of our semantic competence concerning locative talk rather than part of our background understanding or theory of what it takes for medium-sized goods to be located is a more delicate question, however.

can't read off from the fact that things looking that way depends on some object the conclusion that you see that object. Suppose one sees a continuous red wall. The wall itself may be composed of bricks, although the discontinuities between the bricks may not be visible. In this case how things look to one as one stares at the wall depends on how (parts) of each of the bricks are. Had the middle brick been green, for example, and still part of the wall, then the wall would not have been a uniform red expanse. At the moment it looks to you as if there is a red expanse before you, and that holds in virtue of each brick being red and that redness being visible. Do you thereby see any of the individual bricks? Not obviously so. After all, none of the individual bricks is segmented out for you in the visual array as a possible object of visual attention. Now take a case in which one suddenly sees through a slit a vivid flash of turquoise. Behind the slit someone has walked past wearing a turquoise scarf. So how that person was, in wearing such a scarf, and how that scarf was, being turquoise, were responsible for how things looked to one. Nonetheless, we can't simply determine from that whether one has seen the person, or indeed the scarf. Indeed, in this case it seems that what we are inclined to say very much turns on the context: we can imagine a case in which you know that the given individual is liable to wearing such bright colours and that no one else is, so that in the circumstance you would be so placed to determine by sight whether that person had walked past. Against such background assumptions, we can construe a context in which one can truly say one saw the person; as well as a context in which one is prepared only to say that one saw a flash of colour. So there is no simple rule for moving from facts about how things look to a subject to claims about what things they see. We shouldn't hope to explain what it is to see some object in terms of a more fundamental idea of what it is for things to look a certain way to a subject.

Yet that is not what we require given our current purposes. We cannot define what it is for a physical object to be located in a region of space through the notion of excluding other matter. But the connection between the two notions helps us understand how one's location in one region must be constituted by one's location in a sub-region. In parallel, by taking seeing and things looking to one a certain way both as equally basic we can hope to elucidate how the seeing of one object may be constitutive of the seeing of another and thereby the distinction between mediately and immediately seeing.

So consider the kind of case often appealed to in discussion of why one could only be seeing an object through seeing its surface. We compare two situations: in case 1 you see an orange on a table in its full glory; in case 2 you are similarly placed and the surface of the orange is directed towards you as in situation 1, but the rest of the orange has been eaten away. There is some thing which you see in both cases which is the same, the surface of the orange; moreover, the way in which things look to you on both occasions is the same. So the objects absent in case 2 cannot be responsible for how things do look to you on that occasion. Whatever it is that is responsible in case 2 for determining the way things then look must be present on that occasion and be looking to one an appropriate way: we think things look as they do because we see the surface of the orange and the way it looks. But now, if that same thing is present in case 1 as well as in case 2, and there is no difference otherwise in how things look, then doesn't that show that it is the common object between case 2 and case 1, the surface of the orange, that is responsible for how things look in *both* situations? After all, *ex hypothesi*, the additional elements present in case 1 have made no difference to how things look to you given that the scene looks the same both in case 1 and in case 2. That suggests that it is how the surface of the orange is (and the background surfaces), and how it (and they) look to you, that constitute how everything in the scene looks to you. Although we say you see the orange in case 1, the orange itself, as opposed to its frontmost surface, does not play a constituting role in relation to your experience.

This seems to offer us the parallel for the case of vision to the role exclusion of bodies plays in relation to location. A primary role for objects of perception is to make up the array of elements that look some way to us. The immediate objects of sight will then be those that not only look some way, but which, in so looking, fix the way in which all objects we perceive look to us to be. Other objects will count as being seen (and hence as being seen mediately) through their relations to the objects immediately seen. It is through the immediate object of perception, and the way it looks, that these mediate objects come to look some way to us. The relation of part to whole seems to offer the relevant relation in the case of the orange and its frontmost surface, but there are other relations that seem capable of providing for the same. For example, the curtain moves and one sees the burglar enter the room. Perhaps in this case one does see the burglar. Yet matters could look just the same way if no burglar was there (perhaps there was just a sudden gust of wind). So even if you see the burglar in the actual case, the seeing of him does not determine the ways things now look to you. You see the burglar in virtue of seeing how the curtain looks, since across the two situations you see the curtain and in each it looks the same way. We can extend the line of thought further. There is a conceivable situation in which, through over-activity of moths, the curtain is no longer there except for the wisp of its foremost pile. Still, here matters can look the same to you as in the other two cases. So the curtain in turn is seen only in virtue of seeing its surface. This suggests that we might be able to provide an ordering of the objects of vision: immediately seen, seen only in virtue of a distinct, immediately seen object, seen only in virtue of a distinct object, seen only in virtue of another immediately seen object, and so on.

Our primitive idea of what it is for something to be seen, and for it to look a certain way, is for it to fix the way one then experiences, that is, the phenomenal nature of one's experience. Since we do say of other things that we see them too—we are prepared to say this of the whole orange in case 1, for example—we might surmise that, just as topological relations and political concerns can spread out the appropriate location of an object, so too some salient relations of belonging to, being a part of, or being a salient cause of, might play just such a role in the case of perception. There is, it must be said, a notable contrast here with the example of location inasmuch as the ways of specifying what belonging to should amount to as between immediate and mediate objects of perception is not at all clear, a fact that G. E. Moore was very sensitive to in his various discussions. That does not take away from the thought that the intuition driving one in the case of seeing rests with the condition for objects to be immediately visually perceived. And an object will count as an immediate object of perception where that object figures among those that determine the way one's experience currently is.

We started with the question whether one directly or immediately perceives any physical objects. Surfaces of objects are presumably themselves still physical. So the cases we have considered so far would not by themselves lead one to reject the claim that we immediately perceive physical things, even if we do not immediately see the ordinary objects around us that we have an interest in knowing about and interacting with. Still, it is easy to see how the terms of the distinction we have introduced could be extended to cover the proposal that one sees immediately only non-physical entities. Just as we considered in case 2 a situation in which the surface of the orange is present and seen as in case 1, and the manner in which things look is the same, so we might now consider a further situation—case 3. In case 3 not even the surface of the orange is seen. Case 3 is that of a hallucination indistinguishable from actually seeing the orange. Still, one might hypothesize, there is something seen in case 3 that is present in both cases 1 and 2 (just as the surface of the curtain is seen when the burglar is seen and only the curtain is seen): this would be some non-physical expanse that looks some way to the subject. Now, we might hypothesize as above that since the same thing is seen in case 3 as in cases 1 and 2, and how things look in all three is the same, then what constitutes the way in which things look to one in cases 1, 2, and 3 is the same: the presentation of the non-physical expanse and how it appears to be, which is the minimum that is present in case 3. So for this account of immediate seeing to provide the notion needed for the traditional debate, we must suppose that even when no physical objects are perceived, one can still count as seeing things in virtue of seeing some non-physical entities; and in addition we must hypothesize that these non-physical entities always play a role in visual perception, determining how things look to one even where one is also seeing a physical object.

Now this question, whether there are non-physical constituents of visual experience that determine how we visually experience things as being, is one that can be raised whether one appeals to the distinction between direct and indirect objects of perception or immediate and mediated seeing. Moreover, the rationale for claiming that we only immediately see non-physical entities can be understood perfectly well in these more general terms without drawing on the contrast between direct and indirect or immediate and mediate. The general form of those concerns will be addressed in the next section, but we should close this one by asking whether, even if we question the role of non-physical entities in visual perception, we must concede that we see objects only in virtue of seeing their surfaces.

3. 'Now you see it; now you don't': Seeing and Context-Sensitivity

Understanding the distinction between direct and indirect perception (or immediate and mediate perception) in this way does not yet give us the materials properly to interpret the traditional debate. Even if it were clear that one only saw the table before one through seeing a surface (or some surfaces) of the table, as we noted, this still does not show that one only sees the surface or the table because one sees some other non-physical thing. Yet before we even come to address the question of why one might think any non-physical object is also seen and plays a constitutive role in seeing physical things, one may already object to the contrast drawn, however simple and easy to apply it may appear.

The critic here may protest in terms introduced earlier, that it is through seeing things and thereby coming to be aware of them that we typically are placed to single those objects out in thought and come to know various facts about them. Perception plays a central role in our coming to refer to and know about things around us. But it plays this key role through making us aware of the objects and presenting them to us. The means of distinguishing between the immediate objects of perception and mediated ones requires us to recognize that only the immediate ones properly turn up in our experience of a scene and fix the way in which things as a whole appear to us. And this consequence, the critic complains, undermines our conception of how perception is useful to us. We take ourselves to be presented with such ordinary objects as tables and chairs, trees and dogs, cars and buses. But now, the critic continues, the reasoning rehearsed above seems to undermine the advantage we take such experience to give us. For while we start out with the idea that the orange itself is part of the experiential situation for us, when we reflect on case 2, we come to the conclusion that strictly speaking only the surface is an aspect of the experiential situation. We are therefore less privileged than we supposed ourselves to be, if the reasoning really is cogent. It hardly helps that in some other sense we still count as seeing the orange, albeit doing so indirectly, because that was not the sense in which we started out supposing that we stood in a relation to the orange.

Suppose that one were moved by these concerns, and hence inclined to reject Jackson's suggestion that it is obvious that we see tables through just seeing their surfaces, or England through seeing the white cliffs of Dover. Where could one point to where the reasoning goes wrong? The most developed critique is offered by Thompson Clarke (1965).[7] He argues that the discussion here ignores the context-sensitivity of talk of perceiving and appearing. The contrast between direct and indirect perception is a mistaken attempt to render into a context-insensitive vocabulary the irremediably context-sensitive issue of what one counts as perceiving on a given occasion. Given a suitable context and understanding of what is at stake, in staring at what is on the table, one does count as seeing the orange, even though given a differ-ent context and understanding the same situation is one in which one strictly only see the surface of the orange and not the orange itself. If one ignored the role that context plays here, we would simply have a clash of intuitions about what one sees: we both have the intuition that the orange is seen and the intuition that merely the surface is seen. Consistency could be restored by marking a context-independent distinction between immediate and mediate perception, but that would require that we have a context-independent way of fixing what one perceives or, as we saw in the last section, what is apparent to one and responsible for how the scene looks. The contextualist challenge then develops through insisting, first, that there is a prima facie clash in our intuitions and then that there is no context-insensitive way of resolving the clash.

To press this complaint, one needs to do two things. First, one needs to show that there is context-sensitivity that bears on the reasoning rehearsed in the last section. Secondly, one needs to give some reason to suppose that the context-sensitivity in question cannot be removed through suitable revision of the way we talk.

It is clear that what counts as seeing something can vary with context. Lost on an orienteering trip, you may spot a dot on the horizon and be correctly described as seeing the church on the hill—perhaps it is the only salient landmark in the area, and having noted it you are now able to use the map. By contrast, if you are tra-versing the moors inspired by reading a guide to English churches that announces that one's view of English Romanesque architecture will forever be changed on see-ing the church, you will not yet count as having seen the church (i.e. your failure to be impressed as yet does not, as it stands, count against the guide's claim). So in the very same physical circumstances, you can both count and not count as seeing the church. But this example of context-sensitivity does not yet show that anything in the argument we rehearsed above trades on ignoring it.[8]

Better grounds for supposing that context-sensitivity in the original reasoning may be involved comes from reflecting on a tension among the claims in play in our original description of cases 1 and 2, from which we extracted the test for direct versus indirect perception. Consider again case 1: in this the orange is on the table

---

[7] For discussions inspired by Clarke, see Neta (forthcoming) and Travis (2004).

[8] Cf. Neta (forthcoming), who does not appear to note the gap.

before one, and we initially suppose that a proper description of this case is one of seeing the orange. Not only is the orange there on the table, but one can seemingly pay attention to it, pick it out, and wonder whether it would be good to eat, or a bit too dry or sour. We fix on case 2 as one in which the scene as a whole looks just the same to one (for it is by appeal to that thought that we reason that what is seen in both case 2 and case 1 is responsible for how things look, not only in 2 but also in 1). Yet, when we describe case 2, we are inclined to describe this case as one in which all that is apparent to one is just the surface of the orange. In this case the orange does not look some way to one. The surface may well look a certain way, the way such that it is as if there is an orange there, but there is no orange looking some way. Now one might suppose that still in case 2 we have a case of its looking as if there is an orange there when in fact none is present, much as in cases of hallucination. When caught by delirium it may look to a subject as if pink rats are running through the room, but we don't say that there are then any pink rats that look some way to that subject. Yet, we are also reluctant to assimilate case 2 to one of hallucination: in this case one does see all that there is to see; it is not as if some imaginary object occupies one's field of view.

So we now seem to have a tension among three claims concerning our descriptions of the two cases: (*a*) things look the same to one in both cases 1 and 2; (*b*) in case 2 solely the surface (and surrounding background) look some way to one; (*c*) in case 1 the orange and not (or not merely) the surface looks some way to one. No explicit contradiction has been demonstrated across (*a*) to (*c*), but still one may feel a tension between them. Isn't there a difference in the way things look in case 1 from case 2 if we say of case 1 that an orange is an element of how things look while finding no corresponding element to this in case 2?

I speak of tension here, rather than evident inconsistency, because the sense in which things look the same in cases 1 and 2 relates to the scene as a whole. But I have given no account of how the look of a scene should relate to how individual elements of a scene look to one. Inconsistency will follow immediately only if, from the fact that one scene looks exactly the same as another, it follows that there is nothing in one case that looks some way to the perceiver for which there is no corresponding element in the other situation. Once we admit that how a scene looks to one is a complex matter, involving different things looking some way or other to one, this principle no longer looks obvious. After all, it is conceivable that different elements in two scenes could combine so as to look the same overall. Even granting that, a tension remains: for there is an element in case 1, the orange looking some way, for which there is no element or combination of elements corresponding to it in case 2.

The tension would be removed if we could affirm simply that in both cases, strictly speaking, how things look to one is merely a matter of how the surface looks. And that, as we have seen above, is what the defender of the contrast between direct and indirect perception recommends to us. But we should be happy with this recommendation only to the extent that we are sure that it just isn't true of case 1 that the orange as such looks some way to one in this circumstance. This brings us back to the original complaint: that to accept this description of the experience is to construe it in a way involving less than initially we thought it did. It seemed to provide us with experiential access to the orange and not merely its surface.

The contextualist diagnoses the problem in a somewhat different way, and thereby rejects the use of the reasoning rehearsed in the last section. The contextualist will affirm the first claim (*a*) because there is a way of considering case 1 under which one counts as seeing the orange, and under which how things are presented to the subject includes that object. The contextualist will accept claim (*b*) because there is a context under which this is a correct description of how things are in case 2—obviously there is no context relative to which the agent perceives an orange in case 2 since there is no orange there to be seen, but whether the case counts as one in which what one seems to perceive matches with only what is there to be perceived is taken to be context-sensitive. We can construe case 2 as entirely veridical taking the subject to be liable to take in only what is there to be seen; but we can likewise construe it as misleading given its similarity to case 1.

For the contextualist, then, what the tension among the intuitions reveal is not that strictly speaking we don't have visual awareness of physical objects as opposed to their surfaces, but rather that we don't have a context-independent intuition about what one counts as either seeing or having a visual experience of. In the light of this we won't accept as compelling any form of the reasoning that keeps track of the contexts we are concerned with: in the context in which the orange counts as apparent to one in case 1, the appearance of things is not fixed in case 2 just by the way the objects present there look, for there is also the illusory aspect of the presence of the orange in addition. If we take instead the context in which in case 2 the way things look match what is there to be perceived, then there is an aspect of how things can look to be in case 1 that doesn't echo this, namely the perceived orange. This is not to say that it is wrong to suppose that there is a way in which there is nothing more to be seen in case 1 than what is there to be perceived in case 2; when one focuses on this way of thinking of case 2, one can construe what is apparent to one in case 1 also as merely the surface of the orange. What is mistaken, according to the contextualist, is to suppose from this that no truth can be expressed in saying that one sees the orange or that it looks some way to one.

This gives a sketch of how the context-sensitivity of 'see' or 'appears to' may bear on the cogency of the reasoning of the last section. But that is not yet to address the second, and equally important, concern. J. L. Austin complained that there are just different uses for the term 'directly' even in connection with verbs of perception, so there could be no one thing that philosophers could mean by indirect perception.[9] In response, one may simply insist that one aims to introduce a specific and technical usage, such as that suggested by Jackson's definition for specific philosophical

---

[9] See Austin (1962: 15).

concerns. By analogy, one may respond to the contextualist's challenge that while it may be true that our ordinary usage of 'see' or 'looks' is context-sensitive in the ways sketched here, and no doubt in other ways too, still that does not show that we cannot introduce a special technical usage of 'immediately see' which, by stipulation, is intended to be context-independent. It is this that the theorist needs, and which the objector has not yet said anything against.

After all, it is familiar that when one person says 'It is raining' and another utters 'It is not raining', they need not be disagreeing. The first may be talking about the weather in Paris, the latter the state of play in London. Here, implicitly, there is a further parameter that affects the truth of the utterance. It is both a parameter that we can make explicit and which we can fix a specific value for, if, for example, our concern is solely with the weather in London. If the context-sensitivity that the objection appeals to above is anything like this, then we may suppose that there is some further parameter that we fix on in our ordinary use of 'see' or 'look'. The theorist who wishes to introduce a constant and technical sense of these terms would then just need to fix on some relevant value and ensure that this value is held constant in all of our debates. The theorist need not deny that there may be an ordinary context of use under which it is true that we see oranges and that these are manifest to us in visual experience. What they should insist is that for the purposes of a philosophical account of seeing, we need to specify a particular value, and relative to that it is correct to say only that the surfaces of oranges, and not oranges themselves, are manifest to us in visual experience.

The objector may retort that this is not getting the point at all. For the response assumes that there simply is a determinate fact about how the subject is experiencing the situation, or how things look to him or her and what they can thereby take in about the situation. Although we may report on these experiential facts in different ways, depending on the relevant contextual understanding of 'sees', 'looks', or anyway the sentences containing these verbs, what is reported on is much the same fact in each case. But that was not the way that the original complaint developed; there was no assumption that there was a fixed or determinate way in which things must have been looking to the subject. When we describe the sense experience of subjects, we are describing what they take in about the world around them and thereby what is available for them to single out in thought and discover things about. Indeed, the complaint starts from the thought that if the orange is not part of how one experiences things to be and only the surface of the orange is, then one is not properly related to the orange through vision. Now, once the contextualist grants that there is a correct description of the experience under which the subject simply takes in the surface of the orange, then that suggests that when so considered the experiential facts are different: the subject takes in a different and more restricted range of the situation perceptually.[10]

[10] The clearest development of this radical position is developed by Charles Travis in relation to thought content and representation in Travis (2001) and extended to the case of perception in Travis (2004).

Since our conception of sense experience here, or so the contextualist may insist, is just a matter of what aspects of the environment the subject has awareness of, the correct moral to draw from this is that there are not context-independent determinate facts about what one sees or how one experiences things to be. So there would be nothing genuinely experiential for the technical usage to pick up on.

The idea that one's experience does not have a unique, determinate character sounds like a radical response to the initial and quite intuitive thought experiments. Whether or not one follows the contextualist down this route, the disagreement on this matter brings out one of the key points at issue, concerning the significance of sense perception or sense experience within one's broader cognitive economy. In part this takes us back to the traditional division between direct and indirect realism about perception. But it also takes us beyond that, since the underlying disagreement can be raised without having to worry about the contrast between immediate and mediate perception, and hence without having to settle the question whether or not our sense experience is determinate in character.

The contextualist is moved by the thought that our sense experience is the presentation to us of the ordinary objects around us in the world that we normally take ourselves to perceive, and not something less than that, be that the surfaces of these objects, or some non-physical entity.

Now the indirect realist can establish his or her case only if both the indirect–direct distinction can be applied to sense experience, and also the claim that we only perceive the ordinary objects of perception in virtue of being aware of non-physical entities. A common way of understanding this debate is to focus on the positive grounds for supposing that there are non-physical objects of awareness. But the contextualist rejection of the immediate–mediate distinction suggests a different way of understanding this debate: that what is at stake is whether we can make sense of how our sense experience in itself gives us access to the objects we ordinarily take ourselves to perceive and be in a position to think about through perceiving them. If our experience is merely of the surfaces of these objects or of other entities interestingly related to them, then, according to the contextualist conception, we are not related to these things as we took ourselves to be.

The more fundamental question is whether there is any reason to suppose that we just couldn't have experience in the way that the contextualist supposes that we do of the objects around us. The concerns so far raised about the intuitive distinction between immediate and mediate objects of perception cannot establish that result. For, as we have seen, there is as much plausibility to the idea that we do have visual experience of objects as to the idea that we merely experience their surfaces. But, as we shall see in the next section, the traditional concerns about illusion or hallucination can be put to the service of arguing that one couldn't be aware of mind-independent objects in the way the contextualist presupposes.

4. The Argument from Hallucination

The commonest strategy for arguing that we never directly perceive physical objects is to appeal to some form of the argument from illusion or hallucination. That is, writers seek to show that in no case are we ever aware of physical entities as the perceived elements of our sense experience: first, by highlighting some salient cases of illusion, where one misperceives some entity, or by highlighting some cases of hallucination, where all agree one fails to perceive any physical object; then arguing of such cases that they do not constitute sense experience in which we directly perceive physical entities; and then to make a generalizing move and argue that if this holds of the illusions or hallucinations, it must hold of all of the sense experience we enjoy.

Of course, this is only to offer the schematic structure of the argument. And in fact there is no one argument that can be identified as the argument from illusion or hallucination. Rather, there is a whole menagerie of considerations that writers have appealed to; these vary in the examples of illusion or hallucination taken to be critical to the case and how the generalizing move is made from the test cases to all sense experience. In general, presentations of these arguments are enthymematic (at best), or plain invalid. Moreover, it is often difficult to discern what the needed extra premises are that would render the argument valid, or what further support could be offered for the principles required once identified.

Here I will focus on just one variant of the argument from hallucination. First I will assume that the argument is intended in itself to have a purely negative purpose: to show that we do not directly perceive physical objects, or in fact, more narrowly, that what I shall call a *naive realist* conception of sense experience must be false. This negative conclusion is consistent with various different positive conceptions of sense experience. It is consistent, for example, with the view that our sense experience is the awareness of some non-physical entities, sense-data, whose manifest qualities determine what our experience is like. Equally it is consistent with the view that our sense experience is representational in character and does not involve any *relation* of awareness at all. The interest of the argument, though, lies in the significance of rejecting naive realism. For, if it is true that this is the account that best articulates our pre-theoretical conception of how our sense experience is, then we can construe the alternative theories as different attempts to account for this apparent character of sense experience, while avoiding the inconsistency that naive realism falls into.

What then is a naive realist conception of experience? In the last section I suggested that the contextualists like Clarke concerning the verb 'see' are moved by the thought that were the objects of perception not properly part of the perceptual situation from the subject's own point of view, one would be in a much worse position perceptually than we ordinarily take ourselves to be. For Clarke, it wouldn't be enough to respond that even if we don't immediately or directly perceive the orange, we can still see it indirectly or mediately. For Clarke's concern is that when initially we think of our perceptual situation it includes the orange, but when we consider the reasoning that leads to the contrast between immediate and mediate perception, we are left with the thought that strictly speaking we are only aware of the surface, and so at a disadvantage with respect to the position we initially took ourselves to be in.

Elaborating on this, we might suggest that we not only think of perceiving objects, seeing, feeling, hearing, or smelling, as relations to what is perceived, but also that the mental episode or experience involved in so perceiving is a relation. That is to say, first the naive realist supposes that what it is to have a sense experience is for one to be aware of some entity or entities: be that some object, event, or property instance, or other aspect of an object. So conceived, the occurrence of a sense experience is a relational occurrence or state involving both the subject and the entities of which the subject is thereby immediately or directly aware, and hence requiring the existence of both for the experience to occur. Secondly, the naive realist supposes that at least some of the entities to which we are so related in experience are the mind-independent entities around us that we take ourselves to perceive. At the moment I can look out of the window across a north London vista: for the naive realist, the rooftops and chimneys, and the bare trees and the clouds in view, may all be constituents of my current experience. These rooftops, chimneys, trees, and clouds do not depend for their very existence on my current awareness of them: they would remain were I simply to disappear, or less dramatically to close my eyes and no longer be aware of them. So, for the naive realist, my current visual perception of the scene before me is a relation: it is a relation of awareness, between me and the various physical and mind-independent entities in the world around me that I currently directly perceive.

We will return below to the question whether such a picture deserves the epithet 'naive': is this really the best articulation of how our sense experience seems to us to be before we engage in theoretical musing about it? What is of more concern for us now is why such an account could not be correct. One limited strategy for falsifying the account is to argue that various of the qualities that we are naively inclined to attribute to physical objects and which we take these objects to manifest in our experience of them are in fact not exemplified by any physical items. For example, many writers argue that colours as we experience them could not be instantiated by physical objects; or at least, even if instantiated by such objects, could not be perceived by us. If this thought is right, the red of the tiles opposite, which currently I take myself to be aware of, cannot be an example of some aspect of the tiles themselves featuring as part of my experience—because it is not them but something else that exemplifies the redness I am aware of. This strategy is limited in what it can show against the naive view, though. Even if the view of colour is correct and it is also true that no subject ever perceives a physical object as coloured, it still won't have been established that one is aware of no physical object in visual experience. To show that the subject is not directly aware of any physical object, it also needs to be established that the only entities one is aware of in visual experience actually do possess a colour. Doubting the physical reality of colour does not in itself settle this further point. In contrast, the inconsistency highlighted by the argument from hallucination would directly rule out the truth of naive realism with respect to any object of awareness, if the argument is sound.

The argument takes naive realism to be inconsistent with two further assumptions that in themselves seem plausible and are quite widely accepted: one that we might call *experiential naturalism*, that our sense experiences are themselves part of the natural causal order, subject to broadly physical and psychological causes; the other, the *Common Kind Assumption*, that whatever kind of mental, or more narrowly experiential, event occurs when one perceives, the very same kind of event could occur were one hallucinating. The first of these principles constrains what can be the case in regard to certain hallucinatory states, and the latter implies that this result must apply equally to the case of sense experience enjoyed when veridically perceiving.

Our starting point is with the idea of certain kinds of illusion or hallucination. Typically, when clinicians discuss hallucinations, they have in mind the kinds of delusion suffered by psychotics or extremely mentally disturbed individuals: someone might hear the voices of angels, see their loved ones as replaced by aliens, or suppose him- or herself covered by ants. There is no assumption in these discussions that the delusions or hallucinations such unfortunate people suffer are anything in character like what it would be really to perceive these circumstances. Typically delusion leads one to lose a grip on the nature of reality, and that may be a loss of understanding of what one's sense experience is like just as much as it is of what the world is like. When philosophers wish to stress the significance of hallucination or the argument from hallucination, what they typically have in mind, instead, is the possibility of the occurrence of mental episodes that lack the appropriately genealogy to be perceptions of objects in the world around us, but which from the subject's point of view need not necessarily be discernible from such perceptions. That is to say, for our current purposes we need to work solely with the idea of what one might call 'perfect hallucinations'. Consider your current perception of the environment around you. Perhaps you are staring out at a late spring evening, or lying in summer grass, or sitting in a dusky office reading a philosophy paper. It is quite conceivable that there should be a situation in which you could not tell that things were not as they are now: so it might seem to you as if you were staring at an orange on the table, or taking in the smell of new-mown grass, even though unknown to you in that situation you were not doing so. Your perspective on the situation would not, in that situation, distinguish how things were from how they are now. Now we might say that how you are in that situation is a matter of having a sense experience that is not a case of perception.

It seems both conceivable that such sense experience should occur—that is, that there is nothing in our way of conceiving phenomenal consciousness that should rule out the occurrence of such perfect hallucinations—and that they should be brought about through appropriate stimulation of a subject's brain. Experimenters have only been able to induce through direct stimulation of the cortex very simple visual phenomena—the flashes of light or phosphenes, for example, exploited in artificial visual systems for the blind.[11] But this seems a merely practical or medical difficulty. So that we think, as embodied in the assumption of experiential naturalism, that our sense experiences, like other mental episodes, are subject to broadly physical causes.[12] Once one has suitably manipulated the physical and psychological conditions, however, one has done all that can and need be done in order to induce in a subject a suitable sense experience.

But now suppose that we take hallucinatory experience to be relational in form, just as the naive realist takes veridical perception to be. There can be no instance of a relation without appropriate relata: so for the experience to occur, there needs not only to be a subject of the experience, but also the entities of which the subject is thereby aware. Since we are, *ex hypothesi*, dealing with a case of perfect hallucination, we know that there are no candidate physical objects of awareness. If you have the perfect hallucination of an orange, then the existence of this experience does not require that there be any real oranges, or other physical entities that look alike, to exist or to be appropriately situated for you to be aware of them. Nonetheless, if it is relational in nature, the experience can occur only if there is something or other for the subject to be aware of.

If we hypothesize (as the early sense-datum theorists did) that the relevant relata must be mind-independent, then the conditions for bringing about an experience must involve not only suitable manipulation of a subject's body and mind but also a guarantee of correlation between the perceiver and candidate objects of awareness. Given that such entities would be non-physical (since this is a hallucination) and non-mental (being awareness-independent), causing someone to have a hallucination would require causal influence over something neither physical nor psychological: the non-physical object of awareness. Therefore, if one holds to experiential naturalism and countenances only physical and psychological causation, one must deny that any such influence could take place. The only way, therefore, that the physical and psychological conditions could be sufficient for bringing about the experience is through them being sufficient for the existence of its object as well. And that can only be because the kind of occurrence one has brought about, the kind of state of awareness that occurs when one is hallucinating,

---

[11] Phosphenes, little flashes of light, were first investigated by Johannes Purkinje in the early nineteenth century. The effect can be produced just by physical pressure on the eye, but it has often been elicited through electrical stimulation. For its use in creating prosthetic vision systems, see Dobelle *et al.* (1974) and for a recent survey, Tehovnik *et al.* (2005).

[12] And, remaining agnostic of the truth of dualism, psychological causes.

is such that its occurrence constitutively guarantees the existence of an object of awareness.

That is to say: the reason that one might hypothesize that sense-data, or impressions, or percepts should be conceived as mind-dependent entities if they are to exist derives from the causal conditions for bringing about sense experience. It is only if the sense experience is itself constitutively sufficient for the existence of its object that one can assume that the physical and psychological causal conditions for bringing about sense experience are sufficient for bringing it about while also supposing such experience to be relational.

So far, this conclusion is not inconsistent with naive realism as I have characterized it. For that is a view about what we succeed in being aware of in cases of genuine perception. That theorist need have no pretensions about explaining how we can come to have sense experience when merely hallucinating, and so may well be agnostic about whether we are aware of anything at all when hallucinating, or aware instead of some mind-dependent entity. The naive realist need not take a view on whether merely mind-dependent entities could present the same appearance to a subject as a physical object. Ducks and decoy ducks can look the same while being very different in nature; why can't oranges and mental impressions have a common appearance too? Austin (1962) pressed just this question, and since he thought there was no good answer, he summarily dismissed the force of any argument in this area.

However, inconsistency does arise once we suppose that the very same kind of thing must be occurring when one has a perfect hallucination as when one perceives. Why? By the Common Kind Assumption, whatever kind of experience does occur when one perceives, the same kind of experience can be present when one is hallucinating. So if a hallucinatory experience must be of a kind that constitutes the existence of its objects, then since the very same kind of experience is also present when perceiving, that too will constitute the existence of its objects. That is, for any aspect of the perceptual experience the naive realist hypothesizes to be a relation to a mind-independent entity, consideration of the corresponding hallucination shows the entity in that case to be mind-dependent, and hence, any experience of that kind thereby to have a mind-dependent object rather than any mind-independent one.[13] Mind-independent entities cannot, it follows, be constituents of the experience, contra the naive realist.

Suppose, then, that the naive realist seeks to avoid the conclusion by denying that any sense-data or other awareness-dependent entities are involved in hallucination. The alternative is to deny that the hallucination has any constituent elements. What account of hallucination is consistent with this denial? The commonest approach is

---

[13] I assume here, in effect, that there cannot be constitutive over-determination of the veridical perceptual experience such that it is a relation to both the mind-dependent entity and the mind-independent one.

to embrace a representationalist or intentionalist construal of experience. The denial that the experience has any constituent elements must be made consistent with the evident fact that, from the subject's perspective, it is as if there are various objects of awareness presented as being some way or other. That is to say, whenever one has a sense experience such as seemingly viewing an orange on the table, one's experience has a subject matter (as we might say)—there seemingly is a particular kind of scene presented to the subject in having the experience. And it looks as if the description of this subject matter carries with it a commitment to the existence of what the naive realist thinks of as the constituents of experience in the case of veridical perception. Since we deny that there are any such constituents of the experience in the hallucinatory case, our talk here must be lacking in ontological import. We are treating the hallucinatory experience as if it is the presentation of objects when in fact it is not. Intentional theories of experience take the description of the subject matter of an experience to express the representational or intentional content of the experiential state. The experience has its phenomenal character, according to this approach, in virtue of its possession of this content. In general we take ascriptions of representational content to psychological states to lack ontological commitment.[14]

Again, by the Common Kind Assumption, whatever kind of experience occurs when one perceives, that same kind of event will be present when one hallucinates. So if the hallucinatory experience lacks any constituents, then the perceptual experience, being of the same kind, does not have any constituents either. Although there may be objects that do act as appropriate values for our quantifiers, or referents for our terms, when we describe how things are presented as being to the subject of the perceptual state, none of these should be taken actually to be aspects of the experiential state itself, since such a kind of experience can occur when the subject is not perceiving. On this view, even in the case of veridical perception, when we make mention of the particular objects that the subject is perceiving, we do not describe them as parts of the experiential situation, but make mention of them to express the representational import of the experience. Given the naive realist's commitment to thinking of perceptual experience as genuinely relational between the subject and a mind-independent world, this representationalist construal of hallucination is no more amenable to naive realism than the sense-datum conception.

But what is the force of talking of a common kind here? There are ways of construing the Common Kind Assumption on which it is trivially false. If we relax our conception of a kind of event sufficiently, then any true description of an

---

[14] Or rather, more precisely, we may take the ascription to a psychological state of a given representational content to lack the ontological commitment that assertion of that content (or of a proposition corresponding to that content if the content is non-conceptual or non-propositional in form) would involve. Some people, however, question whether one can avoid the ontological commitment inherent in the use of some referential terms in this way, cf. McDowell (1984). I assume that those drawn to intentional theories of perception will posit representational contents for perceptual states that avoid these difficulties. For more on this issue, see Martin (2002).

individual event introduces a kind of event. On such a conception, it is easy to find kinds that some individual events fall under and otherwise matching individuals fail to. You paint your picket fence white on Tuesday and I do so on Wednesday: mine is a Wednesday painting, yours a Tuesday one. Given the different descriptions, these seem to be different kinds of event. Since no party to the debate about perception denies that there are *some* descriptions true only of the perceptual scenario, namely that they are perceptions rather than hallucinations, someone who wants to take the Common Kind Assumption to be a significant addition to the debate cannot be using this broad conception of a kind of event.

For the Common Kind Assumption to be a genuine condition on the argument, and not simply a trivial falsehood, we need some conception of the privileged descriptions of experiences. For it to be a substantive matter that perceptions fail to be the same kind of mental episode as illusions or hallucinations, we need some characterizations of events that reflect their nature or what is most fundamentally true of them.[15] I assume that we can make sense of the idea that there are some privileged classifications of individuals, both concrete objects and events, and that our talk of what is essential to a given individual tracks our understanding of the kinds of thing it is. That is, I assume the following: entities (both objects and events) can be classified by species and genus; for all such entities there is a most specific answer to the question 'What is it?'[16] In relation to the mental, and to perception in particular, I assume that for mental episodes or states there is a unique answer to this question that gives its most specific kind: it tells us what essentially the event or episode is. In being a member of this kind, it will thereby be a member of other, more generic kinds as well. It is not to be assumed that for any description true of a mental event, there is a corresponding kind under which the event falls. The Common Kind Assumption is then to be taken as making a claim about the most specific kind that a perceptual experience is, that events of that specific kind can also be hallucinations.[17]

---

[15] Note that this is not the same thing as to assume that the events we are interested in here are themselves part of the fundamental furniture of the universe. It is quite consistent with what is claimed here that there is a more fundamental level of reality out of which the mental is somehow constructed, or out of which it emerges. All that is rejected is that we explain the salience of this level of reality merely through appeal to an inclination on our part to describe some things as similar and others as different.

[16] The most developed recent treatment of this kind of Aristotelianism about essence and nature is to be found in Wiggins (1980, 1996). For more on the question of essence, see Kit Fine's discussions of these matters (Fine 1994).

[17] Can one formulate the argument, and the resistance to it, by avoiding mention of kinds? The argument from hallucination is often presented in terms of the causal conditions for bringing about a given instance of perceiving. That is, it is sometimes suggested that the issue turns on whether a given perception could have occurred without being a perception (cf. Valberg 1992). But there are many reasons for denying that the very same event could have occurred in a different causal context that have nothing to do with the debate about the nature of perception. (Consider Davidson's original criterion of identity for events: Davidson 1969.) If we do not assume that an individual event of hallucinating a picket fence is identical with a given perception, some additional principle must be appealed to in order to indicate that what is true of the one must be true of the other.

The background concern of the debate, therefore, is with the kind of occurrence that is involved in perceiving. When the naive realist insists that awareness is a form of relation and that we can bear it to mind-independent objects, this brings with it a commitment that relates to all of the kinds of cases in which such episodes can occur. Opponents appeal to the case of perfect hallucination not because they suppose that we can easily bring these states about, or because they think that in general illusions and hallucinations are just like perceptions, but because they want to test what the possible circumstances are for having this kind of awareness.

5. INDIRECT REALISM AGAIN

Experiential naturalism and the Common Kind Assumption taken together rule out naive realism about all aspects of sense experience. What bearing does that have on our original questions about direct perception and the role of sensing in our knowledge of the world? One way of responding to the argument is to hold on to the assumption that sense experience is a relation of awareness, but in the light of the constraints from experiential naturalism, suppose that the only objects of awareness are mind-dependent entities, sense-data, or impressions. If ordinary perception is constituted through one's sensory awareness, such a view will be close to, if not a version of, indirect realism about perception. Sense awareness will be constituted by awareness of mind-dependent entities, and through that one will count as perceiving (some of) the environmental causes of this state of awareness. The view will count strictly as a form of indirect realism, if one supposes that the sensuous awareness one has in having an experience is itself a mode of perceiving or sensing; for then one can apply the contrast between immediate and mediate perception introduced above.[18] On the other hand, the theorist may as easily resist the claim that we perceive these objects of awareness—after all, our sense organs are not affected by them and we don't interact with them in the ways we do with the ordinary objects of perception. The theory will simply claim that what it takes to perceive objects at all is to have a sense experience and then go on to claim that such experience is the awareness of mind-dependent entities and qualities, even though not the perception of them.

On either construal, the original complaint about the position will have force. On initial reflection one's experience would seem to take in the ordinary objects in

[18] Moreover, contra the contextualist, the restriction of sense experience just to awareness of mind-dependent entities will not rest on ignoring the context-dependence of the words 'look' or 'appear'.

the environment around one. But, given reflection on the argument from hallucination above, one realizes that one's sense experience encompasses merely the mind-dependent entities constituted through one's awareness of them. Sense experience takes in less than it did, and hence seems to put one at a disadvantage relative to the position one initially took oneself to occupy.

Note that the worry here is not that one can only think about objects if one can genuinely perceive them, or that one can only know facts that one perceives; or that the objects of perception and the perceptually known facts must somehow be basic to all one's knowledge. Any such claims would be contentious and inconsistent with some familiar everyday examples: we know much about the world that we have learnt through testimony of books or other people; we know of and think about many things that we have never encountered. The worry here turns on a more modest point. When subjects first reflect on what they are in a position currently to find out about their situation and what they can think of, they take sense experience to involve the ordinary objects around them as available to attend to. As a consequence of reasoning through the argument from hallucination, they realize that that is not what sense experience provides them with. So, on one construal their thoughts are really about something different from what they supposed: one judges that that mind-dependent patch is an ink bottle, when supposing that the judgement was initially about the piece of glass five feet away. Alternatively, they do succeed in making the judgements that they supposed themselves to make, but they lack the understanding of how and why they made just that judgement that they originally started with. It seems obvious at first why it should have been that ink bottle that one picked out to think about: it was the one in view, salient within experience. In the light of the argument, however, we are to recognize that no such physical object is salient at all in experience.

6. INTENTIONAL THEORIES OF PERCEPTION AS DIRECT REALISM

But this consequence follows not from the argument from hallucination alone, but from the further commitment that we must conceive of sense experience as relational in character: if not a relation to mind-independent objects like the tables, chairs, trees, or birds around us, then a relation to some entity, sense-datum, impression, or image that is conjured up in our awareness of it. The alternative response is to deny that sense experience has a relational character at all. For if there need be no object of awareness in the case of hallucinatory experience, there is no reason to suppose that there must be anything mind-dependent involved in sense perception at all.

Initially responses to sense-datum theories of sense experience sought to avoid this ontological commitment just by denying that sense experience is a relation to anything: so-called adverbialists about sense experience, for example, claim that to have a visual experience of a red patch is not thereby to stand in any relation to an object, some red thing, that one senses, but rather to have experience in a certain manner, to sense redly.[19] But to put matters this way is to seek to avoid the ontological commitments of the sense-datum approach without necessarily addressing what leads the sense-datum theorist to posit the controversial entities in the first place. The sense-datum theorist posits the mind-dependent entities to play the role in sense experience that the naive realist supposes the ordinary objects of perception to play: those things to which one has access in reflection on what it is like for one now to be perceiving or seeming to perceive. The adverbialist talk of sensing red merely being a manner of sensing does not obviously pick up on this element. Rather it would seem to deny that the sense-datum theorist is right to suppose that there is anything we are thereby aware of when we have sense experience, and hence to reject the naive realist's starting point as well.

A representational or intentional approach to perception, on the other hand, promises to offer an account that addresses these concerns.[20] The minimum commitment of an intentional theory of perception is simply to attribute representational or intentional contents to sense experience: these states represent objects or one's environment as being a certain way, and the sense experience will count as veridical to the extent that how matters are represented coincides with how they are. Typically an intentionalist account of sense experience, however, seeks to account for the phenomenal character of such experience. Some suggest that this requires that the phenomenal character supervene on intentional content such that there can be no difference in character without a difference in intentional content.[21] But in the current context a more substantive commitment is required: that that aspect of experience which the naive realist treats as a relation to the object of perception instead be treated as arising out of the representational or intentional properties of the experience. That is to say, where the naive realist supposes

---

[19] Adverbialism is initially associated with Ducasse (1942), and later developed in very different ways by Chisholm (1959) and Sellars (1968) (it is doubtful whether Sellars's account does raise the question pressed in the text); and more recently defended by Tye (1984) against Jackson's (1977) critique. Tye has subsequently endorsed a form of intentionalism about perception.

[20] Recent defenders of intentionalism include Harman (1990), Peacocke (1983, 1990, 1992), Searle (1983), Tye (1992). In the analytic tradition its popularity can be traced back to Firth's (1965) discussion of the percept theory, on the one hand, and Anscombe's (1965) critique of both sense-datum theorists and their ordinary language opponents, on the other. With some caveats, one can also see it as dominant within the phenomenological tradition. Armstrong's inclination to believe the theory may also be thought of as part of the tradition, although he hesitated to treat it as a form of direct realism about perception; see e.g. Armstrong (1968, ch. 10).   [21] Cf. Byrne (2001).

that to have the sense experience one stands in a relation to the object of perception, the intentionalist suggests instead that the experience represents the presence of the object and that this is not strictly a relation to the object in itself because the same kind of experience can occur with no object there. For the intentionalist, when one has a sense experience it is as if one is related to the objects of perception, as if the kind of awareness or attention to them requires the presence of those objects, but in fact experiences are such that this isn't so: for the same experience could occur and no objects be there.

The intentionalist does not deny the seeming role of the objects of perception in characterizing what the sense experience is like; he or she recognizes that the objects of perception will be part of the sense experience's subject matter. The only possible dispute with the naive realist is over what it takes for an object to be the subject matter of an experience. Therefore, one may conclude that this approach avoids the problems that the sense-datum theory raises. Intentionalism about perception, if it can consistently be fleshed out, seems to offer us a way of understanding how sense experience can be directed on mind-independent objects even given that experience can occur when we hallucinate. Intentionalism, after all, comes to be a way of defending a kind of direct realism about sense perception.

What, then, does the debate between the naive realist and such intentionalism amount to? What could show that sense experience of objects around us was or was not relational in form? One of the ways of thinking about this is to fix on the case of hallucination. In accepting the Common Kind Assumption, the intentionalist supposes that the same kind of thing can occur when one has a hallucination as a veridical perception. So there should be a correct description of your experience that can apply equally to the hallucinatory case and to the veridical perception.

If one is moved by the original thought, one might say that in the veridical case, the experiential situation should be describable in terms of the actual objects perceived: one is aware of the orange on the table and various of its features. If that is the correct description of the veridical case, then it is not directly available in the case of the hallucination given that no object is present there. So there needs to be a description of the hallucinatory case that avoids that commitment. One way, as Strawson (1979) stressed, is to describe it as a case in which it is as if one was presented with an orange. But what is the force of 'as if' here? If we take it as characterizing the hallucination by analogy with the case of veridical perception, then we will have to suppose that there is a distinct characterization to be given of the veridical case by which we can understand the comparison. But that cannot be the intention, since the presupposition is that whatever occurs in the veridical case is also present in the hallucinatory situation, so there should be some description in common that we can give directly of both.

To press this point further one needs to consider what the substance of the debate is between the naive realist insistence that sense experience must be thought of as a relation to the objects of perception, and the intentionalist's denial of this claim. At this stage, one might consider whether there is another way of responding to the argument from hallucination which preserves the naive realist view, namely a way of resisting the argument by rejecting one of its starting assumptions. For example, in different ways, transcendental idealists and early sense-datum theorists suppose that experiential naturalism is false. Merleau-Ponty (1942), for example, uses the causal argument to establish that our experience is not subject to the causal order and hence is outside the natural world, acting as limit on it. On the other hand, G. E. Moore (1957), C. D. Broad (1923, 1925, 1956), and H. H. Price (1932) all insisted that the immediate objects of awareness were non-physical but also not mind-dependent. At least for Moore, the initial impulse for this claim may have been that he wished to use sensing as an example of a mode of knowledge of a world independent of one's awareness of it. He takes it as definitional of knowledge that its objects are independent of the knowing of them, so if the argument from illusion establishes that the objects of sense are not the ordinary objects of perception, it cannot establish that they are mind-dependent. Apart from the oddities involved in supposing the world populated by non-physical entities with which we come into causal commerce only in perception, the resulting picture leaves the sense-datum theorist without a compelling way of showing why we must always be aware solely of such non-physical sense-data. So a naive realist might be untroubled by the hypothesis that hallucination involves the awareness of such strange non-physical entities.

If, though, the naive realist wishes to embrace a more conservative metaphysical picture and allow that we are just part of the normal natural, causal order and that we have no reason to suppose that the causal powers of this realm extend beyond the physical and psychological, then the only other option here would be to reject the Common Kind Assumption: that the very same kind of event that occurs when one perceives could have occurred were one hallucinating.

This approach to perception and appearance states is associated with so-called disjunctivism. The disjunctive theory of appearances (such labelling, I think, is due to Howard Robinson) was first propounded by Michael Hinton; the view was then defended further by Paul Snowdon and separately by John McDowell.[22] In its simplest formulation, disjunctivism affirms that there is no highest common factor between perceiving and illusion or hallucination. Our description of our situation as one in which it seems to the subject as if there is an orange there covers diverse cases: the good case in which one sees the orange and is thereby aware of it as what it is; or a bad case in which this fails to be so, but in which it is as if the former obtains. What consequences would flow from denying the Common Kind Assumption? Does this give a coherent picture of sense experience?

---

[22] See Hinton (1967, 1973); Snowdon (1980–1, 1990); McDowell (1982, 1986, 1994). There are significant differences in the formulation and motivation for each of these approaches. I discuss a little of this in Martin (2004). Robinson's critical discussion can be found initially in Robinson (1985) and is further elaborated in Robinson (1994).

7. DISJUNCTIVISM ABOUT APPEARANCES

In rejecting the Common Kind Assumption, the disjunctivist might be seeking to deny that there is *anything* really in common with respect to being an experience, or being a mental state, that perceptions, illusions, and hallucinations need have in common. This would be to deny even that the idea of a perceptual experience defines a proper mental kind, since all parties to the debate agree that this is a notion we can apply equally to veridical perceptions, illusions, and hallucinations. Yet given that disjunctivism seeks to defend naive realism, the rejection of the Common Kind Assumption only requires that one claim that the most specific kind of experience one enjoys when one perceives not occur when having an illusion or hallucination. This claim is the minimum needed to block the entailment from the claim that hallucinations cannot have mind-independent objects as constituents to the claim that the same is so of veridical perceptions. In this manner, the disjunctivist preserves naive realism through affirming

(I) No instance of the specific kind of experience I have now, when seeing the orange for what it is, could occur were I not to perceive such a mind-independent object as this.

and thereby denying the Common Kind Assumption.[23]

But what does this commit one to saying about the non-perceptual cases? At first sight, it may appear that all that the disjunctivist has to say is something entirely negative: that these are not cases of having the specific kind of experience one has when veridically perceiving. And hence one might think that disjunctivism avoids saying anything general about the nature of sense experience. In fact there is something more to say here that derives from what ought to be common ground to all parties to the debate.

Hinton began the debate about disjunctivism by focusing on a certain kind of locution, what he called 'perception–illusion disjunctions', for example, 'Macbeth is seeing a dagger or under the illusion of so doing'.[24] Hinton's strategy is to argue that there is no good reason to think that these disjunctive statements could not do all the work that our normal talk of appearances and experience do. That is, that there is no good reason from our ordinary ways of talking to suppose that we are committed to the existence of some special kind of experiential event that may be

---

[23] As should already be clear from the naive realist commitment to having entities as constituents of perceptual episodes, the disjunctivist must reject any kind of physicalism that identifies kinds of mental episode with kinds of physical events in the subject's brain. In rejecting the Common Kind Assumption, the disjunctivist does not take a stance on whether the very same kind of local physical conditions can accompany veridical perception and hallucination.

[24] See the works cited above in n. 20.

present equally in cases of perception and hallucination. Now this strategy prompts a question: Why pick on these disjunctions, then, rather than, say, 'Either Macbeth is seeing a dagger, or he is under the illusion of seeing twenty-three pink elephants'? The answer, I take it, is that the disjunction Hinton highlights has the same evidential profile as self-ascriptions of perceptual experience. Someone in a position to make a warranted judgement about their experience can also put forward one of Hinton's perception–illusion disjunctions, but not so the alternative just suggested. One can gloss this, I suggest, by highlighting the connection between our talk of perceptual experience and the epistemic position a subject is in with respect to his or her perceptions and certain illusions or hallucinations, that they are indiscriminable from the perceptions through introspective reflection.

Above I suggested that philosophers' use of the argument from hallucination focuses not on examples of actual hallucination as it occurs in dementia or delusions, but rather on the theoretical possibility of perfect hallucination. The disjunctivist can exploit just that idea to offer an alternative construal to the notion of sense experience implicit in the Common Kind Assumption. Suppose you start out only with the notion of veridical perception: what could introduce you to the idea of sensory experience more generally, to include illusion and hallucination? The idea of perfect hallucination sketched earlier was just that of a situation which from the subject's perspective is just like the veridical perception of a given scene, but which in fact is not a case of veridical perception at all. And surely it is at least cases like these that we have in mind when we think about examples of sensory experience that are not cases of veridical perception. We have a broader conception of sense experience than this, of course. For we allow that we can have illusions and hallucinations which are not veridical perceptions but that are not indiscriminable from perceptions: their character may vary wildly from what the corresponding perception would be like. But for the sake of this chapter, I want to work with the simplifying assumption that throughout we are to deal with what we might call perfect hallucinations. And for the case of perfect hallucinations, one could get someone to track the relevant cases in just the way suggested here.[25]

It is this idea, I suggest, that disjunctivists such as Hinton use in order to explicate their preferred notion of sense experience in general, i.e. that which generalizes across veridical perception, illusion, and hallucination. For in using this methodology, one can introduce, at least as a first approximation, the range of cases in dispute among the parties, without yet having to admit that there is something of the sort in common between perception, illusion, and hallucination of the sort

---

[25] For a (too brief) discussion of how we can generalize away from the case of perfect hallucination to cover illusions and hallucinations more generally, see Martin (2004: 80–1).

that Hinton wishes to dispute. And hence this gives us the second commitment of disjunctivism:

(II) The notion of a visual experience of an orange on a table is that of a situation being indiscriminable through reflection from a veridical visual perception of an orange on a table as what it is.

We should immediately note three points about (II). First, the acceptability of (II) turns on how we are to understand the notion of indiscriminability. The relevant conception of what it is for one thing to be indiscriminable from another is that of not possibly knowing it to be distinct from the other.[26] To be somewhat more precise, since here we are concerned with knowing of individual experiences whether they are among the veridical perceptions or not, we can gloss it as:

$$\neg \lozenge \, K_{[\text{through reflection}]} \, \neg \, x \text{ is one of the Vs.}$$

(That is, x is such that it is not possible to know through reflection that it is not one of the veridical perceptions of an orange on the table as what it is.)[27]

This condition is met whenever x is one of the Vs, but if there are truths that are unknowable through reflection, then the condition can be met in other ways. It should be stressed that it is no part of this discussion that we can analyse or reduce the truths concerning indiscriminability, modal facts concerning the possibility or impossibility of certain knowledge, to claims about the sorting behaviour of individuals, or the functional organization that might underpin such behaviour. There are delicate questions for the disjunctivist concerning the link between a subject's failure to treat differently two situations and the claim that the two are indiscriminable for that subject.

---

[26] The most extensive discussion of indiscriminability is to be found in Williamson (1990). Williamson principally focuses on the case of knowledge or lack of knowledge of identities and distinctness, that $x = y$ or $x \neq y$. As I note in the text, we are concerned with the plural form of whether x is one of the Vs. This form, even more obviously than the case of individual identities and distinctness, raises questions about intensional versus extensional formulations.

[27] Jim Pryor and others have suggested to me that in our normal usage of 'phenomenally indiscriminable' this phrase should *not* be interpreted according to the above schema. The schema is not symmetrical: that hallucinating is not discriminable through reflection from perceiving does not entail that perceiving is indiscriminable from hallucinating (cf. Williams 1978, app.; Williamson 2000, ch. 6). But, the complaint goes, it is just obvious that as we use talk of 'phenomenally indiscriminable', this relation is symmetrical. In response, I would suggest that we should be more respectful of the etymology of the term, which would support the more complex form suggested in the text. That this should lead to a symmetrical relation in the case of phenomenal states is readily explicable without supposing it analytic of the notion. For the vast majority of philosophers in this debate do make further substantive assumptions about the nature of psychological states that would allow experiential states to be indiscriminable in our sense only if they are identical in phenomenal character. And it is just these substantive assumptions that the disjunctivist challenges.

Secondly, the restriction 'through reflection' is an important and central addition here. When we describe the kind of case that fixes what we mean by perfect hallucination, we fix on one in which we unknowingly find ourselves in a situation that we can't know is not one of staring at an orange on the table. But we equally have a conception of sense experiences occurring where one has been tipped off about their non-perceptual status. If I take you into the bowels of William James Hall and subject you to an expensive visual-cortical stimulator so as to induce in you the hallucination of an orange, it seems quite conceivable that I should put you in a situation that in a certain respect is just like seeing an orange. In one important respect it is not: I have told you the experiment you will be subjected to. Since you have that information from my testimony, there is something you know that rules out your situation from being one in which you see the orange. Since we don't want to deny the possibility that this is a case of perfect hallucination, we need to bracket the relevance of the additional information you have acquired through testimony. This is what the appeal to 'through reflection' is intended to do. The situation in which you are knowingly having a hallucination of an orange is like a situation in which you don't know of the hallucination, because, if we bracket that additional information, then what is available to you otherwise, i.e. what is available to you in simply reflecting on your circumstances, does not discriminate between the two situations. The import of this restriction and the consequences that flow from it are central to understanding what disjunctivism is committed to, and how one should characterize one's objections to that picture of experience.

Thirdly, we should note that condition (II) just taken by itself ought to be interpretable as at least extensionally adequate on all theories of perceptual experience. Of course, the disjunctivist's opponent will not think that this properly gives an account of the nature of sense experience, and nor, for the matter, may it really articulate the concept or conception that we all have of what sense experience is. Nonetheless, the condition cannot fail to count as a sense experience anything that genuinely is one. For according to someone who accepts the Common Kind Assumption, the relevant condition for being an experience, being a P-event we might say,[28] will be exemplified by both perceptions and perfect hallucinations. In both cases, then, the x in question will be one of the Vs, namely a P-event, and so it will not be possible for one to know that it is not one.[29] The only way in which the extensions of our concept of sense experience and what is defined by (II) may fail to coincide is if (II) really is too liberal: that is, if it includes as instances of experience episodes that fail to be P-events. Now, as we shall see below, the full

---

[28] That is, for example, an event of being aware of an array of sense-data with such-and-such characteristics, or an event of being in a state of mind with such-and-such representational properties or content.

[29] Note also that, as formulated, (II) takes no stance on whether perceptions ever occur, or whether a subject need believe themselves ever to have perceived anything. All that it requires is that *we* accept that sense experiences have the character at least of seeming to be perceptions.

import of this possibility is a delicate matter. But at first sight, this is not a possibility that a theorist will wish to countenance. For after all, if in meeting (II) we describe a situation which from the subject's own perspective is just as if one is seeing an orange on the table, then how could it fail to count as a visual experience of an orange? For example, if the preferred account of experience is one in terms of sense-data, then this fact is not one entirely evident to us through initial reflection on our experience. As both intentional theorists of perception and naive realists insist, at least some objects of awareness are presented as the mind-independent objects of perception. There seems to be a privilege to the case of veridical perception in our description of any sense experience, whether it be a veridical perception, illusion, or hallucination (inasmuch as these cannot be told apart from veridical perception). Therefore, the theorist won't be able to isolate any feature that a P-event which isn't a veridical perception possesses and which the subject of the experience can tell through introspection that the event possesses but which a non-P-event which meets condition (II) can be known to lack. There would be nothing about the non-P-event that would rule it out from the subject's point of view as a candidate for being a sense experience in contrast to the P-event. Given this, someone who wishes to rule out such a case because it is not a P-event (whatever the particular account of experience is in question) seems to be offering us too restrictive an account of sense experience; for he or she seems to be interpreting what should at best be a sufficient condition for having a sense experience as a necessary condition. The catholicism of (II) in this case would suggest not that the account is too liberal in conditions on what is to count as experience, but rather that the theory in question (be it a sense-datum account, or some form of intentionalism) is just too restrictive in what it countenances as possible ways in which the kinds of sensory experience we have can be realized.

This suggests that the defender of the Common Kind Assumption should agree that there can be no case of one of us being in a situation indiscriminable through reflection from veridical perception, which is not a case of sense experience, whatever exactly the substantive account of sense experience the theorist thereby favours. The consequence of this is to accept certain constraints on the nature of sense experience and our knowledge of it. It is common for philosophers to suppose that conscious states must be (at least to self-conscious beings) self-intimating; such states will indicate their presence and some of their properties to the subject who is in them. What is required here is much more: that there should be no circumstance in which we are awake and there is no possibility for us to detect the absence of such states.

The disjunctivist's opponents need not reject (II) itself, or think of it as obviously implausible. They may even agree that our initial understanding of what sense experience is as (II) dictates, but then offer a more substantive account of what it takes for something to be an experience and so meet the condition in (II). On the other hand, they may think that the condition laid down in (II) itself is too thin, or modest, as an account of our understanding of sense experience. Still, for the reasons rehearsed above, they are unlikely to complain that (II) gets the extension of our concept of sense experience wrong. So (II) itself is unlikely to lead to any counter-intuitive consequences and on its own can hardly be considered a particularly con-troversial commitment of the disjunctivist. The same is not so, though, for the combination of (I) and (II). (I) commits us to thinking that there are some sense experiences that have a distinctive nature lacked by others, while (II) insists that all of these can nonetheless be indiscriminable from each other introspectively. Together this suggests that the phenomenal characters of two experiences can be different even while one of them is indiscriminable from the other. Many have supposed that what we mean by the phenomenal character of an experience is just that aspect of it that is introspectible, and hence that any two experiences that are introspectively indiscriminable must share their phenomenal characters, even if they differ in other ways.[30]

Now while some such complaint may have widespread support in discussions of phenomenal consciousness, it is not clear whether it should be taken as a primitive claim that is somehow obvious, and the rejection of which is incredible. After all, we can make at least some sense of the idea that distinct individuals, distinct events, and distinct scenes can all be perceptually presented to us and yet be perceptually indiscriminable from each other. That is, suppose that the individual experiences we have of the various individuals, events, and scenes we perceive thereby have as part of their phenomenal natures the presentation of those very objects; each of these individual experiences will be different from each other through featuring one object or event rather than another. Since distinct objects can be indiscrim-inable perceptually, it is plausible that these perceptions should be indiscriminable from each other introspectively. If so, distinct experiences will be different in ways that are not necessarily detectable through introspective reflection.[31] It may be right in the end to dismiss such theories of perceptual experience as incorrect. But if there is an incoherence here, it is a subtle one, and not so glaringly obviously a contradiction. So this throws doubt on the idea that we should view the principle that sameness of phenomenal character is guaranteed by phenomenal indiscrim-inability as an evident truth. If we think the conjunction of (I) and (II) generates a counter-intuitive position, then there must be some further principle at work behind our thoughts that forces us to accept this strong condition.

Once one accepts that (I) and (II) are both true, then one must also deny that two experiences, one of which is indiscriminable from the other, must share

---

[30] In effect, this is to press what I called principle (IND) in Martin (1997): 'If two experiences are indistinguishable for the subject of them then the two experiences are of the same conscious character' (p. 81).

[31] I discuss this option for an intentional theory of perception in Martin (2002). There are delicate questions to be raised here about the interrelation between the phenomenology of individual experiences and the ways in which experiences are similar or different from each other.

phenomenal character (that is, one denies: any phenomenal character the one experience has, the other has too). It is consistent with accepting these two principles that one hold that such experiences would nonetheless share *a* phenomenal character. But a disjunctivist ought to reject even that claim, if the common phenomenal character is conceived of independently of (II), in terms of a positive characterization conceived independently of the unknowable difference across cases.

Why so? The problem that the argument from hallucination poses for naive realism relates to hallucinatory experiences that involve purely local causal conditions sufficient to bring about sense experience but which lack more distant conditions, such as the presence of a real orange in one's environment, which would be necessary to count the sense experience as a genuine perception of something in one's environment. The naive realist is motivated to reject the Common Kind Assumption because he or she insists that a necessary condition on having the experience he or she does when perceiving will be absent in such cases of hallucination. But in itself that doesn't determine what is necessary for one to be having a hallucinatory sense experience.

So now suppose that we manage to bring about a hallucination through reproducing the kinds of local causal conditions in someone's brain that otherwise result in the seeing of an orange. If no orange is in the environment, the subject is not seeing the orange, and according to the naive realist, is having an experience of a different kind from that had when perceiving. Still, we can ask, were the causes sufficient in this case to bring about a hallucination equally operative in the case of veridical perception? As we have set things up, this cannot be denied. So now it would appear that whatever occurs when one hallucinates (and the hallucination is brought about through the same local causal conditions as in veridical perception) also occurs when one veridically perceives.

This is strictly consistent with the Common Kind Assumption: one may both claim that the most specific kind of thing that occurs when one perceives does not also occur when one has a matching hallucination; and yet grant that whatever it is that occurs when one hallucinates, that same kind of thing does occur when one perceives. But still there seems to be a tension between the two commitments. Not least because one might otherwise suppose that what the disjunctivist accepts is the common element of perception and hallucination might by others be taken to be what is relevant to all of our explanations and accounts of sensory experience. Since everyone agrees that there is something about the perceptual situation not carried over to the hallucinatory one—it is, after all a case of perception of an orange on the table, while the hallucination is not—this threatens to reduce the disagreement to merely a verbal dispute. All sides agree that there is a common element present in both hallucination and perception, whatever is the kind of thing that can occur in both situations, and an element that is not carried over.

The disjunctivist can block this manoeuvre by adding one further characterization of sense experience:

(III) For certain visual experiences as of an orange on the table, namely causally matching hallucinations, there is no more to the phenomenal character of such experiences than that of being indiscriminable from corresponding visual perceptions of an orange on the table for what it is.

Another way to put this point is to highlight that there are two sides to the disjunctivist's original conception of perception and sensory appearances. On the one hand is the thought that there is something special about the 'good' case, the presence of veridical perception and the apprehension of the mind-independent world. What holds essentially of the mental state or episode present in this case is not reduplicated across illusion and hallucination, so we can hold to the intuition that such states in themselves relate us to the mind-independent world. On the other hand, though, is the thought that in the 'bad' cases, the cases of illusion and hallucination, one is in a situation that fails to be the way that good cases are, but which purports to be the way that the good case is. Were a positive characterization always possible of the bad cases independent of their relation to veridical perception, were the notion of perceptual experience construable independent of this relation, then that these cases were bad would not be something intrinsic to them. This would not be a matter of us seemingly being related to the world but failing to be so, but rather being a certain way that we might also confuse with being perceptually related. So the disjunctivist thinks that there are cases of phenomenal consciousness that are essentially failures—they purport to relate us to the world while failing to do so. Commitment (III) makes this additional element clear in a way that (I) and (II) alone cannot.

But it does so through bringing out what many will take to be the high costs involved in endorsing a disjunctivist proposal. One can defend the naive realist conception of sense experience as applied to the case of veridical perception—that when one perceives, one is thereby in an experiential state that is a relation to the mind-independent objects of perception. The argument from hallucination can be blocked by denying that our conception of sense experience in general is that of a single kind of mental state that either is or is not a relation to something. Rather we conceive of sense experience in general as that which is indiscriminable through introspective reflection from perception. But in turn, when we reflect on certain kinds of case in which one has sense experience, cases of hallucination brought about through the same local causal circumstances as perception, we realize that the disjunctivist must go even further and claim that there is nothing more to having such an experience than being in a situation indiscriminable through reflection from sense experience: there is something necessarily delusive about the situation. Even if other accounts of sense experience really are unbelievable in relation to veridical perception, is the disjunctivist's conception of causally matching hallucination any more acceptable?

8. PERCEPTUAL CONTACT

We started the discussion of this chapter with the idea that perception can relate us to the ordinary mind-independent objects we take ourselves to perceive, and that it is those objects that figure in our sense experience, where that is conceived as what is reflectively accessible to us when perceiving.

If this is construed in terms of naive realism, then the argument from hallucination sketched above, relying on experiential naturalism and the Common Kind Assumption, seems to reveal the falsity of this account of experience. And we can find one kind of motivation for traditional indirect realism in this: the sense-datum theorist embraces the idea that sense experience is relational in character, but in the light of the argument supposes that the objects of awareness must be mind-dependent and hence not the ordinary objects of perception.

An intentional or representational conception of sense experience would seem to promise a way of avoiding this result. For in denying that hallucinatory experience is a relation to any object, the approach can avoid making the claim that in having experience we must be aware of mind-dependent entities. So far, then, it seems as if an intentional or representational view could preserve the common-sense thought that sense perception makes available to us the objects of perception. But that requires that we can make sense of the idea that our perceptual experience, in being a representational state, may be as if a relation to something without really being relational in character.

In contrast to this, a disjunctive approach seeks to preserve the idea that sense experience really is a relation to the ordinary objects of perception in cases of veridical perception. To block the argument from hallucination it denies that we can be having the same kind of experience when hallucinating as when veridically perceiving. For reasons rehearsed above, this leads the theory to deny that there is any positive characterization to be given of certain hallucinatory states: nothing more can be said of them than that they are situations in which it is as if one is veridically perceiving.

This result is certainly one that many find counter-intuitive. But it should also remind us of the question raised earlier in relation to the intentional approach to perceptual consciousness. For that seeks to give a positive account of what hallucinatory experience is like in terms that are consistent with the thought that one is experiencing in just the same way when veridically perceiving and yet allow that veridical perception seemingly does relate us to the objects of perception present. However counter-intuitive the disjunctivist's position, a parallel problem seems to press on the intentionalist: how can we characterize the hallucinatory situation in the same way as that of veridical perception without undermining the thought that distinctively in the perceptual case alone one is aware of the objects of perception?

If the traditional problem of perception is presented in terms of a contrast between direct and indirect perception, the persisting issue we face concerns our understanding of perceptual consciousness. The fundamental reason for resisting an indirect conception of perception is that the mind-independent objects of perception seem to us to feature in the subject matter of our sense experiences. Sense experience could only be a relation to objects in all cases of having experience if the objects in question are mind-dependent. The disjunctivist is moved by the thought that we do conceive of sense experience in the case of veridical perception as just such a relation to mind-independent objects. The cost of this view is to admit that there are other experiences for which a purely epistemological characterization must be given: there are cases simply of its being as if one is related to objects of perception, even when none are there. It might be thought that the intentional approach to perception avoids both this problem and the concerns with indirect realism. But it does so only if it can offer us a positive characterization of sense experience. And at that point the account seems to echo the disjunctivist's proposal that experience is as if one is perceiving.

References

Anscombe, G. E. M. (1965). 'The Intentionality of Sensation: A Grammatical Feature', in R. Butler (ed.), *Analytic Philosophy*, 2nd ser. Oxford: Blackwell.

Armstrong, D. M. (1961). *Perception and the Physical World*. London: Routledge & Kegan Paul.

—— (1968). *A Materialist Theory of the Mind*. London: Routledge.

Austin, J. L. (1962). *Sense and Sensibilia*, ed. G. Warnock. Oxford: Clarendon Press.

Baldwin, Tom (1990). *G. E. Moore*. London: Routledge.

Broad, C. D. (1923). *Scientific Thought*. London: Routledge & Kegan Paul.

—— (1925). *The Mind and its Place in Nature*. London: Kegan Paul.

—— (1956). 'Some Elementary Reflexions on Sense-Perception', in R. Swartz (ed.), *Perceiving, Sensing and Knowing*. Berkeley and Los Angeles: University of California Press.

Byrne, Alex (2001). 'Intentionalism Defended'. *Philosophical Review*, 110: 199–240.

Chisholm, R. (1959). *Perception*. Ithaca, NY: Cornell University Press.

Clarke, Thompson (1965). 'Seeing Surfaces and Physical Objects', in M. Black (ed.), *Philosophy in America*. London: George Allen.

Davidson, Donald (1969). 'The Individuation of Events', in Davidson, *Essays on Actions and Events*. Oxford: Clarendon Press.

Dobelle, W. H., Mladejovsky, M. G., and Girvin, J. P. (1974). 'Artifical Vision for the Blind: Electrical Stimulation of Visual Cortex Offers Hope for a Functional Prosthesis'. *Science*, 183/123: 440–4.

Ducasse, C. J. (1942). 'Moore's "Refutation of Idealism"', in P. A. Schilpp (ed.), *The Philosophy of G. E. Moore*. La Salle, Ill.: Open Court.

Fine, K. (1994). 'Essence and Modality', in J. Tomberlin (ed.), *Philosophical Perspectives*, 8. Atascadero, Calif.: Ridgeview.

Firth, R. (1965). 'Sense-Data and the Percept Theory', in R. Swartz (ed.), *Perceiving, Sensing and Knowing*. Berkeley and Los Angeles: University of California Press.

Harman, G. (1990). 'The Intrinsic Quality of Experience', in J. Tomberlin (ed.), *Philosophical Perspectives*, 4. Atascadero, Calif.: Ridgeview.

Hinton, J. M. (1967). 'Visual Experiences'. *Mind*, 76: 217–27.

—— (1973). *Experiences: An Inquiry into Some Ambiguities*. Oxford: Clarendon Press.

Jackson, F. (1977). *Perception: A Representative Theory*. Cambridge: Cambridge University Press.

Locke, Don (1967). *Perception and our Knowledge of the External World*. London: George Allen & Unwin.

McDowell, J. (1982). 'Criteria, Defeasibility and Knowledge'. *Proceedings of the British Academy*, 68: 455–79.

—— (1984). *De Re* Senses. *Philosophical Quarterly*, 84; 34: 283–94.

—— (1986). 'Singular Thought and the Extent of Inner Space', in P. Pettit and J. McDowell (eds.), *Subject, Thought and Context*. Oxford: Clarendon Press.

—— (1994). *Mind and World*. Cambridge, MA: Harvard University Press.

Martin, M. G. F. (1997). 'The Reality of Appearances', in M. Sainsbury (ed.), *Thought and Ontology*. Milan: FrancoAngeli.

—— (2002). 'Particular Thoughts and Singular Thought', in A. O'Hear (ed.), *Logic, Thought, and Language*. Cambridge: Cambridge University Press.

—— (2004). 'The Limits of Self-Awareness'. *Philosophical Studies*, 120: 37–89.

Merleau-Ponty, M. (1942). *La Structure de comportement*. Paris: Presses Universitaires de France. Trans. A. Fisher as *The Structure of Behavior* (1963). Repr. Pittsburgh: Duquesne University Press, 1983.

Moore, G. E. (1922). 'Some Judgments of Perception', in Moore, *Philosophical Studies*. London: Routledge & Kegan Paul.

—— (1957). 'Visual Sense-Data', in C. Mace (ed.), *British Philosophy in Mid-Century*. London: George Allen & Unwin.

Neta, Ram (forthcoming). 'Contextualism and a Puzzle about Seeing'. *Philosophical Studies*.

Peacocke, C. A. B. (1983). *Sense and Content*. Oxford: Clarendon Press.

—— (1990). 'Perceptual Content', in J. Almog, J. Perry, and H. Wettstein (eds.), *Themes from Kaplan*. New York: Oxford University Press.

—— (1992). *A Study of Concepts*. Cambridge, Mass.: MIT Press.

Pitcher, George (1977). 'Berkeley', in T. Honderich (ed.), *Arguments of the Philosophers*. London: Routledge & Kegan Paul.

Price, H. H. (1932). *Perception*. London: Methuen.

Robinson, H. (1985). 'The General Form of the Argument for Berkeleian Idealism', in J. Foster and H. Robinson (eds.), *Essays on Berkeley: A Tercentennial Celebration*. Oxford: Clarendon Press.

—— (1994). *Perception*. London: Routledge.

Searle, J. (1983). *Intentionality*. Cambridge: Cambridge University Press.

Sellars, Wilfrid (1968). *Science and Metaphysics*, ed. T. Honderich, International Library of Philosophy and Scientific Methodology. London: Routledge & Kegan Paul.

Snowdon, P. F. (1980–1). 'Perception, Vision and Causation'. *Proceedings of the Aristotelian Society*, 81: 175–92.

—— (1990). 'The Objects of Perceptual Experience'. *Proceedings of the Aristotelian Society*, suppl. vol., 64: 121–50.

Strawson, P. F. (1979). 'Perception and its Objects', in G. Macdonald (ed.), *Perception and Identity*. London: Macmillan.

Tehovnik *et al.* (2005). 'Phosphene Induction and the Generation of Saccadic Eye Movements by Striate Cortex'. *Journal of Neurophysiology*, 93: 1–19.

Travis, Charles (2001). *Unshadowed Thought*. Cambridge, Mass.: Harvard University Press.

—— (2004). 'Silence of the Senses'. *Mind*, 113/449: 57–94.

Tye, M. (1984). 'The Adverbial Approach to Visual Experience'. *Philosophical Review*, 93: 195–225.

—— (1992). 'Visual Qualia and Visual Content', in T. Crane (ed.), *The Contents of Experience*. Cambridge: Cambridge University Press.

Valberg, J. J. (1992). *The Puzzle of Experience*. Oxford: Clarendon Press.

Wiggins, David (1980). *Sameness and Substance*. Oxford: Blackwell.

—— (1996). 'Substance', in A. C. Grayling (ed.), *Philosophy: A Guide through the Subject*. Oxford: Oxford University Press.

Williams, Bernard (1978). *Descartes: The Project of Pure Enquiry*. Harmondsworth: Penguin.

Williamson, Timothy (1990). *Identity and Discrimination*. Cambridge, Mass.: Blackwell.

—— (2000). *Knowledge and its Limits*. New York: Oxford University Press.

CHAPTER 25

THE A PRIORI

CHRISTOPHER PEACOCKE

1. INTRODUCTION

The existence and nature of the a priori are defining issues for philosophy. A philosopher's attitude to the a priori is a touchstone for his whole approach to the subject. Sometimes, as in Kant's critical philosophy, or in Quine's epistemology, a major new position emerges from reflection on questions that explicitly involve the notions of the a priori or the empirical. But even when no explicit use is made of the notion of the a priori in the questions addressed, a philosopher's methodology, the range of considerations to which the philosopher is open, his conception of the goals of the subject, his idea of what is involved in justification—all of these cannot fail to involve commitments about the nature and the existence of the a priori. So understanding the a priori is not only of interest in itself. It is also essential for self-understanding, if we are to understand ourselves as philosophers.

More specifically, issues about the a priori lie at the intersection of the theory of justification and the theory of meaning, or the theory of intentional content. Whatever the truths about the existence and nature of the a priori, they should in one way or another be explained by the theory of justification and the theory of content.

I distinguish five general questions about the a priori which must be addressed if we are to reach a sufficiently general and deep understanding of the notion:

1. How is the concept of the a priori to be characterized? What is the correct form to be taken by any true statements about what is a priori?
2. What is the scope or extent of the a priori?

3. What is the source of a priori status?
4. The existence of the a priori has been regarded as incompatible with some compulsory kind of naturalism. Is this so, and are naturalistically motivated surrogates for the a priori adequate?
5. What is the philosophical significance of the a priori, and what further philosophical tasks does it pose?

I will advocate specific answers to each of these questions. So this will not be a neutral discussion. Nor will it be a discussion of the history of thought about the a priori, a rich topic which merits independent discussion (see Coffa 1991; and for a historical discussion bearing on the relations between Frege and Kant, see Burge 2000). But I will try to outline some competing current theories of the a priori, and to do so in ways that are relevant to those who wish to pursue the history further.

2. Characterizing the A Priori

There is a diverse and structured family of notions of the a priori. This necessitates a certain amount of stage-setting in order to formulate the fundamental issues.

One core notion of an outright a priori belief is this: it is a belief for which the thinker's operative justification or entitlement is independent of the content or kind of any of his particular perceptual experiences. Derivatively, we can also speak of a justification or entitlement as being outright a priori, and of a content or proposition as being outright a priori. A thinker's justification or entitlement in forming a particular belief is a priori if it is independent of the content or kind of any of the thinker's particular perceptual experiences. A content or proposition is a priori if it can be known in virtue of a thinker's having an a priori justification or entitlement for it.

A thinker's belief in a generalization like "All bodies are extended" (Kant's example) or the logical principle "If A and B, then A" are paradigmatic cases of the a priori. The belief "That book has a red cover", based on visual perception of the book's cover as red, is paradigmatically a posteriori. This distinction is, however, only one of several in which one may have a legitimate theoretical interest. Diverse theoretical interests have quite properly motivated different theorists to generalize or precisify the characterization of the a priori in different directions.

One distinction of theoretical interest is the difference between perceptual experience and other mental states. If that is the distinction of interest to a theorist, then the fact that a thinker's operative justification or entitlement for a belief is the content or kind of some conscious state other than perceptual experience will certainly not prevent the theorist from classifying that belief as a priori. This was precisely Kant's position on arithmetic. Kant held both that arithmetic is a priori, and that our knowledge of it relies on our faculty of intuition, which, according to Kant, we employ in ordinary arithmetical calculation. Kant (1997: B15–16) said that this is how he reaches the judgement "$7 + 5 = 12$":

For I take first the number 7, and, as I take the fingers of my hand as an intuition for assistance with the concept of 5, to that image of mine I now add the units that I have previously taken together in order to constitute the number 5 one after another to the number 7, and thus see the number 12 arise.

So Kant was interested in the property of having a non-perceptual justification, even if this justification involves other conscious states. He was interested, we may say, in the property of being a priori in the non-perceptual sense. Kant also held that we could never derive the necessity of arithmetical propositions—nor the necessity of a priori propositions more generally—from experience. We will return later on to assess this view.

When one judges that one is in pain because one is experiencing the pain, or that one is in an enthusiastic mood because one is, consciously, in an enthusiastic mood, these are not judgements whose operative justification or entitlement depends on the content or kind of one's perceptual experiences. Yet there is an equally legitimate and different notion of the a priori on which they would not be classified as a priori. This is the notion one would use when one's concern is not with the distinction between perceptual experiences and everything else, but rather with a second distinction: the distinction between all conscious states, and everything else. The salient notion of the a priori under which such judgements as "I am in pain" and "I am in an enthusiastic mood" are not a priori is one under which we generalize from perceptual experience to all conscious states in the original paradigm. Under this more broadly characterized notion, a belief is outright a priori if the thinker's justification or entitlement for it is independent of the content or kind of any of his conscious states. I will call this "being a priori in the broad sense".

A third distinction that may exercise a theorist is the boundary between that which is justified by a specific, particular perceptual experience, and that which is justified by perceptual experience in general. Our belief that our perceptions have spatial representational content is not dependent upon any one perceptual experience, but is supported by all our experiences. One could equally introduce a variant of the a priori to mark this distinction. Truths captured with that variant would equally be a legitimate object of investigation and explanation. In this third case, we can speak of being a priori in the non-specific sense.

The fact that a belief is a priori in the non-perceptual sense, or in the broad sense, does not mean that it is of a kind about which the thinker cannot be mistaken. We make arithmetical and logical mistakes. Similarly and correlatively, an a priori belief need not be certain. Nor need an a priori content be true purely in virtue of content, nor a sentence expressing it be true purely in virtue of meaning.

I will below outline a theory which acknowledges a wide range of a priori truths, but on which they are true in virtue of their standard disquoted truth conditions, just like any other truth. (For critical discussions of the idea of truth purely in virtue of meaning, from opponents of the a priori, see above all Quine 1976b, and the particularly formidable 1976a, and for a more recent discussion, Harman 1996. For more recent critical discussion of the idea of truth purely in virtue of meaning from friends of the a priori, see Peacocke 1993, Boghossian 1996, and BonJour 1998.)

What of the relation of a priori status to necessity? Saul Kripke (1980) and David Kaplan (1989), and others following in their wake, gave convincing examples of the two-way independence of the a priori and metaphysical necessity. Belief in all of the following contents can be a priori, even though the contents are not metaphysically necessary: "If I exist, and I am located somewhere, I am here", "If something is uniquely F, then the actual F is F", "If p, then Actually p". In the other direction, the following are metaphysically necessary, but cannot be known a priori: "Water contains hydrogen", "Tully is Cicero".

Does this two-way independence completely undermine Kant's idea that there is a link between the a priori and necessity, and that the necessity of something cannot be known from perceptual experience? The above examples are indisputable, and Kant's formulations are indeed overly general. Nonetheless, the spirit of Kant's idea survives in at least three respects. First, nothing in these examples establishes that necessity can be learned from perceptual experience. Experience is necessary to establish that Tully is Cicero. To move from that identity to the necessity, however, we need the principle of the necessity of identity. That principle is a priori, and is not learned from perceptual experience.

The second respect in which Kant's idea survives is that it is arguable that the source of metaphysical necessity is always fundamentally a priori. There are theories of the truth conditions of modal statements according to which necessity is a matter of being true under all assignments which meet certain constraints on possibility, the so-called "Principles of Possibility" (Peacocke 1999, ch. 4). These Principles of Possibility include, for instance, the requirement that any genuine possibility involving a concept must respect the same rules for assigning semantic values to concepts as govern that concept's semantic value in the actual world. These fundamental Principles of Possibility all seem to have an a priori status. The a posteriori necessities seem always to result from taking some fundamentally a priori necessity, like the necessity of identity, and then inferring from it, together with empirical but non-modal information ("Tully is Cicero"), some modal proposition. We do not seem to find cases of the necessary a posteriori that cannot be explained in this fashion.

A third source of support for the Kantian idea is that there is a variety of necessity which is much more closely connected with many cases of the a priori than is metaphysical necessity. This more closely connected variety is the property of a content of holding in the actual world, whichever world is labelled as the actual world. In the helpful terminology of Davies and Humberstone (1980), this is the property of holding "Fixedly Actually". "Actually p" holds at a world in a model just in case p holds in the actual world of that model. "Fixedly p" holds at a world in a model just in case it holds at that world in any variant of that model which differs only in which world is labelled as the actual world. So "Fixedly Actually p" holds at a world in a model just in case p holds at the actual world of any variant of that model which differs only in which world is labelled as the actual world. The results of prefixing the propositions "The actual F is F" and "If p then Actually p" with the operators 'Fixedly Actually' are true, even though the propositions so prefixed are not metaphysically necessary. None of the Kripke–Kaplan style examples cited above is a counter-example to the claim that what is a priori is Fixedly Actually true. We can then formulate the claim, still Kantian in spirit, that perceptual experience alone cannot tell one that a proposition is true in the actual world whichever world is actual. This reformulated Kantian claim is highly plausible.

When a belief is reached in a way that is both a priori, and guarantees that what is known is true in the actual world, whichever world is labelled as the actual world, let us say that the belief is *contentually* a priori (Peacocke 2004b). Within the general class of a priori beliefs, we can draw a further intuitive distinction. This is the distinction between those a priori beliefs which are true in part because the thinker is making a certain judgement, and those whose truth is independent of whether the thinker is making the judgement.

Consider the judgement "I am thinking", or "I hereby judge that London is larger than Paris". In both cases, the judgements can be a priori in the non-perceptual sense. They can also be a priori in the broad sense. The judgements can be made not as reports on the contents of the thinker's current stream of consciousness, but can be made by a thinker whose grasp of the concepts involved allows him to appreciate that his making the judgements ensures their truth. These beliefs "I am thinking" and "I hereby judge that London is larger than Paris" are not, however, true in the actual world whichever world is labelled as the actual world. The world labelled as actual might have been one in which the thinker never existed, or is not thinking at the time in question, or is not making that judgement about London and Paris. That is, these beliefs "I am thinking" and "I hereby judge that London is larger than Paris" are not contentually a priori. They may be regarded as *judgementally* a priori, in the sense that they come to be made in an a priori way, and will be true in any world in which they come to be made in that way. But this is a much weaker property than being contentually a priori.

The phenomenon of the contentually a priori poses much more of a theoretical challenge than the judgementally a priori. The explanation of the judgementally a priori status of "I am thinking" is not hard to seek. A judgement with this content is self-verifying, and is establishably so given the nature of the concepts involved. The general phenomenon of the contentually a priori certainly does not have that explanation, and its range far outstrips such relatively unproblematic examples as "The actual F is F", or "If p then Actually p". Even logic, mathematics, and the abstract sciences, let alone the wider range of examples we will consider in the next section, cannot be explained in the way in which we would account for the merely judgementally a priori.

The contentually a priori status of propositions in a given domain also strongly constrains an acceptable metaphysics for that domain. Here I signal just one such issue. If a known truth p about some given domain is contentually a priori, it seems that the property of truth in that domain could not be a mind-dependent matter, or at least not dependent upon any contingent propositions about minds. If there is some world in which those propositions about minds fail to hold, then if that world were actual, p would not hold there either. Hence knowledge of p could not be contentually a priori after all. This simple reasoning identifies just one of several points at which the significance of the a priori is not only epistemological, but metaphysical too (Peacocke 2001a, 2004c).

There are two last pieces of stage-setting before we turn to more substantive issues about the a priori. All of the above distinctions concern the outright a priori. There is also an important, and often neglected, relative notion. We can ask whether, given that a thinker is in a certain state S, he is justified or entitled in judging that p without any further reliance on the content or kind of his perceptual states beyond those included in S. The justification or entitlement in question need not be conclusive. When this condition on S and p is met, we can say that p is relatively a priori, given that the thinker is in state S. In an alternative terminology, we say that the transition from S to p is a priori. To illustrate: it might be argued that the transition to the perceptual-demonstrative content "That shape is square" from a perceptual state which represents that shape as square is an a priori transition. In the relativized terminology, that content is relatively a priori, given the thinker is in that perceptual state. Similarly it may be argued that "I am in pain" is relatively a priori given that the thinker consciously experiences pain. Neither of these contents is outright a priori in the broad sense; and the first is not outright a priori in the non-perceptual sense. It is, evidently, the notion of the relatively a priori, rather than the outright a priori, on which we need to focus when we are considering the epistemic status of transitions in thought from perception and other non-judgemental informational states to judgements.

Since relative a priori justification or entitlement need not be conclusive, we can take this as its canonical form:

> State S a priori justifies or entitles the thinker in judging that p, in the absence of specific reasons for doubt.

Specific reasons for doubt would be evidence which suggests that one of the conditions holds under which being in S is not sufficient for it to be the case that p. Use of this canonical form leaves open substantive questions of whether its true instances are derivative from some other kind of conclusive entitlement, or whether they are themselves fundamental. The form itself can be used by both parties to that discussion. In a longer treatment, we could modify the form to taken account of degrees of belief and a priori principles governing them.

3. The Scope of the A Priori

The range of propositions that are a priori is vast and varied. Even if we confine our attention to the outright a priori, the range of the a priori seems plausibly to include all of the following:

- The axioms and principles of logic, of mathematics, and of the other abstract sciences, such as set theory and category theory, are all plausibly a priori; as are
- the axioms of probability theory;
- the axioms of confirmation theory; and
- the principles of rational decision theory.
- The most fundamental principles of metaphysical necessity do not seem to be empirical.
- There are, famously, many a priori principles about the properties of colours: that no shade is both a shade of red and a shade of green; that orange is closer to yellow than it is to blue; and so forth.
- There seems to be a class of moral principles that do not require empirical evidence, but are a priori. This class seems to contain the principle that every conscious being has a prima facie equal moral claim; that causing avoidable suffering is wrong; that just institutions are, prima facie, better than unjust institutions. It is arguable that every true moral principle either is, or depends in part upon, some such a priori moral claims.
- Much of economics seems to have an a priori status. The proposition that an economy satisfying the specified conditions in some economic model will also display various other properties is frequently derived in a purely a priori way.
- Many true propositions of philosophy are apparently a priori, including apparently principles about the nature of particular concepts, objects, kinds, properties, and relations.

This list just scratches the surface.

The range and diversity of true a priori propositions places demands on any general explanation of the a priori. If any such explanation is possible, it must be sufficiently general to cover this range, and it has also to be sufficiently flexible to be capable of adaptation to the distinctive features of each of these many special kinds of case.

It is often clear that a proposition is a priori, while the nature of the justification or entitlement for belief in the proposition remains unclear. When this combination obtains, it is a task for a philosophical theorist of the a priori to explain what the justification or entitlement is. The task exists even for the a priori propositions of (relatively) clearly understood domains, such as that of logical and arithmetical knowledge. The model of derivation of a priori conclusions by a priori means from a priori axioms is a satisfying model for many examples. It is in the nature of the case, however, that this model cannot be applied to the primitive axioms themselves, nor to the primitive means of derivation. The question of how these are known a priori remains a lively subject of debate. The nature of the entitlement or justification is equally an issue for the striking phenomenon, which rightly so interested Gödel (1995a), of a thinker's ability to come to appreciate, by a priori reflection upon a given domain, new axioms which do not follow from those the thinker accepted hitherto. Indeed the axioms we currently accept will in many cases once have been new axioms, when a form of thought was already in use before its explicit axiomatization. The identification of the full nature of the entitlement that sustains a priori knowledge, as opposed to its existence, is an open question in almost all the domains mentioned above.

The means by which we come to know outright a priori propositions in the above domains may involve any or all of the following: conversations and discussion with others; reading books which archive knowledge achieved many generations ago; our own workings-out on paper; musings and reflection on examples; computer simulations and computer proofs; and much else. Many in this array of methods involve perception at some stage or other. Does this fact undermine the status of knowledge so reached as a priori?

It does not. There is a distinction between what gives us access to the entitling conditions for a priori knowledge, and the entitling conditions themselves. Possession of what the thinker knows to be a proof (a tree-structure of contents) provides an a priori entitlement to accept a logical or an arithmetical proposition. Inscriptions, conversations, rough workings-out on paper may all help a thinker to appreciate that there is such a proof, and what it is. But these perception-involving activities merely facilitate: they are not the entitlement itself. Of two thinkers, one may discover a proof of a given proposition in his head, and the other may have to work it out on paper. The two thinkers may nevertheless have the same justification for their common conclusion. Only their modes of access to that justification differ. Respect for the distinction between a justification or entitlement on the one hand, and what makes it available on the other, is essential to a proper understanding of the a priori.

The distinction between an entitlement and what makes it available operates at the social level, as well as the level of the individual thinker. In his most recent discussion, after many years' consideration of the notion of the a priori, Philip Kitcher argues for what he calls the "tradition-dependence" of contemporary mathematical knowledge. He holds that this tradition-dependence is incompatible with that knowledge having an a priori status (Kitcher 2000, esp. 80–5; for the views of his earlier self, see his 1980). To say that a piece of knowledge is tradition-dependent is to say that its status as knowledge depends upon the history in the knower's society of such matters as the development and acquisition of various axioms and principles of reasoning, and the reliability of their developers' modes of thought. Whether someone now knows something can depend upon matters of intellectual history prior to his birth. The use of unreliable methods or fallacious reasoning in earlier generations could, Kitcher emphasizes, undermine the status of present beliefs as knowledge.

In my view, the friend of the a priori should agree with the thesis of the tradition-dependence of much mathematical knowledge; but he should also insist that it does not make the notion of the a priori inapplicable. It is an empirical matter which institutions, divisions of labour, and more generally psychologically characterized modes of acquiring, storing, and transmitting information result in beliefs for which an a priori warrant exists. This does not make the notion of an a priori warrant inapplicable. It means only that it is an empirical matter which conditions are conducive to the acquisition and transmission of beliefs for which such warrants exist. It is also an empirical matter which conditions are conducive to the acquisition and transmission of a priori warrants themselves.

Doubts about the applicability of the notion of the a priori can also flow from doubts about the very notion of an a priori warrant or entitlement itself. Philip Kitcher also argues that if we use only a defeasible notion of a priori warrant— what he calls the "Weak" conception—'We would have abandoned the traditional thought that a priori knowledge can prescribe to experience, that when we know something a priori we don't have to be concerned about what future experiences may…bring' (2000: 77). Only an indefeasible conception of a priori entitlement will capture that function of the notion of the a priori (ibid.); the Weak conception 'abandons parts of the idea that a priori knowledge is independent of experience' (ibid.). This argument, which also influenced Kitcher's earlier writings on the subject, may seem compelling. Absolutely indefeasible entitlement is simply not to be had. There can always be some evidence that would rationally make us think we had made a mistake in believing something to be a proof. To have indefeasible grounds we would have to be infallible, and indeed to have conclusive grounds that we are so. So it may seem that in accepting there are a priori entitlements, we are committed either to something that is too strong, or that is too weak to be a philosophically interesting notion of the a priori. If Kitcher is right, we are committed either to infallibility, or else merely to defeasible entitlement that, he says, involves an empirical element.

The friend of the a priori should dispute both halves of this dilemma. The first step in doing so is to distinguish two kinds of defeasibility, which I will call *defeasibility of identification* and *defeasibility of grounds*. A ground for accepting a proposition can be conclusive even though our entitlement to believe that we have identified such a ground is defeasible. Identifying something as a conclusive ground is one thing; its being a conclusive ground is another. My confidence that something is a proof can be rationally undermined by the report of mathematicians whose competence I have reason to believe far outstrips my own. Nonetheless, a proof is a conclusive ground. Here we have defeasibility in respect of identification, but not defeasibility in respect of grounds.

By contrast, inductive evidence for a generalization, even evidence drawn from an extensive range of a wide variety of kinds of instance, is never conclusive. In this case we have defeasibility of grounds. If the generalization does not hold, that does not show that the inductive evidence did not hold. The corresponding conditional for proofs would not be true. If the last line of a sequence of propositions is false, it cannot be a sound proof.

With this distinction in mind, we can return to the claim that only indefeasible entitlements can capture a traditional notion of independence from experience, or can "prescribe to experience". Consider the case in which we have a genuine proof, but in which (as is arguably always so) we have defeasibility of identification. It is always possible that some mathematician tells us, mistakenly, that what we have is not a proof. It would then in those circumstances be reasonable for us to accept his word, and not believe that it is a proof. But how does this show that as things actually are we have not properly and knowledgeably identified the proof as a proof? It seems it does not; and if we have properly identified it as a proof, the proof itself provides an experience-independent derivation that its conclusion holds. Once again, we have to distinguish the nature of the entitlement from the question of what may be involved in identifying it as an entitlement. A notion of a priori warrant that displays defeasibility of identification need not import an empirical element into the entitlement for propositions that it counts as a priori.

What of defeasible a priori entitlements? Are they drained of philosophical interest on this approach? In my judgement, the relatively a priori character of some defeasible experience-based warrants is essential to a transition in thought being rational at all. If the supporter of the defeasible a priori is pressed by Kitcher for an explanation of the philosophical significance of these cases, his answer should be as follows. Defeasible entitlement is a notion that must be instantiated if rational thought is to get started at all. Not all warrants can be empirical, on pain of regress. Acceptance of this point does not involve a commitment to infallibility, certainty, or indefeasibility. Kitcher himself (2000: 74) favours a purely reliabilist epistemology, and would find some place for defeasible a priori warrants in that reliabilist framework. By contrast, examples in the literature on epistemology seem to me to establish that pure reliability cannot capture the rationality required for a warrant or entitlement relation (BonJour 1985).

Kitcher was not the only one to argue that any philosophically significant notion of the a priori is not instantiated. One of the most-discussed and influential arguments of twentieth-century philosophy aimed to establish that nothing is a priori (or, in later versions, virtually nothing of philosophical substance). This was the argument of Quine's paper 'Two Dogmas of Empiricism' (1961). His argument started from the premiss that the meaning of a sentence, in so far as the notion is explicable at all, is to be characterized in terms of what would be evidence for the sentence's being correct. But, Quine continued, evidential conditions cannot in fact be associated with sentences one by one. Any piece of evidence is evidence for a given sentence only in the presence of various background conditions. Evidential conditions can be associated only with large classes of sentences. Almost any sentence can be rejected under some background conditions or other. The Quinean conclusion was that almost nothing is a priori.

At first glance, it may seem that Quine was targeting a rather narrow position, one that hardly exists today as a live philosophical position. He himself characterized the second dogma under attack in his famous paper as 'the belief that each meaningful statement is equivalent to some logical construct upon terms which refer to immediate experience' (p. 20). Virtually no one today has that reductionist, phenomenalist belief. But if Quine's argument is sound, it works against a much wider range of positions than that of reductionism. If his argument is sound, it shows that any evidential theory of meaning—whatever notion of evidence it uses—implies that there is no possibility for a widely applicable and theoretically interesting notion of the a priori. Many current theorists of meaning would agree that evidential relations have some part to play in the explication of the meaning of certain sentences, even though they are not believers in a reductive phenomenalism. So Quine's argument still presents a pressing challenge.

Only evidential theories of meaning received a serious consideration in 'Two Dogmas'. From 'Two Dogmas' through to his writings in the 1970s, Quine always held that any explication of meaning or content, in so far as it is possible at all, had to be given in terms of evidential relations (for a statement a quarter-century after 'Two Dogmas', see 1974: 38). But can meaning be exhaustively explained in terms of evidence, and is evidence always relevant to meaning?

We can identify three problems for evidential treatments of meaning. These problems can be formulated even before we turn to issues about the possibility of evidence-transcendent truth, which is also a challenge for evidential theories of meaning.

(i) The first problem is that of the informativeness of evidential relations. Understanding, even full understanding, of a sentence seems sometimes to precede any knowledge of what would be evidence for its truth. At a humble level, I have to work out, and work out from my understanding, and from my other background knowledge, what would be evidence that, say, my son has a French class this afternoon. At a more elevated level, it may be a great intellectual achievement to work out what would be evidence for the hypothesis that there is a new kind of fundamental particle with certain properties. The hypothesis may be understood decades before anyone works out what would be evidence for it. Superstring theory in physics provides another example.

(ii) The second problem concerns the source of evidential relations. In cases in which the evidence for a sentence has to be worked out, and is not primitively written into the identity of its meaning, it seems that meaning must be what the evidence is worked out *from*, rather than consisting in the evidential relations themselves. There is a special problem here for the view that evidential relations are associated only with large sets of sentences. There are infinitely many such large sets. How do our finite minds grasp this association of evidential relations with the infinitely many sets of sentences? We must do so by tacitly using some finite basis. Could the finite basis be the individual word meanings in the sentences making up the sets? That certainly seems incompatible with the Quinean thesis that sentences do not have meanings considered one by one. Yet it is very hard to see what else the finite basis could possibly be.

(iii) The third problem is one of insufficiency, combined with a threat of parasitism on non-evidential accounts. Consider a most basic case, a content in which an observational concept is predicated in the present tense of some object given in a thinker's perception, a perception which represents that object as falling under that concept (or under a suitable corresponding non-conceptual content). Certainly it is part of grasping that whole intentional content that the thinker appreciates that such a perception gives reason for accepting the content. But grasping the content, and understanding a sentence which expresses it, also involves importantly more. The content is an objective one, in the sense that it could have been true without the thinker, or anyone else, perceiving that it is true. How could this feature of the understanding be captured evidentially? Of course one could mention evidence that the condition holds unperceived. But how are we to think of such evidence? What such evidence of unperceived instantiation would be is itself very much an empirical matter, and not something extractable from understanding alone. If the evidence for unperceived instantiation is characterized as evidence that the object in question has, unperceived, the same property required for the intentional content's truth when the content is perceived to hold, that is indeed much more plausibly involved in understanding. But that account then involves the notions of truth and reference in understanding, and is far from being a purely evidential account.

These three problems (i)–(iii) give grounds for thinking that purely evidential theories of meaning or content cannot succeed. Any argument for the non-existence of the a priori which starts from a purely evidential theory of meaning is starting from a false premiss.

4. THE SOURCE OF THE A PRIORI

Understanding-based views of the a priori hold that it is the nature of understanding that makes available ways of knowing which are a priori. The initial, pre-theoretical attraction of understanding-based views lies simply in the fact that when we consider examples of a priori contents, grasp of those contents, and whatever is involved in that grasp, seem sufficient to permit a priori knowledge of those contents. Sometimes a priori knowledge is hard to attain. Attaining it may require deep reflection on concepts in the proposition known. But deeper reflection, when successful, seems always to involve deeper understanding, rather than anything extraneous to understanding. This fact about deeper reflection enhances the intuitive support for understanding-based views of the a priori. An understanding-based view of the a priori is an important strand in rationalist thought, running through Leibniz (1981), Frege (1953), and Gödel (1995a) to such present-day rationalists as BonJour (1998).

To understand an expression, completely or partially, is to know its meaning, completely or partially. So the task of explaining the a priori in terms of understanding is part of the more general task of elucidating the relations between the theory of meaning and the theory of knowledge. On the understanding-based view, the fact that a way of coming to know that p is an a priori way is something to be explained by the nature of the concepts comprising p and their mode of combination. The most satisfying forms of understanding-based views of the a priori will treat a priori entitlement as a special or limiting case of some more general species of meaning-based entitlement. This more general species will include both experience-dependent and experience-independent entitlement. Just as it is intuitive that understanding makes available some a priori ways of coming to know propositions, so it is equally intuitive that in some cases, understanding is sufficient to allow a thinker to appreciate that certain experiential evidence bears on the understood hypothesis (even if, as we have seen in discussion of Quine, such appreciation does not exhaust the understanding of the hypothesis).

An understanding-based theory might be quite minimal. That is, one variety of understanding-based theorist would hold that it is primitively written into the identity of a concept that certain ways of coming to know given contents containing those concepts are a priori ways. This minimalism seems to be available only to those who do not think that any substantive theory of meaning or intentional content is possible. If any substantive theory of meaning or intentional content is possible, then on the understanding-based view, we have to explain the fact that a way of coming to know has an a priori status from features of that content cited in the fundamental theory of meaning or content. If content is a matter of pure conceptual role, then the a priori character of a given way of coming to know must be explained in terms of pure conceptual roles. If content is substantively a matter of contributions to truth conditions, the a priori character of a way of coming to know a content must be explained in terms of the content's truth conditions; and so on. Understanding-based views that reject minimalism are views that have a commitment to the possibility of such explanations.

Here I will be presupposing a substantive theory of intentional content that elucidates content in the first instance in terms of truth conditions. Pure conceptual-role theories have difficulties in explaining which roles determine meanings or genuine concepts. They have difficulties in explaining verification-transcendent truth. In my view (2002), they also have difficulties in explaining the aim of judgement without invoking substantive notions of truth and reference. I will not argue these points here. Readers tempted by pure conceptual-role theories can consider ways—where such exist—in which the arguments below can be adapted to theories that are not truth-conditional. Curiously, Quine's view as described above is an understanding-based view, one based on a substantive evidential conception of meaning. His thesis was simply that not very much of interest is a priori given what that would have to involve on his understanding-based conception thereof.

On the particular points on which I criticized a Quinean evidential conception of meaning, a truth-conditional approach seems to do much better. The truth conditions of a complete sentence are determined by the contribution to truth conditions made by the sentence's constituents and their mode of combination. The truth-conditional approach is intrinsically componential. It has a finite basis lacking in evidential approaches that associate evidence only with large classes of sentences. In short, the truth-conditional approach avoids the problems of a non-finite basis that I summarized under the heading "the source of evidential relations".

In many of the examples I gave of understanding without knowledge of evidential conditions, a truth-conditional theorist will, in explaining understanding, likely appeal to grasp of an identity relation. We are capable of thinking of new particles of a size smaller than anything hitherto detected because we have the conception of them as things of the same general kind (matter, with its causal powers) as things already known about, and as having spatial properties whose instantiation is known in other cases. The truth-conditional theorist certainly has to give some account of what this understanding consists in, and it will have to be a non-evidential account. Some limited progress has been made in this direction (see Peacocke 1999, ch. 3). Though there is much in the general style of approach that remains to be worked out, it seems to me that this classical truth-conditional approach is much the most promising extant treatment of understanding.

How then can a truth-conditional approach explain why certain ways of coming to know a content are a priori? Any fully developed truth-conditional theory must be accompanied by an account of what it is to possess the concepts whose contributions to truth conditions are given in the truth-conditional theory. Without prejudging anything as to its correct form, I will here use the phrase "possession condition" for a true statement of what it is, fundamentally, to possess a given concept. The theory of possession conditions is the crucial resource on which truth-conditional theories need to draw in explaining why certain ways of coming to know are a priori ways.

There also has to be a theory connecting the account of possession conditions for concepts with the determination of the semantic values for those concepts. If sense together with the way the world is determines reference (perhaps relative to certain parameters), and possession conditions individuate senses, possession conditions together with the way the world is must equally determine reference (relative to any parameters involved). It was this theory connecting possession conditions and semantic values that I labelled "Determination Theory" in *A Study of Concepts* (1992).

The task for the truth-conditional theorist is then to use the above resources to coordinate and properly interrelate three apparently diverse things:

> a way of coming to know that *p*;
> the possession conditions for the concepts in *p*; and
> the truth-value of the content *p*.

The task is to do this in a way that explains the distinctive characteristics of the a priori we have already identified.

The core idea of one approach to the a priori coordinates these three elements in the following two claims.

(a) An outright, non-defeasible, way of coming to know *p* is an a priori way if the possession conditions for the concepts in *p*, together with the Determination Theory, jointly guarantee that use of that way leads to a true belief about whether *p* is the case. Similarly, a transition from one set of contents to a given content is an a priori transition if the possession conditions for the contents involved, together with the Determination Theory, jointly guarantee that the transition is truth-preserving.

(b) A content *p* is outright a priori if the possession conditions for the concepts comprising *p*, together with the Determination Theory, jointly guarantee the truth of *p*.

The claims (a) and (b) constitute the *metasemantic* theory of the a priori (this was the name I gave to the theory when proposing it in Peacocke 1993). To illustrate with the most trivial case, consider the possession condition for the concept of conjunction. On any theory, this possession condition will entail that thinkers must find the transition from A & B to A compelling, and must do so without relying on any background information. A plausible Determination Theory will entail that semantic values are assigned to concepts in such a way as to make truth-preserving any transitions which, according to the possession conditions for a concept, must be found compelling without further information. It is thus a consequence of the possession condition for conjunction, together with the Determination Theory, that when A & B is true, A is true. That, according to the metasemantic theory, is why the transition is a priori.

More generally, the metasemantic theory holds that at each line of a valid proof of an a priori proposition, the transition involved is one whose truth-preserving character follows from the possession conditions for the concepts involved together with the Determination Theory for those concepts.

How does the metasemantic theory explain why the use of a priori ways generates not merely true beliefs, but knowledge? The theory of possession conditions and the Determination Theory for the concepts comprising a given content p give an account of what has to be the case for the content p to be true. The semantic values fixed by the Determination Theory and the world must, when combined to fix a truth-value in the way determined by the structure of the content p, determine the truth-value True or the truth-value False. The conditions under which they determine that the truth-value True is a fundamental account of what it is, constitutively, for the content p to be true. According to the metasemantic theory, in using an a priori way of coming to judge that p, a thinker is using a method which guarantees, as a result of the very nature of p and the way in which its truth-condition is determined, that the thinker judges that p only if it is the case that p. When the soundness of a method is thus internally related to what it is for the content to be true, it is hard to see what more could be required for knowledge. Such a constitutive grounding of the soundness of the method goes far beyond merely reliabilist conditions for knowledge.

In providing this connection with knowledge, the metasemantic theory also meets the condition noted earlier, that the account of why a way or method is a priori should be a consequence of some more general thesis relating knowledge and understanding. I just gave an argument aiming to explain why ways whose soundness is underwritten by the possession conditions and the Determination Theory will yield knowledge. The same applies equally in empirical cases. Take a case in which a thinker applies an observational concept to a perceptually given object, in accordance with the possession condition for that observational concept. That is, the thinker's application of the concept to the object is an exercise of exactly that sensitivity to perceptual experience mentioned in the possession condition for the concept. The natural Determination Theory for an observational concept C implies this: the semantic value of C maps any object x to the True if x has the property required for veridicality of a perceptual experience of x of the sort mentioned in C's possession condition. If the thinker is indeed perceiving properly, that fact together with the natural Determination Theory for observational concepts will imply that in such a case the semantic value of the observational concept will map the perceived object to the truth-value True. The truth of the thinker's judgement in this empirical case, when made in accordance with the possession condition for the concept, is equally a consequence of an account of what it is for the content in question to be true. Again, the relation between the way of coming to judge and the account of what it is for the content to be true is so close that this is enough for knowledge. Once again, the relation goes far beyond reliability.

We noted that outright a priori ways of coming to know that p seem to be ways that ensure that p is true in the actual world, whichever is the actual world: that is, we have Fixedly Actually p. The metasemantic account can also explain this apparent datum. Possession conditions hold Fixedly Actually. The statement of the possession condition for a concept specifies what it is to be that concept, and this is something which is invariant under which world is the actual world. The same holds for the principles of Determination Theory. The rule by which the semantic value of a concept depends on the way the world is, and on the nature of the concept's possession condition, does not vary with which world is actual. Logical principles also hold Fixedly Actually.

Now consider the metasemantic theory. In one central kind of case in which a way of coming to know that p is a priori, there is a derivation from the possession conditions and the Determination Theory to the conclusion that the content p reached by use of that way is true. Since the premises of this derivation and its rules of inference all hold Fixedly Actually, it follows that p holds Fixedly Actually. This style of argument can also be carried over to the more general case in which we are concerned with model-theoretic consequence, rather than derivability.

The metasemantic theory does not have any special account of truth for a priori contents. On the contrary, it explains the a priori status of certain contents by considering the consequences of entirely general rules which determine the semantic values of concepts, the rules being exactly the same whether the concept is featuring in an empirical content or in an a priori content. It thus differs from all kinds of conventionalism about a priori contents (or special subsets of them). On the metasemantic account, a single possession condition for each concept, and a uniform Determination Theory, explain the truth conditions and epistemic character of contents of whatever stripe.

In the examples given so far, we have not needed to appeal to mysterious mechanisms connecting thinkers who have a priori knowledge with a third realm of concepts. The metasemantic theory, properly developed, can thus be at the service of a moderate rationalism. The moderate rationalist holds that any case of a priori status can be explained as such by appeal to the nature of the concepts involved in the content known a priori, and without postulating mechanisms connecting thinkers with the third realm (for moderate rationalism in this sense, see Peacocke 2000).

The moderate rationalist who adopts the metasemantic view faces a range of tasks. In any case in which something is known a priori, it ought to be possible to identify the way in which it comes to be known a priori. It ought also to be possible to explain why that way of knowing is a priori on the basis of the possession condition for the concepts that form the content in question. It is precisely because some extreme rationalists have not, on reflection, seen how to do this for certain a priori propositions that they have rejected a merely moderate rationalism. The moderate rationalist does, however, have more extensive resources in defending his position than may be apparent when one thinks only of the simpler and more familiar forms of possession conditions. I indicate two such resources here, each relevant to examples that some have cited against other forms of moderate rationalism.

Not every a priori truth involving a concept follows from the principles that a thinker must find compelling in order to possess the concept. This was the burden of Gödel's (1995a) effective points against Carnap (1937), that we can, on the basis of our understanding, discover new axioms for concepts that do not follow from the principles we have already accepted. The force of this point extends far beyond Carnapian conventionalist theories. The phenomena Gödel identified, concerning as they do the nature of understanding and the phenomenon of new, understanding-based a priori principles, present a challenge to all theories of the a priori. The metasemantic account itself would be unable to explain the phenomenon if the only cases of the a priori it admitted were those that followed from principles whose acceptance by the thinker is already mentioned in the possession conditions for the concepts in question. If that were the case, the metasemantic theorist would have two options. Either he would have to deny the existence of the phenomenon, which would be quite implausible; or he would have to say that not all cases of understanding-based a priori propositions can be captured by appeal to possession conditions, which is to abandon his version of the metasemantic theory.

The correct response to the phenomena is rather to acknowledge the existence of what I call implicit conceptions. In some cases, possessing a concept involves having tacit knowledge of some condition for something to fall under the concept, a condition the thinker may not be able to articulate correctly. Cases of this phenomenon run from the most humble, such as our possession of a condition for something to be a chair (a condition which it is very easy to misarticulate), through understanding of moral and political concepts, which can have a rich, hidden struc- ture, to the early use of mathematical and scientific concepts. That tacit knowledge of one condition rather than another underlies understanding is shown by the thinker's pattern of application of the concept in question. The tacit knowledge of the condition explains that pattern of application. Such implicit conceptions are also capable of explaining the phenomenon of understanding-based a priori knowledge of new principles that do not follow from those previously accepted. Consider an ordinary person's possession of the concept of a whole number. I would say that underlying this person's grasp of the concept is possession of an implicit conception with the content:

> 0 is a whole number;
> the successor of a whole number is a whole number;
> only what is determined to be a whole number on the basis of the preceding two conditions is a whole number.

Now consider the principle that any whole number has only finitely many predecessors. This principle cannot follow from what the ordinary thinker explicitly accepts. What he explicitly accepts has non-standard models, in which some objects within the extension of "whole number" in those models do have infinitely many predecessors. But our ordinary thinker can reflect on his own practice, can think about which things are whole numbers and which are not. By an a priori abduction from cases, he can come to the conclusion that the recursion displayed above, with its limiting clause, fixes what it is to be a whole number. This condition then rules out whole numbers with infinitely many predecessors. Abduction from cases, and thinking of hypotheses that explain the cases, is a creative matter that not everyone who possesses the concept of natural number either can or will engage in; not everyone who has the concept of a whole number needs explicitly to accept that whole numbers do not have infinitely many predecessors. The ordinary thinker who uses the concept of a natural number need not even possess the concept of finiteness or of infinity.

Under this approach using implicit conceptions, we explain the phenomenon of new principles consistently with the metasemantic theory. Unlike Gödel himself, we also remain within the bounds of a moderate rationalism.

The other resource available to the metasemantic theory can be drawn upon in cases in which we are, intuitively, inclined to say that it is because we see the nature of some kind of entity—a set, a colour, a number, a shape—that we appreciate a priori that certain principles about that entity are correct. What, an opponent of moderate rationalism may ask, can this possibly have to do with concepts and understanding? Do we not rather have direct insight into the nature of these entities, an insight that enables us to appreciate a priori that certain principles hold of them? The resourceful metasemantic theorist should agree that there is here a special class of examples of the a priori, but he should say that what distinguishes them is as follows. The conditions which individuate the entity in question (the set, colour, number, shape) actually enter the possession condition for certain canonical concepts of these entities. As one could say, in these cases, the concept is individuated by what individuates the object. The implicit conception detailed above which underlies mastery of the notion of a whole number already exemplifies this phenomenon. The content of that conception specifies what it is to be a whole number. The phenomenon is not restricted to implicit conceptions. There is a way of thinking of the colour green mastery of which involves sensitivity to the rough borders of which shades are shades of green, and which are not, when those shades are actually given in perception to the thinker. From this resource, it is possible to explain why certain principles about the colour green, when so conceived, are a priori. It arguably permits derivation of the principle that no shade is a shade of both red and green, for instance (Peacocke 2000).

If we step back from the data of particular a priori ways and propositions, and ask what more generally we should want of a theory of the a priori, there are two further natural demands. One is that the theory should explain why there should be a priori ways and truths at all. This condition is met by the metasemantic theory. In fact, the metasemantic theory predicts that for any concept at all, there will be a priori principles involving it. This is so because any concept will have some possession condition. By the account given in the metasemantic theory, that possession condition, and the Determination Theory applied to it, will generate some a priori principles, and generate a priori ways of coming to know contents containing that concept. There will be at least one such way for each clause of the possession condition.

The other demand is one which conventionalist theories of the a priori have conspicuously failed. Some properties, considered as subject matter for a philosophical theory, have a distinctive characteristic. It is that any adequate theory of those properties must be self-applicable. For instance, a completely general account of truth must be self-applicable: for we want our account of truth to be true. Similarly, any fully general account of metaphysical necessity should be applicable to itself, if we are trying to provide an account of necessity which is not merely contingent. A theory of the a priori is another case in point. Our philosophical theories of the a priori are not merely empirical. Any theory of the a priori must therefore be applicable to itself, if it is to be acceptable.

Carnapian and other conventionalist approaches do not meet this condition, unless we are prepared to take the extremely unintuitive position that adoption of a philosophical theory is itself a matter of convention, a matter of choice of a framework. On the metasemantic approach, however, the same explanation of the a priori status of philosophical knowledge can be offered as is given for the a priori status of our knowledge of arithmetic, logic, and the rest. The metasemantic theory of the a priori draws upon our understanding of what it is for something to be a concept. To possess the concept of a concept is to have some implicit conception of something individuated by a possession condition. Our philosophical knowledge of the connection between the individuation of a concept and the existence of a priori ways of coming to know certain contents containing that concept results from an a priori abduction from a priori data about concepts. This abduction is not in its general structure and epistemic status any different from a priori abductions that allow us to reach new a priori principles in non-philosophical subject matters.

5.   NATURALISM, THE A PRIORI, AND A SURROGATE NOTION

Is the existence of a priori propositions incompatible with a naturalistic world-view? The impression that there is such an incompatibility is often voiced in the literature by those sympathetic to broadly Quinean ideas. It is, however, surprisingly hard to formulate a credible version of naturalism and a plausible view of the a priori on which there is any incompatibility at all. A neo-Gödelian view that we are in some kind of causal contact with abstract objects, and that this is the source of some of our a priori knowledge, is certainly non-naturalistic. It postulates causal processes which cannot be embedded in our conception of the kinds of things with which minds can interact, which are always things or events in the spatial or temporal realm. But the moderate rationalism I outlined above fully embraces the a priori, and eschews mysterious causal interactions. A reasonable view of the a priori need not be non-naturalistic in the way in which any neo-Gödelian view is non-naturalistic.

Quine, rightly in my view, also objected to Carnap's "internal"–"external" distinction, and insisted in effect that the notion of truth is uniform. Fundamentally the same notion of truth is applied to propositions of mathematics and logic as is applied to empirical sentences. But this doctrine of uniformity is equally endorsed in the metasemantic account of the a priori.

In *Theories and Things* (1981: 21), Quine formulates a broad naturalistic doctrine. He characterizes naturalism as 'the recognition that it is within science itself, and not in some prior philosophy, that reality is to be identified and described'. But it seems to me incoherent to suppose that the empirical ways of knowing employed in reaching empirical theories, including our theory of the layout of the observable world around us, could exhaust the ways of coming to know propositions. Any case of knowledge of an empirical theory exists only because some a priori entitlements also exist. Empirical knowledge is not merely inextricably entwined with the a priori. A better metaphor would be that the a priori provides the girders without which empirical entitlement would collapse.

There are at least three ways in which any empirical theory involves the a priori. First, the methodology which is applied in reaching the theory has a fundamentally a priori status, even if the theory is empirical. The canons of confirmation, of inductive reasoning, and of abduction have an a priori status. Secondly, rational acceptance of any scientific theory rests ultimately upon some persons or other taking perceptual experience and memory at face value. The defeasible entitlement to do so also has an a priori status. Thirdly, almost any theory beyond the rudimentary must include some kind of logic, which also has an a priori status. Though the matter is controversial, in my judgement no one has developed a thorough epistemological and semantical account on which the result of essentially empirical investigation could make it reasonable to revise one's logic. Beyond these three points, there are also more limited but very important respects, identified by Michael Friedman, in which not all elements of a mathematical physics face the tribunal of experience in the same way (Friedman has a series of papers on this theme; see for instance his 2000).

One theorist who is much more explicit about why some naturalists have felt uncomfortable with the a priori is Hartry Field (2000). He identifies empirical indefeasibility as the characteristic they find mysterious. Field presents a radical treatment of the a priori, under which some propositions are said to be "default reasonable", a technical term by which he means that they are reasonably believed without any justification at all (p. 119). According to Field, not all default reasonable propositions are a priori: 'there is no obvious reason why propositions such as "People usually tell the truth" shouldn't count as default reasonable, and it would be odd to count such propositions a priori' (p. 120). Field has a non-factualist account of reasonableness: 'My proposal is that it [reasonableness] is an evaluative property, in a way incompatible with its being straightforwardly factual' (p. 127). '... reasonableness doesn't *consist in* anything: it is not a factual property' (p. 127).

   This approach deserves an extended discussion, but here I will have to confine myself to four comments in favour of a competing position.

   (i) Empirical indefeasibility, the phenomenon Field says is puzzling on a natural-istic world-view, seems to me to be explained by, and made less puzzling by, the metasemantic account. If *p* is guaranteed to be true in the actual world, how-ever the actual world is, by the nature of the concepts in *p*, together with the rules for determining their semantic values and their mode of combination in *p*, then nothing we empirically discover will genuinely refute *p*. (There may always be misleading evidence, of course.) Why should this explanation be thought to be defective? One complaint might be that various rules and axioms, including the possession conditions themselves, are used in the deriva-tion that a certain content is guaranteed to be true. These rules and axioms must themselves be a priori if this explanation is to be fully successful. I agree. The rules of logic and the possession conditions do seem to be themselves a priori. The metasemantic account is intuitively applicable to them too, as we noted. It must be so, if the metasemantic account is to cover all the ground.

   (ii) It seems to me that non-factualism about the reasonableness of choosing one logic rather than another could be sustained only if one were a non-factualist about modality. If one is a factualist about modality, there will be truths about which states of the world are genuinely possible, and which are not. If we are factualists about modality, and if there is a real, and not merely an apparent, problem about indefeasibility, it is not clear to me that the non-factualist account can solve it either. Suppose the selection of one logic rather than another as reasonable is not a factual matter. One theorist, after selecting clas-sical logic, will say that it is a priori that (A→B) v (B→A), and will say that this is guaranteed to be true in the actual world, whichever is the actual world. His intuitionistic colleague will disagree. But if there is fact of the matter of whether it is really possible that the actual world should fail, on empirical investigation, to verify (A→B) v (B→A), it seems very hard to see why the rational choice of logic should not be answerable to this modal fact of the matter. The thoroughgoing non-factualist will say that these remarks simply prove a lemma: non-factualism about the a priori and reasonableness must involve non-factualism about modality. We cannot pursue that here either: here I am just indicating what comes with the territory of non-factualism about reasonableness.

(iii) It is not at all clear that there are default reasonable propositions that are not a priori. In the case of Field's own example—"People normally tell the truth"—I would say that one is default entitled to believe that a rational agent is telling the truth, and that relying on such a default entitlement is rational. But I would also say that it is an a priori entitlement, founded in the nature of rationality and interpretation (Burge 1993). The default entitlement is weaker than the "usually" claim. This parallels other cases of default entitlement. It is not outright a priori that experience is normally veridical; but one is entitled to take (at least the observational content of) experience at face value, in the absence of reasons for doubting it. This too is arguably founded in the nature of the individuation of the content of perceptual states (for some preliminary remarks, see Burge 2003 and Peacocke 2001b, 2004a, 2004b, chs. 2 and 3). I do, however, agree with a conditional which is an implication of Field's position: if one is to defend a factual theory of the a priori, such as the metasemantic theory, one is committed to the possibility of a substantive, though not necessarily reductive, theory of reasonableness and the rationality of methods. A factual theory of the a priori is stable and makes sense only in the context of such a more general account of reason.

6. PHILOSOPHICAL SIGNIFICANCE AND FURTHER TASKS

A philosophical, explanatory account, if such a thing is possible, of the distinction between those ways of coming to know that a priori and those that are not would be of significance in itself. But the significance of an account of the a priori goes beyond that, in raising challenges in areas outside the domain of the a priori considered on its own. I mention in conclusion three such challenges.

(a) If we become convinced that true propositions in a given domain are contentually a priori—say, in the case of morality, or confirmation theory—that will have large effects on our metaphysics and epistemology of that domain. In the case of moral thought, for instance, if true moral propositions are contentually a priori, that is extremely difficult to reconcile with mind-dependent approaches to moral truth. We would need to develop a metaphysics, an epistemology, and a theory of understanding for moral propositions that is consistent with this contentually a priori status (see Peacocke 2001*a*, 2004*c*).

(*b*) The above account has not explained how it is possible that there should be a priori defeasible entitlements to rely on certain informational states, most notably perceptual states. Why are there such entitlements, and what do they have to do with understanding and truth? Can they be accommodated within a natural extension of the metasemantic theory, and if so, how? This is a fundamental issue that needs to be addressed head-on.

(*c*) When we think of truth as a constitutive aim of judgement, and see the rationality of so many transitions in thought as founded in their a priori status, it is natural to conjecture that all instances of the entitlement relation are fundamentally a priori. This conjecture would in effect say that the a priori extends as far as all cases of the normative in epistemology. This too should be a focus of further investigation, both in respect of particular problematic transitions, and in respect of the general principles that would sustain it. Successful defence of the conjecture would, in the context of the metasemantic theory, constitute a case for a generalized rationalism (see also Peacocke 2002, 2004*b*).

References

Boghossian, P. (1996). 'Analyticity Reconsidered'. *Noûs*, 30: 369–91.

BonJour, L. (1985). *The Structure of Empirical Knowledge*. Cambridge, Mass.: Harvard University Press.

——(1998). *In Defense of Pure Reason*. Cambridge: Cambridge University Press.

Burge, T. (1993). 'Content Preservation'. *Philosophical Review*, 102: 457–88.

——(2000). 'Frege on Apriority', in P. Boghossian and C. Peacocke (eds.), *New Essays on the A Priori*. Oxford: Oxford University Press.

——(2003). 'Perceptual Entitlement'. *Philosophy and Phenomenological Research*, 67: 503–48.

Carnap, R. (1937). *Logical Syntax of Language*, trans. A. Smeaton. London: Routledge & Kegan Paul.

Coffa, A. (1991). *The Semantic Tradition from Kant to Carnap*, ed. L. Wessels. Cambridge: Cambridge University Press.

Davies, M., and Humberstone, L. (1980). 'Two Notions of Necessity'. *Philosophical Studies*, 38: 1–30.

Field, Hartry (2000). 'Apriority as an Evaluative Notion', in P. Boghossian and C. Peacocke (eds.), *New Essays on the A Priori*. Oxford: Oxford University Press.

Frege, G. (1953). *The Foundations of Arithmetic*, trans. J. L. Austin. Oxford: Blackwell.

Friedman, Michael (2000). 'Transcendental Philosophy and A Priori Knowledge: A Neo-Kantian Perspective', in P. Boghossian and C. Peacocke (eds.), *New Essays on the A Priori*. Oxford: Oxford University Press.

Gödel, K. (1995*a*). 'Is Mathematics Syntax of Language?', in Gödel (1995*b*).

—— (1995*b*). *Collected Works*, 'iii: *Unpublished Lectures and Essays*, ed. S. Feferman, J. Dawson, Jr., W. Goldfarb, C. Parsons, and R. Solovay, New York: Oxford University Press.

Harman, G. (1996). 'Analyticity Regained?' *Noûs*, 30: 392–400.

Kant, Immanuel (1997). *Critique of Pure Reason*, trans. P. Guyer and A. Wood. Cambridge: Cambridge University Press.

Kaplan, D. (1989). 'Demonstratives', in J. Almog, J. Perry, and H. Wettstein (eds.), *Themes from Kaplan*. New York: Oxford University Press.

Kitcher, P. (1980). 'A Priori Knowledge'. *Philosophical Review*, 89: 3–23.

—— (2000). 'A Priori Knowledge Revisited', in P. Boghossian and C. Peacocke (eds.), *New Essays on the A Priori*. Oxford: Oxford University Press.

Kripke, S. (1980). *Naming and Necessity*. Oxford: Blackwell.

Leibniz, G. (1981). *New Essays on Human Understanding*, trans. P. Remnant and J. Bennett. Cambridge: Cambridge University Press.

Peacocke, C. (1992). *A Study of Concepts*. Cambridge, Mass.: MIT Press.

—— (1993). 'How Are A Priori Truths Possible?' *European Journal of Philosophy*, 1: 175–99.

—— (1999). *Being Known*. Oxford: Oxford University Press.

—— (2000). 'Explaining the A Priori: The Programme of Moderate Rationalism', in P. Boghossian and C. Peacocke (eds.), *New Essays on the A Priori*. Oxford: Oxford University Press.

—— (2001*a*). 'Moralischer Rationalismus. Eine erste Skizze'. *Deutsche Zeitschrift für Philosophie*, 49: 197–208.

—— (2001*b*). 'The Past, Necessity, Externalism and Entitlement'. *Philosophical Books*, 42: 106–17.

—— (2002). 'Three Principles of Rationalism'. *European Journal of Philosophy*, 10: 375–97.

—— (2004*a*). 'Explaining Perceptual Entitlement', in R. Schantz (ed.), *The Externalist Challenge*. Berlin: de Gruyter.

—— (2004*b*). *The Realm of Reason*. Oxford: Oxford University Press.

—— (2004*c*). 'Moral Rationalism'. *Journal of Philosophy*, 101: 499–526.

Quine, W. v. O. (1961). 'Two Dogmas of Empiricism', in Quine, *From a Logical Point of View*. Cambridge, Mass.: Harvard University Press.

—— (1974). *The Roots of Reference*. LaSalle, Ill.: Open Court.

—— (1976*a*). 'Carnap and Logical Truth', in Quine, *The Ways of Paradox and Other Essays*. Cambridge, Mass.: Harvard University Press.

—— (1976*b*). 'Truth by Convention', in Quine, *The Ways of Paradox and Other Essays*. Cambridge, Mass.: Harvard University Press.

—— (1981). *Theories and Things*. Cambridge, Mass.: Harvard University Press.

PART VII

PHILOSOPHY OF THE SCIENCES

CHAPTER 26

SCIENTIFIC REALISM

MICHAEL DEVITT

1. INTRODUCTION

What is scientific realism? The literature provides a bewildering variety of answers. I shall start by addressing this question (Section 2). I shall go on to discuss the most influential arguments for and against scientific realism. The arguments for are the 'success argument' and related explanationist arguments (Section 3). The arguments against are the 'underdetermination argument', which starts from the claim that theories always have empirically equivalent rivals; and the 'pessimistic meta-induction', which starts from a bleak view of the accuracy of past scientific theories (Section 4). My approach is naturalistic.

2. WHAT IS SCIENTIFIC REALISM?

Science appears to be committed to the existence of a variety of unobservable entities—to atoms, viruses, photons, and the like—and to these entities having certain properties. The central idea of scientific realism is that science really is committed and is, for the most part, right in its commitments. As Hilary Putnam once put it, realism takes science at 'face value' (1978: 37). So, for the most part, those scientific entities exist and have those properties. We might call this the 'existence dimension' of realism. It is opposed by those who are sceptical that science is giving us an accurate picture of reality.

Scientific realism is about *un*observable entities. Science appears also to be committed to lots of observable entities—to a variety of plants, molluscs, moons, and the like. Folk theory appears to be committed to observables like stones, trees, and cats. A scepticism that extends to observables is extreme, 'Cartesian', scepticism. It yields the issue of 'realism about the external world'. This issue is both different from and prior to the issue of scientific realism. It addresses doubts about the very clearest cases of knowledge about observables, doubts occasioned by sceptical hypotheses such as that we are manipulated by an evil demon. The issue of scientific realism arises only once such doubts about the observable world have, somehow or other, been allayed. Given the obvious truth of the following weak underdetermination thesis,

> (WU) Any theory has rivals that entail the same actual given observational evidence,

allaying those doubts will involve accepting some method of non-deductive ampliative inference. Not even a theory about observables can be simply deduced from any given body of evidence; indeed, not even the very existence of an observable can be deduced 'from experience'. If we are to put extreme scepticism behind us and gain any knowledge about the world, we need some ampliative method of inference. Armed with that method, and confident enough about the observable world, there is thought to be a further problem believing what science says about unobservables. So the defence of scientific realism does not require that we refight the battle with extreme scepticism, just that we respond to this special scepticism about unobservables. We shall see that this point has not been kept firmly enough in mind.

The general doctrine of realism about the external world is committed not only to the existence of this world but also to its 'mind-independence': it is not made up of 'ideas' or 'sense data' and does not depend for its existence and nature on the cognitive activities and capacities of our minds. Scientific realism is committed to the unobservable world enjoying this independence. We might call this the 'independence dimension' of realism. The very influential philosophers of science Thomas Kuhn and Paul Feyerabend think that scientific entities are not independent but are somehow 'constructed' by the theories we have of them. This 'constructivism' has its roots in the philosophy of Kant and is extremely influential. An important feature of constructivism, for the purposes of this chapter, is that it applies in the first instance to observables: there is no special problem about the independence of unobservables (as there is thought to be about their existence).[1]

---

[1] But what about quantum theory? The notorious Copenhagen interpretation responds to the mysterious picture of the world suggested by quantum theory by taking the quantum world to be observer-dependent. This would offend against the independence dimension of realism. But, of

The struggle between constructivism and realism is appropriately conducted at the level of observables. I shall therefore not engage in it here.[2]

Before attempting a 'definition' of scientific realism, some further clarification is called for. First, talk of the commitments 'of science' is vague. In the context of the realism debate it means the commitments of *current scientific theories*. The realist's attitude to past theories will be the concern of Section 4.2. Secondly, the realist holds that science is right, 'for the most part'. It would be foolhardy to hold that current science is not making any mistakes and no realist would hold this. Thirdly, this caution does not seem to go far enough: it comes too close to a blanket endorsement of the claims of science. Yet scientists themselves have many epistemic attitudes to their theories. These attitudes range from outright disbelief in a few theories that are useful for predictions but known to be false, through agnosticism about exciting speculations at the frontiers, to a strong commitment to thoroughly tested and well-established theories. The realist is not less sceptical than the scientist: she is committed only to the claims of the latter theories. Furthermore, realism has a critical aspect. Theories may posit unobservables that, given their purposes, they need not posit. Realism is committed only to 'essential' unobservables. In brief, realism is a cautious and critical generalization of the commitments of well-established current theories.

More clarification would be appropriate but this will have to do. Utilizing the language of the clarification we can define a doctrine of scientific realism as follows:

(SR) Most of the essential unobservables of well-established current scientific theories exist mind-independently.

With a commitment to the existence of a certain unobservable goes an implicit commitment to its having whatever properties are essential to its nature as that unobservable. But, beyond that, SR is non-committal on the properties of the unobservables, on the scientific 'facts'. Yet the scientific realist is often committed not only to the entity realism of SR but to a stronger 'fact' realism:[3]

(SSR) Most of the essential unobservables of well-established current scientific theories exist mind-independently and mostly have the properties attributed to them by science.

course, this interpretation of the theory is not obligatory. Many interpretations have been proposed that do not involve observer-dependence. I'm told that all of these are somewhat weird in one way or another. Some philosophers respond to the mysteries by taking quantum theory instrumentally and hence not as an accurate guide to reality; so, the existence dimension of realism is not embraced for the theory. But the enormous success of the theory makes this a difficult choice (see Sect. 3 below on the significance of success). In brief, controversy rages (see e.g. the papers in Cushing and McMullin 1989; Cushing *et al.* 1996). This situation is both fascinating and worrying. What conclusions should we draw from it about scientific realism? In my view, we should draw none until the dust begins to settle.

  [2] Elsewhere (Devitt 1991, 1999, 2001) I take a very dim view of constructivism.

  [3] The scare quotes around "facts" are to indicate that the use of the term can be regarded as a mere manner of speaking, not reflecting any commitment to the existence of what many regard as very

The existence dimensions of these doctrines are opposed by those who are sceptical of what science is revealing; the independence dimension is opposed by the constructivists.

Although not generally sceptical of scientific theories, SR and SSR do reflect some scepticism. By varying the amount of scepticism, we could define some other doctrines; for example, instead of claiming that most of the unobservables exist we could claim that *a large proportion* do or, even weaker, that *some* do. Clearly there is room for argument about how strong a position should be defended against the sceptic. Related to this, but less interesting, there is room for argument about which doctrines warrant the label 'scientific realism'. But this does not prepare one for the bewildering variety of definitions of scientific realism in the literature, many of them very different from SR and SSR.

SR and SSR are about what the world is like, they are *metaphysical* (or *ontological*). Some philosophers favour *epistemic* definitions of scientific realism (for example, Kukla 1998: 10; see also Psillos 1999, pp. xix–xxi). Thus, instead of claiming that most of the unobservables of science exist, one could claim that a belief that they do is justified; or, instead of claiming SSR, one could claim that SSR is justified. This illustrates that epistemic definitions are generally parasitic on metaphysical ones. And although the epistemic ones are clearly different from metaphysical ones, they are not different in a way that is significant for the realism debate. For, if one believes that, say, SSR is justified, one should believe SSR. On the other hand, if one believes SSR, one should be able to produce a justification for it. And someone who urges SSR in the realism debate would produce (what she hopes is) a justification because she would argue for SSR. A metaphysical doctrine of scientific realism and the epistemic one that is parasitic on it stand or fall epistemically together.[4]

It is common to propose what may seem to be *semantic* definitions of scientific realism, definitions using the terms "refer" and "true" (e.g. Hesse 1967: 407; Hooker 1974: 409; Papineau 1979: 126; Ellis 1979: 28; Boyd 1984: 41–2; Leplin 1984b; Fales 1988: 253–4; Jennings 1989: 240; Matheson 1989). For example, we might propose: 'Most of the theoretical terms of currently well-established scientific theories refer to mind-independent entities and the theories' statements about those entities are approximately true.' This should be seen as simply a paraphrase of the metaphysical SSR, exploiting only the 'disquotational' properties of "refer" and "true"

---

dubious entities. Ian Hacking (1983) calls this sort of doctrine 'theory realism'. I prefer to talk of 'facts' rather than theories to emphasize that the doctrine is about the world itself not our account of it.

[4] Indeed, one can generalize: $(p)((p$ is justified) is justified iff p is justified). (Talk of justification here should be construed broadly so that 'externalist' accounts of knowledge are not ruled out.) Jarrett Leplin (1997: 26) has defined an epistemic doctrine, 'minimal epistemic realism', that is not parasitic on a metaphysical one. This doctrine does not claim that a belief in any of the claims of science *is* justified, just that such a belief *could be* justified. A realism that concedes this much to the sceptic is indeed minimal (although still too strong for an anti-realist like Bas van Fraassen).

captured in the schemas ' "F" refers iff Fs exist' and ' "S" is true iff S'. Such paraphrases are often convenient but they do not change the subject matter away from atoms, viruses, photons, and the like. They are not *in any interesting sense* semantic. In particular, they do not involve commitment to a *causal theory* of reference or a *correspondence theory* of truth, nor to any other theory of reference or truth. Indeed, they are compatible with a totally deflationary view of reference and truth: a deflationist can be a scientific realist (Horwich 1998).

So there are epistemic and apparently semantic definitions of scientific realism which do not differ in any significant way from straightforwardly metaphysical definitions like SR and SSR. However, there are others that do differ significantly. Most important are the ones that really have a semantic component. "Scientific realism" is often now taken to refer to some combination of a metaphysical doctrine like SSR with a correspondence theory of truth (see e.g. Putnam 1978: 18–20, 123–5; 1987: 15–16; Fine 1986a: 115–16, 136–7; Miller 1987; Kitcher 1993: 127–33; Brown 1994).[5] The combination is strange. Scepticism about unobservables, which is indubitably at the centre of the realism debate, is simply not about the nature of truth. The issue of that nature is surely fascinating but is orthogonal to the realism issue.[6] Of course there may be evidential connections between the two issues: there may be evidential connections between *any* issues (Duhem–Quine). But no doctrine of truth is constitutive of metaphysical doctrines of scientific realism.[7] In what follows I shall be concerned simply with the latter, using SR and SSR as my examples.

---

[5] Arthur Fine dismisses the realism issue altogether because he takes it to involve an issue about truth. Despite this dismissal, Fine urges the mysterious 'Natural Ontological Attitude' (1986a,b), which often seems to be a realist doctrine like SSR! However, some passages (1986b: 163–5) make it hard to take Fine as a realist.

[6] This objection also counts against definitions of realism that include the idea that truth is the *aim* of science (e.g. van Fraassen 1980: 8) *wherever this talk of truth is taken to commit realism to correspondence truth*. Even if the talk does not have that commitment, and so is acceptable to a deflationist, such definitions have problems. On the one hand, if the idea that truth is the aim of science is added to a doctrine like SSR, the addition is uninteresting: if science *is* discovering the truth, nobody is going to propose that it is not aiming to, that truth is a happy accident. On the other hand, if the idea is not added to a doctrine like SSR, the definition will be too weak: realism will require that science aims for truth without any commitment to it ever having achieved that aim. Indeed, if science had never achieved that aim despite the efforts of the last few centuries, it would hardly be rational now to have the aim. In the distant past, of course, the situation was different (as Howard Sankey has emphasized to me). *Then* the realistically inclined philosopher should have had the aim without the commitment. But *now* she should have the commitment with the result that the aim goes without saying.

[7] For more on this and other matters to do with defining realism, see Devitt (1991, particularly chs. 2–4; 1997, pt. I; 1999, pt. I). Here are two excuses for the intrusion of semantics into the definition of scientific realism. (1) We seem to need semantics to capture the 'non-factualist' anti-realism of classical positivistic instrumentalism (for a learned account of the history of this instrumentalism, see Psillos 1999, ch. 3). This instrumentalism is like the moral anti-realism of 'non-cognitivism' in claiming that what appear to be descriptive and factual statements are not really so. So these 'statements' are not really committed to what they appear to be committed to. I argue that these anti-realisms are, nonetheless, at bottom metaphysical not semantic (Devitt 1997, pt. II). Aside from that, positivistic instrumentalism is no longer a player in the dispute over scientific realism (although instrumentalism

We move on to consider the explanationist arguments for scientific realism, and the underdetermination argument and the pessimistic meta-induction against realism.

3. ARGUMENTS FOR SCIENTIFIC REALISM

3.1 The Success Argument

The most famous argument for realism is the argument from the success of science. The argument has its origins in the work of Grover Maxwell (1962) and J. J. C. Smart (1963) but its most influential expression is by Putnam (1978: 18–19) drawing on Richard Boyd. Scientific theories tend to be successful in that their observational predictions tend to come out true: if a theory says that S then the world tends to be observationally as if S. Why are theories thus successful? The best explanation, the realist claims, is that the theories' theoretical terms typically refer—SR—and the theories are approximately true—SSR: the world is observationally as if S because, approximately, S.[8] For example, why are all the observations we make just the sort we would make if there were atoms? Answer: because there *are* atoms. Sometimes the realist goes further: it would be 'a miracle' that theories were so successful if they weren't approximately true. Realism does not just have the best explanation of success, it has *the only good* explanation.

Larry Laudan (1981, 1984, 1996) has mounted a sustained attack on this argument. In the first prong of this attack, Laudan offers a list of past theories—phlogiston theory is a favourite example—that were successful but are now known not to be approximately true. The realist has a number of responses. First, the success of a theory can be challenged: although it was thought to be successful, it was not really so (McAllister 1993). But unless the criterion of success is put so high that not even contemporary theories will qualify, some theories on Laudan's list will surely

---

in general certainly is, for it simply involves doubting the theoretical claims of science without reinterpreting them). (2) Although a doctrine like SSR need not be combined with a correspondence theory of truth, it very likely cannot be plausibly combined with an epistemic theory of truth. But still a non-epistemic theory is not constitutive of SSR (Devitt 1991: 4.3).

[8] Note that although this argument is usually stated using "refer" and "true", this is not essential. And such usage should be seen as exploiting only the disquotational properties of the terms with no commitment to a robust correspondence relation between language and the world. The realist argument should be that success is explained by the properties of unobservables, not by the properties of truth and reference. ('Truth, like Mae West's goodness, has nothing to do with it'; Levin 1984: 124.) So the argument could be urged by a deflationist (Devitt 1991: 113–17).

survive. Secondly, it can be argued that a theory was not, in the appropriate sense, well established and hence not the sort that the realist is committed to; or that entities it posited were not essential to its success (Kitcher 1993: 140–9). But surely some theories on the list will survive this test too. Thirdly, the realist can insist that there are many other past theories, ones not on Laudan's list, for which the realist's explanation of success works fine (McMullin 1984).

Still, what about the theories that survive on Laudan's list? The realist must offer some other explanation of their success. So even if the approximate truth of most theories is the best, perhaps only, explanation of their success, it cannot be so for all theories. But then the realist should not have needed to struggle with Laudan's list to discover this need to modify the success argument. After all, the sensible realist does not suppose that no well-established scientific theory has ever been very wrong in its entities and its claims about them. And some theories that have been very wrong have surely been successful; indeed, scientists sometimes continue to use theories known to be false simply *because* they are so successful. So the realist must offer some explanation of this success that does not depend on the rightness of the theories.

Here is a suggestion that is very much in the spirit of the original success argument. The success of a theory T that is very wrong is explained by the approximate truth of a replacement theory T'.[9] It is because the unobservables posited by T' exist and have approximately the properties attributed to them that T is successful. Indeed, we expect the very same theory that shows T to be wrong also to explain T's observational success.[10] So the realist modifies the success argument: the best explanation of a theory's success is mostly that its unobservables exist and have approximately the properties specified by the theory; otherwise, the best explanation is that the unobservables of a replacement theory exist and have approximately the properties specified by that theory. Furthermore, the realist may insist, the only way to explain the success of a theory is by appeal to its unobservables or those of another theory.

The three earlier realist responses greatly reduce the challenge that Laudan's list poses for the original success argument. Still, some theories on the list will survive these responses. The modified argument offers an explanation of the success of those theories and is sufficient to support SR and SSR.[11]

---

[9] Laudan is scornful of the realists' appeal to the explanatory role of approximate truth. He complains that the notion is undefined. He acknowledges that many scientifically useful notions are undefined, but thinks that approximate truth is so specially unclear that the realists' appeal to it is 'so much mumbo-jumbo' (1981: 32). This is excessive. First, approximately true theories can have fully true parts that do the explaining. Secondly, the talk of approximate truth is simply a convenience (n. 8). The claim that the approximate truth of "a is F" explains an observation amounts to the claim that a's being approximately F explains it. Science and life are replete with such explanations; for example, a's being approximately spherical explains why it rolls.

[10] This expectation should not be construed as a *requirement* on a replacement theory: that no theory should replace T until it has explained T's success. Laudan rightly objects to this requirement (1981: 44–5).

[11] In so far as we have reason to believe that the success of a current theory is to be explained by some as yet unknown future theory, that success provides no reason to believe in the current theory's entities or approximate truth. So the modified success argument's support for SR and SSR does

Now, of course, this modification that accepts past mistakes raises the spectre of the pessimistic meta-induction.[12] We shall consider that later (Section 4.2). Meanwhile, the modification does seem to save the success argument.

But perhaps anti-realists can explain success? There have been attempts.

1. Bas van Fraassen has offered a Darwinian explanation: 'any scientific theory is born into a life of fierce competition, a jungle red in tooth and claw. Only the successful theories survive' (1980: 39). But this explanation is not relevant because it is not explaining the same thing as the realist's success argument. It is explaining why we humans hold successful theories. It is not explaining why those particular theories are successful (Lipton 1991: 170–2; Devitt 1991: 116; Kitcher 1993: 155–7; Leplin 1997: 7–9).

2. Arthur Fine claims that anti-realism can explain success as well as realism can by appealing to a theory's instrumental reliability (1986b; Fine is not committed to this anti-realist explanation). Jarrett Leplin (1987, 1997) develops this proposal and labels it 'surrealism'. The basic idea is that although the world has a 'deep structure' this structure is 'not experientially accessible'. 'The explanation of the success of any theory...is that the actual structure of the world operates at the experiential level as if the theory represented it correctly' (1997: 26). Leplin goes on to argue, in my view convincingly, that the surrealist explanation is not a successful alternative to the realist one.[13]

In the second prong of his attack on realism, Laudan (1981: 45–6) has criticized the realist's success argument for its dependence on *inference to the best explanation*, or 'abduction'. Fine (1986a: 113–22) has made a similar criticism.[14] In presenting this criticism they charge the realist with 'question-begging'. This charge is not apt. The realist argument could be question-begging only if it assumed abduction and the dispute with the anti-realist was over abduction. But the primary dispute, at least, is not over abduction but over a doctrine like SSR. So, presented in this way, the criticism seems to miss its target. (One wonders if the cause of this mistake is that the many definitions of scientific realism have left the target unclear.)

---

depend on the three earlier responses showing that it is mostly the case that the success of a past theory can be explained by the reference of *its* terms and *its* approximate truth. (I am indebted to Mathias Frisch for drawing my attention to this.)

[12] Peter Lewis (2002) summarizes Laudan's discussion as a meta-induction (which differs from the meta-induction we shall be considering):

Many false past theories were successful.
So the success of a theory is not a reliable test for its truth.

Lewis argues persuasively that Laudan's meta-induction exemplifies 'the false positives paradox'. To establish his conclusion, Laudan needs to find periods of science where most theories were successful and yet most were false.

[13] For more on this, see Kukla (1998: 20–4); Psillos (1999: 90–3).

[14] Realists tend to be fond of abduction; e.g. Glymour (1984); Boyd (1984); McMullin (1984); Musgrave (1985); Leplin (1997).

The criticism should be simply that the realist argument relies on abduction and this is a method of inference that an anti-realist might reject. Van Fraassen (1980, 1989), for one, does reject it. Is the realist entitled to rely on abduction? Boyd (1984: 65–75) has argued that the anti-realists are not in a position to deny entitlement because scientists regularly use abduction to draw conclusions about observables.

Boyd's argument illustrates an important, and quite general, realist strategy to defend unobservables against discrimination, to defend 'unobservable rights'.[15] The realist starts by reminding the anti-realist that the debate is not over extreme scepticism: the anti-realist claims to have knowledge of observables (Section 2). The realist then examines the anti-realist's justification for this knowledge. Using this justification she attempts to show, positively, that the epistemology it involves also justifies knowledge of unobservables. And, she attempts to show, negatively, that the case for scepticism about unobservables produced by the anti-realist is no better than the case for scepticism about observables, a scepticism that all parties to the scientific realism dispute have rejected.

So the anti-realist's criticism of the success argument leaves him with the task of showing that he can save his beliefs about observables without using abduction. If he cannot manage this, the criticism fails. If he can—and van Fraassen (1989) has made an attempt—then the realist seems to face the task of justifying abduction.

How concerned should the realist be about this? Perhaps not as much as many suppose. After all, the anti-realist must rely on some methods of ampliative inference, even if not on abduction, to overcome extreme scepticism. How are those methods justified? The anti-realist may well have little to say about this, relying on the fact that these methods are widely and successfully used in science and ordinary life and on there being no apparent reason to abandon them. But, of course, that seems to be true of abduction as well. If further justification for a method is required, where could we find it?[16] The naturalistically inclined will have trouble with any attempt at an a priori justification. And it is hard to see how an a priori approach could be effective either for or against abduction. What about an empirical justification within a naturalized epistemology? Any justification must of course use some methods of inference. If it uses the very method it seeks to justify, circularity threatens. Stathis Psillos argues that this circularity is not vicious (1999: 81–90). Be that as it may, Neurath's famous image of rebuilding a boat while staying afloat on it suggests another procedure for justifying a method: we hold fast to all other methods and use them to justify the method in contention. So, perhaps we can justify abduction using the methods of induction and deduction. Indeed, perhaps the very success of abduction in science and everyday life—its tendency to

[15] For examples of this strategy, see Churchland (1985); Gutting (1985); Musgrave (1985); Clendinnen (1989); Devitt (1991: 147–53); Psillos (1999: 186–91). Van Fraassen (1985) responds to the first three of these.

[16] One problem in finding it is that we cannot give a precise specification of any of these methods: as Georges Rey says, 'no one yet has an adequate theory of our knowledge of much of anything' (1998: 29).

produce conclusions that are later observationally confirmed—provides the basis for such an inductive justification.[17] In any case it is not obvious that the justification of abduction will be more problematic than the justification of the methods of inference relied on by the anti-realists.

3.2 The Success of Methodology Argument

Our scientific methodology is 'instrumentally reliable' in that it leads to successful theories, theories that make true observational predictions. Everyone agrees that our methodology does this. Why does it? What is the explanation? Boyd (1973, 1984, 1985) has posed this question and offered an answer that is both realist and naturalist: the methodology is based in a dialectical way on our theories and those theories are approximately true. He argues that anti-realists of various sorts cannot explain this methodological success satisfactorily and so his realist explanation is the best. I think that he is probably right.

Like the earlier success argument this argument relies on abduction, but it has a different explanandum. Where the earlier argument sought to explain the success of theories, this one seeks to explain the success of scientific methodology in producing successful theories.

3.3 The Basic Abductive Argument

The two abductive arguments for realism that we have considered are somewhat sophisticated. A more basic argument is strangely overlooked: by supposing that

---

[17] The suggestion is that experience, according to the empiricist 'the sole legitimate source of information about the world' (van Fraassen 1985: 286), supports abduction. For arguments in favour of abduction, see Boyd (1984); McMullin (1984); Lipton (1991); Devitt (1991: 111–13); Leplin (1997: 116–20). Analogous problems arise, of course, over the justification of deduction; see Field (1996, 1998); Rey (1998); Devitt (1998).

Van Fraassen (2000: 261–71) seems to misunderstand the relation of naturalized epistemology to science. It goes without saying that epistemology implies the methods of science. But van Fraassen seems to take the naturalist view to be that basic science, or special sciences like biology, medicine, and psychology, imply the methods of science, a view that he rejects. This view misrepresents naturalism. Naturalism holds that epistemology is itself a special science. As such it is no more simply implied by another science than is any other special science: it has the same sort of relative autonomy, and yet dependence on basic science, as other special sciences. Naturalized epistemology, like any special science, applies the usual methods of science, whatever they may be, mostly taking established science for granted, to investigate its special realm. In the case of epistemology that realm is those very methods of science. The aim is to discover empirically how we humans learn, and should learn, about the world (Devitt 1991: 75–9). We have no reason to suppose that the methods that have yielded knowledge elsewhere cannot yield knowledge in epistemology.

the unobservables of science exist, we can give good explanations of the behaviour and characteristics of observed entities, behaviour and characteristics which would otherwise remain inexplicable. This basic argument differs from the success argument in the following way. Where the success argument uses realism to explain the observational success of theories, the basic argument uses realism to explain observed phenomena. This is not to say that observational success is unimportant to the basic argument: the explanation of observed phenomena, like any explanation, is tested by its observational success. So according to the basic argument, realism is successful; according to the popular one, it explains success.[18]

In sum, there are some good arguments for scientific realism provided the realist is allowed abduction. Some critics reject abduction but this rejection seems dubious. Perhaps our knowledge of observables depends on abduction. In any case, abduction seems to be on an equal footing, at least, with other ampliative methods of inference.

4. Arguments Against Scientific Realism

4.1 The Underdetermination Argument

There is an appealing and influential empiricist argument against scientific realism that starts from a doctrine of empirical equivalence.[19] Let T be any theory committed to unobservables. Then,

   (EE) T has empirically equivalent rivals.

This is taken to imply the strong underdetermination thesis:

   (SU) T has rivals that are equally supported by all possible observational evidence
         for it.

---

[18] Devitt (1991: 113–17). Hacking's arguments (1983) for the reality of entities manipulated in experiments and perceived under a microscope are persuasive examples of the basic argument (although he, strangely, does not regard them as abductions). Hacking's point about manipulation is clearly related to Alan Musgrave's (1988) insistence that novel predictions give us the best reason for believing a theory. Ernan McMullin (1991), responding to Fine (1991), provides some nice examples of the basic argument in geology, biology, and astrophysics. An advantage of the basic argument is that it makes clear that, contrary to Fine's frequent claims, the use of abduction to justify realism is not at some 'philosophical' level above science: 'the argument is properly carried on at one level only, the level of the scientist' (McMullin 1991: 104).

[19] My discussion of this argument draws on a more detailed one in Devitt (2002).

So, realist doctrines like SR and SSR are unjustified.[20]

Some preliminaries. First, what exactly is it for two theories to be 'empirically equivalent'? The basic idea is that they have the same observational consequences. We shall later see the importance of looking very closely at this basic idea.

Secondly, where EE talks simply of T having equivalent rivals, the premiss of the argument is sometimes that T has *indefinitely many* rivals (e.g. Kukla 1998: 58) and sometimes that it has *at least one* (e.g. Psillos 1999: 164). For convenience, I shall mostly treat EE as if it were only committed to one rival because its commitment to more does not seem to make a significant difference to the conclusions we should draw.

Thirdly, SU should not be confused with various other underdetermination theses[21] including the weak and obviously true one, mentioned in Section 2, that leads to the challenge of extreme scepticism:

(WU) Any theory has rivals that entail the same actual given observational evidence.

SU is stronger than WU in two respects. First, SU concerns an *ampliative* relation between theories and evidence and not merely a deductive one. Secondly, SU is concerned with T's relation to *all possible* evidence not merely to the given evidence.[22] If we are to avoid scepticism in the face of WU, we noted, some ampliative method of inference must be accepted. But if SU is true, we face a further challenge: ampliative methods do not support T over its rivals on the given evidence nor even on all possible evidence. So what T says about the unobservable world can make no evidential difference. Surely, then, commitment to what the theory says is a piece of misguided metaphysics. Even with extreme scepticism behind us, realism is threatened.

Now, consider EE. A good reason for believing EE is that there is an empiricist algorithm for constructing an equivalent rival to T. Consider T_o, the theory that the observational consequences of T are true. T_o is obviously empirically equivalent to T. Still, it may not count as a rival because it is consistent with T. That is easily fixed: T^* is the theory that T_o is true but T is not. T^* is an empirically equivalent rival to T. So EE is established.

It is tempting to respond that T^* is produced by trickery and is not a *genuine* rival to T (Laudan and Leplin 1991; Hoefer and Rosenberg 1994). But this response

---

[20] The argument has no one clear source. But see Duhem (1906); Quine (1960, 1961 ('Two Dogmas'), 1975); van Fraassen (1980); Putnam (1983 ('Equivalence')).

[21] My presentation reflects the influence of Laudan's excellent discussion of this variety (1996, ch. 2).

[22] So the premiss about empirical equivalence that is supposed to support SU in the underdetermination argument must also concern all possible evidence. Psillos's version of the argument fails on this score. It starts: 'for *any* theory T and *any* body of observational evidence E, there is another theory T' such that T and T' are empirically equivalent with respect to E' (1999: 164). The quantifiers need to be reordered if this is to support SU: for *any* theory T, there is another theory T' such that for *any* (possible) body of observational evidence E, T and T' are empirically equivalent with respect to E.

seems question-begging and unconvincing, as Andre Kukla argues (1998: 66–81). A better response is that, in counting theories generated by the empiricist algorithm as rivals, EE, as it stands, is too weak to sustain SU. For, with extreme scepticism behind us, we are justified in choosing T over T*.

In considering this choice, the first half of T*, T_o, is key. In van Fraassen's terminology, T_o is the claim that T is 'empirically adequate'. He has some famous remarks comparing this claim with the bolder claim that T is true: 'the empirical adequacy of an empirical theory must always be more credible than its truth' (1985: 247); 'it is not an epistemological principle that one may as well hang for a sheep as for a lamb' (p. 254). The extra boldness of T comes, of course, from its realist commitment to certain truths about unobservables. Because van Fraassen thinks that T takes no further empirical risk than T_o, he claims that this extra boldness 'is but empty strutting and posturing', a 'display of courage not under fire' (p. 255). We should prefer the weaker T_o.

Now if van Fraassen were right about this, no evidence could justify a move from T_o to the bolder T. So it could not justify a preference for T over its rival T* ($=T_o$ & not-T). SU would be established.

Here is a reason for thinking that van Fraassen is not right. If it were really the case that we were only ever justified in adopting the weakest theory compatible with the possible evidence for T, we would have to surrender to extreme scepticism. For T_o is far from being the weakest such theory. For example, consider T_e, the theory that T is 'experientially adequate'. Where T_o claims that the observable world *is* as if T, T_e claims only that the observable world *appears to be* as if T. T_e is much weaker than T_o: it does not require that there be an observable world at all; perhaps an evil demon is at work. Those, like van Fraassen, who believe theories of the observable world are displaying courage not under fire all the time.[23]

This argument exemplifies the negative side of the realist strategy described earlier: arguing that the case for scepticism about unobservables produced by the anti-realist is no better than the case for scepticism about observables.

We can apply the positive side of the strategy too. Any methods of ampliative inference that support the move from T_e to T_o and free us from extreme scepticism must justify the dismissal of the evil-demon hypothesis and a whole lot of others. The methods must justify many singular hypotheses about unobserved objects and many general hypotheses that cover such objects ("All ravens are black" and the like). Whether or not these methods alone support the further move to T, hence support scientific realism, they will surely justify the dismissal of T's rival T*, produced by the empiricist algorithm. And they will justify the dismissal of another empirically equivalent rival produced by Kukla's algorithm according to which the world changes when unobserved (1993). It would be nice to know, of course, what these methods are. But it is a strategic error for the scientific realist to attempt to

---

[23] I develop this argument more thoroughly in Devitt (1991: 150–3).

say what they are in responding to the anti-realist. For, the anti-realist believes in observables and *whatever* ampliative inferences support that belief will justify the dismissal of the likes of T*.

The anti-realist might, of course, simply insist that inferences that work for observables do not work for unobservables. Certainly there is no logical inconsistency in this insistence.[24] Nevertheless, the insistence is arbitrary and unprincipled. The realist need say no more.[25]

We conclude that EE as it stands cannot sustain SU: T is indeed justified over empirically equivalent rivals like T*. If the underdetermination argument is to work, it needs to start from a stronger equivalence thesis, one that does not count any theory as a rival to T that can be dismissed by whatever ampliative inferences enable us to avoid extreme scepticism. Let us say that the rivals that can be thus dismissed are not 'genuine'. T* and the output of Kukla's algorithm are surely not genuine. Precisely how far we can go in thus dismissing rivals remains to be seen, of course, pending an account of how to avoid extreme scepticism. And, given the realist strategy, the account that matters is the one given by the anti-realist.

With EE now restricted to genuine rivals, the next step in assessing the underdetermination argument is a careful consideration of how to interpret EE's talk of empirical equivalence. The basic idea is that empirically equivalent theories have the same observational consequences. What does this amount to? A natural first stab at an answer is that the theories entail the same observations. This yields the following version of EE:

(EE1) T has genuine rivals that entail the same possible observational evidence.

Whether or not EE1 is true, it is easy to see that it is inadequate to support SU. This inadequacy arises from the fact that T is likely to entail few observations on its own and yet the conjunction of T with auxiliary hypotheses, theories of instruments, background assumptions, and so on—briefly, its conjunction with 'auxiliaries'—is likely to entail many observations. T does not face the tribunal of experience alone (Duhem–Quine). By failing to take account of these joint consequences, EE1 leaves many ways in which evidence could favour T over its rivals, contrary to SU. To sustain SU and challenge realism, we need another interpretation of EE.

Consider Laudan and Leplin's influential critique of the underdetermination argument (1991). They propose the thesis 'the Instability of Auxiliary Assumptions' according to which 'auxiliary information providing premises for the derivation of observational consequences from theory is unstable in two respects: it is defeasible and it is augmentable' (p. 57).[26] As the accepted auxiliaries that can be conjoined

---

[24] Kukla emphasizes this (1998: 25–6, 84).

[25] However, I think that an examination of the epistemic significance of observation helps to bring out the arbitrariness (Devitt 1991: 143–7).

[26] See also Ellis (1985); Devitt (1991: 117–21).

with T change, so do its consequences. So, any determination of T's empirical consequence class 'must be relativized to a particular state of science', the state that supplies the auxiliary hypotheses. Thus 'any finding of empirical equivalence is both contextual and defeasible' (p. 58). To determine the consequences of T we need more than logic, we need to know which auxiliaries are acceptable, an '*inescapably epistemic*' matter (p. 59).

To avoid the consequences of this argument, Kukla (1993) proposed an answer to our interpretative question along the following lines: for two theories to be empirically equivalent at time *t* is for them to entail the same observations when conjoined with A*t*, the auxiliaries that are accepted at *t*. This yields:

(EE2) T has genuine rivals which are such that when T and any of the rivals are conjoined with A*t* they entail the same possible observational evidence.

Set aside for a moment whether or not EE2 is any threat at all to realism. It is clearly too weak to sustain the threat posed by SU. Let T′ be an empirically equivalent rival to T according to this interpretation. So T & A*t* and T′ & A*t* entail the same observations. This sort of equivalence is *relative to A t*, to the auxiliaries accepted at a certain time. It amounts to the claim that T and T′ cannot be discriminated observationally if conjoined only with those auxiliaries. But this does not show that T and T′ could not be distinguished when conjoined with *any* acceptable auxiliaries at *any* time. And that is what is needed, at least, to sustain the claim that T and T′ cannot be discriminated by *any possible* evidence, as SU requires. SU demands a much stronger answer to the interpretative question: for two theories to be empirically equivalent is for them to entail the same observations when conjoined with any (possible) acceptable auxiliaries.[27] This yields:

(EE3) T has genuine rivals which are such that when T and any of the rivals are conjoined with any possible acceptable auxiliaries they entail the same possible observational evidence.

If T and T′ were thus related they would be empirically equivalent not just relative to certain auxiliaries but *tout court*, absolutely equivalent. Only then would they be observationally indiscriminable. So if EE is to support SU, it must be interpreted as EE3.[28]

[27] This demand arises out of a liberal and, it seems to me, intuitive view of what counts as 'possible evidence'. Quine and van Fraassen have a more restricted view, which I discuss in Devitt (2002, sect. 13).

[28] Tim Williamson pointed out to me a problem with EE3 as it stands. Suppose that T_1 and T_2 are two allegedly equivalent rivals and that A_1 is an acceptable auxiliary *relative to T* but not T_2 and A_2 is an acceptable auxiliary *relative to T_2* but not T_1. Thus A_1 might be a theory of a testing instrument from the perspective of T_1, and A_2 a theory of that instrument from the perspective of T_2. So the acceptability of the auxiliaries is not independent of the theories being tested. Now suppose that T_1 & A_1 and T_2 & A_1 have different observational consequences. That alone should not show that T_1 and T_2 are not empirically equivalent. For, T_1 & A_1 and T_2 & A_2 might have the same observational consequences. Clearly, what needs to be assessed for empirical equivalence are theories *together with their*

The main point of Laudan and Leplin's critique can be put simply: we have no reason to believe EE3.[29] If T and T' cannot be discriminated observationally relative to, say, currently accepted auxiliaries, they may well be so relative to some future accepted auxiliaries. Some currently accepted auxiliaries may cease to be accepted and some new auxiliaries are likely to become accepted. This point becomes particularly persuasive, in my view (Devitt 1991: 119), when we note our capacity to invent new instruments and experiments to test theories. With a new instrument and experiment comes new auxiliaries, including a theory of the instrument and assumptions about the experimental situation. Given that we can thus create evidence, the set of observational consequences of any theory seems totally open. Of course, there is no guarantee of successful discrimination by these means: a theory may really face a genuine empirically equivalent rival. Still, we are unlikely to have sufficient reason for believing this of any particular theory.[30] More importantly, we have no reason at all for believing it of all theories, as EE3 requires. We will seldom, if ever, have a basis for concluding that two genuine rivals are empirically equivalent in the absolute sense required by EE3.

This argument against EE3 does not depend on any assumption about the breadth of T. So EE3 cannot be saved by taking it to apply to 'total sciences' (Boyd 1984: 50). Should such a broad conjunction of theories seem to face an equivalent rival at a certain time, we are unlikely to have sufficient reason for believing that experimental developments will not enable us to discriminate the conjunction from its rival by supplying new auxiliaries. *There is no known limit to our capacity to generate acceptable auxiliaries.*

I have argued that we have no reason to believe EE3. But suppose, nonetheless, that EE3 were true. Would this establish SU and undermine scientific realism? It might well do so.[31] If EE3 were true, realists would have to appeal to 'non-empirical virtues' to choose between empirically equivalent theories. Empirical virtue is a matter of entailing (in conjunction with accepted auxiliaries) observational truths and not entailing observational falsehoods. The non-empirical virtues are explanatory power, simplicity, and the like. For the reason indicated earlier in discussing abduction (Section 3), I think that the realist is entitled to appeal to explanatory virtues, at least. But if it really were the case that all theories faced genuine rivals equally compatible with all possible evidence, the appeal to these virtues would

dependent auxiliaries. And EE3 should be taken as referring to any possible *independently* acceptable auxiliaries.

[29] Note that this is not the claim that EE3 is 'demonstratively false'; cf. Kukla (1998: 58).

[30] For some theories where we may have sufficient reason, and for some past ones where we wrongly thought we had, see Psillos (1999: 166–8 and the works he cites).

[31] Laudan and Leplin (1991: 63–8) think not, arguing that T can be indirectly supported over its rival by evidence that confirms another theory that entails T but not its rival; and that some consequences of T and its rival might support only T. But, as Kukla points out (1998: 84–90), this argument begs the question: if EE3 really were true, this evidential support would seem to disappear.

seem epistemologically dubious.[32] For, in those circumstances, there could be no way to judge the empirical success of these virtues, no way to show, for example, that theories that provide the best explanation tend to be observationally confirmed. So the defence of realism might well depend on there being no good reason for believing EE3.

What about EE2? We have already seen that EE2 will not sustain SU. But perhaps it is otherwise threatening to realism. So, first, we need to consider whether it is true; then, whether, if it were, it would undermine realism.

There are surely some theories that face a genuine rival that is empirically equivalent relative to the accepted auxiliaries at a certain time. But do *all* theories face such rivals at that time, let alone at *all* times? EE2 guarantees that all theories do at all times. But the ampliative methods, whatever they may be, that support our knowledge of the observable world and avoid extreme scepticism will count many rivals as not genuine, so many as to make this guarantee seem baseless. How could we know a priori that T must always face such a genuine rival?

Suppose, nonetheless, that EE2 were true. So, if T and its rivals are restricted to the accepted auxiliaries at a certain time, T could not be justified over some rivals on the basis only of the observations that the theories and auxiliaries entail and the ampliative methods that save us from extreme scepticism. So, without recourse to some further ampliative methods, T would be underdetermined by the evidence that the restriction allows into play. Of course, once new acceptable auxiliaries were discovered and the restriction changed, the further methods might well not be needed to justify T over those old rivals. So this underdetermination would not be as serious as SU, but it would be serious enough: at any time, we would not know what to be realist about. But then perhaps the realist would be entitled to the further ampliative methods that would remove this underdetermination. For the reasons already indicated, and given that the case for EE3 has not been made, I think that the realist might be so entitled.[33]

In sum, we have no reason to believe EE2 or EE3 and so the underdetermination argument fails. However, if EE3 were true, it might well undermine scientific realism and if EE2 were true, it could. Once we have set aside extreme scepticism, then, contrary to received opinion, the non-empirical virtues are not central to defending realism from the underdetermination argument; the rejection of the equivalence

---

[32] I emphasize that since it has not been established that all theories do face such rivals, it might well be appropriate to appeal to explanatory virtues, or indeed to the evidential support mentioned by Laudan and Leplin (1991: 63–8), to prefer some theory that does face such a rival.

[33] In a reply to Kukla (1993), Leplin and Laudan (1993: 10), in effect, doubt EE2 but in any case emphasize that EE3 is what matters to the underdetermination argument. Kukla disagrees, claiming, in effect, that EE2, when applied to total sciences, 'brings in its train all the epistemological problems that were ever ascribed to the doctrine of EE' (1998: 64). According to my discussion, EE2 would bring some epistemological problems if it were true, but they are not as extreme as those that would be brought by EE3 if it were true.

thesis is. In drawing these conclusions I have mostly construed EE2 and EE3 as if they were committed only to T having at least one genuine empirically equivalent rival. Their actual commitment to more rivals does not significantly change the conclusions we should draw.

4.2 The Pessimistic Meta-Induction

The most powerful argument against scientific realism, in my view, is what Putnam (1978) calls a 'meta-induction'. It does not rest on a prejudice against abduction or exaggerated concerns about underdetermination. It rests on plausible claims about the history of science. The basic version of the argument is aimed at an entity realism like SR: the unobservables posited by past theories do not exist; so, probably the unobservables posited by present theories do not exist. Another version, largely dependent on the basic one, is aimed at a 'fact' realism like SSR: past scientific theories are not approximately true; so, probably present theories are not approximately true. (This is an example of the convenience of exploiting the disquotational property of "true" to talk about the world.) Both versions of the argument rest on a claim about past theories from the perspective of our present theory.[34] And the pessimistic suggestion is that, from a future perspective, we will have a similarly critical view of our present theories. Laudan (1981, 1984, 1996) has supported these claims about the past with a list of theoretical failures.

Laudan's list is the one used to discuss the realist's success argument (2.1), but the purpose of the list is different here. The purpose before was to show that past theories were successful without being true, thus undermining the argument for realism that 'realism explains success'. The list's purpose here is to show that past theories were not approximately true and their unobservables did not exist, thus establishing the premiss of an argument against realism, against the view that present theories are approximately true and their unobservables exist.

Scientific realism already concedes something to the meta-induction in exhibiting *some* scepticism about the claims of science. It holds that science is more or less right but not totally so. It is committed only to well-established theories not exciting speculations. It leaves room for a theoretical posit to be dismissed as inessential to the theory. According to the meta-induction, reflection on the track record of science shows that this scepticism has not gone nearly far enough.

The realist can respond to the meta-induction by attacking the premiss or the inference. Concerning the premiss, the realist can, on the one hand, resist the bleak assessment of the theories on Laudan's list, claiming that while some of the

---

[34] So there is a 'tension' in the argument: it seems to rest on a realist view of present science and yet concludes that this realist view is mistaken; see Leplin (1997: 141–5). I suppose that we should see the meta-induction as some sort of *reductio*.

unobservables posited by these theories do not exist, others do; or claiming that while there is a deal of falsehood in these theories, there is a deal of truth too (Worrall 1989;[35] Kitcher 1993: 140–9; Psillos 1999, chs. 5–6). On the other hand, the realist can claim that the list is unrepresentative, that other past theories do seem to be approximately true and to posit entities that do exist (McMullin 1984).

In the light of history, some scepticism about the claims of science is clearly appropriate. The argument is over how much, the mild scepticism of the realist, or the sweeping scepticism of the meta-induction. Settling the argument requires close attention to the historical details. This is not, of course, something that I shall be attempting. However, I shall make some general remarks about the attempt.

How can we *tell* whether Fs, posited by a past theory, exist? Given the disquotational schema ' "F" refers iff Fs exist,' many approach this question by considering another: How do we tell whether "F" refers? This common approach would be harmless if it exploited only the disquotational property of "refer" captured by the schema, a property acceptable to the deflationist. For then the reference question is just a paraphrase of the existence question. However, it is usual (and, in my view, right) to take "refer" to pick out a substantive semantic relation between "F" and the world, a relation that needs to be explained by a *theory* of reference. So it is natural to take the reference question to concern this substantive relation and to be answered by appealing to some theory of reference. But then the common approach is far from harmless.

The first problem is that the theory of reference appealed to on this approach is usually a description theory. According to this theory, the reference of "F" depends on the descriptions (other terms) that its containing theory associates with it: it refers to whatever those descriptions pick out. It is likely that, from our present scientific perspective, those descriptions do not pick anything out. So, the conclusion is drawn that "F" does not refer and hence there are no Fs.[36] Yet, the arguments of Saul Kripke (1980) and others have made it likely that reference for some terms, at least, is to be explained not by a description theory but by a theory that links a term to its referent in a more direct causal way.[37] So it may well be that a description theory is the wrong theory for "F". This points to the second, deeper, problem with the common approach: in attempting to answer the existence question by answering the reference question, the approach has its epistemic priorities all wrong. For, *we know far less about reference*, particularly about when to apply a description theory and when to apply a causal theory, than we know about what exists. In light of this,

[35] Worrall takes the truth to be not about the nature of entities but about structures that contain the entities. For a critical discussion of this 'structural realism', see Psillos (1999, ch. 7).

[36] See Kuhn (1962) for an argument along these lines. Stephen Stich (1983) and others have argued similarly for various forms of eliminativism about the mind. Stich has since recanted (1996: 3–90).

[37] For a summary and development of these and other moves in the theory of reference, see Devitt and Sterelny (1999).

the rational procedure is to let our view of what exists guide our theories of reference rather than let our theories of reference determine what exists.[38]

So, we should not use a theory of reference to answer our existence question. How then should we answer it? Consider how, in general, we argue directly for the non-existence of Fs. On the basis of the established view of Fs, we start, implicitly if not explicitly, with an assumption about the nature of Fs: something would not be an F unless it were G. Then we argue that nothing is G. So, there are no Fs. Very often this argument is persuasive and generally accepted. But someone might respond by denying the assumption about nature. 'Fs do not have to be G, they are just mistakenly thought to be G. So the argument proves nothing.' How do we settle this disagreement? It may be difficult. We can try saying more about the established view of Fs, but this may not do the trick. After all, the responder does not deny that Fs are thought to be G, just that being G is part of the nature of being an F. And the established view may not be clear on the nature issue. We may be left with nothing but a 'clash of intuitions' over that issue. In such a situation, we should wonder whether there is a genuine issue to settle: there may be no determinate matter of fact about the nature issue. If there is not, then there is no determinate matter of fact about whether the absence of G things establishes the non-existence of Fs.

Consider two humdrum examples. Most people are anti-realist about witches because they believe that nothing casts spells, rides on a broomstick through the sky, and so on. Some people may be anti-realist about God because they are convinced by the Problem of Evil that nothing is both all powerful and all good. But these are grounds for anti-realism only if casting of spells, riding on broomsticks, and so on, and being all powerful and all good, are essential to witches and God, respectively. There may be disagreement about that. And there is room for worry that disagreement may not be entirely over matters of fact.

In light of this, we can expect that close attention to the historical details about past unobservables will reveal some ontologically determinate cases but very likely some indeterminate ones too. The determinate cases will surely include some of non-existence; phlogiston is a good candidate. But it will surely also include some of existence; the atoms posited in the nineteenth century are good candidates.[39] So, we should conclude that the premiss of the meta-induction is overstated, at least. But how much is it overstated? That depends on the 'success ratio' of past theories, the ratio of the determinately existents to the determinately non-existents + indeterminates. Where is this ratio likely to leave scientific realism? To answer this we need to consider the meta-induction's inference.

---

[38] In Devitt (1991) I argue for this priority. There is, of course, a truth underlying the mistaken approach: to determine whether the posits of a theory exist we have to know what those posits are and for that we have to understand the language of the theory (pp. 50–3). But understanding a language is a practical skill that does not require theoretical knowledge about the language, else we would understand very little (pp. 270–5).

[39] Also molecules and microbes; see Miller (1987).

I think (Devitt 1991: 162–5) that there is a good reason for being dubious about the inference. Suppose that our past theories have indeed failed rather badly to get the unobservable world right. Why would that show that our present theories are failing similarly? It clearly would show this if we supposed that we are no better at finding out about unobservables now than we were in the past. But why suppose that? Just the opposite seems more plausible: we are now much better at finding out about unobservables. A naturalized epistemology would surely show that science has for two or three centuries been getting better and better at this. Scientific progress is, to a large degree, a matter of improving scientific methodologies often based on new technologies that provide new instruments for investigating the world. If this is so—and it seems fairly indubitable—then we should expect an examination of the historical details to show improvement over time in our success ratio for unobservables. If the details do show this, it will not matter to realism that the ratio for, say, two centuries ago was poor. What will matter is that we have been improving enough to have now the sort of confidence reflected by SR.[40] And if we have been improving, but not fast enough for SR, the realist can fall back to a more moderate commitment to, say, a high proportion of the unobservables of currently well-established theories.

Improvements in scientific methodologies make it much harder to mount a case against realism than seems to have been appreciated. For the appeal to historical details has to show not only that we were nearly always wrong in our unobservable posits but that, despite methodological improvements, we have not been getting significantly righter. It seems to me most unlikely that this case can be made.

5. CONCLUSIONS

Scientific realism is best seen as a straightforwardly metaphysical doctrine along the lines of SR or SSR. Various explanationist arguments for scientific realism succeed provided that the realist is entitled to abduction. I have suggested that the realist is entitled. The underdetermination argument against realism fails because we have no good reason to believe an empirical equivalence thesis that would serve as its premiss. The pessimistic meta-induction, with its attention to past theoretical failures, does pose a problem for realism. But the problem may be manageable.

---

[40] So this realist response does not take the failures of 'immature' science to be irrelevant to the defence of realism, thus threatening the defence with 'vacuity' (Laudan 1981: 34). Rather, it takes the relevance of a science's failures (and successes) to that defence to increase with *the degree of* that science's maturity, a degree assessed by an empirical epistemology.

For, the anti-realist must argue that the historical record shows not only that past failures are extensive but also that we have not improved our capacity to describe the unobservable world sufficiently to justify confidence that the accounts given by our current well-established theories are to a large extent right. This is a hard case to make.[41]

REFERENCES

Boyd, Richard N. (1973). 'Realism, Underdetermination and a Causal Theory of Evidence'. *Noûs*, 7: 1–12.

——(1984). 'The Current Status of Scientific Realism', in Jarrett Leplin (ed.), *Scientific Realism*. Berkeley: University of California Press.

——(1985). 'Lex Orandi Est Lex Credendi', in Paul M. Churchland and Clifford A. Hooker (eds.), *Images of Science: Essays on Realism and Empiricism, with a Reply from Bas C. van Fraassen*. Chicago: University of Chicago Press.

Brown, James Robert (1994). *Smoke and Mirrors: How Science Reflects Reality*. New York: Routledge.

Churchland, Paul M. (1985). 'The Ontological Status of Observables: In Praise of the Superempirical Virtues', in Paul M. Churchland and Clifford A. Hooker (eds.), *Images of Science: Essays on Realism and Empiricism, with a Reply from Bas C. van Fraassen*. Chicago: University of Chicago Press.

——and Hooker, Clifford A. (eds.) (1985). *Images of Science: Essays on Realism and Empiricism, with a Reply from Bas C. van Fraassen*. Chicago: University of Chicago Press.

Clendinnen, F. J. (1989). 'Realism and the Underdetermination of Theory'. *Synthese*, 81: 63–90.

Cushing, James T., and McMullin, Ernan (eds.) (1989). *Philosophical Consequences of Quantum Theory*. Notre Dame, Ind.: University of Notre Dame Press.

——Fine, A., and Goldstein, S. (eds.) (1996). *Bohmian Mechanics and Quantum Theory: An Appraisal*, Boston Studies in the Philosophy of Science, 184. Dordrecht: Kluwer.

Devitt, Michael (1991). *Realism and Truth*, 2nd edn. Oxford: Blackwell.

——(1997). Afterword to Devitt, *Realism and Truth*, 2nd edn. Repr. Princeton: Princeton University Press.

——(1998). 'Naturalism and the A Priori'. *Philosophical Studies*, 92: 45–65.

——(1999). 'A Naturalistic Defense of Realism', in Steven D. Hales (ed.), *Metaphysics: Contemporary Readings*. Belmont, Calif: Wadsworth.

——(2001). 'Incommensurability and the Priority of Metaphysics', in P. Hoyningen-Huene and H. Sankey (eds.), *Incommensurability and Related Matters*. Dordrecht: Kluwer.

——(2002). 'Underdetermination and Realism', in Ernest Sosa and Enrique Villanueva (eds.), *Philosophical Issues*, xii: *Realism and Relativism*. Cambridge, Mass.: Blackwell.

[41] Versions of this chapter have been delivered in many places, starting with a conference, 'Logic and Metaphysics', held in Genoa, Sept. 2001. I am indebted to these audiences for comments. I am also indebted to Radu Dudau for helpful advice on the literature, to Peter Godfrey-Smith for a helpful prior exchange on the topic, to the members of my graduate class on scientific realism in Fall 2001, and to the following for comments on a draft: Jeff Bub, Radu Dudau, Frank Jackson, Mikael Karlsson, Andre Kukla, Jarrett Leplin, David Papineau, Stathis Psillos, and Howard Sankey.

—— and Sterelny, Kim (1999). *Language and Reality: An Introduction to the Philosophy of Language*, 2nd edn. Oxford: Blackwell.

Duhem, P. (1906). *The Aim and Structure of Physical Theory*. Repr. trans. P. Wiener. Princeton: Princeton University Press, 1954.

Ellis, Brian (1979). *Rational Belief Systems*. Oxford: Blackwell.

—— (1985). 'What Science Aims to Do', in Paul M. Churchland and Clifford A. Hooker (eds.), *Images of Science: Essays on Realism and Empiricism, with a Reply from Bas C. van Fraassen*. Chicago: University of Chicago Press.

Fales, Evan (1988). 'How To Be a Metaphysical Realist', in Peter A. French, Theodore E. Uehling, Jr., and Howard K. Wettstein (eds.), *Midwest Studies in Philosophy*, xii: *Realism and Antirealism*. Minneapolis: University of Minnesota Press.

Field, Hartry (1996). 'The A Prioricity of Logic'. *Proceedings of the Aristotelian Society*, 96: 1–21.

—— (1998). 'Epistemological Nonfactualism and the A Prioricity of Logic'. *Philosophical Studies*, 92: 1–21.

Fine, Arthur (1986a). *The Shaky Game: Einstein, Realism, and the Quantum Theory*. Chicago: University of Chicago Press.

—— (1986b). 'Unnatural Attitudes: Realist and Instrumentalist Attachments to Science'. *Mind*, 95: 149–77.

—— (1991). 'Piecemeal Realism'. *Philosophical Studies*, 61: 79–96.

Glymour, Clark (1984). 'Explanation and Realism', in Jarrett Leplin (ed.), *Scientific Realism*. Berkeley: University of California Press.

Gutting, Gary (1985). 'Scientific Realism versus Constructive Empiricism: A Dialogue', in Paul M. Churchland and Clifford A. Hooker (eds.), *Images of Science: Essays on Realism and Empiricism, with a Reply from Bas C. van Fraassen*. Chicago: University of Chicago Press.

Hacking, Ian (1983). *Representing and Intervening: Introductory Topics in the Philosophy of Natural Science*. Cambridge: Cambridge University Press.

Hesse, Mary (1967). 'Laws and Theories', in Paul Edwards (ed.), *The Encyclopedia of Philosophy*, iv. New York: Macmillan.

Hoefer, C., and Rosenberg, A. (1994). 'Empirical Equivalence, Underdetermination, and Systems of the World'. *Philosophy of Science*, 61: 592–607.

Hooker, Clifford A. (1974). 'Systematic Realism'. *Synthese*, 51: 409–97.

Horwich, Paul (1998). *Truth*, 2nd edn. Oxford: Clarendon Press.

Jennings, Richard (1989). 'Scientific Quasi-Realism'. *Mind*, 98: 223–45.

Kitcher, Philip (1993). *The Advancement of Science: Science without Legend, Objectivity without Illusions*. New York: Oxford University Press.

Kripke, Saul A. (1980). *Naming and Necessity*. Cambridge, Mass.: Harvard University Press.

Kuhn, Thomas S. (1962). *The Structure of Scientific Revolutions*. Chicago: Chicago University Press.

Kukla, Andre (1993). 'Laudan, Leplin, Empirical Equivalence, and Underdetermination'. *Analysis*, 53: 1–7.

—— (1998). *Studies in Scientific Realism*. New York: Oxford University Press.

Laudan, Larry (1981). 'A Confutation of Convergent Realism'. *Philosophy of Science*, 48: 19–49. Repr. in Jarrett Leplin (ed.), *Scientific Realism*. Berkeley: University of California Press, 1984.

—— (1984). *Science and Values*. Berkeley: University of California Press.

Laudan, Larry (1996). *Beyond Positivism and Relativism: Theory, Method and Evidence*. Boulder, Colo: Westview Press.

——and Jarrett Leplin (1991). 'Empirical Equivalence and Underdetermination'. *Journal of Philosophy*, 88: 449–72. Repr. in Larry Laudan (ed.), *Beyond Positivism and Relativism: Theory, Method and Evidence*. Boulder, Colo.: Westview Press, 1996.

Leplin, Jarrett (ed.) (1984*a*). *Scientific Realism*. Berkeley: University of California Press.

——(1984*b*). Introduction to Leplin, *Scientific Realism*. Berkeley: University of California Press.

——(1987). 'Surrealism'. *Mind*, 96: 519–24.

——(1997). *A Novel Defense of Scientific Realism*. New York: Oxford University Press.

——and Laudan, Larry (1993). 'Determination Underdeterred: Reply to Kukla'. *Analysis*, 53: 8–15.

Levin, Michael (1984). 'What Kind of Explanation Is Truth?', in Jarrett Leplin (ed.), *Scientific Realism*. Berkeley: University of California Press.

Lewis, Peter J. (2002). 'Why the Pessimistic Induction Is a Fallacy'. *Synthese*, 129: 371–80.

Lipton, Peter (1991). *Inference to the Best Explanation*. London: Routledge.

McAllister, J. W. (1993). 'Scientific Realism and Criteria for Theory-Choice'. *Erkenntnis*, 38: 203–22.

McMullin, Ernan (1984). 'A Case for Scientific Realism', in Jarrett Leplin (ed.), *Scientific Realism*. Berkeley: University of California Press.

——(1991). 'Comment: Selective Anti-Realism'. *Philosophical Studies*, 61: 97–108.

Matheson, Carl (1989). 'Is the Naturalist Really Naturally a Realist?' *Mind*, 98: 247–58.

Maxwell, Grover (1962). 'The Ontological Status of Theoretical Entities', in H. Feigl and G. Maxwell (eds.), *Minnesota Studies in the Philosophy of Science*, iii: *Scientific Explanation, Space and Time*. Minneapolis: University of Minnesota Press.

Miller, Richard W. (1987). *Fact and Method: Explanation, Confirmation and Reality in the Natural and Social Sciences*. Princeton: Princeton University Press.

Musgrave, Alan (1985). 'Realism versus Constructive Empiricism', in Paul M. Churchland and Clifford A. Hooker (eds.) (1985). *Images of Science: Essays on Realism and Empiricism, with a Reply from Bas C. van Fraassen*. Chicago: University of Chicago Press.

——(1988). 'The Ultimate Argument for Scientific Realism', in R. Nola (ed.), *Relativism and Realism in Science*. Dordrecht: Kluwer.

Papineau, David (1979). *Theory and Meaning*. Oxford: Clarendon Press.

Psillos, Stathis (1999). *Scientific Realism: How Science Tracks Truth*. New York: Routledge.

Putnam, Hilary (1978). *Meaning and the Moral Sciences* (London: Routledge & Kegan Paul).

——(1983). *Philosophical Papers*, iii: *Realism and Reason*. Cambridge: Cambridge University Press.

——(1987). *The Many Faces of Realism*. LaSalle, Ill.: Open Court.

Quine, W. v O. (1960). *Word and Object*. Cambridge, Mass.: MIT Press.

——(1961). *From a Logical Point of View*, 2nd edn. Cambridge, Mass.: Harvard University Press.

——(1975). 'On Empirically Equivalent Systems of the World'. *Erkenntnis*, 9: 313–28.

Rey, Georges (1998). 'A Naturalistic A Priori'. *Philosophical Studies*, 92: 25–43.

Smart, J. J. C. (1963). *Philosophy and Scientific Realism*. London: Routledge & Kegan Paul.

Stich, Stephen P. (1983). *From Folk Psychology to Cognitive Science: The Case Against Belief*. Cambridge, Mass.: MIT Press.

——(1996). *Deconstructing the Mind*. Oxford: Oxford University Press.

van Fraassen, Bas C. (1980). *The Scientific Image*. Oxford: Clarendon Press.

—— (1985). 'Empiricism in the Philosophy of Science', in Paul M. Churchland and Clifford A. Hooker (eds.) (1985). *Images of Science: Essays on Realism and Empiricism, with a Reply from Bas C. van Fraassen*. Chicago: University of Chicago Press.

—— (1989). *Laws and Symmetry*. Oxford: Clarendon Press.

—— (2000). 'The False Hopes of Traditional Epistemology'. *Philosophy and Phenomenological Research*, 40: 253–80.

Worrall, J. (1989). 'Structural Realism: The Best of Both Worlds'. *Dialectica*, 43: 99–124.

CHAPTER 27

LAWS

NANCY CARTWRIGHT AND
ANNA ALEXANDROVA
WITH SOPHIA EFSTATHIOU,
ANDREW HAMILTON, AND
IOAN MUNTEAN

1. INTRODUCTION

For a long time the analytic tradition in philosophy of science focused on two main questions about laws: "Can one reasonably take a realist stand about the laws of science?" and "What distinguishes a law from other kinds of truths, especially from universal and statistical truths that are not laws?" For a discussion of the first question, look to the entry on "realism". The second was taken to be important because laws were thought to be ontologically fundamental—the basis responsible for all other natural facts—and to be the source of scientific prediction, explanation, and technology. Nowadays these assumptions are under attack from a variety of vantage points and the second question is overshadowed by a prior one: "Of what use are laws to begin with?" In Section 3 we shall discuss five overlapping positions that downplay the role of laws in science and nature. The slogan of all of these could be Ronald Giere's 'Science without laws!' Before that in Section 2 we describe more traditional views that take laws as central, either as the repository of scientific knowledge (laws of science) or as the basic sources or governors for what happens (laws of nature).

2. TRADITIONAL VIEWS

What we call the *traditional view* takes laws to be a fundamental aim and a crowning achievement of modern science. The problem is only to find an adequate definition of them. What does it mean to be a law of nature? This question dominated metaphysics and philosophy of science in the second half of the twentieth century. Among the accounts of laws the most notable competitors are the *necessitarian theory* and the *systems view*. However, both of these accounts can be viewed as reactions to an older, Humean, view of laws. Hence we begin with a description of the Humean regularity account.

2.1 The Regularity Account and its Critique

David Hume's (1946) empiricist treatment of causality is usually credited as an inspiration for this view. Hume took causal relations to be nothing but relations of constant conjunction between a cause and its effect, plus spatio-temporal contiguity. He granted that we feel a certain necessity in the causal connection between, say, kicking a ball and the ball moving, so that we are able to say that if the ball was not kicked it would not have moved. However, he claimed that the observed constancy of the connection between the kick and the movement of the ball is all that accounts for our feeling that there is a necessary connection between a cause and its effect. The feeling of determination is, for Hume, an addition of the mind, not an indication that there is necessity in the world.

By reducing causation to constant conjunction, Hume opened the possibility for a similar understanding of laws of nature. Laws, for a Humean, are just expressions of universal regularities of occurrent properties, propositions that say, as A. J. Ayer puts it, 'what invariably happens' (1998: 815). Expressed in the language of first-order logic, laws are just the conditions in the world that make expressions like the following true: for all x, if x has a property F then x has a property G.

The account is attractive to empiricists who seek to emphasize the inductive and the a posteriori element in science, as opposed to the deductive and a priori nature of logical knowledge. Empiricists are also keen to economize on their ontology by eschewing all modal notions such as necessity. However, it is not hard to realize that this simple account fails. Two problems are most commonly cited.

First is the problem with *non-instantial* and *vacuous* laws. Vacuous regularities are those whose antecedent is always false, thereby making the universal implication true. Ayer's famous example of such a regularity is "All winged horses are spirited". Obviously, we would like to exclude vacuous generalizations by stipulating that the antecedent of a law has to be realizable. But that would in turn exclude non-instantial laws, such as Newton's law that a body on which no forces act will move inertially.

This problem gets more serious when we consider the implications of the fact that a law, for a regularity theorist, cannot refer to any unrealized possibility. The difficulty was pointed out by, among others, William Kneale (1950, 1961) and George Molnar (1969). The latter reconstructed the argument as follows:

If "Something is F" is a statement of unrealized possibility, then it is false. If it is false, then by the regularity view "Nothing is F" is a law of nature. So "Something is F" is inconsistent with a law of nature and hence is not a statement of unrealized possibility.

Molnar concludes: 'for any contingent unrestricted existential proposition containing only empirical predicates, it logically cannot be the case that the proposition is false and that it is consistent with every law of nature' (1969: 81). This is very counter-intuitive, for we are asked to choose either truth or impossibility. This means that if there never was a chain reaction of plutonium within a strong steel shell containing heavy hydrogen, then there is a law of nature preventing it from happening. It also implies that there is a law of nature that there cannot be a river of Coca-Cola.

The second obstacle is known as the problem of accidental generalizations. "All golden spheres are less than a mile in diameter" is true accidentally, whereas "All uranium spheres are less than a mile in diameter" is true in virtue of a law of nature (van Fraassen 1989: 27). The regularity account can make no sense of this obvious and important distinction.

What is known as the *epistemic* version of the regularity account attempts to address these problems by supplementing the occurrent regularity requirement with a proviso that laws are those universal generalizations towards which scientists have a special *attitude*. This special attitude can be readiness to use a generalization as a tool for prediction, acceptance of the law on the basis of examining only few instances, treating the generalization as a part of a deductive theory, etc. (Ayer 1998). (More on this later.)

The other philosophical accounts of laws can be viewed as reactions to the regularity view, because they seek either to incorporate or to exorcize its empiricist intuitions, and to overcome its obvious failings.

2.2 The Necessitarian View: Motivation, Theory, and Problems

One attempt to overcome the problems associated with the regularity view is to admit that laws of nature are not contingent, but necessary (in some non-logical sense of necessity). Indeed, regularity theorists often slide necessity or other modal notions through the back door when answering the standard objections. Consider

Karl Popper's attempt to rescue the Humean theory. To accommodate Kneale's objections Popper (1959) proposed that a law of nature is a statement deducible from a statement function which is satisfied in all worlds that differ from ours at most in their initial conditions. This, however, is no longer a purely Humean view since it makes use of the modal notion of possible worlds. Many philosophers conclude that we cannot after all make sense of laws of nature without some notion of necessity. But a positive account of this view was not articulated until David Armstrong (1983), Fred Dretske (1977), and Michael Tooley (1977) pioneered their versions of a necessitarian view of laws in the 1970s.

The necessitarians reject the possibility of making sense of laws on any version of the Humean model, epistemic or otherwise. Dretske (1977), for example, argues against all variants of these accounts. He summarizes the attempts to preserve a Humean element by the following formulas:

Law = universal regularity + X, where X can be (a) a high degree of confirmation, (b) wide acceptance within the relevant community, (c) readiness to use this regularity for explanation, (d) deductive relations with a larger theoretical framework, and (e) predictive use.

Nowadays we should also add explanatory power and ability to unify to this list. (See discussion below.)

The first two attempts to supplement the universal regularity are epistemic, and hence, as Dretske points out, are unable to clarify the ontological status of a law of nature. High degree of confirmation and a wide acceptance are characteristics of a *statement* expressing a law of nature; they are not intrinsic characterizations of the law itself. If we take them to be the latter, then we are left with the uncomfortable conclusion that universal truths *become* laws of nature once we begin to treat them as such and that there are no unknown laws.

Being deducible from higher-level statements cannot be definitive of a law either, for this requirement could not be satisfied by the most fundamental laws of a theory. We could, however, postulate that the genuine laws are "nomologically ultimate", or not deducible from other universal generalizations plus some singular statements of initial conditions (Molnar 1969). So if a universal generalization can be shown to be a special case of another such generalization, then it is not a basic law. On this view only basic laws have to be realized, and we thus reduce the problem of non-instantial laws (though we do not solve it). However, this modification won't eliminate the difficulty with accidental generalizations. Molnar asks us to imagine an accidental and an unexplainable (i.e. non-deducible from laws) event such as the death of a lone moa before reaching 50. It is most counter-intuitive that this should be considered a basic law.

In response to these objections, it is often claimed that the main characteristic of a law is its explanatory power with respect to instances as well as lower-level generalizations. Yet, necessitarians claim, a universal regularity cannot suddenly acquire explanatory power, since many universal generalizations patently lack such power. The addition of this condition is ad hoc because we do not know how these generalizations can serve as explanations.

A better theory of laws, necessitarians propose, can be obtained if we postulate properties and connections between them. Since properties are universals, laws of nature are constituted by relations between universals, of the form "F-ness yields G-ness" (Dretske 1977), so that 'something's being F necessitates that same something's being G in virtue of the universals F and G' (Armstrong 1983: 96). For example, the correct way to read Newton's "F = *ma*" is as follows: the properties of being subject to a force *f* and having a mass *m* necessitate the property of accelerating in the direction of this force at *f/m* meters/second (N(F,G)) (Earman 1984). The relation N(F,G) implies and explains a universal association between Fs and Gs, but is not in turn implied by it.

Modern necessitarians take necessitation to be a non-logical relation holding between the universals, but not between the particulars which may have the properties described by those universals. Hence, there is no strong necessitation relation between physical objects in the world, rather the relation holds only between properties and the "mustness" is then "passed on" to the particulars. Necessitarians such as Armstrong also espouse the Principle of Instantiation, which requires that universals be instantiated by real particulars in the world.

The view has some intuitive plausibility. Postulating universals can explain how laws but not accidental generalizations support counterfactuals: laws do so in virtue of an existing relation between the universals which accidental generalizations lack. Nevertheless, many philosophers find the account controversial. Bas van Fraassen's critique (1989) of the necessitarian conception of laws is perhaps the most widely cited. He raises a dilemma. Its two horns are known as the *problem of identification* and the *problem of inference*.

The inference problem is an invitation to explain how the "mustness" at the level of particulars is implied by the relation between the universals whose properties these particulars have. If it is a law that all As are Bs, how do we infer that an A *must* be a B? The inference is not logically straightforward. One could just postulate that lawhood *is* necessity and that all that is necessary is actual. However, then necessity cannot be a *ground* for lawhood, in which case we face the identification problem. What is the nature of the relation between universals such that it yields necessitation at the level of particulars? Just calling the relation necessity does not seem to help. This is the problem that led David Lewis to conclude that "necessitation" cannot just be postulated. 'It [necessitation] cannot enter into them [necessary connections between particulars] just by bearing a name, any more that one can have mighty biceps just by being called "Armstrong" ' (1983).

2.3 Laws as Best Systems

Some necessitarians sought to justify their postulation of universals and relations between them by pointing out the advantages of this view over the regularity theory and claiming that universals are the best explanation for lawhood. However, such metaphysical extravagance did not suit the tastes of more traditional empiricists. The account of laws as best systems can be seen as an empiricist response to necessitarians, motivated to maintain an austere ontology of occurrent facts.

2.3.1 *The Best Balance of Strength and Simplicity*

One such view is known as the Mill–Ramsey–Lewis account. It proposes that laws of nature be regarded as axioms or theorems that appear in those deductive systems that strike the best balance between strength of description and simplicity. The strength of a deductive system is usually defined by the amount of information it carries about the world, while simplicity is measured by how efficiently the system organizes the disparate facts that describe the universe. Its proponents claim that it passes 'the empiricist loyalty test' (Earman 1984) or satisfies *Humean supervenience*, which requires that metaphysical and epistemological priority be granted to occurrent properties and regularities (Lewis 1986, p. ix). It is also argued that the systems account avoids the problems of non-instantiated laws and accidental generalizations. Admitting vacuous laws and accidental generalizations jeopardizes a deductive system's simplicity, while eschewing non-instantiated laws can hurt its strength. Finally, systems theorists contend that the account explains why scientific theories aim at universality, coherence, and parsimony.

Most critics of this account point out that strength and simplicity are far from unproblematic as criteria for lawhood. Both are highly dependent on the language used for theory formulation and lack an objective definition. Could they be more than slogans? Van Fraassen argues that in fact the Mill–Ramsey–Lewis account requires five criteria: theories have to be formulated in "natural predicates", be true, simple, strong, and balanced between strength and simplicity. Can these criteria be maintained in the face of evidence from the history of science? For van Fraassen these criteria are too general for actual use in science, easily defeasible by other criteria, and highly dependent on the starting point of an investigation (1989: 56).

John Earman, a prominent systems theorist, argues that this account can and should be modified by replacing its highly general criteria for lawhood with more pragmatic principles: simplicity and information content can be maximized relative to a certain application of a theory. He also doubts that simplicity and strength as applied to deductive systems can by themselves secure lawhood (1984). It is possible though not obvious, he argues, that considerations of simplicity will necessarily exclude accidental generalizations. Earman thus suggests further constraints based on Mill's notion of indefeasibility.[1] Mill introduced the notion to distinguish between defeasible (or non-lawful) generalizations and the indefeasible (or genuinely lawful) ones. However, most philosophers agree that he failed to secure such a distinction (for an argument to this effect, see Mackie 1974). Earman sees the distinction between fundamental laws and generalizations of fact as one of degree rather than of kind, where the former are set apart from the latter by the fact that their conditions of defeasibility are exceptional rather than generic. The methodology is as follows: take any generalization of fact, and partition its realization conditions into *defeasors* (the states of affairs that guarantee the failure of this generalization) and *enablers* (those that guarantee its success). If the enablers are exceptional, the generalization is accidental; otherwise, it approaches lawhood.

Earman's addendum requires a better articulation. How are we to measure genericness and exceptionality? Simple statistical head-counting seems to be too crude and sample-dependent. The condition is also very demanding and it is unclear that it can be applied to much of contemporary science. Take, for instance, the poor cousins of physics—the special sciences. There we have very little reason to expect a complete theory. As things stand now, the few laws that biologists and social scientists claim to have discovered rely on very specific *ceteris paribus* assumptions and hence, in Earman's language, have rather exceptional enablers. Lawhood in special sciences, on his account, should be characterized by generic defeasors and exceptional enablers. Many would argue that this is not a good reason to deny some principles the status of a law.

2.3.2 *Explanatory Power and Unificationism*

An alternative systems view to taking laws as those generalizations that balance strength with simplicity is to associate lawhood with explanatory power and to see that in turn as a matter of unification.

On this view, perhaps first articulated in contemporary work by Michael Friedman (1974), the growth of understanding and, consequently of science, proceeds by formulating fewer and fewer laws as ultimate and reducing the number of independent phenomena we need to accept as basic. To explain a phenomenon or a law is to show how it follows from more basic laws that also explain very different phenomena and laws. The role of laws on this account is to contain as much information as possible so as to serve as the deductive basis for the rest of our knowledge. For the deduction to count as a genuine unification (i.e. to avoid the reduction of the number of laws just by treating them as conjunctions), the deduced laws have each to be independently acceptable.

Another major proponent of the unificationist view of scientific progress and explanation is Philip Kitcher (1976, 1981). Kitcher criticizes Friedman's account

---

[1] Mill referred to indefeasibility as *unconditionality* (see Mill 1947, book III, ch. 5).

because it seeks to construct unification as a progressive reduction of the *number* of laws and insists that what really counts is 'a reserve of explanatory arguments' that best unifies the statements accepted as true by a scientific community. According to Kitcher, the history of science shows that successful theories offered general patterns of argument that could be applied to many new phenomena. A Newtonian pattern, for example, requires us to specify a force function, mass of the bodies, distance, time, etc. If much of our presently accepted knowledge can be derived using the same argumentative pattern, then the argumentative pattern with the strongest unifying power is the one that should and generally does get accepted.

Although rarely made explicit, the assumption that true laws of nature are few and unifying has been the driving force behind this view. It motivates the claim that unification is the essential feature of explanation. This claim has recently come under fire (Dupre 1993; Cartwright 1999). But a more direct challenge to this account, as both a prescriptive and a descriptive ideal, comes from two directions. On the one hand, the unificationists have been attacked by students of modelling in science. Notice how Friedman uses "laws" and "phenomena" interchangeably. Since he wrote, many detailed case studies of the practice of application of theories in natural science have exposed the very tenuous relationship between fundamental laws and the actual phenomena (Cartwright 1983; Morgan and Morrison 1999). According to this literature laws are, at best, only one element in explanation, an element whose relation to reality is neither deductive nor simple. (More on this later.)

A different challenge to the unificationist programme can be posed by the special sciences, where explanation and modelling is achieved on a much more local and piecemeal basis than the unificationist view allows. Take, for instance, rational choice theory, hailed by its proponents to be the next grand theory of the social world. Unification of all, or almost all, human behaviour under the paradigm of rational choice is seen by many to be the main virtue of this research programme (Frerejohn and Satz 1994). However, when we inspect the few examples of the actual successful application of rational choice theory, the locality and fragility of the conditions under which the theory applies become evident (Guala 2001). The unifying power of this theory thus only conceals its real problems. We will return to these concerns below. Now we proceed to two of the most recent accounts within the traditional approach and a final challenge to the traditional view of laws.

2.4 Recent Revivals of Laws

Two recent approaches that continue to set laws centre-stage in science are Marc Lange's (1997) and Michael Friedman's (1999). The former takes laws to be empirical though necessary principles, while the latter formulates a Kantian view of laws.

2.4.1 *Lange: Laws in Terms of Stability*

Marc Lange aims to make his account 'fit the facts of scientific practice' (2000: 6). If his account lives up to his claims, he will be able to avoid both importing necessity from outside, as do accounts that ground lawhood in relations between universals, and distinguishing law-truths from others by prior metaphysical appeals, such as the assumption that the laws that science discovers must be simple and unifying. The account Lange offers also promises to provide degrees of necessity, which will allow, for instance, that the laws of biology and of the social sciences will be laws, like the laws of physics, but with a lower degree of necessity, as well as the possibility that there are distinct sets of truths that count equally as laws. The trick is in Lange's use of counterfactuals. He takes these for granted and does not suppose they are reducible to or supervene on facts about what actually occurs—thus diverging from all "Humean supervenience" accounts that take what is and is not a law to be fixed by the non-nomic, non-modal facts.

2.4.1.1 *Laws and Counterfactuals*

Although Lange's account of lawhood relies on a close connection between laws and counterfactuals, it does not suppose, as traditional accounts do, that what picks out laws from other truths is the distinctive capacity of natural laws to support counterfactuals. Lange argues, instead, with those who hold a pragmatic view of laws (see below, Section 3.3), that accidental generalizations, just like laws, can support counterfactuals. His work begins rather from the idea central to current invariance accounts of laws (see Section 3.4.2) that what is distinctive about laws is that they would continue to be true under the widest possible variety of circumstances: that is in some sense laws 'collectively possess a maximal range of invariance' (1997: 246). He concludes that any non-nomic claim is a physically necessary non-nomic claim exactly when it is preserved under every counterfactual supposition consistent with the physically necessary non-nomic claims.

However, Lange's ultimate aim is to specify the relation between counterfactuals and laws 'without using the concept of a law' (2000: 10). Saying that no accidental truth is preserved under every counterfactual consistent with the laws is simply trivial and question-begging. The problem is not that the relationship between laws and counterfactuals is stated in terms of laws. The problem is that the relationship between laws and counterfactuals is explained in terms of laws, giving no indication as to why such a relation is special.

The key is the notion of stability. This is a relation to the non-nomic facts borne uniquely by the laws, whose scientific importance can be appreciated without presupposing that the laws are special in the first place. Such a relation, claims Lange, has 'never before been identified' (2000: 99). Lange defines a set S to be *non-nomically stable* if and only if it is a logically closed set of true non-nomic claims that is preserved whenever it *could* be preserved without any logical inconsistencies; in other words, a *non-nomically stable* set is *maximally* invariant. In this parlance, Lange concludes that the set of all physically necessary non-nomic claims is non-nomically stable, i.e. maximally invariant.

Why, though, is the range of invariance of non-nomically stable sets important? Lange shows that besides the trivially non-nomically stable sets of all logically true non-nomic claims and all true non-nomic claims, the set of all physically necessary non-nomic claims is most plausibly the only non-trivially non-nomically stable set. Scientific practice seems to suggest that we accept this set to be *uniquely* non-trivially non-nomically stable as a consequence of a root commitment we make in believing that some hypothesis states a law, that is, that it results from our best set of inductive strategies. Inductive confirmation is simply unavailable to claims that we do not regard as physically necessary. Since we cannot perceive what we believe to be an accident as having been inductively confirmed, no accident could be preserved along with the set of physically necessary non-nomic claims. Consequently, there can be no non-trivially, non-nomically stable set that contains an accidental truth. So, finally, the special and exclusive relation of laws to counterfactuals is this: *the set of physically necessary non-nomic claims is non-nomically stable (maximally invariant) and non-trivially stable (exclusive to accidents).*

2.4.1.2 *Multiple Grades of Physical Necessity (Lawhood)*

Under Lange's scheme it is logically possible that there be more than one non-trivially, non-nomically stable set and, he claims, it is up to science to discover whether this is the case. This logical possibility incites Lange to introduce the notion of multiple grades of physical necessity (1997: 260–1). Physically necessary non-nomic claims are preserved under the range of counterfactuals that they themselves pick out and this preservation must itself not be accidental. In this sense 'there is a grade of necessity corresponding to a set (of non-nomic claims) if and only if that set is non-nomically stable, i.e. is *maximally* invariant' (preserved whenever it logically could be) (p. 260). Associated with the set of all physically necessary non-nomic claims is a grade of physical necessity, which lies between the logical necessity associated with the set of all non-nomic logical truths and zero necessity associated with the set of all non-nomic truths. Since there could logically be non-nomically stable subsets of physically necessary non-nomic claims, there could also logically be multiple grades of physical necessity, the respective grades of necessity increasing when we move closer towards a "kernel" of "most" physically necessary laws (pp. 261–2).

2.4.2 *A Kantian View of Laws*

Michael Friedman (1999) has recently proposed a vision of laws (especially those in mathematical physics) that combines and builds on insights from Immanuel Kant, Rudolph Carnap, and Thomas Kuhn. This account is supposed to fulfil two tasks: to describe both the structure of theories and the rationality of their development. We will concentrate on the first aspect.

The core of a physical theory, according to Friedman, is its constitutive principles. Friedman's examples of these principles include principles of geometry (Euclidean and Riemannian), calculus (including tensor calculus), Newton's laws of motion, and Einstein's principle of equivalence. What unifies these statements is their special status with respect to the rest of our physical knowledge. They are, it is claimed, necessary conditions for the possibility of formulation of empirical problems and their treatment within this theory. The constitutive principles also explain the phenomenon of "conceptual shift", which characterizes scientific revolutions. To explain how Friedman appeals to a Kantian notion of the "synthetic a priori". In its original formulation, the notion encompassed, on the one hand, the necessary preconditions for doing the science of nature, and, on the other, eternal, unrevisable truths. Friedman suggests that we need to reject the second element of the Kantian notion in order to accommodate the possibility of radical revision of the basic principles of mathematical physics, which characterizes the history of science. We are then left with a 'relativized and dynamical conception' of the constitutive a priori: it makes natural knowledge possible but at the same time can change with the development of new physical theories.

On Friedman's theory, the basic laws of physical theories are not empirical principles. Rather they are a priori rules for studying nature. They supply elements of both Carnapian linguistic conventions and Kuhnian conceptual paradigms. The revision of these constitutive principles is not only an empirical but also a philosophical matter (see, for example, Descartes's justification of Galilean physics and Kant's treatment of Euclidean geometry and Newton's laws of motion). The progress of physics, Friedman concludes, is a progressive movement towards more and more general constitutive principles.

2.5 Generality and Connectedness

The traditional empiricist view in almost all its forms supposes that laws must be *general* or *repeatable* in the sense of having a large and varied stock of instances. They must not in general be true of just a handful of objects (as in the non-lawful claim 'All the coins in my pocket are copper') and in particular there are no laws of nature about single specific individuals but only about kinds of individuals. Constancy of conjunction between two features (like "being a coin in my pocket" and "being copper") will admit too many claims as laws if there are too few objects displaying these features. As we have seen, the insistence on wide scope of instances is central to both main versions of the systems view. Erhard Scheibe argues that this assumption must be a mistake because it rules out as laws the esteemed laws of fundamental physics (1995). That is because of the total interconnection (what Scheibe calls "coherence") of physical systems, an interconnection dictated by the laws of physics themselves.

Our world, Scheibe points out, is composed of a vast number of physical systems that are always interacting, and modern physics shows us how to treat their composition and interaction. Our best theories, such as classical mechanics and quantum mechanics, contain dynamical laws that imply that there are *no* completely independent systems.

For example, only perfectly isolated planets would actually orbit in a Newtonian ellipse; real planets' orbits are disturbed by the interfering influences of other planets, comets, and so forth. Are these interfering influences not themselves covered by the inverse square law? Yes indeed, but the point is that Newtonian theory does not describe accurately until *all* influences are taken into account, which means not until the whole universe is taken into account. Hence 'no subsystem of a Newtonian system is itself a Newtonian system' (1995: p. 224). Strictly speaking, only one solution to the gravitational equations can be realized in one space-time. Similar remarks apply to quantum mechanics, where the inseparability of quantum-mechanical states is the general rule.

The implication of these observations is that to require that laws have a large number of instances—indeed more than one—is wrong in principle. In practice we may very well discover systems that are independent or separable enough, and hence the universal quantifier in front of our laws will be a decent approximation. But, as Scheibe points out, it is still important to understand that multiplicity of instances, as far as our best physics is concerned, fails in principle. An implication of Scheibe's argument is that neither constant conjunction nor descriptive strength nor the power to unify can be a characterizing feature of a genuine law wherever the kind of interconnectedness prescribed by basic physics theories obtains. On Scheibe's account, *no* law is non-trivially of the form "All As are Bs"; a true law can only be of the form "The whole universe is C".

If correct Scheibe's argument undermines the strategy of the various systems' views for substituting some kind or another of generality for necessity in distinguishing laws' claims from other true claims about the world.

3. SCIENCE WITHOUT LAWS

Those who attack laws, develop substitutes, or ignore them altogether do so from a great variety of distinct points of view.

3.1 Models

One reason that models play a central role in philosophy of science nowadays is the *semantic view of theories*: the doctrine, popular throughout Anglophone philosophy of science but most articulated and well illustrated by the German structuralists, that a theory is not a set of claims as the Logical Positivists maintained but rather a set of models (Balzer *et al.* 1987; see also Suppes 1977). The semantic view is not, however, in itself opposed to laws. The models that constitute a theory must be specified in some way; the standard way is to list the laws. The models that constitute the theory are the ones that satisfy those laws. Focusing on the models rather than the laws that they satisfy is thought to have a number of advantages, however. For instance, the language and logic used to express the laws becomes unimportant and the relations between theory and the world can be thought of in terms of isomorphism of structure rather than the truth of a proposition.

In opposition to laws some authors are explicit in arguing that the models that constitute theory and that satisfy its laws are not the models that provide our best descriptions of the world (Giere 1999; Cartwright 1983; Cartwright *et al.* 1995; Suarez 1999). The theory is at best a foundation from which more accurate models are built, by improvement and correction, models that in the end no longer satisfy the laws.

The arguments for this view are of two different kinds. The first involves a detailed investigation of the practice of the sciences themselves, which now occupies a great deal of attention in the philosophy of science (Morgan and Morrison 1999; Giere 1999; Humphreys 2004). The second focuses on the abstract and often mathematical nature of laws; the classical source for this kind of view is Pierre Duhem, a historian of science who wrote at the beginning of the twentieth century (1906). If what happens is to be seen as a special case, or an instance, of the laws, then it must be possible to describe—correctly—what happens as a literal *concretization* for the circumstances at hand of the abstract description prescribed by the laws. "Traversing an elliptical orbit" is, for instance, what in more concrete terms constitutes obeying Newton's abstractly stated laws for a system moving subject to the gravitational attraction of another body.

But the *concretizations* of abstract and mathematical vocabulary do not fit properly to the world, Duhem maintains. Our most accurate models are presented in a mix of material and theoretical descriptions, where the theoretical descriptions themselves come from a mix of theories at a mix of levels; and these cannot be squeezed back into the vocabulary that literally concretizes the abstract descriptions from our laws, at least not from our fundamental mathematical laws. At best the theory concretizations form a core that with addition and correction can approximate the accuracy achieved with this more open mix of description. This is why Duhem claims that the laws of mathematical physics provide a mere *symbolic representation* of the facts of our world rather than an accurate abstract description.

More dramatic, though usually less explicit, opposition to laws comes from those who focus on the vast variety of different kinds of models used in science other than models that constitute theory—prototypes, blueprints, animal models of human behaviour, computer simulations, thought experiments, models of toy economies, idealizations, etc. (Morgan and Morrison 1999; Morgan 2001; Guala 2001; Humphreys 2004). These are opposed to laws in the sense that they take away their business, the central functions that laws were thought to serve, or at least most of them: explanation, prediction, accurate and precise description, and the provision of epistemic warrant for technological advance. In constructing and manipulating models we also learn new things not recognized before about the systems modelled, so they are the source of new knowledge of nature as well—yet another job previously assigned to laws. They do not, however, provide unification. Nor can models govern nature in the way that many take laws to do: models may describe, explain, and predict what happens but no one thinks they can necessitate it.

3.2 Symmetries

Symmetries, especially those in contemporary physics, have also recently received attention previously reserved for laws. Symmetries of entities, equations, processes, etc. pick out their *invariances* under certain *groups of transformations*. Basically a symmetry is an operation that leaves some properties of an object unchanged. For example, in the case of a snowflake the unchanged property is the geometrical form. Some of the operations that preserve the geometrical form are rotation of 60 degrees, rotation by a full turn, and reflection through an axis along any spoke. In physics, symmetry principles such as Galilean relativity (roughly, everything is the same if all systems in the universe are represented as if they had moved, say, three feet to the left) and Einstein's more complicated principles of relativity and general covariance (connected respectively with the special and the general theories of relativity), the symmetries in quantum theory, the gauge symmetry, etc. have been widely discussed by philosophers of physics as both sources and consequences of fundamental laws. Some philosophers invoke various symmetries as replacements for laws; others take symmetries to be a way of investigating the status of laws.

Van Fraassen belongs to the first group, arguing that the metaphysical notion of a law of nature should be rejected because all its definitions fail (1989). In its place, he invites us to accept the central role of symmetry arguments and principles, which are neutral between a realist interpretation as fundamental features of nature discoverable through science and a heuristic understanding on which symmetries are a guide to theorizing. (Van Fraassen himself prefers the latter as a part of his instrumentalism about science.) He argues that 'at the most basic level of theorizing, *sive* model construction, lies the pursuit of symmetry' (1989: 233). Symmetry thus is a general ideal to which scientific theories aspire, and different sorts of symmetries can serve as particular clues to the building of models that are supposed to represent phenomena. For example, Galileo's principle that laws of physics are symmetrical between rest and motion with uniform velocity puts constraints on the form of these laws and hence is "deeper" than these laws (p. 223).

Symmetries replace laws in van Fraassen's scheme not only in the sense that they constrain laws but also that they take on a number of the central virtues normally attributed to laws, especially *generality*. When a scientist analyses a problem with the aim of giving it a theoretical treatment, she seeks to isolate the "essential aspects" of the situation at hand. What counts as essential is theory-laden. She can apply existing theory to solve this problem if she establishes that this problem is 'essentially the same' as the one she already knows how to solve within her theory, or 'essentially the same' in all 'relevant aspects' (p. 235). Once this is done, the problem can be thought to be understood *generally*, which means 'we know exactly which transformations do and which do not change the situation in relevant aspects' (p. 236). Thus establishing all the symmetries of a situation leads to abstraction of its essential features and hence to its theory.

Postulations of symmetries is, of course, empirically fallible. We learn as we go which features of the situation are invariant under which transformations, and this, it is claimed, is what model-building is about. "Laws" which are "discovered" in its course are a function of the symmetries, or the generalities we require our theories to obey. For example, the principle of covariance in mechanics serves as a check on the law of conservation of momentum, so that the latter's logical status relative to this symmetry decides whether or not the law can be a basic principle of mechanics.

John Earman pursues a different direction (1993, 2002). He takes symmetries to be important for physical theory, but not in a way that dispenses with laws. For Earman pure philosophical analysis is incapable of providing results relevant to current scientific practice. His arguments start rather from fundamental issues in the foundations of physics. Laws of physics are, for Earman, the 'sets of true principles that form a strong but simple unified system that can be used to predict and explain' (2002: 3). But which these are will depend on the symmetries they display, i.e. on their invariance under various transformations. Symmetries thus function at a meta-level, helping to pick out the set of truths we should count as laws.

3.3 The Special Sciences, *Ceteris Paribus* Principles, and Pragmatic Laws

The traditional empiricist definition of law takes it to be an exceptionless generalization with sufficiently general predicates. Perhaps the most noticeable feature of special sciences is the dearth or sometimes even the lack of such principles. What conclusions should we draw from this fact?

3.3.1 *Biology*

In biology the discussion among philosophers has been less about why laws are laws than about *whether* there are biological laws. Broadly speaking, the discussion has issued in four basic positions. First, some argue that at least some biological generalizations count as laws in the standard sense, for example Dollo's "law", the Hardy–Weinberg "law", and Mendel's "laws" (Sober 1993, 1997). In direct contrast, others argue that there are no laws of biology (Beatty 1995; Gould 1989). A third position is that there are laws of biology, but that they are difficult or impossible for us to uncover due to biology's complexity. Charles Darwin offers a weak version of this position (1859). Stronger versions can be found in Alexander Rosenberg (1995) and Barbara Horan (1994). Finally, others claim that there are laws of biology but want to widen the notion of what laws are (Mitchell 1997, forthcoming).

Elliot Sober's argument for laws of biology turns on a distinction between empirical laws and a priori laws. While he grants, with John Beatty and Alex Rosenberg, that biology has no empirical laws, he argues that 'evolution is governed by models that can be known to be true *a priori*' (1997, S548). A simple, crude example of the kind of models he has in mind can be found in Malthus's claim about the relationship between resources and populations: other things being equal, the latter increases geometrically while the former increases arithmetically. A shortage of resources follows a priori, and this shortage (indirectly) governs certain evolutionary processes. For Sober, evolution—and so at least some of biology—is lawful in the sense that aspects of its path are completely constrained by a priori considerations.

Sandra Mitchell argues that most of the foregoing discussion is wrong-headed because it preserves a logical empiricist notion of law that is no longer defensible. In contrast to the metaphysical view that nature is simple and regular, Mitchell directs our attention to what she takes to be the contingency and complexity of the biological world and argues that our conception of what laws are (or should be) should shift to match this reality.

On her view, it is a mistake to ask whether biology has any laws that resemble those of physics, since to do so is to ignore that in practice, generalizations across science differ in kind, and that the generalizations biologists use are often contingent in nature. Mitchell argues that we should replace the old view of laws as necessary and universal with one that stresses pragmatic virtues like cognitive manageability, degree of accuracy, and simplicity. When we do, she says, we will find that there are a variety of "pragmatic laws" of biology that operate in the explanations biology offers.

3.3.2 *The Social Sciences*

In philosophy of the social sciences the situation is similar: the traditional analyses of laws and their role in explanation have little to say about the successes and failures of economics, political science, sociology, etc. Some have argued that social science is forever doomed to produce only instrumentally justifiable knowledge (Rosenberg 1995). Mitchell (1997), as we have seen, urges a more inclusive and pragmatic notion of lawhood. Still others seek to reject laws in favour of generalizations whose explanatory power derives from more methodologically feasible elements, such as invariance under intervention. (More on this later.)

The notion of a *ceteris paribus* law is well known in philosophy of economics (Hausman 1992). It is perhaps the most common way to cash out the conclusions derived from economic models. However, it is not unproblematic since we rarely know what the *ceteris paribus* clause stands for (for an up-to-date discussion on *ceteris paribus* laws, see Earman *et al.* 2002). "Other things" are never equal in real economies, so the condition carries little information. A more fitting notion is, perhaps, that of a causal tendency originated by J. S. Mill (1947). If Millian tendencies are to replace laws in social science, then we need to understand how they can be, are, and should be studied. Most models in economics derive tendencies a priori, using highly abstract concepts and very restrictive assumptions. Given how sensitive these derivations are to the exact conditions of the model it is hard to defend their empirical status. However, if we look at the practices of applied economists, we can discover some methods for identifying empirically robust tendencies and measuring their stability (Guala 2001; Cartwright 1989).

It is clear that if philosophy of science is to make sense of the practices of the biological and social sciences, it needs to move beyond the traditional view of laws. Social scientists developed methodologies for evaluating different explanations of phenomena and for identifying robust processes on the basis of which we can build institutions and construct policy. Lumping all these practices under the heading of instrumental knowledge or immature science seems unilluminating. What is required instead is a critical analysis of the diverse methods for inferring explanatory principles in social science.

3.4 Causal Principles

A few authors maintain explicitly that explanation, prediction, epistemic warrant for technology, and necessitation all require causal principles rather than laws in any more traditional sense. Others, as with those who work on models, vote with their feet: they spend their time and effort not talking about laws but rather explicating what causal principles are, investigating how they can be confirmed, and showing how they serve the bulk of functions laws are supposed to perform.

Causal principles differ from laws in at least three ways: (i) Causes make their effects happen. So the idea of necessitation is built right into the relation between the antecedent and the consequent in a causal principle; it is not added on as in empiricist-based notions of law. (ii) Causal principles can express themselves in regularities, but these regularities need not be universal—they can be probabilistic, and they need not be exceptionless—they can have a *ceteris paribus* character. (iii) Causal principles need not be eternal nor hold everywhere. This may be because they arise from more "fundamental" eternal unchanging laws which lead to different derivative principles in different contexts or it may be just the way things are; authors writing on causation tend to remain silent on this.

The best attempts to provide a Humean analysis of causal principles that reduces them to facts about conjunctions all fail, even if purely probabilistic conjunctions are admitted. It seems that at some point some causal notion is needed in the analysis itself. So most authors currently restrict themselves to trying to provide an "informative theory" of causation. The idea seems to be that there is some central fact about causal principles that marks them out from other kinds of principles. Interestingly, none of the central attempts to explain what causal principles claim about the world work, but rather just tell us some important characteristics they have.[2] The dominant current views include counterfactual accounts, manipulation accounts, and causal process accounts, all of which are frequently on offer as theories of singular causation as well (read about them under "causation"). There are two central accounts now popular specifically directed at generic causal claims, that is, at the causal principles that stand to replace laws.

3.4.1 *Probabilistic Theories of Causality and Bayes Nets*

Causes make their effects happen. So if there are more cases of a cause occurring, there should be more instances of the effect (or higher levels of the effect)—unless something offsets this expected increase. So causes should increase the probability of their effects, *ceteris paribus*. Can we make this *ceteris paribus* clause explicit?

Standard social science techniques control for the effects of offsetting or confounding factors by looking for increase in probabilities of effects on causes in populations that are homogeneous with respect to the confounding factors. Overweight people tend to smoke and tend to have heart trouble. To study the effects of weight on heart conditions, we look to see if the two are correlated among those who do not smoke at all, or among those who all smoke the same amount. Probabilistic theories of causality, which originated in the work of Patrick Suppes (1970), do the same. 'C causes E' is true iff the probability of E given C is greater than probability of E given ¬C, conditioning on any specific fixed arrangement of all the other causal factors for E. This formula of course is not a reduction of causality to probability because it relies on a causal notion to pick out the conditioning

    [2] Though see Cartwright (1989), who maintains that causal principles make claims about singular causal facts: "C's cause E's" claims that "In the long run, some C's, by virtue of being C's, do cause E's". See also Cartwright (forthcoming) and Christopher Hitchcock (2003) for an attack on the idea that there is any single central feature characteristic of causation.

population. There is also considerable difficulty explicating what is meant by "all" the other causes of E.

Even supposing we know what we mean, we usually do not know all the other causes for a given effect. *Bayes nets methods* can finesse this lack of knowledge (Pearl 2000; Spirtes *et al.* 2000). They suppose essentially what Suppes supposed, that causes always increase the probability of their effect (which may not be true, for instance, if a cause and a counter-cause are correlated) and that this increase persists when we condition on fixed arrangements of the other causes, plus the assumption that the minimal causal structure obtains that is necessary for these other two conditions to hold. The computer programs built using these methods can then generate for a given set of variables every set of causal hypotheses consistent with any given probabilistic information. All three of the assumptions about the relations between causes and probabilities are highly controversial, however, when taken as universally true (Hoover 2001, esp. ch. 7.2; Cartwright 2001; for criticisms and answers, see Spirtes, forthcoming).

3.4.2 *Invariance*

Causal principles give rise to regular associations between the cause and its effect, either a 100 per cent association or a merely probabilistic one. On the basis of such a regular association between two factors, C and E, we can hypothesize the principle that C causes E. On invariance accounts, like that championed by James Woodward (2003), this hypothesis is true just in case the regular association persists when we intervene to change C. This kind of invariance of the related association under intervention is thought to be characteristic of causal principles.

Two lines of thought motivate this claim. The first is close to the pragmatic view of laws described above. Causal principles are supposed to tell us what will happen as we change the cause; if the related regularity breaks down as we do so, we will not be able to predict what happens. The wider the range of interventions across which the regular association remains invariant, the more useful the causal principle is. The second generalizes from features of common-cause situations. Consider the regular association between the barometer dropping and storms, which arises because of a common cause, low pressure. If we manipulate the barometer this association breaks down, whereas we do not expect the association between low pressure and storms to break down were we able to manipulate the low pressure.

Several problems beset this view. If we *define* "intervene" so that in intervening on C by definition we do not change the related association, the invariance account offers only a trivial necessary condition for causal principles. Can we offer a definition of "intervention" that does not trivialize the result but under which causal principles really will be universally invariant under intervention? On the other hand, to defend it as a sufficient condition, we need to be sure that associations will never remain invariant (in the right ways across all the right kinds of intervention) unless they express a causal principle. Showing that is a tall order, not yet fulfilled.

3.5 Powers, Capacities, and Mechanisms

For Aristotle the regularities of the world do not result from the governance of law but rather on account of substances acting according to their natures, which are constituted by their distinctive powers and dispositions (1935). As Eric Watkins reads him, for Kant, too, powers are absolutely central: Kant

> holds that there are permanent substances along with changes of state in these substances and argues that such changes of state are possible only if substances exercise their causal powers in accordance with their natures. By thus accepting substances endowed with causal powers, Kant can grant that they stand in real relations to each other, relations that do not require (or even permit) further analysis, since it is built into the very nature of substances exercising their causal powers that they can determine the state of another substance in this way. (Watkins 2005: 391)

Rom Harré and E. H. Madden were early advocates of powers in the post-war analytic tradition. For them ' "X has the power to A" means "X (will)/(can) do A, in the appropriate conditions, *in virtue of its intrinsic character*" ' (Harré and Madden 1975: 86). A number of more recent authors similarly eschew laws, setting powers in their place, or something very similar such as capacities, mechanisms, or dispositions (Mumford, forthcoming; Ellis 2001; Cartwright 1989, 1999; Machamer *et al.* 2000; Bechtel and Richardson 1993). There are a number of different kinds of advantages powers are supposed to have over laws, as follows.

3.5.1 *Necessitation*

Why are some features regularly associated with each other—say, an object's having a negative charge and any other object that is positively charged being attracted towards it? On a Humean view of law where laws are just, as Dretske says, universal regularities plus some add-on, laws just describe this association; they do not explain why it holds; nor do they necessitate it; nor do they provide any way in which the first feature necessitates the second.

Powers are supposed to do better on all three fronts. The regular association holds because negatively charged objects have the power to attract those that are positively charged, which they exercise continuously (other powers may be exercised spasmodically or only when triggered). The exercise of the power creates the second feature and in that sense necessitates it. This in turn also shows that the regular association of negative charge in one object with the attraction of a positive object is necessitated—so long as the connection between being negatively charged and having the power to attract a positively charged object is itself necessary.

This last is the reason that accounts in terms of powers tend to include something akin to Aristotle's natures, or Harré and Madden's stricture that the object that has the power—in our case the negatively charged object—has that specific power only if in attracting the positively charged object it is acting 'in accordance with its intrinsic character'. This is the source of the necessity in the connection between being a negatively charged object and the attractive force on a positive charge. An object with a negative charge must, because of its character or nature *as* a negative charge, have a very specific power to act in a very specific way—to create an attractive force on a positive charge.

The "necessitarian view" that laws are necessary relations between universals also claims to be able to do these three jobs that the regularity view cannot. A powers view, though, is supposed to be better because it evades the inference problem (recall Section 2.2). The necessary relation between particulars is direct and does not need to be inherited from a necessary relation between universals: it follows from the concept of "power" that the power to X cannot be exercised in the right circumstances without X obtaining. Still, matters are not so clear because of the connection between powers and natures. The power to attract positive charges is part of the nature of, or intrinsic to, negatively charged bodies. What account of necessitation is to be given that makes this relation a necessary one, and will it fare better in being able to meet the challenges raised by law-endorsing empiricists than does the account that takes laws to be relations between universals? That question is still open.

3.5.2 *Exercise versus Achievement*

As John Stuart Mill pointed out, much of modern science—both social science and natural science—operates by the analytic method. The overall cause acting at any time is analysed into components, each of which has its own stable law of action—what Mill call a "tendency law". A tendency law dictates what a particular cause contributes on each occasion it is exercised, and when we are lucky we will also have a law of combination that describes what results when a number of causes all operate at once. Classical mechanics with its separate force laws (the tendency laws) and its law of vector addition (the law of combination) is the paradigm.

How shall we understand these tendency laws? A traditional regularity view will not do since the effect is *not* regularly associated with its cause. One proposal to save the regularity account is to insert between the cause and the result actually achieved a new kind of item, a kind of shadow effect, that occurs each time the cause operates. For instance, a negative charge will not always produce a motion towards itself. So we posit that the charge always produces an *attractive force*, where that force itself, though it exists, has no effects on motion; only the total force, calculated by vector addition, can move an object.

The separate forces, it seems, are idle. They do nothing. Or do they cause the total force? If so, the problem repeats itself. Mill's solution is to suppose that the separate forces *compose* the total force, as parts to the whole. This eliminates the need for a further causal story to explain what produces the total force and also shows how the separate forces themselves can play a causal role in the final result. Whether or not this proposal is reasonable for forces, it does not work where very different kinds of laws of combination are employed. For instance, the total current of a circuit is calculated from the tendency laws about the behaviour of resistors, capacitors, and inductors by "reducing" the actual circuits in which they sit to simple circuits, equivalent in their effect on the current, and even for the simple circuits it is far-fetched to insist that the resulting current is *made up of* separate components, each contributed by one of the elements of the simple circuit.

Here again the ontology of powers and their exercise seems to have an advantage. A system may exercise its power and yet fail to produce the related effect if conditions are not right, for instance if it is interfered with or some other power operates in an opposed way. This is just what happens with causes where the analytic method is in play. If powers are admitted, tendency laws can be read as laws about the powers that a cause has and not about the results that are actually achieved whenever the cause is exercised.

3.5.3 *Practices in Specific Sciences*

Besides general reasons relevant across the sciences, powers or similar non-Humean items have been thought to be necessary to understand the practices and claims in specific sciences, most notably quantum physics, biology, and the social sciences.

3.5.3.1 *Quantum Mechanics*

It is well known that in quantum mechanics we cannot ascribe to a system all the properties we would like to at once. For instance, if a system has a well-defined position, it cannot simultaneously possess a momentum. Nevertheless, were we to measure momentum we would find a definite result and in a long series of such measurements a clear probability distribution across the results will emerge. Karl Popper (1957) postulated that the system has a certain probabilistic *propensity* to produce momentum results, and in the observed distributions. Propensities are like powers, in this case powers that need to be triggered by measurement: the effect (in our case the momentum) is not there all along; still, *something*—i.e. the propensity—is what explains how this kind of outcome results after a measurement and not something totally arbitrary and unsystematic (for discussion, see Suárez 2003).

3.5.3.2 *Biological Sciences*

Recent work on the explanatory practices in the biological sciences emphasizes notions other than law. The most prominent among them is *mechanism*, usually defined as a material system consisting of components with stable properties that produce stable behaviours (Machamer *et al.* 2000; Bechtel and Richardson 1993). A typical example of a mechanism in neurobiology is the phenomenon of action potential, which involves a rapid surge and fall in the electric potential of a cell membrane and is responsible for firing of neurons in the central nervous system. Some mechanism theorists claim that laws necessarily underlie mechanisms, so that it is still laws that are ontologically fundamental (Glennan 1996). Others, like Machamer, Darden, and Craver (2000) take mechanisms (identified with particular entities and its activities) to be the proper ontic commitment for anyone who wants to make sense of neurobiology and molecular biology. Although laws sometimes enter into the description of the mechanism's activities, there are times when the regularities produced by mechanisms are not described by any laws. One could just call these regularities "laws", but, according to Machamer, Darden, and Craver, in the face of the immense explanatory potential of the notion of mechanism, this postulation has no philosophical advantages. In social sciences too, mechanism is invoked as the appropriate notion to understand the models that are supposed to represent and explain social phenomena (Elster 1993).

3.5.3.3 *Game Theory and the Social Sciences*

The dominant way of theorizing in economics nowadays is to offer game theory models to represent or explain economic phenomena, from auctions to labour relations, to the formation of industries. This mode of theorizing is sweeping through the rest of the social sciences as well, especially political science, where game theory is used to study, for instance, bargaining at the international level, formation of political parties, voting, and legislation. For a game model one needs to specify the permitted moves for each player (in the famous Prisoners' Dilemma, for example, these are "remain silent" or "confess" for both players), the structure of the game (do the players move simultaneously or successively? are the moves "one shot" or reiterated? etc.), the characteristics of the players (for instance, that they are perfect calculators) and the pay-offs that the players receive for any combination of moves they are permitted.

The nearest thing to a law anywhere in the offing appears only when we turn to what might be called the *criterion for successful explanation*. A particular kind of behaviour is successfully explained by a game model when the behaviour can be modelled as that set of moves that secures the best pay-offs for a player in light of what the other players do. If we are casting around for laws, it seems then as if the best candidate would be something like this: "In the domain of behaviours to be explained, people always (predominantly?) behave in ways that maximize their gains". That is not, however, how game models are presented. Rather the modellers talk about the *characteristics* of the agents—e.g. that they are perfect calculators, have full information, and aim to maximize their pay-offs. This is language for which the ontology of powers and capacities is ideally suited. The agents have the *power* to do any calculation and they are *disposed* to maximize their own pay-offs.

The behaviour to be explained is the appropriate manifestation of these powers and dispositions in the game with the structure and rules on offer.

As we have seen, throughout the philosophical discussion of laws and powers, the question always arises, "Which is 'more fundamental'? Which explains which?" In game models the answer seems transparent. The powers are fundamental and the laws are derivative. Why (if it is true) is it that people in the situations under consideration behave in ways that maximize their gains? Because they are disposed to maximize their gains and have the power to calculate how to do so. The maximizing behaviour is the natural consequence when these dispositions and powers act unimpeded. Moreover, when we look at claims derived from these models (for example, in international diplomatic bargaining, democracies tend to threaten less but more effectively), they too are not adequately viewed as laws. This is because derivations require a vast number of restrictive theoretical assumptions and hence we very rarely know what conditions in the world make these claims true. In these cases we may have evidence for a power or a disposition, but not for a law. The widespread use of game models suggests, then, that much of social science has abandoned laws in favour of powers and dispositions, at least for the time being.[3]

References

Aristotle (1935). *Metaphysics*, trans. Hugh Tredennick, 2 vols. London: Heinemann.

Armstrong, D. M. (1983). *What Is a Law of Nature?* Cambridge: Cambridge University Press.

Ayer, A. J. (1998). 'What Is a Law of Nature?', in M. Curd and J. A. Cover (eds.), *Philosophy of Science: The Central Issues*. New York: Norton.

Balzer, W. C., Moulines, U., and Sneed, J. D. (1987). *An Architectonic for Science: The Structuralist Program*. Dordrecht: Reidel.

Beatty, J. (1995). 'The Evolutionary Contingency Thesis', in G. Wolters and J. Lennox (eds.), *Theories and Rationality in the Biological Sciences: The Second Annual Pittsburgh/Konstanz Colloquium in the Philosophy of Science*. Pittsburgh: University of Pittsburgh Press.

Bechtel, W., and Richardson, R. C. (1993). *Discovering Complexity: Decomposition and Localization as Strategies in Scientific Research*. Princeton: Princeton University Press.

Cartwright, N. (1983). *How the Laws of Physics Lie*. Oxford: Oxford University Press.

——— (1989). *Nature's Capacities and their Measurement*. Oxford: Oxford University Press.

——— (1999). *The Dappled World: A Study of the Boundaries of Science*. Cambridge: Cambridge University Press.

——— (2001). 'What Is Wrong with Bayes Nets?' *The Monist*, 84: 242–64.

——— (forthcoming). 'Causation: One Word, Many Things', Proceedings of the 18th Biennial Meeting of the Philosophy of Science Association, Milwaukee, 2002.

[3] We would like to thank Robert Northcott for helpful comments on numerous drafts of this chapter. Cartwright's research for this work was carried out in conjunction with the Arts and Humanities Research Board project 'Causality: Metaphysics and Methods' and was supported by a grant from the Latsis Foundation, for both of which she is grateful.

Cartwright, N., Shomar, T., and Suárez, M. (1995). 'The Toolbox of Science: Tools for the Building of Models with a Superconductivity Example'. *Poznan Studies in the Philosophy of the Sciences and the Humanities*, 44: 137–49.

Darwin, C. (1859). *On the Origin of Species*. Repr. Cambridge, Mass.: Harvard University Press, 1975.

Dretske, F. (1977). 'Laws of Nature'. *Philosophy of Science*, 44: 248–68.

Duhem, P. (1906). *La Théorie physique: Son objet et sa structure*. Paris: Chevalier & Rivière. 2nd edn. 1914 trans. P. P. Wiener as *The Aim and Structure of Physical Theory*. Princeton: Princeton University Press, 1954.

Dupré, J. (1993). *The Disorder of Things: Metaphysical Foundations of the Disunity of Science*. Cambridge, Mass.: Harvard University Press.

Earman, J. (1984). 'Laws of Nature: The Empiricist Challenge', in. R. J. Bogdan (ed.), *D. M. Armstrong*. Dordrecht: Reidel.

——(1993). 'In Defense of Laws: Reflections on Bas van Fraassen's Laws and Symmetry'. *Philosophy and Phenomenological Research*, 53: 413–19.

——(forthcoming). 'Laws, Symmetry, and Symmetry Breaking; Invariance, Conservation Principles, and Objectivity', *Philosophy of Science*, suppl. vol., Proceedings of the 18th Biennial Meeting of the Philosophy of Science Association, Milwaukee, 2002.

——Glymour, C., and Mitchell, S. (eds.) (2002). *Erkenntnis*, special issue, 57/3: *Ceteris Paribus Laws*.

Ellis, B. (2001). *Scientific Essentialism*. Cambridge: Cambridge University Press.

Elster, J. (1993). *Political Psychology*. Cambridge: Cambridge University Press.

Frerejohn, J., and Satz, D. (1994). 'Unification, Universalism and Rational Choice Theory', in M. Friedman (ed.), *The Rational Choice Controversy*. New Haven: Yale University Press.

Friedman, M. (1974). 'Explanation and Scientific Understanding'. *Journal of Philosophy*, 71: 5–19.

——(1999). *The Dynamics of Reason*, Stanford University Kant Lectures. Stanford, Calif.: CSLI.

Giere, R. N. (1999). *Science without Laws*. Chicago: University of Chicago Press.

Glennan, S. (1996). 'Mechanisms and the Nature of Causation'. *Erkenntnis*, 44: 49–71.

Gould, S. J. (1989). *Wonderful Life: The Burgess Shale and the Nature of History*. New York: Norton.

Guala, F. (2001). 'Building Economic Machines: The FCC Auctions'. *Studies in History and Philosophy of Science*, 32: 453–77.

Harré, R., and Madden, E. H. (1975). *Causal Powers: A Theory of Natural Necessity*. Oxford: Blackwell.

Hausman, D. (1992). *The Inexact and Separate Science of Economics*. Cambridge: Cambridge University Press.

Hempel, C. G. (1965). *Aspects of Scientific Explanation*. New York: Free Press.

Hitchcock, C. (2003). 'Of Humean Bondage'. *British Journal of Philosophy of Science*, 54: 1–25.

Hoover, K. (2001). *Causality in Macroeconomics*. Cambridge: Cambridge University Press.

Horan, B. L. (1994). 'The Statistical Character of Evolutionary Theory'. *Philosophy of Science*, 61: 76–95.

Hume, D. (1946). *Inquiry Concerning Human Understanding*, ed. L. A. Selby-Bigge. Oxford: Oxford University Press.

Humphreys, P. (2004). *Extending Ourselves*. Oxford: Oxford University Press.

Kitcher, P. (1976). 'Explanation, Conjunction and Unification'. *Journal of Philosophy*, 73: 207–12.

—— (1981). 'Explanatory Unification'. *Philosophy of Science*, 48: 507–31.

Kneale, W. C. (1950). 'Natural Laws and Contrary-to-Fact Conditionals'. *Analysis*, 10: 123–5.

—— (1961). 'Universality and Necessity'. *British Journal for Philosophy of Science*, 12: 89–102.

Lange, M. (1997). 'Laws, Counterfactuals, Stability and Degrees of Lawhood'. *Philosophy of Science*, 66: 243–67.

—— (2000). *Natural Laws in Scientific Practice*. Oxford: Oxford University Press.

Lewis, D. (1983). 'New Work for the Theory of Universals'. *Australasian Journal of Philosophy*, 61: 343–77.

—— (1986). *Philosophical Papers*, ii. New York: Oxford University Press.

Machamer, P., Darden, L., and Craver, C. (2000). 'Thinking About Mechanisms'. *Philosophy of Science*, 67: 1–25.

Mackie, J. L. (1974). *The Cement of the Universe*. Oxford: Oxford University Press.

Mill, J. S. (1947). *A System of Logic*. London: Longmans, Green.

Mitchell, S. (1997). 'Pragmatic Laws'. *Philosophy of Science*, suppl. vol., 64: S468–S479.

—— (2003). *Biological Complexity and Integrative Pluralism*. Cambridge: Cambridge University Press.

Molnar, G. (1969). 'Kneale's Argument Revisited'. *Philosophical Review*, 78: 79–89.

Morgan, M. (2001). 'Models, Stories and the Economic World'. *Journal of Economic Methodology*, 8: 361–84.

—— and Morrison, M. (eds.) (1999). *Models as Mediators*. Cambridge: Cambridge University Press.

Mumford, S. (2004). *Laws in Nature*. London: Routledge.

Nagel, E. (1961). *The Structure of Science*. New York: Harcourt, Brace, & World.

Pearl, J. (2000). *Causality: Models, Reasoning, Inference*. Cambridge: Cambridge University Press.

Popper, K. R. (1957). 'The Propensity Interpretation of the Calculus of Probability, and the Quantum Theory', in S. Körner (ed.), *Observation and Interpretation in the Philosophy of Physics*. New York: Dover.

—— (1959). *The Logic of Scientific Discovery*. London: Hutchinson.

Rosenberg, A. (1992). *Economics: Mathematical Politics or Science of Diminishing Returns*. Chicago: University of Chicago Press.

—— (1995). *Instrumental Biology or the Disunity of Science*. Chicago: University of Chicago Press.

Scheibe, E. (1995). 'Laws and Theories: Generality versus Coherence', in F. Weinert (ed.), *Laws of Nature Essays on the Philosophical, Scientific and Historical Dimensions*. Berlin: de Gruyter.

Sober, E. (1993). *Philosophy of Biology*. Boulder, Colo.: Westview Press.

—— (1997). 'Two Outbreaks of Lawlessness in Recent Philosophy of Science'. *Philosophy of Science*, suppl. vol., 64: S458–67.

Spirtes, P. (forthcoming). 'Inferring Causal Structure: What Can We Know and When Can We Know It?', Proceedings of the 18th Biennial Meeting of the Philosophy of Science Association, Milwaukee, 2002.

—— Glymour, C., and Scheines, R. (2000). *Causation, Prediction, and Search*, 2nd edn. Cambridge, Mass.: MIT Press.

Suárez, M. (1999). 'The Role of Models in the Application of Scientific Theories: Epistemological Implications', in M. Morgan and M. Morrison (eds.), *Models as Mediators*. Cambridge: Cambridge University Press.

Suárez, M. (2004) 'On Quantum Propensities: Two Arguments Revisited'. Erkenntnis, 61: 1–16.

Suppes, P. (1970). *A Probabilistic Theory of Causality*. Amsterdam: North-Holland.

——(ed.) (1977). *The Structure of Scientific Theories*, 2nd edn. Urbana: University of Illinois Press.

Tooley, M. (1977). 'The Nature of Laws'. *Canadian Journal of Philosophy*, 7: 667–98.

van Fraassen, B. C. (1989). *Laws and Symmetry*. Oxford: Clarendon Press.

Watkins, E. (2005). *Kant and the Metaphysics of Causality*. New York: Cambridge University Press.

Woodward, J. F. (2003). *Making Things Happen: A Theory of Causal Explanation*. Oxford: Oxford University Press.

CHAPTER 28

PHILOSOPHY OF BIOLOGY

PHILIP KITCHER

1. ORIGINS AND EVOLUTION

In the middle decades of the twentieth century, biology was hardly visible in twentieth-century philosophy of science. Apart from occasional references to vitalism, a few discussions of teleology, and J. H. Woodger's valiant (but scholastic) attempt to make evolutionary biology fit within the frame provided by standard logical empiricism (Woodger 1937), philosophers concentrated their attentions on physics and psychology, with chemistry, anthropology, and history receiving less discussion, but still substantially more air time than the life (and earth) sciences. Ironically, at the same time, biological science was undergoing major transformations, first in the modern synthesis (the integration of Darwinian evolutionary theory and classical genetics, accomplished in the 1930s and 1940s through the work of R. A. Fisher, Sewall Wright, J. B. S. Haldane, Theodosius Dobzhansky, G. G. Simpson, and Ernst Mayr), and later in the post-war birth of molecular biology. These advances, particularly the latter, made biology the glory science of the second half of the century—at most major universities today there are far more biology students than specialists in other sciences, and, at many, enrolments in biology exceed all other sciences combined. Sooner or later, philosophers of science were bound to notice.

In the 1960s there were early pioneers, Morton Beckner (1959), Marjorie Grene (1959), and T. A. Goudge (1961), but those who established the philosophy of biology as a thriving, independent subdiscipline of philosophy of science came a generation later. In the writings of David Hull, Michael Ruse, and William Wimsatt, philosophers encountered wide-ranging discussions of a variety of problems, informed by technical details of biology at a level that had long been attained in the parallel philosophical study of the physical sciences. By and large, however, the principal philosophical focus was the first major transition in mid-century biology, the forging of the evolutionary synthesis. Molecular biology, despite its obvious increasing hegemony in the life sciences, was relatively neglected.

Philosophers approaching biological materials naturally brought with them tools and concepts that had been fashioned in general studies of science, studies nourished by favourite examples from physics. It was not hard to see that the tools and concepts did not always fit the biological cases, and that casual claims made about science in general often could not be sustained. Hence the turn to biology frequently brought lessons for the general philosophy of science. Sometimes, indeed, the presentation of biological complexities undermined popular claims in metaphysics or in moral philosophy. Most philosophers of biology, however, were not content to regard their field as a new laboratory in which parts of philosophy could be tested. Like their colleagues in the philosophy of physics, they were excited by the opportunity to engage in theoretical disputes within biology—they wrote for biologists as well as for philosophers. From the mid-1970s to the present, there have been serious collaborations between biologists and philosophers, and, in general, practising biologists have tended to see the work of philosophers of biology as relevant to their concerns and to appraise it more favourably than their physicist colleagues welcome work in philosophy of physics. Moreover, because late twentieth-century biology has often been applied to issues of great social concern—as in debates about the genetics of intelligence (and, more broadly, in controversies in behavioural genetics), in human sociobiology, in evolutionary psychology, and the Human Genome Project—philosophers have had the opportunity to help clarify, and even resolve, questions of obvious practical significance.

Philosophy of biology has thus evolved in a number of directions, sometimes attempting to illuminate the general philosophy of science, sometimes offering new perspectives on old philosophical problems, sometimes entering the theoretical fray within biology, sometimes participating in controversies about the social implications of biological findings. Although it's useful to consider these four varieties of philosophical work, it would be artificial and misguided to attempt to classify every article or book as exemplifying just one of them. Authors writing on the character of species, for example, may have an interest both in sorting out a biological controversy and in enriching philosophical discussion about natural kinds. Sometimes, as we'll see below, the attempt to engage a socially vexed question prompts a new theoretical debate that demands philosophical analysis. The evolution of the philosophy of biology has revealed the interaction of different pressures, in many combinations. What follows is a review of what has interested philosophers who have usually started with a focus on evolutionary biology, and have been variously prodded by a philosophical thesis here, a novel piece of biology there, and an arousing of public interest somewhere else.[1]

1.1 The Status (and Structure?) of Evolutionary Theory

One of the obvious reasons for concentrating on Darwin's theory of evolution by natural selection is that it doesn't look much like those respectable theories within physical science that have attracted philosophical attempts at reconstruction. According to logical empiricism, scientific theories are axiomatic systems, some of whose axioms employ special vocabulary ('theoretical terms'), and the best theories are those that generate a broad class of consequences that admit of test ('observation sentences'). Informal attempts to cast Darwin's achievement in this mould tend to view his theory as consisting in a 'principle of natural selection', as if this were the sole axiom of evolutionary theory. Efforts to articulate this principle then proceed to formulate it as the claim

(1) Heritable traits that increase the fitness of their bearers increase in frequency in a population

or something similar. At this point, a decision must be made about the concept of fitness. Philosophers have pursued two main options. The first supposes that "fitness" is a theoretical term, in the classical logical empiricist sense, and that its meaning is specified by correspondence rules (M. Williams, 1970; Rosenberg 1982, 1983); but this faces the obvious difficulty that biological practice rarely, if ever, provides general principles about fitness (even about fitness in types of environments), offering instead a bundle of specific claims about the relative fitnesses of highly specific traits in carefully characterized situations. The second approach attempts a general definition of fitness. Here, an obvious way to identify fitness is to appeal to the measures that field biologists actually employ, and to equate relative fitness with relative number of progeny (and here there are options depending on whether one counts the descendants in the first, or some later, generation). That strategy, however, invites the retort that Darwin's theory has now become a triviality (or, as creationists love to proclaim, a 'tautology')—that what it says is

(2) Heritable traits that increase the number of descendants left by their bearers increase in frequency in a population.

In the 1970s some philosophers attempted to evade this discouraging conclusion by offering a slightly different account of fitness: they took relative fitnesses to be not

---

[1] I should note explicitly that this review is idiosyncratic; I have concentrated on those aspects of contemporary philosophy of biology that have struck me as most interesting. I suspect that others would draw the map rather differently.

actual relative numbers of progeny, but *expected* relative numbers of progeny (Mills and Beatty 1979; Brandon 1990). Thus (1) was transformed into

(3) Heritable traits that are expected to increase the number of descendants left by their bearers increase in frequency in a population.

Darwin's theory now stands as the barely empirical claim that expectation values are actualized.

Partly under pressure from creationist challenges, philosophers have done better, and they have done so by breaking free of the idea that all areas of flourishing science should be reconstructed by viewing them as offering theories in the classical logical empiricist sense. If one wants to insist that the only viable notion of a theory is that of an axiomatic system (with the familiar empiricist conditions about theoretical and observational vocabulary), then the point is that one can have major scientific achievements that don't provide 'theories'. A more common view has been that the logical empiricist conception of theory is too narrow. From the late 1970s on, a number of commentators urged the merits of using the semantic conception of theories (according to which a theory is identified with a family of models) as a means of reconstructing Darwin (Beatty 1980*b*; Thompson 1983; Lloyd 1983, 1988). Others remained closer to the framework of logical empiricism by urging that Darwin offered a pattern of explanation (Kitcher 1982*b*, 1985*a*) or a general causal mechanism (Sober 1984) that was used again and again in the explanation of biological phenomena. Any of these approaches was able to provide a more satisfying account of what Darwin's classic work (1859) accomplishes. The immense detail of the chapters on comparative anatomy and morphology, on embryology, the fossil record, and perhaps most of all on biogeography, serves as the illustration of how Darwin's general framework of viewing all organisms as related by descent with modification and his invocation of natural selection as an agent of transspecific modification can be used to explain phenomena that would otherwise be puzzling. One can develop this approach in terms of the fecundity of an abstract model type, in terms of the unifying power of a few explanatory patterns, or by recognizing the omnipresence of some general causal mechanisms.

So what is the structure of evolutionary theory, either as formulated initially by Darwin or as it emerges in the work of his successors? That strikes me as a bad question, one born of a general logical empiricist project that we ought to abandon. Scientists practise their craft by doing a wide variety of things, observing, experimenting, refining techniques, offering predictions, intervening, giving explanations, sometimes combining apparently disparate phenomena under a single perspective. Philosophers who want to 'reconstruct' this diverse practice can usually do so in a variety of ways, and different modes of reconstruction can be valuable for distinct purposes. The much-maligned logical empiricist conception of theories as axiomatic systems is sometimes useful precisely because axiomatizations lend themselves to discussion about issues of independence of assumptions (to cite one obvious example).

I suggest that there is *no* genuine question about *the* structure of scientific theories. Philosophers have a bundle of techniques that are more or less useful in answering particular purposes. The failure of the logical empiricist conception of theory in the Darwinian case lay in the facts that (*a*) there was no serious question to which it usefully lent itself, and (*b*) it was a disaster for clarifying the epistemological status of Darwinian claims (especially in a context in which religious fundamentalists delighted in making that status as obscure as possible).

2. THE UNITS OF SELECTION DEBATE

One of the first areas in which the philosophy of biology engaged with a debate in theoretical biology was the controversy over the units of selection. The sources of the dispute lay in discussions of the early twentieth century. Darwin's theory seemed to imply that organisms would never have a heritable tendency to behave in ways that promote the reproductive success of other members of their populations at reproductive cost to themselves. Yet behavioural biologists seemed to find recurrent instances of just this type of 'altruistic' behaviour.[2] Hence arose the task of explaining the possibility of altruism in a Darwinian world. An initially attractive solution proposed that the types of behaviour in question endured because of a benefit to the group to which the actor belongs (perhaps conceived as a local population, or as the entire species). During the 1960s that suggestion came under intense scrutiny: a number of writers showed that appeals to group benefits were much more problematic than had been appreciated and that the puzzling phenomena could be understood by taking selection to operate on individuals—or even on genes (Hamilton 1964; Maynard Smith 1964; G. Williams 1966).

The last thought was developed with great rhetorical flair by Richard Dawkins in his widely read book *The Selfish Gene* (1976). There Dawkins summarized the theoretical advances of a fertile decade and recast them as demonstrating that selection really acts on genes. By this he intended not merely that one can keep track of evolutionary changes by recording the frequencies of gene variants (alleles) across the generations, but that the process of selection should be seen as one in which alleles have advantages or disadvantages (in the pertinent environments), and that these advantages and disadvantages are the causes of subsequent differences in allelic frequencies. In Dawkins's vision, the packaging of genes on chromosomes,

---

[2] According to the biological definition, an organism A acts altruistically towards another organism B just in case A's action increases the reproductive success (the number of offspring reaching maturity in the next generation) of B and diminishes the reproductive success of A.

the embedding of the genetic material in cells, and the aggregation of cells into multicellular organisms should all be understood as the expression of good strategies for genes to lever themselves into future generations.

After Dawkins, biologists and philosophers could formulate the general 'units of selection problem'. The 'orthodox Darwinian' view takes organisms to be units of selection; confused pre-1960 discussions often invoked groups (superorganismic entities) as units of selection; radical Darwinians (Dawkins and George Williams) claim that genes are the units of selection; who is right? There were early criticisms of Dawkins's proposal; Stephen Jay Gould argued that genes were not 'visible' to natural selection, suggesting that only manifest traits make a difference to survival, attraction of mates, fecundity, and the other conditions on which the transmission of genes into the next generation depends (Gould 1980a); Robert Brandon subsequently tried to make Gould's concerns more precise, by supposing that manifest traits will typically 'screen off' underlying genetic characteristics (Brandon 1984). Biological discussion quickly attracted philosophical attention to the formulations traded by the contending participants. David Hull (1981) drew a useful distinction between *replicators* (those entities that are transmitted unchanged across generations) and *interactors* (entities that engage in causal processes affecting reproductive success); if the unit of selection is conceived as a replicator, then genes are an obvious candidate; if the unit of selection is conceived as an interactor, then Dawkins's thesis is far less immediate.

An article by Elliott Sober and Richard Lewontin (1982) and the subsequent book by Sober (1984) greatly advanced the discussion.[3] Sober and Lewontin conceded that genes can be used for 'bookkeeping' in processes of natural selection, but they denied that genes can figure as causal agents. In support of their latter claim they introduced an important example. It is possible for there to be two alleles at a locus (A and *a*) so that the homozygotes (AA, *aa*) are lethal (organisms with these combinations die young) while the heterozygotes (A*a*) thrive. Under these circumstances, both alleles will be viewed as having equal fitness (because, in each generation, there are equal frequencies of each), so that a genic view will disclose no selection. In each generation, however, selection is plainly occurring, for all the homozygotes (half the population, since matings between heterozygotes yield each of the homozygotes one-quarter of the time) die before reaching maturity. Dawkins's vision thus obliterates important causal facts about the situation.

Sober continued by developing a causal criterion that he invoked to resolve issues about the units of selection. Causes, he suggests, must raise the probability of effects, and they must do so in all causally relevant background contexts. More exactly:

(4) C causes E only if, for any causally relevant background condition B_i, $Pr(E/C \& B_i) \geq Pr(E/B_i)$, with the inequality holding strictly in at least one case.

---

[3] In my judgement, the importance of Sober's (1984) account of natural selection is comparable to the celebrated monographs by Hans Reichenbach that have been so seminal in philosophy of physics. As will be apparent in what follows, I don't agree with Sober's conclusions.

(4) can be deployed to sharpen the Sober–Lewontin argument, for, as the contrived example shows, the effects of alleles on reproductive success may be positive or negative depending on other genotypic features (the effect of A varies according to whether or not it is accompanied with another A or an a). Moreover, as Sober showed, (4) allows one to make sense of the notion of group selection. His discussion advocated a *pluralistic hierarchical* view of selection. When we consider a natural selection process, the units of selection may sometimes be genes, sometimes organisms, sometimes groups; in some complicated processes, selection can even act at several distinct levels, so that selection for genes is countered (or reinforced) by selection for organisms (or groups).[4]

Although other philosophers and biologists (Gould 1982; Lloyd 1988; Wimsatt 1981; Brandon 1990; Godfrey-Smith and Lewontin 1993) may dissent from the details of Sober's argument, preferring their own substitutes for his framework (centred on the use of (4)), the pluralistic hierarchical view of selection has become the dominant position in the field. Nevertheless, it seems to me to be incorrect. Although his original (1976) accepted the commitment to a *real unit of selection*, Dawkins's (1982) contained hints of a different view, one according to which there is no fact of the matter. Kim Sterelny and I have attempted to articulate this view (Sterelny and Kitcher 1988; see also Waters 1991). In response to Sober's critique of genetic selection, we point out that principle (4) fails to govern the most celebrated examples of natural selection, all of which average across causally relevant background contexts. The famous case of industrial melanism, for example, introduces selective pressures on moth populations that abstract from local details—for even in woods that are polluted there will be clumps of trees that are unaffected and in which the speckled (non-melanic) form has an advantage in escaping predation. Further, as we show, it is possible to attribute genic fitnesses in ways that will capture the causal facts of selection, so long as one is careful to identify the environment in the right way; thus, in Sober's example of the lethal homozygotes, part of the environment of each allele is the allele with which it is paired—an A promotes reproductive success in the context of a, and detracts from reproductive success in the context of another A. (The point is further articulated in the important Godfrey-Smith and Lewontin 1993, although the authors try to defend their hierarchical view by adverting to an ill-defined conception of causation as sometimes acting at different levels.) So, in contrast to the pluralist hierarchical view, Sterelny and I propose a pluralist conventionalism. Where our opponents suppose that for each selection process there is a unique correct causal description, typically invoking a single causal level (with different levels picked out in different instances) and sometimes recognizing multiple levels, we suggest that any selection process can usually be described in a number of different ways, with the genic perspective

---

[4] Strictly speaking, Sober's account treats selection as being 'for' *traits* of genes (or organisms, or groups), but I'll gloss over the niceties here; see Sober (1984) for details.

being most widely available, and that the choice among modes of description is purely pragmatic.

To simplify, one can formulate our position as the claim that the units of selection debate over-interprets Darwin's metaphor. Organisms are born, they mate, they reproduce, and they die.[5] Darwin offered us a way of thinking about the aggregate results of such individual occurrences, and contemporary evolutionary theory has demonstrated how to make precise mathematical models that subsume a myriad of causal details. It seems at least disputable that there should be privileged assignments of fitness values to particular entities, assignments that capture the 'causal facts' about 'levels of selection'; for when a hawk picks a moth off a tree, although we have a causal interaction between a bird and an insect, there's no place at which *selection* points; we can recognize the causal interaction without forgoing the right to describe the general process of which it is a tiny part in any mode that seems most convenient. The talk of selection is a *tool* which we introduce to sum up a complex array of causal facts, and we should fashion the tool so as best to suit our concerns.

For most participants in the debate, however, pluralistic conventionalism is seen not as a way of avoiding dubious metaphysics but as a refusal to respond to the complete causal facts. In recent years, discussions on this point seem to have stalled. The main recent contribution to the units of selection controversy has been the effort by Sober and the evolutionary theorist David Sloan Wilson to rehabilitate the notion of group selection (Sober and Wilson 1998). Sober and Wilson have used their well-articulated account of group selection to generate a synthetic approach to the issue of altruism (see Section 6 below), as well as to advance the claims of the pluralistic hierarchical view. From my perspective, they have offered biologists a richer choice of models of evolutionary processes, adding to the repertoire from which we can legitimately choose in tackling the complexities of birth, reproduction, and death.

3. CONCEPTS AND METHODS OF EVOLUTIONARY THEORIZING

Many other issues concerning evolutionary biology have attracted philosophical attention, either because, like the units of selection controversy, they are debated by prominent biologists, or because they bear on long-standing philosophical questions. In this section I'll briefly look at four that seem particularly important.

In 1979 Stephen Jay Gould and Richard Lewontin published an influential essay suggesting that evolutionary theory was in the grip of a 'Panglossian paradigm'

---

[5] Of course, some organisms are asexual, and don't mate at all. For them the story is simpler.

(Gould and Lewontin 1979). They charged that evolutionary theorists were too keen to see the action of selection everywhere in nature, and in consequence that they were lulled into accepting accounts of the evolution of traits, including forms of behaviour, on the basis of inadequate evidence. Gould and Lewontin were particularly moved by examples from sociobiology (see Section 6 below), where, they suggested, a penchant for 'just so stories' often led researchers astray.

Darwin famously claimed that natural selection has been the chief but not the sole agent of modification (1859: 6). Responses to Gould and Lewontin quite naturally asked what alternative causal mechanisms these authors intended to invoke (Mayr 1983). The ensuing debate identified two main issues: First, when selection acts, can we always think of it as producing an optimal outcome? Secondly, to what extent is the operation of selection supplemented or countered by other causes? Although answers to these questions are often conflated with theses about the units of selection, it is important to recognize that they are logically independent of that debate: one can maintain any position on which entities (if any) are 'real' units of selection, while holding any view about selection and optimality or any view about modes of evolutionary causation. The urge to conflate probably arises from the fact that the most prominent advocate of genic selection, Richard Dawkins, is also one of the most outspoken defenders of the scope and power of natural selection (Dawkins 1987).

Biologists and philosophers have articulated with some care the conditions under which one can deploy optimality models in understanding the operation of natural selection. A succession of articles has clarified the kinds of constraints to which claims of optimization must be subject (Oster and Wilson 1978; Maynard Smith 1978; Beatty 1980a; Dupré 1987; Orzack and Sober 1994; Sober 1998). The second question has been much more controversial. Some biologists and philosophers have insisted on the power of natural selection (Dawkins 1987; Dennett 1995) and have condemned Gould, Lewontin, and their fellow-travellers for mystery-mongering. The strongest claims for alternative agents of evolutionary change have emerged from attempts to expose sources of order not recognized in contemporary Darwinism. Gould and Lewontin had already emphasized the possibility of deeply entrenched patterns of development (Baupläne—a concept introduced by German biologists who are often dismissed by orthodox Darwinians), and Gould's first book (his often neglected 1978) focused on historical and current explorations of that possibility. Subsequent contributions by philosophers (Wimsatt 1986; Beurton et al. 2000) and by biologists (Raff 1996; Meinhardt 1998) have pursued this theme, and Stuart Kauffman (1993) is a particularly thorough and well-developed attempt to investigate whether there are sources of biological order that need to be integrated with Darwinian orthodoxy.

I turn now to a second debate that is closely linked to the adaptationism controversy. One moral that might be drawn from (Gould and Lewontin 1979) is that the connections between evolutionary biology and developmental biology must be more precisely articulated (see also Lewontin 1974a). To ignore the processes of development that underlie a structure or trait is to risk offering an absurd 'just so story'—as if one suggested that jutting chins have been selected for their value in male displays (overlooking the fact that the chin emerges as a by-product of growth in two developmental fields). Scholars incensed by the influence of casual adaptationist thinking on nature–nurture controversies have been particularly moved to suggest that the source of the trouble is the way in which Darwinian theory has ignored development, and they have called for a new synthesis (Ho and Saunders 1984; Ho and Fox 1988). Particularly influential has been Susan Oyama's proposal of 'developmental systems theory' (Oyama 1985), which is explicitly intended to deliver the 'stake-in-the-heart move' to recurrent claims about the limits placed on us by our biological nature.

Oyama's work has inspired biologists like Russell Gray and philosophers such as Paul Griffiths and Kim Sterelny (Griffiths and Gray 1994; Sterelny and Griffiths 1999). In the strongest versions (those of Oyama, Griffiths, and Gray) our standard gene-centred versions of evolutionary theory should give way to a new style of analysis, one that takes the developmental system as central. This new perspective will recognize that what organisms inherit are not only stable chunks of DNA, but also other important molecules (the proteins that play a crucial role in early development, for example) and enduring aspects of the environment. There are connections between the celebration of developmental systems theory and other calls for the reform of evolutionary theory (for example, the 'dialectical biology' of Levins and Lewontin 1985).

At the heart of developmental systems theory is a principle of causal democracy that biologists should be happy to accept. (Indeed one common reaction is to insist that this principle is already well established in orthodox theorizing.) That principle recognizes that the manifest traits of organisms are not products of their genes alone, but emerge from the intricate interactions among pieces of DNA, other molecules, and environmental causes at multiple levels. Developmental systems theory, however, aims to go beyond this undisputed interactionism, and the principal challenge to it consists in asking for a precise specification of just the ways in which orthodox interactionism is deficient. My own view is that the insights of the proponents of developmental systems theory can be accommodated without any serious departure from orthodoxy—other, perhaps, than a commitment to keep interactionism firmly in focus—and that we cannot hope to drive a stake in the heart of all ventures in applying biology in socially harmful ways (Kitcher 2000).

The two issues so far considered have emerged first within evolutionary theory, although resolution of them has consequences for philosophical positions (Dennett 1995). The third topic of this section is a more purely philosophical problem. Biology is full of attributions of functions to traits, structures, organs, and forms of behaviour. Perhaps before the nineteenth century those functional claims could be understood in terms of the design of the creator who intended that plants and animals should be able to satisfy their needs, but, in a post-Darwinian world, they are much harder to understand. This was already appreciated before the philosophy of biology came of age, and C. G. Hempel and Ernest Nagel both devoted some attention to analysing the character of functional explanation (Hempel 1965; Nagel 1979). The task of clarifying what functional claims mean has continued to exercise philosophers.

The two most important rival proposals were both advanced in the 1970s. Robert Cummins (1973) suggested that to give a functional analysis of an item (trait, organ, structure) is to provide a causal decomposition of the production of that item. By contrast, Larry Wright (1973) argued that claims of the form 'The function of X is Y' should be understood as meaning that Y is both an effect of X and also the explanation of why X is there. Both views encounter apparent difficulties. Cummins's account seems to allow for the attribution of function to items that play a causal role in virtually any kind of process—thus we can use his analysis to identify the function that an outcrop of rock plays in the flow of water down a mountainside. Similarly, Wright's proposal licenses some peculiar functional claims; in a telling example offered by Christopher Boorse (1976) if a leaky hose in a laboratory causes a scientist to collapse from asphyxiation before he can fix it, then we're committed to the odd idea that the function of the leak is to asphyxiate scientists.

Although both suggestions were subsequently developed in the philosophical literature, Wright's received the major share of attention and his 'aetiological approach' has become the orthodox treatment of functional and teleological notions. An important elaboration was offered by Ruth Millikan, who presented a complex account of 'proper functions' explicitly linking the notion of function to evolution (Millikan 1984). Thus, for Millikan and her successors (Neander 1991; Godfrey-Smith 1994; Sober 1984; Mitchell 1995; Bigelow and Pargetter 1987), the functions of X are those effects of X whose past instances have played a causal role in the evolution of X under natural selection. Using the hoary example of the heart, we may say that the function of hearts is to pump blood, meaning thereby that pumping blood is one of the things that hearts do and that the ability of past hearts to do that was advantageous to organisms that had rudimentary hearts and thus played a role in the process of natural selection through which hearts evolved.

Although the aetiological account, thus articulated, seems to accord with many features of biological practice (see e.g. Gould and Vrba 1982) it is at odds with a celebrated distinction drawn by the ethologist Niko Tinbergen, who explicitly separated questions about evolutionary origin from questions about function (Tinbergen 1963). Since Millikan's detailed treatment, philosophers have considered the temporal location of the selection process through which the attribution of function is supposed to be grounded. At one extreme, one can demand that the function of X is Y only if Y played a role in the selection process through which X originated; at the other, one can look into the future, and suppose that Y explains the presence of X in the generations that will succeed the present (Bigelow and

Pargetter 1987; for criticism, see Mitchell 1993). Godfrey-Smith has offered a middle view that has the advantage of allowing us to draw Tinbergen's distinction; his 'modern history' theory of functions proposes that the appropriate selective regime be one in the recent past that has maintained X into the present (Godfrey-Smith 1994). Even with this clarification in place, however, the aetiological view still faces questions about the extent to which selection played a role in the maintenance of the appropriate item (Kitcher 1993).

There is a broader concern. Functional attributions abound in areas of biology where evolution is far from the dominant focus, and in which researchers would cheerfully confess their ignorance of evolutionary detail. In molecular studies in physiology, for example, there are routine claims about the function of various enzymes, despite the fact that the evolutionary pressures on the pertinent features of past organisms are swathed in obscurity. Precisely in these areas, the Wright–Millikan approach appears forced, and Cummins's proposal—which would allow researchers to deploy the kinds of causal considerations they typically advance to support their functional ascriptions—seems to do better. Yet, as seen briefly above, Cummins's analysis is too liberal. I've suggested that we can modify that analysis and integrate it with the aetiological view by supposing that functional analysis only proceeds against the background of a general view of selective pressures, whether or not we know how to articulate a history of selection in the case at hand (Kitcher 1993). Godfrey-Smith has countered that a unified vision of functions is not so easily achieved (Godfrey-Smith 1993).

The fourth and last topic from evolutionary theory that I want to discuss here connects both with biological debates and with very broad questions in metaphysics. In 1942 Ernst Mayr remedied an important deficiency in Darwinian evolutionary theory by offering an account of the notion of species (that Darwin had taken for granted). According to Mayr's 'biological species concept', species taxa are clusters of populations each of which would freely interbreed with others (if present in nature at the same place at the same time) and would not freely interbreed with other populations that fall outside the cluster (Mayr 1942, 1963). Although Mayr was successful in convincing most of his biological colleagues to adopt his definition, it has been the object of much discussion from the 1940s to the present. One obvious issue concerns the counterfactual condition: there are instances in which it simply is impossible to bring candidate populations into geographical contact with one another (think, for example, of extinct organisms), and in such cases Mayr's concept is hard to apply with conviction. Another centres on the existence of species that reproduce asexually, with respect to which Mayr has often advised that biologists deploy morphological criteria that have been found to coincide with species divisions among the closest sexually reproducing relatives of the asexual organisms in question.

The biological species concept was embedded within a more general approach to classifying organisms—'evolutionary systematics'—that drew higher distinctions (into genera, classes, families, and so forth) partly on the basis of morphological similarity, partly on the basis of evolutionary relationships. For over four decades, systematists—those who study biological classification—have debated the merits of this approach, and it has come to be seen as a compromise between two polar positions. One of these, 'numerical taxonomy', proposed to classify organisms by using a large number of characteristics for which numerical measures could be assigned and looking for clusters in the high-dimensional space defined by those characteristics. The other, 'cladistics', resolutely insists on evolutionary relationships, even if the resulting classifications turn out to be at odds with morphological similarities or past biological practice. Cladists have developed various precise compendia of rules for identifying how evolutionary kinship is to be assessed, and there are currently a number of different versions of the position.

During the 1970s an evolutionary biologist, Michael Ghiselin, and a philosopher, David Hull, mounted a serious challenge to the biological species concept, one that had ramifications for the more general issues about classification (Ghiselin 1974; Hull 1976). Ghiselin and Hull contended that species are not 'classes' but 'individuals'. As Hull articulated the point in a seminal essay (Hull 1978), we should think of species taxa as individuated by the role they play within the genealogy of living things; they are segments of the tree of life, bound together by actual relations of reproduction and descent. A consequence that Hull explicitly noted is that species, once extinct, cannot recur. The Ghiselin–Hull proposal captured biological attention because of its kinship with cladistic approaches to systematics (although many cladists have developed different concepts of species) and because it seemed to allow for higher-order processes of selection of the sort proposed in articulating an 'expansion' of evolutionary theory (Eldredge 1985; Gould 1980b, 2002). It also provoked considerable philosophical discussion.

One uncontroversial moral for philosophy has been that much of the literature on natural kinds, even some that is most influential, has been ill-designed to cope with the complexities of biological examples (see Dupré 1981, 1993). Beyond this, there has been a wide-ranging debate about the thesis that species are individuals, about how to individuate species taxa, and about the implications of a view of species for our general understanding of evolutionary theory. Although the Ghiselin–Hull thesis has been widely accepted, it seems, at first sight, to rest on a confusion: for it contrasts an ontological possibility (species are individuals rather than collections, or sets) with a semantic possibility (species names can be defined without reference to spatio-temporal markers). I have suggested that the confusion is real, and that the important point is to identify species taxa in ways that make essential reference to their historical origins (Kitcher 1984a, 1989). Framing the issue in this way enables us to make sense of the wide variety of proposals for individuating species (see the essays in Ereshevsky 1992). One option would then be to decide that one of the contending proposals is correct. From my perspective, that would be a mistake, and we ought to honour different approaches to species, advanced with different biological purposes in mind; thus, contra Hull, I think there's a use for a species concept that enables us to make sense of the recurrence of species, and that this concept would naturally be employed by biomedical researchers concerned with the possibility that *the same pathogen* might be produced again (Kitcher 1984*a*).

As I've already noted, the Ghiselin–Hull proposal was linked both to cladistic approaches to classification of organisms and to suggestions about expanding Darwinism. On the latter front, it seems that the logical connections are very loose. Whether or not we can make sense of species selection, and whether or not appeals to species selection are needed to make sense of the history of life, are matters for careful analysis of selection processes and of actual cases in palaeontology; they aren't settled by drawing semantic distinctions and making arguments in ontology. By contrast, the work of philosophers has played a valuable role in the fierce disputes among rival systematists, where Hull has served both as patient elucidator of rival views and as chronicler of the campaigns (Hull 1979, 1988). Cladistic methodology has also benefited from the careful study provided by Elliott Sober of the ways in which various desiderata are deployed in the development of a genealogical account of life (Sober 1988).

For many biologists, probably for almost all, the questions of classification and the principles that should guide it are arcane, even 'philosophical' in the pejorative sense. The discussions of species concepts from the 1970s to the present are probably more important for refining philosophical proposals in traditional areas of metaphysics than they are for reforming or aiding biology (so that Dupré 1993 may be the most enduring contribution of a large literature; see also Splitter 1988). One remarkable feature of the discussion has been the almost invariable insistence on the need to fit classificatory concepts (primarily that of species) to the needs of evolutionary theory, as if there were no other areas of biology whose projects should be considered. The protracted 'species debate' thus highlights the 'evolutionary chauvinism' that has dominated philosophy of biology. I now turn to philosophical ventures in other parts of the life sciences.

4. The Neglected Elephant

As noted in Section 1, philosophy of biology came of age a decade or so after two major transitions in the life sciences, and, as just claimed, it has focused particularly on one of these. Yet, from the 1960s to the present, an increasing proportion of biologists have been working in the areas transformed by the second—the emergence and acceleration of molecular biology—so that today's undergraduate philosophy of biology class often *introduces* most of the students within it to the *scientific* material about which it philosophizes, even though those enrolled have substantial backgrounds in biology. What they know about, of course, is things like DNA replication and the roles of various enzymes in metabolic pathways. Molecular biology sits in the classroom like a neglected elephant.

One possible explanation for this might be that not all parts of the sciences are philosophically interesting. Thus one might claim that evolutionary theory has attracted so much attention because it raises large philosophical issues, that it is a sad fact that evolution occupies less biological attention than it used, and that philosophers should be impervious to this change of fashion. I'll try to argue that the premiss is false, that molecular biology poses interesting philosophical questions, but, even were that not so, philosophers might have important work to do in articulating theoretical issues that arise in molecular studies (as they have done with respect to the units of selection, the adaptationism controversy and to disputes in systematics).

The most prominent philosophical work that touches on molecular biology addresses the issue of whether the life sciences can be reduced to the physical sciences. Since the 1960s philosophers of science have debated issues about the reduction of 'higher-order' sciences to more fundamental disciplines. In pursuing these questions, they typically employed an influential model of reduction articulated by Ernest Nagel (1962): scientific theories are viewed as axiomatic systems, whose axioms consist of laws of nature, and reduction is effected by deriving the axioms of the reduced theory from the axioms of the reducing theory, possibly with the aid of 'bridge principles' that specify the referents of terms in the language of the reduced theory using the language of the reducing theory. Although discussion of general possibilities of reduction often drew on examples from physics, psychology, and social science as test cases, biology provides an especially good domain on which to focus the arguments. For, within molecular genetics, we have a well-established and articulated body of doctrine that uses the language of biochemistry to bear on issues that were previously tackled within classical genetics (the genetics descending from Mendel, worked out by Morgan and his associates in the early decades of the twentieth century). Instead of suggestions about how some vaguely characterized area of psychology might relate to some unknown future piece of neuroscience, we can look at the details of work in pre-molecular genetics and at the ways in which contemporary biologists have transformed it through the use of concepts and principles from biochemistry.

It was quickly apparent that Nagel's model couldn't apply without modification, but philosophers of biology drew different conclusions. In an important article, Kenneth Schaffner (1969) suggested that a modification of Nagel's approach would support the claim that classical genetics is reducible to molecular biology. David Hull (1972; 1974, ch. 1) argued that the reductionist claim was more deeply problematic, and that it represented another misguided effort to force scientific practice into philosophical preconceptions. In two articles (Kitcher 1982a, 1984b), I developed Hull's critique, proposing that the classical account of reduction failed for three reasons: first, because the practices of classical and molecular genetics don't fit the conception of theory presupposed by the Nagel model; secondly, because main concepts of classical genetics, such as *gene*, cannot be specified in purely bio-chemical terms (that is, the pertinent 'bridge laws' aren't available; thirdly, because even if a derivation of some 'law' of genetics from principles of molecular biology were available, that derivation would fail to be explanatory (this point is amplified further in Kitcher 1999). Yet it seemed to me important to provide a framework in which the actual connections between molecular and classical genetics could be made clear, without relying on any concept of reduction. I proposed that the explanatory strategies of classical and molecular genetics are related in that molecu-lar explanations deepen, or extend, those offered by the classical approach, and, in particular, that they allow for the analysis of relations between specific genotypes and specific phenotypes (in particular environments, of course). Kenneth Schaffner has also pursued a project of showing how the classical and molecular practices interrelate, although his preferred account remains closer to the logical empiricist conception of theories and theoretical reduction (Schaffner 1969, 1993).

Although many writers have supposed that attempts to reduce biology to physics and chemistry are thoroughly misguided (see e.g. Dupré 1993), anti-reductionism hasn't gone unquestioned. Alexander Rosenberg (1994) and Kenneth Waters (1990, 1994) have offered probing criticisms of the claims that classical concepts aren't specifiable in biochemical terms and that biochemical derivations wouldn't be explanatory. Similarly, Sahotra Sarkar (1998), while sceptical of reductionist claims, has offered a novel model of reductionism within which to situate the debate.

Unfortunately, attempts to go beyond the debate about reductionism to make philosophical sense of the view of life that emerges from contemporary molecular biology are relatively rare. Kenneth Schaffner has explored some of the ways in which explanations in biomedicine work (Schaffner 1993). William Bechtel and Robert Richardson consider a variety of lines of biological research in their study of complex sciences (Bechtel and Richardson 1992). There are also some discus-sions of experimentation and theory change in molecular biology (Culp 1995; Culp and Kitcher 1989). These endeavours tend to be driven by broader philosophical concerns—questions about scientific explanation, theory change, or the character of emergent properties. There is, however, at least one attempt to view molecular biology as generating an important new puzzle—a pioneering attempt to address the notion of biological information (Rosenberg 1985, ch. 8).

Ironically, this last issue has recently surfaced in philosophy of biology as a side consequence of evolutionary discussions. As I have already noted, some philo-sophers of biology have taken seriously the idea that there needs to be a new synthesis between evolutionary and developmental biology. A recent article by the evolu-tionary biologist John Maynard Smith on the notion of information in biology (Maynard Smith 2000) attracted commentary from several philosophers who are sceptical of the gene-centred perspective that they take to be standard in evolutionary studies (Sarkar 2000; Godfrey-Smith 2000). Independently of how we formulate the theory of evolution, or of how we integrate evolution and development, however, contemporary molecular biology itself raises questions about how to understand the notion of information—which, according to the 'Central Dogma', is supposed to be able to flow from DNA to RNA, and from RNA to proteins, without being able to flow in the reverse directions.[6] Hence, I suggest, there was already a philosophically interesting question (spotted by Rosenberg in 1985), that didn't need the connection with evolution to make it worth pursuing.

Indeed, philosophical concern with an 'evolutionary-developmental synthesis' might better be directed at the prior clarification of developmental biology. During the past decades, molecular approaches to early embryology and to some aspects of development have made enormous strides—as in the work of Christiane Nüsslein-Volhard and her associates (which deservedly won the Nobel Prize in 1996). Providing a synthetic overview of what has already been accomplished would be a serious and important project in the philosophy of biology, one that would require careful delineation of suggestive (but imprecise) concepts of developmental stages and of levels of causation, and it seems evident to me that this project is a necessary precursor to fitting development into evolutionary biology. Further, the detailed molecular analyses raise intriguing questions about how to relate them to more general approaches to development, for example those that try to reconstruct developmental 'software' (Meinhardt 1998; Murray 1989; see Kitcher 1999).

I suspect that we are still only in the middle of the revolution begun in the 1940s with the birth of molecular biology, and the philosophical enterprises just reviewed only scratch the surface of the transformation that has so far occurred. The Human Genome Project has inspired some philosophers to look more closely at molecular biology, although the main discussions of that project centre, quite understandably, on its social implications. I'll now turn from my plea for a molecular turn in philosophical studies to a type of philosophical investigation that cuts across the categories that have been prominent so far, to take a look at philosophical appraisals of socially significant biology.

5. The Uses and Abuses of Biology

During the past decades, prominent biologists and social theorists have sometimes claimed that advances in the life sciences hold dramatic implications for our

---

[6] Since the discovery of retroviruses, it has been appreciated that information can sometimes flow from RNA to DNA, so that a more careful formulation of the Dogma is needed.

understanding of ourselves and our society. In the late 1960s, for example, investigations in behavioural genetics were advertised as showing the existence of a strong hereditary component in human intelligence. That conclusion seemed to have particular relevance in the context of test results revealing a fifteen-point average difference between the scores obtained on IQ tests by American blacks and Americans of Caucasian descent. It was hardly surprising that the title question of Arthur Jensen's famous article asked how much we can boost IQ (Jensen 1969).

The argument advanced by Jensen (and by Richard Herrnstein) began from the premiss that IQ tests provide a reliable measure of intelligence, independently of cultural background. It proceeds by offering estimates of the *heritability* of IQ test performance, taking these to be around 50 per cent. From this, Jensen and his followers draw the conclusion that there is a substantial genetic contribution to intelligence, and, as a result, efforts to modify the environment to raise the average in the black population to that in the white population are doomed to fail.

As Richard Lewontin pointed out in an early critique of this argument (1974b), there seems to be a misunderstanding of the notion of heritability. That notion is part of the technical apparatus of quantitative genetics, and is defined as follows: for any trait that admits of a quantitative measure, the heritability is the ratio of the variance due to genotype to the total variance. Plainly, then, heritability is a *population* statistic: in a population where there's no variance in environment, the heritability of any trait will be 1, whereas in a population in which there's no variance in genotype the heritability will be 0. These population-level features are quite independent of the question whether the trait in question is under stringent genetic control. Building on Lewontin's argument, the philosophers Ned Block and Gerald Dworkin presented a wide-ranging analysis of the flaws in the hereditarian argument (Block and Dworkin 1974). That analysis was later supplemented by Leon Kamin's demonstration that some of the data alleged to support high heritability estimates had been fudged (Kamin 1974), and by Gould's subsequent researches on the ways in which historical uses of IQ tests had been insensitive to cultural differences (Gould 1981).

That ended one round of the IQ debate, but, as so often, bad old arguments have amazing powers of regeneration. In the 1990s Richard Herrnstein, in collaboration with the social theorist Charles Murray, published a widely read book (Herrnstein and Murray 1994). Although the authors appeared to absorb the fundamental point made by Lewontin (and extended in the subsequent discussion), they claimed to reach similar conclusions to those endorsed earlier. A penetrating review by Block (1995) refashioned his original argument to the new context, and a subsequent article by Clark Glymour presented the Herrnstein–Murray claims within a general methodological framework (Glymour 1998).

I doubt that this will be the end of the matter. Contemporary behavioural genetics has crafted new molecular tools for attempting to understand the ways in which human behaviour is constrained by our genotypes. Although the Lewontin–Block

diagnosis shows clearly that heritability estimates alone will not provide information about the extent to which a trait can be modified by altering the environment,
it is quite probable that the new tools (either alone or in combination with estimates of heritability) will be deployed to undergird the old conclusions. The idea
of genetic determination seems endlessly fascinating. One main contribution of
Lewontin and Block is to show us how to think clearly about that idea: for any
given genotype, we can envisage a graph that shows the way in which a trait of
social concern varies as the environment changes; the simplest genetic determinist
theme is to suppose that the variation is relatively slight across the range of environments that we'd consider suitable for members of our species (for other themes,
see Kitcher 2000). The challenge for people who think that our genes set limits to
productive social policies is to amass evidence that enables them to draw the appropriate graph, and to show that it accords with their dismal predictions about the
possibilities. Critics have to scrutinize carefully the methods that are used, and to
identify the points (if any) at which unwarranted conclusions are drawn. That
requires constant attention to the ways in which study of the genetics of behaviour
evolves. Although it's easy to sympathize with those (like Susan Oyama) who yearn
to solve nature–nurture problems at one stroke (by the 'stake-in-the-heart move'),
there's no substitute for piecemeal consideration of the latest arguments.[7]

The same holds for another recurrent controversy of past decades, one that
began with popular work in human ethology, became much more visible in the
human sociobiology of the 1970s and 1980s, and that has metamorphosed into
claims and counter-claims of contemporary evolutionary psychology. In all these
instances, enthusiasts suggest that understanding the evolutionary past of our
species will help us refine our views about who we are, how our minds work, and
what we can aspire to be. I'll illustrate the programme by starting with one of the
most celebrated instances, E. O. Wilson's Sociobiology (Wilson 1975, 1978).

A distinguished entomologist, famous for his ground-breaking work on social
insects, Wilson was impressed by the theoretical developments of the 1960s, and
offered a wide-ranging survey of the evolution of sociality across a wide range of
species. Applying his favoured tools to human beings, he defended a biological
account of behavioural differences between the sexes (both in propensities to various kinds of work and in sexual responses), of xenophobia, of tendencies to aggression, and of the hierarchical structure of human society. Part of the argument
about sexual behaviour can serve as an example. According to Wilson, asymmetries
in numbers and size of gametes (men produce a lot of sperm, women a far smaller
number of eggs), coupled with greater female 'investment' in progeny at the embry-
onic stages, serve as the basis for selection pressures that can be expected to favour

---

[7] So far, philosophers have not paid much attention to the sophisticated work now being done in
molecular behavioural genetics, although the recent work of Kenneth Schaffner (1993, 1998) is a
notable contribution.

different sexual attitudes, men being relatively hasty and promiscuous, women relatively coy. We can thus expect that the differences we observe in male–female behaviour are traceable to underlying genes, and that there's little that can be done to modify these differences (1975, 1978).

Although some philosophers were more impressed by this style of argument (Ruse 1979), it quickly attracted detailed objections. Critics pointed out that evolutionary expectations depend on the provision of detailed models that show how fitness is affected by various factors, that they are also subject to conditions about the ability of genetic variations to modify particular manifest traits (a point that leads into the controversy about adaptationism), that human behaviour has to be understood as responsive to cultural transmission, and, perhaps most importantly, that even granting a genetic basis for a trait, nothing follows about the extent to which the trait is now changeable by altering the environment (Kitcher 1985b; Lewontin et al. 1984).[8] These objections are quite consistent with a positive view of some ventures in sociobiology, for example careful studies of animals that combine field observations with attention to genetic and ecological models and that draw no deterministic conclusions; indeed, Wilson's own work on the social insects can be seen as far more rigorous and cautious than his speculations about our species.

During the late 1980s human sociobiology became almost invisible. A number of researchers continued to insist that a Darwinian perspective could inform anthropology, but this was typically qualified with the recognition that the pitfalls of human sociobiology should be avoided. In the past decade or so, however, more of the old themes have re-emerged. Authors have proposed that evolutionary theory can offer insights into the character of human psychology (Barkow et al. 1992), ranging from our sensitivity to social cheating (Cosmides and Tooby 1992) to the springs of sexual desire (Buss 1994, 2000) and rape (Thornhill and Palmer 2000). The worst excesses of this literature recapitulate the errors diagnosed earlier, and philosophers, as well as scientists, have begun to develop critiques (Cheng and Holyoak 1989; Lloyd 1999; Dupré 2001; Travis 2002).

As with the IQ controversy, it would be desirable to settle matters once for all, but there's no substitute for piecemeal analyses. For the problem doesn't stem from some systematic flaw in evolutionary theory but from the ways in which perfectly good evolutionary tools are applied. Wilson drew on the same arsenal of techniques in his work on ants and in his claims about human behaviour; the difference lay in the care and caution with which those techniques were applied.

Besides focusing on the forms of behaviour just considered, evolutionary studies of human beings are also pertinent to areas of traditional philosophical concern. Since the late nineteenth century, many thinkers have pondered the connection

---

[8] Here we re-encounter a point made in discussing the IQ controversy. Simply supposing that, in some environment, there's a causal connection between a genotype and a trait doesn't tell us whether that connection would also obtain in other environments.

(if any) between evolution and ethics. Human sociobiology took a forthright stand on this issue, claiming that the content of 'ethical imperatives' could be derived from an understanding of our evolutionary heritage. When the claim was made more concrete, it typically amounted either to the idea that we have a moral obligation to promote the replication of human DNA (Wilson 1978) or to moral prohibitions against such things as incest (Ruse and Wilson 1986). It's not hard to show that such simple connections are suspect (Kitcher 1992). Fortunately, some scholars have found more subtle ways of linking evolutionary ideas to our moral and political concerns. Elliott Sober and David Sloan Wilson use their account of the evolution of altruism (in the biologist's sense) as a prelude to giving an account of human psychological altruism and to exploring the possibility that psychological altruism might have evolved under natural selection (Sober and Wilson 1998). Brian Skyrms has drawn on the techniques of evolutionary game theory (Maynard Smith 1982) to show how we can make sense of elementary features of social and political arrangements (Skyrms 1996). These ventures evade my earlier objections because they make precise use of evolutionary concepts and methods, and they are appropriately restrained in drawing their conclusions—in many instances, Sober and Wilson, and Skyrms, are interested in showing how a particular outcome is possible rather than trying to infer something 'deep' about genetic determination of behaviour. From a different direction, philosophers interested in moral theory have found inspiration in evolutionary discussions of altruism and cooperation, and have tried to make biological links with meta-ethical positions (non-cognitivism in Gibbard 1990; Humean expressivism in Blackburn 2000). Although the history of speculations about evolution and ethics isn't encouraging, we may finally have reached a stage in which careful research in this area will bear dividends.

Another important locus of philosophical discussion is the relationship between evolutionary biology and religion (particularly Christianity). Despite the fact that the Church of England made its peace with Darwin in 1882—he was, after all, buried in Westminster Abbey, against the wishes of his family—there have been many people, especially in North America, who have viewed evolutionary biology as antipathetic to religion. In the 1970s and early 1980s such people obtained enough popular support to inspire many authors, including philosophers, to defend evolution against the critiques of fundamentalist 'creation science' (Ruse 1982; Futuyma 1983; Kitcher 1982b). More recently, creationists have articulated a more sophisticated anti-evolutionary position, one no longer committed to the literal truth of Genesis, emphasizing the role of 'intelligent design' (Behe 1996; Johnson 1993; Dembski 1998). In response, a number of philosophers have dissected the arguments supposed to show the presence of design in the universe and the corresponding limitation of orthodox Darwinism (Pennock 1999, 2002).

But the major issue of the compatibility of Darwinism and Christianity remains. A popular approach, defended in (Kitcher 1982b; Gould 2000; Ruse 2001), is to insist that enlightened religious believers can slough off those parts of religious texts for which evolutionary biology causes trouble and preserve the central moral messages. Despite my own earlier advocacy of this compatibilism, it no longer appears so easy. For, as Darwin saw, and as Dawkins has forcefully emphasized, a standard Darwinian view of the history of life exacerbates the traditional problem of evil—Dawkins puts the point by asking us to reconstruct the deity's utility function from the observed phenomena (Dawkins 1995). In my own view, the difficulties of combining Darwinism with religious belief result from a much more general war between various sciences and religion, one that also involves historical reconstructions of major religious texts and of the growth of religious belief, anthropological studies of religious diversity, psychological investigations of the causes of 'religious experiences', and philosophical dissection of the concept of faith. In effect the war is fought on many fronts and although religion's losses in Darwinian battles are extremely severe, the real trouble is that the believer is hard-pressed everywhere (Kitcher, forthcoming).

I'll conclude with a quick look at another socially relevant area of biology, the current research on genome sequencing, with our own species as a special case. The advertisements for the Human Genome Project promise that investment in this research will offer cures for major diseases and disabilities, and, indeed, we would be extremely unlucky if we were not *eventually* to be able to do better with some of the chronic conditions to which major efforts are currently directed (cancer, heart disease, diabetes). In the short term, however, the immediate applications of the power to obtain DNA sequences are likely to lie in techniques of identification (used already to liberate innocent people from prisons) and most of all in predictive testing. The uses of predictive tests have now been thoroughly debated (Holtzmann 1989; Nelkin and Tancredi 1994; Hubbard and Wald 1993; Andrews *et al.* 1994). It's far from clear, however, that the affluent societies in which tests are likely to be available in greatest profusion are yet equipped with the social mechanisms to ensure that people are adequately protected. Already in the United States those testing positive for genetic conditions have found their lives disrupted by loss of jobs and insurance, and this is likely to increase in coming decades as the power to test grows. Moreover, matters will become more complicated with the application of molecular genetics to questions about human behaviour (as noted in Section 5 above), and several authors have recognized the possibility of a new form of eugenics, one that might in principle be benign but that is likely in practice to recapitulate old errors (Duster 1990; Kitcher 1996).

Philosophical work on these social issues ranges from relatively abstract considerations in moral theory (Heyd 1992) to more detailed involvement with the possibilities furnished by contemporary biology (Harris 1992; Kitcher 1996; Buchanan *et al.* 2000). Some issues, especially the threats and promises of molecular behavioural genetics, need to be explored more thoroughly than has been done so far. There is also a broader question about the concentration of biomedical research on the diseases that afflict citizens of affluent nations, especially when the sequencing techniques provide opportunities for developing vaccines that might alleviate the misery of millions in the developing world. A healthy outgrowth of philosophical concern with the Human Genome Project—and socially significant biology more generally—might be a more resolute attempt to pose and answer ethical and political questions about scientific research.

6. An Apologetic Conclusion

Although I have swept through many areas of recent discussion at a brisk pace, there are other questions that are being (or ought to be) addressed, questions that I have neglected. I'll close with a very brief mention of some of these.

The notion of a law of nature was central to logical empiricist philosophy of science, and, since the 1970s, a number of philosophers have attempted to characterize laws without imposing on themselves the Humean scruples that logical empiricists tried to honour. Philosophy of biology has contributed to this debate both by raising questions about the contingency of laws (Beatty 1995), and by reviving the controversy about the sense of "law" in which biology can lay claim to laws of its own (Mitchell 2000). Here, as in other examples I've discussed above, we can recognize the impact of the philosophy of biology on general philosophy of science.

There have also been consequences for other areas of philosophy. Discussions in the philosophy of mind have been transformed by a richer understanding of neurobiology, stemming from Patricia Churchland's pioneering (1985) and more recent work by Kathleen Akins (1996) and Brian Keeley (2002). Within the philosophy of language, attempts to provide a naturalistic account of semantics (and of mental representation) have drawn on conceptions of biological function and on research on animal communication (Dretske 1988; Millikan 1984; Godfrey-Smith 1996).

But some areas of biology that seem to call for philosophical attention have been strangely neglected. Very little has been done to clarify the notion of biodiversity and to elaborate a philosophical foundation for conservation. Although a few philosophers have contributed to debates about artificial life (Boden 1996), this is another area in which there is abundant philosophical work to be done. Yet, as I've insisted in Section 5, the major gap in contemporary philosophy of biology is the failure to come to terms with the many facets of molecular biology, and, in particular, its transformation of physiology, cell biology, and developmental biology.

It would be wrong to end on a note of complaint. The last thirty years have witnessed so many diverse and fruitful interactions between philosophy and biology that it has become impossible for any philosopher of science (perhaps any philosopher) to write in ignorance of the main concepts and themes of the life sciences.

Philosophy owes a debt to the pioneers who saw the importance of biological research. I have tried to provide a sketch of the exciting enterprise they started.[9]

References

Akins, Kathleen (1996). 'Of Sensory Systems and the "Aboutness" of Mental States'. *Journal of Philosophy*, 93: 337–72.

Andrews, Lori, Fullerton, Jane E., Holtzmann, Neil A., and Motulsk, Arno G. (1994). *Assessing Genetic Risks*. Washington: National Academy Press.

Barkow, Jerome, Cosmides, Leda, and Tooby, John (eds.) (1992). *The Adapted Mind*. New York: Oxford University Press.

Beatty, John (1980a). 'Optimal-Design Models and the Strategy of Model-Building in Evolutionary Biology'. *Philosophy of Science*, 47: 532–61.

—— (1980b). 'What's Wrong with the Received View of Evolutionary Theory?', in Peter Asquith and Ronald Giere (eds.), *PSA 1980*, ii. East Lansing, Mich.: Philosophy of Science Association.

—— (1995). 'The Evolutionary Contingency Thesis', in G. Walters and J. Lennox (eds.), *Concepts, Theories, and Rationality in the Biological Sciences*. Pittsburgh: University of Pittsburgh Press.

Bechtel, William, and Richardson, Robert (1992). *Discovering Complexity*. Princeton: Princeton University Press.

Beckner, Morton (1959). *The Biological Way of Thought*. New York: Columbia University Press.

Behe, Michael (1996). *Darwin's Black Box*. New York: Free Press.

Beurton, Peter, Falk, Raphael, and Reinberger, Hans-Jörg (eds.) (2000). *The Concept of the Gene in Development and Evolution*. Cambridge: Cambridge University Press.

Bigelow, John, and Pargetter, Robert (1987). 'Functions'. *Journal of Philosophy*, 84: 181–96.

Blackburn, Simon (2000) *Ruling Passions*. New York: Oxford University Press.

Block, N. J., and Dworkin, Gerald (1974). 'IQ, Heritability and Inequality'. *Philosophy and Public Affairs*, 4: 1–99. Repr. in N. J. Block and Gerald Dworkin (eds.), *The I.Q. Controversy*. New York: Pantheon, 1976.

—— (1995). 'How Heritability Misleads About Race'. *Cognition*, 56: 99–126.

Boden, Margaret (ed.) (1996). *The Philosophy of Artificial Life*. Oxford: Oxford University Press.

Boorse, Christopher (1976). 'Wright on Functions'. *Philosophical Review*, 85: 70–86.

Brandon, Robert (1984). 'The Levels of Selection', in Robert Brandon and Richard Burian (eds.), *Genes, Organisms, Populations*. Cambridge, Mass.: MIT Press.

—— (1990). *Adaptation and Environment*. Princeton: Princeton University Press.

Buchanan, Allen, Brock, Dan, Daniels, Norman, and Wikler, Daniel (2000). *From Chance to Choice*. Cambridge: Cambridge University Press.

Buss, David (1994). *The Evolution of Desire*. New York: Basic Books.

—— (2000). *The Dangerous Passion*. New York: Free Press.

---

[9] Many thanks to Frank Jackson and Michael Smith, for their comments on an earlier version, and, above all, for their patience.

Cheng, Patricia, and Holyoak, Keith (1989). 'On the Natural Selection of Reasoning Theories'. *Cognition*, 33: 285–313.

Churchland, Patricia (1985). *Neurophilosophy*. Cambridge, Mass.: MIT Press.

Cosmides, Leda, and Tooby, John (1992). 'Cognitive Adaptations for Social Exchange', in J. Barkow, L. Cosmides, and J. Tooby (eds.), *The Adapted Mind*. New York: Oxford University Press.

Culp, Sylvia (1995). 'Objectivity in Experimental Inquiry: Breaking Data-Technique Circles', *Philosophy of Science*, 62: 430–50.

—— and Kitcher, Philip (1989). 'Theory Structure and Theory Change in Contemporary Molecular Biology'. *British Journal for the Philosophy of Science*, 40: 459–83.

Cummins, Robert (1973). 'Functional Analysis'. *Journal of Philosophy*, 72: 741–64.

Darwin, Charles (1859). *The Origin of Species*. London: John Murray.

Dawkins, Richard (1976). *The Selfish Gene*. Oxford: Oxford University Press.

—— (1982). *The Extended Phenotype*. San Francisco: Freeman.

—— (1987). *The Blind Watchmaker*. London: Longmans.

—— (1995). *River Out of Eden*. New York: Basic Books.

Dembski, William (1998). *The Design Inference*. Cambridge: Cambridge University Press.

Dennett, Daniel (1995). *Darwin's Dangerous Idea*. New York: Simon & Schuster.

Dretske, Fred (1988). *Explaining Behavior*. Cambridge, Mass.: MIT Press.

Dupré, John (1981). 'Natural Kinds and Biological Taxa'. *Philosophical Review*, 90: 66–90.

—— (ed.) (1987). *The Latest on the Best*. Cambridge, Mass.: MIT Press.

—— (1993). *The Disorder of Things*. Cambridge, Mass.: Harvard University Press.

—— (2001). *Human Nature and the Limits of Science*. Oxford: Oxford University Press.

Duster, Troy (1990). *Backdoor to Eugenics*. New York: Routledge.

Eldredge, Niles (1985). *Unfinished Synthesis*. New York: Oxford University Press.

Ereshevsky, Marc (ed.) (1992). *The Units of Evolution*. Cambridge, Mass.: MIT Press.

Futuyma, Douglas (1983). *Science on Trial*. New York: Pantheon.

Ghiselin, Michael (1974). 'A Radical Solution to the Species Problem'. *Systematic Zoology*, 23: 536–44.

Gibbard, Allan (1990). *Wise Choices, Apt Feelings*. Cambridge, Mass.: Harvard University Press.

Glymour, Clark (1998). 'What Went Wrong?' *Philosophy of Science*, 65: 1–32.

Godfrey-Smith, Peter (1993). 'Functions: Consensus without Unity'. *Pacific Philosophical Quarterly*, 74: 196–208.

—— (1994). 'A Modern History Theory of Functions'. *Noûs*, 28: 344–62.

—— (1996). *Complexity and the Function of Mind in Nature*. Cambridge: Cambridge University Press.

—— (2000). 'On the Theoretical Role of "Genetic Coding"', *Philosophy of Science*, 67: 26–44.

—— and Lewontin, Richard (1993). 'The Dimensions of Selection'. *Philosophy of Science*, 60: 373–95.

Goudge, T. A. (1961). *The Ascent of Life*. Toronto: University of Toronto Press.

Gould, Stephen Jay (1978). *Ontogeny and Phylogeny*. Cambridge, Mass.: Harvard University Press.

—— (1980a). 'Caring Groups and Selfish Genes', in Gould, *The Panda's Thumb*. New York: Norton.

—— (1980b). 'Is a New and General Theory of Evolution Emerging?' *Paleobiology*, 6: 119–30.

—— (1981). *The Mismeasure of Man*. New York: Norton.

—— (1982). 'Darwinism and the Expansion of Evolutionary Theory'. *Science*, 216: 380–7.

Gould, Stephen Jay (2000). *Rocks of Ages*. New York: Ballantine.

—— (2002). *The Structure of Evolutionary Theory*. Cambridge, Mass.: Harvard University Press.

—— and Lewontin, Richard C. (1979). 'The Spandrels of San Marco and the Panglossian Paradigm: A Critique of the Adaptationist Programme'. *Proceedings of the Royal Society of London*, ser. B, 205: 581–98.

—— and Vrba, Elizabeth (1982). 'Exaptation: A Missing Term in the Science of Form'. *Paleobiology*, 8: 4–15.

Grene, Marjorie (1959). 'Two Evolutionary Theories'. *British Journal for the Philosophy of Science*, 9: 110–27, 185–93.

Griffiths, Paul, and Gray, Russell (1994). 'Developmental Systems and Evolutionary Explanation'. *Journal of Philosophy*, 91: 277–304.

Hamilton, W. D. (1964). 'The Genetical Evolution of Social Behavior', I and II. *Journal of Theoretical Biology*, 7: 1–16, 17–32.

Harris, John (1992). *Wonderwoman and Superman*. Oxford: Oxford University Press.

Hempel, C. G. (1965). 'The Logic of Functional Explanation', in C. G. Hempel, *Aspects of Scientific Explanation*. New York: Free Press.

Herrnstein, R., and Murray, C. (1994). *The Bell Curve*. New York: Free Press.

Heyd, David (1992). *Genethics*. Berkeley: University of California Press.

Ho, Mae-Wan, and Fox, Sidney (eds.) (1988). *Evolutionary Processes and Metaphors*. Chichester: John Wiley.

—— and Saunders, Peter T. (1984). *Beyond Neo-Darwinism*. London: Academic Press.

Holtzmann, Neil A. (1989). *Proceed with Caution*. Baltimore: Johns Hopkins University Press).

Hubbard, Ruth, and Wald, Elijah (1993). *Exploding the Gene Myth*. Boston: Beacon.

Hull, David (1972). 'Reduction in Genetics—Biology or Philosophy?' *Philosophy of Science*, 39: 491–9.

—— (1974). *Philosophy of Biological Science*. Englewood Cliffs, NJ: Prentice-Hall.

—— (1976). 'Are Species Really Individuals?' *Systematic Zoology*, 25: 174–91.

—— (1978). 'A Matter of Individuality'. *Philosophy of Science*, 45: 335–60.

—— (1979). 'The Limits of Cladism'. *Systematic Zoology*, 28: 414–38.

—— (1981). 'Units of Evolution: A Metaphysical Essay', in R. Jensen and R. Harré (eds.), *The Philosophy of Evolution*. Brighton: Harvester.

—— (1988). *Science as a Process*. Chicago: University of Chicago Press.

—— and Ruse, Michael (eds.) (1998). *Philosophy of Biology*. Oxford: Oxford University Press.

Jensen, A. R. (1969). 'How Much Can We Boost I.Q. and Scholastic Achievement?' *Harvard Educational Review*, 39: 1–123.

Johnson, Phillip (1993). *Darwin on Trial*. Washington: Regnery Gateway.

Kamin, Leon (1974). *The Science and Politics of IQ*. Potomac, Md.: Erlbaum.

Kauffman, Stuart (1993). *The Origins of Order*. New York: Oxford University Press.

Keeley, Brian (2002). 'Making Sense of the Senses'. *Journal of Philosophy*, 99: 5–28.

Kitcher, Philip (1982*a*). 'Genes'. *British Journal for the Philosophy of Science*, 33: 337–59.

—— (1982*b*). *Abusing Science: The Case Against Creationism*. Cambridge, Mass.: MIT Press.

—— (1984*a*). 'Species'. *Philosophy of Science*, 51: 308–33.

—— (1984*b*). '1953 and All That: A Tale of Two Sciences'. *Philosophical Review*, 93: 335–73.

—— (1985*a*). 'Darwin's Achievement', in N. Rescher (ed.), *Reason and Rationality in Science*. Washington: University Press of America.

—— (1985b). *Vaulting Ambition*. Cambridge, Mass.: MIT Press.

—— (1989). 'Some Puzzles About Species', in M. Ruse (ed.), *What the Philosophy of Biology Is*. Dordrecht: Kluwer.

—— (1992). 'Four Ways of "Biologicizing" Ethics', in Kurt Bayertz (ed.), *Evolution und Ethik. Biologische Grundlagen der Moral?* Stuttgart: Reclam. Repr. in English in Elliott Sober (ed.), *Conceptual Issues in Evolutionary Theory*, 2nd edn. Cambridge, Mass.: MIT Press.

—— (1993). 'Function and Design', in P. French, T. Uehling, and H. Wettstein (eds.), *Midwest Studies in Philosophy*, xviii: *Philosophy of Science*. Minneapolis: University of Minnesota Press.

—— (1996). *The Lives to Come*. New York: Simon & Schuster.

—— (1999). 'The Hegemony of Molecular Biology'. *Biology and Philosophy*, 14: 195–210.

—— (2000). 'Battling the Undead: How (and How Not) to Resist Genetic Determinism', in Rama Singh, Costas Krimbas, Diane Paul, and John Beatty (eds.), *Thinking About Evolution: Historical, Philosophical and Political Perspectives*. Cambridge: Cambridge University Press.

—— (forthcoming). 'The Many-Sided Conflict Between Science and Religion', in William Mann (ed.), *Companion to the Philosophy of Religion*. Oxford: Blackwell.

Levins, Richard, and Lewontin, Richard C. (1985). *The Dialectical Biologist*. Cambridge, Mass.: Harvard University Press.

Lewontin, Richard C. (1974a). *The Genetic Basis of Evolutionary Change*. New York: Columbia University Press.

—— (1974b). 'The Analysis of Variance and the Analysis of Causes'. *American Journal of Human Genetics*, 26: 400–11.

—— Rose, Steven, and Kamin, Leon (1984). *Not in our Genes*. New York: Pantheon.

Lloyd, Elisabeth (1983). 'The Nature of Darwin's Support for the Theory of Natural Selection'. *Philosophy of Science*, 50: 112–29.

—— (1988). *The Structure and Confirmation of Evolutionary Theory*. Westport, Conn.: Greenwood Press.

—— (1999). 'Evolutionary Psychology: The Burden of Proof'. *Biology and Philosophy*, 14: 211–33.

Maynard Smith, John (1964). 'Group Selection and Kin Selection'. *Nature*, 201: 1145–7.

—— (1978). 'Optimization Theory in Evolution'. *Annual Review of Ecology and Systematics*, 9: 31–56.

—— (1982). *Evolution and the Theory of Games*. Cambridge: Cambridge University Press.

—— (2000). 'The Concept of Information in Biology'. *Philosophy of Science*, 67: 177–94.

Mayr, Ernst (1942). *Systematics and the Origin of Species*. New York: Columbia University Press.

—— (1963). *Animal Species and Evolution*. Cambridge, Mass.: Harvard University Press.

—— (1983). 'How to Carry Out the Adaptationist Program?' *American Naturalist*, 121: 324–33.

Meinhardt, Hans (1998). *The Algorithmic Beauty of Sea Shells*. New York: Springer.

Millikan, Ruth (1984). *Language, Thought, and Other Biological Categories*. Cambridge, Mass.: MIT Press.

Mills, Susan, and Beatty, John (1979). 'The Propensity Interpretation of Fitness'. *Philosophy of Science*, 46: 263–86.

Mitchell, Sandra (1993). 'Dispositions or Etiologies?' *Journal of Philosophy*, 90: 249–59.

—— (1995). 'Function, Fitness and Disposition'. *Biology and Philosophy*, 10: 39–54.

Mitchell, Sandra (2000). 'Dimensions of Scientific Law'. *Philosophy of Science*, 67: 242–65.

Murray, John D. (1989). *Mathematical Biology*. New York: Springer.

Nagel, Ernest (1962). *The Structure of Science*. London: Routledge.

—— (1979). *Teleology Revisited*. New York: Columbia University Press.

Neander, Karen (1991). 'Functions as Selected Effects'. *Philosophy of Science*, 58: 168–84.

Nelkin, Dorothy, and Tancredi, Laurence (1994). *Dangerous Diagnostics*. Chicago: University of Chicago Press.

Orzack, S., and Sober, Elliott (1994). 'Optimality Methods and the Test of Adaptationism'. *American Naturalist*, 143: 361–80.

Oster, George, and Wilson, E. O. (1978). *Caste and Ecology in the Social Insects*. Princeton: Princeton University Press.

Oyama, Susan (1985). *The Ontogeny of Information*. Cambridge: Cambridge University Press.

Pennock, Robert (1999). *Tower of Babel*. Cambridge, Mass.: MIT Press.

—— (ed.) (2002). *Intelligent Design Creationism and its Critics*. Cambridge, Mass.: MIT Press.

Raff, R. (1996). *The Shape of Life*. Chicago: University of Chicago Press.

Rosenberg, Alexander (1982). 'On the Propensity Definition of Fitness'. *Philosophy of Science*, 49: 268–73.

—— (1983). 'Fitness'. *Journal of Philosophy*, 80: 457–73.

—— (1985). *The Structure of Biological Science*. Cambridge: Cambridge University Press.

—— (1994). *Instrumental Biology and the Disunity of Science*. Chicago: University of Chicago Press.

Ruse, Michael (1979). *Sociobiology: Sense or Nonsense?* Dordrecht: Reidel.

—— (1982). *Darwinism Defended*. Reading, Mass.: Addison-Wesley.

—— (2001). *Can a Darwinian Be a Christian?* Cambridge: Cambridge University Press.

—— and Wilson, E. O. (1986). 'Moral Philosophy as Applied Science'. *Philosophy*, 61: 173–92.

Sarkar, Sahotra (1998). *Genetics and Reductionism*. Cambridge: Cambridge University Press.

—— (2000). 'Information in Genetics and Developmental Biology'. *Philosophy of Science*, 67: 208–13.

Schaffner, Kenneth (1969). 'The Watson–Crick Model and Reductionism'. *British Journal for the Philosophy of Science*, 20: 325–48.

—— (1993). *Discovery and Explanation in Biology and Medicine*. Chicago: University of Chicago Press.

—— (1998). 'Genes, Behavior, and Developmental Emergentism: One Process, Indivisible', *Philosophy of Science*, 65: 209–52.

Skyrms, Brian (1996). *Evolution of the Social Contract*. Cambridge: Cambridge University Press.

Sober, Elliott (1984). *The Nature of Selection*. Cambridge Mass.: MIT Press.

—— (1988). *Reconstructing the Past*. Cambridge, Mass.: MIT Press.

—— (1998). 'Six Sayings About Adaptationism', in David Hull and Michael Ruse (eds.), *Philosophy of Biology*. Oxford: Oxford University Press.

—— and Lewontin, Richard (1982). 'Artifact, Cause and Genic Selection'. *Philosophy of Science*, 49: 157–80.

—— and Wilson, David Sloan (1998). *Unto Others*. Cambridge, Mass.: Harvard University Press.

Splitter, Laurence (1988). 'Species and Identity'. *Philosophy of Science*, 55: 323–48.

Sterelny, Kim, and Kitcher, Philip (1988). 'The Return of the Gene'. *Journal of Philosophy*, 85: 339–60.

——and Griffiths, Paul (1999). *Sex and Death*. Chicago: University of Chicago Press.

Thompson, R. P. (1983). 'The Structure of Evolutionary Theory: A Semantic Approach'. *Studies in the History and Philosophy of Science*, 14: 215–29.

Thornhill, Randy, and Palmer, Craig (2000). *The Natural History of Rape*. Cambridge, Mass.: MIT Press.

Tinbergen, Niko (1963). 'On Aims and Methods of Ethology'. *Zeitschrift für Tierpsychologie*, 20: 410–33.

Travis, Cheryl (ed.) (2002). *Evolution, Gender, and Violence*. Cambridge, Mass.: MIT Press.

Waters, C. Kenneth (1990). 'Why the Anti-Reductionist Consensus Won't Survive: The Case of Classical Genetics', in Arthur Fine, Micky Forbes, and Linda Wessels (eds.), *PSA 1990*, i. East Lansing, Mich.: Philosophy of Science Association.

——(1991). 'Tempered Realism About the Force of Selection'. *Philosophy of Science*, 58: 553–73.

——(1994). 'Genes Made Molecular'. *Philosophy of Science*, 61: 163–85.

Williams, George C. (1966). *Adaptation and Natural Selection*. Princeton: Princeton University Press.

Williams, Mary (1970). 'Deducing the Consequences of Evolution: A Mathematical Model'. *Journal of Theoretical Biology*, 29: 343–85.

Wilson, E. O. (1975). *Sociobiology*. Cambridge, Mass.: Harvard University Press.

——(1978). *On Human Nature*. Cambridge, Mass.: Harvard University Press.

Wimsatt, William (1981). 'The Units of Selection and the Structure of the Multi-Level Genome', in Peter Asquith and Ronald Giere (eds.), *PSA 1980*, ii. East Lansing, Mich.: Philosophy of Science Association.

——(1986). 'Developmental Constraints, Generative Entrenchment, and the Innate–Acquired Distinction', in W. Bechtel (ed.), *Integrating Scientific Disciplines*. Amsterdam: Nijhoff.

Woodger, J. H. (1937). *The Axiomatic Method in Biology*. Cambridge: Cambridge University Press.

Wright, Larry (1973). 'Functions'. *Philosophical Review*, 82: 139–68.

CHAPTER 29

THE FOUNDATIONS OF PHYSICS

DAVID ALBERT

1

The busiest, most productive, and most conspicuous topic at the foundations of physics over the past several decades has been the quantum-mechanical measurement problem, and the enterprise of trying to fix that problem up (it seems to me) has opened a wide and distinctive new avenue into nature, which exuberantly resists classification as either science or philosophy, and which has important implications for a whole slew of other questions—both within the traditional concerns of the philosophy of physics and elsewhere as well.

That is what this chapter mainly proposes to be about. I will start at the centre—with the measurement problem itself—and then branch out some into stuff about the foundations of statistical mechanics, and about the theory of relativity.

2

Here (to begin with) is what the quantum-mechanical measurement problem is:

Quantum mechanics, as it gets presented in textbooks, more or less boils down to three general principles:[1]

1. A principle of the evolutions of the quantum states of physical systems in time (which is: that the quantum states of physical systems invariably evolve in

[1] See e.g. Albert (2000).

accordance with the linear deterministic quantum-mechanical equations of motion).

2. A principle that connects the physical properties of such systems at any given moment to their quantum states at that moment (which is: that a system S has a determinate value of the physical property P at time T if and only if the quantum state of S at T is an eigenstate of the operator associated with P; that (to put it slightly differently) there literally fails to be any determinate matter of fact whatever about the value of P at T for a system whose state at T is a superposition of differently valued eigenstates of the operator associated with P).

3. A principle that connects the probabilities of given outcomes of given measurements on such systems to their quantum states at the moment just before those measurements occur (which is: that the probability that a measurement at time T of the value of a property P on a system S whose quantum state at the instant just prior to T is $[@>$ will come out P = p is equal to $<@ \, \&>^2$, where $P[\&> = p[\&>)$.

These three principles, taken together, amount to what is by far, and beyond all dispute, the most empirically successful theory in the history of physics.

And yet there are a number of famous arguments in the physical literature to the effect that those principles—together with the truism that measuring devices, whatever else they may be, are physical systems, and so are subject to the same universal physical laws as other such systems are—amount to a contradiction.

It is that situation (which is what's so interesting about the foundations of quantum mechanics) that is referred to in the literature as the *measurement problem*.

The sharpest and clearest and most extreme way of setting that problem up is the story of Wigner's friend (Wigner 1962), which goes like this.

Wigner has a friend who is a competent observer of the x-spins of electrons, and that friend is in possession of a device for measuring the x-spins of electrons, and that device is working properly. What Wigner takes "competent" and "working properly" to mean is something like this: Suppose that Wigner's friend has resolved to measure the x-spin of a certain electron. If it's the case that the x-spin of the electron is with certainty up, then an x-spin measuring device which is working properly will, by definition, once it has completed a measurement of the x-spin of that electron, indicate (by means of some sort of a pointer, for example), with certainty, that the x-spin of that electron is up; and a competent observer, by definition, once she has looked at the measuring device subsequent to that measurement, will with certainty come to believe that the x-spin of the electron is up. Of course, if it's the case that the x-spin of the electron is with certainty down, then a measuring device that's working properly will end up indicating that, and Wigner's competent friend will end up believing that, by definition, with certainty.

Let us put that in more explicitly mathematical terms. What Wigner is supposing is that the quantum-mechanical equations of motion entail that the composite physical system consisting of Wigner's friend and her measuring device and the measured electron will behave like this:

(1) [resolved to measure the x-spin$>_F$ x [ready to measure the x-spin$>_M$ x [x-spin up$>_e$ → [believes that x-spin is up$>_F$ x [indicates that x-spin is up$>_M$ x [x-spin up$>_e$

and like this:

(2) [resolved to measure the x-spin$>_F$ x [ready to measure the x-spin$>_M$ x [x-spin down$>_e$ → [believes that x-spin is down$>_F$ x [indicates that x-spin is down$>_M$ x [x-spin down$>_e$.

These certainly seem like eminently reasonable necessary conditions for character-izing Wigner's friend and her measuring instrument as (respectively) "competent" and "working properly".[2]

OK. Now, suppose that as a matter of fact the initial state of the electron in ques-tion is neither the x-spin up state nor the x-spin down state but rather the y-spin up state; and suppose (as before) that Wigner's friend is resolved to measure the x-spin of this electron. So the state of the composite system that consists of the electron and the x-spin measuring device and Wigner's friend looks like this:

(3) [resolved ...$>$ x [ready ...$>$ x [y-spin up$>$ = [resolved ...$>$ x [ready ...$>$ x {½[x-spin up$>$ + ½[x-spin down$>$}.

Well, it turns out that if Wigner's friend is indeed competent in accord with Wigner's definition, and if her x-spin measuring device is working OK. in accord with Wigner's definition, and if the quantum states of both of those physical sys-tems are taken to evolve strictly in accord with the linear quantum-mechanical equations of motion, then it follows from the linearity of those equations that

(4) [the state in (3)$>$ → ½{[believes that x-spin is up$>$ x [indicates that x-spin is up$>$ x [x-spin up$>$}+{[believes that x-spin is down$>$ x [indicates that x-spin is down$>$ x [x-spin is down$>$}.

The reason is that the initial state here (the state in (3)) can be expressed as a super-position of the two initial states in (1) and (2); and since that's so, the linearity of

---

[2] It hardly needs saying, by the way, that there are immense oversimplifications in the way I've written down the states in (1) and (2). For example, the phrase "resolved to measure the x-spin" certainly doesn't exhaustively describe the quantum state of Wigner's very complicated friend. The physical system called Wigner's friend obviously has many other physical properties too; properties like the positions of her toes, or the positions of those ions in her brain which determine, say, what sorts of ice cream are her favourites. Moreover, I am obviously adopting an absolutely naive account of how mental states supervene on phys-ical states of the brains of sentient beings here. But I don't think that anything important is going to turn out to hinge on any of that. I think that all of what's about to happen would go through in much the same way in the context of considerably more detailed accounts of the physical structures of sentient observers and considerably less naive accounts of the supervenience of the mental on the physical too.

the equations of motion require that the final state here can necessarily be written as the same superposition of the two final states in (1) and (2).

So what comes of supposing that the quantum-mechanical equations of motion give a true and complete account of the dynamical workings of the entire physical world is that we get forced to conclude that measuring processes like the one I've just described invariably and deterministically leave the world in a coherent super-position of two states, in one of which the x-spin of the electron is down and the pointer on the measuring device is pointing to the word "down" and the experimenter sees that that pointer is pointing to the word "down" and consequently believes that the x-spin of the electron is down, and in the other of which the x-spin of the electron is up and the pointer of the measuring-device is pointing to the word "up" and the experimenter sees that the pointer is pointing to the word "up" and consequently believes that the x-spin of the electron is up.

Furthermore, what comes of supposing that quantum mechanics gives a true and complete account of the workings of the entire physical world is that we get forced to conclude that measuring processes like the one I've just described invari-ably and deterministically leave the world in a state in which (on the standard way of thinking about what it means to be in a superposition) there fails to be any determinate matter of fact about (among other things) where the pointer on the measuring device is pointing, and where the experimenter takes the pointer on the measuring device to be pointing.[3]

There are two sorts of pretty obvious troubles with that. One of them (the less important one) is that it flatly contradicts the third of the principles I started out with, and the other (the more important one) is that we're pretty sure that we know that there really are determinate matters of fact about where pointers on those sorts of devices are pointing at the ends of those sorts of measurements, and that at any rate we're absolutely sure (so the story goes) that we know that there are determinate matters of fact about where we *take* those pointers to be pointing at the ends of those sorts of measurements.

The job of figuring out what to do about those troubles is what I take the main job of the foundations of quantum mechanics to be.

There have been two big ideas (or rather, there have been two big ideas which seem to me to have any chance at all of being on the right track, of which more later)

[3] This is worth pausing and wondering over for a minute. Look at what has just happened: substant-ive, non-trivial, and, moreover, radically counter-intuitive conclusions about the behaviours of macro-scopic measuring instruments and about the inner lives of embodied subjects have been drawn directly out of the mathematical structure of a certain proposed set of microscopic fundamental laws of physics. And this sort of a move—this sort of a willingness to entertain the possibility of the most radical imag-inable sort of completeness of physics, this sort of determination to push the general project of a phys-ical account of the world as far away as possible from its originally intended applications, to push it at exactly those points at which it seems most at risk of collapsing—is precisely what is essential, distinctive, and exciting about the way the interrogation of the foundations of physics has lately been pursued.

about how to get that job done. Both of them have been around more or less since the trouble first came up; but a good deal has been learned in the past few years about what each of them really amounts to, and about how to parlay each of them into fully worked-out scientific theories.

One of those ideas is to deny that the standard way of thinking about what it means to be in a superposition is the right way of thinking about it; to deny, for example, that there fails to be any determinate matter of fact, when a quantum state like the one in (4) obtains, about where the pointer is pointing, or about where the experimenter takes that pointer to be pointing.

The idea (to come at it from a slightly different angle) is to construe quantum states as *less than complete descriptions of the world*. The idea is that something extra needs to be added to the quantum state description, something that can broadly be thought of as choosing between the two conditions superposed in (4), something that can be thought of as somehow marking one of those two conditions as the unique, actual, outcome of the measurement that leads up to it.

Probably the most famous and most successful way of parlaying that idea into a full-fledged physical theory is due to David Bohm. In 1952, Bohm wrote down a replacement for standard quantum mechanics which stipulates that the linear quantum-mechanical equations of motion are the correct equations of the time-evolutions of all quantum states at all times and under all circumstances, but on which certain facts over and above the facts about the quantum state of a system need to be specified in order to specify precisely and uniquely what the physical situation of that system is.

What those extra facts are about is the *positions of the particles* of which the system in question is made up, and what Bohm's theory is about is the evolution of those positions in time—what this theory takes the job of physical science to be (and note that this is precisely what classical mechanics took the job of physical science to be) is nothing other than to produce an account of those evolutions. Quantum-mechanical wave-functions come up in this theory only to the extent that we find we need them in order to produce that account.

Quantum-mechanical wave-functions are explicitly conceived of in this theory as concrete physical objects, as something like force fields. The laws of the evolutions of these wave-functions in time are (as I mentioned above) precisely the linear quantum-mechanical equations of motion. The job of these wave-functions in this theory is to sort of push the particles around (as force fields do), to guide them along their proper courses, and there are laws in the theory which stipulate precisely how they do that.

It turns out that the account which Bohm's theory gives of the motions of particles is a completely deterministic one. The positions of all of the particles in the world, and the world's complete quantum-mechanical wave-function, at any time, can in principle be calculated with certainty from the positions of all of the particles in the world and the world's complete quantum-mechanical wave-function at any earlier time. Any incapacity to carry out those calculations, any uncertainty in the results of those calculations, is necessarily (on this theory) an epistemic uncertainty, a matter of ignorance, and not a matter of the operations of any irreducible element of chance in the fundamental laws of the world. Nonetheless, this theory entails that some such ignorance (precisely enough, and of precisely the right kind) exists for us as a matter of principle: some such ignorance is unavoidably forced upon us by the dynamics of the theory. The dynamics acts so as to prevent us from ever knowing enough about the physical state of the world to make those predictions which the standard irreducibly statistical formalism of quantum mechanics can't make for us. There is, on this account, a very real and concrete and lawlike and deterministic physical process, a process which can be followed out in exact mathematical detail, whereby the physical act of measurement unavoidably gets in the way of what is being measured, like your eyeball unavoidably gets in the way of any attempt to look straight down the infinite corridor projected by a parallel pair of mirrors. This theory entails that there is a sort of ignorance which is merely ignorance (merely, that is, ignorance of a certain intelligible fact about the world), and which, nonetheless, could not be eliminated without violation of a physical law; just as your inability to see that infinite corridor of mirrors is merely an inability to see an image that really is (in some naive sense) there, and is nonetheless an inability which could not possibly be overcome so long as your organ of vision remains a physical object.

There are a number of other extra-variable sorts of responses to the measurement problem, newer ones, on the market these days as well. These are referred to in the literature as modal interpretations of quantum mechanics. All of them start off (just as Bohm's theory does) by stipulating that the linear dynamical equations of motion are always exactly right, and that there are certain particular properties of physical systems (let's call them the extra properties of those systems) whose values are determinate even in the event that the quantum state of the world fails to be an eigenstate of the operators associated with them.[4]

On Bohm's theory, those extra properties are the positions of particles.

On modal interpretations, things are a bit more complicated. On those interpretations, the identities of the extra properties can vary from moment to moment. Those identities depend on what the overall quantum state of the world is, and the particular way in which they depend on what that overall quantum state is (that is: the explicit rules whereby they depend on what that overall quantum state is) is cooked up with the aim of guaranteeing that measurements always have outcomes.

Moreover, modal interpretations (unlike Bohm's theory) aren't entirely deterministic. The evolution of the quantum state of the world is of course entirely deterministic on these interpretations (just as it is on Bohm's theory), and the rules whereby the identities of the extra properties depend on what the quantum state of

---

[4] See e.g. Deiks (1991); Healy (1989); van Fraassen (1991).

the world is are deterministic too, but the probabilities associated with the various possible values of the extra properties, on modal theories, are real physical chances.

The second of the two big ideas that I mentioned a few paragraphs back—the second of the two big ideas, that is, about what to do about the measurement problem—is to affirm that the standard way of thinking about what it means to be in a superposition (the so-called eigenstate–eigenvalue link) is the right way of thinking about it, to affirm that a quantum state does amount to a complete description of a physical system, and to deny that the time-evolutions of those states always occur in strict accordance with the standard linear deterministic equations of motion.

The idea here is to somehow alter the equations of motion (without, of course, altering any of the innumerable empirical consequences of those equations which are now experimentally known to be true) so as to guarantee that one of the two conditions superposed in a state like (4) simply, physically, goes away.

There is an enormously long and mostly pointless history of speculations in the physical literature (speculations which have notoriously involved terms like "macroscopicness", "consciousness", "irreversibility", "record", "subject", "object", and so on) about precisely what sorts of alterations are called for here; but there has to date been only one fully worked-out, traditionally scientific sort of proposal along these lines, which is due to Ghirardi, Rimini, and Weber (1986), and which has been developed somewhat further by Philip Pearle and John Bell (1989).

Ghirardi, Rimini, and Weber's idea goes (roughly) like this: The wave-function of any single-particle system[5] almost always evolves in accordance with the linear deterministic equations of motion; but every now and then (once in something like 10^9 years), at random, but with fixed probability per unit time, the wave-function is suddenly multiplied by a narrow bell-shaped curve—a curve (more particularly) whose width is something of the order of the diameter of a single atom of one of the lighter elements—which has the effect of localizing it, of setting its value at zero everywhere in space except within a certain small region. The probability of this bell-curve's being centred at any particular point x depends (in accordance with a precise mathematical rule) on the wave-function of the particle at the moment just prior to that multiplication. Then, until the next such 'jump', everything proceeds as before, in accordance with the deterministic differential equations.

---

[5] Wave-functions, by the way, are just another device for representing the possible physical states of quantum-mechanical systems—a device which is, of course, fully mathematically equivalent to the representation by means of vectors that we've been using so far—but which turns out to be more convenient (for example) in the context of discussions of the GRW theory. In the particularly simple case of a single-particle system, the quantum-mechanical wave-function takes the form of a straightforward function of (among other things) position in space. The wave-function of a particle which is located in some spatial region A, for example, will have the value zero everywhere in space except in A, and will have a non-zero value in A. Similarly, the wave-function of a particle which is located in some other region B will have the value zero everywhere in space except in B, and will have a non-zero value in B. The wave-function of a particle which is in a superposition of being in region A and in region B will have non-zero values in *both* of those regions, and will be zero everywhere else.

That's the whole theory. No attempt is made to explain the occurrence of these 'jumps'; that such jumps occur, and occur in precisely the way stipulated above, can be thought of as a new fundamental law, a beautifully straightforward and absolutely explicit law of the so-called "collapse of the wave-function", wherein there is no talk at a fundamental level of 'measurements' or 'recordings' or 'macroscopicness' or anything like that.

Moreover, the theory can more or less do its job.

Note, to begin with, that for isolated microscopic systems (i.e. systems consisting of small numbers of particles), 'jumps' will be so rare as to be completely unobservable in practice.

On the other hand (and this is the pay-off), it turns out that the effects of these jumps on the evolutions of the wave-functions of macroscopic systems (systems like measuring devices, for example) can sometimes be dramatic. As a matter of fact a reasonably good argument can be made to the effect that these jumps will almost instantaneously convert superpositions of macroscopically different states like {particle found in A + particle found in B} into *either* {particle found in A} *or* {particle found in B}, and that they will do so in very good accordance with the standard quantum-mechanical probabilities governing the outcomes of measurements like that.

A lively and very illuminating debate has been under way for some years now about the various troubles and the comparative merits of these and other related ideas. Modal theories (for example) have been criticized for relying on an unreasonably idealized conception of the operations of measuring devices—and there have subsequently been interesting attempts to show how that sort of reliance might potentially be done without.[6] There have also been much-discussed worries about whether or not it suffices to solve the measurement problem to merely to guarantee—as the GRW theory does—that the spatial positions of macroscopic material bodies are almost always almost determinate.[7] And there has been an enormous literature (of which much more later) on the business of bringing all these ideas into accord with the special theory of relativity.

There has been a third tradition of thinking about the measurement problem as well, which goes back to the work of the late Hugh Everett III. It has for the most part been referred to in the literature as the many-worlds interpretation of quantum mechanics, and seems to me not to have much of a chance of being on the right track. It is worth talking some about, though, because (to begin with) it is surely one of the most thrilling and radical and suggestive ideas ever to have been seriously entertained in the entire history of science, and because it has (as a matter

---

[6] See e.g. Ruetsche (1998) and the many helpful references therein.
[7] See Albert and Loewer (1995).

of fact) generated a great deal of interest among practising physicists over the past several years. It also—even in failure—has much to teach.

The story, then, is that in 1957 a heroic and astonishing paper was published by Hugh Everett III, in which it was announced that a means had been discovered of coherently entertaining the possibility that the linear quantum-mechanical equations of motion are indeed—notwithstanding (say) the story of Wigner's friend—the true and complete equations of motion of the whole world. The paper was very difficult, and everybody who read it seemed to come away with the powerful impression that there was something of immense interest in it, but couldn't quite say—at least at the outset—just exactly what that might be. As time went by, a number of different schools of thought grew up around what it was that Everett had actually had in mind, or what it was that he actually *ought* to have had in mind. The earliest and most famous of these schools of thought goes under the name of the many-worlds interpretation of quantum mechanics.

What Everett announced in his paper (to put things a little more concretely) was that he had discovered some means of coherently entertaining the possibility that the states of things at the conclusions of the sorts of x-spin measurement we were talking about above really *are* superpositions like the one in (4). The idea of the many-worlds reading of Everett's paper is that the means of coherently entertaining that possibility that Everett had in mind is to take the two components of a state like the one in (4) to represent (literally) *two physical worlds* (DeWitt 1970). The idea is that in the course of an interaction like the one that leads from (3) to (4), the number of physical worlds there are literally increases from one to two, and that in each one of those worlds, the x-spin measurement actually has a determinate outcome and the observer actually has a determinate belief about that outcome, and that the linearity of the equations of motion will entail that those two worlds will for all subsequent time be absolutely unaware of one another.

The trouble is that this way of looking at things makes it hard to imagine what it could possibly mean to say (for example) that in the event that Wigner's friend carries out a measurement of the x-spin of an initially y-spin-up electron, the *probability* that that measurement will come out *up* is ½. The trouble (more particularly) is that probabilities are always and invariably and necessarily in one way or another about ignorance of the future, and there just seems not to be any room for that sort of ignorance here: this sort of a measurement, on this interpretation of quantum mechanics, will (after all) with certainty give rise to two worlds, in one of which there is a friend of Wigner's who sees that the outcome of the measurement is up and in the other of which there is a friend of Wigner's who sees that the outcome of the measurement is down, and there isn't going to be any matter of fact about which one of those two worlds is the real one, or about which one of those two friends of Wigner's is the original friend.

There are ways of making many-worlds talk sound less vulgar: there are ways, that is, of making it sound less literal. Sometimes, for example, it is said that there is exactly one physical world, but that (when superpositions like the one in (4) obtain) there are somehow two incompatible stories about that world that are somehow both simultaneously true. Sometimes it is said that there is exactly one physical world, but that (when superpositions like the one in (4) obtain) that world somehow supports two distinct and incompatible phenomenal experiences of itself, simultaneously, within one and the same sentient observer. The rub is that these more high-toned ways of talking are perhaps not even intelligible, and (more importantly) that in so far as they *are* intelligible, they will manifestly run into precisely the same trouble about probabilities as the original many-worlds interpretation did (for a particularly sophisticated attempt at defending these sorts of interpretations against this sort of charge, see Saunders 1998).

Let's try another tack.

The idea here is to read Everett as being sceptical that, when you come right down to it, the problem of measurement has any empirical basis.

It goes like this. Suppose that there is exactly one world, and that quantum states amount to complete descriptions of that world. Suppose also that the standard way of thinking about what it means to be in a superposition is the right way of thinking about what it means to be in a superposition. And suppose that the linear quantum-mechanical equations of motion are invariably true, and (consequently) that observers like the one described above frequently did end up, at the conclusions of x-spin measurements, in states like the one in (4).

Let us see if we can figure out what those equations would entail about how an observer like that, in a state like the one in (4), would respond to questions about how she feels (that is, about what her mental state is).[8] Maybe this will tell us something.

The most obvious question to ask is 'What is your present belief about the x-spin of the electron?' But that question turns out not to be of much use here. Here's why: Suppose that the observer in question (the one that's now in the state in (4)) gives honest responses to such questions; suppose, that is, that when her brain state is [believes that x-spin up> she invariably responds to such a question by saying the word "up", and that when her brain state is [believes that x-spin down> she invariably responds to such a question by saying the word "down". The problem is that precisely the same linearity of the equations of motion which brought about the superposition of different brain states in the state in (4) in the first place will now entail that if we were to address this sort of question to this sort of observer, when (4) obtains, then the state of the world after she responds to the question will be a superposition of one in which she says "up" and another in which she says "down"; and of course it won't be any easier to interpret a "response" like that than it was to interpret the superposition of brain states in (4) that that response was intended to be a description of.

---

[8] The habit of raising this sort of a question (which, once again, is typical of recent investigations into the foundations of physics) is what makes it altogether natural that the foundations of physics should have been the birthplace of the idea of (say) quantum computation, in Deutsche (1985).

But suppose we were to say this: 'Don't tell me whether you believe the x-spin of the electron to be up or you believe it to be down, but tell me merely whether or not *one* of those two is the case; tell me (in other words) merely whether or not you now have any particular definite belief (not uncertain, not confused, not vague, and not superposed) about the value of the x-spin of this electron.'

If we were to ask the observer this question when the state [believes that x-spin up$>_F$[indicates that x-spin up$>_m$[x-spin up$>_e$ obtains, and if she is indeed an honest and competent reporter of her mental states, then she would presumably answer 'Yes, I do have some determinate belief about that at present: one of those two is the case'; and of course she would answer in precisely the same way in the event that [believes that x-spin down$>_F$[indicates that x-spin down$>_m$[x-spin down$>_e$ obtains. And so responding to this particular question in this particular way (by saying yes) is an observable property of this observer in both of those states, and consequently (and this is the punchline) it will also be an observable property of her in any superposition of those two brain states, and consequently (in particular) it will be an observable property of her in (4).

That's really odd. On the one hand, the dynamical equations of motion predict that this observer is going to end up, at the conclusion of a measurement like the one we've been talking about, in the state in (4), and not in either one of the brain states associated with any definite particular belief about the x-spin of the electron; and on the other hand, we have just now discovered that those same equations also predict that when a state like (4) obtains, the observer is necessarily going to be convinced (or at any rate she is necessarily going to report) that she does have a definite particular belief about the x-spin of the electron.

Let us go on. Suppose that the observer carries out a measurement of the x-spin of an electron whose y-spin is initially definite with a x-spin measuring device, and suppose that when that's done (that is, when a state like (4) obtains) she carries out a second measurement of the x-spin of that electron, with a second x-spin measuring device. And suppose that when that is all done, we were to say 'Don't tell me what the outcomes of either of those two x-spin measurements were; just tell me whether or not you now believe that those two measurements both had definite outcomes, and whether or not those two outcomes were the same'. Well, it will follow from the same sorts of arguments as I gave above that Wigner's friend's response to a question like that (even though, as a matter of fact, on the standard way of thinking, neither of those experiments had any definite outcome) will necessarily be 'Yes: they both had definite outcomes, and both of those outcomes were the same'.

It will also follow from the same sorts of arguments that if two observers were both to carry out measurements of the x-spin of some particular electron whose y-spin was initially definite, and were subsequently to talk to one another about the outcomes of their respective experiments (if they were both, that is, to check up on one another), then both of those observers would report, falsely, that the other observer had reported some definite particular outcome of her measurement, and both of them would report that that reported outcome was completely in agreement with their own.

There is something else we can show that is worth mentioning here too. Suppose that an observer is confronted with an infinite ensemble of identical systems in identical states, and that she carries out a certain identical measurement on each one of them. Then, even though there will actually be no matter of fact about what she takes the outcomes of any of those measurements to be, nonetheless as the number of those measurements which have already been carried out goes to infinity, the state of the world will approach (as a well-defined mathematical limit) a state in which the reports of this observer about the statistical frequency of any particular outcome of those measurements will be perfectly definite, and also perfectly in accord with the standard quantum-mechanical predictions about what that frequency ought to be.

The upshot of all this is that it turns out not to be altogether impossible (even if the standard way of thinking about what it means to be in a superposition is the right way of thinking about it) that the state we end up in at the conclusion of a measurement of the x-spin of a y-spin-up electron is the one in (4).

It turns out (that is) that the quantum-mechanical equations of motion can function as a scientific instrument for being radically sceptical even about the determinateness of the most mundane and everyday features of the external macroscopic physical world, and even about the most mundane and everyday features of our own mental lives.

The conventional formulation of the measurement problem (that is, the one rehearsed at the outset of this chapter—the one according to which there is some particular point in the course of the sort of measurement we've been discussing here at which the hypothesis that the quantum-mechanical equations of motion are the true and complete equations of motion of the whole world somehow flatly contradicts something that we know, with certainty, by pure introspection, about our own thoughts) is therefore all wrong.

The hope, of course, is that this might amount to an argument that there just isn't any such thing as a measurement problem. The hope, that is, is that this might make it entertainable that, even if the standard way of thinking about what it means to be in a superposition is the right way of thinking about what it means to be in a superposition, the linear dynamical laws are nonetheless the complete laws of the evolution of the entire world, and all of the appearances to the contrary (like the appearance that experiments have outcomes, and the appearance that the world doesn't evolve deterministically) turn out to be just the sorts of delusions which those laws themselves can be shown to bring on.

But there turn out to be all sorts of reasons why this hypothesis (call it the bare theory[9]) can't be quite right. Note, for example, that if the bare theory were true,

[9] The physicist Sydney Coleman, who concocted much the same hypothesis himself, calls it 'Quantum Mechanics in your Face'.

then there would be matters of fact about what we think about (say) the frequencies of x-spin-up outcomes of measurements of the x-spins of y-spin-up electrons only (if at all) in the limit as the number of those measurements goes to infinity. And so, if the bare theory were true (and since only a finite number of such measurements has ever actually been carried out by any one of us, or even in the entire history of the world), then there couldn't now be any matter of fact (notwithstanding our delusion that there is one) about what we take those frequencies to be. And so, if the bare theory is true, then there can't be any matter of fact (notwithstanding our delusion that there is one) about whether or not we take those frequencies to be in accordance with the standard quantum-mechanical predictions about them. And so, if the bare theory is true, then it isn't clear what sorts of reasons we can possibly have for believing in anything like quantum mechanics (which is what the bare theory is supposed to be a way of making sense of) in the first place.[10]

As a matter of fact, if the bare theory is true, then it turns out to be extraordinarily unlikely that the present quantum state of the world is one of those on which there's even a matter of fact about whether or not any sentient experimenters exist at all. Of course, in the event that there isn't any matter of fact about whether or not any sentient experimenters exist, then it becomes unintelligible even to inquire (as we've been doing here) about what sorts of things such experimenters will report.

And then (as far as I can tell) all bets are off.[11]

It now seems to me not to be entertainable (in any of the ways we have lately been considering, or in any other way I know of) that the linear quantum-mechanical equations of motion are the true and complete equations of motion of the whole world. What I think this stuff about what superpositions feel like does show, though, is that precisely that feature of those equations which makes it clear that they cannot possibly be the true and complete equations of motion of the whole world—that is, their linearity—also makes it radically unclear how much of the world and which parts of the world those equations possibly can be the true and complete equations of motion of.

What I think it shows (to put it another way) is that there can be no such thing as a definitive list of what there have absolutely got to be matters of fact about which is scientifically fit to serve as an "observational basis" from which all attempts at fixing quantum mechanics up must start out.

What I think it shows is that what there are and what there aren't determinate matters of fact about, even in connection with the most mundane and everyday

---

[10] This is worth mulling over a bit. What we're running into here is a very general and very fundamental and heretofore not much noticed principle of scientific theorizing—a principle which it has become necessary to state very explicitly and to put to very concrete sorts of work in the context of recent work in the foundations of physics—to the following effect: One of the conditions of the possibility of entertaining any particular scientific hypothesis (entertaining it, that is, as a genuinely scientific hypothesis, as opposed to a merely sceptical one) is that it be consistent with that hypothesis that beings like us could in principle have good scientific reasons for believing it.

[11] There are very helpful discussions of all of the issues of the last several paragraphs, by the way, in Barrett (1999).

macroscopic features of the external physical world, and even in connection with the most mundane and everyday features of our own mental lives, is something which we shall ultimately have to learn (in some part) from whatever turns out to be the best way of fixing quantum mechanics up.

Let me say something, just by way of finishing (and which is going to have to be absurdly brief), about the business of seeking out the best way of fixing quantum mechanics up.

To begin with, there are all sorts of non-observational criteria of theory choice (various sorts of simplicity, various sorts of economy; stuff like that) which have been much discussed in the philosophy of science, and which will of course come into play in choosing the best way of fixing quantum mechanics up. We shall of course require that any acceptable way of fixing quantum mechanics up make the correct predictions about the values of those observable properties of the world whose values it entails there are matters of fact about. We shall also want to adopt some generally conservative principle on the question of what there are matters of fact about; we shall want, that is, to adhere as closely as we can (all other things being equal) to the commonsensical position that there are invariably determinate matters of fact at least about the most mundane and everyday features of our own mental lives, and of the macroscopic external physical world.

The lesson about what superpositions feel like, I think, is just that the linearity of the quantum-mechanical equations of motion can function as a scientific instrument for injecting some slack into that conservative principle, more or less at any point we like, if we find we need some.

3

Let us change the subject.

There is a famous tension between fundamental microscopic physical theory and everyday macroscopic human experience about the question of precisely how the past is different from the future.

Let us set it up—as simply as can be done—in a streamlined version of the Newtonian mechanics of particles.

The physical furniture of the universe, on this picture, consists entirely of point particles. The only dynamical variables of such particles—the only physical attributes of such particles that can change with time—are their positions; consequently, a list of what particles exist, of what sorts of particles they are,[12] and of what their

---

[12] That is, of their non-dynamical properties: their masses and their charges and so forth.

positions are at all times, is a list of absolutely everything there is to say about the physical history of the world.[13]

What Newtonian mechanics has to say about the motions of particles, the entirety of what it has to say about the motions of particles, is that a certain breathtakingly simple mathematical relation, $F = ma$, invariably holds between the force on any particle at any particular instant, its acceleration at that instant, and its mass.

One of the consequences of the previous sentence is that Newtonian mechanics is deterministic. Given a list of the positions of all of the particles in the world at any particular time, and of how those positions are changing at that time, as time flows forward, and of what sorts of particles they are, what sorts of interactions they have, and what sorts of forces they exert on one another, the universe's entire history, in every detail, from that time forward, can in principle be calculated (if this theory is true) with certainty.

Now, Newtonian mechanics has a number of what are referred to in the literature as fundamental symmetries. What that means is that Newtonian mechanics entails (that $F = ma$ entails) that there are certain sorts of facts about the world which—as a matter of absolutely general principle—don't make any dynamical difference.

Suppose, for example, that we are given the present positions and velocities of all of the particles in the world, that we are told what sorts of particles they are, and that we should like to calculate their positions and velocities (say) two hours from now. It is an extremely straightforward consequence of the Newtonian picture of the world that that calculation can be carried through in perfect ignorance of what time "now" is. If the classical laws of motion entail that a certain set of positions and velocities at 4.02 evolves into a certain other set of positions and velocities at 6.02, then those laws will necessarily also entail that the first set at 4.07 will evolve into the second set at 6.07, and that the first set at 12.23 will evolve into the second at 2.23, and so on. Any sequence of position and velocity values for every particle in an isolated collection which is in accord with classical mechanics and which begins at time t would necessarily (to put all this slightly differently) also be in accord with classical mechanics if it were to begin instead at t'. And in virtue of all that, Newtonian mechanics is said to have time-translation symmetry—it is said to be invariant under translations like that.

It also has a number of other significant invariances. Absolute positions don't play any role in Newtonian mechanics (although the positions of particles relative to one another certainly do), and neither do absolute directions in space, or absolute velocities.[14]

---

[13] This is certainly not to deny that there are such things in the world as extended objects; the idea is just that all of the facts about objects like that (facts, say, about where the tables and chairs are, and about who punched whom, and about who said what, and so on) are determined, in principle, by the facts about the particles of which those objects are composed.

[14] And all of these invariances are (by the way) also invariances of Maxwellian electrodynamics, and of relativistic quantum string theories, and of every other fundamental theory in the canon.

And neither does the direction of time.

Think (say) of watching a film of a baseball which is thrown directly upwards, and which is subject to the influence of the gravitational force of the earth. Then imagine watching the same film in reverse. The film run forwards will depict the baseball moving more and more slowly upwards, and the film run in reverse will depict the baseball moving more and more quickly downward. What both films will depict, though, is a baseball which (whatever its velocity) is accelerating, constantly, at the rate of 32 feet per second per second, in the direction of the ground.

This is, of course, an absolutely general phenomenon. The apparent velocity of any particular material particle at any particular frame of any film of any classical physical process run forwards will be equal and opposite to the apparent velocity of that particle at that frame of that film run in reverse; but the apparent acceleration of any particular particle at any particular frame of the film run forwards will be identical, both in magnitude and in direction, to the apparent acceleration of that particle at that frame of the film run in reverse.[15] $x(-t)$ is (by definition) $dx(-t)/dt$, which is equal (by the chain rule) to $-v(-t)$, which is, of course, the negative of the velocity of the particle (at the frame in question) depicted in the film run forwards. On the other hand, the apparent acceleration of a particle whose apparent trajectory is $x(-t)$ is (by definition) $(d/dt)(dx(-t)/dt)$, which is equal (by the upshot of the previous sentence) to $(d/dt)(-v(-t))$, which is equal (by the chain rule) to $-(-a(-t))$, which is equal (because (-1) times (-1) is $(+1)$) to $a(-t)$, which is (of course) the *same* as the acceleration of the particle (at the frame in question) depicted in the film run forwards.

Now, the Newtonian law of motion (which is, remember, the entirety of what the Newtonian picture of the world has to say about the motions of particles) is that a certain mathematical relation holds, at every instant, between mass and force and acceleration. And of course the mass of any particular particle at any particular frame of the sort of movie we've been talking about depends on nothing other than what particular particle it is; and the force on any particular particle at any particular frame of the sort of movie we've been talking about depends on nothing other than what particular set of particles happens to exist, and what their spatial distances from one another at that frame happen to be; and what we've just seen is that the acceleration of any particular particle, at any particular frame of such a movie, will be entirely independent of the direction in which the film is run. And

---

[15] The proof is trivial. Let $x(t)$ represent the apparent trajectory (that is, the apparent position as a function of time) of the particle depicted in the film run forwards; let $v(t)$ represent the apparent velocity (that is, the apparent derivative of the position with respect to time) of that particle; and let $a(t)$ represent the apparent acceleration (that is, the apparent derivative of the velocity with respect to time) of that particle. Then the apparent trajectory of the particle depicted in the film run in reverse will be $x(-t)$. And of course the apparent velocity of a particle whose apparent trajectory is $x(-t)$ will be the opposite of the velocity of a particle whose trajectory is $x(t)$ for all t.

so if a certain film, run forwards, depicts a process which is in accord with Newtonian mechanics, then, necessarily, the same film run in reverse will depict a process which is in accord with Newtonian mechanics as well.[16]

It is therefore a consequence of Newtonian mechanics that nothing in the laws of nature can be of any help whatever in deciding which way any film is ever being run. It is also a consequence of Newtonian mechanics that whatever can happen can just as easily, just as naturally, happen backwards.[17]

So the Newtonian-mechanical instructions for calculating future physical situations of the world from its present physical situation turn out to be identical to the Newtonian-mechanical instructions for calculating past physical situations of the world from its present physical situation. The instructions for calculating (say) the positions of all of the particles in the world ten minutes from now are that the present positions of all those particles, and the rates at which those positions are changing as time flows forwards, be plugged into a certain algorithm; and the instructions for calculating the positions of those particles ten minutes ago are that their present positions, and the rates at which those positions are changing as time flows backwards, be plugged into precisely the same algorithm.

Thus if we are told the positions of all the particles in the world at present, and if we are told the rates at which those positions are changing as time flows towards some other moment M, and if we are told the size of the time-interval that separates M from the present, then we can in principle calculate the positions of all of the particles in the world at M, with certainty, without our ever having been told (and also without our ever learning, as the calculation proceeds) whether M happens to lie after the present or before it.

So (if the laws of Newtonian mechanics are all the fundamental natural laws there are) there can be no lawlike asymmetries whatever between past and future.

But the thing is that all this is wildly at odds with our everyday experience.

To begin with, every corner of the world is positively swarming with ordinary physical processes that don't, or don't regularly, or don't naturally, or don't familiarly,

---

[16] Let us put this a bit more formally. Consider a history $\{x_1(t) \ldots x_N(t)\}$ of some isolated collection of N particles. What's just been shown is that if

$$d^2x_i(t)/dt^2 = F_i(x_1(t) \ldots x_N(t))$$

for all i (where x_i is the position of particle i, and F_i is the force on particle i), then, necessarily

$$d^2x_i(-t)/dt^2 = F_i(x_1(-t) \ldots x_N(-t)),$$

which is to say that if $\{x_1(t) \ldots x_N(t)\}$ is a solution to the Newtonian equations of motion, then, necessarily, $\{x_1(-t) \ldots x_N(-t)\}$ is as well.

[17] Maybe a few of the standard illustrations are in order here. Think, then, of watching films, run forwards and run in reverse, of a single particle, alone in the universe, moving (say) to the right; or of two billiard balls colliding; or of a rock moving downward, and accelerating downward, in the gravitational field of the earth.

happen backwards (the melting of ice, say, or the cooling of soup, or the breaking of glass, or the passing of youth; whatever).[18]

On top of that there's an asymmetry of epistemic access: our capacities to know what happened yesterday, and our methods of finding out what happened yesterday, are as a general matter very different from our capacities to know and our methods of finding out what will happen tomorrow.[19]

And on top of that there's what you might call an asymmetry of intervention: it seems to us that we can bring it about that certain things occur—or that they don't—in the future, but we feel absolutely incapable of doing anything at all about the past.[20]

That is the tension I mentioned before. It is (as I said at the outset) a tension which has stubbornly and astonishingly persisted, in more or less the same form, from the Newtonian beginnings of modern physics through the great nineteenth-century investigations of analytical mechanics and electromagnetism and the revolutionary twentieth-century developments of the special and general theories of relativity, of quantum mechanics, of quantum field theory, of quantum string theory, and (as a matter of fact) of virtually every one of the serious candidates for a fundamental physical theory of the world which has come up over the past several hundred years.

The question of precisely what to do about this tension is the subject of far too rich and busy and open a scientific and philosophical literature to be summarized here.[21] Let it suffice for the moment, then, merely to mention a few of the main themes.

Note (to begin with) that the fact that a certain set of dynamical laws is symmetric under a certain transformation certainly does not entail that all of the individual

---

[18] Maybe this is worth belabouring a bit further. Take soup. It isn't that soup never heats up; it is rather that occasions when soup does heat up never look anything at all like mere temporal inversions, like films watched backwards, of occasions when soup cools off. The former occasions are always different, somehow. They involve fires or electrical currents or parabolic mirrors or something like that. And that's the point here: that you can bet your life that a tepid pot of soup, in (say) an otherwise empty, cold, closed, insulated room, is invariably and ineluctably in the process of getting colder.

[19] The mere recognition of this asymmetry of epistemic access as amounting to anything along the lines of a problem for physics, by the way, is yet another instance of the brave new willingness I was talking about in note 3—the willingness to entertain the possibility of the most radical imaginable sort of completeness of physics. This asymmetry, according to the new way of thinking, is no less a physical business than the stuff about the cooling of soup: this too is about the sequences in which the states of physical systems occur; this is about the fact that (say) detailed and accurate depictions of freak accidents (photographic depictions, or tape-recorded ones, or written ones, or ones stored in the physical states of human brains, or whatever) almost never precede those accidents themselves.

[20] Everything I said in note 20 about the asymmetry of epistemic access obviously goes double for the asymmetry of intervention. To insist that even this—even our conviction that by acting now we can affect the future but not the past—has got to point to some feature of the world which it is the task of a fundamental physical theory of the world to explain, is of the very essence of the approach to the world by way of the promising new avenue I mentioned in the first paragraph of this chapter.

[21] There is, happily, an excellent, up-to-date, and breathtakingly exhaustive summary of it in Sklar (1998).

trajectories which those laws allow have that sort of symmetry as well. (A single particle moving in some single particular direction in space, for example, is perfectly compatible with the Newtonian laws of motion, notwithstanding that there is no single particular direction in space which those laws in and of themselves pick out as in any way special.) The canonical way of coming to grips with the tension we have just been talking about (the tradition associated with the names of Boltzmann, Ehrenfest, and Riechenbach) is to exploit precisely that: to see the asymmetry of our macroscopic experience under time-reversal, that is, as entering into the world not by way of the dynamical laws (which, as we have just seen, seem to have no such asymmetry in them), but rather by way of the particular trajectory the world is on, by way, that is, of the world's initial conditions. Moreover (and this is a way of sum-ming up the achievement, over the past century and a half, of the science of statist-ical mechanics), it turns out that the sorts of initial conditions in question here—the sorts of initial conditions, that is, which, in combination with the dynamical laws, can arguably generate precisely the sorts of ordinary physical asymmetries under time-reversal that characterize our everyday macroscopic experience—have a strik-ingly simple, elegant, and plausible form. And the same may well apply, by the way, to the above-mentioned asymmetries of intervention and epistemic access—but these questions are as yet a good deal more open, and are only now beginning to receive the careful and detailed kind of attention they deserve.

A number of things about all this, however, have almost always made almost everybody uneasy.

The initial conditions in question, to begin with, include some statistical elements—some probabilistic elements, whose exact conceptual status has been the subject of what now amounts to more than a century of intense debate.

There is something ineluctably awkward about the whole strategy of explaining the utterly familiar, fundamental, ubiquitous time-asymmetries of our everyday experience in terms of the world's initial conditions. The time-asymmetries of our everyday experience—the fact, say, that if two bodies at different temperatures are put into thermal contact with one another, heat will flow from the hotter body to the cooler one—are, on the one hand, the very models and paradigms (if anything ever was) of physical law. And, on the other, we have long been used to thinking of initial conditions in physics as falling under the category of the accidental, of the contingent, of what might have been otherwise, of how things merely happen to be.

And so there have always been alternative traditions out there as well.

Ilya Prigogine and his collaborators, for example, have been working away for decades, and with prodigious mathematical sophistication, on a proposed cure for this tension (there's an excellent account and critique of this proposed cure, along with voluminous references, in Sklar, 1998). Prigogine's idea is that the very busi-ness of representing the history of the world as a trajectory, the very business, that is, of thinking of the world as having any particular precisely defined set of initial conditions, is somehow oversimplified or misleading or false. The world (so the story goes) does not have an initial condition, but (rather, somehow) a little continuous group of them. This, so it is said, somehow renders the above-mentioned puzzling statistical features of the canonical picture an entirely natural and transparent and expected sort of thing, and this (if everything works out, and taken together with the chaotic structure of the Newtonian dynamics of certain paradigmatic sorts of physical systems) is supposed to point the way to the ultimate resolution of the tension about the direction of time. The trouble (or rather, one of the troubles) is that it has never been made particularly clear what it might mean, or what it might amount to, to think of the world as having a multiplicity of initial conditions; and, moreover, that all of the arguments that have been offered on behalf of this idea (which invariably seem to come down to the fact that whenever we perform an experiment, we are dealing with situations in which the initial conditions are given with a finite precision) seem to mix up epistemic considerations with metaphysical ones.

Finally, there has been a vague and mostly unspoken idea in the back of the collective mind of theoretical physics for as long as anybody can remember—and which is only now beginning to receive a detailed and rigorous and quantitative sort of examination—to the effect that the statistical character of our everyday experience, and its asymmetry under time-reversal, may have something deep to do with the statistical character and asymmetry under time-reversal of a number of proposed solutions to the infamous quantum-mechanical problem of measurement. As of this writing, for example, there is reason to hope that if anything along the lines of the GRW theory of the collapses of quantum-mechanical wave-functions should turn out to be true, then the melting of ice and the cooling of soup and the breaking of glass and the passing of youth could be shown to represent genuine stochastic time-asymmetric dynamical laws; there is reason to hope, that is, that if that sort of a theory should turn out to be true, then the melting of ice (etc.) could be shown to be the sorts of transitions which are overwhelmingly likely to occur, and overwhelmingly unlikely to occur in reverse, completely irrespective of what the initial conditions of the universe may happen to have been.[22]

4

The deepest, most involved, and longest-running conversation about the philosophy of the modern physical picture of the world is surely the one about the ontological structure of space and time. This goes back, of course, to the debates between Newton and Leibniz about the character of motion, and was enriched and

---

[22] For details, see the last chapter of Albert (2001).

reconfigured in the twentieth century by investigations into the foundations of the special and general theories of relativity, and is at present a galaxy of fascinating individual questions.

We shall have only space (needless to say) for a few tiny seductive opinionated representative snippets of that conversation here.

Let us start with something very simple, something conceptually prior, as it were, even to the seminal and original and paradigmatic debate about the character of motion in Newtonian mechanics.

Suppose, for the moment, that the physical furniture of the universe consists entirely of particles. Then, as everybody knows, there is a reasonably compelling empiricist sort of an intuition to the effect that the only spatial facts about the world are the ones about the distances between arbitrary pairs of particles—that there *are* no facts, say, about the position of any particular particle *simpliciter*.

There is a famous argument of Kant to the effect that the above position, the empiricist position, the so-called relationalist position, cannot be right; an argument, that is, to the effect that it recognizes fewer spatial facts about the world than (if you think it over) there manifestly are. It goes like this: Consider a pair of possible universes, in one of which the only material object is a right-handed glove and in the other of which the only material object is an (otherwise identical) left-handed one. The two universes (so says Kant) manifestly differ, but, as a moment's reflection will show, they do not differ in terms of any of the complete list of spatial facts recognized by the relationalist. And so (the argument goes) relationalism is false.

The canonical relationalist response—at this point in the game—is to bite the bullet and simply deny that there is any difference whatever (notwithstanding immediate intuitions to the contrary) between the two universes described above.

Let us spell that out in just a bit more detail.

Note, to begin with, that among the set of all mathematically possible material shapes (which is to say: among the set of all mathematically possible relationalist arrangements of particles, among the set of all mathematically possible sets of interparticle distances) there are those which can, and those which can not, be made to coincide perfectly with their mirror images by means of ordinary three-dimensional translations and rotations. Call the second sort *handed*. Gloves are handed, then, and shoes are; trousers and hats, for example, aren't.

While right-handedness and left-handedness are, of course, not kosher relationalist predicates, handedness *simpliciter* surely is. Whether or not a certain shape is handed, again, depends exclusively on the distances between its constituent particles; and whether the handednesses of any two relationally identical handed shapes are the same or the opposites of one another (whether, that is, any two relationally identical handed objects—any two gloves, say, or any two shoes—can be translated and rotated in such a way as to coincide perfectly with one another in space) can be read off from nothing over and above the distances between corresponding elements of their two sets of constituent particles. For any two relationally identical handed objects (to put it a bit more formally) there will necessarily exist some two-valued mathematical function—which is a function exclusively of the distances between corresponding elements of their two sets of constituent particles—and which takes on the value (say) 1 if and only if the handedness of the two objects are the same and −1 if and only if their handednesses are opposite.

The relationalist strategy is just to run with that. The relationalist idea, that is, is that relative handedness itself, relative handedness in its essence, is nothing over and above the peculiar exclusively spatial relation picked out by precisely this relative-handedness function, and that our impression to the contrary, our impression that (say) two oppositely handed gloves are somehow intrinsically different from one another, can be traced to the fact that the particular sort of relation in question here—notwithstanding that it is a perfectly and exclusively spatial relation—is a relation which, as it happens, no combination of three-dimensional rotations and translations can ever alter. It will follow from all this (as promised above) that there just can't be any matter of fact as to whether two relationally identical gloves in different possible universes have the same handedness or not—precisely because there can be no matters of fact about the spatial distance between any particular particle in one glove and any particular particle in the other.

This was more or less how things stood all the way up until the middle of the twentieth century, when new fundamental physical laws were discovered which (it seems to have been thought) simply cannot be written down in kosher relationalist language, and so decide the question in favour of absolutism.

The laws in question concern the decays of certain elementary particles; they concern, that is, processes in which certain individual such particles fall apart into collections of others, of so-called products. The spatial configurations in which those decay products appear are sometimes handed, and, moreover, it turns out to be a law that certain sorts of particles are more likely to fall apart into (say) the right-handed version of the configuration in question than the left-handed one. This last phrase is, of course, just not sayable in the vocabulary of the relationalist.

It seems somehow not to have been all that widely noticed that the relationalist can now, of course, bite the bullet yet again and say that the law should rightly read just that the configuration of the decay products of the sort of particle in question here is invariably the same, single, handed one; that the configurations of the decay products of any large group of such particles is likely to fall into two oppositely handed classes (which, according to the relationalist, is to say nothing other than that those decay products are going to be at certain particular sets of spatial distances from one another); and that those two classes are likely to be unequal in size. Period.[23]

---

[23] Simon Saunders and I discovered some years ago that this option had previously and independently crossed both of our minds. We wondered why we had never come across it in the literature, as it must surely have crossed many other minds before ours.

At this point the whole business is manifestly beginning to harden into a stalemate. The internal consistency and the empirical adequacy of the relationalist position is (by construction) unassailable, but it comes at a conceptual price: it comes along with a certain new offence to intuition, which is that the laws of the decay of the sorts of particles we've been talking about here now look curiously non-local, both in space and (even less familiarly) in time. On this construal of the world, that is, what those laws apparently require of each new decay event is that it probabilistically have the same handedness as—that it probabilistically line itself up with—the majority of the decays of the sort of particle in question which happen to have taken place else-where and before. The entirety of what any relationalist reading of those laws can have to say about (say) the first such decay which happens to have occurred in the history of the world, or about any particular such decay considered in isolation, is (of course) that it deterministically assumes the handed configuration in question.

The reason for going through all this is that it seems to me to contain the essence of the much larger, more complicated, and more seminal dispute—the one we started off with a few pages back—about the character of motion in classical mechanics, the dispute (more particularly) about whether or not there can be a satisfactory relationalist account of the dynamical effects of rotation.

The business gets started like this: Consider a universe which consists of nothing whatever over and above two balls affixed to opposite ends of a spring. Stipulate that the length of that spring, in its relaxed configuration, in its unstretched and uncompressed configuration, is L. And imagine that there is some particular tem-poral instant in the history of that universe at which it happens to be the case that (1) the length of the spring is greater than L, and (2) there are no two material com-ponents of this contraption—there are no two material components, that is, of this universe which are, at the instant in question, in motion relative to one another.[24] Suppose that we should like to know something about the dynamical evolution of this universe in the future of that instant; and that we should like to know (say) whether or not this spring is fated, in the future, to oscillate.

Well, the thing (as everybody knows) is that on Newtonian mechanics, or at any rate on the conventional way of understanding Newtonian mechanics, or at any rate on the conventional way of writing Newtonian mechanics down, whether or not this spring is fated to oscillate will depend on whether or not, and to what extent, at the instant in question, the contraption is rotating with respect to absolute space.[25]

---

[24] Imagine, that is, that for every pair of material components of this contraption, the first derivat-ive with respect to time of the spatial distance between the two components in that pair, at the instant in question, is zero.

[25] If, for example, the angular velocity of the contraption with respect to absolute space is zero, then the spring will immediately commence oscillating about its relaxed configuration. And there will necessarily be some possible value of that velocity at which no oscillations at all will occur, and there will manifestly be still others at which the spring will oscillate about any one of an infinity of its unrelaxed configurations.

The trouble with that, of course, is that on a relationalist picture of the world there can simply not be any *fact of the matter* about rotations relative to absolute space.

Thereby (as they say) hangs a curious and still unfinished tale—the full telling of which would take us much too far afield at present[26]—of attempts at coming to grips with this, of attempts, as it were, at fixing it up, by means of baroque and ingenious Machian speculations about the ultimate origin of inertia. And these speculations invariably empirically disagree (which is to say: they invariably disagree about the time-evolutions of proper, kosher, relationalist interparticle distances) with standard Newtonian mechanics.[27]

It also seems not to have been widely enough noticed, or mentioned sufficiently prominently, or taken sufficiently seriously, that there is, as above, an absolutely straightforward relationalist reading of the world, unassailable in its internal consistency and its empirical adequacy, and fully in agreement with all of the standard Newtonian predictions about the evolutions of the distances between material particles, which is that all and only those sequences of interparticle distances are physically possible which can be embedded into a Newtonian space-time in such a way as to satisfy $F = ma$.

The price, again (as this is now a theory not of the evolutions of the positions of particles relative to a local background of absolute space, but directly of the evolutions of the spatial separations between the particles, particles whose spatial separations from one another may of course be arbitrarily large) is that the world turns run on a curious sort of action at a distance.[28]

And this, of course, is only the beginning. One needs to decide, for example, what to make—in connection with these sorts of questions—of the existence of fields, and of the theory of relativity, and of gauge theories,[29] and of God knows what else.

Quite apart from these discussions of the relativity of motion, there has been a magnificent flowering over the past few decades in our understanding of a host

[26] Anyway, it's been told, well and recently, elsewhere (Sklar 1977; Earman 1989; and especially and particularly Barbour 2000).

[27] That, by the way, might not be such a bad thing. These sorts of speculations will typically entail, for example, that the total angular momentum of the universe will necessarily be zero; and so far as we can tell at present, the angular momentum of our universe is (approximately) zero. So the sorts of speculations we have just now been thinking through would have the advantage of providing an explanation of that fact, rather than having to chalk it up (as Newtonian mechanics does) as a merely contingent feature of the universe's initial conditions.

[28] The sort of non-locality that comes up here, however, is a great deal less pernicious than the kind you have to deal with in the Machian theories. The laws of this theory, for example, apply both to the universe as a whole and to any one of its dynamically isolated subsystems. The laws of this theory (to put it another way) render it impossible to determine, by means of observations of the behaviour of any dynamically isolated subsystem of the universe, whether there are any other systems in the universe or not. Not so on the Machian theories. But this is matter for another paper.

[29] There is, by the way, a particularly novel and wonderful, recent and as yet unpublished, paper of Tim Maudlin's on the metaphysics of general relativity and gauge theories, which isn't directly about questions of the relativity of motion but which very much bears on those questions, and which, I suspect, is still a good deal less well known than it ought to be.

of philosophically interesting consequences of the general theory of relativity, particularly in connection with the development of space-time singularities, and with the possibility of time-travel into the past,[30] and (more recently) with the vanishing of the canonically quantized general-relativistic Hamiltonian.

Still, it seems to me, there is a question about space and time beside which all these others may yet pale, which has never yet fully, directly, and unflinchingly been looked in the face, and which concerns the compatibility of the sorts of attempts at solving the measurement problem that we were talking about earlier on with the special theory of relativity.

The business of genuinely coming to grips with this question is, as I said, still almost entirely ahead of us—but we know something of the general lie of the land.

It turns out, to begin with, that compatibility with special relativity is the sort of thing that admits of degrees. We will need (as a matter of fact) to think about five of them—not (mind you) because only five are logically imaginable, but because one or another of those five corresponds to every one of the fundamental physical theories that anybody has thus far taken seriously.

Let's start at the top.

What it is for a theory to be metaphysically compatible with special relativity (which is to say: what it is for a theory to be compatible with special relativity in the highest degree) is for it to depict the world as unfolding in a four-dimensional Minkowskian space-time. And what it means to speak of the world as unfolding within a four-dimensional Minkowskian space-time is (1) that everything there is to say about the world can straightforwardly be read off a catalogue of the local physical properties at every one of the continuous infinity of positions in a space-time like that, and (2) that whatever lawlike relations there may be between the values of those local properties can be written down entirely in the language of a space-time like that—that whatever lawlike relations there may be between the values of those local properties are invariant under Lorentz-transformations. What it is to pick out some particular inertial frame of reference in the context of the sort of theory we're talking about here—what it is, that is, to adopt the conventions of measurement that are indigenous to any particular inertial frame of reference in the context of the sort of theory we're talking about here—is just to pick out some particular way of organizing everything there is to say about the world into a story, into a narrative, into a temporal sequence of instantaneous global physical situations. And every possible world on such a theory will invariably be organizable into an infinity of such stories—and those stories will invariably be related to one another by Lorentz-transformations. And note that if even a single one of those stories is in accord with the laws, then (since the laws are invariant under Lorentz-transformations) all of them must be.

---

[30] The most authoritative, comprehensive, balanced, and up-to-date account of these matters is surely Earman (1995).

The Lorentz-invariant theories of classical physics (the electrodynamics of Maxwell, for example) are metaphysically compatible with special relativity; and so (more surprisingly) are a number of radically non-local theories (completely hypothetical ones, mind you—ones which in so far as we know at present have no application whatever to the actual world) which have recently appeared in the literature.[31]

But it happens that not a single one of the existing proposals for making sense of quantum mechanics is metaphysically compatible with special relativity, and, moreover, it isn't easy to imagine there ever being one that is. The reason is simple: What is absolutely of the essence of the quantum-mechanical picture of the world, in so far as we understand it at present—what none of the attempts to straighten quantum mechanics out have yet dreamed of dispensing with—is wave-functions. And wave-functions just don't live in four-dimensional space-times; wave-functions, that is, are just not the sorts of objects which can always be uniquely picked out by means of any catalogue of the local properties of the positions of a space-time like that. As a general matter, they need bigger ones, which is to say higher-dimensional ones, which is to say configurational ones. And that (alas!) is that.

The next level down (let us call this one the level of dynamical compatibility with special relativity) is inhabited by pictures on which the physics of the world is exhaustively described by something along the lines of a (so-called) relativistic quantum field theory—a pure one, mind you, in which there are no additional variables, and in which the quantum states of the world invariably evolve in accord with local, linear, deterministic, Lorentz-invariant quantum-mechanical equations of motion. These pictures, once again, must depict the world as unfolding not in a Minkowskian space-time but in a configuration one—and the dimensionalities of the configuration space-times in question here are (of course) going to be infinite. Other than that, however, everything remains more or less as it was above. The configuration space-time in question here is built directly out of the Minkowskian one, remember, by treating each of the points in Minkowskian space-time (just as one does in the classical theory of fields) as an instantaneous bundle of physical degrees of freedom. So what it is to pick out some particular inertial frame of reference in the context of this sort of picture is still just to pick out some particular way of organizing everything there is to say about the world into a temporal sequence of instantaneous global physical situations. Every possible world on this sort of a theory will still be organizable into an infinity of such stories, and those stories will still be related to one another by means of the appropriate generalizations of the Lorentz point-transformations. And it will still be the case that if even a single one of those stories is in accord with the laws, then (since the laws are invariant under Lorentz-transformations) all of them must be.

---

[31] Tim Maudlin and Frank Artzenius have both been particularly ingenious in concocting theories like these, which, notwithstanding their non-locality, are entirely formulable in four-dimensional Minkowski space-time. Maudlin (1994) contains extremely elegant discussions of several such theories.

The trouble is that there may well not *be* any such pictures that turn out to be worth taking seriously. All we have along these lines at present is the many-worlds pictures (which, for the reasons we discussed in some detail above, I fear will turn out not to be coherent) and the many-minds pictures (which is yet another of the numerous attempts at making sense of Everett—one that I concluded wasn't worth bringing up here, because I fear it will turn out not to be plausible).

And further down things start to get ugly.

We have known for more than thirty years now—since the seminal work of Bell—that any proposal for making sense of quantum mechanics on which measurements invariably have unique, particular, and determinate outcomes (which covers all of the proposals I know about, or at any rate the ones I know about that are also worth thinking about, other than many worlds and many minds) is going to have no choice whatever but to turn out to be non-local.

Now, non-locality is certainly not an obstacle in and of itself even to metaphysical compatibility with special relativity. There are now, as I mentioned before, a number of explicit examples in the literature of hypothetical dynamical laws which are radically non-local and which are nonetheless cleverly cooked up in such a way as to be formulable entirely within Minkowski-space. The thing is that none of them can even remotely mimic the empirical predictions of quantum mechanics; and nobody I talk to thinks that we have even the slightest reason to hope for one that will.

What we do have, on the other hand, is a very straightforward trick by means of which a wide variety of theories which are radically non-local and, moreover, are flatly incompatible with the proposition that the stage on which physical history unfolds is Minkowski-space can nonetheless be made fully and trivially Lorentz-invariant; a trick, that is, by means of which a wide variety of such theories can be made that you might call formally compatible with special relativity.

The trick[32] is just to let go of the requirement that the physical history of the world can be represented in its entirety as a temporal sequence of situations. The trick, more particularly, is to let go of the requirement that the situations associated with two intersecting space-like hypersurfaces in Minkowski-space must agree with one another about the expectation values of local observables at points where the two surfaces coincide.

Consider, for example, an old-fashioned non-relativistic projection-postulate, which stipulates that the quantum states of physical systems invariably evolve in accord with the linear deterministic equations of motion except when the system in question is being 'measured'; and that the quantum state of a system instantaneously jumps, at the instant the system is measured, into the eigenstate of the measured observable corresponding to the outcome of the measurement. This is the sort of theory that, as I mentioned above, nobody takes seriously any more, but

---

[32] See Aharonov and Albert (1984).

never mind that; it will serve us well enough, for the moment, as an illustration. Here's how to make this sort of a projection-postulate Lorentz-invariant. First, take the linear collapse-free dynamics of the measured system—the dynamics which we are generally in the habit of writing down as a deterministic connection between the wave-functions on two arbitrary equal-time hyperplanes—and rewrite it a deterministic connection between the wave-functions on two arbitrary space-like hypersurfaces. Then stipulate that the jumps referred to above occur not, as it were, when the equal-time hyperplane sweeps across the measurement-event, but whenever an arbitrary space-like hypersurface undulates across it.

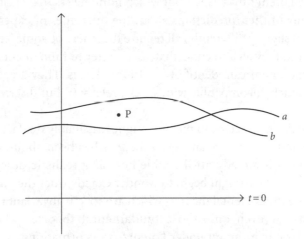

FIG. 29.1.

Suppose (say) that the momentum of a free particle is measured along the hypersurface marked $t = 0$ in Figure 29.1, and that later on a measurement locates the particle at P. Then our new projection-postulate will stipulate, among other things, that the wave-function of the particle along hypersurface a is an eigenstate of momentum, and that the wave-function of the particle along hypersurface b is (very nearly) an eigenstate of position. And none of that (and nothing else that this new postulate will have to say) refers in any way, shape, or form to any particular Lorentz-frame. And this is pretty.

But think for a minute about what's been paid for it. As things stand now, we have let go not only of Minkowski-space as a realistic description of the stage on which the story of the world is enacted, but (so far as I can see) of any conception of that stage whatever. That is, we have let go of the idea of the world's having anything along the lines of a narratable story at all! And all this just so as to guarantee that the fundamental laws remain exactly invariant under a certain hollowed-out set of mathematical transformations, a set which is now of no particularly deep conceptual interest, a set which is now utterly disconnected from any idea of an arena in which the world occurs.

Never mind. Suppose we had somehow managed to resign ourselves to that. There would still be trouble, since it happens that notwithstanding the enormous energy and technical ingenuity has been expended over the past several years in attempting to concoct a version of a more believable theory of collapses—a version (say) of GRW theory—on which a trick like this might work, even that (paltry as it is) is as yet beyond our grasp.

Let us descend still further, then. There are proposed solutions to the measurement problem (Bohm's theory, say, or modal theories) on which the special theory of relativity, whatever it means, is unambiguously false—theories, that is, which explicitly violate Lorentz-invariance, but which nonetheless manage to refrain from violating it in any of their predictions about the outcomes of experiments. These theories (to put it slightly differently) all require that there be some legally privileged Lorentz-frame, but they all also entail that, as a matter of fundamental principle, no performable experiment can identify what frame that is. They are, you might say, utterly and absolutely incompatible with special relativity, but discreetly so.

Now, one of the things it seems to me one might reasonably do, faced with all this, is to begin to wonder exactly what the all the fuss has been about. Given that the theory of relativity is already off the table here as a realistic description of the structure of the world we might begin to wonder exactly what the point is of entertaining only those fundamental theories which are strictly invariant under Lorentz-transformations, or even only those fundamental theories whose empirical predictions are strictly invariant under Lorentz-transformations.

Consider, for example, the case of GRW-like theories of the collapse of the wave-function. The stuff we've just been through seems to me to offer very little hope of anybody's ever cooking up a theory like that which has any of the sorts of compatibility with special relativity worth wanting. Why not, then, start to experiment with theories which are only approximately so? Why not have a look at theories which violate Lorentz-invariance in ways which we would be unlikely to have noticed yet? Theories like that, and, more particularly, GRW-like theories like that, turn out to be simple to cook up.

Let's think one through. Take (say) standard, Lorentz-invariant, relativistic quantum electrodynamics—without a collapse. Add to it some non-Lorentz-invariant second-quantized generalization of a collapse-process which is designed to reduce—under the appropriate circumstances, *and in some particular preferred frame of reference*—to a standard non-relativistic GRW Gaussian collapse of the effective wave-functions of electrons. And suppose that the frame associated with our laboratory is some frame other than the preferred one. Then consider what measurements carried out in that laboratory will show.

This needs to be done with some care. What happens in the lab frame is certainly not (for example) that the wave-function gets multiplied by anything along the lines of a Lorentz-transformation of the non-relativistic GRW Gaussian I mentioned a minute ago, for the simple reason that Gaussians are not the sorts of things that are susceptible of having a Lorentz-transformation carried out on them in the first place.[33] And it is, as a more general matter, not to be expected that a theory like this one is going to yield any straightforward universal geometrical technique whatever—such as we have always had at our disposal, in one form or another, throughout the entire modern history of physics—whereby the way the world looks to one observer can be read off the way it looks to some other one, who is in constant rectilinear motion relative to the first. The theory we have in front of us at the moment is simply not like that. We are, it seems fair to say, in infinitely messier waters here. The only absolutely reliable way to proceed on theories like this one (unless and until we can argue otherwise) is to deduce how things may look to this or that observer by explicitly treating those observers and all of their measuring instruments as ordinary physical objects, whose states change only and exactly in whatever way it is that they are required to change by the microscopic laws of nature, and whose evolutions will presumably need to be calculated from the point of view of the unique frame of reference in which those laws take on their simplest form.

That having been said, remember that the violations of Lorentz-invariance in this theory arise exclusively in connection with collapses, and that the collapses in this theory have been specifically designed so as to have no effects whatever, or no effects to speak of, on any of the familiar properties or behaviours of everyday localized solid macroscopic objects. So, in so far as we are concerned with things like (say) the lengths of medium-sized wooden dowels, or the rates at which cheap spring-driven wristwatches tick, everything is going to proceed, to a very good approximation, as if no such violations were occurring at all.

Let us see how far we can run with just that.

Two very schematic ideas for experiments more or less jump right out at you: one of them zeros in on what this theory still has left of the special-relativistic length-contraction, and the other on what it still has left of the special-relativistic time-dilation.

The first would go like this: Suppose that the wave-function of a subatomic particle which is more or less at rest in our lab frame is divided in half—suppose, for example, that the wave-function of a neutron whose z-spin is initially up is divided, by means of a Stern–Gerlach magnet, into equal y-spin-up and y-spin-down components; and suppose that one of those halves is placed in box A and the other half in box B. Suppose then that those two boxes are fastened onto opposite ends of a little wooden dowel and that they are left in that condition for a certain interval—an interval which is to be measured (by the way) in the lab frame, and by means of a co-moving cheap mechanical wristwatch. Suppose that at the end of that interval the two boxes are brought back together and opened, and that

---

[33] The sort of thing you need to start out with, if you want to do a Lorentz-transformation, is not a function of three-space (which is what a Gaussian is) but a function of three-space and time.

we have a look—in the usual way—for the usual sorts of interference effects. Note (and this is the crucial point here) that the length of this dowel, as measured in the preferred frame, will depend radically (if the velocity of the lab frame relative to the preferred one is sufficiently large) on the dowel's orientation. If, for example, the dowel is perpendicular to the velocity of the lab relative to the preferred frame, its length will be the same in the preferred frame as in the lab, but if the dowel is parallel to that relative velocity, then its length—and hence also the spatial separation between A and B—as measured in the preferred frame, will be much shorter. Of course, the degree to which the GRW collapses wash out the interference effects will vary (inversely) with the distance between those boxes as measured in the preferred frame.[34] And so it is among the predictions of the sort of theory we are entertaining here that if the lab frame is indeed moving rapidly with respect to the preferred one, the observed interference effects in these sorts of contraptions ought to vary observably as the spatial orientation of that device is altered. It is among the consequences of the failure of Lorentz-invariance in this theory that (to put it slightly differently) in frames other than the preferred one, invariance under spatial rotations fails as well.

The second experiment involves exactly the same contraption, but in this case what you do with it is to boost it—particle, dowel, boxes, wristwatch, and all—in various directions, and to various degrees, but always (so as to keep whatever this theory still has in it of the Lorentzian length-contractions entirely out of the picture for the moment) perpendicular to the length of the dowel. As viewed in the preferred frame, this will yield interference experiments of different temporal durations, in which different numbers of GRW collapses will typically occur, and in which the observed interference effects will (in consequence) be washed out to different degrees.

The sizes of these effects are, of course, going to depend on things like the velocity of the earth relative to the preferred frame (which there can be no way of guessing[35]), the degree to which we are able to boost contraptions of the sort I have been describing, the accuracies with which we are able to observe interferences, and so on. The size of the effect in the time-dilation experiment is always going to vary linearly in $(1 - v^2/c^2)$, where v is the magnitude of whatever boosts we find we are able to produce artificially. In the length-contraction experiment, on the other hand, the effect will tend to pop in and out a good deal more dramatically. If, in that second experiment, the velocity of the contraption relative to the preferred frame can somehow be raised to the point at which $(1 - v^2/c^2)$ is of the order of the width of the GRW Gaussian divided by the length of the dowel—either in virtue of the motion of the earth itself, or by means of whatever boosts we find we are able to produce artificially, or by means of some combination of the two—whatever washing-out there is of the interference effects when the length of the dowel is perpendicular to its velocity relative to the preferred frame will more or less discontinuously vanish when we rotate it.

Anyway, it seems to me that it might well be worth the trouble to do some of the arithmetic I have just been alluding to, to inquire into some of our present technical capacities, and to see if any of this might actually be worth going out and trying.[36]

REFERENCES

Aharonov, Y., and Albert, D. (1984). 'Is the Usual Notion of Time Evolution Adequate for Quantum-Mechanical Systems?', pt. II: 'Relativistic Considerations'. *Physical Review*, D29: 228–34.

Albert, David (2000). *Quantum Mechanics and Experience*. Cambridge, Mass.: Harvard University Press.

—— (2001). *Time and Chance*. Cambridge, Mass.: Harvard University Press.

—— and Loewer, B. (1995). 'Tails of Schrödinger's Cat', in R. Clifton (ed.), *Perspectives on Quantum Reality*. Dordrecht: Kluwer.

Barbour, Julian (2000). *The End of Time*. Oxford: Oxford University Press.

Barrett, Jeff (1999). *The Quantum Mechanics of Minds and Worlds*. Oxford: Oxford University Press.

Bell, J. (1989). 'Are there Quantum Jumps?', in Bell, *Speakable and Unspeakable in Quantum Mechanics*. Cambridge: Cambridge University Press.

Bohm, David (1952). 'A Suggested Interpretation of Quantum Theory in Terms of "Hidden Variables"', pts. I and II. *Physical Review*, 85: 166–93.

Deiks, Dennis (1991). 'On Some Difficulties in the Interpretation of Quantum Mechanics'. *Synthese*, 86: 77–86.

Deutsche, David (1985). 'Quantum Theory, the Church–Turing Principle and the Universal Quantum Computer'. *Proceedings of the Royal Society*, A400.

DeWitt, B. (1970). 'Quantum Mechanics and Reality'. *Physics Today*, 23.

Earman, John (1989). *World Enough and Spacetime*. Cambridge, Mass.: MIT Press.

—— (1995). *Bangs, Crunches, Whimpers, and Shrieks*. Oxford: Oxford University Press.

Everett, H., III (1957). 'Relative State Formulation of Quantum Mechanics'. *Reviews of Modern Physics*, 29.

Ghirardi, G. C., Rimini, A., and Weber, T. (1986). 'Unified Dynamics for Microscopic and Macroscopic Systems'. *Physical Review*, D34.

Healy, Richard (1989). *The Philosophy of Quantum Mechanics*. Cambridge: Cambridge University Press.

[36] All of this, of course, leaves aside the question of whether there might be still simpler experiments, experiments which might perhaps have already been performed, on the basis of which the theory we have been talking about here might be falsified. It goes without saying that I don't, as yet, know of any. But that's not saying much.

Maudlin, Tim (1994). *Quantum Non-Locality and Relativity*. Oxford: Blackwell.

—— (n.d.). 'Suggestions from Physics for Deep Metaphysics'. Rutgers University.

Ruetsche, Laura (1998). 'How Close Is Close Enough?', in D. Dieks and P. E. Vermass (eds.), *The Modal Interpretation of Quantum Mechanics*. Dordrecht: Kluwer.

Saunders, S. (1998). 'Time, Quantum Mechanics, and Probability'. *Synthese*, 114.

Sklar, Lawrence (1974). *Space, Time and Spacetime*. Berkeley: University of California Press.

—— (1998). *Physics and Chance*. Oxford: Oxford University Press.

van Fraassen, Bas (1991). *Quantum Mechanics: An Empiricist View*. Oxford: Oxford University Press.

Wigner, E. P. (1962). 'Remarks on the Body Question', in I. J. Wood (ed.), *The Scientist Speculates*. New York: Basic Books.

INDEX

a posteriori: knowable 402, 405, 685
  necessities 407–10, 412–13, 415–16, 420, 423,
    742; *see also* Kripke, Saul;
    two-dimensionalism
a priori 22, 23, 93, 407, 416, 455, 460, 685, 739,
    807–8
  beliefs 740
  contentually a priori 743–4, 761–2
  the contingent a priori 405–7, 409–13,
    415–17, 423–4
  conventionalist theories of 756, 758
  and defeasibility 747–8
  and determination theory 753–5, 758
  and empirical indefeasibility 759–60
  judgementally a priori 743–4
  justification or entitlement 740–1, 744, 746–8
  knowable 406, 408, 410–11, 415, 751
  knowledge 400, 418, 754–5, 758–9
  meta-semantic theory of 753–62
  and naturalism 758–9; and necessity 741–2
  propositions 740–1, 744, 746, 754, 756–8
  and rationalism 751, 755–7, 759, 762
  scope of the 745
  and truth in virtue of meaning 742
  synthetic 802; *see also* Kant, Immanuel
  truths 406, 742, 756, 758
  understanding-based views of 751–2, 756
aboutness:
  attitude 363–4
  indicator 362–3; *see also* cognitive science
  subdoxastic 363; *see also* cognitive science;
    personal versus subpersonal level of
    description and explanation
  teleological function and 362–4
  see also intentionality
Ackrill, J. L. 547 n
actions 12, 15, 50, 87, 270, 334–55
  and common-sense psychology 334
  Davidsonian reasons for 337–8, 349
  desirability characteristic of actions 11, 15
  folk concept of intentional 353–4
  individuation of 335–6
  intentional 88, 102, 104–5, 334, 336–40, 345,
    352–5
  and moral assessment 353–5

reasons for 14, 17, 19–21, 69, 86, 88, 92, 95,
    102, 117, 204, 336–7, 345, 347, 349, 352
  side-effect 353–5
  theory of the explanation of 334, 338, 347
  theory of the nature of 334, 338, 347
  see also causalism (in philosophy of action)
actualism in ethics 55 n
Adams, F., and Mele, A. 346
Adams, Robert 38 n
Adler, Matthew, and Dorf, Michael 187 n
adverbalists about sense experience 724
agent-neutrality in ethical theories 35, 41 n
Aharonov, Y., and Albert, D. 874 n
Aimola, Davies, A. M. 390
Akins, Kathleen 841
Albert, David 848 n, 867
  and Loewer, B. 855 n
Albritton, Richard 102
Alexander, Larry, and Sherwin, Emily 196 n
Alexandrescu, Sorin 542 n
alienation (and moral psychology) 99–100, 102
Alston, W. P. 456 n
Altman, Jack, and Ziporyn, Marvin 541 n
analytical social and political theory 259
  see also normative social and
    political theory
Anderson, Alan Ross 569
  and Belnap, Nuel, D. 564, 566, 595
Anderson, C. Anthony 564 n, 569
Anderson, Elizabeth 237
Andrews, Lort, Fullerton, Jane, E., Holtzmann,
    Neil A., and Motulsk, Arno G. 840
androcentrism 232, 237–42
  see also feminism
An-Na'im, Abdullahi 172
Annas, J. 117 n
Annis, D. 79 n
Anscombe, G. E. M. 11, 14–15, 19, 54, 122, 506,
    724 n
Anscombre, Jean-Claude, and Ducrot, Oswald
    475, 493 n
anthropology and ethics 114, 129–32
anti-descriptivist theories, *see* non-descriptivist
    theories
anti-rationalism in ethics 8

anti-realism (in philosophy of science) 774–6,
    780, 787
Antony, L. 75, 241–2
applied ethics 76
Aquinas, T. 45 n 182, 192
argument for asymmetrical skepticism in
    moral epistemology 65–7, 77–81
argument from illusion or hallucination 329,
    715, 717, 722, 726, 728, 733, 735
Aristotle 43, 98, 106 n, 117–18, 120, 336, 811–12
Armstrong, D. M. 313, 323 n, 326 n, 346, 456 n,
    506, 510–13, 515–19, 522, 525, 621, 703 n,
    724 n, 795–6
Arneson, Richard 210 n
Arpaly, Nomy 6 n, 101 n, 103
Arrow, Kenneth 216, 217 n, 218, 220, 262
Arrow's 'impossibility theorem' 262
Asher, Nicholas, and Lascarides, Alex 469, 475
associations 160, 163–5
    non-voluntary 162, 164, 169, 172–4
    right to exit from 163–4, 167, 169, 172–3
    voluntary 161, 164, 166, 169–70, 172–4
Astell, Mary 233–4, 242, 254
Athanassoulis, N. 119–20, 123
Atherton, Margaret 233 n
Atlas, Jay 471, 483 n, 493 n
Atran, S. 304
Audi, Robert 69 n, 71–2
Audi, Robert, and Sinnott-Armstrong,
    Walter 41 n, 104, 117 n
Augustine 192
Austin, J. L. 242, 433–6, 438, 440, 456 n, 468,
    491, 712, 719
Austin, John 182–3
autonomy (and moral psychology) 99, 101
autonomy affirmation 232, 244, 250–1, 253
    see also feminism; objectification; treating
        someone as an object
autonomy denial 232, 244, 246, 248–53
    see also feminism; objectification; treating
        someone as an object
autonomy violations 246, 248–53
    see also feminism; objectification; treating
        someone as an object
Ayer, A. J. 4 n, 65, 565 n, 794
Ayers, I., and Braithwaite, J. 272

Bach, K. 288 n, 471 n, 475, 476 n, 481 n, 491
    and Harnish, Robert Michael 475
Bacon, John 584 n
badness 11–12, 20, 26
Baier, K. 69, 77 n, 96
Bailenson, Jeremy N., Shum, Michael S.,
    Atran, Scott., Medin, Douglas L., and
    Coley, John D. 304
Bailhache, Patrice 601 n
Baker, G. P., and Hacker, P. M. S. 367, 369

Baker, Lynne Rudder 671–6
Baldwin, Thomas 703
Bales, Eugene 31
Barba Escriba, J. 541
Barbour, Julian 871 n
Barkow, J. H., Cosmides, L., and Tooby, J. 387,
    838
Baron J. 140 n
Barrett, Jeff 860 n
Barron, Marcia 43
Barry, Brian 157–60, 162–4, 166, 168, 170–3
Barry, Brian, and Hardin, Russell 216 n
Baumeister, Roy 249 n
Bayesianism 265, 684 n
Baynes, Kenneth 224 n
Bealer, G. 697 n
Beatty, J. 807, 822, 827, 841
Bechara, A., Damasio, H., and
    Damasio, A. R. 126
Bechtel, W., and Richardson, R. C. 811, 814, 834
Becker, L. C. 116 n
Beckner, Morton 819
Beebee, Helen 528
Begemihl, B. 239
behaviourism 312, 358–9
Behe, Michael 839
belief 4–10, 12, 21–5, 64, 294, 681–2
    falsity indicative 685–8, 690
    justified true 686, 693, 696; see also
        Gettier, E.
    perceptual 697–8; suspension of 681–3, 688,
        see also scepticism
    truth-indicative 685–6
    see also justification of beliefs; moral beliefs
belief ascriptions 421, 423
    de se reading of 422; see also de se
    see also propositional attitude reports
Bell, J. 874
Bender, Edward D. 544 n
Bennett, Jonathan 103, 508, 514
Bennett, W. J. 120
Bentham, Jeremy 33 n, 35, 182–3, 192, 259
Berlin, Isaiah 259
Beurton, Peter, Falk, Raphael, and Reinberger,
    Hans-Jörg 827
Bezuidenhout, Anne, and Morris, Robyn 472 n
Bigelow, John, and Pargetter, Robert 583 n, 585,
    592, 829
    and Dodds, Susan, and Pargetter, Robert 105
biology 807, 813
    see also philosophy of biology
Bishop, J. 335 n, 336, 339, 340 n
Bittner, Rüdiger 89, 109
Blackburn, Simon 4 n, 5 n, 6 n, 8 n, 22, 23 n,
    63 n, 64, 94 n, 116 n, 301, 535, 592, 839
Blair, R. J. 127–8
Blakemore, Diane 476 n, 493

Blamey, Stephen, and Humberstone, Lloyd 556
Blanchard, B. 456 n
Blanché, Robert 542, 548–9, 551–3, 568, 598–9, 605
blindsight 387–9
  and superblindsight 388; *see also* consciousness, access versus phenomenal consciousness distinction; Block, N.
Block, N. 301, 313, 319 n, 324, 332, 361, 388
  and Dworkin, Gerald 836–7
Blum, L. A. 118 n, 121, 138 n
Blutner, Reinhard, and Zeevat, Henk 469, 475, 495
Boden, M. 387, 841
Bohm, David 852
Bohman, James, and Rehg, William 222 n
Bok, H. 116 n
Bolinger, Dwight 538 n, 539
BonJour, L. 692 n, 693 n, 742, 748, 751
Boolos, George 563 n
Boorse, Christopher 829
Bork, Robert 188
Boyd, Richard 4 n, 5 n, 66 n, 77–8, 131, 136
Boyd, Richard N. 770, 772, 774 n, 775–6, 782
Braddon-Mitchell, David, and Jackson, Frank 332 n
Bradley, F. H. 456 n, 534
Braithwaite, J. 272
Brand, M. 335–6, 339, 340 n, 341 n
Brandom, R. 458 n, 464
Brandon, Robert 822, 824–5
Brandt, Richard 10, 39, 118 n, 129–30, 131 n, 132, 138
Bratman, Michael 100, 143 n, 186, 352–5
Braun, D. 289 n, 291–2, 294, 424
Breheny, Richard, Katsos, Napolean, and Williams, John 472
Brennan, Geoffrey 260, 272
  and Buchanan, J. 269
  and Pettit, Philip 209 n, 275
Brennan, Samantha 57
Brentano, Franz 283–4, 289 n
Brentano's problem 283–4, 286–7, 293
  see also intentionality
Brink, David O. 4 n, 5 n, 22 n, 34 n, 65 n, 70 n, 74–5, 78, 130–1, 135 n, 136–7
Brison, Susan 236
Broad, C. D. 16, 619, 703, 726
Brock, Stuart 593–4
Brooks, R. A. 387
Broome, John 33 n, 95
Brown, James Robert 771
Brown, Mark, A. 543 n, 544
Bruxelles, Sylvie, Ducrot, Oswald, and Raccah, Pierre-Yves 493 n
Buchanan, Allen, Brock, Dan, Daniels, Norman, and Wikler, Daniel 840

Buchannan, Allan 214 n
Bull, Robert A. 570, 580
Burge, Tyler 300 n, 302, 693 n, 740, 761
Burgess, John A. 537
Burgess, John P. 561 n, 563
Burke, Michael 666–9
Burks, A. W. 565
Buss, David 838
Buss, Sarah 104
Butterfield, J. 626, 633
Butler, Judith 242
Byrne, Alex 724 n

Campbell, J. 116 n
Campbell, Keith 314
Campbell, Richmond, and Sowden, Lanning 22
Campbell, Tom 192
Capgras delusion 390
Caramazza, A. 379–80
Carnap, Rudolf 468, 605, 756, 759, 801
Carritt, E. F. 36 n
Carroll, Lewis 24, 94 n
Carruthers, P. 370
Carston, Robyn 472 n, 473, 475 n, 478 n, 480, 481 n, 483 n, 489
Cartwright, Nancy 510, 799, 804, 808, 809 n, 810–11
  and Shomar, T., and Suárez, M. 804
Casati, Robert, and Varsi, Achille 647
categorical imperative 22, 42–3
  see also Kant; Kantian ethics
Caulfield, Mina 242 n
causalism (in philosophy of action) 334–6, 338–9, 341, 345–6, 355
  and free will 336, 352
  and the mind–body problem 336, 352
  and negative actions 345–9, 351
  problem of causal deviance for 338–9, 341, 345
  problem of vanishing agents for 351–2
  and trying 346–7, 349
  see also actions
causally explanatory versus causally efficacious properties 375
causation 505–31
  causal relata as events versus causal relata as facts 508, 524–6
  as constant conjunction 505, 630, 793, 809; *see also* Hume, David; laws, Humean regularity account of
  counterfactual accounts of 505–6, 509, 518, 523, 808; *see also* Lewis, David dependency accounts of 524, 526, 529–30
  folk theory of 521–2
  and laws of nature 508–9, 511, 514, 516–17, 519; *see also* laws (in philosophy of science)
  intuitions about 512–14, 519

causation (*cont.*):
  lawful regularity accounts of 505–6
  level-neutral constraint on accounts of 515,
    518, 521, 523
  nomological entailment accounts of 509–11,
    514, 520–1, 523–5, 531
  and non-discriminating conception of
    properties and relations 516, 522
  non-reductionist accounts of 506, 508, 510,
    512–14, 518–19, 521
  by omission 513, 524, 527–9, 531
  and normative considerations 527–8
  and pre-emption cases 520, 522, 524, 526–7,
    529–30
  physical connection accounts of 506, 509,
    511, 514, 519–21, 523, 525
  and primary versus secondary causal
    locutions 507–8
  probabilistic accounts of 506, 809–10
  reductionist accounts of 506, 508, 511–12,
    515–18, 521
  Shoemaker–Cartwright style non-
    reductionism 510, 515–16
  and sparse conceptions of properties and
    relations 516–17, 522
  sufficiency approach to 524–5, 528–30
  Tooley–Armstrong style non-reductionism
    510, 512–13, 515–19, 522, 525
  topic-neutral constraint on accounts of 514
  transitivity of 513–14, 523–4, 529–30
central state materialism 359
Chafe, Wallace, and Nichols, Johanna 541
Chagrov, A. V., and Zakharyaschev, M. 572 n,
  576
Chalmers, David 314, 317 n, 407–10
Chellas, B. F. 556
  and Segerberg, K. 560, 562–3
Cheng, Patricia, and Holyoak, Keith 838
Chierchia, Gennaro, Crain, Stephen, Guasti,
  Maria Teresa, Gualmini, Andrea, and
  Meroni, Luisa 472 n
Chihara, Charles 592, 595 n
Chisholm, R. 283, 543, 724 n
Chomsky, Noam 359, 365–9
Christiano, Thomas 209 n, 210 n, 218 n,
  219 n, 261
Churchland, Patricia 841
Churchland, Paul 319, 775 n
Cicero 182
Clark, A. 387, 389
Clark, Herbert, H. 475, 483 n
Clarke, Thompson 710, 715–16
Clendinnen, F. J. 775 n
Coffa, A. 740
cognitive neuropsychology 379–80, 382
  challenge of connectionism to, *see*
    connectionism

  and double dissociation arguments 381–2,
    385–6
  and the dual-route theory of reading aloud
    380–1, 385–6
cognitive neuroscience 362
cognitive science 358, 360, 362–4, 367, 375–6,
  390, 494
  classical 384, 386–7
  connectionist 383, 385–6; *see also*
    connectionism
  and homunculi 361–2; and intentionality
    361
  and 'as if' intentionality 361–3
  relationship with philosophy 364–5, 387–90;
    see also philosophy of cognitive science of
    spatial representation 387
cognitivism (in ethics) 4, 6 n, 21
  about normative judgements within the
    domain of reason 25
  about moral judgements 25; *see also*
    non-cognitivism (in ethics)
Cohen, G. A. 167–8
Cohen, Joshua 210 n, 225–7
Cohen, Rachel 92–3
Cohen, S. 688 n
coherentism (in epistemology) 73–4, 76, 79
coherentism (in moral epistemology) 64, 69,
  73, 82
  realist coherentism 73–8; *see also* moral
    epistemology
Coleman, Jules 185, 189–90, 192, 203
Coleman, Jules, and Ferejohn, John 217–18
Coleman, Sydney 859 n
collective principle of beneficence 37
  see also Murphy, Liam
colour experience 318
Coltheart, M. 380, 386
  and Davies, M. 382, 386
  and Rastle, K., Perry, C. Langdon, R., and
    Ziegler, J. 386
communitarian critics of Rawls 52
  see also Rawls, John; Sandel, Michael
communitarianism 155, 174–7
  see also liberalism; minorities;
    multiculturalism
compliance problem 50
  see also Gauthier, David
computational theory of mind 374–5,
  378–9, 382
  see also language of thought hypothesis;
    modularity of mind; tacit knowledge
concepts 125, 295, 297, 300, 303, 305, 330–1
  see also empty concepts; moral concepts;
    name-concepts; natural kind concepts
conceptual analysis 125, 192, 696–7
  see also thought experiments
conceptual versus non-conceptual content 330

connectionism 382–7
  as alternative to the computational theory of mind 382
  as challenge to the methodology of cognitive neuropsychology 382, 385–6
  as a challenge to nativism 382, 385
  and modularity 385–6
  and syntactically structure representations 383–4; *see also* tacit knowledge
consciousness 310–14, 316, 330
  access versus phenomenal consciousness distinction 388; *see also* Block, N.
consequentialism 26, 33 n, 34, 35 n, 36–7, 41–2, 45–7, 49, 53, 56, 58
  act consequentialism 40
  demandingness problem for 38, 41, 46
  global versus local 37, 38 n
  indirect forms of 38–9
  motive consequentialism 38
  objective consequentialism 38, 40, 46; *see also* Railton, Peter
  rule consequentialism 38–40
  satisficer accounts 37
  self-defeating objection to 39
  schizophrenia objection to 39, 41; *see also* Stocker, Michael
  subjective consequentialism 40, 44
  two-levels view 38–9; *see also* Hare, R. M.
constitution 636–7, 642, 650, 657, 666, 670–2, 674–6
  and co-occupancy 652, 657, 666–8, 670, 674
  and d-parts 639–46, 653, 655, 658, 665–6, 670
  and identity 639, 642, 647–8, 661–2, 666, 670
  immediate 642, 670, 676
  material 642, 648, 670
  and mereology 636–7, 647, 651, 654, 657, 665, 672–3
  and principles of division 639–42, 650, 665
  and principles of unity 638–9, 641, 642–3, 646, 648–55, 657, 659–61, 663–5, 667, 669, 672, 675
  and real kinds 638–9, 649–50, 660, 663, 671
  and reductionism 639, 642–3
  and simples 639, 644, 651, 656
  and sortals 667–8, 670–1
  and u-parts 639, 642, 644–8, 650–1, 653–5, 657–8, 664–6, 670, 672–6
constructivism (in philosophy of science) 768–9
constructivism (in ethics) 64 n, 66
contextualism (in epistemology) 79, 686 n, 688–9, 694–5, 697
contextualism (in moral epistemology) 64, 69, 79–83
  see also Timmons, Mark
continuity theorists (in ethics) 67
contractarian ethics 41, 49–51, 53–4

contractualist ethics 34 n, 41, 45, 49–54, 97
contractualist principles of just outcomes 225, 228
conventions (in relation to legal philosophy) 182, 184, 187, 190–1, 204
  and disagreement 185–6
convergence of moral views or judgements 129–32, 135, 137
Cooper, J. M. 117
coordination problems (in relation to legal philosophy) 184–5, 204
Copeland, B. J. 570
Copp, D. 68 n, 69
Cornell-style moral realism 67
Cosmides, Leda, and Tooby, John 838
Craig, E. J. 633, 686 n
Cresswell, M. J. 568 n
Crimmins, Mark 424
Cronin, Ciarin, and De Greiff, Pablo 223 n
Cullity, Garrett, and Gaut, Berys 6 n
Culp, Sylvia 834
  and Kitcher, Philip 834
culture of honour 132–7
  see also Nisbett, R. E., and Cohen, D.
Cummins, Robert 829–30
Cummiskey, David 36 n
Cushing, James T., and McMullin, Ernan 769 n
  and Fine, A., and Goldstein, S. 769 n
Czezowski, Tadeusz 569

D'arms, Justin, and Jacobson, Daniel 6 n, 128 n
Damasio, A. R., and Tranel, D. and Damasio, H. 126
Dancy, Jonathan 4 n, 5 n, 6 n, 64 n, 70 n, 71, 89, 560
Daniels, Norman 3 n, 68 n, 75
Darley, J. M., and Batson, C. D. 118
Darwall Stephen 71 n, 124 n
  and Gibbard, Allan, and Railton, Peter 14, 67, 69 n, 75, 78 n, 114–16, 129
Darwin, Charles 807, 823–4, 826–7
Dascal, Marcelo 475
Davenport, W. 240
Davidson, Donald 9, 11, 14–15, 19, 88, 104, 313 n, 335–6, 338, 345 n, 353 n, 449 n, 450, 456–8, 469, 505–6, 508, 633, 698 n, 721 n
Davidson's scepticism about meaning 457–8
Davies, M. 373
  and Coltheart, M., Langdon, R., and Breen, N. 390
  and Humberstone, Lloyd 411–12, 413 n, 414, 743
Davis, Steven 469
Dawkins, Richard 823–5, 827, 840
de Gelder, B., and Vroomen, J., Pourtois, G., and Weiskrantz, L. 388
de Lavalette, G. R. Renardel 553

De Paul, M., and Ramsey, W. 697 n
de se 416, 422
   see also indexicals; Lewis, David; Perry, John
decision theory 105
deep deliberative democracy 210, 214, 222,
   224–5, 227–8
   see also deliberative democracy
deep versus superficial necessity distinction
   411
   see also Evans, Gareth; two-dimensionalism
definite descriptions 287–8
definitionally basic concepts 12, 17, 21, 23–4
   see also deontic concepts; evaluative
      concepts; normative concepts, norms of
      reason and rationality
Deigh, John 98, 124
Deiks, Dennis 853 n
deliberative democracy 210, 214, 222
   see also deep deliberative democracy
Dembski, William 839
democracy 209–11, 213–14, 217–20, 222, 226–8,
   259, 261
   see also deep deliberative democracy;
      deliberative democracy
democratic: decisions 208, 210–11, 213, 224
   procedures 211–18, 222, 225–7; *see also*
      political procedures
   see also political decisions
Dennett, D. C. 138, 142, 312 n, 313 n, 319, 330,
   359–61, 363, 631, 827–8
Dent, N. J. H. 118 n
deontic concepts 10–13, 16–17
   see also evaluative concepts
deontic the 11–12, 14
deontological ethical theories 31–2, 34 n, 41–2,
   44–6, 48–50
   see also contractarianism; contractualism;
      intuitionist approaches to deontological
      ethics; Kantian ethics
DePaul, M. 120
DeRose, K 79 n, 684 n, 686 n, 688 n
   and Warfield, T. 698 n
Descartes, René 232, 234, 236, 254, 802
descriptivism 403, 406–7, 413, 417, 422–3, 785
   about meaning of names 397, 399, 401, 408,
      413
   about natural kind terms 402, 408, 413, 418,
      422; *see also* natural kind terms
   about reference determination of names
      397, 400–1, 408, 418, 422
   as *a priori* irrefutable 407, 417–18
   causal version of 408–10, 419, 421–2; *see also*
      Chalmers, David; Jackson, Frank; Kroon,
      Fred; Lewis, David; Searle, John
   challenge of indexicals to 403–5, 414, 417–18;
      see also Kaplan, David; Perry, John;
      two-dimensionalism

Kripke's epistemological argument against
   399, 408, 417, 420; *see also* Kripke, Saul
Kripke's modal argument against 398–9,
   408, 417, 420, 423; *see also* Kripke, Saul
Kripke's objections to 288–9, 397, 400, 408;
   see also Kripke, Saul
Kripke's semantic arguments against 401,
   408, 410, 417; *see also* Kripke, Saul
and metalinguistic descriptions 419–20
and reference fixing descriptions 408–9,
   417–19, 420–3
   see also two-dimensionalism
desires 4–25, 33, 43, 104
   for esteem and to avoid disesteem (in
      economics and political philosophy) 258,
      275–8; *see also* economics; political
      philosophy
   and reason 90–5
   phenomenal 91, 100–1
   hierarchy of 99–100
determinism and responsibility 141–5
Deutsche, David 857 n
Devitt, Michael 769 n, 771 n, 772 n, 774, 775 n,
   776 n, 777 n, 779 n, 780 n, 781 n, 782,
   786 n, 787
   and Sterelny, Kim 785 n
DeWitt, B. 856
diaphanousness of experience 321–2, 326–7
   see also phenomenal experience
discontinuity theorists in ethics 67–8
discrimination 156–7, 165
diversity 155–6, 163–4
Dixon, R. M. W. 539
Dobelle, W. H., Mladejovsky, M. G., and
   Girvin, J. P. 718 n
doctrine of doing and allowing 46
   see also doing versus allowing harm
      distinction
doctrine of double effect 46–8
   see also intending versus merely foreseeing
      harm distinction
doing versus allowing harm distinction 45, 47
   see also consequentialism; doctrine of doing
      and allowing; deontological ethical
      theories
Doris, J. M. 116 n, 118, 120 n, 121, 143 n
   and Stich, S. P. 116 n, 119 n, 120, 123
Dowe, Phil 506
Dreier, James 4 n, 5 n, 20 n, 26, 63 n, 64 n, 80 n
Dretske, F. 335 n, 362, 686 n, 688 n, 795–6,
   811, 841
Driver, Julia 3, 44 n, 55 n, 56
Dryzek, John 209 n, 222 n
   and List, Christian 210 n
dualism 311, 314, 643, 718 n
Ducasse, C. J. 724 n
Ducrot, Oswald 475, 493

Duhem, P. 771, 778 n, 780, 804
Dummett, Michael 409, 431, 456 n
Dunn, J. Michael 546, 556 n, 587 n
Dunne, J. W. 315
Dupré, J. 303, 799, 827, 831–2, 834, 838
Duster, Troy 840
duties 43, 45
   negative versus positive 46; *see also* Foot,
     Philippa
Dworkin, Andrea 250
Dworkin, Ronald 8–9, 50, 52, 66 n, 168, 182, 185,
   190, 192, 196–8, 200–2

Earman, J. 618, 684 n, 686 n, 796–8, 806, 871 n,
   872 n
   and Glymour, C., and Mitchell, S. 808
economics 258, 263–8, 271, 273–5, 278, 808, 814
Eells, Ellery 506
egocentric goods 3
egoism in ethics 16
Ehring, Douglas 506, 520
Eilan, N., McCarthy, R., and Brewer, B. 387
Einstein, A. 615, 633, 805
Elder, Crawford L. 586
Eldredge, Niles 831
Ellis, B. 811
Ellis, Brian 770, 780 n
Ellis, H. D., and Young, A. W. 390
Ellsworth, P. C. 132
Elster, J. 223 n, 814
   and Hylland, A. 216 n, 224 n
emotions 57
   lack of intrinsic worth or moral significance
     of 43
empirical claims 22
empirical claims and ethics 115, 120–2, 125, 127,
   145–6
empty:
   concepts 284
   definite descriptions 287; *see also* definite
     descriptions
   expressions 286–7, 292
   names 294, 422
   singular concepts 294–5
   see also Russell's problem of negative
     existentials
Endicott, Timothy 189
Engel, P. 458 n
epistemic norms 64, 80–2
epistemology 63–4, 79, 688–9, 695, 775
   see also coherentism (in epistemology);
     contextualism (in epistemology);
     externalism (in epistemology);
     internalism (in epistemology); moral
     epistemology; naturalized epistemology
equality of opportunities 155, 157–9
equality of resources 159–60

Ereshevsky, Marc 831
error theory about morality 74 n
Estlund, David 209 n
ethics of care 57, 239
   see also Gilligan, Carole; Noddings, Nel
Euthyphro question 210
evaluative, the 14, 16
evaluative concepts 10–14, 16
   see also deontic concepts
Evans, Gareth 286 n, 287, 291 n, 296, 297 n,
   368–9, 387, 411, 564
Everett, H., III 855–7, 874
Ewing, A. C. 17
externalism (in epistemology) 688, 693
externalism (in philosophy of mind), *see*
   psychological states, externalism about
   the content of
extrinsic good or value 32 n–33 n
   and instrumental good 32 n–33 n
   and relational good 33 n

Fair, David 506, 519
Fales, Evan 770
Fauconnier, Gilles 475
Feinberg, Joel 244–5
Feldman, Fred 33
Feldman, R. 688 n
female experience 57–8
feminism 231–55
   and accounts of female orgasm in
     evolutionary biology 232, 238
   and epistemology 238, 241–2
   and dualism 232–7, 242, 254–5
   and metaphysics of personal identity 232,
     234–7
   and moral epistemology 66, 75–6, 81–2, 234
   and philosophy of science 232, 238, 240
   and political philosophy 156, 163–4, 234
   and pornography 242, 244, 246–8, 251, 253
   relationship with philosophy 231–5
   and speech act theory 242–3; *see also* speech
     acts
feminist ethics 57–8
feminist philosophy 52, 54, 57, 232
feminist philosophy of science 241–2
Feyerabend, P. 694 n, 768
Field, H. 293 n, 456 n, 457 n, 459 n, 465, 759–61,
   776 n
filtering problem in moral epistemology 75–6
   see also input objection
final good 33 n
Fine, Arthur 771, 774, 777 n
Fine, Kit 663, 673, 721 n, 537, 572, 587–8, 591
Finnis, John 8, 45 n, 181 n, 193
Firth, Roderick 17, 129 n, 724 n
Fish, Stanley 197 n
Flanagan, O. 116 n, 118–19, 122

Flax, Jane 234
Fleischer, Isidore 570
Flood, R., and Lockwood, M. 633
Fodor, J. 125, 289 n, 291–2, 295, 300–1, 359,
    370–2, 376–9, 478, 495
folk-biology 304
Foot, Philippa 4 n, 5 n, 9, 46–7
Forbes, Graeme 567–8, 588, 591–2, 594–5
Foster, John 322 n, 323 n
foundationalism (in epistemology) 70, 73, 79
foundations of physics, the 848–79
    and absolutism versus relationism about
        space 868–71
    and asymmetries of human experience
        865–7
    and the bare theory 859–60
    and Bohm's theory 852–3, 876; see also
        Bohm, David
    and GRW theory 854–5, 867, 876, 878
        see also Ghirardi, G. C., Rimini, A., and
        Weber, T.
    and the measurement problem in quantum-
        mechanics 848–61, 872, 874; see also
        quantum mechanics
    and the linear quantum-mechanical
        equations of motion 849–54, 856–7,
        859–61; and the many worlds
        interpretation of quantum-mechanics
        855–6, 874; see also Everett, H., III
    and measuring devices 849–51, 855
    and modal interpretations of quantum
        mechanics 853–5, 876
    and statistical mechanics 866
    and superpositions 850–2, 854, 856–61
    and wave functions 852, 854–5, 873, 876
    and Wigner's friend 849–50, 856, 858; see also
        Wigner, E. P.; see also Newtonian
        mechanics; special theory of relativity
Frankena, William 4 n, 5 n, 124 n
Frankfurt, H. 336, 345, 352
Frankfurt, Harry 99–101, 103, 105 n, 109, 141–3
Frazier, R. L. 70
freedom to govern oneself versus freedom to
    govern others distinction 156, 161
Freeman, Samuel 160
Freeman, Samuel 222 n
Frege, Gottlob 284–7, 289, 397, 462, 468, 740,
    751
Frege's puzzle (or problem) of failures of
    substitution of co-referential names in
    opaque contexts 285–7, 294, 402, 406, 409,
    417, 421–2, 424
Fregean thoughts 285–6, 289
Frerejohn, J., and Satz, D. 799
Freud, Sigmund 97
Frey, Bruno 272
    and Jegen, R. 272

Friedman, Michael 759, 798–9, 801–2
Fuller, Lon L. 182
Fumerton, R. 693 n
functionalism 359
Futuyma, Douglas 839

Gabbay, Dov M. 581, 583–5
Gale, R. M. 624
Gallois, André 559
Gallup, Gordon, and Suarez, Susan 240
Galston, William, A. 161, 163–4, 166–7, 176
game theory 814–15
    evolutionary 839
Gardner, H. 358
Garson, James W. 595
Gaut, B. 72–3
Gauthier, David 50–1, 54 n, 69, 265–6
Gazdar, Gerald 471–2, 476, 493 n
Geach, P. T. 545 n, 546
Geerts, W., and Melis, L. 548 n
Gelman, S., and Hirschfield, L. 304
gender differences in moral thinking 57, 75
    see also feminist ethics
generic-species concepts 304
George, Robert 45 n
Gert, Bernard 41
Gettier, E. 686, 687 n, 696
Gewirth, A. 69
Ghez, Claude, Krakauer, J., Sainburg, R., and
    Ghilardi, M. 344–5
Ghirardi, G. C., Rimini, A., and Weber, T. 854
Ghiselin, Michael 831–2
Gibbard, Allan 4 n, 5 n, 6 n, 22, 63 n, 107–8,
    116 n, 839
Gibbons, J. 693 n
Gibbs, Ray 485, 487
Giere, R. N. 804
Gilbert, D. T., and Malone, P. S. 120 n
Gilligan, Carole 57, 75, 237–8
Ginet, C. 335 n, 337, 354
Glennan, S. 814
Glucksberg, Sam 485, 487
Glymour, Clark 774 n, 836
Goble, L. F. 587 n
Gödel, K. 746, 751, 756–7
Godfrey-Smith, Peter 829–30, 835, 841
    and Lewontin, Richard 825
Goldbatt, Robert 570, 574, 577
Goldie, Peter 107
Goldman, A. 80, 116 n, 335 n, 336, 339, 688 n,
    693 n
Goldsworthy, Jeff 9
Good, I. J. 506
good, the 3, 32, 36, 41, 103
    greater good 45
    hedonism and desire satisfaction
        accounts of 32

maximizing of 34–7, 39–40, 42 n, 46, 96, 98
    see also Sidgwickian definition of the good
Goodin, Robert 222 n, 260
goodness 11–12, 17–18, 20, 26
    as metaphysically simple 16, 18
Goranko, Valentin 601 n
Gottschalk, W. H. 542, 544
Goudge, T. A. 819
Gould, S. J. 807, 824–6, 831, 839
    and Lewontin, Richard 827
    and Vrba, Elizabeth 829
Grabosky, P. N. 272
Gray, John Chipman 194
Gray, Russell 828
Greco, J., and Sosa, E. 698 n
Green, Mitchell 472 n
Greenawalt, Kent 195–6
Greenspan, P. S. 108
Grene, Marjorie 819
Grice, H. P. 197, 428–33, 468–70, 471 n, 472–3,
    475–9, 481 n, 483 n, 484–7, 493 n, 494
Griffiths, Paul, and Gray, Russell 828
Groenendijk, Jeroen, and Stokof, Martin 538 n
Gross, Steven 488
Grover, D. 463
    and Camp, J., and Belnap, N. 458 n, 463
Grünbaum, A. 630
Guala, F. 799, 808
Gupta, A. 462 n
Gutmann, A., and Thompson, D. 226 n
Gutmann, Amy 160, 163, 177
Gutting, Gary 775 n

Habermas, Jurgen 223–5
Hacker, Edward, A. 597–9, 601
Hacking, Ian 770 n, 777 n
Haidt, J., Koller, S., and Dias, M. 140–1
Hall, Alison 493
Hall, Ned 514, 527, 529
    and Paul, L. A. 524, 526
Halldén, Sören 563, 575–6
Halley, Janet E. 172
Halpern, Joseph Y. 560 n, 561 n, 567 n
Hamblin, C. L. 561
Hamilton, W. D. 823
Hamlyn, D. 355
Hampton, Jean 54
Haney, C., Banks, W., and Zimbardo, P. 118
Hardin, Russell 217 n
Harding, Sandra 241
Hare, R. D. 127
Hare, R. M. 3 n, 4 n, 5 n, 38–9, 65, 115, 538 n
Harman, Gilbert 4 n, 49 n, 65, 77, 116 n, 118,
    119 n, 123, 129, 321–2, 353–5, 687 n, 724 n,
    742, 561 n
Harnish, Robert Michael 475, 491

Harré, R., and Madden, E. H. 811–12
Harris, John 840
Harstock, Nancy 241
Hart, D., and Killen, M. 121
Hart, H. L. A. 182–3, 185–6, 192–3, 195, 202
Haslanger, Sally 243
Hausman, D. 808
Hayek, F. A. 200
health care ethics 57
Healy, Richard 853 n
hedonism 32–3, 35
Hempel, C. G. 829
Herman, Barbara 243
Herman, Barbara 42, 43 n, 75, 98
Herrnstein, Richard, and Murray, C. 836
Hesse, Mary 770
Heyd, David 840
Higginbotham, James 446
Hilbert, David 319
Hill, C. S. 458 n, 461
Hill, Thomas E., Jr 106 n, 122 n
Hilpinen, Risto 543
Hintikka, Jaakko 536, 539–40, 543, 557, 567
Hinton, J. M. 322 n, 726–9
Hirschberg, Julia 472 n
Hitchcock, C. 526–7, 809 n
Hite, S. 240
Ho, Mae-Wan, and Fox, Sidney 828
    and Saunders, Peter, T. 828
Hoadley, Bishop 194
Hobbes, Thomas 41, 50, 192, 227
Hobbesian approach to morality 41
    see also natural law theory
Hobbs, Jerry 475
    and Stickel, Mark, Appelt, Douglas, and
        Martin, Paul 475
Hoefer, C., and Rosenberg, A. 778
Holmes, Oliver Wendell 204
Holton Richard 9 n
Holtzmann, Neil A. 840
Hooker, Brad 39–40, 92–3
Hooker, Clifford A. 770
Hoover, K. 810
Horan, B. L. 807
Horn, Laurence 471, 481 n
    and Ward, Gregory 469, 472 n, 493 n
Horn, Laurence R. 542 n, 544 n, 549 n, 552 n
Hornsby, Jennifer 242, 353 n, 457 n
    and Langton, Rae 242 n
Horowitz, Tamara 49 n, 140
Horty, John F. 543, 556 n
Horwich, Paul 455 n, 458 n, 460 n, 461 n, 462 n,
    466 n, 633, 771
Howson, C., and Urbach, P. 684 n
Hrdy, Sarah Blaffer 242 n
Hubbard, Ruth, and Wald, Elijah 840

Huemer, Michael 559 n
Hughes, G. E., and Cresswell, M. J. 557 n, 562,
    566, 568 n, 572, 576, 585, 590
Hull, David 819, 824, 831–3
Humberstone, Lloyd 543, 549 n, 550, 556, 558,
    566, 568, 575 n, 589, 595, 596, 601 n
  and Williamson, Timothy 546 n
Hume, David 8, 23 n 115, 129 n, 271, 274, 505,
    519, 630, 793
Hume's 'knave principle' 271–4, 278
  see also economics; incentive-comparability
    approach; political philosophy
Hume's 'sensible knave' 124, 127
  see also moral motivation; motivation
Humean supervenience 797, 800
Humphreys, P. 804
Hurka, Thomas 16, 34
Hursthouse, Rosalind 55, 121–2
Husserl, Edmund 284 n
Hutcheson, F. 129 n
hypothetical imperatives 42
  see also categorical imperative; Kant;
    Kantian ethics
hypothetical social contracts or
    agreements 50, 52
  as opposed to actual social contracts or
    agreements 50; see also contractarian
    ethics
    ideal language philosophy 468; see also
      Carnap, Rudolf; Frege, Gottlob; Russell,
      Bertrand; Tarski, A.

idealized psychology 17
ideal-theory assumption (in political
    philosophy) 258–9, 261–3, 267, 274, 277
identification (and moral psychology) 99–102
Ifantidou, Elly 492
illiberal groups 161, 164–5, 176–7
  see also liberalism
incentive-comparability approach
    (in economics) 258, 263–7, 269, 271–4,
    276, 278
incentives 258, 264, 268, 272–6, 278
inclusion problem for contractarianism-
    contractualism 53–4
  see also contractarian ethics; contractualist
    ethics
indexicals 403–5, 414
  meaning of 403–4
  reference of 403
indigenous peoples 18–23
  see also liberalism; minorities;
    multiculturalism
inference to the best explanation 65
inferential capacities 24, 94
input objection in moral epistemology 75, 78

  see also filtering problem
institutional design and compliance
    constraints 260
  see also compliance (in political philosophy)
institutional design 267, 272–3, 275–6, 278
institutional principles 259
institutions 258–60, 264, 267–73, 275–8
intangible hand of esteem (in economics and
    political philosophy) 276
  intending versus merely foreseeing harm
    distinction 47; see also doctrine of double
    effect
  see also desires: for esteem and to avoid
    disesteem
intentional objects 283–4, 322, 326–7
  see also Brentano's problem
intentional states 323
intentionalism about experience 321–2, 326–9
intentionality 283–4, 360, 363
  see also Brentano's problem
internalism (in epistemology) 688, 693
internalism (in ethics) 45, 55, 65, 89, 92–6, 104,
    124–8
internalism (in philosophy of mind), see
    psychological states
intrinsic bad 32
intrinsic good or value 32, 35 n
intuitionism in moral epistemology 64, 67,
    70–3
  generalist accounts of 64, 67, 69–71; see also
    moral epistemology
  particularist accounts of 64, 67, 69, 71–2, 80 n
intuitionist approaches to deontological
    ethics 44
  monist version of 45
  pluralist version of 44–5, 70; see also
    Ross, W. D.
invisible hand explanations (in economics)
    266, 274–6
Irigaray, Luce 234
iron hand explanations (in economics) 275–6
Irwin, T. H. 118
Isen, A. M., Levin, P. F. 118
Iten, Corinne 493 n

Jackson, Frank 4 n, 5 n, 6 n, 22, 105, 125, 139,
    141, 315 n, 322 n, 323 n, 329, 332, 407–10,
    417–18, 469, 558, 702–5, 710, 712, 724 n
  and Pargetter, Robert 55 n, 316, 558
  and Pettit, Philip 4 n, 139, 375
  and Smith, Michael 26
Jacob, P., and Jeannerod, M. 389
Jaggar, Alison 234, 241
Jaggar, Alison 57–8
James, Susan 232, 235–7
James, W. 456 n

Jennings, R. E. 542, 568
Jennings, Richard 770
Jensen, Arthur 836
Johnson, M. 116 n
Johnson, Phillip 839
Johnston, Mark 17
Johnston, Mark 642 n, 643
Jones, Andrew, J. L., and Pörn,
    Ingmar 558, 584 n
Jones, E. E. 120 n
Jones, K. 4, 70 n, 234
Jordan, M. 341 n
Joyce, Richard 5 n
Juola, P., and Plunkett, K. 386
jurisprudence 8–9, 182, 185–6, 188–9, 191–3,
    203–5
justice 3, 35–6, 39, 52, 54, 155, 157, 176, 181,
    190–1, 194, 201, 203–4, 209–11, 214–17, 221,
    225–6, 259
  distributive 159, 167
  historical 174–5
justification of belief 67, 688–90, 693, 695, 697
  analyses of 696–7
  circular 70 n
  closure principle on 687, 690–1
  doxastic 68–9
  inferential 73
  non-inferential 70 n, 71, 73, 79
  propositional 68
  structure of 73
  see also belief; knowledge; moral beliefs;
    moral epistemology; scepticism
justified constraint 50
  see also Gauthier, David

Kadmon, Nirit 469, 493 n, 495
Kagan, Shelley 34 n, 36, 45 n, 46 n, 49, 145
Kahneman, David and Slovic, P. and
    Tversky. Amos 140 n
  and Tversky, Amos 49 n
Kamin, Leon 836
Kamm, F. M. 48–9
Kane, R. 141 n, 142
Kant, Immanuel 8, 39, 42–3, 51, 56, 122, 243,
    249, 254, 260, 622, 631–2, 739–42, 768,
    801–2, 811, 868
Kantian ethics 22, 39, 41–4, 45, 49, 52–3, 97–8,
    116, 117 n, 122, 124, 126, 127 n, 128, 243–5
Kaplan, D. 287 n, 293 n, 403–5, 412, 417–18, 627,
    742–3, 592 n
Kaplan, M. 686 n
Karttunen, Lauri, and Peters, Stanley 476 n,
    493 n, 540–1
Kasher, Asa 469, 475
Katz, J. 288 n, 475, 491
Kauffman, Stuart 827

Kavka, Gregory 51, 227 n
Keeley, Brian 841
Kenneally, T. 122
Kennett, Jeanette 105 n, 106
  and Smith, Michael 106–7
Kenny, A. 540, 559, 568 n
Keynes, J. N. 597, 599
Khamara, E. J. 547, 606 n
Kim, J. 115, 525, 526
Kinsey, A. C., Pomeroy, W. B., and
    Martin, C. E. 240
Kirkham, R. L. 458 n
Kitcher, P. 746–748, 771, 773–4, 785, 798–9, 822,
    828, 830–3, 835, 837–40
Kittay, Eva 53 n
Klein, P. 691 n
Kneale, W. C. 794–5
Kneale, William 565
  and Kneale, Martha 542 n
Knobe, Joshua 354
know-how 320
knowledge 65, 684–5, 690, 692, 695
  analyses of 696–7
  closure principle on 686–7, 690
  as a mental state 693; see also Williamson, T.
  see also belief; justification of belief;
    scepticism
knowledge argument, the 314–21, 328
  objection from egocentric knowledge to
    317–18
  knowing one thing under different guises
    objection to 318–19
  fallacy of inferring new properties from
    new concepts objection to 319
  objection from hard-to-spot-patterns to
    319–20
  the ability reply to and recognitional
    capacities 320–1, 328–9
  and intentionalism 328–9; see also
    intentionalism about experience
  see also Jackson, Frank
knowledge-that 321
Kohlberg, Lawrence 57, 126, 237
Kolodny, Niko 109 n
Kornblith, H. 685 n
Korsgaard, Christine 5 n, 6 n, 8 n, 9, 32 n–33 n,
    43 n, 44, 92
Kracht, Marcus 587 n, 601 n
Kratzer, Angelika 538
Kripke, Saul 288–9, 297, 397–402, 406–10, 417,
    420, 423–4, 558, 564, 569, 570, 572–3, 576,
    577, 579, 582, 586, 587 n, 591, 595, 602 n,
    742–3, 785
Kroon, Fred 409
Kuenne, W. 458 n, 461
Kuhn, Steven, T. 542, 561 n, 585–6, 595 n

Kuhn, Thomas S.   78, 768, 785 n, 801
Kukathas, Chandran   162–3, 176–7
Kukla, Andre   770, 774 n, 778–81, 782 n, 783 n
Kupperman, J. J.   120, 122 n
Kvanvig, J.   68
Kvart, Igal   506
Kyburg, H.   687 n
Kymlicka, Will   157–9, 163, 165, 167–7

Lakoff, George   485
Lakoff, Robin   538, 539 n, 543
Larmore, C. E.   118 n
Lange, M.   799–801
Langton, Rae   242 n, 243 n, 253 n
   and Lewis, David   621
language of thought hypothesis, the   292,
      369–73
   and concept possession   373–4
   and compositionality   371
   and intentional realism   370–1
   and syntactic properties   370–1, 373
   see also Fodor, J.; mentalese; mental syntax
LaPorte, J.   303
Larson, R:
   and Ludlow, Peter   424
   and Segal, G.   287, 295
Laudan, Larry   772–4, 778 n, 784, 787 n
   and Leplin, Jarett   778, 780, 782, 783 n
law, the:
   normativity of   183
   concept of   193
   interpretation of   193–199
   rule of   193, 200
laws (in philosophy of science)   792–815, 841
   and ceteris paribus principles   806, 808–9
   best systems accounts of laws of nature   793,
      797–9, 802–3
   and empiricism   793, 797, 802, 806, 809
   Friedman's Kantian view of laws of nature
      799, 801–2; see also Friedman, Michael
   Humean regularity accounts of laws of
      nature   793–7, 811–12; see also causation, as
      constant conjunction; Hume, David
   laws of nature in terms of stability   800–1; see
      also Lange, M.
   Mill–Ramsey–Lewis account of laws of
      nature   797–8
   and models   804–8
   necessitarian views of laws of nature   793–7,
      812
   and powers   811–13, 815
   pragmatic   806–8
   of science   792
   and symmetries   805–6
   and unificationist view of scientific progress
      798–9

   see also causation; philosophy of science
Le Poidevin, R.   630, 632–3
   and Macbeth, M.   633
Leeds, S.   459 n
legal judgments   7–8
   separability from moral judgements   190,
      192; see also separability thesis
legal norms   181, 204
   reduction of legal norms to moral norms   9;
      see also moral norms
legal philosophy   181, 191
legal positivism   8, 181–2, 185–7, 191–3, 204–5
   exclusive   188–90
   inclusive   189–90
legal precedent   199–203
   enactment force of   200
   gravitational force of   200
legal rules:
   constructivist approach to purpose of   197–9;
      see also Dworkin, Ronald
   normativity of   183
   practices theory of   183
   of procedure   186
   primary   182–3
   purpose of   196–7, 199
   of recognition   188, 190–1
   secondary   182–5, 187–8;
      see also Hart, H. L. A.
legal standards versus legal rules distinction
      187, 189
legal systems   181–5, 188–91, 193–4, 197, 204
Le-Grand, J.   272
Leibniz,, G. W., and Clarke, S.   618, 751
Leming, J. S.   121
Lemmon, E. J.   563, 565, 567, 569
   and Scott, D. S.   561, 579 n, 580 n
Lenzen, Wolfgang   557, 567
Leonard, Henry, and Goodman, Nelson   636,
      638
Leplin, Jarett   770, 774, 776 n, 784 n
Lesniewski, Stanislaw   636, 638, 651
Levesque, Hector, J.   601 n
Levin, Michael   772
Levins, Richard, and Lewontin,
      Richard, C.   828
Levinson, Stephen   471–2, 478, 481 n
Levy, Jacob T.   156, 177
Lewis, C. I., and Langford, C. H.   561–2, 567
Lewis, David   9, 17, 125, 129, 139, 264, 288 n,
      407–10, 416, 419, 421–2, 456 n, 473, 475,
      483, 488, 505–6, 509, 510, 514, 516, 521, 523,
      526, 529, 543, 560, 562, 564, 567, 591–3, 595
      630, 636, 647 n, 688 n, 796–7
Lewis, Peter   774 n
Lewontin, Richard   826, 828, 836
   Ross, Steven, and Kamin, Leon   838

liberal democracies 161–2
liberal principles 156, 161, 172–4, 176
    of freedom of association 163, 165–6, 169; see
        also associations
    of freedom of religion 160
    of liberty 161, 163, 166
    of neutrality 157–8, 161, 162, 165, 167
    see also equality of opportunities
liberal states 171, 173, 175
liberal values 160–1, 176–7
liberalism 155–7, 159, 161–5, 167, 169, 171, 173,
        175–7
    communitarian critiques of 156
    feminist critiques of 156
    multiculturalist critiques of 156
libertarianism 162
Linsky, Leonard 556
Lipton, Peter 774, 776 n
Little, Margaret 6 n, 71
Lloyd, Elisabeth 822, 825, 838
Lloyd, Elizabeth A. 232, 238–41
Lloyd, Genevieve 235 n
Loar, B. 302, 319 n
Locke, Don 703 n
Locke, John 275, 660, 663
Lockhart, Ted 33 n
Loeb, D. 130, 132, 137
Longino, Helen 241
Lorde, Audre 254
Louden, R. B. 116 n
Lowe, E. J. 354
Lucas, J. R. 564
Luce, R. Duncan, and Raiffa, Howard 185
Luper-Foy, S. 684 n
Lycan, W. G. 313, 325, 326 n, 332
Lyons, David 39 n
Lyons, John 540 n

MacCormick, Neil 192
Macedo, Stephen 163
Machamer, P., Darden, L., and Craver, C. 811, 814
MacIntyre, A. 122
Mackenzie, Catriona and Stoljar, Natalie
        247 n, 248
Mackie, Gerry 217 n
Mackie, J. L. 4 n, 5, 22 n, 65, 70, 72, 78, 130,
        505–6, 509, 525, 529, 569 n, 630–1, 798
McAllister, J. W. 772
McCann, H. 339, 346
McClelland, J. L., and the PDP Research
        Group 382
McCloskey, H. J. 36 n
McConnell, Michael W. 160
McDermott, Michael 514, 529–30
McDowell, John 4 n, 5 n, 17, 64 n, 66 n, 70 n,
        71 n, 92–3, 117, 118 n, 193, 286 n, 291 n,
        297 n, 693 n, 720 n, 726

McFetridge, Ian 565 n, 586 n, 592 n
McGinn, Colin 54 n, 346, 588, 591–2
McGowan, Mary Kate 242 n
McGrath, Sarah 508, 527–8
McIntyre, Alison 48, 103–4
McKenna, M. 141 n
MacKinnon, Catherine 242–3, 244 n, 247,
        251, 253
    and Dworkin, Andrea 244 n, 246, 248
McKeown-Green, Jonathan 419–20
McLaughlin, B. P., and Warfield, T. A. 384
McMullin, Ernan 773, 774 n, 776 n, 777 n, 785
McNaughton, D. 70 n
McTaggart, J. M. E. 615, 618, 620–4, 633
Madison, J., and Hamilton, A., et al 274
Maguire, A. M. 390
Maher, P. 684 n
Makin, G. 286 n
Makinson, David 543, 556, 568, 587
male experience 58
Malm, Heidi 49 n
Mandeville, B. 272, 274
Manning, John 197
Margalit, Avishai, and Halbertal, Moshe 166–7
    and Raz, Joseph 166
Margolis, E., and Laurence, S. 125
market deregulation 261–2
Markus, H. R., and Kitayama, S. 132
Marr, D. 375–6
Marr's three levels of explanation 375–6
    see also cognitive science; personal versus
        sub-personal levels of description and
        explanation distinction
Marshall, J. C., and Halligan, P. W. 389
Martin, M. G. F. 720 n, 726 n, 728 n, 732 n
Marx, Karl 66, 243 n
Marxism 155, 241
Masters, W. H., and Johnson, V. 240
materialism, see physicalism
Matheson, Carl 770
Mathews, K. E., and Cannon, L. K. 118
Matsui, Tomoko 483 n
Matsumoto, Yo 472 n
Maudlin, Tim 871 n, 873 n
Maxwell, Grover 772
Maynard Smith, John 823, 827, 834, 839
Mayr, Ernst 827, 830
meaning 427–433, 446, 449, 451, 457–458
    and communication 427–8, 433, 435–6, 438,
        451–2
    change 302–3
    evidential theory of 749–50, 752
    and phemes 434–6, 440; see also Austin, J. L.
    and relational phatic acts 434, 436
    sentence meaning 429–33, 452, 469, 473, 475,
        477, 494–5; see also Grice, H. P.
    and speakers' intentions 429–30, 435, 437

meaning (*cont.*):
  and speech 427–8
  and speech acts, *see* speech acts
  theory of 428–9, 431
  and understanding, *see* understanding
    utterances
  and uptake 433–4, 436; *see also* Austin, J. L.;
    speech acts
  utterer's meaning 429–32; *see also*
    Grice, H. P.; pragmatics, and speaker's
    meaning word meaning 429–30, 475;
    see also Grice, H. P.
  see also aboutness; intentionality;
    pragmatics; semantics; understanding
    utterances
Meinhardt, Hans 827, 835
Meinong, A 284 n
Melden, A. I. 351
Mele, Alfred R. 104, 106–7
Mele, Alfred, R. 336–9, 340 n 341–2, 345, 351–5
  and Moser, P. 339, 355
  and Sverdlik, S. 353–5
Mellor, D. H. 506, 621, 625–8, 631–2
mental dossiers 295–6, 304
mental states 283, 311, 315, 323, 329, 364
  beliefs about one's current mental states
    691–2
  conscious 313, 325; *see also* consciousness
  indiscriminable 692, 729, 732
  phenomenal 312–14; *see also* phenomenology
  non-phenomenal 312
  realism about 311–12
  sensory 325
  see also psychological states
mental syntax 292–3
mentalese 292–3
Menzies, Peter 521–3
  and Pettit, Philip 593
Merleau-Ponty, M. 726
Merritt, M. 116 n
meta-ethical questions 6, 8
meta-ethics 3–26, 63, 68, 839
meta-legal questions 7–8
meta-level questions 8–10
  about how evaluative and deontic concepts
    are to be defined 11–12
  about reasons and rationality 7–10, 14
  see also meta-ethical questions; meta-legal
    questions
metaphysics 63–4
Milgram, Elijah 92
Milgram, S. 118, 120
Mill, John Stuart 35, 165, 259, 289, 335 n, 798,
  808, 812
Miller, G. A. 358
Miller, R. 66

Miller, Richard W. 771, 786 n
Millikan, R. 289 n, 303, 829–30, 841
Mills, Susan, and Beatty, John 822
Milner, A. D., and Goodale, M. A. 389
minimax concession principle 50
  see also Gauthier, David
minorities 158, 172–3, 176
  ethnic 156–7
  linguistic 170
  national 169, 172–6
  religious 158, 160, 168, 171
Mintoff, Joe 51
Mischel, W. 118–19
Mitchell, S. 807–8, 841
Mitchell, Sandra 829–30
modality 534–606
alethic modal logics 536, 540, 543, 550–1, 555,
    560–1, 563, 567, 581, 588–90; Blanché's
    hexagon 548, 551, 553
  and deontic logics 540, 543, 555, 558, 560,
    567–8, 584 n, 586, 601
  and epistemic logics 536, 538–40, 543, 557,
    559–60, 567, 578, 592, 601 n
  hexagon of opposition 542–3
  Kripke semantics 558, 569, 570–80, 587 n,
    595; *see also* Kripke, Saul
  modal squares of opposition 535–37, 542–4,
    548–9, 551, 552, 55, 556 n, 558, 560–1, 569,
    598, 601
  possible world semantics 535, 541, 548, 557,
    570, 591–2, 594–5
modularity of mind 376, 385
  and belief fixation 378
  and central systems 377–9
  and cognitive neuropsychology 379–81
  and domain specificity 376–9
  and information encapsulation 376–7
  massive modularity 379
  nine marks of 376–7
  see also Fodor, J.
Molnar, G. 794–5
Moltmann, Frederika 639
monists about the good 3
Montague, Richard 469, 535, 584, 595 n
Montgomery, H., and Routley, R. 542 n, 562
Moody-Adams, M. 78 n
Moore, G. E. 4 n, 5 n, 13–19, 21, 34, 115, 321,
  457 n, 689, 703, 708, 726
Moore, Michael 182 n
Moorean definition:
  of deontic concepts 13–17, 20
  of an all-things-considered reason to act
    25–6; *see also* reasons; Sidgwickian
    definition of the evaluative; Sidgwickian
    definition of the good
moral autism 55

moral beliefs 5, 43, 63, 67, 74, 77–8, 142, 264–5
    justification of 68–70, 79–80, 83
    non-inferential justification for 69, 70–1
    social factors in production of 76
    social factors in justification of 81–2; see also
        epistemology; justification of beliefs;
        moral epistemology
moral development in children 57
moral dilemmas 32
moral disagreement 129–31, 135–7, 140, 146,
        129–37, 189, 204
moral discourse 64–5, 67, 87, 204, 269
moral emotions 107–9
moral epistemology 64, 67, 69, 74, 76, 79
moral evaluation 31, 44
moral facts 4–5, 63, 65–6, 77–8
moral intuitions 33–5, 37–9, 41, 42, 44–7, 49, 52,
        58–9, 72–3
moral irrealism 63, 80
moral judgements 4–5, 8, 25, 66, 72, 74–6,
        78, 124 6, 129, 131–2, 138 n, 181, 187–8,
        191, 204
moral knowledge 63–7, 70 n
    ideological function of claims to 66, 76, 82
    non-inferential 69, 71
    presupposition of 76
    sociality of 68, 78
moral luck 44, 56
moral motivation 87, 95–9, 123–8
    problems presented by psychopathy and
        sociopathy for internalist theories of
        124–8; see also internalism in ethics
    see also motivation
moral norms 8–9, 25–6, 49 n, 86, 98, 107,
        109, 181
    see also norms of reason and rationality
moral observations 65–6, 77–8
moral principles 31, 51, 53, 66, 68, 70, 86,
        182, 203
moral properties 63, 64 n, 66–7
moral psychology 9, 49, 55, 86–8, 96, 98–9, 107,
        117, 119, 122, 124
    cognitivist and non-cognitivist approaches
        to 100
moral realism 63, 74, 80, 131–2, 135–7, 182
moral reasons 36 n, 87–8
moral sensibilities 66, 71, 77–8
moral status of animals 44, 53, 130
    see also Kantian ethics; utilitarianism
moral versus conventional distinction 127–8
Moran, Richard 100
Morgan, M., and Morrison, M. 799, 804
Morris, Charles 468
Morris, Christopher 54 n,
Morris, Desmond 238–40
Morris, Herbert 109

Mortensen, Chris 567
motivation and desire 87–90
    Humean theory of 88, 104–5; see also moral
        motivation
Mulgan, Tim 37 n
multicultural accommodation 156, 159–60,
        169, 176
multiculturalism 156–7, 161, 163, 167, 176–7
multiculturalists 157–60
Mumford, S. 811
Murphy, Liam 37
Murray, John, D. 835
Musgrave, Alan 774 n, 775 n, 777 n

Nagel, Ernest 829, 833–4
Nagel, Thomas 4 n, 5 n, 22 n, 32, 44, 89, 142 n,
        313, 351–2
name-concepts 288, 295–7, 301, 303–4
names, meaning of 288–9, 300, 304, 397, 399,
        400–2, 405, 408, 413, 419
    see also descriptivism; non-descriptivist
        theories
narrow content 297–8, 300–1
narrow properties 298–9
natural kind concepts 297–9, 302
    and dubbing ceremonies 302–4
natural kind terms 299–300, 302, 402, 405, 408,
        413, 418, 422, 424, 519
    see also descriptivism; non-descriptivist
        theories
natural kinds 302–4, 831
natural law theory (in ethics) 41, 45 n
    see also Gert, Bernard; Hobbesian approach
        to morality
natural law theory (in philosophy of law) 8, 9,
        181–2, 186, 191
naturalized epistemology 685, 739, 775,
        776 n, 787
    see also Quine, W. V.
Neale, S. 287, 471 n, 475, 478 n
Neander, Karen 829
negative existentials, see empty names; Russell's
        problem of negative existentials
Nelkin, Dorothy, and Tancredi, Laurence 840
neo-Russellianism (about propositional
        attitude reports) 289–96
    see also propositional attitudes; propositional
        attitude reports
Nerlich, G. 618–19
Neta, Ram 710 n
neuroscience 311
Newcomb's problem 22
Newtonian mechanics 616, 802–3, 861–68,
        870–1
Nichols, S. 124–8
Nietzsche, Friedrich 5 n, 97

Nisbett, R. E. 132
    and Cohen, D. 132–7
    and Ross, L. 140 n
Noddings, Nel 57
non-cognitivism (in ethics) 4, 6 n, 21, 63, 64,
        771 n, 839
    see also cognitivism (in ethics)
non-descriptivist (or anti-descriptivist)
        theories 406–8, 421–4
    about the semantics of names 405, 424; see
        also Kripke, Saul
    about the semantics of natural kind terms
        405, 424; see also Kripke, Saul; Putnam,
        Hilary
non-existent objects 284 n
non-ideal normative theory (in political
        philosophy) 258–9, 260 n, 273, 278
non-tuism (in economics) 265–6
Noonan, H. 300, 593
normative democratic theory 209–10,
        213, 228
normative ethics 3–5, 31–2, 35, 50, 58–9
normative social and political theory
        259–60, 263
    see also analytical social and
        political theory
normative social choice theory 210, 216–19,
        221–5, 227–8
    see also social choice theory
normative:
    concepts 12, 54, 87
    judgements 4, 7, 21, 25, 103
    reasons 86, 88–90, 92–5, 97, 100–1
norms of equality 161
    see also equality of opportunities
norms of etiquette 9
    see also legal norms; moral norms
norms of reason and rationality 8–10, 14, 21,
        23–6
    see also legal norms; moral norms
Noveck, Ira 472 n
    and Bianco, Maryse, and Castry, Alain 487
Nowell-Smith, P. H. 72
Nozick, Robert 22 n, 33, 560, 566 n, 567 n,
        684 n, 686 n
Nozick's experience machine 33
Nucci, L. 127
Nussbaum, Martha 107, 117, 160–1, 166, 232,
        243–8, 250–1, 254, 262–3

O'Connor, T. 335 n
O'Leary-Hawthorne, John, and Cortens,
        Andrew 655
O'Neill, Onora 43 n, 248 n
O'Shaughnessy, B. 355
Oaklander, L. N., and Smith, Q. 623, 626

objectification 243–6, 248, 250, 254
    see also autonomy affirmation; autonomy
        denial; feminism; treating someone as an
        object
objects of thought 284
Okin, Susan Moller 54, 163–7, 172
Olson, E. T. 632
ontology 636–7, 639, 667, 670
Open Question Argument 14
    see also Moore, G. E.
Oppy, Graham 563
ordinary language philosophy 468–9, 479
    see also Austin, J. L.; Strawson, P. F.;
        Wittgenstein, Ludwig
Orzack, S., and Sober, Elliott 827
Oster, George, and Wilson, E. O. 827
Oyama, Susan 828, 837

Palmer, F. R. 541 n
Pap, Arthur 567
Papafragou, Anna, and Musolino, Julien 472 n
Papineau, D. 456 n, 770
Parekh, Bhikhu 159
Paretian assumption of welfare economics
        266–7
Parfit, Derek 35, 36 n, 40 n, 92–4, 235, 254
Pargetter, Robert 583–6
Parry, William T., and Hacker, Edward A. 598
particularism in ethics 31, 64
Pateman, Carole 52 n
Peacocke, C. A. B. 287 n, 305, 325, 373, 387, 389,
        592, 724 n, 742, 744, 752, 753, 755, 757, 761–2
Pearl, J. 810
Pearl, Judea 506, 531
Pearle, P., and Bell, J. 854
Pelletier, F. J. 537, 542 n
Penfield, W. 343
Pennock, Robert 839
perception 701–36
    and awareness 702
    and the common kind assumption 717,
        719–22, 725–8, 730–1, 733, 735;
        contextualism about talk of 710, 712–715,
        722 n
    direct perception or direct objects of 702,
        708–10, 716, 736
    direct realism about 701, 714, 723
    and disjunctivism 702, 726–8, 730–1, 733–6
    and experiential naturalism 717, 722, 726, 735
    and illusions or hallucinations 708, 710, 714,
        717–18, 722, 725, 727–8, 731, 734; see also
        arguments from illusion or hallucination
    immediate perception or immediate objects
        of 701, 703–8, 710, 713–14, 716, 722
    indirect perception or indirect objects of
        702, 708–10, 712, 722, 736

indirect realism 701, 714, 736
and knowledge 701–2, 709, 726
mediated perception or mediated objects of
701, 703, 705–8, 710, 714, 716, 722; and
naive realism 715–18, 720, 722, 724–7, 731,
733, 735
of non-physical entities 708–9, 714–15,
718, 726
phenomenalists about 701
representational or intentionalist approach
to 702, 715, 720, 723–5, 731, 735–6; and
sense-experience 714–17, 719–20, 722–3,
725, 727, 730, 732, 734
and sense-data 322, 702–3, 715, 718–19, 722–4,
726, 730 n, 731, 735
see also philosophy of perception
perceptual:
experiences 323–4
representations 323
states 313
Perry, John 287 n, 317 n, 403, 416, 557, 628
Perry, Ruth 233 n
Perry, Stephen 192
personal versus sub-personal levels of
description and explanation (in
cognitive science, philosophy of mind,
philosophy of psychology and
psychology) 359–60, 364
and intentionality 360, 363
and the intentional stance 360; see also
Dennett, D. C.
personal level notions 363
personal level intentionality 363–4
metaphorical use of personal level notions in
sub-personal level descriptions 361
sub-personal level representation 363–4;
sub-personal level systems 360, 363, 369
see also Dennett, D. C.
Peterson, D. R. 118
Pettit, Philip 35 n, 37, 54 n, 220 n, 264, 268 n,
272–3
and Smith, Michael 37 n, 38 n, 90, 101 n
phenomenal experiences 314, 320–1
phenomenology 313–14, 322, 324–5, 332
philosophy of action 334, 338, 355
philosophy of biology 819–42
and altruism 823, 826, 839
and Darwinian evolutionary theory 819–24,
826, 831, 833, 838
Darwinism and religion 839–40
and developmental systems theory 828, 833
evolution and ethics 839; and evolutionary
systematics 830–2
and functions 828–9
and the Human Genome Project 820, 835,
840–1
and IQ tests 836; and molecular biology
819–20, 832–5
and the notion of biological information
834–5
and the notion of a species 830–2
and pluralist conventionalism 825–6
and the pluralist hierarchical view of
selection 825
and reduction 833–4
and the relation between molecular and
classical genetics 833–4
and sociobiology 827, 837–9
and units of selection 823–7, 833
philosophy of causation 506, 508, 511, 514
and research on statistical data and causal
structures 530–1
see also causation
philosophy of cognitive science 359
prospects for 387–90
philosophy of language 306, 371, 428, 478, 485,
487, 494–5, 633
philosophy of linguistics 478
philosophy of mind 284, 311, 359–60, 364, 494,
841
philosophy of perception 388
see also perception
philosophy of physics 805, 820
see also foundations of physics
philosophy of psychology 298
philosophy of science 792–3, 804, 808,
819–20, 841, 861
see also antirealism; constructivism; laws (in
philosophy of science); scientific realism
philosophy of the social sciences 807
philosophy of time 615, 632
see also time
physical sciences, the 310–11
physicalism 310–11, 313, 315–16, 318, 330, 517
Pidgen, Charles 74 n
Pierce, C. S. 456 n
Pinker, S. 304
Pitcher, George 703 n
Plato 66, 209, 418
Platts, Mark 265
Plaut, D. C. 385–6
pleasure 32, 33
Pocock, J. 264
political philosophy 50, 156, 211, 216, 258–9
political:
decisions 209–11, 223–4, 227–8; see also
democratic decisions
procedures 209, 212–13, 215–16, 219, 224; see
also democratic procedures;
proceduralism; procedural values
Popper, K. R. 795, 813
Pörn, Ingmar 556 n

Port, R. F., and van Gelder, T. 387
Porte, Jean 580 n
Posner, Richard 203 n
possibility:
  epistemic 407
  metaphysical 407–8
  see also modality
Postema, Gerald J. 9 n, 192
Pouget, A., and Sejnowski, T. J. 383
pragmatics 468–95
  and explicatures 479–84, 489, 491–2
  formal 469, 472
  and Grice's cooperative principle 470–1,
    484, 486
  and Grice's maxims of manner 470–1
  and Grice's maxims of quality 470–1, 486–7
  and Grice's maxims of quantity 470–1
  and Grice's maxims of relation 470–1
  Gricean approaches to 469, 473, 475–6,
    484–5; see also Grice, H. P.
  and implicatures 468, 472–3, 476–7,
    479–484, 486, 489, 493; see also
    Grice, H. P. inferential 478, 491
  and the literal versus figurative meaning
    distinction 485–7
  and metaphor 485–7, 489–90
  Neo-Gricean approaches to 471–3,
    475–6, 484
  relevance theory approach to 473–5, 479,
    481–5, 488–9, 491, 493, 495
  and speech act theory 491–4; see also speech
    acts
  and speaker's meaning 469, 473–5, 479–81,
    491–2, 494–5; see also Grice, H. P.;
    meaning, utterer's meaning
  and tropes 485–7
  and vagueness 487–8
  see also Grice, H. P.; meaning; meaning,
    sentence meaning; semantics
preference utilitarianism 15
  see also utilitarianism
preferences 218–23
  and action 264–5
  egocentric 265
  other-regarding 266–7
  self-regarding 266–7
Price, H. 535, 633
Price, H. H. 703 n, 726
Prigogine, Ilya 866
principle of permissible harm 48
  see also Kamm, F. M.
principle of utility 35
  see also utility; utilitarianism
Prior, A. N. 537, 563, 568, 570, 574, 581–3, 619,
  626
prisoner's dilemma, the 266

probability 683–6, 690
  conditional 683
  subjective probabilities 684
problem of apocalyptic retaliation strategies 51
  see also contractarian ethics; Gauthier,
    David; Mintoff, Joe
problem of incentive-compatibility (in
  economics) 264
procedural values (in democratic theory) 209,
  211, 215–16, 222, 224–5
  instrumental 212, 217–19, 221–2, 225–6
  intrinsic 209, 212–13, 223, 225–6
  non-instrumental 212, 223; prospective
    212–13, 215–16, 222, 224
  retrospective 212–13, 215–16, 221, 224
proceduralism (in democratic theory) 211, 213,
  217–18, 222, 227
propositional attitude reports (or 'PARs') 289,
  293–4, 296, 301
propositional attitudes 286, 289, 292, 294, 404,
  480 n, 693 n
propositional fragments 294
prosopagnosia 388–9
prudence, accounts of 32
Pryor, J. 79 n, 688 n, 698 n, 729 n
Psillos, Stathis 770, 771 n, 774 n, 775, 778, 782 n,
  785
psychological explanation 289–91, 293, 297,
  300, 304–5
psychological states 291, 298
  internalism about the content of 300–1; see
    also narrow content
  externalism about the content of 300–2; see
    also wide content
  see also mental states
psychology 293–5, 316, 358
  cognitive 375, 485
  cognitive revolution in 358; see also cognitive
    science
  computational 374–5; see also computational
    theory of mind
  and ethics 6, 41, 49, 55, 58, 87, 114–15, 117–20,
    122–4, 132; see also moral psychology
  information-processing 363, 370
Purkinje, Johannes 718 n
Putnam, Hillary 297–300, 302, 305, 402, 456 n,
  684 n, 693 n, 767, 771–2, 778 n, 784

qualia 330
quantum-mechanics 631, 768 n, 769 n, 803,
  805, 813
  see also foundations of physics
quasi-Fregeanism 291, 293, 295, 302
  about name-concepts 295–6; see also
    name-concepts
  see also Frege, Gottlob; sense; reference

Quine, W. V. 115, 294, 367–9, 459 n, 465, 617, 622, 685, 739, 742, 749, 751–2, 759, 771, 778 n, 780, 781 n
Quinn, Warren 47, 49 n, 89
Quinton, Anthony 236

Rabinowicz, W., and Segerberg, K. 578 n
Rabinowicz, Woldek, and Rønow-Rasmussen, Toni 17
Rachels, James 47
Radin, Margaret Jane 195
Raff, R. 827
Railton, Peter 4 n, 5 n, 6 n, 33, 38, 40–1, 99, 115 n, 116 n, 120, 129, 131
Ramsey, F. 458 n, 461
Ramsey, W., and Stich, S., and Garon, J. 385
rational nature 42
rationalism in ethics 8
rationality 692
  see also reason and rationality
Rawls, John 3–4, 10, 32 n, 36 n, 52–4, 70, 75, 98, 108 n, 138, 165, 175 n, 176, 211, 213–16, 225–7, 259–60, 262–3
  see also reflective equilibrium
Raz, Joseph 8, 93, 97, 100, 166–7, 172, 190, 193, 197 n
reason and rationality:
  accounts of 32
  desirability characteristic of reasons 14
  domain of 10–12, 25–6
  requirements and ideals of reason 20–5; see also desirability characteristic of actions; norms of reason and rationality
reasons: agent-neutral reason 35 n
  agent–relative reasons 35
  all-things considered reason 15
  all-things considered reason to act 17–18
  explanatory 88–90
  motivating 90; see also action, reasons for
Recanati, François 468, 471 n, 475, 478 n, 481 n, 491 n, 493
Redhead, M. L. G. 618
Redstockings Collective 66
reference 285–8, 292–7, 397, 400, 433, 436–8, 461, 470, 682, 697, 786
  and baptism or dubbing ceremonies 289, 299, 401–2
  causal theory of 771, 785
  direct 403–5
  and causal–historical chains of reference determination 401–2, 406, 419–20; see also Kripke, Saul; McKeown-Green, Jonathan
  see also descriptivism; Frege, Gottlob; sense
reflective equilibrium 3–5, 52, 73–4, 76, 138 n, 259

wide reflective equilibrium 66–8, 74–5, 77; see also Rawls, John
  see also Rawls, John
regress problem in epistemology 70, 73, 79, 683
  see also belief; scepticism
Reichenbach, H. 616, 630, 632, 824 n
relativism in ethics 58, 78 n, 129–31
reliabilism (in epistemology) 748, 754
representationalism about experience 322, 326
  and externalism 331–2; see also psychological states, externalism about the content of
  minimal 323–4, 326–7
  and narrow content 332; see also narrow content
  strong 323–6; weak 323
  and wide content 332; see also wide content
responsibility 10–11, 13–14, 37–8
Rey, Georges 775 n, 776 n
Richard, M. 289 n, 290, 424
Richards, David 52 n
Richardson, Henry 221 n, 222 n
Ridge, Michael 54 n
right action 39, 51, 53, 55–6, 121
right, the 32, 36, 41
rights: positive versus negative 47
  feminist accounts of 58
  see also Quinn, Warren
rigid designation 400, 404–5
Riker, William 217, 220–1
Risse, Mathias 210 n
Rivière, Claude 538 n
Robb, A. A. 630, 632
Roberts, Robert C. 106 n
Robinson, H. 726
Robinson, Richard 537–40
Rolls, E. T. 383
Rorty, Amèlie Okensberg 103
Rosati, C. S. 129 n
Rosen, Gideon 592–3, 596
Rosenberg, A. 807–8, 821, 834–5
Rosenberg, J. 288 n
Rosenblum, Nancy 164–7
Roskies, A. 126–7
Ross, L., and Nisbett, R. E. 120 n
Ross, W. D. 10, 45, 70–1
Rousseau 98
Routley, Richard, and Meyer, Robert K. 573 n
  and Plumwood, V. Meyer, R. K., and Brady, R. T. 567
  and Routley, Valerie 566
Ruetsche, Laura 855 n
Rumelhart, D. E. 382
  and McClelland, J. L. 383–4
Rumfitt, Ian 450
Ruse, Michael 819, 838–9
  and Wilson, E. O. 839

Russell, Bertrand 13, 287–9, 397, 401, 404, 468, 535, 556
Russell's problem of negative existentials 406, 417, 421–22, 424
    see also empty expressions; empty names
Russellian propositions 289–91, 293
Ryle, Gilbert 336, 448

Sadock, Jerry 491 n
Sainsbury, R. M. 286 n, 288 n
Saito, Setsuo 583 n
Salmon, N. 284 n, 289 n, 290, 292, 294, 405, 424, 469, 567, 619
Salmon, Wesley 506
Sandel, Michael 52–3
Sanford, D. H. 550
Sankey, Howard 771 n
Sarkar, Sahorta 834–5
Sartre, Jean-Paul 250
Saul, Jennifer 237 n, 238 n, 239
Saunders, S. 857, 869 n
Sauriol, Pierre 542
Saver, J. L., and Damasio, A. R. 126
Sayre-McCord, G. 64 n, 73 n, 74 n
Scalia, Antonin 188 n, 189
Scanlon, T. M. 6 n, 17, 53–4, 88, 92–4, 96–7, 100, 141, 337
scepticism (in ethics):
    about moral knowledge 63, 64 n, 65–7, 70, 76–7, 81, 182
    about normative ethics 3–5
scepticism 65, 80, 681, 683, 688–9, 704–5
    and intuitions 694–5, 697
    about justified true belief 686;
        see also belief, justified true;
        justification (of beliefs)
    about knowledge 686–7; see also knowledge
    nd sceptical scenarios 684–8, 690–3, 697
    see also scientific realism, and scepticism
Schaffer, Jonathan 519
Schaffner, Kenneth 833–4, 837
Schauer, Frederich 196 n
Scheffler, Samuel 46 n, 98
Scheibe, E. 802–3
Schick, F. 265
Schiffer, Stephen 471, 688 n, 690 n, 697 n
Schotch, P. K. 558, 560, 568
Schueler, G. F. 88
Schumm, George F. 576
Schurz, Gerhard 580 n
scientific concepts 304
scientific realism 517, 767–88
    and abduction 774–7, 782, 784, 787
    and ampliative inferences 768, 775, 779–80, 783
    and anti-realism, see anti-realism
        (in philosophy of science)

epistemic definitions of 770–1
metaphysical definitions of 770–1, 787
pessimistic meta-induction argument against 767, 774, 784–7; see also Putnam, Hilary
and scepticism 768, 770–1, 775, 778–80, 783–5
semantic definitions of 770–1
strong version of 769–74, 778, 784
success arguments for 767, 772–4, 776–7, 784
underdetermination argument against 767, 777–84, 787
and unobservable entities 768–70, 773, 775, 780, 785–8
Searle, J. 335 n, 364, 409, 432, 434–5, 437–8, 470–1, 473, 475, 491, 724 n
Segal, Gabriel 287 n, 291, 294–5, 297 n, 300–3
Segerberg, Krister 556
Sehon, S. 337, 341–2
Seidenberg, M. S. 386
self-government rights or powers 156, 161, 167, 169–75
self-regard (in economics and political philosophy) 266–71
Sellars, Wilfrid 724 n
semantics 63–64, 468, 479, 488
    contextualist approach to 470, 477–8, 491
    linguistic versus conceptual 478
    literalist approach to 470, 475–9
    semantics versus pragmatics distinction 475–8, 494; see also pragmatics
    see also meaning
Sen, Amartya 216 n, 262, 265–6
Sen's 'liberal paradox' 262
sense 285–6, 292–3, 296, 433, 436, 470
    quasi 293, 296–8, 301–2; see also quasi-Fregeanism
    see also Frege, Gottlob; reference
sensory experience 321, 330
    see also perception; phenomenal experience
sensory states 316, 325
    see also mental states
separability thesis 186, 188
    see also legal judgments; legal positivism
Seuren, Pieter 540
Shafer-Landau, Russ 4 n, 5 n
Shallice, T. 380
Sher, G. 117 n
Sherman, N. 117 n
Shoemaker, Sydney 327 n, 510, 586
Shope, R. 696 n
Shweder, R. A., and Bourne, E. J. 132
Sider, Ted 676
Sidgwick, Henry 16, 18, 35 n, 259
Sidgwick's rational egoist 35 n
Sidgwickian definition 16–21
    of the evaluative 16

of the good 16–21, 25–6
of the bad 16, 20, 26
Simmons, A. John 202, 214 n
Simon, Herbert 271
Simons, Peter 544 n, 548 n, 552, 569, 576, 621, 646 n
Singer, Peter 3 n, 36, 138 n, 145
Sinnott-Armstrong, Walter 32 n–33 n, 67, 70, 140
Skinner, B. F. 312 n, 358
Skinner, Q. 264
Sklar, L. 630, 865 n, 866, 871 n
Skorupski, John 35 n, 41 n, 448
Skyrms, B. 563, 631, 839
Slote, Michael 37 n, 55–7
Smart, J. J. C. 39 n, 142, 616, 628, 630, 772
  and Williams, Bernard 35, 39 n
Smiley, T. J. 578 n, 580, 586
Smith, Adam 129 n, 275
Smith, Michael 4 n, 5 n, 6 n, 9 n, 17–18, 20, 41 n, 63 n, 65 n, 88, 92, 94, 124–5, 131
Smith, P. 684 n
Smith, P., and Jones, O. R. 633
Smith, Q. 619, 622, 624, 627
Smolensky, P. 383–4
Snowdon, P. F. 726 n
Soames, Scott 289 n, 401–2, 405, 408, 413, 421, 423–4
Sober, E. 807, 822, 824–5, 827, 829, 832
  and Lewontin, Richard 824–5
  and Wilson, David Sloan 826, 839
social choice theory 210, 216–23, 225
  see also normative social choice theory
social epistemology 64, 81
  see also moral epistemology
social externalism 301–2
  see also psychological states, externalism about the content of; wide content
social sciences, the 807–8, 812–15
societal cultures 17–23
Socrates 117, 273
Sorensen, Roy 565 n, 578
Sosa, Ernest 80
source thesis 186–7, 191
  see also legal positivism
special theory of relativity 616, 848, 855, 871–3, 876
  see also Einstein, A.
speech acts 476, 480 n
  communicative 433–4, 437
  locutionary 433–4
  illocutionary 433–4, 439
  perlocutionary 433–5, 440; relational 432–3, 435
  see also Austin, J. L.; Grice, H. P.; meaning; Searle, J.; understanding utterances

Spelman, Elizabeth 57
Sperber, Dan 379
Sperber, Dan, and Noveck, Ira 472 n, 483 n
  and Wilson, Deirdre 471 n, 472 n, 473, 478 n, 479–80, 483 n, 486 n, 489, 492, 493 n
Spinner-Halev, Jeff 164–5, 173
Spirtes, P. 810
  and Glymour, C., and Scheines, R. 810
Splitter, Laurence 832
Stalnaker, Robert 330, 408, 412 n, 469, 475, 493 n, 557
Stampe, Dennis 92
Stanley, Jason 478 n, 481 n
  and Szabó, Zoltan 478 n
stare decisis 199–200, 202
  see also legal precedent
Sterelny, Kim, and Griffiths, Paul 828
  and Kitcher, Philip 825
Stevenson, Charles 4 n, 115
Stich, Stephen P. 115, 116 n, 363, 785 n
  and Warfield, T. A. 364
Stocker, Michael 39 n, 40, 43, 99, 107, 109
Stoerig, P., and Cowey, A. 388
Stoljar, Daniel, and Nagasawa, Yujin 317 n
Stone, T., and Davies, M. 389
  and Young, A. W. 390
Stratton-Lake, P. 71 n, 72 n
Strawson, G. 138 n, 142–3
Strawson, P. F. 107, 138 n, 142 n, 145, 249, 427–8, 468, 470 n, 491 n, 725
strength of will 102, 106
Sturgeon, Nicholas 4 n, 5 n, 70, 77, 78 n, 130–2, 135–6
Suárez, M. 804, 813
Suarez, Susan 239
sub-doxastic states 363, 370
  see also aboutness: subdoxastic; Stich, Stephen P.
Sumner, W. G. 130
Sunstein, C. R. 223 n
Sunstein, Cass R. 166
Suppes, Patrick 506, 804, 809–10
Suzumura, Kotaro 216 n, 217 n
Svavarsdòttir, S. 124 n
Svensson, Frances 176
Swaine, Lucas A. 160
Swanton, Christine 106 n
Sweetser, Eve 475, 538 n
Swinburne, R. G. 619
Symons, Donald 241
Szabó, Zoltan 475 n, 478 n

tacit knowledge 756
  and explicitness 384
  Evan's dispositional response to Quine's challenge to 368

tacit knowledge (*cont.*):
  of grammar 359, 365–9; *see also* Chomsky,
    Noam
  and I-languages 365–6
  and linguistic competence 365–6, 369
  and linguistic performance 365–6, 369
  and innateness 367
  Quine's challenge to 367–8
  of rules 372–4, 378, 382
  of rules of inference 373
  of semantics 368–9
  of syntactically structured representations
    372–3, 387
  Wittgensteinian concerns with 367, 369
Tamir, Yael 172
Tarski, A. 457–8, 460–1, 468
Taylor, Charles 166
Taylor, Gabriele 108 n
Tehovnik *et al* 718 n
teleological ethical theories 31–2, 34, 50
  see also consequentialism; utilitarianism
Tetlock, P. E. 137 n
Thalberg, I. 335 n, 339, 340 n
theory acceptance in ethics 67–70
  see also moral beliefs; moral epistemology
Thomason, S. K. 572, 582 n, 587 n
Thompson, J. 335 n
Thompson, Janna 175
Thompson, Judith Jarvis 46–7, 655, 673
Thompson, R. P. 822
Thornhill, Randy, and Palmer, Craig 838
thought experiments 138–41, 145
time 615–33
  and A-beliefs 625–6, 628–30, 633
  and A-concepts 625–6
  and A-facts 621, 624
  A-series of 615, 618, 620–3, 625, 627, 630;
    see also McTaggart, J. M. E.
  and B-beliefs 625–7, 629
  and B-facts 624, 628, 630, 633
  B-series of 615, 618, 620, 622–3, 625–6, 630–1;
    see also McTaggart, J. M. E., and C-facts
  C-series 622; *see also* McTaggart, J. M. E.
  and causation 630–3; *see also* causation
  and change 620–1, 630, 632
  and cosmology 618–19
  the flow of 621, 630, 633
  as the form of inner sense 631–2; *see also*
    Kant, Immanuel
  the new theory of 626–8
  and reference frames 618–19
  and seeing events as present 626
  and the special theory of relativity 615–19,
    631; *see also* Einstein, A., special theory of
    relativity
  and space 615, 618, 621–2, 630, 633

  and space–time 616–20, 622, 632
  and simultaneity 618–20, 624
  and successful action 628–30
  and theories that contain reality to the
    present 619–20; *see also* Prior, A. N.
  and theories that contain reality to the past
    and present 619–20; *see also* Broad, C. D.
Timmons, Mark 4 n, 63 n, 67–69, 74 n, 79–83
Tinbergen, Niko 829–30
Tooley, Michael 506, 510, 512–19, 522, 525, 592
  n, 619, 630–1, 795
tort law, philosophy of 203–5
  see also jurisprudence; legal philosophy
toxin puzzle 51
  see also Kavka, Gregory
Travis, Charles 475, 710 n, 713 n
Travis, Cheryl 838
treating someone as an object 232, 243–54
  see also autonomy affirmation; autonomy
    denial; feminism; objectification
trolley problem in ethics, the 46–7
truth 454–66
  anaphoric theory of 464; *see also* Brandom,
    Robert
  correspondence theory of 456–7, 771, 772 n
  Davidson's theory of 456–7; *see also*
    Davidson, Donald
  deflationary theories of 454–9, 466, 771
  disquotation theory of 459, 465–6
  explicit definitions of 460, 462–3
  minimalist theory of 454, 456 n, 458–60, 463,
    465–6
  non-deflationary theories of 455 n, 456–7
  pragmatic theory of 456–7
  proof theory of 456–7
  prosentential theory of 458, 463–5
  redundancy theory of 458–60
  sentence-variable analysis of 458, 461–3
  as a substantive property 454–5, 458
  Tarski's theory of 458, 460–2;
    see also Tarski, A.
  the truth predicate 454–5, 459–60, 462–5
Tsohatzidis, Savas 491 n
Turiel, E., Killen, M. and Helwig, C. 127
Turner, Kenneth 475 n
Tversky, A., and Kahneman, D. 139
Twin Earth 297–9, 301, 305–6, 421 n
two-dimensionalism 408–9, 412–13, 422–3, 743
  criticisms of 413–17; *see also* Soames, Scott
  and primary intensions 412, 414–16
  and secondary intensions 412, 415–16
  strong version of 410–11, 413–16, 423
  weak version of 410, 416–17, 420–1
  see also descriptivism
Tye, Michael 322 n, 323 n, 324, 326 n, 330, 724 n
Tyler, T. R. 272

understanding utterances 427, 432, 436, 439, 441, 446, 448
and communicative intentions 438
of declarative sentences 440
gaining knowledge on the basis of 443–4
of non-declarative sentences 440, 433
and reasons for belief 441–4, 447
and reasons for disbelief 442
and reasons for taking them to be false 442
and reasons for taking them to be true 441–2
rhetic understanding: of utterances 436, 438–40, 444–8, 450–1; as similar to an inferential capacity 444–5, 449; as practical knowledge 444; as propositional knowledge 444; and truth 440
of WH-questions 440–1, 449
see also meaning
Unger, P. 687 n, 688 n
unilateral visual neglect 389–90
utilitarianism 16, 31, 34–7, 43–5, 96, 98, 116, 117 n, 122, 138, 145, 228, 259
act utilitarianism 35, 38–9
all-pervasive problem for 36
overriding problem for 36
demandingness problem for 36
rule utilitarianism 39
utility 33, 50
average utility versus total utility 35
function 265
maximizing utility 39, 265; *see also* good, the

Valberg, J. J. 721 n
Vallar, G. 390
values 31, 43, 97, 103, 105
of actions 93–4
buck-passing theory of 17–18
desire satisfaction theories of 34
dispositional theories of 17, 129
evaluative hedonism theory of 32
fitting attitude theory of 17
ideal observer theory of 17
incommensurability of 32
objective list theory of 34
perfectionism about 34
pluralism of 32, 97
response dependent theories of
subjective or quasi-subjective accounts of 33, 623
unconditional value 42
unified theory of 32
theory of 31–2
values are like secondary qualities theory of 17
van Benthem, Johan 541, 544–5, 572–4, 576, 595 n, 601 n
van der Auwera, Johan 475
van Dyke, Vernon 176

van Fraassen, Bas 595, 770 n, 771 n, 774–5, 776 n, 778 n, 779, 781 n, 796–7, 805–6, 853 n
van Roojen, Mark 49 n
van Rooy, Robert 475
van, Inwagen, P. 336, 559, 592, 640, 656, 658
Vanderveken, Daniel 475
Velleman, J. David 92, 95, 99, 101, 109, 143 n, 336, 351–2
Veltman, Frank 541
Vernon, P. E. 118
vice 31, 117, 122, 274
Viroli, M. 264
virtue 31, 55–8, 97
in political philosophy 258, 273–4
virtue ethics 31, 43, 49, 54–7, 116
and character 116–18, 119 n, 121–4, 146
Humean approach to 55
and moral education 120–2
neo-Aristotelian approach to 55
sentimentalist form of 55
situationist critique of 118–23
volitional necessities 102, 109
von, Wright, G. H. 535, 543, 560 n, 568

Waldron, Jeremy 176–7, 182 n, 185, 190, 192, 195, 197, 201 n, 263
Walker, M. 75, 77 n, 82, 104
Walker, R. C. S 456 n
Wallace, R. Jay 5 n, 6, 89, 92–3, 95, 101, 107, 109, 138 n, 337
Wansing, Heinrich 556
Waters, C. Kenneth 825, 834
Watkins, E. 811
Watson, Gary 34 n, 99–102, 106, 116 n, 143 n
Watson, J. B. 358
Waulchow, W. J. 187
weakness of will (or *akrasia*) 102–6, 122 n, 124
Weinberg, J., Nichols, S., and Stich, S. 141 n
Weinrib, Ernest J. 203 n
Weiskrantz, L 388
Wertheimer, Roger 538, 539 n
Westermarck, E. 130
Wharton, Time 493 n
White, Alan R. 538
Whyte, J. T. 629
wide content 298, 300–1, 304–5
Widerker, David 559 n
Wiggins, David 4 n, 5 n, 17, 105, 449 n, 632, 660, 663, 671, 721 n
Wigner, E. P. 849
Williams, Bernard 20, 37, 44, 70, 71 n, 92–3, 96, 97 n, 98, 102, 108–9, 116–17, 120, 122, 132, 136, 138, 145, 558 n, 729 n
Williams, C. E. 622
Williams, George, C. 823–4
Williams, John, N. 540, 578 n

Williams, M. 688 n
Williams, Mary 821
Williams, S. G. 578 n
Williamson, T. 305, 546 n, 564 n, 567 n, 684 n, 687 n, 688 n, 689 n, 692 n, 693 n, 694, 698 n, 729 n, 781 n
Wilson, Deirdre 489, 493 n
    and Matsui, Tomoko 483 n
    and Sperber, Dan 473, 475 n, 478 n, 483 n, 486 n, 487, 489, 492, 493 n
Wilson, E. O. 837–9
Wilson, G. 335 n, 337, 341
Wilson, M. 303
Wimsatt, William 819, 825, 827
Wiseman, C. 544
Wittgenstein, Ludwig 195, 231, 336, 346–7, 367, 369, 440–1, 445–6, 456 n, 468, 510

Wolf, Susan 36 n, 109
Wolheim, Richard 97, 107–8
Woods, M. 117 n, 337
Woodward, J. F. 810
Woolfolk, R. L., and Doris, J. M. 116 n
    and Darley, J. M. 143–5
Worrall, J. 785
Wright, C. 686 n
Wright, Larry 829–30
Wundt, Wilhelm 358

Yablo, Stephen 526–7
Young, A. W. 388

Zapf, Christian, and Moglen, Eben 195
Zimmerman, Dean 676
zombies 314